THE CELTIC WORLD

THE CELTIC WORLD

Edited by

Miranda J. Green

London and New York

First published 1995
by Routledge
11 New Fetter Lane, London EC4P 4EE

First published in paperback in 1996

Simultaneously published in the USA and Canada
by Routledge
29 West 35th Street, New York, NY 10001

Reprinted 1996, 1997

Typeset in Stempel Garamond by
Florencetype Ltd, Stoodleigh, Devon

Printed and bound in Great Britain by
Redwood Books Ltd, Trowbridge, Wiltshire

British Library Cataloguing in Publication Data
A catalogue record for this book is available from the British Library

Library of Congress Cataloguing in Publication Data
A catalogue record for this book is available from the Library of Congress

ISBN 0-415-05764-7 (hbk)
ISBN 0-415-14627-5 (pbk)

CONTENTS

——— .◆. ———

— Contents —

— Contents —

PART IX: THE CELTS IN EUROPE

PART X: ON THE EDGE OF THE WESTERN WORLD

PART XI: CELTIC BRITAIN POST AD 400

PART XII: THE SURVIVAL OF THE CELTS

ILLUSTRATIONS

———— •◆• ————

TABLES

CONTRIBUTORS

——— •◆• ———

Martin Bell is a Senior Lecturer in Archaeology at the University of Wales, Lampeter. He is currently directing the Experimental Earthwork Project, and a programme of intertidal wetland archaeology in the Severn Estuary. He is author (with Dr M.J.C. Walker) of *Late Quaternary Environmental Change* (1992) and editor (with Dr J. Boardman) of *Past and Present Soil Erosion* (1992).

Daphne Nash Briggs was an Assistant Keeper in the Heberden Coin Room, Ashmolean Museum, Oxford, and part-time University Lecturer in Roman, then Greek numismatics at Oxford University, from 1976[-]85. Her publications include (as Daphne Nash) *Coinage in the Celtic World* (1987).

Olivier Büchsenschütz is Director of the Centre National de la Recherche Scientifique, Archéologies d'Orient et d'Occident, in Paris, and is Associate Professor at the University of Paris. He has published *Structures d'habitats et fortifications de l'âge du Fer en France Septentrionale* (1984); *Architectures des âges des metaux* (1988); he is co-author (with Françoise Audouze) of *Towns, villages and countryside of Celtic Europe* (1989), and has published reports on his excavations at Levroux.

Barry C. Burnham is a Senior Lecturer in Archaeology at the University of Wales, Lampeter. His publications include a joint-authored volume on *The 'Small Towns' of Roman Britain* (1990), and an edited work on *Conquest, Co-existence and Change: Recent Work in Roman Wales* (1991).

Sara Champion is Visiting Senior Lecturer in the Department of Archaeology at the University of Southampton. Her publications include *A Dictionary of Terms and Techniques in Archaeology* (1980) and numerous articles on coral, enamel, craft production and its relationship to social organization in iron age Europe.

Timothy Champion is Reader in Archaeology and Head of the Department of Archaeology at the University of Southampton. His publications include *Prehistoric Europe* (1984) and *Centre and Periphery* (1989).

Thomas Charles-Edwards is Fellow and Tutor in Modern History at Corpus Christi College, Oxford. He is the author of *Early Irish and Welsh Kinship* (Oxford, 1993)

John Collis is Professor in the Department of Archaeology and Prehistory, University of Sheffield. He has published extensively on the Iron Age in Europe, and his books include *The European Iron Age* (1984), and *Oppida, earliest towns north of the Alps* (1984). His main field project is investigating the changes in settlement pattern and social and economic organization in central France.

Jeffrey L. Davies is Senior Lecturer in Archaeology in the Department of History, University of Wales, Aberystwyth. His publications include *Conquest, Co-existence and Change* (1991); *Excavations at Segontium (Caernarfon) Roman Ford, 1975–9* (1993); and *Cardiganshire County History Vol. I: From the earliest times to the coming of the Normans.*

Sioned Davies is a lecturer in the Department of Welsh, University of Wales College of Cardiff. Her works include *The Four Branches of the Mabinogi* (1993) and a volume in Welsh on the art of the medieval story-teller (in press). She has published many articles on the *Mabinogion*, especially on issues relating to orality and literacy.

D. Ellis Evans is Jesus Professor of Celtic and Professorial Fellow of Jesus College, Oxford. He is a Fellow of the British Academy and Foreign Honorary Member of the American Academy of Arts and Sciences. His publications include *Gaulish Personal Names, A Study of some Continental Celtic Formations* (1967), and numerous articles on Continental Celtic and early Insular Celtic. He co-edited the *Bulletin of the Board of Celtic Studies*, and is now Chief Editor of *Studio Celtica*.

Otto-Herman Frey is Professor of Pre- and Protohistory at the University of Marburg/Lahn. His works include several papers on the pre-Roman Iron Age, especially in central and southern Europe, and he was co-editor of the Catalogue of the Venice Exhibition, *The Celts*.

Alex Gibson is Projects Manager with the Clwyd-Powys Archaeological Trust. He is author of *Neolithic and Bronze Age Pottery*, and co-author of *Prehistoric Pottery for the Archaeologist.*

Miranda J. Green is a Senior Lecturer in Archaeology at Gwent College of Higher Education (a University of Wales Associate College), and she also lectures in Celtic Studies at the University of Wales, Cardiff. She is an Honorary Research Fellow at the Centre for Advanced Welsh and Celtic Studies at the University of Wales, Aberystwyth. Her publications include *The Gods of the Celts* (1986); *Symbol and Image in Celtic Religious Art* (1989); *Dictionary of Celtic Myth and Legend* (1992); *Animals in Celtic Life and Myth* (1992); and *Celtic Myths* (1993). A new book on Celtic goddesses is in press.

Elizabeth Jerem is a researcher at the Archaeological Institute of the Hungarian Academy of Sciences and former Rhys Fellow of Jesus College, Oxford. She is a member of the Celtic Commission of the Austrian Academy of Sciences and editor in chief of the Series *Archaeolingua*. She is the author of numerous works on the Iron Age in eastern Europe, in many languages. An important new monograph entitled *Iron Age Settlement of Sopron-Krautacker: archaeological and environmental investigations* (Archaeolingua Main Series) is in press.

Martyn Jope is Professor Emeritus of Archaeology at Queen's University, Belfast, and a Fellow of the British Academy. He has long worked on Celtic problems, collaborating closely in earlier years (1942[-]57) with Paul Jacobsthal in Oxford. *Early Celtic Art in the British Isles* is in press.

Majolie Lenerz-de Wilde is Professor in the Department of Prehistory at the University of Münster, Westfalia. She is a specialist in later Spanish prehistory.

Wynne Lloyd, formerly a radio and subsequently a television producer with BBC Wales, is a television columnist, music reviewer and commentator on the Welsh scene.

Glenys Lloyd-Morgan was formerly Archaeological Assistant at the Grosvenor Museum, Chester. She currently works as a freelance lecturer and small finds specialist in Lancashire. Her publications include *Description of the Collections in the Rijksmuseum G.M. Kam at Nijmegen IX: the mirrors* (1981)

Proinsias Mac Cana is Senior Professor in the School of Celtic Studies, The Dublin Institute for Advanced Studies. He has published widely on the subject of Irish mythology, and his works include *Celtic Mythology* (1970, 1983).

Euan W. MacKie is Senior Curator in Archaeology and Anthropology at the Hunterian Museum, University of Glasgow. His main research interests are in the North British Iron Age and the late Neolithic period in Britain. His publications include *Dun Mor Vaul, an Iron Age broch on Tiree* (University of Glasgow 1974); and *Science and Society in Prehistoric Britain* (Elek, 1977).

Sean McGrail was Chief Archaeologist at the National Maritime Museum, Greenwich (1976–86), and Professor of Maritime Archaeology, University of Oxford (1986–93). He is now Visiting Professor in Maritime Archaeology at the University of Southampton. His publications include *Logboats of England and Wales* (1978); *Rafts, Boats and Ships* (1981), *Ancient Boats in North-West Europe* (1987); and *Medieval Boat and Ship Timbers from Dublin* (1993).

W.H. Manning is Professor of Archaeology in the University of Cardiff, and is a specialist on later prehistoric and Roman Britain. One of his major interests is the early Roman army and, in particular, the legionary fortress at Usk: seven volumes of his excavation report on Usk have already been published. His other main specialism is early ironworking: publications on this subject include the *Catalogue of the Romano-British iron tools, fittings and weapons in the British Museum.*

Ruth Megaw was trained as am American historian and has a longstanding interest in cultural history. She is a former member of the UK Diplomatic Service, and has taught at the Universities of New South Wales and Sydney. She is a former head of American Studies at the Nene College, Northampton. Currently, she is a part-time Lecturer at Flinders University in Adelaide, sharing with her husband, Vincent Megaw, topics in early Celtic art and archaeology and contemporary Aboriginal art. She is working with him on the preparation of a Supplement to Paul Jacobsthal's seminal *Early Celtic Art*, to be published by Clarendon Press.

Vincent Megaw, formerly Professor of Archaeology at the University of Leicester, has taught European archaeology and prehistoric art both there and previously at the University of Sydney. In his present position at Flinders University, he teaches Visual Arts and Archaeology. His central concern with Celtic art was established first as an undergraduate at the University of Edinburgh which recently awarded him a D.Litt. for his contributions to the field. He has published widely, most recently together with Ruth Megaw, and their joint works include *Celtic Art from its beginnings to the Book of Kells* (1989) and *The Basse-Hutz (1927) Find: masterpieces of Celtic art* (1990).

Peter Northover is leader of the Materials Science-Based Archaeology Research Group in the Department of Materials, University of Oxford. He has made a particular study of bronze age and iron age gold and bronze, and has published widely on these subjects.

Stuart Piggott is Professor Emeritus of Archaeology at the University of Edinburgh, and a Fellow of the British Academy. He has published numerous books and articles on aspects of prehistory, including *The Earliest Wheeled Transport* (1983).

Glanville Price is a Research Professor in the Department of European Languages, University of Wales, Aberystwyth, where he was formerly Professor of French. From 1979–90 he was Chairman of the Committee of the Modern Humanities Research Association. His publications include *The Present Position of Minority Languages in Western Europe: a selective bibliography* (1969); *The French Language, Present and Past* (1971); *The Languages of Britain* (1984); *A Comprehensive French Grammar* (1986); and (as editor) *A Comprehensive French Grammar* (1988); and (as editor) *The Celtic Connection* (1992).

Barry Raftery is Associate Professor of Archaeology at University College, Dublin. He is a Member both of the Royal Irish Academy and of the German Archaeological Institute. He is also a Fellow of the Alexander von Humboldt Foundation. His principal publications include *A Catalogue of Irish Iron Age Antiquities* (1983); *Le Tène in Ireland* (1984) and *Pagan Celtic Ireland* (1994).

Ian Ralston is a Senior Lecturer in Archaeology and the Director of the Centre for Field Archaeology at Edinburgh University. He is the author of *Les enceintes fortifi[ae]ees du Limousin* (1992) and of a range of papers on the archaeology of France and Scotland. He was co-editor of *Archaeological Resource Management in the UK; an introduction* (1993) for the Institute of Field Archaeologists.

David Rankin is Professor of Ancient Philosophy at the University of Southampton. His publications include *Plato and the Individual* (1964); *Petronius the Artists* (1971); *Archilochus of Paros* (1978); *Sophists, Socratics and Cynics* (1983); *Antisthenes Sokratikos* (1986); and *Celts and the Classical World* (1987).

Mark Redknap gained his Ph.D. from the University of London in 1987, and is currently Medievalist of the Department of Archaeology and Numismatics at the National Museum of Wales, Cardiff. He has published articles on medieval artefacts, underwater archaeology, and the archaeology of the medieval period. Publications include *The Cattewater wreck; the investigation of an armed merchantman of the early 16th century* (1984); *Eifelkeramik and Mayen Ware; the Roman and medieval pottery industries of the Eifel* (1987); and *The Christian Celts: treasures of late Celtic Wales* (1991).

Peter J. Reynolds has been Director of the Butser Ancient Farm Project since its inception in 1972 to the present. He was Visiting Professor in the Department of Medieval History and Palaeography at the University of Barcelona (1993[-]4); and is a former Editor of the Archaeological Journal. He has published widely on prehistoric agriculture and experiment in archaeology, and is the author of *Iron Age Farm* (1979) and *Ancient Farming* (1987).

J.N.G. Ritchie is on the staff of the Royal Commission on the Ancient and Historical Monuments of Scotland, and Deputy Curator of the National Monuments Record of Scotland. His publications include joint authorship (with W.F. Ritchie) of the Shire book *Celtic Warriors* (1985).

W.F. Ritchie was formerly Principal Teacher of Classics and then Deputy Rector of Arbroath High School. He is a member of the Scottish Classics Group which produces the Latin Reading Course, *Ecce Romani*. He is co-author of *Celtic Warriors*.

Anne Ross was formerly a Senior Research Fellow at the School of Scottish Studies, Edinburgh University, and Research Fellow at the Department of Archaeology, University of Southampton. Her many publications include *Pagan Celtic Britain* (1967, reprinted 1992); she is actively pursuing research into aspects of Celtic religion.

Gerald A. Wait is Senior Archaeologist with Gifford and Partners, Chester. His doctoral research at Oxford culminated in *Ritual and Religion in Iron Age Britain* (1985). He has maintained his research interests in Celtic religion and Iron Age and Roman Britain, whilst working as a Consulting Archaeologist.

Graham Webster was a Reader and Senior Tutor in Archaeology in the Extra-Mural Department of the University of Birmingham. He is Honorary Vice-President of the Royal Archaeological Society and of the Council for British Archaeology. His seventeen books include *The Roman Imperial Army* (1985); and *The British Celts and their Gods under Rome* (1986).

Jane Webster gained her Ph.D. at the University of Edinburgh. She lectures at the School of Archaeological Studies, University of Leicester.

Colin Wells is T. Frank Murchison Distinguished Professor of Classical Studies and Chair of the Department of Classical Studies at Trinity University. San Antonio. He is the author of *The German Policy of Augustus* (1972) and *The Roman Empire* (2nd edn 1992). He has been excavating at Carthage since 1976, and has published many articles on Roman Gaul, Germany and Africa.

Peter S. Wells is Professor of Anthropology at the University of Minnesota. His recent publications include *Settlement, Economy, and Cultural Change at the End of the European Iron Age; excavations at Kelheim in Bavaria, 1987[-]1991* (1993).

PREFACE

———— •◆• ————

The Celts have long been the subject of intense interest and speculation not only in Britain, Ireland and the European continent, but worldwide. The purpose of this book is to present a collection of contributions by people who are currently in the forefront of Celtic research. With forty authors from all over the world, there is inevitably a diversity of approach, methodology and treatment which, to my mind, enriches and enlivens the subject: scholars from varied disciplines examine aspects of Celtic culture from the differing perspectives of archaeology, language, literature and anthropology.

The book is divided into twelve main sections, each comprising a major theme; every section is subdivided into chapters. Part I explores the origins of the continental Celts and the spread of their traditions over most of non-Mediterranean Europe. Miranda Green's introductory chapter examines the problems of how Celtic culture may be identified; David Ellis Evans looks at the evidence of early Celtic languages; and David Rankin discusses the way in which the Celts of the late first millennium BC are depicted through the media of classical art and literature.

Parts II–VIII are thematic in approach: in Part II, Graham and William Ritchie and Ian Ralston present the evidence for Celtic warfare, in terms of both the way armies functioned, and the different forms of defensive installation employed. In Part III, Timothy Champion discusses political organization and the hierarchical nature of society, while Glenys Lloyd-Morgan takes a closer look at the Celts themselves, the stereotype and reality of their appearance, and aspects of daily life. Barry Burnham's analysis shows how Celtic and Roman cultures interacted and merged to become a new, hybrid society. Parts IV and V explore environment, rural and urban settlement, trade and industry: Martin Bell sets the environmental scene and shows how it changed through time; John Collis examines the emergence of urban centres in the second and first centuries BC; and Peter Reynolds discusses rural life and its agricultural base. The latter chapter leads naturally to consideration of economic themes. Here, in Part V, Peter Wells contributes two chapters on the closely related subjects of resources, industry and trade; Daphne Nash Briggs examines the use of coinage both as a trading tool and as an indicator of the evolving relationship between classical and Celtic Europe; and Sean McGrail discusses the vital issue of how goods and people were transported. Parts VI and VII are concerned with technology, craftsmanship and Celtic art: bronze- and goldworking are examined by Peter Northover, whilst William Manning explores the extraction of iron and the blacksmith's craft. The use of wood for building and, in particular, for making vehicles is dealt with by Stuart Piggott. The craft of the Celtic potters is treated by Alex Gibson, who is especially interested in technological and artistic development. Ruth and Vincent Megaw discuss the enigma of Celtic art, its nature, function and interpretation; Martyn Jope concentrates on the Celtic artist; Sara Champion analyses the specific art forms associated with personal ornament, as found in both settlements and graves, and argues that such items are important not only intrinsically but as indicators of rank and relationships within society. In Part VIII Anne Ross discusses priests and aspects of ritual, including festivals; Jane Webster's chapter explores the concept of sacred space and, in particular, expresses doubts about the usual interpretation of the literary evidence. Miranda Green's survey of the evidence for divinities and for Celtic perceptions of the supernatural is balanced by Gerald Wait's examination of burial ritual and the implications that may be drawn from this material about beliefs concerning the dead and the afterlife.

The Celts in their different geographical settings are considered in Parts IX and X: in the former, Celtic settlement in Italy and Spain is discussed by Otto-Herman Frey and Majolie Lenerz-de Wilde respectively; surveys of the Celts in France and eastern Europe are presented by Olivier Büchsenschütz and Elizabeth Jerem; the problems of ethnicity in identifying the relationship between Celts and Germanic peoples in the Rhineland regions are explored by Colin Wells. Part X is concerned with the western Celts: here, the Britons under the influence of romanization are surveyed by Graham Webster but, by contrast, Barry Raftery looks at Ireland, an area virtually free from the overlay of Roman tradition. The evidence from Scotland and Wales, discussed by Euan Mackie and Jeffrey Davies respectively, presents aspects of Celtic culture in lands which were frontier zones, areas with a Roman military presence but never fully integrated into the Roman Empire.

Finally, although the central focus of the book deals with ancient Celtic Europe between 600 BC and AD 600, Parts XI and XII extend the chronological framework to examine Celtic culture in the early medieval period and to look at Celtic traditions in the modern world. In Part XI, Thomas Charles-Edwards explores the relationships both between language and nationality and between language and status among British and Irish Celts from AD 400 to AD 1000; he looks also at the wider perspective of connections between Britain/Ireland and the wider world. Mark Redknap specifically studies the evidence for early Christianity in the Celtic West, focusing upon religious centres and monuments. This chapter is balanced by appraisals of the vernacular mythological tradition in Wales and Ireland, presented by Sioned Davies and Proinsias Mac Cana. This mythic literature was compiled in the medieval period but draws on pagan material which may well incorporate pre-Christian oral tradition. The concluding section, Part XII, deals with present-day Celts: Wynne Lloyd discusses the inextricable links between language and Welsh identity from the perspective of a Welsh-speaking Welshman; Glanville Price surveys the six surviving Celtic languages, their respective status in modern culture and the dangers of their extinction. It is for the reader to decide whether or not it is possible to make links between the Celts of the first millennium BC and the present day.

Contributors have been given the freedom to approach their own subjects as they have wished, and no attempt has been made to introduce any kind of academic uniformity nor to impose the views of the editor: indeed, it is felt that the retention of individuality is an important aspect of a multi-author work of this kind. The different viewpoints of each writer mean that any points of overlap between contributions have caused no concerns over repetition. There is, too, a certain diversity in bibliographical referencing: most authors have adopted the Harvard system, but a few chapters are supported by footnotes. In addition, the varied nature of the disciplines involved means that, whilst the chapters which deal with archaeology and art may be fully illustrated, the more literary contributions often require little, if any, visual material.

I should like to offer my warmest thanks to all the authors for their valuable contributions, and to the staff at Routledge, particularly Andrew Wheatcroft, Moira Taylor, Diana Grivas, Joanne Tinson and Margaret Deith.

Miranda J. Green
June 1994

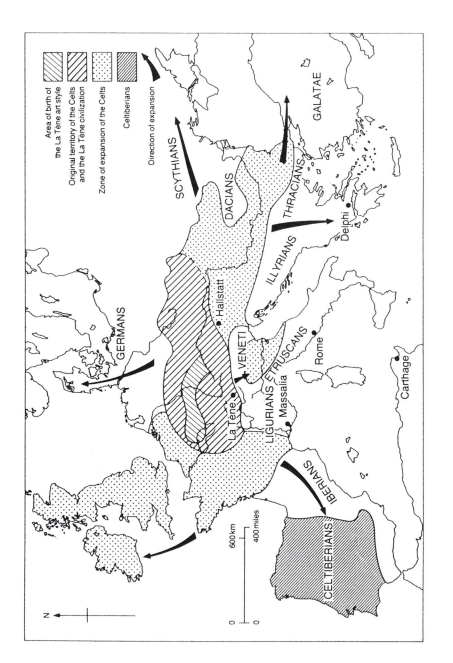

Figure 0.1 The territories occupied by Celts from the fifth century BC until the Roman conquest. (After R. and V. Megaw, *Celtic Art*, London:Thames & Hudson, 1989.)

PART I

CELTIC ORIGINS

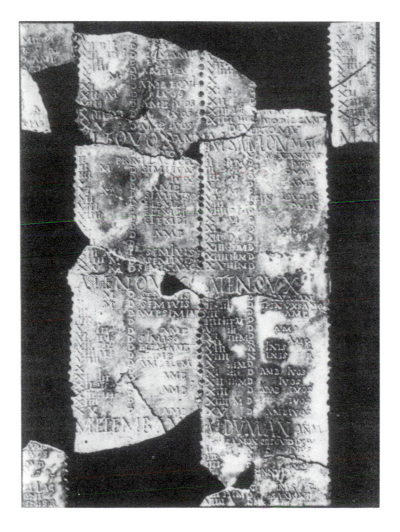

INTRODUCTION
Who were the Celts?

——— .◆. ———

Miranda J. Green

The decision to produce an international exploration of the Celtic world between 600 BC and AD 600 rests upon the premiss that the ancient Celts existed in some manner, whether self-defined or as a group of peoples who were classified as such by communities who belonged to a separate cultural – and literate – tradition. The area of temperate Europe north of the Alps and beyond the Mediterranean littoral generally referred to as Celtic was virtually non-literate until it came fully within the orbit of the classical world at the end of the first millennium BC. It was observers from the Mediterranean lands of Greece and Rome who called their northern neighbours Celts. But are we, as modern investigators, justified in speaking of the ancient inhabitants of 'barbarian' Europe as Celts? Who were the Celts? How should we define this term? It is interesting that the same questions do not tend to be asked of – say – the Roman world. We are secure with Romans because they identified themselves as such: *Civis Romanus sum* ('I am a Roman citizen'). We cannot tell whether a comparable Celtic consciousness ever existed.

It is pertinent to pose these questions in a survey such as this because the existence of Celts in any meaningful sense in antiquity continues to be a focus of controversy and debate. Many prehistorians (including some contributors to this volume) argue that it is spurious to identify iron age Europeans as Celts. Other investigators are more comfortable with this nomenclature, as long as its meaning is specifically defined. On the opposite pole to the sceptics are the committed Celticists who perceive a genuine continuity of tradition between the ancient peoples of northern Europe and the modern inhabitants of Ireland, Scotland, Wales, Cornwall, the Isle of Man and Brittany. The debate is active and well-nourished, and present contributors exhibit its diversity in both methodology and approach. No attempt has been made on the part of the editor to 'iron out' controversy or to present a unidirectional approach. It is important to reflect academic debate as it exists.

The problem of defining what is (or should be) meant by the terms 'Celt' and 'Celtic' centres around the relationship, if any, between material culture, ethnicity and language. Any construction of later prehistoric Europe is based upon information which is both fragmentary and ambiguous. The evidence is (like many Celtic gods) triple-headed and consists of archaeology, documentary sources and linguistic material. These three categories of evidence combine to present us with a Celtic world which, by the last few centuries BC, appears to have stretched from Ireland to eastern Europe and beyond, to Galatia (see map p. XXIV). The term 'Celts' is one to which we are introduced by Greek and Roman observers of their 'barbarian' neighbours north of the Alps. But did these people think of themselves as Celtic? Did they have an ethnic consciousness of themselves as possessing any kind of homogeneity within ancient Europe? With what degree of precision did Mediterranean commentators apply this descriptive label? Some scholars would argue that 'Celt' was maybe little more than a loose term for people different from those of the classical world: 'foreign', 'less civilized', 'marginal', 'fringe', 'other' people. Was there more to Celticness than that? In my opinion, this is an interesting but rather too extreme viewpoint: the Greek historian Herodotus made a clear distinction between those non-Greek peoples whom he called Celts and others, such as Scythians and Ethiopians. But the precision with which the term 'Celt' was used by writers from the Mediterranean world may well have varied widely: Herodotus, Livy and Caesar may well all be speaking of different groups even though they used the same word.

Classical commentators on the Celts reflected a school of thought in the Graeco-Roman world which appears to have recognized a group of peoples to their north as possessing sufficient cultural features in common to justify their endowment with a common name, the 'Celts'. We need to raise the question of how far we can trace this commonality of tradition in both archaeological evidence for material culture and in language. But for the moment let us remain with the contemporary documentary sources. Allusion is first made to Celts by name in the writings of such Greek historians as Hecataeus of Miletus in about 500 BC and Herodotus in the fifth century BC. These authors speak of *Keltoi*. Later Mediterranean writers such as Livy and Polybius chronicle the expansion of the Celts during the fourth and third centuries. These writers inform us that by the later third century BC the Celts were heavily defeated by the Romans and thereafter suffered a series of setbacks and reversals, until the Celtic heartlands of Gaul were annexed by the Romans in the mid-first century BC. Britain is never referred to by ancient authors as Celtic but Caesar recognized the similarities between Britain and Gaul. Tacitus and other Roman authors record the conquest of Britain, which was more or less complete by the later first century AD.

Early linguistic evidence for the Celts is extremely sparse before the Roman period because northern Europe was virtually non-literate during most of the first millennium BC. When writing was adopted in the Celtic world in the late first millennium, it appeared almost entirely in Greek or Latin. Early Celtic linguistic evidence, such as it is, consists of inscriptions, coin legends and the names of people and places contained within classical documents. These early sources suggest that by the time of the Roman occupation, at the end of the first millennium BC, Celtic languages were spoken in Britain, Gaul, north Italy, Spain, central and eastern Europe.

Material culture perhaps offers the best hope of approaching and identifying the ancient Celts. In archaeological terms, Celtic Europe is distinguished from previous prehistoric cultures by the adoption of iron as a commonly utilized metal. The archaeological record of later European prehistory suggests that the historical Celts (those named as such in documentary sources) may have had their origins within the cultures of the later Bronze Age. In terms of their archaeological presence, it does not make sense to think of the Celts as suddenly appearing on the European stage in the mid-first millennium BC. It is more likely that groups of people living in Europe became 'Celtic' by accretion, through process of time.

The material culture of central and northern Europe in the later Bronze Age of the mid–late second millennium BC is known to archaeologists as the 'Urnfield' tradition, a term derived from a distinctive burial rite in which some members of the population were cremated, their burnt bones being interred within pots, in flat cemeteries. In addition, this Urnfield tradition is characterized by the new ability of metalsmiths to fashion bronze into thin sheets which were formed into vessels, body-armour and shields. The new technology may have been stimulated by the collapse of the great hegemonies of southern Europe, namely the Mycenaean and Hittite Empires, the demise of which perhaps released onto the market large supplies of metal for central European use. The Urnfield tradition occurred widely in regions later occupied by iron age Celts and some scholars would go so far as to apply the label of 'proto-Celts' to the people to whom this Bronze Age culture belonged.

During the eighth century BC, new elements in material culture began to manifest themselves in central Europe. New metal types associated with horse-gear and riding are indicative of the presence of warrior-horsemen, who might be regarded as the antecedents of the Celtic *equites*, the horse-owning knights alluded to by Caesar in his *Gallic War*. These early iron age cavalrymen used long slashing swords, sometimes made of bronze, sometimes of iron. This new material culture has been called 'Hallstatt', after the so-called type-site, a great cemetery at Hallstatt in Austria, which housed the bodies of local people involved in salt-mining, trading and the control of the 'Salzkammergut' (salt-route) of the region around modern Hallein. This cemetery was first used during the later Bronze Age, but also produced large quantities of rich metalwork belonging to the earliest Iron Age. The same distinctive artefact-types found at Hallstatt have been recognized over wide areas of Europe. The bronze age material from the site has been designated Ha A and B and that of the Early Iron Age, Ha C and D. It is the material culture of the later Hallstatt, Iron Age, phases which is often considered to be the earliest evidence of the European Celts. This Hallstatt tradition is distinctive in the archaeological record for its wealth and its clear evidence for close trading links with the classical world. The upper echelons of society in the seventh and sixth centuries BC are represented by rich inhumation burials, like those of Hohmichele and Hochdorf in Germany and Vix in Burgundy, the dead often being interred in wooden mortuary houses, accompanied by four-wheeled wagons, weapons and luxury goods, including jewellery and feasting equipment, some of which came from the Mediterranean world. Little is known of the smaller settlements inhabited by these early iron age communities, but large fortified centres, like the Heuneburg near the Hohmichele grave and Mont Lassois near Vix, are presumed to have been the dwelling-places, and perhaps the power bases, of the high-ranking individuals buried nearby.

Archaeological evidence suggests that, by the early fifth century BC, the centres of power and wealth had shifted north and west to the Rhineland and the Marne. This may have occurred because, at a time when Etruria was becoming a major power, the trade-routes were perhaps reorientated to facilitate direct trading between the Celts and the Etruscans. This geographical shift is marked by the appearance of new elements in material culture, which archaeologists call La Tène, after the metal-work from the site of the same name on Lake Neuchâtel in Switzerland. Precious items of war-gear and other implements, together with animals, were deliberately deposited in the water over a long period, presumably as a series of votive acts. The La Tène phase of the European Iron Age demonstrates the presence of a warrior-aristocracy, some of whom were still buried with vehicles, but now with a light, two-wheeled cart or chariot replacing the heavy wagon of the later Hallstatt period. The La Tène tradition is above all characterized by a fine art, essentially an aristo-cratic art which was employed principally for the embellishment of metalwork. La Tène artists owed much to their Hallstatt forebears but they were also heavily influenced by themes and art forms from both the classical world and the Near East. Celtic art was dominated by abstract, geometric designs, but images from the natural world – foliage, animals and human faces – were often incorporated as integral components of these designs. The material culture of the La Tène phase represents the *floruit* of Celtic civilization. The archaeological record presents us with a picture of a heroic society in which war, feasting and display were important, a society which is recognizable as that alluded to by classical chroniclers of their 'Celtic' neighbours.

Celtic culture *per se* is generally considered to come to an end around the end of the first century BC, when most of temperate Europe was subjected to the domina-tion of the Roman world. The new hybrid culture resulting from the interaction between Roman and indigenous Celtic ideas retained many elements of pre-Roman tradition, whilst at the same time adopting new influences from Graeco-Roman Europe. The new 'Romano-Celtic' culture is nowhere better represented than by religious imagery which manifested itself in stone and other media. Here, Graeco-Roman iconographic traditions of depicting divine figures in human form were imported to Celtic lands and used by the native inhabitants of those regions to represent their own distinctive religious vision of the supernatural world. Deities essentially alien to the classical pantheon were now depicted for the first time in Gaul, the Rhineland, Britain and elsewhere, and the Celtic and Roman cult systems combined to form a rich, dynamic new Romano-Celtic religion.

It will be clear from the foregoing discussion that there are major problems in defining Celts and Celticness. The difficulties arise partly from the fact that 'Celts' and 'Celtic' are terms which mean different things to different people. The archaeo-logical approach to the Celtic question is different from that of the linguists and perhaps also from that of anthropologists. So the varied types of evidence at our disposal – archaeological, linguistic and literary – themselves cause problems of determination. The only way to deal with this conflict of approaches is to recognize that they are, to an extent, irreconcilable. There is a lack of congruence between language, material culture and ethnicity so that direct correlations cannot be made between the evidence for the distribution of language and that of archaeological indicators. It is equally impossible to make precise links between these categories of evidence and actual peoples. Ethnic boundaries are fluid, blurred and mutable; language cannot be used to define populations with any precision; specific artefacts and settlement types can spread through channels other than those of their use by ethnically definable groups. The three main categories of evidence for the ancient Celts may overlap or correlate in certain respects, but each contains its own parameters specific to itself.

Ancient literary sources, archaeological evidence and, to a lesser extent, language, all contrive to present us with a picture of a Celtic world which, in its heyday (the later first millennium BC), stretched from Ireland and Spain in the west and Scotland in the north to Czechoslovakia in the east and northern Italy in the south and even beyond Europe to Asia Minor. But we need to examine the nature of that Celtic culture and how it expanded from its original central European heartlands. When we speak of Celtic expansion over Europe, how far do we perceive this in terms of vast folk movements? Classical writers refer to marauding bands of Celts sacking Rome in the early fourth century BC, Delphi in the early third century, and to the establishment of the Celtic Galatians in Asia Minor at the same time. But some Celtic expansion was surely the result of the spread of fashions, ideas and traditions at least as much as of actual ethnic Celts.

A problem which is of the same order of magnitude as the origin of the Celts is what happened to this great European culture. The Roman Empire in the west disintegrated during the fifth century AD and with that collapse of centralized power the Celts also apparently disappeared from all but a few peripheral regions in the extreme west. The areas of Europe previously under Roman influence, and in which Celtic and Roman culture had merged, were overrun by a new Germanic culture which seems largely to have obliterated Celtic tradition in central Europe, Gaul and much of Britain. But it is questionable how different these 'free' Germanic peoples were, in ethnic terms, from the original Celts, although they spoke a different language. After the collapse of Roman power, the western areas that had been on the fringe of Celtic tradition became its focus and remain its focus: Ireland, Scotland, Wales and Brittany. Only there (together with Cornwall and the Isle of Man) did Celtic languages survive, and it is these areas which, during the later first and earlier second millennium AD, produced a vernacular Celtic mythic tradition on the one hand, and literary and archaeological evidence for early western Christianity on the other.

CHAPTER TWO

THE EARLY CELTS
The evidence of language

—— •❖• ——

D. Ellis Evans

The study of the testimony of language concerning the early Celts has in recent years reached a new and exciting stage of vitality, for all the difficulty and uncertainty surrounding the interpretation of a relatively high proportion of the extant sources. Work on the earliest Celtic linguistic data, both Continental and Insular, has been carried forward by a distinguished array of leading scholars. This interest reflects in part the continuing attraction of the earliest evidence available concerning the languages of the Celts of antiquity, the precursors of the modern Celtic languages. This interest has also been fired anew in part through the discovery of valuable new sources (especially fairly long inscriptions) which, by and large, have helped scholars to gain a better understanding of Old Celtic overall. We have had several fresh attempts at tracing the emergence and interrelationship of Celtic languages, both in general and in detail. We have also had a remarkable spate of scholarly writing reflecting the abiding concern for establishing new archaeo-linguistic models. Several of these have been applied to the world of the Celts, in the enduring quest for a clearer understanding of Celtic origins and the celticization of lands which came to be parts of that wide world.

I will admit at once that this scholarly activity has, by and large, not produced results that are generally acceptable and enlightening. The labyrinthine and frustrating nature of the subject discussed here must not be denied or disguised, for all the new insights gained from caring concentration on it. Its fascination and importance remain undiminished for both Celtic and non-Celtic scholars alike. It is, for all its hazards, significant for the study of linguistics and the early history (also to some extent the prehistory) and culture of Europe.

In this short section we can briefly describe only some of the relevant evidence and some of the ways in which it has been handled as part of the testimony concerning the early Celts.[1] I wish to stress at the outset that we would do well to heed the insistence of the social anthropologist, Edwin Ardener,[2] on how difficult it is to identify a people as 'part of an imaginary world' and, in relation to Celtic and other peoples, how 'the expropriation of an image of another is a puzzling thing', and also how (in Kirsten Hartrup's words) 'peoples are named and defined according to selected criteria, reflecting a semantic density centring around only a minority of the actual population'.[3]

When we consider in what way and to what extent the linguistic evidence of the
ancient world, concentrating on the linguistic evidence of Old Celtic, can play a role
in our understanding of the patterns observable in the fabric of society among Celtic
peoples, we have here to be ruthlessly restrained. However, we cannot avoid alluding
to some theoretical constructs, definitions, models and divisions of opinion and
we have to take account of some overpedantic, even misleading, studies of certain
language-related aspects of the history and culture of the Celts. There is no need
to repeat here comments made elsewhere on matters connected with the origins of
the Celts and the connotation and usage of the terms 'Celts' and 'Celtic', crucially
important though both of these topics must be.[4] Tied in with the question of the
ethnogenesis of the Celtic peoples are most difficult matters relating to nebulous
proto-cultures and proto-languages, the urge to locate old cradles or homelands
and to trace the spread and mix of peoples and of cultures probably over several
millennia. The great abundance of work published in recent years seeking to harmo-
nize the evidence of language and archaeology in relation to the so-called
Indo-European (and pre-Indo-European) complex and to evaluate various traditions,
myths and models, new and old, relating to that complex has not produced anything
approaching a consensus or convincing synthesis.[5] Lord Renfrew has interestingly
and frankly conceded that 'It is perhaps fair to say that the enterprise of relating
linguistic data to archaeological data is a more difficult one than has hitherto been
appreciated' and this for sure still applies in the area of Early Celtic studies.[6] Models
'acceptable to all parties' (to quote Dr Stefan Zimmer's phrase)[7] have not been
established. It is, in any case, a truism that the quest for the ultimate origin of a
particular language or particular groups or families of languages is futile if we have to
delve far into prehistory for our tentative answers.

The term 'Celtic' is at best vague and it has too easily, but improperly, been
claimed by some scholars that it should, strictly speaking, have a linguistic connotation only. It has been used in the modern period,[8] certainly, to denote a group or
family of languages surviving chiefly on the north Atlantic seaboard of Europe in
Scotland, Ireland, Wales and Brittany, but with related precursors attested over
far-flung tracts of territory the length and breadth of Europe in the ancient world.
It is well recognized that in the evidence preserved in epigraphic sources, graffiti,
coin legends, pottery and tile stamps, in the writings of historians and geographers,
ethnographers and naturalists and many others in antiquity, in contact languages and
in substrata in later languages, there is a very rich and greatly varied reflection of Old
Celtic languages, from Galatia in Asia Minor to Celtiberia in the Iberian peninsula,
from Italy (especially in the region of the north Italian lakes), Danubian or central
European regions and ancient Gaul to Britain and Ireland.

The date, range, density and quality of the evidence vary from area to area. A comprehensive analysis of this evidence has not hitherto been achieved, partly because
it is so varied and extensive and partly because it is not always securely identified or
(for various reasons) securely analysed. Nevertheless, in recent decades scholars have
been inclined to attach names to particular areas or groupings of evidence, especially
for Continental Celtic.[9] There has been the view that we can identify fairly securely
some variant Celtic languages for continental Europe. This is true, up to a point. But
these variants have had certain tags overconfidently attached to them. The name

Gaulish is sometimes made to embrace both Cisalpine and Transalpine Gaulish, although it is now fashionable (but somewhat misleading or unfruitful) to separate out, for northern Italy, a Lepontic or Luganian sector and (less commonly) for Transalpine Gaul sectors or variants such as Narbonensian and Aquitanian. For Hispano-Celtic the term 'Celtiberian' finds favour for an area of Celtic linguistic prominence or concentration in central Spain, especially along the upper and middle reaches of the rivers Douro and Tagus, and the name 'Lusitanian' is used for a more westerly area (this is applied to a range of sources concerning the Celticity of which there has been a lot of controversy). 'Galatian' is used for the Celtic of Asia Minor. The identification of Celtic in central and eastern Europe and in the Balkans is problematic, not least because it is scanty and limited to proper names; the manipulation of Roman imperial province names here for the identification of Celtic and other contact languages is probably unavoidable, but it is by and large unrewarding.[10]

Leo Weisgerber's claim[11] that we should exercise caution in many cases before we allocate epigraphic sources to particular languages is still valid. We should also heed Michel Lejeune's warning[12] that in speaking of Celtiberian, Gaulish and Lepontic (these are the three dominant identifying tags) we can only speak very generally of the languages or dialects of particular groups of people who used in various sites or areas various alphabets (forms of the Iberian, Etruscan, Greek and Latin alphabets in continental Europe) in their inscriptions and that we really cannot speak (even for the Celts of the Iberian peninsula or of ancient Gaul) of people constituting 'groupes d'une complète unité linguistique'. This is the case in spite of the discovery during the last twenty-five years or so of a number of relatively long inscriptions, especially in Gaul and Celtiberia, which are demonstrably Celtic and (for all their difficulty) valuable because of the quite considerable amount of additional information they provide.

At best the earliest linguistic evidence concerning the Celts reflects fragmentary languages.[13] But it would be wrong nowadays to accept Zeuss's statement that we cannot hope to find linguistic variation in this early evidence.[14] That there were divergences or cleavages in a linguistic group attested over such a wide area is not surprising, however partial or unsatisfactory our demonstration of the differences observed up to now continues to be.

The broad division of the Celtic family of languages into Continental and Insular sectors is still, in my opinion, essentially a convenient geographical one, despite all the interconnections bridging that general divide which have been viewed by scholars in various ways. Here we should note that the Breton language is usually regarded as being an Insular Brittonic language, although the case has been argued in various ways for recognizing in it the partial survival of a northern or north-western form of Gaulish.[15] The ways in which scholars view the status of Insular Celtic as distinct from Continental Celtic should have an important bearing on our understanding of the emergence and interrelationship of Celtic languages, of the proper approach to the interpretation of early Celtic linguistic evidence overall, and indeed our perception of the relationship of Celtic to other Indo-European and non-Indo-European or pre-Celtic languages.[16]

There is disagreement on the nature and significance of the Continental/Insular Celtic linguistic divide. This stems in part from the different range of evidence available for each sector and in part from the fact that the Insular evidence, by and large – and this holds true even for the earliest sources – belongs to a considerably later date than the bulk of the primary Continental sources, the earliest of which take us back several centuries BC.[17] Also a lot of the Continental evidence (especially recently discovered inscriptions such as those of Botorrita, Peñalba de Villastar, Chamalières, Lezoux and Larzac) provides a fuller range of evidence, for all the uncertainty still surrounding many readings, formations and patterns, than has hitherto emerged from the very earliest Insular records, and this information relates to syntax as well as phonology and morphology.[18]

Professor Karl Horst Schmidt has on several occasions sought to establish the order of emergence of the individual Celtic languages and indeed tried to demonstrate the means whereby one can exploit the evidence of individual Celtic languages in order to reconstruct some of the features of a notional Proto-Celtic.[19] Relying especially on his view of the well-known development of the Indo-European labio-velar $*k^w$ (and the cluster $*kw$) and the more controversial patterning of the development of the Indo-European syllabic nasals in Celtic languages he has assumed that Goidelic (the parent language of Irish) and Celtiberian broke away from Proto-Celtic before the change of the labio-velar $*k^w$ to the bilabial $*p$ in other parts of the Celtic linguistic domain. Evidence of the sporadic preservation of the labio-velar in Gaulish is thought of as 'basically archaic'. He also concedes that this is in part a mark of the 'dialectal diversity of ancient Gaul'. He sees an opposition between what he believes to be a change of the Indo-European syllabic nasals $*\m$, $*\n$ into Goidelic $*em$, $*en$, ($*im$, $*in$) as distinct from Gallo-Brittonic and Celtiberian $*am$, $*an$. In this highly selective analysis, controversial in itself, it is claimed that the supposed 'unique development of the vocalic nasals is Goidelic' means that 'this language was the first to break away from Proto-Celtic'. Moreover, Schmidt affirms that we can recognize the character of Proto-Celtic, up to a point, insofar as 'any Indo-European archaism preserved in one or other of the Celtic languages must have been a feature of Proto-Celtic as well' and that the identification of innovations shared by Celtic and other Indo-European languages mark them off as features of Proto-Celtic. Part of the trouble with this analysis is that it does not question the validity of the concept of a reconstructed Proto-Celtic language or model, and, more seriously, that it makes too few more or less controversial analyses of certain phonological features carry too much weight in the urge to perceive the 'order of emergence of the individual Celtic languages'.[20]

V.P. Kalygin and A.A. Korolev have taken a different stance on this front in their consideration of what they have termed 'The classification of the Celtic languages'.[21] They stress that 'the differences between the Insular and Continental Celtic languages cannot be explained by built-in differences in an original linguistic structure', that these differences do not 'enable us to judge whether the Insular Celtic languages had a single source or several' and that 'it is difficult to find any individual criterion on whose foundation one might build a single classification for all Celtic languages'. Although they declare their interest in *Ursprachen* and Common Languages they rightly reject the concept of a monolithic kind of early Celtic linguistic unity ('without any signs of dialectal articulation'). On the other hand they, to my mind, strangely favour a panorama in which 'Disagreement over the reconstruction of particular features of the Ursprache should not be discouraged, because even an idealized model reconstruction should not be deprived of the features present in any living language'.[22]

Schmidt's quest for criteria to enable us to recognize the order of emergence of the historically attested Celtic languages has attracted considerable attention, interesting with regard to methodology and important for our subject. Professor Oswald Szemerényi remarked on the fragility of views concerning the incidence of a vocalic element *a* and *e* in the development of the syllabic nasals.[23] This criticism has been embroidered of late by Professor Kim McCone.[24] He has been obliged to concede that the testimony of the termination of the Gaulish form δεκαντεμ (/-εν) (acc. sing.) 'tithe'[25] may still be anomalous, not to say decisive, in his detailed review of the development of the syllabic nasals in Celtic. The development of $*k^w$ to $*p$ (altogether characteristic of both British and Gaulish) is dismissed by him a little too summarily as being 'not at all reliable as a criterion for the genetic classification of Celtic languages'. He plausibly assumes that Celtic (*recte* British?) Britain received its *p*-isogloss (structurally motivated, as he thinks) from northern Gaul, possibly through Belgic incursions in the second or third century BC. For McCone the occurrence of the change $*k^w > *p$ 'in both Gaulish and British falls well short of necessarily implying a Gallo-British subfamily, from which Irish must then have already separated at some earlier stage'.[26] He has consistently tended to favour the view that there was at one time a Common Insular Celtic (he has not declared any good reason for arguing that there was a Common Continental Celtic, and this is understandable). For me McCone's argument is inconclusive[27] and seems to strain overmuch to see patterns in Insular Celtic evidence inherited from an underlying commonality pre-dating the separating out of Goidelic and British (e.g. in the augment morphology of the verb, in the absolute/conjunct contrast in verb forms and in the Old Irish and Brittonic *s*-preterite forms – all concentrating on morphology), with patterns allegedly distinct from those reflected in the Continental Celtic evidence hitherto available.[28] He then claims that this indicates that the notional Common Celtic from which this alleged dialectal split, which he claims we have here, arose must be assumed to have been in place a long time before the historically attested 'Gaulish' migrations to the south and west in the fifth century BC. This kind of allure, favouring an early Insular/Continental linguistic divergence or split, should be approached with all due caution. The dating of the divergence is bound to be uncertain (it must precede the earliest attested linguistic evidence) and the overriding notion of a Common Celtic subsumed by it all is, for me, vague and unsatisfactory.[29] McCone's hypothesis that 'within the Celtic family Irish and British are particularly closely related through a shared Insular Celtic intermediary'[30] is in no way surprising and should not be discounted. But it is uncertain. There is no way of proving or disproving it on the basis of the linguistic evidence available to us.

Moreover, McCone sees no difficulty in claiming that 'the "La Tène" migrations into North Italy and along the Danube as far as Asia Minor from the fifth to the third centuries BC are more correctly considered Gaulish [than Celtic]' and that this phase was preceded by 'Celtic migrations westwards and northwards to Spain, France, Belgium and Britain' entailing 'the spread of a Gaulish variety of Celtic certainly characterized by *p* for k^w from a centre not far north of the Alps'. After positing the spread of the *p* (> *kʷ*) isogloss to Celtic Britain from northern Gaul (spreading throughout British Celtic), he suggests that it was 'prevented from going further by the Irish Sea rather as the barrier of the Pyrenees hindered its penetration from Gaul into Spain'.[31] This is a quite risky analysis and appears to stem in part from the questionable view that we can identify a commonality of language in various areas of the Celtic terrain in late prehistory or in the early historic period. Comparable with McCone's approach, but differently argued, is Professor John T. Koch's revision of his 1983 Oxford Celtic Congress paper in a paper in the Léon Fleuriot Festschrift,[32] in which he argues that Celtic speech was established in Ireland and Britain 'very early in the Iron Age, before the penetration of La Tène influences' (here he relies heavily on an ingenious reconsideration of the significance of the earliest place and ethnic names) and assumes a gradual separating out of the languages of Britain and Gaul. He too claims that the archaeologists' 'La Tène' influences correspond to what the linguists would term 'Gallicization'. He has now distanced himself from the view that European mainland iron age proto-languages (later than Proto-Celtic) are a significant factor in divergences from Gaulish in what he calls 'the Insular Celtic phenomenon'.

My discussion has in part drawn particular and deliberate attention to some of the recent proliferation of generally inconclusive hypotheses and syntheses based on some of the earliest extant evidence concerning the Celtic languages.[33] However, I am certain that the commitment of so many scholars to contribute towards a more reliable and comprehensive analysis of this evidence indicates a growing awareness of its primacy and importance. Those who are well informed about it know that it can no longer be said to be insubstantial or arid. Recent detailed work on it includes, for example, discussion of the local and ethnic names of Roman Britain, the language of early British coin legends, a whole range of aspects of the study of Ogam inscriptions, the gathering in and careful editing of large corpora of primary sources, detailed discussion of a host of often very difficult texts, the study of various early epigraphic traditions, the development of mixed languages and the erosion and demise of Old Celtic in so many areas. All this work has added much to our knowledge of early Celtic linguistic patterns. It has shown anew, more often than not in confirmatory fashion, the wide dispersion of speakers of Celtic languages in antiquity. Increasingly it has revealed for the first time comparatively early linguistic features which could not be recovered by processes of linguistic reconstruction from the study of later sources.

The complex early linguistic evidence is of great importance. It is a vital part of our knowledge of the early history and culture of the Celts and, treated cautiously and critically alongside the testimony of so many other sources, it greatly enriches our understanding of that many-faceted history and culture.

NOTES

1   Here I can note only a small selection of references to general surveys relevant for our
    discussion: de Bernardo Stempel 1991; Eska and Evans 1993; Evans 1977, 1979, 1983a,
    1983b, 1988, 1990, 1992b, 1993; Fleuriot 1981, 1988, 1991; de Hoz 1986, 1988; Kalygin and

Korolev 1989; Koch 1983a, 1983b, 1985, 1992; Lambert 1994; McCone 1991a, 1991b, 1992; McManus 1991; Meid 1989a, 1989b, 1992; 1993; Schmidt 1977a, 1977b, 1979, 1981, 1983, 1988a, 1990a, 1990b, 1993; Tovar 1986, 1987; Untermann 1983. This highly selective list has, perforce, been limited to some recent work only.

2   See Ardener 1989: 217.

3   In Ardener 1989: 226.

4   See, for example, Evans 1988, 1992.

5   See, *inter alios*, Gamkrelidze and Ivanov 1984, 1990; Mallory 1989; Markey and Greppin 1990; Meid 1989b; Zimmer 1990a, 1990b.

6   In Markey and Greppin 1990: 24.

7   In Markey and Greppin 1990: 338. See also Zimmer 1990a and 1990b.

8   On the identification of Celtic, also on the rise of modern Celticism, see Evans 1992b and 1993.

9   There are similar difficulties with early Insular Celtic. See, for example, Evans 1990; Schmidt 1993.

10 See especially Evans 1979: 511–23 on some of the problems connected with the identification and labelling of early Celtic linguistic areas. For Hispano-Celtic see, for example, Schmidt 1976; Gorrochategui 1991; Evans 1993.

11 See Weisgerber 1931: 173; 1969: 33f.

12 See Lejeune 1971: 122f.; 1972a: 265; 1972b.

13 On fragmentary languages see Untermann 1980.

14 See Zeuss 1871: vi.

15 See especially Fleuriot 1978, 1980, 1981, 1982, 1991; Fleuriot and Giot 1977; Evans 1979: 525; Schmidt 1992: 193f. For the views of Falc'hun see also Jackson 1967: 30–2.

16 The complex question of relationship with non-Indo-European and probably pre-Celtic languages cannot be faced here. See Wagner 1959, 1969, 1976, 1977, 1982, 1987; Evans 1983b: 951–4; Kalygin and Korolev 1989: 20f.; Shisha-Halevy forthcoming: chapter 4, section 7 ('Celtic typology and affinities: a personal standpoint').

17 The dating of the continental evidence overall is uncertain. For a general statement see Lejeune 1972a: 266 (see also 265); Lambert 1985.

18 Here one has to be exceedingly careful as to what one regards as the earliest Insular evidence. For all the challenging work on archaisms in relatively early Insular sources (e.g. work on early Welsh poetry and on Archaic and Early Old Irish), the difference in date of these sources from that of so many of the most important Continental Celtic sources needs to be recognized and respected more than it has been in some recent work in the quest to set up new linguistic syntheses. See, for example, Evans 1990; Koch 1992; Schmidt 1993.

19 See, for example, Schmidt 1976, 1977a, 1980, 1986a, 1988b.

20 I quote here from Schmidt 1988a: 235–6.

21 See Kalygin and Korolev 1989: 6. I am much indebted to Mr David Howells for his kind permission to quote from his full English version of Kalygin and Korolev's work.

22 See Kalygin and Korolev 1989: 8–9.

23 See Szemerényi 1978: 296.

24 See McCone 1991a, 1992.

25 This form, on which there is by now an extensive literature, was first identified by Professor Oswald Szemerényi in a brilliant resegmentation of an Old Gaulish formula (see Szemerényi 1974).

26 See McCone 1991a: 50; also 1992. McCone has consistently tended to favour the view that there is a fundamental division between Insular and Continental Celtic. Warren Cowgill had placed some emphasis on the distinctive character of Insular Celtic in general in his

renowned 1973 Regensburg discussion of 'The Insular Celtic conjunct and absolute verbal endings' (see Cowgill 1975). With regard to the very complex issue of determining the relative importance of particular features and trends in languages in connection with Celtic (in relation to both internal and external relationships) the picture we have, for all the attempts at refinement, is still blurred and in general unsatisfactory. Here I refer only to Schmidt 1986a, 1986b, 1986c, 1988a; McCone 1991a, 1991b, 1992; Kalygin and Korolev 1989; 27–44 (see especially 27).

27 The additional evidence adduced in Professor McCone's Leiden lecture (see McCone 1992) is, it seems to me, too limited and may again be underplaying the significance of the earlier Continental Celtic evidence (not only in its archaisms but also in some secure and close correspondences with the testimony of Insular Celtic).

28 The differences in location and date and genre of various Continental Celtic sources are important and the same is true for Insular Celtic, but they all need to be used in conjunction with each other (and with relevant evidence in other languages) whenever that produces coherent and/or enlightening results. For just one recent instance of a highly sophisticated exploitation of a very full range of Celtic evidence by McCone, seeking to relate that evidence to its ancestry in notional earlier phases (postulated with the vital additional aid of the testimony of other non-Celtic languages), see McCone 1991b: 115–36 (chapter 6: 'Old Irish *beith*, *-bé*, Gaulish *bueti(d)* and the Old Indic root-aorist subjunctive *bhúvat*'). Compare McCone 1986.

29 We should recall Wagner's by no means mischievous comment again, that

> The basic error of comparative grammar is the reconstruction of undivided or homogeneous *Common Languages* or *Ursprachen*. In reality language or dialect diversity is always primary, while language unity is the secondary result either of the expansion of a language over wider territories or the creation of an oral literary standard language.
>
> (see Wagner 1969: 228, n.9a)

30 See McCone 1991a: 69.

31 See ibid.: 49–50.

32 See Koch 1992. Compare also now Waddell 1991a and 1991b.

33 My views on the great value of so much of this complex and tantalizing evidence and on the need for delicacy and caution in dealing with them in general syntheses (see, for example, Evans 1979: 536–7; 1990: 172–7) remain essentially unchanged.

REFERENCES

Ardener, E. (1989) *The Voice of Prophecy and Other Essays*, ed. M. Chapman, Oxford: Basil Blackwell.

Bammesberger, A. and Wollmann, A. (eds) (1990) *Britain 400–600: language and history*, Heidelberg: Carl Winter.

Beekes, R., Lubotsky, A. and Weitenberg, J. (eds) (1992) *Rekonstruktion und relative Chronologie. Akten der VIII. Fachtagung der indogermanischen Gesellschaft. Leiden, 31. August–4. September 1987*, Innsbrucker Beiträge zur Sprachwissenschaft 65, Innsbruck: Institut für Sprachwissenschaft der Universität Innsbruck.

de Bernardo Stempel, P. (1991) 'Die Sprache altbritannischer Münzlegenden', *Zeitschrift für celtische Philologie* 44: 36–55.

Campanile, E. (ed.) (1983) *Problemi di lingua e di cultura nel campo indoeuropeo*, Pisa: Giardini.

Cowgill, W. (1975) 'The origins of the Insular Celtic conjunct and absolute verbal endings', in H. Rix (ed.) *Flexion und Wortbildung. Akten der V. Fachtagung der Indogermanischen Gesellschaft. Regensburg 9.–14. September 1973*, Wiesbaden: Dr Ludwig Reichert, 40–70.

Eska, J.F. (1989) *Towards an Interpretation of the Hispano-Celtic Inscription of Botorrita*, Innsbrucker Beiträge zur Sprachwissenschaft 59, Innsbruck: Institut für Sprachwissenschaft der Universität Innsbruck.

Eska, J.F. and Evans, D.E. (1993) 'Continental Celtic', in M.J. Ball and J. Fife (eds) *The Celtic Languages*, London: Routledge.

Evans, D.E. (1977) 'The contribution of (non-Celtiberian) Continental Celtic to the reconstruction of the Celtic "Grundsprache"', in K.H. Schmidt (ed.) *Indogermanisch und Keltisch*, 66–88.

—— (1979) 'The labyrinth of Continental Celtic', *Proceedings of the British Academy* 65: 497–538.

—— (1983a) 'Continental Celtic and linguistic reconstruction', in G. Mac Eoin with A. Ahlqvist and D. Ó hAodha (eds) *Proceedings of the Sixth International Congress of Celtic Studies (University College, Galway, 6–13 July 1979)*, Dublin: Dublin Institute for Advanced Studies, 19–54.

—— (1983b) 'Language contact in pre-Roman and Roman Britain', in W. Haase (ed.) *Aufstieg und Niedergang*, 949–87.

—— (1986) 'The Celts in Britain (up to the formation of the Brittonic languages): history, culture, linguistic remains, substrata', in K.H. Schmidt (ed.) *Geschichte und Kultur der Kelten*, 102–15.

—— (1988) 'Celtic origins', in G.W. MacLennan (ed.) *Proceedings*, 209–22.

—— (1990) 'Insular Celtic and the emergence of the Welsh language', in A. Bammesberger and A. Wollmann (eds) *Britain 400–600*, 149–77.

—— (1992a) 'Ar drywydd y Celtiaid', in G.H. Jenkins (ed.) *Cof Cenedl* VII, Ysgrifau ar Hanes Cymru, Llandysul: Gwasg Gomer, 1–30.

—— (1992b) 'Celticity, identity, and the study of language – fact, speculation, and legend', *Archaeologia Cambrensis* 140: 1–16.

—— (1993) 'The identification of Continental Celtic with special reference to Hispano-Celtic', in F. Villar (ed.), *Actas del V coloquio sobre lenguas y culturas prerromanas de la península ibérica, Köln, 25.–29. September 1989*, Salamanca: Universidad de Salamanca, 545–90.

Evans, D.E., Griffith, J.G. and Jope, E.M. (eds) (1986) *Proceedings of the Seventh International Congress of Celtic Studies Held at Oxford, from 10th to 15th July, 1983*, Oxford: D. Ellis Evans.

Fleuriot, L. (1978) 'Brittonique et Gaulois durant les premiers siècles de notre ère', in *Étrennes de septantaine. Travaux de linguistique et de grammaire comparée offerts à Michel Lejeune par un groupe de ses élèves*, Paris: Klincksiek, 75–83.

—— (1980) *Les Origines de la Bretagne. L'émigration*, Paris: Payot (2nd edn 1982).

—— (1981) 'Du gaulois au breton ancien en Armorique', *Bulletin de la Société Archéologique du Finistère* 109: 165–94.

—— (1982) 'Toponymes contenant des dérivés de *Brittanus, Britto* . . . ', *Etudes Celtiques* 19: 259–61.

—— (1988) 'New documents on ancient Celtic and the relationship between Brittonic and Continental Celtic', in G.W. MacLennan (ed.) *Proceedings*, 223–30.

—— (1991) 'Celtoromanica in the light of the newly discovered Celtic inscriptions', *Zeitschrift für celtische Philologie* 44: 1–35.

Fleuriot, L. and Giot, P.-R. (1977) 'Early Brittany', *Antiquity* 51: 106–16.

Gamkrelidze, T.V. and Ivanov, V.V. (1984) *Indoevropejskij jasyk i Indoevropejcy. Rekonstrukcija i istoriko-tipologičeskij analiz prajasyka i protokul'tury*, Tbilisi: Tbilisskogo University.

—— (1990) 'The early history of Indo-European languages', *Scientific American* (March): 82–9.

Gorrochategui, J. (1991) 'Descripción y posición lingüística del celtibérico', in J.A. Lakarra and I.R. Arzallus (eds) *Anejos del Anuario del Seminario de Filología Vasca 'Julio de Urquijo'* 14, Memoriae L. Mitxelena magistri sacrum, Donostia: Gipuzkoako Foru Aldundia/San Sebastian: Diputación Foral de Gipuzkoa, 3–31.

Gorrochategui, J., Melena, J.L. and Santos, J. (eds) (1987) *Studia palaeohispanica. Actas del IV coloquio sobre lenguas y culturas paleohispánicas (Vitoria/Gasteiz, 6–10 mayo 1985)*, Vitoria/Gasteiz: Victoriaco Vasconum.

Haase, W. (ed.) (1983) *Aufstieg und Niedergang der römischen Welt*, II: *Principat* 29.2, Berlin: Walter de Gruyter.

de Hoz, J. (1986) 'La epigrafía celtibérica', in G. Fatás (ed.) *Actas de la reunión sobre epigrafía hispánica de época romano-republicana (Zaragoza, 1–3 de diciembre de 1983)*, Zaragoza: Consejo Superior de Investigaciones Científicas, 43–102.

—— (1988) 'Hispano-Celtic and Celtiberian', in G.W. MacLennan (ed.) *Proceedings*, 191–207.

Jackson, K.H. (1967) *A Historical Phonology of Breton*, Dublin: Dublin Institute for Advanced Studies.

Jordá, F., de Hoz, J. and Michelena, L. (eds) (1976) *Actas del I coloquio sobre lenguas y culturas prerromanas de la península ibérica (Salamanca, 27–31 mayo 1974)*, Salamanca: Ediciones Universidad de Salamanca.

Kalygin, V.P. and Korolev, A.A. (1989) *Vvedenie v kel'tskuju filologiju*, Moscow: Nauka.

Koch, J.T. (1983a) 'The sentence in Gaulish', *Proceedings of the Harvard Celtic Colloquium* 3: 169–215.

—— (1983b) 'The loss of final syllables and loss of declension in Brittonic', *Bulletin of the Board of Celtic Studies* 30: 201–33.

—— (1985) 'Movement and emphasis in the Gaulish sentence', *Bulletin of the Board of Celtic Studies* 32: 1–37.

—— (1992) '"Gallo-Brittonic" vs. "Insular Celtic": the inter-relationships of the Celtic languages reconsidered', in G. Le Menn (ed.) *Bretagne et pays celtiques: langues, histoire, civilisation. Mélanges offerts à la mémoire de Léon Fleuriot 1923–1987*, Rennes: Presses Universitaires Rennes/Skol: Saint Brieuc, 471–95.

Lambert, P.-Y. (1985) 'A propos des inscriptions gauloises récemment découvertes', *Celtic Cultures Newsletter* 3: 19–24.

—— (1994) *La langue gauloise. Description linguistique, commentaire et inscriptions choisies*, Paris: Editions Errance.

Lejeune, M. (1971) *Lepontica*, Paris: Société d'Editions 'Les Belles Lettres' [(1970–1) 'Documents gaulois et para-gaulois de Cisalpine', *Etudes Celtiques* 12: 357–500].

—— (1972a) 'Celtibère et lépontique', in *Homenaje a Antonio Tovar*, Madrid: Gredos, 265–71.

—— (1972b) 'Un problème de nomenclature: lépontiens et lépontique', *Studi Etruschi* 40: 259–69.

McCone, K. (1986) 'From Indo-European to Old Irish: conservation and innovation in the verbal system', in D.E. Evans, J.G. Griffith and E.M. Jope (eds) *Proceedings*, 222–66.

—— (1991a) 'The PIE stops and syllabic nasals in Celtic', *Studia Celtica Japonica* 4: 37–69.

—— (1991b) *The Indo-European Origins of the Old Irish Nasal Presents, Subjunctives and Futures*, Innsbrucker Beiträge zur Sprachwissenschaft 66, Innsbruck: Institut für Sprachwissenschaft der Universität Innsbruck.

—— (1992) 'Relative Chronologie: Keltisch', in R. Beekes, A. Lubotsky and J. Weitenberg (eds) *Rekonstruktion und relative Chronologie*, 11–39.

MacLennan, G.W. (ed.) (1988) *Proceedings of the First North American Congress of Celtic*

Studies (Ottawa, 26–30 March 1986), Ottawa: Chair of Celtic Studies of the University of Ottawa.

McManus, D. (1991) *A Guide to Ogam*, Maynooth Monographs 4, Maynooth: An Sagart.

Mallory, J.P. (1989) *In Search of the Indo-Europeans. Language, archaeology and myth*, London: Thames & Hudson.

Markey, T.L. and Greppin, J.A.C. (eds) (1990) *When Worlds Collide: Indo-Europeans and pre-Indo-Europeans*, Linguistica Extranea, Studia 19, Ann Arbor: Karoma.

Meid, W. (1989a) *Zur Lesung und Deutung gallischer Inschriften*, Innsbrucker Beiträge zur Sprachwissenschaft: Vorträge und kleinere Schriften 40, Innsbruck: Institut für Sprachwissenschaft der Universität Innsbruck.

—— (1989b) *Archäologie und Sprachwissenschaft. Kritisches zu neueren Hypothesen der Ausbreitung der Indogermanen*, Innsbrucker Beiträge zur Sprachwissenschaft: Vorträge und kleinere Schriften 43, Innsbruck: Institut für Sprachwissenschaft der Universität Innsbruck.

—— (1992) *Gaulish Inscriptions: their interpretation in the light of archaeological evidence and their value as a source of linguistic and sociological information*, Archaeollingua, Series Minor 1, Budapest: Archaeological Institute of the Hungarian Academy of Sciences and the Linguistic Institute of the University of Innsbruck.

—— (1993) *Die erste Botorrita-Inschrift. Interpretation eines keltiberischen Sprachdenkmals*, Innsbrucker Beiträge zur Sprachwissenschaft 76, Innsbruck: Institut für Sprachwissenschaft der Universität Innsbruck.

Rivet, A.L.F. and Smith, C. (1979) *The Place-Names of Roman Britain*, London: Batsford.

Schmidt, K.H. (1976) 'The contribution of Celt-Iberian to the reconstruction of Common Celtic', in F. Jordá, J. de Hoz and L. Michelena (eds) *Actas del I coloquio*, 329–42.

—— (1977a) *Die festlandkeltischen Sprachen*, Innsbrucker Beiträge zur Sprachwissenschaft: Vorträge 18, Innsbruck: Institut für Sprachwissenschaft der Universität Innsbruck (1979) 'On the Celtic languages of continental Europe', *Bulletin of the Board of Celtic Studies* 28: 189–205.

—— (ed.) (1977b) *Indogermanisch und Keltisch*, Colloquium of the Indogermanische Gesellschaft am 16. und 17. Februar 1976 in Bonn, Wiesbaden: Dr Ludwig Reichert.

—— (1980) 'Continental Celtic as an aid to the reconstruction of Proto-Celtic', *Zeitschrift für vergleichende Sprachforschung* 90: 172–97.

—— (1981) 'The Gaulish inscription of Chamalières', *Bulletin of the Board of Celtic Studies* 29: 256–68.

—— (1983) 'Grundlagen einer festlandkeltischen Grammatik', in E. Vineis (ed.) *Le lingue indoeuropee di frammentaria attestazione: die indogermanischen Restsprachen*, Proceedings of the conference of the Società Italiana di Glottologia and of the Indogermanische Gesellschaft (Udine, 22–24 septembre 1981), Pisa: Giardini, 65–90.

—— (1986a) 'The Celtic languages in their European context', in D.E. Evans, J.G. Griffith and E.M. Jope (eds) *Proceedings*, 199–221.

—— (1986b) 'Zur Rekonstruktion des Keltischen. Festlandkeltisches und inselkeltisches Verbum', *Zeitschrift für celtische Philologie* 41: 159–79.

—— (ed.) (1986c) *Geschichte und Kultur der Kelten*, Vorbereitungskonferenz 25–28 October in Bonn, *Vorträge*, Heidelberg: Carl Winter.

—— (1988a) 'On the reconstruction of Proto-Celtic', in G.W. MacLennan (ed.) *Proceedings*, 231–48.

—— (1988b) 'Zu den phonologischen Differenzierungmerkmalen in den keltischen Sprachen', *Studia Celtica Japonica* 1: 1–12.

—— (1990a) 'Late British', in A. Bammesberger and A. Wollmann (eds) *Britain 400–600*, 121–48.

—— (1990b) 'Gallo-Brittonic or Insular Celtic', in F. Villar (ed.) *Studia indogermanica*, 255–67.

—— (1992) 'La romanité des îles britanniques', in D. Kremer (ed.) *Actes du XVIIIᵉ Congrès International de Linguistique et de Philologie Romanes* I, Université de Trèves (Trier) 1986, Tübingen: Max Niemeyer, 188–210.

—— (1993) 'Insular Celtic: P and Q Celtic', in M.J. Ball and J. Fife (eds) *The Celtic Languages*, London: Routledge, 64–98.

Shisha-Halevy, A. (forthcoming) 'Structural sketches of Middle Welsh syntax (I)'.

Szemerényi, O. (1974) 'A Gaulish dedicatory formula', *Zeitschrift für vergleichende Sprachforschung* 88: 246–86.

—— (1978) Review of Schmidt 1977a, *Zeitschrift für celtische Philologie* 36: 293–7.

Tovar, A. (1986) 'The Celts in the Iberian peninsula: archaeology, history, language', in K.H. Schmidt (ed.) *Geschichte und Kultur der Kelten*, 68–101.

—— (1987) 'Lenguas y pueblos de la antigua Hispania: lo que sabemos de nuestros antepasados protohistóricos', in J. Gorrochategui, J.L. Melena and J. Santos (eds) *Studia palaeohispanica*, 15–34.

Untermann, J. (1980) *Trümmersprachen zwischen Grammatik und Geschichte*, Vorträge/ Rheinisch Westfälische Akademie der Wissenschaften: Geisteswissenschaften, G 245, Opladen: Westdeutscher Verlag.

—— (1983) 'Die Celtiberer und das Keltiberische', in E. Campanile (ed.) *Problemi*, 109–46.

—— (1987) 'Lusitanisch, Keltiberisch, Keltisch', in J. Gorrochategui, J.L. Melena and J. Santos (eds) *Studia palaeohispanica*, 57–76.

Villar, F. (ed.) (1990a) *Studia indogermanica et palaeohispanica in honorem A. Tovar et L. Michelena*, Salamanca: Ediciones Universidad de Salamanca/Vitoria: Universidad del País Vasco.

—— (1990b) 'Indo-européens et pré-indo-européens dans la peninsule ibérique', in T.L. Markey and J.A.C. Greppin (eds) *When Worlds Collide*, 363–401.

Waddell, J. (1991a) 'The celticization of the west: an Irish perspective', in Ch. Chevillot and A. Coffyn (eds) *L'Âge du bronze atlantique: ses faciès, de l'Ecosse à l'Andalousie et leurs relations avec le bronze continental et la Méditerranée*, Proceedings of the first Colloque du Parc Archéologique de Beynac, Beynac-et-Cazenac: L'association des Musées du Sarladais, 349–66.

—— (1991b) 'The question of the celticization of Ireland', *Emania. Bulletin of the Navan Research Group* 9: 5–16.

Wagner, H. (1959) *Das Verbum in den Sprachen der britischen Inseln*, Tübingen: Max Niemeyer.

—— (1969) 'The origin of the Celts in the light of linguistic geography', *Transactions of the Philological Society* 1969: 202–50.

—— (1976) 'Common problems concerning the early languages of the British Isles and the Iberian peninsula', in F. Jordá, J. de Hoz and L. Michelena (eds) *Actas del I coloquio*, 388–407.

—— (1977) 'Wortstellung im Keltischen und Indogermanischen', in K.H. Schmidt (ed.) *Indogermanisch und Keltisch*, 206–35.

—— (1982) 'Near Eastern and African connections with the Celtic world', in R. O'Driscoll (ed.), *The Celtic Consciousness*, Portlaoise: Dolmen Press/Edinburgh: Canongate Publishing, 51–67.

—— (1987) 'The Celtic invasions of Ireland and Great Britain – facts and theories', *Zeitschrift für celtische Philologie* 42: 1–40.

Weisgerber, L. (1931) 'Die Sprache der Festlandkelten', *Bericht der Römisch-Germanischen Kommission* 20: 147–226.

—— (1969) *Rhenania Germano-Celtica* (ed.) J. Knobloch and R. Schützeichel, Bonn: Ludwig Röhrscheid.

Zeuss, I.C. (1871) *Grammatica Celtica*, Editio altera curavit H. Ebel, Berolini: apud Weidmannos.

Zimmer, S. (1990a) *Urvolk, Ursprache und Indogermanisierung*, Innsbrucker Beiträge zur Sprachwissenschaft, Vorträge und kleinere Schriften 46, Innsbruck: Institut für Sprachwissenschaft der Universität Innsbruck.

—— (1990b) 'On Indo-Europeanization', *Journal of Indo-European Studies* 18: 141–55.

—— (1990c) 'The investigation of Proto-Indo-European history: methods, problems, limitations', in T.L. Markery and J.A.C. Greppin (eds) *When Worlds Collide*, 311–44.

CHAPTER THREE

THE CELTS THROUGH
CLASSICAL EYES

————— ·◆· —————

David Rankin

Visual evidence in ancient art is scarce but striking. The well-known statues of the dying Gaul and his wife and that of the wounded Gaulish warrior are widely photographed and most poignant: the former is in the Terme Museum in Rome, the latter in the Capitoline. In seeing them, we see how the Roman and probably the Hellenistic world saw the Celts: giants of violent pathos, survivors of a heroic age long past, but still dangerous. The Terme group shows a man in the act of killing himself with his sword. His wife, whom he supports with one hand, is sinking in death, for he has killed her, we presume, so that she may avoid capture and defilement. The Capitoline warrior wears a torque, an unmistakable ethnic marker. He sits, awaiting death from a body-wound. He is heroically naked, and at his side is a curved war-horn. From a Mediterranean viewpoint, the faces of the men are alien. The profiles are concave, facial bones high, and the orbits narrow. The warriors have moustaches but no beards, and their hair is thick and wild.

The statues are probably copies of Hellenistic originals. They may be copies of statues commissioned by Attalus, king of Pergamon (reigned 241–197 BC), in honour of his victories over the Tolistobogii, a subgroup of the Galatians, a Celtic people who had been troublesome to his and other Hellenistic kingdoms since their arrival in Asia Minor several decades earlier (Pliny, *Naturalis Historia* XXXIV.38; Pollitt 1986: 65, 84–5). They were part of a great outpouring of Celtic invaders through Italy, the Balkans and Greece, which made its first terrible impact early in the fourth century BC in the devastation of Etruria and the partial destruction of Rome (391–390 BC). In 278 BC their invasion of Greece threatened the destruction of peninsular Greek civilization and presented an analogy with the Persian invasions two hundred years earlier. The Celts defeated by Attalus became the Galatian tetrarchy. In time this was a composite, partly Hellenized nation, and it was to the Greek portion, most likely, that Saint Paul addressed his epistle. The Celtic element, which still preserved some of the traits of a warrior aristocracy, would scarcely have appreciated his tone. The Galatians still retained some traces of Celtic identity down to the fifth century AD.

The ethos of high classical art allows little representation of emotion, but at the time when the putative originals of these statues were made, individual feeling and character could be shown. The strong features are contorted in the agony of death. They are

21

individual as well as being ethnically typical. There is no racial disrespect, but an animadversion on wild, emotional and tragic human nature. Other representations of the Celts are those on the Cales seals and the frieze from Civit'Alba. These also commemorate victories over the Celts. Fierce-looking warriors are seen being expelled from temples by presiding deities. In some cases they appear only to be approaching the precinct (Bienkowski 1908). They are also depicted on pottery, not dignified like the marble moribund heroes, but satyr-like, denizens of the wilderness.

The Celts left a lasting impression of their sheer physical bulk and power. In the second century BC, when Dio Cassius describes Boudica, he refers to her size, fierce expression of countenance, and harshness of voice (LXII.2.3). It seemed unnatural to the Greeks and Romans that the women of the Celts should be as big and aggressive as the men. Poseidonios, the Stoic philosopher and anthropologist of the time of Cicero, also noted this (Diodorus V.30). They were a race of Titans: Callimachus, the distinguished Greek poet who was librarian at Alexandria (c. 260–240 BC), describes them as such in his Delian Hymn. Elsewhere he calls them a mindless people, mindful himself of the barbarian impetuosity which during his lifetime had almost enabled them to destroy Greece. Likening Celts to Titans was happily in tune with the deeply rooted Greek mythopoeic custom of assimilating the terrifying and the unknown to Greek notions of a prehistoric past. The name Galatea, which belonged to a heroine of Greek mythology, strikingly resembles Galatai, the familiar ethnic term for Celts in the Hellenistic world. This soon ceased to be a coincidence. The Greeks equipped the Celts with an eponymous heroic ancestor called Galatos, who was the son of the Cyclops Polyphemus and Galatea (*Etymologicum Magnum*). Polyphemus was the savage, repulsive, cannibalistic, one-eyed giant whom Odysseus bested in the *Odyssey*, and he was seen as an archetype of primitive wildness, ignorant of civic and civilized living. What better ancestor could be found for a people who behaved in so cyclopean a fashion? Callimachus wrote a poem called 'Galatea' which may have included this story. It appears also in a fragment of the work of the Greek historian Timaeus (*Fragmenta Graecorum Historicorum* I 200), who was in Athens during the Celtic emergency of 279/8 BC. He also mentions an ancestry stemming from Keltos. Another version tells how Heracles begat Keltos or Galatos (Diodorus X.24; Ammianus XV.9.36). He is also supposed to have fathered Iberos, the ancestor of the Iberians, on the nymph Asterope. In the first century BC, Parthenius of Apamea transmits these two versions in his Love Stories (*Erotika Pathemata*).

So far we have been discussing impressions left by the Celts in Graeco-Roman visual art and in an assimilative mythopoeic tradition. Let us now turn to more rationalized evidence of ancient awareness of the Celtic peoples. Our earliest notices are of Greek origin, though some of them are transmitted by Latin authors. This information tends to be geographical rather than a commentary on the way of life or national character of peoples who had not yet become a threat. By a paradox, the earliest information of all may come from Avienus, a Latin writer of the fourth century AD. A didactic geographical poet, he claims to have at his command material going back to the sixth century BC. His *Ora Maritima* refers to Albion and Hibernia, and also to islands called Oestrymnides, which may possibly be a reference to Cornwall. A really old source, which may be Skylax, who wrote in the sixth century

BC in the time of Dareios the Great, may have enabled Avienus to tell of a people whom he calls Ligurians, who were being pushed southwards into Spain from their north European homeland by the Celts (vv. 130ff.). Celts are by this account not yet in Spain. At the end of the sixth century BC the geographer Hecataeus of Miletus says in his work *Europe* that Massalia (Marseilles) is in Ligurian territory which is close to land occupied by Celts (Timaeus LVI). Celts had not in his account arrived at the Mediterranean coast at the time of which he speaks, which is not the time in which he is writing. Hecataeus is aware of differences in language and culture between Ligurians and Celts. *Europe* also has a reference to a Celtic city called Nyrax. A reasonable guess is that this settlement is Noreia in Austria, where there seems to have been a concentration of Celtic peoples. Hecataeus would not have been in a position, nor would his sources, to know that the Celts did not construct cities in the sense of city-states. Celtic lack of interest in city-states would strike the Greeks forcibly when they met Celtic peoples face to face. When the 'father of history', Herodotus (fifth century BC), refers to Celts, his comments are geographical in character (II.33): the Danube rises in Celtic territory and the city of Pyrene and flows through Europe dividing it in two. Without going into delicate speculations about the identity of Pyrene, it would seem reasonable to suppose that the passage refers in a shadowed way to the coming of Celts into Iberia. I recommend John Hind's interesting article on the question of Pyrene (1972). The Herodotean passage may be an extension of Hecataeus or based on some such earlier writer as Skylax. We know that Hecataeus was a source used by Herodotus (IV.42). We may regret that Herodotus's remarks are so austerely geographical. So must his sources have been. If information about cultural peculiarities of the Celts had been available to him, we may depend upon it that Herodotus would certainly have imparted it to us. There are several other geographical references, but I shall mention only one more. Pytheas of Massilia (the Latin spelling of Massalia), who lived in the late fourth century BC and was the author of the famous *Periplous*, seems actually to have circumnavigated the British Isles (Fr 6a Mette). He distinguishes Celts from Germans, and thinks that Britain lies to the north of the Celtic lands (Fr 11 Mette). However, this need not be taken to mean that there were no Celtic people in Britain at the time of which he speaks.

Celts appear as mercenary soldiers in the Greek world in the second quarter of the fourth Century BC. Xenophon tells us that Dionysius I of Syracuse lent 2,000 of these to the Spartans to help them against Thebes in 369 BC (Hellenica VII.1.20). We note that this force also contained Iberes (VII.1.31). Diodorus (XV.10) also refers to this transaction. In his *Laws* (637dff.), Plato comments on the national character of the Celts, classifying them with Scythians, Persians and Carthaginians as hard-drinking and belligerent people. This is the first culturally descriptive comment we have on the Celts in ancient literature. Aristotle thinks that the peculiar temperament of the Celts enables them to show courage whatever the situation: this is absence of fear rather than true courage. In his view a person is mad or completely insensitive who fears nothing, neither earthquake nor wave of the sea. This, he says, is reputed of the Celts (*Ethica Nicomachea* 1115b.28ff.). Some people know how dangerous thunder and lightning can be, but like the Celts, face it *dia thymon* (*Eudemian Ethics* 1229b.28). *Thymos* is the spirit of aggressive fearlessness, a distinguishing quality in both Homeric heroes and the soldier 'guardians' who protect the state from enemies external and within society in Plato's *Republic*. A state of mind in which *thymos* predominates without the restraints of reason is not approved either by Plato or Aristotle. Under its influence, Aristotle tells us, Celts have been known to take arms against the sea. This practice, which remains enshrined in one version of the death of Cú Chulainn, is not fully understood to this day, but it may have had a ritual significance (Rankin 1987: 58). The fourth-century BC historian Ephorus attributes like behaviour to the Cimbri and Teutones (*Timaeus* XLVI). These were northern tribes, not definitively Celtic, who troubled the Romans considerably in the second century BC. Aristotle's student Alexander of Macedon (reigned 336–323 BC) was told by a Celtic delegation that they feared nothing except that the sky might fall (Arrian, *Anabasis* I.4.6; Strabo VII.83). He thought they were empty boasters, but felt that they were worth treating politely, since he wanted to avoid Celtic incursions from the Balkans while he was engaged in the conquest of Asia. His attitude exemplifies Greek cultural misapprehension. What they said was probably a formula of apotropaic prayer rather than heroic assertiveness. The Celts seemed to think that sooner or later the world as they knew it would come to an end (Livy XL.58.4–6). Aristotle mentions the prevalence of homosexual attachments amongst the Celts, in contrast to the female dominance usual amongst barbarians (*Politics* 1269b.27). Athenaeus (*Deipnosophistai* 603a) echoes this view. If it is a true report this may refer to the achievement of a ritual distance from females as a preparation for battle in some primitive warrior groups (Tiger and Fox 1972: 110). In contrast to writers who criticize Celtic lack of stamina, Aristotle regards the Celts as a tough people who condition their children early to the endurance of cold (*Politics* 1336a). The object of Celtic society is warfare, as it is in the case of Scythians, Persians and Thracians (*Politics* 1324b).

The Romans had already experienced the warlike qualities of the Celts (whom they called Galli: Rhys 1905–6) in 390 BC when their city had almost been eliminated by an invading horde. Further incursions occurred in 367, 360, 350 and 348 BC. Aristotle may have known of an invasion in 322 BC (Plutarch, *Camillus* XXII.44). Roman resources and capacity for organization, which increased as the city grew to be the dominant power in the peninsula, rendered each subsequent attack less dangerous to the existence of the Roman state, but the Romans never cast aside the memory of their early terror, and even the passage of centuries did not dissolve the prejudice into which it crystallized. It is fair to say that growth of Roman power was stimulated by the Celtic threat. A large tract of northern, transpadane Italy became Celtic land as a result of these early assaults, and the Etruscan culture in that area was virtually overwhelmed. The power of the Etruscan cities in peninsular Italy was broken, and Rome, although she was a beneficiary of this development, feared a similar fate for herself A special word, *tumultus*, was deployed to designate the Gallic threat. It can reasonably be translated as 'emergency'. We may understand that Roman attitudes towards foreign peoples, never from the outset notably tender, were hardened by these experiences. Fear of Celts at least partially explains the savage treachery of Roman policies towards the Celts and Celtiberians of Spain. There were several more Celtic threats to the security of Italy subsequent to those which have been mentioned. Nor can we omit to mention the participation of Celts in Hannibal's invasion of Italy in 218 BC. For many years after this the Gauls of northern Italy were capable of disturbing Roman peace of mind. Rome was strategically vulnerable from the north. Julius Caesar knew this as well as anybody. In 49 BC he led into Italy an army which had been trained, developed and hardened in Gaul.

Celtic peoples spread over the eastern alpine zone towards the end of the fifth century BC. We have encountered them negotiating with Alexander in 335 BC. They seem to have advanced into Thrace about 281 BC. Macedonian military power, which had subdued the Greek world as well as considerable portions of Asia, failed to impress them. The Macedonian king Ptolemy Keraunos was killed by them in 281 BC. He was the first leader of a Greek or near-Greek people to be killed by Celts. His tenure as successor to Alexander was short. In any case it had been obtained by ruthless chicanery and murder. In 279 BC a Celtic war-horde under the leadership of Brennus and Achichorius was in a position to invade Greece itself. After the defeat of 278 BC, remnants of this group occupied south-eastern Thrace and formed a kingdom which had its capital at Tulis, until in 213 BC the original inhabitants rose against them successfully. Three tribes had already made their way to Asia Minor and become the Galatians. According to Polybius (IV.65) some settled in Egypt. They were greatly in demand as mercenaries throughout the Greek and Near Eastern world. An inscription on a temple wall in Upper Egypt tells us that some mercenaries caught a fox (presumably a jackal). The names, with a possible exception, are Greek, but they describe themselves as Galatians (Hubert 1934: 53).

The Celtic attack on peninsular Greece was in fact a most serious threat to Greek civilization, especially since the invaders seemed interested only in destruction and robbery. The Persians, whose invasions early in the fifth century BC were predictably compared to this attack, had wanted to assert suzerainty as well as uprooting the bases of Greek resistance.

The Celtic incursion was in no respect so large or so organized as the Persian invasions of 490 and 480–79 BC. It was more like the irruption of a large raiding party than a systematic campaign. On an individual or local level it would appear no less terrifying. Peninsular Greece was a less energetic and confident congeries of states than it had been at the beginning of the fifth century BC. For nearly half a century the heavy burden of Macedonian overlordship had lain upon it. Continuous wars before that had destroyed men and prevented the birth of a national spirit. The defeat of the Celtic invaders, in which Athens, as if by tradition and right, played so prominent a part, raised Greek confidence and ushered in a period of renewed freedom which Rome ultimately crushed. Freedom was now regained not only by the defeat of the Celts and the exhilaration this inspired but also because the Celts had so significantly weakened the strength of Macedon.

We shall not narrate blow by blow this apparent replay of the Persian Wars. Yet the Celtic war contained all the requisite elements of myth: instant and inexplicable panic on the part of the attackers; their sudden speaking in tongues and killing each other in a frenzy of misunderstanding; divine apparitions to the advantage of the Greeks: thunderbolts, oracles and unexpected snowstorms. Delphi seems to have been attacked and may well have been looted. Brennus is said to have mocked the anthropomorphic statues of the gods he saw in Delphi (Dio XXII.97). The Cos inscription commemorating the cessation of the Celtic threat maintains that the Celts never reached Delphi. On the other hand, Callimachus, in his *Hymn to Delos*, has

Apollo speaking of the Celts as 'already amongst my tripods'. Whatever way the matter stands, Greek sources knew that it was against Celtic sentiments to make naturalistic likenesses of the gods. There had been another battle of Thermopylae, as the Celts made their way towards Delphi and its wealth, but this time the defenders were taken off by ship when the invaders took the same path to circumvent the position that had been pointed out to the Persians in 480 BC (Pausanias I.35). Brennus's army was weary as it came towards Delphi, and was almost ready to break. He himself was wounded, and many of his comrades had been killed by guerrilla warfare on the part of the Phocians. A depleted Celtic horde withdrew from Greece leaving the victors to quarrel over the honours of a victory they were to commemorate with a Panhellenic ceremony called *Soteria*, 'Salvation' (Nachtergael 1977).

The history of the war was written by Hieronymus of Cardia (third century BC), and by Timaeus, who was resident in Athens during the war. They seem to have been the main sources of the account of the war we have from Pausanias, who lived in the Antonine period. This writer of travel narrative decided to imitate Herodotus's epic history of the Persian invasions. Like Herodotus, he glorified the part played by Athens. In his time many relics of the Celtic war were still to be seen in Athens. Pausanias even attributes to the Celts an atrocity identical to one which, according to Herodotus, was perpetrated by the Persians, namely the murder by multiple rape of a number of women in Phocis (VIII.33).

Polybius (II.19) writes that after their defeat in Greece there was an outbreak of fights at feasts amongst the Celts due to recriminations and reproaches about responsibility for the disaster. He thinks excess of food and drink was the cause of this. Clearly a warriors' ritual feast would be a time when heated exchanges in a time of stress would be likely to lead to violence, as each individual anxiously tried to shift his share of the dishonour on to somebody else. The Greeks learned how to manipulate this Titanic fighting temperament of the Celts to their own advantage. Ptolemy Philadelphus (reigned 283–246 BC) got rid of unwanted Celtic mercenaries by hemming them in an island where he could be sure that shortage of supplies would soon prompt them to find excuses for fighting each other. We also learn from Polybius (III.62) that Hannibal set up bouts of personal combat between Celtic warriors to entertain his troops who were weary from their long march over the Alps into Italy. It appears that single combat, according to Celtic custom, could be a substitute for the usual determination of a war in open battle. Notable illustrations of this are the victories won over Gallic chieftains by Messala Corvinus and Manlius Torquatus. Apparently the Romans, with their small stature and short up-thrusting swords, had some advantage over their heroic challengers.

We may be reminded by some of this evidence of scenes from the *Táin* or *Fled Bricrend*. To the Greeks, the Celts seemed to resemble the Cyclopes of the *Odyssey* in their uncouthness and ferocity, their ignorance of the ways of the *polis*, their pastoral life-style (more apparent than actual in wandering tribes) and their corresponding contempt for agriculture. On the other hand, Herodotus takes the view that the absence of a civic market-place in the way of life of any people leaves less room for the growth of dishonesty. The classical and Hellenistic Greeks, and after them the Romans, believed in an age of primal innocence, now lost to them, but perhaps still surviving amongst the barbarians (Lovejoy and Boas 1935). Cleitarchus (c.280 BC) took this view of the inhabitants of India. Later, Julius Caesar says it of the Galli (*De Bello Gallico* VI.19.3). Poseidonios, whose lectures had once been attended by Cicero, followed this line of opinion by adapting to a description of the Celts what Herodotus had said of the Scythians. And this distinguished Stoic had actually visited Celtic lands. However, the theme of primitive simplicity had become a rhetorical *topos* too powerful to resist. Caesar was influenced by Poseidonios. Tacitus (*Germania* XVIII.19.21) applied a similar template to his account of the German tribes in his *Germania*.

Celtic religion, in being apparently an imprecise and abstract worship of natural forces with no seeming emphasis on one prominent god, had a certain philosophical attraction for Greeks, especially Stoics. The complexities of this aspect of Celtic life would come home to the Romans in due course when they encountered the druids, particularly those of Britain. The Greeks in all of this were harking back to their own traditions about their early ancestry who, according to Thucydides (1.5), lived very much as the barbarians lived in his own time (fifth century BC), pursuing a life of rapine.

The Romans had more continuous contact with Celtic peoples than had the Greeks. Greek sources are flavoured with philosophical and anthropological preconceptions, which tend to see elements of a universal philosophy in the customs and ideas of the people studied. Stoics like Poseidonios are representative of this line of thought. In the historian Polybius we see a Greek intellectual whose wonder at the growth of Roman power certainly does not lead him to underestimate the menace of the Celts, since the Celts were capable of spreading alarm amongst Romans, who, after all, had themselves been able to dominate Greece. The Romans came to see the Celts as having a coherent culture, with some similarities to their own, but marked by a violent primitivism which was entirely alien and a temper of mind which they could not understand.

Polybius was a leading citizen of Megalopolis and a prominent person in the Achaean League Greek city-states. He was forcibly removed to Rome after the Battle of Pydna (168 BC), which brought an end to Greek hopes of a renewal of their former glory and influence. He was the son of one of the League's generals, Lycortes, and a friend of Philopoemen, who has been described as the last great Greek leader. Polybius was treated honourably, in accordance with his status. Friendship with the family of Aemilius Paullus, his captor, gave him not only personal security, but intimate knowledge of Roman government and acquaintance with members of leading families. Rome was to him a social, political and military phenomenon. His history attempts to explain its remarkable growth to world power. He sees the Celtic threat, which was urgent in 226 BC, and was to revive again and again, as an important stimulus of Rome's military development over the centuries. Its recurrence itself was a shaping influence. He never forgets his national origins. His description of Celtic incursions into Italy is intended to inform and alert those who are responsible for defending Greece. More advanced elements of Celtic culture receive little attention from him. He is more concerned with its sharp end, its war-making capacity, which has been, and still may be, directed at Rome, and possibly Greece.

In contrasting the cultures of Rome and the Celts, he mentions that Celts are ineffective planners, volatile in mentality, and lacking in cohesion. This volatility (*athesia*) is their greatest defect, and is connected with their being a nomadic people, without organized political or social basis, and having little cultural or intellectual tradition. Where they are settled, they live in straw-roofed cottages. Their main property is portable, cattle and gold rather than land and buildings, and friendship is the moral quality on which they set the highest value (II.17, 18). According to Polybius, this *athesia* made the Romans unwilling to use the help of an allied tribe, the Cenomani, against the Insubres in 223 BC (II.31). It is understandable that he should attribute to a whole culture characteristics which the invaded particularly notice in an invading horde. The historian Livy, no warm friend of the Celts, adopts Polybius's skewed perspective. Yet Polybius could appreciate that, while the Celts were lacking both in the steadfastness that characterized Rome and the rational intellect (*logismos*) of civilized Greece, they represented an ancient spirit of warlike aggressiveness, the *thymos* of antique heroism (II.22). This is illustrated by the noise, impetus and colour of the Celtic battle-charge, and the frenzy of the warrior group called *gaisatai*, who fling themselves naked into the fight (II.27). The nakedness he rationalizes as the warrior's means of preventing himself from being impeded by thorns and brambles which could catch on his clothes. This must surely be some Roman legionary's yarn. In his opinion the Celtic shield is inadequate, and the sword (possibly an ancestor of the *cleideamh mor*) unwieldy in battle conditions. He acutely observes that the unreliability of Celtic mercenaries was connected with their old raiding habits (II.7).

The Romans remained basically terrified by the prospect of Celtic *tumultus*, which they had experienced so often. Preoccupation with the Celtic threat diverted the attention of the Romans from the more serious menace represented by the accumulation of Carthaginian power in Spain (II.22). They thought that in the Celts they faced a superpower of unlimited resources. In reality, as Polybius saw, it was they who were the superpower. Yet he seems to realize that the Galli might have succeeded in extinguishing Rome at an early stage of her development. Polybius's history from 145 BC to 82 BC is continued by Poseidonios. We possess his work only in fragments. Polybius visited Celtic territory. So did Poseidonios, but he observed with the investigative eye of the philosopher and anthropologist. Not only was he in Gaul, he also visited Spain, and may possibly have gone to Britain. Julius Caesar's famous account of his wars in Gaul (*De Bello Gallico*) makes use of Poseidonios's histories. The fact that Poseidonios did not regard the Celts as mere primitives was grist to Caesar's propagandist mill, since he could represent himself as the conquerer of no mean people.

Poseidonios's distaste for Celtic drinking, boasting, superstition and human sacrifice is only to be expected in a member of the Hellenistic intellectual élite (Strabo V.28). We may admire him for drawing a parallel between the custom of the champion's portion in Celtic feasts and a similar custom in the *Iliad* (Strabo VII.21; Tierney 1960: 221). The custom of headhunting also gave him pause, but after a time he became accustomed to the sight of heads nailed up on the doors of houses. His hosts made it a point of politeness to draw his attention to those which had belonged to special enemies (Strabo IV.98). Livy records that the Boii took the head of Postumius (XXIII.24.11). We have mentioned that the head of Ptolemy Keraunos ended on the tip of a Celtic spear. Both Poseidonios and the *Fled Bricrend* mention the champion's contract whereby a man may agree to be killed for some price or reward (Mac Cana 1972: 89–90). Possibly both Poseidonios and the *Fled Bricrend* represent a state of affairs current in some parts of the Celtic domain in the first century BC. Some of his descriptions may be based on hearsay rather than autopsy. The custom of fighting from chariots reminds Poseidonios of the Trojan War. Chariots were not used by the Celts on the European mainland at this time, though we know they were still in use in Britain. Poseidonios was aware of the crucial importance of the first wild charge of a Celtic host: if that failed, all was lost (Strabo IV.43). This feature of Celtic war-culture was still practised at Culloden, and perhaps also on the part of Confederate forces in the American Civil War, many of whom were of Scots or Scots Irish derivation.

Poseidonios also remarks on the hospitality of the Celts. A feature of this was their reluctance to ask questions of a newly arrived guest, which may remind us of the tact shown by King Alcinous to Odysseus in Book VII of the *Odyssey*. Poseidonios tells us that the Celts ate and drank in a leonine fashion, but were clean in their table manners. Armed men were in attendance at the feasts, and a distinct order of precedence was observed amongst the guests. Wine was drunk, and only seldom blended with water. The native drink was mead (*korma*). Hospitality could assume the form of conspicuous consumption for political purposes (Athenaeus 151e–152f). In a bid for leadership, an Arvernian chief, Louernius, scattered gold and silver to crowds of people with extraordinary lavishness, and set up enormous feasts.

There is evidence (Diodorus V.31) that Poseidonios respected the intellectual quickness and imagination of the Celts. He mentions the learned orders of druids, bards and seers. In a lost work Aristotle or one of the Peripatetics may have mentioned druids and another priestly class (Diogenes Laertius I.1). The druids take the auspices and divine from the inspection of entrails. Another method of divination is the observation of the dying twitches of human sacrifices. Druids are present at such ceremonies, but are not mentioned as conducting them. Poseidonios gives the still largely honourable name of *philosophos* to the druids, whom he sees as having a learned understanding of the universe as well as mediating between the world of the gods and that of men. Their view of the nature of the world seemed sympathetic to that of the Stoics: the cosmos was animate, animated and purposed. Celtic hardihood, amounting to indifference in the face of death, impressed both Greeks and Romans and was attributed to druidic teachings (Strabo IV.1.97). Poseidonios may have overemphasized the philosophical aspects of druidism. Caesar may have exaggerated its political influence, at least in mainland Gaul. Julius Caesar did not come into contact with Celtic life as it was lived. His purpose was to dominate Gaul and exploit it for his own purposes, not to comprehend Celtic society in any greater depth than seemed conformable to the achievement of his ends. His propagandist intent did not require him to see the Celt as natural man unaffected by any vice but that which was inborn. The druids were preoccupied with secrecy and, like the Pythagoreans, committed nothing to writing. We recall that in his lifetime there was a resurgence of Pythagoreanism in Rome, and several prominent intellectuals were tried for belonging to this potentially subversive secret society. Later writers such as Hippolytus (fifth century AD) compare druidic teaching with that of the Pythagoreans. This tradition would appear to be separate from that which derives from Poseidonios (Chadwick

1966: 60ff.). Its origins cannot be traced back sufficiently to allow the hypothesis that Caesar was aware of it. Yet the similarities were obvious. Julius Caesar initiated a policy which eventually would destroy the druids and other learned orders. At the same time, we must remember that Divitiacus, a druid of the Aedui, and brother of that tribe's leader Dumnorix, was a friend of Julius Caesar and stayed with him in his headquarters for a number of years.

Octavian took steps against the druids. Tiberius suppressed them and the other orders (Tacitus, *Annales* III.40). Claudius abolished their order (Suetonius, *Divus Claudius* 25). Most of the druids of Britain (according to Caesar the home of druidism) perished in the massacre at Anglesey in AD 60 (Tacitus, *Annales* XIV.29). No doubt the druids increasingly gave cohesion to a supra-tribal 'national' opposition to Roman encroachments. No doubt also they were a cultural and ideological nuisance on a local level. The destruction of learned orders became a matter of policy (Chadwick 1966: 4–5; Ross 1967: 462). Ruthless conquest involves the excision of the intellectual leadership of the conquered. Spreading information about human sacrifice was a useful instrument towards this end, and Roman authors make use of it (*De Bello Gallico* VI.16; Lucan I.151; VIII.445; Suetonius, *Claudius* 25). They were able to dissociate their ideas on this subject from the cruel acts of human sacrifice which constituted their own gladiatorial games. What remained of druidism was undermined by classical education, which produced a new intellectual class into which members of druidic families were sometimes absorbed (Ausonius, *Praefatiunculae* IV.10; X.27).

Another strange property of the Celts was that the women were as large as the men and as strong. Diodorus Siculus, following Poseidonios, is probably our earliest authority for this fact. Diodorus lived in the time of Julius Caesar. When Cassius Dio (praetor *c.* AD 194) wants to give us an impression of Boudica, he refers to her great size, her grimness of expression, and her harsh voice (LXII.2.3). The ferocity and aggressiveness of Celtic women is confirmed four centuries later by Ammianus Marcellinus (XV.12.1). This information, agreeing with the Poseidonian report, seems also to be based on eyewitness accounts (Thompson 1949: 4). We cannot be entirely sure how far the needs of rhetoric preserved this view as a commonplace.

On the whole, Poseidonios's account of the Celts is rational and scientific, even though he is to some extent influenced by primitivistic notions about a past golden age. He could understand that the differences between peoples were possible reflections of differing environmental factors. This was a line of thinking which had its origins in the fifth century BC and the Hippocratic treatise on *Airs, Waters, and Places*. Julius Caesar is prepared to set up Ariovistus as a vicious and primitive, though politically shrewd, Cyclops (*De Bello Gallico* I.44; II.15), but he speaks with some respect of his most formidable enemy Vercingetorix (VII.89). He presents another leader, Critognatus, making a comparison between the methodical exploitation inflicted on the Gauls by Roman tax-officials and the transient plague of invading raiders like the Cimbri and Teutones (VII.77). Tacitus similarly allows Calgacus, the leader of the Caledones (*Agricola* 30–3), to put his case; and also the famous Caratacus. Boudica too expounds her wrongs (*Annales* XIV.35). There are other examples and their speeches are presented in the style of Roman oratory. The traditions of ancient rhetoric encouraged such antiphony, and authorial openness of mind should not be exaggerated. It may be said that there is no flavour of a biologically racist contempt. If Celts were inferior, it was in their social organization and culture, not natural talent.

Yet Romans at large preserved an inherited fear of the Celts. Cicero was quite capable of playing the anti-Celtic card in his *Pro Fonteio*, a speech he made in defence of a Roman official accused of extortion by the people of Narbonese Gaul, where he was praetor in 75–73 BC. He speaks of the Gauls as wild men, potential invaders of Italy, useless at finance, and not even at their best to be considered on the same level as the lowest Roman (27). They almost destroyed Rome in 390 BC. They attacked Delphi; they wear trousers, their speech is uncouth. In his accusation of Piso, he mentions the defendant's Insubrian grandfather as if it were a point of legal relevance, and there is another derogatory reference to trousers. Yet he speaks of Divitiacus as a civilized expert on natural philosophy (*De Divinatione* I.90). He is prepared to make a speech before Julius Caesar in order to reconcile the dictator to Deiotarus, the wicked and wily old king of Galatia who had chosen the wrong side in the civil war of 49–45 BC. Nor does he show hostility to the Allobroges, whom the conspirator Catiline tried to recruit: after all they chose the loyalist side. Sallust (86–55 BC), who wrote an account of the conspiracy, has these Gauls speaking with the egotistic overbearingness of ancient heroes. Cicero, by the way, has no good to say of the Celtic accent (*Brutus* 171).

In his long rhetorical history of Rome from its foundation, Livy (69/54 BC–AD 17/12) loses no opportunity of proclaiming Roman superiority (VI.42). He has contempt for their barbarous warfare, colourful clothes, boasting, gold ornaments, and noisy clashing of arms before battle. Much of his material on the Celts is adapted from Poseidonios. He relishes accounts of single combat in which Celtic leaders are bested by Romans, quiet in the face of spells and vainglory (VII.9), which he is not concerned to understand. He recalls their ferocity, their instability in battle (LIX.77), their lack of stamina. They are essentially soft (XXII.2). Their temper is over-aggressive (*fervidum ingenium* XXVIII.17). They are unpredictable (XXI.39, 52; XXII.1). As a people they are born to create ineffectual emergencies (*vanos tumultus* V.37–9; XXXVIII.17).

Livy may not have had Celtic connections himself but his origins were in northern Italy, and he would have had some knowledge of the Celts whom, in spite of considerable effort and subsequent self-deception on the matter, the Romans had not been able to eliminate (Chilver 1941: 71). Several distinguished Roman writers came from this region. Possibly some had Celtic roots in spite of their Roman names (Rhys 1905–6; Chevallier 1962). The poet Catullus (*c*.85–55 BC) may have been of Celtic origin, but he does not mention it. His family seems to have been prosperous, assimilated upper middle-class. He ridicules a Celtiberian called Egnatius for his permanent rictus (Poem 37) and the bad ethnic mannerism of washing his teeth in urine (Poem 39). Compatriots of Catullus and fellow members of the school of 'New Poets' were: Valerius Cato, Helvius Cinna, Furius Bibaculus and Caecilius. The philosopher-poet Lucretius (Holland 1979: 15, 48f.), who was about ten years older than Catullus and died *c*.54 BC, may have had some Cisalpine connections. Amongst later writers associated with this area were the elder (AD 23/4–79) and younger Pliny (AD 51–112) and possibly Tacitus (AD 56–*c*.115). The first writer to proclaim his Celticity was Martial (AD 40–*c*.104), who mentions the outlandish place-names of his native Bilbilis in Spain and refers to himself as Celtiberian (IV.55). We may note that it was only by the persuasion of the emperor Claudius (emperor AD 51–54) that Celts from Gallia Comata were admitted to the senate in AD 48 (Tacitus, *Annales*, XI.24), a move which provoked some satire ([Seneca,] *Apocolocyntosis* 6). The advice he received against this essentially liberal move was in political terms not entirely misplaced. These new senators were princes in their own land, which suggested to some a danger which was abundantly realized a couple of decades later in the revolt of Vindex (Syme 1958: 450–64).

Celtic boorishness and insensitivity are mentioned by the Emperor Julian (emperor AD 360–363) in his *Misopogon* 342. Later, S. Jerome, in his commentary on the Epistle to the Galatians (Migne, *Patrologia Latina* 26357), ridicules their incapacity to learn. Their wildness rather than their intelligence seems to be the point of his strictures. The reputation of Britons seems to have remained relatively unchanged from the time of Catullus, for whom they are remote, bristling barbarians (Poem 11 lines 10–11), to Ausonius in the fourth century AD, who questions the plausibility of a Briton having the name 'Bonus': he thinks 'Matus' (drunk) would be more suitable (Poem 11). Gaul was effectively the core of the Roman Empire of the West at this time, a development which would have seemed as remarkable to Julius Caesar as the Tarasque monster. Ausonius, a poet and academic working in Burdigala, saw Britons as wild Celts. Yet some of his friends traced their ancestry from druidic families.

There is a noteworthy consistency in the evidences we have for Graeco-Roman attitudes to the Celts, who remained archaic, heroic, *kataplektikoi*, 'terrific' (Poseidonios in Diodorus V.30), eloquent, volatile. No doubt one of the main factors which helped to crystallize this view was the persistence over the centuries of a rhetorical scheme of education. This placed great emphasis on the learning and deployment of *topoi* (*communes loci*), or common themes. Once the picture of the Celts had congealed, it would be difficult for detailed observation to modify it. The use of other commonplaces can be seen in the speeches given to Celtic leaders by such writers as Caesar, Sallust and Tacitus. The romantic view of the Celts and their culture owes much to these ancient attitudes. However, our attempts to see the Celts through classical eyes are focused through the lens of a literature written by an educated class whose understanding was in many ways shielded from the input of factual information by the influence of rhetorical training.

REFERENCES

Bienkowski, P.R. von (1908) *Die Darstellungen der Gallier in der hellenistischen Kunst*, Vienna: A. Holder.

Chadwick, N. (1966) *The Druids*, Cardiff: University of Wales Press.

Chevallier, R. (1962) 'La Celtique du Po, position des problèmes', *Latomus* 21: 356–70.

Chilver, G.E.F. (1941) *Cisalpine Gaul, a Social and Economic History from 49 BC to the Death of Trajan*, Oxford: Oxford University Press.

Hind, John (1972) 'Pyrene and the date of the Massiliot sailing manual', *Rivista Storica dell'Antichità* 2: 39–52.

Holland, L.A. (1979) *Lucretius and the Transpadanes*, Princeton: Princeton University Press.

Hubert, H. (1934) *The Greatness and Decline of the Celts*, London: Routledge & Kegan Paul.

Lovejoy, Arthur O. and Boas, George (1935) *Primitivism and Related Ideas in Antiquity*, Baltimore: Johns Hopkins University Press.

Mac Cana, P. (1972) 'Conservation and innovation in early Celtic literature', *Etudes Celtiques* 13: 61–119.

Mette, H.J. (1952) *Pytheas von Massilia*, Berlin: De Gruyter.

Nachtergael, G. (1977) 'Les Galates en Grèce et les Sôteries de Delphes; recherches d'histoire et d'épigraphie hellénistiques', *Académie Royale de Belgique: Memoires de la Classe de Lettres* 63.1.

Pollitt, J.J. (1986) *Art in the Hellenistic Age*, Cambridge: Cambridge University Press.

Rankin, H.D. (1987) *Celts and the Classical World*, London: Croom Helm.

Rhys, J. (1905–6) 'Celtae and Galli', *Proceedings of the British Academy* 6: 71–133.

Ross, Anne (1967) *Pagan Celtic Britain*, London: Routledge & Kegan Paul.

Syme, R. (1958) *Tacitus*, Oxford: Oxford University Press.

Thompson, E.A. (1949) *The Historical Works of Ammianus Marcellinus*, Cambridge: Cambridge University Press.

Tierney, J.J. (1960) 'The Celtic ethnography of Poseidonius', *Proceedings of the Royal Irish Academy* 60: 189–246.

Tiger, L. and Fox, Robin (1972) *The Imperial Animal*, New York: Delta.

PART II

WARRIORS AND WARFARE

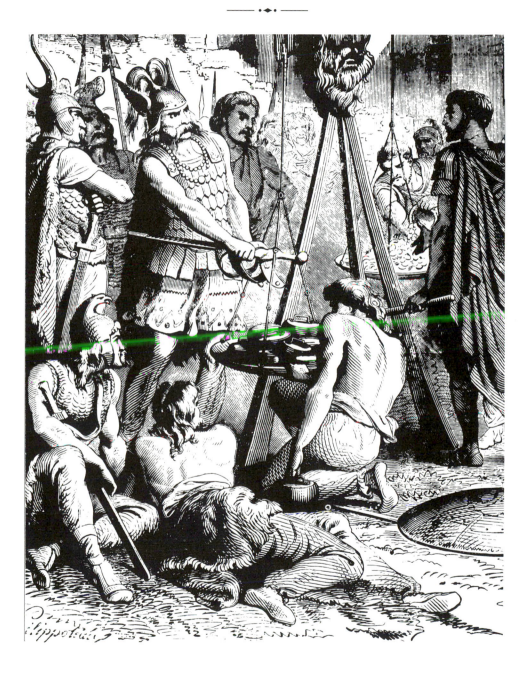

THE ARMY, WEAPONS
AND FIGHTING

——— •◆• ———

J.N.G. and *W.F. Ritchie*

INTRODUCTION

Ceremonial uniform and weaponry today would give but a poor impression of the realities of modern warfare, armament and battle formations; second-hand news-paper accounts would offer an unreliable picture of the background to a territorial skirmish or the social customs of the participants. The archaeological and literary information relating to Celtic warfare is equally partial and one-sided, for the arms discovered in a burial or a ritual deposit may not reflect those of the warrior class as a whole; classical writers were neither dispassionate nor necessarily knowledgeable reporters, frequently collating snippets of received information from a variety of sources. From such evidence it would be wrong to try to present even a series of snapshots for the wide chronological span or geographical range of Celtic activity in Europe. In most cases classical writers were evoking events in areas where archaeo-logical evidence is sparse, and we have no knowledge of how stylized their apparent descriptions are. In other areas our evidence comes from weaponry itself, but in contexts that may involve special selection either to accompany a burial or as a religious offering. The choice of weapons may equally represent particular regional burial traditions (Lorenz 1986). Thus although our canvas is as wide as possible throughout the Celtic world, we have inevitably focused on certain areas where the results of research may be fuller than others; thus the detail of our tapestry leaves intervening parts unworked. The literature on Celtic warriors is too extensive to review, for, if we are to believe Strabo that the whole race was madly fond of war, warriors and the panoply of war enter many aspects of Celtic life, art, technology and religion.

Our knowledge is also skewed by the differential survival in the archaeological record of the various components: a mass of ironwork is known, although only a tiny proportion is fully conserved; wood survives more rarely, although spears and shields are known to have played important parts in regular armament; leather and other fittings are, like the clamour and trumpeting of the battlefield, largely matters for the imagination.

Déchelette offered one of the first detailed accounts of the archaeology of the warrior (1927: 612–710). The broad sequence of armament has been reconstructed visually in popular form by Connolly (1978: 49–69); Rapin, in bringing together illustrations of weapons at consistent sizes, has shown the development of swords, spears and shields from the fifth to the first century BC (1983a). Weaponry and warfare in Gaul has been most recently discussed and illustrated by Brunaux and Lambot (1987). Several recent exhibitions and museum displays have evoked the Celtic warrior through full-scale reconstructions and drawings (e.g. Zeller 1980; and the Museum of the Iron Age at Andover in Hampshire); the magnificent volume accompanying an exhibition in Venice in 1991 explores many aspects of warrior activity throughout the Celtic world (Moscati *et al.* 1991).

The two strands of evidence, the archaeological and the literary, that must be interwoven in any discussion of Celtic warriors can be evoked so vividly that the popular notion of the Celtic barbarian is second only to that of his Hunnic or Viking successor as the scourge of classical or later Christian civilization. Barbarity is conjured up through noise and an absence of discipline; physical stature is enhanced by shagginess of hair or by helmets apparently designed to instil terror into the person to whom the story is being told – horns in the case of the Celts, wings in that of the Vikings. Unusually, our picture of the warrior Celt is also affected by two groups of monumental sculpture: the first, nearly contemporary, includes Roman arches such as the Arc de Triomphe at Orange and is designed to commemorate Roman military victory and the defeat of dejected barbarians (Amy *et al.* 1962); the second and more disparate group is of nineteenth-century date and belongs to a period when Europe was discovering its Celtic rather than its classical past (see Figure 4.1) – statues of Ambiorix at Tongres, Vercingetorix at Alésia, and Boudica in her scythed chariot on the Embankment in London are among the most famous, and are perhaps the most important, in perpetuating past images of warrior leaders. Today, of course, the cartoon creation of Asterix has provided new generations with expectations of Gallic invincibility and bombast, as well as a sense of humour, an essential part in relating the past to the present to contemporary audiences. When myth becomes an inevitable part of popular culture, archaeology has an unusually important part to play in presenting a rounded picture of the material evidence. In broad terms this chapter will take a site or a group of sites to form the focus of the exploration of a theme, incorporating material from sculptural or classical sources where this adds clarity to the picture. Illustrations and reconstruction drawings have thus been chosen to reflect general themes.

LA GORGE MEILLET AND CHARIOT BURIALS

One of the most extraordinary snapshots of princely Celtic weaponry is that offered by the excavation report of the chariot burial of La Gorge Meillet, in the French department of Marne, discovered in 1876 (see Figure 4.2); it is partly the economical presentation of the illustrations, laying out, as they do, the results of a nineteenth-century excavation with a beguiling simplicity that readily allows the reader to reconstruct the panoply of the buried warrior (Fourdringier 1878). The grave pit, measuring 3.2 m by 2.4 m, had been dug into the chalk subsoil to a depth of some 1.7 m; the floor of the pit was stepped, with a lower portion with two deeper slots to receive the wheels of a chariot, and a rather higher ledge at one end, on which the

Figure 4.1 Gaulish chieftains, as evoked in nineteenth-century France.

yoke and harness rested. The body of a warrior had been laid on the floor of the chariot with the legs on either side of the pole; a series of weapons had been laid ceremoniously to accompany the body, four spears with iron heads and butts, a long iron knife, and a magnificent bronze helmet. The clothing did not survive, apart from a bronze brooch and four bronze buttons decorated with rosettes, to which slight traces of a woven woollen garment still adhered. Nor did the organic parts of the chariot survive, but the iron tyres and the bronze axle bands and hub caps still remained to indicate that the diameter of the tyres was about 1 m and that they were set about 1.3 m apart. The horse harness comprised bronze bits and chains inlaid with coral. The burial was accompanied by joints of pork, fowl and eggs, as well as by a bronze wine flagon of Etruscan manufacture, the latter providing the dating evidence for the burial within the later fifth century BC. In the upper part of the filling of the grave pit a second burial had been inserted, that of a man accompanied by a sword. The principal burial suggests the armament of a warrior leader, the practical weapons of sword and spears as well as a resplendent bronze helmet, tall and pointed, but offering only limited protection to the head. The function of the helmet is for parade and display, to show that its bearer is a person apart. In shape and decoration, however, the helmet is part of a scattered group with examples in the Marne, Dürrnberg in the Austrian Alps, and in Slovakia; the decorative palmettes on the helmet from Berru (Marne) point to Italy as one source of inspiration (Schaaff 1973; 1988: 315; Megaw and Megaw 1989: 63–4; Duval 1989: 45–6, 51).

A burial comparable to that of La Gorge Meillet, excavated at Somme-Bionne in 1873, also illustrates the careful layout of objects round a chariot including a long sword in an engraved bronze scabbard and a red-figure Greek pottery cup dating to about 420 BC (Stead 1991a). Jacobsthal, in evoking the princely nature of such deposits, dubbed the burial that of Monsieur le Comte de Somme-Bionne. Such burials represent on the one hand the potential for reconstruction of a warrior fully armed – helmet, sword suspended from a chain at the waist, spears at the ready, as well as the two-wheel chariot, doubtless with wicker sides, and the richly decorated harness for the two horses; on the other hand such burials are found only in distinct groups and at discrete periods within the Celtic world. There are, for example, some 250 burials in the Champagne area of France which date to the La Tène period. Another distinct group has been found in the Rhineland with that from Bescheid Tumulus 6, for example, containing the two wheels from a dismantled vehicle, a sword with an anthropoid handle, a coral-decorated suspension chain, three spearheads, three arrowheads, a knife and a drinking horn with a gold mouthpiece (Haffner and Joachim 1984: 78, fig. 7).

In eastern Yorkshire there is another discrete group of burials with chariots, or less grandly, carts. Evaluation of the finds from the last century has been refined as further burials are revealed, largely in advance of gravel extraction (Stead 1984; 1991b: 58–61). In some cases the vehicle had been dismantled before deposition, whereas in others the vehicle was laid over the body. The Yorkshire burials seem to represent a distinctive religious tradition rather than being in every case the burial of a warrior, for there are few associated weapons. However, at Kirkburn, a burial with a two-wheel vehicle was accompanied by a shirt of mail, which may be reconstructed in a style that finds parallels elsewhere in Europe (Stead 1991b: 54–6).

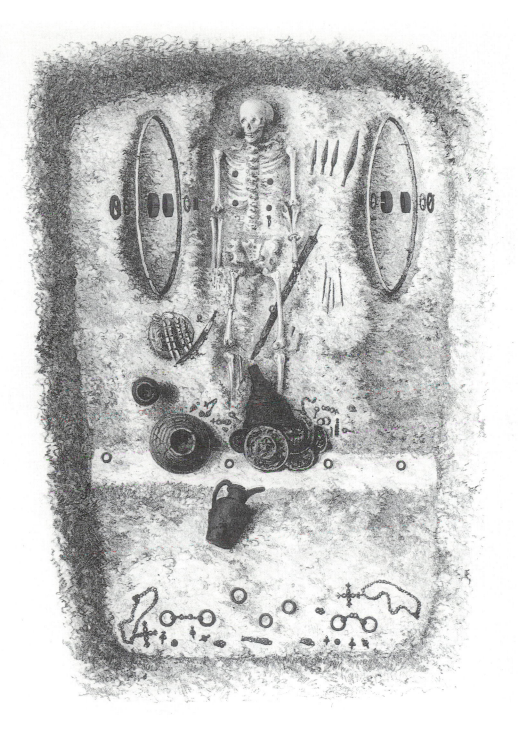

Figure 4.2 La Gorge Meillet, Marne; excavated in 1876. (Fourdringier 1878.)

The evidence from many excavations of chariot burials, coupled with that from depictions on coins and notably on a stele from Padua (Frey 1968; Harbison 1969), has allowed the reconstruction of Celtic chariots to be undertaken both as models and as full-size artefacts (e.g. Furger-Gunti 1991); the recent reconstruction by the Schweizerisches Landesmuseum incorporated longitudinal suspension, without which it would have been virtually impossible to throw a spear from a moving chariot with any accuracy.

CHARIOTS IN CLASSICAL SOURCES

Classical sources stress that chariots were used not in the heat of battle but as a means of getting to the fray. Roman armies encountered Gaulish chariots at Sentinum, and, as Arrian avers (*Res Tactica* XIX.2) that the Romans never practised fighting from chariots themselves, the foot soldiers particularly must have been thoroughly terrified when they met the Gauls. Standing erect in their chariots, the armed enemies came rushing at them with a great clattering of hooves and wheels, frightening the Roman horses by the unfamiliar din. Once the mad rush was over, the warriors dismounted and fought on foot. The attendant kept the chariot at the ready, in order to effect, if necessary, a speedy retreat (Livy, *History* X.28). A thousand chariots took part in the battle of Sentinum; at Telemon, perhaps the last battle on the Continent in which chariots were used, they were stationed on the wings (Polybius, *Histories* II.28).

Diodorus Siculus (*History* V.29.1; 21.5) explains that, when going into battle, the Gauls used two-horsed chariots that carried the charioteer and the warrior. The use of chariots, however, decreased as their prowess and agility as mounted soldiery increased, and chariots were certainly no longer common when Caesar was campaigning in Gaul, although there are a few late chariot burials. His army must have been surprised when, after crossing the Channel, they saw the British chariots drawn up against them. He described the scene. 'They drive all over the field, hurling javelins and throwing the enemy-ranks into confusion by the terror inspired by the horses and the noise of the wheels. Then they jump down from their chariots and engage on foot.' Caesar continues, 'Their daily training and practice have made them so expert that they can control their horses at full gallop on a steep incline and then check and turn them in a moment ...' They 'can run along the chariot pole, stand on the yoke, and get back into the chariot very speedily' (*De Bello Gallico* IV.33).

At the battle of Mons Graupius in north-east Scotland (AD 83) Tacitus describes the Caledonians as receiving Calgacus's speech (a literary device created by Tacitus himself) with an uproar of war-cries and confused shouting, as is their custom. Before the battle began, the charioteers (*covinarii*) filled the intervening space with noisy manoeuvring. They did not have much success, however, probably because the terrain did not suit that kind of warfare (*Agricola* 35–6).

Finally, as a picture of the Celtic love of flamboyant display, there is the appearance of Bituitus, king of the Arverni, in the Roman triumphal procession after his defeat (121 BC). There the most conspicuous figure was the king himself in his vari-coloured arms and silver-plated chariot, just as he had been when he fought in battle (Florus, *Epitome of Roman History* I.37).

CELTIC HELMETS

At the Gorge Meillet and at Dürrnberg Grave 44/2, the early La Tène chieftain was accompanied by an array of grave goods that illustrated transalpine contacts, as well as objects denoting princely or warrior status, including stout swords, spears, arrowheads and pointed helmets with attachments for chin-straps (Penninger 1972). Helmets are found in small numbers throughout the Celtic world, in some cases in distinct chronological or geographical groups. Was it because they were proud of their elaborate hairstyles that Celtic warriors did not generally wear helmets, or were there more fundamental religious reasons? Neither the Britons nor the Germans had helmets, writes Tacitus, but the Cimbri had helmets like the maws of frightful beasts or the heads of animals, with crests that made them look larger than they really were (Plutarch, *Marius* XXV.2). Only in Italy in the region of the Senones have helmets been found in great numbers, in a style named after the burial ground of Montefortino and characterized by a back peak to protect the neck and a top knob.

Richly ornamented helmets which show Italian influence in shape or decoration occur in France, including Amfreville (Eure) and Agris (Charente); both are magnificent artistic achievements of iron, bronze, gold and coral and date from the fourth century BC. From Canosa (Apulia) a helmet of iron, bronze and coral (of earlier fourth-century date) bears side mountings to allow the addition of a crest. The helmet from Agris has a finely wrought cheek-piece, while that from Amfreville has a decorative motif on the side of the cap that may originally have been mirrored by a cheek-piece that no longer survives. Excavations at Monte Bibele (Bologna) have uncovered several warrior burials that provide archaeological contexts for such helmets with decorated bronze cap decorations and cheek-pieces with triple rosettes, e.g. Grave 14 (Vitali 1985: 40–9; 1990: 202–6). A simpler helmet with a chin-strap and a top-knob was associated with a late fourth-century cremation burial from Varenna, Como, with sword and decorated scabbard and leech brooches (de Marinis 1977: 32, pl.2).

In Celtic areas in south-eastern Europe and on sculpture at Pergamon, in Asia Minor, a small class of helmets continues the pattern of a side decoration that mirrors a cheek-piece (Schaaff 1988: 300). The most spectacular example comes from Ciumesti in Rumania, in a grave excavated in 1961, in which a cremation deposit was accompanied by a helmet, a mail shirt with decorated bronze rosettes, and a spear (Rusu 1969). The helmet was surmounted by a bronze bird with hinged wings that would have flapped as the warrior rode to battle. Few other helmet mountings survive, but there are examples of bronze boars, and the Celtic helmets shown on the Arc de Triomphe at Orange have a wide variety of motifs including horns and wheels. The warriors on the Gundestrup Cauldron bear helmets with crests, horns, boars and a bird. Two carefully fashioned objects of sheet bronze from La Tène have sometimes been tentatively interpreted as helmet crests, but it is possible too that they formed part of the battle standards (*militaria signa*) described by classical writers (Vouga 1923: 63–4).

'They wear bronze helmets with large projecting figures which give the wearer the appearance of enormous size. In some cases horns are attached so as to form one piece, in others the fore-parts of birds or quadrupeds worked in relief,' recorded Diodorus Siculus (*History* V.30.2).

The flamboyant helmets of the first phases of La Tène are well known, but the practical weapons of Late La Tène are part of a warrior panoply that is less frequently described. Iron helmets, for example, from Port bei Nidau (Bern), Giubiasco (Ticino) and Novo mesto (Slovenia) (Schaaff 1974; 1980; 1988: 302–9) have stout neck protection and practical cheek-pieces. The weaponry of the warrior burial from Grave 169 at Novo mesto has been reconstructed by André Rapin (Figure 4.3), a researcher whose illustrations of Celtic warriors has done much to inform recent work in France; Rapin has kindly brought the illustrations up to date in the light of his research on sword-belts and using the evidence of the helmet from Smarjeta-Vinji (also in Slovenia). The cheek-pieces of such helmets, and doubtless the crests, retain some of the decorative ideals of earlier types, but there is no doubt that these are pieces of defensive armour appropriate to the grim reality of the battlefield. It is to the armourers' credit that aspects of the design were adopted in the Roman legionary helmet of the first century AD.

The famous Waterloo Bridge helmet dredged from the Thames in 1868 demonstrates that pieces of parade gear still had a place in the first century BC in eastern England (Megaw 1970: 170). The bronze head-piece, decorated in repoussé and applied roundels of red enamel or cupric glass, is a unique piece of flamboyant headgear like that from La Gorge Meillet, and it is unfortunate that it has found such a firm place in many popular reconstructions of British warriors. The helmeted heads on the bucket from Aylesford in Kent, however, surmounted with luxuriant crescentic crests, may serve to illustrate how illusory any search for the norm may be (Megaw 1970: 119–20).

CELTIC HORSEMANSHIP

Prowess in horsemanship is difficult to evoke from the archaeological record alone; certainly bridle bits and harness fittings show a love of finery and display. Spurs are shown on the Gundestrup Cauldron. It is as horsemen that Celtic warriors made their greatest impression on classical authors. 'The whole race of Gauls is madly fond of war,' writes Strabo (*Geography* IV.4.2). 'Although they are all fighters by nature, they are better as cavalry than as infantry. . . . The best of the Roman cavalry is recruited from among them.' Another tribute comes from Plutarch: 'The Gauls are particularly formidable at fighting on horse-back and they are reputed to be excellent in this arm above any other' (*Marcellus* 6).

According to Pausanias there was at the time of the Celtic invasion of Greece a certain cavalry exercise called *trimarcisia* (*marca* is the Celtic word for a horse). It involved three horsemen, a chieftain and two grooms. The grooms would stay behind ready to supply their master with a fresh horse if his were wounded; one groom would take his place if he were injured or killed, and the other would take him back to camp if he were wounded. The idea behind this was to keep the number of their horsemen complete (279 BC) (Pausanias, *Guide to Greece* X.19).

At the battle of Ticinus the Roman javelin-throwers fled, terrified by the approaching charge and of being trampled underfoot by the horsemen. The cavalry forces met head-on and soon so many had dismounted that it became a mixed action of cavalry

NOVO MESTO. T. 169.

A. RAPIN. 1982.

Figure 4.3 The warrior panoply of burial 169, Novo mesto, Slovenia.
(Drawn by André Rapin.)

and infantry. At Cannae there was none of the usual advance and withdrawal: as soon as the two forces met they dismounted and fought on foot, man to man (Polybius, *Histories* III.65 and 115). Such actions were forced upon the opposing units because of lack of space for any outflanking or skirmishing manoeuvres (Livy, *History* XXII.47).

The German cavalry used to dismount and fight on foot; they had trained their horses to remain on the spot so that they could return to them quickly in case of need. The Celtiberians had a similar manoeuvre, but they had a small peg attached to their reins which they fixed to the ground when they dismounted to keep the horses on that spot until they returned (Polybius, *Fragment* 21). Other warrior bands clearly fought from horseback rather than dismounting; a skilful horseman armed with a stout lance as well as a sword, shield and perhaps a helmet would have been an effective member of any charge. The use of spears by mounted warriors is attested by representations on coins and on the Gundestrup Cauldron.

When Caesar crossed the Rhine, he discovered that the Germans thought it rather shameful to use saddles and that they dared to engage with any number of saddled horsemen regardless of how many they were outnumbered by (Caesar, *De Bello Gallico* IV.2).

The Roman and Celtic squadrons had horses which were bridled (*frenati*) and saddled (*instrati*). When the Numidian cavalry came on the scene they were always referred to as unbridled (*sine frenis*). Neither the Romans nor the Celts had knowledge of stirrups. The fullest appreciation of the Celtic skills in horsemanship is provided by Arrian writing in AD 136 in a manual of cavalry training. 'The Romans have adopted the exercises of the Celtic horsemen who, in their opinion, had the highest reputation in battle.' He describes fully how these were used in a special cavalry school whose patron was the Emperor Hadrian (Arrian, *Res Tactica* 33–4).

BURIALS AND VOTIVE DEPOSITS

By beginning our discussion with the most prestigious and individual aspects of the archaeological record, warrior burials with chariots, and then following such themes as helmets and horsemanship, we have concentrated on the unusual rather than on the mass of the evidence. Such a course is compounded both by the archaeological richness and by the predilection for the unusual among the classical authors, perhaps a natural partiality of reportage. But the large numbers of burials belonging to the core of any warrior band, which have been found in particular areas of Celtic Europe (though not in others), is in itself remarkable. Almost no other group represented in the archaeological and historical evidence from such a wide geographical spectrum commands comparable respect from its peers (and it is perhaps worth noting that burials of mercenary Celts are almost unknown). This respect may also be sensed in the absence of evidence for grave-robbing, although the location of many burials must have been evident.

The ritual and religious aspects of Celtic warfare and weapons may seem at some remove from the essentially practical aspects of this chapter, but the richness of the preservation of organic material from votive deposits in many parts of the Celtic world and the large numbers of weapons discovered in watery circumstances make this an important source of information. Did such deposits represent dedication before the battle, with the casting of swords, shields, spears and bronze objects into the waters of the river Thièle near its confluence with the Lac de Neuchâtel at La Tène or into the pool of Llyn Cerrig Bach in Anglesey? Were such rituals part of a thanksgiving after a successful campaign with the deposit of weapons gathered from the battlefield? The circumstances of such offerings can never be known, but the preservation of evidence for the shape and make-up of shields as at La Tène or identification of the ash of spear shafts make them a valuable source of practical information. Ritual dedication of weapons may be an answer at Gournay-sur-Aronde (Oise), a ditched enclosure with an internal stockade; the stockade appears to have been decorated with trophies of warrior gear (sword, scabbard, shield, spearhead), particularly on the eastern side of the enclosure. Skulls too appear to have been displayed. The ritual aspects of the site are obviously one reason for its importance: the large numbers of weapons recorded in stratified deposits – over 200 shields for example – are among the most extensive in the Celtic world (Brunaux *et al.* 1985; Brunaux and Rapin 1988).

SPEARS, SWORDS AND SHIELDS

A brief examination of the development of the sword (and suspension chain), spear and shield of the foot soldier illustrates the panoply and hints at the tactics of the mass of the Celtic warrior band. Volleys of spears were thrown at the start of an engagement; such volleys were clearly an important first stage, striking at the heart of any opposing band, as well as causing havoc if the spears became embedded in an enemy's shield. A considerable range of shapes of spearhead has been found from burials and ritual deposits; throwing spears – javelins (the word coming from the Gaulish *gabalaccos/gabalottus*) – had lighter heads and presumably shorter shafts than the lances, which might be both thrown or used in hand-to-hand or mounted combat. The large number of spearheads from Gournay-sur-Aronde has allowed a typological sequence to be proposed illustrating fashions in shape from before 300 BC to about 100 BC; spearheads of classic lanceolate form occur throughout the period, but more oval forms are present in the third century and more bayonet-like heads, particularly suitable as thrusting weapons, are present in the second century (Brunaux and Rapin 1988: 132–4). From La Tène itself come two complete spears measuring over 2.4 m in length from tip to butt with shafts of ash from which the bark has been stripped (Vouga 1923: 54). Ash was also favoured for the shafts of the spears at Llyn Cerrig Bach, Anglesey (Fox 1947: 6), and ash, willow and hazel in Yorkshire (Stead 1991b: 75).

In Champagne swords of the Early La Tène period taper to a long sharp point, while those of La Tène II have a longer blade, which tapers only towards the tip to a more rounded point (Stead 1983: 490). From the late second century the typical sword is longer and wider than its La Tène II predecessor. In his studies of weaponry Rapin has convincingly shown that the evolution in the combat gear demonstrates the determination of Celtic armourers to ensure the lightest and the most effective use of the materials at their disposal, iron and wood primarily. Such work can be illustrated in typological study of belt-chains and shield fittings for example (Rapin 1987). Armourers used a hot welding process that ensured that the blade was strong but retained a degree of elasticity; the forged blades were surmounted with a hilt of organic material, probably with additional embellishments; in some cases armourers stamped their weapons with an individual mark. The decoration on sword scabbards falls beyond the essentially practical scope of this chapter, but the fine detail shows that the artistic skills that were employed for the weapons of the élite, on helmets for example, found a more widespread expression on the bronze scabbards of a greater number of warriors (de Navarro 1972; Megaw and Megaw 1989:126–35). Sword scabbards from Britain were also on occasion individually decorated in insular styles (Piggott 1950), and superb examples from Little Wittenham in Oxfordshire, and Isleham in Cambridgeshire, among others, have added to the artistic range in more recent years (Stead 1991b: 64–74). In both Britain and on the Continent a distinct accessory weapon, a short sword with an anthropoid handle, has been found; at North Grimston, in Yorkshire, a burial found in 1902 was accompanied by a long slashing sword and a short sword with an anthropoid hilt, perhaps a stabbing weapon.

Classical authors found the length of the Celtic sword remarkable: 'Instead of the short sword they carry long swords held by a chain of iron or bronze and hanging along their right flank,' recorded Diodorus Siculus (*History* V.30.3). The Celtic sword can be used only for cutting and not for thrusting: the Celts raise their arms to slash; this is the stroke peculiar to them, as their swords have no point (Polybius, *Histories* II.33). Polybius also implies that after the first slash the edges became blunted and the blades so bent that, unless the warrior had time to straighten the blade with his foot, the second blow had no effect. The Celtiberians excel in the making of swords, for their point is strong and effective and they can cut with both edges (Polybius, *Histories* III. 114; *Fragment* 22.4). Tacitus describes the Caledonian swords as unwieldy and unsuited to fighting at close quarters (*Agricola* 36). The Gauls had very long slashing swords, says Dionysius of Halicarnassus. They raised their arms aloft and smote, throwing the whole weight of their bodies into the blows as if they intended to cut the bodies of their opponents into pieces (*History of Rome* XIV.10).

Celtic shields used several different materials in their manufacture: wood for the shield itself and for the midrib or spine, which formed a boss over the horizontal handgrip (birch and lime may have been favoured for lightness, oak for strength); leather as an overall covering; and in some cases iron as a binding round the edge, as part of the hand-grip and as additional protection to the central spine. The wooden midrib was an important part of the shield for it bore the brunt of the pressure from any charge, and the midrib was often strengthened by iron cladding, ultimately in the form of a horizontal strip boss with a single rivet on either flank. Additional decoration might include rosettes of bronze or painted motifs. In many burial deposits, only the metal parts now survive, and the shape and make-up of the shield has to be inferred from the disposition of the shield's constituent metal parts in the grave. The proportions of the shield offered protection to between half and two-thirds of the height of the buried warrior. A small number of metal fittings is known from La Tène I, but many are known from La Tène II both from burials and from votive depositions. Several waterlogged deposits have allowed the preservation of organic remains, but only on sculpture do we have any impression of the variety of painted or applied decoration. One third-century burial, chosen from many because of a careful reconstruction drawing of the warrior, is that from Rungis, Val-de-Marne (Figure 4.4) (Andrieux and Rapin 1984; Kruta and Rapin 1987); here an oval shield with central midrib was furnished with a strip boss with semi-circular side flanges with central rivets and a longitudinal rib across the boss. The warrior had been armed with a sword hanging from a chain from his belt and a spear. In many burials the shape of the shield may be determined by the outline of fragments of the binding strip. Excavations in recent years have also revealed a considerable variety of individual decorative motifs as well as the binding strip; that from Grave 14 at Ménfocsanak, in Hungary, for example, appears to have had four matching rosettes and criss-cross metal covering to the central spine rather like the topping of a hot cross bun (Horváth *et al* 1987: 23–5, pl.xv–xvi; Szabó 1988: fig. 13). Ritual deposits at La Tène show the use of a series of vertical planks pinned together to form the board. The sculpture of a warrior from Mondragon, Vaucluse, illustrates a more complex form of diagonal planking. The large numbers of bosses found at Gournay-sur-Aronde allow a local sequence of boss shape to be proposed, illustrating changing fashions throughout the third and second centuries BC (Rapin 1983b; Bruneaux and Rapin 1988). Local sequences from weapons associated with burials have been worked out for several discrete geographical areas, notably Bohemia where there are changes in style of sword, shield-boss, spear and butt at a similar period (Waldhauser *et al*. 1987: 34, fig. 3). Circular bosses are found in first-century BC contexts and are represented on sculpture, for example on the Arc de Triomphe at Orange. The circular boss does not, however, necessarily betoken a circular shield, as those on the Arc de Triomphe, on the model from Saint-Maur-en-Chaussée (Oise) and on the Gundestrup Cauldron demonstrate. The representations of shields at Orange illustrate many decorative motifs, either as appliqué or painted patterns, evidence of which has not so far been found elsewhere. The outline figure of an elongated boar can still be made out on the shield from Witham, in Lincolnshire, as well as the rivet holes by which this appliqué decoration was fixed to the surface of the bronze shield; the shield was subsequently refashioned and the figure was replaced by the famous boss, spine and roundels which are the most noteworthy features today. Among the few examples of decorated bronze bosses from continental Europe are those from Nogent-sur-Seine, Aube (Rapin 1983c).

Although the shields of Celtic warriors were clearly effective on the battlefield, classical authors were not always complimentary; Diodorus Siculus, for example: 'For arms they have man-sized shields decorated in a manner peculiar to them. Some of them have projecting figures in bronze, skilfully wrought not only for decoration but also for protection' (*History* v.30.2), whereas other authors mention that the Celts had no other defensive armour than their traditional oblong shields and assert that the Gallic shield would not cover the whole body. Their shields were long but not wide enough for the size of their bodies, and moreover, because they were flat, they offered poor protection to the bearers. Wooden shields were thought to be a

Figure 4.4 Warrior burial, Rungis, Val-de-Marne. (Drawn by André Rapin.)

disadvantage because they might be pierced or even pinned together by spears and thus become too heavy to wield. The Gauls are also reported to have used shields made of bark or wickerwork, hastily covered with skins.

British shields stand apart from the European examples not only because of the range of shape and use of richly decorated bronze bosses, but also because of the discovery of shields with elaborate bronze sheeting and bosses from Witham (Lincolnshire) and Battersea (London) as well as a complete shield from Chertsey (Surrey) (Stead 1985, 1987, 1991c). Discussion of British shields highlights the dilemma outlined at the beginning of this chapter: everyday examples are very few, whereas exquisitely decorated pieces such as the boss from Llyn Cerrig Bach (Anglesey) and fittings from Tal y Llyn (Merioneth) could not have been appreciated on the battlefield, and the objects they represent may have been visual metaphors of warrior status for ceremonial occasions (Fox 1947; Savory 1964). Similarly, the magnificent bronze shields from Witham, Battersea and Chertsey may be symbols of position and wealth as well as demonstrating the importance of weaponry in religious depositions; several examples of model shields are miniature versions, perhaps for religious or votive dedications (Cunliffe 1991: 514; Stead 1991c). Of the small number of British burials with weapons, very few have surviving parts of a shield, the most remarkable being that from Owslebury, in Hampshire, which has a bronze boss with a central point (Collis 1973; Dent 1983).

MAIL AND BODY ARMOUR

Varro records that the invention of the shirt of mail of interlocking rings belongs to Celtic armourers, although doubtless its use was very restricted. A small number of pieces is known, including Ciumesti and Kirkburn, as well as representations at Pergamon and Vachères. Mail shirts protected the torso to below the waist and often had broad shoulder straps with decorative rosettes; the shoulder pieces must not only have provided additional protection but also helped to spread the weight that a warrior would have to bear in the field. The use of mail clearly ran counter to traditions of disregard for body armour and the pride in nakedness noted by Diodorus Siculus: 'Some of them have iron breast plates wrought in chain, while others are satisfied with the arms nature has given them and fight naked' (*History* V.30.3). The sculpture from Entremont has been interpreted as showing either mail shirts with shoulder and pectoral decoration or leather body armour with bronze rosettes and figural decoration (Benoit 1955). A delightful small bronze figure from Gutenberg (Liechtenstein) wears what is more certainly a leather cuirasse with well-marked shoulder pieces and a fringed hem. Such model figures as that from Saint-Maur-en-Chaussée (Oise) and Gutenberg were clearly figures of warrior gods, but there is no reason to think that the representation of the tunics is not accurate. Only the Gundestrup Cauldron offers more detailed representation with the foot soldiers and carnyx-blowers wearing long-sleeved singlets and tight trousers akin to cycling shorts and the horsemen have waist-length tunics of similar material (Klindt-Jensen 1961).

SLINGS

The use of slings is attested from southern Britain, Brittany, and for example at le Puy du Tour (Corrèze) (Ralston 1992: 52), but it is a custom that may be difficult to recognize in the archaeological record. The defence of Maiden Castle (Dorset) and Danebury (Hampshire) was in part undertaken by slingers (Cunliffe 1991: 489). Piles of sling stones made ready for use at Maiden Castle were found to have been chosen to be broadly the same weight (50 grams). Less organized use of material hurled at the enemy is recorded from Gaul where Caesar describes an incident in the course of which a Gaul who was throwing lumps of tallow and pitch was killed by an arrow from a catapult. During one siege the Gauls began slinging (*fundis iacere*) moulded bullets of red-hot slag and hurling incendiary darts (Caesar, *De Bello Gallico* VII.25).

ARCHERY

Archery too played a part in Celtic life, Strabo recording that some Celts 'also use bows and slings', and during sacrifices 'they used to shoot men down with arrows' (Strabo, *Geography* IV. 4.3, 4.5). Vercingetorix, during his war against Caesar, ordered all the archers, and there was a very large number in Gaul, to be sought out and brought to him. The cavalry was sent out daily with archers dispersed among their ranks to help them if they were yielding and to check the enemy's advance (Caesar, *De Bello Gallico* VII.31,36,80). Arrowheads have been found among other locations at Alésia (Duval 1970), Gournay and Manching (Sievers 1989: 101).

CELTS IN BATTLE

Classical authors, in creating a picture of contrasts between the Celts and their own audiences, told stories of noise, of naked combat and of head-taking. Such accounts still have an important role in our understanding of the way in which the warrior bands of the third century were to make such an impact on the mythology and art of subsequent centuries. The two largest Gallic tribes in north Italy, the Insubres and the Boii, persuaded the Gaesatae who lived beyond the Alps and near the Rhone to join them in attacking Rome. The combined armies, which are said to have consisted of some 50,000 infantry and 20,000 cavalry and chariots, marched south in high spirits and advanced on Etruria. In Rome the people were filled with dread, for they had heard rumours of the approach of the Gauls; the old fear of the Gallic uprising and invasion had not yet been dispelled. The feelings of humiliation and terror inspired by the Gallic warriors lingered on. Each time they approached, it is said, the Roman authorities suspended municipal business and enrolled an army.

The historian Polybius gives a full account of the Celts in action at the battle of Telamon (225 BC), and it is worth quoting certain passages which highlight recurring features of Celtic customs and manoeuvres (*Histories* II.28). It is sometimes said that the charge was the centrepiece of Celtic offensive tactics, in which they relied on unbounded fury, strength and dexterity. The charge succeeded because of the emphasis on individual effort, but if the attack failed, it became clear that the Celts lacked the essential skills of military organization.

> The Insubres and the Boii wore trousers and light cloaks, but the Gaesatae, in their love of glory and defiant spirit, had thrown off their garments and taken up their position in front of the whole army naked and wearing nothing but their arms. . . . The appearance of these naked warriors was a terrifying spectacle, for they were all men of splendid physique and in the prime of life.

In later times, however, when the Celts were acting as mercenaries, they had to make some modifications in their dress and movements to fit in with the regulations of the army in which they were serving. At the battle of Cannae (216 BC) the Celts were naked from the navel up and the Iberians wore dazzling white linen shirts bordered with purple. But some Celts in Asia Minor still fought naked, and their wounds were plain to see, because their bodies were white, never exposed except in battle (Livy, *History* XXII.46 and XXXVIII.21). Dionysius of Halicarnassus wrote in scorn, 'Our enemies fight naked. What injury could their long hair, their fierce looks, their clashing arms do us? These are mere symbols of barbarian boastfulness' (*History of Rome* XIV.9). But the Celts were fighting naked, not because they were boastful and arrogant, but in accordance with religious and social customs.

TRUMPETS AND NOISE

> The fine order and the noise of the Celtic host terrified the Romans, for there were countless trumpeters and horn-blowers, and since the whole army was shouting its war-cries at the same time there was such a confused sound that the noise seemed to come not only from the trumpeters and soldiers but also from the country-side which was joining in the echo.
>
> (Polybius, *Histories* II.29)

This tactical use of noise is variously described as wild outbursts, hideous songs, and a thoroughly terrifying sound; in Asia Minor, their yells and their leaping, the dreadful noise of arms as they beat their shields in some traditional custom was orchestrated to terrify the enemy. The Carthaginians also, when attempting to cross the Rhône, saw the Gallic warriors come surging to the bank howling and singing as was their custom, shaking their shields above their heads and brandishing their spears (Livy, *History* I.37; XXXVIII.17; XXI.28).

According to Caesar's description of the Gauls they were no less demonstrative. 'In their usual custom they raised their shout of triumph (*ululatus*) and broke our ranks; elsewhere the same words are used in a less triumphant situation when the Gauls encouraged their comrades with shouts and yells (*clamore et ululatu*)' (Caesar, *De Bello Gallico* V.37; VII.80). There was also the noise of the trumpeters and horn-blowers. 'They had trumpets peculiar to them and barbaric in sound: for when they blew upon them, they produced a harsh sound, suitable to the tumult of battle' (Diodorus Siculus, *History* V.30.3). The trumpet (or carnyx) is represented on Celtic coinage, on classical sculpture, notably at Pergamon in Asia Minor, at Orange, on an

altar from Nîmes, both in southern France, as well as on the Gundestrup Cauldron;
a few fragments have survived, most notably the boar-shaped trumpet-mouth from
Deskford in Banffshire (Piggott 1959) and a bronze duck-shaped carnyx from
Castiglione delle Stiviere, Mantua (de Marinis 1977).

HEAD-TAKING

'The consul Gaius fell fighting desperately ... and his head was brought back to the
Celtic kings.' Polybius mentions very briefly the custom of decapitation (*Histories*
II.28). After a battle between the Senones and the Romans near Clusium, the consul
had no news of the battle until some Gallic horsemen came in sight with heads
hanging from their horses' breasts or fixed on spears. The riders were singing their
customary song of triumph (Livy, *History* X.26). Once when the Boii had caught a
Roman army in an ambush, they cut off the head of the leader and carried it to their
most hallowed temple. There the head was cleaned out, and the skull gilded and used
as a sacred vessel (Livy, *History* XXIII.24). The taking of an adversary's head is
described by Diodorus Siculus:

> When the enemies fall, the Gauls cut off their heads and fasten them to the
> necks of their horses. . . . They nail up the heads in their houses. They embalm
> in cedar-oil the heads of the most distinguished of their enemies and keep them
> carefully in a chest: they display them with pride to strangers. They refuse to
> accept for them a large sum of money or even the weight of the head in gold.
>
> (Diodorus Siculus, *History* V.29.4–5)

The religious significance of the practice is not explored by classical authors, and to
the Romans it was a sign of barbarism. They put an end to it, says Strabo, and to the
acts of divination and to the sacrifices which were contrary to Roman customs. There
is no mention of the practice of head-taking in Caesar's Commentaries.

SINGLE COMBAT

Several tales mention the Celtic custom of single combat. 'It was their custom,' says
Diodorus Siculus,

> when drawn up for battle to come forward before the front line and challenge
> the bravest of their enemies drawn up opposite them to single combat.
> Whenever one accepts the challenge, they praise in song the manly virtues of
> their ancestors and also their own brave deeds. . . . Then reviling and belittling
> their opponents they try to rob them by their words of their boldness of spirit
> before the contest.
>
> (*History* V.29.3)

The exploits of Roman leaders and Celtic giants became famous. Titus Manlius
killed the leader of the Senones in a battle near the river Anio (361 BC). Marcus Valerius
overcame the Gallic champion with the help of a raven (349 BC). Marcus Claudius

Marcellus killed Britomarus, the Insubrian leader, at Clastidium (222 BC). It is told that in the battle Britomarus advanced, and picking out Marcus Claudius Marcellus by means of his badges of rank, shouted a challenge and brandished his spear. He was an outstanding figure not only for his size but also for his adornments; he was resplendent in bright colours and his armour shone with gold and silver.

MERCENARIES

In 369–368 BC some 2,000 Celtic soldiers were hired by Dionysius I of Syracuse and sent to Greece to help his ally Sparta against Thebes; they received pay for five months. Celtic mercenaries played an important part in the wars of the western Mediterranean, in Asia Minor and in Egypt from the fourth century BC; from these encounters we learn something of the warfare and tactics of the Celts themselves, even if it is only in comparison to contrasting approaches (Xenophon, *Hellenica* VII.1.20; Diodorus Siculus, *History* XV.70.1). Pyrrhus with a host of Celtic soldiers defeated Antigonus of Macedonia and his Celtic followers. Later Pyrrhus captured Aegae, the cult centre of the royal house and left the Celts to garrison the city. Driven by their insatiable appetite for money, they dug up the tombs of the rulers and stole their treasures (Pausanias, *Guide to Greece* I.13.2; Plutarch, *Pyrrhus* 26.6). From this time on it could be said that no eastern king waged war without Celtic warriors. Such was the terror of the Celtic name, and so sure the success of their arms that the kings thought they could not protect their royal power nor recover it, if lost, without the support of Celtic valour. Ptolemy II Philadelphus brought in 4,000 Gauls (277–276 BC), but he caught them plotting to take over Egypt. He put them on an uncultivated island where they murdered one another or perished from hunger. In another unsuccessful campaign the Celts who were serving with Attalus I, King of Pergamon, became discontented with the hardship of the march, chiefly because they were accompanied by their wives and children, and refused to go on. Attalus made all sorts of offers to make them stay, but finally led them back to the Hellespont (Polybius, *Histories* V.77–8).

The Carthaginians recruited Celts for their army in Sicily (250–241 BC), and during the Punic Wars Gauls and Iberians (usually cavalry) fought in all the major battles of Hannibal. Army leaders of both camps were aware of the fickleness and treachery of the Gauls. Scipio remembered the perfidy of the Boii. Hannibal, constantly on guard against attempts on his life, even had various wigs made to give the impression of a man of a different age (Polybius, *Histories* I.43, 67, 77).

To make a list of the mercenary groups and to marvel at the large numbers involved is easy; to explain how the system, begun by Dionysius of Syracuse in 369 BC and lasting three centuries, worked is quite baffling. It is important to give an account of mercenary activity, however, for even if the numbers are widely exaggerated, the readiness of large bands of warriors to travel over great distances is well recorded – movements that are for the most part undetected from archaeological evidence. Mercenary groups such as these must also be among the first where financial gain rather than political or economic pressures was paramount – with consequential effects on the economies around them. But they must often have become so detached from the original heartlands of Celtic tribes that their importance lies as much in their ability to retain a recognizably Celtic identity as in their prowess as warriors. The relationship between payment and military activity is also raised by the possibility of standing armed forces in first-century Gaul based on both the evidence of Caesar and that of the production of gold coinage; but there is as yet no general agreement on the importance of the social divisions outlined by Caesar, the *pagus* for example, and the military organization of Gaulish forces (Ralston 1992: 142–3).

The era of stylized warfare and ceremonial, symbolized by La Gorge Meillet for example, the age of myth and single combat evoked by the tales of Titus Manlius, Marcus Valerius and Marcus Claudius Marcellus gave way in the first century BC to the reality of warfare for political freedom. Perhaps the record of the dedication and eventual deposition over two centuries of many hundreds of weapons at Gournay-sur-Aronde gives the most telling indication of the endemic nature of warfare among the Celtic tribes themselves. The weapons of Caesar's protagonists in Gaul, for example, were thus made in workshops and armouries with several centuries of tradition in maintaining a high order of manufacture; something of the respect in which the Romans held their adversaries may be sensed in the careful way such arms are depicted on such monumental statements of victory as the Arc de Triomphe at Orange. In the end it was superior military organization and tactics that won the day rather than superior weaponry, for, as Tacitus says of the Caledonians after Mons Graupius, 'they would try to concert plans, then break off'.

ACKNOWLEDGEMENTS

We should like to thank Dr Ian Ralston, André Rapin and Dr Anna Ritchie for their support and advice throughout the preparation of the chapter.

REFERENCES

Amy, R. *et al.* (1962) 'L'Arc d'Orange', *Gallia* Supplément 15, Paris: CNRS.

Andrieux, P. and Rapin, A. (1984) 'La sépulture du guerrier gaulois de Rungis, Val-de-Marne (iiie siècle av. J.-C.)', in *Lutèce: Paris de César à Clovis*, Paris: Musée Carnavalet, Société des Amis de Musée Carnavalet, 65–71.

Benoit, F. (1955) *L'Art primitif méditerranéen de la vallée du Rhône*, Gap: Annales de la Faculté des Lettres d'Aix-en-Provence.

Brunaux, J.-L. and Lambot, B. (1987) *Guerre et armement chez les Gaulois*, Paris: Editions Errance.

Brunaux, J.-L. and Rapin, A. (1988) *Gournay II: boucliers et lances, dépôts et trophées*, Paris: Revue Archéologique de Picardie, Editions Errance.

Brunaux, J.-L., Meniel, P. and Poplin, F. (1985) *Gournay I: Les fouilles sur le sanctuaire et l'oppidum (1975–1984)*, Amiens: Revue Archéologique de Picardie.

Collis, J.R. (1973) 'Burials with weapons in iron age Britain', *Germania* 51: 121–33.

Connolly, P. (1978) *Hannibal and the Enemies of Rome*, London: Macdonald.

Cunliffe, B.W. (1991) *Iron Age Communities in Britain* 3rd edn, London and New York: Routledge.

Déchelette, J. (1927) *Manuel d'archéologie préhistorique celtique et gallo-romaine*, IV: *Second âge du fer ou époque de la Tène*, Paris: Picard.

Dent, J.S. (1983) 'Weapons, wounds and war in the Iron Age', *Archaeological Journal* 140: 120–8.

Duval, A. (1970) 'Les pointes de flèche d'Alésia au Musée des Antiquités Nationales', *Bulletin des Antiquités Nationales* 2: 35–51.

—— (1989) *L'Art celtique de la Gaule au Musée des Antiquités Nationales*, Paris: Réunion des Musées Nationaux.

Fourdringier, E. (1878) *Double sépulture gauloise de la Gorge Meillet, territoire de Somme-Tourbe (Marne)*, Paris and Châlons-sur-Marne: privately published.

Fox, Sir C. (1947) *A Find of the Early Iron Age from Llyn Cerrig Bach, Anglesey*, Cardiff: National Museum of Wales.

Frey, O.-H. (1968) 'Ein neue Grabstele aus Padua', *Germania* 46: 317–20.

Furger-Gunti, A. (1991) 'The Celtic war chariot: the experimental reconstruction in the Schweizerisches Landesmuseum', in S. Moscati *et al.* (eds) *The Celts*, 356–9.

Guštin, M. (ed.) (1977) *Keltske Studije*, Ljubljana: Brežice.

Guštin, M. and Pauli, L. (eds) (1984) *Keltski Voz*, Ljubljana: Brežice.

Haffner, A. and Joachim, H.-E. (1984) 'Die keltischen Wagengräber der Mittelrheingruppe', in M. Guštin and L. Pauli (eds) *Keltski Voz*, 71–87.

Harbison, P. (1969) 'The chariot of Celtic funerary tradition', *Fundberichte aus Hessen* 1: 34–58.

Horváth, L., Kelemen, M., Uzsoki, A. and Vadász, É. (1987) *Corpus of Celtic Finds in Hungary*, Transdanubia 1, Budapest: Académiai Kiadó.

Klindt-Jensen, O. (1961) *Gundestrupkedelen*, Copenhagen: National Museum.

Kruta, V. and Rapin, A. (1987) 'Une sépulture de guerrier gaulois du iiie siècle avant Jésus-Christ découverte à Rungis (Val-de-Marne)', *Cahiers de la Rotonde* 10: 5–35.

Lorenz, H. (1986) 'Association d'armes dans les sépultures de la Tène ancienne en Europe de l'ouest – un reflet de l'armement', *Revue Aquitania* Supplement 1: 281–4.

de Marinis, R. (1977) 'The La Tène culture of the Cisalpine Gauls', in M. Guštin (ed.) *Keltske Studije*, 23–50.

Megaw, J.V.S. (1970) *Art of the European Iron Age*, Bath: Adams & Dart.

Megaw, R. and Megaw, V. *(1989) Celtic Art: from its beginnings to the Book of Kells*, London: Thames & Hudson.

Moscati, S. *et al* (1991) *The Celts*, London: Thames & Hudson.

de Navarro, J.M. (1972) *The Finds from the Site of La Tène I: scabbards and the swords found in them*, London: British Academy.

Penninger, E. (1972) *Der Dürrnberg bei Hallein I*, Munich: C.H. Beck'sche Verlagsbuchhandlung.

Piggott, S. (1950) 'Swords and scabbards of the British Early Iron Age', *Proceedings of the Prehistoric Society* 16: 1–28.

—— (1959) 'The carnyx in early iron age Britain', *Antiquaries Journal* 39: 19–32.

Ralston, I.B.M. (1992) *Les Enceintes fortifiées du Limousin*, Documents d'Archéologie Française 36, Paris: Editions de la Maison des Sciences de l'Homme.

Rapin, A. (1983a) 'L'armement du guerrier celte au 2e âge du fer', in *L'Art celtique en Gaule*, Collections des Musées de Province; exhibition Marseille, Paris, Bordeaux and Dijon, 1983–4.

—— (1983b) 'Les umbos de bouclier de Gournay-sur-Aronde (Oise)', *Revue Archéologique de Picardie*, 1: 174–80.

—— (1983c) 'Les umbos de bouclier celtiques décorés de Nogent-sur-Seine au Musée des Antiquités Nationales', *Bulletin des Antiquités Nationales* 14/15: 70–7.

—— (1987) 'Le système de suspension des fourreaux d'epées latèniens aux iii siècle av. J.-C. . . .', in D. Vitali (ed.) *Celti ed Etruschi*, Bologna: Bologna University Press, 529–30.

Rusu, M. (1969) 'Das keltische Fürstengrab von Ciumesti in Romanien', *Berichte der Römisch-Germanische Kommission* 50: 267–300.

Savory, H.N. (1964) 'The Tal-y-lyn hoard', *Antiquity* 38: 18–31.

Schaaff, U. (1973) 'Frühlatènezeitliche Grabfunde mit Helmen vom Typ Berru', *Jahrbuch Römisch-Germanisch Zentralmuseum* 20: 81–106.

—— (1974) 'Keltische Eisenhelme aus vorrömischer Zeit', *Jahrbuch Römisch-Germanische Zentralmuseum* 21: 149–204.

—— (1980) 'Ein spätkeltisches Kriegergrab mit Eisenhelm aus Novo mesto', *Situla* 20-1: 397–413.

—— (1988) 'Keltische Helme', in A. Bottini, *et al.*, *Antike Helme: Sammlung Lipperheide*, Mainz. Römisch-Germanisches Zentralmuseum, Monograph 14, 293–317.

Sievers, S. (1989) 'Die Waffen von Manching unter Berücksichtigung des Übergangs von LTC zu LTD', *Germania* 67: 97–120.

Stead, I.M. (1979) *The Arras Culture*, York: Yorkshire Philosophical Society.

—— (1983) 'La Tène swords and scabbards in Champagne', *Germania* 61: 487–510.

—— (1984) 'Cart-burials in Britain, in M. Guštin and L. Pauli (eds) *Keltski Voz*, 31–41.

—— (1985) *The Battersea Shield*, London: British Museum.

—— (1987) 'The Chertsey shield', *Surrey Archaeological Collections* 78: 181–3.

—— (1988) 'Kirkburn: a Yorkshire chariot burial – with a coat of mail', *Current Archaeology* 111: 115–17.

—— (1991a) 'Somme Bionne', in S. Moscati *et al.* (eds) *The Celts*, 174–5.

—— (1991b) *Iron Age Cemeteries in East Yorkshire*, London: English Heritage, Archaeological Report 22.

—— (1991c) 'Many more iron age shields from Britain', *Antiquaries Journal* 71: 1–35.

Szabó, M. (1988) *Les Celtes en Pannonie: contribution à l'historie de la civilisation celtique dans la cuvette des Karpates*. Etudes d'Histoire d'Archéologie 3, Paris: Presses de l'Ecole Normale Supérieure.

Vitali, D. (1985) 'Monte Bibele (Monterenzio) und andere Fündstellen der keltischen Epoche in Gebiet von Bologna', *Kleine Schriften aus dem Vorgeschichtlichen Seminar Marburg* 16.

—— (ed.) (1990) *Monterenzio e la valle dell'Idice: archeologia e storià di un territorio*, Bologna: Bologna University Press.

Vouga, P. (1923) *La Tène*, Leipzig: Hiersemann.

Waldhauser, J. *et al.* (1987) 'Keltische Gräberfelder in Böhmen', *Bericht der Römisch-Germanische Kommission* 68: 25–179.

Zeller, K.W. (1980) 'Kriegswesen und Bewaffnung der Kelten', in L. Pauli (ed.) *Die Kelten in Mitteleuropa*, Hallein: Salzburger Landesregierung, 111–32.

FORTIFICATIONS AND DEFENCE

——— •◆• ———

Ian Ralston

Amongst the most conspicuous remains datable to later prehistoric times in many of the varied landscapes of temperate Europe are the enclosures which define hill- and promontory-forts. Generally set on elevated or other locations conferring natural defensive advantages, their complete or partial circuits envelop areas varying from less than one hectare to, in extreme cases, in excess of 1,000 ha. Compared to the internal structures within such sites, often now difficult to discern at ground level without excavation, the walls and ramparts which surround them are frequently readily appreciable, even where they are now cloaked in woodland, as is more commonly the case in continental Europe than in the British Isles (Audouze and Büchsenschütz 1992).

The cropmark aerial photographic record, however, provides intimations of works in the arable lowlands which may have been of similar strength initially, but which have since been entirely eradicated as above-ground, three-dimensional monuments. One of the most fully excavated examples in such a location in the United Kingdom occupied a slight knoll on the coastal plain at Broxmouth near Dunbar, East Lothian (Hill 1982). On the Continent, the most thoroughly examined of the massive late iron age enclosures, at Manching in Bavaria, Germany, equally sits (untypically for such sites) in a lowland setting, close to a tributary of the Danube (Maier 1986, with earlier literature). Thus, whilst man-made works normally enhance a naturally defensive location, this is not invariably the case; the topographic settings of some sites often classed with hill-forts may confer little or no altitudinal advantage. There is thus, particularly in the absence of excavation evidence, considerable scope for haziness at the interface between the classification, in English usage, of 'fort' (with its implications of defensive considerations) and 'enclosure', where the enveloping works are not interpreted in this way (Avery 1976).

Some of these constructions represent the most visible surviving testimony of large-scale civil engineering effort on the part of iron age communities. Conventionally, their enclosing features may be considered in terms of requirements for defence; but their characteristics, including the variety in their scales, detailed topographic settings (especially the emplacement of the earthworks relative to the configuration of the hill on which they sit) and architectural forms, suggest that this need falls far short of providing a wholly adequate *raison d'être* for all of them

(Harding 1979). Although the sequencing of the construction of southern British hill-fort defences in terms of a perceived response to invasion from continental Europe played an important role in the fieldwork programmes of major students of such sites like Hawkes (1931) and Wheeler (1943; Wheeler and Richardson 1957), this paradigm of invasion and response has generally fallen from favour.

Other factors, regional or more local in impact, can certainly be argued to have been of significance, on continental Europe as in the British Isles. These include the demonstration of prestige or status on the part of their builders, or more particularly the decision-makers who controlled their activities, and perhaps the need to give physical definition to the limits of jurisdictions, social, ritual, economic or political. More prosaic functions would include the separation of domestic livestock from living and other quarters (Cunliffe 1991).

The enclosure of sites, and by extension the idea of fortification, developed in Europe from the Neolithic period (Mercer 1989). During that timespan, enclosing works already displayed considerable variation in their apparent strengths: from simple palisades or stockades to massively enclosed sites. Neolithic archaeologists have interpreted the purposes of enclosed sites as fulfilling a range of functions, of which defence is but one.

By the Iron Age, enclosed sites, equally of variable apparent strength, were already a recurrent feature of many areas of the Continent, and were constructed by groups who, in so far as archaeological evidence permits their definition, were Celtic speakers, as well as others which were not. The writer's guesstimate is that in excess of 20,000 such sites survive unevenly distributed across non-Mediterranean Europe south of Scandinavia, excluding the 40,000 or so raths and related works in Ireland (see Raftery, Chapter 33).

Accruing evidence suggests that, in some areas, the construction, maintenance, upgrading and use of fortified sites was near-continuous; in others such activities appear to have been much more episodic (Cunliffe 1991; Audouze and Büchsen-schütz 1992; Biel 1987). Instances of settlement preceding the act of enclosure, as well as the contrary sequence, are both demonstrable archaeologically although in many cases the evidence is not clear-cut. In some regions, enclosed upland settlements are complemented by unenclosed sites (the *Höhensiedlungen* of German terminology) in similar topographic locations. Nor is there any straightforward correlation between fortification types and what can be discerned about styles of warfare, lending credence to current doubts that military requirements were always uppermost in the constructors' perceptions. Here a fundamental note of caution needs to be inserted, for almost all detailed evidence is based on rampart cuttings which represent the slightest of incisions relative to the overall length of enceintes, and the presumption that the remainder of the fortification was built in equivalent style is no more than that.

In general, although some fortifications may have had lean-to structures backed against their inner margins, they served to enclose free-standing buildings. In other cases, the internal areas show few traces of occupation and in these the enclosed areas are considered to have served a variety of purposes including a range of agri-cultural uses (such as the corralling of livestock), settings for ritual or display, and as temporary refuges.

It should be acknowledged that, given the passage of centuries of erosion and deposition, there is no straightforward way from the surface examination of earthworks in many instances readily to distinguish between a deliberate desire for fortification on the part of the original builders and enclosure primarily for other purposes. The topographic setting of lines of enclosure may, however, offer some assistance to speculation. Thus the now-diminutive and unexcavated banks which define the site of White Meldon in Tweeddale District, Scotland, are surmised to have been defensive not from their surviving stature but from their hilltop location on a prominent summit (Royal Commission on the Ancient and Historical Monuments of Scotland 1967): a 'high eminence' site, in Avery's terminology (1976: 8). In other cases, such as Scratchbury (Wiltshire), the establishment of the defences well down-slope, rendering much of the interior of the site visible from the adjacent lowland, may indicate a largely non-military purpose (Bowden and McOmish, 1987, 1989) (Figure 5.1). In many areas, including those dominated in more recent times by Celtic speakers, the building of fortifications in broadly similar architectural traditions continued well into the first millennium AD. Radiocarbon dates demonstrate this unequivocally for Scotland, for example (Alcock 1987). Earlier sites were also reoccupied and their enclosures remodelled in the Early Historic period, as at South Cadbury in Somerset (Alcock 1972, 1982). The fortifications of Celtic Europe are thus best regarded as a subset of a vast series, which is more extensive both in space and in time.

The materials used in the construction of fortifications are dominated by those standardly employed in temperate European protohistory: timber, stone and earth (Büchsenschütz 1984; Audouze and Büchsenschütz 1992). Reliance on wood, particularly in cases where structural elements were exposed to weathering, may be assumed to have produced fortifications generally of lesser durability; in some instances, these seem to have been serviceable for a few decades at most. The focus here on the architecture of fortifications mirrors the primary attention that has been devoted to this aspect of them in the archaeological literature.

The fortifications fall into three basic categories: palisades; walls, intended to have a near-vertical external face; and ramparts, in essence linear mounds fronted by an artificial slope or glacis. Fence, wall and dump, as Hawkes (1971) would have it.

Walls include those of simple dry-stone construction, employing either surface-gathered stone or quarried and, in some instances, roughly shaped blocks: on occasion, these may be imported to the site, as for the eastern gate at Maiden Castle, Dorset (Wheeler 1943). A variant form, marked by the presence of additional facings within the thickness of the core, is sometimes termed the *murus duplex*, the descriptor taken from Caesar's account of his subjugation of Gaul (*De Bello Gallico* II.29): at Worlebury in Somerset walls built in this style reach 11 m in width (Figure 5.2). Avery has proposed the descriptor 'shell construction' for this type of wall (1976: 14). Other examples, however, demonstrate substantial use of earth or even domestic detritus in their cores, and considerable components of structural timberwork, as will be discussed further below.

The most sophisticated achievement in terms of dry-stone architecture is that represented by the hollow-wall construction employed in brochs, best considered as a variant on the complex Atlantic round-houses of north-western Scotland

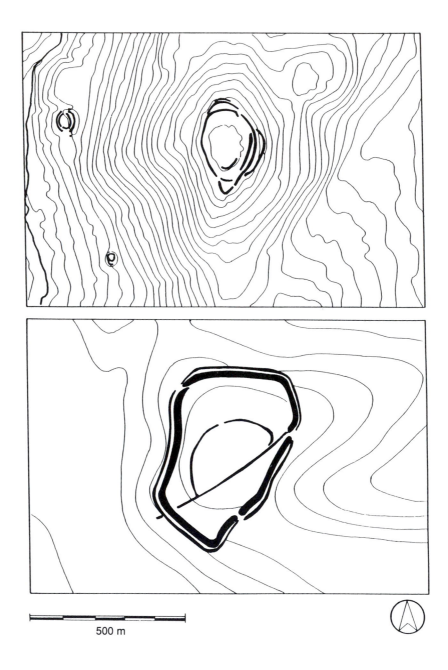

Figure 5.1 Comparative plans of rampart lines in relation to topography on White Meldon, Tweeddale District, Borders Region, Scotland and Scratchbury, Wiltshire, England. (Former redrawn from the Royal Commission on the Ancient and Historical Monuments of Scotland 1967 and Ordnance Survey NT 24 SW; the latter from Bowden and McOmish 1989: fig. 1. Drawn by Gordon Thomas.)

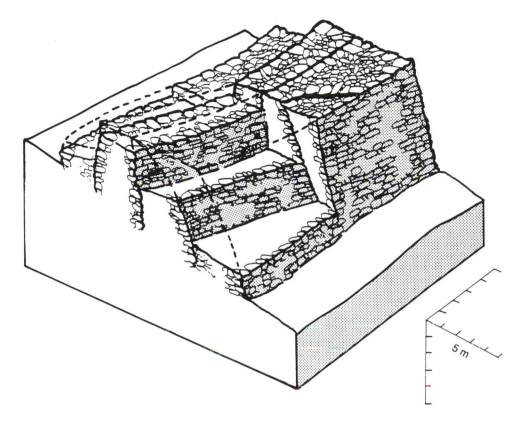

Figure 5.2 Block diagram illustrating the multiple built faces of the *murus duplex* construction, based on Worlebury, Somerset, England. (Drawn by Gordon Thomas after Hogg, 1975.)

constructed during the second half of the first millennium BC (Armit 1990). In these elaborate circular and near-circular towers, superimposed lintelled galleries, linking internal and external wall-faces, enabled heights in excess of 10 m to be attained (see MacKie, Chapter 34). In these, the monumental walls served to support the roof over the domestic living space, to signal their inhabitants' importance (in a very visible way in largely treeless landscapes) and to dissuade attack. A less spectacular version of such wholly roofed, heavy-walled enclosures may be represented by circular duns and related structures in Atlantic Britain. Such sites, in which individual walls arguably served both domestic and defensive ends, are best considered as elaborated versions of individual homesteads.

Many excavated examples of defences demonstrate heavy use of wood (Cunliffe 1991 for Britain; Büchsenschütz and Ralston 1981; Ralston 1981, 1992) as a structural component. Whilst characteristic of many fortifications in Celtic-speaking areas, this trait is in fact represented more widely both in space and in time in Europe. The earliest examples are again neolithic: as at Hambledon Hill, in south-western England (Mercer 1980) and Moulins-sur-Céphons in Berry, central France, the latter representing a precocious use of the Kastenbau technique, most commonly recorded further east. Iron age instances of the employment of wood in multi-material fortifications are recorded from Dacian areas of east-central Europe (Glodariu 1983) to Iberia, where rare examples have been identified (de Palol 1964). One of the fortification lines at the Castelo de Monte Novo in the Evora region of Portugal displays evidence of vitrified stone (Burgess, pers. comm.), discussed further below.

Within the later Hallstatt and La Tène areas, numerous constructional variants employing timbers are recorded. A primary distinction can be proposed between examples which have earth-fast vertical timbers exposed in the front face, either as components of continuous wall-faces or interspersed with panels of dry-stone work, and those which have only, in effect, an internal lattice-work of horizontal timbers anchoring the core materials. The first suite may also have a second earth-fast alignment of timbers on their inner margins. Grossly to simplify matters, the former set is tentatively considered more characteristic of central, and the latter of more westerly regions of the Continent. In the United Kingdom, an equivalent distinction can be drawn between the south and north, although in the last-mentioned area in particular such sites are complemented by those surrounded by earth-fast palisades, including some with closely set pairs of stockade lines which may initially have formed the front and rear faces of narrow box-walls. Variations in architectural detail may be expected to complicate the picture particularly in the vicinity of gateways (Figure 5.3).

The aforementioned distinction, and exceptions to it, can be illustrated by reference to the wood-using fortification types present in the later (primarily La Tène C2/D) Iron Age of continental Europe (Collis and Ralston 1976; Audouze and Büchsenschütz 1992). In south Germany, the dominant series (Kelheim type) of this period is a simplified form of the vertical-post-and-stone-panelwork arrangement, in which the external timbers are no longer anchored by cross-members to an inner row of posts set into the ground, but are believed to have been tied back simply into the wall-core. Isolated examples of this type occur as far west as the site of Castillon in Normandy, France.

In the west, the principal series takes its name from a description (*De Bello Gallico* VII.23) provided by Julius Caesar of the defences he encountered at the siege of Avaricum (Bourges, in Berry) in 52 BC. This, the *murus gallicus* type, is characterized by an internal framework of transversal and longitudinal beams, fronted by a near-vertical external skin of stonework through which the ends of the transversal beams projected. The timber lattice was infilled with a variety of core materials. The inner margin of such walls can consist either of a vertical face, or of a sloping ramp. The technique is thus that of *la terre armée*, used by French military engineers as recently as the 1950s in Indochina, and still employed in civil engineering projects. A major innovation, comprised in the archaeological definition of this type although not recorded by Caesar, is the incorporation of long, quadrangular-sectioned iron spikes, augered into at least some of the intersections between timbers. This conspicuous consumption of iron, given that the spikes seem to confer little advantage in terms of structural stability, is an important element in the demonstration of the significant upturn in production which corresponds to the so-called 'civilisation des oppida'

Figure 5.3 Set of isometric drawings of variant usages of wood in iron age defences. *Left-hand column:* Kastenbau type; box rampart with earthfast vertical timbers in front and rear faces; Hod Hill variant, with small internal ramp and inner wall-face verticals no longer earthfast. *Right-hand column:* Ehrang timber-laced type; inset: variant (of Ehrang type) called the *murus gallicus* of Avaricum type, with long iron spikes inserted, probably in augered holes, at the intersections of the timberwork; Altkönig-Priest type; Kelheim type, lacking an internal wall-face, but with an internal earthen ramp; the elaborate wall on Cathedral Hill, Basle, Switzerland (*at bottom*) combines elements of various traditions. (After Audouze and Büchsenschütz 1992: fig. 49; Büchsenschütz and Ralston 1981. Drawn by Gordon Thomas.)

(see Collis, Chapter 10). The majority of *muri gallici* occur in non-Mediterranean France, with outliers occurring in Belgium (at Rouveroy and Lompret, province of Hainaut: Cahen-Delhaye 1982; Cahen-Delhaye and Jadin 1990) and in Germany, where the most easterly example known is the final fortification, replacing earlier defences of Kelheim type, at Manching (van Endert 1987). The elaborate fortification discovered on the promontory fort which occupied the Cathedral Hill, adjacent to the Rhine at Basle, Switzerland, melds elements from these two traditions (Fürger-Gunti 1980) and provides a good indication of the increasing variation which can be expected as a result of large-scale excavations of (rather than narrow cuttings through) such remains.

Professor Dehn, more recently supported by Frey (1984), has hypothesized that elements of the architecture of *muri gallici* forts derive from Italian and other southern models, noted by Celts during their presence as settlers or mercenaries in such areas. Against this has to be set the quantitatively preponderant evidence, which indicates that the construction of versions of such stone, earth and wood fortifications was a long-lived tradition in temperate Europe. However, on the southern fringes of the hill-fort area, in Provence and Languedoc, the dry-stone-built forts characteristic of that area display different borrowings from Mediterranean traditions (Dedet and Py 1985), including in areas at least latterly occupied by groups bearing Celtic names.

A particular problem is set by some of the fortifications which show evidence of intense burning. These may usefully be subdivided into two series, on the basis of differences in their geological make-up. Vitrified forts are characteristic of igneous and metamorphic zones, and appear particularly numerous in France (Ralston 1981, 1992) and Scotland (MacKie 1976); calcined examples occur in limestone and related sedimentary areas. A key question which has attracted attention since the eighteenth century is whether the resolidified but distorted masses of stonework (implying the application of temperatures in the vicinity of 1,000 degrees Celsius) visible in the vitrified walls represent the outcome of deliberate constructional intent on the part of their builders or not. If the former perspective is upheld, the technology is certainly not narrowly delimited spatially or in time; a wide date range for such works is suggested by radiocarbon determinations, and an even wider one by the thermoluminescence dating of Scottish examples (Sanderson *et al.* 1988).

In the case of the vitrified forts, a number of strands of evidence may be adduced to argue that vitrification is rather a product of the destruction, intentional or not, by fire of timber-laced walls. In a number of instances, only a small proportion of the enceinte displays the characteristic evidence. Further, excavation at Dun Lagaidh, Ross and Cromarty District, Scotland (MacKie, 1969), demonstrated vitrifaction overlying the slots of timbers which have simply rotted *in situ*. Experimental evidence shows that it is possible to replicate the characteristics of the vitrified walls by igniting timber-laced replicas (Ralston 1986) (Figure 5.4). In some instances, the deliberate destruction of fortifications by fire either in the aftermath of conflict or in other circumstances would have provided, in the walls glowing red-hot against the night sky, a spectacular advertisement of power or intimation of the site's abandonment.

Whilst the vitrification of fortifications seems thus adequately explicated, there are

Figure 5.4 The vitrified wall experiment at Aberdeen, Scotland. The wall on successive days in April 1980. (Copyright: Jim Livingston, Geography Department, Aberdeen University.)

increasing signs that monocausal explanation will be insufficient in the case of the defences that have been described as calcined. At least three causes can be advanced, one being essentially the same process as that just described. In other examples, the calcined cores of fortifications may simply be a product of the materials employed, and natural changes to them, as Nicolardot (1974) has proposed for examples near Dijon, Burgundy, France. The argument that, in some instances, the solidification of the wall-core materials represented by calcination may have been deliberately intended has been given renewed impetus by observations and analyses during excavations at the Cité d'Affrique in Lorraine, France, where the charcoal-free calcined mass, consisting of limestone and clay locally heated to 1,200 degrees Celsius, is underpinned by a heavily burnt network of timbers. It is argued to have been formed intentionally as the foundation for a vertically faced wall which surmounted it (Duval *et al.* 1991).

Dump ramparts, contrastingly, necessitate much less by way of formal internal structure, and constructional materials may have been varied, although not with complete indifference to the engineering consequences of settling and slumping. The range of skilled labour required to construct them would also have been much reduced. Individually, some of the most massive and imposing of such earthworks are to be found in France, where ramparts of the Fécamp series (see Büchsenschütz, Chapter 29), initially identified north-east of the Seine by Sir Mortimer Wheeler (Wheeler and Richardson 1957), on occasion comfortably exceed 10 m in altitude. There are a few comparable sites in southern Britain (Cunliffe 1991). Many of the most substantial of such enclosures seem relatively close in date to the local appearance of the Roman army, and may be argued to relate to missile, especially artillery-launched, warfare; but the techniques of constructing glacis banks are demonstrably far older in some areas (Cunliffe 1991).

At many sites, the present-day surface configuration of fortifications is, however, an inadequate guide to the constructional methods originally employed. In numbers of instances, this may simply be due to subsequent collapse and slumping. However, present-day profiles may result from remodelling during the Iron Age which saw dump ramparts erected over the delapidated remnants of antecedent walls, both in Britain and in continental Europe (Ralston 1981; 1992 for instances in France).

In other areas, it can be argued that the desire for protection from sling-warfare in particular was achieved by multiplying the number of individually less grandiose fortification lines in close proximity; such multivallate works reach their apogee in southern British sites like Maiden Castle (Dorset) (Figure 5.5). This argument, that multivallation provides defence in depth, has never been wholly satisfactory, for example because the outer ditches, shielded from defenders within the fort by the intervening banks, effectively provide dead ground in military terms. In the case of the Chesters fort in East Lothian, Scotland, a small multivallate fort is overlooked by a higher ridge in close proximity (Megaw and Simpson 1979, fig. 7.76). In such instances, the rationale behind the construction of these close-set barriers may well lie outside the purely military domain.

Fortifications were frequently fronted by ditches, which penetrated either only superficial deposits or were dug down into the living rock. These, and other less formal quarry-scoops, often (although not universally) formed a principal source

Figure 5.5   The southern ramparts at Maiden Castle, Dorset, England, lit by low sun in 1935. (Copyright: Society of Antiquaries, London.)

of material employed in fortification-building, as is most elegantly demonstrated at unfinished sites (Figure 5.6) (Feachem 1971) like Ladle Hill, Hampshire, with its evidence for gang work. In some instances, a counterscarp bank is visible beyond the external lip of the ditch. On excavation, some hill-fort ditches display evidence of recutting; in others they seem to have been permitted rapidly to infill.

Ancillary features include gateworks of varying degrees of elaboration, and – although rarely evidenced within temperate Europe – bastions and towers on the walls. The former range from simple entrance-gaps, barred by gates fixed on a minimal number of earth-fast posts recoverable archaeologically, through the elaborate timber gate-house structures reconstructed on the basis of the post-hole arrangements present in the inturned entrances (*Zangentore*) of continental oppida (see Collis, Chapter 10), as at Gate A of Závist, Czechoslovakia (Motyková *et al.* 1990) and the east gate of Manching, Bavaria (van Endert 1987: ill.14). The biggest gateway of this type is that at the Porte du Rebout, Mont Beuvray, Burgundy. Flanked by inturned works in *murus gallicus* style, the longer inturn of this offset gateway was 46 m long; and the entrance passage was *c.*20 m wide. It lacks an elaborate gate-structure, which, coupled with its great width, again suggests a configuration meant to impress rather than to be defensible.

Less grandiose versions of elaborate entrances appear early, around the transition to the First Iron Age, in the Lausitz culture province to the north of the Celtic world, as at Biskupin in Poland, and in the British Isles, as at Crickley Hill, Gloucestershire, and Dinorben in Clwyd. In certain southern British forts in particular, the defensive appearance of gateways is enhanced by accompanying hornworks of considerable

Figure 5.6 Aerial photo of Durn Hill, near Portsoy, Banff and Buchan District, Scotland, showing marking-out lines and short sectors of bank as constructed. (Copyright: Aberdeen Archaeological Surveys.)

complexity, designed to confer advantage to the defenders, as at Danebury, Hampshire, and again at Maiden Castle. Cells or chambers, set on the margins of entrance passages, are another feature of a restricted number of sites and are assumed to have housed guards (Cunliffe 1991; Forde-Johnston 1976).

Additional external protection is offered at a few sites by the emplacement of offset rows of vertical stones (or, on rare occasions, timbers) outside the defences in arrangements termed *chevaux-de-frise* (Harbison 1971). Seemingly designed to break up frontal assaults on defences, the locations of some examples in fact square ill with a primarily military purpose, manifestly at Dun Aengus on the Aran Islands (Co. Galway, Eire; Raftery 1991), but also at Spanish Celtiberian examples, as at Chamartín de la Sierra, in the province of Avila (Cabré 1950), where a *chevaux-de-frise* occurs in the interior in the vicinity of one of the gates.

The presence of towers or bastions attached to the enceinte has normally been taken to be indicative of Mediterranean influence, if not the presence of a southern architect. The most celebrated instance is provided by the serried bastions attached to the clay-brick wall – itself an unusual constructional material this far north – erected on a stone footing and forming one phase of the defensive sequence at the late Hallstatt Heuneburg in Baden-Württemburg, Germany (Bittel *et al.* 1981). The replacement of this innovative defensive work was marked by a return to a more traditional wall incorporating horizontal timberwork. Towers surmounting ramparts remain difficult to discern archaeologically, although timber-built examples occur at Altburg-bei-Bundenbach near Trier and on the late La Tène wall of Mont Vully, near La Tène, Switzerland (Kaenel and Curdy 1988), and have been surmised from tumbled material at Mont Boubier, in Wallonia, Belgium (Papeleux *et al.* 1988, fig. 43) (Figure 5.7). Further instances are recorded in the Lausitz province. In general, archaeological evidence for the arrangements on the wall-heads does not survive; parapets and breastworks are likely, but few walls preserve the necessary evidence to allow generalization. In the United Kingdom, arguably late examples of stone-built parapets are evidenced at Tre'r Ceiri (Caernarvonshire, Wales) (Hogg 1975) and the Mither Tap o'Bennachie (Gordon District, Grampian Region, Scotland). At Crickley Hill, Gloucestershire, stone paving on the top of the period 3 defences may provide a rare secure indication of their original height (Dixon 1976); and Wheeler (1943) identified a palisade line, presumably for a breastwork, near the summit of one of Maiden Castle's dump ramparts.

Generally speaking, the lines of fortification conform to the topography of the terrain on which they are set. Thus, in contour forts, the enceinte usually occupies a narrow altitudinal band around the hill, only departing from this in cases where not to have done so would leave dead ground, not capable of surveillance from the enceinte, in its immediate vicinity, because of the changing convexity of the external topography for instance. Such military common sense is not, however, universal. In extreme cases, a contrary arrangement prevails, in which the form of the enclosure appears to have been dictated at least partially by the materials employed. Examples include some of the seemingly gateless, oblong forts of eastern Scotland north of the Forth–Clyde isthmus, such as Finavon, Angus and Tap o'Noth, Gordon District (Figure 5.8). The subsequent vitrification of these is a good indication that these constructions originally contained straightish lengths of timber in quantity.

Figure 5.7 Photo of reconstruction model of timber-built defences at Mont Boubier, Wallonia, Belgium, showing tower. In the foreground is the stone capping on the internal ramp. (Copyright: Professor Pierre Bonenfant, Université Libre de Bruxelles.)

Figure 5.8 Aerial photo of Tap o'Noth, Gordon District, Grampian Region, Scotland, showing the gateless, oblong and heavily vitrified fort on the summit, and the external stone bank, with platforms on the intervening slopes. (Copyright: Aberdeen Archaeological Surveys.)

In the other main series, promontory forts, which occur in both inland and coastal locations, the defences are normally at their most substantial on the side of easiest approach. They may be slighter, or indeed absent, elsewhere: indeed the writer is surprised by how few coastal promontory forts in exposed locations show signs of enclosure at their seaward margins. The young, the elderly, the frail must have been tethered to prevent them being blown off! Other topographic settings are also employed, although less frequently: some ridges are barred by walls at both accessible ends; river meanders and peninsulas jutting into lakes are employed; and in some instances arcs of walling back onto cliffs (Forde-Johnston 1976; Audouze and Büchsenschütz 1992).

One subset of sites, attributable broadly to the last two centuries BC (La Tène IIb and III or C2 and D1–2), includes numerous examples which depart from the locational generalizations sketched above. In these, defensive lines career across slopes (most spectacularly at Velem Sankt Vid in western Hungary), on occasion to enclose the heads of watercourses (as at Mont Beuvray, Burgundy, France), and in other examples to cross low-lying tracts between neighbouring enclosed summits (as at

Heidetränk near Frankfurt-am-Main in the Taunus, Germany; Maier 1985). There are clear intimations in such practices (and others, including the frequency of gates) that defensive requirements were not of paramount significance.

Another indication of this non-military dimension is provided from the northern extremity of the range. The Shetland blockhouses, in themselves elaborate constructions, none the less fail to isolate the promontories on which they are set, as at Ness of Burgi. Here, even allowing for erosion over the intervening millennia, the blockhouse is out of all proportion to the area thus enclosed (Figure 5.9). It is perhaps not altogether fanciful to see such features as platforms for display, by individuals, bombastic or otherwise, or of trophies.

Figure 5.9 Aerial photo of Ness of Burgi promontory fort and blockhouse (showing cells), Shetland Islands, Scotland. The rectangular area of stonework is modern. (Copyright: RCAHMS.)

There can be little doubt that the most extensive of the hill-fort defences were highly consumptive of resources. For example, the principal wall at Mont Beuvray, Burgundy, encloses 135 ha and is some 5.5 km long. If, like the excavated portion, it were entirely built in *murus gallicus* style, up to 100 tonnes of iron spikes and the product of the clear-felling of 40–60 ha of mature oak woodland would have been required to build it. The external wall-face, at a minimal height of 4.5 m, would have needed approximately 7,500 cubic metres of facing stone (some of which was imported to the site). The core of the wall may have required over 100,000 cubic metres of fill materials. The organizational requirements underpinning such an undertaking are manifest. None the less, there is no simple correlation between the existence of technically elaborate fortifications of this kind and the topmost sites in apparent settlement hierarchies; in Berry, France (broadly corresponding to the *civitas* of the Bituriges cubi in the first century BC), for example, *muri gallici* occur on small as well as more extensive sites. Many smaller fortifications were of course much less resource- and labour-demanding: Hogg's calculations (1975) for some north British examples suggest the task could have been achieved by small communities of the size that seemingly inhabited them (perhaps fifty strong) in a few months.

Celtic fortifications may be considered to have faced military threats of two kinds: that offered by other, relatively local, communities and, more particularly latterly, against the assaults mounted by the armies of late Republican and Imperial Rome. In the former case, amongst the weaponry employed, swords, spears and javelins (see Ritchie and Ritchie, Chapter 4) seem to predominate as assault weapons over much less plentiful evidence for archery and the use of the sling in the archaeological record of the La Tène period. Caution has to be exercised, however, since weaponry that has been recovered most frequently comes from burial or ritual contexts. Fire was clearly also used (although the wholesale vitrification of some forts is very unlikely to have been achieved in the heat of battle). Classical written sources – which have unsurprisingly little to say about Celtic assault tactics – record simple, if effective, methods, like the massed throwing of stones all around the perimeter, as in the attack on Bibrax of the Remi, again described by Caesar (*De Bello Gallico* II.6; Rivet 1971). Gates were clearly weak points (Avery 1986), although indubitable evidence of their destruction during conflict is relatively rare. There are no indications that iron age warfare was at all mechanized.

The advent of Roman armies, as well as pitting Celtic troops against organizationally superior forces, seems to have represented a new departure in terms of the technologies and styles of warfare in temperate Europe. Artillery pieces, such as the ballista, were employed. Written sources make reference to the use of other techniques, such as sapping and battering-rams, although it is not precluded that these latter may have been in use earlier. The panoply of siege warfare, including investing works, as most celebratedly around Mandubian Alesia in Côte d'Or, France, equally seems to have been a product of Roman intervention (Le Gall 1985). Interestingly, whilst Caesar makes direct reference to the capacity of the *murus gallicus* – a wall built in a variant of a long-established style – to resist assault by the battering-ram and by fire in the passage referred to previously, it was the newer style of massive bank, fronted by its broad, canal-like ditch, at Noviodunum of the Suessiones (most likely to have been the fort at Pommiers, Aisne, France) which actually frustrated his assault (*De Bello Gallico* II.12).

In this treatment, the author has attempted to cast doubt on the universality with which iron age fortifications can straightforwardly be interpreted as defensive, in the narrowly military sense, in intent. Lacking firepower, of course, direct protection could in any case be extended only to people and goods within their compass, and not to facilities and resources in their vicinities. This is not to dispute that they may have had considerable 'deterrent value' in societies where the possibility of armed conflict (to judge, for example, from the availability of weaponry) was ever-present, an argument cogently advanced by Sharples (1991). Equally, in the labour- and resource-demands in terms of both construction and, importantly, maintenance they represent, elaborate walls and massive ramparts were clearly symbols of latent power.

That power was established on bases other than simply the control of armed force seems clear for many Celtic-speaking societies. The wish to demonstrate status, the need to monitor access to markets, to industries, to food, or to luxuries, or the desire to control participation in ritual activities, are amongst many factors which may equally have contributed to the decision to erect such earthworks, as well as influencing the form they took. In this regard, the kilometres-long defences of certain continental oppida, frequently built in elaborate variants of a traditional (and, arguably, militarily outmoded) style, and set anew – in some cases at some distance from the preceding settlement – in formerly favoured topographic positions, like hill-tops, seem to highlight the 'contradictions' contained in many such earthworks.

This is not to deny that the defence of forts on occasion played a substantial role in conflict. This is most clear in the case of documented wars with Rome, but even in such campaigns there are plentiful indications that holding defensible sites was far from a general strategy. In northern Italy, for example, Peyre (1979, 1985) has demonstrated that, whilst the collapse of resistance in some groups followed the taking of their principal settlements (as is the case with the Insubres in 222 BC), the Boii a generation later contrastingly did not defend Felsina and surrounding fortifications, but instead dispersed into the countryside, thereby prolonging the conflict. In the Gallic War, significant fighting certainly took place at forts (Rivet 1971). None the less, Deyber's (1987) analysis of the conduct of the war demonstrates the substantial extent to which resistance was based on the landscape: the characteristics of terrain, the opportunities provided by forest, and the application of scorched earth policies. It may be concluded that, in these admittedly special circumstances, the existence of forts did not necessarily entail their defence. The Early Irish literature, composed in a later and arguably different Celtic world, and which is of such importance in discussions of the 'heroic' nature of warfare, seemingly makes no mention of the role of fortifications therein (Avery 1976). Contrastingly, the besieging and taking of forts is a recurrent subject in the Annals (Alcock 1981).

In conclusion, the construction of fortifications in the Celtic world is one token of the internal stresses that made the resort to arms a distinct possibility. That they were the arena of armed conflict in some cases is certain; but it would be excessive both to envisage any straightforward correlation between hillfort-building and particularly troubled times and to consider that the existence of what contemporary archaeologists term fortifications necessarily implied a defensive strategy founded on them.

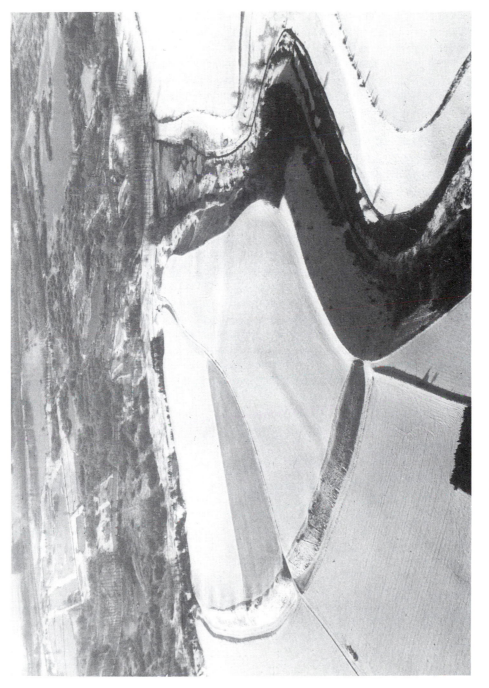

Figure 5.10 Aerial photo of La Chaussée Tirancourt, Somme, France, highlighting defences. (Copyright: Roger Agache.)

Recent work at one of the major forts on the Somme valley, France, has added a novel dimension to consideration of these sites. The Camp de César at La Chaussée Tirancourt, from superficial evidence, belongs to Wheeler's series of major forts defended with Fécamp-specification defences (Wheeler and Richardson 1957) (Figure 5.10). Recent excavations demonstrate that this is not entirely so (the dump rampart is in this case fronted by a stone-faced wall tied back to an earlier and smaller dump which it surmounted), and that the chronological span indicated by comprehensive excavations in the elaborate gateway occupies the period between about 40 and 20 BC. On presently available evidence, then, the fort is entirely post-conquest. Whilst this is, in itself, by no means exceptional, the character of the finds from the gateway assuredly are. These are strongly dominated by non-local material, including imported pottery and coins from Provence. The excavators (Brunaux and Marchand 1990) are confident that the material represents troops in the service of Rome, probably auxiliaries. Whilst it is recorded that Roman forces were elsewhere quartered in native forts, La Chaussée Tirancourt appears to have been constructed *ex nihilo* by soldiers, perhaps recruited amongst the Volcae Arecomici. If the construction and use of the other Fécamp-style forts along the Somme valley mirrors that of La Chaussée Tirancourt, these forts, as Brunaux and Marchand propose, may represent an early Roman *Limes*. Their work is, in any case, a salutary reminder of how excavation evidence can radically alter the standard perception of the defensive and other significance of seemingly 'classic' iron age hill-forts.

Somewhat over half a century thereafter, in Dorset, the capitulation of the fort on Hod Hill, marked by some accurate fire-power directed at what may have been the chieftain's house, was followed by the insertion of a Roman fort of more conventional appearance into one corner within the slighted hill-fort defences (Richmond 1968). Rather later, the tumbled defences of an abandoned hill-fort were used for Roman missile practice, as evidence from Burnswark, Annandale and Eskdale District, Scotland indicates (Jobey 1978). Thus, even for their best-documented period, the relationships between hill-forts and external aggression demonstrate considerable variation.

REFERENCES

Alcock, L. (1972) *By South Cadbury is that Camelot . . . The excavation of Cadbury Castle 1966–70*, London: Thames & Hudson.

—— (1981) 'Early historic fortifications in Scotland', in G. Guilbert (ed.) *Hill-fort Studies*, 150–80.

—— (1982) 'Cadbury-Camelot: a fifteen-year perspective', *Proceedings of the British Academy* 68: 355–88.

—— (1987) 'Pictish studies: present and future', in A. Small (ed.) *The Picts: a new look at old problems*, Dundee: University of Dundee, 80–92.

Armit, I. (1990) 'Broch building in northern Scotland: the context of innovation', *World Archaeology* 21: 435–45.

Audouze, F. and Büchsenschütz, O.E. (1992) *Towns, Villages and Countryside of Celtic Europe*, London: Batsford.

Avery, M. (1976) 'Hillforts of the British Isles: a student's introduction', in D.W. Harding (ed.) *Hillforts*, 1–58.

—— (1986) '"Stoning and firing" at hillfort entrances in southern Britain', *World Archaeology* 18: 216–30.

Biel, J. (1987) *Vorgeschichtliche Höhensiedlungen in Südwürttemburg-Hohenzollern,* Forschungen und Berichte zur Vor- und Frühgeschichte in Baden-Württemburg 24, Stuttgart: Konrad Theiss Verlag.

Bittel, K., Kimmig, W. and Schiek, S. (eds) (1981) *Die Kelten in Baden-Württemburg,* Stuttgart: Konrad Theiss Verlag.

Bowden, M. and McOmish, D. (1987) 'The required barrier', *Scottish Archaeological Review* 4: 76–84.

—— (1989) 'Little boxes: more about hillforts', *Scottish Archaeological Review* 6: 12–16.

Brunaux, J.-L. and Marchand, C. (1990) 'Le "Camp César" à la Chaussée-Tirancourt (Somme)', in G. Leman-Delerive (ed.) *Les Celtes en France du Nord,* 90–5.

Büchsenschütz, O.E. (1984) *Structures d'habitats et fortifications de l'âge du fer en France septentrionale,* Paris: Mémoires de la Société Préhistorique Française 18.

Büchsenschütz, O.E. and Ralston, I.B.M. (1981) 'Les fortifications des âges des métaux', *Archéologia* (Dijon) 154: 124–36.

Cabré, J. (1950) *El castro y la necrópolis del Hierro Céltico de Chamartín de la Sierra (Avila),* Madrid: Acta Arqueologia Hispanica 5.

Cahen-Delhaye, A. (1982) 'Découverte d'un murus gallicus à Rouveroy', *Archaeologia Belgica* 247: 55–9.

—— (1984) 'Fouilles récentes dans les fortifications de l'âge du fer en Belgique', in A. Cahen-Delhaye *et al.* (eds) *Les Celtes en Belgique et dans le nord de la France: les fortifications de l'âge du fer,* Actes 6ème Coll Assoc franç Et. Ages Fer. Lille, Revue du Nord special no., 151–65.

Cahen-Delhaye, A. and Jadin, I. (1990) 'La place forte de Lompret (sud de Hainaut belge)', in G. Leman-Delerive (ed.) *Les Celtes en France du Nord,* 51–5.

Collis, J.R. and Ralston, I.B.M. (1976) 'Late La Tène defences', *Germania* 54: 135–46.

Cunliffe, B.W. (1991) *Iron Age Communities in Britain* (3rd edn) London and New York: Routledge.

Dedet, B. and Py, M. (eds) (1985) *Les Enceintes protohistoriques de Gaule méridionale,* Caveirac: Cahier Assoc Recherche Archéol en Languedoc Oriental 14.

Deyber, A. (1987) 'La guérilla gauloise pendant la Guerre des Gaules (58–50 avant J.-C.)', *Etudes Celtiques* 24: 145–83.

Dixon, P.W. (1976) 'Crickley Hill, 1969–72', in D.W. Harding (ed.) *Hillforts,* 161–75.

Duval, P. *et al.* (1991) 'L'âge du fer en Lorraine. Les remparts calcinés de la Cité d'Affrique', *Archéologia* (Dijon) 274: 52–9.

van Endert, D. (1987) *Das Osttor in Manching,* Die Ausgrabungen in Manching 10, Wiesbaden: Franz Steiner Verlag, for Römisch-Germanische Kommission des Deutschen Archäologischen Instituts.

Feachem, R.W. (1971) 'Unfinished hill-forts', in D. Hill and M. Jesson (eds) *The Iron Age and Its Hill-Forts,* 19–39.

Forde-Johnston, J. (1976) *Hillforts of the Iron Age in England and Wales: a survey of the surface evidence,* Liverpool: Liverpool University Press.

Frey, O.-H. (1984) 'Die Bedeutung der Gallia Cisalpina für die Entstehung der Oppida-Kultur', in O.-H. Frey and H. Roth (eds) *Studien zu Siedlungsfragen der Latènezeit,* Marburg: Veröffentlichung des Vorgeschichtlichen Seminars Marburg 3: 1–23.

Fürger-Gunti, A. (1980) 'Der *Murus gallicus* von Basel', *Annuaire de la Société Suisse de Préhistoire et d'Archéologie* 63: 131–84.

Glodariu, I. (1983) *Arhitectura Dacilor, civila si militara,* Cluj-Napoca: Editura Dacia.

Graham, A. (1953) 'Archaeological gleanings from Dark Age records', *Proceedings of the Society of Antiquaries of Scotland* 85: 64–91.

Guilbert, G. (ed.) (1981) *Hill-fort Studies: essays for A.H.A. Hogg*, Leicester: Leicester University Press.

Harbison, P. (1971) 'Wooden and stone *chevaux-de-frise* in central and western Europe', *Proceedings of the Prehistoric Society* 37: 195–225.

Harding, D.W. (ed.) (1976) *Hillforts: later prehistoric earthworks in Britain and Ireland*, London: Academic Press.

—— (1979) *Celts in Conflict: hillfort studies 1927–77*, Edinburgh: Department of Archaeology, University of Edinburgh, Occasional Papers 3.

Hawkes, C.F.C. (1931) 'Hillforts', *Antiquity* 5: 60–97.

—— (1971) 'Fence, wall, dump, from Troy to Hod', in D. Hill and M. Jesson (eds) *The Iron Age and Its Hill-Forts*, 5–18.

Hill, D. and Jesson, M. (eds) (1971) *The Iron Age and Its Hill-Forts*, Southampton: University of Southampton Monograph Series 1.

Hill, P.H. (1982) 'Broxmouth Hillfort excavations 1977–1978: an interim report (2nd edition)', in D.W. Harding (ed.) *Later Prehistoric Settlement in South-east Scotland*, 141–94, Edinburgh: Department of Archaeology, University of Edinburgh Occasional Papers 8.

Hogg, A.H.A. (1975) *A Guide to the Hill-Forts of Britain*, London: Hart-Davis MacGibbon.

Jobey, G. (1978) 'Burnswark Hill', *Transactions of the Dumfries and Galloway Natural History and Antiquarian Society* 53: 57–104.

Kaenel, A. and Curdy, P. (1988) *L'Oppidum du Mont Vully*, Fribourg: Guides Archéologiques de la Suisse 22.

Le Gall, J. (1985) *Alésia*, Paris: Ministère de la Culture, Guides Archéologiques de la France.

Leman-Delerive, G. (ed.) (1990) *Les Celtes en France du nord et en Belgique VIe–Ier siècle avant J.-C.*, Valenciennes: Crédit Communal.

MacKie, E.W. (1969) 'Timber-laced and vitrified walls in iron age forts: causes of vitrifaction', *Glasgow Archaeological Journal* 1: 69–71.

—— (1976) 'The vitrified forts of Scotland', in D.W. Harding (ed.) *Hillforts*, 205–35.

Maier, F. (1985) *Das Heidetränk-Oppidum*, Führer zur Hessischen Vor- und Frühgeschichte 4, Stuttgart: Konrad Theiss Verlag.

—— (1986) 'Vorbericht über die Ausgrabung 1985 in dem spätkeltischen Oppidum von Manching', *Germania*, 64: 1–43.

Megaw, J.V.S. and Simpson, D.D.A. (eds) (1979) *Introduction to British Prehistory*, Leicester: Leicester University Press.

Mercer, R.J. (1980) *Hambledon Hill – a neolithic landscape*, Edinburgh: Edinburgh University Press.

—— (1989) 'The earliest defences in western Europe: Part I, Warfare in the Neolithic', *Fortress* 2: 16-22.

Motyková, K., Drda, P. and Rybová, A. (1990) 'Oppidum Závist – Prostor Brány v Predsunutém Sijovém Opevneni', *Památky Archeologické* 81: 308–433.

Nicolardot, J.-P. (1974) 'Structures d'habitats de hauteur à caractères défensifs dans le Centre-Est de la France', *Antiquités Nationales* 6: 32–45.

de Palol, P. (1964) 'La muralla céltica del poblado "El Soto de Medinilla"', Zaragoza: VIII Congreso Nacional de Arquelogia, Sevilla-Malaga, 1963, 275–6.

Papeleux, J. and de Boe, G. (eds) (1988) *Forteresses celtiques en Wallonie*, Archaeologicum Belgii Speculum 14, Brussels: Service des Fouilles.

Peyre, C. (1979) *La Cisalpine gauloise du IIIe au Ier siècle avant J.-C.*, Paris: Presses de l'Ecole Normale Supérieure.

—— (1985) 'Felsina et l'organisation du territoire des Boïens selon l'historiographie antique', in D. Vitali (ed.) *Celti ed Etruschi nell'Italia centro-settentrionale dal V secolo a.C. alla romanizzazione*, Fonti e Studi 10, Bologna: Bologna University Press, 101–10.

Raftery, B. (1991) 'Dun Aengus, Inishmore, Aran, County Galway, Ireland', in S. Moscati *et al.* (eds) *The Celts*, Exhibition catalogue, Palazzo Grassi, Venice. Milan: Bompiani, 613.

Ralston, I.B.M. (1981) 'The use of timber in hill-fort defences in France', in G. Guilbert (ed.) *Hill-Fort Studies*, 78–103.

—— (1986) 'The Yorkshire Television vitrified wall experiment at East Tullos, City of Aberdeen District', *Proceedings of the Society of Antiquaries of Scotland*, 116: 17–40.

—— (1992) *Les Enceintes fortifiées du Limousin: les habitats protohistoriques de la France non-méditerranéenne*, Documents d'Archéologie française 36, Paris: Maison des Sciences de l'Homme.

Richmond, I.A. (1968) *Hod Hill II*, London: British Museum.

Rivet, A.L.F. (1971) 'Hillforts in action', in D. Hill and M. Jesson (eds) *The Iron Age and Its Hill-Forts*, 189–202.

Royal Commission on the Ancient and Historical Monuments of Scotland (1967) *Peebles-shire*, 2 vols, Edinburgh: HMSO.

Sanderson, D.C.W., Placido, F. and Tate, J.O. (1988) 'Scottish vitrified forts: TL results from six study sites', *Nuclear Tracts Radiation Measurements* 14: 307–16.

Sharples, N. (1991) 'Warfare in the Iron Age of Wessex', *Scottish Archaeological Review* 8: 79–89.

Wheeler, R.E.M. (1943) *Maiden Castle*, London: Research Reports of the Society of Antiquaries of London 12.

Wheeler, R.E.M. and Richardson, K.M. (1957) *Hill-forts of Northern France*, London: Research Reports of the Society of Antiquaries of London 19.

PART III

SOCIETY AND SOCIAL LIFE

POWER, POLITICS AND STATUS

——— •◆• ———

Timothy Champion

In modern society it is normal to distinguish different areas of activity such as the political, the economic and the social. These divisions, however, are the product of a historically specific set of recent and contemporary societies and should not be used automatically as appropriate categories for the discussion of other social groups; the division, for instance, between a public sphere of political activity and a private sphere of social life is predominantly a recent one. It has been common in recent years for archaeologists to talk of the economy being 'embedded' in society; to use another metaphor, we should perhaps think of political, economic and social as being three different facets of the same set of activities.

Nor should we be tempted to think of a uniform type of Celtic society. Whether it is right to think of the Celts as a homogeneous ethnic group with a common descent, language and culture, or merely as a language group, or even more minimally as a grouping imposed by others, it is unrealistic to think that their social organization was the same throughout the whole of the time and space in which they are recorded. The enormous differences in settlement and economy shown by archaeology, between the Late Iron Age in central Europe and the Early Christian period in Ireland for instance, suggest that the scale of social organization and its degree of complexity must equally have varied. There may have been some features which recurred from time to time throughout this large geographical and chronological range, and may have been derived from a common origin, but we should not start out with the expectation of a uniform pattern of Celtic society and a common set of social practices.

THE EVIDENCE

As with other aspects of our knowledge of the Celts, we are dependent for our understanding of their social organization upon two types of evidence, the archaeological and the documentary. Questions about social organization are much harder to answer than those about material culture or technology, and both of these types of evidence raise special problems of interpretation, of rather different sorts.

The documentary evidence requires double interpretation; in other words there is a question about our own understanding of the written record, and also about the author's understanding and treatment of the available evidence. Despite the superficial appearance of the written records as a more reliable testimony to past social organization than archaeology, their evidence needs very careful appraisal. There are two main bodies of written evidence for the social organization of the Celts, the works of the Greek and Roman authors who mention them, and various writings, especially legal tracts, surviving from early medieval Ireland.

References to the Celts in the classical authors are fragmentary, and none of them is concerned primarily with a discussion of Celtic society. One major source would have been the ethnographic work of Poseidonios, but this survives only in scattered references in later authors (Tierney 1960); he seems to be recording the position, perhaps specific to particular parts of France, around 100 BC. Julius Caesar has a particular value as an eye-witness to events in Gaul in the middle of the first century BC (Nash 1976), but though his military and political activities brought him into contact with powerful leaders, and there are many references to them in his works, he does not offer us a sustained account of Celtic society. His evidence is also specific to a particular period, and he is best informed about central France and Switzerland, though mentioning conditions elsewhere. The differences between the versions of Celtic social organization given by Poseidonios and Caesar are a clear reminder that Celtic society was changing through time, especially during the period of intensifying contact with the expanding Roman world, and indeed that such contact may itself have been a potent force for change.

In addition to the limitations of such evidence, there is a problem in understanding the references that do survive. When Caesar, for instance, uses the Latin word *rex* (king) to refer to a Celtic social institution, it is important not only to ask how well informed he could have been, and how well he understood the social conditions, but also to appreciate that both he and his readers were conditioned by the prevailing ideology of the classical world towards the non-classical or barbarian peoples, and that he was interpreting Celtic institutions in the linguistic terms of the Latin language; he would have to choose the most appropriate term, despite what may have been major differences in the real nature of the social institutions he was trying to describe. Constraints of language may therefore lead to an assimilation of social institutions, and a blurring of real cultural differences. In our own turn, modern readers of Caesar have to come to terms with contemporary attitudes towards the classical world and imperial conquest, as well the difficulty of interpreting his language, as in the translation of *rex* as king.

The early medieval Irish literature may seem to escape one of these layers of interpretative difficulty, since it comprises documents written by a society about itself, but they still require a very careful understanding of the social context in which they were produced. Some of the most interesting are a wide variety of legal texts dealing with early Irish law (Kelly 1988); unlike the classical authors, some of these early Irish sources are specifically concerned with social organization, even obsessively so. The *Crith Gablach*, for instance, spells out in great detail the possessions of various grades of farmer. The writing down of hitherto traditional wisdom is a sign not just of the adoption of literacy but of a fundamental change in the nature of authority, and a detailed concern for the definition of social rank indicates a period when social ranking is in a state of flux; many of the legal tracts date originally to the seventh and eighth centuries AD, when the power of the church was expanding and the nature of Irish kingship was changing dramatically. Some of the documents contain references that are clearly archaic, and it is necessary to ask whether we are dealing with the definition of a social organization as it actually was, or as it was ideally wished for. Much of early Irish literature, including the law tracts, was the product of a highly educated clerical élite, well versed in classical and biblical scholarship, writing documents for the contemporary context, which should not therefore be taken simply as giving an accurate reflection of earlier society (McCone 1990).

The archaeological evidence also clearly needs to be subjected to a process of theoretical interpretation, since the aim is to relate the contemporary record of material finds to the past pattern of social organization, and a set of ideas is needed to form the basis of such inferences. Early iron age hill-forts in southern Germany, for instance, have been compared to medieval castles, and their occupants therefore equated to medieval nobles and their social organization to the feudal system. There is, however, no reason to accept such a comparison, whether the pattern is thought to be continuous or not, simply on the grounds of geographical identity. Appropriate principles for such inferences can be derived from a wider consideration of anthropological and ethnographic evidence. These might be based on arguments for recurring types of social institution found frequently in Indo-European society, or on an even wider consideration of the known nature of societies of an approximately similar type.

Three categories of evidence have been particularly interpreted as indicators of social organization. Burial traditions in the Iron Age were often marked by a considerable variation in the treatment of the dead, including the wealth of the goods interred with the body, and wealthier and more elaborate graves can be read as a sign of higher social status. The nature of that enhanced social standing needs definition; it has often been seen as a status based on political power, but it could also perhaps be based on the authority of factors such as age. In any case, the burials were part of the active process of social readjustment after a death, and they may tell us more about the ideas of the survivors than the real identity of the deceased. Though they cannot be taken as a simple record of social status, they do give us a valuable insight into Celtic society. The burial traditions, however, were not uniform throughout the Celtic world, and in some parts of western Europe there are long periods with few known burials.

Archaeologists have long been recovering high quality artefacts of the Iron Age, especially decorated jewellery of gold or bronze, often found in elaborate graves, and have taken these as symbols of social distinction. Such use of prestige goods is a well-documented strategy in many societies with differences of social ranking, and the flourishing of craftsmanship in the Celtic world must owe much to the demand for such symbols.

The evidence of settlements is rather more problematic. There is little sign that domestic architecture was used as a means of displaying social difference, as it has been in more recent times in Europe, but there are some sites which seem more elaborately built, especially ones with impressive defences. There are also many areas of iron age Europe with large defended hill-forts, which have often been taken as centres of political power and of developing social hierarchies. Some of the most massively fortified sites in prehistoric Europe, however, were built by the early farming societies of the Neolithic, societies which we like to think were much less differentiated than those of the Iron Age. It is essential, therefore, to avoid inappropriate analogies with the medieval and later world and to recognize that the world of the Celts was fundamentally different from our own.

Taken together, these lines of evidence suggest that Celtic society was marked by important differences of social status, but the basis on which the authority and power of those enjoying higher status rested needs to be further explored. The degree of such differentiation can easily be exaggerated, and we must resist the temptation to reconstruct Celtic society as we would like it to have been.

SOCIAL GROUPS AND IDENTITIES

There is no evidence to suggest that anyone in prehistoric or early historic times thought of himself or herself as a Celt. On the contrary, names such as Celt, Gaul or Gael were given by outsiders, whether Greek geographers, Roman historians or Anglo-Norman conquerors, according to their own perceptions of themselves and other peoples. Such large-scale identities were never shared by the so-called Celts themselves, despite a certain similarity of material culture, especially in such areas as art and prestige goods, throughout much of Europe, nor was there ever any political unity at such a scale.

The largest social or political groupings that may have been meaningful were much smaller. The classical authors refer to many groups such as the Arverni, the Helvetii or the Iceni; Caesar's regular word in Latin for such groups is *civitas*, usually translated into English as 'tribe', and though they may have been very different in internal organization from the classical city-state, his use of the term shows that he recognized them as political entities. At their largest, they could number several hundred thousand people; when Caesar conquered the Helvetii, he gave their population as 263,000 and, although there may be some doubt about the exact figure, the general order of magnitude must be correct (*De Bello Gallico* I.2–30).

Some of these tribes are known to have comprised a number of smaller groups, for which Caesar's term is a *pagus*; it is not clear, however, whether these were equal subdivisions, perhaps on a territorial basis, or whether they were groups subordinate to the dominant one which gave its name to the larger entity. Whether they had an ideology of identity, at the level of either the *civitas* or the *pagus*, based on concepts of ethnicity or descent rather than just on political allegiance to a common élite and a single individual, is obscure. Archaeology has had little success in identifying common traits in sites or material to match these political groups. In the Late Iron Age, the production and distribution of coinage has often been attributed to a tribal origin (e.g. Nash 1978a), but that may merely reflect the political purpose of the coins; otherwise, the very rarity of such apparently tribal traits as the gold neck-rings of the Iceni in eastern England or the distinctive inhumation burial tradition of the Parisi in east Yorkshire simply emphasizes how little such identities were signalled in ways that archaeology has yet been able to recover, if indeed they were signalled at all.

In Early Christian Ireland, the fundamental unit of social organization was the *tuath* (Kelly 1988: 3–6), of which there were at least 150, each comprising up to several thousand people; it was larger than a kin-group, and it was a political rather than an ethnic or cultural entity. Membership of a *tuath* was an important part of an individual's identity, not least because of the political obligations that it entailed. Individual *tuatha* varied considerably in size and prestige, and their power fluctuated over time; at times one *tuath* could exercise dominance over a few others. By the eighth century AD some dynasties were beginning to be able to exert more stable authority over even larger territories. As with the prehistoric groups, archaeology has had little or no success in identifying the extent of the *tuatha*.

There have been various attempts to define political groups on archaeological grounds alone, mainly by defining territories around hypothetical political centres. One of the most successful concerns the late Hallstatt fortified sites with rich burials of the sixth century BC in southern Germany (Härke 1979); if these really were the centres of independent polities, then each one dominated a territory about 100 kilometres across, much bigger than the Irish *tuath*. On the other hand, the rich burials of the fifth-century Early La Tène period in the Rhineland have a much closer spacing, suggesting a very different sort of social organization.

It would be dangerous to extrapolate uncritically from the few areas and periods for which we have good documentation, whether archaeological or historical, because the patterns they reveal are so different. There is no reason to think that political groups of the size of the larger late iron age tribes described by Caesar or of the Irish kingdoms of the late first millennium AD were typical of other periods. These may well have been the product of unusual historical circumstances, and we should expect the more common pattern to have been one of much smaller political units, perhaps of the scale of the *tuath*. Such political groupings may therefore have offered what was generally only a very small stage for the political activities which took place within and between them.

Perhaps the most important form of identity for an individual was as a member of a kin-group. According to the early Irish literature, the most informative source for this, many social rights and obligations were exercised by the *derbfine*, or four-generation descent group sharing a common patrilineal great-grandfather (Kelly 1988: 12–16). The group held land in common; it was responsible for offences committed by any of its members, and likewise sought retribution in common for grievances. By the eighth century AD a three-generation group with a common grandfather was beginning to be a more important social unit, but kinship was still an important basis for social relationships. It is highly likely that kinship was the dominant factor in social relationships in earlier periods also, but the classical authors tell us little of social organization at this level, and archaeology has not been good at exploring social organization in such fine detail.

We know even less about the fundamental forms of social identity within the kin-group, in particular concepts of male and female or adult and child. It is clear that categories of male and female were well established; prehistoric burial traditions regularly show distinctive sets of personal ornaments and possessions which are correlated with sexual identification of the skeletons to show gender divisions in society. The Irish laws also treat men and women differently, in terms that seem familiar to modern readers. It would be tempting to think that these categories were unproblematic, but we do not really know the conceptual structure that underlies them.

The difference between the categories of adult and child is more varied. The best archaeological evidence is from cemeteries; most regions show a significant under-representation of young people, which may suggest that the very young were thought of as a separate category not to be treated in the same way as older people. The treatment of older children also differs from place to place; in some cases they are buried with the same rites and accompanying goods as adults, but in others they have distinct rites and sets of ornaments, suggesting a variability in the way that differences between adults and children were constructed.

The Irish laws show the practice of one particular region. Until the age of 7, children were reared in their parents' household, but then left to join the family of foster-parents; this was a common practice, but we do not know whether it was universal or limited only to particular levels of Irish society. After the end of fosterage at the age of 14, females were ready to join new households through marriage, but young males could not establish themselves as full members of the adult community with their own household until they had inherited land. There were thus large numbers of young landless males of intermediate status who joined together in bands or *fianna*, which engaged in hunting, fighting and on occasion acts of brigandage. Such age-grade institutions can be found in other Indo-European societies, and may originally have been more widespread (McCone 1990: 203–17). They are not documented for the prehistoric Iron Age, but the regular occurrence of Celts as mercenaries in the armies of the Mediterranean states may well be connected with such a tradition of young men's wandering and fighting.

SOCIAL DIFFERENCES

All the archaeological and literary evidence suggests that, within whatever social groups may have existed at any time and place, Celtic society was hierarchical and inegalitarian. Individuals were not equal before the law; it was, rather, a society based on variations of status and honour, and the preservation or enhancement of that honour was a vital concern. The most rigid formulation of this structure is to be found in the early Irish law tracts, where each grade of society is assigned its honour-price (Kelly 1988: 8–10). This value established the limits of the legal rights of an individual, so that no one could offer a surety beyond the level of his honour-price, and an oath was outweighed by the oath of a person with a higher honour-price. It also set the level of compensation for an offence to be paid by the offender to the victim or the victim's kin, for the severity of a crime, and hence the extent of recompense due, was judged by the honour-price of the victim.

At a more general level, both the classical and the Irish sources agree in recognizing the existence of free and unfree classes, and of a higher rank of more exalted status. The unfree class was of little interest to the classical geographers and historians, and even the Irish laws cannot add much. There certainly were slaves who seem to have been regarded as chattels without legal rights; they were prisoners of war, those unable to pay their debts, or else, like St Patrick, people captured abroad by slave traders. Slavery was of considerable economic importance, and one system of measuring value in early Ireland used as its unit the value of a female slave. In early medieval Ireland there were also serfs, who were bound to their lords and could not renounce their tenancy.

The majority of individuals must have fallen within the free class, able to exercise their legal rights within their own community but subject to the authority of those of higher status. Roman authors such as Caesar, using Latin terminology, separate the *equites* (nobles), as well as some special categories such as the druids, from the ordinary people, and the Irish literature distinguishes the *nemed* (privileged person); as with the classical account of Celtic society, this term applies not only to the nobles, but also to those with certain special skills or knowledge.

The special groups mentioned in the classical authors include druids, bards and prophets (Piggott 1975), though it is possible that craftsmen may also have enjoyed a privileged status. Bards were particularly important, since singing the praises of a noble was a public way of honouring his status in society. By the time of the early Irish laws, the role of the pagan druids had declined, and the most important of the skilled classes was the poets, who rehearsed the traditional lore and praised the nobles for their achievements or satirized them for their failures (McCone 1990). Other groups of valued specialists included lawyers and physicians, as well as hospitallers, who owed their status to the generosity of the hospitality they offered to visitors. Others who enjoyed special status included skilled craftsmen such as carpenters and metalsmiths, as well as entertainers such as harpists.

The highest status was that of the king. Kings are attested in western Europe in the prehistoric period by the classical authors, although the institution was in decline in some parts by the early first century BC, as will be described below. Kingship was also the normal form of political authority in early medieval Ireland (Byrne 1973), and comparison with other parts of Europe suggests that there was an underlying tradition of sacral kingship common to the Indo-European world, and perhaps of considerable antiquity. The king was supposed to be wise, successful in battle and without physical blemish, and the well-being of his people was closely tied to these qualities. By the seventh and eighth centuries AD, the time when many of the legal tracts were first being written down, the nature of kingship was already being transformed into something altogether more powerful and more secular, and the spread of Christianity had eclipsed its pagan religious connotations.

The possibility of women holding positions of high status in their own right, rather than by virtue of their male relatives, seems to have varied. Some of the richest graves of the early Iron Age in central Europe were certainly the burials of women, and in the first century AD in Britain two women held power as queens over their tribes, Boudica of the Iceni and Cartimandua of the Brigantes. The picture given by early medieval Ireland, however, is very different. Neither the laws nor the Annals suggest that women were able to exercise political power, either in theory or in practice. They had no independent legal rights, but took their status from their fathers and husbands. The qualities valued in a woman were the traditional patriarchal ones of virtue, reticence and industry.

THE SOURCES OF SOCIAL POWER

Celtic society was based on status and honour, and status was based partly on birth and partly on individual achievement. Kinship and descent were vitally important; early Irish literature contains a vast mass of genealogies designed to celebrate the nobility of the present and legitimate their claims to power by an appeal to their distinguished ancestry in the past. Kingship passed within a closely defined lineage, and the lower grades of noble and free status were likewise hereditary. The special skills of poets, musicians and craftsmen, as well as any equipment needed, may also have been passed from one generation to the next in a family.

Status was not immutably fixed at birth, however, and it was possible to rise or fall in society by virtue of one's acts. The early Irish law tracts provide examples of such social mobility. A king who failed in battle would lose the respect of his people, as well as having perhaps to accept the domination of his conqueror; a noble who acted unbecomingly or failed to meet the obligations of his rank would similarly have his honour-price reduced. Failure to meet one's debts could result in slavery. On the other hand, conspicuous success in farming or in the accumulation of wealth could result in an ordinary free man acquiring greater authority and even aspiring to the status of a noble; after three generations his grandson could achieve a noble status.

The most important social institution which structured the relationship between individuals of different status in Celtic society was that of clientship. It is known in the prehistoric period from the evidence of the classical authors, and in more detail from the early Irish laws (Kelly 1988: 29–33), and was probably to be found throughout the Celtic world. It was a relationship which embraced social, military, political and economic obligations, and can be seen as lying at the heart of the power of the Celtic nobility as well as conferring benefits on the client.

Although there were obligations on both sides, the relationship was a fundamentally unequal one. The patron provided his clients with legal support, political protection and the possibility of sharing in the fruits of his success, for instance in raiding and looting; he also supplied his clients with a fief comprising the essentials for farming, especially livestock, but also tools and equipment, and sometimes land. In return, the client paid to the patron an annual food-rent based on the size of the fief, as well as manual labour, political support and military service. The early Irish laws contain details of different types of clientship, but the basic principles of the relationship are clear.

Clientship was fundamental to Celtic society, and a patron's status was measured by the number of his clients. It structured all levels of Celtic society. A noble could be a patron of his own clients, and in turn be a client to another more powerful noble; even a king could be a client to another king. It provided an opportunity for economic success in farming to be put to use in the promotion of social standing, and was the most important mechanism for the exercise of power by one person over another. Its political importance is demonstrated by Caesar's account of Orgetorix of the Helvetii; when brought to court on a charge of murder, he turned up with 10,000 of his household and followers, and was acquitted (*De Bello Gallico* 1.2–4).

Another important factor in the acquisition and enjoyment of social status was wealth, and the two main sources of wealth were cattle and treasure. The early Irish laws preserve three methods of counting the value of anything, in which the units of value were respectively a female slave, a cow and an ounce of silver. Cattle were central to the economy of early medieval Ireland (Lucas 1989), and may have had a similar importance in prehistory, at least in some parts of western Europe. Treasure was accumulated not just to be hoarded, but also to be displayed and used. It could be in the form of gold or silver, especially for personal adornment, but also in more utilitarian products of skilled craftsmen. Success in agriculture and in obtaining material goods came together in the activity of feasting; lavish entertainment was a favoured means of demonstrating and reinforcing social status. Throughout the first millennium BC the archaeological record is marked by a recurring theme of prestige goods comprising buckets and cauldrons, cups and jugs, spits, firedogs and other hearth furniture, all associated with the entertaining of guests and the serving of food and drink.

THE COMPETITION FOR STATUS

It would be wrong to think in terms of a sphere of political activity in Celtic society clearly separate from economic or social concerns, but in a social structure characterized to such an extent by a concern for status, social relationships were focused on attempts to maintain or enhance it. Where supreme power was in the hands of a king, succession to this office was confined to the royal lineage, but without a rule of primogeniture. Within the royal line succession was open to any suitable adult male; often a brother or nephew succeeded, but where there was more than one suitable contender, a struggle could ensue.

Caesar records a different political structure which had emerged in Switzerland and central France by the middle of the first century BC. Though the institution of kingship still survived in other regions of France, here it had been eclipsed by the adoption of a system based on a council and magistrates elected according to known laws, not unlike the consuls and senate of Rome (Nash 1978b). Political conflict revolved around factions which were trying to maintain the new structures and those which sought to restore the kingship; among the Aedui, for instance, the noble brothers Dumnorix and Diviciacus were the rival leaders, respectively for and against restoration of the kingship.

Political relationships between groups were likewise characterized by competition for power. Depending on the particular circumstances, this could be achieved either by hostile or by amicable means. Armed warfare could be aimed at the defeat and subjugation of other polities; by accepting an inferior status, they would augment the authority and power of the victor. Such an arrangement could also be symbolized by payment of tribute, and the offering of hostages by the defeated. Alternatively, raiding could be intended for the acquisition of booty; early Irish history records many such raids, sometimes to avenge a wrong, but often just for loot. Cattle were often the target, since they were a prime source of wealth, and could easily be driven off to the victor's home (Lucas 1989: 125–99); in the Christian period, monasteries were also a target, as a source of valuable treasure.

In other circumstances, treaties and alliances could provide an alternative source of political support. Their mere existence could be a source of power, but their ultimate value lay in the possibility of mobilizing allies for political or military activity. Such alliances were often sealed by a dynastic marriage; Caesar describes how Dumnorix of the Aedui had arranged a web of such alliances: 'he had given his mother in marriage to the noblest and most powerful man among the Bituriges, he had himself taken a wife from the Helvetii, and had married his half-sister and female relations to men of other states' (*De Bello Gallico* I.18).

REFERENCES

Byrne, F.J. (1973) *Irish Kings and High Kings*, London: Batsford.

Härke, H.G.H. (1979) *Settlement Types and Patterns in the West Hallstatt Province*, Oxford: British Archaeological Reports, International Series 57.

Kelly, F. (1988) *A Guide to Early Irish Law*, Dublin: Institute for Advanced Studies.

Lucas, A. (1989) *Cattle in Ancient Ireland*, Kilkenny: Boethius Press.

McCone, K. (1990) *Pagan Past and Christian Present in Early Irish Literature*, Maynooth: St Patrick's College.

Nash, D. (1976) 'Reconstructing Poseidonius' Celtic ethnography: some considerations', *Britannia* 7: 111–26.

—— (1978a) *Settlement and Coinage in Central Gaul, c.200–50 BC*, Oxford: British Archaeological Reports International Series 39.

—— (1978b) 'Territory and state formation in central Gaul', in D. Green, C. Haselgrove and M. Spriggs (eds) *Social Organization and Settlement*, 95–133, Oxford: British Archaeological Reports, International Series 47.

Piggott, S. (1975) *The Druids* (2nd edn) London: Thames & Hudson.

Tierney, J. (1960) 'The Celtic ethnography of Posidonius', *Proceedings of the Royal Irish Academy* 60C: 189–275.

APPEARANCE, LIFE AND LEISURE

———— ·•· ————

Glenys Lloyd-Morgan

Despite our growing knowledge of the ancient world, through excavation and the reassessment of the evidence from surviving texts, inscriptions, small objects of daily use and traces of structures within the landscape, there are still many popular misapprehensions about the past. Within the Celtic world we are hampered in that the surviving descriptions are all drawn in the main from the pens of Graeco-Roman writers and not from the people of the tribes and countries who were in various ways drawn into contact and conflict with the Mediterranean world. Some of the earliest descriptions, as for example Tacitus in his *Germania*, are not unbiased, as he contrasts the valour and rectitude of the tribes with what he saw as the declining moral strength and virtues of contemporary society in Rome. The attitude towards the northern tribes of Celts, as well as the Germans, as the Noble Savage and as a worthy and honourable opponent in war, is found not only in the literature but can also be seen reflected in the sculptures dedicated by King Attalus I in the late third century BC. The original bronzes showed dying Gauls, and the dramatic composition depicting, amongst others, a warrior with his dead wife, killing himself rather than submit to the conqueror, is known from numerous Roman copies (Figure 7.1). This same romantic image of the 'natural man' is also found in the eighteenth- and nineteenth-century writers, such as Jean Jacques Rousseau in the essays, as for example 'Discours sur les sciences et les arts' (1751); 'Discours sur l'origine de l'inégalité' (1755), and his novel *Emile* (1762); and in sculptures like the bronze statue of Ambiorix, joint king of the Eburones, made by Jules Bertin and erected in 1866 in the Grote Markt at Tongres, Belgium; or, more familiar to British eyes, the chariot group of Boudica and her daughters by Thomas Thornycroft designed between 1856 and 1871 but which was not cast and raised on to its site at Westminster Bridge until 1902.[1] The details of the piece, especially the presence of scythes on the wheels,[2] do nothing to dispel the popular misconceptions surrounding the Celts; rather, they reinforce the legend from one generation to the next.

Despite this fictitious but amusing nonsense, there are genuine, contemporary representations of Celts and their deities from the pre-Roman as well as the Roman Imperial periods. The sub-Roman period is somewhat less well represented. Warriors, for example the surviving three-quarter-length statue of the Warrior of Grezan (Gard) (Figure 7.2), and the third-century BC bust of a helmeted warrior

Figure 7.1 The Dying Gaul and his wife: a marble copy of one of the original bronze sculptures by Epigonos, dedicated by King Attalus I (241–197 BC) to celebrate a series of victories over the Gauls who had attacked the Pergamene state. The original monument was set up on the acropolis at Pergamon, whilst a similar smaller scale version in bronze was a gift to Athene at Athens. (Museo Nazionale Romano, Rome, inv. no. 8608; copyright: Soprintendenza Archeologica di Roma.)

Figure 7.2 Pre-Roman bust of a warrior, known as *Le Guerrier de Grezan*, probably part of a statue. (From Grezan (Gard), now in the collections of the Musée Archéologique de Nîmes; copyright: Musée Archéologique de Nîmes.)

97

from Sainte Anastasie (Gard) may not be very sophisticated in style,[3] but the preserved detail, especially in the former piece, is more immediate in its impact than the emotive style of the Dying Gauls of Pergamon. They also conjure up a more realistic impression of the Gauls who came into such bloody contact with Caesar's legions. These warriors from Gard can be compared with the Roman interpretation of a Celtic warrior, with sweeping moustache, long hair, and holding a sword and shield (Figure 7.3).[4] The other side of the picture, the defeated warrior killed or captured by the Romans, can be seen on the left-hand side panel of the Bridgeness distance slab from the Antonine Wall (Figure 7.4);[5] or the late Augustan frieze showing a battle between Romans and Gauls, and now in the Palazzo Ducale, Mantua.[6] On a smaller scale, there are bronze figurines showing individual captives, for instance the standing Gaulish prisoner with hands behind his back.[7]

DRESS AND APPEARANCE

Unfortunately, the remains of organic materials are preserved only where the optimum conditions obtain, either in a dry, well-drained soil, as for example in Egypt; where the conditions are waterlogged and anaerobic; or where the material, whether it is textile or made of wood, has come into contact with metal and left its imprint in the corrosion products, or has itself become partly mineralized.[8] Even some human remains may be found to have completely disappeared from the grave in which they were laid, where the soil conditions are adverse.[9]

Textiles, however, have occasionally been preserved, and in some cases even complete garments, such as the tunics, cloaks, caps, even hairnets, which were found in burials of bronze age date in Denmark.[10] Most garments would have been made from the raw materials most readily to hand, of which wool would be the most common and versatile of fibres that could be spun into threads of various thickness for weaving or netting, or could be felted.[11] Other animal hair was also used, though it would very much depend on the type of land available to support the most appropriate beasts. Goat hair, though coarse, could be used for fabrics which could be put to rough use, and Wild notes an insole sock of hare's wool from Basle, as well as fragments of textile made from the fibres secreted by the *Pinna nobilis* (a variety of mollusc).[12] Of plant fibres, the most common was the flax which could be spun and woven into clothes, from the finest grades – with some fabrics having up to as many as 200 threads per inch in examples from Egypt – to the heavier coarser materials.[13] Silk and cotton would either be unavailable or totally beyond the reach of the majority of people, but hemp and other plant fibres could be used, including those of the nettle.[14] Once the fibres had been cleaned and prepared, the next task was to spin them into thread using the spindle and whorl. Most spindles and distaffs would have been of wood, but some jet examples have been found in Roman contexts.[15] In general, the finer the thread to be spun, the lighter in proportion the weight of spindle and whorl must be. Spindle whorls of stone, baked clay, reutilized potsherds, antler and bone, including unfused epiphyses of cattle femurs, have been found.[16] The tombstone of Regina of the Catuvellauni, set up at South Shields by her husband, show her with distaff and spindle on her lap, and a basket with balls of

Figure 7.3 Terracotta figure of a Celtic warrior with oval shield, sword and characteristic long hair and flowing moustache. Height 17 cm. Unprovenanced, probably early Roman period. (Copyright: Ashmolean Museum, Oxford.)

Figure 7.4 Left-hand panel of the distance slab found at Bridgeness, West Lothian, 1868, marking the eastern terminus of the Antonine Wall, and erected by the Second Augustan Legion early in the reign of Antoninus Pius (AD 138–61). The scene shows a fully equipped cavalryman triumphantly overcoming four native warriors (*RIB* no. 2139). (Copyright: The Trustees of the National Museums of Scotland.)

wool by her side.[17] Other evidence for the preparation of thread and its manufacture into cloth is given by the so-called weaving-combs of bone and antler, as for example the pieces from Hunsbury hill-fort, Northants; Danebury, Hants; and from Padua in the Venetia region of north-east Italy.[18] Loom weights of baked clay, as used on the upright warp-weighted loom, were triangular in shape and pierced across the angles during the Iron Age, and, like the spindle-whorls, were of a weight appropriate to the type and grade of warp and weft threads. Examples have been found at Hunsbury hill-fort, Danebury and Verulamium.[19]

The work of Dr Michael Ryder over the last thirty years or so has been of considerable importance in establishing the colours of the natural fibres of fleece as well as goat and other animal hair. Finds from Hallstatt in Austria have shown the presence of white and coloured sheep wool in cloth which had not been dyed.[20] One sample of white cloth had woven into it 'a rectangular pattern of bands of black or dark brown wool, which was reminiscent of a Scottish tartan'.[21] He also suggests that grey sheep were predominant during the European Iron Age. The use of grey and black wools is also attested by Tacitus's description of the women who stood with the druids against Suetonius Paulinus and his army, on the southern shore of Anglesey in AD 61 *in modum Furiarum veste feriali* – like Furies in funereal garb.[22] Pollux, writing in the late second century AD, notes that for mourning the Greeks wore 'grey and black very like one another',[23] which tends to bear out Ryder's conclusions. Pliny the Elder also noted a natural 'reddish' coloured wool as well as yellow or tan, black, white and brown.[24] White sheep appear increasingly to have been selectively bred to produce a yarn and cloth which could be dyed to extend the range of colours naturally available. Amongst the remains of textiles from Scythian burials found at Pazryk and Bashadar dated to *c*.400 BC, woollen yarns coloured pink, blue, yellow, yellow/ginger and brown have been identified.[25] Other colours would have depended very much on the availability of berries, bark and lichens which could produce a pleasing and relatively stable dye. Woad, for example, produces a useful blue,[26] whilst oak bark can be used to produce a range of light to darker browns depending on the length of time the cloth is left in the vat. Madder and Lady's bedstraw both produce orangey reds. Some descriptions of clothing worn by the Celts are give by classical sources. Dio Cassius describes Boudica as wearing 'a multicoloured tunic folded round her, over which was a thick cloak fastened with a brooch. This was how she always dressed.'[27] The warriors of Gaul were described by Diodorus Siculus as wearing 'a striking kind of clothing, tunics dyed and stained in various colours, and trousers, which they call by the name of bracae'.[28] The Gaulish aristocracy was described by Strabo as wearing 'clothes that have been dyed and shot through with gold',[29] whilst Martial says the 'Gaul dresses mostly in reds'.[30] The presence of coloured patterning on garments is suggested by simple incised and punched decoration on some of the surviving figurines (see n. 7). Other recorded garments include the Gallic *sagum*, a coarse woollen cloak or mantle; and the famous *burrus Britannicus* which was priced at a maximum of 6,000 denarii in the Prices Edict of Diocletian.[31]

Animal skins have been used from early prehistoric times for clothing and other uses; in the form of leather, as well as complete with the original wool, hair or fur, for instance the sheepskin cape from Huldremose, Randers, in Denmark dated to the Iron Age;[32] and from Hallstatt have come caps made of brown and black undyed sheepskin, and a white sheepskin bag.[33]

Whether the description of Boudica is based on an eyewitness account or not,[27] the use of brooches and pins to fasten garments or hold them together is witnessed by finds from archaeological sites, and more importantly from inhumations where the dead were laid to rest with a range of possessions appropriate for the afterlife,

Figure 7.5 Reconstruction of the head of Lindow Man, found during peat-cutting near Wilmslow, Cheshire in 1984, by Richard Neave, Unit of Art in Medicine and Life Sciences, University of Manchester. Investigation of samples of skin from this body and a further one discovered in 1987 have revealed traces of iron and copper colourants in a clay-based pigment. These results are discussed and compared with comments from classical authors (Pyatt *et al.* 1991).

and in accord with the family resources. The position of brooches and other hooks and fasteners, where the grave is well excavated and recorded and both skeleton and finds adequately preserved, can add considerably to our knowledge of the way individuals dressed.[34] One of these pioneer studies has been Jochen Garbsch's survey of women's dress from Noricum and Pannonia in the first and second century AD, using tombstone reliefs to augment and clarify the finds.[35]

Probably the best known item of jewellery to be associated with the various Celtic tribes is the neck torque. One of the earliest references to the torque comes in *c.*361 BC when Titus Manlius, in command of the Roman army, accepted the challenge of the Celtic chieftain who had brought his warriors into Italy, killed his opponent and took the torque as spoils of war, gaining for himself and his descendants the name Torquatus.[36] Boudica is also specifically described as wearing 'a great gold torque'.[27] It is useful to note the increasing numbers of gold torques which have been found in East Anglia over recent years, for example the six pieces from Ipswich;[37] and the finds from Snettisham found at different dates between 1948 and 1990.[38] One of these gold torques has been compared with a similar piece from Mailly-le-Camp (Aube), though bronze pieces seem to have been generally more common within that region of France.[39] Probably the largest, most exotic gold piece is the so-called diadem from the rich burial at Vix (Côte d'Or) dated to the sixth century BC, which also included a modest copper alloy torque, two anklets still virtually *in situ*, bracelets, six fibulas and a number of beads.[40] Another rich grave, of the late fourth century BC in Waldalgesheim in the Hunsrück mountains, included a gold torque and three gold bracelets.[41] Other gold torques have been found, for example in another rich grave at Filottrano near Ancona, similar to the Waldalgesheim piece in style and date;[42] and a third-century BC example from Gasic, Vojvodina, in what was Yugoslavia.[43] These ornaments not only represented items for securing clothes but were also evidence for the wealth and status of those wearing them. They could be given as gifts to favoured kinsmen and supporters, as well as providing a useful source of bullion in times of emergency; they could be given as offerings to the gods and their intermediaries, such as Veleda, prophetess of the Bructeri;[44] or offered to them as spoils of war.[45]

Other examples of personal jewellery that have been found in settlements and cemeteries are beads, for instance in the burials at Vix;[46] Arras, Burton Fleming, Danes Graves, Garton Slack and other sites in the East Riding of Yorkshire have yielded examples of jet, amber, bronze and more commonly glass, both plain and with applied decoration:[47] whilst there have also been the occasional finds of gold beads.[48] One of the better known series of finds from a burial in late iron age Britain is that at Welwyn Garden City (1965) which produced one amber bead and two glass ones.[49]

For warriors and other wealthier persons, personal appearance was always important. Strabo relates not only that he had seen Celts in Rome towering as much as half a foot above the tallest people in the city, but that the Celts of transalpine Gaul tried to avoid becoming stout and pot-bellied, and that any young man whose girth exceeded the standard length of belt was punished.[50] Some men shaved their faces, though the moustache was often allowed to grow to a luxuriant length (see Figure 7.3). Examples of metal razors have been found from the Late Bronze Age on, as witnessed by a number of finds from Verona and the region around;[51] and the perhaps better known crescent-shaped examples of Iron Age date.[52] An earlier, more unusual subrectangular piece from Croson di Bovolane was decorated with patterns of swimming ducks.[53] By the Late Iron Age, in Britain, and more commonly in the north-western parts of Europe, razors had taken on a triangular shape with an iron blade, and a small handle or grip of copper alloy at the apex, sometimes with an ornamental gryphon or leopard's head as decoration.[54] One of the more recent finds with a gryphon-head terminal came from excavations at Canterbury in 1982.[55] Hair was also well groomed and an object of note; see, for instance, the description of Boudica, who is said to have a mass of very yellow hair growing down to her hips.[27] Julius Civilis, who led the revolt of the Batavians in AD 69–70, swore to dye his hair red and let it grow until he had wiped out the Roman legions;[56] whilst Diodorus notes that Celtic warriors had blond hair and used limewash to enhance its appearance. The hair was then pulled back from the forehead towards the top of the head and back towards the nape of the neck.[57] This style is illustrated on the obverse of a denarius of L. Hostilius Saserna struck *c.*48 BC which shows a bearded and moustachioed warrior in right profile with a miniature shield behind his head and a chain round the neck. He has been identified as Vercingetorix, King of the Arverni, who led a loose confederation of Gaulish tribes against Caesar from 52 BC until his capture after the fall of Alesia.[58] Hair colouration was probably much the same as is seen on any cross-section of the modern northern European populace. Black was the colour of Noisiu's hair, who was to be the chosen lover of Deidre of the Sorrows, whilst in the story of 'The Destruction of Da Derga's Hostel' Conaire Mor sees three other worldly horsemen riding before him, 'red of body, hair and clothing'.[59] Few pre-Roman representations survive which show the type of hairstyle worn by both sexes, as compared with those from the Imperial period. Men seem to have worn their hair to about shoulder length. As has been mentioned, Boudica and probably most noble women would have grown their hair to show status, as well as being attractive for its length and colour. This can be compared with the Japanese appreciation of female beauty during the Heian period (*c.*950–1050), when length of hair and its appearance was not only a woman's crowning glory but could also incite passionate admiration and infatuation.[60] It seems highly likely that most women working in the home and on the land with their family would, for purely practical purposes, want to tie it or fasten it back so that it didn't get in the way of the task in hand. The advent of the Romans as occupying force and administrators, with their families, would have influenced hairstyles amongst the local populace (Figure 7.6), and seen the adoption of ornamental hairpins of precious metals, copper alloy as well as bone, antler, glass and jet.[61] Some rare actual examples of hair preserved on heads of the dead have survived. One skull from the peat bog at Osterby, in the district of Eckernförde, Schleswig-Holstein, has the hair coiled into a knot on the right side of the head, in the same fashion as described by Tacitus as being typical of Suebian freemen and warriors.[62] From York come a number of burials where gypsum was poured over the body, and in two cases the whole head of hair was preserved: one was a woman's auburn hair in ringlets; the other, found in a lead coffin, came from the body of an adolescent girl with auburn hair fastened up in a bun by two jet pins.[63] As hairbrushes do not appear to have been made or used until the seventeenth century or later,[64] combs were the only practical way of untangling the knots and grooming the hair into simple neatness or elaborate styles. Some double-sided combs had a set of coarse teeth, and a very much finer set, which could be used not only to produce a smooth glossy appearance, but also to extract unwelcome inhabitants such as nits and lice. Combs of this type and other designs were made of antler, bone, wood – especially boxwood – and, less common, horn or metal. Two small bone combs have been recorded from Scotland, both with incised Celtic-style ornamentation on the solid semicircular section above the line of teeth.[65] Ivory was also used for combs, and it is particularly interesting to note that Pope Boniface V sent a gilded ivory comb to Ethelburga, Queen to King Edwin of Northumbria.[66] It seems unlikely that this was a unique incident, and other noble or wealthy women may also have been honoured by such a gift, perhaps marking a special event, or from individuals hoping to gain favours or advancement in return.

Figure 7.6 Copper alloy head of a young girl, said to have been found at Silkstead quarry in the parish of Otterbourne, Hampshire. The pupils of the eyes are small black pebbles. Partly Roman in style, the hatching round the eyes and ears is found in late iron age art, and into the late first and early second centuries. (Copyright: Winchester Museums Service Collection.)

One of the other luxuries for wealthier members of this society was the mirror. Queen Ethelburga received a silver mirror to go with the ivory comb that the pope had sent, but comparatively few silver examples have survived in comparison with the copper alloy ones known from the early prehistoric period down to the Middle Ages. One of the earlier types was found in the La Tène 'Princess's Grave' found at Reinheim in 1954.[67] Although the mirror disc is badly damaged and incomplete, the handle, which is in the form of a stylized janiform person, has the disc slotted into the deep cut across the head, whilst arms, ending in hands stylized as roundels ornamented with studs, appear to hold the disc steady. The style of the head with its comma-shaped horns or locks of hair is closely related to the damaged stone head from Heidelberg.[68] However, in all other respects, it most closely resembles the caryatid mirrors of Greece and Magna Graecia, which had their origins and inspiration from the stand mirrors of Egypt which show gods and mortals supporting the mirror disc. The earliest date for these Greek mirrors is towards the end of the seventh century BC, with the latest examples being dated towards the end of the fifth century BC.[69] Some of these mirrors appear to be held on top of the head by a caryatid figure, or her male equivalent, and supported on the outstretched hands. It seems highly unlikely that the Reinheim mirror, along with the more naturalistically modelled caryatid on the Hochheim mirror, is a Celtic version of a mirror type which had already become established in the Greek heartland.[70] Other mirrors which owe their basic design to the inspiration of examples from the classical lands are the Celtic mirrors in the British series, now totalling some eight iron examples with, in some cases, copper alloy fittings; and thirty-four copper alloy pieces complete or represented either by a handle or a disc in varying states of preservation, with one outlier now in Nijmegen, the Netherlands.[71] The handles of the Celtic mirrors can be divided into two major groups. The first has a grip with a series of loops along its length, as for example on the Desborough, Birdlip and Colchester mirrors,[72] which can be compared with the elegant silver example from Villa Boscoreale, Campania,[73] and less elaborate pieces from Vaison-la-Romaine, Aquileia, Nîmes and Nijmegen.[74] The second group has a more rod-like grip with a small terminal ring, for instance the handle from Mount Batten, Stamford Hill I, Ingleton, Yorkshire, and more recently the fragment from Thetford, Norfolk,[75] which can be compared with examples including ones from the Casa del Menandro, Pompeii, the Villa Boscoreale, and three other close parallels.[76]

DAILY LIFE, LEISURE AND OTHER ACTIVITIES

Within the household of individual families there were certain items which would have been used on a daily basis. These would be the millstones for the grinding of grain into flour for bread-making; buckets for carrying water, or milk from domesticated animals, for instance the pre-Roman examples from Aylesford (Kent), Marlborough (Wiltshire)[77] and the less elaborate example from a cemetery at Roanne (Loire) with a suggested date of the first century BC.[78] These were made of wooden staves with copper-alloy binding strips, some plain, others decorated, a base which was held in grooves cut into the lower section of the staves, and a movable copper-alloy handle. Three longer staves would have acted as rudimentary feet. A cauldron suspended by a chain from the rafters, or from a tripod, would have been used in the preparation of food on a regular basis.[79] Its importance in practical terms is witnessed by the number of times it is mentioned in histories, folklore and the legendary exploits of the gods and heroes.[80] Storage jars to keep dried fruits, berries and other useful foodstuffs would not have been uncommon, though in areas lacking suitable clays for potting, other materials such as wood for platters, bowls and boxes, wicker for storage baskets, and soft stone which could be cut into bowls or saucers, would be utilized. Drinking vessels could be small bowls, or made of animal horn whilst tankards, such as the perfectly preserved Trawsfynydd (Merioneth) find, is another instance of what the wealthier classes could afford as objects for use and display.[81] The display of exotic imported vessels for the serving of wine or beer, at banquets on formal occasions, was, as in classical lands, one aspect of conspicuous consumption. The enthusiasm for wine drinking amongst the Gauls was particularly noted, and is confirmed by the presence in south-east Britain of wine amphorae in the late iron age burials (Figure 7.7).[82] Beer was well known as a beverage, and drunk throughout the Roman period, as is confirmed not only by finds from the potteries of Britain, but also by the closely related silver example from the Villa Boscoreale.[83] Mead was also made,[84] though poorer families may have depended more heavily on milk, and water.

Figure 7.7 The La Tène III period rich burial found at Welwyn Garden City, Herts., in 1965 included five wine amphorae, pottery vessels, beads, fragments of glass bracelet, twenty-four glass gaming-pieces and a wooden board, a silver cup and two bronze vessels, handles and bindings for wooden vessels, an iron razor, studs and a 'straw' mat. The dating for the group is most probably within the last quarter of the first century BC. (Copyright: The British Museum, London.)

The wealth of any family or group was dependent on the size and well-being of the stock. Cattle were particularly important for the production of milk, meat, leather and bone, all of which could be utilized for a variety of domestic and semi-industrial uses.[85] Pigs were important to the humbler farmer, as they could be turned out to forage on less tractable forest, scrub or moorlands, farrowed easily with multiple offspring, and after the autumn cull meat, bone and leather could be used, with the blood made up into puddings or sausages for winter use (Figure 7.8). Joints of pork as well as complete skeletons were not uncommon as part of the offerings to the dead (Figure 7.9).[86]

Although a certain proportion of animal meat was raised through the breeding of domesticated stock, hunting produced further supplies to supplement the diet with its wider variety, and conserve the best breeders for as long a period as possible. Hunting would, as in the medieval world, include horsemen, who would need the speed to keep up with deer, or to sidestep the dangers of attack from a cornered wild boar whose tusks could wreak such havoc on men, horses and dogs.[87] Other hunters would track down their prey on foot, set traps, lime twigs, or set nets to catch

Figure 7.8 Members of Y Ddraig, a branch of The Vikings (Norse Film and Pageant Society), and a pig with wild boar ancestry recreate a scene from the sub-Roman period at Bridgemere Wild Life Park, near Nantwich, Cheshire (November 1991). (Copyright: John Eagle.)

Figure 7.9 Iron age chariot burial found at Garton Slack near Driffield, Yorkshire, by T.C.M. Brewster in 1971. The skeleton of a male of about 30 years was laid out over the dismantled wheels, with the remains of two horse-bits, five terrets, two strap-links and other fragments. Part of the pole shaft can be seen in the upper part of the photograph. Food, in the form of half a pig's head, was placed on the body. (Copyright: Hull City Museums and Art Galleries.)

birds or fish in streams, rivers and the sea (Figure 7.10). Children could be set to collecting shellfish on the sea shore.[88] Many of the weapons used for hunting, the bows and arrows, spears of various types, slings with shot, nets, and all the skills of the chase which were used for food-gathering, or ensuring that larger animals, deer, wild boar, wolves, foxes, and bears in mountainous regions, did not trample and destroy crops or steal and kill young stock, could prove excellent training for the young men who might one day have to show their mettle in local skirmishes or major battles.[89]

The majority of Celts would have lived within a mainly agricultural village community, growing crops and raising beasts, as often as not having little contact with the larger political or religious centres except at festivals or times of trouble. Few families would have had either the two- or four-wheeled carts which have been identified from burials (Figure 7.9).[90] Only the wealthier members of society could have afforded the lightweight chariots with the elaborate sets of trappings for the horses, and other ornamental fittings such as terrets, finials and linchpins.[91] Britons, a well as Gaulish Celts, were noted for their use of chariots which were drawn by two horses and carried the warrior and his charioteer.[92] One source describes the fighting man as being armed with a shield, short spear and daggers, and that they were remarkable for their endurance; another that they put bronze helmet on their heads and had long shields as high as a man.[93] They were also noted for taking the heads of their foremost enemies and preserving them as trophies

Figure 7.10 Castor-ware beaker with hunting scene, showing a hare pursued by dogs. Found at Verulamium, Herts., dated late second or early third century AD height *c.*22.8 cm. (Copyright: St Albans Museums.)

in cedar oil,[94] which practice is also recorded on Trajan's column, completed in c.AD 113.[95]

In many respects society was structured, with nobles, princes and kings guiding the tribe or smaller social group under their control. Hence the shock felt when Cartimandua, Queen of the Brigantes, set aside her husband Venutius, and took his armour-bearer Vellocatus for her lover.[96] Below the noble classes, but no less important to the whole society were the druids with their various skills, intermediary between ordinary mortals and the gods, and custodians of the laws and traditions, and whose influence could sway the decisions of kings and warriors, and bind the people more closely together during times of conflict.[97]

Artisans and craftsmen, especially the smith, were accorded high honour and status, for what must have seemed the almost magical transformation of lumps of earth and rock into pure molten iron, bronze or the precious gold and silver, and thence into weapons, tools and things of great beauty. The skills of the smith were jealously guarded and kept within the family, or passed on to a trusted apprentice who had shown aptitude. The importance of the smith's trade is also reinforced by representations of the tools of his trade on pottery,[98] but the secrecy and accompanying ritual during the process of smelting and manufacture continued well into the Middle Ages.[99] Less is known of the other, lesser members of society, the farmers, traders, servants and slaves, or of their families. As elsewhere in the ancient world where medicine and a true understanding of disease and its causes were little understood, life must have been a hard grind to keep body and soul together. Infant mortality and death in childbirth was not uncommon. As was pointed out by Birley in 1979, life expectancy was short when compared with the comparative longevity of today.[100] Parents would have tried to raise a large family in the hope that some of their offspring would be strong enough to survive until adulthood. War and agricultural accidents, especially if suffered by the stronger members of the family, could ruin a household where children were too young to cope with the vital heavier tasks. Failure of crops through unseasonable weather, infestation by pests or fungal attack were also to be greatly feared.

Not all prospects were bleak. The Celts of the historic period down to the present have always been able to entertain themselves. Visits from traders travelling between farmsteads, villages and towns, and the fortified and strategically defensible places that were establishing themselves, would have been welcomed for their news and gossip. Bards were made much of for their music and songs, and their stories would have been suitably rewarded, especially during the dark days of winter and at festival time. Board games were played, as demonstrated by the gaming-pieces and (?)board from the Welwyn Garden City burial 1965;[101] and at important gatherings young men would compete against each other in different sports and contests to prove their prowess before their elders.

Gradually under external influences over the centuries, the various Celtic tribes adapted to the outward trappings of Graeco-Roman civilization. Members of the upper classes became part of the administration from G. Julius Alpinus Classicianus, who became procurator of the province of Britain in AD 61 following the revolt of Boudica;[102] to the fourth-century Attius Patera of Bayeux, who claimed descent from a druidical family. He was the son of a priest of Apollo Belenus and friend to the poet Ausonius.[103] It was people like these, who could compromise and adapt themselves to a changing world, who were able to hand on the most important aspects of their culture and tradition which has, even though grievously fragmented, survived down to the present day.

ACKNOWLEDGEMENTS

Thanks are due to the following friends and colleagues for kindly supplying the photographs for this chapter, namely: Adriano La Regina, Soprintendente at the Soprintendenza Archeologica di Roma; Mlle Dominique Darde, Conservateur, Musée Archéologique de Nîmes (Gard); Dr Andrew Foxon, Keeper of Archaeology at the Hull and East Riding Museum, Hull; Mr Geoffrey Denford, Keeper of Antiquities, and Karen Parker, Keeper of Records, Winchester Museum Service; Dr D.V. Clarke, Department of Archaeology, and Mrs W. Henderson, National Museums of Scotland, Edinburgh; Mr Arthur MacGregor, Assistant Keeper, Department of Archaeology, Ashmolean Museum of Art and Archaeology, Oxford; Mr Sam Mullins, Assistant Director, and Hazel Simons, Assistant Keeper, Verulamium Museum, St Albans; Mr Ralph Jackson and colleagues, Department of Prehistoric and Romano-British Antiquities, British Museum, London; Mr John Eagle, East Molesey, Surrey KT8 0BL.

Particular thanks are due to Caroline David and colleagues at the Bridgemere Wild Life Park, for permission to borrow Floyd the Pig, and for use of the Park's facilities during the photographic session; and to all members of Y Ddraig who gave their time to take part, including Deidre de Goldthorpe Hanson; Deborah White; Duncan Probert; Michael Hughes; Andrew McCallum; Nick and Diane McGee; Ken Jackson; Phaedra Kaine; and especially Fon Matthews for help with transport, local organization, and her continuing support, enthusiasm and friendship. To Mrs M.J. Morgan for discussion of Rousseau's work, and the references; Mr Peter J. Boughton, Grosvenor Museum, Chester, for supplying the name of the sculptor of the Ambiorix statue at Tongres, and other useful details; and all the friends and relations who have given help and encouragement over the years, not the least of whom Miranda Aldhouse Green for inviting me to contribute a chapter to this volume.

NOTES

1 Warner 1985: 49–50.
2 Rivet 1979.
3 Pobé and Roubier 1961: 55–6 pl. 44; 55 pl. 41, both in the Musée Archéologique, Nîmes.
4 Now in the Ashmolean Museum, Oxford, no. 1970.1059, terracotta, ht 17 cm, unprovenanced.
5 Keppie 1979: 9, no. 1, pl. 1 and fig. 1; Collingwood and Wright 1965: 657–8, no. 2139, pl. XVIII, now in the National Museums of Scotland, Edinburgh.
6 Strong 1980: 88, pl. 40.
7 Stead 1981: 18, no. 92 with plate, British Museum, Department of Greek and Roman Antiquities no. 59.11–26. 1, ht 7.2 cm.

8 Wild 1970: Chapter 5, pp.. 41–58.

9 Compare the curious note in Pliny, *Naturalis Historia* XXXVI.131 and the comment in Bailey 1932: 117 and notes pp. 251–2.

10 Broholm and Hald 1935.

11 Wild 1970: 4–10; Olschki 1949.

12 Wild 1970: 20.

13 Hall 1986: 9.

14 For silk see Wightman 1985: 9 n. 12, 336; Wild 1970: 10–13, 17–19 (cotton), 15–17 (hemp), 21 (mallow and nettles). It is interesting to note Andersen's story 'The Wild Swans', where eleven princes, transformed into swans, were released from the spell when their sister Elissa wove them shirts made of fibres from nettles gathered from a churchyard at night.

15 Lawson 1976: 272, fig. 14 nos. 105, 106; RCHM 1962: 143–4, pl. 69, nos. H314.1, H314.2; Pirling 1986: 59–60, Abb. 34 from Grave 3918 at Krefeld dated late second century AD.

16 Cunliffe 1984: 395, fig. 7.39 nos. 3.211–3.213, for bone whorls; 401, fig. 7.46 nos. 7.31–7.50, for baked clay and one sherd whorl; Fell 1936: 69–70, fig. 5 no. 2.

17 Collingwood and Wright 1965: 356, pl. 15 no. 1065; Phillips 1977: 90–1, pl. 68 no. 247.

18 Fell 1936: 69, pl. 8 no. 1, 12 no. 7; Cunliffe 1984; 371–8, figs 7.27–7.30, nos. 3.1–3.29; Fogolari *et al.* 1976: 131, fig. 28 nos. 223–8, showing examples in course of manufacture, complete, and with damaged teeth.

19 Fell 1936: 91, pl. 11a no. 1. Twelve examples were reported with only one illustrated; Cunliffe 1984: 401, 403, 406, figs 7.47, 7.48 nos. 7.51–7.67; Wheeler and Wheeler 1936: 150, pl. 52 no. 5.

20 Ryder 1990a: 38.

21 ibid: 38–9.

22 Tacitus, *Annales* XIV.30.

23 Abrahams 1908: 101; Pollux, *Onomasticon* VII.56.

24 Pliny VIII.73.191; Ryder 1991: 59.

25 Ryder 1990b: 316.

26 Wild 1970: 81.

27 Dio Cassius, *Epitome* LXXII.2; the adjective describing her hair colour is ξανθοτατην, from ξανθοδ, which covers all shades of yellow from the palest to a red or auburn (Liddell and Scott 1964: 470).

28 Diodorus Siculus V.30.1; quoted in Stead 1981: 17.

29 Strabo, *Geographia* IV.5.

30 Martial, *Epigrammates* XIV.129 'Canusinae Rufae': 'Roma magis fusci vestitur, Gallia rufis, et placet hic pueris militibusque color.'

31 Roueché 1989: 284, chapter XIX line 48.

32 Wild 1988: 8, fig. 1.

33 Ryder 1990a: 39.

34 Stead 1979: Danes Graves no. 43 excavated 1897, p.20, fig. 5, p. 68 skeleton A oriented south-west to north-east, had an iron and bronze brooch.

35 Garbsch 1965: fig. 1 nos. 8, 10, 13; figs 6, 7; fig. 12 nos. 2, 4; fig. 13 nos. 5, 10, 17; fig. 14 nos. 10, 11, 13, 17, 22; fig. 15 nos. 32, 23; fig. 16 nos. 1, 2 all show the characteristic use of local brooch types to fasten the overdress at the shoulder.

36 Livy, *Ab Urbe Condita* VII.9.6; also Aulus Gellius, *Attic Nights* IX.13.18–19.

37 Brailsford 1975: 44–52, pl. 59, 60, 64, 67, 70, 75, colour pl. IV.

38 Brailsford 1975: 55–61, pl. 77, 81–6, colour pl. V–VII; Stead 1991: 447–64.

39 Stead 1981: 39, pl. 37 no. 307.

40 Joffroy 1962: chapter 6, see pp. 105, 106 with pl. pp. 102, 104, 107; for plan of finds from the burial see p. 40. Note also the statuette, British Museum, Department of Greek and

Roman Antiquities nos. 67.5–8.748, Stead 1981: 20, pl. 12 no. 113, showing a seated Gaulish woman wearing a torque and bracelets.

41 Jope 1971: pl. 21; Megaw 1970: 95–6 no. 127 with pl.

42 Megaw 1970: 96–7, no. 128 and pl.

43 Ibid.: 105–6, no. 151 and pl.

44 Tacitus, *Historiae* IV.61, 65.

45 Diodorus Siculus V.27.1; Trogus Pompeius in Justin III.3.36. Note the treasures found in sacred lakes at Tolosa in 106 BC, after the defeat of the Tectosages by the Roman army under the consul Q. Servilius Caepio: see Scullard 1965: 54.

46 Joffroy 1962: 100–1, plan of tomb on p. 40 where item no. 18 are the beads in the region of the neck and upper part of the body.

47 Stead 1979: 78–81, fig. 31; compare also the necklaces from burials in the Department of Marne, France: Stead 1981: 37, nos. 282, 283, pl. 35.

48 Megaw 1970: 59 no. 38, one bead from the seventh-century BC barrow at Strettweg, Judenburg, Austria; 96 no. 128 fourth century BC, two beads from Grave NZ, Filottrano, S. Paolina, Ancona, Italy; 112 no. 170 third century BC from Mal Tepe, Mezek, Bulgaria; and 130–1 no. 208 first century BC from Szárad, Regöly, Hungary, hoard I.

49 Stead 1967: 17, section iv, fragments A–C: fig. 10 and frontispiece pl. 1b. Note also the discussion of the pre-Roman beads in Guido 1978: 19–89.

50 Strabo, IV.5.2 and IV.4.6.

51 Aspes *et al.* 1976: 133 no. 1, fig. 2 no. 7, damaged and incomplete, from S. Michele, near Caprino Veronese in 1973.

52 Aspes *et al.* 1976: 187 nos. 24, 25; fig. 47 nos. 9, 10 for the region of Verona; for the damaged piece from S. Briccio di Lavagno see p. 193 no. 6; fig. 50 no. 8.

53 Aspes *et al.* 1976: 190 no. 2; fig. 50 no. 2.

54 Mariën 1971: 213–27; 1973: 71–8.

55 Garrard and Sellwood 1983: 333–4, fig. 143, pl. XXXVII.

56 Tacitus, *Historiae* IV.61.1.

57 Diodorus Siculus V.28.1.

58 Toynbee 1978: 102, pl. 173; Sydenham 1952: 159, pl. 26 no. 952; Caesar, *De Bello Gallico* VII.

59 Rees and Rees 1961: 280, 328 respectively.

60 Morris 1964 [1979]: 215, with references to the writing of Murasaki Shikibu (AD 975–1025).

61 Cool 1990; Crummy 1979, 1983: 19–30.

62 Jankuhn 1958: 254, fig. 6; Tacitus, *Germania* 28.

63 RCHM 1962: 79b; Region IV, Area (b), burial (vi), p. 81b reported August 1840; Area (d), burial (i), p. 83a found in May 1875.

64 MacGregor 1985: 183, fig. 99.

65 MacGregor 1976: 1,143; II no. 274 from Ghegan Rock, Seacliff, East Lothian found before 1865–70; no. 275 from Langbank, Renfrewshire, found 1903; MacGregor 1985: 73–98.

66 Bede, *Historia Ecclesiastica Gentis Anglorum* II.11. Boniface V of Naples, pope from 23 December 619 to 25 October 625.

67 Now in the Museum für Vor- und Frühgeschichte, Saarbrucken, diam. disc 18.9 cm, Keller 1958: 158; 1965: 41 no. 15 fig. 28.1 plan of grave fig. 4 on p. 16; 1966: 156.

68 Megaw 1970: 64 no. 49 and pl., dated late fifth/early fourth century BC.

69 Congdon 1981: see fig. 3, discussion pp. 7–12; dating on pp. 96–106.

70 Behrens 1933; Nahrgang 1934: 40 no. T.3, fig. 13, diam. mirror 12.5 cm.

71 Lloyd-Morgan 1981, Appendix I pp. 111–16, pl. 30a, b, fig. 10.

72 Desborough, Northants, mirror now in the British Museum, Department of Prehistoric and Romano-British Antiquities no. 1924.1–9, Smith 1909; Birdlip, Glos., now in the City

Museum and Art Gallery, Gloucester, Bellows 1880–1; Colchester, Essex, Laver 1905; Fox 1948a, in the Colchester and Essex Museum.

73 de Villefosse 1899: 88–90, no. 21 pl. XIX, figs. 20, 47; Strong 1966: 158, pl. 37B, now in the Louvre, cat. no. 2158.

74 Vaison-la-Romaine mirror now in the Musée Archéologique, Nîmes, cat. no. 908.51.55 with maximum date range *c*.23 BC–AD 37; Museo Archeologico, Aquileia, inv. no. 15848; Musée Archéologique, Nîmes, no. 1053, from a tomb in the Boulevard de la République, Nîmes, 1872; Nijmegen inv. no. XXI.f/L.4, Lloyd-Morgan 1981: 60, pl. 13a, b.

75 Mount Batten: Spence Bate 1866: 501–2, pl. XXX; Cunliffe 1988: 90, no. S3 figs. 48, 49; Ingleton, Yorkshire, now in the British Museum, Department of Prehistoric and Romano-British Antiquities inv. no. 1945.11–3.1; Fox 1948b: 24, 26–7, 35, 38, figs 1.4, 2, 3, pl. II; Thetford, Norfolk, found in a Neronian context: Lloyd-Morgan in Gregory 1991: 132, fig. 116 no. 10.

76 de Villefosse 1899: 90–2, 190–1, 277 and note on p. 91; no. 22 pl. XX, now in the Louvre cat. no. 2159 from the Villa Boscoreale; from the Casa del Menandro, Pompeii, Maiuri 1932: 350 no. 15 figs 135–6, pl. XLVII–XLVIII, which with the following examples is housed in the Museo Archeologico Nazionale, Naples, no. 25716: Ward Perkins and Claridge 1976: no. 69 with pl; nos. 25717, 74926.

77 Fox 1958: 68–71 pl. 33a–36; Brailsford 1975: 83–9, pl. 124, 126–31; Hawkes 1951: 191–8, pl. VII–IX, figs 50–2.

78 Feugère 1984–5; note also seven examples of iron bucket fittings in Manning 1985: 102–3.

79 Note the elaborately worked example from Great Chesterford, Essex: Fox 1958: 110–1, pl. 67a, 68; Manning 1985: 100–2, no. P9, arm of a cauldron hanger from Water Newton, Huntingdonshire, BM cat. no. 1882.6–21.80; P10, pl. 46, head of a chain from Dorn Farm, near Moreton-in-the-Marsh, Glos., BM inv. no. 1938.10–8.2; fig. 27 shows the reconstruction of an example from Butley, Suffolk, and Great Chesterford, Essex: Stead 1967: 55, no. 18 on fig. for an iron tripod from Stanfordbury, Beds., now in the Museum of Archaeology and Ethnology, Cambridge.

80 For example, in the story of Branwen, daughter of Llyr, in the second branch of the *Mabinogion*, the Cauldron of Regeneration given by Bendigeidfran to Matholwch, King of Ireland, in compensation for insult, was later used to revive the Irish warriors who were slain in battle by Bran's men. In the *Chwedl Taliesin*, Ceridwen prepares a magical brew in her cauldron, from which three drops would be swallowed that would reveal secrets of past, present and future. Compare the actual examples in Hawkes 1951, figs 46–7, 49 dated first century BC/AD, pp. 172–91.

81 Fox 1958: pl. 63a, tankard from Shapwick Heath, Somerset; pl. 64a from the Thames at Kew; also Corcoran 1952.

82 See Megaw and Megaw 1990: 91 for discussion on purpose and use; Diodorus Siculus V.26.1; Stead 1967: 7–8, fig. 5 and fig. on p. 59.

83 Dioscorides, *De Medica Materia* II.88; Booth 1980: 18, fig. 11 nos. 3, 4; Carrington 1977: 151 nos. 36, 37; fig. 10.2 dated second to third century; de Villefosse 1899: 102 no. 43, pl. XXIII no. 1 with concave sides engraved with a feather pattern.

84 Strabo IV.5.5.

85 Leather for caps, shoes, belts, harness and other straps and bindings, containers for liquids, crude hinges, piping, bellows for use in metalworking, construction of carts, chariots, boats, coracles, sails and rigging as used by the Veneti on their ships (Caesar, *De Bello Gallico* III.13), sword and knife sheaths, etc.

86 Note the finds of pork joints and complete skeletons in burials, Brewster 1975: 110; Lethbridge 1953: 28 and bone report p. 37; Stead 1979: 17, 18, 20, 22, 36–7, 39, who notes similar finds in the cart burials from the champagne area of France on pp. 25–6; also the presence of horse, goat, sheep and other food bones in these and other burials.

87 Hunting the wild boar proved fatal to both Adonis and Meleager in classical mythology
(Rose 1965: 124–5 and 258 respectively). In the story of Culhwch and Olwen, Ysbaddaden
the giant, Olwen's father, sets Culhwch the task of hunting down Twrch Trwyth to take the
comb, razor and shears between his ears. All of which was accomplished with the slaying of
the boar, but not without loss of the lives of men and animals. Note the model of a horseman with spear chasing a boar on a four-wheeled cart from Merida, Spain – Megaw 1970:
58–9, pl. 37, dated second to first century BC; and the triumphant votive inscription set up
at Bollihope Common, Stanhope, Co. Durham to commemorate the capture of a 'wild boar
of remarkable fineness' by G. Tetius Veturius Micianus, prefect of the Sobosian cavalry
(Collingwood and Wright 1965: I, no. 1041 p. 346) dated to *c.* the third century AD; and the
boar's tusk amulet now damaged, from Segontium–Boon 1975: 62–4, fig. 6.

88 Shell middens are not uncommon on coastal sites in Britain and its offshore islands, in the
Orkneys, Hebrides, etc.; Ynys Seiriol, off the south-east coast of Anglesey (Hughes
1901); Hilbre Island off the western coast of the Wirral peninsula, Cheshire; Twlc Point,
Llangennith, West Glamorgan, with potsherds in the midden dated second to fourth
century AD (Penniman 1936).

89 Celtic mercenaries were recruited from Cisalpine Gaul by Dionysos, Tyrant of Syracuse,
*c.*369–368 BC, and included cavalry, Xenophon, *Hellenica* VII.1.20–22 and VII.1.31; Caesar
VI.15; also Strabo's comment on the Celtic fondness for fighting (IV.4.6).

90 Stead 1979 for fittings from the two-wheeled carts found in the East Riding, Yorkshire,
graves; also Dent 1985 ; Joffroy 1962: 111–20, fig. on p. 40 for plan of tomb with remains
of the four-wheeled cart.

91 Davies and Spratling 1976. Note especially p. 129 fig. 6 no. 16; p. 131 figs 7, 8 no. 17; fig.
8, no. 18; fig. 8 no. 19; fig. 7, no. 20.

92 Strabo IV.5.2; Tacitus, *Agricola* 12; Cassius Dio XXXIX.51. In the Táin Bó Cualnge, Lóeg
is charioteer to the great hero Cú Chulainn. see Fox 1945 for the chariot fittings and horse
furniture from Llyn Cerrig Bach, Anglesey, pp. 12–19 nos. 19–43 pl. III, VI, VII; and pp.
19–30 nos. 44–58 pl. IV, IX–XIV respectively. Tacitus, *Historiae* III.45.

93 Dio Cassius LXXVI.12.1–5; Diodorus Siculus V.30.2.

94 Strabo IV.4.5.

95 Lepper and Frere 1988: 70–1, pl. XVIII cast 58; 15–16 for date of completion and dedication of the column.

96 Strabo IV.5.2; Tacitus, *Historiae* III.4.5.

97 Caesar VI.13.

98 Toynbee 1964: 401, 403–4, pl. XCI.C; note also the story of Weland Smith (Davidson 1986:
131); also Webster and Backhouse 1991: 101–3: Franks Casket no. 70 (with three plates).
The left half of the front panel shows a scene from the story of Weland Smith, casket dated
to the second half of the eighth century.

99 Pliny the Elder discusses metallurgy in Book XXXIV of the *Naturalis Historia*;
Theophilus, *c.*1100, described casting and metalworking, but the works of Agricola from
1530, and Vannoccio Biringuccio's *Pirotechnia* of 1540, were amongst the first modern
treatises to discuss the processes involved clearly and without mystification.

100 Birley 1979: 19, 147.

101 Gaming-pieces, Stead 1967: 14–17, 18–19, fig. 10, on left, frontispiece pl. Ia, c, d; board
pp. 31–6, figs 19, 20, 21 and fig. on p. 59. Note also the story of 'The Dream of Macsen
Wledig' in the *Mabinogion*, where the emperor sees two young men playing *gwyddbwyll*
on a silver gaming-board.

102 Collingwood and Wright 1965: I, 5–6, no. 12 and fig.

103 Ausonius, *Commemoratio Professorum Burdigalensium* IV.7–14; Henig 1984: 66–7;
Rankin 1987: 233.

REFERENCES

Abrahams, Ethel B. (1908) *A Study of the Costumes Worn in Ancient Greece from Pre-Hellenic Times into the Hellenistic Age*, London: John Murray.

Andersen, Hans Christian (c.1906) 'The Wild Swans', in *The Fairy Tales*, London and Glasgow: Collins Imperial Library, 7–24.

Aspes, Alessandra *et al.* (eds) (1976) *3000 anni fa a Verona. Dalla fine dell'eta del bronzo all'arrivo dei Romani nel territorio veronese*, Catalogue of the exhibition held 1 July–31 December 1976, at the Museo Civico di Storia Naturale, Verona. Verona: Museo di Storia Naturale di Verona.

Bailey, Kenneth C. (1929, 1932) *The Elder Pliny's Chapters on Chemical Subjects*, 2 vols (1929, 1932), London: Edward Arnold.

Bate, C. Spence (1866) 'On the discovery of a Romano-British cemetery near Plymouth', *Archaeologia* 40(2): 500–10.

Behrens, Gustav (1933) 'Bronze spiegel und flasche der Frühlatènezeit von Hochheim a.M.', *Germania* 17: 81–7.

Bellows, John (1880–1) 'On some bronze and other articles found near Birdlip', *Transactions of the Bristol and Gloucestershire Archaeological Society* 5: 137–41.

Birley, Anthony (1979) *The People of Roman Britain*, London: Batsford.

Boon, George C. (1975) 'Segontium fifty years on, I: A Roman stave of larchwood and other unpublished finds mainly of organic materials together with a note on late barracks', *Archaeologia Cambrensis* 124: 52–67.

Booth, Paul M. (1980) *Roman Alcester*, Warwick: Warwickshire Museum.

Brailsford, John W. (1975) *Early Celtic Masterpieces from Britain in the British Museum*, London: British Museum.

Brewster, T.C.M. (1975) 'Garton Slack', *Current Archaeology* no. 51 (July) vol. 5(4).

Broholm, H.C. and Hald, Margrethe (1935) 'Danske Bronzealders Dragter', *Nordiske Fortisminder* 2 (5, 6): 215–347.

Carrington, Peter (1977) '"Severn Valley" ware and its place in the Roman pottery supply at Chester: a preliminary assessment', in J. Dore and K. Greene (eds.) *Roman Pottery Studies in Britain and Beyond*, Oxford: British Archaeological Reports, Supplementary Series 30, 147–62.

Collingwood, R.G. and Wright, R.P. (1965) *The Roman Inscriptions of Britain I*, Oxford: Oxford University Press.

Cool, H.E.M. (1990) 'Roman metal hairpins from southern Britain', *Archaeological Journal* 147: 148–82.

Corcoran, J.X.W.P. (1952) 'Tankards and tankard handles of the British early Iron Age', *Proceedings of the Prehistoric Society* 18: 85–102.

Crummy, Nina (1979) 'A chronology of Romano-British bone pins', *Britannia* 10: 157–63.

—— (1983) *Colchester Archaeological Report 2: The Roman Small Finds from Excavations in Colchester 1971–9*, Colchester: Colchester Archaeological Trust.

Congdon, Lenore O. Keene (1981) *Caryatid Mirrors of Ancient Greece*, Mainz am Rhein: Verlag Philipp von Zabern.

Cunliffe, Barry W. (1984) *Danebury. An Iron Age Hillfort in Hampshire 2: The Excavations 1969–1978: the finds*, London: CBA Research Report no. 52.

—— (1988) *Mount Batten: Plymouth. A prehistoric and Roman port*, Oxford: Oxford University Committee for Archaeology, Monograph 26.

Davidson, H.R. Ellis (1986) *Gods and Myths of Northern Europe*, Harmondsworth: Penguin Books.

Davies, Jeffrey L. and Spratling, Mansel G. (1976) 'The Seven Sisters hoard: a centenary study', in George C. Boon and J.M. Lewis (eds) *Welsh Antiquity. Essays mainly on prehistoric topics presented to H.N. Savory upon his retirement as Keeper of Archaeology*, Cardiff: National Museum of Wales, 121–47.

Dent, John (1985) 'Three cart burials from Wetwang, Yorkshire', *Antiquity* 59(226): 85–92.

de Villefosse, A. Heron (1899) *Le Trésor de Boscoreale*, Paris: Monuments et Mémoires Eugène Piot 5.

Fell, Clare I. (1936) 'The Hunsbury hillfort, Northants: a new survey of the material', *Archaeological Journal* 93(1): 57–100.

Feugère, Michel (1984–5) 'Le seau en bois de la nécropole gauloise et gallo-romaine de Roanne', *Cahiers Archéologiques de la Loire* 4–5: 71–8.

Fogolari, Giulia *et al.* (1976) *Padova Pre-Romana*, Catalogue of the exhibition held at the Nuovo Museo Civico agli Eremitani, Padua 27 June–15 November 1976. Venice: Comune di Padova, Soprintendenza della Venezia.

Fox, Cyril (1945) *A Find of the Early Iron Age from Llyn Cerrig Bach, Anglesey, Interim Report*, Cardiff: National Museum of Wales.

—— (1948a) 'The incised ornament on the Celtic Mirror from Colchester, Essex', *Antiquaries Journal* 28: 123–37.

—— (1948b) 'Celtic mirror handles in Britain', *Archaeologia Cambrensis* 100(1): 24–44.

—— (1958) *Pattern and Purpose: a survey of early Celtic art in Britain*, Cardiff: National Museum of Wales.

Garbach, Jochen (1965) *Die Norisch-Pannonische Frauentracht im 1 und 2 Jahrhundert*, Munich: C.H. Beck'sche Verlagsbuchhandlung.

Garrard, P. and Sellwood, Lyn (1983) 'Appendix X: a razor from the St George's Street bath-house site', in S.S. Frere and Sally Stow, *The Archaeology of Canterbury*, VII: *Excavations in the St George's Street and Bargate Street Areas*, Maidstone: Kent Archaeological Society, 333–4.

Gregory, Tony (1991) *Excavations in Thetford 1980–1982, Fison Way*, Gressenhall: East Anglian Archaeology Report 53.

Guido, Margaret (1978) *The Glass Beads of the Prehistoric and Roman Periods in Britain and Ireland*, London: Reports of the Research Committee, Society of Antiquaries of London 35.

Hall, Rosalind (1986) *Egyptian Textiles*, Aylesbury: Shire Egyptology Series 4.

Hawkes, C.F.C. (1951) 'Bronzeworkers, cauldrons and bucket animals in iron age and Roman Britain', in W.F. Grimes (ed.) *Aspects of Archaeology and Beyond. Essays presented to O.G.S. Crawford*, London, 172–99.

Henig, Martin (1984) *Religion in Roman Britain*, London: Batsford.

Hughes, Harold (1901) 'Ynys Seiriol', *Archaeologia Cambrensis* 6th series 1(2): 85–108.

Jankuhn, Herbert (1958) 'Moorfunde', *Neue Ausgrabungen in Deutschland*, Römisch-Germanische Kommission, Berlin, 243–57.

Joffroy, René (1962) *Le Trésor de Vix. Histoire et portée d'une grande découverte*, Paris: Librarie Anthème Fayard.

Jope, E.M. (1971) 'The Waldalgesheim master', in John Boardman, M.A Brown and T.G.E. Powell (eds) *The European Community in Later Prehistory. Studies in honour of C.F.C Hawkes*, London: Routledge & Kegan Paul, 165–80.

Keller, Josef (1958) 'Das Keltisch Fürstengrab von Reinheim', *Neue Ausgrabungen in Deutschland*, Berlin: Römisch-Germanische Kommission 146–60.

—— (1965) *Das Keltische Fürstengrab von Reinheim*, Mainz am Rhein: Römisch-Germanisches Zentralmuseum.

—— (1966) *Das Keltische Fürstengrab von Reinheim, kreis St. Ingbert*, Mainz am Rhein: Führer zu Vör und Frühgeschichtlichen Denkmälern vol. 5, Saarland.

Keppie, Lawrence J.F. (1979) *Roman Distance Slabs from the Antonine Wall*, Glasgow:

Hunterian Museum, University of Glasgow.

Laver, Henry (1903–5) 'On a discovery of a late Celtic burial at Colchester', *Proceedings of the Society of Antiquaries of London* 2nd ser., 20: 212–4.

Lawson, Andrew J. (1976) 'Shale and jet objects from Silchester', *Archaeologia* 105: 241–75.

Lepper, Frank and Frere, Sheppard (1988) *Trajan's Column. A new edition of the Cichorius plates*, Gloucester: Alan Sutton.

Lethbridge, T.C. (1953) 'Burial of an iron age warrior at Snailwell', *Proceedings of the Cambridge Antiquarian Society* 47: 25–37.

Liddell and Scott (1964) *Greek–English Lexicon*, Oxford.

Lloyd-Morgan, G. (1981) *Description of the Collections in the Rijksmuseum G.M. Kamm at Nijmegen IX: the mirrors*, Nijmegen: Rijksmuseum, G.M. Kamm, The Netherlands.

MacGregor, Arthur G. (1985) *Bone, Antler Ivory and Horn. The technology of skeletal materials since the Roman period*, Beckenham: Croom Helm.

MacGregor, Morna (1976) *Early Celtic Art in North Britain. A study of decorative metalwork from the third century BC to the third century AD*, Leicester: Leicester University Press.

Maiuri, A. (1932) *La casa del Menandro e il suo tesoro di argenteria*, Rome.

Manning, W.H. (1985) *Catalogue of the Romano-British Iron Tools, Fittings and Weapons in the British Museum*, London: British Museum

Mariën, M.E. (1971) 'Rasoir romain découvert dans la Grotte de Han (Han-sur-Lesse) prov. Namur', *Helinium* 11: 213–27.

—— (1973) 'A propos de rasoirs romains', *Helinium* 13: 71–8.

Megaw, J.V.S. (1970) *Art of the European Iron Age*, Bath: Adams & Dart.

Megaw, J.V.S. and Megaw, M. Ruth (1990) *The Basse-Yutz Find: masterpieces of Celtic art. The 1927 discovery in the British Museum*, London: Reports of the Research Committee, Society of Antiquaries of London no. 46.

Morris, Ivan (1979) *The World of the Shining Prince. Court life in ancient Japan*, Oxford (1964); Harmondsworth (1969).

Nahrgang, Karl (1934) 'Archäologische Fundkarte des Mainmundungsgebietes', *Mainzer Zeitschrift* 29: 40.

Nicholson, Susan M. (1980) *Catalogue of the Prehistoric Metalwork in Merseyside County Museums*, Liverpool: University of Liverpool, Department of Prehistoric Archaeology, Worknotes 2.

Olschki, Leonardo (1949) *The Myth of Felt*, Berkeley and Los Angeles: University of California Press.

Penniman, T.K. (1936) 'Twlc Point shell-heap, Broughton Bay, Llangennith, Gower', *Bulletin of the Board of Celtic Studies* 8: 275–6.

Phillips, E.J. (1977) *Corpus Signorum Imperii Romani: Great Britain*, vol. I fasc. 1: Corbridge. Hadrians Wall east of the north Tyne, London: British Academy.

Pirling, Renate (1986) *Römer und Franken am Niederrhein*, Mainz am Rhein: Verlag Philipp von Zabern.

Pobé, Marcel and Roubier, Jean (1961) *The Art of Roman Gaul. A thousand years of Celtic art and culture*, London: Gallery Press.

Pyatt, F.B. *et al.* (1991) 'Non isatis sed, vitrum, or the colour of Lindow Man', *Oxford Journal of Archaeology* 10: 61–73.

Rankin, H.D. (1987) *Celts and the Classical World*, London and Sydney: Croom Helm.

Rees, Alwyn and Rees, Brinley (1961; reprinted 1978) *Celtic Heritage. Ancient tradition in Ireland and Wales*, London: Thames & Hudson.

Rivet, A.L.F.(1979) 'A note on scythed chariots', *Antiquity* 53: 130–2.

Rose, H.J. (1965) *A Handbook of Greek Mythology*, London: Methuen.

Roueché, Charlotte (1989) *Aphrodisias in Late Antiquity*, London: Journal of Roman Studies Monograph 5.

Royal Commission on Historical Monuments (1962) *An Inventory of the Historical Monuments in the City of York*, vol. I: *Eburacum. Roman York*, London: Royal Commission on Historical Monuments.

Ryder, Michael L. (1990a) 'Skin and wool textile remains from Hallstatt, Austria', *Oxford Journal of Archaeology* 9(1): 37–49.

—— (1990b) 'Wool remains from Scythian burials in Siberia', *Oxford Journal of Archaeology* 9(3): 313–21.

—— (1991) 'The last word on the golden fleece legend', *Oxford Journal of Archaeology* 10(1): 57–60.

Scullard, H.H. (1965) *From the Gracchi to Nero. A history of Rome 133 BC–AD 68*, London (1st edn 1959, 2nd edn 1963): Methuen.

Smith, R.A. (1909) 'On a late Celtic mirror found at Desborough, Northants, and other mirrors of the period', *Archaeologia* 61: 329–46.

Stead, I.M. (1967) 'A La Tène burial at Welwyn Garden City', *Archaeologia* 101: 1–67.

—— (1979) *The Arras Culture*, York: Yorkshire Philosophical Society.

—— (1981) *The Gauls. Celtic antiquities from France*, Catalogue of the exhibition held in the British Museum, London: British Museum.

—— (1991) 'The Snettisham treasure: excavations in 1990', *Antiquity* 25(248): 447–64.

Strong, D.E. (1966) *Greek and Roman Gold and Silver Plate*, London: Methuen.

—— (1980) *Roman Art*, Norwich: Fletcher & Son (Harmondsworth: Penguin 1976).

Sydenham, E.A. (1952) *The Coinage of the Roman Republic*, London: Spink.

Toynbee, J.M.C. (1964) *Art in Britain under the Romans*, Oxford: Oxford University Press.

—— (1978) *Roman Historical Portraits*, London: Thames & Hudson.

Ward Perkins, J. and Claridge, Amanda (1976) *Pompeii AD 79*, Catalogue of the exhibition held at the Royal Academy of Arts, Piccadilly, London 20 November 1976–27 February 1977, London: Royal Academy of Arts.

Warner, Marina (1985) *Monuments and Maidens. The allegory of the female form*, London: Weidenfeld & Nicolson.

Webster, Leslie and Backhouse, Janet (eds) (1991) *The Making of England. Anglo-Saxon art and culture AD 600–900*, Catalogue of the exhibition held in the British Museum London: British Museum.

Wheeler, R.E.M. and Wheeler, T.V. (1936) *Verulamium, a Belgic and Two Roman Cities*, Oxford: Reports of the Research Committee, Society of Antiquaries of London no. 11.

Wightman, Edith Mary (1985) *Galla Belgica*, London: Batsford.

Wild, John Peter (1970) *Textile Manufacture in the Northern Roman Provinces*, Cambridge: Cambridge University Press.

—— (1988) *Textiles in Archaeology*, Aylesbury: Shire Archaeology Series.

CELTS AND ROMANS
Towards a Romano-Celtic society

—— ·◆· ——

Barry C. Burnham

Rome's expansion in the west brought her into contact with diverse peoples, not least those traditionally grouped together as the 'Celts'. This raises interesting questions about native and Roman interaction and the emergence of hybrid cultures as conquest, assimilation and romanization took place, questions which are appropriate to a volume on the 'Celtic world'. Detailed comments will be confined to southern Britain, with appropriate references where necessary to continental material, principally for the period between the first century BC and the early third century AD; the significant changes wrought in the third and fourth centuries lie beyond the scope of this paper. Key questions include: (i) how did the process of interaction and romanization work? (ii) how far did things actually change under Roman rule? and (iii) how deep did the veneer of romanization percolate?

Caution is necessary at the outset about terminology. Terms like 'Celts' and 'Romans' carry the notion of two identifiable cultural entities, a notion which may hinder rather than help the analysis of change. 'Roman culture' was not itself a 'pure' entity, rather a progressive synthesis of many different strands. Initially these were of Greek, Etruscan and Italian origin, overlaid by contact with other Mediterranean peoples. This amalgam progressively developed as it spread northwards and westwards into Gaul and Britain from the first century BC onwards. The notion of 'Celtic culture' is even more problematical, bound up as it is with historical issues of ethnic identity and the nature of the classical sources, and with the modern debate over 'Who were the Celts?' Views range from outright scepticism about the value of classical sources and the reality of Celtic identity (Hill 1989; Taylor 1991) to the somewhat 'homogenized' portrayal of the Celtic world in recent works (Audouze and Büchsenschütz 1991), with its overtones of the Celts as the 'first Europeans'. This homogeneity may be more apparent than real, serving to mask important variations in the society and economy of north-west Europe on the eve of the conquest, variations which are vital to our understanding of the processes of interaction (Haselgrove 1991).

The material impact of romanization is self-evident in the north-west provinces, stretching from southern Gaul to northern Britain. It is most clearly seen in the emergence of distinctive urban centres, all conforming to a recognizable Graeco-Roman model, the essential foundations of which were laid in the context of Rome's expansion into north Italy during the third and second centuries BC (Ward Perkins 1974). This had witnessed the establishment of various military colonies in recently conquered Celtic lands, among them Piacenza (218 BC) and Bologna (189 BC), all characterized by the later norm of square or near square street grids. Such sites and their developing public buildings and amenities provided the models for urban development elsewhere in the west, where Rome had to take a more active role in promoting city growth as the focus of local self-government (Bedon *et al.* 1988; Duby 1980; Wacher 1974). The resulting cities were planned from the outset with a street grid which conformed to the north Italian norm, providing a unity of plan which was further emphasized by the provision of public buildings and amenities, most notably a forum–basilica complex, bath-houses and markets, theatres and amphitheatres, official guesthouses, and a water supply and sewerage system, together with temples, wealthy private housing, shops and workshops (Figure 8.1). Such features help to explain the family likeness of most cities in the north-west provinces, from Arles and Nîmes in the south, to Augst, Trier and Silchester further north. Such cities were not mass-produced, however, and did not appear overnight, each one being the dynamic end product of essentially local circumstances, as regional variations show (Drinkwater 1985).

Figure 8.1 Reconstruction view of Silchester in the third century from the south-east by Alan Sorrell. The street grid, public buildings and amenities of a romanized administrative centre are clearly apparent. (The original is housed in the Reading Museum and Art Gallery; photo courtesy of English Heritage Photo Library.)

Romanization is also clearly seen in the emergence of the villa, which symbolizes the injection of surplus wealth into romanized country houses, elaborate mosaics, bath-houses and underfloor heating (Percival 1976; Ferdière 1988: 157–200). For Gaul, a good starting point has to be Agache's work in Picardy (1975, 1978), which located a large number of sites with a double courtyard, one containing the principal residence, the other surrounded by subordinate buildings serving various functions (cf. Estrées-sur-Noye and Warfusée-Abencourt – Figure 8.2). This type of plan is not unique to Picardy, however, being equally common in the Rhineland and Aquitaine (Wightman 1975, 1985; King 1990). Most seem to have emerged in the first century AD, generally earlier in the south than the north. Not all villas were of this double courtyard type, nor were they all as regular, as sites like Köln-Mungersdorf and Mayen demonstrate. In Britain, courtyard villas are exceptional in the first and second centuries, the norm being a relatively small and simple cottage or winged corridor house, as at Park Street, Cox Green and Ditchley (Percival 1976: 91–105). Few such sites had elaborate mosaics, bath-houses or underfloor heating at an early date. Exceptions do exist, however, along the south coast, in Essex and in north Kent, reflecting different emphases in the speed with which romanized country housing appeared (Cunliffe 1973; Detsicas 1983; Rodwell 1978).

Figure 8.2 Aerial photo of the extensive courtyard villa complex at Warfusée-Abencourt (Nord) in Picardy. The main residential complex lies to the left of an extended courtyard over 400 m long, along the sides of which are the clear traces of numerous subsidiary buildings. (Photo courtesy of R. Agache.)

Another obvious feature of provincial romanization is the road system, tying town and country together and also linking frontier zones with civilian hinterlands. According to Strabo (*Geography* IV.6.11), the Gallic system was developed from scratch under Agrippa, who was left in charge after Octavian's first visit to the area in 39–38 BC. It involved three major routes fanning out from Lugdunum, one west to the Atlantic, another north-north-west to the Channel, and a third north-north-east to the Rhine (Drinkwater 1983: 124–5). All three clearly provided a co-ordinated military network for rapid communication and troop movement. A similar framework was developed in Britain, focused on the emerging centre at London, with major supply routes leading north, north-west and south-west (Fulford 1989: 180). These roads formed the basis for more localized networks in and around the emerging *civitas* centres.

Such roads encouraged economic growth, a process facilitated by the introduction of Roman coinage as a medium of exchange and taxation and by the growth of the new towns as market centres, clearly distinguished by their possession of *fora* and occasional, subsidiary market buildings (*macella*), by the range of shops and workshops fronting their main streets and by the evidence for increasing specialization. Through such channels, romanized goods and ideas passed into the socio-economic network, which explains the widespread distribution of mass-produced pottery and metal objects down the settlement hierarchy.

Romanization is also self-evident in other material objects, especially in terms of religious interaction and art, the two often inextricably interlinked (Henig 1984). Roman and native gods were widely found side by side, and frequently became hybridized in both epigraphic and artistic terms (Figure 8.3). The artwork itself took on new forms, providing new media and new symbols for the artists to work with. Further indicators of romanization include the progressive adoption of the Latin language (Evans 1987) – so clearly illustrated by the range of epigraphic material from official inscriptions to simple graffiti and by the presence of writing implements at a wide variety of sites – and perhaps also the progressive shift in the composition of the diet reflected in the bone assemblages (King 1984).

Although such material symbols are often regarded as self-evident indicators of romanization within the Celtic provinces, they do not actually 'speak for themselves' about the nature of 'Romano-Celtic' interaction, nor about the processes of continuity and change at work. Instead, the archaeological evidence has to be interpreted, a process which very much depends upon an individual's perspective and the scale of the analysis. One very common interpretation has been to emphasize the symbolic importance of the presence of Mediterranean-style towns and villas and of the adoption of Roman customs in art, religion, language, diet and clothing, as evidence of an underlying ideological unity linking the provincials (especially the élites) of Roman Britain with their counterparts elsewhere, a unity which became more pronounced with time; but one has to be aware that too simple an equation of the material evidence with acculturation to a Roman ideal risks obscuring significant regional trends, whereby the same symbols may have been used in various subtle ways not just to demonstrate acceptance of the new order but, more importantly, to reinforce existing socio-cultural traditions and hierarchies. This emphasizes the importance of studying continuity and change at a regional level, as the basis for a fuller understanding of Romano-Celtic interaction. What follows will be primarily focused on southern Britain.

Figure 8.3 Sculptural relief of Mercury and Rosmerta from Shakespeare's Inn, Gloucester, reflecting the hybridization of Roman and native cults in art. The Roman god is represented with his caduceus, cockerel and a purse, while his native consort has an axe, patera and a wooden bucket. (Photo courtesy of Gloucester Museum.)

One of the commonest approaches to the problem of native and Roman interaction in Britain has been to adopt a somewhat myopic perspective, often against the backcloth of Britain's own colonial and imperial past. This has usually had the effect of (i) treating Roman Britain as a chronological package in relative isolation from the pre-existing native background; (ii) giving undue prominence to the limited historical sources at the expense of the archaeological; (iii) seeing 'change' as a direct consequence of the Roman presence, and equating it with notions of civilization and improvement; and (iv) giving undue attention to the visible superstructure of romanization, the roads, towns, villas and so on, as evidence of acculturation to a Roman ideal (cf. Barrett 1989: 235–6). Thus the conquest in AD 43 heralded significant change (cf. Salway 1981; Frere 1987). Towns emerged out of the civil settlements spawned by military sites, their subsequent elaboration as centres of administration with the appropriate public buildings and amenities being guaranteed by military assistance and government encouragement. Money and taxation facilitated the growth of towns and the appearance of a developed economic infrastructure based around a full market economy, accompanied by intensified economic, industrial and specialized productive capacity and the widespread appearance of shops and workshops and of extensive distributions of goods in town and country. Villas, too, formed part of this socio-economic symbiosis, acting as the centres of large, profitable estates along classical lines involved in specialized production for new markets and for the army and as a focus for change in agriculture and the countryside. Parallel developments also occurred in religion, art, language, culture and dress.

Such an approach necessarily focused excavation and research on the visible Roman superstructure at the expense of the native. More importantly, the emphasis lay on 'change' within the Roman period, facilitated by a number of factors, most of them of Roman origin or external to the province (cf. Salway 1981: 505–16; Frere 1987: 296): (i) the presence of a large army and a retinue of specialists and followers; (ii) the presence of traders, merchants and entrepreneurs; (iii) the establishment of model colonies and other islands of romanization; (iv) the intervention of influential governors, like Agricola, or emperors, like Hadrian; (v) the activities of influential rulers like Cogidubnus and, to a lesser extent, the élite of the newly emerging *civitates*; (vi) the spread of the Latin language and Roman law. Surprisingly little attention was paid in this to the existing native infrastructure, nor the reasons behind the apparent 'backwardness' of the north and west of the province.

This approach to native and Roman interaction has come under scrutiny in the last fifteen years or so, not least from a generation of post-imperial scholars with different world perspectives. This has caused some extreme reactions, especially in north Africa, where a particular brand of 'decolonized' history written by African scholars has emphasised *resistance*, both military and civilian, to the Roman presence (Bénabou 1976); by contrast in the north-west provinces, and especially in Britain, recent work has seen a greater emphasis on the way in which native societies adapted to the proximity of Rome and to eventual assimilation within the empire. Romanization is now seen less as a one-way than as a two-way process (Figure 8.4). The publication of Burnham and Johnson (1979) was an important turning point, followed by Blagg and King (1984), Millett (1990) and Jones (1991c); this is

Figure 8.4 Native resistance or romanization as a two-way process? (Cartoon courtesy of Albert Rusling.)

paralleled by works on broader continental issues like Brandt and Slofstra (1983), Barrett *et al.* (1989) and Blagg and Millett (1991). Various factors lie behind this shift in emphasis.

The first has been the significant increase in the number of new sites being discovered in the countryside, with considerable implications for the size of the provincial population. One of the most influential surveys was that undertaken in Northamptonshire in the 1970s (Royal Commission on Historical Monuments 1980), which recorded some 900 sites or find spots, including just 59 villas and over 600 rural sites. To put this into perspective, Taylor (1975) quantified the rate of discovery in just one area, the Nene valley south-west of Water Newton; here there were 36 sites on the 1931 Ordnance Survey map of Roman Britain, 130 by the 1956 edition, and 434 by 1972 – a twelvefold increase in discoveries over 40 years (Figure 8.5). The density of sites across the county as a whole was one per 3.6 square km; in the Nene valley this rises to one per 1.5 square km. Comparable densities have been noted elsewhere (Millett 1990, table 8.3). The implications for the population are enormous, with past estimates progressively moving upwards from Collingwood's conservative estimate of half a million (1929) to Smith's inflated figure of 5 to 6 million (1977). The modern consensus favours a figure of 3 to 4 million, with Millett (1990: 185) suggesting 3.7 million, certainly more than Domesday levels, but not as high as estimates for the fourteenth century prior to the Black Death.

A second factor has been the realization that something like 90 per cent of the population occupied the diverse range of non-villa settlements now known in the countryside, outside the romanized towns and villas. This point has been emphasized by Hingley (1989: 4) who calculated from the ratio of villa to non-villa settlements in three counties that, even in the south and east, villas may have formed no more than *c*.15 per cent of the total of rural sites. This increasing emphasis

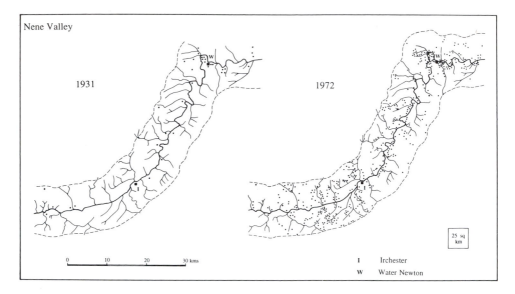

Figure 8.5 Rural settlement in the Nene valley. Comparative distribution maps of the known sites in 1931 and 1972, the dramatic increase being the result of intensive aerial reconnaissance and field survey. (After Taylor 1975.)

on non-villa sites is matched by growing evidence for settlement continuity from the Iron Age into the Romano-British period. High levels of continuity have of course long been known for the north and west of the province, where villas are absent (e.g. Cefn Graeanog and Thorpe Thewles), and likewise even for some areas of the south and east (e.g. Rotherley and Woodcutts on Cranborne Chase); increasingly also in areas with villas, other forms of rural settlement have become better known through excavation, many of them demonstrating either clear evidence of continuity from an iron-age predecessor, or failing that, a layout and design clearly perpetuating iron-age rather than Roman traditions (e.g. Odell and Wakerley). A similar process of continuity can be argued for villas and many larger nucleated and urban sites which emerged out of the existing native infrastructure.

A third factor has been the increasing study of the Roman Empire within a wider chronological framework, with the realization that it is difficult to distinguish between changes resulting directly from conquest and assimilation and those which were merely intensifications of processes already under way. As will become clear later, this has had a marked impact in Roman Britain in the key spheres of agriculture and economy, but in the wider context, it is reflected in the increasing importance now attached to the existence of an already 'romanized' native infrastructure as a foundation upon which successful post-conquest interaction and assimilation could be constructed and upon which it ultimately depended. The clearest statement of this principle is to be found in Groenman-van Waateringe (1980), but it was first elaborated for central and east Gaul by Nash (1978a, 1978b), who argued for a process of significant socio-political change amongst the native communities in direct response to the proximity of Roman Provence and the dramatic increase in the wine trade in and after the later second century BC (Tchernia 1983). Similar changes have been identified by Haselgrove (1982, 1984, 1987) in south-east Britain, involving diplomatic links between known British rulers and the emperor, intensified trade (particularly in prestige items) and the emergence of political centres (*oppida*) at key sites for trade and exchange.

Such changes have traditionally been explained in terms of core–periphery models and prestige goods economies in which native élites were progressively drawn into the Roman orbit by virtue of their dependence on trade for prestige items (Roymans 1983; Haselgrove 1984; Cunliffe 1988). It is clearly not as simple as this, to judge from recent criticisms by Fulford (1985a) and Fitzpatrick (1989), but that does not deny the key point that interaction with the Roman world, directly or indirectly, before the conquest, via diplomacy and trade, provided a vital infrastructure upon which romanization could be built. It is also clear that the key to the process lay in the attitude of the native élite in any given area.

All these factors have opened up new avenues for research into the development of a 'Romano-Celtic' society, not just in Britain, but elsewhere in the north-west provinces. In particular, the wider perspective has had the effect of (i) placing Roman Britain firmly into a wider chronological perspective spanning the Iron-Age to Anglo-Saxon periods; (ii) emphasizing the importance of the archaeological evidence as a primary source for the study of interaction; (iii) seeing change as an intensification of processes already under way within the native infrastructure; (iv) stressing the importance of 'continuity' in many aspects of the substructure (agriculture, economy, rural settlement) and the emergence of the romanized superstructure (towns, villas) out of the existing framework. Romanization is seen to be about the way in which the natives reacted to the Roman presence, not the way in which Rome wrought cultural change.

A new perspective is thus beginning to develop, within which it is possible to identify several strands. First is the existence in south-east Britain of a developed native infrastructure already in contact with and influenced by romanized communities across the Channel. Second is the increasing evidence for a well-developed agricultural and economic substructure supporting the native communities of the south and east, both articulated by a native élite whose habits were already 'romanized' through diplomatic and trading activity. This native infrastructure was the basis for romanization in the south and east; its absence or less well-developed character further north and west made progress less easy, leaving aside the overwhelming military presence in the north, which may have vitiated it altogether.

In considering how Romano-Celtic society emerged after AD 43, it is important to stress that, at the level of agriculture and economy, Rome does not seem to have brought any significant or dramatic changes. As far as farming techniques are concerned, Jones (1981, 1982, 1989) has made it abundantly clear that the Roman impact is very difficult to disentangle from broader trends spanning the later first millennium BC and the early first millennium AD (Figure 8.6). In particular, he could identify no specific innovations in crop production in the half-century or so following the invasion, while the iron-age staple crops continued to predominate with few, if any, significant new introductions. Iron tools certainly became more widely available across the settlement spectrum, but without any major innovations

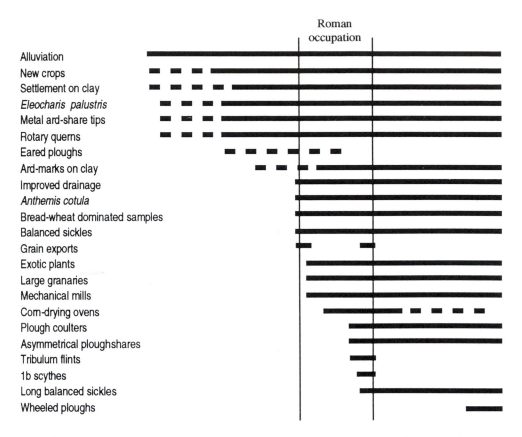

Figure 8.6 Comparative evidence for the date of significant introductions and innovations in British agriculture. Few major changes in agricultural practice can be identified in the period immediately after the Roman conquest. (After Jones 1981.)

in design. Indeed, Jones has argued forcibly for the early Roman period being one of 'stagnation' in agriculture, a term which is perhaps a little too derogatory; presumably the key point is that the agricultural system was sufficiently well-developed in its surplus potential to support the emergence of a romanized society based on towns and villas without any further need for innovation. Some longer term changes have been noted in animal husbandry, including the appearance of larger breeds of cattle, sheep and horse and distinctive changes in the composition of the diet, to which we will return later (King 1984; Grant 1989).

A similar consensus is beginning to emerge regarding the Roman contribution in the economic sphere, though much here depends upon one's position in the debate over the extent to which the economy remained embedded (i.e. socially articulated) or disembedded (i.e. money-using), especially in the Late Iron Age of south-east Britain (Hodder 1979; Greene 1986: 45–66; Fulford 1989). Although it is commonly agreed that the initial conquest would have been disruptive – a large army had to be supplied, crops and assets had been destroyed and people killed, existing social networks and administrative systems had been dislocated, especially after the Boudican revolt – there is a growing consensus that many aspects of the iron-age embedded economy could have been retained after AD 43 even within an obviously less embedded Roman system. Reciprocal exchange, for instance, is unlikely to have changed overnight; and once the surviving élite became fully responsible for local self-government and the collection of taxes, this would have strengthened rather than diminished their stranglehold on the redistribution ties within society. At this level, it can perhaps be argued that Rome merely added an extra tier of tribute and obligation onto the old redistributive hierarchy.

That said, iron-age agriculture and embedded economic systems could hardly have continued totally unchanged, largely because so many new opportunities were available to those with an eye to profit. Thus even in the first century, and progressively in the second, there were several areas of potential romanization which must have helped to stimulate change and to disembed the native economies of the south and east. These included: (i) the activities of the state and the army in encouraging and expanding exchange outside the social sphere; (ii) the introduction of imperial currency and its key roles in the collection of taxes and in the development of market exchange; (iii) the appearance of foreign traders and entrepreneurs with money to invest in the development of the extractive and productive industries; (iv) the establishment of model centres like the *colonia* at Colchester and the development of the trading port and centre at London; (v) the promotion and development of a series of administrative urban centres which created demand and opened up new markets. Such agents of change have often been seen as fundamental to the process whereby Britain was absorbed into the Roman world, but there is an emerging consensus that their impact must be qualified in the face of greater provincial conservatism arising from the continued power and influence of the native élite upon whom Rome relied so heavily (Millett 1990).

Indeed it is becoming clear that the integration of local communities into the Roman world order and the process of romanization was heavily dependent upon the cultural attitude and sympathy of the native élites, both those who survived the conquest and those who emerged in its wake. Such élites were vital to the process of Roman management, since the imperial system was dependent upon them taking up the reins of local government, focused henceforth on new administrative centres within individual *civitates*. These élites in the Celtic west had a tradition of competition for status within society, coupled with conspicuous consumption and display, which is well attested by the classical sources. It is also emphasized by the way in which the leaders maintained control over access to prestige goods arriving from the Continent, by the coins they minted and by the prestige items they commissioned, many with deliberate martial overtones. This competitive instinct was harnessed by Rome and effectively redirected at the development of the administrative centres, by providing the élite with an alternative stage upon which to act out their status-building activities and with a new medium of architectural display for reinforcing their traditional position in the social hierarchy (Drinkwater 1983: 190; King 1990: 64–6; Millett 1991); an additional incentive included the possibility of achieving citizenship. *De facto* and *de jure*, they became the new curial class and, as Jones (1991b: 119) has emphasized, rapidly became integrated into the Roman system, acting as the link between the majority of the population and the empire, in such a way as to maintain the traditions of an older social order whilst also collaborating in and focusing the creation of the new. Such competition and conspicuous displays of status were not just confined to public buildings and amenities in the cities, however; they also found an outlet in the adoption of the villa in the countryside, and in time they percolated down throughout society in other material ways. All this means that towns and villas, two key features in the process of romanization, grew out of the competitive instincts of the existing native élites and their desire to conform, rather than being symbols of radical change in themselves.

The traditional view of most urban development in Britain has usually emphasized its military origins (Webster 1966), coupled with some form of deliberate official encouragement by central government; this relied very largely on Tacitus (*Agricola* 21), underpinned by Rivet's (1977) assertion that virtually all *civitas* capitals (let alone the *coloniae*) could be shown to have had a military presence at or very near to their sites. Official designation is thus implied as the key to the subsequent development of the cities, involving a mixture of official help and encouragement and local participation and patronage. Cirencester has long served as a model for this process, with at least one phase of military activity acting as an economic magnet for a civilian *vicus* which was sufficiently well developed to survive the army's departure and so take on the new administrative role assigned by central government (Wacher 1974: 30–2).

Such explanations have a powerful appeal for those areas which were uncentralized in the later Iron Age, hence perhaps their applicability in the cases of Wroxeter and Exeter; but where there was a well-developed infrastructure on the eve of the conquest, fort location must be viewed in the context of pre-existing settlement networks and centres of power (Cunliffe 1976; Millett 1984). Thus in the south-east alone, significant levels of continuity can be identified at sites like Canterbury, Verulamium, Silchester, Winchester and Leicester, not forgetting the *colonia* at Colchester, all lying on or near an existing iron-age predecessor; incidentally, the same is true of many small towns like Braughing and Baldock (Burnham 1986). Where a military presence is known (with the exception of Colchester), it is both short-lived and peripheral to the main focus, suggesting at best a secondary role in a wider process. Even at sites like Cirencester, the sequence is likely to be more complex, the emphasis resting on the relocation of an existing focus from an inconvenient site at Bagendon to one more suited to the needs of the developing road network.

This continuity of existing native centres within their respective tribal areas, and their emergence as romanized cities, clearly emphasizes the way Rome sought to work through and reinforce the status quo, of those already in power. It is for this reason that the new cities became the focus for patronage, because they provided the vehicle for continued competition and display within the new political order. This process could even begin before official designation as a *civitas* centre, as the evidence of early patronage and romanization at the native site of Silchester clearly demonstrates, presumably within the client kingdom of Cogidubnus; indeed, the baths, the timber phase of the amphitheatre and the earliest of the massive timber buildings on the site of the later forum all originated in the Neronian period, the baths even incorporating tiles of Nero, suggestive of an imperial interest (Boon 1974; Fulford 1985b).

The clearest evidence for competition and patronage across the empire is to be found in epigraphic material, though even this seems to betray marked variations between the more romanized areas and the more peripheral provinces like northern Gaul, the Germanies and Britain (Blagg 1990). There is clear evidence also in the provision of street grids, public buildings and amenities, and wealthy private housing – the distinctive features of the developed Mediterranean town. It is vital to stress, however, that such distinctive features did not emerge overnight; close analysis of the archaeological evidence reveals significant variations in the speed with which the individual building complexes were provided (Todd 1989a; Wacher 1989). This is much as one would expect, given the lengthy time-span over which the *civitates* were created, and, more importantly, the varying levels of public-spiritedness or private enterprise which the local élites exhibited in their development.

It now seems clear that at most sites during the first and early second centuries, the only stone buildings were public structures, though not all sites had even these; instead the majority of buildings were timber-framed structures, most of them of strip-building type, associated with commercial or industrial activities (Perring 1987); these clearly reflect the early economic growth of the cities within their respective *civitates*, as illustrated by the shops in Insula XIV at Verulamium and elsewhere at Chichester, Colchester and London. Even the most important of the public buildings, the forum-basilica, provides a surprising date range for the known stone structures (Table 8.1). On the surface this is an interesting reflection of the speed at which money was committed to public buildings, but the picture is somewhat complicated by the evidence for two phases of timber building (both apparently fora) pre-dating the Silchester complex (Fulford 1985b), and suggestive traces of a similar wooden phase at Exeter in the 80s (Bidwell 1979: 73). Such material advises caution elsewhere for the general level of first-century developments, even though the picture for other public buildings generally conforms to the prolonged sequence identified for fora (Table 8.1). An even starker picture is provided by the evidence for private housing which is such a prominent feature in the developed urban plans. In this context, Walthew (1975) has argued that, generally speaking, rich town houses may not have appeared in any great numbers until the second century, somewhat later than their villa counterparts, suggesting perhaps that the élite were slow to move into the town.

Despite this generally slow and piecemeal development of romanized urban centres, most had been provided with a basic range of public buildings and related facilities by the end of the second century (Wacher 1989). Some measure of official encouragement must have been available under the Flavian governors, and again in the wake of Hadrian's visit, which would help to explain the surge of second-century activity. In general terms, Britain conforms with trends identified elsewhere in the Roman world; but like northern Gaul and Germany, there is increasing evidence to suggest a more restricted level of provision in terms of public buildings, statuary and inscriptions recording individual civic benefactions, by comparison with

Table 8.1 Dates of major public buildings

Building type	Site	Date (AD)
Forum-basilica	London proto-forum	60–90
	main complex	90–110
	Verulamium	79–81
	Silchester	second century
	Wroxeter	Hadrianic
	Leicester	Hadrianic
	Caistor by Norwich	Antonine
Market places	Verulamium	Flavian
	Cirencester	Hadrianic
	Leicester	late second/early third century
Bath houses	Silchester	Neronian
	Canterbury	late first century
	Leicester	mid-second century
Theatres/amphitheatres	Canterbury	80–90
	Cirencester	late first century
	Verulamium	mid-second century
(in timber)	Silchester	50s–60s

the more romanized provinces of central and southern Gaul and the Mediterranean littoral (Blagg 1990). This has often been explained as the result of a lack of wealth or of remoteness, but it is more probably related to a reduced level of competitive munificence amongst the native élites. In this context, Millett (1990: 81–2) has argued that power within the British *civitates* remained in the hands of a limited oligarchy with far fewer outsiders, who had much less need to compete with each other because power was already theirs; this may have led to collective rather than individual displays of wealth in the central cities (cf. Wroxeter) and, thereby, to an adequate rather than an excessive level of provision in terms of buildings and amenities. More than likely, the real competition lay between *civitates*, not within them, except in those cities with a clearly cosmopolitan element outside the system, such as London or the colonies, or a more sharply defined social hierarchy, such as early Silchester.

The growth of *civitas* centres in the first and second centuries was very distinctive in morphological terms, but also had a significant functional impact, as has already been indicated, in opening up new markets, witness the appearance of fora, *macella*, and large numbers of shops and workshops. Despite such evidence for economic expansion, it need not necessarily have occurred entirely within the sphere of free market forces; rather, early *civitas* organization and taxation system may have been such that it reinforced the power of the native élites (who controlled taxation), enabling them to exercise considerable control over where and how the economy developed.

This would help to explain the apparent primate importance of the *civitas* centres during the later first and second centuries (Jones 1991a: 59–60), and the relatively slow development at all but a few 'small towns' (Burnham and Wacher 1990: 10–14).

In the countryside, the villa has traditionally been seen as a symbol of change, usually involving a more capitalistic approach to agriculture and a close economic symbiosis with the cities (Applebaum 1972). For reasons already outlined, it now seems less easy to link villas directly with innovation in agriculture and as such they are best seen not so much as evidence of successful and profitable exploitation of large estates, but rather as symbols of surplus wealth and conspicuous display. More important, perhaps, the increased emphasis on continuity in the landscape and among rural settlements spanning the later Iron-Age to Romano-British periods has influenced modern opinion on early villa development, with a growing acceptance that many villas must have emerged out of, rather than being imposed upon, the existing native infrastructure. This has long been known or suspected for sites like Park Street and Lockleys, but has recently been further reinforced by the evidence from Rivenhall (Rodwell and Rodwell 1986) and Gorhambury, where the villa was clearly constructed on a site previously occupied by a native settlement in close proximity to the dykes associated with the oppidum of Verulamium (Neal *et al.* 1990); a similar link between an existing centre of power and an early villa has also been noted at The Ditches, part of the oppidum complex at Bagendon (Trow 1988). Although the question of ownership is hard to establish with any certainty, such examples serve to reinforce the notion that most belonged to natives, thereby helping to explain the rash of villas which emerged in the vicinity of such towns as Verulamium at a time when the city itself was being progressively elaborated with public buildings and amenities (Neal 1978). This would be the simplest interpretation as well of the early and large villas which developed along the south coast at sites like Fishbourne, Angmering and Southwick, in what had probably been the client kingdom of Cogidubnus, though the direct association of Fishbourne with Cogidubnus now seems far less secure than was once thought (Cunliffe 1973). Similar concentrations are known in Kent (Detsicas 1983) and Essex (Rodwell 1978), likewise in areas with a well-developed native infrastructure on the eve of the conquest. This would reinforce the argument that the élite adopted the villa as a convenient vehicle for expressing their attachment to the new romanized order (much as they were doing in the towns), while still retaining their power within the existing socio-economic and agricultural landscape (Blagg 1991).

Moreover Smith's (1978, 1984) work on villas has consistently identified distinctive types of villa which do not conform easily with the traditional classical norm of individual ownership. The most important from the point of view of early villa development and the emergence of a Romano-Celtic society, is his recognition of so-called 'unit system villas' involving two houses set at an angle, two or more houses focused around a courtyard with no obvious, axially placed entrance, and elongated villas incorporating groups of rooms seemingly forming separate units. Smith has argued that such villas reflect some form of multiple land ownership enshrined within the plan, even though it can sometimes be skilfully hidden beneath the classical veneer. Although there are problems with this interpretation, there seems to be little doubt that the explanation lies firmly in the native social order and infrastructure, further emphasizing the power this had over the ultimate direction and character of romanization.

Towns and villas clearly represent the visibly romanized superstructure of the new province, set alongside the obviously imposed aspects represented by the colonies and the administrative capital and trading centre at London. Quite how the two elements, the conservative and the progressive, articulated remains unclear, but one might expect that if the native élite did retain a stranglehold over existing socio-economic and redistributive networks, they would also have sought to integrate, neutralize or marginalize the potentially disruptive influence of the 'external' islands, whilst at the same time seeking to demonstrate their participation in the new world order which these very same islands represented. Indeed, during the early stages of the romanizing process and the emergence of a distinctive new Romano-Celtic society, the élite in the towns and in their villas (aided and abetted by traders, entrepreneurs and the army) must have set the standards for others to follow, commencing a process whereby romanization gradually percolated to varying degrees down the settlement hierarchy and the social order.

This process is clearly discernible in a variety of ways in the archaeological record of the south and east, reflecting a gradient from highly romanized to less or non-romanized, although the full details need considerable clarification. Perhaps the clearest such gradient is to be found in the evidence for diet (King 1984). At the top of the scale come the military sites and highly romanized cities which have a high percentage of pig and cattle bones by comparison with sheep (up to 90 per cent on some sites), followed lower down the scale by the major *civitas* centres and the villas (Figure 8.7); below this the balance progressively shifts in favour of sheep down the non-villa spectrum, though the gap narrowed in the third and fourth centuries. This seems to be clear evidence for a shift towards a romanized diet, yet it had already been happening in the later Iron Age as part of the 'pre-romanization' of the progressive élite; now it was being extended further down the scale as romanization bit deeper. The same is arguably true of romanized artefacts, which progressively became available within society. Fulford (1982) has certainly suggested that, type for type, the most extensive range of finds (especially in terms of luxury items) is concentrated in the cities and towns, closely followed by the villas, whilst further down the scale the range is less extensive and the balance of functional to luxury items more pronounced. This balance is typical of the sort of gradient which might be expected, though there are obviously chronological trends which need detailed elaboration. Comparable gradients seem to be recognizable for sculptural and artistic features, not least for the different categories of 'small town' considered by Millett (1977); this impression can be extended to other sites in the settlement hierarchy (especially the rural sanctuaries and temple sites), where the number of pieces with a clearly identifiable, romanized symbolism is highly suggestive of the desire to appear romanized well down the order. The same may well be true of the adoption of the Latin language (Mann 1971; Evans 1987). Romanization may also be measured in other ways, including such things as the shift from timber to stone and from circular to rectangular structures, the adoption of better building technologies, the use of more effective storage systems and wells.

The clear suggestion in all this is that the native élite, together with incomers, set

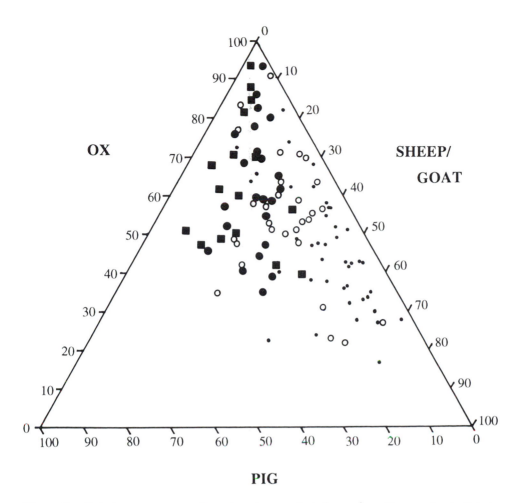

Figure 8.7 Relative percentages of ox, sheep/goat and pig bones from Roman sites in Britain, ranging from military sites (■), through towns (●), villas (○), to rural settlements (•). The more 'romanized', the higher the percentage of ox to sheep/goat. (After King 1984.)

the pace, competing with each other to establish their position in the new system, but at the same time providing models for others to follow. The relative degree of romanization which resulted clearly depended on their level of commitment, hence the regional variations in the south and east. This process had begun before the conquest, in the later Iron Age, and continued throughout the first and second centuries, the only real difference being that it was now far easier to participate lower down the social order and to acquire, albeit in a limited way, access to romanized goods and practices. What happened in the third and fourth centuries to change this picture lies beyond the scope of this chapter.

REFERENCES

Agache, R. (1975) 'La campagne à l'époque romaine dans les grandes plaines du Nord de France d'après les photographies aériennes', *Aufstieg und Niedergang der Römischen Welt* 2(4): 658–713.

—— (1978) *La Somme pré-romaine et romaine*, Amiens.

Applebaum, S. (1972) 'Roman Britain', in H.P.R. Finberg (ed.) *The Agrarian History of England and Wales* I, ii.

Audouze, F. and Büchsenschütz, O. (1991) *Towns, Villages and Countryside of Celtic Europe*, London.

Barrett, J.C. (1989) 'Afterword: render unto Caesar', in J.C. Barrett *et al.* (eds) *Barbarians and Romans*, 235–41.

Barrett, J.C., Fitzpatrick, A.P. and Macinnes, L. (eds) (1989) *Barbarians and Romans in North-West Europe*, Oxford: British Archaeological Reports S471.

Bedon, R., Chevallier, R. and Pinon, P. (1988) *Architecture et urbanisme en Gaule romaine*, vol.2 *L'Urbanisme*, Paris.

Bénabou, M. (1976) *La Résistance africaine à la romanisation.*

Bidwell, P. (1979) *The Legionary Bath-House and Basilica and Forum at Exeter*, Exeter: Exeter Archaeological Reports 1.

Blagg, T.F.C. (1990) 'Architectural munificence in Britain: the evidence of inscriptions', *Britannia* 21: 13–32.

—— (1991) 'First-century Roman houses in Gaul and Britain', in T.F.C. Blagg and M. Millett (eds) *The Early Roman Empire*, 194–209.

Blagg, T.F.C. and King, A.C. (eds) (1984) *Military and Civilian in Roman Britain: cultural relationships in a frontier province*, Oxford: British Archaeological Reports 136.

Blagg, T.F.C. and Millett, M. (eds) (1991) *The Early Roman Empire in the West*, Oxford.

Boon, G.C. (1974) *Silchester, the Roman Town of Calleva*, Newton Abbot.

Brandt, R. and Slofstra, J. (eds) (1983) *Roman and Native in the Low Countries*, Oxford: British Archaeological Reports S184.

Burnham, B.C. (1986) 'The origin of Romano-British small towns', *Oxford Journal of Archaeology* 5: 185–203.

Burnham, B.C. and Johnson, H.B. (eds) (1979) *Invasion and Response: the case of Roman Britain*, Oxford: British Archaeological Reports 73.

Burnham, B.C. and Wacher, J. (1990) *The 'Small Towns' of Roman Britain*, London.

Collingwood, R.G. (1929) 'Town and country in Roman Britain', *Antiquity* 3: 261–76.

Cunliffe, B. (1973) *The Regni*, London.

—— (1976) 'The origins of urbanisation in Britain', in B.W. Cunliffe and T. Rowley (eds) *Oppida: the beginnings of urbanisation in barbarian Europe*, Oxford: British Archaeological Reports S11, 135–62.

—— (1988) *Greeks, Romans and Barbarians: spheres of interaction*, London.

Detsicas, A. (1983) *The Cantiaci*, Gloucester.

Drinkwater, J. (1983) *Roman Gaul*, London.

—— (1985) 'Urbanization in the three Gauls: some observations', in F. Grew and B. Hobley (eds) *Roman Urban Topography in Britain and the Western Empire*, London: CBA Research Report 59, 49–55.

Duby, G. (ed.) (1980) *Histoire de la France urbaine 1: La Ville antique*, Seville.

Evans, J. (1987) 'Graffiti and the evidence of literacy and pottery use in Roman Britain', *Archaeological Journal* 144: 191–204.

Ferdière, A. (1988) *Les Campagnes en Gaule romaine, 1: Les hommes et l'environment en Gaule rurale*, Paris.

Fitzpatrick, A.P. (1989) 'The uses of Roman imperialism by the Celtic barbarians in the later republic', in J.C. Barrett *et al. Barbarians and Romans*, 27–54.

Frere, S.S. (1987) *Britannia* (3rd edn), London.

Fulford, M. (1982) 'Town and country in Roman Britain – a parasitical relationship?' in D. Miles (ed.) *Romano-British Countryside*, 403–19.

—— (1985a) 'Roman material in barbarian society', in T.C. Champion and J.V.S. Megaw (eds) *Settlement and Society*, 91–108.

—— (1985b) 'Excavations on the sites of the amphitheatre and forum-basilica at Silchester, Hampshire: an interim report', *Antiquaries Journal* 65: 39–81.

—— (1989) 'The economy of Roman Britain', in M. Todd (ed.) *Research on Roman Britain*, 175–201.

Grant, A. (1989) 'Animals in Roman Britain', in M. Todd (ed.) *Research on Roman Britain*, 135–46.

Greene, K. (1986) *The Archaeology of the Roman Economy*, London.

Groenman-Van Waateringe, W. (1980) 'Urbanisation and the north-west frontier of the Roman Empire', in W.S. Hanson and L.J.F. Keppie (eds) *Roman Frontier Studies 1979*, Oxford: British Archaeological Reports S71, 1037–44.

Haselgrove, C.C. (1982) 'Wealth, prestige and power: the dynamics of political centralisation in south-east England', in A.C. Renfrew and S. Shennan (eds) *Ranking, Resource and Exchange*, 79–88.

—— (1984) 'Romanisation before the conquest: Gaulish precedents and British consequences', in T.F.C. Blagg and A.C. King (eds) *Military and Civilian*, 5–63.

—— (1987) 'Culture process on the periphery: Belgic Gaul and Rome during the late Republic and early Empire', in M. Rowlands *et al.* (eds) *Centre and Periphery in the Ancient World*.

—— (1991) 'The romanisation of Belgic Gaul: some archaeological perspectives', in T.F.C. Blagg and M. Millett, *Early Roman Empire*, 45–71.

Henig, M. (1984) *Religion in Roman Britain*, London.

Hill, J.D. (1989) 'Re-thinking the Iron Age', *Scottish Archaeological Review* 6: 16–24.

Hingley, R. (1989) *Rural Settlement in Roman Britain*, London.

Hodder, I. (1979) 'Pre-Roman and Romano-British tribal economies', in B.C. Burnham and H.B. Johnson, *Invasion and Response*,189–96.

Jones, M. (1981) 'The development of crop husbandry', in G.W. Dimbleby and M. Jones (eds) *The Environment of Man: Iron Age to Anglo-Saxon*, Oxford: British Archaeological Reports 87, 95–127.

—— (1982) 'Crop production in Roman Britain', in D. Miles (ed.) *Romano-British Countryside*, 97–107.

—— (1989) 'Agriculture in Roman Britain: the dynamics of change', in M. Todd (ed.) *Research on Roman Britain*, 127–34.

Jones, R.F.J. (1991a) 'The urbanisation of Roman Britain', in R.F.J. Jones (ed.) *Roman Britain*, 53–65.

—— (1991b) 'Cultural change in Roman Britain', in R.F.J. Jones (ed.) *Roman Britain*, 115–20.

—— (ed.) (1991c) *Roman Britain: Recent Trends*, Sheffield.

King, A. (1984) 'Animal bones and the dietary identity of military and civilian groups in Roman Britain, Gaul and Germany', in T.F.C. Blagg and A.C. King (eds) *Military and Civilian*, 187–217.

—— (1990) *Roman Gaul and Germany*, London.

Mann, J.C. (1971) 'Spoken Latin in Britain as evidenced in inscriptions', *Britannia* 2: 218–24.

Miles, D. (ed.) (1982) *The Romano-British Countryside: studies in rural settlement and economy*, Oxford: British Archaeological Reports 103.

Millett, M. (1977) 'Art in the "small towns": "Celtic" or "Classical"', in J. Munby and M. Henig (eds) *Roman Life and Art*, Oxford: British Archaeological Reports 41, 283–95.

—— (1984) 'Forts and the origins of towns: cause or effect?', in T.F.C. Blagg and A.C. King (eds) *Military and Civilian*, 65–74.

—— (1990) *The Romanization of Britain*, Cambridge.

—— (1991) 'Romanization: historical issues and archaeological interpretation', in T.F.C. Blagg and M. Millett (eds) *Early Roman Empire*, 35–41.

Nash, D. (1978a) *Settlement and Coinage in Central Gaul c.200-50 BC*, Oxford.

—— (1978b) 'Territory and state formation in central Gaul', in D. Green, C.C. Haselgrove and M. Spriggs (eds) *Social Organisation and Settlement*, Oxford: British Archaeological Reports S47, 455–76.

Neal, D. (1978) 'The growth and decline of villas in the Verulamium area', in M. Todd (ed.), *Romano-British Villa*, 33–58.

Neal, D., Wardle, A. and Hunn, J. (1990) *Excavation of the Iron Age, Roman and Medieval Settlement at Gorhambury, St Albans*, London.

Percival, J. (1976) *The Roman Villa*, London.

Perring, D. (1987) 'Domestic buildings in Romano-British towns', in J. Schofield and R. Leech (eds) *Urban Archaeology in Britain*, London: CBA Research Report 61, 147–55.

Rivet, A.L.F. (1977) 'The origins of cities in Roman Britain', in P.M. Duval and E. Frezouls (eds) *Thème de recherches sur les villes antiques d'occident*, Colloques Internationaux du CNRS 542, 161–72.

Rodwell, W.J. (1978) 'Rivenhall and the emergence of first-century villas in northern Essex', in M. Todd (ed.), *Romano-British Villa*, 11–32.

Rodwell, W.J. and Rodwell, K.A. (1986) *Rivenhall: investigation of a villa, church and village, 1950–1977*, London: CBA Research Report 55.

Royal Commission on Historical Monuments (1980) *Northamptonshire: an archaeological atlas*.

Roymans, N. (1983) 'The north Belgic tribes in the first century BC: a historical-anthropological perspective', in R. Brandt and J. Slofstra (eds) *Roman and Native*, 43–70.

Salway, P. (1981) *Roman Britain*, Oxford.

Smith, C. (1977) 'The valleys of the Tame and the middle Trent – their populations and ecology', in J.R. Collis (ed.) *The Iron Age: a review*, Sheffield, 51–61.

Smith, J.T. (1978) 'Villas as a key to social structure', in M. Todd (ed.), *Romano-British Villa*, 149–73.

—— (1984) 'Villa plans and social structure in Britain and Gaul', *Caesarodunum* 17: 321–36.

Taylor, C.C. (1975) 'Roman settlements in the Nene valley: the impact of recent archaeology', in P.J. Fowler (ed.) *Recent Work in Rural Archaeology*, 107–20.

Taylor, T.F. (1991) 'Celtic art', *Scottish Archaeological Review* 8: 129–32.

Tchernia, A. (1983) 'Italian wine in Gaul at the end of the Republic', in P.D.A. Garnsey, K. Hopkins and C.R. Whittaker (eds) *Trade in the Ancient Economy*, 87–104.

Todd, M. (ed.) (1978) *Studies in the Romano-British Villa*, Leicester.

—— (1989a) 'The early cities', in M. Todd (ed.) *Research on Roman Britain*, 75–89.

—— (ed.) (1989b) *Research on Roman Britain 1960–89*, London: Britannia Monograph 11.

Trow, S.D. (1988) 'Excavations at Ditches hillfort, North Cerney, Gloucestershire, 1982–83', *Transactions of the Bristol and Gloucestershire Archaeological Society* 106: 19–85.

Wacher, J.S. (1974) *The Towns of Roman Britain*, London.

—— (1989) 'Cities from the second to fourth centuries', in M. Todd (ed.) *Research on Roman Britain*, 91–6.

Ward Perkins, J.B. (1974) *Cities of Ancient Greece and Rome*, London.

Walthew, C.W. (1975) 'The town house and villa house in Roman Britain', *Britannia* 6: 189–205.

Webster, G. (1966) 'Fort and town in early Roman Britain', in J.S. Wacher (ed.) *The Civitas Capitals of Roman Britain*, Leicester, 31–45.

Wightman, E.M. (1975) 'Rural settlement in Roman Gaul', *Aufstieg und Niedergang der Römischen Welt* 2(4): 584–647.

—— (1985) *Gallia Belgica*, London.

PART IV

SETTLEMENT AND ENVIRONMENT

PEOPLE AND NATURE IN THE CELTIC WORLD

—— •◆• ——

Martin Bell

The prehistoric environment is often perceived as natural and wild. By later prehistory, however, few environments were passive backcloths to human activity; most had been, or were being, fundamentally changed by people. Here we are concerned with the environments of the first millennia BC and AD over much of Europe, extending from the British Isles to the Black Sea and from southern Germany to the Mediterranean. Most of the evidence reviewed is from the western half of this area, in parts of which humanly created 'cultural landscapes' had come about thousands of years before with the activities of the first farmers. In other instances major changes resulted from deliberate actions during the period in question.

Past environments can be reconstructed using many sources of evidence. Lakes, peat bogs, valleys and occupation deposits on archaeological sites provide sequences of sediment containing biological evidence, such as pollen, seeds, wood, snails, insects and animal bones, which document landscape change during the period whilst the deposits were accumulating. For further discussion of sources of evidence see Evans (1978) and Bell and Walker (1992).

The geographical area in question exhibits remarkable diversity in terms of both its natural and cultural landscapes. There is not something inherently identifiable as a distinctive 'Celtic environment'. The area is defined, not by environmental criteria, but in terms of that geographical area which classical writers described as Celtic (Chapter 1); the distribution of Celtic place-names and linguistic elements; and various aspects of material culture which are regarded as Celtic. Each of these criteria defines an entity at differing points in time. Where we place the geographical boundaries varies according to the criteria we adopt and the date in question. This chapter takes rather a wide geographical view and includes evidence from the Netherlands and some reference to work in Denmark.

Geographically loosely defined as the Celtic world may be, it none the less represents a significant entity for the investigation of particular issues concerning people–environment relationships. There are, for instance, the environmental consequences of the relationship between the politically and economically powerful so-called 'core' areas of classical societies, Greece, Etruria and Rome to the south, and the 'periphery' of the Celtic world to the north. It is a period of dramatic social and political change, the environmental consequences of which are examined. These changes relate first to the geographical expansion of the Celtic world in the first millennium BC, then to the northward expansion of the Roman Empire over most of the area and then in the fifth century the empire's collapse, the southward migrations of Germanic people and the resurgence in the wreckage of the Roman Empire of pre-Roman Celtic traditions which were strongest in the peripheral areas of Ireland, Wales and Brittany. These are issues which have traditionally been examined through historical sources, art history, place-names, material culture, etc. Environmental archaeology also has a distinctive contribution to make in evaluating the degree of continuity and change over this period. Its contribution is sometimes independent of the vicissitudes in the lives of individual settlements which dominate many aspects of the archaeological record. It may tell us whether there was continuity of land-use in the wider surrounding environment.

CLIMATIC CHANGE

The extent of human environmental impact by this date makes it difficult to disentangle the role of natural factors such as climate. Even so, the first half of the first millennium BC experienced one of the most widely accepted climatic changes of the Postglacial, with evidence for higher precipitation and lower temperatures during the climatic episode known as the Sub-Atlantic. This can be seen as the culmination of a long-term climatic deterioration which began around 3000 BC. In the Greenland ice caps changing ratios of the oxygen isotopes ^{16}O and ^{18}O represent a palaeo-climatic record which shows that the deterioration was progressively more marked between 1000 and 500 BC (Dansgaard *et al.* 1982). A pronounced change around 500 BC is also indicated by the oxygen isotope content of lake carbonates in Götland, southern Sweden, where mean summer temperatures may have been as much as 3.7°C lower (Mörner 1980). Alpine glaciers re-established themselves and advanced between 900 and 300 BC (Grove 1988). The most widespread evidence of climatic change comes from peat bogs. The preceding Sub-Boreal climatic phase was relatively dry, with slow peat growth and humification. Many bogs then show a renewed and rapid peat growth recurrence horizon, known as the *Grenzhorizont*. Radiocarbon dates show the onset of climatic deterioration, particularly in the more maritime western areas, from about 1250 BC, with most of the dates from the British Isles clustering between the eighth and fifth centuries BC (Turner 1981). Boulton Fell Moss in Cumbria became much wetter in the ninth century BC and a detailed study by Barber (1981) gives good reason to infer that changes in the growth of this bog provide a faithful record of climatic change. Danish bogs indicate wetter conditions from around 500 BC (Aaby 1976). In the Netherlands the Bourtanger Bog grew rapidly as a result of increased precipitation then burst catastrophically around 530 BC, destroying a recently built trackway (Casparie 1986).

Glacier advances indicate that the temperature reduction may have been in the order of 1–2°C (Grove 1988). That change, and indeed the glacier movements themselves, is comparable to that which occurred in the Little Ice Age between AD 1550 and 1850, which was a partial cause of the abandonment of farms in uplands. The onset of the Sub-Atlantic may have had similar effects, especially in high rainfall areas of the west and in the north where the growing season was short. This may be an important factor in the late bronze age abandonment of moorland, particularly Dartmoor and the Scottish moors.

Subsequent climatic changes during the period in question are not as clearly marked or widespread. Slow peat growth and a lack of recurrence horizons indicates relatively dry conditions from c.400 BC to AD 450. Around AD 550 several upland blanket mires have recently been identified as showing evidence of wetter conditions (Blackford and Chambers 1991). The Greenland ice core evidence shows that around c.AD 700 there was a warmer episode with temperatures 1–2°C higher than present (Dansgaard *et al.* 1975). This was the Little Climatic Optimum, a period of reduced sea ice in the north Atlantic and the possibly related Viking expansion which impacted on the Celtic world.

VEGETATION

Before the advent of farming, virtually all the area with which we are concerned had a forest cover. The character of this natural 'wildwood' (Rackham 1980) can be re-constructed from the sequence of pollen in peat bogs and lakes. Huntley (1990) has collated the results of pollen analyses across Europe, to prepare maps of its vegetation at thousand-year intervals over the last 13,000 years. Figure 9.1 shows the vegetation map at around the birth of Christ. The west (the British Isles, the Netherlands, France and Spain) had vegetation in which the predominant plants were hazel, oak, and alder. The alpine area and southern France were characterized by oak, beech and chenopods. Southern Germany and the Balkans had beech, spruce and hornbeam woods. Parts of the Italian and Yugoslav coasts had oak, pine, heath and chenopods. This map provides a useful picture of broad-scale vegetation patterns; what it does not bring out is the extent to which individual pollen studies demonstrate that the vegetation had, by this time, been changed by human activity.

THE CULTURAL LANDSCAPE

Mainland Europe

Authors offer very different perceptions of the extent to which woodland survived in mainland Europe into the Iron Age. Piggott (1975) speaks of the great uncleared 'Celtic jungle', a view based on classical authors who noted its contrast with the more open landscapes of the Mediterranean. Palaeoenvironmental evidence paints a different picture. By the time of the Roman conquest many areas had been cleared and in the more densely settled areas the forest had been broken into small woods and copses in a largely agricultural landscape (Audouze and Büchsenschütz 1991). Parts of Brittany were deforested well before the Iron Age but deforestation increased greatly during the period and settlements are set within an agricultural landscape containing scattered trees and wooded areas (Marguerie 1990). In the Paris

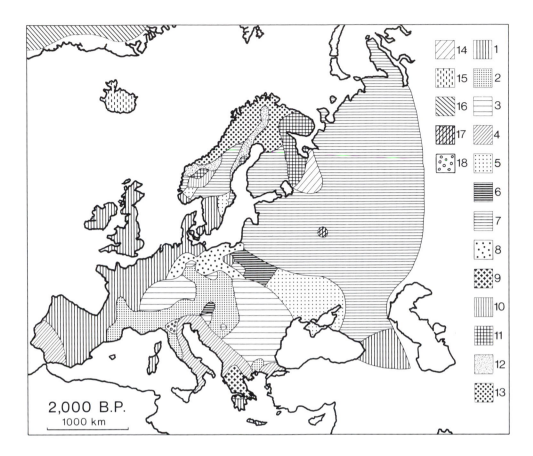

Figure 9.1 The predominant vegetation types in Europe 2,000 years ago. (After Huntley 1990. Reprinted by permission of John Wiley & Sons, Ltd.).

KEY

(1)hazel-oak-alder; (2)oak-beech-chenopods; (3)beech-spruce-hornbeam; (4)oak-pine-beech; (5) hazel-oak-elm; (6) pine-chenopods; (7) spruce-pine-birch-alder; (8)oak-hazel-grasses; (9) oak-chenopods-*Ostrya*; (10) pine-birch-chenopods-oak; (11) spruce-pine-birch; (12) pine-birch-alder; (13) birch-pine-alder; (14) pine-birch; (15) birch-willow-juniper-heaths; (16) ice sheets; (17) spruce-lime-elm-birch; (18) pine-beech-sclerophyll taxa.

Basin pollen diagrams show uninterrupted clearance from *c.*200 BC, though some forest remained (van Zeist and Spoel-Walvius 1980). A similar story of land-use intensification in the later Iron Age comes from the valleys of the Massif Central, although here, as in many parts of France, extensive clearance continued into the Roman period (van Vliet-Lanoe *et al.* 1992). The rare occurrence on French iron age sites of wild animals such as aurochs, wildcat, lynx, wolf and bear shows that areas of wild habitat survived, but Meniel (1987) argues that the more commonly found wild animals such as deer and boar were killed in order to protect crops in an increasingly agricultural landscape.

Along the Mediterranean coast of France and Italy the earlier deciduous forest was being replaced by evergreen trees and shrubs and by the expansion of the characteristic Mediterranean scrubby macchia and garrigue vegetation. Human activity is generally believed to be the main factor in these changes (Behre 1988), although climatic changes may also have played a part (Huntley 1990).

In the environs of Manching, Bavaria, oak woodland had been cleared well before the Iron Age and had given way to an open landscape with scattered pine and juniper trees, with denser woods remaining only in the damper parts of the Danube valley (Kuster 1991). Construction of Manching's 7km long defences c.200 BC required vast numbers of mature oak trees, which pollen analysis shows must have been transported from beyond the immediate vicinity of the site. By this period some woodland was being managed: there is evidence for the conversion of beech forest in Westphalia into coppice before the birth of Christ (Pott 1986). Another form of management, which can be seen as a response to declining woodland for pasture and leaf foliage, is the appearance of mown meadows in central Europe in the Early Iron Age, a practice which increased considerably during the Roman period (Behre 1988).

On the Atlantic fringes of the area, the Landes, Brittany, Normandy and the sandy soils in Belgium and the Netherlands, as well as sandy and coastal areas of the British Isles, areas of heathland developed. This can be seen as a specific type of cultural landscape created and maintained by particular regimes of grazing and burning. Heathland expanded in Brittany during the Iron Age (Marguerie 1990). In Germany and the Netherlands barrows were constructed of podsolized heath turves (Behre 1988) and heathland continued to increase in the Roman period and later during the tenth century AD.

The intensity of iron age agriculture in some areas led to erosion. Sandy soils of the Netherlands experienced wind erosion which buried iron age fields (van Gijn and Waterbolk 1984). Major erosion of loessic soils on the chalk of Champagne, France, occurred during the period when La Tène cemeteries were in use (Beal *et al.* 1980).

Wetlands in Mainland Europe and Britain

In this period of increasing human impact on nature, those inhabiting coastal areas remained subject to natural changes in the extent of marine influence. At the beginning of the Iron Age, settlement on the Assendelver Polder in the Netherlands was restricted to slightly higher areas of peat or river levees (Brandt *et al.* 1987). Clay areas subject to marine influence were exploited seasonally until c.250 BC when reduced marine influence enabled settlement. By the first quarter of the first century AD ditched fields were laid out, peat was drained and converted to grass pasture. The ditches manifest greater control over the natural and social environment, and human activity created a more homogeneous agricultural landscape, masking some of the wetland's natural diversity, but only within temporal limits set, by variability in the extent of marine influence. Eventually water-tables rose, peat growth resumed and settlement on the polder was abandoned in the second and third centuries AD.

On the Somerset Levels, England, the first millennium BC saw renewed construc-tion of wooden trackways, sometimes prompted by particular episodes of flooding and designed to maintain existing communication routes in wetter conditions (Coles and Coles 1986). In the later Iron Age settlement was established for the first time on the wetland itself, taking the form of an artificial palisaded island of clay mounds at Glastonbury and seasonal settlement on clay mounds on a raised bog surface at Meare. Pollen diagrams show that this was a time of major clearance on the dry ground, with herb pollen accounting for 30–40 per cent and representing a fully agricultural landscape.

Excavations at Goldcliff in the neighbouring Severn Estuary provide a further indication of the specialized nature of iron age wetland exploitation, and the capacity of these communities to exploit every niche of their environment. Here rectangular wooden buildings and trackways dating to the fourth and third BC are found in a thin peat band within marine clays (Bell 1992). The peat represents a brief period when settlement of the wetland was possible, though for what purpose, whether grazing, fishing or ritual activity, remains unclear. Despite the substantial nature of these structures, their use was temporary: there were no hearths or artefacts apart from a few bones, and the site had been subject to periodic marine inundation during its use. In the later Iron Age, marine influence in the Severn Estuary and Somerset Levels was reduced and in the Roman period the coastal clays were drained and presumably embanked from the sea (Allen and Fulford 1986). This Roman-inspired drainage takes place almost a millennium before large-scale drainage and dyke construction in the Netherlands north of the *Limes*, which finally insulated those communities from the effects of all but the most severe storm surges.

British Lowland Zone

Palaeoenvironmental evidence for this period is particularly abundant in the British Isles and has already been reviewed by Turner (1981) and Bell (forthcoming). Current evidence indicates more widespread clearance, both before and during the period, than on the Continent but reveals some marked contrasts between the British Highland and Lowland Zones. The latter is the southern and eastern part of the British Isles with mostly fertile soils, modest topography and rainfall, and much evidence of intensive clearance before the Iron Age. This is most clearly shown on the chalk where, for instance, the environs of Maiden Castle, Dorset (Evans 1991), and iron age settlements on the M3 motorway (Evans and Williams 1991) were already cleared, although some woodland regeneration occurred during an abandonment phase at Danebury (Evans 1984). 'Celtic' fields show that arable agriculture was extensive in the Iron Age and Romano-British periods and this led to soil erosion represented by lynchets and dry valley fills (Bell 1983). Seed assemblages from iron age sites confirm the increasing intensity of land-use during the period, with greater use of heavier and poorly drained soils and some evidence of soil exhaustion (Jones 1981). At Danebury crop growing was taking place in a range of surrounding habitats including the river valleys (Jones 1984). By the Iron Age river valleys in the Lowland Zone were mostly open and farmed. Tree pollen values were low in the Thames valley, and at Farmoor seasonal occupation and grazing took place on the floodplain, which was inundated in winter (Lambrick and Robinson 1979). Similarly, at Fisherwick in the Tame valley, a settlement was surrounded by ditched and hedged pasture with some cultivated land and beyond that rough grazing. Woodland that remained was secondary and probably managed (Smith 1979). In the Severn and Avon valleys of the Midlands there is evidence of greatly increased soil erosion in the first millennium BC at a time of increased clearance (Shotton 1978; Brown 1987).

British Highland Zone

This area of old hard rocks, with mostly poor soils and high rainfall in the west and north of the British Isles was, in general, cleared significantly later than the Lowland Zone, much of it in the mid- to late Iron Age. Earlier prehistoric clearances were mostly small, localized and temporary. In north-east England these gave way between c.100 BC and AD 200 to much more widespread clearances (Turner 1979). As Figure 9.2 indicates, on some sites clearance certainly began before the Roman conquest and is of native iron age origin. It also occurs at a range of altitudes and topographic locations, encouraging the impression that it was widespread. Roman military sites in the Central Lowlands of Scotland were also constructed in an essentially pastoral heath landscape which can sometimes be shown to have formed as a result of grazing pressure in the preceding couple of centuries (Robinson 1983; Boyd 1985). Other sites, especially along Hadrian's Wall, show increased clearance during the Roman period but elsewhere woodland survived later. Major deforestation in parts of the Lake District occurred around AD 400 and in south-west Scotland later in the first millennium AD (Turner 1981; Dickson *et al.* 1978). On the exposed coastal areas in the north and west of Scotland and the islands, heathland, moorland and blanket bog communities had developed well before the first millennium BC. By then virtually no woodland remained and the environmental evidence from broch settlements reflects an open landscape with much pastoral and arable activity (Mackie 1974; Dickson and Dickson 1984).

In Wales, many upland areas had developed moorland and blanket bog plant communities before the Iron Age. Environmental evidence from the Breiddin hill-fort (Musson 1991) reveals several episodes of human impact before the final removal of trees in the first millennium BC. In the more remote parts of Wales, however, as in northern England, many areas remained wooded. The environs of Tregaron Bog were cleared around 400 BC as a result of pastoral activity during the period of hill-fort building. Once established, the largely pastoral environment continued until the Medieval period (Turner 1964). Despite the pollen evidence for a largely pastoral landscape, plant remains from iron age enclosures in both Wales (Caseldine 1990) and northern England (van der Veen 1992) show that crop growing was widespread, although limited in scale, indicating that the old model (Piggott 1958) of an almost entirely pastoral Highland Zone can no longer be sustained.

Ireland

By the first millennium BC moorland was extensive on the high-rainfall west coast and peats were increasingly blanketing the landscape, covering, for instance, former bronze age fields on Valencia Island (Mitchell 1989). Several areas which had been

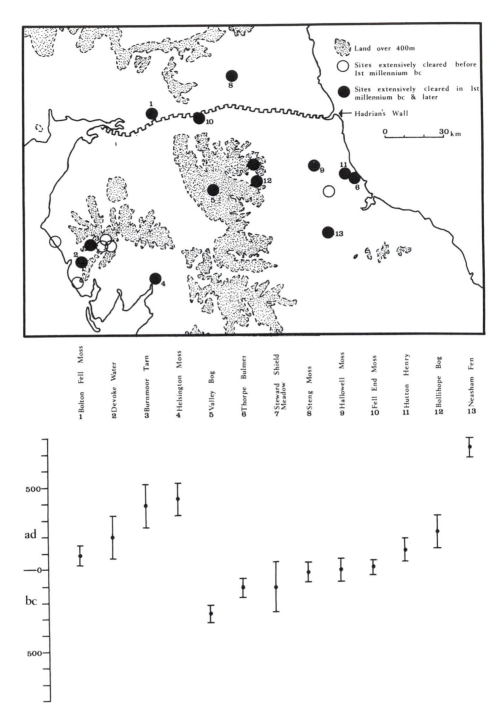

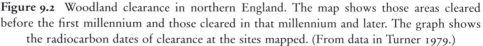

Figure 9.2 Woodland clearance in northern England. The map shows those areas cleared before the first millennium and those cleared in that millennium and later. The graph shows the radiocarbon dates of clearance at the sites mapped. (From data in Turner 1979.)

partly cleared and cultivated in the Bronze Age were subject either to regeneration or moorland development in the Iron Age, indicating reduced agricultural activity (Mitchell 1986; Lynch 1981), which is in contrast to most of the other areas discussed. There are, however, individual sites which show marked clearance in the first millennium BC (Turner 1981). The Corlea trackway, dendrochronologically dated 148 BC, ran across a very large bog, the surroundings of which were still essentially wooded, although there was clearance at the time of trackway construction (Raftery 1990). Significantly, a number of sites recently dated by dendrochronology show that this period was one of major social change and monument construction, yet the contemporary environmental impact seems to have been more limited than in northern Britain and many other parts of western Europe.

In Ireland the really significant change takes place after about AD 300 in the Early Christian period, when there is much evidence for permanent clearance and arable activity throughout Ireland. This is confirmed by dating and environmental evidence from raths and crannogs and by a series of dendrochronologically dated horizontal grain mills (Mitchell 1986; Baillie 1982), which are of seventh- to tenth-century date and indicate a high level of arable activity. In the case of Ireland, the environmental evidence seems to support the traditional picture of the flowering of Celtic culture and agriculture in the wake of the Roman Empire's collapse.

CONTINUITY AND CHANGE

As the number of sites with palaeoenvironmental evidence grows, it becomes increasingly possible to evaluate the extent to which environmental changes are coincident with, or independent of, the major periods of change attested in historical sources, settlement patterns or artefact assemblages. In addressing this issue we need to consider to what extent current dating is sufficiently accurate to distinguish, for instance, iron age and early Roman clearances. In this regard the growing number of dendrochronological dates (Baillie 1982) will, in future, assume particular significance.

On present evidence there are few sites which show dramatic environmental change at the beginning of the Iron Age. Many, however, show marked, sometimes permanent, clearance in the two centuries preceding the Roman conquest. In northern Britain, at least, the dating evidence seems solid enough to support this inference (Turner 1979). There may be a connection between these changes and the increasing social complexity and nucleation of the later Iron Age. It is, however, a pronounced phenomenon well to the north and west of the area where, for instance, oppida occur. In some areas the late iron age environmental changes seem to be more dramatic than those consequent upon the Roman conquest. In the Manching area of Bavaria botanical evidence indicates continuity across this key interface and the Mediterranean plants which the Romans introduced were largely confined to the towns (Kuster 1991). During the Roman period clearances in many areas were extended and land-use intensified but the interesting thing about this phenomenon is that it is also present north of the *Limes* (Behre 1988). It could therefore be argued that it is a continuation of the native-inspired changes of the later Iron Age, albeit encouraged by the increasing proximity of Roman markets.

It is often suggested that the collapse of the Roman Empire led to large-scale wood-land regeneration. There is late and post-Roman expansion of beech in regenerated woodland in many parts of Europe (Behre 1988). In Brittany a reduction in agriculture occurs in the third century, apparently as a result of Roman-inspired population movements (Marguerie 1990). In the British Isles some sites show post-Roman regeneration, but sometimes centuries after the collapse of Rome (Turner 1979). Generally, however, the extent of regeneration has been exaggerated, partly because, where dating evidence is poor, there is a temptation to make simplistic correlations between vegetation changes and the inferred cultural sequence in an area. There is a surprising number of sites with pollen evidence of continuity of agricultural activity, indeed sometimes continuity in the growing of specific crops, from Roman to post-Roman times (Bell 1989).

CELTIC PERCEPTION OF NATURE

Increasingly archaeologists have the technical ability to reconstruct the environment of the Celtic world, but there remains the more difficult, and largely unaddressed, question of how the Celtic communities perceived their environment and how and why they reacted to aspects of its changing nature. Their reaction was not to the environment which we can reconstruct, with more or less accuracy, from the palaeoenvironmental record. They were reacting to the perceived environment, itself reflecting their own lived world of experience. Our own perception inevitably impinges: do we see the Celtic world as the beginning of an essentially familiar Europe, as implied by the 1991 Venice exhibition entitled 'The Celts, the Origins of Europe' (Moscati *et al.* 1991)? In support of this view we can point to the emergence of an increasingly familiar agricultural landscape. On the other hand, a conflicting view is put by Hill (1989), who contends that it was 'a very different past from the one which our common sense expects or allows'. Particular aspects of the environment do seem to have been perceived in what, to us, are unfamiliar ways. Bog bodies are an example. Many are ritual killings. Some were inserted into remaining natural places within an increasingly controlled cultural landscape. Lindow Man was deposited in a shallow bog pool at the beginning of a phase which, on the neighbouring dry ground, was marked by forest disturbance and cereal cultivation (Stead *et al.* 1986). There is a great deal of other evidence for ritual iron age and Romano-Gallic deposition in bogs, lakes and rivers, for example the deposition of weaponry at La Tène (Dunning 1991) and the numerous wooden figures of people and animals from the Sources de la Seine (Deyts 1983). Such ritual deposition does seem to be a unifying theme across much of Celtic Europe and north into Germania. An example is the Gundestrup Cauldron from Denmark (Bergquist and Taylor 1987), the decoration on which includes Celtic motifs. It was deposited in a dis-mantled state on the relatively dry surface of a small bog. Glimpses of the particular significance of some aspects of the botanical world are provided by classical references to the significance of oak trees for the druids and the excavation of a model tree at Manching (Maier 1991).

Evidence of ritual deposition involving human and articulated animal bone occurs in up to a quarter of pits on some British sites (Hill 1989). At Danebury the animals forming special deposits are all domestic, with the exception of a significant association with ravens (Grant 1984), birds which feature in Celtic iconography (Green 1992). A recent survey of the French evidence (Meniel 1987) indicates that bone assemblages from shrines are overwhelmingly of domesticates in comparable proportions to those which occur on domestic sites. That boars were of particular ritual significance is suggested by bronze figurines, occurring widely across the Celtic world (Foster 1977), as well as bones in sacrificial deposits and burials, although there is sometimes uncertainty as to their wild or domestic status (Meniel 1987; Bökönyi 1991).

At a wider environmental scale Parker Pearson (forthcoming) argues that the layout and orientation of iron age enclosures and huts may reflect the cosmology of the groups concerned, thus providing important clues to their relationship with the natural world. The most obvious aspect of this is the easterly orientation of most roundhouses and enclosures, which could reflect the sunrise and daily rebirth of light.

Celtic ritual activity seems to have been particularly concerned with wild places: bogs, lakes, springs and groves. These may have assumed particular significance at a time when the environmental evidence shows that the landscape was being quite dramatically transformed by cultural activity. Such an hypothesis echoes current emphasis on the opposition between wild and domestic in earlier prehistory (e.g. Hodder 1990). Probably, however, the relationship between people and nature in the Celtic world was much more complex than is suggested by simple binary oppositions, for instance. In the animal world domesticates account for most ritual deposits in Britain and France. The full complexity of the Celtic perception of the natural world may gradually be clarified as archaeologists give greater emphasis to issues such as perception, the spatial organization of sites, associations of material in contexts, and the relationship between archaeological and palaeoenvironmental evidence.

ACKNOWLEDGEMENT

I am grateful to Jennifer Foster for stimulating my interest in the Iron Age and for her comments on an earlier version of this chapter.

REFERENCES

Aaby, B. (1976) 'Cyclical climatic variations over the past 5,500 years reflected in raised bogs', *Nature* 263: 281–4.

Allen, J.R.L. and Fulford, M.G. (1986) 'The Wentlooge level: a Romano-British saltmarsh reclamation in south-east Wales', *Britannia* 17: 91–117.

Audouze, F. and Büchsenschütz, O. (1991) *Towns, Villages and Countryside of Celtic Europe*, London: Batsford.

Baillie, M.G.L. (1982) *Tree-ring Dating and Archaeology*, Chicago: University of Chicago Press.

Barber, K.E. (1981) *Peat Stratigraphy and Climatic Change*, Rotterdam: Balkema.

Beal, C.J., Buckland, P.C. and Greig, J.R.A. (1980) *Late Holocene Environmental Change in the Champagne, France*, Birmingham: University of Birmingham Department of Geography, Working Paper 6.

Behre K.-E. (1988) 'The role of man in European vegetation history', in B. Huntley and J. Webb (eds) *Vegetation History*, Dordrecht: Kluwer, 633–72.

Bell, M. (1983) 'Valley sediments as evidence of prehistoric landuse on the South Downs', *Proceedings of the Prehistoric Society* 49: 119–50.

—— (1989) 'Environmental archaeology as an index of continuity and change in the medieval landscape', in M. Aston, D. Austin and C. Dyer (eds) *The Rural Settlements of Medieval England*, Oxford: Blackwell, 269–86.

—— (1992) 'Goldcliff excavation 1991', in *Severn Estuary Levels Research Committee Annual Report 1991*, 13–23.

—— (forthcoming) 'The environment in the first millennium BC', in T.C. Champion and J.R. Collis (eds) *Iron Age Britain: recent trends*, Sheffield: University Department of Archaeology and Prehistory.

Bell, M. and Walker, M.J.C. (1992) *Late Quaternary Environmental Change: physical and human perspectives*, London: Longman.

Bergquist, A. and Taylor, T. (1987) 'The origin of the Gundestrup Cauldron', *Antiquity* 621: 10–24.

Blackford, J.J. and Chambers, F.M. (1991) 'Proxy records of climate from blanket mires: evidence for a Dark Age (1400 BP) climatic deterioration in the British Isles', *The Holocene* 1(1): 63–7.

Bökönyi, S. (1991) 'Agriculture: animal husbandry', in S. Moscati *et al.* (eds) *The Celts*, 429–35.

Boyd, W.E. (1985) 'The problem of the time span represented by pollen spectra in podzol turves with examples from Roman sites at Bar Hill and Mollins, central Scotland', in N.R.J. Fieller, D.D. Gilbertson and N.G.A. Ralph (eds) *Palaeobiological Investigations*, Oxford: British Archaeological Reports, International Series 266, 189–96.

Brandt, R., Groenman-van Waateringe, W. and van der Leeuw, S.E. (1987) *Assendelver Polder Papers I*, Amsterdam: van Griffen Instituut.

Brown, A.G. (1987) 'Longterm sediment storage in the Severn and Wye catchments', in K.J. Gregory, J. Lewin and J.B. Thornes (eds) *Palaeohydrology in Practice*, Wiley: Chichester, 307–32.

Caseldine, A. (1990) *Environmental Archaeology in Wales*, Lampeter: St David's University College.

Casparie, W.A. (1986) 'The two iron age wooden trackways XIV (Bou) and XV (Bou) in the raised bog of southeast Drenthe', *Palaeohistoria* 28: 169–210.

Coles, B. and Coles, J. (1986) *Sweet Track to Glastonbury*, London: Thames & Hudson.

Cunliffe, B.W. (1984) *Danebury: an iron age hillfort in Hampshire* II, London: Council for British Archaeology Research Report 52.

Dansgaard, W. *et al.* (1975) 'Climatic changes, Norsemen and modern man', *Nature* 255: 24–8.

Dansgaard, W. *et al.* (1982) 'A new Greenland deep ice core', *Science* 218: 1273–7.

Deyts, S. (1983) *Les Bois sculptés des Sources de la Seine*, Paris: *Gallia* Supplement 42.

Dickson, C.A. and Dickson, J.H. (1984) 'The botany of Cross Kirk Broch site', in H. Fairhurst (ed.) *Excavations at Crosskirk Broch, Caithness*, Edinburgh: Society of Antiquaries of Scotland Monograph 3, 147–55.

Dickson, J. *et al.* (1978) 'Palynology, palaeomagnetism and radiometric dating of Flandrian marine and freshwater sediments in Loch Lomond', *Nature* 274: 548–53.

Dunning, C. (1991) 'La Tène', in S. Moscati *et al.* (eds) *The Celts*, 366–8.

Evans J.G. (1978) *Introduction to Environmental Archaeology*, London: Elek.

—— (1984) 'Land snail analysis', in Cunliffe, *Danebury*, 476–80.

—— (1991) 'The environment', in N.M. Sharples, *Maiden Castle*, London: English Heritage Archaeological Report 19, 250–3.

Evans, J.G. and Williams, D. (1991) 'Land mollusca from the M3 archaeological sites – a review', in P.J. Fasham and R.J.B. Whinney, *Archaeology and the M3*, Hampshire Field Club Monograph 7, 113–42.

Foster, J.A. (1977) *Bronze Boar Figurines in Iron Age and Roman Britain*, Oxford: British Archaeological Reports, British Series 39.

Gijn, A.L. van and Walterbolk, H.T. (1984) 'The colonisation of the salt marshes of Friesland and Groningen: the possibility of a transhumant prelude', *Palaeohistoria* 26: 101–22.

Grant, A. (1984) 'Animal husbandry', in B.W. Cunliffe, *Danebury*, 496–548.

Green, M. (1992) *Dictionary of Celtic Myth and Legend*, London: Thames & Hudson.

Grove, J.M. (1988) *The Little Ice Age*, London: Methuen.

Hill, J.D. (1989) 'Re-thinking the Iron Age', *Scottish Archaeological Review* 6: 16–23.

Hodder, I (1990) *The Domestication of Europe*, Oxford: Blackwell.

Huntley, B. (1990) 'European vegetation history: palaeoenvironmental maps from pollen data – 13,000 yr BP to present', *Journal of Quaternary Science* 5: 103–22.

Jones, M. (1981) 'The development of crop husbandry', in M. Jones and G. Dimbleby (eds) *The Environment of Man: the Iron Age to the Anglo-Saxon period*, Oxford: British Archaeological Reports, British Series 87, 95–127.

—— (1984) 'The plant remains', in B.W. Cunliffe, *Danebury*, 483–95.

Kuster, H. (1991) 'The history of vegetation', in S. Moscati *et al.* (eds) *The Celts*, 426.

Lambrick, G. and Robinson, M. (1979) *Iron Age and Roman Riverside Settlement at Farmoor, Oxon*, London: Council for British Archaeology Research Report 32.

Lynch, A. (1981) *Man and Environment in Southwest Ireland*, Oxford: British Archaeological Reports, British Series 76, 233–41.

Mackie, E.W. (1974) *Dun Mor Vaul: an iron age broch on Tiree*, Glasgow: Glasgow University Press.

Maier, F. (1991) 'The oppidum of Manching', in S. Moscati *et al.* (eds) *The Celts*, 530–1.

Marguerie, D. (1990) 'L'environment a l'âge du fer en Armorique', in A. Duval, J.P. de Bihan and Y. Menez, *Les Gaulois d'Armorique*, Revue Archéologique de l'Ouest Supplement 3, 115–20.

Meniel, P. (1987) *Chasse et élevage chez les Gaulois*, Paris: Editions Errance.

Mitchell, F. (1986) *Reading the Irish Landscape*, Dublin: Country House.

—— (1989) *Man and Environment in Valencia Island*, Dublin: Royal Irish Academy.

Mörner, N.-A. (1980) 'A 10.7 year palaeotemperature record from Götland and Pleistocene/ Holocene boundary events in Sweden', *Boreas* 9: 283–7.

Moscati, S. *et al.* (eds) (1991) *The Celts*, Milan: Bompiani.

Musson, C.R. (1991) *The Breiddin hillfort*, London: Council for British Archaeology Research Report 76.

Parker Pearson, M. (forthcoming) 'Food, fertility and front doors in the first millennium BC'.

Piggott, S. (1958) 'Native economies and the Roman occupation of north Britain', in I.A. Richmond (ed.) *Roman and Native in North Britain*, Edinburgh: Nelson, 1–27.

—— (1975) *The Druids*, London: Thames & Hudson.

Pott, R. (1986) 'Der pollenanalytische Nachweis extensiver Waldbewirtschaftungen in den Haubergen des Siegerlandes', in K.-E. Behre (ed.) *Anthropological Indicators in Pollen Diagrams*, Rotterdam: Balkema, 125–34.

Rackham, O. (1980) *Ancient Woodland*, London: Arnold.

Raftery, B. (1990) *Trackways through Time: archaeological investigations on Irish bog roads 1985–1989*, Dublin: Headline Publishing.

Robinson, D. (1983) 'Pollen and plant macrofossil analysis of deposits from the iron age ditched enclosure at Shiels, Govan, Glasgow', in M. Jones (ed.) *Integrating the Subsistence Economy*, Oxford: British Archaeological Reports, International Series 181, 123–34.

Shotton, F.W. (1978) 'Archaeological inferences from the study of alluvium in the lower Severn–Avon valleys', in S. Limbrey and J.G. Evans (eds) *The Effect of Man on the Landscape: the Lowland Zone*, London: Council for British Archaeology Research Report 21, 27–31.

Smith, C. (1979) *Fisherwick*, Oxford: British Archaeological Reports, British Series 61.

Stead, I.M., Bourke, J.B. and Brothwell, D. (1986) *Lindow Man: the body in the bog*, London: British Museum Publications.

Turner, J. (1964) 'Anthropogenic factors in vegetation history', *New Phytologist* 63: 73–89.

—— (1979) 'The environment of north east England during Roman times as shown by pollen analysis', *Journal of Archaeological Science* 6: 285–90.

—— (1981) 'The Iron Age', in I. Simmons and M. Tooley (eds) *The Environment in British Prehistory*, London: Duckworth, 250–81.

Veen, M. van der (1992) *Crop Husbandry Regimes*, Sheffield: University of Sheffield Archaeological Monographs 3.

Vliet-Lanoe, B. van *et al.* (1992) 'Soil erosion in western Europe: from the last interglacial to the present', in M. Bell and J. Boardman (eds) *Past and Present Soil Erosion*, Oxford: Oxbow Books, 101–14.

Zeist, W. van and Spoel-Walvius, M.R. van der (1980) 'A palynological study of the Lateglacial and the Postglacial in the Paris Basin', *Palaeohistoria* 22: 67–109.

THE FIRST TOWNS

—— •◆• ——

John Collis

Whether one accepts that urban settlements existed before the Roman conquest or not, it is certain that the second and first centuries BC represented a period of radical change in settlement pattern and social, political and economic organization in central and western Europe. By the time Caesar reached Gaul (Figure 10.1), the predecessors of Roman and modern towns were already in existence as administrative and trading centres – Vesontio (Besançon), Durocortorum (Reims), Lutetia (Paris), Avaricum (Bourges) and others. In the Celtic-speaking parts of Spain sites such as Numantia formed the major centres of resistance, while Camulodunum (Colchester) was considered the capital of Britain, sufficiently important for the Emperor Claudius himself to take part in its capture. Over a broad zone, Portugal, central Spain, southern Britain, France, southern and central Germany, the Alpine zone, Hungary and Czechoslovakia major settlements, often labelled by ancient authors and modern archaeologists alike as 'oppida', had come into existence (Collis 1984).

But this term 'oppidum' covers a wide range of different sorts of defended settlements, very variable in size, character of occupation, and presumably function. It does also exclude a number of open settlements or partially defended sites which share many of the characteristics of the oppida, and which demonstrate that, although nucleation for reasons of defence was the major factor in urban origins, economic and social factors also played a role; indeed, without physical resources and centralized political control, the oppida themselves could not have been founded.

In this chapter I will start by considering the evidence region by region before considering the general processes which were going on.

SLOVAKIA AND HUNGARY

This region, which includes the Puchov culture of the Tatry Mountains and parts of the Hungarian Plain, is characterized by a plethora of small hill-forts which appear sometime in the first century BC. Like Roman forts or medieval castles, some of these became the nucleus for more extensive occupation, loose agglomerations of farmsteads and industrial zones, extending up to a kilometre or more from the central nucleus, what I have termed the Zemplín type of settlement (Collis 1972). What lay

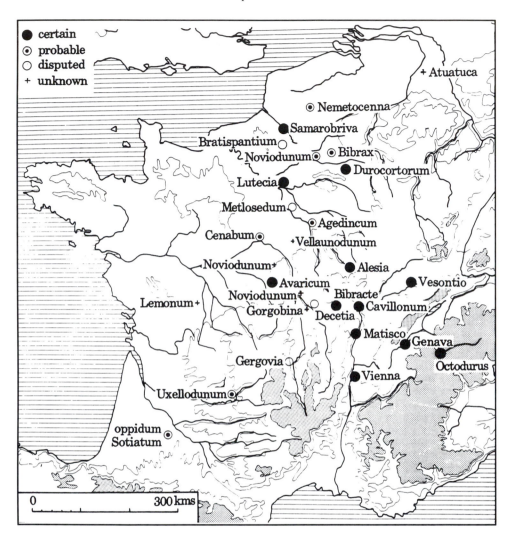

Figure 10.1 Location of sites mentioned by Julius Caesar in Gaul. (From Collis 1984, fig. 2.1.)

in the central enclosed nucleus seems to have varied. Logically the size of the ramparts at Zemplín suggests a defensive function. Nitriansky Hrádok contained a cluster of unpretentious houses overlying an earlier cemetery. At Liptovská Mara in northern Slovakia the primary function was ritual: from the entrance a stone path, strewn with burnt offerings (bronzes, fibulae, burnt animal bones and cereals), led to a pit which contained fragments of female human remains (Pieta 1982). From the two phases remains of eight individuals were found, several of whom suffered from genetic abnormalities. On the slopes of the hill and around its foot were clusters of occupation, including farm enclosures, but also plentiful evidence of industrial production – glass, coinage, iron and other metals. Liptovská Mara was only one of a number of defended settlements in the Liptov Basin, but it seems to have acted as a central place. Several such semi-nucleated sites are known in the region with evidence of industrial activity – extensive ironworking at Zemplín, and pottery production, including painted wares, at Budapest.

BOHEMIA AND MORAVIA

In 1984 I drew a contrast between the small defended sites of Slovakia with their surrounding open settlements, and the nucleated oppida of Bohemia and Moravia in which the whole of the defended area was occupied. An overlap area existed around Bratislava. This contrast still exists, but the boundary is less marked. The oppida in Bohemia are generally large, up to 180 ha or more at Závist, whereas the largest oppidum in Moravia, Staré Hradisko, is only 30 ha, still larger than the Slovakian sites, but like them it has extensive occupation outside its defences (Čižmář 1989).

The Czech sites are still generally the earliest oppida in temperate Europe, belonging to the early second century BC – Závist, Stradonice, Hrazany, Staré Hradisko. Despite the apparently rational distribution along trade routes, the appearance of the oppida was not a unitary phenomenon. Trísov has long been accepted as a later addition to the system some time in the first century BC (La Tène D1–2), and Drda (pers. comm.), considering the evidence for reconstruction of sites and the subtle changes in construction techniques for the defences, believes that a sequence can be detected, with Závist as the oldest. Their end is, however, synchronous, some time in La Tène D2, late in the first century BC, with violent destructions at Závist and Hrazany, whereas certainly in Slovakia, and perhaps in Moravia, the sites continued later, in places into the first century AD. Despite one or two suggestions, no oppida have been definitely identified in northern Bohemia, though major open settlements such as Lovosice (Salač 1990), and many small farming settlements on the loess, are now beginning to be identified. The concept of the oppida being established to stem hostile Germanic invasion from the north can no longer be sustained by the archaeology.

In both size and the complexity and elaborate sequence of its defences, Závist is obviously a key site, controlling, like Prague, the geographical centre of Bohemia (Motyková *et al.* 1990). Despite the evidence of a massive late bronze age settlement, and the Hallstatt – La Tène A settlement with its religious centre on the 'Akropolis' (Motyková *et al.* 1986), the La Tène C2 oppidum is a new foundation after a couple of centuries of abandonment. But the wealth of finds, especially coins, is still less impressive than those plundered in the nineteenth century from its smaller neighbour Stradonice (Rybová and Drda 1989), and the relative status of the two sites in the economic and political hierarchy is unclear. But concentrations of iron working, coin production, bronze-working and other industrial activity is a feature of all the oppida which have been extensively explored.

GERMANY AND THE ALPS

Oppida occur from the Swiss plateau in the south to the German Mittelgebirge in the north, but present no coherent pattern in chronology, construction, distribution, density of occupation or size. The extensive excavations at Manching make it the best known site, but in few respects does it have parallels, and those – open settlement on a river bank, *murus gallicus* defences – lie more with western than with central Europe.

Small centres of trade and production were already appearing at the beginning of La Tène D around 120 BC, sites such as Basle, Berne and Breisach, or specialist settlements such as the salt-producing site of Bad Nauheim. Typically these sites are undefended and lie on river routes. Already Manching (Figure 10.2) was something of an exception. It was huge in comparison to other open settlements, and it started much earlier, around 300 BC. When other sites were abandoned for more defensive locations, Manching stayed where it was, and was given ramparts around 120 BC. Though the area enclosed by the defences was large, around 350 ha, it was not exceptional – the Heidengraben bei Grabenstetten and Kelheim were larger, but in terms of the area of dense occupation and its size (around three times the size of Roman London), it seems to have had no peer. It is also exceptional in terms of its longevity, as most sites were occupied for only a generation or two at the most. Even after the construction of its ramparts, Manching survived for another seventy-five years, finally being abandoned or destroyed around the middle of the first century BC.

In the Mittelgebirge, many sites which had been occupied in Hallstatt D and La Tène A were reoccupied and refortified. Some, like the Staffelberg, were only

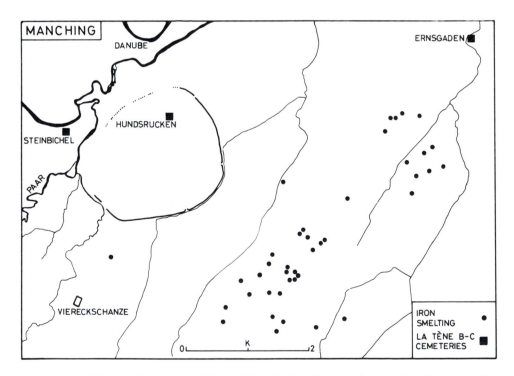

Figure 10.2 The oppidum of Manching and its relationship to earlier La Tène flat cemeteries, iron smelting sites, and religious enclosure (*Viereckschanze*).

sporadically occupied; others like the Steinsberg bei Römhild have produced plentiful finds. In the latter case the extensive, but limited, range of the ironwork (for instance large numbers of ploughshares) may be connected with some ritual deposition, and hoards are also known from the Dünsberg in Hesse and from Tiefenau, in the later oppidum on the Engehalbinsel in Berne.

The date of abandonment of these sites too presents no coherent picture. Excepting Switzerland, which properly forms part of Gaul, no sites in the areas later conquered by Rome survived as Roman towns. Most, like Manching, had been abandoned a generation or more before the conquest. But further north, in the Mittelgebirge, some sites such as the Alteburg bei Arnstadt were still extensively occupied, perhaps as late as Augustan times, like the oppida in Bohemia. Thus, though they did not form a cohesive defensive, economic and trading system, individual sites could survive in apparent isolation.

GAUL

The Mediterranean littoral has a very different history from the areas to the north. It came under early influence from the developing cultures of the classical world, of the Greeks, the Phoenicians and Etruscans, as early as the seventh century BC, and this process of contact was accelerated with the foundation of the Greek colonies, of which Massalia, founded around 600 BC by the Phocaeans, quickly gained supremacy. Inland a wide variety of small defended sites appeared, some such as the Cayla de Mailhac as early as the eighth to seventh century.

The majority of sites, however, start after the period of the Greek colonies, and their earliest levels produce Attic black- or red-figure ware, and from the fifth century onwards the settlement pattern was highly nucleated with, it appears, most, if not all, the population living in nucleated defended sites. In character these might vary from small defended villages such as Les Pennes near Marseilles, to sophisticated urban settlements such as St Blaise or Entremont, the former hardly distinguishable from its Greek contemporaries. In comparison to the central and western European oppida, they are small, rarely exceeding 15–20 ha, and often much smaller. Many of the characteristics of classical towns are present on these sites – elaborate stone ramparts, rectilinear road layout, and monumental architecture, especially for temples with their stone sculpture, sometimes aping Greek prototypes with, for instance, friezes of horses' heads, but more often with local themes such as the *têtes coupées* or monstrous beasts. With such a centralized settlement system, naturally trade and industry were also centred on these sites, though these are aspects which have been little studied in comparison to the art and architecture. Many sites continued in occupation up to and beyond the Roman conquest in 125–123 BC, and its urban system rapidly adapted to the Roman system.

Ostensibly the area north of Provence between the Rhine and the Atlantic presents a consistent pattern. The small open settlements ('industrial villages') such as Levroux and Aulnat have long been known, like those in southern Germany. But they are now beginning to emerge along the valley of the Garenne, the Rhône–Saône corridor, and in the valley of the Aisne. Most are small isolated settlements of about

4–5 ha; Levroux is large at about 20 ha (Büchsenschütz *et al.* 1992). The sites around Clermont-Ferrand in the central Massif, however, present a different picture in both the density of sites and chronology (Malacher and Collis 1992). In addition to the three or four sites at Aulnat, surface finds hint at a number of other sites, one of which, Gerzat, 5 km north of Aulnat, has been extensively excavated. Though these sites lack the nucleated population of Manching (the individual clusters of houses are separated from one another by 500 metres or so, within an area of about 10 square kilometres), they represent the same concentration of industrial activity as Manching. The site of Aulnat-La Grande Borne was extensively involved in working of iron, gold, silver and bronze, including coin manufacture, as well as bone- and glass-working, and probably textiles. Gerzat was more specialized in ironworking, but had glassworking as well. This settlement pattern was already coming into existence in the third century BC.

During La Tène D1 these open settlements were abandoned over much of Gaul. Only in exceptional cases such as Roanne was there continuous development into a Roman town. Instead there was a shift to defensive situations on hilltops, peninsulae or islands, the oppida encountered by Caesar. Only rarely is there a case of straight displacement of the settlement – Levroux and Berne are examples. More normally the new defended sites are much larger than the earlier open settlements and more densely occupied, implying that several settlements combined to defend themselves, similar to the Greek process of synoecism. However, we know little of the effect of this process on the overall settlement pattern. The Aulnat sites were abandoned, whereas Gerzat seems to have survived longer, but there is little comparable data from elsewhere in France.

The revolution in settlement pattern occurred while the Nauheim brooch was in fashion for female dress – these brooches are generally the earliest types from the major oppida such as Mont Beuvray, and have actually been found in the ramparts of some oppida such as Berne. In absolute dates the change occurs around 120 BC. We have dendrochronological dates from the earliest levels at Besançon and Yverdon (Orcel *et al.* 1992), and there is a similar date from one of the phases at Manching. The Roman conquest of Provence in 125–123 BC and the subsequent explosion in trade may not be unconnected.

Not all sites date back this early; indeed ramparts continued to be refurbished, and even new sites founded, as at Gergovie, as late as the Augustan period. In some areas such as Brittany and Normandy the enclosures were constructed, but no major occupation took place. In other areas such nucleation may not have taken place, as there are great gaps in the distribution, for instance in western France. In some cases this may be because sites are masked by modern towns. The archaeology of some sites mentioned by Caesar has yet to be found – Arras and Paris are examples – and previously unknown sites are emerging as urban archaeology develops – Chartres, for example. Nevertheless, urbanization was by no means universal even in areas where social and political development seems to be relatively advanced, and especially in northern areas such as Belgium and the Netherlands.

Another peculiarity is the ephemeral nature of some of the sites. Though some sites, like Besançon and Reims, and presumably Paris, once founded, have remained in permanent occupation ever since, others, though densely occupied, were abandoned within a generation or so. The best documented cases of this are in the Auvergne and in the Aisne valley. In the former case, at the time of the abandonment of the open settlements such as Aulnat in the Grande Limagne, a plateau settlement of some 40 ha was founded at Corent. This seems to have been occupied for about a generation, and was replaced by a lowland site of about 35 ha on the river terrace of the Allier at Gondole. With its massive earthen dump rampart of Fécamp type, this site should date to about the time of the Roman conquest, and the finds from in and around it belong to the decades just after 50 BC. It was a short-lived site, and around 30 BC a new defended site was established on the imposing spur of Gergovie. This too was abandoned after a generation, with the foundation of the Roman town of Augustonemetum on the site of modern Clermont-Ferrand.

In the Aisne valley the sequence is less complicated, and is most complete around Soissons, centre of the tribe of the Suessiones. The earliest site in this case is a poorly defended settlement of about 30 ha at Villeneuve St Germain (Audouze and Büchsenschütz 1992). This was replaced by the hilltop oppidum of Pommiers, with Fécamp ramparts, itself replaced by the Roman town at Soissons. Villeneuve has been extensively excavated, revealing a densely occupied planned settlement. One peculiarity is that the interior was divided into four quadrants by cross-ditches (Figure 10.3). In fact, these ditches may have been the substructure for a massive roofed timber structure for which no parallels can be found. In part the division was functional – one quadrant has palisaded enclosures (Figure 10.4), either high-status dwellings or farm enclosures; another area seems to have been industrial. Limited work on Pommiers suggests that it too had this internal division. The other major excavation in the valley of the Aisne is the oppidum of Guignicourt. About 9 ha has been excavated, revealing another planned layout on a rectilinear pattern, with a wide range of different-sized houses and enclosures. With the exception of one or two buildings which lie at an angle to the main orientation, and seem to belong to a different period, the layout is unitary, and short-lived, as none of the houses was repaired or replaced.

The sites in central and southern Gaul – Toulouse, Palais d'Essalois, Corent and Mont Beuvray – are characterized by large quantities of wine amphorae. At Toulouse they are found in large quantities in the *puits funéraires*, pits up to 10 m deep filled with broken amphorae, and often containing other imported or prestige items such as bronze vessels and helmets. Some contain cremation burials, but burial may not be their only function. These quantities of amphorae have often been taken as evidence that they were important trade centres, but rather we are seeing here large-scale consumption of wine. Figures are not yet available, but the ratio of wine amphorae to other pottery on these sites seems to be exceptional. In the case of Mont Beuvray, the ancient Bibracte, it was an administrative centre where the 'senate' met, and though certainly it was a centre of industrial production, and permanently occupied (Caesar himself stayed there over winter), the amount of wine consumed is more than one would expect on an ordinary domestic site, suggesting some sort of ceremonial or social/political activity which involved wine and food consumption.

In many cases tribal territories can be approximately defined, so oppida can be assigned to specific tribes. Some, like the Bituriges and the Helvetii, possessed

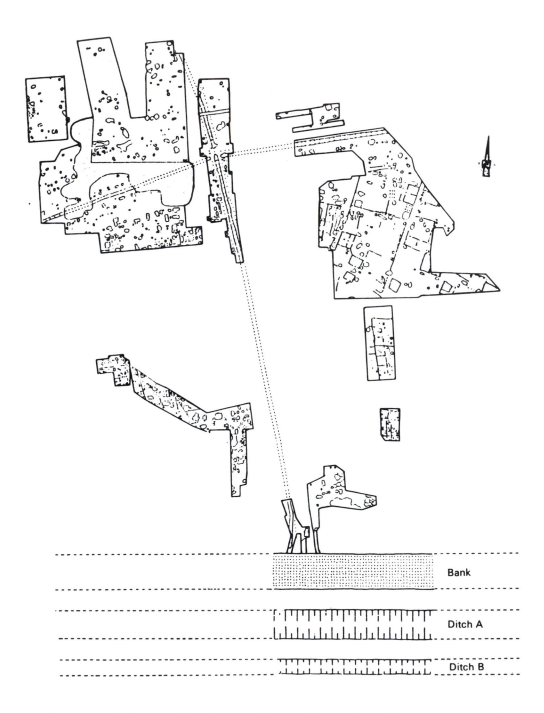

Bank

Ditch A

Ditch B

Figure 10.3 Villeneuve-Saint-Germain, Soissons. General plan of the excavated area, showing the ditches which divide the site into quarters. (From Audouze and Büchsenschütz 1989, fig. 141.)

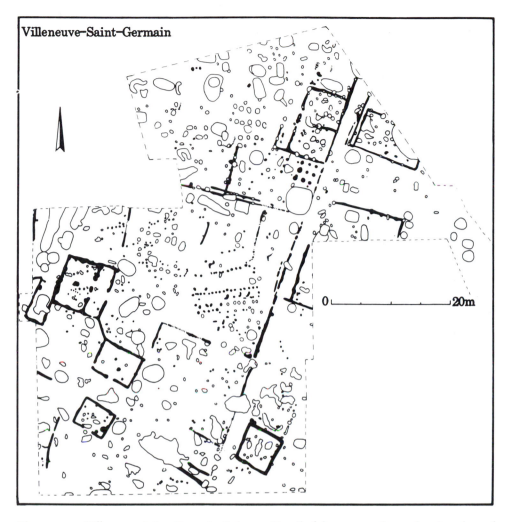

Figure 10.4 Villeneuve-Saint-Germain, Soissons. Detail of the excavated area showing plans of palisaded enclosures aligned along a street. (From Collis 1984, fig. 8.20.)

several oppida, of which one may be the primary site, Bourges (Avaricum) in the case of the Bituriges. The Aedui possessed different types of site, Bibracte (Mont Beuvray), the main oppidum, or φρούριον (defended outpost) as Strabo termed it; and a major trading port at Cabillonum (Châlons-sur-Saône). In contrast, other tribes seem to have had only a single massive site, like the oppidum of Villejoubert in the territory of the Lemovices, while others may have had only one, but not especially large (Corent and its successors among the Arverni).

Caesar mentioned, in addition to oppida, *vici* and *aedificia*, presumably villages and estates. Archaeologically, little is known of such sites, and this may not only be due to lack of fieldwork, as two extensive field-walking exercises failed to produce settlements around known oppida. Some secondary settlements are known in Gaul, but generally they are associated with cult sites, for instance the settlement at Nuits St Georges in Burgundy (Pommeret 1992). Generally small industrial or market settlements are features of the Roman countryside, rather than the pre-Roman.

THE IBERIAN PENINSULA

In many ways the Iberian peninsula mirrors Gaul and Britain. The pattern of urban settlement shows a general trend from south to north, starting with a zone of small nucleated urban settlements along the Mediterranean coast, occupied by speakers of Iberian languages. The central area was controlled by tribes collectively referred to as Celtiberians, who were certainly speakers of Celtic languages. Their area is dominated by large defended sites, some of the same massive dimension as Gallic oppida. To the north and west, though some large sites do exist, the majority are small hill-forts generally termed 'castros'.

The southern coast of Spain came under early east Mediterranean influence with the arrival of the Phoenicians early in the first millennium BC, followed after 600 BC by Greek colonists moving into the north via southern France, and founding the colonies of Emporion (Ampurias) and Rhode (Rosas). Subsequently Carthaginian control was replaced by Roman conquest, which started in the north-east from 218 BC, and spread southwards along the coast, and then inland to the north and west. In fact it took nearly 200 years for the conquest to be completed in the early years of Augustus's reign, Galicia finally being conquered by Agrippa in 19 BC.

The chronology of the Celtiberian sites is far from clear, but many were certainly in existence by the time of the Roman conquest in the second century BC. Most sites are known only from their bronze coinage – individual towns are named on the inscribed bronze coins. The most famous site, both historically and archaeologically, is Numantia, site of the siege by Scipio in 133 BC, but the extensive finds still await modern analysis. In places the size and concentration of these oppida are impressive. For instance, around the plain of Ávila (Alvarez Sanchís 1990; Fernández Gómez 1990) there are five or six sites: Cillán, Las Cogatas, Chamartín de la Sierra, Sanchorreja, and probably Ávila itself. Each was certainly occupied, and had its own cremation cemeteries adjacent to the main gateways, with typically small stone cairns. The major site in the group, however, is Ulaca, on a dominating and inaccessible hill. At the centre of the site is a cult boulder and an associated cult building or sauna. Part of the enclosed site was laid out with rectangular buildings fronting on to one of the main thoroughfares, but there was also occupation outside the site at the bottom of the hill. Rectangular houses are typical of the Celtiberian area, often grouped together either as a continuous terrace of houses along a street, or backing on to the defences.

In the north and west circular houses are the norm in the castros of Galicia and northern Portugal. Cult boulders and saunas are regularly recurring features on the major sites, but the layout of even the larger sites tends to be irregular. At many sites such as the Citânia de Sanfins or the Citânia de Briteiros there are also rectilinear structures, but in part the explanation for this is chronological as often occupation continued into the Roman period; indeed many sites were substantially reconstructed in the fourth and fifth centuries AD. The role of these sites in the total settlement pattern, and for trade and production, is still unclear.

BRITAIN

Much of Britain lies outside the area for which urbanism might be claimed (Cunliffe 1991). Though defended sites with concentrations of population are not uncommon, by continental standards they are small, and excavation generally reveals only a small range of building types as well as limited evidence for trade and industry. This points to a relatively simple economic and social structure, and more recent analogies with over-nucleated societies suggest an inefficient agricultural production which would have inhibited growth and development.

Only along the southern and eastern coasts and their hinterlands can any sites be found which warrant the epithet 'urban', even though most of these sites seem very different from contemporary continental or later, Roman, urban settlements. Contemporary with continental sites, only one site can seriously be put forward, Hengistbury Head (Cunliffe 1987). Even so, in its major period as a port at the end of the local Middle Iron Age (late second – early first century BC), its fairly standard round-houses hardly distinguish it from other contemporary settlements. Apparently contemporary with these buildings (it is not clear from the report), an extensive range of foreign goods was being imported – ceramics and coins from northern Brittany and Normandy, Italian wine and, reportedly, figs. Glass and bronze were worked, and probably iron. However, as has been suggested for equally industrialized 'villages' at Meare in Somerset, occupation may have been seasonal; indeed this can be suggested for other evidence for industrial production at this period, like the coastal salt production, or the chariot construction at Gussage All Saints. The later phases at Hengistbury, with palisaded enclosures (also known at Cleavel Point in Poole Harbour, Woodward 1987), are more reminiscent of continental oppida, but trade and industry are less in evidence at that period in the late first century BC, early first century AD.

The nature of British 'oppida' which appeared in eastern England at the end of the first century BC has been the subject of much debate. They are very different from the similarly labelled continental sites, first in their valley or lowland situation and their discontinuous dykes, which seem non-defensive and more for prestige; and second in their vast scale, usually enclosing several square kilometres, but with only localized nuclei of population within them. Their associations with dynastic leaders has led to suggestions that they may have been royal estates. Both St Albans (Verulamium) and Colchester (Camulodunum) have produced burials which deserve the epithet 'royal', with a range of imported goods that transcends the normal range of imported bronze and silver vessels and wine amphorae found in other rich burials. The Lexden tumulus, for instance, produced bronze statuettes and silver ears of corn which were apparently originally sewn on to a cloak or some such garment (Foster 1986). The names of these major settlements also appear alongside the names of the rulers on their inscribed coins.

The earliest of these sites which can claim a large agglomeration of settlement is

Braughing, perhaps the royal residence of Tasciovanus (Partridge 1981). Though it has an exceptionally rich range of imported continental pottery and amphorae for wine and garum (fish paste) from Italy and Spain, it lacks the prestigious dykes found elsewhere. As on later sites, one of the nodal points is a subrectangular enclosure which may mark the royal residence. In the case of Gosbecks at Colchester there is a temple site immediately adjacent. The major centres of population were elsewhere within the enclosed area, but most of these sites are badly eroded or excavated in only a limited way, so their true nature is unclear; the supposed industrial activity is more assumed than demonstrated.

In addition to these top-level 'royal' sites there are secondary centres, of which Baldock is the most extensively explored. It too has a dyke system, and rich burials, with buckets, chain mail, etc., but certainly not of the highest class. Similar centres seem to have existed along the Thames, as at Dorchester on Thames or Abingdon. In Wessex even smaller agglomerations are now being identified which seem to ape on a small scale the eastern oppida – sites like Gussage Hill in Dorset with its short lengths of dykes and ditched burial enclosure. But the larger sites are also found in the west (Bagendon in Gloucestershire) or in the north (Stanwick in North Yorkshire).

Many of these sites were subsequently to develop into Roman towns. Colchester was initially selected as the capital of the new province, though it was quickly eclipsed by London. St Albans rose rapidly to the status of *municipium*; Braughing became a 'small town'. Other towns such as Leicester or Canterbury have more shadowy iron age origins. To what extent this was a natural outcome of an already developing process, or rather the imposition of an entirely new system from outside, is still a matter of discussion.

OVERVIEW

Urbanization among the Celtic-speaking tribes of continental Europe and Britain is essentially a phenomenon of the third to the first centuries BC, occurring in a wide arc from central Spain and Portugal in the west to the Carpathian Basin in the east. The urban sites in this zone form a contrast to those of the Mediterranean countries, in that generally they are large in size and small in number, in contrast to the small but densely spaced sites of the Mediterranean littoral, be they Greek, Etruscan, Roman, Gallic or Iberian. This in part seems to be connected with social and political organization: the Mediterranean towns generally start their life as city-states, whereas, in Gaul at least, we are dealing with tribal states covering much larger territories. Inscribed coinage usually bears the name of an individual ruler or aristocrat, in contrast to the city's name in the Mediterranean. Celtiberian inscribed coinages are among the few exceptions (Blanco García 1991).

Chronologically the appearance of these sites is not homogeneous – probably third century in Spain, early second century in Czechoslovakia and southern Germany, late second century in Gaul, later first century in Slovakia, and early first century AD in Britain (Figure 10.5). Nor can we look for a common cause for their appearance. Defence and nucleation of the population within a defended site is a

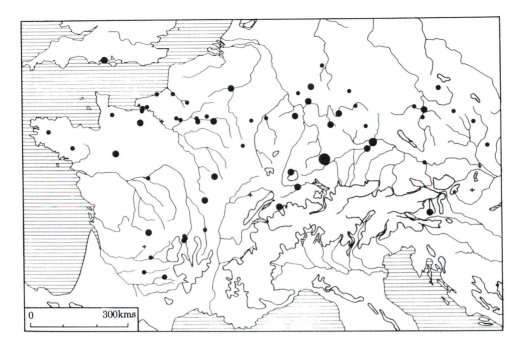

Figure 10.5 Defended sites larger then 30 ha of the second to first century BC in central and western Europe. (From Collis 1984, fig. 1.8, with additions.)

major factor for many sites and areas, but not all. There are open sites in Gaul and southern Germany which precede the defended oppida; in Slovakia and perhaps Moravia, much if not all the population lived outside the 'defended' site; in Britain the dyke systems are hardly defensible; and even some of the oppida in Gaul, such as Villeneuve St Germain, are not in ideal defensive situations. In Britain the element of display and prestige is an important aspect of the size of the ramparts. In any case, the organization politically and economically to 'found' a site implies a developed tribal organization capable of sustaining urban settlements even before they were established.

The spatial arrangement of this arc of urban sites in the hinterland of the Mediterranean urbanized zone would imply some sort of causal relationship, but what this was is not immediately apparent. Trade might seem to be an obvious cause, but this was not highly developed at the time when the earliest oppida were being founded in Czechoslovakia, and the same may be true for the Iberian peninsula as well – we are poorly informed about the earliest phases there. However, in Gaul the major period of the foundation of the oppida does coincide with the enormous upsurge in trade, just preceding, and especially just after, the Roman conquest of Provence in 125–123 BC, which is documented in the huge quantities of amphorae which were being imported (Figure 10.6). The conflict for resources, especially slaves, to meet the trade demands of the Mediterranean, would provide a scenario for the conflicts between the Gallic states mentioned by Caesar, and a context for the establishment of defended sites.

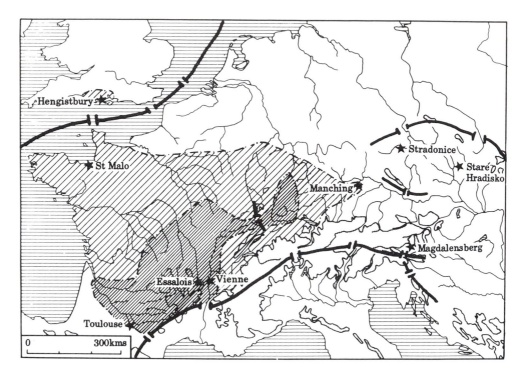

Figure 10.6 Generalized plan showing the density of traded Mediterranean objects (amphorae, Campanian wares, etc.) in central and western Europe, and the relationship of key settlements to major through routes (rivers, passes, sea crossings). (From Collis 1984, fig. 9.22.)

The third and second centuries BC saw enormous strides in production and exchange in central and western Europe. There are two industries which document this development most clearly, but similar things were probably happening in other industries as well. In iron production we can demonstrate both a qualitative and a quantitative leap, and huge quantities of iron objects suddenly become common on all types of settlement. Something similar happens in the pottery industry, and this can be characterized first in the increased importance of wheel-turned pottery over hand-made, and second in the construction of elaborate kilns for mass-production. They are indicators of increased specialization in a broad range of other industries – wood- and leather-working, glass, metallurgy, textiles, and at Manching Jacobi (1974) has identified the specialist tools that accompanied these changes (Figure 10.7).

We do not yet understand much of the interrelationship between industrial and agricultural production, but in some areas one element may have been the appearance of low-value coinage, notably the cast bronze 'potin' coins whose relatively early date, late second century BC, has now been generally recognized. In many areas they pre-date the foundation of the oppida, but there are areas in central Europe where coinage was not common even after the oppida had been established. In Gaul these coins are exceptionally common, and the use of low-value coins may have been more

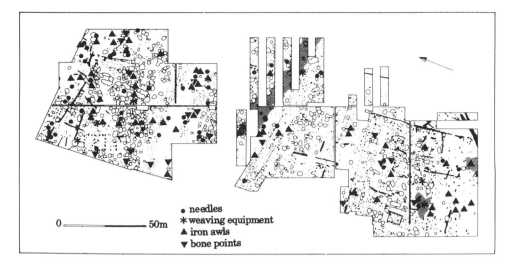

Figure 10.7 Distribution of leather and textile working from Manching. (From Collis 1984, fig. 8.23.)

advanced than in the Roman world. Py (1990) has demonstrated how the numbers of coins lost, and so presumably in circulation, drop in the Augustan period in southern France, and the same is probably true for central France and south-east Britain as well.

It would thus seem that the industrial revolution was a prerequisite for the foundation of urban settlements, and it is noteworthy that major settlements do not generally occur outside the main areas where wheel-turned pottery, glass and coinage were in common use. The failure of urban settlements to appear, for instance, on the North European Plain seems more connected with the failure of that area to develop technologically. Some of the innovation of this period, for instance the advances in pottery production, can be traced back to the Mediterranean world, but some aspects, like the iron industry and coin use, were more advanced than in the Mediterranean, and indicate indigenous changes.

In conclusion, urbanization in the Celtic-speaking world seems mainly to be connected with an upsurge in production, partly due to contacts with the Mediterranean world, but partly indigenous. This increased production in turn stimulated increased trade contacts with the Mediterranean, bringing in luxury goods such as wine, and the upsurge in trade itself became a factor in urbanization. However, this development was not maintained everywhere. In the areas north of the Danube, almost all the urban sites had been abandoned by the end of the first century BC; in contrast, in Gaul, Britain and Spain it laid the foundations for subsequent urban development, and many major settlements were already well established by the time of the Roman conquest.

REFERENCES

Alvarez Sanchís, J. R. (1990) 'Los "verracos" del valle de Amblés (Ávila): del análisis espacial a la interpretación socio-económico', *Trabajos de Prehistoria* 47: 201–33.

Audouze, F. and Büchsenschütz, O. (1989) *Towns, Villages and Countryside in Celtic Europe*, London: Batsford.

Blanco García, J.F. (1991) 'Las acuñaciones del la Celtiberia', in J.A. García Castro (ed.) *Los Celtas*, 123–5.

Büchsenschütz, O., Krausz, S. and Soyer, C. (1992) 'Le village celtique des Arènes à Levroux (Indre): état des recherches', in D. Vuaillat (ed.) *Le Berry et le Limousin*, 245–52.

Čižmář, M. (1989) 'Erforschung des keltischen Oppidums Staré Hradisko in den Jahren 1983–1988 (Mähren, CSSR)', *Archäologisches Korrespondenzblatt* 19: 265–8.

Collis, J.R. (1972) 'The Dacian horizon – settlements and chronology', *Slovenská Archeologia* 20: 313–16.

—— (1984) *Oppida: earliest towns north of the Alps*, Sheffield: Department of Prehistory and Archaeology.

Cunliffe, B.W. (1987) *Hengistbury Head, Dorset*, vol. 1: *The prehistoric and Roman Settlement, 3500 BC – AD 500*, Oxford: Oxford University Committee for Archaeology, Monograph 13.

—— (1991) *Iron Age Communities in Britain*, 3rd edn, London: Routledge & Kegan Paul.

Fernández Gómez, F. (1990) 'Los poblados y las casas', in J.A. García Castro (ed.) *Los Celtas*, 42–51.

Foster, J. (1986) *The Lexden Tumulus: a re-appraisal of an iron age burial from Colchester, Essex*, Oxford: British Archaeological Reports, British Series 156.

García Castro, J.A. (ed.) (1991) *Los Celtas en la peninsula iberica*, Madrid: Zugarto Ediciones, S.A.

Guilhot, J.-O., Lavendhomme, M.-O. and Guichard, V. (1992) 'Habitat et urbanisme en Gaule interne aux IIe et Ier siècles av J.-C. L'apport de deux fouilles récentes: Besançon (département du Doubs) et Roanne (département de la Loire)', in G. Kaenel and P. Curdy (eds) *L'Age du fer dans le Jura*, 239–62.

Jacobi, G. (1974) *Werkzeug und Gerät aus dem Oppidum von Manching*, vol.5 of *Die Ausgrabungen in Manching*, Wiesbaden: Steiner.

Kaenel, G. and Curdy, P. (eds) (1992) *L'Age du fer dans le Jura*, Proceedings of the 15th Colloquium of the AFEAF, Pontarlier (France) and Yverdon-les-Bains (Suisse), May 1991.

Malacher, F. and Collis, J. (1992) 'Chronology, production and distribution of coins in the Auvergne', in M. Mays (ed.) *Celtic Coinage*, 189–206.

Mangin, M. (ed.) (1992) *Colloque Bliesbruck-Reinheim – Bitche: les agglomerations secondaires de Gaule belgique et des Germanies, 21–24 octobre 1992, Atlas*, Metz: Département de la Moselle.

Mays, M. (ed.) (1992) *Celtic Coinage: Britain and beyond. The Eleventh Oxford Symposium on Coinage and Monetary History*, Oxford: British Archaeological Reports 222.

Motyková, K., Drda, P. and Rybová, A. (1988) 'Die bauliche Gestalt der Akropolis auf dem Burgwall Závist in der Späthallstatt- und Frühlatènezeit', *Germania* 66: 391–436.

—— (1990) 'Oppidum Závist – prostor brány A v předsunutém šíjovém opvnení, *Památky Archeologické* 81: 308–433.

Orcel, A., Orcel, C. and Tercier, J. (1992) 'L'état des recherches dendrochronologiques concernant l'âge du fer à Yverdon-les-Bains (canton de Vaud)', in G. Kaenel and P. Curdy (eds) *L'Age du fer dans le Jura*, 301–8.

Partridge C. (1981) *Skeleton Green: a late iron age and Romano-British site*, London: Britannia Monograph Series 2.

Pieta, K. (1982) *Die Púchov-Kultur*, Nitra: Archeologický Ustav S.A.V.

Pommeret, C. (1992) 'Nuits-St Georges, Les Bolards (Côte d'Or)', in M. Mangin (ed.) *Colloque Bliesbruck-Reinheim*, 123–5.

Py, M. (1990) 'Considérations sur la circulation monétaire', in M. Py (ed.) *Lattera 3*, 377–90.

—— (ed.) (1990) *Lattera 3: fouilles dans la ville antique de Lattes*, Lattes.

Rybová, A. and Drda, P. (1989) 'Hradište de Stradonice – nouvelles notions sur l'oppidum celtique', *Památky Archeologické* 80: 384–404.

Salač, V. (1990) 'K poznání laténského (LTC2-D1) výrobního a distribučního centra v Lovosicích, *Archeologické Rozhledý* 42: 609–39 (German summary).

Sunter, N. and Woodward, P.J. (1987) *Romano-British Industries in Purbeck*, Dorset Natural History and Archaeological Society, Monograph 6.

Vuaillat, D. (ed.) (1992) *Le Berry et le Limousin á l'âge du fer; artisanat du bois et des matières organiques*, Proceedings of the 13th Colloquium of the AFEAF, Guéret, May 1989, Guéret: Association pour la Recherche Archéologique en Limousin.

Woodward, P.J. (1987) 'The excavation of a late iron age settlement and Romano-British site at Ower, Dorset', in N. Sunter and P.J. Woodward *Romano-British Industries*, 44–124.

RURAL LIFE AND FARMING

— ·•· —

Peter J. Reynolds

In just the same way as it is impossible to isolate the Celts, so it is to determine a specific kind of agriculture which might be described as 'Celtic'. That agriculture formed the basic economy of Europe and the Mediterranean zone by the first millennium BC is not in question. However, outside the classical world our knowledge of the nature of agriculture is severely restricted by the lack of any significant documentary sources. A few tantalizing references occur in the works of Greek and Roman commentators but they are barely enough to construct any kind of coherent picture. The practice of agriculture, probably more than any other industry, is constrained by the nature of the soil and vicissitudes of climate. It is, therefore, important to recognize that agriculture in Europe and particularly in Britain is quite different from the agriculture of the Mediterranean zones. In consequence the classical works on agriculture cannot be used to provide any kind of generalized insight into what happened in northern Europe. This applies equally to soil preparation and treatment and to the particular crops cultivated. Bearing in mind that agriculture in the sense of food production probably began in the latter part of the seventh millennium BC in the fertile crescent at the eastern end of the Mediterranean and gradually spread throughout Europe to include Britain and Ireland by the fourth millennium BC, specific Mediterranean practice would have been adapted and changed quite significantly as man responded to soil and climate change. Similarly within the Celtic world of the first millennium BC, arguably the land area stretching from the Pyrenees to the Rhine and from Ireland to Romania, contemporary farming practice would have varied quite considerably from one zone to another: differences would have been dictated by the varied climatic zones and soil types. Until quite recently, with the advent of agrochemicals, farmers have been able to grow only those crops which any particular landscape will allow them to cultivate. The ability to influence the natural prevailing conditions was extremely limited.

The construction of a picture of agriculture in the Celtic world has to be based upon the data extracted by archaeological excavation. Inevitably these data are fundamentally inadequate. Agricultural practice and its produce are by definition ephemeral and annual: ephemeral in the sense that agricultural operations are carried out day by day, ploughing, manuring, planting, hoeing and reaping; and annual in that the fruits of farming depend upon the seasons of the year to reach maturation.

To isolate an annual event in the archaeological data is virtually impossible. It is also true to say that climatically each year is a unique event having quite specific challenges and responses which normally defy clear identification. The data range from pollen grains, impressions of seeds fired into pottery, carbonized seed more often than not the result of an accident, desiccated and waterlogged plant remains, the former virtually non-existent in Europe, traces of ploughing left in underlying rock or subsoil of soil layers identified to the period, ancient fields surviving as monuments in the landscape, occasional tools and implements or fragments thereof and a limited range of iconography. In fact, it is this last type of data which gives some of our best source evidence for agricultural practice in north-west Europe, but the majority of it is to be found in Scandinavia rather than in the limited 'Celtic' zone. However, the close similarity of the other surviving data suggests that the agricultural responses were the same then and it would be foolish to deny such useful evidence simply because it falls marginally beyond the Celtic lands.

In any approach to understanding the remote past it is critically important that the argument or interpretation is directly driven by the archaeological evidence. Where there is an assumption of a practice which must have occurred to sustain the existing data, every effort must be made to identify such a practice by exploring the processes which might have left physical traces previously unrecognized or not linked with such a practice. The provision of winter feed for livestock is such an example and is examined below. The following discussion will demonstrate how little is known for this period and how much there is yet to discover.

Agriculture is traditionally divided into two general categories of arable and pastoral farming. There seems little doubt that the great majority of farms, with minor exceptions, practised a mixture of these two categories, any emphasis on one or the other being dictated by soil and climate. In broad terms Britain can be divided into two agricultural zones; the region south-east of a line from the Bristol Channel to north Yorkshire but including south-east Scotland is primarily devoted to arable farming while north-west of that line pastoral farming is the norm. Given the minimal change in climate between the present day and two thousand years ago, the same constraints would have obtained for the Celtic farmers.

The single most significant element of arable farming is the plough itself. A full understanding of the technology of tillage is regarded as an indicator of successful arable farming. The normal appreciation of Celtic or iron age farming falls somewhat short of this state, the plough being discussed simply as a stick ard which does little more than scratch the surface of the soil; hence the farmers merely scratched a living from the soil.

To compound the issue the assumption has normally been that the soil must also be light and therefore relatively poor. From the peat bogs of Denmark a number of these so-called stick ploughs have been recovered which, on close examination, rather belie their dismissive description. One typical example is referred to as the Donneruplund ard, named after its find location. The reason for its deposition in the bog is generally thought to be ritualistic but, since the tool was actually worn out and broken, it was most probably dumped there with a curse rather than a blessing. The simple difference between an ard and a plough is that the latter is fitted with a curved mouldboard which inverts the soil. Its probable introduction occurs in the tenth century AD. Nevertheless, it is a complex tool comprising a main share which is in fact a pointed stick, a heart shaped undershare fitted with spigots which hold the main share in position, a curved handle or stilt, all of which pass through a mortise joint cut in the foot of the main beam and locked into place with wedges (Figure 11.1). The wear pattern on the undershare (one side was worn away to the spigot, thus causing the ard to be abandoned) strongly suggests that the ard was used in a particular and specific manner. One side was continually in undisturbed soil, the other in disturbed soil. If this is the case, the ploughman must have ploughed the soil in 'lands' or blocks rather than going up and down the field laying one furrow immediately against another one. The interpretation of this sophisticated technique has been enhanced by the construction and testing of a full-scale replica. The angle of presentation of the main share (the pointed stick to the soil surface) is c.29° from the horizontal, which ensures it neither bounces along the surface nor digs itself into the ground. Quite simply, it holds the implement at a steady level in the body of the soil. The heart-shaped undershare lifts the soil, which then flows past the foot of the main beam of the ard, having been thoroughly stirred. In practice it is extremely efficient and is able to cope with a wide range of soils including heavy loams as well as the light rendzinas. A large number of iron socks or sheaths designed to protect the end of the main share from excessive wear have been found on iron age sites throughout Europe. Without such a protection (none was found for the Donneruplund ard), the main share wears away at an average rate of c.625 mm per hectare. Given the ease of adjustment for the main share this hardly represents a problem.

Figure 11.1 Replica of the Donneruplund ard. (Copyright: Peter Reynolds.)

In addition to the actual ard itself there are a number of rock carvings, primarily in the region of Bohuslan in Sweden, which show such an ard being drawn by a pair of horn-yoked cattle. The great majority of these rock carvings date from the Late Bronze Age to the Early Iron Age. Some even show the vertical bar between the main beam and the share, suggesting either a method of adjusting the angle of penetration or the presence of a coulter, in effect a vertical knife. One major problem encountered in the use of the Donneruplund replica was the bulk of vegetation and roots which collected between the angle of the share and the main beam. A coulter would have been a useful addition. An edged iron bar, however, even should it survive, is unlikely to be identified as a coulter out of context. A replica of this so-called stick plough has become an extremely successful and useful implement, so successful in the lighter soils, in fact, that it produced furrows in the ploughsoil up to 300 mm deep, which meant that the field area had to be smoothed or levelled out before it became a seed bed.

A second ard of totally different design was recovered from another peat bog in Denmark at Hvorslev. Quite simply, the main beam is an appropriately curved tree branch and the trunk from which the branch grew was fashioned into a horizontal share. At the rear a mortise joint was cut into which the handle was fixed. This ard, too, was worn out and most probably thrown away. Trials with a full-scale replica proved quite disconcerting in that it failed totally as a tillage implement. However, it too is represented on a rock carving scene from Littlesby in Sweden. This depicts as a ritual what can only be a spring sowing scene. Both the ploughman and the bulls are shown with rampant phalluses, a bag the ploughman carries is interpreted as a bag of seed and two horizontal lines below are thought to be the furrows waiting to be sown. Changing the kind of trials with the Hvorslev ard from ploughing the soil to drawing seed-drills in a previously ploughed soil demonstrated quite clearly that this was its primary function. The furrow it produced averaged just 200 mm deep, the ideal depth for seeding in north-west Europe. If such a practice was the norm, first ploughing and then seed drills, another major reassessment is necessary. If the seed is sown directly into a prepared drill, the total germinability of the seed, normally in excess of 95 per cent, is enjoyed by the farmer. In other words the input is total, unlike broadcasting the seed, which has a loss rate of up to 75 per cent, as both biblical parable and practical trials confirm, requiring considerable over-input to achieve the same end product. Without increasing the input, lower production is the inevitable result.

There remains yet a further problem posed by the archaeological data. This is the plough or ard marks found on prehistoric and later sites in all types of soil. They comprise interrupted score marks in the underlying rock, whether that is chalk, clay, sand or loam. They often indicate multiple ploughing and occasionally cross-ploughing. Repeated trials with the above ards completely failed to produce any kind of comparative evidence. Indeed, only when things went terribly wrong, when the ard tip buried itself in the soil, with commensurate risk and danger to the ploughman, did any kind of mark in the subsoil occur.

Unfortunately no physical plough or ard like those above has yet been discovered but further prehistoric rock-art scenes perhaps hold the key. There are three specific examples, one from Sweden, one from southern France and one from northern Italy, which depict an ard scene with a share set at an extremely steep angle to the ground.

None of these could be used as a regular plough to create a tilth because the angle of presentation is such that the implement would bury itself almost immediately. In north-west Spain in the province of Galicia a similar type of plough or ard was in use in this century. In effect it was an oak hook, the point tipped with an iron sheath, the upper curve attached to a straight plough beam fitted at the rear with two grab handles. It was used specifically to break up ground previously uncultivated or which had lain fallow for many years. The manner of use is especially interesting. The implement was attached to a pair of bulls (each district kept such a pair for this purpose as well as the more prosaic reasons of husbandry), a ploughman firmly grasped the handles at the rear of the beam, the point of the hook just locked into the ground surface, two further men armed with goads simultaneously jabbed the bulls' rumps. They in turn lunged forward to escape the goads, the hook was driven fiercely through the ground, effectively burying itself in uprooted vegetation and soil, and the whole ensemble came to a juddering halt after 2 to 4 metres' progress. At this point the hooked share, for such it was, was wrestled out of the soil and the operation repeated again and again. The resulting upheaved clods were broken down with mattock hoes into the semblance of a tilth which was then ploughed with the regular ard. Excavation of this process revealed a typical plough or ard mark in the underlying surface.

Re-examination of the actual prehistoric ard marks indicates the average length to be between 2 and 4 metres, often with an area of greater disturbance at one end. It would seem that these marks rather correlate with the kind of action of what can best be described as a rip ard or sod buster. It is most unlikely they are the result of regular ploughing, which can occur several times a year since, within a relatively short time, they would be cancelled out. The implication of the ard marks, however, does not cease with the argument for a rip ard but also supports the idea of fallowing land to allow it to recover.

Finally with regard to ards and ploughing, if the evidence of the rock art is admissible, then a remarkable ploughing scene from Krokholmen in Bohuslan discovered in 1971 but previously unpublished gives even more insight into agricultural practice (Figure 11.2). The scene clearly shows a double team of cattle, undoubtedly cows, pulling an ard, with a ploughman at the rear holding the stilt of the ard and another figure midway between the teams seemingly in close attendance to help steer the cattle. The major importance of this scene is the use of a double team of cattle, in effect increasing the traction power presumably to cope with a heavier soil. Apart from this one example to date, the increasing of the cattle to two or more spans is thought not to have occurred until the Middle Ages. The evidence is quite clear that a panoply of ploughs or ards existed in the Celtic period, raising the level of tillage technology far above that implied by the description of a stick ard. Given this level of equipment and skill, there is clearly no particular landscape or soil type which could not be tackled successfully.

There is an abundance of evidence for prehistoric fields and field systems to be found in Britain. As a general rule they have survived as field monuments on hillslopes delineated by the low banks or lynchets which formed through soil creep at the lower side of the field, during their use. Abandonment has allowed them to become stabilized by vegetation, and subsequent grazing means that the majority are under grass.

Figure 11.2 Rock carving from Krokholmen in the region of Bohuslan, Sweden, showing a double team of cattle pulling an ard. (Copyright: Peter Reynolds.)

Unfortunately, the agrochemical revolution of the past forty years has seen great swathes of these fields destroyed by the plough. Many can still be seen outlined by soil marks where once the lynchets stood but even these are disappearing at a depressing rate. Ironically, the prehistoric fields had survived on the poor light soils particularly in Wessex and Yorkshire, and without chemical boosting of these soils they would survive still. The fact that iron age farmers were cultivating the poor soils themselves raises a question about the extent of land under cultivation at that time. The distribution of iron age sites across all soil types in all regions clearly denies that the fields which survive as monuments were the only areas cultivated. Undoubtedly the whole landscape was under intensive and necessarily diverse use. Because these fields have survived on the poor soils rather implies that during the Iron Age pressure on cultivable ground was greater than at any other time until the present century.

The fields themselves tend to be square rather than rectangular in shape, and given the ard marks described above, were probably cross-ploughed as a rule. Certainly a better tilth is gained by cross-ploughing, the clods of earth being attacked from two directions. Also because the organic content in the soil is high, the roots and plant material tend to be streamed in the direction of the plough. Turning at right angles to the stream does break the material down more successfully and in addition brings persistent root masses to the surface, allowing them to be pulled out more easily. One of the greatest enemies to the farmer, a great colonizer of cereal fields is couch grass (*Agropyron repens*), which needs continuous rooting out if the cereals are to thrive. The field sizes range in extent from 0.16 to 0.25 hectares and broadly represent an agricultural day's work. Such an area can be ploughed, sown, hoed and reaped within a working day. There is seemingly no other reason to offer for their size since the farmers were technologically fully equipped to make much larger fields. The larger fields of the Roman period, for example, were cultivated with exactly similar equipment.

Very few fields have been examined archaeologically and evidence for field boundaries is extremely slight. Some fields have been edged with a continuous wattle fence. Perhaps hedges were set between the fields. Recent evidence supports the possibility of hedges on top of enclosure banks around settlement sites. Perhaps the cultivated fields were simply left without specific physical boundaries like those to be seen in Galicia in north-west Spain. Alternatively, blocks of fields may have been fenced in. By the same token, if the fields were fenced, no clear evidence of gateways has yet come to light.

Our knowledge of the crops cultivated in the latter part of the first millennium BC comes almost exclusively from carbonized seed, seed accidentally burned and turned into charcoal within the settlement zone, except for representations on the reverse of some Celtic coins. In this latter case there is a stylized ear of cereal which is most probably emmer wheat rather than barley, which is the more usual interpretation. Because both are bearded cereals, the confusion is easily understood. If the representation is to indicate wealth or even to advertise a product like the representation of vines on Roman coins, the likelihood of its being emmer wheat is reinforced by Strabo's comment that this was a major export from Britain to the Continent. The seed evidence, however, is comparatively slight and gives at best only a presence and absence listing. The critical point is that carbonized seed is invariably recovered from the settlement zone, and therefore has had to have been moved from the production zone, the fields, into the settlement area, probably during harvesting, before it could have suffered the accident which led to its carbonization. That representatives of all the plants within the cultivated areas were brought back into the settlement is extremely unlikely.

The list of cereals available to the Celtic farmer differs little from that of today. There were four types of wheat, four types of barley, oats, rye and probably millet.

Wheat
      Emmer   *Triticum dicoccum*
      Spelt   *T. spelta*
      Club   *T. aestivo-compactum*
      Bread   *T. aestivum*

Barley
      Two-row naked   *Hordeum distichum* var. *nudum*
      Six-row naked   *H. hexastichum* var. *nudum*
      Two-row hulled   *H. distichum*
      Six-row hulled   *H. hexastichum*

Other
      Oats   *Avena sativa*
      Rye   *Secale cereale*
      Millet   *Panicum miliaceum*

The finds argue for wheat and barley as the predominant crops. Their presence and diversity, however, give no insight into how they were actually cultivated, nor is there any documentary evidence. Britain has a climate distinctly different even from that of the near Continent and undoubtedly this would have been exploited to the full. Caesar describes our winters as less severe (*remissioribus frigoribus*) (v.12) and the humid temperate climate, driven as it always has been by low pressure from the Atlantic, provided ideal conditions for cereal production. The principle of autumn sowing is traditional in the Mediterranean zones and presumably with the arrival of the first farmers to Britain in the Neolithic this practice was continued. However, because the winter here tends to be over by early March and summer is considerably less severe and barely arrives until late June or even July, spring sowing of cereals is a positive option. The advantages of two sowing seasons are not inconsiderable since the harvesting time is staggered, the winter-sown crops being ready before the spring ones; the work load similarly is spread and – of economic interest – the yield from autumn-sown crops (because of winter frosts checking growth and subsequently increased tillering by the plants) is greater. In addition some cereals, like millet, are frost-sensitive and can be sown only in the spring. Specifically, it allows for greater areas of land to be cultivated and therefore for greater returns.

The evidence of the seed-drill ard discussed above suggests that seed potential was maximized but it gives no real indication of seed input. The fundamental assumption must be that an adequate seeding rate had evolved in the sense of minimum expedient input to perceived maximum output. Research into prehistoric crop yields at Butser Ancient Farm (Figure 11.3) spanning more than twenty years has been based upon this premise. The minimum input assumed in the research programme is a mere 50 kilos per hectare, approximately a quarter of the modern sowing rate. The other issue of paramount interest with regard to crop yields is whether fields were manured or not. The general assumption is that manuring was practised from the Bronze Age onwards, based upon abraded sherds of pottery being recovered from field areas. Tantalizingly, however, very little evidence has been found for the presence of middens or manure heaps within enclosures, though present research into the trace evidence of lipids may alter this in the future. The difficulty lies in the very organic nature of the material and its rapid dissolution and disappearance. In consequence the Ancient Farm research programme has examined a range of treatments including manuring and non-manuring practice. The results averaged across two decades suggest surprisingly good yields of both emmer and spelt for manured fields of 3.5 tonnes per hectare and non-manured fields of 1.7 tonnes per hectare for autumn-sown fields and slightly less for spring-sown fields. These figures correlate favourably with modern yields prior to the introduction of chemicals. All of which suggests that surplus production was well within the grasp of the Celtic farmer, especially as the results quoted are gained from a worst option, since the trials were conducted on the poorest of soils, a friable rendzina over middle chalk on a north-facing hill slope. Given a good soil in a protected river valley, the results would have been commensurately improved. In addition to the cereals, the evidence from carbonized seed indicates the presence of several legumes in the Late Iron Age. Primarily the Celtic or tic bean (*Vicia faba minor*) is represented along with vetch (*V. sativa*) and with the very occasional pea (*Pisum sativum*).

Figure 11.3 General view of Butser Ancient Farm, nr Chalton, Hampshire.
(Copyright: Peter Reynolds.)

Conditions for the accidental carbonization of vegetables are seemingly more rare. The presence of these leguminous crops, well attested, of course, in subsequent periods, rather complicates the treatment options open to the prehistoric farmer. Crop rotation must be regarded as a likely treatment, with the legume crop fixing nitrogen in the soil to the advantage of any following cereal crop. Results from this treatment at the Ancient Farm suggest a regular cereal return year on year of 2.6 tonnes per hectare. A third option is also not unlikely: the growing of beans in particular inter-rowed with the cereal. The major benefit from this is not only the simultaneous deposit and utilization of nitrogen after the first year but also the stouter stalks of the bean plants literally holding up the cereals in bad weather conditions and preventing lodging. This symbiosis of crops can be extended to include both vetch (*V. sativa*) and tufted vetch (*V. cracca*), though if the growth of the vetch is excessive it can actually cause lodging. Traditionally rye (*Secale cereale*) and vetch (*V. sativa*) have been grown together but in recent times primarily as a fodder crop for livestock.

Besides the major food crops, evidence abounds for the growing of flax (*Linum usitatissimum*). Whether this was specifically for the stem fibres to manufacture into linen or for the oil which was obtained by crushing the seeds is difficult to assess, since there is virtually no surviving evidence in Britain for the post-harvest processing. In all probability flax was grown for both purposes. Another oil-producing plant, gold-of-pleasure (*Camelina sativa*), is also found, though it may have been a weed of the flax crop itself.

One particular plant, fat hen (*Chenopodium album*), occurs very regularly in the seed evidence from iron age sites. Today it is universally regarded as a weed but in times past the young plant has been used as a vegetable like spinach for human consumption; the mature plant can be treated like hay for winter animal fodder and the seeds can be ground up into a flour for bread-making. Its frequency suggests it could well have been a serious crop plant in prehistory, especially with regard to its germination time and short life-cycle. It normally germinates in early June and can be harvested in early September. Given its diversity of uses, it could have been employed as a catch crop, being planted when a cereal crop had failed. Alternatively it could have held its place as a cropping plant in its own right.

The wealth of cereals, legumes and other plants clearly indicates that the Celtic farmer had a wide variety of choice. In addition, given the knowledge of the micro-climate and soil types available to him, there can be no doubt that land was used optimally. It requires but little experience not to plant specific crops where they won't thrive.

The methods of harvesting crops, especially cereals, offer a number of choices in that the resources a crop offers are quite considerable. A reference by Strabo which describes the Celtic practice of specifically harvesting the ears of the cereals focuses attention upon the problem. No doubt Strabo mentions the practice simply because it was so different from the Roman harvesting methods. If he was correct in his observation, and the subsequent Celtic invention of the harvesting machine (*vallus*) in the second century AD which strips the heads off the cereals supports him, then the direct result (substantiated by experiment) is a virtually pure harvest of the cereal in question. When both emmer and spelt wheats are ripe and ready to harvest, the joint between the cereal stem and ear, the rachis internode, becomes extremely brittle and breaks off very easily (Figure 11.4), so easily, in fact, that the use of a sickle is made redundant since the ears literally come off in the hand. Impurities in the crop are represented primarily by black bindweed (*Polygonum bilderdykia*) amd common cleavers (*Galium aparine*) which entwine themselves around the cereal and its ears and are extremely difficult to separate during harvesting. These too are found with carbonized cereal grains. Common cleavers is particularly interesting since it might well be an indicator of the autumn sowing of cereals. It rarely appears as a weed of a spring-sown crop.

The obvious second crop of a cereal field is the straw itself. In the case of barley straw, the crop is a significant source of winter fodder, while the wheat straw, less palatable to livestock, is important for thatching, animal bedding, perhaps for matting and even basket-making. But there is potentially a third crop to be con-sidered. Inevitably the fields were infested with arable weeds even if the spaces between the rows were carefully hoed during the growing season. A common ratio of arable weed to cereals even in a managed field, as revealed by experiment, is 2:3. Of these arable weeds all of which germinate after sowing and come to fruition before harvest, quite a percentage are food plants. The vetches, cleavers, oraches, bindweeds and fat hen, amongst others, are all worth collecting as storable food supplies. It is not unreasonable, therefore, since all these seeds are found in the carbonized seed record, to suppose a triple harvesting, first for the 'sport' food plants, second for the cereal itself and finally for the straw.

Figure 11.4 Emmer wheat (*Triticum dicoccum*) at harvest time. (Copyright: Peter Reynolds.)

The harvest, whether it was double or triple, spanned most of August and September and involved its transfer from the fields into the settlement area. Bearing in mind that the focus of archaeological attention is invariably upon the settlement, only that plant material which is transferred from the fields has any chance of being represented in excavated data. The incompleteness of that data is emphasized when one examines a harvested field after the removal of the crop. A large range of low-growing arable weeds is present but unrepresented in the harvest itself. Typical examples include the corn pansy (*Viola arvensis*) and scarlet pimpernel (*Anagallis arvensis*). In fact, the overall view of a harvested field immediately suggests its value as animal fodder, especially as the grass grows only poorly at this time of year. The principle of turning livestock out into the stubble, both to clean the fields and manure them at the same time, is self-evident. The other alternative of burning the stubble is a real possibility but to prove it further work needs to be done in examining surviving and undisturbed prehistoric fields.

Similarly it is, as yet, impossible to identify the methods or zones of treatment of the harvest itself. The critical process is the preparation of the cereals, in particular for storage. All the cereals in question are bearded, and for practicable storage it is necessary to remove the beards or awns to reduce the bulk. The beards may have been singed off or alternatively beaten or flailed off. The presence of the flail is argued as early as the Neolithic in Switzerland. The former system might well lead to carbonized seed as the result of too enthusiastic processing and certainly leaves the ears entire, which means a second breaking-down process into seeds or spikelets. The second and more likely system, certainly if the traditional treatment of cereals has its beginning in prehistory, achieves both ends in one process. The cereal is heaped up and beaten with flails or even sticks and subsequently winnowed. Thereafter it can be stored. The archaeological evidence for storage is of two major types. For the Middle Iron Age in particular there is an abundance of pits which have been determined to be grain-storage pits. These are generally cylindrical or beehive-shaped with a diameter of *c.*1.50 m and a depth between 1.0 m and 2.0 m. Exceptionally, pits deeper than 3.0 m have been found. Long series of experiments have demonstrated that storing grain in such pits is extremely successful. The practice is referred to by both Tacitus and Pliny. Quite simply, the pit is filled with grain and the mouth is sealed with clay or even dung and covered with soil. The clay or dung, provided it is kept damp, makes an hermetic seal for the pit. The grain immediately adjacent to the seal and the walls of the pit begins to germinate, using up the oxygen and giving off carbon dioxide. Within the space of three weeks the atmosphere within the pit has become loaded with carbon dioxide which inhibits any further germination in the bulk of the grain. The loading by volume can reach as much as 20 per cent (in air the normal carbon dioxide content is 0.006 per cent by volume). The germinated grain dies and forms a thin skin against the pit surface, representing a loss rate of less than 2 per cent of the quantity stored. Provided the seal remains intact, grain can be stored in this way for long periods. However, in all probability it was stored only for the winter period. Again experiment has shown that grain stored in this way retains its germinability quite remarkably at levels over 90 per cent. In consequence these storage pits require careful consideration. The average pit volume holds approximately 1.5 tonnes of grain. That grain can be either food grain, enough to feed at the least thirty people eating a mixed diet or seed grain, enough at the assumed sowing rate above to seed 25 hectares. What is certain is that the whole contents of the pit have to be removed once the pit is opened, since resealing is impossible. These pits, therefore, may represent the safe warehousing of grain, probably seed grain, for the export to which Caesar refers. Major sites like Danebury hill-fort, where great numbers of pits were found, could represent collection centres, although most minor sites of this period have one or more such pits. More mundanely the major sites could be controlling grain supplies in the sense of collection and redistribution. Whatever the management might have been, the pits clearly represent the storage of grain surplus for the immediate requirements of the ensuing winter and underline the success of arable farming.

It has been argued that the other system of storage comprised small granaries set on large posts above ground very much like the small buildings set on staddle-stones still to be seen in the modern landscape. The primary purpose of these buildings is to allow air circulation all around the structures and secondly to inhibit access to rodents. These buildings are likely to have been storage sheds not only for grain but also for other materials. Their average size is some 2 m × 2.5 m, giving a potential capacity of over 7 cubic metres, which is virtually impossible to exploit fully because of problems of access and management. It is also likely that any grain stored in such buildings was kept in sacks or bins. With regard to the actual bulk of the grain needed for human consumption, half a tonne is small enough to keep within the domestic house, the grain being ground into flour as required.

Livestock was without doubt important to the Celts but it is virtually impossible to quantify that importance. The documentary evidence is slight and devolves primarily upon Caesar's comments that grain and leather were two principal exports. Britain lends itself to both cereal production in the south-east and pastoralism or stock-raising in the north-west. Perhaps it is not beyond the realms of possibility that in Celtic Britain prior to the Roman conquest cattle drives were made from the northern regions to the south-east ports. If stock is raised for leather only, it is much easier to move on the hoof and process at the latest possible stage. Perhaps the return trade was in cereals, needed but difficult to produce in the north-west. Leather, of course, need not imply only cattle. Sheep and goatskins are equally of value and wool would logically have been another trading item.

Archaeological evidence is restricted to the usual principal sources: bones, coprolites, representations like rock carvings and figurines. Occasional discoveries of hoofprints have been made but these are more curiosities rather than specific evidence. The bone evidence itself, discovered during site excavations, is not unexpectedly relatively sparse. In fact, it is surprising that any does survive, given the ways in which all parts of an animal carcass can be put to good use. Though quantification of bone evidence is carried out with painstaking care and skill, it is difficult to relate the actual evidence itself with the organized running of an agricultural unit. Since it is virtually impossible to date the bone assemblages to a particular century, let alone assign any contemporaneity within the assemblage itself, it is important to remember that a decade in farming, like a week in politics, is a long time, certainly long enough to see shifts of emphasis in a farm's livestock holding – whether by choice or by external constraint, like disease or extreme climatic conditions or a combination of both. In recent cool humid summers in the 1990s farmers have lost 50 per cent and more of a flock to fly strike. Other fatal diseases, not yet eradicated, could well have been present in the Iron Age. Lung worm and liver fluke were certainly present; if they are unchecked, these diseases will debilitate sheep to the point of death. Less dramatic in terms of maintaining livestock numbers is the sheer necessity of providing winter fodder. If the summer harvest of grass and leaf hay is inadequate, then stock numbers most certainly would have been reduced in the autumn. There is little point in eating an animal which has starved to death rather than culling it at its prime in the early autumn.

If the bones cannot give a realistic idea of proportions of stock, at least they tell us what kind of stock was kept. That it was ultimately kept for food is shown by the occasional discovery of butchery marks.

The cattle were by modern standards relatively small. The medium-legged Dexter cattle are the modern equivalent of the Celtic shorthorn. The Dexter, bred in the nineteenth century from the Kerry cattle of Ireland and the Welsh Black cattle, themselves probably descendants of the Celtic cattle, has a number of characteristics likely to have been present in its remote ancestor. It is a tough, powerful animal capable of thriving on relatively poor pasture in challenging conditions. Experience in training Dexters to the yoke ard to ploughing with replicated iron age ards has shown them quite capable of ploughing a fifth of a hectare a day. Cattle management can only be guessed at in the context of the prehistoric period. From the many rock carvings it can be seen that both bull and cow were horned, which, while useful for yoking, leads to difficulties in winter housing. On the Continent the long-houses indicate the use of individual stalls. In Britain evidence of indoor overwintering is inconclusive. The reason for separating cattle when they are kept in close proximity is the dominance factor. In every herd of cattle or any other group of farm livestock there is a strict order of dominance, with usually a lead cow. Even with a yoked pair of cattle, one of the pair will dominate the other, a fact exploited by the ploughman by putting the dominator on the land side of the work. The working pair of cattle undoubtedly received different treatment from that of the general breeding herd. They were probably housed within the farmstead, specially fed and watered and, most importantly, they were tame. They represented the power unit of the farm. The remainder were kept for milk, beef and hides. Cows mature at about two and a half years old, at which time they can be put in calf and subsequently provide milk. The gestation period is nine months and most cows will calve annually if managed in that way. To obtain all the dairy products, there must have been some kind of organized management. Critically, those animals deemed to be worth keeping, as opposed to culling as calves, had to be kept as unproductive animals for over two years. It is likely that the working pair, probably cows rather than bulls or steers, were selected from the herd at 5 or 6 years old to maximize their value. It is interesting that in the Celtic legends of a thousand years later cattle were regarded as being at their prime at 7 years of age.

Gourmet connoisseurs of today bemoan the modern tendency to describe 3-year-old cattle as beef and indeed 3-year-old sheep as mutton. It would seem neither beef nor mutton grace the modern table as they surely did the Celtic feast.

The difficulty of distinguishing sheep and goat bones has led to a strange hybrid referred to in specialist reports as a caprovid. However, sufficient evidence has been recovered to identify both bronze age and iron age sheep. The typical sheep of the Bronze Age was the Soay, a breed which has survived in the Hebrides. Finds of both wool and bone identify it accurately. It is a small but athletic animal, both female and male usually horned, and the wool is plucked or rooed in the early summer. Wool colour ranges from dark brown to oatmeal with occasional white. In the Iron Age the sheep were slightly heavier boned and larger. The probable breeds were the Hebridean and the Manx Loughton, survivors respectively in the Hebrides and the Isle of Man. Both breeds occasionally have four horns in male and female. The wool colour of the Hebridean is normally dark brown and for the Manx a fawn; their fleeces, a longer staple than that of the Soay, are shorn. Their arrival coincides with finds of sheep shears. At the end of the first millennium BC the Shetland sheep is identified: it has a much longer stapled wool ranging in colour from white to moorit. While it is neat to docket each breed into a specific time slot, the reality was probably entirely otherwise. A flock of sheep at the end of the Iron Age would have been a mixture of all three breeds, some characteristic of just one type, others crosses between the breeds.

The primary value of sheep is for meat and wool, though they might have been milked as well. In terms of bone survival it is quite remarkable that any escaped the omnivorous attentions of self-respecting dogs. Breeding maturity for sheep is normally reached in the second year, along with the first fleece. Like cattle, sheep need to be foddered over winter and the same considerations apply for them.

The probable descendant of the prehistoric goat is the breed known as the Old English goat. Relatively small and tough, the goat undoubtedly had its place in the Celtic farmstead. Far less fussy than cattle or sheep, the goat will eat almost anything. In addition, having kidded, it will continue to produce milk well beyond the kid's weaning time.

The management of sheep and goats is difficult to assess with any accuracy. There is a need to excavate areas beyond settlements in order to attempt to discover the presence or absence of grazing paddocks. It would seem from the abundance of settlement sites and their close juxtaposition, along with the focus upon cereal production, especially in the south, that open grazing areas where flocks of sheep and herds of goats might browse were at a premium. The pastoral idyll has the shepherd or goatherd wandering about the landscape with his charges, perhaps playing a note or two on the pipe, returning to the fold each evening: the sort of thing to be seen to this day in the Mediterranean where the maquis abounds. In temperate Europe, however, there is no maquis. By the same token sheep and goats must be kept off cereal fields and, indeed, freshly coppiced woodland too, where they will, if given the opportunity, destroy tree shoots with relish. The question focuses upon the nature of the landscape. Was it ordered and totally managed or was it farmed in tiny pockets surrounded by rough uncultivated land? The evidence to date indicates the former. In consequence it is likely that cattle, goats and sheep were kept in some form of paddock system, which in turn led to grazing management regimes.

The pig, both domestic and wild, was equally important in the Celtic world. A large number of figurines of wild boar have been found, including on shields as emblems. There is no doubt that it was revered for its ferocious fighting characteristics as well as it wondrous feasting qualities. The later legends of boar hunts suggest that the chase was an important element of the boar's status. Perhaps the wild boar was particularly important because the hunt for it represents a major leisure activity, a time within the welter of farming activities when a man could choose a particularly dangerous way to prove his manhood. The domesticated version of the wild boar was undoubtedly kept but exactly how remains a problem for archaeologists to solve. Pig bones are regularly well represented in assemblages but evidence for housing or control is at present lacking.

Bone evidence for poultry is meagre. Caesar remarks that geese were kept for pleasure (*animi causa*) but makes no reference to chickens. Since chickens were widespread throughout the Mediterranean countries, their presence in Britain probably warranted no special mention. Geese, however, held a special place in what for Caesar was contemporary Roman history. Exactly what is meant by *animi causa* is difficult to interpret since the real meaning is about spiritual pleasure. Our knowledge of the importance of birds in the Celtic spiritual world barely ranks the goose as especially significant. Nonetheless the image of a Celtic farmyard must be populated by free-range chickens and geese. As for specific types it is attractive to think of the chickens as being Old English game fowl. These birds have a reputation for hardiness and aggression. The cocks have been much sought after as fighting birds. It is interesting to speculate whether some of the circular buildings were not houses but cock pits. This would, indeed, have been *animi causa* and fits into a long tradition of the sport. The geese could well have been the grey lag, an elegant, medium-sized bird also given to a degree of territorial aggression but not against its own kind as in the case of fighting cocks.

Poultry management is an area of pure speculation. The basic requisite is protection from predators, particularly the fox. Perhaps the fouls were rounded up each evening and housed safely. Interestingly, in contrast to modern poultry which lay virtually all the year round, these early types lay eggs only in the Spring. Egg collection lengthens the laying period slightly but not enough to include eggs in the Celtic diet as other than a seasonal luxury. The approach might well have been not to collect eggs but allow the hens to sit and produce more birds.

Finally, with regard to livestock mention must be made of the horse. There is no doubt that the horse played an important role in the Celtic world especially with regard to the warrior aristocracy. It is most unlikely to have been an agricultural animal in the sense of working on a farm. Caesar refers in his battles with Cassivellaunus to being faced by 4,000 chariots. Numbers are always to be treated with a degree of suspicion, especially when they are referring to battles won and lost. However, given the size of the Caesarian legion, this figure is not unreasonable. The implication is for 8,000 trained war horses. To keep such a number in the field, at least another 8,000 must be in reserve in the sense of breeding stock, foals and animals in training. And this specifically in south-east England. The raising of horses, therefore, must have been a not insignificant agricultural operation. The infrastructure needed to produce such numbers argues for specialist ranches with all the problems of grazing, winter foddering, housing and necessarily breaking in and training. That they were status animals and were held in high esteem is evidenced at the very least by the chariot burials both in Britain and elsewhere in Europe. The animal itself was probably very similar to the Exmoor pony, a tough, uncompromising beast capable of carrying a man all day across rough country.

Mention was made above of coprolites or faeces as an important source of archaeological evidence for livestock. The analysis of the faeces allows insight into feeding regimes. It has proved possible, for example, to prove that both hay and leaf foddering, including twigs of hazel and alder, were used as early as the Neolithic in Switzerland. This kind of evidence has implications for the way in which the total landscape was employed.

Farming is, by definition, a system devised to produce a reliable and organized food supply throughout the year. With regard to plants it involves the growing of essentially storable foodstuffs, fruits which can be dried and kept in reasonable condition for at least a year. For human consumption these broadly comprise cereals, pulses and legumes. The maintenance of livestock for food as well as other products requires similar attention for the provision of fodder with virtually the same rules. The material must be capable of being dried and stored successfully, this time for a minimum of six winter months, i.e. hay, some cereals, straw (especially barley and oat straw and leaf fodder). Given all the archaeological evidence for the prehistoric Celtic period, it is certain that the Celtic farmer not only grew all these products and maintained a healthy herd of livestock, but that he did it remarkably successfully. One suspects the real economic reason for the Roman conquest of Britain in the first century AD was the agricultural wealth of the country.

Celtic farmsteads and farmhouses present us with yet more difficulties inasmuch as what could be described the average, the typical for any region, has yet to be established. A considerable number of enclosures have been excavated in Britain, ranging in size from great hill-forts or hill towns of many hectares to small banjo-shaped enclosures of less than a hectare. These latter, the small enclosures, are the target sites in that the few that have been examined carefully are usually associated with traces of field systems and often, though not invariably, contain elements of what one might expect of a farmstead. The problem lies in the size of the sample, which is too small to allow generalizations. Ironically, in 1993 at Lavant in West Sussex, in the shadow of the Trundle hill-fort a totally unenclosed group of several iron age round-houses and four- and six-post structures were discovered prior to the extension of a reservoir. The site extends beyond the limit of the excavated area, so further research is planned. The nature of the evidence, in fact, comprised the bases of postholes, arguing for an overburden of some 450 mm of topsoil and therefore the greatest percentage of the evidence will be earthfast. The disturbing aspect of this particular site lies first in the lack of an enclosure ditch, a feature that is likely to be picked up in aerial photographs, and second, that the evidence lay in the soil overburden. Identification of such sites by present prospection methods is virtually impossible. A major area survey of the region around the Danebury hill-fort in Hampshire is currently in train following the intensive excavations of the hill-fort itself. The objective is to determine the nature of the feeder landscape for the hill-fort where considerable provision for grain storage in the form of pits and four-post granaries were identified (Figure 11.5). If the typical feeder farms were unenclosed sites like that of Lavant, the difficulties of executing such a survey so that it has real significance have been immediately compounded if not made insurmountable. Logic would suggest that within the purview of a major powerful site like the Danebury hill-fort farmers might well have dispensed with any enclosure ditches and even perhaps have initiated an early form of monoculture in response to supply and demand, some perhaps specializing in cereal production where enclosure ditches were not needed, while others concentrated upon livestock where ditches and banks provide valuable stock control elements. The normal enclosure ditch is usually 1.50 m wide and 1.50 m deep with a 'v' section. The bank is made from the upcast material and most likely surmounted by a wattle or living fence. Such a ditch can hardly be regarded as a significant military defence of any kind and is best regarded as a system of livestock control which has even survived as a recommended system into the nineteenth century.

Although it is virtually impossible to identify archaeologically the typical farmstead, there is an abundance of evidence for Celtic houses. In contrast to the prehistoric long-house found on the Continent, the Celtic houses of Britain and Ireland are traditionally round. This particular feature, a round house with a conical thatched roof, has unfortunately led to the rather dismissive description of such dwellings as 'huts' and, given the normal walling material of wattle and daub the description worsens to 'mud huts', a definition which is belied by the sheer scale and intricacy of some of the houses. Construction materials, in fact, vary considerably

Figure 11.5 Two four-post overhead granaries under construction.
(Copyright: Peter Reynolds.)

according to the region and range from dry-stone walled houses in Cornwall, Wales, the Cotswolds and Scotland to plank walls and wattle and daub in other areas and even chalk walls in southern England. However, the reality of such houses needs to be fully appreciated if the description of mere 'hut' is to be dispelled.

In general terms there are three basic forms of house construction revealed by excavation and, indeed, tested by empirical constructs. The evidence, with rare exceptions, is normally in negative form in that all that is found are the stake holes, postholes and foundation layers of stones or chalk blocks. The simplest form of round-house is evidenced by a single ring of stakeholes, the doorway only being distinguished by a pair of postholes. The regular occurrence of daub fragments, occasionally burned and thus preserving the impressions of wattles, argues that such houses were made of a wicker wall in the form of a circular basket, the break for the doorway comprising two major posts surmounted by a lintel mortised and tenoned into place. The doorway, in fact, has to be substantial to counteract the outward thrust exerted by the interwoven wall. The height of the walls of such houses is to a large extent conjectural although an experimental construct of the second type of house discussed below indicated a height of 1.50 m. The waterlogged remains of an Early Christian round-house in Northern Ireland supports this estimate. In practical terms such a height obviates unnecessary stooping within the building. Of particular note is the sheer strength of this type of wall, especially when newly built.

Although the component elements are themselves relatively weak, the stakes average 80–100 mm while the hazel rods or willow withies at the thickest point are no more than 25 mm in diameter; once woven into place, the opposing tensions create an extremely powerful structure. Over time the wattles dry, become brittle and lose their strength but the power of the wall now lies in the brittle strength of the daub which is plastered into the wattles both inside and out. Daub itself is a specific amalgam of 30 per cent clay, 60 per cent earth and 10 per cent straw, grass, hair or any other fibrous material. Initially it is mixed with water to apply to the walls. Gradually it dries out and provided the mixture is correct, there is little cracking and ultimately the fibres both hold it together and reinforce it. It is not unlikely that a lime wash was finally applied to give a waterproof and, incidentally, an attractive finish. The roofs of such houses described by Caesar as thatched perforce have to have been conical. The other alternative of a domed roof, inspired by the native houses of Swaziland in South Africa, is most unlikely given the average rainfall in Britain. The Swazi houses leak abominably when it rains. There is unfortunately no archaeological evidence for roof construction but a cone presents only a limited number of variables. The greatest problem is offered by the peak or point of the cone in that only a certain number of rafters can actually form it. If too many meet at the apex the point of the roof is lost in a jumble of timber and becomes impossible to thatch. In addition, because a thatched roof has to have a minimum pitch of 45° and a maximum pitch of 55°, then there is a tendency for the rafters to sag along their length under the weight of the thatch. A device which is critical to counteract any potential sag is a ring-beam made of hazel rods set one-third down the slant height of the roof. This also serves to support the supplementary rafters which make up the rest of the cone. All the rafters are secured in place by concentric rings of hazel rods tied to each rafter. These are correctly determined as purlins, since they are contructional and physically hold the cone together. An equally strong alternative is to interweave the rafters with hazel rods, creating a conical basket. The final effect is to convert any lateral thrust exerted by the rafters on the wall stakes, to which they are simply notched, into vertical thrust. All the weight of the roof including the thatch is directly downwards onto the wall. This type of house has, therefore, the same life expectancy as the walls of the house. Once the wall deteriorates the building will collapse. How long that should take is difficult to determine. There is no real reason why such a building should not last many decades provided the thatch is replaced at regular intervals. The type of thatch rather dictates its own lifespan: wheat straw, for example, lasts usually for fifteen years or so before it needs either to be replaced or another layer applied, river reed (commonly known as Norfolk reed) can last as long as eighty years, and ling or heather forty years or more. In none of the excavated examples to date is there a central post to hold up the roof. Where one would logically be found is the normal location of the hearth. The size of this type of house ranges from 4 metres to 9 metres in diameter. However, to put this into a more comprehensible context, the floor areas range from 12.6 square metres to 63.6 square metres. An average modern house has a ground-floor area of *c*.54 square metres. There are many perfectly adequate houses with smaller floor areas.

The second major type of Celtic round-house is widened by a double ring, an outer ring of close-set stakeholes and an inner ring of more widely set substantial postholes. Usually on the south-eastern quadrant is an arrangement of postholes suggesting the presence of a porch, the width of the doorway being twice the depth of the porch. This suggests a pair of doors which swing back into the porch flat against the walls. These houses range in size from 10 metres to over 15 metres in diameter, with respective floor areas excluding the porch of 78 square metres to over 180 square metres. The latter would accommodate one and a half average modern houses!

The construction of these houses can be conjectured in that, like the single wall buildings, the number of possible variations on a round wall and a cone-shaped roof are limited. The writer has, in fact, built several constructions based upon specific excavated plans of double-ring houses. The construction depends very largely upon the inner ring of posts. The postholes invariably indicate individual posts of 300 mm or greater in diameter. These are veritable tree-trunks averaging, in the case of oak trees, an age of sixty plus years, for ash trees forty-five years. In simple terms, they are columns which must be turned into a powerful cylinder by having a horizontal rail of timber mortised and tenoned on to their tops, the individual components of the ring each spanning a pair of posts. Once completed, this cylinder looks rather like Stonehenge and utilizes exactly similar joinery techniques. The outer wall of stakes is directly equivalent to the single-wall houses being made of wattle and daub. At this stage the building is the form of a double cylinder with a break in the outer wall for a four-post rectangular structure which will become the porch. The greatest problem lies in establishing the height of the outer wall and the inner ring and spanning the roof with a cone of timbers. Given the need for a 45° pitch these roof timbers were also mature trees some 11 m long.

The excavation of a great round-house at Pimperne Down in Dorset afforded the answer to this particular problem (Figure 11.6). Beyond the outer wall at the same distance as the inner ring from the outer ring was a series of six curving slots set at regular intervals around the building. The butts of the principal rafters were set into a slot at an angle of 45°. The reason for using a slot rather than a hole emerges later. The outer wall height is the same distance between the ring and the slot, in effect a height of 1.50 m, the inner ring height in this case being exactly twice that. With six approximately straight ash trees set in position, the apex of the roof had to be exactly over the centre of the building. In order to make this adjustment the butts of the main rafters had to be moved by main force, the moving of which replicated almost exactly the archaeological evidence of curved slots. Thereafter these rafters were notched onto the outer wall, seated and attached with a wooden peg onto the inner ring and lashed together at the apex. The need for a ring-beam a third of the way down the slant height of the roof became immediately obvious because even at this stage the sag was noticeable. With six principal rafters, a hexagonal ring-beam was lashed into place and subsequently cross-braced. All the supplementary rafters were attached to the outer wall, the inner ring and the ring-beam. None of these actually reached the apex.

There is, of course, no evidence for such a ring-beam at all other than the building itself. It is the simple argument of 'without which then nothing'. Such a device or something similar is fundamental to such a roof. Incidentally all subsequent roof trusses on rectangular houses are similarly stressed. As in the single-ring houses, concentric rings of hazel rods were tied to the rafters as functional purlins. Once complete, all the considerable lateral thrust of the component timbers in the roof was

Figure 11.6 The Pimperne Down round-house. Over 13 m in diameter. More than 200 trees were required for its construction. The roof weighs over 25 tonnes with a free span of over 10 m. (Copyright: Peter Reynolds.)

converted to vertical thrust and sustained primarily by the inner ring of timbers. At this stage and subsequently it is possible to remove and replace the outer wall. Similarly, the principal rafters no longer depend upon having the butts on the ground and can be sawn off at the eave level along with the other rafters.

The porch is in essence a straightforward rectangular building with a pitched roof attached to the round-house. The primary observation is that the pitch of the porch roof is dictated by the joint between it and the main house roof having to subtend an angle of 45°. This inevitably leads to a steeper pitch for the porch of some 55°. Details of doors are virtually non-existent but there is little doubt but that such a structure would have had a fine pair of doors to complete it.

The reason for dwelling upon the detail of such a conjectured building lies in its forbidding complexity. The materials alone would have comprised over 200 trees, nearly one hectare of coppiced hazel, over 10 tonnes of clay and twice that of soil, 15 to 20 tonnes of thatching straw, a kilometre or so of binding and lashing material. Such houses are not round huts lived in by rude natives struggling to survive until history catches up with them. In architectural engineering concept they are more complex than the average Greek or Roman temple, which only comprises stone blocks laid upon one another. Furthermore, to have such a house built, since surely such complexity argues for service industries of builders, joiners and thatchers, implies great wealth and status. How such houses were fitted out we have little or no real idea other than those glimpses afforded by the Celtic legends. If these can be used as a guide, the interior would have been richly adorned with brightly coloured hanging brocades shot through with silver and gold. Chairs, settles and low tables, a great bronze cauldron hanging on a chain over a central hearth, the broth bubbling over great joints of beef, mutton and pork, withdrawing rooms set opposite the porch and beyond the 'great hall', for such it must have been. Above these rooms maybe there was a gallery for bard and minstrel. Such a house would have lent itself to the legendary Celtic feasting, the chieftain opposite the great doors, the champions and guests seated in descending order of rank in a circle around the central hearth. These images are dealt with more expertly elsewhere but at least the archaeology provides real evidence for great houses. Having actually built structures based upon the archaeological data and handled the materials, especially the straight-stemmed trees, it is easy to understand the Celtic love of overstatement, 'great wooden pillars beyond the compass of a man's arms and heavy enough to make the strongest champion grunt under the strain'.

The life expectancy of these houses is often regarded as extremely short, simply because they are built in timber. In fact, the reverse would seem to be the case. During the dismantling of the Pimperne house several interesting features came to light. The outer wall stakes had virtually rotted away to ground level and beneath the wattle-and-daub wall, still in perfectly good condition after fifteen years, a gully had been created by rodents. The gully itself penetrated more deeply than the original stakeholes and thus removed all trace of them. In addition, directly below the edge of the roof eave, the expected location for the drip gully, the opposite had occurred. In practice, because no one walks there, a special little habitat is afforded which in time creates a humic lump which encircles the house. Only when there is bare earth, a difficult state to achieve in the British climate, will a drip gully be found.

Of greater specific interest were the posts and postholes which formed the inner ring and upon which the whole house depends. In all cases the pithwood had rotted away below the ground surface and in most cases the heartwood had started to rot. The ensuing cavities formed between stone packing and the remains of the heartwood had begun to fill with debris from the house floor, primarily soil dust but including ring-pulls from beer-cans, a 10p piece dated 1974, a hair-grip and a plastic toy soldier – an American GI. They are, of course, the direct equivalent of prehistoric bronze and gold brooches and pins. In one particular case the whole post butt had powdered away leaving a cavity directly beneath a seemingly perfectly good post above ground. The logical deduction to be made from this discovery is that if, as the timber rots in its posthole, the cavity is carefully filled, ultimately the post will be standing on the ground surface, at which time rotting will cease. Because the weight thrust of the building is vertical it will remain perfectly stable. In effect the building will outlive its foundation postholes and material found within those postholes will necessarily be coeval with the building rather than marking the time after its destruction.

That there was a good knowledge of how timber posts rot in the ground is attested by the regular renewal of the two outer porch posts. These particular postholes invariably show great disturbance with even evidence of levers being used to prise old stumps from the posthole. The experience of the construct showed the average life of these posts to be no more than eight or nine years before they had to be replaced. This was achieved by raising the lintel of the porch free of the tenons, replacing the uprights and lowering the lintel back into position.

The third type of Celtic house, still a round-house, is one with a solid wall of stone. Remains of these houses can still be seen in the classic stone country of Cornwall, Wales and Scotland. With the exception of Chysauster in Cornwall where the walls survive to a considerable height, the remainder survive as barely discernible circles of stone rubble. This type of house hardly challenges the great double-ring houses for size and splendour. Rather they perhaps reflect the poverty of their landscape in so far as they have to use stone simply because the traditional timber building materials are in extremely short supply. Nevertheless, these houses still hold a deep fascination, surviving as they do in the final romantic Celtic landscapes. One house, the evidence for which was excavated on Conderton Hill in Gloucestershire, an outlier of the Cotswolds, has been built as a structure on two separate occasions by the writer. The evidence comprised just the foundation layers of the stone wall, its width being just under 1.0 m. The external diameter of the house was just over 7 m. Experiments during the excavation led to a conjectural wall height of about 1.0 m. The doorway was a mere 600 mm wide. The actual construction of this type of house wall is relatively straightforward in that it is a standard dry-stone wall with an inner and outer face. The only observation to be made is that in the original and in normal practice the inner part of the wall is not rubble-filled. Each and every stone is carefully positioned. What was remarkable was the sheer quantity of stone needed to build a relatively modest structure. On both occasions the wall absorbed in excess of 80 tonnes of stone.

The real challenge, however, lay in erecting a cone-shaped roof on top of a dry-stone wall. The lateral thrust of each rafter butt during building was enough to dislodge the upper courses of stonework. Again one has to use the argument of 'without which, then nothing'; the only obvious way was to use a wall-plate around the inner edge of the wall to spread the thrust, each rafter being simply notched into place onto the wall-plate. The roof construction follows exactly the same sequence as the single-wall houses described above. For each of the two structures a different method of thatching the eaves was employed. The first made the thatch protrude over the edge of the wall by some 200 mm, the other started the thatch over the centre of the wall but with an under layer of sloping flat stones to shoot the rain-water to the edge of the wall. This latter type of eave thatching is traditional in both west Wales and the highlands of Scotland. The final aspect makes the houses look dramatically different: the former with its thatched eaves looks wide and comfortable while the latter appears narrow and quite prim. Which is the more accurate is a matter of debate; perhaps they both are and reflect regional differences which survive even into the present. The longevity of such a house is incalculable and, provided the roof is kept in good order, it makes a snug and comfortable dwelling against whatever extreme the climate chooses to provide.

Finally, with regard to solid-walled Celtic houses there is every likelihood, though conclusive evidence has yet to be found, that the houses could have been built of turf walls. Traditionally turf houses or soddies are known from Wales and Ireland and were even taken to the prairies of America. But what traces would structures like these leave? A scatter of pottery, enhanced phosphate and magnetic susceptibility zones would be the most likely if only one knew where to look. Indeed it is this last point which is significant for the future. Although we do have a considerable body of disparate archaeological evidence, perhaps this is all it will ever be, increased of course but always disparate and disjointed. With the exception of the third category of house described above, all the other types of house, including the great double-ring houses, can be perfectly well built with just earthfast timbers. Given a considerable overburden of topsoil of 600 mm, there is absolutely no need whatsoever for a builder of a round-house to penetrate further into the subsoil and thus leave foundation traces as potential archaeological evidence. To underline this observation the Pimperne house posts, except for an arc of seven, were all earthfast. To hypothesize such a structure from so little evidence would be a not inconsiderable challenge to credibility.

What should be our image of a Celtic farm? Should it be like the Celtic village constructed by the author for the National Museum of Wales at St Fagans? There the overall view of three houses, one from each category, along with ancillary buildings nestling within an enclosure, makes it an unlikely candidate. Alternatively, should it be like the Butser Ancient Farm site, where the enclosure is dominated by a great round-house over 15.00 m in diameter with lesser round-houses, granaries and haystacks around its skirts? Outside the enclosure are fields and paddocks where Celtic crops and livestock are raised. In a sense both are extremely useful but because they are so isolated they serve to reinforce the disparity between the archaeological data and the popular perception of pockets of population in the Celtic period. It is the translation of these images into the *creberrima aedificia* of Caesar in his description of south-east England: 'there are buildings everywhere' or 'the landscape bristles with buildings' and, therefore, Celts.

In concluding this chapter on prehistoric agriculture it is perhaps worth considering the nature of the farming year in the light of the archaeological evidence we have. The general view held of the rural life is idyllic in any age: the shepherd tending his flocks; white fleecy clouds in an azure sky; the harvesters nearly always depicted drawing a jar of cider or some other inspiring liquid with a backdrop of sun-drenched golden fields; the farmer leaning on a gate contentedly puffing on his pipe and no doubt thinking beautiful thoughts gazing at cows happily grazing on the green green grass. These are the pictures of the countryside and farming that are most commonly held, reinforced, of course, by artist and poet. Would that it were true today, in the recent or even the remote past! The real picture of agriculture is one of pressure, stress and tension, an ongoing battle against weather and nature with all the odds stacked against the farmer. It is ironic that when most people think of prehistory, their instant thought is generally that of pouring rain, a state which has perhaps been engendered by all those reconstruction drawings in which dark clouds and pouring rain mask the things we don't understand. Yet this first thought is quickly abandoned when farming becomes the focus of attention. Similarly, since the rural landscape is least visited during the winter, this should be the starting point of an analysis of the farming year.

The depths of winter were a critical time for the farmer of the past. It was at this time that foundations were laid not only for the coming growing season but also for seasons, even generations, into the future. The primary tasks of this period lay in the woodland. There was, of course, the need to provide kindling and stores of firewood for the domestic hearth. In order to avoid living in a continually smoky atmosphere it was critical to collect and store fuel not for the current winter but the one following and preferably the one two winters away. That wood stocks were a common feature in any homestead has to be a truism. Obvious places for their storage are between the ubiquitous four-post settings. Alternatively the fuel could have been stacked beneath the projecting eaves of the round-houses where it could be kept dry and also provide greater insulation and protection for the daubed walls. Wood stocks are notorious for harbouring rodents. On several occasions, on the dismantling of round-houses, beneath the line of the wall a gully has been formed by the activities of these fellow travellers. Where wood has been stacked against the outside of the wall the gully is most pronounced, often going beneath the stakes of the wall itself, literally removing all archaeological trace of their presence. This gully, without clear evidence of any wall structure, has been regularly observed. Its presence, however, does not undermine the wall in such a way that it will fracture; the daub and the wattle work it protects hold the wall firmly in place even on houses which do not depend upon an inner construction ring.

The provision of fuel, however, one suspects is a side product from the real work in the woodlands. This work can be divided into two major elements: the provision of timber for building and the provision of working wood. In the case of the farmer, we know from all the excavations of the gargantuan appetite of iron age groups for specific types of timber. Any general analysis of the posthole evidence will show three broad categories of post normally used, a diameter of 0.30 m and greater, a diameter of 0.20 m and a diameter of 0.10 m. In order to create the structures we believe they built, their need was for straight lengths of timber of at least 3 m and occasionally 6 or 7 m in length, in other words, trees grown in a carefully managed plantation where judicious thinning and felling are critical. An oak tree with a diameter of 0.30 m, from this type of plantation which today is extremely rare, can range in age from fifty to ninety years old. An ash tree can reach the same girth in slightly less time but certainly a time spanning at least three, if not four, generations. The logic, therefore, suggests that the timber woodland being managed was an investment for future generations, just as the trees felled were an investment from generations in the past. Given the spread of agriculture from the Neolithic through the Bronze Age and the land clearance we know to have taken place, the presence of any 'wildwood' to which the Celtic farmer may have had recourse is clearly unlikely, if not impossible. In any event the 'wildwood' would be unlikely to provide the kind of timber required and which we know was used. For the lesser timbers of 0.10 m to 0.20 m in diameter it is not unreasonable to believe that the typical hardwoods, oak, ash and elm, were coppiced. This process involves the cutting out of the main stem, allowing suckers to form into stout stems. From one tree coppiced in this way it is possible to obtain from three to seven good timbers. Virgil, writing in the first century BC, speaks of living tree boughs and stems being trained into specific shapes for the manufacture of ploughs. This is, of course, one further refinement in woodland management. While the coppicing of ash trees particularly can produce by accident the right curved shape for a plough beam, it is far easier to train just a stem for the future – in this particular instance at least twenty years.

The fact that woodland has been managed, of course, does not necessarily give any indication of timber quality, of how many trees were required at a time. A large round-house of double-ring construction required more than 200 trees in its construction. Of these at least thirty of 15–16 m in diameter belong to the largest category. Even a more modest home of 9–10 m in diameter needs over 100 trees. If one were to consider the construction of a timber-faced or box rampart, the requirement for such trees reaches quite remarkable proportions. A simple blockhouse or log cabin structure uses several hundred trees while a simple four-post structure will use at least a dozen trees. Whatever may have been the requirements in any one year, even in the unlikely event of none at all, the woodland would still have to be tended. In normal conditions the assumption must be that timber was felled, cleaned, the brush and logwood set aside for fuel, the timber cut to length and then hauled back to the settlement, where again it would have to be stocked against its future use.

One annual requirement would undoubtedly have been fencing stakes which average a diameter of 0.10 m. Farm fences require regular replacement and refurbishment, especially for the control of stock. The average length of time a post or stake will last in the ground is ten to twelve years. In passing, hardening the points of stakes with fire has no effect whatsoever in lengthening the life of a stake in the ground; if anything, it hastens the rotting process because its own moisture content has been radically reduced and in consequence it is more susceptible to moisture from the ground. From the archaeological evidence, scant though it is for fence lines, stakes seem to have been set slightly less than 1 m apart. Thus, given a normal replacement of fences on a settled farm, it would not be unreasonable to hypothesize a programme of some 500 m of new fencing a year. This would need in excess of 600 stakes, plus one for the end, or a minimum of 300 trees, probably of ash. These, too, would have to be cut, trimmed, sharpened and hauled from the woodland to the appropriate location. It is most likely that the fences would actually have been built during the winter, the task of obtaining the materials and building being regarded as one.

The second element, the provision of working wood essentially refers to coppicing hazel for wattling of fences and walls. Like many agricultural processes, it has a specific rotation. It takes an average of seven years for a hazel stool to produce good usable wattles of sufficient length and strength. The use of such wattles is of course attested as early as the Neolithic in the Somerset trackways and elsewhere. Some 4,000 years and a huge increase in the population later, one has to assume that large tracts of land were set aside for hazel coppice. Given the natural growth pattern, each coppice area would have been divided into sevenths, yielding an annual winter crop. Just as with timber, it is normal practice to cut when the leaves are off and the sap down. Cutting at other times of year is possible but damaging to the rootstock. Again, it is interesting to calculate the scale of the annual requirement. Above a 500-m length of fencing was hypothesized; if this were closely wattled to a height of 1.5 m approximately 12,000 wattles would be needed, the average product of one hectare of woodland. It is unwise to calculate the time it would take to harvest this quantity but it can be seen that a modest product in terms of fencing required a considerable impact of man-time and investment in land management.

There are alternatives to hazel which were also exploited and in a probably similar manner. Osier beds and pollarded willows also provided materials for wattling. There are, too, the myriad baskets and mats for which materials like reeds, rushes and sedges as well as young osiers and willow wands had to be collected.

One further winter harvest evidenced in the archaeological record as river reeds, which were used as a better alternative to straw for thatching rooves. A roof thatched with reed has a life span approximately three times that of wheat straw. Given that the river valleys were considerably wetter than they are today, the water fringes would have naturally sustained considerable reed beds providing, in the sense that the farmer had neither to plant it nor to manage it, a free harvest. However, a regularly cut reed bed invariably provides a better harvest. The normal time for harvesting reed is the most unpleasant months of January and February. Again, it is significant to consider the quantities of material required to thatch a roof. A modest round-house of 7 m in diameter needs well over a tonne of reed to thatch the roof. Increase the diameter and the weight increases proportionally. A round-house of 15 m in diameter needs nearly 15 tonnes.

Timber, wattle, fuel and reed, all attested in the archaeological record, spell a long hard winter of toil. Far from the settlement being idle, by the arrival of spring, the ploughing and sowing of the fields would have seemed a welcome release. As a final postcript to this winter work, not the least of the tasks was the loading and hauling of the materials back to the settlement. The ephemeral traces recovered in the archaeological record do little justice to what must have been a harsh reality.

The spring is a time of gradual awakening of the plant world. By the time one actually realizes it has arrived, it is too late for the farmer. Cereals sown late barely cope with the vigorous and hostile growth of the arable weeds. How exactly the prehistoric farmer recognized the time to plant, whether he used the stars in the night sky or measured the lengthening days, we have no certain knowledge. Nevertheless, the real gamble of farming lies in the springtime, the recognition of the moment when the soil conditions and weather are right. Every spring there is such a moment, followed by the decision to plough the land and prepare the seedbed. The ploughs or ards he had were ideally suited to the preparation of the soil and it must be assumed that on a settled farm the fields would have been well worked and therefore tractable. The actual process of ploughing does depend upon the ground being neither too wet nor too dry. The evidence suggests that fields were cross-ploughed (hence their square rather than rectangular shape) and that the fields were ploughed in lands, the most economical method of manoeuvring cattle around the headlands. Field sizes range from about a quarter to half an acre, the sort of area on which all agricultural operations can be completed within a working day. Again we have no real insight into the number of fields a farmer might cultivate but, given that experimental results of approximately one tonne per acre achieved from cropping trials, a planned yield of between 7 and 10 tonnes would not be an unreasonable estimate. Given capacities of storage pits and four-post granaries, a total expected yield of 14 tonnes from both autumn and spring sowing would allow for food supplies for human and animal, seed resources and trade surplus. If these suppositions are correct, an area of 7 or 14 acres would need to have been ploughed and cultivated in the spring: two weeks of solid work followed by a further week of planting. Not even then is the ploughing at an end. The planting of the more frost-susceptible crops must be prepared for in advance. Peas and flax and even spring beans are likely to be severely damaged, if not destroyed, by frost. It is important to realize also that planting fields is not quite as simple as it sounds. The Celtic farmer had at his disposal at least ten different types of cereals and doubtless the proportions of each type planted depended upon the overall requirements of the farm and its stock, both human and animal. In addition the exact field in which each type of crop was planted depended upon the farmer's understanding of the microclimate of his land. Barley will prosper where wheat will struggle; beans and other legumes, as well as flax, are best planted away from a frost hollow in case of a late cold spell in April or May. The permutations are not endless but everything needs to be taken into account.

Once the fields are planted in late March and early April, attention invariably switches to the livestock. At this time the grass begins to grow vigorously. The cattle, apart from the plough team which in all probability received special treatment at all times, need to be turned out to pasture. Whether they were taken daily and herded back each evening or left out in field enclosures we have yet to prove. The basic question is relatively straightforward. Were the crop fields fenced or were the stock fields fenced? The evidence, sparse though it is, suggests the latter, in which case careful rotation of such paddocks would have been necessary to avoid poaching of the grass. The benefit of bringing stock back to the farmstead each evening lies in the steady acquisition of manure and of course the tractability of the animals. Cattle defecate normally each evening and morning. Along with the midden acquired over the winter while all the stock are contained and fed, this nightly increase would be invaluable come the following autumn. The sheep and goats were undoubtedly kept together and treated in a similar way, if only to obtain the milk during the appropriate times. Cattle, sheep and goats provide milk for only a limited period after parturition. Management undoubtedly varied during the year as options changed but the springtime was the major time of change.

Lambing, kidding and calving are also the hallmarks of spring. In the case of cattle this has to be carefully arranged, since mating has to occur the previous June. In normal conditions with the hardy breeds in question, although there are few problems, inevitably there are some and it is the task of the farmer to be on hand to help the process. Failure can lead to the loss of both dam and progeny and, therefore, of measurable wealth.

Towards the end of spring the crops have begun to grow and now require urgent attention. If the interpretation of the ploughing implements is correct and the crops are sown in drills for subsequent management, now is the time for that management. The timing of planting is arranged quite critically to give the crops a favourable advantage over the arable weeds. For that advantage to be maintained, especially against pernicious weeds like charlock, hoeing is essential. Given the average size of the fields at half an acre, inter-row hoeing with a mattock hoe represents one man-day. The hypothesis of a gross produce yield of 14 tonnes implies twenty-eight fields and therefore, twenty-eight man-days. No doubt all able-bodied members of the farmstead were brought into action for this task. It is normally necessary to hoe through the crops twice, once in late April to take out the early competitors, once in mid- to late May to take out the secondary growth. After this time hoeing probably ceased for fear of damaging the rootstock of the crops. One interesting aspect of hoeing concerns the method of dealing with hoed weeds. Were they left where they were cut in the rows, thus shielding the soil from moisture loss through evaporation and adding to the fibre content of the soil and enriching it? Or were the weeds cast onto the field edges, contributing towards lynchet formation? The former is probably the case.

Early June is the time for shearing the sheep and dealing with the harvest of wool. Given the different breeds of sheep evidenced by the bones from archaeological excavations some, like the Soay, were plucked or combed while others, like the Manx Loughton, Hebridean and Shetland, were sheared. Sheep shears make their appearance in the middle of the first millennium BC. The processing of the wool was undoubtedly the role of the women of the settlement and probably carried on throughout the year. Even today it is a common sight in peasant economies to see the women spinning wool on a drop spindle even as they walk along. No doubt any excess wool represented a trading resource.

With the completion of shearing there might have been a brief period of rest and relaxation, perhaps the only one in the farming calendar because in late June and early July comes the time for haymaking. In a very real sense the major purpose of farming is to provide during the growing months food supplies for those months when nothing grows. This truism involves grassland as well. Normally grass grows vigorously in the spring, flushing the landscapes with a healthy green coat. However, come July the growth radically slows as seeding takes place and only begins again with a late flourish at the end of August to the first frost in late September/early October. Grazing of livestock in restricted areas can severely damage and even destroy grassland after this time. The actual process of poaching the grass down to root level allows the mosses to take hold and thereafter dominate. Getting rid of moss is an extremely difficult process whether now or 2,000 years ago. The best approach is to avoid it happening. In consequence haymaking for winter fodder for livestock has to have been a priority. Again our knowledge is slight. Single postholes within a circular depression of 2 or 3 m in diameter may well have been haystacks. Experimental trials support this interpretation, and there is a wealth of ethnographic evidence for such haystacks in this country and the near Continent. The source of the hay, however, is a subject for considerable conjecture. Perhaps areas of grassland were specifically set aside, and with an average yield of a tonne or so per acre, the area would be dominated by the stock held on the farm. A mature cow needs approximately 1 tonne of hay per winter to maintain condition. A tonne will feed perhaps five sheep. For a herd of half a dozen cattle including the plough team, perhaps thirty to forty sheep and goats, the hay provision must approach 14 to 15 tonnes. Within the farmyard this means as many as five or six circular haystacks. An alternative and in more recent times a traditional source of hay was the water-meadows, the grassland which flourishes within the flooding zones of rivers and streams. Those areas are too much at risk of flash floods to cultivate for cereals, too wet to graze in the early part of the year for stock susceptible to footrot on the one hand and liver fluke on the other. Not that this would have been necessarily recognized other than by trial and disaster. Sheep, especially if grazed on low-lying wet ground, can die mysteriously! Folklore will take care of the reason. Nevertheless, these areas provide lush growth and an ideal resource for haymaking at the ideal time of year when the grass and other herbs are about to seed. The cutting of hay in sufficient quantities, its drying in the sun and its subsequent carting back to the farm and stacking into ricks must have been a major work programme involving all the able-bodied labour available. It would have taken at least a month to six weeks to complete the harvest. The culmination of haymaking is the thatching of the stacks to protect them from rainfall. During Winter as the stacks are used they take on the unusual appearance of an apple core. Of course, once the hay is off the water-meadows they become ideal grazing areas to cover the non-growing period in the normal grazing paddocks.

One other probable source of winter fodder that may have been collected almost immediately after the haymaking was tree leaves. Traditionally in north-west Europe leaves of ash and elm trees were cut in high summer, sun-dried on racks and stored in barns or sheds. Many of the pairs of postholes excavated on iron age farms may represent drying racks for leaf fodder. The appeal of dried leaves as a fodder for stock is beyond question. Cattle, goats and sheep, offered an uncomplicated choice in trials between prime hay and dried tree leaves, have shown a marked preference for the dried leaves. In reality this should only be expected since all are naturally browsers rather than grazers. Any tree in a regular pasture shows evidence of heavy browsing of those boughs within reach and it is not an uncommon sight to see cattle straining on their hind legs to reach the higher boughs. This alternative fodder means an ongoing task for the farmer at this time around the woodland fringes where leaf growth is greatest and most accessible. It may well be that trees scheduled for felling the following winter were systematically stripped of their leaves the preceding summer. There is little doubt that stripping a tree of its leaves doesn't enhance the appearance or the expected life span of the tree. The process of cutting, bundling, hauling, drying on racks and final storage of the leaf harvest neatly fills the time until the cereal and legume harvest is ready.

The early cereal types all require a slightly longer growing season than the modern hybrid cereals. Nowadays autumn cereals are currently ready in mid-August and the spring cereals in late August, early September. Of all the tasks of the farmer this is the most critical and labour-intensive. We have little real evidence of exactly how the harvesting was achieved. The Roman historian Strabo refers to the Celtic practice of cutting off the heads of the cereals, which has led to an abundance of representations of one hand grasping a bunch of straws, the other poised with a sickle about to deliver in one smooth movement a fistful of ears. Countless experiments in grasping the prehistoric cereals have delivered a different reality. Because the prehistoric cereals are stable hybrids, each ear-bearing stalk does not grow to the same height. In fact, some can grow as tall as 1.80 m while others grow to a mere 0.40 m. The disparity in height over the whole crop is regularly over 1 m. The second natural element which denies the above picture is that the grasping hand often comes away with the ears, which break off from the stem without even a glancing blow from the sickle. In fact, when the cereal is ripe the internode between the ear and straw stalk becomes very brittle and snaps off easily. It is, of course, the natural way in which the plant distributes its own seed. The other aspect, of course, equally doesn't work too well. If the straw is sickled off close to the ground and bundled into sheaves a considerable number of ears is lost in the process. Perhaps Strabo is right in his observations but the translation should rather be 'picks the ears of the cereals'. While tedious, this has proved experimentally to be far the best harvesting system and leads to a virtually pure harvest. Very few arable weeds manage to find their way into the harvesters' sacks. The notable exception is the black bindweed, itself harmless and in subsequent periods recorded as a food plant. If this was the system then transport of the crop back to the farmyard is relatively straightforward. The obvious problem thereafter is a field full of standing straw, itself a valuable commodity for thatching, fodder supplement and bedding. Sickling, bundling and cutting and then stacking in the farmyard represent an investment of many man-hours. The straw couldn't be left in the field simply to rot down and be ploughed in. The major difficulty is the length of time straw takes to rot, usually many months, and the impossible conditions it would provide for the ard, which was not necessarily fitted with a coulter to cut through the fibrous material. An abundance of chickweed left behind in the stubble of the crop can bring an ard to a grinding halt. Harvesting, therefore, would seem to be a twofold process but there might even have been a third harvest which preceded the other two. Many of the so-called arable weeds are, in fact, food plants and from the carbonized seed evidence their presence on sites is attested. This clearly indicates they were either deliberately or accidentally brought into the farmstead; if deliberately, then the ideal time to collect them is just prior to the harvest itself. Plants like the wild vetches, common orache and bindweeds all make an excellent contribution to and variation in diet. If they were brought accidentally then it must be assumed these plants made their way into the settlement amongst the straw harvest and became separated out in the later processing of straw, perhaps in its preparation for thatching.

Of all the crops for which we have evidence, the most difficult for the prehistoric farmer must have been the flax crop. This plant provides a double yield: oil from the crushed seeds and fibres from the stems when they are retted. The crop had to be cut just before the seed pods were completely ripe, put into bundles and probably taken back to the farmstead. It could be left for final ripening and treating in the field but the risk of rain spoiling the crop was hardly worth taking. Once the pods were completely ripe, the seed was crushed to extract the linseed oil. For the fibres to be stripped off the stems, the bundles have to be steeped in water for several days to loosen the fibre threads. Then the stems are raked down their length with combs to pull away the fibres which can subsequently be washed, teased and then spun into linen thread.

Harvesting includes the legumes as well. No doubt quantities of these were picked during the season for immediate consumption but the bulk of the crop would no doubt have been left until the seeds were hard and dry. The legumes included the field bean, pea and the vetch. Probably these were harvested by picking the pods, which would be further processed prior to storage. If they are left in the pod, all legumes tend to deteriorate through dampness and the inevitable presence of the bean weevil, whose appetite knows no bounds. Because ripening time for legumes is not consistent, unlike that for cereals, the legume harvest could well have meant at least two pickings, if not more. To leave it to a single harvest would have meant losing a fair proportion of the harvest because the ripe pods burst open and spill the seeds onto the ground.

One usual crop which may have been grown is fat hen (*Chenopodium album*). Several collections of pure seed have been recovered from excavations, suggesting that it was either deliberately collected from wild plants, perhaps the third harvest mentioned above, or that it was a standard crop. The plant itself has many good qualities: the young leaves can be eaten like spinach; the whole mature plant can be cut and sun dried as fodder for livestock; and when the seeds are ripe they can be harvested and ground into a fine flour for bread-making. It has one further major benefit beyond these important qualities. Its primary germination period is in June with fruiting in mid- to late September. In the event of crop failure this plant could be sown late on in the season and provide a useful fail-safe harvest. If it was, in fact, grown, then the harvest would have stretched on for at least a further two weeks to the end of September.

Once the crops were off, the fields would be a mess of stubble and arable weed, some beginning to grow quite quickly with the competition removed. Doubtless all the livestock of the farm were turned out into the stubble, when there would be plenty to eat for several days. The beneficial side-effect would be the natural dunging of the fields at this time.

With the harvest in, the attention would focus upon the farmyard and the inevitable processing of the crops for their safe storage. The cereals share a common characteristic in that all of them without exception are bearded cereals. The minimim treatment needed for storage is the removal of the beards so that the bulk is reduced and the chance of moisture penetration is limited. This can be achieved either by beating the ears with a flail or similar tool or alternatively by the judicious use of fire. The awns or beard will quickly flame off, leaving the ear untouched by the fire, but the risk of conflagration is ever-present. The former method is the safer and in some ways better because it reduces the ear to spikelet form. To reduce it still further to the naked seed is necessary only for food preparation, a process which in all likeli-hood was essentially domestic and on a 'need only' basis.

This raises the whole question of storage methods, and of the proportions in which the cereals were divided. A standard method of grain storage through a major part of the Iron Age was in underground silos or pits. The average holding capacity of the pit was some 1.5 or 2 tonnes. The only drawback to pit storage was that the complete contents of a pit had to be used immediately once the seal was broken. This rather suggests the pit was entirely set aside for bulk storage either for seed grain or trade or for both. Food grain would have to be stored separately. No doubt the cereal types were also kept separate from one another in bulk storage. Given the variety of crops and expected tonnage maybe as many as five storage pits would be in use in any one winter. For successful storage, experiment has shown that the removal of the awns from the ears is quite critical and we can therefore be sure that the harvest was processed more or less as soon as it reached the farmstead from the fields. The filling and sealing of the pits with dung or clay is quite straightforward and removes the physical problem of surface storage. Food grain was undoubtedly stored above ground, perhaps in one of the ubiquitous four-post structures which are normally interpreted as granaries. However, the actual bulk of food grain in comparison to the pits is quite small. Given the average annual consumption of flour in a mixed diet as 60 kilos, supplies for ten people would occupy just over a cubic metre. Ideally such a small quantity would best be kept within the kitchen area where it could be under constant surveillance against deterioration. Also it would be far less tedious to reduce to pure seed form from the spikelets only as much as was needed each day. Seed grain, of course, can be planted in spikelet form.

Within the context of the harvest there was no doubt an autumn cull of livestock, the very old and the very young being the most likely victims. Not that a wholesale slaughter was in any way necessary or desirable. The stock to be carried through the winter would be dictated by the success of the hay, straw and leaf harvests. Those that were slaughtered would have been carefully jointed and salted down or hung from the rafters and gently smoked above the domestic hearth. Nothing would be wasted, hides and skins being cured, sinews kept for binding and bones used for pins, combs and toggles.

The successful gathering in of the harvest was naturally celebrated at the Festival of Lughnasa. Probably the very next day, thick of head, the preparation for autumn sowing began with the carting of the midden, so carefully collected throughout the previous winter and now nicely matured, out to the autumn fields and then spread evenly over the ground. Then the Autumn round of ploughing would begin in earnest. Concentration would focus upon the fields to be sown but the ambition undoubtedly would be to plough all the arable land to open it up and allow the frost to do its work in breaking down the soil and killing off any build-up of microbes. It is unlikely that this was recognized but experience taught that ensuing crops were better after a number of heavy frosts had got to the soil. By the same token it would have been experience which dictated the autumn was only finished by mid-October. And so the agricultural year comes full circle. There are myriads of jobs around the farm and the fields not included in this conjectural review, like the refurbishment of ploughing tackle, mending barns and byres, repairing ravaged thatch: the list is endless. On a farm of any time or place there are always jobs to be done outside the normal flow of the seasonal work. That some jobs never get done indicates the nature of the work load. All the above and much more in a sense 'must have happened' for us to have the archaeological evidence we have. All that is conjectured here is the deductive story behind the carbonized seed, the bone pins, empty pits and patterns of postholes. It is a simple, perhaps simplistic, attempt to understand the agricultural round of the Celtic year in the late first millennium BC.

FURTHER READING

Bowen, H.C. (1961) *Ancient Fields*, London: British Association for the Advancement of Science.

Clarke, A. (1990) *Seeing Beneath the Soil*, London: Batsford.

Fowler, P.J. (1983) *The Farming of Prehistoric Britain*, Cambridge: Cambridge University Press.

Glob, P.V. (1951) *Ard og Plov*, Aarhus Eniversitetsforlaget. Jysk Arkaeologisk, Selskabs Skrifter, vol. 1.

Green, M.G. (1992) *Animals in Celtic Life and Myth*, London: Routledge, 5–43.

Harding, D.W., Blake, I.M. and Reynolds, P.J. (1993) *An Iron Age Settlement in Dorset: excavation and reconstruction*, Edinburgh: University of Edinburgh, Department of Archaeology Monograph Series 1.

Meniel, P. (1987) *Chasse et élevage chez les Gaulois (450–2 av J.-C.)*, Paris: Errance.

Reynolds, P.J. (1978) 'The experimental storage of grain in underground silos', Ph.D. thesis, Leicester University.

—— (1979) *Iron Age Farm*, London: British Museum.

—— (1987) *Ancient Farming*, Princes Risborough: Shire Archaeology, no. 50.

—— (1988) 'Arquelogia experimental. Una perspectiva de futur', Euro Editorial, Universitaria de Vic, Catalonia.

PART V

THE ECONOMY

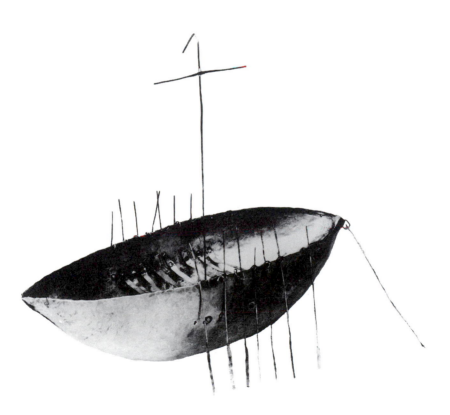

RESOURCES AND INDUSTRY

— •◦• —

Peter S. Wells

INTRODUCTION

Under 'resources' I consider the materials that Celtic peoples extracted from their natural environment for purposes of manufacturing and building. Under 'industry', I treat the manufacturing processes by which they transformed raw materials into finished goods.

The resource procurement and industrial activities of the Celtic peoples must be understood in the context of social and economic changes taking place at the end of the Iron Age. We can distinguish three main periods of development, though we must bear in mind that these are constructs that we impose upon continuous cultural processes. Between 600 and 400 BC, centres of economic activity emerged in temperate Europe that formed foci for these activities. Between 400 and 200 BC, during a time for which we have historical and archaeological evidence of Celtic peoples moving to other regions of Europe, centres were few in number. Starting around 200 BC, the great fortified settlements known as oppida served as focal points for large-scale resource procurement and manufacturing.

Most of the resources that Celtic peoples exploited had been utilized earlier (Clark 1952; Jankuhn 1969). In some cases, traditional patterns of resource procurement and industrial activity were intensified, in other cases new technologies were developed. Links to bronze age and neolithic practices are always apparent.

RESOURCES

The peoples of iron age Europe exploited a wide range of resources, including different kinds of stone, timber, clays and mineral ores, as well as salt and graphite, jet, lignite and sapropelite.

Stone was quarried for use in fortification walls and, particularly in the period of the oppida, for pavings for streets and house floors (e.g. Meduna 1970). Different kinds of stone, including sandstone and limestone, were employed for sculpture, many examples of which survive (Megaw and Megaw 1989). Some special kinds of stone were used for decorative and household purposes, for example shale from

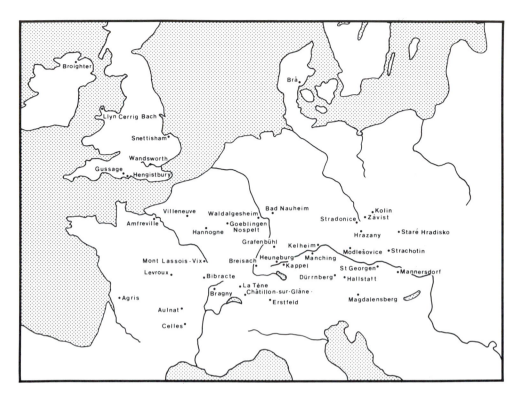

Figure 12.1 Map showing some of the principal sites mentioned in Chapters 12 and 13.

which ornaments, vessels and spindle-whorls were made at Hengistbury Head in Britain (Cunliffe 1987) (Figure 12.1). Stone was also important for grinding grain. Waldhauser's (1981) study of rotary querns in Bohemia demonstrates the complex system of quarrying and trade (Figure 12.2) that brought this important device into general use during the third and second centuries BC.

Wood was the primary substance for construction of buildings of all kinds, and at the oppida large quantities of timber were employed for building the walls. Wood was important for weapons (especially spear shafts and shields), tools, furniture, vessels and vehicles, including wagons, carts and boats, as well as for sculpture. In most environments in temperate Europe, wood does not survive from the Iron Age; only under special circumstances is wood preserved, as in the marshy lakeshore at La Tène (Vouga 1923).

Clays were extracted from the ground for the manufacture of pottery and for daub for the walls of buildings, as well as for constructing ovens, kilns and furnaces. In most regions of temperate Europe, good clays were readily available, and technical studies (Cumberpatch and Pawlikowski 1988) indicate that most communities used local clays rather than bringing material in from outside.

In contrast to copper and tin, iron was available locally to most communities in temperate Europe. In the hilly uplands of central and western Europe that formed

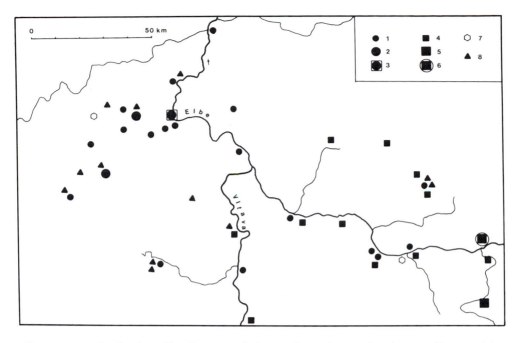

Figure 12.2 Distribution of late iron age grindstones in northern Bohemia, according to origin of raw material: 1 – quartz porphyry, one object, 2 – two or more objects, 3 – source; 4 – phonolite of Kunětická Hora type, one object, 5 – two or more objects, 6 – source; 7 – basalt of Mayen type, from the Middle Rhineland of Germany; 8 – other. (Adapted from Waldhauser 1981: 198, map 2.)

the heartland of the Celtic world, rich surface deposits of iron ore often required little mining technology for their extraction. Iron began to replace bronze as the principal material for tools and weapons at the start of the Iron Age, in the period 800–600 BC, and in the fourth and third centuries BC the exploitation of iron deposits increased greatly. By the time of the oppida, beginning around 200 BC, very sizeable quantities of iron ore were mined and smelted (Pleiner 1980). At virtually all of the oppida, we have indications of iron-making. At Manching, for example, bog iron ore was extracted (Jacobi 1974), and at Kelheim, iron was mined by means of pits dug into the limestone covering layer (Schwarz *et al.* 1966).

Although iron replaced bronze for tools and weapons, bronze continued in use for ornaments such as fibulae, pendants and bracelets; vessels including cauldrons and jugs; figurines; and coins. Some of the new bronze objects may have been made from old metal still in circulation or discovered in hoards dating from the Bronze Age, but copper and tin mining continued in the Iron Age at deposits that had been exploited earlier (Pittioni 1976). Unlike iron, these metals do not occur widely in nature, and most communities had to rely on trade systems to obtain them.

Gold was probably obtained principally from mountain streams. At Modlešovice near Strakonice in Bohemia, remains of gold-washing operations, including wooden troughs, dated to La Tène B2 (about 300–250 BC), have been identified (Pauli 1974).

In the final centuries of the Iron Age, much of the gold used in coins and rings may have derived from gold imported from the Mediterranean world, partly in the form of payment to Celtic mercenaries who served in armies in east Mediterranean lands (Szabo 1991).

Silver is rare in iron age temperate Europe until the latter half of the second century BC, when silver coinage began north of the Alps (Krämer 1971). Much of the silver probably arrived through interaction with the Roman world. Celtic and Roman silver coins are common north of the Alps during the final century and a half before Christ.

Salt was procured through underground mining and through evaporation. Maier (1974: 328) indicates 350 known sites of salt extraction in Europe dating from Neolithic times on. The best evidence from the Celtic period comes from the salt mines at Hallstatt and at the Dürrnberg in the Austrian Alps. Those mines yield information about technology and scale of mining, from about 1000 BC to the end of the prehistoric Iron Age. The evidence from the mines and the associated cemeteries demonstrates a relatively large-scale and highly organized procurement technology, as well as a profitable enterprise, to judge by the trade goods present in the graves (Pauli 1978). There is evidence of salt evaporation at numerous sites throughout Europe (Nenquin 1961), for example at Seille in France, Bad Nauheim in Germany, and Hengistbury Head in Britain.

A substantial industry developed in the extraction of graphite-bearing clays for the manufacture of pottery. In the Bronze and Early Iron Ages, graphite was favoured as a surface decoration on fine pottery, and in the Early La Tène period some communities began making pottery of a natural graphite–clay mix. During the second and final centuries BC, pottery of this composition was very actively manufactured in the Celtic lands east of the Rhine (Figure 12.3). At Manching, 24 per cent of the sherds studied came from graphite–clay vessels, and comparable quantities appear at other oppida east of the Rhine, as well as at smaller settlements (Kappel 1969).

Different forms of coal were mined for the manufacture of personal ornaments. Jet and lignite were extracted and cut into ring jewellery and beads, especially in the Early Iron Age (Rochna 1961), and sapropelite was used for bracelets in the Late Iron Age (Rochna and Mädler 1974).

INDUSTRY

Most of the goods manufactured by the iron age Celts that survive archaeologically can be divided into four main functional categories – tools, weapons, containers and personal ornaments. Discussion here focuses on these. Other categories of manufactured objects are not as well represented in the archaeological record, principally because they are less well preserved. They include textiles (Hald 1980), furniture (Biel 1985), wheeled vehicles (*Vierrädrige Wagen der Hallstattzeit* 1987) and boats (Ellmers 1969).

Manufactured objects belonging to the four principal categories served two main kinds of purpose. One was utilitarian – iron axes were used for cutting wood,

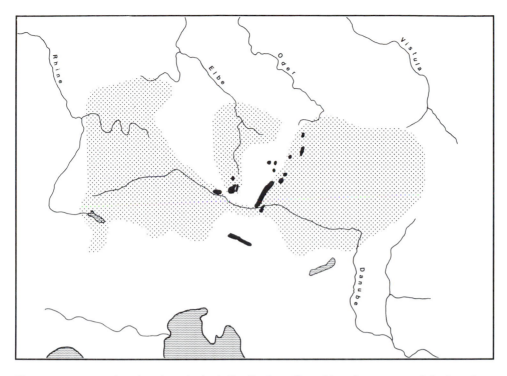

Figure 12.3 Map showing the principal distribution of graphite–clay pottery of the Late Iron Age (shaded areas) and natural deposits of graphite–clay (black areas). (Adapted from Kappel 1969: 40, fig. 11 and map 2.)

weapons for fighting, and pots for holding food. The other purpose was expressive – to communicate information (Douglas and Isherwood 1979). Fibulae and bracelets were often highly ornate and individualized – no two were exactly alike. Pauli (1972) has shown that particular items of personal ornamentation were associated with specific categories of persons, a pattern conforming to what we know about the role of costume in folk traditions (Bogatyrev 1971). Tools in iron age Europe are rarely ornamented, yet Rybová and Motyková (1983) have presented arguments for interpreting hoards of iron tools as votive deposits, used to communicate with supernatural powers rather than for purely utilitarian purposes. Weapons, especially swords, frequently bear decoration. Both pottery and metal containers are often ornamented in ways that communicated information.

Tools

Most of the tools that survive from the Iron Age are made of iron. By the time of the oppida, in the second and final centuries BC, some 200 distinct types of iron tools can be identified, serving a wide range of purposes (Jacobi 1974). These include metalworking, carpentry, agriculture, mining, fishing, hunting, textile production, leatherworking and cooking. Other implements include medical instruments, equipment for the hearth, locks and keys, and fittings for harnesses and wagons. Metallographic analyses indicate techniques employed in the manufacture of tools. Pleiner (1968) has shown that already at the start of the Iron Age, around 800 BC, some smiths had mastered the techniques for producing fine, hard and sharp cutting-edges by carburizing blades to make the iron–carbon alloy, steel. By the final centuries before Christ, smiths were regularly applying specialized welding techniques for producing sharp steel blades and utilizing other properties of iron, such as the toughness of wrought iron, for implements such as nails. Pleiner (1962) provides an overview of the techniques utilized by Celtic smiths.

Weapons

At the start of the Iron Age, some swords, spearheads and helmets were still made of bronze, but several centuries later, iron had nearly completely replaced bronze for weapons. The principal categories were swords, spearheads and shields (the body of the shield was usually of wood, the boss and rim of iron); and, less frequently, helmets. The characteristic burial practice of the period between 400 and 150 BC included placement of weapons in many of the men's graves (Figure 12.4) – typically in between 25 per cent and 75 per cent of men's burials – indicating that a very large number of iron weapons were manufactured. Some weapons, especially swords, were decorated, and the helmets – restricted to a small number of individuals – were sometimes elaborately ornate. Helmets from Agris and Amfreville, both in France, are intricately decorated in gold over iron bases, and the Agris specimen is further ornamented with coral, that from Amfreville with enamel (Megaw and Megaw 1989: 72, pl. X, XI; 112, fig. 154).

The technology of sword manufacture deserves special attention. Swords from about 400 BC to the end of the Celtic Iron Age were long, two-edged, with straight parallel blades and hilt of organic material (Figure 12.4, 1). Analyses show that complex techiques such as packet-welding were employed in manufacture, and the result was characteristically an excellent piece of military hardware. Many of these weapons, especially a group from Switzerland, bear stamped signs, most often symbols but in one case the Celtic name KORISIOS written in Greek letters (Wyss 1956). These signs may identify the smiths who made the swords, and suggest a high degree of specialization in this craft. The scabbards were frequently decorated (De Navarro 1972).

In the final three centuries BC in the British Isles, some weapons were objects of particularly rich adornment. Parade shields, scabbards, helmets, spearheads and harness fittings were often decorated extravagantly, with fine engraved line ornament and enamel inlay (Raftery 1991). These objects were intended to display status. They are often found in wet places, for example the Wandsworth shield bosses from the Thames River and the Lisnacrogher scabbard-plates from a bog in Northern Ireland. The fine craftsmanship suggests a highly organized community of metalworkers that produced special display items for an élite group (Raftery 1991: 557, 562). A large assemblage of weaponry, including many ornate pieces, was found in a bog at Llyn Cerrig Bach in Anglesey, Wales (Fox 1946).

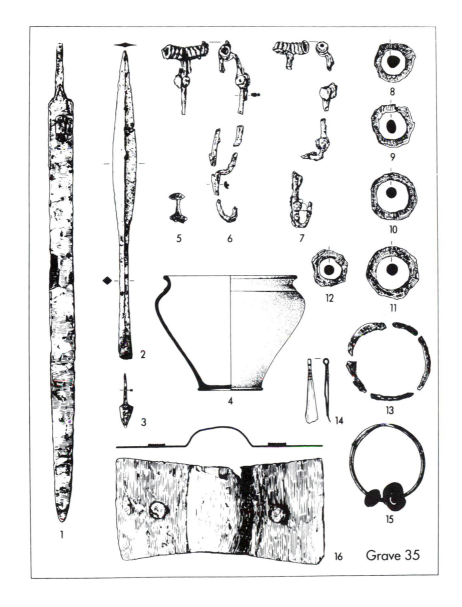

Figure 12.4 Manufactured goods in Grave 35 of the Steinbichl cemetery at Manching, Bavaria, Germany. 1 – iron sword; 2 – iron spearhead; 3 – iron spear shoe; 4 – ceramic vessel; 5–7 – fragmentary iron fibulae; 8–13 – iron rings, probably part of the suspension system for the sword; 14 – bronze tweezers; 15 – bronze ring with two blue glass beads; 16 – iron shield boss. (From Krämer 1985: pl. 21; reproduced with permission from Franz Steiner Verlag, Stuttgart.)

Containers

Pottery is the most common artefactual material recovered on settlement sites in Celtic Europe, and ceramic vessels occur in graves as well. Analyses of clays indicate that most pottery was locally made, and finds of kilns (e.g. Meduna 1970) provide information about scale and character of pottery manufacture. Already at the beginning of the Celtic Iron Age, ceramics included a wide range of different forms, such as large storage vessels, large and small bowls, jugs, plates, dishes and cups, each piece with its specific function (Kossack 1964). The potter's wheel was introduced about 500 BC and became a general piece of pottery-making equipment around the start of La Tène D, about 120 BC (Roualet and Charpy 1987). By the period of the oppida, in the second and final centuries BC, several distinctive categories of pottery were made and used on the large settlements. These included coarse 'domestic' ware, fine wheel-thrown pottery, a special cooking vessel of graphite–clay mix, and thin-walled, highly fired ceramics with often intricate polychrome painted patterns (Figure 12.5). For Manching, we have good statistical data on types. Of 175,142 sherds studied, Stöckli (1979: 3) provides the following percentages: 35 per cent smooth wheel-turned pottery, 25 per cent coarse domestic ware, 24 per cent graphite–clay, 11 per cent fine painted, and 5 per cent non-graphite–clay comb-decorated pottery.

Celtic craftworkers also made metal vessels, especially of bronze, but also, in the early period, of gold. The few gold bowls recovered were apparently intended for display (Kimmig 1991), but the bronze containers served a range of purposes. Common among the metal containers were large, round-bodied vessels called cauldrons or kettles. Bronze cauldrons are found in many richly outfitted burials and in deposits in wet contexts suggestive of votive offerings (Rybová and Motyková 1983). Only at the oppida do we have evidence for their manufacture (Jacobi 1974; Hachmann 1990). Cauldrons may have been used for boiling large quantities of meat or for brewing beer, but it is clear from the evidence of myths and legends that they also served ritual purposes in feasts and other ceremonies (Green 1992: 57–8).

Personal Ornaments

The most common ornaments worn on the person during the Celtic Iron Age can be divided into four main categories – fibulae, ring jewellery (bracelets, leg-rings, finger-rings, ear-rings), belt-hooks and beads. Fibulae were most often of bronze, though in the oppidum period iron fibulae were also common, and iron fibulae are often found in men's graves (Figure 12.4, nos. 6 and 7). In the earlier part of the Celtic period, inlay and attached ornaments of enamel, glass and coral were common on bronze fibulae. Gold and silver fibulae occur infrequently. We have evidence for on-site manufacture of fibulae from throughout the Celtic Iron Age. The evidence includes moulds in which the fibula bows were cast, and partly finished fibulae. Fibulae occur in graves, especially in women's burials (Figure 12.6, 3), on settlements and in hoards and votive deposits. Their utilitarian purpose was to hold together garments at the shoulder, but they played an important communicative function too, in transmitting information about the wearer, as Pauli (1972) has shown. For the archaeologist, fibulae are important as chronological markers, because the fashion for particular types changed rapidly.

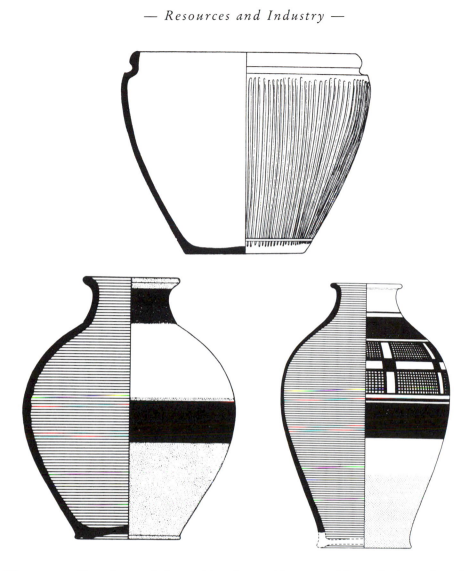

Figure 12.5 *Top:* characteristic graphite–clay cooking pot with comb decoration, from Manching. (From Kappel 1969: pl. 1, no. 4.) *Bottom left:* jar of fine pottery with painted band decoration, from Manching. (Maier 1970: pl. 5, no. 120.) *Bottom right:* high jar of fine pottery with painted band and cross-hatch decoration, from Manching. (Maier 1970: pl. 82, no. 1177.) (All reproduced with permission from Franz Steiner Verlag, Stuttgart.)

Ring jewellery was common and is found particularly in burials, but also in hoard deposits, especially in the final two centuries before Christ. Bronze is the most common material (Figure 12.6, no. 4), but iron rings also occur, and gold rings are found in special contexts, in rich burials of the period 550–400 BC and in hoard deposits from 150–50 BC. In Britain, of special significance are large numbers of gold torques made in East Anglia during the final century BC. At Snettisham, eight sets of

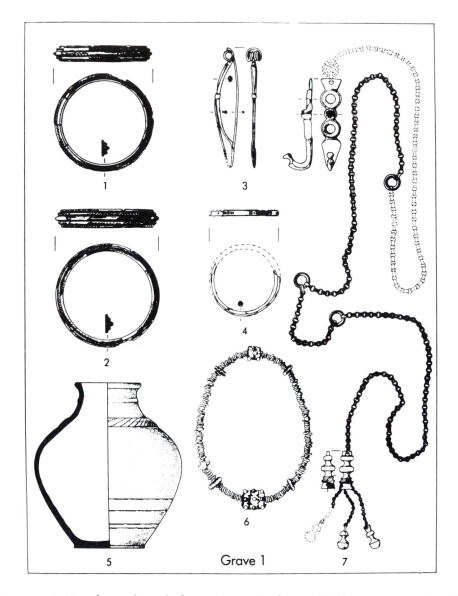

Figure 12.6 Manufactured goods from Grave 1 in the Steinbichl cemetery at Manching, Bavaria, Germany. 1, 2 – blue glass bracelets; 3 – bronze fibula; 4 – bronze bracelet; 5 – ceramic vessel; 6 – 201 glass and two amber beads; 7 – bronze chain belt. (From Krämer 1985: pl. 1; reproduced with permission from Franz Steiner Verlag, Stuttgart.)

objects were found on a field, containing a total of at least sixty-one torques, as well as numerous coins, some bracelets and pieces of gold and tin (Raftery 1991: 565–6). Silver rings are less common than gold. Bronze rings, especially neck-rings, are often ornamented with enamel inlay. Glass rings came into fashion around the middle of the third century BC. They are frequent in women's burials (Figure 12.6, nos. 1 and 2), and fragmentary rings are numerous on settlement sites (Gebhard 1989; Venclová 1990). Sapropelite bracelets are common burial goods and occur in fragmentary form on oppidum settlements (Rochna 1961).

Chain belts made of bronze links are a form of ring jewellery. Like the glass bracelets, they are common in women's graves (Figure 12.6, no. 7) of La Tène C (about 250–120 BC). The decorative hooks are often ornamented with enamel.

Belt-hooks of both bronze and iron are common in men's and women's graves. Many are highly ornamental, especially in the earlier periods. Like other categories of personal ornament, they were worn in visible locations on the body and probably served to communicate information about the wearer.

Glass beads of many different forms, sizes and patterns are common, especially in graves of women (Figure 12.6, no. 6) and children, but also on settlements (Haevernick 1960; Venclová 1990). Amber was also a favoured material for beads, as were bone and antler.

THE ORGANIZATION OF RESOURCE PROCUREMENT AND INDUSTRY

In order to gain information about the organization of resource exploitation and industry during prehistoric Celtic times, we need to examine available archaeological evidence at the production sites, and consider it in the context of economic and social patterns. For discussion here, I divide the Celtic Iron Age into three periods, Early (600–400 BC), Middle (400-200 BC) and Late (200 BC–Roman conquest). During each of these periods, most Celtic communities across Europe shared certain features of economic and social organization. Common types of objects found, and similar settlement and burial patterns throughout much of Celtic Europe, suggest roughly similar economic, social and political structures. In every period, each household carried out craft activities to fill the needs of the family unit. My concern here is rather with community-level production.

Early Celtic Iron Age (600–400 BC)

The clearest evidence for production in this period is at the salt mines at Hallstatt and at the Dürrnberg. In both places, the evidence indicates large-scale, specialized mining. For both sites, the question of leadership and command is difficult to answer. Although there are variations in the wealth of individual graves, in neither cemetery are there any exceptionally richly outfitted burials, as might befit a potentate who gave orders and profited from the enterprise. The skeletal evidence at the Dürrnberg shows that the people buried in well-equipped graves were the ones who did the physical labour. This physical anthropological evidence supports Pauli's (1978) use of the analogy of medieval mining communities in central Europe, where the miners were free workers who contracted out their labour to landowners in exchange for a share of the profits. Maier (1974: 338) interprets the evidence from the two salt-mining sites to indicate the existence of family enterprises operating side by side at the two locations.

From this period, a number of centres have been identified that represent the first towns north of the Alps. They are characterized by more abundant habitation remains, indicating larger populations, than other settlements, and by evidence of substantial manufacturing and trade activity in a variety of materials. Well-documented examples include Mont Lassois (Joffroy 1960) and Bragny (Feugère and Guillot 1986) in France, Châtillon-sur-Glâne in Switzerland (Schwab 1975), and the Heuneburg in south-west Germany (Kimmig 1983). These sites yield evidence for on-site iron-smithing and bronze-casting, bone and antler carving, lignite and jet cutting, and working of exotic substances such as amber and coral. Mansfeld's (1973) study of fibulae and Dämmer's (1978) research on painted pottery suggest that workshops at these centres produced goods for the surrounding countryside (Wells 1987). The richly outfitted burials associated with the centres have been interpreted as reflecting a marked social hierarchy. Links between craft production and rich graves (special craft products, including bronze vessels and gold ornaments, occur in the graves) make it likely that craftworkers at the centres were under the control of the local élite group. In regions where there were no such centres, ironworking and bronze-casting were carried out by many small communities, as for example at Niedererlbach in Bavaria (Koch and Kohnke 1988).

For extractive industries in iron, Driehaus (1965) has called attention to the association between ore deposits and rich Early La Tène (500–400 BC) burials in the western Middle Rhineland, and has suggested that the wealth in southern imports, local fine crafts products and gold ornaments in these graves derived from exploitation of the iron resources and from trade in the metal. Pauli (1974) proposed a similar model of early La Tène wealth based on exploitation of resources in Bohemia, drawing on potentially analogous evidence from the medieval period.

Middle Period (400–200 BC)

Few centres of the kind cited above existed during this period in temperate Europe. Small communities characterized all of the landscapes (on community size, see Wells 1984: 133), and expression of marked status differences in burials decreased. The activities of the crafts industries that had produced such special goods as bronze vessels and gold ornaments declined.

The two industries that are best represented are ironworking and bronze-casting. In the thousands of cemeteries known from this period, men's graves are character-istically equipped with iron weapons, women's with bronze jewellery, sometimes in substantial quantities (Bujna 1982; Krämer 1985). Much more iron was produced than before, and the techniques of manufacture were refined. Since iron is widely available in temperate Europe, most communities probably produced their own metal. Bujna (1982: 421) attributes the great increase in quantities of iron produced to the needs of military expeditions that Celtic peoples made to Italy, Greece and eastern Europe. Even though communities were small, the practice of burying weapons meant regular consumption of metal – buried swords, spears and shields required replacement. Smiths working in the small communities of this period are unlikely to have been full-time specialists, unless they made iron implements for other communities besides their own.

Similarly, the occurrence of sizeable amounts of bronze jewellery in women's graves indicates ongoing production of personal ornaments. Much of the jewellery shows highly skilled workmanship, suggesting part-time if not full-time specialist bronzesmiths.

Late Period (200 BC–Roman conquest)

The final two centuries before Christ represent the culmination in resource extraction and industrial activity in Celtic Europe. The quantities of many materials extracted from the environment, especially iron for tools and weapons and stone and wood for the construction of oppidum walls, was much larger than ever before. Many of the products of manufacturing activity indicate a level of specialization that researchers believe results from a profound change in the organization of manufacturing, from a largely domestic, kin-based system to one based instead on specialized occupational activity (Meduna 1980: 157; Audouze and Buchsenschutz 1989: 303; Gebhard 1989: 185).

The oppida were centres for resource exploitation and industrial production of goods. The evidence is most abundant at Manching, but similar results are emerging from other sites, especially among the intensively researched Bohemian and Moravian oppida. Serial or mass-production is first evident at the oppida with large quantities of objects such as knives, axes, hammers, nails and clamps forged of iron (Jacobi 1974). Gebhard (1989) interprets the great quantities of glass bracelets manufactured as indicating mass-production aimed at export trade.

The fast-turning potter's wheel came into general use late in the second century BC, and led to mass-production of ceramics at the oppida and to increased standization of vessel forms across Celtic Europe (Arcelin 1981; Roualet and Charpy 1987). In the large quantities and striking uniformity of vessels at the major oppida, Pingel (1971: 82) sees evidence for centralized pottery production.

For Bibracte, Hrazany, Manching, and some other oppida, investigators have interpreted spatial evidence on the excavated surfaces as indicating special areas where production activities were concentrated (Capelle 1979). Yet others challenge this interpretation. For Bibracte, it is not clear whether the workshop quarter belonged to the pre-Roman or to the post-conquest settlement (Duval 1991). At other oppida, not enough evidence has been collected to speak confidently of industrial areas within the settlements. Current results from Staré Hradisko (Meduna 1970; Čižmář 1989a) and Závist (Čižmář 1989b; Motyková, Drda and Rybová 1990) seem to indicate instead many small-scale production areas within the oppidum. At many sites, such as Hrazany in Bohemia (Jansová 1987: 71), ironworking and bronze-casting locations have been identified near gates in the walls, presumably because metal production generates noxious fumes that people wanted to keep away from the middle of the settlement. The accumulating evidence for industry at the oppida suggests full-time industrial specialists at some sites. Since at present we know little about the leadership structure at the oppida, it is difficult to suggest who directed, and benefited from, the work of the specialists.

Fundamental to the growth of the oppida and of the industries that they housed was the great increase in agricultural productivity during this period. The proliferation of new iron tools made that change possible (Meduna 1980: 154). The iron ploughshare, coulter, and scythe first came into regular use, and they made possible faster ploughing, opening of heavier, more fertile soils, and more efficient harvesting of grasses for fodder. The rotary quern increased the efficiency of grinding grain several hundred per cent, according to modern experiments (Waldhauser 1981).

Recent discovery of evidence for manufacturing, often on a substantial scale, at smaller, unenclosed settlements necessitates a rethinking of the organization of industry at the end of the Iron Age. At a growing number of excavated small settlements such as Aulnat (Collis 1980) and Levroux (Audouze and Buchsenschutz 1989: 306–7) in south-western France, and Berching-Pollanten in northern Bavaria (Fischer, Rieckhoff-Pauli and Spindler 1984), ironworking, bronze-casting, and coin-minting were carried out. Mšec in Bohemia was a specialized iron-smelting site (Pleiner and Princ 1984). At Strachotin in Moravia (Čižmář 1987), iron-working and textile production are apparent, and pottery appears to have been manufactured on a large scale, suggestive of specialized production for export. In Britain, the small settlement of Gussage All Saints (Wainwright 1979) yielded abundant evidence for the casting of bronze harness ornaments, almost certainly for use by persons who did not live in the community. It is apparent now that the oppida, while clearly focal points for intensive and specialized production for surrounding landscapes, did not maintain monopolies on such production. Considerably more excavation, on both oppidum and smaller settlements, as well as more detailed comparison of the products of different communities, is needed, before we can develop a better understanding of the organization of industry in this period.

It is significant that in this final stage of the Celtic Iron Age, metal tools appeared in graves (Krämer 1985: 34). At St Georgen in Lower Austria (Taus 1963), a set of smith's tools, including tongs, a hammer and shears, accompanied a burial. (The find at Celles in south-western France, long considered contents of a smith's grave outfitted with a large quantity of iron tools, has been reinterpreted recently as a possible settlement find [Guillaumet 1983]). The burial of tools with deceased workers may be symbolic of the increased specialization of such crafts as iron production, pottery manufacture and jewellery-making in the final two centuries before Christ.

The large-scale, specialized industrial activity at the major settlements of the Late Iron Age was targeted, at least in large part, at export trade (Bujna 1982: 421). Distributions of such products of Celtic workshops as painted pottery, graphite–clay ceramics, glass bracelets, bronze cauldrons and iron swords, in lands beyond the Celtic territories, illustrates the important connection between industry and trade at the end of the Iron Age.

REFERENCES

Arcelin, P. (1981) 'Les céramiques de type celtique en Provence', *Revue Archéologique de l'Est et du Centre-Est* 32: 33–66.
Audouze, F. and Buchsenschutz, O. (1989) *Villes, villages et campagne de l'Europe celtique*, Paris.

Biel, J. (1985) *Der Keltenfürst von Hochdorf*, Stuttgart.

Bogatyrev, P. (1971) *Functions of Folk Costume in Moravian Slovakia*, The Hague.

Bujna, J. (1982) 'Spiegelung der Sozialstruktur auf latènezeitlichen Gräberfeldern im Karpathenbecken', *Památky Archeologické*, 73: 312–431.

Capelle, T. (1979) 'Bemerkungen zum keltischen Handwerk', *Boreas* 2: 62–75.

Čižmář, M. (1987) 'Laténské Sídliště ze Strachotína, Okr. Břeclav' ('Eine latènezeitliche Siedlung aus Strachotín, Bez. Břeclav'), *Památky Archeologické* 73: 205–30.

—— (1989a) 'Erforschung des keltischen Oppidums Staré Hradisko in den Jahren 1983–1988 (Mähren, ČSSR)', *Archäologisches Korrespondenzblatt* 19: 265–8.

—— (1989b) 'Pozdně Laténské Osídlení Předhradí Závisti' ('Die spätlatènezeitliche Besiedlung der Vorburg von Závist'), *Památky Archeologické* 80: 59–122.

Clark, J.G.D. (1952) *Prehistoric Europe: the economic basis*, London.

Collis, J. (1980) 'Aulnat and urbanisation in France', *Archaeological Journal* 137: 40–9.

Cumberpatch, C.G. and Pawlikowski, M. (1988) 'Preliminary results of mineralogical analyses of late La Tène painted pottery from Czechoslovakia', *Archeologické Rozhledy* 40: 184–93, 237–40.

Cunliffe, B. (1987) *Hengistbury Head Dorset, 1: The Prehistoric and Roman Settlement, 3500 BC–AD 500*, Oxford.

Dämmer, H.-W. (1978) *Die bemalte Keramik der Heuneburg*, Mainz.

De Navarro, J.M. (1972) *The Finds from the Site of La Tène: the scabbards and the swords found in them*, London.

Douglas, M. and Isherwood, B. (1979) *The World of Goods: towards an anthropology of consumption*, New York.

Driehaus, J. (1965) '"Fürstengräber" und Eisenerze zwischen Mittelrhein, Mosel und Saar', *Germania* 43: 32–49.

Duval, A. (1991) 'Celtic society', in S. Moscati *et al.* (eds) *The Celts*, 485–90.

Ellmers, D. (1969) 'Keltischer Schiffbau', *Jahrbuch des Römisch-Germanischen Zentralmuseums* 16: 73–122.

Feugère, M. and Guillot, A. (1986) 'Fouilles de Bragny', *Revue Archéologique de l'Est et du Centre-Est* 37: 159–221.

Fischer, T., Rieckhoff-Pauli, S. and Spindler, K. (1984) 'Grabungen in der spätkeltischen Siedlung im Sulztal bei Berching-Pollanten', *Germania* 62: 311–63.

Fox, C. (1946) *A Find of the Early Iron Age from Llyn Cerrig Bach, Anglesey*, Cardiff.

Gebhard, R. (1989) *Der Glasschmuck aus dem Oppidum von Manching*, Wiesbaden.

Green, M. (1992) *Dictionary of Celtic Myth and Legend*, London.

Guillaumet, J.-P. (1983) 'Le materiel du tumulus de Celles (Cantal)', in J. Collis, A. Duval and R. Périchon (eds) *Le Deuxième Age du fer en Auvergne et en Forez*, Sheffield, 189–211.

Hachmann, R. (1990) 'Gundestrup-Studien: Untersuchungen zu den spätkeltischen Grundlagen der frühgermanischen Kunst', *Bericht der Römisch-Germanischen Kommission* 71: 565–903.

Haevernick, T.E. (1960) *Die Glasarmringe und Ringperlen der Mittel- und Spätlatènezeit auf dem europäischen Festland*, Bonn.

Hald, M. (1980) *Ancient Danish Textiles from Bogs and Burials*, Copenhagen.

Jacobi, G. (1974) *Werkzeug und Gerät aus dem Oppidum von Manching*, Wiesbaden.

Jankuhn, H. (1969) *Vor- und Frühgeschichte vom Neolithikum bis zur Völkerwanderungszeit*, Stuttgart.

Jansová, L. (1987) *Hrazany. Das keltische Oppidum in Böhmen, 1: Die Befestigung und die anliegende Siedlungsbebauung*, Prague.

Joffroy, R. (1960) *L'Oppidum de Vix et la civilisation hallstatiene finale dans l'Est de la France*, Dijon.

Kappel, I. (1969) *Die Graphittonkeramik von Manching*, Wiesbaden.

Kimmig, W. (1983) *Die Heuneburg an der oberen Donau*, Stuttgart.

—— (1991) 'Edelmetallschalen der späten Hallstatt- und frühen Latènezeit', *Archäologisches Korrespondenzblatt* 21: 241- 53.

Koch, H. and Kohnke, H.-G. (1988) 'Neue Ausgrabungen in Niedererlbach, Lkr. Landshut (Niederbayern)', *Bayerische Vorgeschichtsblätter*, 53: 47–75.

Kossack, G. (1964) 'Trinkgeschirr als Kultgerät der Hallstattzeit', in P. Grimm (ed.) *Varia Archaeologica*, 96–105, Berlin.

Krämer, W. (1971) 'Silberne Fibelpaare aus dem letzten vorchristlichen Jahrhundert', *Germania* 49: 111–32.

—— (1985) *Die Grabfunde von Manching und die latènezeitlichen Flachgräber in Südbayern*, Wiesbaden.

Maier, F. (1970) *Die bemalte Spätlatène-Keramik von Manching*, Wiesbaden.

—— (1974) 'Gedanken zur Entstehung der industriellen Grosssiedlung der Hallstatt- und Latènezeit auf dem Dürrnberg bei Hallein', *Germania* 52: 326–47.

Mansfeld, G. (1973) *Die Fibeln der Heuneburg*, Berlin.

Meduna, J. (1970) 'Das keltische Oppidum Staré Hradisko in Mähren', *Germania* 48: 34–59.

—— (1980) *Die latènezeitlichen Siedlungen in Mähren*, Brno.

Megaw, R. and Megaw, V. (1989) *Celtic Art*, London.

Moscati, S. *et al.* (eds) (1991) *The Celts*, New York.

Motyková, K., Drda, P. and Rybová, A. (1990) 'Die Siedlungsstruktur des Oppidums Závist', *Archäologisches Korrespondenzblatt* 20: 415–26.

Nenquin, J. (1961) *Salt: a study in economic prehistory*, Bruges.

Pauli, L. (1972) *Untersuchungen zur Späthallstattkultur in Nordwürttemberg*, Hamburg.

—— (1974) 'Der goldene Steig: Wirtschaftsgeographisch-archäologische Untersuchungen im östlichen Mitteleuropa', in G. Kossack and G. Ulbert (eds), *Studien zur vor- und frühgeschichtlichen Archäologie*, Munich, 115–39.

—— (1978) *Der Dürrnberg bei Hallein III*, Munich.

Pingel, V. (1971) *Die glatte Drehscheiben-Keramik von Manching*, Wiesbaden.

Pittioni, R. (1976) 'Bergbau: Kupfererz', in J. Hoops (ed.) *Reallexikon der germanischen Altertumskunde*, 2nd edn, II, Berlin, 251–6.

Pleiner, R. (1962) *Staré Evropské Kovářství (Alteuropäisches Schmiedehandwerk)*, Prague.

—— (1968) 'Schmiedetechnik der Hallstattzeit im Lichte der Untersuchung des Hortfundes von Schlöben', *Archeologické Rozhledy* 20: 33–42.

—— (1980) 'Early iron metallurgy in Europe', in T.A. Wertime and J.D. Muhly (eds) *The Coming of the Age of Iron*, New Haven, 375–415.

Pleiner, R. and Princ, M. (1984) 'Die latènezeitliche Eisenverhüttung und die Untersuchung einer Rennschmelze in Mšec, Böhmen', *Památky Archeologické* 75: 133–80.

Raftery, B. (1991) 'The island Celts', in S. Moscati *et al.* (eds) *The Celts*, 555–72.

Rochna, O. (1961) 'Zur Herkunft der Manchinger Sapropelit-Ringe', *Germania* 39: 329–54.

Rochna, O. and Mädler, K. (1974) 'Die Sapropelit- und Gagatfunde vom Dürrnberg', in F. Moosleitner, L. Pauli and E. Penninger (eds) *Der Dürrnberg bei Hallein II*, Munich, 153–67.

Roualet, P. and Charpy, J.J. (1987) *La Céramique peinte gauloise en Champagne*, Epernay.

Rybová, A. and Motyková, K. (1983) 'Der Eisendepotfund der Latènezeit von Kolín', *Památky Archeologické* 74: 96–174.

Schwab, H. (1975) 'Châtillon-sur-Glâne: ein Fürstensitz der Hallstattzeit bei Freiburg im Uechtland', *Germania* 53: 79–84.

Schwarz, K., Tillmann, H. and Treibs, W. (1966) 'Zur spätlatènezeitlichen und mittelalterlichen Eisenerzgewinnung auf der südlichen Frankenalb bei Kelheim', *Jahresbericht der bayerischen Bodendenkmalpflege*, 6/7: 35–66.

Stöckli, W.E. (1979) *Die Grob- und Importkeramik von Manching*, Wiesbaden.

Szabo, M. (1991) 'Mercenary activity', in S. Moscati *et al.* (eds) *The Celts*, 333–6.

Taus, M. (1963) 'Ein spätlatènezeitliches Schmied-Grab aus St. Georgen am Steinfeld, p.B. St. Pölten, NÖ', *Archaeologia Austriaca*, 34: 13–16.

Venclová, N. (1990) *Prehistoric Glass in Bohemia*, Prague.

Vierrädrige Wagen der Hallstattzeit (1987) Mainz.

Vouga, P. (1923) *La Tène*, Leipzig.

Wainwright, G.J. (1979) *Excavations at Gussage All Saints*, London.

Waldhauser, J. (1981) 'Keltské Rotacni Mlyny v Čechách' ('Keltische Drehmühlen in Böhmen'), *Památky Archeologické*, 72: 153–221.

Wells, P.S. (1984) *Farms, Villages, and Cities: commerce and urban origins in late prehistoric Europe*, Ithaca, NY.

——— (1987) 'Sociopolitical change and core–periphery interactions: an example from early iron age Europe', in K.M. Trinkaus (ed.) *Polities and Partitions: human boundaries and the growth of complex societies*, Tempe, AZ, 141–55.

Wyss, R. (1956) 'The sword of Korisios', *Antiquity* 30: 27–8.

TRADE AND EXCHANGE

— ·•· —

Peter S. Wells

INTRODUCTION

Trade and exchange – peaceful means by which people obtain goods not available to them in their local environments – are mechanisms complementary to resource procurement and industry. Together they constitute the means by which people acquire things they want. Here I define 'trade' as the peaceful transmission of goods for other goods, and 'exchange' as the transmission of goods primarily for social or political purposes, as in gift exchange or tribute payment. The two blend together in real life, and archaeologically it is not always possible to distinguish between them.

Archaeological evidence demonstrates the regular transmission of goods between peoples inhabiting different regions of Europe at least from the Early Neolithic period onward (Jankuhn 1969), and by the Celtic Iron Age, systems of trade and circulation operated intensively and extensively throughout Europe.

The results of trade are often very apparent archaeologically, in the presence of goods in a context that is foreign to that cultural or physical environment (Stjernquist 1985). Less apparent are the mechanisms of circulation and the meaning of the trade or exchange for the people involved. All systems of trade and exchange depend upon the social and economic structure of the participating communities. The close connection between social systems and circulation of goods is especially clear in the rich burials of Celtic Europe – exotic trade goods from distant lands often distinguish these graves from the majority of burials.

One reason for trade is to obtain raw materials not available in the local environment. We have good evidence during the Celtic Iron Age for trade in iron, copper and tin, graphite, salt, coral, stone, lignite, jet, sapropelite, amber, gold and silver. Communities that did not inhabit lands where these materials were naturally available had to acquire them through trade, though other less peaceful means were probably used sometimes. At the salt-mining sites of Hallstatt and the Dürrnberg, iron deposits in the middle Rhineland, and graphite–clay sources in south-east Bavaria and Bohemia, communities developed to produce raw materials for trade (see Chapter 12 for discussion and references).

The second main reason for trade in Celtic Europe was to acquire manufactured goods. This trade included both circulation between production centres and outlying rural communities, and long-distance trade that supplied exotic goods from other culture-areas. Most such trade in iron age Europe served primarily social purposes – to provide objects to express and enhance status relations – rather than strictly economic purposes. To understand the motives behind most of the circulation of materials in prehistoric Celtic Europe, we have to think of goods in terms of their social and communicative value, as Douglas and Isherwood (1979) have argued.

INTERNAL AND EXTERNAL TRADE AND EXCHANGE: THE GOODS

It is important to distinguish between circulation of goods within the Celtic lands and that between Celtic lands and those of other peoples. For the period between 600 BC and the birth of Christ, similarities in material culture and human behaviour throughout the Celtic lands make it apparent that we are dealing with a single 'culture' on some level (Pauli 1980; Hachmann, Kossack and Kuhn 1962; Moscati *et al.* 1991), though regional variations in style of ornament and in features of burial practice and settlement structure are always present.

Trade within the Celtic lands is apparent both in a variety of raw materials (see above) and in manufactured goods. Metals, salt and substances used for ornaments (lignite and jet, for example) were traded throughout the period, and commerce intensified in the final two centuries of the Iron Age. Circulation of manufactured goods increased greatly at that time, and the evidence shows that pottery, glass ornaments and coins produced at the centres were traded to smaller communities in the countryside. Each category of material provides insight into the character of these trade systems (Kappel 1969; Maier 1970; Gebhard 1989), and coins are among the most informative (Kellner 1990). The place of origin of many Celtic coins can be determined, and large quantities are recovered on settlements and in hoards through-out Europe, providing excellent insight into trade during the final centuries of the Iron Age (Nash 1978; Allen 1980).

In trade and exchange between Celtic lands and other culture-areas, amber from the Baltic region and coral from the Mediterranean are raw materials that were regularly imported. Both were used for ornamentation, carved into beads and as inlay for metal jewellery, and both possessed magical meaning for the Celtic peoples (Pauli 1975). Aside from these substances, trade with foreign lands was primarily in finished goods.

Most striking is the complex of objects from the Mediterranean world that arrived in substantial quantities from the sixth century BC to the time of the Roman conquest. The interaction between Celtic Europe and the Mediterranean societies, of which this trade was a part, was important for economic, social and artistic developments in the second half of the Iron Age (*Les Princes celtes et la Mediterranée* 1988). Predominant among the southern imports are various kinds of bronze and ceramic vessels associated with wine-drinking that were made in Greek, Etruscan and Roman workshops. Ceramic amphorae in which wine was transported occur at the centres of the sixth century BC and at the oppida of the final two centuries BC, as well as in some graves of both periods. The distribution of amphorae (Figure 13.1; Fitzpatrick 1985) reflects primarily the availability of water routes for transportation rather than the distribution of traded wine. Ancient writers mention wooden barrels and skin bags for use in wine transport (Wells 1980: 66), and these containers would have been much more efficient for overland travel.

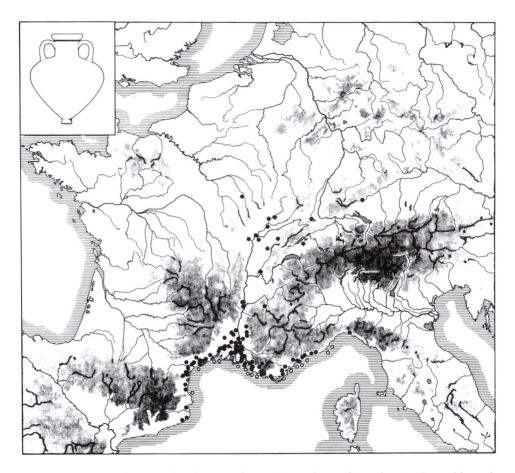

Figure 13.1 Map showing distribution of ceramic amphorae from the Greek world on the shores of the Mediterranean Sea. Profile in upper left indicates shape of the amphorae. Solid dots: land finds. Open dots: amphorae on shipwrecks. Note especially the locations in eastern France, Switzerland and south-western Germany. (From Kimmig 1983: 36, fig. 27; reproduced with permission from the Römisch-Germanisches Zentralmuseum, Mainz.)

The series of imported bronze vessels began with the so-called Rhodian jugs that appear in graves of the first half of the sixth century BC, and continued into the Roman period. The vessels included unique objects such as the Grächwil hydria, the Vix krater and the Hochdorf cauldron, all dating to the sixth century BC, but also undistinctive objects that belong to larger groups such as the Etruscan

Schnabelkannen, mostly of the fifth century BC (Figure 13.2), and the Kelheim and Kaerumgaard-type jugs of the final century BC (Werner 1978). These wine-associated vessel imports, both bronze and ceramic, are most abundant during the sixth and fifth centuries BC and again during the second and first centuries BC (Fischer 1985; Svobodová 1983), but objects such as the bronze buckets from Waldalgesheim in the middle Rhineland and Mannersdorf in Austria, and the two glass masks from St Sulpice on Lake Geneva in Switzerland (Wyss 1989: 167–8) show that this import trade was maintained on some level throughout the Iron Age.

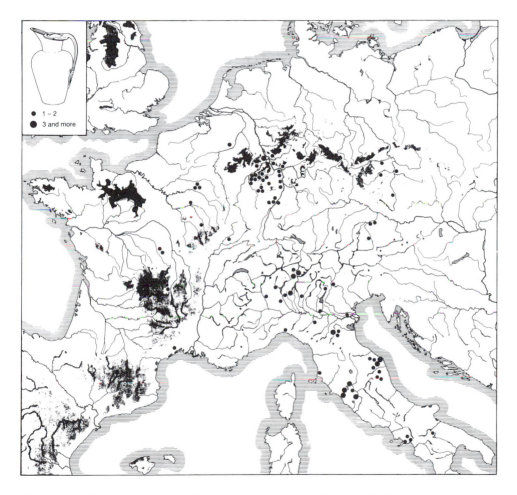

Figure 13.2 Distribution map of Etruscan bronze *Schnabelkannen*. Profile in upper left shows shape of the jugs. Most are believed to have been manufactured at Vulci on the Tyrrhenian coast of Central Italy. Note the dense concentration in the middle Rhineland, and other finds in France to the west and Bohemia and Austria to the east. (From Kimmig 1983: 41, fig. 32; reproduced with permission from the Römisch-Germanisches Zentralmuseum, Mainz.)

Because of the spectacular nature of the Vix krater and other wine-associated imports, the wine trade has attracted considerable research attention, but other categories of imports show that the interaction between the Mediterranean world and central Europe was diverse. For example, the Grafenbühl grave of around 500 BC (Zürn 1970) contained ornamental sphinxes of amber, bone and ivory, and remains of furniture from the Mediterranean world. Grave 6 in the Hohmichele tumulus at the Heuneburg included silk textiles (Hundt 1969), from the East. At the oppida, surgical instruments, balances, mirrors, fibulae, finger-rings, cameos, glass vessels and bone writing implements from the Roman world are well represented (Svobodová 1985). Archaeological evidence for the goods that were traded for all of the Mediterranean imports is sparse. Textual evidence suggests that the Celtic communities were supplying raw materials and organic products – things that would not survive archaeologically in recognizable form (Wells 1984).

Export trade from the Celtic lands in other directions is attested archaeologically, however. Glass ornaments, probably manufactured at the major oppida, are well represented north of the Celtic regions, for example in the Netherlands (Peddemors 1975) and in Thuringia (Lappe 1979), and Gebhard (1989: 185) suggests that the Celtic glass industry was producing specifically for export trade in the final phase of the Iron Age. Graphite–clay pottery has been found at sites in regions north of the Celtic lands as well (Kappel 1969) and was probably an export item. Fine painted pottery of late La Tène type occurs north of the Celtic production areas (Figure 13.3) and apparently was traded into those regions. Iron weapons made by Celtic smiths were traded northward (Eggers 1951: 38; Frey 1986), as were bronze cauldrons, which are well represented on the North European Plain (Redlich 1980) and occur even further north (Hachmann 1990: 652, fig. 24). The stylistically 'Celtic' cauldrons from Denmark, such as those from Brå, Gundestrup and Rynkeby, may have been manufactured in Celtic workshops in central Europe (Frey 1985: 257; Hachmann 1990), but many investigators now argue for a Danish or, in the case of Gundestrup, south-eastern European origin (Megaw and Megaw 1989: 176).

CONTEXT OF TRADE AND EXCHANGE

I distinguish here two levels of context for consideration of trade and exchange. One is the historical and economic context of the Greater Mediterranean world, including the Celtic regions north and west of the Alps, during the second half of the final millennium BC. The other is the specific context of the archaeological sites on which evidence for trade is found.

Peoples of Europe traded with one another regularly from at least the Neolithic period on, but during the Iron Age, trade intensified within temperate Europe, and trade became much more extensive from central Europe outward. In order to understand this growth in trade, we need to view developments in Europe in the context of change in the Greater Mediterranean world, in the sense used by Braudel (1972) in his study of that great geographical entity in late medieval times. By the Iron Age, the peoples of temperate Europe, like others bordering on the civilizations of the

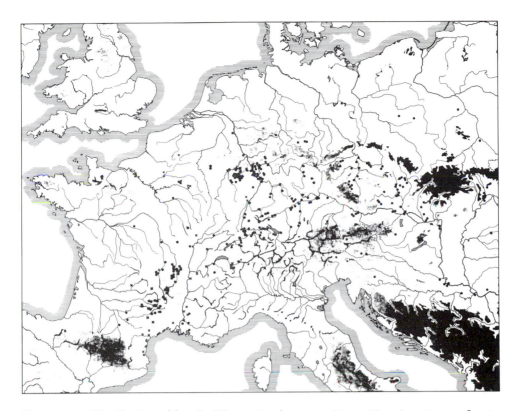

Figure 13.3 Distribution of late La Tène painted pottery. (From Kimmig 1983: 75, fig. 64, adapted from Maier 1970; reproduced with permission from the Römisch-Germanisches Zentralmuseum, Mainz.)

Mediterranean shores, were in contact with peoples such as Greeks, Etruscans and Romans. Similar developments in trade and technology occurred in many different lands on the fringes of the Mediterranean at about the same time. North of the Black Sea and in Iberia, for example, patterns of change were similar to those in Celtic Europe (Boardman 1980).

Amidst growth of connections between the Mediterranean world and temperate Europe, trade interactions intensified during two periods in particular, one in the latter half of the Early Iron Age, 600–450 BC, the other in the final two centuries before Christ. The first was contemporaneous with Greek colonial expansion throughout the Mediterranean Basin (Kimmig 1983; *Les Princes celtes* 1988), the second with the development of mass-production in the Roman world (Dyson 1988) and Roman expansion into southern Gaul during the second century BC (Timpe 1985: 271, 280; Rivet 1988). The changes in trade in Celtic Europe need to be viewed in the context of these related developments (Wells 1984).

Trade goods are found in the context of three principal types of archaeological sites in Celtic Europe – settlements, graves and hoards.

Settlements

During the Iron Age, trade within temperate Europe is evident at most settlements in bronze objects, graphite used for surface colouration and mixed with clay in pottery, glass beads, and other materials. This evidence indicates that virtually all communities were involved in trade on a regular basis. The early iron age centres such as the Heuneburg in south-west Germany and Bragny in France, and the oppida of the Late Iron Age probably manufactured goods for trade to the smaller communities in the countryside (see p. 224), perhaps in a system that brought foodstuffs and other farm and forest products into the centres. But we need to be cautious in hypothesizing such relationships between centres and small communities, because many of the smaller sites also yield evidence of manufacturing (see p. 226). Until we have more information about the small settlements, and technical analyses that indicate the origins of particular goods, we will remain uncertain as to the organization of this internal trade.

The importation of goods from outside Celtic Europe is apparent at many of the centres. The Heuneburg, Mont Lassois and other settlements have yielded sherds of Attic painted pottery, ceramic amphorae from the Mediterranean world, coral, and amber from the Baltic region. These goods are not common on smaller sites, though the recent discovery of Attic red-figure pottery at a small settlement at Hochdorf in south-west Germany (Biel 1991) indicates that further research may change substantially our present view.

The oppida of the final two centuries BC were centres of commerce (Timpe 1985: 267–8), as is apparent in the quantities of Roman imports recovered at them (Svobodová 1983, 1985) and in the growth of industries that operated for export trade. The manufacture of pottery, glass jewellery, sapropelite ornaments, bronze vessels and iron weapons seems to have been geared to some extent towards export trade in this late period. The major oppida are characterized as market-places (Maier 1991) at which local and long-distance commerce were concentrated. Silver and bronze coinage may have developed to serve the needs of the large, commercially focused communities for a standard of exchange (Kellner 1990: 15). Coins are good indicators of trade, because their places of origin can often be determined (Figure 13.4). For example, of the 886 coins recovered at Manching, 58 per cent were minted in southern Germany, 28 per cent in regions to the west, 5 per cent in regions to the east, 3 per cent were Roman, and 6 per cent were unidentifiable (Kellner 1990: 16). At other oppida, too, substantial numbers of coins are of foreign origin.

Graves

The evidence for trade activity from graves parallels that from settlements. Bronze objects, graphite-decorated pottery and glass beads and bracelets frequently occur in graves and reflect local patterns of circulation within temperate Europe. Elaborately constructed graves that contain more and finer local products than most also often have in them imported objects from outside the Celtic area. The Vix grave at Mont Lassois and Grafenbühl at the Hohenasperg, for example, contained many imported luxury goods from the Mediterranean world, including the enormous bronze krater,

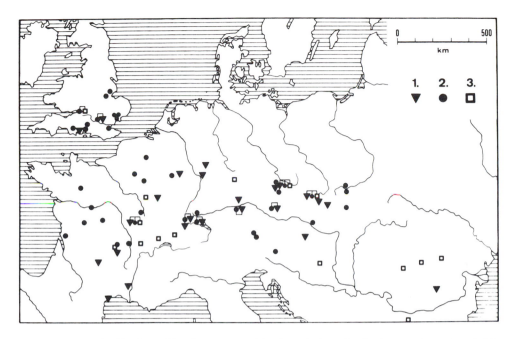

Figure 13.4 Distribution of implements used in the minting of coins in Late Iron Age Celtic Europe. 1 – balances; 2 – moulds for casting coin blanks; 3 – coin dies. (From Steuer 1987: 413, fig. 1; reproduced with permission from Vandenhoeck & Ruprecht, Göttingen.)

two Attic kylikes and an Etruscan jug and basins at Vix, and a bronze tripod, bone, ivory and amber sphinxes and fragments of furniture at Grafenbühl. For unique objects such as the Vix krater, the Grafenbühl tripod and the Grächwil hydria, an exchange mechanism such as gift-giving is more likely than barter trade (see below) to account for their presence in Celtic graves. Lavish and unique Mediterranean imports are less common in the later Iron Age, but wealthy graves then were still characterized by luxury imports from the south. At Hannogne in eastern France, a grave that contained an iron sword and local ornaments also had a bronze jug and pan, pottery and an amphora, all of Roman manufacture (Flouest and Stead 1977). Graves at Goeblingen-Nospelt in Luxembourg (Haffner 1974) and at Welwyn in southern Britain (Stead 1967) dating from the middle and late first century BC (fig. 7.7), contained a large quantity of Roman imports, including ceramic amphorae, many bronze vessels and large quantities of fine pottery.

Hoards

Hoards often contain objects that were made in other regions, and they are some-times interpreted as travelling merchants' deposits. The Erstfeld hoard, from the northern end of an Alpine pass in Switzerland, contained gold rings manufactured in the middle Rhine area (Wyss 1975). Whether the find represents a merchant's cache that was never collected, or an offering for safe passage through the mountains, the find is an important reflection of transmission of precious objects over sizeable distances within temperate Europe.

Hoards of iron ingots are different. They represent the transport of smelted and forged iron from sites of production to places where the metal was to be further processed into needed implements. Several different forms of ingots are known, each concentrated in a particular region of Europe (Jacobi 1974a: 248–53).

During the Late La Tène period, about 120–50 BC, two different types of hoards provide important information about trade. One group contains metal objects, including iron tools and bronze ornaments and vessels. The hoard from Kappel in southern Württemberg had in it a bronze jug from an Italian workshop, along with other bronze vessels and many iron tools (Fischer 1959). Hoards of the other group contain gold and silver, in the form of coins and ring jewellery. The gold and silver coins in these hoards often reflect long-distance trade (Krämer 1971; Furger-Gunti 1982).

MECHANISMS

The archaeological evidence of the results of trade and exchange is relatively straight-forward, and changes in the intensity and directionality of commerce can be identified. Less clear are the mechanisms and organization of Celtic trade. Renfrew's (1975: 42, fig. 10) diagram provides useful models for thinking about the way trade systems work. In order to identify specific mechanisms, we need to use ethnographic and ethno-historic information to generate models for examining prehistoric trade situations. I distinguish here five main categories of trade and exchange mechanisms. Until we develop a better understanding of how to recognize the different mechanisms through their material correlates, using analogy, these suggestions must remain tentative.

Barter Trade

Barter is the exchange of goods for other goods perceived by the participants to be of equal value. The purpose of the transaction is acquisition of goods, and interaction is peaceful. For trade in raw materials, barter trade was probably the predominant mechanism, to judge by what we know of historical cases in medieval Europe and elsewhere. We have archaeological evidence for the use of packhorses (Wyss 1989) and freight boats (Ellmers 1969) to transport materials, and ancient writers emphasize the importance of the river systems of Gaul for Celtic trade (Timpe 1985: 260). Payment of tolls in the course of such trade seems to have been a regular practice (Timpe 1985: 276), at least at the end of the Iron Age.

The gold, silver and bronze coinage of the final two centuries BC provides good information about barter trade. The regular sizes and weights of coins, and especially the balances for weighing precious metals – more than thirty have been found at Stradonice in Bohemia – indicate that coins served as standards of value in a barter system (Steuer 1987). The recovery of balances, as well as moulds for casting coin blanks, at small settlements, as well as at oppida, suggests that this early monetary system permeated the late iron age countryside.

Gift Exchange

Fischer (1973) has outlined arguments for interpreting unusual and particularly valuable (in labour investment and transportation) objects in Celtic Europe in terms of gifts given between powerful members of societies. Drawing on classical literary sources and anthropological studies of gift exchange, Fischer argues that such special objects as the Grächwil hydria and the Vix krater can be understood as political gifts, presented to potentates in Celtic Europe for the purpose of establishing congenial relations for political or economic reasons.

The special objects that lend themselves to this interpretation are more common in the Early Iron Age than in the Late. In the later context, nearly all of the imports are objects that were produced in large quantities in Roman workshops, even though they were apparently highly regarded in Celtic Europe and are found associated with high-status individuals.

Booty

Reinecke (1958) addressed the problem of distinguishing archaeologically between objects of trade and those seized as booty. The distinction is not always easy. As Grierson (1959) argues for the early medieval world, we need to think in terms of a range of different mechanisms of goods transmission. For the fourth and third centuries BC, during the time of the Celtic raids and migrations to other parts of Europe, Bujna (1982: 421–2) envisions a major role being played by the seizing of booty. Later, to account for the abundance of bronze cauldrons on the Saale and lower Elbe rivers, Redlich (1980) suggests that some were obtained through Germanic raids into Celtic territory, though the large number of such cauldrons found in similar contexts suggests that barter trade may have been the principal mechanism of their transmission.

Mercenary Activity

The service of Celts as mercenaries in armies of east Mediterranean lands is well documented in ancient historical sources (Szabo 1991). The introduction of coinage into Celtic Europe has been connected with this mercenary activity. The earliest Celtic coins were gold, fashioned after the gold staters of Philip of Macedon (359–336 BC) and his son Alexander the Great (336–323 BC), and it is likely that these proto-types were brought into Celtic central Europe by mercenaries returning home (Mannsperger 1981: 234). Much of the gold jewellery from the fourth century BC onwards in Celtic Europe, as well as the local gold coinage from the early third century, may have been made of remelted gold brought by returning mercenaries.

Exogamy as Exchange

During the final 150 years before the birth of Christ, numerous personal ornaments, including fibulae and belt decorations, were brought from non-Celtic lands into the Celtic regions. The objects are characteristic of women's costume, and the finds, which occur in sets, may reflect the movement of women from outside Celtic territories into Celtic communities as marriage partners (Krämer 1961; Polenz 1982: 214–15). Textual sources at the end of the Iron Age attest to the practice of such inter-group marriage, and the foreign jewellery may be the archaeological reflection of that practice. This mechanism of exchange would involve transmission of cultural information between Celtic and other peoples too, along with the material signs of the exchange.

ORGANIZATION OF TRADE

We can distinguish at least three systems of goods circulation in the Celtic Iron Age. The luxury objects, best represented by the Mediterranean imports, are associated with élite groups, as is apparent from the grave assemblages in which they occur. A second category consists of everyday manufactured articles, such as bronze fibulae and bracelets, and glass beads and arm-rings. These objects were much more widely distributed through the social system, and they occur in graves of differing degrees of wealth. The third category is trade in raw materials – iron, copper and tin, salt, graphite–clay and stone.

In the period 600–450 BC, circulation of Mediterranean luxury goods was in the hands of élites at the centres. The products of the centres' workshops circulated into the countryside, where they are found in the graves of the small communities (Wells 1980: 38–46; 1987). Trade in raw materials such as metals and salt was handled differently, because their extraction and circulation had to be managed at the locations where they occurred. We do not have the same evidence suggestive of élite control of the circulation of these materials as we have for the manufactured goods at the centres.

For trade at the oppida between 200 BC and the Roman conquest, there is no clear archaeological evidence for control by élites. The coin evidence points to a profound change in the organization of trade (Haselgrove 1988), from circulation of personal ornaments that was in the control of élites at small centres of the earlier period, to export of large quantities of mass-produced goods by specialist industrial workers who were increasingly controlling their own output and the resulting commerce, in the late period.

The lack, in the rich graves of the Late Iron Age, of unique foreign imports comparable to the Vix krater and the Grafenbühl tripod, and their replacement by mass-produced Roman bronze jugs, basins and pans, indicates the profound change in the relation between élites and trade during the Iron Age. The presence of the mass-produced Roman vessels may indicate that even the circulation of Mediterranean wine paraphernalia was by this time in the hands of professional merchants, not transmitted through personal relationships involving the élites. In the final century BC, Roman writers distinguished between the large-scale merchant (*negotiator*), who dealt in such bulk goods as grain, and the merchant who traded on a smaller scale (*mercator*). According to those authors, persons of high social status were sometimes involved in the large-scale trade, but not in the more modest undertakings (Timpe 1985: 273–4). These circumstances may have been peculiar to Gaul, brought about in part by the intensive interactions with the Roman world.

In addition to the concentrated commercial activities evident at the oppida, many small, unfortified settlements were situated at fords on rivers, such as Aulnat, Basel-Gasfabrik and Breisach-Hochstetten, and they too show evidence of considerable commercial activity (Fischer 1985: 288–9). The pattern supports the suggestion by Duval (1983) and others that, as commerce expanded during the second century BC, new groups of artisans and merchants emerged into positions of wealth and prominence, their economic activities and social positions based on the growing commerce.

The excavated oppida yield evidence of writing in the final two centuries before Christ, both in the form of writing implements – *stili* and bronze frames from wooden writing tablets (Jacobi 1974b), and in inscriptions in Greek characters scratched into pottery, as at Manching (Krämer 1982) and in central and southern Gaul (Laubenheimer 1987). This writing was probably introduced in the context of trade between the oppidum communities and the Mediterranean world and provides another indication of the increasingly specialized role of the Celtic merchants in the expanding commerce of the late iron age centres.

REFERENCES

Allen, D. (1980) *The Coins of the Ancient Celts*, Edinburgh.
Biel, J. (1991) 'Fortsetzung der Siedlungsgrabung in Eberdingen-Hochdorf, Kreis Ludwigsburg', *Archäologische Ausgrabungen in Baden-Württemberg 1990*, 89–93.
Boardman, J. (1980) *The Greeks Overseas* (3rd edn) London.
Braudel, F. (1972) *The Mediterranean and the Mediterranean World in the Age of Philip II*, New York.
Bujna, J. (1982) 'Spiegelung der Sozialstruktur auf latènezeitlichen Gräberfeldern im Karpathenbecken', *Památky Archeologické* 73: 312–431.
Douglas, M. and Isherwood, B. (1979) *The World of Goods: towards an anthropology of consumption*, New York.
Duval, A. (1983) 'Autour de Vercingétorix: de l'archéologie à histoire économique et sociale', in J. Collis, A. Duval and R. Périchon (eds) *Le deuxième âge du fer en Auvergne et en Forez*, Sheffield, 298–335.
Dyson, S.L. (1988) 'Rise of complex societies in Italy', in D.B. Gibson and M.N. Geselowitz (eds) *Tribe and Polity in Late Prehistoric Europe*, New York, 193–203.
Eggers, H.J. (1951) *Der römische Import im Freien Germanien*, Hamburg.
Ellmers, D. (1969) 'Keltischer Schiffbau', *Jahrbuch des Römisch-Germanischen Zentralmuseums* 16: 73–122.
Fischer, F. (1959) *Der spätlatènezeitliche Depot-Fund von Kappel (Kreis Saulgau)*, Stuttgart.
—— (1973) 'KEIMHΛIA. Bemerkungen zur kulturgeschichtlichen Interpretation des sogenannten Südimports in der späten Hallstatt- und frühen Latène-Kultur des westlichen Mitteleuropa', *Germania* 51: 436–59.
—— (1985) 'Der Handel der Mittel- und Spät-Latène-Zeit in Mitteleuropa aufgrund archäologischer Zeugnisse', in K. Düwel et al. (eds) *Untersuchungen zu Handel und Verkehr der vor- und frühgeschichtlichen Zeit in Mittel- und Nordeuropa* I, Göttingen, 285–98.
Fitzpatrick, A. (1985) 'The distribution of Dressel 1 amphorae in northwestern Europe', *Oxford Journal of Archaeology* 4: 305–40.

Flouest, J.-L. and Stead, I.M. (1977) 'Une tombe de La Tène III à Hannogne (Ardennes)', *Mémoires de la Société d'Agriculture, Commerce, Sciences et Arts de Département de la Marne* 92: 55–72.

Frey, O.-H. (1985) 'Zum Handel und Verkehr während der Frühlatènezeit in Mitteleuropa', in K. Düwel *et al.* (eds) *Untersuchungen zu Handel und Verkehr der vor- und frühgeschichtlichen Zeit in Mittel- und Nordeuropa* I, Göttingen, 231–57.

—— (1986) 'Einige Überlegungen zu den Beziehungen zwischen Kelten und Germanen in der Spätlatènezeit', *Marburger Studien zur Vor- und Frühgeschichte* 7: 45–79.

Furger-Gunti, A. (1982) 'Der "Goldfund von Saint-Louis" bei Basel und ähnliche keltische Schatzfunde', *Zeitschrift für schweizerische Archäologie und Kunstgeschichte* 39: 1–47.

Gebhard, R. (1989) *Der Glasschmuck aus dem Oppidum von Manching*, Wiesbaden.

Grierson, P. (1959) 'Commerce in the Dark Ages', *Transactions of the Royal Historical Society*, 5(9): 123–40.

Hachmann, R. (1990) 'Gundestrup-Studien: Untersuchungen zu den spätkeltischen Grundlagen der frühgermanischen Kunst', *Bericht der Römisch-Germanischen Kommission* 71: 565–903.

Hachmann, R., Kossack, G. and Kuhn, H. (1962) *Völker zwischen Germanen und Kelten*, Neumünster.

Haffner, A. (1974) 'Zum Ende der Latènezeit im Mittelrhein', *Archäologisches Korrespondenzblatt* 4: 59–72.

Haselgrove, C. (1988) 'Coinage and complexity: archaeological analysis of socio-political change in Britain and non-Mediterranean Gaul during the later Iron Age', in D.B. Gibson and M.N. Geselowitz (eds) *Tribe and Polity in Late Prehistoric Europe*, New York, 69–96.

Hundt, H.-J. (1969) 'Über vorgeschichtliche Seidenfunde', *Jahrbuch des Römisch-Germanischen Zentralmuseums* 16: 59–71.

Jacobi, G. (1974a) *Werkzeug und Gerät aus dem Oppidum von Manching*, Weisbaden.

Jacobi, G. (1974b) 'Zum Schriftgebrauch in keltischen Oppida nördlich der Alpen', *Hamburger Beiträge zur Archäologie* 4: 171-81.

Jankuhn, H. (1969) *Vor- und Frühgeschichte vom Neolithikum bis zur Völkerwanderungszeit*, Stuttgart.

Kappel, I. (1969) *Die Graphittonkeramik von Manching*, Wiesbaden.

Kellner, H.-J. (1990) *Die Münzfunde von Manching und die keltischen Fundmünzen aus Südbayern*, Wiesbaden.

Kimmig, W. (1983) 'Die griechische Kolonisation im westlichen Mittelmeergebiet und ihre Wirkung auf die Landschaften des westlichen Mitteleuropa', *Jahrbuch des Römisch-Germanischen Zentralmuseums* 30: 5–78.

Krämer, W. (1961) 'Fremder Frauenschmuck aus Manching', *Germania* 39: 305–22.

—— (1971) 'Silberne Fibelpaare aus dem letzten vorchristlichen Jahrhundert', *Germania* 49: 111–32.

—— (1982) 'Graffiti auf Spätlatènekeramik aus Manching', *Germania* 60: 489–99.

Lappe, U. (1979) 'Keltische Glasarmringe und Ringperlen aus Thüringen', *Alt-Thüringen* 16: 84–111.

Laubenheimer, F. (1987) 'De l'usage populaire de l'écriture grecque dans la Gaule du Centre-Est', *Revue Archéologique de l'Est et du Centre-Est* 38: 163–7.

Maier, F. (1970) *Die bemalte Spätlatène-Keramik von Manching*, Wiesbaden.

—— (1991) 'The Celtic oppida', in S. Moscati *et al.* (eds) *The Celts*, 411–25.

Mannsperger, D. (1981) 'Münzen und Münzfunde', in K. Bittel, W. Kimmig and S. Schiek (eds) *Die Kelten in Baden-Württemberg*, Stuttgart, 228–47.

Megaw, R. and Megaw, V. (1989) *Celtic Art*, London.

Moscati, S. *et al.* (eds) (1991) *The Celts*, New York.

Nash, D. (1978) *Settlement and Coinage in Central Gaul c. 200–50 B.C.*, Oxford.

Pauli, L. (1975) *Keltische Volksglaube*, Munich.

—— (1980) 'Das keltische Mitteleuropa vom 6. bis zum 2. Jahrhundert v. Chr.', in L. Pauli (ed.) *Die Kelten in Mitteleuropa*, Salzburg, 25–36.

Peddemors, A. (1975) 'Latèneglasarmringe in den Niederlanden', *Analecta Praehistorica Leidensia* 8: 93–145.

Polenz, H. (1982) 'Münzen in latènezeitlichen Gräbern Mitteleuropas aus der Zeit zwischen 300 und 50 vor Christi Geburt', *Bayerische Vorgeschichtsblätter* 47: 27–222.

Les Princes celtes et la Mediterranée (1988) Paris.

Redlich, C. (1980) 'Politische und wirtschaftliche Bedeutung der Bronzegefässe an Unterelbe und Saale zur Zeit der Römerkriege', *Studien zur Sachsenforschung* 2: 329–73.

Reinecke, P. (1958) 'Einführ- oder Beutegut?', *Bonner Jahrbücher* 158: 246–52.

Renfrew, C. (1975) 'Trade as action at a distance', in J.A. Sabloff and C.C. Lamberg-Karlovsky (eds) *Ancient Civilization and Trade*, Albuquerque, 3–59.

Rivet, A. (1988) *Gallia Narbonensis: southern France in Roman times*, London.

Stead, I.M. (1967) 'A La Tène III burial at Welwyn Garden City', *Archaeologia* 101: 1–62.

Steuer, H. (1987) 'Gewichtgeldwirtschaften im frühgeschichtlichen Europa', in K. Düwel *et al.* (eds) *Untersuchungen zu Handel und Verkehr der vor- und frühgeschichtlichen Zeit in Mittel- und Nordeuropa* IV, Göttingen, 405–527.

Stjernquist, B. (1985) 'Methodische Überlegungen zum Nachweis von Handel aufgrund archäologischer Quellen', in K. Düwel *et al.* (eds) *Untersuchungen zu Handel und Verkehr der vor- und frühgeschichtlichen Zeit in Mittel- und Nordeuropa* I, Göttingen, 56–83.

Svobodová, H. (1983) 'Bronzové Nádoby z Keltských Oppid v Čechách a na Moravě' ('Bronzegefässe aus keltischen Oppida in Böhmen und Mähren') *Archeologické Rozhledy* 35: 656–77.

—— (1985) 'Antické Importy z Keltských Oppid v Čechách a na Moravě' ('Antike Importe aus den keltischen Oppida in Böhmen und Mähren') *Archeologické Rozhledy* 37: 653–8.

Szabo, M. (1991) 'Mercenary activity', in S. Moscati *et al.* (eds) *The Celts*, 333–6.

Timpe, D. (1985) 'Der keltische Handel nach historischen Quellen', in K. Düwel *et al.* (eds) *Untersuchungen zu Handel und Verkehr der vor- und frühgeschichtlichen Zeit in Mittel- und Nordeuropa* I, Göttingen, 258–84.

Wells, P.S. (1980) *Culture Contact and Culture Change: early iron age central Europe and the Mediterranean world*, Cambridge.

—— (1984) *Farms, Villages, and Cities: commerce and urban origins in late prehistoric Europe*, Ithaca, NY.

—— (1987) 'Sociopolitical change and core–periphery interactions: an example from early iron age Europe', in K.M. Trinkaus (ed.) *Polities and Partitions: human boundaries and the growth of complex societies*, Tempe, AZ, 141–55.

Werner, J. (1978) 'Zur Bronzekanne von Kelheim', *Bayerische Vorgeschichtsblätter* 43: 1–18.

Wyss, R. (1975) *Der Schatzfund von Erstfeld*, Zurich.

—— (1989) 'Handel und Verkehr über die Alpenpässe', in H. Jankuhn *et al.* (eds) *Untersuchungen zu Handel und Verkehr der vor- und frühgeschichtlichen Zeit in Mittel- und Nordeuropa* V, Göttingen, 155–73.

Zürn, H. (1970) *Hallstattforschungen in Nordwürttemberg*, Stuttgart.

COINAGE

—— ·◆· ——

Daphne Nash Briggs

When Julius Caesar published a brief account of what he observed and accomplished during his invasions of Britain in 55 and 54 BC, one of the first things he mentioned in a general description of the island and its inhabitants was that 'they use either bronze or gold coinage, or else iron bars of definite weight instead of coins' (*De Bello Gallico* V.12.4).

A Roman military commander attempting to justify a dangerous and speculative war of foreign conquest to an educated Roman audience had, perhaps, a natural preoccupation with money and supplies, and this observation was in fact part of a short list of the most important resources of Britain as he perceived them: a vast population, multitudes of livestock, gold and bronze coinage, and ores of tin and iron. But as the geographer Strabo remarked a couple of generations later (*Geography* IV.5.3), Caesar did not in fact achieve very much, although he brought back 'hostages, slaves, and quantities of other booty'. In Strabo's time, early in the first century AD, the Romans were finding it more profitable to trade with the island and tax the traffic than to try to conquer and administer warlike and politically labile tribesmen; it was not until the 40s AD that conquest became both feasible and attractive, with the growth of several large and relatively stable kingdoms in southern Britain after a century of lively contact with the Roman provinces of Gaul.

The history of Celtic coinage is intimately connected with the evolving relationship between Celtic Europe and the Mediterranean between the fourth century BC and the mid-first century AD, and the geographical location of the most influential centres of Celtic coinage production tended to move outwards from the margins of the Mediterranean world with the passage of time.

Britain was in fact the last major region of ancient Celtic Europe to adopt coinage, and the earliest British coins were indeed of gold and a tin-rich bronze alloy, in line with Caesar's description. The cast bronze (potin) coins in fact came first, in the later second century BC, followed by the earliest gold between *c.*80 and 60 BC (Haselgrove 1993). At the time of Caesar's invasions, however, British coinage was still at an early stage in its development, and its expansion into one of the most intricate and potentially informative of all Celtic coinage systems took place during the following century when the Roman conquest of Gaul had temporarily brought the north-western frontier of the Roman Empire to the Channel coastline. On the Continent,

Celtic coinage began much earlier, during the third century BC in places, and by the early second century was in existence over an enormous geographical area, from Picardy, southern Germany, Bohemia and Transylvania in the north, to Languedoc, Provence, northern Italy, Hungary, Austria and Bulgaria in the south.

Although a few overall regularities can be observed in the pattern of adoption and development of Celtic coinage in many different areas, coinage was not in reality a single, uniform phenomenon subject to the same interpretation in widely separated times and places. Instead, it was one among many expressions of the social and economic priorities of the élites who issued it, and the interpretation of any given coinage inevitably depends upon some understanding of the particular cultural context within which it was used. For this reason, Celtic coinage should always be studied in the context of the general archaeological record of its times.

Almost without exception, the earliest coinages in each region were of silver and gold, and of relatively large denominations. Such coinage was treasure, and as such belonged to the sphere of élite circulation: official payments, taxes, tribute, and fines, religious offerings, dowries, and other customary payments. The alloy, weight and designs of gold and silver coinage were always carefully adjusted and controlled.

By contrast, small change, whether in the form of very small silver coins, some-times weighing a mere fraction of a gramme, or low-value copper and bronze coins, generally made its first appearance rather late in any given region's history of coinage use. Early British potin (cast bronze) coinage is only an apparent exception to this rule, as the way it was used suggests that, despite its appearance, it was treated as a valuable material, with a special and essentially restricted range of uses (Haselgrove forthcoming). Small change proper seems generally to have been used for a much wider range of transactions than the larger denominations of silver and all gold coinage, and probably by a much larger number of people. It tends, for instance, to be found amidst general settlement debris, suggesting use in the course of everyday life on nucleated settlements (cf. Kraay 1964).

Rare glimpses by Mediterranean observers of Celtic societies before and around the time at which they first began to strike coinage of their own afford valuable insight into the social environment within which the earliest Celtic coinages were used.

The second-century BC historian of Roman affairs, Polybius, describing some of the early Celtic immigrants to northern Italy, long before the introduction of coinage, said,

> Their possessions consisted of cattle and gold, because these were the only things they could carry about with them everywhere according to circumstances and shift wherever they chose. They treated comradeship as of the greatest impor-tance, those among them being the most feared and most powerful who were thought to have the largest number of attendants and associates.
>
> (*Histories* II.17)

A later observer, Poseidonios, writing in around 80 BC, described how in the mid-second century BC, King Louernios of the Arverni in central Gaul, 'in an attempt to win popular favour, rode in a chariot over the plains distributing gold and silver to the tens of thousands of Celts who followed him', and in addition laid on a lavish feast to entertain all comers that lasted for many days on end (in Athenaeus, *Deipnosphists* IV.37).

Although largesse could be distributed in many different ways, coinage was a particularly convenient medium for making relatively small but conspicuous gifts or payments to large numbers of people. Something like the social organization that Polybius's sources or Poseidonios himself observed was probably universal in early Celtic societies. Powerful nobles needed to attract and entertain personal retinues, dependants, craftsmen and poets (Poseidonios also mentioned that a poet turned up late to the feast, but flattered his way into a bag of gold all the same), foreign guests, and armies of warriors. It was within a world such as this that coinage was integrated during the third and early second centuries BC into many communities throughout Celtic Europe.

But striking coinage was an expensive way to maintain dependants, make gifts, and pay armies. Gold and silver coinage consisted of actual pieces of treasure, and at the rate of, for instance, 7 grammes of gold per early Celtic alloyed stater and perhaps 5 staters per soldier per season, 1,000 men would cost 35 kg of gold, a lot by any standards. Their leaders would of course cost more. This is not an entirely fanciful calculation, as we do have a little evidence for relevant rates of pay (cf. Nash 1987: 14 ff.). The Macedonian stater contained over 8.50 grammes of pure gold, and King Perseus of Macedon (179–168 BC) is known to have hired a large contingent of Danubian Celtic Bastarnae for a season's campaign at a rate of 5 gold staters apiece for infantry warriors, 10 each for the cavalry, and 1,000 for their king Claodicus (Livy, *History of Rome* XLIV.26).

Enormous quantities of Mediterranean gold passed into Celtic Europe in the hands of returning warriors during the fourth and third centuries BC as the rulers of the Hellenistic Mediterranean spent their resources on wars of conquest, competition and defence. The Celts were the most popular barbarian soldiers of the day (Griffith 1935), having earned a reputation with the Greeks for being almost insanely courageous, prepared to fight even the ocean waves, and alleging no fear of death. The Celts, particularly those of central and western Europe, preferred their salaries in gold at a time when silver was the normal currency medium in the Mediterranean sphere, and colossal amounts of Hellenistic gold coinage were struck to meet their demands.

It is therefore no surprise to find that it was coinages struck by the main Mediterranean employers of barbarian mercenary soldiers that inspired the types of the earliest native coinages of Celtic Europe (Table 14.1). There is in fact reason to think that some Celtic groups travelled enormous distances to participate in Mediterranean wars. In third-century Picardy, far remote from southern Italy, successive coinages of Tarentum were copied with such accuracy, and in the correct order, that it is difficult to escape the conclusion that these Celts were in direct contact over a relatively long period with some source of Tarentine coinage (Scheers 1968, 1981). It is difficult to make out a convincing case for coinage having played any important part in trading relations between the Mediterranean world and northern Europe at that period, and even more difficult to account for such apparently consistent trading contact between Tarentum and Picardy in particular. But coinage *was* the unique and universal medium of payment for mercenary soldiers, whom the Tarentines, among many others, did employ. It is tempting to see in the

Table 14.1 Principal Mediterranean prototypes for Celtic coinage

Model	Where copied
	1 Third–early second century BC
Philip II of Macedon (359–336 BC) gold staters (+ posthumous types until 3rd century BC)	Switzerland gold Rhineland gold Central Gaul gold
Philip II lifetime + posthumous silver tetradrachms	Romania/Danube Basin silver
Alexander III (356–32 BC) gold staters	Central Europe gold
Alexander III silver tetradrachms	Danube Basin silver
Massalia 4th-century BC silver drachmae	Northern Italy silver Languedoc/Aquitaine silver
Massalia 4th-century BC silver obols	Rhône valley/Alps silver
Philip III (323–316 BC) silver tetradrachms	Bulgaria silver
Tarentum (*c.*334–272 BC) gold and silver	Picardy gold
Syracuse (Agathokles: 317–289 BC) gold	Normandy gold
Rhodes 3rd-century BC silver drachmae	Languedoc silver
Emporion silver drachmae (*c.*246–218 BC)	Languedoc/Aquitaine silver
	2 Mid–late second century BC
Roman Republican denarii (after *c.*150 BC)	Noricum silver Rhône valley silver
	3 First century BC
Roman Republican silver	Britain, all metals (after *c.*20 BC)

history of the first coinages of north-western France early evidence for the martial prowess of the ancestors of the Belgae whom Julius Caesar was much later to encounter as formidable, almost invincible, opponents.

Celtic warriors did not enter mercenary service only for pay, but for the sake of any booty to be won and for the prestige that would accrue to success. They not only served for Mediterranean employers during the century of continuous warfare that culminated in the wars between Carthage and Rome of 264–241 and 218–201 BC, but also for one another. Roman conquests in the Mediterranean sphere provoked not only the Greeks and Carthage, but also the Cisalpine Celts to hire transalpine mercenaries.

> The two largest tribes [of Cisalpine Gaul], the Insubres and Boii, made a league and sent messengers to the Gauls dwelling among the Alps and near the Rhône, who are called Gaesatae because they serve for hire. . . . They urged and incited their kings . . . to make war on Rome, offering them an immediate large sum in gold, and for the future pointing out the great prosperity of the Romans, and the vast wealth that would be theirs if they were victorious. They had no difficulty in persuading them . . .
>
> (*Polybius*, Histories II.22ff.)

The leaders of the Gaesatae collected a richly equipped and formidable force which descended into the Po valley in 225 BC for what turned out to be an ill-fated expedition.

The Cisalpine Celts had no gold coinage of their own, so if they paid the Gaesatae their advance in coin, it can only have been in that of other communities, especially the ubiquitous Macedonian currency struck in the name of Philip II long after his death, but popular with foreign mercenary soldiers. It was in fact posthumous types of Philip II gold staters that furnished the prototypes for nearly all the most influential early coinages in the Gallic sphere, including the Alps, Rhineland and central Gaul, areas from which Polybius's 'Gaesatae' (whose name actually only means 'spearsmen') were recruited (Nash 1987: 84 ff.).

Celtic coinage therefore originated during the third century BC, in a period of intensified military contact with the rulers of Macedon, Tarentum, Rhode and Carthage as the latter fought losing struggles with Rome, and Syracuse, Massalia and probably Emporion as they supplied military and naval assistance to their Roman allies. This was followed by a new epoch in economic relations with the Mediterranean world, since Rome did not employ mercenary soldiers, but had an enormous and growing need for trade goods from Celtic Europe – above all, slaves and metals. This would not in itself have led to the adoption of coinage in Celtic Europe, but its impact upon a Celtic world that was already integrating coinage into its social functioning for other reasons did give an enormous spur to further development.

We have good documentary evidence from contemporary observers that the Celts' eagerness to import wine was at least as great as their greed for gold, and that in Gaul during the second and first centuries BC, the slaves that the Romans needed in ever increasing numbers were being purchased from Celts with amphorae of wine by Mediterranean merchants based at Narbonne and other cities in southern Gaul (Diodorus Siculus, *World History* V.26).

In the Danube Basin, where the Celts had for centuries mingled with other native communities, and had by the early first century BC evolved a distinctive hybrid regional culture, silver in the form of Republican denarii does actually seem to have been the preferred medium of exchange for slaves, and Roman Republican coinage flooded into the area in extremely large quantities when the suppression of piracy in the eastern Mediterranean enforced the development of other avenues for slave procurement (Crawford 1977).

This unusual situation only emphasizes by contrast what an insignificant role Roman, or any other, coinage played in long-range external trading activity elsewhere. Outside the Danube Basin, trade between the Celts and the Mediterranean world was conducted by means of direct exchange, in which wine certainly played an important part. There is clear archaeological evidence that from the mid-second century BC onwards, Italian wine amphorae were being imported in rising numbers into almost every area of Gaul and even southern Britain (Cunliffe 1991: 434 ff.), betraying local accumulation of wealth, prestige and power; and within this social context Celtic coinages began to proliferate and spread, with increasingly well-differentiated designs that are sometimes far removed from their remote Mediterranean models.

As the use of coinage spread from its earliest centres, therefore, a number of discrete regional groupings took shape, each with its own characteristic repertoire of types and styles, weights and metals (Allen and Nash 1980; Nash 1987). There are still many areas, particularly in parts of continental Europe, in which coinage is almost the only source of information for the Celts in the second century BC. This is no accident: at that time many Celtic communities, like the immigrants to northern Italy described by Polybius, seem to have invested a disproportionate amount of their wealth in the sorts of movable or perishable goods and livestock that were necessary to maintain social relationships and political hierarchies, but spent relatively little on the sort of monumental building that readily attracted archaeological attention in the past. In very recent years, however, painstaking archaeological research, aided by aerial surveys, is gradually filling in the picture in selected areas.

One of the things that makes the absolute dating of Celtic coinages so difficult is that they were almost certainly never issued on a regular annual basis, but were instead produced in a series of discontinuous episodes, as and when they were needed, to make distributions, mark special occasions, make customary payments or alliance gifts, pay soldiers, and so on. Crises in political life, perhaps especially surrounding changes of ruler, and periods of civil or external warfare were all likely to be expensive times with very high coinage output, but almost nothing is known for certain about the detailed history of the societies concerned that would help in interpreting apparent fluctuations in the production of individual coinages. The Gallic War with Caesar (58–51 BC) is one of the few adequately documented periods of crisis that certainly did provoke enormous quantities of coinage in almost every area of Gaul. It is therefore a valuable landmark in attempting to determine the chronology of late Gaulish and early British coinage.

Caesar's successful conquest of Gaul in 52–51 BC brought an end to its independent coinages. Gold went out of use immediately, and documentary evidence suggests that a lot of what was then in existence was actually confiscated. The Imperial biographer Suetonius reported the tradition that

> in Gaul [Caesar] plundered large and small temples of their votive offerings, and . . . as a result collected larger quantities of gold than he could handle, and began selling it for silver, in Italy and the provinces, at 750 denarii to the pound, which was about two-thirds of the official exchange rate.
>
> (*Lives of the Twelve Caesars, Julius Caesar* 54)

Suetonius may be suggesting that the price Caesar got for his gold was due to its excessive quantity, but it should also be remembered that the standard Celtic gold stater of the Gallic War period was debased by around one-third, which would also account for a realistic lowering of bullion prices (Castelin 1974: 13). Within the new Gallic provinces, several rather Romanized silver coinages and many local bronze issues went on being produced until close to the end of the first century BC, when Augustus's mint at Lugdunum took over as the sole official source of new coinage in Gaul. At least another century was to elapse, however, before the last of the old Celtic bronzes went completely out of circulation for everyday use.

Across the Channel, meanwhile, as Roman trading networks for slaves and raw materials extended ever further afield, new centres of accumulated wealth emerged in southern Britain, and the history of British coinage reveals some very interesting aspects of the evolving relationship between northern Gaul and Britain at the end of the first millennium BC. Two very different regions of northern Gaul were routinely involved with Britain; both had well-developed coinages of their own in the second and first centuries BC, but their impact upon Britain was strikingly different.

The first was Armorica, modern Brittany. Here, some of the most beautifully and independently designed of all Celtic coinages were issued first in alloyed gold and eventually in silver and debased silver, from at least the early second century BC onwards, to meet the internal needs of the Armorican communities. Although the Armoricans were renowned sea-traders, and were actively involved in the distribution of Mediterranean trade goods to Britain (Cunliffe 1991: 434ff.), their coinages were neither issued to facilitate trade, nor evidently used except very incidentally in the course of intertribal or cross-Channel trading activity.

From the outset, therefore, Armorican coinages tend to have rather compact and well-localized geographical distributions, seldom straying far from their communities of origin on the Continent. Compared with their abundance in Gaul itself, very few Armorican coins have been found in Britain, despite the very well-attested and long-standing sea-trade that went on between Armorica and south-western Britain. In Britain, Armorican coins, mainly of the Coriosolites, who seem to have been the most active carriers of trade goods on this route, tend to cluster in and around Channel ports of trade such as Hengistbury Head, Mount Batten and Selsey Bill, where foreign traders may well have resided. Elsewhere, finds of Armorican coins are only sparsely distributed, mainly in western counties of southern England (Cunliffe 1991: 544, map). Compared with the density of distribution of contemporary Belgic coins in south-eastern Britain, this is the merest scattering.

There is at present no reason to think that any Armorican coinage was actually struck in Britain, and none of the Armorican coinages was directly imitated in Britain either, although the Durotriges of Dorset (in most direct contact with Armorica) did eventually adopt the Armorican custom of using debased silver for coinage, and a few other central-southern communities displayed some Armorican influence in the flamboyant design of their earliest silver coinages in the mid-first century BC. There could hardly be a better demonstration that even centuries of trading contact with a coin-using people was seldom, if ever, in itself of much importance in inspiring the adoption of coinage.

For a Celtic community to do that, it had to be against a background of more complex social involvement.

This was the case in the relationship between Belgic Gaul and Britain. Here, coast-to-coast trading activity, although it probably went on, was only one, and by no means the most important, of the ties that had linked the Celts of Belgic Gaul and the Seine Basin with southern and eastern Britain for centuries. There is, for instance, both archaeological and documentary evidence for at least some degree of direct immigration from Gaul before and during the period when coinage was first introduced to the island. Julius Caesar himself observed that the inhabitants of Kent were almost indistinguishable from the Belgae of adjacent areas of Gaul, and that in other parts of Britain too there were colonial settlements with the same names as their communities of origin on the Continent (*De Bello Gallico* V.12.1–2, V.14.1).

Perhaps Belgic immigrants in such settlements were always in a small minority compared with resident native populations, but they seem to have been influential among their new neighbours all the same. They were almost certainly instrumental in maintaining a current of social contact that involved all manner of traditional inter-change with Picardy and the Seine Basin, in the course of which Belgic coinage was introduced into south-eastern Britain. Only four examples of the earliest types of third- or early-second-century Belgic gold coinage have been found in Britain, three of them in Kent, but later Belgic coinage entered Britain in enormous quantities starting in the mid- or late second century BC (Haselgrove 1992). The Belgae estab-lished ties with non-Belgic British communities as well, and during Caesar's wars in Gaul, British tribes gave military assistance to the Gauls, paid for, undoubtedly, in the Belgic gold coinage of the day, which flooded into Britain.

The process of introduction of Belgic coinage to Britain and subsequent British adoption of their own types based on Belgic prototypes (Table 14.2) has therefore much in common with the way in which Mediterranean coinage gave rise to Celtic continental coinages in the first place. By contrast with Armorican coinage, that of Belgic Gaul and its immediate neighbours had a profound and lasting impact upon British coinage, suggesting a quite different level of involvement between the two areas of northern Gaul and Britain.

Having begun to produce coinage of their own during the late second and early first century BC, the native communities of southern Britain went on to develop one of the most sophisticated coinage systems anywhere in the Celtic world. This took place above all during a period of lively diplomatic and trading contact with the Romans in Gaul between c.50 BC and AD 43 which fostered dynastic expansion among the leading tribes of central-southern and eastern Britain (Haselgrove 1992; cf. Mack 1975; Van Arsdell 1989).

The relentless advance of the Roman Empire affected relations among the Celts not only by promoting the internal development of allies, favoured trading partners, and other members of their supply networks, but also by conquest of successive Celtic societies close to their borders, starting with Cisalpine Gaul in 191–100 BC, then Provence and Languedoc in 121 BC, the rest of Gaul in 58–52 BC, Noricum in c.35–16 BC, the Alps in 14 BC, and finally southern Britain in AD 43–60. In each case, native gold coinage, which had no place in the Roman economy, came promptly to an end. Some version of native silver and bronze coinage often went on being produced for a generation or so in the new Roman provinces, until metropolitan Roman coinage was fully established in circulation (Nash 1987: 23 ff.).

When the Roman conquest of Britain finally extinguished native coinage in the 60s AD, it also brought the entire history of Celtic coinage to an end. Beyond the Roman frontier in Britain, Celtic societies that had never used coinage of any sort took their turn to be the closest neighbours of the Roman Empire, making alliances, doing trade, being preyed upon, and accumulating wealth and prestige, but without ever adopting coinage for their own use. The Romans did not employ mercenary soldiers, nor did they, or their British provincial subjects, ever seem to use coinage in any other very systematic way in dealing with the Scots and the Irish. Although, therefore, plenty of Roman coinage did cross the imperial frontier in the course of three and a half centuries, it almost certainly did so in a haphazard, incidental way. Unlike the continental Celts and the southern British who had evidently already integrated foreign coinage into their own systems of social relations during the generations preceding the introduction of coinages of their own, the Scots and the Irish had little or no such history of exposure to the use of coinage, and continued to prosper without it.

Table 14.2 Principal prototypes for British coinage

Origin in Gaul	British coinage
Picardy earliest gold (late 3rd/early 2nd century BC)	A few found, esp. Kent, but not copied
Picardy wide flan gold staters (=Gallo-Belgic A, mid-2nd–early 1st century BC)	Numerous imports, centre of distribution probably Kent; some late issues probably struck in Britain; not copied
Gaulish potin (2nd century BC)	Imported, mainly Kent, then first British potin coinage begins by late 2nd century (focus in Kent)
Picardy Gallo-Belgic C gold (c.100–60 BC), the single most influential prototype for early British gold coinage	Imports same area; first gold copies c.80–60 BC on periphery of areas of distribution of Picardy coinages
Belgic gold quarter-staters, geometric design (Gallo-Belgic DC), uncertain coastal origin (c. 100–60 BC)	Numerous imports, inspired coastal British gold and silver types c.80/60 BC and later
Belgic silver coinages (late 2nd/1st century BC)	Few known imports, but inspired British silver types from mid-1st century BC onwards
Picardy uniface staters (= Gallo-Belgic E, c.60–50 BC)	The main Belgic coinage of the Gallic war; imported in huge quantities into Britain, some probably struck there, but only slightly influential with subsequent British coin design (some uniface staters of eastern Britain)
Suessiones gold staters (= Gallo-Belgic F, c. 60–50 BC)	Few known imports, but inspired early gold of Atrebatic dynasty and neighbours
Aulerci Eburovices gold (c.70–50 BC)	Few known imports, but inspired silver types of central-southern and western Britain
Ambiani under Roman control (after 50 BC)	Some imports, and inspired bronze types, esp. in Kent from c.20 BC onwards
Roman coinage current in Gaul (50 BC–AD 40)	Modest imports; influenced coinage types in all metals in dynasties of southern and eastern Britain, c.15 BC onwards

REFERENCES

Allen, D.F. and Nash, D. (eds) (1980) *The Coins of the Ancient Celts*, Edinburgh.

Castelin, K. (1974) 'Galliens Gold und Cäsar', *Money Trend* 10: 11–14.

Crawford, M.H. (1977) 'Republican denarii in Romania: the suppression of piracy and the slave trade', *Journal of Roman Studies* 67: 117–24.

Cunliffe, B. (1991) *Iron Age Communities in Britain* (3rd edn) London/New York.

Griffith, G.T. (1935) *The Mercenaries of the Hellenistic World*, Cambridge.

Haselgrove, C. (1992) 'Coinage in iron age Britain', in J. Collis and T. Champion (eds) *Iron Age Britain: recent trends*, Sheffield.

—— (1993) 'The development of British iron age coinage', *Numismatic Chronicle* 153: 31–64.

Kraay, C.M. (1964) 'Hoards, small change, and the origin of coinage', *Journal of Hellenic Studies* 84: 76–91.

Mack, R.P. (1975) *The Coinage of Ancient Britain* (3rd edn) London.

Nash D. (1987) *Coinage in the Celtic World*, London.

Scheers, S. (1968) 'Le premier monnayage des Ambiani', *Revue Belge de Numismatique* 114: 45–73.

—— (1981) 'The origins and evolution of coinage in Belgic Gaul', in B.W. Cunliffe (ed.) *Coinage and Society in Britain and Gaul: some current problems*, London: CBA Research Report 38: 18–23.

Van Arsdell, R.D. (1989) *Celtic Coinage of Britain*, London.

CELTIC SEAFARING AND TRANSPORT

——— •◦• ———

Sean McGrail

In this chapter I plan to review the evidence for Celtic boats and ships, the landing places these vessels were operated from, and the way goods were moved inland from beach, river foreshore and lakeside. I shall also describe some of the seafaring and navigational techniques the Celts needed to use on overseas voyages.

The precise bounds of the Celts in time and space are difficult to define. In certain parts of Europe, for example, there is a degree of cultural continuity archaeologically visible from the second millennium BC, through to Roman times (Audouze and Büchsenschütz 1991). Furthermore, in Ireland and in other western regions of the archipelago of islands off the north-west coast of continental Europe, Celtic cultural traits, including boatbuilding techniques, continued into the medieval period and beyond. The core period of this book is, however, 600 BC to AD 600, and this chapter will therefore generally be restricted to that date range. It will also concentrate on the heartlands of the Celtic peoples (Figure 15.1) and not follow them to the eastern Mediterranean.

Environmental conditions such as sea-levels, the shape and character of coastlines, river courses and the general climate, all of which have an effect on maritime affairs, have not always been as they are today (McGrail 1987: 258–60). However, off north-west Europe in the period from the mid-first millennium BC to the mid-first millennium AD, the mean sea-level was well within today's tidal range, at c.1.5 to 0.7m below the AD 1950 tidal datum; the tidal regime was probably comparable with that we experience today; and the climate, including the predominant wind, must have been not unlike that of the twentieth century, apart from the 300 years or so from AD 100 to 400, when it was somewhat warmer and drier (Heyworth and Kidson 1982; Lamb 1977: 372–4, 384–5). The main environmental differences are that, in the period under discussion, there would have been less silting of estuaries, and spits and bars across river mouths would not have been as prominent as they are today. Furthermore, rivers, especially in their lower reaches, would not have been restricted to the one well-defined channel to which they are nowadays generally constrained.

WATER TRANSPORT

By the Bronze Age the technological 'environment' in Europe was such that, in theory, almost any type of raft and boat ever known could have been built (McGrail

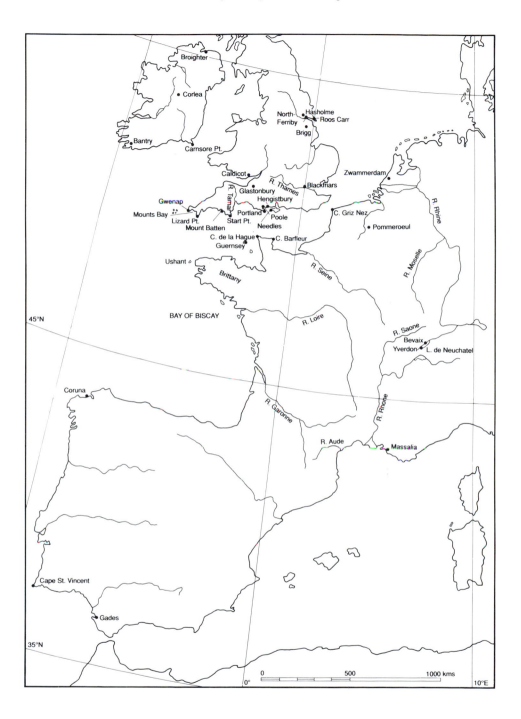

Figure 15.1 Map of Atlantic Europe showing sites named in the text. (Institute of Archaeology, Oxford.)

1990b: table 4.1). Those most likely to have been built are: bundle rafts, log rafts, hide boats, logboats and plank boats. All these could have been used on inland waters for hunting, fishing and the gathering of reeds, for the movement of animals and goods, and for social intercourse.

Rafts, however, cannot generally be used at sea north of latitude 40° to 45°N, even in the summer months. People cannot endure for long the chilling and wetness effects of low sea temperatures, combined with wind and spray, which soon produce numbness and indeed hypothermia. Thus boats, in which there is some protection from the elements, had to be used for seafishing, and for coastal and cross-Channel voyages in European waters outside the Mediterranean.

Propulsion

Paddles capable of propelling rafts and boats are known from the fourth millennium BC in Europe, whilst the earliest evidence for oars is a fifth-century BC gold model boat (Figure 15.2) from Dürrnberg (Ellmers 1978). There is both documentary and iconographic evidence for indigenous sail in north-west Europe from the first century BC (Caesar, *De Bello Gallico* III.13; Farrell and Penney 1975). However, embedded within the fourth-century AD poem *Ora Maritima* by Avienus (Murphy 1977) are extracts from a *periplus* (a coastal pilot's 'handbook') which Hawkes (1977: 19) has dated to the late-sixth century BC. This *periplus* mentions two-day voyages by hide boats from the region of Ushant in western Brittany to Ireland, which almost certainly must have been made under sail.

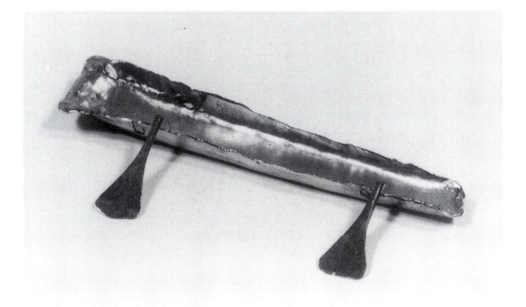

Figure 15.2 A fifth-century BC gold model boat with two oars from Dürrnberg (Germany). (Photo: Keltenmuseum, Hallein.)

Steering

A first-century BC gold model boat from Broighter in the north of Ireland (Figure 15.3) has a steering oar pivoted near the stern as have the boats depicted on the first-century AD monument to Blussus (a Celt) now in Mainz Museum (Ellmers 1975) (Figure 15.4), and on a third-century AD altar to the Celtic deity Nehalennia from Colijnsplaat (Ellmers 1978: fig. 5). A steering oar, some 10 m in length, and dated to the second/third century AD, has been recovered from Lake Neuchâtel, Switzerland (Eglofff 1974); a 5.15 m steering oar from the first/second century AD boat site at Zwammerdam, Netherlands (de Weerd 1988); and one of 4.10 m in length with the second/third century AD Bruges boat (Marsden 1976: fig. 6). As the boat depicted on the eighth-century AD Kilnaruane Pillar near Bantry, Co. Cork, also has a steering oar (Hourihane and Hourihane 1979), the total evidence seems to suggest that steering oars were widely used on Celtic boats. There is no mention of the steering arrangements of the Veneti seagoing plank ships described by Caesar (*De Bello Gallico* 111.13) and by Strabo (IV.4.1) and perhaps we may conclude that they had side rudders as in Roman ships, possibly only one rather than a pair. Side rudders are, indeed, shown on the starboard side of seagoing plank vessels depicted on two

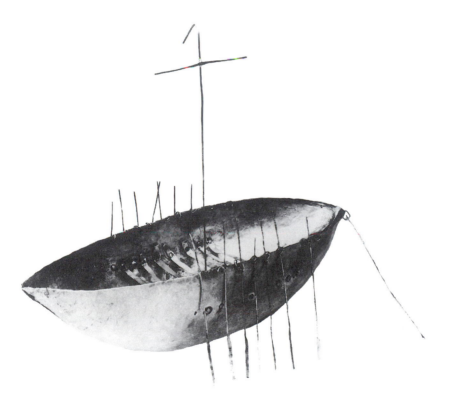

Figure 15.3 A first-century BC gold model boat from Broighter (Ireland). (Photo: National Museum of Ireland.)

Figure 15.4 Relief on first-century AD Blussus monument (Mainz).
(Drawing: Landesmuseum, Mainz.)

first-century AD coins (Figure 15.5) of the Celtic ruler Cunobelin found at
Canterbury and at Sheepen near Colchester (McGrail 1990b). This is some 500 years
before the first evidence for side rudders on vessels of the pre-Viking/Nordic
tradition of northern Europe (McGrail 1987: 244–6).

Rafts

In the first century BC Caesar (*De Bello Gallico* I.12) noted that the Celtic Helvetii
used log rafts to cross the river Saône, a tributary of the river Rhône, whilst the
Sugambri used them to cross the river Rhine (*De Bello Gallico* VI.35). Parts of two
log rafts dated to the second century AD were found at Strasbourg near the river
Rhine in 1938 (Ellmers 1972: 106, figs 83, 84).

Bundle rafts have not been excavated and as they are generally made of ephemeral
materials which can readily be reused, perhaps early examples will never be found.
However, simple rafts of reed bundles have been used in recent times on inland
waters in Ireland and elsewhere in Europe (McGrail 1987: 163) and it seems likely
that they were widely used in earlier times wherever reeds were readily available.

Logboats

Logboats – that is boats made by hollowing out a log and sometimes known as
'dugout canoes' – have been found throughout north-west Europe (McGrail 1978:
4–13). The circumstances of their discovery usually mean that dating by association or
by stratigraphy is not possible. Furthermore, research is insufficiently advanced at
present to permit accurate dating by technological criteria. It is necessary therefore to

Figure 15.5 A first-century AD coin of Cunobelin from Canterbury. (Photo: Canterbury Archaeological Trust.)

use other methods, such as radiocarbon assay, to obtain reliable dates. Apart from a few Swiss logboats (Arnold 1992), however, there is at present only one European region, southern Britain, where a sizeable group of logboats has been dated and technologically recorded. The Godwin Laboratory in the University of Cambridge has recently published 81 radiocarbon dates for 57 British logboats; of these, ten boats are dated between 600 cal. BC and cal. AD 600 and also come from sites which can clearly be identified as having been occupied by Celtic peoples at the time of deposition (Table 15.1). Four logboats dated from before 600 BC (Peterborough, Short Ferry, Brigg and Appleby), which appear to have technological similarities with those of the core Celtic period, are also included in Table 15.1.

Raw Material

All the logboats in Table 15.1 were of oak (*Quercus* sp.), as are the great majority of those reported elsewhere in Europe. In general terms the tabled data show that the length of parent tree of these logboats becomes less with time, either because smaller logboats were able to carry out the functions required of them, or because larger oaks were no longer available. From the Appleby logboat of 1525 to 1205 BC to Holme Pierrepont 3 of 410 to 135 BC twelve parent logs averaged 9.3 ± 2.9 m in length, whilst the five parent logs from Shapwick (795 to 80 BC) to Wisley (110 BC to AD 345) averaged 5.6 ± 1.5 m.

Table 15.1 Logboats from Southern Britain dated AD 600 or earlier

Logboat	Date range BC cal.	Region	Size[d] (m)	Deadweight[e] coefficient	Volumetric[f] coefficient (× 10³)
Appleby	1525–1205	Humber/Ancholme	>7.5 × 1.35		
Short Ferry	1255–805	Wash/Witham	>7.3 × 0.85		
Brigg 1	1245–800	Humber/Ancholme	14.78 × 1.37 × 1	0.67	1.54
Peterborough	875–530	Wash/Nene	>9.8 × 0.78		
Hasholme[a]	750–390	Humber/Foulness	12.78 × 1.4 × 1.25	0.57	3.00
Ellesmere	465–200	Severn/Parry	3.35 × 0.73 × 0.44	0.67	11.3
Clifton 1	450–195	Humber/Trent	8.55 × 0.76 × 0.36	0.43	1.9
Clifton 2	415–95	Humber/Trent	9.25 × 0.76 × 0.38	0.47	1.7
Poole	410–190	Poole Harbour	10.01 × 1.52 × 0.5	0.57	1.94
Holme Pierrepont 1	410–135	Humber/Trent	>6.5 × 0.86		
Holme Pierrepont 2[b]	—	Humber/Trent	>5.3 × 0.82		
Holme Pierrepont 3[b]	—	Humber/Trent	>10.0 × 1.28		
Shapwick[c]	795–80	Brue	>6 × 0.75		
Glastonbury 1	340–30	Brue	5.4 × 0.69 × 0.42	0.60	4.6
Woolwich	205–105 AD	Thames	>4.75 × 0.55		
Baddiley Mere	100–110 AD	Mersey/Weaver	5.49 × 0.92 × 0.61	0.66	14.8
Wisley	110–345 AD	Thames/Wey	>3.66 × 0.7		

Notes

a Dated by dendrochronology (Sheffield) to 322–277 BC (Millett and McGrail 1987: 79–84).
b Undated but considered contemporary with HP1.
c The one date for this boat (Q–317) has a high uncertainty (±120), hence the large date range. It is possible that this boat has a similar date to Glastonbury 1.
d Sizes are given as length × max. breadth × max. height of hull, for those boats which have been theoretically reconstructed. For the others, with less remains, a minimum length and breadth are given.
e Deadweight coefficient = weight of crew and cargo/displacement at standard draft (60% height of sides). The greater this coefficient, the better the boat is for carrying high density loads (McGrail 1978: 137).
f Volumetric coefficient = displacement/cube of waterline length (when carrying maximum crew and no cargo). A value $\leq 2 \times 10^{-3}$ indicates a hull of potentially high speed.

Sources

Dates: Switsur, R.V. (1990) Results of Boat Dating Programme, Cambridge (unpublished). The dates have been calibrated using the curves published by Pearson and Stuiver (1986). The felling dates of the parent logs of these boats (close to the building date) could be an estimated 25 to 70 years later than the calibrated dates given above.

Other data: McGrail, S. (1978) Logboats of England and Wales, Oxford: British Archaeological Reports 51.

Woodworking Techniques

The techniques used to fasten fittings or to make repairs to logboats may be listed in chronological order:

- sewing from *c*.1525 to 800 BC
- wooden treenails from *c*.1525 BC to AD 345 (and onwards)
- dovetailed joints from *c*.1255 to 135 BC (and onwards)
- cleat and transverse timbers from *c*.1245 to 277 BC.
- iron nails from *c*.410 to 135 BC (and onwards)

Large, mature oaks tend to develop heart rot which spreads up the centre of the tree from the butt end. Every logboat over 7 m long in Table 15.1 had been fitted with a transom board set into a groove near the stern – this was probably necessary because of heart rot at that end. In the case of the Brigg parent log this rot extended almost to the bow end (Atkinson 1887: 367); in the Hasholme tree, rot probably extended along the whole of the usable length, for a composite bow of two large timbers had to be fastened to the main log (Figure 15.6). Extending the bow of a logboat as in Hasholme is almost unique: the only comparable cases are Pommeroeul 2 (de Boe and Hubert 1977) and Zwammerdam 3 (de Weerd 1988), both dated to the first/second centuries AD.

Estimates of the age of the Hasholme tree when it was felled range from 600 to 820 (Hillam 1987: 84) to 810 to 880 years (Millett and McGrail 1987: 107). This log, without branches, would have weighed more than 20 tonnes, whilst the Brigg parent log would have weighed over 30 tonnes, both sizeable objects to move from the forest to the river: that the Celts could do this testifies to their competence in this field.

Performance

Details of the loads eight logboats could carry are given in Table 15.2 where it can be seen that, in a state of adequate transverse stability, the smallest one could carry a useful load of 337 kg whilst the logboats from Brigg and Hasholme could carry nearly 6 tonnes.

The volumetric coefficients in Table 15.1 were calculated at the 'maximum men' condition given in Table 15.2, that is, when maximum paddling power was available. Four logboats, Brigg, Clifton 1 and 2 and Poole, have coefficients $\leqslant 2 \times 10^{-3}$: in theory these boats have high speed potential. For reasons of stability, however, the Clifton boats were probably only able to embark around half the crew there was room for and thus they are unlikely to have developed sufficient power to achieve more than, say, 3 kts. On the other hand, both Brigg and Poole were able to carry a full complement of paddlers, who, in reasonable conditions, may have been able to make the boat semi-plane and thus achieve extraordinary speeds, say up to 7 kts for a short while.

The Use of Logboats at Sea

A simple logboat, generally speaking, has insufficient freeboard (height of sides above waterline) and transverse stability to be safely used at sea except in the calmest

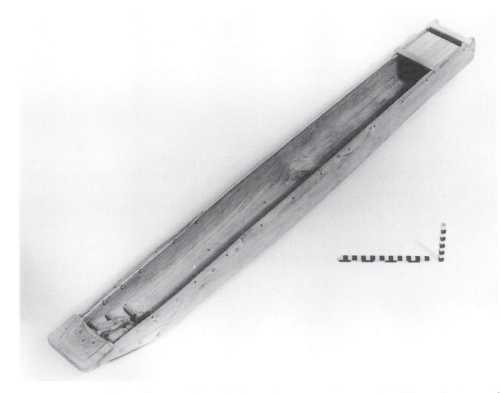

Figure 15.6 Model of the Hasholme logboat of *c*.300 BC (1:10 scale). (Photo: Institute of Archaeology, Oxford.)

of conditions. It is possible, however, to gain extra stability by increasing the water-line breadth (beam measurement) of a boat; and to increase freeboard by adding extra planks to the sides. Washstrakes were, in fact, added to the Hasholme logboat but only over a limited length towards the bow and no effective extra freeboard was gained overall.

One way of increasing the waterline breadth of a logboat is to force the sides apart after heat treatment. There is, however, no sign that any of the boats in Table 15.1 had been so expanded. Indeed, it is only certain species of tree that can be expanded safely, and oak seems unlikely to be one of these (McGrail 1978: 38–41).

A second method of increasing the waterline breadth measurement and hence improving stability is to pair two boats side by side. Clifton 1 and 2 are very similar to one another and could have readily been paired; however, there is no sign on the surviving remains of any appropriate fittings or fastenings. On the other hand, the three logboats from Holme Pierrepont, also from the river Trent, do have a number of holes along their sides which *might* be where each one was fastened to another boat of similar form. Nevertheless, these boats were incomplete when found, the accounts of their recording do not always agree with the published drawings, and they have never since been made available for re-recording and so the evidence remains ambiguous (McGrail 1978: 205–18, figs 20–2).

Table 15.2 Load-carrying estimates for eight logboats from southern Britain

Boat	Description	Draft (m)	Freeboard (m)	%age[a]	Dwt[b] (tonnes)
Brigg	maximum men (2 + 26)	0.35	0.65	35	1.44
	5 men + 5491 kg cargo	0.60	0.40	60	5.79
Hasholme	Maximum men (2 + 18)	0.46	0.79	37	1.20
	5 men + 5502 kg cargo	0.75	0.50	60	5.80
Ellesmere	maximum men (1)	0.13	0.31	28	0.06
	1 man + 277 kg cargo	0.26	0.18	60	0.38
Clifton 1	maximum men (1 + 5)	0.17	0.19	46	0.36
	2 men + 361 kg cargo	0.21	0.15	60	0.48
Clifton 2	maximum men (1 + 6)	0.19	0.19	50	0.42
	2 men + 533 kg cargo	0.23	0.25	60	0.65
Poole	maximum men (2 + 16)	0.29	0.21	59	1.08
	4 men + 898 kg cargo	0.30	0.20	60	1.14
Glastonbury 1	maximum men (1 + 2)	0.18	0.24	42	0.18
	1 man + 345 kg cargo	0.25	0.17	60	0.41
Baddiley Mere	maximum men (1 + 6)	0.25	0.36	41	0.42
	1 man + 832 kg cargo	0.37	0.24	60	0.89

Notes
[a] Ratio of draft to height of sides expressed as a percentage. 60% is used for international comparison of seagoing vessels.
[b] Deadweight = weight of crew and cargo.
Source McGrail 1978.

Glastonbury 1 has notches worked in the top edges of both sides, near one end (McGrail 1978: fig. 62) which may have been where a transverse fitting was fastened to pair this boat to a similar one. However, at least one more fastening point would be needed and there is no clear sign of this.

Thus there is no unambiguous evidence that Celtic logboats from Britain were paired and the continental evidence is also insubstantial. On the other hand, we know from Caesar (*De Bello Gallico* I.12) that the Celtic Helvetii used paired boats as river ferries. Detailed recording of future finds from this period may provide more convincing artefactual evidence for this practice than is available from the logboats known to date.

Another stability-enhancing method is to fasten longitudinal timbers to both sides of individual boats at the waterline. The only early British logboats with holes through their sides are those from Holme Pierrepont, Hasholme and Brigg, but these holes appear to be either too high or too low for stabilizers.

In sum then, there is no unchallengeable evidence from this group of logboats from southern Britain that any were modified to increase stability or freeboard. Nor is there any good evidence for these practices in any other of the north-west

European logboats from this period. Nevertheless, paired boats were clearly used by the Celts on rivers and thus, providing that these boats had increased freeboard, they may also have been used at sea.

Hide Boats

Hide boats, sometimes known as skin boats, are essentially a hide or leather water-proof covering fastened to a framework of light timbers. These are insubstantial materials, not surviving well over the years, and there is little excavated evidence of them to date. Reappraisal of the evidence from an early bronze age grave at Barns Farm, Dalgety, Fife, has suggested to Watkins (1980) that the body had been buried in a coracle; Sheppard (1926) noted a 'coracle like vessel' containing a 'skeleton' found in Lincolnshire near the confluence of the river Ancholme with the river Humber and possibly of Roman date; whilst a bronze or iron age 'coracle burial' was said to have been excavated in 1961 at Corbridge near the Roman Wall (Bishop and Dore 1988: 7); and from a tenth-century crannog site at Ballinderry, Co. Westmeath, a short length of timber has been interpreted as part of a currach's framework (Ellmers 1972).

The literary evidence from the late first millennium BC onwards is more promising. The sixth-century BC *periplus* extract incorporated within Avienus's fourth-century AD poem *Ora Maritima* (Hawkes 1977; Murphy 1977) tells us that the 'hardy and industrious peoples' of western Brittany used hide boats (*netisque cumbis*) to obtain tin and lead from Ireland and Britain, whilst Pliny (IV.104) quoting the early third-century BC historian Timaeus, describes how Britons used seagoing boats of 'osiers covered with stitched hides'. Other references to British hide boats, used both at sea and on inland waters, are made by Roman authors of the first century BC to the third century AD including Caesar (*De Bello Gallico* I.54), Pliny (VII.206), Lucan (*Pharsalia* IV.130–8) and Solinus (*Polyhistor* II.3).

The Broighter Model

A small gold model from Broighter on the margins of Lough Foyle, Co. Derry, Ireland, probably represents such a seagoing hide boat of the first century BC (Figure 15.3). This vessel could be propelled by a square sail on a mast stepped near amidships, or by oars – nine oarsmen each side – or in the shallows by poles ('punted'). She was steered by a steering oar which could be pivoted through a grommet (of rope?) on the port or starboard quarters. Other equipment with this model includes a grapnel anchor and a spar which may have been used to bear out the sail thus improving windward performance. If we assume that the thwarts (cross-beams) are spaced at 3 ft (0.914 m) intervals, the minimum distance for sea-rowing (McKee 1983: 139) then this model represents a hide boat which was *c*.20 m in overall length: that is, about twice the size of T. Severin's hide boat *Brendan* (1978). The largest Inuit seagoing hide boat (umiak) ever recorded is said to have been *c*.18 m in length (Adney and Chapelle 1964: 175–6), so 20 m would not be an unreasonable estimate for the length of the Broighter prototype.

Hide Boat Structure

Recent umiaks and currachs have not had keels, and their wooden framework has been made of laths fastened together by lashings, wooden pegs or iron nails. However, a late seventeenth-century drawing, now in the Pepys Library of Magdalene College, Cambridge, shows a large Irish sailing currach with prominent keel and stem outside the hide, and with a woven wickerwork hull underneath the hide. From medieval authors such as Adamnan, in his sixth/seventh-century *Vita St Columba* (Anderson and Anderson 1961; Marcus 1953–4: 315) and from classical authors such as Caesar (*De Bello Gallico* 1.54), Lucan (*Pharsalia* IV.136–8), Pliny (*Naturalis Historia* VII.205–6) and Dio Cassius (*Epitome* XLVIII.18–19) we get a similar picture of early British and Irish hide boats built on an osier or woven wicker framework and having prominent keels.

With such a keel an ancient currach would have been able to sail somewhat closer to the wind than its keel-less twentieth-century equivalent; and the woven basketry framework would have been stronger and more resilient than the frameworks of twentieth-century hide boats.

Performance

The lightweight structure of a hide boat, only half the weight of a planked boat of similar capacity, gives it good freeboard even when loaded: however, the consequent light draft means less resistance to leeway, and modern currachs and umiaks have a strong tendency to drift downwind. On the other hand, the prominent keel on the ancient currach and the use of a steering oar rather than a rudder mean that Celtic seagoing hide boats probably experienced less leeway than their keel-less twentieth-century equivalents. The other main drawback of the hide boat is that, although hide on a woven framework results in a resilient and energy-absorbing hull, the hide cover contributes little to structural strength: thus hide boats are limited in length and could never have been developed into ships. They would, however, have fitted well into the environment and economy of the western Celts in France, Britain and Ireland for fishing and for transport both at sea and on rivers and lakes. It is much to be regretted that, as yet, we have no excavated example of this 'workhorse' of the maritime Celts.

Plank Boats

Sewn Boats

The oldest known plank boats in Europe, and indeed in the world outside Egypt and the eastern Mediterranean, are from Britain: the so-called Brigg 'raft', actually a flat-bottomed boat, from the river Ancholme, a tributary of the river Humber, dated *c*.800 cal. BC (McGrail 1981b, 1985; Switsur and Wright 1989); the remains of three, possibly four, boats from North Ferriby on the northern foreshore of the Humber, dated *c*.1300 cal. BC (Wright 1990; Switsur and Wright 1989); and a plank fragment from a former bed of the river Neddern, a tributary of the river Severn at Caldicot Castle, Gwent, dated 1594–1454 cal. BC (Parry and McGrail 1991). These boats were built in the shell sequence from oak (*Quercus* sp.) planks which were fastened together by yew (*Taxus* sp.) lashings (Caldicot and Ferriby) or by continuous willow (*Salix* sp.) stitching (Brigg), with moss caulking between the planking held in position by longitudinal laths. Another common feature is that the planks in these boats were linked together by transverse timbers wedged within mortises in cleats that were proud of, but integral with, the planking. This technique was also used in a repair to the Brigg logboat and to fasten the lower bow to the hull of the Hasholme logboat – a tradition lasting from *c.*1500 to *c.*300 BC.

After the time of the Brigg 'raft', sewn plank boats are known only from the Baltic region: the plank boat from Hjortspring, Als, Denmark of *c.*350 BC (Rosenberg 1937); and medieval and later sewn plank boats of Finland, Sweden, Norway, Estonia and Russia (McGrail and Kentley 1985: 195–268). A similar survival at the margins may be seen in the Mediterranean: sewn planking is known from the third millennium BC through to the mid-first millennium BC in the eastern and central Mediterranean region, but from then on appears to be restricted to the Adriatic, in the Po estuary and on the Dalmatian coast, where it survived until at least the eleventh century AD (Pomey 1985; McGrail 1981a: 21).

The Caldicot, Ferriby and Brigg boats were all narrow, relatively long and full-bodied (Caldicot and Ferriby) or flat-bottomed (Brigg), without stems or significant keels. They were probably propelled and steered by paddles or, in shallow water, by poles. The Brigg boat would have been used within the river Ancholme, whereas the Caldicot and Ferriby boats could have been used along and across tidal estuaries and their associated rivers. Examples of loads that could be carried are given in Table 15.3. With a length:breadth ratio at the waterline of *c.*6:1, the Ferriby estuary boats were designed for speed, possibly up to 6 kts, which would be necessary when crossing the tidal Humber at times other than slack water.

In autumn 1992 there were further finds of early sewn plank boats in Britain: two fragments of planking, dated to *c.*1000 BC, at Goldcliff, Gwent, on the foreshore of the Severn estuary; and the substantial remains of a boat at Dover, Kent, in a former freshwater stream. The Goldcliff fragments have features also found in the Brigg 'raft', whilst the Dover boat has some similarities with the boats from North Ferriby.

Another Tradition?

One of the bronze age logboat-shaped coffins from Loose Howe, North Yorkshire, has a pseudo-keel and stem worked in the solid (Elgee and Elgee 1949; McGrail 1978). Furthermore, the Poole, and possibly Holme Pierrepont 3, logboats of the period 410–135 BC have similar 'stems'. Such fittings are non-functional in a logboat: the idea may well have been copied from a plank boat; this suggests that there may have been an early tradition of plank boats with keels and stems for which there is, as yet, no direct archaeological evidence.

Romano-Celtic Boats and Ships

Towards the end of the Iron Age and during late Roman times, between the first century BC and the third century AD, there is evidence for Celtic plank boats and ships, both riverine and seagoing. Caesar (*De Bello Gallico* III.13) and Strabo

Table 15.3 Load-carrying estimates for the Ferriby and Brigg plank boats

Boat	Load[a]	Draft (m)	Freeboard (m)	%age[b]	Dwt[c] (tonnes)	Dwt coeff.[d]
Ferriby 1	20 crew + 30 passengers + 2.9 tonnes of cargo[e]	0.58	0.40	60	6.70	0.60
Brigg 2	4 crew + 26 sheep	0.25	0.09	74	1.54	0.23
	6 crew + 17 cattle	0.46	0.09	84	7.16	0.57

Notes
[a] Assumes each man weighs 60kg; sheep 50kg; cattle 400 kg.
[b] Ratio of draft to height of sides expressed as a percentage.
[c] Weight of crew + cargo.
[d] Deadweight/displacement.
[e] If this was not high-density cargo, then the weight carried would be less.

Sources
   Coates 1981, 1990: 113–16.

(*Geography* IV.4.1) describe the seagoing sailing ships of the Veneti Celts of south-west Brittany, which were more seaworthy and better suited to the difficult seas off north-west France than were Caesar's own vessels, for they could sail closer inshore and take the ground readily in those tidal waters. They had flush-laid oak planking which was caulked with 'seaweed' – possibly moss (Wright 1990), or even reeds (*harundines*), which Pliny (*Naturalis Historia* XVI.158) tells us were used for caulking by the Belgae in the first century AD. The Veneti planking was fastened to 1 ft (30 cm) thick framing timbers by iron nails 1 inch (2.5 cm) in diameter. These Veneti ships were propelled by sails of leather and were used for cross-Channel voyages to Britain. A Gallic merchant ship known as a *ponto* is mentioned elsewhere by Caesar (*Bellum Civile* III.29), but it is not clear whether this is a reference to the Veneti ships or to another Celtic seagoing type (McGrail 1990b: 41–3).

   A Celtic sailing ship is featured on a gold coin of the first century BC Atrebates (McGrail 1990b: fig. 4.9), but this representation is stylistic and difficult to interpret. Vessels with more readily recognizable features are depicted on two bronze coins of the first century AD issued by Cunobelin of the Catuvellauni of south-eastern Britain (Figure 15.5). These two vessels have the relatively deep hull of a merchant ship, were propelled by a square sail set on a mast stepped near amidships, and steered by side rudder. Braces to the yard suggest a weatherly performance, as do the protruding forefoot and the spar at the stem head which may have taken a bowline. If these Cunobelin ships were broad in the beam to match the depicted depth of hull, they would have been stable, seaworthy ships with good cargo capacity, albeit only moderate speed potential.

   A dozen or more boats from the second and third centuries AD, some seagoing, some for inland waters, from the Thames estuary, the lower reaches of the Rhine (Figure 15.7) and nearby rivers, from Guernsey, and from the Swiss lakes, have several boatbuilding features in common which differentiate them as a group from both the contemporary Mediterranean tradition and from the late Roman/early

Figure 15.7 A Zwammerdam barge during excavation.
(Photo: I.P.P. University of Amsterdam.)

medieval proto-Viking tradition of northern Europe (McGrail 1981a: 23–4). Some of the boats in this group do have anomalous features: for example Zwammerdam 2 and 6 have some overlapping planking fastened by nails, comparable with proto-Viking techniques; whilst Zwammerdam 6 also has flush-laid planking fastened by loose-tongue joints similar to those in the Mediterranean tradition; and Zwammerdam 6 and Pommeroeul 5 have flush-laid planking fastened by obliquely driven spikes (de Weerd 1988; de Boe and Hubert 1977). Nevertheless, in all the boats of this group, the greater part of the planking is flush-laid and is not edge-joined, but fastened to the heavy framing timbers by large iron nails clenched by turning the point back through 180° so that it re-enters the frame.

This strongly suggests that these boats and ships were built in the skeleton sequence, possibly the earliest known use of this technique in the building of plank boats. Arnold (1992) has, however, argued that boats of this tradition designed for use on inland waters (in particular those from Yverdon and Bevaix, Switzerland) were neither skeleton nor shell construction, but 'bottom-based construction'. It is true that shell and skeleton concepts are more difficult to apply to barge-like boats with flat-bottomed transverse sections and hard chines, than to round-hulled vessels; and it is also true, as Arnold says, that 'the flat bottom constitutes a base for the entire construction'. However, the shape of the sides of such a boat is determined either by the shape of the first side strakes (the side timbers subsequently conforming to that shape), in which case the shell sequence has been used; or initially by the shape of the floor-timber ends and subsequently by the side timbers (the planking conforming to this shape), in which case the skeleton sequence has been used. Which of these two sequences was used is not clear from the publications of the great majority of boats in this tradition, but it *is* clear for the ship Blackfriars 1 (Figure 15.8) (Marsden 1991): floor timbers were fastened to the two longitudinal planks forming the keel of this ship, and the shape of the hull (full form with rounded bilges) was determined by these floors and by the subsequently erected side framing – thus Blackfriars 1 was built in the skeleton sequence, as also probably was the Romano-Celtic ship from St Peter Port, Guernsey (Rule 1990).

The idea of using a framework or skeleton to give the form of a boat had been familiar to north-west European hide-boat builders from prehistoric times (McGrail 1987: 173–86). To transfer this technique to the building of plank boats and ships may well have been a major contribution by the Celts to nautical technology. There are, however, those who would not give the name 'Celtic' to this distinctive type of boatbuilding: see, for example, Parker (1991); and Haywood (1991: 17–21) has argued that, by the second and third centuries AD, the land near the Rhine mouth, where several of these boats were excavated, was occupied by Germanic tribes. Nevertheless, most of these boats were excavated from regions which were undoubtedly occupied by Celts at the date attributed to the boats. Furthermore, the general similarity between Caesar's description of the Veneti vessels and features of the Blackfriars 1 and St Peter Port ships is undeniable. It does not therefore seem unreasonable to call this tradition 'Celtic' although perhaps 'Romano-Celtic' (or 'Gallo-Roman' to Franco-phones) is to be preferred, as the nucleus of the boats and ships of this tradition are of Roman date; moreover, this term draws attention to the possibility of some Roman technological influence on this Celtic tradition.

Figure 15.8 Blackfriars boat 1 during excavation. (Photo: P. Marsden.)

De Weerd (1988, 1990) has taken an extreme view on this question and argues that the Zwammerdam boats and related ones were built under strong Roman influence. He has sought to demonstrate that their planks were of standard lengths and that their frames were spaced out in multiples of the standard Roman unit the *pes monetalis*. As Arnold (1991) has pointed out, de Weerd's sample is small, there are inconsistencies in his choice of data for analysis, and his use of 1:20 scale drawings rather than direct measurement cannot give the necessary accuracy of measurement. Moreover, such data, even when precisely measured, must be investigated statistically to determine the numerical value of the unit most likely to have been used, rather than assuming, as de Weerd has done, that the *pes monetalis* was the unit and then showing that it more or less fits the data.

Another distinctive feature of these Romano-Celtic boats and ships is that, where a mast step has survived to be excavated, it is found to be positioned at *c.*one-quarter to one-third the waterline length from the bow (McGrail 1987: 217–18, table 12.5; Rule 1990). For barge-like boats used on rivers this is the ideal position for a towing mast, but for the two seagoing ships (Blackfriars 1 and St Peter Port) such a mast must have carried a sail. A square sail so far forward would induce steering problems if the wind was other than from the stern sector (McGrail 1987: 225–7). This suggests that these two ships may therefore have had a fore-and-aft sail such as a sprit or lugsail, rather than a square sail (McGrail 1990b: 45). Support for this hypothesis comes from Rhinelands representations of Romano-Celtic river boats of the second/third century AD, which Ellmers (1969, 1975, 1978) believes have leather lugsails with battens.

Here again is another strong suggestion of a Celtic innovation, as lugsails are otherwise not known in European waters until post-medieval times. Such fore-and-aft sails would have enhanced the windward performance of Celtic boats and ships, and as the mast was well forward, the cargo hold would have been free of obstructions. Both river barges and seagoing ships of this Romano-Celtic tradition were capable of carrying sizeable quantities of cargo: the barges 18 to 20 tonnes; the Blackfriars ship up to 60 tonnes (Table 15.4).

In autumn 1993 a third-century AD boat of the Romano-Celtic tradition was excavated at Barland's Farm, Magor, Gwent, from the bed of a stream which formerly flowed southwards into the Severn estuary. This boat has a mast-step well forward and other features characteristic of this tradition. In general terms she may be thought of as a boat one-fifth the size in volume of Blackfriars 1.

CELTIC BOATBUILDING AND SEAFARING

Similarities between the logboats and plank boats of the period 600 BC to AD 600 and those of earlier times suggest that the roots of Celtic boatbuilding lie in the second millennium BC or earlier. From this time onwards increasing competence is shown in boatbuilding and woodworking techniques, for example, the movement of large logs from felling site to river and their transformation into cargo-carrying logboats; the ingenious system of interlocking planking seen in the Ferriby boats, particularly towards the bow and stern; and the range of techniques used in the Hasholme logboat of *c.* 300 BC. Iron began to be used in boats in the period 410–135 BC or even earlier, culminating in the great iron nails used to fasten planking to framework in Romano-Celtic seagoing ships: these nails were up to 0.79 m (2 ft 7 in) in length and weighed up to 1.5 kg (3.3 lbs), a very clear indication of the Celtic smith's abilities (see Chapter 17).

Table 15.4 Load-carrying estimates for three Romano-Celtic vessels

Vessel	Load	Draft (m)	Freeboard (m)	%age[a]	Dwt[b] (tonnes)	Dwt coeff.[c]
Blackfriars 1	12 barrels of wine	1.02	1.83	36	15.33	0.30
	grain	1.07	1.78	37	18.36	0.35
	stone	1.18	1.67	41	26.00	0.45
	mixed load	1.71	1.14	60	63.30	0.66
Bevaix	mixed load	0.50	0.40	55	10.00	0.61
	mixed load	0.70	0.20	77	18.00	0.74
Yverdon 1	mixed load	0.80	0.20	80	20.00	0.71

Notes
[a] Ratio of draft to height of sides, expressed as a percentage. Bevaix and Yverdon 1 are boats from inland waters and therefore they have been assessed at drafts deeper than the seagoing standard of 60%.
[b] Weight of cargo.
[c] Deadweight/displacement.

Sources
Marsden 1991; Arnold 1992.

On rivers and lakes the Celts used log rafts (and possibly bundle rafts), plank boats (barges) of (near) rectangular cross-section and logboats. In estuaries they had plank-built ferry boats designed for speedy crossings. At sea, from early times, they seem to have used hide boats and possibly paired logboats. There are signs in the Bronze Age that plank boats may also have been used at sea, and in the first century BC there is clear evidence for Celtic seagoing planked ships specifically designed for operations in the difficult waters of the Channel and the south-western approaches.

The evidence at present available strongly suggests that the Celts were innovative boatbuilders and seamen. From 500 BC or earlier they were undertaking open sea voyages of two days' duration on which they had to use specialized navigational techniques: these voyages are the earliest known, indigenous, ocean-going voyages in northern Europe. By this date too, they were using sail – again the earliest known European use outside the areas of Mediterranean influence. Furthermore, by the first century AD the Celts had developed both hull and rigging to improve weatherly performance: and their probable use of fore-and-aft sails from the second century AD is also the earliest known use outside the Mediterranean. By this time too, if not earlier, they were using side rudders rather than steering paddle or oar, the earliest indigenous use in northern Europe.

Perhaps the most striking Celtic innovation is their use of the skeleton sequence of building ships, from the early years of the first millennium AD. For it was only by using this technique, rather than the shell sequence, that the large ocean-going ships of the fifteenth century could be built. Although there is a hint in Herodotus (1.194) that plank boats were built by a form of skeleton building in the eastern Mediterranean in the fifth century BC (Morrison 1976: 165–6), the first clear steps towards a skeleton-built seagoing ship do not seem to have been taken in that region until the seventh century AD, some 500 years after its use in Celtic Europe. This Celtic innovation seems to disappear from archaeological sight by the fourth century AD, apparently swamped by the widespread use of the shell sequence in the Viking/Norse tradition. It is not noted again until the eleventh century when it re-appears in the lower hull of the Cog tradition (Ellmers 1979): future finds of the fourth to eleventh century may clarify what happened during this hiatus.

CELTIC NAVIGATIONAL TECHNIQUES

Today, navigation is regarded primarily as a science, and seafarers have many aids to help them find their way and keep a reckoning of their position in the seas off north-west Europe. Before the twelfth century AD this was not so: the only instrument in use was the sounding lead, and navigation was more of an art in that personal skills were used. Being essentially non-instrumental, there is no artefactual evidence for the methods used by the Celts. There is, however, indirect archaeological evidence and some documentary evidence, and we can also draw on comparative evidence from other times and places with a generally similar technological background (Olsen 1885; Lewis 1972; Waters 1978: 3–38; Binns 1980: 79–80; McGrail 1989).

The alignment of neolithic and bronze age megalithic structures in Britain, Ireland and France indicates a knowledge of the sun's movements and possibly those of the moon (Wood 1978: 184–8; Heggie 1981: 222–3). The Celtic world inherited this learning and extended it: Caesar (*De Bello Gallico* VI.14) describes the Celts' knowledge of astronomy, 'the stars and their movements', and there was particular emphasis on the moon (Piggott 1974: 104–5): being the chief arbiter of tides, the moon would be of particular importance to maritime Celts. Recent analysis of the fragments of a second century AD calendar, found in 1897 in a vineyard at Coligny, north of Lyons, has shown that it was primarily a lunar calendar adapted to the solar cycle, with an error of only 1 day in 455 years (Olmsted 1992). This further emphasizes the Celts' ability to study the heavens systematically, an ability which would have been especially needed by Celtic navigators.

Precisely how directions and distances at sea were measured and described by the Celts is not clear, but contemporary Roman usage and comparative evidence from such diverse sources as the Vikings (McGrail 1987) and Homer in his account of Odysseus's voyages (McGrail forthcoming), suggests that distances would have been in units of a standard day's sail. Directions, when land was out of sight, would probably have been estimated relative to the wind, the swell, sunset and sunrise, and at night from the Great Bear (Ursa Major) or even the Little Bear (Ursa Minor) or other constellations (McGrail 1983) for in those times there was no star actually at the North Pole (the null point about which the heavens appear to revolve).

Celtic navigators would have 'plotted' these estimates of distances and directions travelled on their 'mental sea charts' and so determined their position relative to their home base or to their overseas destination (McGrail 1983).

The Celts paid great attention to memory training and oral instruction for the transmission of learning (Caesar, *De Bello Gallico* VI.14; Chadwick 1970: 45–7; Ross 1970: 125–6). The motions of the heavenly bodies, the phases of the moon and the ebb and flow of the tides, the weather sequences, descriptions of coastal landscapes, safe channels and sailing marks leading to the main landing places, the direction and distance between point of departure, and landfalls for each overseas route used – all these would have had to be memorized by Celtic seamen, encapsulated in easily remembered phrases and rules of thumb, possibly in verse form, which medieval Arabs are known to have used (Tibbetts 1981).

We can theorize that the following oral sailing directions might have been learned and used by a fifth-century BC seaman crossing from Mounts Bay, Cornwall, to Ushant off Brittany:

> Leave Mounts Bay in the afternoon on an ebb tide and with a westerly wind (as is often the case in the sailing season). Keep this wind as far forward of the starboard beam as is practicable and steer away from land, noting your track by reference to memorized landmarks and seamarks; use the sounding lead if necessary.
>
> Take departure from land before sunset by noting your position relative to Lizard Head or Gwenap Head, and maintain or turn to that heading which puts the wind just forward of the starboard beam. Note the relative direction of the sea swell. Confirm the boat's heading at sunset when the sun should be on or near the starboard beam. When dark, keep the Great Bear constellation fine on the starboard quarter. Check wind and swell direction against this bearing. At dawn check them against the bearing of sunrise which should be on the port quarter.
>
> Certain types of cloud or the flight line of birds may give early warning of the French coast. If the standard speed [4 kts in twentieth-century terms] has been maintained, and visibility is good, high ground beyond the French coast should be seen on the port bow at around the time of day when the sun is at its highest. The island of Ushant will be sighted fine on the port bow during the afternoon, well before sunset.
>
> Use landmarks and seamarks to identify your position, and plan your approach to the land so that you have a flood tide for entering your destination haven; use the sounding lead.

Celtic seamen had solved the problems of deep-sea voyages in some of Europe's most dangerous waters by the fifth century BC or even earlier. As the evidence stands at present, in their use of these skills they were well ahead of their contemporaries in northern Europe.

OVERSEAS ROUTES AND HARBOURS

From the first century BC there is confirmation in the writings of Caesar, Pliny, Strabo and Diodorus of cross-Channel routes between the Continent and Britain and Ireland suggested by contemporary and earlier distribution patterns of artefacts (Cunliffe 1982; McGrail 1983). These are (Figure 15.9):

- The Rhine to the Thames
- In the region of the Strait

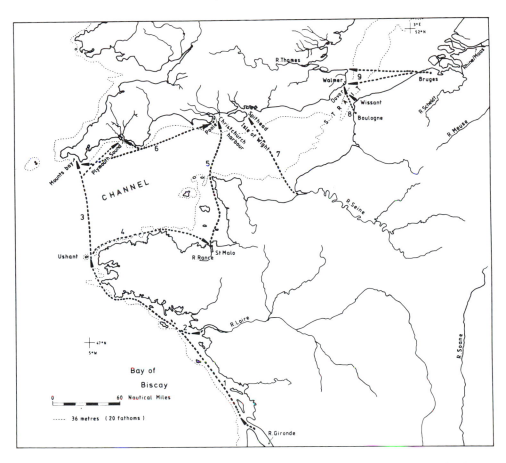

Figure 15.9 Map of cross-Channel trade routes. (Institute of Archaeology, Oxford.)

- Mid-Channel routes
- Western Brittany to south-west Britain and south-east Ireland

Mediterranean maritime trade routes were linked to these Channel crossings and their associated coastal routes in one of three ways:

- Up the river Rhône, then portages to the upper reaches of the rivers Loire, Seine and Rhine.
- Up the river Aude, then a portage across the Carcassonne gap to the river Garonne and Gironde; thence via the coastal route to western Brittany.
- Through the strait at Gibraltar and then the Iberian coastal route to western Brittany. This Atlantic route seems to have been used by Mediterranean merchants in the late sixth century BC and also by Pytheas on his late fourth-century BC exploration of northern waters (Hawkes 1977, 1984; Murphy 1977; McGrail 1990b: 36). This would have been an arduous passage, especially outbound from the Mediterranean, with a strong eastward setting current in the Strait and generally foul winds and currents along the Iberian Atlantic seaboard.

Furthermore, there were prominent headlands to be rounded which could have caused considerable delays during the wait for favourable winds and tidal streams. That this difficult route was indeed used in Roman times seems to be confirmed by the lighthouse built at Corunna in north-west Spain (Hague 1973).

Landing Places

Vessels on cross-Channel voyages would have taken departure from, and made a landfall off, a prominent landmark such as the island of Ushant, Cap de la Hague, Pointe de Barfleur, Cap Gris Nez or the Needles, Portland Bill, Start Point and the Lizard. The beginning and end of these voyages would, however, have been natural havens such as the Gironde, the Loire estuary, the Baie de St Malo, the Seine, Rhine and Thames estuaries, the Solent, Christchurch and Poole harbours and Plymouth Sound. Landing places within these havens were informal ones with little, if any, man-made protection or facilities. Only on soft muddy strands, where a beached boat might stick despite a rising tide, were artificial structures (hards) needed, as at Hengistbury with its gravelled area on the foreshore (Cunliffe 1990) or at North Ferriby where Wright (1990) found light timbers and hurdles pegged to the beach in the intertidal zone.

Carts and Wagons

Boats were beached on a falling (ebb) tide or they were anchored in the shallows below low-water mark off these beaches, and goods unloaded into smaller boats (logboats?). Horse or oxen-drawn wagons or carts were also probably used to load and discharge beached and anchored boats (Ellmers 1985). Logboat 1 from Holme Pierrepont on the river Trent, Nottinghamshire, was found lying on a 12-spoked wheel (Musty and McCormick 1973). Fragments of wheels have also been excavated from Glastonbury (Bulleid and Gray 1911) in the vicinity of the find-spot of Glastonbury logboat 1 (Bulleid 1893, 1894). Timbers from the village at Glastonbury have been dated by radiocarbon to the period 80 BC to AD 150 (J.M. Coles 1989: 64) whilst the date range of Glastonbury 1 logboat is 340 to 30 BC. Cart or wagon wheels have also been found at similar sites in the Netherlands and in Lower Saxony (Piggott 1983; Coles and Coles 1989: 162; see also Chapter 18).

In the first century BC Diodorus (v.22.1–4) described how the inhabitants of Belerion (the Devon/Cornwall peninsula) used wagons to take tin to an island Ictis; Pliny (*Naturalis Historia* IV.16.104), quoting Timaeus of the third century BC, gives a similar account about an island Mictis which may be in the Solent region. The two places considered most likely to be Ictis are the island of St Michael's Mount, Cornwall, and the peninsula of Mount Batten in Plymouth Sound (Cunliffe 1983; Hawkes 1984). Tin and copper could have been brought by wagon from north and central Cornwall to Mount's Bay and thence to the island at low water. On the other hand, Mount Batten seems archaeologically more likely as there are a number of finds from there which indicate it was prominent in international trade from the fourth century BC until the first century AD (Cunliffe 1988). Tin and copper from the Dartmoor and Callington deposits would, however, more easily have been brought to Mount Batten by boats down the rivers Tavy and Tamar, whereas wagons could have been used to take ingots from a 'warehouse' at Mount Batten to beached or anchored ships.

INLAND TRAVEL

Rivers

Celtic lands are well endowed with rivers and streams which become natural routes for travel, trade and social intercourse: by raft or boat in favourable circumstances, or by riverside tracks when the water level was too low, the river bed encumbered with obstacles, or the river flow too fast. Thus the preferred inland routes to and from international landing places would have been the rivers. From Hengistbury Head within Christchurch harbour, for example, the rivers Stour and Avon give access to a large tract of Wessex including Cranbourne Chase and Blackmore Vale in the west and much of Wiltshire as far north as the Vale of Pewsey. The Thames, Humber, Rhine, Seine, Loire and Gironde have even greater catchment areas.

Roads

In the wet seasons rivers could still be used, though with more difficulty, but riverside and valley bottom tracks would often have been impassable, and travellers by foot, cart or wagon would have used alternative routes along higher ground. The lowlands were sometimes connected to these ridgeways by sunken roads created in part as banks were built to define fields, and in part by the repeated passage of cattle (Audouze and Büchsenschütz 1991: 145–7). These were natural roads with, generally speaking, no man-made structures. However, where wetlands had to be traversed, as in marshy areas, or on the approaches to a river or the coast, causeways – roads raised above their general surroundings – had to be built (Coles and Coles 1989: 151–69).

Evidence from the Somerset levels, the Irish midlands, the Netherlands and Lower Saxony suggests that there were two main types of built roads: simple, relatively narrow footpaths for foot travellers, built of brushwood, or hurdles or planking laid longitudinally – examples are the Garvins, Eclipse and Sweet causeways of Somerset (Coles and Coles 1986); and broader, heavy-duty roads built of large timbers (often oak) laid transversely in corduroy fashion, which could be used by carts and wagons – examples are the bronze age causeway on the approaches to the river Ancholme near Brigg, Lincolnshire (McGrail 1981b); the 148 BC causeway at Derraghan and Corlea, Co. Longford, Ireland (Raftery 1986); and the Bohlensweg XCII of 129 BC which crossed the Wittemooor in Lower Saxony and was probably used by wheeled vehicles transporting bog iron to boats in a tributary of the river Weser (Coles and Coles 1989: 167–8).

ACKNOWLEDGEMENTS

I am grateful to Dr Roy Switsur of the Godwin Laboratory, University of Cambridge, for allowing me to refer to radiocarbon dates before their definitive publication; to Dr Peter Marsden of the Museum of London for data from his forthcoming book, *Ships of the Port of London*, English Heritage; and to Owain Roberts of the University of Wales, Bangor, for discussion of seafaring problems.

REFERENCES

Adney, E.T. and Chapelle, H.I.(1964) *Bark Canoes and Skin Boats of North America*, Washington: Smithsonian Institution.

Anderson, A.O. and Anderson, M.O. (eds) (1961) *Adamnan's Life of St Columba*, London.

Arnold, B. (1977) 'Some remarks on caulking in Celtic boat construction and its evolution in areas lying northwest of the Alplne arc', *International Journal of Nautical Archaeology* 6: 293–7.

—— (1990) 'Some objections to the link between Gallo-Roman boats and the Roman foot (*pes monetalis*)' *IJNA* 19: 273–7.

—— (1992) *Batellerie gallo-romaine sur le lac de Neuchâtel*, 2 vols, Saint Blaise: Editions du Ruan, Archéologie neuchâteloise 12 and 13.

Atkinson, A. (1887) 'Notes on an ancient boat found at Brigg', *Archaeologia* 50(2): 361–70.

Audouze, F. and Büchsenschütz, O. (1991) *Towns, Villages and Countryside of Celtic Europe*, London: Batsford.

Binns, A. (1980) *Viking Voyages*, London: Heinemann.

Bishop, M.C. and Dore, J.N. (1988) *Corbridge: excavations of the Roman fort and town 1947–80*, London: English Heritage, Archaeological Report 8.

Bonino, M. (1985) 'Sewn boats in Italy', in S. McGrail and E. Kentley (eds) *Sewn Plank Boats*, 87–104.

Brusić, Z. and Domjan, M. (1985) 'Liburnian boats', in S. McGrail and E. Kentley (eds) *Sewn Plank Boats*, 67–86.

Bulleid, A. (1893) 'Ancient canoe found near Glastonbury', *Somerset and Dorset Notes and Queries* 3: 121.

—— (1894) 'The lake village near Glastonbury', *Proceedings of the Somerset Archaeological and Natural History Society* 40: 141–51.

Bulleid, A. and Gray, H. St G. (1911) *Glastonbury Lake-Village* 1, Glastonbury: Glastonbury Antiquarian Society.

Chadwick, N. (1970) *The Celts*, Harmondsworth: Penguin Books.

Coates, J. (1981) 'Safe carrying capacity of the hypothetical reconstruction', in S. McGrail (ed.) *Brigg 'Raft'*, 261–70.

—— (1990) 'Performance', in E. Wright (ed.) *Ferriby Boats*, 113–16.

Coles, B. and Coles, J. (1986) *Sweet Track to Glastonbury*, London: Thames & Hudson.

—— (1989) *Peoples of the Wetlands*, London: Thames & Hudson.

Coles, J.M. (ed.) (1975–89) *Somerset Levels Papers* 1–15, Exeter: University of Exeter, Somerset Levels Project.

Cuniffe, B. (1982) 'Britain, the Veneti and beyond', *Oxford Journal of Archaeology* 1: 39–68.

—— (1983) 'Ictis: is it here?' *Oxford Journal of Archaeology* 2: 123–6.

—— (1988) *Mount Batten, Plymouth*, Oxford: Oxford University Committee for Archaeology Monograph 26.

—— (1990) Hengistbury Head: a late prehistoric haven', in S. McGrail (ed.) *Maritime Celts*, 27–31.

de Boe, G. and Hubert, F. (1977) 'Une installation portuaire d'époque romaine à Pommeroeul', *Archaeologia Belgica* 192: 1–57.

de Weerd, M. (1988) *Schepen voor Zwammerdam, Bouwwijze en herkomst van enkele vaartnigtypen in West – en Midden europa uit de Romeinse tijd ende Middel-eeuwen in archeologisch perspectief*, Amersterdam: Universiteit van Amsterdam.

—— (1990) 'Barges of the Zwammerdam type and their building procedures', in S. McGrail (ed.) *Maritime Celts*, 75–6.

Egloff, M. (1974) 'La barque de Bevaix, épave gallo-romaine du lac de Neuchâtel', *Helvetia Archaeologica* 19/20: 82–91.

Elgee, H.W. and Elgee, F. (1949) 'An EBA burial in a boat-shaped wooden coffin from north-east Yorkshire', *Proceedings of the Prehistoric Society* 15: 87–106.

Ellmers, D. (1969) 'Keltischer Schiffbau', *Jahrbuch des Römisch-Germanischen Zentralmuseums Mainz* 16: 73–122.

—— (1972) *Frühmittelalterliche Handelsschiffahrt in Mittel und Nordeuropa*, Neumunster: Karl Wachholtz Verlag.

—— (1975) 'Antriebstechniken Germanischer schiffe im 1 Jahrtausend N. CHR.', *Deutsches Schiffahrtsarchiv* 1: 79–90.

—— (1978) 'Shipping on the Rhine during the Roman period', in J. du P. Taylor and H. Cleere (eds) *Roman Shipping and Trade*, London: CBA Research Report 24, 1–14.

—— (1979) 'The Cog of Bremen and related boats', in S. McGrail (ed.) *Medieval Ships and Harbours in Northern Europe*, Oxford: British Archaeological Reports S66, 1–15.

—— (1985) 'Loading and unloading ships using a horse and cart standing in the water: the archaeological evidence', in A.E. Herteig (ed.) *Conference on Waterfront Archaeology in North European Towns no. 2*, Bergen: Historisk Museum Bergen, 25–30.

Farrell, A.W. and Penney, S. (1975) 'Broighter boat: a re-assessment', *Irish Archaeological Research Forum* 2(2): 15–26.

Hague, D.B. (1973) 'Lighthouses', in D.J. Blackman (ed.) *Marine Archaeology*, London: Butterworth, 293–316.

Hawkes, C.F.C. (1977) *Pytheas*, 8th J.N.L Myres Memorial Lecture, Oxford, published privately.

—— (1984) 'Ictis disentangled and the British tin trade', *Oxford Journal of Archaeology* 3: 211–33.

Haywood, J. (1991) *Dark Age Naval Power*, London: Routledge.

Heggie, D.C. (1981) *Megalithic Science*, London: Thames & Hudson.

Heyworth, A. and Kidson, C. (1982) 'Sea level changes in southwest England and in Wales', *Proceedings of the Geologists' Association* 93: 91–111.

Hillam, J. (1987) 'Tree-ring dating', in M. Millett and S. McGrail 'Archaeology of the Hasholme logboat', 79–84.

Hourihane, C.P. and Hourihane, J.J. (1979) 'Kilnaruane Pillar Stone, Bantry, Co. Cork', *Journal of the Cork Historical and Archaeological Society* 84: 65–73.

Lamb, H.H. (1977) *Climate* vol. II, London: Methuen.

Lewis, D. (1972) *We the Navigators*, Canberra: National University Press.

McGrail, S. (1978) *Logboats of England and Wales*, Oxford: British Archaeological Reports 51.

—— (1981a) *Rafts, Boats and Ships*, London: HMSO.

—— (1981b) (ed.) *Brigg 'Raft' and her Prehistoric Environment*, Oxford: British Archaeological Reports 89.

—— (1983) 'Cross-Channel seamanship and navigation in the late-first millennium BC',

Oxford: *Oxford Journal of Archaeology* 2: 299–337.

—— (1985) 'Brigg 'raft' – problems in reconstruction and the assessment of performance', in S. McGrail and E. Kentley (eds) *Sewn Plank Boats*, 165–94.

—— (1987) *Ancient Boats in North-West Europe*, London: Longman.

—— (1989) 'Pilotage and navigation in the times of St Brendan in de Courcy Ireland', in J. and D.C. Sheehy (eds) *Atlantic Visions*, Dun Laoghaire: Boole Press, 25–35.

—— (ed.) (1990a) *Maritime Celts, Frisians and Saxons*, London: CBA Research Report 71.

—— (1990b) 'Boats and boatmanship in the late-prehistoric southern North Sea and Channel region', in S. McGrail (ed.) *Maritime Celts*, 32–48.

—— (forthcoming) 'Navigational techniques in Homer's *Odyssey*', Athens Conference (1991) Proceedings.

McGrail, S. and Kentley, E. (eds) (1985) *Sewn Plank Boats*, Oxford: British Archaeological Reports S276.

McKee, E. (1983) *Working Boats of Britain*, Conway: Conway Maritime Press.

Marcus, G.J. (1953–4) 'Factors in early Celtic navigation', *Etudes Celtiques* 6: 312–27.

Marsden, P.R.V. (1976) 'A boat of the Roman period found at Bruges, Belgium in 1899, and related finds', *International Journal of Maritime Archaeology* 5: 23–55.

—— (1990) 'Re-assessment of Blackfriars 1', in S. McGrail (ed.) *Maritime Celts*, 66–74.

—— (1991) 'Shipping in the port of London from Roman times to the 13th century AD', D. Phil. thesis, University of Oxford.

Millett, M. and McGrail, S. (1987) 'Archaeology of the Hasholme logboat', *Archaeological Journal* 144: 69–155.

Morrison, J.S. (1976) 'Classical traditions', in B. Greenhill *Archaeology of the Boat*, London: A & C. Black, 155–73.

Murphy, J.P. (1977) *Rufus Festus Avienus' Ora Maritima*, Chicago.

Musty, J. and MacCormick, A.G. (1973) 'Early iron age wheel from Holme Pierrepont, Notts.', *Antiquaries Journal* 5: 275–7.

Olmsted, G. (1992) *Gaulish Calendar*, Bonn: Habelt.

Olsen, O.T. (1885) *Fisherman's Seamanship*, Grimsby: O.T. Olsen/London: Imray, Norrie & Wilson.

Parker, A.J. (1991) Review of *Maritime Celts, Frisians and Saxons*, *International Journal of Nautical Archaeology* 20: 363.

Parry, S. and McGrail, S. (1991) 'Prehistoric plank boat fragment and a hard from Caldicot Castle Lake, Gwent, Wales', *International Journal of Nautical Archaeology* 20: 321–4.

Pearson, G.W. and Stuiver, M. (1986) 'High precision calibration of the radiocarbon time scale 500–2500 B.C.', *Radiocarbon* 28: 839–62.

Piggott, S. (1974) *The Druids*, Harmondsworth: Penguin.

—— (1983) *Earliest Wheeled Transport*, London: Thames & Hudson.

Pomey, P. (1985) 'Mediterranean sewn boats in antiquity', in S. McGrail and E. Kentley (eds) *Sewn Plank Boats*, 35–48.

Raftery, B. (1986) 'Wooden trackway of Iron Age date in Ireland', *Antiquity* 60: 50–3.

Rosenberg, G. (1937) *Hjortspring fundet*, Copenhagen: Nordiske Fortidsminder.

Ross, A. (1970) *Everyday Life of the Pagan Celts*, London: Batsford.

Rule, M. (1990) 'Romano-Celtic ship excavated at St Peter Port, Guernsey', in S. McGrail (ed.) *Maritime Celts*, 49–56.

Severin, T. (1978) *Brendan Voyage*, London: Hutchinson.

Sheppard, T. (1926) 'Roman remains in north Lincolnshire', *East Riding Antiquarian Society Transactions*, 25: 170–4.

Steffy, J.R. (1982) 'Reconstruction of the 11th century Serçe Liman vessel', *International Journal of Nautical Archaeology* 11: 13–34.

Switsur, V.R. (1990) 'Results of boat dating programme' (unpublished).

Switsur, V.R. and Wright, E.V. (1989) 'Radiocarbon ages and calibrated dates for the boats from North Ferriby, Humberside – a reappraisal', *Archaeological Journal* 146: 58–67.

Tibbetts, G.R. (1981) *Arab Navigation in the Indian Ocean before the Coming of the Portuguese*, London: Royal Asiatic Society.

Waters, D. (1978) *Art of Navigation in England in Elizabethan and Early Stuart Times*, Greenwich: National Maritime Museum.

Watkins, T. (1980) 'Prehistoric coracle in Fife', *International Journal of Nautical Archaeology* 9: 277–86.

Wood, J.E. (1978) *Sun, Moon and Standing Stones*, Oxford: Oxford University Press.

Wright, E. (1990) *Ferriby Boats*, London: Routledge.

PART VI

TECHNOLOGY AND CRAFTSMANSHIP

THE TECHNOLOGY OF METALWORK
Bronze and gold

——— ·◆· ———

Peter Northover

The Celtic world covers such a large extent in both time and space that it is impossible in this short essay to explore in any comprehensive manner the way in which copper alloys were used. The focus is in any case immediately restricted by the limited range of metallurgical research applied to Celtic material when compared with, say, the bronze age and classical worlds. The most extensive work has been done in Britain, although similar research is now taking place in France, in Switzerland and in Spain, and also in areas on the fringes of the ancient Celtic world such as Denmark, Bulgaria and Romania. This work has been concentrated in the pre-Roman Iron Age although some technical studies have been made of the metalwork of the late Celtic Christian West (see Youngs 1989). This discussion must therefore concern itself mainly with the pre-Roman Iron Age in western and alpine Europe and in particular with the British Isles because that is where the majority of metallurgical research has been carried out.

The definition of the Celtic Iron Age itself is not without its difficulties. The conventional archaeological division into Hallstatt and La Tène eras (First and Second Iron Ages to use French terminology) and the distribution of the styles and technology associated with them form the most useful basis for exploring the copper and bronze metallurgy of the period. This is not surprising given that these cultural groupings were defined on the basis of their metalwork.

BRONZE AND IRON

Iron came late to north-west Europe. It did not reach Britain until the end of the eighth century or beginning of the seventh century BC, appearing in company with objects of Hallstatt C type. In Britain, at least, it has been impossible to confirm the presence of iron in any earlier association. The key find, after which the period is named in Britain, is a votive deposit from the bed of Llyn Fawr, a small lake in South Wales (Savory 1975, 1976). This find combines elements of the local final bronze age tradition, such as specific types of bronze socketed axes and chisels, types which had a wide European distribution such as razors and belt and harness fittings, with both local and continental types of iron object. The last mentioned is the only example of a Hallstatt iron sword in Britain and certainly an import (O'Connor 1980). The local production of an iron socketed sickle is indicated by the fact that it is an exact replica in iron of the contemporary bronze type. The find is completed by two large and elaborate bronze cauldrons which exemplify the changes which were taking place in bronzeworking during this period.

During the preceding, Ewart Park, phase of the Late Bronze Age in many areas of Britain metal was abundant and basic tools and weapons such as socketed axes and plain spearheads were mass-produced and of relatively poor quality. Specialized tools and the more important and expensive weapons, such as swords, were better finished but even the most elaborate of bronze products, the cauldrons, are rather crude in detail and simple in construction. The bronzes of the Llyn Fawr are more carefully made and even the most basic show a high standard of finish. At the same time the prestige products show greatly increased inputs of time and skill. The body of a Ewart Park-period cauldron is made from three sheets of bronze in two tiers with plain rivets and one-piece cast handle fittings. The Llyn Fawr-period cauldron has as many as five tiers of sheets with as many as 500 decorative rivets, with the handle fittings incorporating as many as ten separate components, all carefully finished. The vessels as they survive are generally in good order and not extensively patched and repaired as were their predecessors. Clearly there has been a significant change in the élite who could support this type of production, with display becoming as important as function.

Other changes were occurring in the way bronze was perceived and used. A considerable weight of metal was removed by the manufacture of non-utilitarian forms, as in the many thousands of heavily leaded, non-functional Armorican socketed axes occurring in hoards in north-west France. The British equivalent is the production of thin-walled castings of socketed axes and other tools in high tin-bronzes with up to 20 per cent tin, possibly associated with an increase in the votive deposition of metal. At the same time the quantity of bronze in daily circulation appears have declined quite rapidly during this period. It is tempting to relate this to the increasing importance of iron but this is much too simplistic a conclusion (Northover 1984). In fact, in the British Isles and in adjacent parts of Atlantic Europe, the overall quantity of metal in use was rapidly approaching a minimum it reached in the sixth century BC, contemporary with Hallstatt D in central Europe. There is little more than a handful of iron objects, and gold has disappeared altogether in most of the area. In other words the impact of iron was not instant and dramatic and it occurred during a time in which the existing metal industry was being greatly affected by other social and economic changes.

Nevertheless, it was during the seventh and sixth centuries BC that iron replaced bronze in Britain as the metal of choice for most tools and weapons, and by the beginning of the fifth century at the latest the change was complete. The uncertainty over chronology comes from the lack of associated finds and the difficulty of determining what tool types were in use in the sixth century BC. We should take brief notice here of why iron and iron alloys such as steel came to achieve their dominant position. The principal factor must be economic and geographical, that is the general availability and accessibility of iron ores compared with those of copper and tin. Where the making of copper alloys required the mixing of two separate metals (or three with lead), iron alloys either derived directly from a single ore with iron–phosphorus alloys or from reactions between iron and carbon in the form of charcoal when iron–carbon alloys (steel) were being made. Once the technology was widely disseminated, most areas had a local supply of metal, although there is also sufficient evidence of long-distance trade in iron for special purposes. Indeed, it is almost certainly the way in which the technology was controlled and transferred that dictated the pace at which iron was adopted, a process for which we have minimal archaeological evidence. For many purposes the actual properties of iron alloys offered little advantage over their copper-based competitors but their superior toughness or resistance to brittle fracture would have been attractive in daily use; cast bronze is brittle and fracture was a common mode of failure in bronze tools. Finally, although the blacksmith's skills of forging, welding and carburizing are as complex as those of the bronze founder and bronzesmith, being able to dispense with the paraphernalia of casting – crucibles and moulds – was probably regarded as another improvement.

RESOURCES

Many years of effort, not always successful, have been invested in locating the copper, tin and lead resources exploited in the Bronze Age and linking them with objects derived from those ores. Recently, for example, considerable excitement has been generated by the identification and dating of bronze age copper mines in Britain and Ireland. Similarly, the exploration and excavation of Roman mines has been a topic of research since work of Oliver Davies in the 1930s (Davies 1935). Possibly because interest has naturally been focused on the new metal, iron, there has been very little investigation of the non-ferrous metal resources used by Celtic smiths and, outside Britain, only a limited amount of scientific analysis of iron age copper alloy metallurgy. As yet no iron age copper mine has been found in Britain. However, there is good evidence for the exploitation of British copper and, probably, tin resources during the La Tène period and some of the earliest raw copper yet found on metalworking sites (Musson *et al.* 1993).

Although it makes good sense to assume that British copper ores were being mined and smelted during the Late Bronze Age, there is no direct evidence. The copper ingots, common in the ninth–eighth centuries BC in southern and eastern England, appear to have been exported from the Continent, although a few may come from the south-west, where there is also a limited distribution. A dependence on scrap bronze from the Continent, and also from Ireland, is also evident. For the seventh–sixth centuries there are even fewer clues and it is quite possible that by the end of the sixth century BC copper and tin extraction had virtually ceased in Britain. Lead mining probably stopped even earlier as the alloys of this period are mainly lead-free.

Even in the earliest La Tène period there were the beginnings of a revival in metallurgical activity and new, previously unused copper deposits were opened up. The best example of this is in the area of the Llanymynech hill-fort and the Tanat valley, just on the Welsh side of the Powys/Shropshire border. Two hearths excavated on the hill-fort ramparts date to the second/first centuries BC and were used for processing a zinc- and lead-rich copper. The hill-fort itself stands over a copper mine which could have supplied the right ore to produce this metal, a mine, moreover, that is believed to have been exploited in Roman times. The same raw copper and associated slag have been excavated from a metallurgical context at the small hill-fort of Llwyn Bryn-dinas in the Tanat valley with a C-14 date that takes the use of this metal back at least to third century BC, perhaps even further. Together with other excavated material and the analysis of bronze objects it is possible to demonstrate the existence of a copper extraction industry based on the ores of this area, with products mainly distributed in north and east Wales, although examples are known from as far away as Llyn Cerrig Bach in Anglesey (Northover, 1991a; Musson *et al.* 1993). It appears that the source was not used before the fifth–fourth centuries, and it may have come to an end in the first century BC.

The same chronology applies to a second source for which the evidence is rather more circumstantial. A large quantity of bronze has now been analysed, with a very characteristic impurity pattern in which arsenic, cobalt and iron are the most important elements; where nickel is present there is always more cobalt than nickel. This metal is most common in southern and south-western England and on several sites, for example Maiden Castle hill-fort (Northover 1991b), all the metalworking waste is of this composition. The distribution of this metal hints at a source in the south-west and there is some confirmation from analyses of bronze age metalwork. In about the fourteenth century BC there is a type of bronze axe specific to Devon and Cornwall and those examples clustered around Dartmoor have the same arsenic/cobalt/iron impurity pattern (Northover unpublished). A source in this area also has the benefit of being close to major tin sources. There has always been speculation about the exploitation of the mineral wealth of Devon and Cornwall in prehistory. Both tin and copper were certainly produced there in the Bronze Age, but it is impossible to gauge how much was mined. An industry of significant size in that region seems to be a creation of the Iron Age so it can be argued that classical writers did actually have knowledge of a real industry that was in a position to export both tin and bronze. There is a long way to go in testing the evidence but it may well be more than coincidence that the sheet bronze in the cauldrons found at La Tène itself are made of the same type of bronze. It is also noteworthy that the same impurity pattern appears in both the earliest cast bronze Celtic coins made in Britain and their Massiliote prototypes (Northover 1992).

These are two of the best characterized metal types in the British Iron Age. There are several others and some at least must represent imported metal coming from either the Continent or Ireland. We have seen that there was a change in the utilization of metal resources at the beginning of the La Tène period. The demise of the two metal groups detailed above in the mid-first century BC and the increasing importance of others shows that further major changes occurred at that time. It is tempting to associate them with the events of, or consequent upon, either supposed Belgic migrations to Britain, or the Roman occupation of Gaul and the Romans' first incursions into Britain but it is impossible to be that precise in the dating of any site or artefact. Both literary evidence and events after the conquest show that the Romans were interested in British resources, so it is curious that what appear to have been flourishing British mines were abandoned when they were. It is, of course, possible that the decline was caused by the British market being invaded by the potential surplus of metal brought into Gaul by the Romans and then increased by the occupation.

LOCATION

Apart from the mines there is very little tangible evidence of bronze age metallurgical sites and processes until the beginning of the Late Bronze Age in the eleventh–tenth centuries BC. From that period until the end of the eighth century a considerable number of metalworking sites has been excavated, yielding crucibles, moulds and casting waste (Howard 1983). There is quite clearly an association of bronze-working with late bronze age occupation of hill-fort sites, for example at the Breiddin, Powys, Wales (Musson 1991); this is typical in producing ceramic piece moulds for weapons, crucible fragments, metalworking tools, notably a hammer, and metal waste. In areas without hill-forts, from south Devon to Yorkshire, other types of settlement have produced the same evidence, generally with ceramic moulds. The use of this technology demanded some degree of permanence for the workshop as the various stages such as pattern-making and the forming and drying of the moulds all took time and space and were not particularly portable. Even so, the episodes of bronze casting at sites like the Breiddin often seem to have occupied a very short space of time.

Ceramic moulds were impermanent and could only be used for a single cast each; the mass-production of axes that developed in the later Bronze Age was dependent on permanent moulds of stone and bronze. Hoards with up to eleven axes from the same mould survive from this basic bronze-founding (Stanton 1984) but no associated production sites are known. This need not be a surprise because extensive facilities for mould preparation are not needed and, with one mould able to cast as many as fifty objects, accumulations of discarded moulds will not be common. The major constraints on the axe-maker would have been his ability to make or acquire new moulds and the availability of a fuel supply. Technology has thus ordered a separation of tasks between different types of bronzeworking sites and the evidence they leave behind. As society became more hierarchical these different levels of site could have responded to different levels in society.

During the transition to a fully developed Iron Age we have very few traces of metalworking, but as the intensity of metallurgical activity picked up again during the La Tène period there is again an association of particular types of metalworking with particular types of site. For what a metalworking site might have looked like in the Hallstatt period we must look at two sites in France: Choisy-au-Bac, Aisne (Blanchet 1984), and Bragny-sur-Saône, Saône-et-Loire (Flouest 1991). Both these sites are on terraces close to the confluence of important rivers, the Aisne and the Oise for the former, the Saône, the Doubs and the Dheune for the latter. Both sites are clearly connected with the working of both bronze and iron and Bragny provides evidence for a variety of processes: ceramic *cire perdu* and stone bivalve moulds, tools for the shaping and decoration of bronze sheet, and tin and lead for soldering and plating. Choisy-au-Bac also produced ingot copper, and a touchstone and other traces of goldworking. These two sites are only one category and others, from hill-forts to small villages, may also have been the home of bronzesmiths. A British equivalent of the two river-confluence sites may be Weybridge, where the Thames and the Wey meet (Hanworth and Tomalin 1977). The metalworking evidence is scanty but there was some very early ironworking there and an exotic, imported ribbed bucket was found nearby. There is not too much evidence of metalworking sites but debris from Dinorben shows that bronzeworking was a feature there as early as this (Guilbert pers. comm.).

During the La Tène Iron Age in Britain the remains of metalworking become much more abundant and there is a very distinct pattern to the location of different types of process. Analysis L of the metal waste from three important hill-forts – Danebury (Northover 1991c), Maiden Castle (Northover 1991a) and South Cadbury (Northover unpublished) – showed it to be dominated by fragments of sheet, either off-cuts, scrap, carefully folded packets or even partially fused masses. Much of the debris at Maiden Castle was identified as coming from a workshop involved with the repair or demolition, or even manufacture of typical La Tène bronze and iron cauldrons. South Cadbury (Spratling 1970) has also been associated with sheet metalworking and the hill-fort at Bredon Hill (Hereford and Worcester) yielded iron hammers suitable for sheet metalworking. The metalworking evidence from Danebury is much more limited but there was a remarkable find of what had been a small cloth or leather bag filled with swarf from a number of copper alloys, either from drilling or from engraving (Northover 1991c). Crucibles or crucible fragments have been found at all these sites but there appears to have been no significant casting industry.

The classic La Tène period foundry site in England is at Gussage All Saints, Dorset (Foster 1980). The excavators uncovered a pit filled with the debris of moulds and crucibles used for the *cire perdu* casting of numerous items of horse harness. Other similar sites have been found, for example at Beckford (Hereford and Worcester) and Grimsby (Lincolnshire), both in course of preparation for publication. All of these sites are simple settlements, at most with a simple ditched enclosure surrounding them. None are hill-forts although there are such sites in the neighbourhood of Gussage All Saints and Beckford. Clearly casting operations of this type were not part of the economy of hill-forts. Village-scale industry of this type persisted until the Roman conquest at least, as seen at a small iron age site at Stanton Harcourt near Oxford (Oxford Archaeological Unit, unpublished). Other types of site were involved in bronzeworking: on the Continent the great oppida such as Manching and Mont Beuvray were certainly most important but such semi-urban sites came late to Britain. Where they have been explored, as at Bagendon (Clifford 1961) and Silchester, a varied metal economy is evident with signs of the working of all metals, including the use of precious metals for the coinage. A new feature at Silchester, Colchester and Hengistbury Head is the use of matte, otherwise copper sulphide, a semi-smelted product brought to the site for further processing. These sites are far removed from copper mines and the implications of the matte are still being worked out (Salter and Northover 1992). Other special sites were also important. The published data show a wide range of metallurgical activity at Glastonbury; at the trading port of Hengistbury Head the metallurgy was more specialized and, besides the casting of bronze objects, much of the metallurgy appears to have been involved with silver and, perhaps, the coinage of the Durotriges. The production of the cast bronze (potin) and struck copper coinages must also have taken place at a number of sites in Britain but none have so far been identified. The oppidum of the Üetliberg near Zürich in Switzerland has, however, produced extensive debris from the casting of potin coins (Northover 1992). We still have to locate workshops used for such items as sword scabbards, which would have involved both cast and sheet components, and brooches, although brooch blanks have been found at Baldock, Hertfordshire (Stead and Rigby 1986), and deposits of Roman brooch moulds have come from Prestatyn in North Wales (Blockley 1989) and Compton Dando, Somerset (Bayley pers. comm.).

TECHNIQUES AND TYPES: CAST AND WROUGHT PRODUCTS

Late bronze age bronzework in Britain is almost always cast close to its final shape and finished with a minimum of working. For a socketed axe this might simply mean removal of flash and sprue and then cold-working and annealing cycles applied to the cutting edge. For mass-produced items the annealing might be carried out at a low temperature and the area worked be very limited. The castings for ornaments and weapons might be cleaned up in the same way but in many cases finishing might consist entirely of grinding and polishing. The only important exceptions in the British Bronze Age to this casting-dominated technology were the cauldrons and shields (Gerloff 1991; Coles 1962) with their large-scale use of sheet bronze. The shields always show exemplary skill in handling this material but the cauldrons are much more mundane until the Llyn Fawr period when they became both more elaborate and finished to a much higher standard (see the introduction to this chapter discussing the Late Bronze Age). Indeed the general quality of all metalwork improved greatly at this time.

In the Hallstatt Iron Age in Britain, and elsewhere in Europe, the separation of bronzes into cast and wrought products intensified and wrought products increased in importance. As shown on page 5, the achievements of the sheet metalsmiths supported by the Hallstatt princes could be spectacular, for example the bronze couch and cauldron from the Hochdorf tomb, showing how they could produce large and durable structures in gold. There is nothing on this scale in Britain and even the cauldrons become simplified (Gerloff 1991; Meany 1990), but even so there are some striking items such as the dagger sheaths from the Thames (Jope 1983). Pins and the first fibulae in Britain also point the way to the ascendancy of wrought or part-wrought products.

The introduction of La Tène styles to the British Isles made a revolution in bronzeworking. Apart, possibly, from highly specialized objects like the handle fittings of some cauldrons, there is no evidence for the use of *cire perdu* casting at any earlier date. Even a find such as the eleventh/tenth century BC hoard from Isleham, Cambridgeshire, with its host of thin-walled scabbard chapes, parade spearheads and ornaments, was based on the use of bivalve ceramic moulds, as is demonstrated by many flash lines round unfinished castings (Northover 1982). One possible reason for this was that beeswax of sufficient quality was very scarce. Although bee products are known from the Bronze Age, it is possible that they are from wild or forest bees; some effort is required to refine beeswax from them, and the product from the domesticated honeybee may have been seen as essential. It may be coincidence but the earliest remains of honeybees from British sites are no earlier than La Tène either.

The freedom of modelling given by the use of *cire perdu* investment casting liberated the bronzesmith. Casting by means of piece moulds never achieved the fantastic skill and three-dimensionality that it did, say, in China and it was only the new technique that permitted anything similar. Initially the most complex shapes were small, as in the fibulae, and larger, ornamental castings still tended to be relatively two-dimensional. For small, flat items simple bivalve moulds, often of stone, remained in use (e.g. Savory 1976: 104). One of the greatest expressions of this is the openwork bronze castings designed to ornament a wooden jug from Brno-Maloměřice in former Czechoslovakia, a work so expressive of Celtic art that part of it was used for the cover illustration of the catalogue for the great Celtic exhibition in Venice in 1991 (Tanzi 1991; Meduna and Peškař 1993). Lesser pieces, such as highly complex armlets, appeared in many parts of the Celtic world and continued to develop in areas as remote as Scotland until the second century AD. In Britain the most typical products of Celtic casting must be the many elements of horse harness which allowed the smiths to show all their decorative skills.

Although the basic elements of the casting technique remained the same, the technology did gradually evolve with time, sometimes in surprising ways. Crucibles from about the fifth to third centuries BC were deep, narrow cups with a thick handle; they were placed in the hearth with the draught directed at their base so the exterior became heavily slagged while the charge was quite well protected from oxidation. There was then a change to a shallow triangular type without a handle, characteristic of the industry at Gussage All Saints already mentioned. Here the draught was directed at the rim of the crucible, which became heavily slagged. Certainly it was possible to melt small charges of metal very quickly in this way but this had to be balanced against the considerable losses of metal through oxidation. From the first century BC new types, generally in the form of hemispherical bowls with pouring lips, became standard in the south and gradually spread northwards over the next century or so. This slow spread is seen with some aspects of iron technology as well and a series of isochrones can be drawn across Britain to chart the adoption of several techniques. Moulds changed as well with developments in the provision of runners and gates. The Gussage All Saints terret moulds from the late second to early first centuries BC have a single runner serving a single terminal, while those from Silchester of a century later have two, one for each terminal. The Silchester moulds also show how multiple matrices were included in one mould flask. Another odd feature at Silchester is that the matrix surfaces are not smooth but have a ribbed pattern; the rough surface would only have increased the work of finishing the casting unless it was designed to provide a substrate for some form of cladding (Northover unpublished).

COMPOSITE STRUCTURES

The existence of two major structural metals, bronze and iron, seems to have stimulated the inventiveness of many craftsman to produce composite structures. In the western European Bronze Age opportunities were limited because, in effect, only tin and the precious metals were available: gold inlays and tinned decoration do exist but only in small numbers. In the Iron Age bronze and iron were combined for functional purposes in the typical La Tène cauldrons, or for decorative purposes, as in the bronze inlays in some iron spearheads (Raftery 1991). Replacing the bottom of a bronze cauldron with iron produced a vessel much better able to stand the heat, while the colour contrast between polished copper alloys and iron is startling and attractive, as recognized by the makers of Renaissance parade armour. Iron could be bonded to other metals as well: iron pins could have tin heads while the use of iron armatures in the tubular torcs at Snettisham required the bonding of gold to iron.

A large part of the greatly expanded use of bronze sheet at this time was due to its application for cladding a variety of materials, organic as well as metallic. The late iron age graves of Aylesford, Kent, or, for example, Goeblingen-Nospelt in Luxembourg (Vidal 1976), show how elaborate wooden buckets were assembled and decorated with bronze sheet. Similarly, bronze sheet was used in other icons of Celtic art such as the Battersea and Witham shields, where it in turn could be inlaid with opaque coloured glass (Stead 1985). In all these cases a functional purpose has been elevated to give the appearance of luxury. Sheet bronze and other metals could be combined in many ways and the variety of effects increased with time. In Britain this is particularly true of the metalwork of the first century BC and first century AD and perhaps even later in Scotland and Ireland. Examples include the combination of sheet brass and tinned copper in the roundels from the Tal-y-llyn, Gwynedd, hoard (Savory 1964), and a torque combining differently patinated cast and sheet components from Dinnington, Yorkshire, with the sheet formed round a lead core (Beswick *et al.*1991). The mixing of metals extended to precious metals with, for example, combinations of gold and silver; discussion of the use of metallurgy for decorative purposes is continued below.

DECORATIVE METALWORKING TECHNIQUES

The decorative techniques of the Celtic smiths can be divided in to the mechanical manipulation of the metal itself, from engraving to casting, the mechanical addition of other materials such as enamel/glass inlays or bronze claddings, and the use of metallurgical or chemical techniques for plating, etching and patination. The first two of these are well-known elements of Celtic art but the third has seen much less study and, because of the limited space available, will be the topic dealt with at greatest length here.

The mechanical decoration of bronze can be split between three categories, the first involves the removal of metal, for example in engraving (Lowery *et al.* 1976). The classic example of this in Britain is the decoration of the mirror plates of the Late Iron Age, where engraving techniques were used to produce the linear outlines of the design and to fill in parts of it with textured surfaces such as basketwork. Another application was in shield plates: in the Tal-y-llyn hoard already referred to this is combined with the shaping of sheet bronze and brass in repoussé. Repoussé and chasing imply that metal is moved rather than removed. Some of the best known examples are in the shields (Stead 1985) but might also be seen, for example, in scabbards such as that from Little Wittenham, Oxfordshire. The main panel of the front plate has been textured with a ladder-like pattern of narrow, closely packed repoussé rungs (Raftery 1991) while the upper and lower ends have a panel of typical curvilinear Celtic decoration, also in repoussé, with added ornament in the form of studs and appliqués. The same styles of decoration might also be created by casting them directly. This is particularly associated with Snettisham gold art but was also repeated in bronze. Inserted into both sheet and cast bronze might be inlays of other materials. This might be anything from coral to tin to glass. The use of coloured opaque glasses is especially favoured in later iron age art in Britain, with some spectacular effects (Haseloff 1991; Brun and Pernot 1992). The use of bronze as a cladding has already been described, but bronze or brass might also be used as a fretwork against a contrasting backing, which might be tinned copper in the Tal-y-llyn hoard or, perhaps, patinated bronze in the Lochar Moss collar (MacGregor 1976).

Plating techniques could also be used to effect, either covering an object completely or just forming part of the design. Study of the corroded remains of a sword scabbard from a warrior grave at Kelvedon, Essex, England, datable to *c*.10 BC, showed that an otherwise plain faceplate was decorated with a longitudinal strip of tin plating thick enough to stand proud of the surface. When newly made and polished, the tinning would show as a silver strip against the golden background of a medium tin bronze; the strip itself has accurately straight and parallel edges. It was created by masking the outer parts of the faceplate with clay, heating the bronze sheet, fluxing the exposed strip with resin, and then rubbing the hot bronze with a stick of tin. Above the melting point of tin (232 °C) reaction between the bronze and tin is instant, a series of compounds of copper and tin being produced, with excess tin remaining on the outside. The plate was then heated to a higher temperature approaching 600 °C; the bronze–tin reactions continued, although in this case they did not go to completion. Some unreacted tin remained on the surface but this is now corroded away, exposing the underlying compound layers (Northover and Salter 1990; Jones 1992).

This is one example of the way in which Celtic craftsmen used metallurgical and chemical techniques to decorate, conceal, texture or patinate bronze surfaces. The decorative use of tin plating goes back to the Early Bronze Age (Meeks 1986) but its appearance is intermittent. Within the period we are reviewing here one of its earliest uses is on some brooches of the sixth–fifth centuries BC; excellent examples come from the Dürrnberg in Austria (Moosleitner 1991). It then disappears from the Celtic west for a long period but the technique was not forgotten elsewhere. It can be seen on south Italian bronze armour of the fifth century, for example (Born *et al.* 1990). As far as is known at present, tinning in the form of plating reappeared in Britain in the second half of the first century BC but tin had been used for inlays early in the La Tène period. A La Tène I brooch from Flag Fen (Jones 1992) has its bow deeply hollowed and filled with tin metal, while an iron pin from Llwyn Bryn-dinas, Powys, Wales, has a tin bead cast onto its head (Musson *et al.* 1993). The sword scabbard just described is one of the earliest surviving examples of true tin-plating after its reintroduction but the technique became very popular in the years around the Roman conquest, with tinned brooches, vessels and decorative elements such as the Tal-y-llyn plaques already mentioned.

Bronze itself was used as a plating, now on iron. If iron is hot-dipped into molten bronze there is a fast reaction and a strong and coherent plating is formed. This method was used particularly to plate iron horse-harness but the motivation is not clear (Northover and Salter 1990). It may have been done simply for the sake of appearance but equally it could have been used to improve the wear resistance of the iron. There are several good examples in the Llyn Cerrig Bach, Anglesey, votive deposit (Savory 1976; Lynch 1991). For the use of precious metals in plating on copper and bronze see the section on gold.

THE IMPACT OF THE ROMANS

Any discussion of the later stages of iron age metallurgy and metalworking in western Europe must review the effects of the Roman conquest of Gaul and the Alps and the arrival of the Romans at the Channel. Here we have space to be concerned only with the effects in Britain and its century of continued independence. We have already seen major changes in the metal economy around the middle of the first century BC but the exact causal relationship with the Roman expansion is not known. Celtic art styles continued to evolve vigorously in Britain and metallurgy was fully exploited in this development. Some techniques, such as tin-plating, become apparent only in this period. The major contribution of the Romans was a new copper alloy, brass, combining copper and zinc (Bayley 1990). Initially brass was imported in two forms, as fibulae, and, probably, as coinage then being recycled into the coinage of the Trinovantes (Northover 1992). Brass brooch blanks from Baldock with a date close to the conquest show that brass came to be worked in Britain (Bayley 1990) but it was probably not made there until after the Roman occupation had started. Brass then spread to smiths continuing to work in the Celtic tradition; for example, there are brass ingots and Celtic-style objects in the Seven Sisters, Glamorgan, hoard deposited in the 80s AD (Davies and Spratling 1976). Romanization of style spread with the romanization of technology but in northern Britain objects continued to be made in developed Celtic forms into the second century AD and some of the most elaborate achievements date to this period (MacGregor 1976), in the south the Celtic techniques became completely submerged by the Roman.

GOLD AND SILVER IN THE CELTIC WORLD

Gold and silver and their alloys are metals just as bronze and iron are. The way in which they are worked will reflect the general level of metallurgical knowledge and skill attained by a society's craftsmen, and the habitual technical style. Their work will also be influenced by the specific properties of gold and silver alloys, in particular their ductility and colour as well as their potential for being formed into complex shapes and textured surfaces.

Our appreciation of the place of gold and silver in Celtic art and of the way in which their properties were adapted to the Celtic aesthetic is inevitably coloured by a small number of spectacular finds, such as the Snettisham treasure (Clarke 1954; Stead 1991), the Vix collar (Joffroy 1979; Chaume *et al.* 1987; Eluère 1987a: 114–18), the Broighter boat (Raftery 1984: 181–91), or the gold in the Hochdorf tomb (Biel 1987; Hartmann 1987). There is a natural tendency to assume that these master-works are at the summit of a pyramid of lesser, plainer objects. In many ways this is not the case and these finds often do represent the whole achievement of Celtic goldworking. Even when there is evidence of a hierarchy of gold or silver alloy pieces from the elaborate to the simple, as at Snettisham, then their context itself makes them highly distinctive. The question of context forms one of two major themes in this section of the chapter, as might be expected over a period of time as long as a millennium, there were several radical shifts in the social and economic position of gold and silver. The second derives from the metals themselves: their sources, the ways in which the alloys were made and used and the special skills of the goldsmiths and how these skills influenced their artistic ambitions. Any discussion of gold and silver in the Celtic world should also look at these points in relation to the coinage (Voûte 1985; Cowell 1992; Northover 1992). This discussion also confines itself to the period before the end of the first century AD when Celtic art in Britain was finally being overlaid by Roman styles; late iron age and early Christian gold and silverwork in the Celtic west is another story.

LATE BRONZE AGE

The use of gold in the first cultures we specifically label 'Celtic', those of the princes of 'Hallstatt' central Europe from the seventh into the fifth centuries BC, is radically different from what went before. We must therefore start this review of the goldwork with that of the preceding centuries of the Late Bronze Age in Europe. From the latter part of the second millennium BC the centre of gravity of gold and gold-working in western Europe is in the lands adjoining the Atlantic and the North Sea. Three major provinces within this large area have extensive gold industries, each with a highly distinctive range of products: Spain (e.g. Gonzalo 1989; Ruiz-Gálvez 1989), the Highland and Island regions of the British Isles together with Brittany (Taylor 1980; Eluère 1982), and Denmark (e.g. Hartmann 1982). The first two of these had sufficient gold reserves of their own to provide for the probable level of production. Denmark, on the other hand, was dependent entirely on imported metal, as it was for bronze, but nevertheless stamped its own style on the gold objects made there.

In the British Isles one of the most prominent and characteristic forms of gold artefact is the flange-twisted gold torque and its lighter, wire-twisted cousins (Eogan 1983b; Northover 1989). Although superficially flamboyant, the metalworking skills they employ are straightforward and require only a few specialist tools. On the other hand they do display a good knowledge of the properties of the gold alloys used and an eye for accuracy and regularity in their shape and dimensions. They were probably made and used from the thirteenth to the eleventh centuries BC, a time when the British Isles and other parts of western Europe experienced a rapid development of wrought-metal techniques with the introduction of sheet-metal armour and vessels and, possibly, the development of wire drawing. Some of the small hoards of gold torques and bracelets that survive suggest that the users of the gold had some notion of its having an intrinsic value: often the weights of the objects in a hoard show a simple relationship with each other. For example, in hoards with a pair of torques one is generally twice the weight of the other; on occasion these weight relationships can be very exact. For some examples there is also a strong ritual element in their deposition.

Because of the great importance of gold in Ireland through much of the Bronze Age it was thought that these torques, too, were typical of Ireland. In fact they are distributed fairly widely across England, Wales and north-western France but are almost absent from Scotland. In the succeeding century, the beginning of the Late Bronze Age in Britain, there is something of a hiatus and the amount of goldwork surviving is very small (Needham 1990). At the same time there is a marked change in the character of the finest quality bronzeworking, from wrought products to elaborate castings, and the skills which formed the torques might well have been in abeyance. After that, through the main span of the Late Bronze Age in Britain, the quantity of gold, both by weight and number of objects, is very small in relation to the amount of copper and copper alloys in circulation. In contrast, in Ireland there was a great increase in the number of gold objects produced in the Late Bronze Age although we have no absolute dating for the start of this process. Some of the gold hoards were very large, such as that from Mooghaun, Co. Clare, with 146 gold objects (Eogan 1983a: esp. 69–72). Reflecting the relative simplicity of contemporary bronze types, many of the gold ornaments are very simple combinations of casting and forging. A small proportion, such as 'lock-rings', gorgets and boxes, are fabricated from sheet with stamped, engraved or chased decoration; however, the technology is still simple with all joints being mechanical. A greater degree of metallurgical complexity is seen in the 'ring-money', some of which has striped decoration formed from precious alloys of contrasting colours formed round a base-metal core; the methods by which the patterns were created have still to be determined (Green 1988).

Developments in the British Isles have been described in some detail to give an idea of the major changes which could have taken place in both the use of gold and the craft techniques involved in shaping it during the half-millennium of the later Bronze Age. The other regional industries had their own distinct identities. For example, the Danish tradition is very much associated with gold wire and gold vessels, while in Iberia the goldsmiths were by this time coming under the influence of the Mediterranean civilizations, initially that of the Phoenicians (Almagro Gorbea 1989).

RESOURCES

The Celtic goldsmith had access to three basic sources of gold: vein or reef gold, i.e. gold mined from the ground, alluvial or placer gold panned or washed from streams, and the recycling of gold already in circulation either within the Celtic world or from outside it, often in the form of Greek or Macedonian gold coins. Gold naturally contains a variable amount of silver, ranging from a fraction of 1 per cent to 30 per cent or more, the higher silver natural alloys often being referred to as electrum (Lehrberge forthcoming). During the later Bronze Age it had become standard throughout most of Europe to alloy gold with up to 10 per cent copper, perhaps to improve the mechanical properties, perhaps to counteract the whitening effect of the silver naturally occurring in the gold.

As we will see, from the eighth century BC onwards there was a change in the use of gold across much of Europe with a gradually increasing tendency to deposit it with burials. The large late bronze age hoards disappear and the gold alloys used in them were no longer available. The gold used in the Hallstatt period is unalloyed and, depending on area, could be either vein gold or placer gold (e.g. Hartmann 1987; Hofmann 1991). From the beginning of the La Tène period the copper content begins to rise again but seldom exceeds 5 per cent (e.g. Eluère 1987a; Voûte 1991) until the first century BC when both coinage alloys and many of the alloys used at Snettisham must be described as ternary alloys with up to 40 per cent or more copper (Stone 1987; Northover 1992). Similar ternary alloys appear in the rather separate development of gold alloys in Iberia (Pingel forthcoming).

Around the middle of the first millennium BC the process of parting gold–silver alloys with salt to remove the silver was discovered, probably in Mesopotamia. Combined with the process of cupellation to remove base metals, this meant that gold could now be refined to better than 99.5 per cent purity (Eluère 1989a). As far as we know at present these techniques were not known to Celtic goldsmiths but high-purity gold could enter the system via the Macedonian gold coinage and some natural high purity sources (Eluère 1987b). Little thought has been given so far to the origins of silver used in the Celtic world and we await the application of lead isotope analysis more extensively. The final precious metal known to the Celts was mercury, attested by several mercury-gilded torques and other objects at Snettisham.

HALLSTATT

Metallurgical issues surrounding the end of the conventionally defined Bronze Age and the adoption of iron as a utilitarian metal in what became Celtic Europe are complex and often misconstrued. The period is also one of considerable social change. There are stark contrasts between the increasing wealth and power of the chiefdoms in the core area of the Hallstatt culture, evidenced by the princely graves, and the periphery, where regions such as the British Isles saw a rapid decline in the availability of finished metal despite apparently adequate resources of copper, tin, iron and even gold. The production of gold, and the uses to which it was put have to be seen against this background. One of the principal effects was that the accumulation of large numbers of near-identical objects in hoards, as in late bronze age Ireland, ceased and gold begins to be deposited in high-status graves. In other words gold has ceased to be a measure of wealth with, perhaps, a primitive value system attached to it, and has become a symbol of power. No one has ever made any calculations but a casual impression is that the weight of gold available for use was much less than in the Late Bronze Age. Silver, virtually absent from much of the Bronze Age in northern and western Europe, also begins to make an appearance.

Metalworking in the later Bronze Age, especially in Atlantic Europe, was dominated by casting technology: objects were cast close to their finished shape with often only minimal mechanical working and finishing. The transition to the iron-using system of the Hallstatt C–D periods significantly increased the emphasis on wrought products, especially of sheet, culminating in such enormous pieces as the cauldron and couch from the Hochdorf tomb (Biel 1987). The same is true of much Hallstatt gold with embossed and decorated gold sheet the dominant form: the Hochdorf tomb again is prominent with the sheet-gold mounts for drinking-horns, shoes and a dagger sheath and hilt (Eluère 1987a; Furger and Müller 1991). There may have been several reasons for this shift. If gold was indeed now a symbol of power rather than simply of wealth, then the display of gold, and the cladding of large objects in gold, would have been more important than the quantity of gold actually owned, which might anyway have been more restricted than before. The contemporary aesthetic for fine metalwork also shifted to the sort of embossed, chased or engraved figures, patterns and textures that could be made in thin sheet (e.g. *Situlenkunst*). Finally, there was, perhaps, some affinity with the forming of the new metals, iron and steel, which at that time could only be forged; with these tendencies it may have happened that the availability of moulding and casting skills became much more limited. An extensive use of sheet-gold was not new; the earliest bronze age gold in north-west Europe was almost entirely sheet (Taylor 1980) and bronze age gold in Denmark was dominated by sheet and wire products.

Besides the sheet appliqués and scabbard plates exemplified by the Hochdorf tomb, more three-dimensional objects were being made. Many are in the form of bracelets and collars made up from the same embossed, thin gold sheet, for example in the tomb of Hundersingen, Baden-Württemberg (e.g. Eluère 1987a: pl. 85–8), but new ideas and techniques are beginning to enter the world of the Celtic goldsmith. Finds in Switzerland, notably at Ins and Jegenstorf in Canton Bern, show jewellery with wire loop-in-loop chains and the embossed textured surfaces of the sheet-metal replaced by the application of granulation and filigree (for bibliography see Furger and Muller 1991: 114–17). These may have been made by the Celts' neighbours south of the Alps, the Etruscans, who had learned these new skills from the Greek and eastern Mediterranean civilizations. It is also possible that one or two Celtic smiths had also mastered the new style and that some of the items were made in Switzerland. One of the finest and most controlled applications of filigree is in the terminals of the Vix collar. This collar, with a thick, smooth sheet body and complex multi-component terminals with cast, chased, punched and filigree ornaments, is unique but contains several pointers to developments in the La Tène period, the classic period of Celtic art from the fifth century BC onwards (Eluère, 1989b).

LA TÈNE

There are changes in goldworking and gold use associated with the evolution of the traditions to which we have given the label La Tène although there is also a degree of continuity with Hallstatt traditions and techniques. The first of these concern deposition. The rich Hallstatt graves are those of princes but, by the end of the sixth century BC, a tomb with contents as elaborate as those from Vix was prepared for a princess. This rite developed in the fifth/fourth centuries BC and graves such as Waldalgesheim in the Rhineland and Reinheim in the Saarland, which contain truly sumptuous gold jewellery, were also those of women of the highest status (Eluère 1991). Gold in male graves seems to be reduced to ornamental gold-clad plaques, sometimes decorated with amber and coral, which may have been no more than a military decoration. More elaborate examples of the same style can be seen in the fourth-century BC helmets from Agris, Charente and Amfréville, Eure, in France, where gold cladding and filigree, silver rivets, coral and red enamel feature in a kaleidoscope of materials (Eluère 1987a: pl. 99–100). These helmets seem garish to modern taste and a more elegant application, this time of openwork gold sheet, is the decoration of a wooden bowl from Schwarzenbach, also in the Saarland (Frey 1971).

The gold from the tombs of the princesses shows how the goldsmiths extended the idea of more solid and three-dimensional objects; a key find is that of Waldalgesheim, a tomb group that is also important for defining a stage in the evolution of Celtic art (for bibliography see Megaw and Megaw 1990). The buffer-terminal torque and bracelets are elaborate gold versions of bronze examples which were also a common offering in female graves. The hoops of these are solid with the deeply moulded decoration cast with them, but the terminals are separate components soldered on (cf. Echt forthcoming). These same graves also show the revival of torques with twisted bodies, either two bars twisted together or, as at Reinheim, a flanged body reminiscent of bronze age examples. The Reinheim group is also remarkable for having both torque and bracelets with terminals in the form of cast human figures.

These torques and bracelets were among the last to be used as grave goods. From then on deposition occurred either singly or, more often, in hoards, usually with a strong sense of a ritual motive behind it. An early example is the Erstfeld hoard from Switzerland, concealed late in the fourth century BC on a remote mountain pass. The Erstfeld torques are also remarkable for their fantastic animal decoration and the mortise-and-tenon fastenings with securing pins used to assemble their hoops (Müller 1990). Later hoards, from the second and first centuries BC, were frequently deposited with gold Celtic coins (e.g. Tayac, Gironde (Boudet 1987)).

The design of torques from then until the arrival of the Romans achieved many variations. The solid, smooth bodies of the Waldalgesheim and Erstfeld torques were replaced by tubes of gold sheet, either slender as at Niederzier in Nordrhein-Westfalen (Joachim 1991), Germany, and Clonmacnois, an import from Germany into Ireland (Raftery 1984: 175–80, or thick as at Mailly-le-Camp in France, Frasne-lez-Buissenal in Belgium, and Snettisham in Norfolk, England (for bibliography see Eluère 1987b; Furger-Gunti 1982). Some of these torques were built up over a resin/sand core supported by an iron armature, and several of the later examples had bodies with elaborate repoussé decoration. There is not space here to go into all the details of their construction. Torques with twisted bodies increased in prominence through the same centuries and several variations of the theme have been found in French hoards. They might be formed from a single, twisted square bar at Montan, Tarn; from a square bar chiselled into a cruciform section and then twisted, as at Soucy, Aisne; from two plain twisted bars with simple buffer terminals at Fenouillet, Haute-Garonne, or larger numbers of twisted, square- or round-section wires twisted together, for example at Civray, Indre-et-Loire (Eluère 1987b). The culmination of forming a deeply textured torque body from varied patterns of twisted wires is seen at Snettisham, discussed below. The torques from Montan and Civray are also part of a remarkable phenomenon which was a speciality of Gallic goldsmiths in the second century BC. This was the *cire perdu* casting of collars, terminals and even torque bodies into deeply moulded, three-dimensional abstract vegetal forms, the sections so produced usually being hollow with thin walls, a triumph of contemporary casting technology. Although apparently the results of French skills, one example has been found as far away as Gajić-Hercegmárok in former Yugoslavia, a reminder of the geographical extent of Celtic culture (Eluère 1985).

THE PERIPHERY

We have seen how, along the Atlantic coast of Europe, the use of gold contracted dramatically at the end of the Late Bronze Age. In southern Britain it seems to have vanished altogether but there was a limited survival to the north and west in the form of ribbon torques. There is some difficulty in deciding exactly which of these torques belong to this period. There was a limited vogue for simple, loosely twisted versions in the Middle Bronze Age and these match other contemporary goldwork in composition. Those that can be assigned to the Iron Age with some certainty on grounds of either composition or association tend to be much more tightly twisted from carefully shaped gold strips with a variety of terminals soldered on (Eogan 1983b). The two groups of torques may have no ancestral relationship at all; after all, twisting a strip of gold alloy is a simple and obvious thing to do with it; certainly there are no associations with late bronze age objects. The key iron age associations are Somerset, Co. Galway, with a Navan-type fibula and other obviously La Tène bronze, and at Clonmacnois, Co. Offaly, with an elaborate, tubular, buffer-terminal torque almost certainly made in the middle Rhine area around the beginning of the third century BC (Raftery 1984: 175–81). These finds not only confirm the La Tène date of the ribbon torques, but show that even areas as remote as central Ireland had some links with important areas of the Continent. How long this peripheral gold industry lasted is unknown. There are two or three ribbon torques of uncertain provenance made of refined, almost pure gold, which could be dated as late as the Roman period (Northover unpublished). There are no associations with iron age Celtic metalwork on the mainland of Britain, and certainly none in either the Snettisham treasure or in the Broighter hoard, which must date to the first century BC.

The Broighter hoard is a remarkable assemblage whose find circumstances have been the subject of controversy, although it is now accepted as a genuine hoard. It contains undoubted imports in the form of wire bracelets from the Eastern

Mediterranean but the other objects are more difficult to assess. Two twisted rod bracelets may be local copies of Roman types but in the apparent absence of a substantial gold industry in Ireland at this time this must be uncertain. The famous tubular torque uses techniques, such as the use of beaded wires joined to small gold beads, which are not part of Celtic goldworking anywhere in Britain but, on the other hand, it is decorated in a distinctly Irish style. The most plausible answer is that the torque has a continental origin and its body was either renewed or at least decorated in Ireland. The boat must have been modelled on typical Celtic ships, such as those of the Veneti referred to by Caesar. Model boats in precious metal have a long history, with a fourth-century BC model canoe from Hallein in Austria and the twelfth–eleventh-century BC gold ornamented shale model from Caergwrle in north-east Wales (for illustration see Eluère 1987a: 29, 98). The analyses of the Broighter gold show a significant platinum impurity which has been associated with both European and Mediterranean sources.

In contrast to this small-scale use of gold on the north-western fringe of the Celtic world, two other areas, the lower Danube and the Balkans in the east, and Iberia in the south-west, were major consumers of precious metal. There is an important parallel between the two in that a large proportion of the work was in silver, barely known in the core area. The most magnificent and enigmatic creation in silver of this period must be the Gundestrup Cauldron (Bergquist and Taylor 1987; Kaul 1991). For just over a century this vessel has been one of the principal icons of Celtic art throughout Europe. The evidence for its Celticity is chiefly its iconography, for example the wearing of torques, the blowing of a Celtic form of carnyx, and the attributes of some of the deities apparently portrayed, such as the horned god Cernnunos. The cauldron, found dismantled, is composed of thirteen silver sheets worked in repoussé, assembled in two friezes facing outwards as well as to the interior. The base is bowl-shaped with a gilded ornamented plaque in the bottom. A rim with a circular section is clipped on while the plates themselves are soldered together with pure tin (Northover unpublished).

Since its discovery, numerous theories for the origin of the cauldron have been put forward; the two most favoured are Gaul and the lower Danube area. The former region was proposed because of the specifically Celtic motifs on the cauldron, a number of which are most frequently found in Gaul. However, present opinion, for good reason, has settled on the area of present-day Romania and Bulgaria. The use of high-relief designs in partially gilded silver sheet with distinctive styles of chasing and engraving are typical of Thracian craftsmanship. The mixing of this with a partly Celtic iconography has led to the inspiration for the cauldron's being attributed to the territory of the Scordisci, a Celtic group living on the south-eastern borders of the Celtic world in a close relationship with the Thracians (e.g. Moscalu 1990). Other products of the silversmiths of this area were brought west, one of the best known being the iron-cored silver torque from Trichtingen, Baden-Württemberg (Fischer 1987; Eichhorn 1987).

In Iberia, too, the styles of precious metalworking represent a fusion of Celtic designs and motifs with local ideas and influences from the Mediterranean civilizations of the Phoenicians and the Greeks. The result, often referred to as Celtiberian, was stylish and inventive. As in the lands of the lower Danube, silver was probably the more important metal. Familiar forms are re-interpreted in silver, such as torques formed from twisting silver bars alternating with beaded or twisted wires. Some of the silver torques make more inventive use of their component bars and wires, with knots, side-loops and other ornaments incorporated into the hoops. Such features are not unique to the Celtiberian silver but appear in Switzerland and in some Roman jewellery. Copper alloy types are also repeated in silver, for example fibulae, spiral armlets and small vessels. Gold is particularly characteristic of the smaller jewellery, fibulae and earrings, where the basic forms are embellished with wire wrapping, filigree, soldered beads and granulation. Some large hoards, such as Arrabalde I, Zamora, Spain, display the full range of techniques (Delibes de Castro and Esparza Arroyo 1989; Perea Caveda and Rovira Llorens forthcoming).

SNETTISHAM

The phenomenon of the Snettisham treasure is remarkable in many ways: in its chronology, the clear association of the bulk of the material with one workshop and one style of metalworking, the remarkable nature of some of the imports, and the special nature of its deposition (Clarke 1954; Sealey 1979; Stone 1987; Stead 1991). As discussed in the previous paragraphs, goldwork in the British Isles during the Hallstatt and most of the La Tène Iron Ages seems to have been confined to the production of ribbon torcs in Scotland and Ireland and the acceptance of a small number of imports such as the Clonmacnois torque, clearly a continental type. The evidence available today suggests that gold vanished completely from southern England between the seventh and second centuries AD. The first hint of a return is the arrival of imported Gallo- gold coins, particularly the Gallo-Belgic types towards the end of the second century BC (Fitzpatrick 1992).

To metalsmiths working in southern England the metallurgy of gold and gold alloys would have been completely unknown, as would the range of techniques that depend on their specific properties (thin foils, filigree, granulation, soldering, etc.), and there is no evidence that they acquired this knowledge. The techniques that can be attributed to the Snettisham smiths are simply those common to La Tène bronzeworking in the same area. As discussed in the chapter on bronze, the introduction and extensive use of *cire perdu* casting techniques was the major innovation of that period. The necessary skills were developed to a high degree in the manufacture of fibulae, weapon fittings and horse-harness. These were adapted very well to make the patterned and textured surfaces of the ring terminals of the most elaborate torques. The art developed for the Snettisham-style gold castings was then transferred back to bronze, where, for example, a sword pommel from a neighbouring parish in Norfolk exhibits it (Gregory pers. comm.).

At the same time the workshops had great experience in the forging of copper alloys, both as wire in brooches and pins, and as sheet in everything from cauldrons to scabbards and shield fittings, with particular skill in the production of abstract, three-dimensional geometric designs in repoussé. This ability is repeated in some of the torque terminals from the new discoveries at Snettisham (Stead 1991) and in the bracelet from the earlier finds. One thing that characterizes these pieces is the use of rather thick sheet-metal, as thick as, or thicker than the bronze sheet they would have known. The same solidity applies to the wires and bars used for the wide variety of twisted torque bodies. The most elaborate show great inventiveness in creating different, regularly patterned, surface textures from twisting and bundling the wires in different ways. The Snettisham smiths seem to have had casting-on as their only technique for joining terminals to torques, or for adding extra decorative elements. This last is plainly exhibited in the Ipswich torques, where the decoration has been applied to plain torque terminals by building up a wax model on the surface and casting on more gold alloy (Brailsford and Stapley 1972).

These torques contrast strongly with the tubular torques in the same treasure which are typical members of the continental class reviewed earlier (Eluère 1987b) and exhibit the same, more delicate techniques. It was possible for such torques to be altered locally, as with the redesign of the body of the Broighter torque, but the Snettisham examples are largely unaltered. Several, as at Snettisham, are deposited in close association with gold coins. There are other possible imports at Snettisham, for example the torques with square-section wires and mercury-gilt terminals. Wires with non-circular cross-sections appear not to be native to the Snettisham tradition, and where the technique of mercury gilding was acquired is not known (Stone 1987; Stead 1991). Indeed, the Snettisham material represents some of the earliest dated mercury gilding in the west so that pursuing its antecedents will be of great interest.

The alloys used in the Snettisham workshops tell us a great deal about the way in which the smiths understood the properties of gold–silver–copper alloys, and also about the effects of the political and economic events of the first century BC (Northover 1992). The tubular torques and some of the finest quality torques and bracelets of other types use the same range of natural golds with a small percentage of copper that appear in continental La Tène pieces. From this starting-point the rest of the gold alloy material is increasingly debased until a point is reached where gold has effectively disappeared from the alloy. Down to 25–30 per cent gold, a consistent path is followed, with a 65 per cent silver to 35 per cent copper alloy being added; the resulting ternary alloys will be close to the minimum melting-point for a given gold content and the colour change from yellow to white gold is retarded. The same process was followed in the Gallo-Belgic (Ambiani) coinage which was both the inspiration and a major source of bullion for the British Celtic coinage. This imported bullion was recycled into the British coinage without being re-refined so it too exhibits the same debasement process, and it is reasonable to conclude that the same bullion sources supplied the Snettisham smiths (the Snettisham area is host to a number of important Celtic coin hoards). This conclusion is reinforced by the fact that many of the smaller Snettisham items, such as rings and 'ingot' bracelets, are exact multiples of coin weights.

The continued debasement of these gold alloys beyond the 25–30 per cent level indicates that the available gold supply was finite, and decreasing as more was taken out of circulation by the creation and deposition of new objects. The most likely cause for this disruption of the gold supply is the final conquest of Gaul by Rome and the consequent suppression of the Gallic gold coinage and the cutting off of Gallic purchases of British assistance. Within the Snettisham treasure and other hoards there was clearly a hierarchy of torques from the most elaborate gold creations to basic bronze examples. The aim of the smiths was to make sure that the most prestigious items always had the most golden appearance, both by reserving high-quality gold scrap or withdrawn coins for these pieces, and by the employment of such techniques as depletion gilding; the ultimate expression of this process may have been the mercury gilding of base metal and, for silver, the silver-alloy plating of copper (Northover and Salter 1990). At the same time the coinage alloys used by those tribes still issuing gold coins underwent a major reform, with a raising of the standard to 40–45 per cent gold and the use of a red, copper-rich alloy rather than the earlier white alloys. The Iceni, the tribe in whose territory Snettisham lay, at this stage abandoned the use of a gold coinage.

We cannot leave any discussion of the Snettisham treasure without considering its function or functions. The recent excavations have shown that the great majority of it was concealed in a series of pits carefully excavated into the subsoil. Several possibilities can be offered and it is probable that the whole structure of the find involves several of them. The tubular torques, by analogy with some of the continental examples, may imply an element of ritual deposition. The large caches of scrap, including stock alloy bars (the 'ingot' bracelets – in fact billets) and remains of work in progress (e.g. freshly cast ingots and crucible waste), point to a close connection with a nearby workshop. The way in which the other objects were deposited suggests a desire for long-term security rather than a reaction to a short-term emergency. It could be the caches were designed for periodic access and reuse on ceremonial occasions. The alloys in the ingot material are some of the most debased and, taken with the whole range of intact torques suggest continuing manufacture over a lengthy period. The occasion for making a new torque may have been a ceremonial one, i.e. a particular event demanded one. This was achieved by recycling whatever bullion was made available, adding silver and bronze, and then rendering the product as golden as possible by, for example, depletion gilding. This torque could then be added to the store. How long this process of extending the life of a finite bullion supply went on is not at all clear, possibly for only a few years. What is certain is that no red golds comparable to the reformed coinages of other tribes occur in the treasure.

THE AFTERMATH

The Snettisham treasure is the final point in the use of gold alloys for large objects in the La Tène tradition. From then on in southern England gold was almost entirely reserved for the coinage, while across the English Channel in romanized Gaul there was a transition to Roman styles of jewellery. Celtic-style fibulae might be made of silver but any large pieces of plate used by the kings and princes would now be Roman. The torques themselves did not entirely pass out of sight: a second century AD jeweller's hoard from Snettisham contains small fragments of torc as well as the Roman silver coins which were his main source of silver. Meanwhile, Celtic artistic traditions continued in the north and west of Britain but the only use of gold is for gilding.

REFERENCES

Almagro Gorbea, M. (1989) 'Orfebreria orientalizante', *Revista de Arqueología* 198.

Bayley, J. (1990) 'The production of brass in antiquity with particular reference to Roman Britain', in P.T. Craddock (ed.) *2000 Years of Zinc and Brass*, London: British Museum Occasional Paper 50, 7–28.

Bémont C. (ed.) (1987) *Mélanges offerts au Docteur J.-B. Colbert de Beaulieu*, Paris: Editions de Léopard d'Or.

Bergquist, A. and Taylor, T. (1987) 'The origin of the Gundestrup Cauldron', *Antiquity* 61: 10–24.

Beswick, P. *et al.* (1991) 'A decorated iron age torc from Dinnington, South Yorkshire', *Antiquaries Journal* 70(1): 16–33.

Biel, J. (1987) 'Catalogue', in J.-P. Mohen *et al. Trésors des princes celtes*, 164–88.

Blanchet, J.-C. (1984) *Les Premiers Métallurgistes, en Picardie et dans le Nord de la France*, Paris: Société Préhistorique Française, Mémoires 17, 413–19.

Blockley, K. (1989) *Prestatyn 1984–5*, Oxford: British Archaeological Reports 210, esp. 171–94.

Boon, G.C. and Davies, J.L. (1976) *Welsh Antiquity*, Cardiff: National Museum of Wales.

Born, H., Metzen, H.J. and Ruthenberg, K. (1990) 'Antike Herstellungstechniken: Oberflächenuntersuchungen an einem süditalischen Muskelpanzer', *Acta Praehistorica et Archaeologica* 22: 157–68.

Boudet, (1987) 'A propos du dépôt celtique de Tayac (Gironde)', in C. Bémont (ed.) *Mélanges*, 107–20.

Brailsford, J.W. and Stapley, J.E. (1972) 'The Ipswich torcs', *Proceedings of the Prehistoric Society* 38: 219–34.

Brun, N. and Pernot, M. (1992) 'The opaque red glass of Celtic enamels from continental Europe', *Archaeometry* 34(2): 235–52.

Castelin, K. (1985) *Keltsiche Münzen – Katalog der Sammlung des Schweizerisches Landesmuseum Zürich* 2 vols, Zurich: Schweizerisches Landesmuseum.

Chaume, B. *et al.* (1987) 'Vix', in J.-P. Mohen *et al. Trésors des princes celtes*, 207–30.

Clarke, R.R. (1954) 'The early iron age treasure from Snettisham, Norfolk', *Proceedings of the Prehistoric Society* 20: 27–86.

Clifford, E.M. (1964) *Bagendon – a Belgic oppidum*, Cambridge: Heffers.

Coles, J.M. (1962) 'European bronze age shields', *Proceedings of the Prehistoric Society* 28: 156–90.

Cowell, M.R. (1992) 'An analytical survey of the British gold coinage', in M. Mays (ed.) *Celtic Coinage* 207–35.

Cunliffe, B.W. (1991) *Danebury: an iron age hillfort in Hampshire: The Excavations 1979–1988: the finds*, London: CBA Research Report 73.

Cunliffe, B.W. and Miles, D. (eds) (1984) *Aspects of the Iron Age in Central Southern Britain*, Oxford: Oxford University Committee for Archaeology Monograph 2.

Davies, J.L. and Spratling, M.G. (1976) 'The Seven Sisters hoard, a centenary study', in G.C. Boon and J.M. Lewis (eds) *Welsh Antiquity*, 121–48.

Davies, O. (1935) *Roman Mines in Europe*, Oxford: Oxford University Press.

Delibes de Castro, G. and Esparza Arroyo, A. (1989) 'Los tesoros preromanos de la Meseta Norte y la orfebreria Celtiberica', *Revista de Arqueologia*.

Echt, R. (forthcoming) 'Sintering, welding, brazing and soldering as bonding techniques in Etruscan and Celtic goldsmithing', in G. Morteani and J.P. Northover (eds) *Prehistoric Gold*.

Eichhorn, P. (1987) 'Neue technische Untersuchungen am Ring von Trichtingen', *Funderbichte aus Baden-Württemberg* 12: 213–25.

Eluère, C. (1982) *Les Ors préhistoriques, L'Age du bronze en France* II: Paris: Picard.

—— (1985) 'Goldwork of the Iron Age in barbarian Europe', *Gold Bulletin* 4: 144–55.

—— (1987a) *L'Or des Celtes*, Fribourg: Office du Livre.

—— (1987b) 'Celtic gold torcs', *Gold Bulletin* 20(1/2): 22–37.

—— (1989a) *The Secrets of Ancient Gold*, Düdingen: Trio Verlag.

—— (1989b) 'L'or et l'argent de la tombe de Vix', *Bulletin de la Société Préhistorique Française* 86(1): 10–32.

—— (1991) 'The Celts and their gold', in C. Tanzi (ed.) *The Celts*, 349–55.

Eogan, G. (1967) 'The associated finds of gold bar torcs', *Journal of the Royal Society of Antiquaries of Ireland* 97: 129–75.

—— (1983a) *Hoards of the Irish Later Bronze Age*, Dublin: University College Dublin.

—— (1983b) 'Ribbon torcs in Britain and Ireland', in A. O'Connor and D.V. Clarke (eds) *From the Stone Age to the 'Forty-Five*, 87–126.

Fischer, F. (1982) 'Der Trichtinger Ring der in der Forschung', *Funderbichte aus Baden-Wüttemberg* 12: 206–12.

Fitzpatrick, A. (1992) 'The roles of Celtic coinage in south-east England', in M. Mays (ed.) *Celtic Coinage*, 1–33.

Flouest, R. (1991) 'Bragny-sur-Saône (Saône-et-Loire) – metallurgy center', in C. Tanzi (ed.) *The Celts*, 118–19.

Foster, J. (1980) *The Iron Age Moulds from Gussage All Saints*, London: British Museum Occasional Papers 12.

Frey, O.-H. (1971) 'Die Goldschale von Schwarzenbach', *Hamburger Beiträge zur Archäologie* 1: 85–100.

Furger, A. and Müller, F. (eds) (1991) *Gold der Helvetiker – keltische Kostbarkeiten aus der Schweiz*, Zurich: Schweizerisches Landesmuseum.

Furger-Gunti, A. (1982) 'Der "Goldfund von Saint-Louis bei Basel" und ähnliche keltische Schatzfunde', *Zeitschrift für Schweizerische Archäologie und Kunstgeschichte* 39: 1–47.

Gerloff, S. (1991) *The Cauldrons and Buckets of Atlantic Europe*, Berlin: Habilitiationsschrift, Freie Universität.

Gonzalo, A.H. (1989) 'Inicios de la orfebreria en la peninsula Iberica', *Revista de Arqueologia*.

Green, H.S. (1988) 'A find of bronze age "ring-money" from Craianog, Llanllyni, Gwynedd', *Bulletin of the Board of Celtic Studies* 35: 87–91.

Hanworth, R. and Tomalin, D. (1977) *Brooklands, Weybridge: the excavation of an iron age and medieval site 1964–65 and 1970–71*, Guilford: Surrey Archaeological Society, Research Volume 4.

Hartmann, A. (1970) *Prähistorische Goldfunde aus Europa I*, Studien zu den Anfängen der Metallurgie 3, Berlin: Gebr. Mann Verlag.

—— (1982) *Prähistorische Goldfunde aus Europa II*, Studien zu den Anfängen der Metallurgie 5, Berlin: Gebr. Mann Verlag.

—— (1987) 'Objets en bronze et en or de la tombe princière de Hochdorf', in J.-P. Mohen *et al. Trésors des princes celtes*, 160–3.

Haseloff, G. (1991) 'Celtic enamel', in C. Tanzi (ed.) *The Celts*, 638–42.

Hofmann, F. (1991) 'Gold seiner Lagerstätten und seine Gewinnung', in A. Furger and F. Müller (eds) *Gold der Helvetiker*, 35–40

Howard, H. (1983) 'The bronze casting industry in later prehistoric Britain: a study based on refactory debris', Ph.D. thesis, University of Southampton.

Joachim, H.-E. (1991) 'The votive deposit at Niederzier', in C. Tanzi (ed.) *The Celts*.

Joffroy, R. (1979) *Vix et ses trésors*, Paris: Editions Tallandier.

Jones, O.B.C. (1992) 'Ancient tin-plating', unpublished dissertation for Part II of BA degree, Metallurgy and Science of Materials, Department of Materials, University of Oxford.

Jope, E.M. (1983) 'Hallstatt D daggers: Britain and Europe', *Bulletin of the Institute of Archaeology, University of London* 19: 83–90.

Kaul, F. (1991) *Thracian Tales on the Gundestrup Cauldron*, Publications of the Holland Travelling University 1, Amsterdam: Najade Press.

Lehrberger, G. (forthcoming) 'Gold deposits of Europe – gold sources over 4000 years', in G. Morteani and J.P. Northover (eds) *Prehistoric Gold in Europe*.

Lowery, P.R., Savage, R.D.A. and Wilkins, R.L. (1976) 'A technical study of the designs on the British mirror series', *Archaeologia* 105: 99–126.

Lynch, F. (1991) *Prehistoric Anglesey*, Llangefni: Anglesey Antiquarian Society.

MacGregor, M. (1976) *Early Celtic Art in North Britain*, 2 vols, Leicester: University of Leicester Press.

Mays, M. (ed.) (1992) *Celtic Coinage: Britain and beyond*, Proceedings of the 11th Oxford Symposium on Coinage and Monetary History, Oxford: British Archaeological Reports 222.

Meany, A. (1990) 'Iron age cauldrons', MA thesis, Department of Archaeology, University College, Dublin.

Meduna, J. and Peškař, I. (1993) 'Ein latènezeitlicher Fund mit Bronzebeschlägen von Brno-Maloměřice (Kr. Brno-Stadt)', *Bericht der Römisch-Germanisch Kommission* 73: 181–268.

Meeks, N.D. (1986) 'Tin-rich surfaces on bronze – some experimental and archaeological considerations', *Archaeometry* 28(2): 133–62.

Megaw, R. and Megaw, J.V.S. (1990) *Celtic Art*, London: Thames & Hudson.

Mohen, J.-P., Duval, A. and Eluère, C. (1987) *Trésors des princes celtes*, Paris: Editions de la Réunion des Musées Nationaux.

Morteani, G. and Northover, J.P. (eds) (forthcoming) *Prehistoric Gold in Europe, Proceedings of a NATO Advanced Research Workshop*, Amsterdam: Cluwer.

Moscalu, E. (1990) 'Das thrako-getische Fürstengrab von Peretu in Rumaniën', *Bericht der Römisch-Germanisch Kommission* 70: 129–90.

Mossleitner, F. (1991) 'The Dürnberg near Hallein, a center of Celtic art and culture', in C. Tanzi (ed.) *The Celts*, 167–73.

Müller, F. (1990) 'Zur Datierung von Goldschatzes von Erstfeld', *Jahrbuch der Schweizerischen Gesellschaft für Ur- und Frühgeschichte* 73: 83–94.

Musson, C.R. (1991) *The Breiddin Hillfort*, London: CBA Research Report 76.

Musson, C.R. *et al.* (1993) 'Excavations and metalworking at Llwyn Bryn-dinas hillfort, Llangedwyn, Clwyd', *Proceedings of the Prehistoric Society* 58: 265–83.

Needham, S.P. (1990) 'The Penard-Wilburton succession: new metalwork finds from Croxton (Norfolk) and Thirsk (Yorkshire)', *Antiquaries Journal* 70(2): 253–70.

Northover, J.-P. (1982) 'The metallurgy of the Wilburton hoards', *Oxford Journal of Archaeology* 1(1): 69–110.

—— (1984) 'Iron age bronze metallurgy in central southern England', in B.W. Cunliffe and D. Miles (eds) *Aspects of the Iron Age in Central Southern Britain*, Oxford: Oxford University Committee for Archaeology Monograph 2, 126–45.

—— (1989) 'The St Helier gold torc', *Annual Bulletin of the Société Jersiaise* 25(1): 112–37.

—— (1991a) 'Analysis of bronze age and iron age metalwork from Anglesey', in F. Lynch *Prehistoric Anglesey*, Appendix 1, 386–93.

—— (1991b) 'Non-ferrous metalwork and metallurgy', in N. Sharples, *Maiden Castle*, 159–65.

—— (1991c) 'Non-ferrous metalwork and metallurgy', in B.W. Cunliffe, *Danebury*, 407–12.

—— (1992) 'Materials issues in the Celtic coinage', in M. Mays (ed.) *Celtic Coinage*, 235–300.

Northover, J.P. and Salter, C.J. (1990) 'Decorative metallurgy of the Celts', *Materials Characterisation* 25(1): 47–62.

O'Connor, A. and Clarke, D.V. (eds) (1983) *From the Stone Age to the 'Forty-Five*, Studies presented to R.B.K. Stevenson, Edinburgh: National Museums of Scotland.

O'Connor, B. (1980) *Cross-Channel Relations in the Later Bronze Age*, Oxford: British Archaeological Reports International Series 91.

Perea Caveda, A. and Rovira Llorens, S. (forthcoming) 'The gold from Arrabalde', in G. Morteani and J.P. Northover (eds) *Prehistoric Gold in Europe*.

Pingel, V. (forthcoming) 'Technological aspects of prehistoric gold objects on the basis of material analyses', in G. Morteani and J.-P. Northover (eds) *Prehistoric Gold in Europe*.

Raftery, B. (1984) *La Tène in Ireland*, Marburg: Veröffentlichung des vorgeschichtlichen Seminars, Marburg, Special issue 2.

—— (1991) 'The island Celts', in C. Tanzi (ed.) *The Celts*, 554–72.

Ruiz-Gálvez Priego, M. (1989) 'La orfebrería del bronce final: el poder y su ostentación', *Revista de Arqueología*.

Salter, C.J. and Northover, J.P. (1992) 'Reconstructing metallurgical processes at Hengistbury Head, Dorset, an iron age and Roman trading port', in P. Vandiver *et al.* (eds) *Materials Issues*.

Savory, H.N. (1964) 'A new hoard of La Tène metalwork from Merionethshire', *Bulletin of the Board of Celtic Studies* 20: 449–75.

—— (1975) 'Some Welsh late bronze age hoards – old and new', *Archaeologia Atlantica* 1(2): 111–26.

—— (1976) *A Guide Catalogue to the Iron Age Collections*, Cardiff: National Museum of Wales.

Sealey, P.R. (1979) 'The later history of the Icenian electrum torcs', *Proceedings of the Prehistoric Society* 45: 165–78.

Sharples, N. (1991) *The Excavations at Maiden Castle, 1985–6*, London: English Heritage.

Spratling, M.G. (1970) 'The smiths of South Cadbury', *Current Archaeology* 188–91.

Stanton, Y. (1984) 'The hoard of South Wales or "Stogursey" axes from St. Mellons, South Glamorgan, a preliminary statement', *Bulletin of the Board of Celtic Studies* 31: 191–5, pl. 1.

Stead, I.M. (1985) *The Battersea Shield*, London: British Museum Publications.

—— (1991) 'The Snettisham treasure, excavations in 1990', *Antiquity* 65: 447–65.

Stead, I.M. and Rigby, V. (1986) *Baldock, the Excavation of a Roman and Pre-Roman Settlement 1968–72*, London: Britannia Monograph Series 7.

Stone, E.C. (1987) 'Iron age metalcraft in southern Britain', unpublished dissertation for Part II of BA degree in Metallurgy and Science of Materials, Department of Materials, University of Oxford.

Tanzi, C. (ed.) (1991) *The Celts – catalogue of an exhibition at the Plazzo Grassi, Venice*, Milan: Bompiani.

Taylor, J.J. (1980) *Bronze Age Goldwork in the British Isles*, Cambridge: Cambridge University Press.

Vandiver, P., Druzik, J., Williams, G. and Freestone, I.C. (eds) (1992) *Materials Issues in Art and Archaeology III*, Pittsburgh: Materials Research Society Proceedings, 267.

Vidal, M. (1976) 'Le seau de bois orné de Vielle Toulouse (Haute Garonne) étude comparative des seaux de la Tène III', 34: 167–200.

Voûte, A. (1985) 'Die Feingehaltbestimmung des Goldmüzen', in K. Castelin, *Keltische Münzen*, 55–68.

—— (1991) 'Die Analysenverfahren für Goldgegenstände', in A. Furger and F. Müller (eds) *Gold der Helvetiker*, 49–52, 164–7.

Youngs, S. (1989) *The Work of Angels – masterpieces of Celtic metalwork, 6th–9th centuries AD*, London: British Museum Publications.

IRONWORKING IN THE CELTIC WORLD

—— ·•· ——

W.H. Manning

Although the Iron Age did not begin north of the Alps until the eighth century BC, occasional iron artefacts had been appearing in central and western Europe for some centuries before then. Some of these may have been made of meteoric iron; others of metal acquired by a series of exchanges from the Hittite kingdoms of Anatolia, where iron was being produced in appreciable amounts from at least the middle of the second millennium BC, and in small quantities probably a millennium earlier. But in some cases the iron may have been produced locally, for the furnaces used to smelt copper could produce iron at only slightly higher temperatures. Indeed, if iron ores were mixed with copper ore as fluxes to increase the copper yield, metallic iron could be produced without any increase in temperature.

However, the ability to produce a material does not mean that it can or will be utilized. For that to happen it must be possible to work it, and there must be a demand for the products made from it; a requirement which may involve overcoming cultural as well as technological barriers. The main difficulty in utilizing iron in a technological regime accustomed to working with copper alloys is that these were normally shaped by casting the molten metal, whereas in European prehistory iron was a solid worked by forging and welding at red-heat.

Two main changes may occur in the furnace when a metal is smelted. The first, which is invariable, is the chemical reduction of the ore to the metal; in the case of both copper and iron this occurs at $c.800°C$. At that temperature the metal is still a solid and is intermixed with the siliceous residue of the ore. The second change, which is not invariable, is the melting of the metal, which frees it from the siliceous residue and concentrates it as a pool of molten metal. Pure copper melts at $1083°C$, pure iron at $1535°C$. A third process, whereby the silica from the ore combines with some of the metal to form a molten slag, usually takes place at much the same temperature. This has the advantage of partially freeing the metal from the non-metallic residue but the disadvantage of reducing the yield, as a percentage of the metal, often a high one, is lost in slag formation. In relatively sophisticated metallurgical regimes this loss is reduced by adding a flux, another metal oxide, with which the silica combines in preference to the metal being smelted. Whether this was done in iron age Europe remains debatable.

The melting-point of pure iron is well above the maximum temperature attainable in a simple furnace. However, in the same way that the addition of tin to copper produces an alloy with a lower melting point than that of pure copper, so the addition of between 2 per cent and 5 per cent carbon produces an alloy, cast iron, which may melt at a temperature as low as *c.*1250 °C, which was within the capabilities of the furnaces used in the later Iron Age. Since iron is smelted with charcoal, a pure form of carbon, this alloying process will occur spontaneously in the furnace if the conditions are right, and there can be little doubt that cast iron will have been produced from time to time in the Iron Age. Indeed, had the will been there, it could probably have been made on a regular basis in the later Iron Age. But cast iron has two great disadvantages as a raw material: it is extremely brittle, and, unlike bronze, it cannot be hot- or cold-worked; defects so fundamental that Celtic technology found no use for it. Instead, what was utilized was wrought iron (in modern terminology, low-carbon steel), an alloy containing less than 0.5 per cent carbon, which lacks the defects of cast iron. At the temperature at which wrought iron is formed (*c.*800°C) it is so intermixed with the siliceous residue of the ore as to be almost unworkable. To free it from this residue it is necessary to raise the temperature of the furnace to about 1200°C, when some of the iron reacts with the silica to form a molten slag which runs off leaving a spongy 'bloom' containing a high proportion of wrought iron. At no point does the metal itself melt.

For such a bloom to be used it has to be freed from the slag intermixed with the iron, and then forged into shape. As this cannot be done by hammering the cold bloom it has to be made red-hot and then hammered on an anvil, a technique alien to the early bronzesmith accustomed to casting and cold-working technique. Not only would such smiths have been unfamiliar with this aspect of working hot metals, but they would also have lacked the toolkit, most notably the tongs and long-handled, heavy hammers, needed to process red-hot blocks of metal; a lack which would have prevented them from utilizing any wrought iron which they produced either by accident or as a result of the experimental smelting of iron ore, a process which must surely have occurred from time to time.

The critical change came late in the Middle Bronze Age with the development of the techniques of working sheet-bronze. Although bronze can be cold-worked, prolonged hammering causes it to harden and become brittle before eventually fracturing; a problem which prevented the development of sheet-bronze for many centuries after the use of the cast metal had become commonplace. The solution lies in annealing the metal, a process whereby bronze which has been stressed by hammering is restored to malleability by heating to red-heat and then cooling. The development of this process, and the consequent production of sheet-bronze, will have accustomed the bronzesmith to handling hot metals and must have led to the development of the smith's hearth for reheating the metal, as well as tongs, heavy hammers and a suitable anvil. From there it was but a short technological step to working wrought iron.

Iron had been used in the Near East and Aegean region for some centuries before it appeared in central and western Europe. In the middle years of the second millennium BC the Hittites appear to have enjoyed a virtual monopoly of the production of iron, although the amount which they actually produced seems to have been relatively small. The conventional view is that it was the collapse of the Hittite empire in the twelfth century BC which spread the techniques of iron working to their neighbours, including the Greeks. Certainly iron was being produced in Greece by the eleventh century BC, and in the following centuries we find it becoming more common and more widespread. By the eighth century it had reached Italy, and it appears in the Hallstatt areas of Europe soon after, probably around 700 BC, the date customarily accepted for the beginning of Hallstatt C. Whether the Hittites really had such a complete monopoly of ironworking may be doubted. Enough pieces are known from earlier contexts in Europe to suggest that occasionally it was both produced and worked, but even if this was the case, such discoveries were not followed up, and it was not until the end of the second millennium BC in sub-Mycenaean Greece (Late Helladic III) that iron was produced and used on any scale in Europe. Initially it was used for small prestige items such as rings, brooches and knife blades, but within a relatively short time, certainly before 1000 BC, larger objects, such as swords, were being made. The route by which mastery of the new metal reached the Hallstatt area is still debated; the most favoured ones are from Italy into the east Alpine region, or from Greece through the Balkans, although it is possible that more than one route was involved. Once the Mediterranean cultures which were in contact with the Urnfield peoples of central Europe had begun to use iron, it was probably inevitable that it would be introduced into central Europe, in the same way that the use of sheet-bronze had been introduced some centuries before.

Wrought iron is often compared unfavourably with bronze; it is more malleable, rather softer and, to modern eyes, lacks the aesthetic appeal of bronze. Wrought-iron swords were notoriously liable to bend. Polybius (*Histories* II.33) records, no doubt with some exaggeration, that at the Battle of Telamon in 225 BC the Celtic swords became as bent as strigils after a few blows. Nor could wrought iron hold an edge as well as work-hardened bronze. But these disadvantages were offset by the fact that iron weapons were less likely to shatter than bronze, and iron has other advantages. Copper is a relatively rare metal, while tin is extremely rare. Iron, however, is common and few areas were far removed from an ore source suitable for use by prehistoric man, whose requirements were measured in kilograms rather than tons. The elaborate exchange networks needed to supply much of Europe with bronze were largely unnecessary for iron, and where they were needed they were usually more limited; facts which may have had a considerable effect on contemporary social structures. Iron is a remarkably versatile material which is easily cut, shaped and welded at red-heat. Taken together, these properties meant that it was relatively easy to produce a wide range of artefacts, from simple pins to the great anchor chains used by the Veneti of Brittany, many of which could only be produced in cast bronze with the greatest difficulty.

The iron age smelter normally used oxide and carbonate ores, both of which were readily available in most parts of Europe. Sulphide ore were generally avoided as the sulphur could be carried into the raw iron with deleterious results. In most areas, including Britain, the ores could be obtained from opencast workings or pits without the need for the deep mines necessary for mining copper ores, although literary references, such as Caesar's *De Bello Gallico* (VII.22), suggest that mines were used in parts of Gaul in the Late Iron Age.

Our knowledge of the furnace technology of this period is fragmentary. The earliest furnaces used for smelting iron were probably based on the furnaces used for smelting copper. The superstructure of such furnaces is rarely well preserved, unless, as was sometimes the case, they were sunk into the ground, probably to reduce heat loss. Recent work has confirmed that many furnaces which appear to be bowl furnaces were almost certainly the bases of low shaft furnaces, 30 to 40 cm in diameter, with a cylindrical superstructure half a metre or so in height. Experimental reconstructions have shown such furnaces to be relatively efficient in producing iron, whereas there are considerable problems with bowl furnaces. Such furnaces lacked arrangements for tapping the slag, and this will have accumulated in the furnace; the bloom could be removed through the top.

The taller shaft furnaces, standing some 2 metres high and often with an adjacent pit into which the slag was tapped, may have been introduced in the later Iron Age, although the best evidence for their use is in the Greek and Roman world, and they do not appear in any numbers in Celtic areas until after the Roman conquest.

If the low shaft furnace dominated the western Celtic tradition, two alternative types were in common use in the eastern part of the Celtic world. The first was a short shaft furnace placed above a deep pit in which the slag was collected. In North Africa, where similar furnaces have remained in use until modern times, it was possible to move the furnace shaft to another pit when the first was full, but the sheer weight of most of the east European examples would probably have prevented this. Such evidence as we have suggests that this type of furnace did not appear until relatively late in the Iron Age. Another form, commonly found in Bavaria and Austria, had a dome rather than a shaft. With a diameter of a metre or more and standing about 80 cm high, it was larger than most of the other types. Although essentially a central European form, isolated examples have been claimed as far west as northern England.

By modern standards such furnaces were highly inefficient; not only did a large part of the iron end up in the slag, but great effort was expended to produce a relatively small piece of iron. Experimental work by Mr Peter Crew based on late iron age iron production sites in Snowdonia, suggests that a low shaft furnace could be used for up to twenty smelts, each producing a bloom weighing about 2 kilograms. Thus the entire production of the ironworking settlement at Crawcwellt, where a total of fifteen furnaces were used, was probably no more than 600 kilograms of raw iron, which, after lengthy processing to expel the slag, would have left about 300 kilograms of workable iron. Experiments using replica furnaces suggest that the production of this amount of metal would have required 30,000 kilograms of charcoal and taken some 7,500 man-days, up to four years' work for a team of six men if we allow for occasional holidays. By comparison the time taken to make a simple iron stool would have been quite short, not more than a few hours.

Even if we allow for the uncertainties in such calculations, the effort required to produce iron artefacts assumes its true proportions. Such objects were prized because they represented weeks or months of work, and the great quantities of ironwork found at cult sites throughout the Celtic world can be seen as offerings of real munificence. The fact that for much of the Iron Age even the smallest scrap of iron was collected and reprocessed is understandable when the effort of producing the raw material is appreciated.

Unlike bronze, wrought iron is only slightly hardened by hammering; only by alloying it with another element is it possible to produce a markedly harder metal. In a few cases such alloys are produced naturally from ores which contain suitable impurities; phosphorus and manganese are the commonest. Of these, phosphorus is the more common and is found in some British ores, but it has the disadvantage of making the iron brittle as well as harder. Despite this, many iron age artefacts do contain appreciable quantities of phosphorus. Manganese alloys have no such disadvantages, but manganese-rich ores are less common. However, they are found in Austria, and a reference in Pliny's *Natural History* (XXXIV.145) shows that the iron produced there was exceptionally highly regarded.

The commonest alloy is with carbon, of course, and the percentage of carbon has a profound effect on the physical properties of the metal. Wrought iron, with less than 0.5 per cent carbon, is almost unaffected, while cast iron, with more than 1.5 per cent carbon, is so brittle as to be unforgeable. Between these two lies steel, an alloy which is not only harder than wrought iron, but one whose properties can be controlled by heat treatment to produce a metal which is easily forged when red-hot but extremely hard and resilient when cold.

Until relatively recent times the only way of producing carbon steel was by carburization, where iron is heated with carbon, normally in the form of charcoal, for many hours during which the carbon diffuses into the iron and alloys with it. Unfortunately, it does not diffuse very far into the iron and the end-product usually is not pure steel, but a bar of wrought iron with a coating of steel. To what extent this process was practised by the Celtic smith is still an open question, although current opinion is that some steel was produced by controlled carburization. To some extent this process occurs naturally in the smith's hearth, but the coating of steel so formed is too thin to be of great value, although in an object which was repeatedly heated during forging the cumulative amount of steel formed could be appreciable. However, the conditions necessary for the production of steel exist in the smelting furnace itself, for the iron which is produced at the beginning of a smelt remains in contact with the burning charcoal for several hours before the process is ended, during which time some of it may be converted into steel. An experienced smith would be quite capable of differentiating those parts of a bloom which were steel from those which were wrought iron by their relative hardnesses, and the two could be separated easily.

The use of untreated steel produces a stronger and harder artefact than does wrought iron, but to utilize its properties to the full it needs to be quenched and tempered. In quenching, the steel is raised to white-heat and then rapidly cooled by being plunged into water or some other liquid. With pure steel this produces a very hard and brittle material, so hard and brittle that these qualities are usually modified by tempering. This involves reheating the metal and allowing it to cool gradually; the higher the temperature reached in the reheating, the softer the metal becomes. By combining quenching and tempering a smith can control the hardness of steel with great precision. In reality the Celtic smith hardly ever used pure steel but rather a mixture of wrought iron and steel. The effect of quenching this is to harden and embrittle the steel while leaving the wrought iron unaffected. Tempering such a piece is unnecessary for the brittleness of the steel is effectively counterbalanced by the resilience of the iron. The idea of quenching the metal may have come from working sheet-bronze which, after being heated to anneal it, is cooled by being plunged in water. Similarly, tempering is so similar to the annealing of work-hardened bronze that it might have been thought an obvious method of softening steel which had been overhardened by quenching.

The existing evidence suggests that by the later Celtic period the advantages of quenching were appreciated by some smiths producing edged tools and weapons. Metallographic examination of iron age ironwork has shown that the amount of steel used varies considerably; most smiths worked with wrought iron containing very little steel, a perfectly satisfactory metal for most purposes. Where steel had great advantages was for weapons and edged tools, and the evidence indicates that by the end of the first millennium BC it was being used for these, although not invariably.

Perhaps the simplest way of utilizing steel in weapons was to weld bars of steel and wrought iron together to produce alternating bands across the blade, a technique seen in one of the sword blades from the late iron age hoard from Llyn Cerrig Bach, Anglesey (Figure 17.1). Even without quenching, such blades had advantages over wrought-iron blades, and metallographic examination shows that often they were not quenched. A more advanced technique was to weld the bars together to form a blade with a steel edge sandwiched between layers of wrought iron, or a thick steel skin encasing a core of wrought iron. Here quenching enhanced the effectiveness of the blade by hardening the steel, but the wrought iron in it made tempering unnecessary. Such blades have been found in central European oppida dating from the end of the first millennium and mark a high point of Celtic smithing.

It is important to remember that the Celtic smith lacked our knowledge of the mechanisms which controlled these changes. He was aware that certain actions produced certain results, but how far the knowledge of processes such a carburization and quenching was disseminated remains uncertain. The fact that pieces of almost pure wrought iron were quenched, while pieces of steel were left unquenched, suggests that confusion was common. For most smiths working with wrought iron containing little or no steel, quenching, let alone tempering, would have been an irrelevancy.

The evidence which we have suggests that the Celtic blacksmith acquired his raw material in a prepared form, and that the smelting and preparation of the iron was separated from the fabrication of the artefacts. Much of the newly prepared metal was traded in the form of bars. On the Continent these usually took the form of square-sectioned bars tapering into a long spike at each end. In Britain they were the so-called currency bars, named from a passage in Caesar's *De Bello Gallico* (v.12) where he refers to the Britons using iron bars as a form of currency. The commonest form is a long, flat bar with a flanged socket with, in some cases, its tip folded back and welded to the body of the bar. Both forms seem unnecessarily elaborate for metal which would have been reworked as soon as the smith had acquired it, but, as Peter Crew has noted, the fact that the iron had been thinned, turned and welded guaranteed its quality, and in a period when bad as well as good ores were smelted, smiths would have welcomed such assurances. As well as material obtained from the smelters, large amounts of scrap iron would have been utilized. This was always an important source of material for the smith. Iron artefacts are

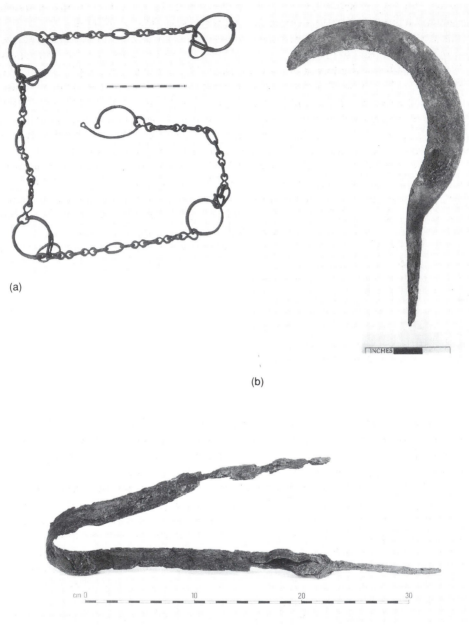

Figure 17.1 Iron artefacts from the late iron age metalwork deposit found in a former pool at Llyn Cerrig Bach, Anglesey, North Wales: (a) gang chain, (b) sickle, (c) sword with the remains of the sheath. The bending may be the result of ritual destruction. (Photo: National Museum of Wales, Cardiff; by permission of the National Museum of Wales.)

largely absent from habitation sites of the earlier Iron Age, so thorough was the collection for reprocessing. Only towards the end of the period does this situation change and ironwork begin to appear on domestic sites in any amount.

The earliest iron artefacts generally have the same form as contemporary bronze ones. Thus the Mindelheim sword is found both in bronze and iron, as are harness fittings, especially bridle bits, and some tools, such as axes and reaping-hooks. There is little doubt that these weapons and tools were designed primarily for production in bronze; they stand at the end of a long series of bronze types and have all the hallmarks of objects which were designed to be cast. The gently swelling, grooved sword blades, or the elaborate mouldings around the sockets of the axes and reaping-hooks were easily executed in the models which formed the basis of late bronze age castings, but they required the most laborious work when forged in iron. The closeness with which the iron artefacts follow the old design has led some writers to suggest that they were produced by bronzesmiths who had turned to the new metal, or by blacksmiths who had not mastered the capabilities of iron and lacked the skill to do more than blindly reproduce existing forms. The former may be true, but the latter is manifestly wrong, for the greatest technical skill was required to copy in wrought iron forms which were originally designed to be cast in bronze. As far as technical skill is concerned, Celtic ironworking appears in the archaeological record as a fully developed craft. If lack of skill does not explain the copying of bronze types, we must assume that it was required by custom. Both the craftsman and his patron would have viewed an implement as the total of its parts, and those parts included form as well as function. It was to be many generations before the Celtic smith was able to free himself from the restraints of design concepts which were essentially alien to his craft.

Our knowledge of the Celtic smith is derived almost entirely from his products, and this requires some consideration of the processes by which such material was preserved, processes which were neither random nor likely to provide a cross-section of all of the types in use. For much of the Iron Age we have two main sources of ironwork, hoards and burials. Unfortunately hoards become increasingly rare as the Iron Age progresses and only reappear in large numbers relatively late in the period. Graves provide a more even chronological coverage, but they produce a limited range of types, mainly prestige pieces such as weapons, horse gear and vehicle fittings. Relatively little ironwork is known from the habitation sites of the earlier Iron Age. As a result we must be very cautious in assuming that the absence of an artefact type, or even a whole class of artefacts, from the archaeological record means that they really were unknown in the Iron Age. Indeed, had that been the case, we would have no ironwork at all, for we lack many of the tools necessary to produce the ironwork which does survive.

We have relatively little knowledge of the organization of the iron industry in the Celtic world, although most major settlement sites produce evidence of bronze- and iron-working. We know of it at such important late Hallstatt sites as the Heuneburg and Mont Lassois, while at Bragny-sur-Saône metalworking debris covers several hectares. The interpretation of such discoveries depends to a considerable extent upon our interpretation of the sites themselves. If they are accepted as being the strongholds of princes, then the craftsmen working there form part of the entourage of those princes, producing work for them and fully integrated into the elaborate system of client–patron relationships which cemented Celtic society. It would have been at such places that the prestige ironwork, such as the swords and the iron fittings of the funerary vehicles found in the contemporary tombs, was made. The control of these craftsmen and the use of their products as gifts to equals and clients would have been an important element in establishing the status of such rulers. Whether ironworking was confined to such prestigious establishments is debatable. The production of the more utilitarian pieces may well have been left to less skilled smiths integrated into the lower levels of society.

As the Iron Age progressed the blacksmith came increasingly to exploit the properties of his metal. The fact that each piece is an individual creation allows it to be designed for its specific purpose, while the ability to join pieces by welding allows the smith to build up large and elaborate objects in a way which was almost impossible with bronze. An early example of the use of these techniques was the development of iron tyres for wheels. Casting a large tyre in bronze would have been no easy feat, but constructing one in iron was a relatively simple operation. Iron tyres are found from the beginning of the Iron Age, although for some centuries it was thought necessary to secure them with nails, but by the later La Tène period the great force exerted by a hot iron hoop as it cools and contracts was recognized and nails were dispensed with.

A similar progression can be seen in the evolution of the socket for attaching tool hafts. In cast bronze it was relatively easy to produce a socket but making one in iron was more difficult and involved forming 'wings' which were then folded over and their edges welded together. Functionally much of this work is unnecessary; simply folding the wings over forms a perfectly effective socket, and by the later La Tène period we find sockets of this type being used for many tools. At much the same time the advantages of the shaft-hole, as opposed to the socket, for securing the hafts of axes and adzes was appreciated and such tools assume the form which they have retained to the present day. It may seem surprising that it took several centuries for such apparently obvious changes to be made, or in some cases to be accepted from the Greek and Roman world, but change is social as well as technological and this is often a more formidable barrier to innovation.

In the last few centuries BC two changes occurred which greatly increase our knowledge of later Celtic ironwork. The first was the reappearance of the custom of making votive offerings in water – rivers, lakes and peat bogs; a custom which greatly increases the quantity and range of material which has survived. At the same time there appears to have been a spectacular rise in the amount of iron produced, a rise which not only led to more objects being sacrificed but to many more surviving on habitation sites. We may question how new some of the utilitarian types which now appear for the first time in the archaeological record really were. At least in some cases new patterns of deposition are probably preserving types, such as tools and structural fittings, which had had no place among the prestige pieces which had dominated the funerary traditions that provided the main mechanism of preservation in the earlier Iron Age. None the less, all the evidence does indicate a vast increase in the production of iron in the later Iron Age; the enormous quantities which were required for the nails used in the *murus gallicus* defences of the late Celtic oppida, perhaps 300 tons in the case of Manching, provide proof enough of that. Nor is there any reason to question the profound effect this increase in production would have had on all aspects of Celtic life. Not only was it now possible for iron to be used for such basic agricultural implements as ploughshares, but there was a great increase in the availability of all kinds of tools, although it is clear that it was still necessary for the metal to be used economically. This is seen in the smith's own tools. Anvils are still relatively small, while tongs have a simple jaw form which enabled them to be used for most work, unlike the more specialized forms, which appear later, and which were designed for the efficient execution of a limited range of tasks. Similarly, some of the more massive tools are multifunctional. Thus anvils and sledge hammers may have grooves on them to enable them to be used as swages for forming round-sectioned rods, a tradition which can be traced back to the Late Bronze Age. That such multipurpose tools were used throughout the Celtic world is shown by the discovery of virtually identical hammers with swage grooves from Waltham Abbey, near London and the Nikolausberg in Austria.

It is at this time that the absolute ascendancy of iron as the metal for weapons, tools and fittings was established in the Celtic world, and the technical ability of the Celtic smith becomes fully apparent. The consummate skill of the weapons smiths is obvious, and their pride is shown by the custom, derived from the classical world, of stamping the maker's mark or name on some of the finest pieces. The advances in offensive weapons are paralleled by the development of the mail shirts known from a few prestige burials and from sculpture. The technical skill shown by such pieces fully matches the more flamboyant craftsmanship seen in the contemporary bronzework. It is probably inevitable that our appreciation of the work of the Celtic blacksmith should be dominated by those pieces which were intended for patrons of the highest social levels, work which includes not only weapons and armour, but the elaborate firedogs and cauldron chains which were a necessary adjunct of the Celtic feast from Wales to Czechoslovakia. But these prestige pieces should not blind us to the fact that it was in the application of iron to more utilitarian objects that the new metal had its greatest effect on the whole Celtic world. It was this which must have revolutionized most aspects of life by making a wide range of functional tools and implements available to all levels of society. The more spectacular achievements of the later Celtic world were firmly underpinned by their ability to produce and work iron on a vast scale.

FURTHER READING

On the Technology of Working Iron

Ehrenreich, R.M. (1985) *Trade, Technology and the Ironworking Community in the Iron Age of Southern Britain*, Oxford.

Scott, B.G. and Cleere, R.F. (eds) (1984) *The Craft of the Blacksmith*, Belfast.

Tylecote, R.F. (1986) *The Prehistory of Metallurgy in the British Isles*, London.

—— (1992) *A History of Metallurgy* (2nd edn) London.

Tylecote, R.F. and Gilmour, B.J.J. (1986) *The Metallography of Early Ferrous Edge Tools and Edged Weapons*, Oxford.

General

Kruta, V. *et al.* (eds) (1991) *The Celts*, London.
Schutz, H. (1983) *The Prehistory of Germanic Europe*, New Haven and London.

Products

Jacobi, G. (1974) *Werkzeug und Gerät aus dem Oppidum von Manching* (*Die Ausgrabungen in Manching* vol. 5), Wiesbaden.

WOOD AND THE WHEELWRIGHT

———— ·◆· ————

Stuart Piggott

The Celtic world from the sixth century BC inherited a very long and sophisticated tradition of woodworking, in continental Europe and Britain going back to at least the beginning of the fourth millennium. The recovery of this fundamental episode in the history of technology has been a product of the exploitation over the last three decades of the potentialities of what has become known as wetland archaeology, where waterlogged conditions provide a medium for the preservation of wood, otherwise a fugitive natural substance save in exceptional circumstances such as extreme aridity or permafrost. An early example of wetland investigation was of course that of the Swiss lakeside sites first revealed in the 1850s and increasingly with the lowering of water levels in 1870–5; the great iron age site of La Tène was first discovered in 1858. In Britain the Glastonbury and Meare wetland iron age sites were excavated from 1892 (Coles and Coles 1986), but the co-ordinated work of archaeologists and natural scientists on the Somerset peat bogs and their contained artefacts, which has given us such astonishing new information, dates from the early 1960s, supplemented by similar projects in the Cambridgeshire Fens. We can now talk with some confidence about the salient facts of prehistoric European woodworking shared by the Celts before the Roman period.

All woodworking demands one or other of two types of timber, heavy or light (Coles *et al.* 1978; Piggott 1983: 16–21, 28 with refs). Traditionally, from medieval Latin to modern English, 'timber' denotes heavy stuff for posts and beams, or split into planks of appropriate thicknesses; 'wood' small-diameter poles which can themselves be split for hurdling or basketry. Already by the early fourth millennium BC in neolithic Britain there is evidence of conscious woodland management both in the selection of trees (usually oaks) for heavy timber posts up to a metre in diameter, log-boats from halved hollowed stems, and planks split or riven 'on the chord' and along the natural medullary rays for, among other things, single-piece or composite disc wheels and plank-built boats. More surprising is the neolithic achievement of the techniques of coppicing and pollarding for the controlled production of pole wood and its use when split for hurdling, the wattle element in wattle-and-daub walling, and basket-making. All this was the product of stone tools, to be replaced first by a bronze and in the Celtic world by an iron toolkit of axe and adze, chisels, gouges and knives. The saw was a late-comer to European prehistory, and from the Late

Bronze Age and the iron-working Celtic world usually small joiners' tools, but the planks of the burial chamber of the Hohmichele, of sixth-century Hallstatt D date, over 6 m long and 0.35 m wide, appear to have been not split, but sawn by a large timber-yard saw. The other technological innovation, also sixth-century in the Celtic world of west Europe, was the adoption of the lathe for wood-turning, to which we will return later.

In the meantime, heavy timber posts and beams were extensively used in the Celtic world, especially in fortifications (Figure 5.3). The problems of felling and handling massive tree stems had been faced and mastered by neolithic societies building in Britain the ceremonial and burial monuments of henges and long barrows by the third millennium BC, when oaks of up to a metre in diameter were worked into posts up to an estimated 3.25 m in height and a weight of over 2,000 kg. Such timber could be split and hollowed into log-boats (Ellmens 1969; McGrail and Switsur 1975) as detailed in Chapter 15 (Figure 15.6), but Chapter 5 describes the vast amount of timber used in the facing and internal lacing of so many types of defensive ramparts of forts and the later oppida of the Continent, where timber-laced walls with lengths of 5 or 6 km in circuit must have drawn heavily on the natural resources of woodland. All types of wood, from heavy timber to brushwood, and including discarded worked pieces, were used to make up the artifical islands for settlement in lakes or marshes, as at Glastonbury and the crannogs of Ireland and Scotland, as well as piles which could be massive posts driven into the lake bed (Morrison 1985). In the Milton Loch crannog in Scotland the woodwork included the plough-head and stilt of an ard which gave a radiocarbon date coincident with a structural pile of c.450–500 BC (Guido 1974). An ard beam from 45 km away is of the first century BC and the type goes back to the second millennium in Italy and south Russia. Heavy timber again was needed for the single-piece or composite wheels of ox-wagons, as we shall see on pp. 324–6, on the craft of the Celtic wheelwright, but before this we may consider two minor forms of woodworking, figural sculpture and wooden containers, which may involve raw material of varying dimensions.

Such human representations as survive seem to fall into two classes (Coles 1990). The first comprises seven dated figures from Britain and Ireland, all naked and some ithyphallic, and ranging from the early second millennium to the fourth century BC. Those from the sixth-century could include the large Ballachulish female nearly 1.5 m high of 728–524 BC, the contemporary little figures holding round shields and standing in a boat from Roos Carr, and the 34 cm ithyphallic figure from Kingsteignston, of 426–352 BC. Later prehistoric figures from the Nordic world beyond the Celts provide vague parallels. The second class is formed by an enormous number of Gaulish or Gallo-Roman wooden votive figures from two sanctuary sites at sacred springs, 300 or so from Sources-de-la-Seine near Dijon, and up to about 5,000 at the twin springs at Chamalières in the Massif Central. Some of the wood carvings are ex votos of human organs, but the complete human figures are clothed, and at Sources-de-la-Seine less romanized than at Chamalières (Megaw and Megaw 1989: 172–3, with references). Animal sculpture survives from one site, a waterlogged well or shaft within a ritual enclosure of the *Viereckschanze* type at Fellbach-Schmiden near Stuttgart with a tree-felling date of 123 BC, where a spirited stag protome and an antithetical pair of rams or goats originally flanking a human figure show us how much Celtic art in fugitive substances we must have lost (Megaw and Megaw 1989: 162–3).

Small pole-wood obtained by coppicing was extensively used for building trackways across bogs and marshes from the early third millennium BC, and in later prehistory in the Somerset Levels and the Cambridgeshire fens and the Dutch bogs, and in late prehistory in north Germany, sometimes flanked by highly stylized human figures cut from planks. Planks were used for shields of long oval type from the third century BC at Hjortspring on the Danish island of Als and at La Tène (Rosenberg 1937; Vouga 1923: pl. XVI–XVIII) and of course for arrows and spear-shafts, bows, and the handles of domestic tools from Neolithic times onwards. Woodwork was also freely used for vessels and containers of various types and it is here we must consider the early use of the lathe in prehistoric western Europe.

The earliest evidence for lathe-turning is in the ancient Orient and Aegean, and a lathe is technologically the application of the principle of the long-established bow-drill to a horizontal spindle driven into intermittent rotation by a wrapped-round cord or strap. This motion needed an assistant strap-puller or the return of the slack obtained by a springy upright in the pole lathe, common to most European peasant contexts, and in Britain surviving until modern times among, for instance, the chair-bodgers of the Chiltern beech woods. In prehistoric Europe the lathe must derive from Mediterranean sources, either Aegean or Etruscan. There is inferential evidence for the lathe finishing of bronze bowls in late bronze age central Europe, but general agreement puts the first real use of the wood-turner's lathe to sixth-century Hallstatt craftsmen in south Germany (Piggott 1983: 162), and a rapid adoption of the pole lathe or its equivalent throughout the Celtic world. The true lathe with continuous rotation had to await the invention of the crankshaft around AD 1400 (White 1978: 305).

Despite their importance in the Celtic world, wooden containers for liquids or dry stuffs have scarcely been discussed by archaeologists and the only technical study seems to be that made on the Glastonbury material (Earwood 1988; 1993). Lathe-turning may play a part, but vessels hollowed from the solid by axe and adze, chisel gouge and knife are part of the neolithic ancestry of woodcraft: at the lakeside settlement at Chalain in the Jura, for instance, hand-carved wooden bowls copy the contemporary early third-millennium neolithic pottery styles. In late prehistory finds from Northern Ireland are remarkable feats of carving from the solid wood block: one such cauldron is over half a metre in diameter (Coles *et al.* 1978) and another, from Altatarte, Co. Monaghan, and 30 cm across, is decorated with incised La Tène ornament and has free ring-drop handles (e.g. Raftery 1931: fig. 256). Some of the bowls and platters from La Tène itself were certainly turned (Vouga 1923: pl. XXIX) and in the third-century Hjortspring find were elegant little turned boxes with knobbed lids (Rosenberg 1937: fig. 34). From Glastonbury came the two well-known shallow flat-bottomed bowls with incised La Tène ornament, turned from solid blocks some 35–40 cm across. Decorative lathe-turned bases were incorporated in some British stave-built vessels, a class of construction of widespread employment in the Celtic world (Earwood 1993).

The stave-built hooped cask or barrel (Figure 8.3) to hold liquids was a Celtic invention, a northern barbarian counterpart to the Mediterranean amphora. Such a barrel is shown on the well-known Gallo-Roman relief from Langres, a huge cask, perhaps a couple of metres long, mounted on a mule drawn-wagon and usually taken to indicate the bulk transport of wine (Eydoux 1962: fig. 232). Such casks have been found reused as well linings in Roman Gaul and Britain (e.g. at Silchester). A series of late iron age stave-built vessels, often with decorative bronze bindings, occur in the Celtic world of Britain and the Continent. The great straight-sided stave-built vessel from Marlborough in Wiltshire, 60 cm in diameter and height (Fox called it a 'vat') has elaborate repoussé bronze decorative hoops and panels, and may be a Gaulish import, but unquestionably insular are stave-built tankards, banded or sheathed in bronze (e.g. Trawsfynydd and Shapwick), with decorative lathe-turned bases (Fox 1958: 68–70, 108–10). A distinctive series of stave-built buckets with hoop handles and decorative bronze mountings, in which three or four staves are prolonged into feet, are known from Belgic Britain (e.g. Aylesford and Baldock) and the Continent (Luxembourg) (Megaw and Megaw 1989: 184–7). Fragments of undecorated vessels of this type come from Glastonbury. From this site too come fragments of the walls of boxes made from very thin (3–5 mm) split and adzed strips of wood bent into a cylinder up to 15 cm in diameter and with incised geometric ornament. The technique was known in bronze age Denmark.

An important branch of wood technology in the Celtic world was that of the wheelwright and builder of four-wheeled wagons and two-wheeled carts or their specialized versions, chariots for parade and war. The writer surveyed the subject on a European basis twelve years ago and, where not otherwise documented, detailed references will be found in this source (Piggott 1983). It should be noted at the outset that our knowledge of Celtic vehicles from the sixth century BC to Roman times is very unequal and largely consists of wheels alone. The four-wheeled carriages from the Hallstatt D princely graves in the sixth century can be reconstructed in some detail (Pare 1992) from their elaborate bronze or iron sheathing and ornamentation, which allowed full-sized replicas to be built (Barth 1987), whereas our factual knowledge of the Celtic chariot, despite recent excavations of chariot graves in Belgium (Piggott 1983: 205) and Yorkshire (Stead 1991) depends on soil stains of the basic plans, and assumptions based on two or three representations on coins or sculpture (Piggott 1983: figs 127–9).

The earliest wheeled vehicles, from 3000 BC, were ox-drawn wagons and carts with simple disc wheels, either one-piece or of tripartite plank construction. Both demand adze and chisel work of heavy timber split on the chord: a single-piece, 90 cm diameter wheel, as in the Dutch Neolithic, would need a plank of 3 cubic metres weighing 322 kg. The wheel of three dowelled planks, the central twice the width of the lateral members, was early achieved and lasted not only throughout prehistory but until the 1950s in rural Ireland (Piggott 1983: 19–26).

In the Celtic world tripartite disc wheels presumably associated with heavy ox-drawn vehicles occur, as in the Nordic world beyond the Celts (Piggott 1983: 197–9; Schvosbo 1987), as early as 490–430 BC at Doogarymore in Ireland, 530 BC in Nordic Dystrup. Celtic examples continue on the Continent (200 BC at Mechanich-Antweiler, second–first century BC at Ezinge in Holland).

A novel type of vehicle, of light construction and drawing on small timber and the produce of coppicing, is that associated with paired horse draught, having four, but more often two, spoked wheels, when it takes the form of the chariot for parade, hunting or warfare. Such chariots were highly developed in the Near East from early in the second millennium BC, and their counterparts are known in Europe in the Urals and the Carpathians from the middle of the millennium. Immediately antecedent to our Celtic period are the Hallstatt C (seventh-century) graves of central Europe such as those in the Grosseibstat cemetery (both wagons and a chariot) or the Czechoslovakian wagon graves such as the Hradenin cemetery. It is, however, in Hallstatt D, from 600 BC, that the great series of wagon or carriage burials belong, to be replaced from the fifth century by chariot burials (Piggott 1983: 138–70; 1992).

The Hallstatt D graves with four spoked-wheeled wagons or carriages (Figure 26.8) which have been excavated number nearly 250, distributed from the Alps to Alsace, from Burgundy to Bohemia (Pare 1992; Barth 1987); the timber burial chambers have often been plundered in antiquity, but occasionally have survived, as at Vix or the staggering intact burial at Hochdorf (Biel 1985). The vehicles, many with elaborate bronze or iron sheathing and decoration on the basic woodwork, have a surprising uniformity in their structure and even dimensions. The axle-trees have a separation (wheelbase) averaging about 1.8 m, and a wheel track or gauge of about 1.3 m. This average track goes back to the earliest ox-wagon of the third millennium BC in south Russia, continues in the La Tène chariots and survived to determine the 'standard gauge' of 4 ft 8½ in for English railways and their continental derivatives of the nineteenth century (Piggott 1992). The Hallstatt D axles were joined by a Y-shaped perch and there was an articulated draught pole for a pair of horses under a yoke in the manner of oxen, a system of harnessing replaced in western Europe by collar and shafts only in the early Middle Ages.

The Hallstatt undercarriage supported a shallow and narrow body, only about 10 cm deep, with bronze-decorated sides and something under a metre wide. The long (40–45 cm) wheel naves allowed for a pivoted front axle with a quarter-lock of 20° and a turning circle of about 8.5 m, but most examples seem to have had a pair of fixed axles, as in all four-wheeled vehicles up to the later fourteenth century AD.

The spoked wheels used on horse-drawn vehicles in the Celtic world demand a fuller discussion. As we saw, the spoked wheel as opposed to the single or tripartite disc is an invention of the second millennium BC in the ancient Orient and eastern Europe as a part of the creation of a lightly built vehicle suitable to paired equid traction at high speeds compared to the lumbering ox-cart. Already by Hallstatt C in the seventh century such wheels were made with nail-studded iron tyres on wooden felloes which could be of complex construction incorporating both bent wood and segmental elements with elaborate iron clasps. By 600 and the beginning of Hallstatt D, wheel types had become simpler, with a single-piece bent felloe around 80 cm diameter, made from a coppiced pole 6–7 cm in diameter, over 3 m long, heat-bent into a true circle with an overlapping scarf joint, a type of construction in the Celtic world until Roman times. Iron hoop-tyres became a constant feature, the nails diminishing in number until about the second century BC, when the shrunk-on tyre with no nails was achieved (Piggott 1983: 216).

All vehicles, from the earliest disc wheels through to spoked wheels of all types, had wheels rotating freely of their axles, and held in place by linchpins of bronze or iron often made into decorative features. The long cylindrical naves of the sixth-century Hallstatt wheels were frequently completely sheathed in bronze or (as at Hochdorf) iron. One vehicle, that from Vix of just before 500 BC, has bronze-sheathed naves in an elegant double-curved classical moulding, the *cyma recta*, which, without sheathing, became standard in La Tène, and here we must look for ultimate origins in the western Greek world (Piggott 1983: 165, 214). All these naves imply lathe-turning on a massive scale, initial shaping with adze and chisel, as the unfinished nave from Glastonbury shows (Earwood 1988: 89; 1993).

The question of wooden horse-yokes for paired draught is a little obscure. In the seventh-century Hallstatt C there was a short-lived fashion for very elaborate bronze-studded, leather-covered wooden yokes, but in the following century they were unknown. The maplewood yoke from Hochdorf is a simple affair with bronze bands and a pair of little cast bronze horse figures. The finely carved yoke from La Tène and simpler versions from Ezinge and unassociated bog finds have all been classed by Fenton as ox-yokes but an equine use is not excluded for some, at least (Piggott 1983: 218).

The body of the 'Celtic' chariot above its axles is, as we have seen, wholly unknown except for inferential double-hooped screens of some material suggested by representations on the third-century BC Padua reliefs and Roman coins of 50–60 BC.

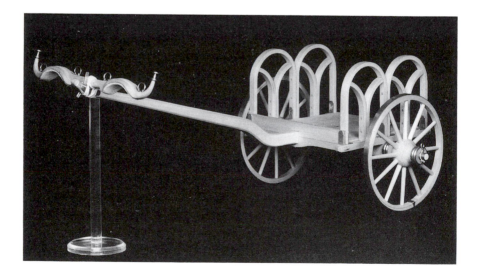

Figure 18.1 Reconstruction model of a chariot, based on fittings from Lynn Cerrig Bach, Anglesey. By courtesy of the National Museum of Wales.

REFERENCES

Barth, F.E. (ed.) (1987) *Vierradige Wagen aus Hallstattzeit*, Mainz.

Biel, J. (1985) *Dr Keltenfürst von Hochdorf*, Stuttgart.

Coles, B. (1990) 'Anthropomorphic wooden figures from Britain and Ireland?', *Proceedings of the Prehistoric Society* 56: 315–53.

Coles, B. and Coles, J. (1986) *Sweet Track to Glastonbury*, London and New York.

Coles, J.M. *et al.* (1978) 'The use and character of wood in prehistoric Britain and Ireland', *Proceedings of the Prehistoric Society* 44: 1–45.

Earwood, C. (1988) 'Wooden containers and other wooden artifacts from the Glastonbury lake village', *Somerset Levels Papers* 14: 83–90.

—— (1993) *Domestic Wooden Artifacts in Great Britain and Ireland*, Exeter.

Ellmers, D. (1969) 'Keltisch Schiffbau', *Jahrbuch Römisch-Germanische Zentralmuseum Mainz* 16: 73–122.

Eydoux, H.-P. (1982) *La France antique*, Paris.

Fox, C. (1958) *Pattern and Purpose*, Cardiff.

Guido, M. (1974) 'A Scottish crannog re-dated', *Antiquity* 48: 54–6.

McGrail, S. and Switsur, R. (1975) 'Earliest British boats and their chronology', *International Journal of Nautical Archaeology* 4(2): 191–200.

Megaw, V. and Megaw, R. (1989) *Celtic Art*, London and New York.

Morrison, I. (1985) *Landscape with Lake Dwellings*, Edinburgh.

Pare, C.F.E. (1992) *Wagons and Wagon-graves of the Early Iron Age in Central Europe*, Oxford.

Piggott, S.L. (1983) *The Earliest Wheeled Transport . . .* , London and New York.

—— (1992) *Wagon, Chariot and Carriage*, London and New York.

Raftery, J. (1931) *Prehistoric Ireland*, London.

Rosenberg, G. (1937) *Hjortspringfundet*, Copenhagen.

Schovsbo, O. (1987) *Oldtidens vogne i Norden*, Bangsbomuseet.

Stead, I. (1991) *Excavations at Burton Fleming*, London: English Heritage Archaeological Reports.

Vouga, P. (1923) *La Tène*, Leipzig.

White, L. (1978) *Medieval Religion and Technology*, Berkeley and London.

THE ART OF THE POTTER

——— •◆• ———

Alex Gibson

INTRODUCTION

In southern Britain, the start of the second millennium BC, the end of the conventional Bronze Age, is marked by a series of large, bucket- and barrel-shaped pots with abundant applied cordon and fingernail- and fingertip-impressed decoration. Though the fabrics are frequently coarse with large, angular calcined flint opening agents, the vessels are generally well made and often highly, if simply, decorated. If these large urns are, rightly or wrongly, termed the coarse ware, then the fine wares take the form of smaller, globular closed vessels in a finer fabric with broad scored lines and chevron motifs around the base of the neck. These pots form part of the Deverel-Rimbury tradition or complex (Calkin 1962) now datable from *c.*1000 BC (Barrett 1976) (Figure 19.1). Elsewhere in Britain, similar regional ceramic equivalents pertain; a tradition of relatively coarse, bucket- and barrel-shaped urns with limited decoration found on domestic sites as well as with cremation burials (Gibson 1986a: 52). These vessels are in marked contrast to the preceding richly decorated ceramic repertoire of Food Vessels, Collared Urns and Biconical Urns of the earlier Bronze Age from which the barrel and bucket urn series evolve.

In the earlier Bronze Age, a great variety of decorative techniques was used, mainly in geometric motifs, to adorn the often high-quality ceramics. Three broad classes of technique were found – incised, impressed and plastic – and frequently a combination of techniques was used on a single vessel. Incised decoration may have been made with a blunt or sharp, narrow or fine point. Impressed decoration employed any tool, from string or cord to fingertips, from toothed comb to reed, stick or the bones of small animals. Plastic decoration formed cordons or knobs on the surface of the vessels, either raised from the surface of the pot or applied to it. There are instances of coloured inlay having been used to highlight the decoration, as in the case of a small accessory cup from Breach Farm, Glamorgan (Clarke *et al.* 1985: 297–8), but painted decoration *sensu stricto* has not been identified.

The richness of the decoration of the early bronze age ceramics was lost by the first millennium BC to the extent that some parts of the British Isles became almost aceramic. In most areas of Britain, however, ceramics regained their importance within both the domestic and artistic spheres. Coarse wares, evolving from the

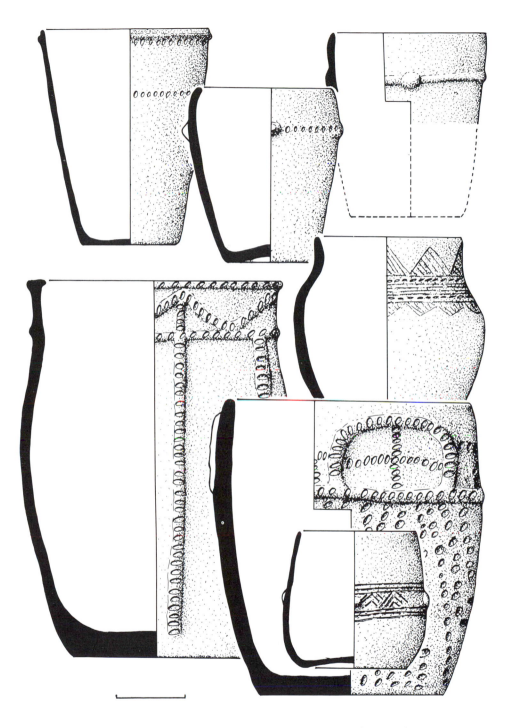

Figure 19.1 Pottery of the middle bronze age Deverel-Rimbury tradition.

Deverel-Rimbury tradition and continuing to develop though time, continue to form the bases of the domestic repertoires but fine wares are often extremely well made and highly decorated, tending to capture and monopolize archaeological attention.

TECHNOLOGY

The technology of prehistoric has been well summarized recently by Ann Woods (Gibson and Woods 1990) and no reiteration of that work is necessary here save some short, introductory remarks.

In iron age Britain, as in the preceding Neolithic and Bronze Age, until the Roman occupation, only a limited number of techniques was used to build a pot: pinching, ring-building, coil-building, strap-building or slab-building. No wheel-thrown vessels are present in the British archaeological record until the introduction of Gallo-Belgic wares in the first century BC. This does not preclude the use of a wheel in the pre-Belgic Iron Age, however, and a wheel or a turntable could well have been used for the building or finishing of a vessel. Nevertheless, the technique of wheel-throwing does not appear in the British ceramic repertoire until the Roman conquest and is consequently outside the scope of this chapter.

Pinching, the first-mentioned of the other pot-building techniques, is the simplest method of manufacture, involving pinching the clay outwards and upwards from a single ball to raise the sides of a simple pot. The technique is best suited to small cups or closed bowls but need not be confined to these forms; pinched bowls may well form a basis for larger vessels if supplemented by another technique. Woods has already clearly described the difficulties of recognizing this technique and the ease with which pinched vessels can be confused with similar but differently constructed vessels (Gibson and Woods 1990: 40–2).

Ring-, coil- or strap-building are closely related techniques and it is by these methods that the majority of iron age pottery vessels were made. In the first two techniques, cylinders of clay are rolled out and joined, one on top of the other, to build up the shape of the pot. In ring-building the pot is built up using distinct layers and in coil-building the cylinders overlap and spiral upwards. The technique of strap-building is similar save that the cylinders of clay are first flattened and joined together on edge so that greater height is given to the rings. The surfaces of the vessel are then smoothed over by the fingers or some other tool so that the rings or coils are hidden. Frequently many vessels are found to have broken along the line of a poorly bonded join (Figure 19.2) and the round surface of the clay ring or coil will be visible in the breaks. Join voids between poorly bonded cylinders may also be visible in the sections of large sherds. It is frequently impossible to differentiate between these closely related techniques in sherd material (Woods 1989).

Slab-building, as the term implies, involves the building of the walls of a pot from a number of slabs of clay: prefabricated pottery! Once more this is a difficult technique to recognize amongst sherd assemblies and its apparent rarity amongst the British material may be a direct result of the inability of scholars readily to identify its use, in stark contrast to the ease with which ring-building can be recognized.

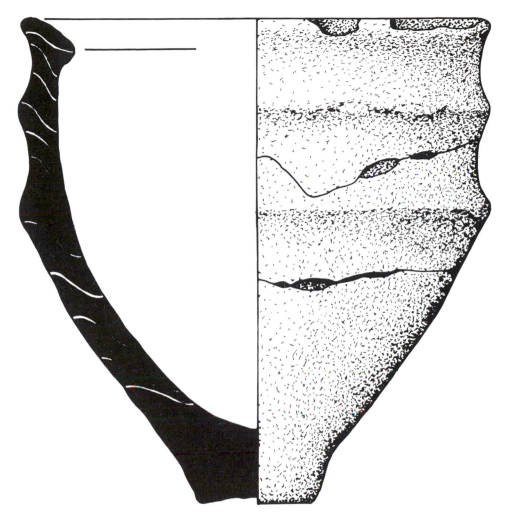

Figure 19.2 Early bronze age food vessel showing join voids in the fabric and breakage lines along incompletely bonded coils or rings. (From Gibson and Woods 1990.)

The frequent softness, blotchy surfaces and dark core of many fabrics indicate that iron age pottery was open-fired in shallow pits or scoops or in surface bonfires. However, actual firing sites are difficult to detect with any certainty. Open-firings tend to be short with a rapid rise and fall in temperature (Woods 1989). Such flash-firing will leave little trace in the archaeological record even if the sites are used on several occasions (Gibson 1986b). Firing sites for Durotrigian Wares and the later Romano-British Black-Burnished Ware, which develops from the native tradition, have been located at Purbeck in Dorset (Farrar 1976). These firing areas were associated with firing wasters (vessels damaged in the firing process) and extensive areas of burnt soil: however, even here it was noted that the 'natural surface did not present obvious signs of subjection to heat' (Farrar 1976: 49). The absence of any evidence for kiln furniture and/or kiln superstructures further strengthens the argument that the vessels were open-fired in bonfires, as in the previous two millennia.

Finds of this nature are rare. Despite a growing body of evidence for regional ceramic manufacture (Peacock 1968, 1989), production centres are elusive, presumably leaving few tangible archaeological traces. The discovery of the Durotrigian sites can most probably be seen to be a direct result of the industrial nature of the manufacture of Durotrigian and later Black-Burnished Wares exploited by the Roman invaders (Gillam 1957).

Despite the lack of archaeologically recognized manufacturing sites, open-firings, as mentioned above, can be attested by the ceramics themselves, which are often blotchy in their surface colouration, ranging from red to black. This uneven surface colour is a distinctive characteristic of open-firings and is a direct result of the constantly changing atmospheric conditions within a bonfire which are difficult to control (Woods 1989). Generally, an open-fired vessel will be basically yellow, red or brown in base colour as the iron oxides in the clay oxidize in the firing process. However, some portions of the pot may be subject to different firing conditions, depending on their contact with smoking flame, partially burnt wood or burial in ash. These portions will tend towards a grey or black colour, giving the vessel a blotchy appearance (see Gibson and Woods 1990: 44–56; Woods 1983, 1989).

SURFACE TREATMENTS

The ways in which the surface of a vessel may be altered or modified are, on prehistoric ceramics, fairly limited, comprising generally colouring, addition or extraction of clay or the raising or compression of the surface to a greater or lesser extent. Though usually decorative, not all surface treatments need to be entirely so. Raised or applied cordons or the roughening of the surface using incision or impressed decoration may be purely functional, allowing better and safer handling of the vessels. This said, the majority of surface treatments on iron age ceramics are decorative, often elaborately so, even imitating the fine metalwork of the later phases of the period (Grimes 1952).

Uniformity of colour of open-fired vessels is difficult to achieve and, in instances where this uniformity is found, it is usually a result of a distinctive surface treatment such as a slip, a pigment such as haematite or the coating of the vessel in carbon by smoking or smudging after the main firing process. Once more Durotrigian and Black-Burnished Ware ceramics can be quoted as an example of this post-firing treatment. At the firing site, Farrar (1976: 50) noted that the water sherds were 'black-burnished ware oxidised tile-red to light grey'. As a result of the difficulties in producing a uniform surface colour in a bonfire and from the presence of red wasters, Farrar concluded that the blackening process may have been a secondary technique.

Slip, a suspension of clay in water, appears to have been comparatively little used in iron age ceramics. However, pigments do seem to have been employed, particularly in the cases of haematite bowls. The bright red colour of some bipartite furrowed and cordoned bowls of later bronze age and early iron age Wessex (Avery

1981) led previous writers to assume that this redness was the result of a deliberately added haematite-rich slip which had been burnished onto the outside of the leather-hard vessel (Elsdon 1989: 18). Using scanning electron microscopy and X-ray analysis, however, Middleton (1987) demonstrated that the red or reddish-brown surface colour had been achieved by burnishing, either with or without an iron-rich pigment or by coating the vessel in a ferruginous slip: different techniques were used to produce an ostensibly similar desired end-product. Occasionally this red pigmentation may be highlighted. In Kent, for example, white or off-white paint may be used to highlight panels of, or paint designs on areas of, haematite coating (Macpherson-Grant 1991). This all serves to highlight the contrasts between the artificial and natural, untreated surface colours.

Burnishing is the most obvious instance of compression of the clay and is found extensively on iron age ceramics over the whole or just part of the pot (Figure 19.3). By rubbing a smooth, rounded tool such as a pebble over the surface of the leather-hard vessel, the surface clay is compacted and takes on a high gloss, the facets caused by the burnishing still clearly visible. Burnishing can be regarded as both functional and decorative. It may help reduce the permeability of a vessel and thus be functional but it also clearly gives a better finish to the vessel and it may also be used as a background against which to highlight other decorative schemes (Elsdon 1989: pl. 11).

A

B

Figure 19.3 (A) Burnishing marks on the neck of a bowl from Glastonbury, Somerset. (B) Burnishing facets on a bowl from Hambledon Hill, Dorset.

Related to burnishing yet significantly different is the execution of linear decoration by a technique known meaninglessly as tooling. More properly, the decoration is scored on the surface of the pot using a smooth, rounded instrument (Figures 19.4A and B; 19.5B). The resulting effect is that the clay is lightly compressed and the decoration is therefore very slightly sunk into the surface of the vessel. This differs dramatically from incised decoration, where the motifs are cut into the surface (Figure 19.4C and D). The lack of ridges of dislodged clay and the uniformity of the depth of the scoring suggest that this decoration was executed when the vessel had reached the leather-hard state. This technique is particularly indicative of pottery in the Glastonbury style and related southern decorated wares.

One of the most common methods of decorating prehistoric pottery generally is impression. This technique takes a variety of forms and motifs and is simply formed by impressing an object into the clay while the vessel is still wet or at any rate not fully leather-hard. Although iron age ceramics do not benefit from the large variety of impressed techniques and motifs used in the later Neolithic and earlier Bronze Age, nevertheless a large variety of tools and points, some specifically made, are used to create impressed decoration.

The simplest 'tool' whose use is demonstrated on iron age pottery is the potter's own nail or fingertip (Figure 19.5A). This form of decoration is particularly common on earlier iron age ceramics such as the large open jars from Staple Howe (Brewster 1963: figs 50–2), where the fingertip impressions are often used to highlight carinations or rims. Although arguably one of the simplest forms of impressed technique, fingernail impressions can also be quite subtle, such as on the cable cordons of earlier iron age ceramics. Here, the fingernail is rotated to produce an S-shaped impression, resulting in a cordon's having the appearance of having been twisted like a rope or cable.

Natural artefacts such as sticks, reeds or quills (Figure 19.6C) all seem to have been used to create a variety of different impressions in the clay, from random dots (Figure 19.5B) to complex geometric patterns; however, other tools seem to have been specifically made for pottery decoration. Broadly S-shaped stamps (Figure 19.6A) were used to decorate ceramics, most notably from hill-forts in the lower Severn valley, and were thought to be derived from continental 'duck-stamped' wares (Hencken 1938), although there is little real evidence for this (Kenyon 1953: 33). As well as S-shaped stamps, a variety of semicircular and wedge-shaped impressions, possibly made with the fingernail or a blunt, rounded stick, are also found on ceramics from this area (Figure 19.6B).

Stamps bearing concentric circles (Figure 19.6A) are used frequently on later decorated wares and actual examples of the stamps have been recovered from the waterlogged deposits at Glastonbury. The same cannot be said for 'rouletting wheels', whose use is frequently invoked to explain lines of 'hyphenated' impressions (Figure 19.6A) used to infill or delineate zones of decoration. These lines of short, square, rounded or oblong impressions recall closely the combed decoration of early bronze age ceramics where examples of the actual combs have been found (Gibson and Woods 1990: fig. 19) and whose careful use can be used to create lines of varying length (Ward 1902; Gibson and Woods 1990: figs 80–2). There seems no reason why similar simple but effective tools could not have been used for iron age ceramics.

Figure 19.4 Differing degrees of scoring, incision and tooling on iron age vessels from (A) Corfe Mullen, Dorset; (B) Llanmelin, Gwent; (C) Subdrook, Gwent; (D) Hambledon Hill, Dorset.

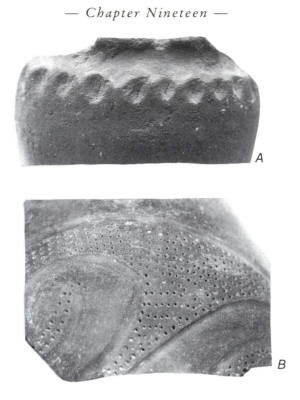

Figure 19.5 (A) Fingertip impressions on a vessel from Ponders End, Essex; (B) 'tooled' decoration and dot-stabs on a vessel from Margate, Kent.

Indeed, if combs rather than roulette wheels were employed, then they might have been used not only to impress but to score the surfaces of pots, in which case a very different effect of multiple parallel incision could be created (Figure 19.7A) and used functionally to rusticate the surfaces of some larger vessels: this usage would facilitate better handling. Random linear incisions are also used (Figure 19.7B).

In comparison to preceding periods, the used of plastic decoration, that is decoration which is raised or applied to the vessels' surface, is rare in the iron age repertoire. Cable cordons of the earliest iron age ceramics have already been mentioned. A horizontal cordon, usually round the upper third of the vessel, is raised from the surface of the pot and decorated with S-shaped fingernail impressions. This decorative motif is particularly common on vessels from Staple Howe (Brewster 1963), though by no means restricted to northern England. Raised cordons are used also to emphasize changes in direction of a pot's profile and to emphasize zones of decoration. This is particularly common on the late haematite bowls. In Scotland, elaborate impressed cordons, both raised and applied, are found in the later iron age ceramics of the Northern and Western Isles, such as from the broch sites of Clettraval (MacKie 1971) and Clickhimin (Hamilton 1968). But the best known examples of cordons are those on the cordoned ware jars and bowls of the later Iron Age in the south-west peninsula (Threipland 1957).

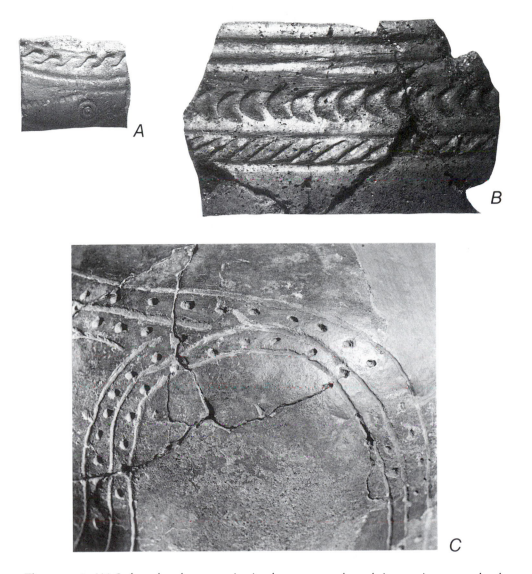

Figure 19.6 (A) S-shaped and concentric circular stamps and comb impressions on a sherd from Merthyr Mawr, Glamorgan; (B) incisions and impressions on a vessel from Twyn-y-Gaer, Gwent; (C) curvilinear incision and complementing stabs on a vessel from Breedon-on-the-Hill, Leicestershire. (Photo: Leicestershire Museums and Art Galleries.)

Arguably the most common decorative technique to be employed on iron age ceramics is incision, where blunt objects (perhaps 'scoring'?) blades or points are drawn through the wet or leather-hard clay (Figures 19.3A; 19.4; 19.6C; 19.7). These lines can be broad or narrow, deep or shallow, uni- or multidirectional, forming orthogonal or curvilinear motifs. The tools employed may be the same as those used

Figure 19.7 (A) Parallel multiple incision to facilitate handling on a vessel from Walmer, Kent; (B) random linear incision to achieve the same effect on a sherd from Breedon-on-the-Hill, Leicestershire. (Photo: Leicestershire Museums and Art Galleries.)

for impression, there being a simple difference in their usage. Incision is perhaps the simplest but most effective and versatile way to decorate the surface of a pot, an argument supported by the frequency with which the technique is encountered amongst iron age ceramic assemblages.

As with all decorative techniques, there is often a grey area between ostensibly different and distinct methods. This is most pertinent with incision, whether it is coarse and haphazard and is best assigned to the repertoire of rustication techniques or whether it is light and well-executed, when it is best described as 'scoring'. The distinction is, perhaps, irrelevant, being only a matter of degree. The difficulty of definition serves only to illustrate the multiplicity and versatility of the technique. Compare, for example, the finely and lightly scored cross-hatching of Durotrigian Wares (technically a cross between incision and burnishing) (Figure 19.4A) with the concisely and deeply executed cross-hatching of Glastonbury ceramics (Figure 19.3A). Similarly, its use can be singular, forming simple motifs in a single technique, or complementary, forming areas of contrast to undecorated or burnished zones or indeed defining zones decorated in other techniques. The best illustrations of this latter usage were presented forty years ago by Professor Grimes in his discussion paper on 'The La Tène style in British early iron age pottery' (Grimes 1952).

Arguably the floruit of the potters' art in pre-Belgic Britain is to be found in the curvilinear decorated bowls of southern Britain (Figures 19.4D; 19.5B; 19.6C; 19.8). On these ceramics the decoration is usually by incision, with some circular impressions frequently forming dimples which augment and complement the design. The motifs can be formed by either single curvilinear lines, as in the case of the Hunsbury bowls, or by larger areas of curvilinear incised infilling commonly found in vessels of the Glastonbury or South-western style. Both styles play roughened against smooth surfaces to contrast light and shade and thus to highlight these non-plastic two-dimensional motifs (Figure 19.5B). Finding clear parallels in the metalworking art of the period, the frequently raised or embossed designs of the metalwork become translated into the two-dimensional planes of the pots' surfaces.

A study such as this cannot do justice to the complexities and quality of the art of the iron age potters. Great varieties of patterns, motifs and effects are produced from a limited repertoire of techniques and tools. Not all the pottery can be claimed to be

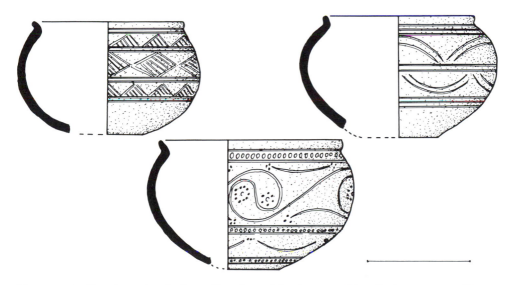

Figure 19.8 Hunsbury bowls from Hunsbury, Northamptonshire. Scale = 10 cm. (From Gibson and Woods 1990.)

fine ware or carefully decorated, and crude, poorly executed decoration is present in all assemblages, but nevertheless, the finer pieces may rightly claim their place amongst the artistic masterpieces of the first millennium BC.

ACKNOWLEDGMENTS

I am most grateful to Dr Stephen Aldhouse-Green and Mr Kenneth Brassil, National Museum of Wales and to Dr Ian Kinnes and Ms Gill Varndell of the British Museum for allowing me to photograph material in their collections. Mr Bob Rutland, Jewry Wall Museum, Leicester, organized the photography of Figures 19.6C and 19.7B.

REFERENCES

Avery, M. (1981) 'Furrowed bowls and carinated Hawkes A pottery', in G. Guilbert (ed.) *Hill-fort Studies: essays for A.H.A. Hogg*, Leicester: Leicester University Press, 28–64.

Barrett, J.C. (1976) 'Deverel-Rimbury: problems of chronology and interpretation', in C.B. Burgess and R.F. Miket (eds) *Settlement and Economy in the Third and Second Millennia BC*, Oxford: British Archaeological Reports 33, 289–307.

Brewster, T.C.M. (1963) *The Excavation of Staple Howe*, Wintringham: East Riding Archaeological Research Committee.

Calkin, J.B. (1962) 'The Bournemouth area in the Middle and Late Bronze Age with the Deverel-Rimbury problem reconsidered', *Archaeological Journal* 119: 1–65.

Clarke, D.V., Cowie, T.G. and Foxon, A. (1985) *Symbols of Power at the Time of Stonehenge*, Edinburgh: HMSO.

Elsdon, S.M. (1989) *Later Prehistoric Pottery in England and Wales*, Princes Risborough: Shire Archaeology 58.

Farrar, R.A.H. (1976) 'Interim report on excavations at the Romano-British potteries at Redcliff near Wareham', *Proceedings of the Dorset Natural History and Archaeology Society* 97 (1975): 49–51.

Fox, C. (1927) 'An encrusted urn of the Bronze Age from Wales with notes of the origin and distribution of the type', *Antiquaries Journal* 7: 115–33.

Gibson, A.M. (1986a) *Neolithic and Early Bronze Age Pottery*, Princes Risborough: Shire Publications.

—— (1986b) 'The excavation of an experimental firing area at Stamford Hall, Leicester, 1985', *Bulletin of the Experimental Firing Group* 4: 5–14.

Gibson, A.M. and Woods, A.J. (1990) *Prehistoric Pottery for the Archaeologist*, Leicester: Leicester University Press.

Gillam, J.P. (1957) 'Types of Roman coarse pottery vessels in northern Britain', *Archaeologia Aeliana* 35: 180–251.

Grimes, W.F. (1952) 'The La Tène art style in British early iron age pottery', *Proceedings of the Prehistoric Society* 18(2): 160–75.

Hamilton, J.R.C. (1968) *Excavations at Clickhimin, Shetland*, Edinburgh: HMSO.

Hencken, T.C. (1938) 'The excavation of the iron age camp on Bredon Hill, Gloucestershire', *Archaeological Journal* 95: 1–111.

Kenyon, K. (1953) 'Excavations at Sutton Walls, Herefordshire, 1948–51', *Archaeological Journal* 110: 1–87.

MacKie, E.W. (1971) 'English migrants and Scottish brochs', *Glasgow Archaeological Journal* 2: 39–71.

Macpherson-Grant, N. (1991) 'A re-appraisal of prehistoric pottery from Canterbury', *Canterbury's Archaeology, 1990–1991*, Canterbury: 15th Annual Report of the Canterbury Archaeological Trust Ltd, 38–48.

Middleton, A.P. (1987) 'Technological investigation of the coatings on some "haematite-coated" pottery from southern England', *Archaeometry* 29(2): 250–61.

Peacock, D.P.S. (1968) 'A petrological study of certain iron age pottery from western England', *Proceedings of the Prehistoric Society* 34: 414–27.

—— (1969) 'A contribution to the study of Glastonbury Ware from south-western Britain', *Antiquaries Journal* 49: 41–61.

Threipland, L.M. (1957) 'An excavation at St Mawgan-in-Pydar, North Cornwall', *Archaeological Journal* 113: 33–81.

Ward, J. (1902) 'Prehistoric interments near Cardiff', *Archaeologia Cambrensis* 2: 25–32.

Woods, A.J. (1983) 'Smoke gets in your eyes: patterns variables and temperature measurement in open firings', *Bulletin of the Experimental Firing Group* 1: 11–25.

—— (1989) 'Fired with enthusiasm: experimental open firings at Leicester University', in A.M. Gibson (ed.) *Midlands Prehistory*, Oxford: British Archaeological Reports 204, 196–226.

PART VII

THE ART OF THE CELTS

THE NATURE AND FUNCTION OF CELTIC ART

—— ·◆· ——

Ruth and Vincent Megaw

Elusive, curvilinear, ambiguous, shape-changing, miniaturist, often abstract and minimalist, symbolic and non-narrative, the art of the pre-Roman peoples we know as Celts is one of the glories of the European past. It is quite different from, but just as important as, the art of Greece and Rome. Clearly visible for half a millennium before the Christian era, it survived the Roman conquest to re-emerge as the Hiberno-Saxon art of the Early Christian gospel books, and continued to influence Romanesque art. Partially eclipsed by the Renaissance rediscovery of all things classical, it has, in the twentieth century, appealed to Modernists and Surrealists, since it goes beyond external appearance to probe the underlying meanings of reality.

THE NATURE OF ART

Debates about definitions of art have filled many library shelves. Distinctions common in our own post-Renaissance western society between 'high' art, popular art and craft are and have been alien to most other peoples at most other times: in many contemporary indigenous cultures of the Third and Fourth Worlds there is no word equivalent to 'art'. The art of the Celts was not 'art for art's sake', but was deeply embedded in the context of their economic, social, intellectual and religious life, as well as being influenced by available technology and the range of accessible materials. There is some evidence that general estimations of what constitutes quality in technical skill are transcultural (e.g. Jopling 1971), yet it is uncertain that what we today find attractive about the 'art' of peoples thousands of years ago is the same as those qualities which they themselves valued. We have in the past offered a definition of Celtic art as encompassing 'elements of decoration beyond those necessary for functional utility' (Megaw and Megaw 1989a: 19).

Our perceptions of the nature of Celtic art are undoubtedly skewed by having to rely largely on a limited range of artefacts. While it is obvious that textiles and wood-working played an important role in the European Iron Age, we have tantalizingly little tangible evidence since they rarely survive. Again, the difficulty of finding early La Tène settlements means that much material comes from graves, and this biases our sample. Little statuary or architecture remains and most painting is confined to pots.

Much of the remaining art is thus made of ceramics and metal, which survive, though it is worth emphasizing that, save in eastern Europe, Celts rarely used silver, though they did use gold, bronze and iron extensively.

DEFINITIONS OF THE CELTS

In recent years there has been considerable discussion among British archaeologists as to the applicability of the terms 'Celts' and 'Celtic' to the archaeological remains of the later prehistoric cultures of much of Europe (Merriman 1987; Megaw and Megaw 1992). Since this is a matter taken up by several other contributors to this volume, it will suffice to note here that we are employing in this chapter 'Celtic' to describe that art style which is the tangible evidence for a continuity of cultural tradition during the last five centuries BC and into the early historic era. This does not of course deny the strictly historical but vague geographical use by our classical sources of those they named 'Keltoi', nor the regional variations detectable in the archaeological record of the later Iron Age. Nevertheless, since art styles can be universally accepted as clear evidence of self-image or cultural (though not necessarily ethnic) identity, 'Celtic' is a term which is just as valid as the no less conventional – and arguably equally inapposite – archaeological labels 'Hallstatt' and 'La Tène' for, respectively, the earlier and later phases of the European pre-Roman Iron Age. So, for the remainder of this chapter, readers may assume that 'Celtic art' is synonymous with 'La Tène' art of the period c.500 BC to AD 100. This is a vast span of time, comparable to that of the whole development of post-Renaissance Europe, and covering a territory which extends from the lower reaches of the Rhine (and sometimes even Denmark) to the Po Basin and from the west coast of Ireland to the mouth of the Danube and into Asia Minor (Kruta *et al.* 1991).

PHASES OF EARLY CELTIC ART

Despite more recent attempts to construct alternative systems for classifying early Celtic art (Duval 1977), especially in Britain and Ireland (De Navarro 1952; Stead 1985), scholars continue basically to employ the phases established more than half a century ago by the late Paul Jacobsthal (1944). His seminal book *Early Celtic Art*, completed and published in Oxford in 1944, still remains the starting-point for all serious study of the nature of Celtic art. Jacobsthal was by training a classical archaeologist who had first been attracted to Celtic studies by observing the classical imports found in graves north of the Alps. In considering the existence of various 'styles' in the material record, he used the term to describe what are often strictly no more than general artistic tendencies, some of which overlap chronologically. Thus, Jacobsthal defines his 'Early Style' predominantly by the classically-derived ornament found on rich burial goods of the fifth and earlier fourth century 'chieftains' graves' in the Rhineland and applies the term also to north-eastern France and as far east as Bohemia. Style more properly defined is the 'totality of conventions which make up the art of a particular area at a particular period of time' while 'the variation of style in a culture or group is often considerable within the same period' (Schapiro 1953). Because of Jacobsthal's classical training and the existence of Greek and Roman written sources, early Celtic art has been largely defined according to what it borrowed from Greek or Italic art, and its phases divided according to what we know of Celtic history from classical commentators. Much of the dating of Celtic material also depends on finds of classical imports in temperate Europe. What is unique about Celtic art has often been described in terms of its differences from classical art and several writers have seen changes in forms and styles as essentially deriving from contact with Mediterranean peoples (e.g. Kruta 1982). Again, some writers see 'truly' Celtic art as that which is most abstract and least representational, or perhaps least 'Mediterranean'. The internal economic, political, intellectual and religious dynamics of non-literate Celtic society are harder to locate than the classical connections, except by means of such crude tools as processual archaeology. Thus we often know less about the relationship of change within La Tène society to Celtic art than about external influences upon it.

The first stage, or Early Style, of this art, according to Jacobsthal, emerged from a triple root in the middle of the fifth century BC. First is the immediately preceding, largely non-representational, angular geometric material typical of the fine metalwork and decorated pottery associated with high-status burials of the so-called Western Hallstatt group in the sixth to mid-fifth centuries BC. In Early Style this is reduced to a background role. The second root of the art of the chieftains' graves is represented by plant-based motifs such as the palmette and lotus flower (Figures 20.1(1), 20.7, 20.8) borrowed by the Celts from the Greeks and Etruscans who used them chiefly as bordering or fill-in decorative elements on fine painted pottery and on metal vessels. Some human faces also derive from Mediterranean metalwork (von Hase 1973). The importance of highly developed trade networks in this Early La Tène phase is underlined by the presence of imports – usually Etruscan or Greek drinking-vessels of one kind or another – and also by the use of foreign materials such as Mediterranean coral (Figures 20.1(1), 20.6, 20.8, 20.10 (top right)) and occasionally Baltic amber, African ivory, and shells from the Indian Ocean. The third strand has been described by Jacobsthal and others as 'orientalizing', referring to the strange, often fantastic, bestiary occasionally employed by local craftsmen basing themselves on models sometimes considered to originate from the semi-nomadic world of the eastern Scythians and related groups (Figures 20.9, 20.10 (below right), 20.15). Some scholars even look to the art of the Achaemenian Persians who, under first Darius and then Xerxes, invaded the Balkans in the course of the fifth century BC (Powell 1971; Sandars 1971, 1976, 1985; Fischer 1983, 1988; Luschey 1983). It seems more likely, however, that the 'orientalizing' element in early Celtic art was transmitted through the intermediary once more of Italy and the orientalizing phases of Etruscan art which in turn influenced northern Italy and the head of the Adriatic. In the absence of any evidence of contact between royal Scythians and the Celts, some similarities between Celtic and Scythian art are also more probably due to the contacts of both peoples with Mediterranean material, in the case of the Scythians with the East Greek colonies on the Black Sea (Castriota 1981; Megaw 1975; Hüttel 1978; Megaw and Megaw 1990a). In addition, it has often been assumed that even the widespread use of compass design on over a quarter of known decorated metalwork (Figure 20.1(2)) must also have been adopted from classical sources (Lenerz-de Wilde 1977).

Figure 20.1 Art styles: (1) gold-leaf covered, coral-inlaid Early Style bronze and iron plaque from Weiskirchen barrow 1, Kr. Merzig-Wadern, Germany; (2) Early Style compass-drawn decoration on a bronze mount from Chlum, okr. Rokyčany, Czech Republic; (3) Waldalgesheim or Vegetal Style decoration (*right*) on a silver brooch from Schosshalde, Kt Bern, Switzerland, and (*left*) its suggested classical forebear, a detail of acanthus tendril on a Greek red-figure vase; (4) detail of Vegetal Style decoration on a stamped bronze sword scabbard from Sanzeno, northern Italy, showing chain of linked triskels; (5) detail of Swiss Sword Style iron scabbard from La Tène, Switzerland; (6) Disney three-dimensional style as seen on an owl-shaped cauldron mount from Brå, Denmark; (7) British 'mirror' style on the back of an engraved bronze mirror from Holcombe, Devon, laid out with compasses. (Drawing: A.C. Bartlett.)

348

This early stage of artistic development can be related to the archaeologically visible collapse of the western late Hallstatt centres of power in southern Germany and the Rhône valley of France, and the shift of political and economic importance to more dispersed warrior élites in the Champagne area (Charpy and Roualet 1991b), the Rhineland and Bohemia. It is also increasingly clear from recent archaeological excavations of major cemeteries that, in the later fifth and early fourth centuries BC, groups with closely related art styles were already installed as far east as Slovakia and eastern Austria as well as in northern Italy (Megaw, Megaw and Neugebauer 1989). Such groups were the forerunners of the expansion documented by classical writers such as Livy, which brought Celts to settle in northern Italy and move gradually eastwards into what is now Transdanubian Hungary and beyond (Szabó 1992). This period of displacement has its artistic reflection in the development of the so-called 'Waldalgesheim' or 'Vegetal' style which by the end of the fourth century can be found decorating pottery, metal and even some of the few pieces of sculpture known from this period (Figures 20.1(3, 4), 20.2, 20.11a).

Typified by an evolution from the stricter, more static use of classical plant motifs found in the art of the chieftains' graves into freer, more continuously flowing patterns, the Vegetal style sometimes incorporates elusive face-like forms – dubbed the 'Cheshire [Cat] style' after the disappearing and appearing feline in *Alice in Wonderland* (Jacobsthal 1944; Megaw 1970b; Lenerz-de Wilde 1977). Yet the style has clear forerunners in Early Style art and is still based upon compass layout (Castriota 1981; Verger 1986, 1987). The close similarity in the decoration of a range of objects across much of Europe is witness to the wide dispersal of iron age iconography and its ready acceptance by disparate groups serviced by artisans with a shared artistic background. There can be no doubt that fresh settlement in Italy, by several peoples, possibly from the Marne and from Bohemia among others, offered a stimulus to the exchange of ideas for the development of this new 'style'. The fine wheel-turned pottery of the Champagne region east of Reims also exhibits in this period painted variations of the 'Vegetal' motifs (Figure 20.11a), including some in reserved red-figure style (Charpy and Roualet 1991a), while other areas of Champagne and Bohemia appear to become depopulated (Bataille-Melkon and Charpy 1985; Charpy and Roualet 1987: 70–86; 1991b; Kruta 1991b; Corradini 1991). In the third century BC, after a further expansion eastwards as far as Anatolia, Celts from central Europe seem to have resettled the same French area, introducing new fashions in decorated arm- and foot-rings and brooches (Kruta 1985; Charpy and Roualet 1991b: 161–96). The fourth and early third centuries saw the adoption in several regions of a more standardized 'set' of ornaments as witnessed by male and female grave goods found in smaller and more dispersed cemeteries.

From the beginning of the third century, Jacobsthal envisaged the development of two 'sub-styles'. One of these was associated chiefly with the decoration of sword scabbards – mostly of iron – obviously important status symbols amongst a warrior-dominated society (Figures 20.1(5), 20.3, 20.16, 20.17). This Sword Style can now be seen to have a series of regional centres in parts of France, western Switzerland, Italy, Serbia and Hungary (De Navarro 1972; Szabó 1977, 1991; Petres and Szabó 1974; Szabó and Petres 1992). In Hungary and Serbia especially, local smiths showed continuing reliance on complex variations on Italo-Greek plant motifs, outgrowths

Figure 20.2 Vegetal Style tendrils on (*top*) bronze and iron scabbard from Filottrano, Ancona, Italy, Grave 22, with Cheshire-cat face. W c.4.6 cm. Later fourth century BC (Photo: Univers des Formes) and (*bottom*) two torques, one with a face in the foliage under the buffer terminals, from the Collection Goury, Musée de Nancy. Max. D 16 (*left*) and 15.4 cm. Early third century BC. (Photo: Gilbert Mangin, Nancy.)

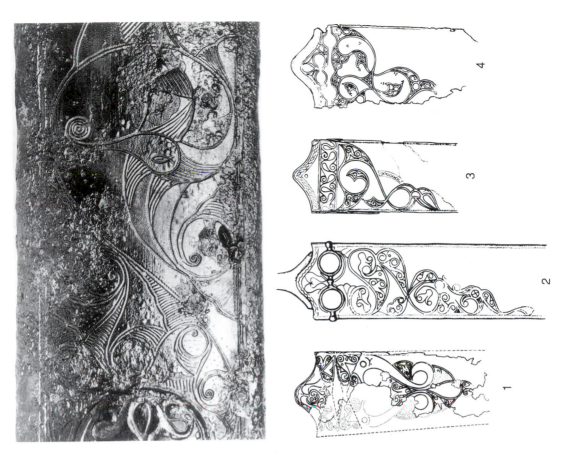

Figure 20.3 Sword Style decorated iron scabbards: (*above*) detail of Hungarian Sword Style scabbard found at Cernon-sur-Coole, Marne, France. W. *c*.5.2 cm. Second half third century BC. (Photo: Centre de la Recherche de la Siderurgie, Nancy, courtesy Professor P.-M. Duval) and (*right*) from (1)? Sremska Mitrovica, Serbia, with vestigial dragon pair. W. *c*.5.5 cm; (2) Batina, Croatia (formerly Kisköszeg, Hungary), with vestigial dragon pair below the scabbard entry. W. 6 cm; (3) Tapolca, Haláphegy, Veszprém m., Hungary, with triskel frieze; (4) Bölscke-Madocsahegy no. 2, Tolna m., Hungary, with triskels and figures-of-eight. W. 9.1 cm. third century BC. (Drawings: Mária Ecsedi.)

of the 'Vegetal style', while in France and Switzerland the decoration is simpler and less extensive. This 'Style' was contemporary with the stage of maximum Celtic expansion which brought several groups from central Europe into contact with the Hellenistic world of Greece and western Turkey, with consequent influence on both pottery and metalwork (Szabó 1973, 1975; Kruta and Szabó 1982). This is the period represented by the massive deposit of objects at the La Tène type-site on the shores of Lake Neuchâtel in Switzerland and marks the beginning of the Middle La Tène phase of conventional iron age chronology (Kaenel 1990).

Jacobsthal's 'Plastic style' also begins around the start of the third century BC and shows a penchant for three-dimensional forms in metal, such as the bronze ankle- and arm-rings and false filigree objects in bronze and gold (Figures 20.1(6), 20.4). A small but striking group of bronze objects, mostly horse and chariot fittings or flagon mounts possibly originating in central Europe, displays an almost film-cartoon-like stylization of animals and human faces giving rise to the name 'Disney style' (Figure 20.1(6)) (Megaw 1970b). Throughout the Middle La Tène period, particularly in eastern and central Europe, one can observe the production of specialized ornaments for women, not only ankle-rings but also complex girdle-chains incorporating enamel inlay (Stanczik and Vaday 1971; Challet 1992).

Figure 20.4 Hinged cast bronze 'Plastic' Style ankle-ring, decorated with triskels, from Straubing-Alburg, Stadtkr. Straubing, Germany, Grave 4. D. 12 cm. Later third century BC. (Photo: Römisch-Germanische Kommission, Frankfurt, J. Bahlo.)

Greater centralization and the further development of regional skilled technologies such as the near mass-production of fine wheel-made pottery, iron and steel and the production of rings and other objects in both glass and sapropelite – a form of shale – is evident from the latter part of the second century BC onwards. This was inextricably connected with the establishment of defended tribal centres, called oppida by Julius Caesar, and as large as most medieval towns. This phase is characterized by extensive renewed trade between Mediterranean civilizations and the north, and increasing contact with the Romans is reflected in the greater naturalism of Celtic art of the period. The establishment of a 'common market' right across continental Europe is seen in a greater degree of standardization and a reduction in the range of fine objects produced. Objects in precious metals became comparatively rare save for a number of gold and electrum torques found in isolated contexts in western Europe, almost always with native coinage (Furger and Müller 1991). Such local coinages, based on a range of Hellenistic, Greek colonial and Republican Roman prototypes, began in the Balkans in the late fourth century and spread westwards from the end of the third century until the establishment of the Roman Empire. Like other manifestations of stylistic borrowings in the European Iron Age, coins exhibit that typical tendency to reduce natural forms to a complex and abstract patterning.

BRITAIN AND IRELAND

As far as insular Celtic art is concerned, the problem of establishing firm dates is even more difficult than on the Continent, since even Mediterranean imports are lacking as chronological markers until late on. In Britain and Ireland a new art style, related to the styles of continental Europe, appeared at least as early as the beginning of the third century BC (Raftery 1983, 1984; Stead 1985, 1991; Megaw and Megaw 1986). A number of isolated finds in eastern England, and Ulster, notably decorated shields and sword scabbards of basically early La Tène form, exhibit elements of both the 'Vegetal' and 'Sword' styles (Figure 20.5). Only in north-east Yorkshire, however, is such material found in closed contexts, notably in the rich graves of the so-called 'Arras culture' which include cart or chariot burials similar but not identical to those of the Marne (Dent 1985; Stead 1979, 1991). Despite indications of the influence of continental styles and burial customs, there is, however, no such certain evidence for major groups of new settlers. Links between Britain and Ireland seem highly probable and direct links with the Continent from both areas possible. New art styles may represent the introduction of new belief systems and certainly, in view of the evidence for a continuity of settlement patterns in Britain from the previous Late Bronze Age, one may envisage a process whereby native communities adopted, through the agency of a few foreign – or at least foreign-trained – missionaries and craftworkers, a new range of symbols of spiritual and temporal power.

From the second century BC until the occupation of southern Britain by the Romans in the mid-first century AD a number of regional stylistic groups develop, although it is not until the late first century BC that there are firm archaeological contexts, such as datable graves or settlements, for such specialized classes of objects as horse harness or engraved bronze mirrors (Figure 20.1(7)). In the later Iron Age of Ireland, untouched by Roman settlement but exhibiting sporadic trading contacts with the new overlords of Britain from the first to the fifth centuries AD, the fine products of the 'Ultimate La Tène' period lack datable context but are not likely to be much later than the second century AD.

Figure 20.5 Incised bronze scabbard plate no. 2 from Lisnacrogher, Co. Antrim, Northern Ireland, showing birds' heads. W. 4.1 cm. ? Third–second century BC. (Photo: Belzeaux-Zodiaque.)

THE NATURE OF CELTIC ART

Celtic willingness to import forms and techniques as well as trade objects has given rise to the view that, particularly in the late Hallstatt and Early La Tène periods, much of Europe north of the Alps was on the periphery and at the mercy of the 'core' cultures of the Mediterranean world. As much as anything it is the art which belies this dependent role since it continued to evolve and spread long after political and economic events brought a halt to southern imports. Unlike classical art, that of the early Celtic world is not so much aniconic as non-narrative and small scale, often almost miniaturist. There is little or no continuity with the occasional representations of dancing, weaving or burial rites illustrated on some of the funerary pottery and sheet metalwork of the late Hallstatt period. Such rare depictions as, for example, a military procession of warriors on an early La Tène sword from one of the later graves associated with the salt-working site of Hallstatt itself (Figure 20.6) (Dehn 1970) have sources in this case in the eastern Hallstatt area and the long-lasting local tradition around the headwaters of the Adriatic of decorating bronze vessels (situlae) with scenes of feasting and military prowess. Local artists clearly used only those foreign elements which suited their visual grammatical syntax (Castriota 1981).

Figure 20.6 Detail of engraving on a bronze and iron scabbard, with remains of coral studs, from Hallstatt Grave 994, showing rare human figures. W. 5 cm. 400–350 BC. (Photo: J.V.S. Megaw.)

Side by side with a continuing concern for patterning runs a tendency for visual punning. In a manner reminiscent of the oral traditions of the Old Irish and Welsh myths, forms are not always what they seem. Reverse, for example, what at first glance appears to be a faithful copy of a fifth-century Etruscan silen head and it transmogrifies into a clean-shaven, perhaps female, face (Megaw 1969); what seems a comma-like motif on closer inspection turns out to be a stylized bird's head (Figures 20.5; 20.7). Shape-shifting in which foreground and background become interchangeable can also be seen in the intricate and mathematically precise compass-based ornamentation of the fifth- or fourth-century BC openwork harness mounts produced by a number of specialized crafts-centres in eastern France or on the incised backs of the first century BC/AD southern British bronze mirrors. Asymmetry is also a feature; even in those objects which at first sight appear balanced, there are slight differences which mean that the viewer is constantly discovering new details (Figure 20.8). The use of lost-wax casting, where the clay mould has to be broken to extract the finished object and thus cannot be reused, also contributed to this lack of uniformity by making each object unique.

We have stated our view that Celtic art is the visible expression of a system of ideas, where even the most seemingly non-representational motifs may have a precise, perhaps religious, meaning. The very absence of the complete human form or of narrative art may indicate a taboo like that of Jewish or Moslem art on the making of certain types of representation. Working with Aboriginal artists in central desert

Figure 20.7 Openwork sheet-gold fragments with reversible faces from Bad Dürkheim, Kr. Neustadt, Germany. Max. ht of heads 1.7 cm. Later fifth to early fourth century BC. (Photo: Historisches Museum der Pfalz, Speyer.)

regions of Australia has made it clear to us that paintings which look 'decorative' or 'abstract' may contain very specific Dreamtime narratives and refer to precise geographic features, as well as serving as assertions of ownership. Recent work on ritual sites of the pre-Roman Iron Age has, however, shown how rarely such sites include objects of artistic note. Among major exceptions is the Celto-Ligurian region of the south of France where the influence of the classical world, particularly from the Greek colonies of the region such as Massalia, permeates everything from settlement plans to stone-carving (Duval and Heude 1983: 128–46). Yet much of the surviving wooden carving is in the form of votive offerings thrown into healing springs or wells in France and Germany in the early Roman period (Figure 20.12) (Planck *et al.* 1982; Deyts 1983; Romeuf 1986). Importantly, the ditched enclosures of northern France such as Gournay-sur-Aronde, with its evidence for sacrifice of horses and cattle along with the ritually destroyed weapons of those killed in battle, or the human ossuary at Ribemont, also include fine ornaments and other distinctive pieces (Brunaux *et al.* 1985; Rapin and Brunaux 1988; Brunaux 1988). The decoration found on swords may have had specific, perhaps apotropaic, meaning for warriors.

WORKSHOPS AND REGIONAL GROUPINGS

The social organization of production of art and the location or even existence of regional styles or workshops can be hard to pinpoint with precision. The greatest amount of regional variation in styles and the objects decorated is evident in the Early Style and, to a lesser extent, in the third- to second-century Sword and related styles.

Style in the oppida period, by contrast, is relatively similar throughout Celtic Europe, despite regional specialization in different classes of material – iron and steel, glass, salt, and the like – with craft production areas visible within oppida (Collis 1984b).

Hierarchical workshops serving princely patrons have been postulated for the rich Early Style products, based in part on a 'feudal' model of society (Champion 1976, 1977, 1982, 1985; Collis 1984a; Pare 1991). In the periods of major Celtic expansion in the fourth to second centuries BC, it seems that production of decorated metalwork was scattered and decentralized, as were settlements and cemeteries, with iron- and bronzesmiths itinerant and sometimes part-time. Even in Early La Tène it seems highly likely that, while some craftworkers were fixed, others travelled considerable distances to execute particular commissions; the complex trading networks of the time meant that ideas as well as individuals and objects were widely exchanged. Especially in this early stage, the production of specific prestige pieces required the bringing together of a range not only of raw materials but also of technical skills. For example, the unique pair of wine flagons found at Basse-Yutz on the Moselle required knowledge of bronze-casting as well as sheet-metal and openwork techniques, metal engraving and chasing, the production of red glass for inlay (Challet 1992), and access to large supplies of imported coral (Figure 20.8) (Megaw and Megaw 1990a, 1990b).

Material evidence for the location of specialized workshops is tantalizingly vague. Attempts to distinguish different traditions in the fine goldwork associated with the early chieftains' graves of the Saar and middle Rhine region are thus still tentative (Megaw 1972). Recent studies using metal analysis and tool marks suggest two separate 'schools', one continuing late Hallstatt goldworking practices (Figure 20.7) and a second, more innovative, group, some of whose most spectacular products, such as the Erstfeld find (Figure 20.9) (Wyss 1975), found their way to the Alpine regions far to the south (Figure 20.6) (Rudolf Echt, pers. comm.). As well as specialist goldsmiths, there seems to have been a group of engravers capable of producing with the use of compasses highly intricate and mathematically precise patterns decorating both imported and local wine flagons, the most common vessel of the funerary symposium which accompanied the noble dead (Frey 1955, 1984; Megaw 1968; Lenerz-de Wilde 1979). In southern Germany and neighbouring western Austria tiny cast bronze brooches were made, decorated with animals such as horses, sheep and boars as well as a range of a fantastic, almost nightmarish, creatures, which also appear on larger objects. These 'mask brooches' are particularly numerous at such important industrial centres as the Dürrnberg south of Salzburg where the wealth of the local salt-mining population could command the skills of the best metalsmiths (Figure 20.10) (Moosleitner, Pauli and Penninger 1974; Pauli 1978; Moosleitner 1985, 1987). Of slightly later date are the 'enamel'- or occasionally coral-inlaid cast bronze disc torques with decoration in the Vegetal style. These occur as imports in Hungary and Champagne; the extremely worn condition of some of the easternmost examples suggests that they were brought by new groups of settlers, though their concentration in the Upper Rhineland strongly suggests an association with a distinctive local ethnic group, served by at least two 'workshops' (Müller 1989).

The production of fine pottery was, as with many other cultures past and present, a matter for even more localized production and distribution, since it is both bulky

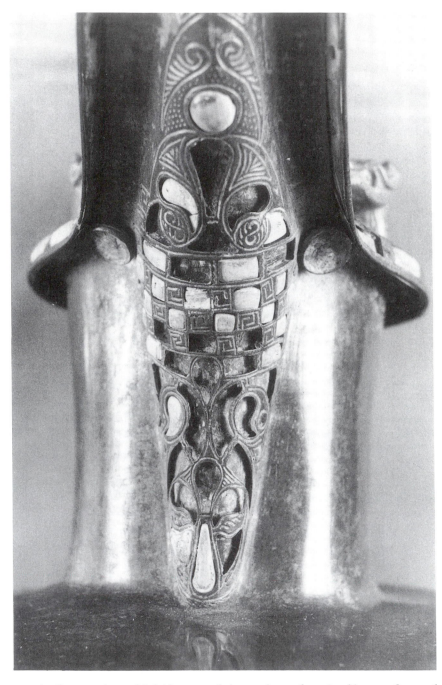

Figure 20.8 Openwork coral-inlaid engraved throat plates of a pair of bronze flagons found at Basse-Yutz, Moselle, France: *left*, flagon 1; *right*, flagon 2. W. *c.*5 cm. Date *c.*400 BC. (Photos: J.V.S. Megaw.)

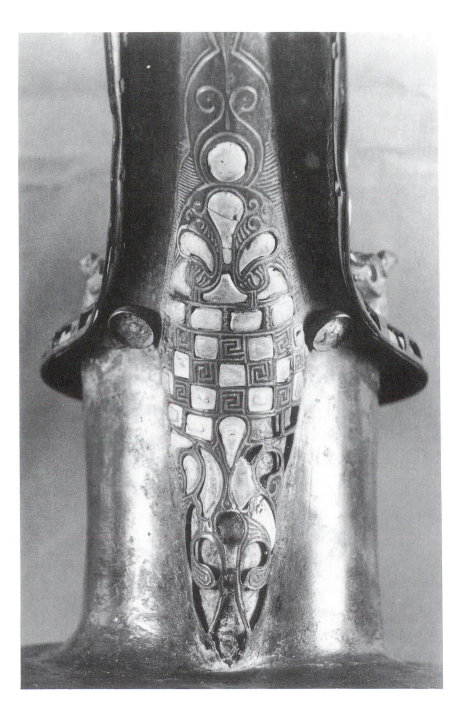

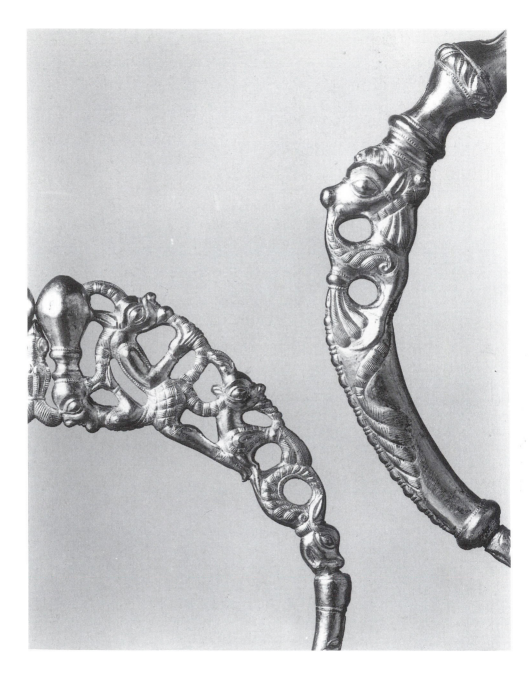

Figure 20.9 Details of two gold torques, part of a hoard found at Erstfeld, Kt Uri, Switzerland. D. *c.*15 cm. Late fifth to early fourth century BC. (Photo: Schweizerisches Landesmuseum.)

Figure 20.10 Bronze brooches found in female inhumation grave 70/2 at Dürrnberg bei Hallein, Ld. Salzburg, Austria. Length of brooch in form of a flying bird. 3.1 cm. Fifth century BC. (Photo courtesy Dr Ing. Fritz Moosleitner.)

and fragile. In the Early Style period, little fine pottery comes from rich Rhineland graves, and the pottery of the Champagne-Ardennes area of France shows forms derived from Greek pottery and geometric designs related to those of the preceding Jogassian period (Charpy and Roualet 1987: 26–69; Roualet 1991; Charpy 1991). We have already mentioned the fine painted pottery of the Marne which developed in the fourth century BC (Figure 20.11a) (Bataille-Melkon and Charpy 1985; Charpy and Roualet 1987: 70–86; 1991b; Kruta 1991a; Corradini 1991). In Bohemia indeed, the introduction of the potter's wheel seems to have made pottery distribution even more localized (Gosden 1983). Several centuries later, pottery workshops associated with the regional defended centres or oppida of the late La Tène period were established in the Massif Central of France, the Swiss plateau, southern Germany and western Hungary (Maier 1970; Charpy and Roualet 1991a: 173–294). While these oppida pots kept decoration in the main to simple geometric designs, a few vessels exhibit the long-lasting tradition of vegetal-based designs and others have friezes of painted animals (Figure 20.11b).

One group of decorated pottery, mostly made in the Early La Tène period, used stamps to build up repeating patterns mainly found on shallow bowls and fine slender-necked wheel-turned flasks with a distribution from the Rhineland to western Hungary (Schwappach 1973a, 1973b, 1974, 1977). The discovery of a number of kilns in the region of a major settlement at Sopron and the close comparison of the stamped motifs used in their decoration have allowed detailed plotting of the local trading networks which exported vessels from this region across into eastern Austria (Jerem 1984). Further fabric analysis has also indicated that the so-called 'Braubach' bowls of the area around Bonn in western Germany were the subject of local trading networks. The designs employed most commonly on such stamped pottery include combinations of concentric circles, S- or lyre-like forms, arcs and double-petalled floral motifs. The petalled motifs are really simplified lotus-flowers and these and other stamped designs are adapted versions of the palmettes and lotus-buds found on metalwork of the western Early Style, and the arcs and petals also reflect the use of compasses in a different medium (Figure 20.1[2]). In slightly later Brittany there is a

Figure 20.11a Painted pottery: wheel-turned pedestalled vase with black Vegetal Style design on red slip from Caurel, 'La Fosse Minore', Marne, France, Grave 46. Ht. 29.5 cm. Fourth–third century BC. (Photo: C. Bedoy.)

Figure 20.11b Pot with plant-based design from Basel gasworks site, Kt Basel, Switzerland. Ht. *c.*37 cm. Late second century BC. (Photo: Héman, Basel.)

far bolder translation of palmettes and the like onto pottery. The general sharing of motifs on disparate materials underscores the common visual vocabulary of the early Celts, despite attempts to distinguish between eastern and western groups by what is basically a comparison of pottery designs with those on metal.

SCULPTURE

Too little carved wood or datable stone survives for much discussion. Often it looks crude compared to the metalwork, but this is sometimes due to decay or weathering.

Wooden votive offerings in springs in France (see p. 356), appear to have been made by local carvers, with those at Chamalières more Roman-influenced than the examples from Sources de-la-Seine. A unique if fragmentary group of a stag and a human figure with goat supporters from a well, within a square ritual enclosure at Fellbach-Schmiden near Stuttgart, is dated by dendrochronology to the late second century BC (Figure 20.12). The presence, however, of turned wooden vessels and other wooden objects in waterlogged situations of much earlier date within a settlement area on the Dürrnberg, and evidence for the skilled production of wheeled vehicles (Piggott 1983: 195–238), are clear indications of how incomplete is our knowledge of the use by early Celtic craftsmen of such perishable materials. A small group of stylized human heads, mostly sandstone, of the late Hallstatt and early La Tène periods is scattered through the Rhineland and south-western Germany (Kimmig 1985, 1987). Except for those of the Celto-Ligurians in the south of France, most other stone sculptures are usually isolated finds of sometimes dubious antiquity, such as the 'Tarasque' or monster of Noves from the Bouches du Rhône (Duval and Heude 1983: 138). The splendid if damaged ragstone head of a torque-wearing, moustachioed male, found buried outside the Bohemian ditched sanctuary

Figure 20.12 Wooden stag from well within square ritual enclosure (*Viereckschanze*) at Fellbach-Schmiden, Kr. Rems-Murr, Germany. Ht. 77 cm. Last quarter second century BC. (Photo courtesy Landesdenkmalamt Baden-Württemberg, Stuttgart.)

Figure 20.13   Ragstone head from Mšecké Žehrovice, okr. Rakovník, Czechoslovakia. Ht. 23.5 cm. Date third century BC. (Photo: Aú ČSAV, Prague.)

site of Mšecké Žehrovice, is an exception which can be dated to at least the third century BC (Figure 20.13) (Megaw and Megaw 1988). Comparison with contemporary or near-contemporary classical sculpture such as the well-known depictions of naked Celtic warriors, originally commissioned by the Hellenistic rulers of Pergamon, demonstrates most clearly the absence of anything approaching naturalistic or even idealized portraiture in early Celtic art.

ICONOGRAPHY AND MEANING

To reconstruct the bases of pre-Roman iron age belief systems is a hazardous task. At best we have to rely on classical descriptions which, even when contemporary with the cultures they describe, clearly see things in terms of their own society's ideas. Use of much later Insular, if authentically Celtic, Welsh and Irish sources also carries the obvious dangers of projecting back in time and space concepts of probably limited regional and chronological applicability. Such as it is, the archaeological record suggests as much regional diversity in belief systems as in more tangible categories of material culture. Nevertheless, there are certain symbolic common denominators in La Tène visual art which support a view of its incorporation of ideas which are long-lasting and widely disseminated in space. A few examples must suffice.

From its very beginnings early Celtic art is concerned to depict not the whole human form – which in fact rarely occurs – but rather the human head either explicitly or ambiguously, as in the Cheshire Cat-like formulations of the later fourth century (Figures 20.1(1), 20.2, 20.6, 20.10 (below right), 20.13, 20.14). Even the insular material, generally abstract or aniconic, shows a few fleeting faces before the more definite first-century BC heads (Lambrechts 1954; Megaw 1965–6; Megaw and Megaw 1993). This recalls what we know from Insular tradition about the Celts' veneration of the human head as the centre of the intellect and the spirit, the heart and soul of the individual. Then there is the frequent depiction of a restricted range of relatively naturalistic animals, longest lasting being the bull, the boar and the horse. It is the boar or, as a substitute, the pig, which is frequently found as the champion's share in early Celtic burials and which occurs right through to the Roman conquest as a common symbol on coinage as well as in the form of free-standing figurines and helmet crests. Cattle, in later prehistoric Europe an economic staple and, one may again surmise from later evidence, a recognized form of wealth, are represented from even before the early Hallstatt period, as are, if less commonly, sheep or goats and deer (Figure 20.12). Birds – where identifiable in particular water-birds and birds of prey – also have a long iconographic life from the bird-headed brooches of Early La Tène onwards (Figures 20.5, 20.10, 20.15, 20.17) and the highly stylized bird's head-comma is particularly significant in the the pre- and post-Roman Celtic art of Britain and Ireland.

Combinations of humans and animals either in composite forms or associated one with the other are most clearly to be found in the strange imagery of the 'Early Style' gold rings (Figure 20.9) and the mask brooches (Figure 20.10), the latter reasonably interpreted as talismans to protect the wearer from an uncertain world populated by threats perceived and imagined (Pauli 1975, 1985). Imported imagery of Italo-Greek

Figure 20.14 Silver phalera with eighteen human heads and central triskel from hoard found at Villa Vecchia, Manerbio sul Mella, Brescia, Italy. D. 19.2 cm. ?First century BC. (Photo: Museo Civico, Brescia.)

Figure 20.15 Openwork 'Ticino'-type bronze belt-hook with water-birds and 'dragons' from San Polo d'Enzo, Reggio Emilia, Italy. L. 8.1 cm. First half fourth century BC. (Photo: Museo Civico 'G. Chierici', Reggio Emilia.)

orientalizing origin includes sphinxes, animals devouring a human head or arm and the human figure supported by a 'tree of life' comprising writhing bird- or 'dragon'-headed lyre-shaped forms. Clearly symbolic and certainly not narrative in its intent this 'master (or mistress) of the beasts' is largely confined to one group of objects, the so-called 'Ticino' openwork belt-hooks of the early fourth century mainly from Switzerland and northern Italy; the ultimate oriental origin is 'the ram in the

Figure 20.16 Iron scabbards with incised dragon pairs: *top*: type II (the earliest) from Taliándörögd, Veszprém, Hungary. W. 6.8 cm. *c*.300 BC. (Photo: E. Neuffer Archive, courtesy Römisch-Germanische Kommission, Frankfurt); *bottom*: type I dragons from Marnay, Saône-et-Loire, France. W. 5 cm. Earlier third century BC. (Photo: Musée Denon, Chalon-sur-Saône.)

thicket' first depicted in ancient Sumer (Figure 20.15). It is less certain that this heraldic group represents, as has been claimed, a trinity of sacred elements of Mediterranean origin which includes coral and the products of the vine (Kruta 1986, 1988). Equally, it is hard to interpret the meaning on early La Tène pieces – but also again on much later coinage – of such foreign beasts as the winged griffin or the sphinx, not to mention in at least one case a pair of lions. Do these simply represent the continuing attraction of the strange and new to a society clearly fascinated by the unusual and other-worldly?

Some motifs seem to be long-lived. Variations on the master of the beasts or the ram in the thicket resurface throughout La Tène times. The so-called dragon-pair scabbards of the fourth to second centuries BC certainly do not show dragons but variations on the bird-headed lyre seen on the Ticino belt-hooks, but without the central tiny figure (Figures 20.3 (left: 1, 2), 20.16; cf. 20.15) (De Navarro 1972; Petres 1982; Megaw 1971; Megaw and Megaw 1989b, 1991; Szabó and Petres 1992). The 'inter-Celtic' currency of these symbolic scabbards occurs from Romania to the Thames and even, in one locally adapted but clearly imported example, in Iberia, a region which had its own particular iron age but partially Celtic culture (Lenerz-de Wilde 1991: fig. 58:2). Whatever its origin, the dragon-pair sword may perhaps be regarded as an apotropaic symbol of special significance to people in new lands

Figure 20.17 Swiss Sword Style iron scabbard with chagrinage and bird-headed triskel found in a surgeon's grave at Obermenzing, Kr. München, Germany, Grave 7. W. *c*.4.8 cm. *c*.200 BC. (Photo: Prähistorische Staatssammlung, Munich.)

in which fierce and exotic beasts may well have protected the owner; subsequently it may have become a symbol of rank and proven prowess in battle. Descendants of such creatures appear on items of the Ultimate La Tène style in Ireland such as the Petrie Crown, as well as the dragonesque brooches of Roman Yorkshire.

Finally, triplism is ubiquitous in early Celtic art (Green 1989). The writhing three-armed triskel, sometimes with bird-headed finials, is another motif which begins in fifth-century BC La Tène art and continues into the imagery of the early Christian gospel books (Figures 20.1(4), 20.3(3, 4), 20.11a, 20.14, 20.17). The Waldalgesheim or Vegetal Style is essentially based on linked triskels (Verger 1986, 1987). Three human heads or simply a triple roundel like a pawn-broker's sign are particularly common as the chief feature of a class of neck-ring peculiar to the southern Champagne region, as appendages to the spring on a subgroup of early mask brooches and on continental coinage, while triple-headed deities abound in the only partly romanized culture of later Celtic Britain and beyond.

It is hardly surprising that the makers of such magical material should have distinctive status in early Celtic society. An early La Tène skeleton grave in the Marne has, in addition to the arms typical for male graves of the period, a set of woodworking tools (Legendre and Piechaud 1985). Metalworkers' implements have been found in a number of other central European graves while the status of another key figure amongst basically peasant societies, the healer, is confirmed by the discovery at Obermenzing near Munich of a middle La Tène surgeon's burial marked by his ownership of a fine iron sword, manufactured in western Switzerland and decorated with a bird-headed triskel (Figure 20.17).

The chief elements of Celtic society seem to be those of a disparate collection of regional communities, often embracing many traits of the territories in which they found themselves but nevertheless largely sharing aspects of a similar economy and technology. Amongst all this variety, the binding element appears to be the art which, as material evidence for their belief systems, in many ways is the one common factor which best defines the Celts as a real identity in the making of Europe.

REFERENCES

Note: The references contain, in addition to works specifically referred to in the text, additional sources for the history of early Celtic art.

Bataille-Melkon, Aline and Charpy, Jean-Jacques (eds) (1985) *Les Celtes en Italie et en Champagne* (exh. cat.), Musée Municipal, Epernay 19 October–8 December 1985; Ancien Collège des Jésuites, Reims 3 May–29 June 1986.

Brunaux, Jean-Louis (1988) *The Celtic Gauls: gods, rites and sanctuaries* trans. Daphne Nash, London: Seaby.

Brunaux, Jean-Louis, Meniel, Patrice and Poplin, François (1985) *Gournay I: Les fouilles sur le sanctuaire et l'oppidum (1975–1984)*, Revue Archéologique de Picardie, special no.

Castriota, D.R. (1981) 'Continuity and innovation in Celtic and Mediterranean ornament: a grammatical-syntactic analysis of the processes of the reception and transformation in the decorative arts of antiquity', Ph.D. thesis, Columbia University [University Microfilms 1982].

Challet, Virginie (1992) *Les Celtes et l'émail*, Documents Préhistoriques 3, Paris: Editions du Comité des Travaux Historiques et Scientifiques.

Champion, Sara T. (1976) 'Coral in Europe: commerce and Celtic ornament', in P.-M. Duval and C.F.C. Hawkes (eds) *Celtic Art*, 29–40.

—— (1977) 'The use of coral and other substances to decorate metalwork in central and western Europe in the middle and later centuries of the first millennium B.C.', D.Phil. thesis, University of Oxford.

—— (1982) 'Exchange and ranking: the case of coral', in A.C. Renfrew and S.J. Shennan (eds) *Ranking, Resources and Exchange*, Cambridge: Cambridge University Press, 67–72.

—— (1985) 'Production and exchange in early iron age central Europe', in T.C. Champion and J.V.S. Megaw (eds) *Settlement and Society*, 133–60.

Champion, T.C. and Megaw, J.V.S. (eds) (1985) *Settlement and Society: aspects of west European prehistory in the first millennium B.C.*, Leicester: Leicester University Press.

Charpy, Jean-Jacques (1991) 'Les situles du Ve siècle en Champagne: formes et décors', in J.-J. Charpy and P. Roualet (eds) *Les Celtes en Champagne*, 41–57.

Charpy, Jean-Jacques and Roualet, Pierre (1987) *Céramique peinte gauloise en Champagne du VIe au Ier siècle avant Jésus-Christ* (exh. cat. 10 June–30 October), Musée d'Epernay.

—— (eds) (1991a) *La Céramique peinte celtique dans son contexte européen; Actes du Symposium International d'Hautvilliers 9–11 Octobre 1987*, Memoires de la Société Archéologique Champenoise 5.

—— (1991b) *Les Celtes en Champagne* (exh. cat. 23 June–3 November 1991), Musée d'Epernay.

Collis, John (1984a) *The European Iron Age*, London: Batsford.

—— (1984b) *Oppida: earliest towns north of the Alps*, Sheffield: University of Sheffield, Department of Prehistory and Archaeology.

Corradini, Nathalie (1991) 'La céramique peinte à décor curviligne rouge et noir en Champagne: approche technologique et chronologique', in J.-J. Charpy and P. Roualet (eds) *Les Celtes en Champagne*, 109–42.

Dehn, Wolfgang (1970) 'Ein keltisches Häuptlingsgrab aus Hallstatt', in *Krieger und Salzherren: Hallstattkultur im Ostalpenraum* (exh. cat.) Römisch-Germanisches Zentralmuseum Mainz Ausstellungskataloge 4: 72–81.

De Navarro, J.M. (1952) 'The Celts in Britain and their art', in M.P. Charlesworth *et al. The Heritage of Early Britain*, London: G. Bell & Sons, 56–82.

—— (1972) *The Finds from the Site of La Tène: scabbards and the swords found in them*, London: Oxford University Press for the Society of Antiquaries.

Dent, John (1985) 'Three chariot burials from Wetwang, Yorkshire', *Antiquity* 59: 85–92 and pl. XVIII–XXI.

Deyts, S. (1983) *Les Bois sculptés des sources de la Seine*, Paris: *Gallia* Supplement 42.

Duval, Alain (1989) *L'Art celtique de la Gaule au Musée des Antiquités Nationales*, Paris: Editions de la Réunion des Musées Nationaux.

Duval, Alain and Heude, Danielle (eds) (1983) *L'art celtique en Gaule: collections des musées de Province*, Paris: Direction des Musées de la France.

Duval, Paul-Marie (1977) *Les Celtes*, Paris: Gallimard.

Duval, Paul-Marie and Hawkes, C.F.C. (eds) (1976) *Celtic Art in Ancient Europe: five protohistoric centuries*, London/New York: Seminar Press.

Duval, Paul-Marie and Kruta, Venceslas (eds) (1979) *Les Mouvements celtiques du Ve au Ier siècle avant notre ère*, Paris: CNRS.

—— (eds) (1982) *L'Art celtique de la période d'expansion, IVe et IIIe siècles avant notre ère = Actes du colloque organisé sous les auspices du Collège de France et de la IVe Section de l'Ecole pratique des Hautes Etudes, du 26 au 28 septembre 1978, au Collège de France à Paris*, Paris.

Filip, Jan (1976) *Celtic Civilization and its Heritage*, Prague: Academiâ.

Finlay, Ian (1973) *Celtic Art: an introduction*, London: Faber & Faber.

Fischer, Franz (1983) 'Thrakien als Vermittler iranischer Metallkunst an die frühen Kelten', in

R.M. Boehmer and H. Hauptmann (eds) *Beiträge zur Altertumskunde Kleinasiens: Festschrift für Kurt Bittel*, Mainz: Philipp von Zabern, 191–202.

—— (1988) 'Celtes et Achéménides', in A. Duval *et al.* (eds) *Les Princes celtes et la Méditerranée*, Paris: La Documentation Française, 21–31.

Frey, O.-H. (1955) 'Eine etruskische Bronzeschnabelkanne', *Annales littéraires de l'Université de Besançon*, 2nd series, II, 4–30.

—— (1976) 'Du Premier style au style de Waldalgesheim: remarques sur l'évolution de l'art celtique ancien', in P.-M. Duval and C.F.C. Hawkes (eds) *Celtic Art*, 141–63.

—— (1984) 'Zur Bronzeschnabelkanne in Besançon', *Annales littéraires de l'Université de Besançon* 294 = H. Walther (ed.) *Hommages à Lucien Lerat* I, 293–308, pl. 1, and figs 1–7.

Furger, Andres and Müller, Felix (eds) (1991) *Helvetian Gold: Celtic treasures from Switzerland* (exh. cat.), Zürich: Eidolon/Swiss National Museum.

Gosden, C.H. (1983) 'Iron age pottery trade in central Europe', Ph.D. thesis, University of Sheffield.

Green, Miranda (1986) *The Gods of the Celts*, Gloucester: Allan Sutton.

—— (1989) *Symbol and Image in Celtic Religious Art*, London: Routledge.

Hüttel, Hans-Georg (1978) 'Keltische Zierscheiben und thrakischer Pferdegeschirrschmuck', *Germania* 56(1): 150–71.

Jacobsthal, Paul (1944) *Early Celtic Art*, Oxford: Clarendon Press.

Jerem, E. (1984) 'An early Celtic pottery workshop in northwestern Hungary: some archaeological and technical evidence', *Oxford Journal of Archaeology* 3: 57–80.

Jopling, Carol F. (ed.) (1971) *Art and Aesthetics in Primitive Societies: a critical anthology*, New York: Dutton.

KEATOI: Kelti in njihovi sobobnikina ozemljn Jugoslavije (1983) (exh. cat.) Narodni Muzej Ljubljana.

Kaenel, Gilbert (1990) *Recherches sur la période de La Tène en Suisse occidentale: analyse des sépultures*, Lausanne: Cahiers d'Archéologie Romande 50.

Kimmig, W. (1985) 'Eisenzeitliche Grabstelen in Mitteleuropa', in *Studi di paleoetnologia in onore di Salvatore M. Puglisi*, Rome: Università di Roma 'La Sapienza', 591–615.

—— (1987) 'Eisenzeitliche Grabstelen in Mitteleuropa', *Fundberichte aus Baden-Württemberg* 12: 251–97.

Kruta, Venceslas (1982) 'Aspects unitaires et faciès dans l'art celtique du IVe siècle avant notre ère: l'hypothèse d'un foyer Celto-Italique', in P.-M. Duval and V. Kruta (eds) *Les Mouvements celtiques*, 35–49.

—— (1985) 'Le port d'anneaux de cheville en Champagne et le problème d'une immigration danubienne au IIIe siècle avant J.-C.', *Etudes Celtiques* 22: 27–51.

—— (1986) 'Le corail, le vin et l'arbre de vie: observations sur l'art et la religion des Celtes du Ve au Ier siècle avant J.-C.', *Etudes Celtiques* 23: 7–32.

—— (1988) 'L'art celtique laténien du Ve siècle avant J.-C.: le signe et l'image', in A. Duval *et al.* (eds) *Les Princes celtes*, 81–92.

—— (1991a) 'La céramique peinte de la Champagne dans le contexte de l'art celtique', in J.-J. Charpy and P. Roualet (eds) *Les Celtes en Champagne*, 143–58.

—— (1991b) 'The first Celtic expansion: prehistory to history', in V. Kruta *et al.* (eds) *The Celts*, London: Thames & Hudson, 195–215.

Kruta, Venceslas and Szabó, Miklos (1978) *Les Celtes*, Paris: Hatier.

—— (1982) 'Canthares danubiens du IIIe siècle a.n.è.: un exemple d'influence hellénistique sur les Celtes orientaux', *Etudes Celtiques* 19: 51–67.

Kruta, Venceslas *et al.* (eds) (1991) *The Celts*, London: Thames & Hudson.

Lambrechts, P. (1954) *L'Exaltation de la tête dans la pensée et dans l'art des Celtes*, Dissertationes Archaeologicae Gandenses 2.

Legendre, Rose-Marie and Piechaud, Simon (1985) 'Une sépulture à outils du début de La Tène à La Chaussée-sur-Marne (Marne)', *Préhistoire et Protohistoire en Champagne-Ardenne* 9: 57–66.

Lejars, T. (1994) *Gournay III: Les fourreaux d'épée*, Paris: Errance.

Lenerz-de Wilde, Majolie (1977) *Zirkelornament in der Kunst der Latènezeit*, Münchner Beiträge zur Vor- und Frühgeschichte 25, Munich: C.H. Beck.

—— (1979) 'Zur Verzierung der Röhrenkanne aus dem Fürstengrab von Waldalgesheim', *Archäologisches Korrespondenzblatt* 9: 313–16.

—— (1982) 'Le Style du Cheshire Cat: un phénomène caractéristique de l'art celtique', in P.-M. Duval and V. Kruta (eds) *Les Mouvements celtiques*, 101–14.

—— (1991) *Iberia Celtica: archäologische Zeugnisse keltischer Kultur auf der Pyrenäenhalbinsel*, 2 vols, Stuttgart: Franz Steiner Verlag.

Luschey, Heinz (1983) 'Thrakien als Ort der Begegnung der Kelten mit der iranischen Metallkunst', in R.M. Boehmer and H. Hauptmann (eds) *Beiträge zur Altertumskunde Kleinasiens: Festschrift für Kurt Bittel*, Mainz: Philipp von Zabern, 313–29.

MacGregor, Morna (1976) *Early Celtic Art in North Britain*, 2 vols, Leicester: Leicester University Press.

Maier, Ferdinand (1970) *Die bemalte Spätlatène-Keramik von Manching. Die Ausgrabungen in Manching* III, Wiesbaden.

Megaw, J.V.S. (1965–6) 'Two La Tène finger rings in the Victoria and Albert Museum, London: an essay on the human face and early Celtic art', *Praehistorische Zeitschrift* 63–4: 96–166.

—— (1968) 'Une épée de La Tène I avec fourreau décoré', *Revue Archéologique de l'Est et du Centre-Est* 19: 129–44.

—— (1969) 'Doppelsinnigkeit in der keltischen Kunst, dargestellt an einem Beispiel aus dem Fürstengrab von Bad Dürkheim', *Pfälzer Heimat* 3: 85–6.

—— (1970a) *The Art of the European Iron Age: a study of the elusive image*, Bath: Adams & Dart.

—— (1970b) 'Cheshire Cat and Mickey Mouse: analysis, interpretation and the art of the European Iron Age', *Proceedings of the Prehistoric Society* 36: 261–79.

—— (1971) 'An unpublished early La Tène *Tierfibel* from Hallstatt, Oberösterreich', *Arch. Austriaca* 50: 176–84.

—— (1972) 'Style and style analysis in continental early La Tène art', *World Archaeology* 3: 276–92.

—— (1975) 'The orientalizing theme in early Celtic art: East or West?', in J. Fitz (ed.) *The Celts in Central Europe. Papers of the II Pannonia Conference, Székesfehérvár 1974* = *Alba Regia* 14: 15–33.

Megaw, J.V.S. and Megaw, M.R. (1986) *Early Celtic Art in Britain and Ireland*, Princes Risborough: Shire Publications.

—— (1988) 'The stone head from Mšecké Žehrovice: a reappraisal', *Antiquity* 62: 630–41.

—— (1989a) *Celtic Art from its Beginnings to the Book of Kells*, London: Thames & Hudson.

—— (1989b) 'The Italian job: some implications of recent finds of Celtic scabbards decorated with dragon-pairs', *Mediterranean Archaeology* 2: 85–100.

—— (1990a) *The Basse-Yutz (1927) Find: masterpieces of Celtic art*, Society of Antiquaries Research Report 46.

—— (1990b) 'Italians and Greeks bearing gifts: the Basse-Yutz find reconsidered', in Jean-Paul Descoeudres (ed.) *Greek Colonists and Native Populations*, Oxford: Oxford University Press, for the Australian Academy of the Humanities, 579–605.

—— (1991) '"Semper aliquid novum . . ." Celtic dragon-pairs re-reviewed', *Acta Archaeologica Academiae Scientificarum Hungaricae* 42: 55–72.

—— (1992) 'The Celts: the first Europeans?', *Antiquity* 66: 254–60.

—— (1993) 'Cumulative Celticity and the human face in insular pre-Roman iron age art', in J. Briard and A. Duval (eds) *Les Représentations humaines du néolithique à l'âge du fer = Actes du 115ᵉ Congrès National des Sociétés savantes* (Avignon, 1990), Paris: Editions du Comité des Travaux Historiques et Scientifiques, 205–18.

Megaw, J.V.S., Megaw, M.R. and Neugebauer, J.-W. (1989) 'Hervorragende Produkte frühlatènezeitlicher Kunsthandwerkes in Ostösterreich', *Germania* 67: 477–517.

Merriman, Nick (1987) 'Value and motivation in pre-history: the evidence for "Celtic spirit"', in Ian Hodder (ed.) *The Archaeology of Contextual Meanings*, Cambridge: Cambridge University Press, 110–16.

Moosleitner, Fritz (1985) *Die Schnabelkanne vom Dürrnberg: ein Meisterwerk keltischer Handwerkskunst*, Salzburg: Schriftreihe des Salzburger Museums C.A. 7.

—— (1987) *Arte Protoceltica a Salisburgo: Mostra della Regione di Salisburgo, Museo degli Argenti, Palazzo Pitti, Firenze*, Salzburg: Salzburger Landesregierung.

Moosleitner, Fritz, Pauli, Ludwig and Penninger, Ernst (1974) *Der Dürrnberg bei Hallein* II, Müncher Beiträge zur Vor- und Frühgeschichte 17, Munich: C.H. Beck.

Müller, Felix (1989) *Die frühlatènezeitlichen Scheibenhalsringe*, Römisch-Germanische Forschungen 46.

Pare, C. (1991) '*Fürstensitze*, Celts and the Mediterranean world: developments in the west Hallstatt culture in the 6th and 5th centuries BC', *Proceedings of the Prehistoric Society* 57(2): 183–202.

Pauli, Ludwig (1975) *Keltischer Volksglaube: Amulette und Sonderbestattungen am Dürrnberg bei Hallein und im eisenzeitlichen Mitteleuropa*, Münchner Beiträge zur Vor- und Frühgeschichte 28, Munich: C.H.Beck.

—— (1978) *Der Dürrnberg bei Hallein* II: 1–2, Münchner Beiträge zur Vor- und Frühgeschichte 18:1, Munich: C.H. Beck.

—— (1985) 'Early Celtic society: two centuries of wealth and turmoil in central Europe', in T.C. Champion and J.V.S. Megaw (eds) *Settlement and Society*, 23–44.

Petres, Éva f. (1982) 'Notes on scabbards decorated with dragons and bird-pairs', in P.-M. Duval and V. Kruta (eds) *L'Art celtique*, 162–74.

Petres, Éva f. and Szabó, Miklós (eds) (1974) *A Keleti Kelta Muvészet /Eastern Celtic Art* (exh. cat.), Székesfehérvár: István Király Múzeum.

Pieta, Karol (1982) *Umenie dobe železnej*, Bratislava: Tatran.

Piggott, Stuart (1983) *The Earliest Wheeled Transport from the Atlantic Coast to the Caspian Sea*, London: Thames & Hudson.

Planck, Dieter *et al.* (1982) 'Ein neuentdecktes Viereckschanz in Fellbach-Schmiden, Rems-Murr-Kreis: Vorbericht der Grabungen 1977–80', *Germania* 60: 105–91.

Powell, T.G.E. (1971) 'From Urartu to Gundestrup', in J. Boardman, M.A. Brown and T.G.E. Powell (eds) *The European Community in Later Prehistory*, London: Routledge & Kegan Paul, 183–210.

Raftery, Barry (1983) *A Catalogue of Irish Iron Age Antiquities*, 2 vols, Marburg: Veröffentlichung des Vorgeschichtlichen Seminars Marburg, Sonderband 1.

—— (1984) *La Tène in Ireland: problems of origin and chronology*, Marburg: Veröffentlichung des Vorgeschichtlichen Seminars Marburg, Sonderband 2.

—— (ed.) (1990) *Celtic Art*, Paris: Unesco.

Rapin, André and Brunaux, Jean Louis (1988) *Gournay II: dépôts et trophées*, Paris: Errance.

Romeuf, Anne-Marie (1986) 'Ex-votos en bois de Chamalières (Puy-de-Dôme) et des Sources de la Seine: essai de comparaison', *Gallia* 44: 65–89.

Roualet, Pierre (1991) 'Les vases peints marniens de La Tène ancienne I dans leur contexte funéraire', in J.-J. Charpy and P. Roualet (eds) *Les Celtes en Champagne*, 9–39.

Sandars, N.K. (1971) 'Orient and orientalizing in early Celtic Art', *Antiquity* 45: 103–12.

—— (1976) 'Orient and orientalizing: recent thoughts reviewed', in P.-M. Duval and C.F.C. Hawkes (eds) *Celtic Art*, 41–60.

—— (1985) *Prehistoric Art in Europe* (2nd edn), Harmondsworth: Penguin Books.

Schwappach, Frank (1973a) 'Floral-decorations and arc-designs in the "Early Style" of Celtic art: ornaments of the western and eastern centres of La Tène', *Etudes Celtiques* 13: 710–31.

—— (1973b) 'Frühkeltisches Ornament zwischen Marne, Rhein und Moldau', *Bonner Jahrbuch* 173: 53–111.

—— (1974) 'Ostkeltisches und westkeltisches Ornament auf einem älterlatènezeitlichen Gürtelhaken von Mühlacker, Kreis Vaihingen', *Fundberichte aus Baden-Württemberg* 1: 337–72.

—— (1977) 'Die Stempelkeramik aus den Gräbern von Braubach', *Bonner Jahrbuch* 177: 119–83.

Stanczik, Ilona and Vaday, Andrea (1971) 'Keltische Bronzegürtel "ungarischen" Typs im Karpathenbecken', *Folia Archaeologica* 22: 7–27.

Stead, I.M. (1979) *The Arras Culture*, York: Yorkshire Philosophical Society.

—— (1985) *Celtic Art in Britain before the Roman Conquest*, London: British Museum Publications.

—— (1991) *Iron Age Cemeteries in East Yorkshire*, London: English Heritage Archaeological Report 22.

Szabó, Miklós (1973) 'Eléments régionaux dans l'art des Celtes orientaux', *Etudes Celtiques* 13: 750–74.

—— (1975) 'Sur la question du filigrane dans l'art des Celtes orientaux', *Alba Regia* 14: 147–65.

—— (1977) 'The origins of the Hungarian sword style', *Antiquity* 51: 211–19.

—— (1989) 'Contribution au problème du style plastique laténien dans la cuvette des Carpathes', *Acta Archaeologica Academiae Scientificarum Hungaricae* 41: 17–32.

—— (1991) *Les Celtes de l'est: le second âge du fer dans la cuvette des Karpates*, Paris: Centre Archéologique Européen du Mont Beuvray with Errance.

—— (1992) *Les Celtes de l'est: le second âge du fer dans la cuvette des Karpates*, Centre Archéologique Européen du Mont Beuvray, Paris: Errance.

Szabó, Miklós and Petres, Eva f. (1992) *Decorated Weapons of the La Tène Iron Age in the Carpathian Basin*, Inventaria Praehistorica Hungariae V, Budapest: Magyar Nemzeti Múzeum.

Verger, Stéphane (1986) 'La formation des styles végétaux du IVe siècle avant J.C.', Master's thesis, Université de Paris I.

—— (1987) 'La genèse celtique des rinceaux à triscèles', *Jahrbuch des Römisch-Germanischen Zentralmuseums Mainz* 34: 287–339.

Von Hase, Friedrich-Wilhelm (1973) 'Unbekannte frühetruskische Edelmetallfunde mit Maskenköpfen: mögliche Vorbilder keltischer Maskendarstellungen', *Hamburger Beiträge zur Archäologie* 3(1): 51–64.

Wyss, René (1975) *Der Schatzfund von Erstfeld: Frühkeltischer Goldschmuck aus der Zentralalpen*, Zurich: Gesellschaft für das Schweizerisches Landesmuseum.

Zachar, Lev (1987) *Keltische Kunst in der Slowakei*, Bratislava: Tatran.

THE SOCIAL IMPLICATIONS
OF CELTIC ART
600 BC to AD 600

———— •◆• ————

Martyn Jope

Artwork, which here must include costume, is full of social implications. First, it has given a fluid, often vivid, means of communication between people, as individuals (sometimes eyeball-to-eyeball; Jope 1987: pls: xia, viiia; fig. 3b), as groups, or as institutions. Second, Celtic art has been a means of displaying social rank (or aspiration thereto); there can be no doubt of the hierarchic nature of societies who possessed display works like the Agris helmet (p. 380). It can give some guidance concerning social level and context within the changing structure of Celtic communities through more than a millennium, not least during the complex processes of conurbanization (often oversimplified in discussion) in 'barbarian' Europe from the sixth to first centuries BC. Artwork has further been a potent factor in expressing cultural taste and human relations with the supernatural, which profoundly affect relations between people. It can sometimes also give clues to the life style and living conditions of different social strata.

Artwork is one of the few means we have of penetrating the social and higher cultural infrastructure of non-literate or non-recorded peoples, and it can give some clues to the amount of leisure time available to people of differing social levels (Jope 1983). The taste shown in everyday items, such as knife handles, can reveal whole facets of humbler personal taste, as, for higher levels, do the grander works for aristocratic display and ceremony. The latter, whether earthly or supernatural, have been powerful agents in persuading unity in a common cause, such as allegiance to a chieftain, or subtribal unity. The carved monoliths atop the 'princely' burial mounds could be examples (Figure 21.1; Jacobsthal 1944: pl. 6–15; Bittel *et al.* 1981: 90–1, 121; Moscati *et al.* 1991: 88, 126).

The very concept of 'Celtic art' seems itself to carry a certain coherence, as though distilling an essential social ethos, to represent the visual sensitivity of 'Celticity', a common cause among those 'barbarian' peoples who had the urge to feel themselves 'Celtic' (Jope 1987: 120; Bodmer 1993). It arose from a profound feeling of dissent from the often rather staid conventions of Greek-style ornament (Jope 1987; Megaw and Megaw 1990), thereby seeming to assert ethnic individuality.

The artwork itself can sometimes tell us directly about the life style, occupation, costume or social position of individuals depicted. This may be through the eyes and minds of classical or near-classical artists, or of Celts themselves (Figures 21.2;

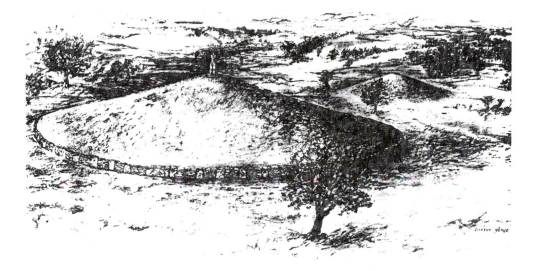

Figure 21.1 Monolith figure atop a princely burial mound
(Bittel *et al.* 1981: 121).

Bienkowski 1908; Piggott 1965: 197–9). We see the proud nudity of Gauls in battle or ceremonial (Bittel *et al.* 1981: 91, fig. 28), Celtic dress (e.g. Jacobsthal 1944: 11, pl. 6, 59–60; Megaw 1971: pl. 24, 25, 231 (brooch holding cloak)); east Celts (Szabó 1971: pl. 72–5); formal processions (Moscati *et al.* 1991: 538f.); horse-play (Jope 1983, probably situla-inspired, cf. Bittel *et al.* 1981: 167), or a Celtic ideal of feminine beauty (Powell 1958: 236, pl. 6). A coin of Cunobelin (Figure 21.3; Allen 1958: 53, pl. v.38) shows a fully accoutred, very un-Roman-looking foot-soldier (perhaps the best view we shall ever have), with animal-crested helmet and Celtic side-seamed trousers bunched under the knees. Various forms of multiple and single human sacrifice are shown by Jacobsthal (1944: 8f., 165, pl. 2, 4; see also Moscati *et al.* 1991: 362–3), though Rome's true motives in suppressing druidism – politically civilizing urge, or merely security – can only be assessed through contemporary writings (Last 1949). Celtic artists had their own subtle ways of portraying their very distinctive nature; note the profoundly un-Greek mouths of the Roquepertuse heads (third century BC; Jacobsthal 1944: pl. 2, 4, pp. 4, 105; Jope 1987: 98, pl. III); witness also the supremely economical expression of Celtic aristocratic aloofness in Britain of the third century BC (Figure 21.2: the Wandsworth 'mask' shield; Jope and Jacobsthal in press: pls 70–5; Jope 1987: 108, pl. v). A similar manner of arrissed modelling has been used to emphasize a very non-aristocratic strain in the little face on the pottery vase from Novo Mesto in Yugoslavia (Moscati *et al.* 1991: 116).

Some items of artwork have overt (or accepted) status implications (e.g. a crown, a neck-ring, a dagger, a brooch – for the kind of dress it implies (Hawkes 1982), or the luxury silks of the Hohmichele (Hundt 1969). Others are meaningful for the connections with wealth or authority they imply (e.g. vehicles and horse gear, or

Figure 21.2 'Celtic aristocracy through Celtic eyes'; face in relief beaten bronze at top of spine of shield from river Thames at Wandsworth. Later third century BC. (Restoration S. Rees-Jones. Photo: R.E.H. Reid, Queen's University, Belfast. British Museum.)

hand mirrors Jope and Jacobsthal (in press): pls 238–49). Control and authority over material resources, and over skilled ateliers is also revealed through artwork.

Gold itself seems to have a special status among Celts already in the seventh century BC (at Halstatt marking off an élite of about 5 per cent of females: Hodson 1990: 80). In early Celtic Britain gold hardly appears before the first century BC; it is all concentrated in East Anglia, above all at and around Snettisham in Norfolk, which must have been a royal repository and where alone in Britain we find a good gold-working tradition in the third–second centuries BC (Stead 1991b; Jope and Jacobsthal in press: 123, map). The Snettisham deposits show the systematic burial of gold treasure as a form of banking (Stead 1991b). The full political significance of this East Anglian concentration of the gold has yet to be assessed (see also Chapter 18). Here the world of coinage must be considered also (Chapter 14).

Figure 21.3 Coin of Cunobelin. A British foot-soldier – the best view we are likely to get –
early first century AD. (Photo courtesy of D.F. Allen; Allen 1958: pl. V.38.)

SOCIAL RANKING

Artwork has played a major part in showing just how sensitive early Celtic peoples
could be to the hierarchical ordering of society. This is well shown by Hodson's
(1990) analysis of the grave contents in the large cemetery of the salt-producing and
salt-trading community at Hallstatt (Kromer 1959). No habitations have, however,
so far been located for this prosperous and specialized close-knit community, living
under restrictive conditions in a precipitous, fragmented terrain. This Hallstatt
community of the seventh–fifth centuries BC has provided an invaluable yardstick of
social grading for barbarian Europe in this age (Figure 21.4 a, b), and we shall return
to this.

We start at the top, with the élite among these early 'Celtic' people, from eastern
Europe to the Atlantic, from Italy to Scandinavia, from the sixth century BC to well
into the Christian era. Their wealth, as displayed through funerary rites, is (in the
earlier centuries) eloquent of power and authority, emphasizing the separateness of
the élite (Kromer 1982; Moscati *et al.* 1991: 72–123). Frankenstein and Rowlands
(1978: 100ff.), following Kimmig (1969), invoking medieval analogies (cf. Radford
1935 and pers. comm.), have marshalled the available evidence into a hypothesis of
hierarchical levels of chieftaincy – paramount, vassal, subchief and lower levels,
and also their domains, as reflected in material wealth, artwork and control over
production of luxury goods, such as fine cloth, etc. All the wine-drinking, the
symposia, followed southerly example (though sometimes with a Celtic flavour)
and continued (with some dilution of exuberance) well into the Christian era, as
imported amphorae in the first centuries BC–AD in Britain, and somewhat later, as
capital places like Tintagel (Thomas 1993) or Lydford in Devon (Saunders 1990: 62)

seem to tell us. No less impressive is the spacious round assembly-place or feasting-hall at Navan near Armagh in Ulster, constructed about 90 BC (Lynn 1991; Moscati *et al.* 1991: 610–11, 614–15), its floor evidently swept free of the discards that would have told us so much (cf. Cadbury-Camelot six centuries later (Alcock 1982)), though for Navan the nearby finds of the great sounding-horns (Fox 1946: pl. XII) on the edge of Lough-na-Shade make high ceremonial practice among this community very clear.

Sacred works for temple or shrine could reach out to a wider clientele, and this was to be greatly expanded in the Christian era in the dichotomy of wealth in secular and church hands, where the church's power over the whole populace was intended to fascinate and embrace even the humblest.

The imposing artworks of the sixth–fifth centuries BC in south-west Germany and eastern France, both exotics of distant origin and more local Celtic products (often just as sumptuous and maybe more intriguing (e.g. Megaw 1971: 10, 15; Megaw and Megaw 1990; Jacobsthal 1944: *passim*), reveal a confident, hierarchical society, probably with widely accepted conventions of prestige gift-exchange (Kromer 1982); it is even suggested that exotic raw materials – coral, etc. – might have travelled as exchange gifts (Megaw 1984: 160–1). But within this display of often overweening élitism, actual markers asserting ultimate authority are elusive, at least until the second century BC, when the minting of coinages in the name of specific rulers indicates the emergence of statecraft (Nash 1976). Among the 'princely' tombs of the seventh–sixth centuries BC, for instance, we might be tempted to see authority shared (or agreed) among near equals (Frey in Moscati *et al.* 1991: 74–92), though we do get an occasional hint of individual authority, as with the one very large iron drinking-horn hanging with four pairs of smaller drinking-horns in the Hochdorf tomb chamber (Moscati *et al.* 1991: 86; Bittel *et al.* 1981: 123), though here perhaps is an uneasy hint of a leader with a band of high-class brigands. Hodson also finds difficulty in identifying supreme authority at Hallstatt, though he comes close to it (Hodson 1990: 82, 99–100; G.259 helmet).

Yet continuity of strong authority there must have been, to devise and organize the massive constructional works such as the Heuneberg or Mont Lassois (Moscati *et al.* 1991: 114–23) and maintain extensive tribute and distant trading systems or a trading and noble-gift-exchange protocol. Some substantial material emblem might be expected to mark the status of 'kingship' (like the crown of state in later times) and indeed the resplendent gold-covered iron helmet of the fourth century BC found at Agris in the Charente (too far west for the Arverni) (Gomez de Soto 1986; Moscati *et al.* 1991: 292–3, reconstituted in Mainz) might be a candidate – it seems too magnificent to be the insignia of a mere 'domain' (cf. Frankenstein and Rowlands 1978: 82ff.), especially as it was found not in a burial (where it would have been lost as a symbol of immediate succession) but in a grotto. For just this reason, burials cannot be expected to clarify this problem of succession insignia very much, and most often fine helmets of this age come from tomb groups (Jacobsthal 1944: pl. 75–89; Moscati *et al.* 1991: 224, 250–1). Hencken (1952) argued that helmets and body armour were royal prerogatives, but this could have extended to the royal bodyguard.

The rich tomb 953 in the Benacci cemetery at Bologna with its crown of gold leaves (Moscati *et al.* 1991: 225f.) indicates a person of high position among the Boii, but not necessarily the ruler. The flat conical hat of birch-bark in the Hochdorf princely tomb (a southerly influence) has been seen as a mark of highest rank (cf. also the Hirschlanden warrior statue). We should note that the 'end-of-dynasty' concept may be occasionally invoked to explain material in rich burials which might otherwise be taken as regalia of succession (as for Vix; Griffith 1988: 8f., 20).

There was clearly a whole lesser sub-ranking within the nobility (e.g. Figure 21.4). Some information concerning hierarchy may perhaps be derived from study of the secondary burials in the 'princely' burial mounds (Frankenstein and Rowlands 1978: 90–1; Bittel *et al.* 1981: 90).

SOCIAL STANDING: THE HALLSTATT CEMETERY EVIDENCE

This ostentation of the sixth and fifth centuries BC could only have existed if it was backed by well-organized productive communities through much of the Celtic world. Hodson's (1990) study of the great Hallstatt cemetery (Kromer 1959) of over 2,500 graves (902 informatively analysed for ranking therein) reveals something of the infrastructure of one such community, one primarily concerned with trading its product, salt, distantly across much of temperate Europe, as seen through its burial conventions. In this, the artwork for both female and male dress adornment, as well as the male weaponry, and the luxury ceremonial items, though not all that gracious, is the major evidence. Figures 21.4a and b show the accepted ranking of female and male burial attire among this specialized community. It ranges from almost no metal accessories to ornate weapons and luxury items such as specialized tools, feasting gear, and metal vessels (many imported from the south) in the top-status graves. The élite tended to be buried in a secluded part of the cemetery (Hodson 1990: 98). There seems a dearth of leading males in the later phase (H2), and no obvious leader among them, which has suggested a rising female dominance (Hodson 1990: 99), but it must be remembered that more males would tend to meet their end on distant journeys. A composite diagram can be conceived to fill the missing highest ranking male for H2 (e.g. Sm4 (H2); Hodson 1990: 83, fig. 29). This would stress the emergence of the snake brooch (*Schlangenfibel*) a design perhaps of southerly inspiration (Mansfeld 1973: 4, 154–82) seen in e.g. G116, G749, G207, and some twenty other graves at Hallstatt. This snake brooch is a main brooch type at the Heuneburg fortress in the later sixth to early fifth century (Mansfeld 1973: 160–81) and in the very rich burials of Hochdorf (Moscati *et al.* 1991: 110). These brooches of the earlier fifth century were a herald of the softly curving shapes (Megaw 1971: pl. 1, 2) which were to become so essential in the ensuing Celtic art from the mid-fifth century BC onwards, the age of the chariot burials, when artwork became more flowing (Megaw 1971: pl. 1, 2, 6).

In the Hallstatt cemetery many juveniles were buried with their symbols of family rank, which suggests that in the eyes of the community they carried their status as a family inheritance, and that status was lineage-related (Hodson 1990: 89–90). This

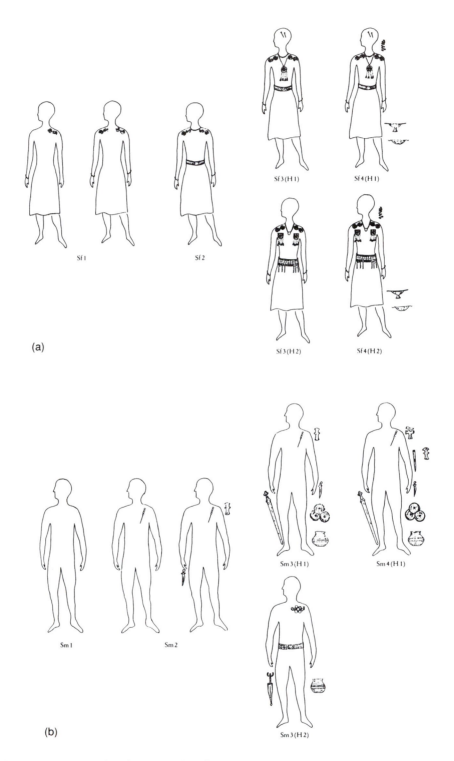

Figure 21.4 Hierarchic diagrams of (a) female and (b) male burials in the Hallstatt cemetery, sixth–fifth centuries BC. (After Hodson 1990: figs 19 and 20 (pp. 81, 83).

can be seen also in later Celtic cemeteries (e.g. Münsingen-Rain, Switzerland (Hodson 1968); Dürrnberg-Hallein (Pauli 1978). Hodson (1990: 90f.) estimates the ritually burying population here as about 400 at any one time, around its peak in the sixth century BC. He sees a small élite – salt-barons, both male and female, who controlled the mining and the trading of the salt – and a more numerous but still privileged group, and then a yet larger number who were allowed some sort of ritual burial.

There remains a non-ritually-burying residuum (comparable perhaps to the serf populations in England of AD 1086, some 15–20 per cent of total population (Darby *et al.* 1952–72, indices under 'serfs'). These people perhaps had no metal artwork, but their clothing might have been held with thongs and bone or wood pins, and some of their wood or bone knife and tool handles might be pleasingly shaped; such people were not always insensitive to graceful things.

Salt production was technologically much developed around 700 BC with a Europe-wide network, around the time of the beginning of the Hallstatt cemetery (Hodson 1985: 198 ff.). The decline of Hallstatt as a wealthy power in the later fifth century was probably also economic; the Dürrnberg-Hallein community farther to the west with its more easily accessible salt resources gradually took over the trade (Barth 1983; Pauli 1978).

Hodson has shown social ranking at burial by highlighting status-significant items such as wrist-rings, pin-and-coil head-dresses, belt- and shoulder-ornaments buried with the women (with gold and animal symbolism marking off an élite upper 5 per cent), and weaponry and other items of iron with the men (Hodson 1990: 99), imported luxury items such as sheet-bronze vessels, again marking off an upper élite. But were the armed men a deliberate force intended to protect the commercial value and safe passage of the distant salt trade? Or were the weapons (daggers particularly) more a mark of personal prestige (note Moscati *et al.* 1991: 84)? Some of the daggers at Hallstatt were probably locally made (Hodson 1990: 66; Sievers 1982: 24) but most were not, and Grave 555 shows that the salt-traders could draw upon the crack weaponsmiths of Swabia in the sixth–fifth centuries BC (Figure 21.5; Jope 1983), as well as the cista-makers of the Kurd area of Hungary (Stjernquist 1967; Jope and Jacobsthal in press: pl. 12 notes), and other graves (e.g. G696–7, 507) display the skills of the Este engravers (Megaw 1971: pl. 7; Jacobsthal 1944: pl. 59–60; Hodson 1990: 68–9).

Daggers were numerous in the Hallstatt cemetery (Kromer 1959, n. 67; Sievers 1982: pl. 8, 10, 55). They can be very instructive as prestige indicators, some worthy of a Hochdorf chief (Bittel *et al.*, 143, 1981: fig. 70). They were carried widely across Europe, as personal weapons, exchange gifts, or in pursuit of trade, and their ranking in the Hallstatt cemetery may be cautiously exploited (Figure 21.4; cf. Hodson 1985: 197, fig., quoting Barth's work).

One of the earliest daggers in the Hallstatt cemetery (a 'dirk' in Grave 555, about 650 BC; Sievers 1982: pl. 1.1) has a hand-grip of intricate construction made of very thin iron, exactly like that of a dagger from the Thames at Mortlake (Hodges, in Jope 1961: 309, 329–30, pl. XVII–XVIII). This kind of hilt construction seems to have been produced by the craft tradition of the Swabian area (Jope 1983).

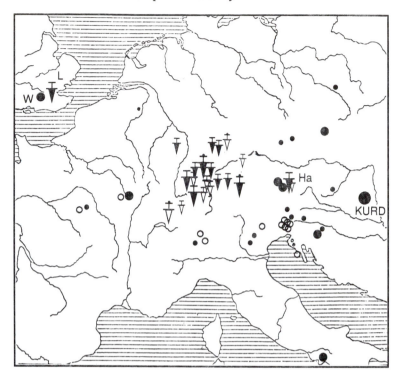

Key:
Iron daggers and bronze cordoned buckets with swing-handles.   Daggers with composite spindle-shaped handgrip (as from Mortlake and Hallstatt grave 555).   Other relevant broad-bladed daggers: with bi-cone ornaments: on sheaths; on pommel.   Cordoned swing-handle buckets, type as from Weybridge (Brooklands, Surrey) and Kurd, Hungary (after Stjernquist, with additions).   Cordoned buckets of closely related variant types. L, London (Mortlake); W, Weybridge (Surrey); Ha, Hallstatt, Austria. The concentrations of black in the Swabian area of the Upper Danube suggest the production area of daggers with these features. Large spot indicate numerous buckets.

Figure 21.5 Map showing distribution of iron daggers across Europe, late seventh–third centuries BC. Some of these daggers had been carried great distances, partly through the custom of prestige gift-exchange. (Jope 1983 with additions.)

This weapon from the Thames had, however, been carefully re-sheathed in the distinctive British manner (retaining just the top bar of the old sheath), with twin-loop suspension and fold-over bronze strips (Jope 1961: pl. XVII), as though handed on as a family possession, perhaps a mark of chieftaincy, a symbol of rank and perhaps of territorial domain. In Britain we have no cemeteries of this age, and it is quite possible that élite body-disposal might have been in some ways riverine (Jope 1961: 320–5; Bradley 1990; Torbrügge 1972; Cunliffe 1974: 269).

This dagger at once suggests that the social standing of some chiefs from the Thames valley lands of the seventh–sixth centuries BC would have been acceptable among the higher rankings of the Hallstatt community (e.g. Figure 21.4b, Sm3 (H2)), and that it was realized through a convention of distant prestige gift-exchange

(Kromer 1983). A sword from the London reaches of the Thames (Brailsford 1953: 60, 65, fig. 23.1; Sievers 1982: pl. 38.2; but note Stead 1984b), and the Weybridge (Brooklands) bucket (made probably in the Kurd region of Hungary, Jope and Jacobsthal in press: pl. 12 notes) are other pieces that might have travelled for the purpose of gift-exchange. This seems to speak of a prosperous southern Britain at this time in continental Celtic eyes. Further away in the north of Ireland the enigmatic two swans and three cygnets confronting two ravens on the Dunaverney flesh-hook could be additions to a native implement (Brailsford 1953: pl. IV; Jope and Jacobsthal in press: pl. 7, cf. Figure 21.6b; Spindler 1976: pl. 21) and are perhaps best explained as exotics coming by gift-exchange (as also the roundel from Danebury).

In Europe these daggers have come mostly from burials. In Britain, as we have noted, there are virtually no rich burials of this age and nearly all these daggers come from the Thames (or its tributaries). The Thames system has yielded twenty-seven iron daggers (some nearer 'dirks'), many with their sheathing of thin sheet- or strip-bronze, lined with wood (or bark), of the seventh to third centuries BC. Only two were imports, and one of these (from Mortlake), as we have noted, had been carefully re-sheathed in distinctive British manner, presumably as a prized family possession, to be passed on through the family line, as a symbol of rank and privilege and perhaps of specific territorial rights. At least ten of these Thames daggers might be seen as denoting rank comparable with the Mortlake piece. If we suggest that about 5–10 per cent of all the daggers made and used during this time-span might be known to us today (the Thames has been well dredged), this would mean that about 100–200 such daggers were made during these four centuries (say about five to ten dagger-chieftains per generation) for territory bordering on some 70 miles of the Thames (all seven of the earliest come from the east London reaches). This hints at something of the order of 500 square miles of varied terrain (some wooded, some open downland, other areas with water-meadow) as a chieftain's subtribal domain in the fifth–third centuries BC in southern Britain.

The seventeen daggers with the specifically British twin-loop suspension reveal a continuity of British armourers' craft practice along the Thames valley area, and hence of life style at chieftain level through four centuries. This is about the same time-span through which the hill-fort at Danebury 50 miles to the south has shown similar stable continuity of life (Cunliffe 1989: 199). It is difficult to surmise relations between chieftainry centred upon the Thames valley and a hill-fort community 50 miles away, but someone at Danebury in the fifth century BC does seem to have had a small openwork disc (Figure 21.6c), made in Celtic Europe (probably in the Taunus region north of Wiesbaden), which had probably graced a small cylindrical box of fine wood (Jope, in Cunliffe and Poole 1991: 331–2), which could have been a small prestige gift for a lady of rank commensurate with the Thames valley chieftain, and who, it seems, lived (at least part of the time) in Danebury (for its houses, see Cunliffe and Poole 1991). Another remarkable exotic piece of this age (which could also have been a prestige gift) is the Weybridge bucket, made probably in the Kurd region of Hungary (Jope and Jacobsthal in press: pl. 12; cf. Hodson 1990: pl. 18–19).

There are only three other examples of this distinctively British Thames dagger-sheath with twin-loop suspension outside the Thames area, one from upland peat in

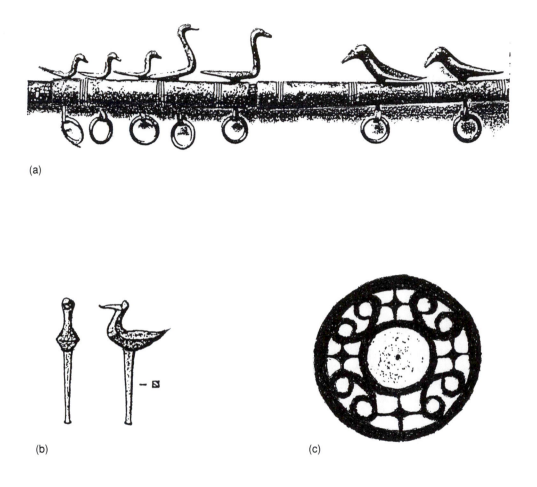

(a)

(b)   (c)

Figure 21.6 Possible prestige exchange gifts: (a) Flesh-hook of bronze, from Dunaverney, Co. Antrim, Northern Ireland: sixth century BC. The five swans, cygnets and ravens seem separately added through newly made holes in the shaft; they are quite unusual in the British Isles at such a date: they seem to have been added to this native type of flesh-hook, and perhaps they came by gift-exchange from Celtic Europe; (b) shows a similar bird (to be similarly fitted) from the princely burial at the Magdalenenberg, in the Black Forest; (c) Bronze openwork disc, 9 cm across, from Danebury, Hants; probably of Continental making, later fifth to earlier fourth centuries BC. The only means of attachment is a very slender pin at centre, which suggests it may have been the central mount on the top of a trinket box of very fine wood, the fineness of the pin intended to avoid splitting the wood (no sign of resin to hold it in place was detected). Such a piece might well have been a prestige gift to a lady of rank. ((a) Photo: British Museum; *c* 1:2; (b) Spindler 1976: pl. 2; (c) E.M. Jope)

Somerset (Jope 1961: 311, 336; Stead 1984a), another from 'Hertford Warren' near Saffron Walden in Suffolk (with analogies for the dagger hand-grip across the North Sea; Clarke and Hawkes 1955: 200f., 208, 226; Jope and Jacobsthal in press: pl. 22), and one in Belgium (Marien 1963). Perhaps exchange gifts are again a likely explanation for these exotic pieces. Much, indeed, could be said about the distant human relationships implied by such items as the Mortlake dagger.

We still do not know where any British dagger-chief had a *Herrensitz* or what his residence might have been like (but see p. 393), or his relations with hill-forts; the Heath Row 'temple' was presumably not a residence, but there might have been one nearby. The occupation site near the find-spot of the Weybridge bucket (cf. Moscati *et al.* 1991: 84) certainly merits further exploration for such evidence.

So we see how in several ways the daggers and other artwork can shed light on the social infrastructure of Celtic Britain in the seventh to second centuries BC.

In the latter years of the Hallstatt cemetery, in the later fifth century BC, there is one of the finest Celtic long swords with decorated scabbard, with a lively scene of warriors, clearly showing its Atestine sources as well as Celtic items of dress (Megaw 1971: pl.; Jacobsthal 1944: pl. 60). Fighting prowess was so much admired among Celtic peoples that fine swords might be expected to reveal some social grading. Such long swords with ornate scabbards must have denoted high rank (e.g. the armed medical specialist of the small Obermenzing family burial-ground (Megaw and Megaw 1989: pl.; Megaw 1971: 17; de Navarro 1955; Moscati *et al.* 1991: 372f.), but it seems hardly possible to discern any widely accepted sword protocol (Pleiner 1993: 35–70). The wide dispersal across the Celtic world (and through a long time span) of scabbards with dragon- or bird-pairs at the head (Megaw 1971: pl. 16) we might like to associate with mercenary activity, but this cannot be justified (Stead 1984b; Megaw and Megaw 1989: 99f.; Moscati *et al.* 1991: 333–6). The emergence of the belt-chain sword suspension systems in the third century BC (Moscati *et al.* 1991: 324–7) is really a manifestation of the upper-middle class levelling of Celtic noble society.

The social patterns of Celtic Europe changed greatly during the sixth–second centuries BC. The swaggering Celtic nobility gave way in the fifth–fourth centuries to less prodigiously wealthy chiefs (but still often buried with a chariot), and Duval 1986: 21) feels already able to write of 'peaceful village chieftains'. Even this more modest wealth steadily became plebeianized in the fourth–third centuries: we see the growth of large mainly middle-class cemeteries, e.g. Münsingen-Rain (Hodson 1968); they were highly organized, of almost urban character, yet apparently serving a scattered rural population, the artwork plainly showing their middle-class bourgeois manners. Yet we know almost nothing of their dwellings; perhaps these cemeteries provided the places (and occasions) for such a rural population to meet.

During the second century BC the well-fortified quasi-urban settlements, the oppida, proliferated over Celtic Europe; we really know little of how these grew up. Manching is too large a site to clarify this problem by itself. Their existence seems based on industry and trade – was the ritual bough with gold leaves at Manching (Moscati *et al.* 1991: 530) a 'civic' emblem? A smaller site might be more informative on origins, such as Pont Maure, a small rectangular enclosure in the Corrèze, but with nevertheless some show of distant trade: Campanian glossy black ware (Ward Perkins 1941: 49–51, 79–81), and part of a La Tène iron brooch (identified by the author while working on site and finds with the excavator, N. Lucas-Shadwell, in 1938); this brooch must have come from far away to the north-east (cf. the Dux-type brooch with Agris helmet (Moscati *et al.* 1991: 292). Then we still need to know much more about oppidan relations with the hinterland, in economy and cultural matters (see Nash 1976: 111–14). They do seem to have consolidated Celtic Europe into a politically viable pattern of tribal territories, as Caesar later recognized, and as the coinage (its art charged with meanings) can demonstrate.

SOCIAL LEVELS, ARTWORK AND HABITATION MODES

We must now enquire into the life style and dwellings of the various levels in Celtic communities which we have sampled so far only through burial evidence, so little of which in Celtic Europe can be directly related to any feeder habitation sites. Many of those burials have shown rich and excellent artwork, stylistically distinctively Celtic.

At Hallstatt itself we as yet know nothing of the habitations in which these prosperous salt-producing and salt-trading people lived through three centuries (as the cemetery shows). Were the dwellings grouped, or scattered among this precipitious inaccessible mountain terrain? The same lack of relation between cemeteries and habitations is largely true for most of Celtic Europe until the second century BC, with a few possible exceptions in areas of north Italic contact, directly influenced by the ways of the southerly world (Moscati *et al.* 1991: 220–30; see also Sopron, Hungary, ibid.: 379). The problem is seen at its most acute for the Hohenasperg (north of Stuttgart), where a core defensive habitation site has to be inferred from the ring of rich burials ranged within some 10 km round the eminence (e.g. Klein Aspergle (Jacobsthal 1944: pl. 16–17, 26–7)), and Greifenbühl with the clothing embroidered with gold thread (Bittel *et al.* 1981: 390–3; Moscati *et al.* 1991: 108–13; Frankenstein and Rowlands 1978: 98–103), or the luxury silks of Hohmichele (Hundt 1969), and Hochdorf-Eberdingen with the nine drinking-horns (Bittel *et al.* 1981: 395–8; Moscati *et al.* 1991: 86). The suggestion that the Hohenasperg chieftains commanded territory from the Black Forest and the Schwäbischen Wald to the Albvorland may be not unreasonable, but it is quite suppositious (Moscati *et al.* 1991: 113; Frankenstein and Rowlands 1978: 98–103).

But where did this swaggering élite of the sixth–fifth-century 'princely' tombs such as Hochdorf or Vix (Moscati *et al.* 1991: 103–7) actually live? Their precise relations with nearby fortresses such as the Heuneburg or Mont Lassois are still largely inferred, though reasonable in the light of items such as the Heuneburg gold strainer (Bittel *et al.* 1981: fig. 265). However, burial mound IV, 200 m north of the Heuneburg, proved to have been piled up over the remains of a rectangular, three-chambered plank-built structure, which with two hearths and an oven (all set inside a lightly palisaded enclosure) might well have been just such a dwelling (Figure 21.7). It had been burnt before the 4 m-square burial chamber had been dug within it, and would have been modest living accommodation for what Zürn (1970: 108) saw as the

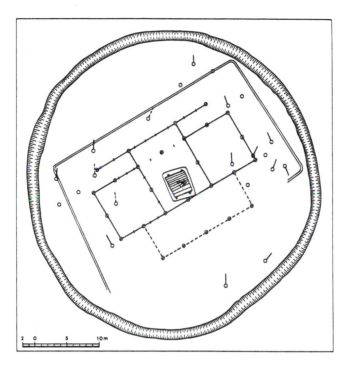

Figure 21.7 Plan of chieftainly residence under Talhau mound IV, close by the Heuneburg. (From Bittel *et al.* 1981: 124.)

Sitz (residence) of a subchief (Bittel *et al.* 1981: 294–5), whose insignia might have been a fine dagger (cf. Moscati *et al.* 1991: 79, 84). Indeed it is quite spacious compared with the private quarters appropriate to a medieval knight (e.g. Jope and Threlfall 1959: 270–3; Jope in Colvin 1963: 129f.). The stone house at Ascot Doilly was built in the early thirteenth century AD, probably as a short-stay residence for the use of the d'Oilli family and of their successors, the earls of Warwick (Jope and Threlfall 1959: 223, 224, 214). This is an instructive example of how the detailed interlocking of medieval archaeological and documentary evidence can be used by analogy to help interpret the evidence of prehistoric archaeology. The overlord of the supposed Celtic subchief at the Heuneburg was perhaps the individual buried in mound IV with appropriate honours such as gold items and a vehicle. Whether such a subchief had additional personal accommodation within the fortress we may never know. The prime overlord must surely have had some establishment a little more like a *palatium*.

Another *Herrensitz* (chief's dwelling) of this age (early fifth century BC) was found at Kyberg just south of Munich (Pätzold 1963). A palisaded enclosure about 80 m square was set on the end of a spur; there were several short-lived building phases; in a later phase was a half-sunk house 6 × 7 m. But there were few objects.

The site still most quoted as an early Celtic chieftain's dwelling (*Herrensitz*) is the Goldberg, on a 100 ft rise near Aalen, 60 km east of Stuttgart, well known through the plan Bersu gave to Childe (Childe 1950: 224; Piggott 1965: 199–200; cf. Bittel *et al.* 1981: 451–2; Schröter 1975). This level hilltop had been occupied from Neolithic times (Goldberg I–III), and again systematically during the early sixth–fifth centuries BC (Goldberg IV), and later (Goldberg V), as Bersu's plans and publications (1911–31) showed. Bersu's own interpretations of his evidence have never been presented, but have now been assembled (Jope 1995), through the kind collaboration of Dr C.A. Ralegh Radford, who had discussed the evidence in detail with Gerhard Bersu from 1932 onwards (I had also discussed it with him in the early 1950s). All this is here summarized, to give a realistic view of Goldberg IV, fifth–sixth centuries BC.

The plan in Childe (1950: 224) runs together all the evidence for Goldberg IV, but the plan itself is composite, and Bersu's evidence confirms this. The 'citadel' area is of primary interest: Bersu saw building 2 (phase IVA) as a post-built tower 13 m square outside (timber posts 1 m across in very deep holes); but a 'tower' would have been at least 13 m high, needing 14 m tree-trunks at 1 m thick, weighing some 7 tons. A hefty stockade some 4 m high is more likely (and note the 4 m-wide ground level entrance). In phase IVB the massive timbers were removed from their sockets and an earth 'wall' made around the whole settlement, covering the 'stockade' position; and some of its material had fallen into the recently emptied stockade post-holes. At this time a post-built ridge 'hall' (10 × 6 m inside) was put up (perhaps re-using the stockade posts), and outside it an oblong entrance complex with projecting entrance structure, the foundation trenches of its enclosures all ending abruptly at what must have been the inner line of the new 'wall' (IVB). Stockade and hall were thus not existing together.

The 'Holz und Erde Mauer' probably had a timber outer facing (any evidence of postholes and slots has now slid down the hillsides); along this inner face were very few postholes, so there was probably no vertical inner face, only a sloping bank.

In the interior were oblong post-built houses of this age (phase IV, so judged by Bersu from pottery and metalwork fragments): some were probably of retainers (e.g. with hearths), others for storage. These structures were not all standing at the same time. Some lay under the line of the defensive wall and must therefore be assigned to IVA (e.g. 17, very like the 'ridge-hall', 1, of IVB). Some buildings were clearly succeeded by others (e.g. 43 replaced 42, and others similarly by analogy). A few groups look as though they had grown by accumulation (e.g. 32–7). On our two plans houses have thus been accorded to IVA and IVB, though rebuilding will not necessarily all have been done at exactly the same time (Figure 21.8). Bersu judged that these timber structures had a short life, thirty years or less, being entirely replaced when dilapidated rather than repaired. This house-building tradition persisted long, at least from IVA through into Middle La Tène (Bersu 1930).

Dating for IVA and IVB rests on Bersu's assessment of pottery and metal fragments, seen now in the light of more up-to-date chronologies. While there was a little use of the hilltop in Ha C (Schröter 1975: 111, fig. 14, no. 13), the bulk of IVA and IVB seems to lie within the later sixth to early fifth centuries. 'Metalwork did not well survive on this site' and the better of the brooches, now labelled 'Goldberg' in museums, probably did not come directly from the settlement itself (e.g. the 'snake', Mansfeld 1973: 170 (note also 185); Bittel *et al.* 1981: 452). But Bersu knew (and photographed) many of these, and had reason to believe that they came from a burial

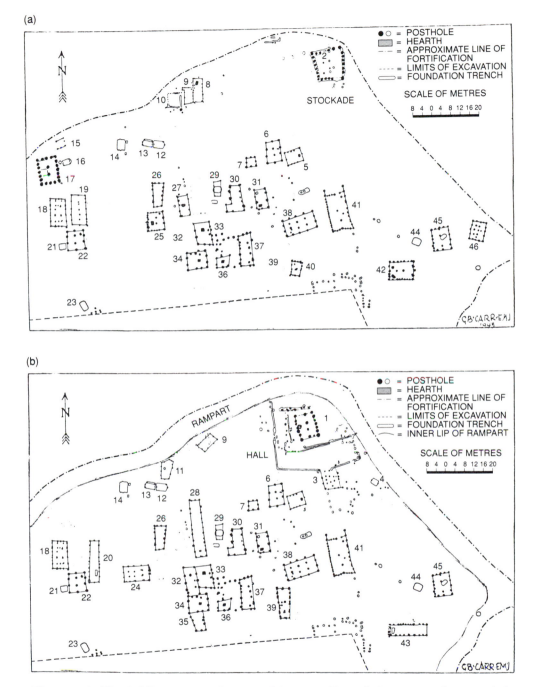

Figure 21.8 The Goldberg, near Aalen, east of Stuttgart. Plans of phases IVA and IVB: (a) sixth century BC; (b) later sixth to early fifth century BC. Probably the residence of an early Celtic subchief. (Worked from Childe 1950: 224, with the collaboration of C.A. Ralegh Radford.)

site very close by, excavated privately but without proper record, probably the burial-ground of a leading Goldberg family; no 'princely tomb' is known that we can associate with the Goldberg settlement.

Bersu considered that at Goldberg he was dealing with the *Herrensitz* of a subchief (no higher); but it had in the German press of 1935 been dubbed *Führenpalast*, a status dangerous for him to refute at that time. We have here evidence of a person whose cloak was held with a single snake brooch (no matching pair); he might have carried a dagger such as in G116 at Hallstatt (a male grave which had a snake-bow brooch, Hodson 1990: 107, 118, 83, fig. 14, showing its Sm2/Sm3 mid-range status, Figure 21.4), or as in the male burial at Wolfegg in Bavaria, with its snake brooch and belt-plate (Hundt in Rieth 1969: 18–23; Sievers 1982: pl. 44, 45). It is thus through such artwork that we are able to place the social level of the Goldberg hierarchy – who evidently had command of the local timber resources.

In the IVA–IVB change from isolated strong 'stockade' to hall-with-enclosures in the 'citadel' area, we may perhaps see a significant change in social outlook, from personal defence to more organized administration of the community, which Radford (pers. comm.) would suggest as the spread of the 'acropolis' concept into 'barbarian' Europe.

Current work in Bohemia is also revealing sites of chiefs' dwellings of the later fifth century, the beginning of the age of chariot burials. At Drougkovice in north-west Bohemia is a stoutly timber-palisaded enclosure 90 m square, with a small oblong enclosure off one corner, at one end of which was an unpretentious half-sunk house 7 × 6.5 m, which did, however, provide a very small bronze model dog with head turned back biting at a ram's head (Smorz, in Moscati *et al.* 1991: 185). This model dog gives a clue to the standing of people using this place, for the stylistic comparanda are many of them from rich chariot burials (Jacobsthal 1944: nos. 289–318). Low soil phosphate suggests, however, that the site was not used very intensively, perhaps intermittently, as might befit this rather unlordly house, the chief moving round with his retainers between several such houses. The courtyards might have housed the retainers for short stays in tents, for such were widely used even for royal retinues on the move in medieval times (e.g. Edward I in Scotland. (Jope *et al.* 1952: 118) and the Field of the Cloth of Gold in France in 1520 (Harvey 1947: pl. 159).

In Britain, by contrast with Celtic Europe, we have almost no cemeteries for the sixth–second centuries BC (except for Yorkshire and the south-west: see below) and modes of body disposal are a problem (see Chapter 29), but instead a range of informative habitation sites (Cunliffe 1974: chs 11 and 12). Most people living in such a rural population may have had little time for real art, but their visual taste can be detected, mainly in pottery, bone, wood, leather and textiles (of which latter a little high-class material is preserved, e.g. Crowfoot, in Stead 1991a; and refs in Stead 1991a: 232). At the top of the scale we are just beginning to recognize the kinds of dwellings lived in by the chieftain class in Britain and Ireland.

Many sites are *Einzelhofe* (single dwellings), but many clusters ('villages') are also known. Almost all dwellings were round (or oval), though there is some evidence for oblong buildings in hill-forts (e.g. Crickley Hill, Glos. (Dixon 1976: 172–4, figs 2, 8).

Some socially informative artwork does survive, some even in meaningful contexts, on habitation sites. In Yorkshire, at Staple Howe, a small oval enclosure on a hill-top had round or oval houses about 8 m across, in one of which someone had left two razors (sixth–fifth centuries BC), one bronze – an exotic from across the North Sea – the other a native piece (Brewster 1963; Piggott 1965: 199; Cunliffe 1974: 204–5, fig. 133). This gives some idea of a minor chief's accommodation towards the north of Britain at this time, the exotic iron razor perhaps an item of prestige gift-exchange. At Coygan, on the south-west coast of Wales, a small defended pro-montory was a farmstead from the fourth century BC; the pair of simple bronze arm-rings might by European Celtic standards suggest a lady of modest rank, a member of the family who controlled this coastal farming estate in the third century BC (Wainwright 1967: 83–5; cf. a lady buried at Trevone on the opposite north Cornish coast: Dudley and Jope 1965).

Little Woodbury in Wiltshire, a ring-work whose interior was fully excavated by Bersu 1940) had a substantial round house 13 m across, producing an iron ring-headed pin and iron brooch of the third century BC (Brailsford 1949: 165) and good pottery; it was set one among a group of prosperous farmsteads (but with very modest artwork), developing in use through some ten generations (Harding 1974: 21–3). At Gussage All Saints in Dorset, inhabitants from the third century BC secured their clothing with simple brooches; but here in the later second–first centuries BC some intensive bronze-founding was producing items of horse and vehicle harness (Spratling in Wainwright 1979; Foster 1980) which ranks with that of the Yorkshire chariot-burial chieftains with their display swords (see pp. 394–5), thereby revealing Gussage as probably an establishment of chieftain class. We should, however, be cautious in not too readily upgrading farmsteads of this kind without specific evidence (e.g. Harding 1974: 21–7; Pimperne, Harding and Blake 1993, Little Woodbury, etc.). Gussage illustrates the kind of evidence needed to upgrade to higher rank; note also the refined balance-arm which the metal-workers at Gussage were using (Wainwright 1979; cf. Stradonice in Moscati *et al.* 1991: 541).

A mirror with decorated back must have been a fine possession for a British lady in the early first century AD. These mirrors are mostly confined to Britain, from the later first century BC for about a century, and those with decorated backs seem to recall faraway Etruscan ways of some centuries earlier. They have nearly all been found in burials, but one of the finest and heaviest, from Holcombe near Lyme Regis in south Devon, gives a rare instance of such a mirror in domestic context, for it must be associated with the native house underlying the romanized farm (Fox and Pollard 1973; Jope and Jacobsthal in press, pls 236–55).

The rivers among the extensive farmlands of the upper Thames have yielded fine daggers and swords of the fourth–first centuries BC (Jope 1961; Jope and Jacobsthal in press:, pls 12–27; Harding 1972). These may in fact be part of a body-disposal custom (see p. 384), the men who owned these weapons actually living as residents up on the chalk rather than on the damp river-plain. A group of horse and vehicle gear at Hagbourne, on the chalk (Harding 1972: 41, 91; Leeds 1933: 133, 124), suggests that it is up there that the chieftainly residences should be sought, even among the hill-forts (cf. Hod Hill, Dorset (Richmond 1968: 21ff., figs 12–14). Hill-forts imply high-ranking leadership and organization of manpower and material resources (note also Cherbury camp, with its marshland defences down in the plain (Bradford 1940; Arkell 1939)).

Horse and vehicle gear similar to that being made by the mobile workers at Gussage (note the distribution of the types to the north-west as far as Yorkshire) can be found in context in hill-forts. At Hod Hill in Dorset, terrets were found as though once hanging at the entrances to oblong huts (Richmond 1968: 20, fig. 13; Piggott 1986: 27); but these houses were not necessarily those of the charioteers – they may have been those of men of more like ostler ranking. Richmond argued that huts 36A–37 were a chief's group as they had attracted concentrated ballista-fire (Richmond 1968: 21f., fig. 14, and pers. comm.). It seems clear that extensive excavation of hill-fort interiors (cf. Danebury; Cunliffe 1986) is needed to clarify Celtic social organization of the sixth century BC to first century AD.

In Somerset, the Glastonbury and Meare lakeside clustered settlements of the third–first centuries BC seem again to have been specialized production communities, Glastonbury for agricultural products, Meare more for industrial ones (especially vitreous materials); but each has its individual ceramic tradition, and both are most valuable for their well-preserved organic materials (Earwood 1993; Harding 1974: 35–6; Henderson 1989). There must be more such sites, but, as usual for Britain, we have no hint of cemeteries used by these communities of, say, a dozen or more families at any one time. It is difficult to interpret artwork at Meare, where items may be slightly faulty in making, or for reuse, rather than in current use by inhabitants. Glastonbury may be better as evidence, with daggers, many brooches, horse and vehicle gear comparable with Gussage and that of the Yorkshire chieftains (see pp. 383, 395); both these lakeside sites are of great value for their well-preserved organic materials, which are now providing valuable, fairly precise dating evidence for pieces of artwork (e.g. wooden statuettes (cf. Megaw 1971: pl. 12) and bowls (Jope and Jacobsthal in press: pl. 313).

In Gaul, Duval (1986) feels able to speak of 'peaceful village chieftains' already by the fifth century BC, and the flamboyant society was beginning to become plebeianized, based more on a people's economy, all gradually working towards the oppida. Among smaller grouped settlements some may have had the necessary corporate organization to merit the term 'village', though this is difficult to show from purely archaeological evidence. It is most clearly to be seen in immediately pre-Roman Britain, and in Gaul a century earlier (Rivet 1958; Hallam 1964), the position perhaps rather obscured by the 'villa-estate' system of the Roman world. In the Celtic world the nobility were presumably countrymen – Rome tried to make them townsmen, with limited success; only in the fourth century in Britain do we see the real luxurious villas, the homes of the *curiales* and repositories of fine art, such as the group centred on Cirencester, a provincial capital with rich town houses (Rivet 1958; Toynbee 1964: 86–7, 145 ff.). Under Roman administration we can see the character of Celtic Britain changing.

In mid-Yorkshire we have one region where cemeteries and coeval settlements of the fourth–second centuries BC lie closely together (Dent 1982, 1985; Stead 1991a). At and around Wetwang and adjacent Kirkburn are cemeteries, large and small, of uniformly middle-ranking people with their monotonously uniform iron involute brooches (Dent 1990), but with a few much more special entombments of the nobility standing aloof. Two young men had been buried with 'carts' and their magnificent (but locally made) swords in their scabbards with red enamel embellishment, of the third century BC. These men had been laid on either side of the tomb of a youngish lady, who had a small cylindrical box of sheet-bronze with line ornament exactly like that on the men's scabbards, a family group (Dent 1985). One small detail, the central wavy relief ring on top of the bean-box, links this nobility with the great Wandsworth and Lincolnshire shields, among the finest displays of aristocratic wealth in third–second century Britain. Only a quarter of a mile away another man had been buried with similar fine sword and covered by a chain-mail tunic (placed upside-down), not a local product and most likely a prestige gift from a potentate visiting from a distance, even perhaps from east Celtic lands (cf. Ciumeşti, Romania: Rusu 1969; Stead 1991a: 54–6). But why should such a potentate visit a Yorkshire chief? Do we see here the early rise of the Yorkshire wool and cloth trade (Crowfoot, in Stead 1991a: 119–22), or was there some other staple source of Yorkshire wealth, such as horse-breeding? But much further research is still needed to show the kind of houses in which this Yorkshire Celtic aristocracy actually lived.

These examples are enough to illustrate how artworks can show the interrelations between the Celtic aristocracy and their various kinds of residence, temporary or less so, in the country, in hill-forts or oppida; they have shown us chiefs and their retainers on the move, the relation between their sumptuous tombs, their artwork and their living quarters.

ROMANIZATION OF THE CELTIC WORLD

As in Gaul a century earlier, so in Britain from the mid-first century AD onwards, expression of Celtic self-awareness was curbed, and some Gauls and Britons would no doubt have wished to be seen as much abreast of new life styles from the southerly world as wedded to old Celtic ways. Their dress and eating habits saw some changes, with better class utensils and crockery (platters, from which few Britons had previously taken their food). But even then there were under-currents of resistance to change: at Colchester, for instance, at the Sheepen site the old huts seem to have been left standing through the 40s and 60s and occupied by natives (probably as a source of labour for the citizens of the nearby Roman *colonia* (started in AD 49). But though they increasingly used good crockery and had some table- and window-glass (Hawkes and Hull 1947: *passim*), the food-refuse bones are mostly cattle, and old butchering habits show that the British had retained their old eating ways (H.M. Jope 1984). Here we see the fluctuations of personal taste in visual art (mainly ceramic) in relation to lifestyle operating in day-to-day life.

In both Gaul and Britain 'Celticity' had a subtle persuasive influence on Roman provincial artistic work (as indeed it must have done in more easterly Celtic provinces). We see this in the Bath gorgon (Cunliffe and Davenport 1985; Toynbee 1962: 161–4; 1964: 130–3), in capitals at Cirencester (Toynbee 1962: 165, pl. 97–100) or among the rural temples of Gaul and Britain. A stone head from Corbridge in Northumberland, second–third century AD (Figure 21.12; Toynbee 1962: 146, pl. 49) shows well how in Roman Britain people who esteemed themselves 'Celtic' could cherish their identity visually, for nothing could have been less acceptable to real Roman visual taste than this hyper-fastidious face, more subtly sensitive than anything purely Roman (cf. the Wandsworth 'mask' shield, Figure 21.2). The strength of surviving feeling for old Celtic ways is summed up in the head of an antlered god with torques hanging from its antlers, named Cernunnos, on an altar found beneath Nôtre Dame in Paris (Brogan 1955: 173, pl. 47a). And not for nothing did the outlaws in Gaul in the 280s band together, choosing a Celtic title Bagaudae, 'the valiant'.

In rural Roman Britain many Britons continued to live in round-houses, as *Einzelhofe*, or grouped in more communal settlements or hill-forts, and occasional pieces of artwork tell us something about the status and lifestyle of inhabitants. At Coygan on the south-west Welsh coast (where we have already looked at earlier inhabitants, see p. 393) a round-house on a defended promontory (first used in the third–second century BC, see above p. 393) yielded from second–third century AD occupation debris a simple iron dagger with ball hand-grip (Wainwright 1967) and a small twisted double-snake bead of bronze, apparently from a collar of Lambay type (Jope and Jacobsthal in press: pls 259–61; cf. Beswick *et al.* 1990), showing such 'lairds' at home with their status markers in immediate context. And the inhabitants of a small rural establishment at Lower Slaughter in fourth-century Gloucestershire did at least have table- and window-glass, and two fine little statuettes hidden away in a nook with three little altars to show their rustic taste; and votive tablets were in a well filling (O'Neil 1961; note that the famed earliest of the ogams (Chapter 37) came from a well of this age at Silchester).

In Caledonia, for instance, romanization did not penetrate very deeply into the ways of a native society, which might retain old individual ways. Terrets, the rein-guide rings on paired-draught vehicles, could illustrate this, for during the second-third centuries AD a group of distinctive designs (e.g. 'Donside'; Simpson 1943: 78-9; Jope and Jacobsthal in press: pl. 291) have a distribution extending northwards far beyond any other items of evidence for wheeled vehicle use at this time (linchpins, bridle-bits, etc.). There terrets must therefore presumably have been non-functional (and indeed some have little brazed-on loops for hanging), but emblematic of some legal rights, e.g. territorial, hunting or judicial (Jope and Jacobsthal in press: pl. 291 notes), giving at last a window on the ways of old Celtic administration in a pre-literate society.

The art of writing was itself a mark of social distinction (Prosdocimi and Kruta, in Moscati *et al.* 1991: 51–9, 491–8) in Celtic Europe, to be found from the third century BC onwards. In Britain there was little evidence of it before romanization, for coins hardly counted in this context.

SOCIAL CHANGE INTO THE FIRST MILLENNIUM AD

We must now see what continental Celtic art can tell us about the changing social life and structure during the first six centuries of the Christian era. Celtic lands and life, once autonomous, were much eroded by Roman domination, first in Gaul (from early first century BC) and the rest of Europe, then in Britain from AD 43 onwards, leaving unromanized only Ireland and parts of Wales, northern Britain, Brittany, and probably small pockets almost anywhere in old Celtic lands, though it is clear that by later Roman times Britain had developed its own high level of higher culture (Henig 1989: 14–19).

Christianization largely robs us of a main source of evidence, for deposition of grave goods receded to almost nothing among Christian communities. Harden (1955: 134, 157) notes what a disadvantage this is for glass studies, and east–west oriented inhumation graves, with no grave goods, can be found (e.g. at Cologne) by the mid-second century (Krämer 1958: 329–39). But Christianity changed social outlook in subtler ways: poverty became a virtue, and much private wealth was channelled into the hands of the church, creating a dichotomy of aristocracy, the ecclesiastic probably stronger than that achieved by priestly classes among pagan Celtic communities. Without our documentary records it would be difficult to give a true account of this new sociological situation; here artwork can, however, still help considerably (Alcock 1963, 1982; Bruce-Mitford 1989: 189).

The Celtic peoples who had been suppressed or thrust out of Europe by Roman power were by the sixth century creeping back in a different guise, as evangelists of Christianity and of the ancient traditions of scholarship. For both, artwork was a potent agent. Art can mark the change with great eloquence; by the late sixth century Clovis's grandson Chilperic appeared as Apollo (with lyre) on a portal of Nôtre Dame; the model was perhaps a Gaulish coin or medallion (Brogan, 1953: 188–9). About 590, Columbanus, a monk of Bangor on Belfast Lough on the north-east coast of Ireland, travelled into Europe and set up a monastery first at Luxeuil (in the remains of a Roman spa), to thrive and become a spiritual centre in eastern Gaul. He moved on over the Alps to Bobbio (south of Milan), where he founded a monastery and died in 615. Bobbio was one of the great early centres of manuscript art and this connection with Ireland was bound to be fruitful.

In Britain in later Roman times social information can still be extracted from artworks left on habitation sites. The continuing elaboration of dress-pins suggests the persistence of the cloak rather than brooch-held dress: indeed, the elaborate brooches were worn more as marks of rank and social position, as set out in the Irish Laws (Henry 1965: 102). Evidence accumulates to show the attire of those who lived in the residences and strongholds in the middle part of the first millennium AD; Figure 21.9 shows a fine one-piece shoe of thin leather that once walked the neatly split oak boards lying on hazel wattle-work in the fifth to seventh centuries AD at Dundarn at the head of Strathearn in Perthshire, the capital of the Pictish province of Fortrenn (Alcock *et al.* 1989: 189ff. esp 200, 217–19; for the high status of shoes in earlier Celtic contexts see Hochdorf, Moscati *et al.* 1991: 108).

Above all, Ireland, never romanized, must show the continuity through from the pagan to the Celtic Christian world. In pagan context the horse and vehicle gear show us a chieftaincy with its processionals (note the uniquely Irish leading pieces: Jope, 1955: 38; Raftery 1982: figs 47–80, 95–8) passing imperceptibly into the Christian tradition as seen on the art of crosses from the seventh century onwards (Chapter 37). One cross (Henry 1965: pl. 79) shows such processions more in a Christian context.

With the rise of pen and brushwork on vellum, art among Celtic communities of

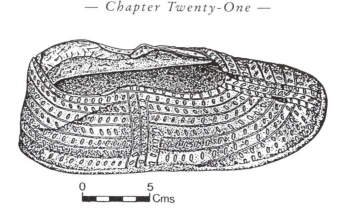

0   5
Cms

Figure 21.9 Openwork leather shoe. Sixth–seventh century AD; 23.5 cm long. (Alcock *et al.* 1989: 219.)

the fifth–seventh centuries AD was brought more within the orbit of early Christian scholarly life, and we can see the Lindisfarne *scriptorium* as a working unit, where the master Eadfrith produced the Lindisfarne Gospels in the early eighth century (Bruce-Mitford 1989: 184–6). Eadfrith by his name was no Celt; yet the Celtic and Saxon traditions can be seen cheek by jowl in symbols and craft traditions already on the Sutton Hoo hanging-bowls (Bruce-Mitford 1972: 85–6). Nearby, at Burgh, was Irish missionary influence and surely there must have been also an eclectic atelier that could use both garnet and millefiori settings and produce the jewelry and hanging-bowls and their escutcheon settings, so deeply eloquent of old Celtic tradition.

The material evidence seems only rarely to reveal the occupation of a Celt (but note Sopron, Hungary; Piggott 1965: 197–9), though we may learn the profession of the bearer of the Obermenzing sword (Figure 30:3, from a grave in a small family cemetery of the third century BC near Munich), who was a medical man with many specialized implements implying up-to-the-minute contact with Alexandrian practice (de Navarro 1955; Moscati *et al.* 1991: 269, 372–3). Celtic artists sometimes had an intellectual bent, as shown for instance by the sense of space into which the water-birds rise obliquely, created by the workers of the Wandsworth shield roundel in the second century BC (Jope 1978: 54, pl. 7; Jope and Jacobsthal in press: pl. 68–70), or the wit of the Aylesford pantomime horses (Jope 1983), or the esoteric designs on British mirror-backs (Jope 1987: 106–10). Celtic intellectual independence is well shown by the Coligny calendar, of the second century BC (Moscati *et al.* 1991: 25, 494–5).

And what of the standing of art workers themselves in Celtic society? Many would be no more than artisans, but a few had held a more special place. Moneyers could name themselves on their coins, for fiscal purposes. For a time a swordsmith (or his workshop) was marking KORISIOS (in Greek letters) at the head of the blade (Megaw 1971: 191–2, nos. 190–3). Rarely, a brooch-maker might give his name, and a skillet-maker gives a very Celtic name BODVOGENUS in the early first century AD (Toynbee 1964: 320, pl. LXXV). A bronzeworker might in the second century AD even take part alongside the patrons in presentation of a work (Toynbee 1962: 131, pl. 19, no. 16). And with some of the finer, wittier pieces (e.g. Figure 21.2; Megaw

1971: 16, 15; Jacobsthal 1944: pls. 70, 101, 111) it is difficult not to see artist and patron relaxing in mutual enjoyment over the result.

The craft thus took its place in developing design for use at all social levels, and had thus a socially moulding role. We now devote a few pages to exploring this theme at practical levels.

TECHNIQUE, DESIGN AND ARTISTRY 600 BC–AD 600: THE CRAFT CONTRIBUTION TO SOCIAL LIFE

These three were closely interlinked in the output of Celtic craftsmen and artworkers, who were making luxury goods as well as utility equipment. Manipulation of materials sometimes preferentially promotes particular shapes, which may then get fossilized in a different material. Some horse-bits of the first century BC, and later, illustrate this: the sidelinks were made first in wrought iron, bent over and welded, leaving a small projection; such bit designs were then made in cast bronze (from a wax model and clay mould); play with the junction (now a solid bronze casting) has yielded a variety of bird-bills (Jope 1950; Scott 1991: 3–4), which must have led an Irish craftsman to try a few rare essays in anthropic faces (Raftery 1983). Something similar, though involving only bronze, must have led, in the early fifth century Celtic heartlands, to the attractive bird-head brooch designs (Jacobsthal 1944: pl. 153–9).

This influence of technique on design is illustrated even more instructively in the developing design of the chapes made to protect the tips of dagger sheaths and sword scabbards during the sixth to third centuries BC. Here we can see how experiment with loose-part constructions of iron and bronze (composite chapes), as guy-wires or twisted strips, gradually consolidated the structure into one-piece units of cast bronze (Figure 21.10), to give the basic design for one particular type of early La Tène chape, one which pervaded most of the Celtic world during the fifth–third centuries BC. Figure 21.11 shows how this experimental phase began among the armourers of the headwater lands of the rivers Aisne and Marne in the fifth century BC (Jope 1974). The map further shows how this design, consolidated as a one-piece construction, spread during some two centuries through much of the then Celtic world, to Hungary in the east, and Ireland in the west (Jope and Jacobsthal, in press, 51). Rarely do we have the birth and evolution of a cultural type set out before us so fully and with such clarity.

In a lesser way, armourers of middle Europe in the third century BC devised an ingenious sword suspension-chain system, allowing the body to twist freely in fighting, and they exploited the technical processes of hammering the links and texturing them with punchwork (Moscati *et al.* 1991: 325, 364; Szabó 1971: pl. 43) but this pleasing result had no future because just at that time such sword-suspension became irrelevant in fighting (Rapin, in Moscati *et al.* 1991: 323–6).

Early Celtic craftsmen were remarkably skilful in manipulating very thin sheet (or strip) iron (Jope 1961). They made innumerable sword blades of varied quality, the best (about half of them) with cutting edges of carbon steel, sometimes welded on to a softer blade (an operation needing the very highest skill), the finest of all being pattern-welded even in the fourth century BC (Pleiner 1993: 117–18, 167, 183–4).

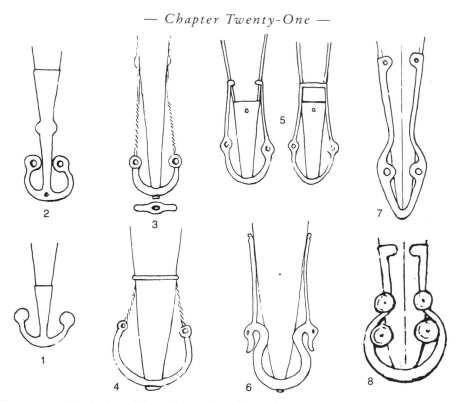

Figure 21.10 Evolution of the La Tène chape design from constructional beginnings. Key: 1, 2 – tube chapes with anchor ends; 3, 4 – initial experimental phase of composite chape construction, with separate strainer bands from anchor tips to sheath sides; 5, 6 – one-piece chapes closely following the design developed in the composite construction phase; 7 – sword-chape design derived from the above developments, as seen in Gaul, the progenitor of the chape design as seen in Hungary, and in Ulster in the second century BC; 8 – shows another La Tène I chape design similarly derived.

Finish and edge preparation were by grinding. Skilled butt-welding had been developed already in north-east France and Britain by the fifth century BC (Pleiner 1993: 138–9, 142–3; cf. Jope 1961: nos. 20–22). This fine ironwork, often on a very small scale, must imply great skill in controlling directed heating-jets.

Celtic ironsmiths most effectively exploited the fibrous surface quality of their wrought iron for decorative purposes (Jope 1987), and in fact iron was in early times treated as a rather special material, used even for prestige items like anklets or neck-rings (Jope and Jacobsthal in press: pl. 310), and often for brooches, which were evidently made by skilled rural smiths (Jope and Jacobsthal in press: pls. 32–4; Musson 1972; Hull and Hawkes 1987: 159–60).

Tools, moreover, were during this time span overwhelmingly made of iron, because of its potential hardness; this demand in itself led to the prodigious development of ironworking skills. And good tools and skilled use gave pleasing shapes, and could imply status. The development of saw blades from the sixth century onwards must be considered, as the extensive use of planking and massive squared beams for socially superior work already in the sixth century BC (pp. 388–9) would

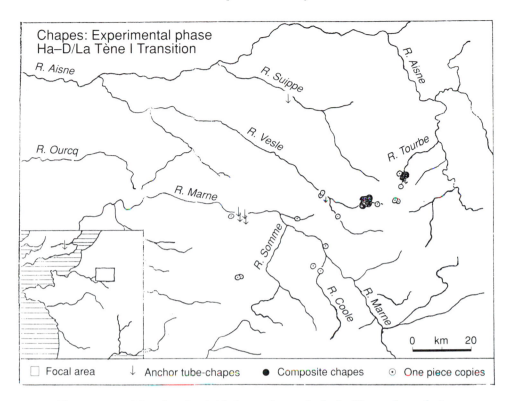

Figure 21.11 Map showing initiation and spread of a La Tène I chape design.

seem to imply two-man sawing, and even precisely set teeth to prevent sticking (Piggott 1965: 186–7; Riek and Hundt 1962; Rieth 1958); such early long saw blades are, however, still to be found. There are also some ingenious specialized tools to be seen in iron, such as the leatherworker's half-moon knife, seen at La Tène itself in a leather bag containing the whole kit of a saddler and harness-maker (Vouga 1907: pl. XLVI).

Combinations of metals have been used for decorative effect. Note the flashing of iron or bronze with tin, or the frequent fusing-on of bronze to iron often for constructional purposes. In more precious metals parcel-gilt was effectively used: note the vigorous British development in the early first century AD (Jope and Jacobsthal in press: 123, pl.).

Organic materials were a far more important factor in earlier times than we sometimes remember, due to poor and erratic preservation; here recent wetlands research is of great importance (Earwood 1993), but there is still an arsenal of earlier evidence to be used.

In wood, we have already noted the early sixth-century BC use of planking (pp. 388–9), and stave-built vessel construction should also be noted (Jope and Jacobsthal in press: pl. 136–47, 31), perhaps first developed in Celtic Europe (Clark 1962: 212ff.), and vessels hollowed from one piece, such as cups or cauldrons, are to be seen. Plastic soft-shaped carving in wood was erratic through the Celtic world (as also with plastic clay), but there are occasional surprises (e.g. the shrine statues from the source of the Seine or from the first-century BC shrine at Feldbach (Megaw and Megaw 1989; Moscati *et al.* 1991: 534; Pittioni 1982). New radiocarbon dates are revealing some enigmatic pieces, particularly in the British Isles, as being within our time span (Jope and Jacobsthal in press: pl. 312–13; Earwood 1993). Wood was used with elaborate metal fittings (e.g. the Maloměřice flagon, Moscati *et al.* 1991: 376 fn; Meduna *et al.* 1992; cf. Jacobsthal 1944: 203, pl. 188–99, nos. 395; cf. ibid.: 203, no. 395, pl. 198–9), and even more unusual organic materials were occasionally used, such as bark, resins and waxes (e.g. Megaw and Megaw 1990). Wood was also used as the basis for most shields, single-plank, tripartite, or in one famed case from the Fayum, in plywood (Kimmig 1940), which implies skilled use of glues. Limitless quantities of well-prepared seasoned timber were constantly needed for all these purposes, as well as for sophisticated vehicle- or ship-building (Piggott 1976; Ellmers 1969; Muckelroy *et al.* 1978; Stead 1991a; Chapter 15 this volume).

Leather, used for so many purposes, had to be prepared by long obnoxious processes of tanning, about the early techniques of which we know too little; the very survival of so much leather in wet conditions shows, however, that the early tanning processes were effective. The pleasing surfaces of leather were sometimes stretched over wood, as on shields (Raftery 1983), and the effect of sewn leathers was even occasionally imitated in bronze (Jope and Jacobsthal in press: pl. 270). We have already seen the well-preserved shoe of c.AD 600 (Figure 21.9); as another example we might cite the Stonyhurst Gospels as a treasure of ninth-century insular decorative book-binding deposited in St Cuthbert's coffin (Kendrick 1938: pl. 53). And we have seen the widely ranging leatherworker's toolkit from the third–second century BC at La Tène (Vouga 1907: pl. XLVIII.18).

The range of cloth fabrics (including luxury silks) that became available to Celts during our time span is now emerging, and evidence for patterning is being derived both from colouring (Hundt 1961, 1969) and, where that has faded, from varied weaves (Crowfoot in Stead 1991a; Hundt 1969).

Early Celtic craftsmen made use of resins, waxes, fats and glues, well illustrated by the Basse-Yutz flagons (J. Evans in Megaw and Megaw 1990: 69f. 74–6), showing for instance how important it could be to use resins and waxes in conjunction with metals on works of high social status.

Celtic craftsmen led the way in Europe in vehicle design and construction (many words on this topic in Latin are of Celtic derivation). Vehicles served a wide range of Celtic societies and vehicle-building drew upon the highest craft skills, and the very finest materials, such as carefully chosen, regular, fine-grained wood; the makers were indeed well versed in using varied wood species. They also exploited the varied properties of metals, as seen in the shrinking-on of iron tyres to wooden wheels by the second century BC (Piggott 1986: 216–17). And the roller-bearings of the Dejbjerg carriages of the first century BC are an ultimate refinement (Klindt-Jensen 1950: 89; Piggott 1986: 213, 227; Moscati *et al.* 1991: 236–7).

Celtic craftsmen also took every opportunity to add to the visual interest of their work. Intertwining of strands (as on the Waldalgesheim work of the fourth century BC: Jacobsthal 1944; Jope 1971) and the cleverly worked intertwining effect in the iron openwork ornaments of the fifth century BC at Hochscheid, Rhineland (Moscati *et al.* 1991: 158) hint at a local background for the genesis of this Waldalgesheim manner – the case for southerly development is not good, for the Filottrano gold neck-ring (Jacobsthal 1944) shows a total misunderstanding of the prototype axillar flowers (Jope 1971: 175; cf. Moscati *et al.* 1991: 286). Heightening of interest away from the Hellenic is well shown by the Celtic flagons of the fifth century BC imparting a subtle, gracious incurving to the straighter body-line of the Etruscan examples (Jacobsthal 1944:, pl. 178–88, 196; Megaw and Megaw 1990: 37–9, 41, 45).

Animalizing or floralizing of finials (Moscati *et al.* 1991), in structure or ornament, or using animals or birds as a living part of a construction, was another way of heightening interest widely used by Celtic people. This continued on into the Christian world, as seen for instance in the inhabited scroll (Toynbee and Ward Perkins 1950). The intensive expressive exploitation of asymmetry is another further illustration of this quest for heightened interest, giving in Britain of the second–first century BC a vitalizing of ornament so that the eye cannot resist the dynamism, as in the springing yo-yo effect on the Battersea shield (Jope 1978: 33).

We know a little of the instruments Celtic artists used for working metal and other materials, and there are hints that designs were sometimes transmitted through 'pattern-books' (Raftery 1983, 1984).

A steadily growing interest in colour was yet another way in which Celtic people heightened the interest of their visual scene. First natural-coloured materials, above all the precious foreign pink-red coral, from the fifth century BC (Champion 1976), were used, and hard on their heels incessant experiment in producing artificial colours with vitreous materials. Most widely used, from the fifth century onwards, was 'red enamel', a lead glass given its red opacity with cuprous oxide. This could indeed have been a Celtic invention, for it seems first encountered in European Celtic work of the fifth century BC (Megaw and Megaw 1990: 40–1, 43). Celtic workers somewhat later seem to have been responsible for using this red opaque vitreous material more readily as a true enamel, taking advantage of its coefficient of expansion properties between bronze and glasses to effect an efficient graded junction between glass and bronze even on pre-Romano-British pieces, such as the Westhall terrets (Jope 1953), a good example of Celtic expertise in applied science.

Yellow glasses particularly have been instrumental in showing up the locations of workshop or craft-tradition spheres of influence, as also have red opaque glasses (Henderson 1989; Jope and Jacobsthal in press: maps 9 and 10). Cobalt was used to produce blue glasses in iron age Europe (Henderson 1989: 34–6), but in a way the blues produced from copper can be of more interest here. The pigment 'Egyptian Blue' (arguably man's earliest artificial material) is a copper-calcium silicate forming a deep blue only when cooled from between $550°$ and $600°C$; when ground up it gives a pale blue powder used in Roman wall-paintings – it was being made as raw material even in Roman Britain (Jope and Huse 1940a, b) by native British artworkers (who clearly had some hand in the development of wall-painting in Roman Britain (Henig 1985; 14ff.; Toynbee 1964: 213–31)). This blue pigment was being made at Woodeaton near Oxford in the third–fourth century AD and used in the wall-paintings in buildings around the Romano-British temple (successor to a Celtic temple), and the walls of several other villas, as far as 30 miles north (Jope and Huse 1940b). Britons of this time evidently knew of this early piece of experimental industrial science, the production of 'Egyptian Blue' (cf. also p. 403, the use of red 'enamel' to make a fusion between blue glass and bronze (Jope 1953)).

It is in Ireland that the real continuities into the Christian world are increasingly being sought, and this is so for vitreous materials. The red opaque glass can illustrate this (Henderson 1989) and we have already seen how this material was used on the Sutton Hoo hanging-bowl escutcheons (p. 398).

The first sign we have of the written word *in extenso* in the Irish Christian record is of the later fifth century, scored in Latin on wax tablets in recessed wood covers

Figure 21.12 'Celtic nobility through Celtic eyes': Stone head from Corbridge, third century AD. A god modelled (in native sandstone) in the image of a living British nobleman, as the mouth and expression seem to show. (Corbridge Museum. Photo Courtesy of J.M.C. Toynbee, 2:3 natural size.)

(Armstrong and Macalister 1920); it is known in Roman Britain from London, (Wheeler 1930: 54–8), and now Vindolanda. The earliest writing on vellum (which has already been shown so important in the rise of flowing ornament, pp. 397–8) is on a psalter of around AD 600, the 'Cathach of St Columba', of which 58 folios survive out of probably about 110 when complete (Lawlor and Lindsay 1916). This would have needed the skins of at least sixty or so calves, very skilfully prepared (for processes, see H. Saxl in Singer and Holmyard 1956: 187–90). Within the century the Irish and North British monastic scriptoria between them were producing vast quantities of illustrated manuscripts on vellum; the Codex Amiatinas alone (stopped short in Florence through the death of its bearer) on its way for presentation as a triple gift to the Pope from a Northumbrian monastic house, was 1,030 folios of calfskin 27 ½ × 20 ½ inches; the whole would have needed the skins of at least 1,545 calves (Bruce-Mitford 1969: 2). Only the richest monastic houses could work on this scale; was this quantity of vellum, with all the skills involved, really being produced locally by and for the Irish monastic houses, or was some being imported? The answer might give a slightly different slant to our cultural and economic view of such institutions (Bruce-Mitford 1989).

These examples will have been enough to show how the Celtic craftsman, as he fashioned a work, would feel ahead to its user, and also back to other designs he remembered, all the time being conditioned by the material under his hand and by his tools. The information thus stored in the artefacts, if read fully, can tell us so much about Celtic life and thinking. Treating the story from 600 BC to AD 600 shows us the Celtic command of technology in its progress into industrialized Europe (a major Celtic contribution to European civilization), and Celtic intellect emerging into a fully literate scene.

REFERENCES

Alcock, L. (1963) *Dinas Powys*, Cardiff: University of Wales Press.
—— (1982) 'Cadbury-Camelot: a fifteen year perspective', *Proceedings of the British Academy* 68, 355–88.
Alcock, L., Alcock, E.A. and Driscoll, S. T. (1989) 'Reconnaisance excavations on early historic fortifications and other royal sites in Scotland', *Proceedings of the Society of Antiquaries of Scotland* 119: 189–226.
Allen, D.F. (1958) 'Belgic coins as illustrations of life in the Late pre-Roman Iron Age of Britain', *Proceedings of the Prehistoric Society* 24: 43–63.
Arkell, W.J. (1939) 'The site of Cherbury camp', *Oxoniensia* 4, 196–7.
Armstrong, E.C.R. and Macalister, R.A.S. (1920) 'Wooden box with leaves indented and waxed, found near Springmount Bog, Co. Antrim', *Proceedings of the Royal Irish Academy* 1920C.
Barth, F.E. (1983) 'Prehistoric saltmining at Hallstatt', *Bulletin of the Institute of Archaeology London* 19: 13–44.
Bersu, G. (1930) 'Fünf Mittel-La-Tène-Häuser von Goldberg', in P. Reinecke (ed.) *Schumacher Festschrift*, Mainz.
—— (1940) 'Excavations at Little Woodbury, Wiltshire', *Proceedings of the Prehistoric Society* 6: 30–111.
Beswick, P., Megaw, J.V.S. and Megaw, M.R. (1990) 'A decorated late iron age torc from

Dinnington, S. Yorkshire', *Antiquaries Journal* 70: 16–33.

Bienkowski, P. (1908) *Die Darstellung der Gallier in des hellenistisch Kunst*, Vienna: Hölder.

—— (1928) *Les Celtes dans les arts mineurs graeco romains*, Cracow: Cracow University Press.

Bittel, K., Kimmig, W. and Schiek, S. (1981) *Die Kelten in Baden-Württemberg*, Stuttgart.

Bodmer, W. (1993) 'The genetics of Celtic populations', Rhys Memorial Lecture: *Proceedings of the British Academy* 82: 37–57.

Bradford, J.S.P. (1940) 'The excavation of Cherbury camp 1939', *Oxoniensia* 5: 13–20.

Brailsford, J.W. (1948) 'Excavations at Little Woodbury', *Proceedings of the Prehistoric Society* 14: 1–23.

—— (1949) 'Excavations at Little Woodbury', *Proceedings of the Prehistoric Society* 15: 156–68.

—— (1953) *Later Prehistoric Antiquities of the British Isles*, London: British Museum.

Brewster, T.C.M. (1963) *The Excavation at Staple Howe*, Malton.

Brogan, O. (1953) *Roman Gaul*, London: Bell.

Brogan, O. and Desforges, E. (1941) 'Gergovià', *Archaeological Journal* 97: 1–36.

Bruce-Mitford, R.L.S. (1948) 'Saxon Rendlesham', *Proceedings of the Suffolk Institute of Archaeology* 24: 228–51.

—— (1969) 'The art of the Codex Amiatinus', *Journal of the British Archaeological Association* 32: 1–25.

—— (1972) *The Sutton Hoo Ship Burial*, London: British Museum Guide.

—— (1983) *The Sutton Hoo Ship Burial*, 3 vols, London: British Museum.

—— (1989) 'The Durham-Echternach calligrapher', in R. Bonner *et al.* (eds) *St Cuthbert and his Cult and his Community*, Boydell Press.

Champion, S.T. (1976) 'Coral in Europe: commerce and Celtic ornament', in P.M. Duval and C.F.C. Hawkes (eds) *Celtic Art in Ancient Europe*, London: Seminar Press.

Childe, V.G. (1950) *Prehistoric Migrations*, Oslo/ London: Kegan Paul.

Clark, J.G.D. (1962) *Prehistoric Europe: the economic basis*, London: Methuen.

Clarke, R.R. and Hawkes, C.F.C. (1955) 'An iron age anthropoid sword from Shouldham, Norfolk', *Proceedings of the Prehistoric Society* 21: 198–227.

Coles, J.M. (1987) 'Meare village east', *Somerset Levels Papers* 13, Exeter: Exeter University Press.

Collis, J.R. (1975) *Defended Sites of the Late La Tène in Central and Western Europe*, Oxford: British Archaeological Reports, Supplementary Series 2.

Colvin, H.M. (1963) *A History of Deddington, Oxfordshire*, London: SPCK.

Cunliffe, B.W. (1974) *Iron Age Communities in Britain*, London: Routledge.

—— (1984) *Danebury: an iron age hillfort in Hampshire*, London: CBA Research Report 52.

Cunliffe, B.W. and Davenport, P. (1985) The Temple of Sulis Minerva at Bath I, Oxford: Oxford Committee for Archaeology, 115–16.

Cunliffe, B.W. and Poole, C. (1991) *Danebury, 5: The Excavations 1979–88: the finds*, London: CBA Research Reports.

Darby, H.C. *et al.* (eds) (1952–72) *Domesday Geography of the Counties of England*, 6 vols, Cambridge: Cambridge University Press.

Dent, J.S. (1982) 'Cemeteries and settlement patterns of the Iron Age on the Yorkshire Wolds', *Proceedings of the Prehistoric Society* 48: 437–57.

—— (1985) 'Cart burials from Wetwang, Yorkshire', *Antiquity* 59: 85–92.

Dixon, P. (1976) 'Crickley Hill, Gloucestershire', in D.W. Harding, *Hillforts*, London: Academic Press.

Dudley, D. and Jope, E.M. (1965) 'An iron age cist burial at Trevone, north Cornwall', *Cornish Archaeology* 4: 18–23.

Duval, P.M. (1986) 'Sources and distribution of chieftaincy wealth in ancient Gaul', *Proceedings of the VIIth International Congress of Celtic Studies (Oxford 1983)*, Oxford:

Oxford University Press.

Earwood, C. (1993) *Domestic Wooden Artefacts*, Exeter: Exeter University Press.

Ellmers, D. (1969) 'Keltischer Schiffbau', *Jahrbusch Römisch-Germanische Zentralmuseum Mainz* 16: 73–122.

Fischer, F. (1967) 'Alte und neue Funde der La Tène Periode aus Württemberg', *Fundbericht aus Schwaben* NS 18: 61–105.

Foster, J. (1980) *The Iron Age Moulds from Gussage-All-Saints*, London: British Museum Occasional Papers.

—— (1986) *The Lexden Tumulus*, Oxford: British Archaeological Reports 156.

Fox, C. (1946) *A Find of the Early Iron Age from Llyn Cerrig Bach, Angelsey*, Cardiff: National Museum of Wales.

Fox, A. and Pollard, S. (1973) 'A decorated bronze mirror from an iron age settlement at Holcombe, Dorset', *Antiquaries Journal* 53: 16–41.

Frankenstein, S. and Rowlands, M.J. (1978) 'The internal structure and regional context of early iron age society in south-western Germany', *Bulletin of the Institute of Archaeology London* 15: 73–112.

Gomez de Soto, J. (1986) 'Le casque du IVème siècle avant notre ère de la grotte des Perrats à Agris, France', *Archaeologisches Korrespondenzblatt* 6: 179–83.

Griffith, J.G. (1988) 'Two passages from Herodotus and the bronze crater from the royal tomb at Vix-sur-Seine', in *Festinat Senex*, Oxford: Oxbow Books.

Hallam, S.J. (1964) 'Villages in Roman Britain: some evidence', *Antiquaries Journal*: 19–32.

Harden, D.B. (ed.) (1955) *Dark Age Britain: studies presented to E.T. Leeds*, London: Methuen.

—— (1955) 'Glass vessels in Britain and Ireland AD 400–1000', in D.B. Harden (ed.) *Dark Age Britain*, 138–70.

Harding, D.W. (1972) *The Iron Age in the Upper Thames Basin*, Oxford: Clarendon Press.

—— (1974) *The Iron Age in Lowland Britain*, London: Routledge.

—— (ed) (1976) *Hillforts*, London: Academic Press.

Harding D.W. and Blake, I.M. (1993) *An Iron Age Settlement at Pimperne, in Dorset: excavations and reconstruction*, Edinburgh: University of Edinburgh, Department of Archaeology.

Harvey, J.H. (1947) *Gothic England*, London: Batsford.

Hawkes, C.F.C. (1982) 'The wearing of the brooch: early iron age dress among the Irish', in *Studies in Early Ireland: essays in honour of M.V. Duignan*, Belfast: Belfast Institute of Irish Studies.

—— (1938) 'An unusual find in the New Forest potteries at Linwood, Hants', *Antiquaries Journal* 18: 113–36.

Hawkes, C.F.C. and Hull, M.R. (1947) *Camulodunum*, London: Society of Antiquaries of London Research Report 14.

Hencken, H. (1932) 'Beitzsch and Knossos', *Proceedings of the Prehistoric Society* 18: 36–46.

Henderson, J. (1989) 'The scientific analysis of ancient glass, and its archaeological interpretation', in J. Henderson (ed.) *Scientific Analysis in Archaeology*, Oxford: Oxford University Committee for Archaeology, Monograph 19.

Henderson, J. and Ivens, R.J. (1992) 'Dunmisk and glassworking in Early Christian Ireland', *Antiquity* 66: 52–64.

Henig, M. (1989) 'Graeco-Roman art and Romano-British imagination', *Journal of the British Archaeological Association* 138: 1–22.

Henry, F. (1965) *Irish Art in the Early Christian Period to AD 800*, London: Methuen.

Hodson, F.R. (1968) *La Tène Cemetery at Münsingen-Rain*, Berne: Acta Berninsia 5.

—— (1990) *Hallstatt: the Ramsauer graves: quantification and analysis*, Römisch-Germanische Zentralmuseum Mainz, Bonn: Habelt.

Hull, M.R. and Hawkes, C.F.C. (1987) *Corpus of Ancient Brooches in Britain*, Oxford: British

Archaeological Reports, British Series.

Hundt, H.J. (1961) 'Neunzehn Textilreste aus den Dürrnburg in Hallein', *Jahrbuch Römisch-Germanische Zentralmuseum, Mainz* 8: 7–25.

—— (1969) 'Über vorgeschiebtliche Seidenfunde', *Jahrbuch Römisch-Germanische Zentralmuseum, Mainz* 16: 39–71.

Jacobsthal, P. (1944) *Early Celtic Art*, Oxford: Clarendon Press.

Jope, E.M. (1950) 'Two iron-age horse-bits from the North of Ireland', *Ulster Journal of Archaeology* 13: 57–60.

—— (1951) 'A bronze butt or ferrule from the river Bann', *Belfast Museum and Art Gallery Bulletin* 1: 1–8.

—— (1953) 'The enamelled brooch form a souterrain in Angus', *Antiquaries Journal* 33: 69–71.

—— (1955) 'Chariotry and paired draught in Ireland', *Ulster Journal of Archaeology* 18: 37–44.

—— (1961) *Studies in Building History*, London: Odhams.

—— (1971) 'The Waldalgesheim Master', in J. Boardman *et al.* (eds) *The European Community in Later Prehistory*, London: Routledge.

—— (1974) 'Iron age dagger and sword chape construction: technology, taxonomy and prehistory', *Irish Archaeological Research Forum* 1: 1–8.

—— (1978) 'The southward face of Celtic Britain 300 BC–AD 50: four British parade shields', *Quaderno Accademico Nazionale dei Lincei* 237: 27–36.

—— (1983) 'Torrs, Aylesford and the Padstow hobbyhorse', in A. O'Connor and D.V. Clarke (eds) *From the Stone Age to the 'Forty–Five*, Edinburgh: Edinburgh University Press.

—— (1987) 'Celtic art: expressiveness and communication through 2500 years', *Proceedings of the British Academy* 73: 97–123.

—— (1995) 'Bersu's Goldberg IV: a subchief's residence in the sixth–fifth centuries BC', *Oxford Journal of Archaeology* (forthcoming).

Jope, E.M. and Huse, G. (1940a) 'Examinations of Egyptian Blue by X-ray power photography', *Nature* 147: 26.

—— (1940b) 'Blue pigment of Roman date from Woodeaton', *Oxoniensia* 5: 167.

Jope, E.M. and Jacobsthal, P. (in press) *Early Celtic Art in the British Isles*, Oxford: Oxford University Press.

Jope, E.M. and Threlfall, R.I. (1959) 'The twelfth century castle at Ascot Doilly, Oxfordshire', *Antiquaries Journal* 39: 119–273.

Jope, E.M., Dunning, G.C. and Hodges, H.W.M. (1952) 'Kirkcudbright Castle, its pottery and iron work', *Proceedings of the Society of Antiquaries of Scotland* 91: 117–38.

Jope, H.M. (1984) Review of R.M. Luff, 'A zoological study of the Roman N.W. Provinces', *Antiquaries Journal* 64, 464–5.

Kendrick, T.D. (1938) *Anglo-Saxon Art*, London: Methnen.

Kimmig, W. (1940) 'Ein Keltenschild aus Ägypten', *Germania* 24: 106–11.

—— (1969) 'Zur Problem späthall stattischer Adelssitze', in *Siedlungen, Burg und Stadt*, Berlin: Festchrift R. Germ.

Klindt-Jensen, O. (1950) 'Foreign influences in Denmark's Early Iron Age', *Acta Archaeologica* 20.

Krämer, W. (ed) (1958) *Neue Ausgrabungen in Deutschland*, Berlin.

Kromer, K. (1959) *Das Gräberfeld von Hallstatt*, Florence: Sansoni.

—— (1982) 'Gift exchange and the Hallstatt courts', *Bulletin of the Institute of Archaeology London* 19: 21–30.

Last, H. (1949) 'Rome and the Druids: a note', *Journal of Roman Studies* 39: 1–5.

Lawlor, H.J. and Lindsay, W.M. (1916) 'The Cathach of St Columba', *Proceedings of the Royal Irish Academy* C241.

Leeds, E.T. (1933) *Celtic Ornament*, Oxford: Oxford University Press.

Lynn, C.J. (1991) 'Emania' and 'Navan', in S. Moscati *et al.* (eds) *The Celts*, 610–11.

Mallory, J.P. and McNeill, T.E. (1991) *The Archaeology of Ulster from Colonization to Plantation*, Belfast: Queen's University, Institute of Irish Studies.

MacDonald, J. (1978) 'An iron age dagger in the Royal Ontario Museum' in *Collectanea Londoniensis: essays presented to R. Merrifield*, London: Middlesex Archaeological Society, special paper 2: 44–51.

Mansfeld, G. (1973) *Die Fibeln der Heuneberg*, Berlin: Römisch-Germanische Forschungen.

Marien, M.E. (1963) 'Poignard hallstattente trouvé à Luttre, Hainault, Belgique', in S. Genouces (ed.) *A Pedro Bosch-Gimpera*, 307–12.

Meduna, J., Poškař, I. and Frey, O.-H. (1992) 'Ein latènezeitlicher Fund mit Bronzebeschläger von Brno-Maloměřice', *Bericht der Römisch-Germanischen Kommission* 73: 181–267.

Megaw, J.V.S. (1971) *Art of the European Iron Age*, London: Harper & Row.

—— (1984) 'Meditations on a Celtic hobby-horse: notes towards a social archaeology of iron age art', in T.C. Champion and J.V.S. Megaw (eds) *Settlement and Society*, Leicester: Leicester University Press.

—— (1989) 'The Italian Job: some implications of recent finds of Celtic scabbards decorated with dragon-pairs', *Mediterranean Archaeology* 2: 85–100.

Megaw, J.V.S. and Megaw, M.R. (1990) *The Basse-Yutz Find: masterpieces of Celtic art*, London: Society of Antiquaries Research Report 45.

Moscati, S. *et al.* (1991) *The Celts*, London: Thames & Hudson.

Musson, C. (1972) 'The Breiddin', *Current Archaeology* 33: 293–302.

Nash, D. (1976) 'The growth of urban society in France', in B.W. Cunliffe and T. Rowley (eds) *Oppida*, Oxford: British Archaeological Reports, Supplementary Series, 95–134.

de Navarro, J.M. (1955) 'A doctor's grave of the Middle La Tène period from Bavaria', *Proceedings of the Prehistoric Society* 21: 231–48.

O'Neil, H.E. (1961) 'Some features of building construction in a rural area of Roman Britain', in E.M. Jope, *Studies in Building History*, 27–38.

Pätzold, J. (1963) 'Ein späthallstatzeitlicher Herrnsitz im Alpen Vorland bei München', *Germania* 41: 101–3.

Pauli, H. (1978) *Der Dürrnberg bei Hallein*, Munich.

Perler, D. (1962) 'Der Antennendolch von Estavayer-le-Sac', *Jahrbuch der Schweizer Gesellschaft Urgeschichte* 49: 25–35.

Piggott, S. (1965) *Ancient Europe*, Edinburgh: Edinburgh University Press.

—— (1986) 'Horse and chariot: the price of prestige', in D.E. Evans, J.G. Griffith and E.M. Jope (eds) *Proceedings of the IIIrd International Congress of Celtic Studies (1983)*, 25–30.

Pittioni, R. (1982) 'Über zwei keltische Götterfiguren aus Wurttemberg', *Veröffentlichungen der Keltischen Kommission* I, Vienna: Verlag der Österreichischen Akademie der Wissenschaften, 338–51 and figs 1–4.

Pleiner, R. (1993) *The Celtic Sword*, Oxford: Oxford University Press.

Radford, C.A.R. (1935) Review of K. Bittel, 'Die Kelten in Württemberg', *Antiquaries Journal* 15: 365–6.

Raftery, B. (1982) *A Catalogue of Irish Iron Age Antiquities*, Marburg: Vorgeschichtlichen Seminars, special vol. 1.

—— (1983) *La Tène in Ireland*, Marburg: Vorgeschichtlichen Seminars, special vol. 2.

Richmond, I.A. (1968) *Hod Hill II*, London: British Museum.

Riek, G. and Hundt H.J. (1962) *Der Hohmichele*, Römisch-Germanische Forschungen 25, 199ff.

Rieth, A. (1958) 'Werkzeuge der Holzbearteitung: Sägen ans vier Jahrtausend', *Saalburg-Jahrbuch* 17: 67–70.

—— (1969) 'Zur Herstellungs technik der Eisendolche der späten Hallstattzeit', *Jahrbuch Römisch-Germanischen Zentralmuseum Mainz* 16: 17–58.

Rivet, A.L.F. (1958) *Town and Country in Roman Britain*, London: Hutchinson.

Rusu, M. (1969) 'Das keltische Fürstengzab von Ciumeşti in Rumania', *Bericht der Römisch-Germanischen Kommission* 50: 267–300.

Saunders, A.D. (1990) 'Lydford: Saxon burgh and Stannary prison', *Archaeological Journal* 147 (supp.): 61–4.

Schröter, P. (1975) 'Zur Besiedlung des Goldbergs im Nördlinger Ries', in *Ausgrabungen in Deutschland, 1950–1975*, Römisch-Germanischen Zentral Museum, Mainz, 98–114.

Scott, B.G. (ed.) (1982) *Studies in Early Ireland: essays in honour of M.V. Duignan*, Belfast.

—— (1991) *Early Irish Ironworking*, Belfast: Ulster Museum.

Sievers, S. (1982) *Die mitteleuropäischen Hallstattdolche*, Praehist Bronzefunde VI.

Simpson, W.D. (1943) *The Province of Mar*, Aberdeen: Aberdeen University Press.

Singer, C. and Holmyard E.J. (eds) (1956) *A History of Technology* II, Oxford: Oxford University Press.

Spindler, K. (1976) *Magdalenenberg IV*, Villingen: Neckar Verlag.

Spratling, M.G. (1979) 'The debris of metal working', in G.J. Wainwright, *Gussage-All-Saints*, 123–49.

Stead, I.M. (1982) 'The Cerrig-y-drudion "hanging bowl"' *Antiquaries Journal* 62: 221–34.

—— (1984a) 'Some notes on imported metal work in iron age Britain', in S. Macready and F.H. Thompson (eds) *Cross Channel Trade*, London: Society of Antiquaries, Occasional Papers N34: 43–66.

—— (1984b) 'Celtic dragons from the river Thames', *Antiquaries Journal* 64: 268–79.

—— (1991a) *Iron Age Cemeteries in East Yorkshire*, London: English Heritage/British Museum.

—— (1991b) 'The Snettisham Treasure, excavations in 1990', *Antiquity* 65: 447–84.

Stjernquist, B. (1967) *Ciste e cordoni (Rippenzisten)*, Lund: Univ. Scrip. Misio.

Szabó, M. (1971) *The Celtic Heritage in Hungary*, Budapest: Corvina Press.

Thomas, A.C. (1993) *Tintagel, Arthur and Archaeology*, London: Batsford.

Torbrügge, W. (1972) 'Vor- und frühgeschichtliche Flussfunde', *Bericht der Römisch-Germanischen Kommission* 51–2: 1–146.

Toynbee, J.M.C. (1962) *Art in Roman Britain*, London: Phaidon.

—— (1964) *Art in Britain under the Romans*, Oxford: Oxford University Press.

Toynbee, J.M.C. and Ward Perkins, J.B. (1950) 'Inhabited vine scrolls', *Journal of Hellenic Studies* 50: 1–33.

Vouga, P. (1923) *La Tène*, Leipzig: Hiersemann.

Wainwright, F. (1953) 'A souterrain identified in Angus', *Antiquaries Journal* 33: 65–71.

Wainwright, G.J. (1967) *Coygan Camp*, Cardiff: Cambrian Archaeol. Association.

—— (1979) *Gussage-All-Saints, an Iron Age Site in Dorset*, London: Department of the Environment Archaeological Report 10.

Ward Perkins, J.B. (1941) 'The pottery of Gergovia in relation to that of other sites in central and south-west France', *Archaeological Journal* 97: 37–87.

Wheeler, R.E.M. (1930) *London in Roman Times*, London: London Museum.

Zürn, H. (1941) 'Die Hallstattzeit in Württemberg', unpublished thesis, University of Tübingen.

—— (1970) 'Hallstattforschungen in Nordwürttemberg', *Veroffentlichung des Stadtslichen Amies für Denkmalpflege*, series A, Stuttgart.

JEWELLERY AND ADORNMENT

—— ·•· ——

Sara Champion

It is not currently possible to prove that any of the iron age peoples who lived in central and western Europe in the first millennium BC definitely spoke a Celtic language or defined themselves as Celts. Because of that I have eschewed the use of the term 'Celtic' in this chapter, and propose to discuss the personal ornaments found in those areas of continental Europe where 'cultures' defined by archaeologists as the Hallstatt and La Tène were located, and in those parts of the British Isles and Ireland where comparable cultural material is found.

Recent years have seen an increasing number of studies of personal ornament and the way it appears to have been distributed in society. Questions of gender, social status, age and regional differentiation have been approached through the examination of the evidence for patterns of ornament use, largely from inhumation cemeteries, and various stimulating and persuasive answers have been offered to some, though not all, of these questions. In particular the work of Herbert Lorenz (1978, 1980) has shown that detailed analysis of the way rings (for the neck, arm, leg and finger) were worn in different parts of Europe allows the tentative identification of women who have moved from one group to another, perhaps demonstrating exogamy. In areas like the British Isles where most of such artefacts do not come from graves but are generally found unstratified, or at the very best on settlement sites, separated from the person who would have worn them, similar questions are almost impossible to answer.

Déchelette referred in 1914 to writers in classical antiquity who mentioned the Celts' passion for jewellery, and he proceeded himself to examine the wide range of necklaces, bracelets, pendants, earrings, belts and brooches which he attributed to the taste for self-decoration which had developed since the mid-Hallstatt period. Then as now, care must be exercised in the interpretation of burial deposits: while some rings, particularly certain solid bronze neck-rings, must have been introduced on to the body in childhood and must therefore have been carried throughout life and into the grave, other items, such as the very large numbers of brooches deposited with some bodies in graves on the Swiss plateau, could well represent the total number owned by the deceased or her family rather than items worn together in life. Similarly, there is evidence from some graves that certain items were made specifically for the burial, which may confuse the ascription of a status assumed to be carried in life.

One further aspect of ornament studies needs to be mentioned. Skeletal, and sometimes cremated, remains from early excavations were frequently sexed on the nature of the ornaments found with them. When better standards of skeletal analysis allowed sexing without reference to associated artefacts, some 'male' bodies were found to be associated with 'female' ornaments. Transvestism was one explanation offered for such occurrences, but it is as likely that some correlations that had been suggested, such as paired fibulae with female gender, were not as simple as at first thought. Many combinations of ornaments have become part of the grammar of gender and status ascription, and it is certainly time for a full-scale reanalysis of the bones themselves (where they survive – unfortunately, those from some of the largest and most representative cemeteries have been lost or mixed together since excavation in the nineteenth and early twentieth centuries), together with the artefacts, so that questions such as the status of women, or the possibility of cross-dressing males, can be addressed in a context free from circular argument.

HEAD AND HAIR

Long-shanked pins with a variety of styles of head are found in the general area of the skull, more frequently during Hallstatt C and D than in the La Tène periods. These have been generally assumed to be hair pins, though they may rather have served to attach or decorate hairnets or other head-covering. Some have a hollow head constructed of two hemispheres of sheet bronze, while others have a solid head of a decorative organic material such as amber, jet or coral. Some of the better-furnished graves of eastern France and south-west Germany contain pins with very large and highly decorated heads up to 4 cm in diameter, which may also be of organic material (for example amber, decorated with patterns of concentric lines and rows of inlaid dots; and segments of Mediterranean red coral, formed into spheres), as well as bronze, or more spectacularly, decorated gold foil.

Pins are found in La Tène graves, though rarely in a similar position near the head, and it is likely that the function of these is as a fastener for a garment such as a cloak (or possibly a shroud). There is thus an implication of a change in hairstyle or head-gear fashion at some point in the fifth century BC, at least among those who would at an earlier period have sported such decoration. Current knowledge does suggest that these hair/headgear pins were worn by women, though their very presence has led to the identification of graves containing them as female, and there has as yet been no study of such pins which looks also at the anatomical sexing of the bones.

EARRINGS

Earrings are found in male and female graves, though more frequently, and occasionally in greater numbers, in the latter. Hollow gold or bronze crescents, sometimes with attached pendants, occur in the Hallstatt period, while a variation of this form with an open upper side, i.e. boat-shaped, is found in richer graves of the Early La Tène period, sometimes decorated with linear geometric ornament and occasionally with beaded lines imitating granulation. There are rare examples of exceptionally decorated gold earrings, such as the pair from La Butte, Ste Colombe (Côte d'Or), with two rows of profiled cups, found in association with other gold-work of high quality. Also known in the Hallstatt period are bronze band rings, frequently with hook-and-eye fastening (the long hook presumably ran through the pierced ear), decorated with geometric or punched circle ornament.

These earrings generally occur in pairs, though they also come singly or in sets of up to six (and exceptionally, as at Esslingen-Sirnau, eighteen); some scholars believe it unlikely that large sets like this could have been worn in the ears at any one time, and have suggested that such rings may rather have been attached to headgear such as a hairnet or shawl. Ethnographic parallels show that sets of rings may well be worn in the ear; alternatively, the placing of sets in the grave does not necessarily mean that all the rings were worn simultaneously. The possibility that sets of rings were attached to some kind of headgear or indeed formed part of a hairstyle ('lock rings') cannot, however, be ruled out.

NECK-RINGS/NECKLACES

The neck-ring or torque has been characterized as a major identifying feature of the Celt, both in representations by classical artists and sculptors, and in the archaeological literature. In some parts and in some periods of iron age Europe there were certainly large numbers of these ornaments being worn (or at least deposited, whether in graves or in potentially ritual contexts such as rivers or 'hoards'); and there are representations, such as the head from Mšecké Žehrovice or the male statue from Hirschlanden, which are likely to be the work of indigenous sculptors. It is therefore of some interest that in the Hallstatt period the neck-ring is not in wide-spread use, though it occurs in rich graves, often in gold, associated with both males and females.

The broad decorated band of gold worn round the neck by some incumbents of the 'princely graves' of later Hallstatt Europe has been characterized as a status symbol, and it is true that both female (e.g. Vix, Reinheim) and male (e.g. Eberdingen-Hochdorf, La Motte d'Apremont) burials with these or similar neck-rings are amongst the most richly equipped inhumations of the Hallstatt world. Other burials may have hollow or solid, open or closed bronze rings, and there are rare instances of iron rings too.

In the La Tène period in many areas the gold or bronze neck-ring (often called a torque because some were made by twisting a rod or band of metal: the word has become a generic term for the neck-ring) did become a widespread form of personal adornment. There are chronological and apparently gender differences, however: in La Tène I the neck-rings, particularly those in bronze, are found mainly (though not exclusively) in female graves, whereas in La Tène II and III they are frequently in gold and, where associated with human remains at all, are largely (though again not exclusively) in male contexts. It is from this period onwards that many of the stone sculptures of male warriors or gods wearing buffer-ended neck-rings probably date.

The range of morphological and decorative types is very large indeed. Such rings may be closed (in some cases implying acquisition in infancy) or open, or may have a closing device such as a mortise-and-tenon joint, a hook and eye, a covering sleeve, or a complicated key-twist mechanism. They may be hollow or solid, twisted or smooth, with engraved linear and geometric decoration or cast 'plastic' relief decoration. Some have buffer terminals with curvilinear decoration around the buffers. One group found in south-west Germany, eastern France and the Swiss plateau cemeteries has coloured decoration in the form of discs (generally three or five, though and one and seven are known) of opaque red glass, sometimes alternating with cast bronze knots or lobes with deep-cut S- or spiral decoration filled with the same red substance. These disc-torques often occur in graves with matching fibulae (disc on foot) and disc-bracelets (with one to four discs). In other areas, for example elsewhere in Germany, northern France and Hungary, neck-rings of similar style were decorated with Mediterranean red coral enhanced by pins and small decorative plaques of gold.

In the later La Tène periods some tubular gold neck-rings are covered with wild rococo ornament that must have made them very uncomfortable to wear, and there are also large loop- and buffer-ended gold neck-rings with complex repoussé or engraved decoration. To this latter group belong the famous Snettisham torque from Suffolk and the Broighter torque from Co. Offaly, Ireland, both of which were found in circumstances which may suggest votive offering or deliberate concealment. The Snettisham area has in recent years produced a large number of gold neck-rings of various types, again probably from deposits of ritual significance.

Necklaces made from a variety of bead types are known in both Hallstatt and La Tène periods. In some rich graves of the earlier period complex necklaces made of strands of beads held apart by spacers occur in jet, amber, bone and coral, as well as bronze and glass. Single-string necklaces have similar beads, often in combination. Glass beads include blue ones with white zigzag decoration and yellow ones with blue and white 'eyes'. Amber beads include large lathe-turned disc-shaped examples up to 6 cm across or more, and biconical beads of similar length. Coral beads may be spherical, or composite in a similar style to the pin-heads described above, and in some rare cases may be branches of coral longitudinally pierced.

A common combination in La Tène I, particularly in the Marne region of France, is of blue glass and coral beads, the latter being either spherical, or raw branches, occasionally with linear decoration to the stem. A wider range of glass beads, including pale green translucent examples, in La Tène I and II leads in La Tène III to polychrome ring-shaped beads of the type found at Stradonice (Bohemia).

PENDANTS AND AMULETS

Pendants should be discussed alongside necklaces, for frequently they are hung in groups around the neck, and they can be attached to solid neck-rings as well as being incorporated in 'standard' necklaces. Their positioning is not restricted to the neck area, however: they are often found at the hip or waist, suggesting that they were suspended from a belt. Though found in both male and female graves, they appear to be most frequently associated with children, who are, however, generally under-represented in most cemeteries, which makes statistical analysis difficult. Bronze pendants include such shapes as shoes or boots, figures (frequently ithyphallic), faces, wheels, birds, baskets, axes, open bronze triangles or squares, etc., the significance of most of these being currently beyond our comprehension. Amber occurs in the form of large beads or shaped pieces, and in some graves there are pieces of broken glass bracelet and fragments of bronze arm-ring, animal teeth (such as bear), naturally pierced stone (e.g. chalk, sandstone), pieces of stone axe and whole or broken glass beads. The use of raw branches of coral in the late Hallstatt and early La Tène periods has been explained as being apotropaic, for there are later classical references to its use to ward off the evil eye.

Also found in the breast area in some burials are highly ornamented openwork discs, usually of bronze, which may have been worn as pendants or perhaps have been sewn to clothing. They are heavy, and are usually two-sided, so the latter is less likely than the former; but there are rarely signs of suspension or the wear patterns associated with it, so the real nature of such ornaments is unclear. Gold-decorated iron plaques and discs with coral and/or amber inlay found in some rich graves are also difficult to classify in terms of function.

ARM-RINGS/BRACELETS

These are found in bronze, iron, lignite, shale and occasionally gold, as well as (later) in glass. The gold examples normally come from rich graves, frequently associated with male burials (and in these cases found singly) but also with female (usually, as with bronze, paired). In late Hallstatt times these may be similar to the neck-bands, of beaten gold with linear decoration, but in the fifth century BC there are some with animals or human heads on them, and others decorated in the early style of La Tène art. In the latter part of the La Tène period gold arm-rings occur again, often with parallel decoration to the gold neck-rings of the same period, with flamboyant, highly plastic decoration.

Bronze arm-rings come in a wide variety of styles throughout the Iron Age, from hollow and solid rings to bands and bangles, the latter usually closed but many of the previous types open. Many in the Hallstatt period are open, with expanded terminals, and they can have heavy cast decoration or be engraved after casting in geometric style. Similar types continue into the La Tène period, but there are also twisted and serpentiform types, and closed or open rings with curvilinear decoration on them. Disc bracelets with attached discs of red opaque glass are found in some Swiss and south-west German graves. In female graves such arm-rings tend to appear in pairs, while male graves generally have only one arm-ring, if any. The narrow bangles with fine engraved decoration were worn in sets. There is a certain amount of evidence to suggest that sometimes an arm-ring was worn on the upper arm in both male and female graves.

Very heavy armbands are known from the north of England and southern Scotland belonging to the end of the Iron Age and the beginning of the Roman period. These have cast decoration and areas of coloured enamelling at the terminals.

One particular form of arm adornment is the barrel armband, made of bronze (occasionally gilded) or jet/lignite. Characteristic of the Hallstatt period in eastern France, south-west Germany and Switzerland, the bronze examples can reach a height of 20 cm, and are usually heavily decorated with engraved geometric designs. In some cases it is clear that they cannot have been removed during life, and though many show signs of repair and therefore wear and tear, it has been suggested that they would have been almost impossible to work in; does this imply that they were worn by women who were of such a status that they did not need to work?

Jet or lignite barrel armbands are rarely decorated, but they belong to the same chronological phase and are found further east into Austria as well as in the area mentioned above. Shale bracelets of simple rounded cross-section are found in Britain as well as in continental Europe, where such forms are also manufactured in sapro-pelite, jet and lignite.

From the very end of La Tène I plain glass arm-rings begin to appear in some graves in France and Switzerland, but during La Tène II and III they become more widespread and more diverse in their form and decoration. Whitish or greenish, blue or yellowish, they may have plastic or at least raised decoration in another colour – yellow zigzags on blue, or blue lines on a clear or greenish base.

A small number of iron arm-rings is known, though the use of this substance in general for ornaments is restricted. They are found mainly in male graves.

Bracelets of glass, coral and less frequently amber beads are known from the later Hallstatt and early La Tène periods in those areas where necklaces of a similar nature are found.

LEG-RINGS

Where found these are normally plain bronze rings, hollow or solid and always closed, though other types are found in some areas such as the heavy hinged *Hohlbuckelringe*, worn in east-central Europe. They were worn in pairs, and seem to be an entirely female ornament (though we should remember that graves containing leg-rings are invariably classified as female graves when no sexing of the bones has been carried out).

FINGER-RINGS

These are rare in the Hallstatt period, but become more numerous during La Tène I. In gold, silver and bronze, and occasionally in iron, they are found with males and females: the rich graves at Rodenbach and Horovice have highly decorated gold examples, while the males in the Marnian chariot burials at Châlons-sur-Marne and Somme-Bionne both had simple gold rings on their right hands. During La Tène I and II, particularly in Switzerland, finger-rings occur relatively frequently, and often in precious metal – one female in the Münsingen cemetery had a silver ring on her right thumb, and gold, silver and electrum ones on the third finger of her left hand. The use of silver is unusual in iron age Europe, though there are fibulae in this material from Swiss cemeteries. One form of finger-ring is the 'bent' or elbow ring, characteristic of the Swiss cemeteries but also found in Britain, and there are other forms such as the meander ring and the wire ring with a knot; plain or decorated bronze bands are also known. From La Tène II there are also a few intaglio rings inlaid with glass, amber or stone.

BROOCHES/FIBULAE

The brooch and the safety-pin-like fibula are the most widespread personal ornaments in the Iron Age; their variety and their constructional changes and technological refinements through time have made them sensitive regional and chronological indicators, and their large numbers have allowed considerable analysis into various aspects of production and exchange. In the Hallstatt cemetery itself so-called spectacle brooches were found in earlier iron age graves, mostly female; there seems to have been a complete change in type from these to the series of fibulae which start in Hallstatt D in the western Hallstatt zone with boat and leech types and those with a serpentiform bow. Furnished with unilateral, short bilateral spring or stop disc, these types develop and mutate into Certosa, kettledrum, double drum and decorated foot varieties with genuine and false springs. Some of these are inlaid with coral, and some with amber, but most are not heavily decorated. Though more than one can be found in a grave, male or female, they are less obviously paired than in later graves. They were probably used normally to fasten clothing, though in some graves they may have been used to secure the shroud, and in Eberdingen-Hochdorf gold serpentiform fibulae were used to pin hangings to the wall of the burial chamber. In at least one grave a small fibula is up by the head, perhaps implying the fastening of a scarf or shawl.

At the end of the Hallstatt period and at the beginning of the La Tène there appears a series of fibulae decorated with plastic representations of animals, animal heads or human faces or masks; these can be highly stylized or quite naturalistic, and some have coral inlay in the eyes or along the top of the bow. They are normally in bronze, though there are a few examples in gold.

From the beginning of the La Tène period there is a proliferation in the number and type of fibulae present both in graves and, increasingly, on settlement sites. In graves it is possible to see patterns in the way that some types are deposited – for example, on some skeletons there are pairs of identical fibulae, occasionally linked with a bronze chain, on the shoulders, suggesting a particular form of clothing or style of display. It has been suggested that these may represent married women, though subsequent identification of some of the skeletons as probably male has introduced difficulties, as discussed above.

Very widespread is the fibula with bilateral spring and returned foot, which may be decorated with plastic or profiled ornament or with a disc, inlaid with coral or, for a short period in La Tène I, with the same red opaque glass as seen on disc torques and disc bracelets. The disc may be fairly small, up to 1 cm diameter, inlaid with a single piece of coral or red glass, or a disc made up of three or four pieces; or it may be large, up to 3 cm across, filled with a number of highly decorated wedge-shaped pieces of coral. Coral is also found in the bow, as occasionally is red opaque glass pressed into an S-shaped or geometric cut-out area. While most graves may only have two or three or a handful of fibulae, there are others with over a dozen, and these may represent the contents of the incumbent's 'jewel box' rather than reflect the way in which the fibulae were worn or displayed in life. Although the vast majority of these fibulae, at least those which have survived, were made in bronze, they also occur occasionally in silver and gold, and rather more frequently in iron. In the case of the latter, they are often single fibulae in male graves with weapons.

A characteristic of many La Tène II fibulae is that the foot reaches back to and is joined to the bow. Although on the continent these are frequently less decorated than their predecessors, in Britain they develop into the involuted brooches with an inwardly curved bow and expanded footplate which carries engraved, plastic or inlaid decoration. In La Tène III the bow and foot are cast together; the catchplate may be ornamentally pierced, but the bow of the fibulae has generally little or no decoration until the eve of the Roman era when a certain amount of polychrome enamel may be inlaid into discs or cut-out areas.

In Ireland and Britain, and to a lesser extent on the Continent, penannular and annular brooches develop during the later La Tène period; in Ireland, uninterrupted development of this style through the early centuries of the first millennium AD leads to the massive and highly ornate silver quoit brooches of the Early Christian period, with their long pins and occasional inlays of semi-precious stones.

BELTS AND BELT-HOOKS

Although these items should perhaps be seen less as jewellery than as decorated functional items of clothing, they clearly served as part of the display of personal adornment and are justifiably included in this chapter. In the Hallstatt period most of the belts themselves were of leather, with hooks and sometimes decorative plates attached. The hooks on male belts were frequently in iron, with minimal or no decoration, but bronze hooks often have geometric designs engraved on them. Perhaps the most spectacular belt decorations of this earlier Iron Age phase are the bronze belt-plates attached to broad leather belts, found mainly in female graves, with their rows of highly decorative stamped patterns, mostly geometric but some incorporating bird and flower motifs. These can reach widths of 20 cm, and though they are generally limited to the front part of the belt, and a length of up to 60 cm, there are examples which are much longer – one from Hallstatt itself is over a metre long including the hook. In the late Hallstatt period there are also belts decorated with rows of bronze studs.

In La Tène I the most common belt ornament is a highly decorative, usually bronze, belt-hook, frequently openwork with a vegetal or animal design, such as the opposed animals at Somme-Bionne (Marne). Among belt-hooks from some of the rich graves in the middle Rhine there are also some extraordinarily ornate pieces with plastic, openwork and/or engraved designs and sometimes coral inlay, such as that from Weiskirchen. There also develops a series of belt-chains formed of bars with loops at either end, joined by link-rings, and less frequently plain chains.

In La Tène II and III the decorated belt-chain becomes much more widespread, and is worn by females from the Marne to Hungary. Though in some cases the chain is just a series of linked rings, in many there are decorated elements which involve the use of red enamel in patterned cut-out areas.

BODY DECORATION

Given the wide range of personal adornment represented by these artefacts, and the increasing evidence of colour and design incorporated into textiles and clothing, it is not unlikely that some people painted or tattooed their bodies. There are hints of this in the classical literature, and at a similar time in Siberia there is archaeological evidence of highly decorative tattooing from frozen iron age tombs where the skin has survived (Rudenko 1970). Although these particular environmental circumstances are not available in the areas of Europe under discussion here, other preservative environments, such as bogs, are, and increased cutting and utilization of these landscapes has begun to yield iron age bodies. The most recently discovered, 'Lindow Man', had no evidence of tattoos, but there remains the possibility that the recorded use of woad was as a regular and decorative form of body adornment.

CONCLUSION

In the past the sometimes spectacular objects associated with personal adornment in the Iron Age have frequently been studied as art objects, largely divorced from their context and function. Recent work has shown the potential for using such finds in studies of status, gender, family relationships, craft organization and political structures. This enhances rather than diminishes our appreciation of them, and allows a deeper understanding of the society whose specialists produced them and whose members wore, displayed and eventually deposited them.

REFERENCES

Lorenz, H. (1978) 'Totenbrauchtum und Tracht. Untersuchungen zur regionalen Gliederung der frühen Latènezeit', *Bericht Römisch-Germanische Kommission*, 59: 144.
—— (1980) 'Bemerkungen zur keltischen Tracht', in L. Pauli (ed.) *Die Kelten in Mitteleuropa*, Salzburg, 133–1.
Martin-Kilcher, S. (1973) 'Zur Tracht und Beigabensitte im keltischen Gräberfeld von Münsingen-Rain (Kt. Bern)' *Zeitschrift für Schweizerische Archäologie und Kunstgeschichte* 30: 26.
Rudenko, S. (1970) *Frozen Tombs of Siberia*, London.
Spindler, K. (1983) *Die frühen Kelten*, 265–99.

PART VIII

PAGAN CELTIC RELIGION

RITUAL AND THE DRUIDS

——— ·◆· ———

Anne Ross

The Lives of the Irish Saints are written in Latin and in early medieval Irish. The latter are of special interest in that they seem to utilize local oral tradition in order to elucidate and illuminate their subject. Many miracles are attributed to the early Irish saints, and powers which vied with those of the druids in magic and cunning. For example, the druids were accredited with the ability to transform themselves, or others, into the form of certain animals; the saints on occasion manifest similar powers. At times natural phenomena obeyed the dictates of the druids – winds, fires, mists yielded to their commands. The same magical powers were brought into play by their saintly successors. Many such miracles are associated with the late sixth-century Irish saint Mochuda, who had his religious foundation at Rahan, County Offaly. The following example comes from his Irish Life, or *Betha*:

> On a certain day in early springtime there came to tempt him a Druid (*draoi*), who said to him 'In the name of your God cause this apple-tree branch to produce foliage.' Mochuda knew that it was in contempt of the divine power the Druid proposed this, and the branch put forth leaves on the instant. The Druid demanded 'In the name of your God put blossom on it.' Mochuda made the sign of the Cross over the branch and it blossomed presently. The Druid persisted 'What profits blossom without fruit?' For the third time Mochuda blessed the branch, and the fruit, fully ripe, fell to the earth. The Druid picked up an apple off the ground and, examining it, he understood it was quite sour, whereupon he objected. 'Such miracles as these are worthless, since the fruit is left uneatable.' Mochuda blessed the apples, and they became as sweet as honey. And in punishment for his opposition the Druid was deprived of his eyesight for a year. He went away, and at the end of the year he came back to Mochuda and did penance, whereupon he received his sight back again, and he returned home rejoicing.
>
> (Power 1914: 93)

The choice of an apple branch with which to test the magical powers of the saint was not random. The apple tree, according to the native tradition, grew prolifically in the Celtic Otherworld, putting forth leaves, blossom and fruit without cessation. In the story of *Cormac's Adventures in the Land of Promise* (translated in Dunn

1969: 503ff.) a stranger approaches the king of Tara, County Meath, who is looking out over the countryside at dawn. The season is Beltain, May, a time of magic. Later the king learns that his visitor is the god Manannan, an important deity in the Insular Celtic world. He carries on his shoulder a silver branch on which there are three apples of gold. 'Delight and amusement enough was it to listen to the music made by the branch.' A similar story is told in the tale *The Adventures of Connla the Fair*. Connla, son of Conn, high-king of Ireland, was with his father at the druidic centre Uisnech, in modern County Westmeath, ancient centre of all Ireland. A beautiful young woman approached him, invisible to all except Connla. She was a goddess from the Otherworld. Although she could not be seen, her voice could be heard. 'Whereupon the Druid (Corann) sang a magic incantation against the voice of the woman, so that no one could hear her voice.' But before the young woman departed 'before the potent chanting of the Druid', she threw an apple to the boy. He lived on the flesh of that apple alone for a whole month. 'What he ate of the apple never diminished it, but it remained always unconsumed' (Dunn 1969: 489). These are but two examples of the occurrence in early Irish of magical apples, and their connection with a god or a druid or both. In his choice of the apple branch in order to work his spells against Mochuda, the druid must have felt himself to be on fairly safe ground; his dismay at the superior magic of his enemy must have been considerable. Here, at the very beginning of our investigation, we witness a scene which would doubtless have been familiar to a much earlier Celtic world (Figure 23.1).

The passage from the Life of Saint Mochuda is of especial interest in that it demonstrates the survival of an active paganism in Ireland in the late sixth century, some one and a half centuries after the Patrician mission, and several centuries after Tiberius issued a decree against the druids and learned classes in Gaul in the first century AD. Even at this late date Irish druidism offered an alternative-belief-system. While the origins of druidism and the earliest religious rites of the druids remain obscure, the survival of druidic influence and the continuing role in some form of the druid immediately after the introduction of Christianity in Ireland is not in question. Druids figure in early Irish hagiographies, in certain of the Penitentials, and in prayers for protection known as *loricae* (Bieler 1953; Mac Eoin 1962; O'Lochlainn 1961). The constant druidic presence in the orally transmitted sagas demonstrates the original integral role of this order in pagan Irish society; and the huge corpus of native learning and tradition was dependent in its written form upon the early churchmen, who tried to record it as faithfully as possible.

The complex laws of medieval Ireland likewise testify to the continuing presence in some form of the druids and druidic beliefs, until the eighth century. At the same time, their elevated place in society would seem to have been usurped by the *filid*, the *vātis* of Gaul, the scholarly poets with certain original powers of a priestly and prophetic nature. These powers were shared by another class of learned men stemming from the pre-Christian druidic order, the so-called *brehons* (from Old Irish *brithemain*, 'judges'). In these two learned orders a great deal of the ancient teachings of the druids must have survived. Later still, the blacksmith in Celtic society, with his alleged powers of healing, his spells, and his mastery of iron, the magical metal, and the itinerant soothsayers replaced the influence of the old learned orders to some extent. For example, this is reflected in the great corpus of spells,

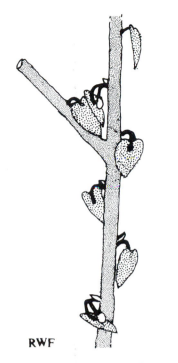

RWF

Figure 23.1 Part of the cult tree, 2 ft 3½ in (70 cm) high, of wood, bronze and gold leaf, found in 1984 in Manching, Bavaria, on a wooden platter plated with richly decorated gold plating. (V. Kruta *et al.* (eds) *The Celts*, London 1991: 530–1.)

prayers for protection, incantations and charms in Scottish Gaelic current until early in the twentieth century and known as *Carmina Gadelica*, as collected and recorded by Alexander Carmichael. This remarkable compilation of material from the rich oral tradition of Gaelic Scotland further testifies to the longevity of the ancient beliefs which were once under the aegis of the druidic orders.

Tradition preserved in the hagiographies, in sagas and poems and early historical tales, reveals unequivocally the high status of the pre-Christian druids of Ireland which equalled that enjoyed by the druids in Britain and on the Continent, according to the classics. In addition to the pre-eminent priestly functions, the druid deployed magical powers, as attested by his incantations, and the ability to foresee the future and to predict the outcome of events. His knowledge of astrology must have been considerable, as was his skill in calendrical computation. He was believed to have powers of shape-shifting, and to be able to change the shapes of others, turning humans into animals or birds at will. Thus he must have been a master of illusion. He was also a skilled healer, with a wide knowledge of the therapeutic properties of herbs and substances. Most importantly, perhaps, he was a teacher of the sons of noblemen, guardian of the hereditary learning and oral tradition.

By the time the Irish law books were compiled in the seventh and eighth centuries the druid still had a place in the legal codices, but under the increasing influence of Christianity he had come to be regarded as a sort of witch-doctor or sorcerer. But while he was discriminated against in the medieval Irish laws, he was not ignored. An impressive example of this discrimination occurs in the Old Irish law text entitled *Bretha Crólige* (Kelly 1988:60). The druid, together with the satirist (*cáinte*) and the brigand (*díberg*) is entitled to sick-maintenance (*othrus*) only at the level of the *bóaire*, 'cow-noble, owner of stock', '*no matter how great his rank, privilege or other rights*' (ibid.). He did, however, still have sufficient influence to be included among the *doernemeds*, dependent or privileged people, of the legal tract known as *Uraicecht Becc*, 'Small Primer'. The druids then had a definite if elusive role in Irish society at this period. Just as the satirist's words were feared, so were the spells of the druids a continuing source of unease. The druids still seem to have practised sorcery, adopting a position reminiscent of a crane's, standing on one leg with one arm outstretched and one eye closed. This was called *corrguinecht*, which may mean something like 'crane-wounding' (ibid.). The crane played a sinister role in Celtic mythology and religion.

This mode of sorcery seems to have included the chanting of a satire. An eighth-century hymn asks for God's protection against the spells of women and blacksmiths and druids. This same word for spells – *brichtu* is used on the Chamalières tablet in the form *bricti*.

It also seems likely that the druids continued to concoct love-potions, which are referred to in legal texts. In the early Irish saga *Serglige Con Culainn*, 'The Wasting Sickness of Cú Chulainn', the druids come to the assistance of the hero Cú Chulainn and his mistress the goddess Fand by giving them draughts of a potion which would make them totally forget their passion. Then the god Manannan, Fand's husband, 'shook his cloak between them so that they might never meet together again throughout eternity' (Dunn 1969: 198).

The undoubted magical powers of the druids could also be employed in war. The classics tell us that this was the case in Gaul. Diodorus Siculus, writing in the late first century BC, says that druids and chanting bards would come between armies lined up for battle, charming them and so averting combat (Kendrick 1927: 83). The Annals of Ulster of 561 note the use of a druid fence (*erbe ndruad*) in the battle of Cúil Dremne. Any warrior leaping over it was killed. Druids could also ensure victory in battle for the weaker side, according to the law *Bretha Nemed toísech*. This states: 'a defeat against odds . . . and setting territories at war confer status on a Druid' (Kelly 1988:61) (Figure 23.2).

DRUIDES, VATES, BARDOS

The classics record a threefold learned order for the Gauls. Chief among these are the druids, whose period of training lasted for some twenty years. They were priests, they alone knew the will of the gods, with whom they could communicate directly. They were also known as philosophers; their specialist knowledge included astrology and astronomy, medicine, magic, legal expertise and skill as teachers and historians (Figure 23.3).

Closely related are the *vates*, whose disciplines took up to twelve years to master. They too were accredited with the power of prophecy, they played some priestly part

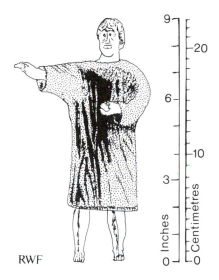

Figure 23.2 Bronze figure apparently representing a priest or druid, found at Neuvy-en-Sullias, Loiret, France. (J. Debal, *Les Gaulois en Orléanais*, Orleans 1974: 98–104, fig. 39.)

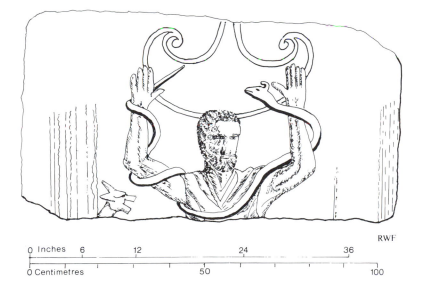

Figure 23.3 Upper half of relief of a male brandishing a snake and accompanied by a dog; possibly a druid. OROLAVNVM, Arlon, Luxembourg, Belgium. (E. Espérandieu, *Recueil général des bas-reliefs, statues et bustes de la Gaule romaine* V, Paris 1913: 4018.)

427

in the sacrifices, and like the other learned orders they were masters of poetry and the complex metres in which this was expressed. The Gaulish word *vátis* is cognate with the Latin *vatis* into which language it may have been borrowed.

The bards, the most enduring of the threefold order, had their own considerable powers and status. Their period of training was seven years. One of their most important functions was the composition of praise-poetry, which could bring great benefits to their patrons and so to the people in general. They also had the much-feared power of satire, which could cause physical blemish, bad luck, or even death to the person against whom it was sung. Satire continued to be feared in Celtic society down to the twentieth century.

Thus the three orders of Celtic men of erudition shared, in varying degrees, the powers of prophecy, magic and religion. It is noteworthy that these three learned orders appear in early Irish contexts having the same, or cognate, names and functions. The druid, Irish *druí*, had much the same powers as his counterpart in Gaul. The *vátis* of Gaul has as his equivalent the Irish *fili*, which originally connoted 'seer', 'diviner', later, esoteric poet. Another word which is an exact cognate of *vátis* is *fáith*, 'seer, prophet'. The Welsh words for these three learned orders are *dryw* or *derwydd*, 'druid'; *gweledydd*, 'prophet', 'seer', 'poet', *bard*. The nearest Welsh equivalent to the word *vátis* is *gwawdawr*, 'poet'.

The Irish *bard* (Welsh *bardd*) had similar functions to those of his Gaulish counterparts. Unlike the bards of Wales, however, whose status as learned poets seemed to increase, the Irish bards were replaced as praise-poets by the *filidh*, and came to be regarded as mere story-tellers, entertainers and rhymers.

The classics tell of a chief druid, while Caesar states that all the druids met together in assembly at a certain time of the year in the tribal territory of the Carnutes, which was regarded as the centre of all Gaul. The Irish druids likewise had a chief druid and, later, a chief *fili*. They used to assemble at Uisnech, in modern County Westmeath. The Assembly of Uisnech, which was regarded as the 'navel' of Ireland, was held on Beltain, 1 May, and the period before and after this date (see p. 437). The whole druidic system would seem to have been common to all the Celts. There is some evidence for female druids and prophets which is not considered here.

In Wales the situation is somewhat different. There would seem to have been a druidic centre on Anglesey (Môn), where the druids were attacked and virtually destroyed by the troops under Suetonius Paulinus in AD 61. Tacitus gives a graphic description of the conflict between the cursing druids (and wild, black-clad women who may have been druidesses or female prophets) and the disciplined soldiers to whom the sight must have been unnerving to a degree. The Romans were victorious; and although druidism clearly continued in some form outside the 'pale', it was effectively disrupted as a formal system in Britain.

This historical event does not necessarily mean that the druids entirely lost their identity and influence among the people of Britain, especially those removed from the centre of imperial activity. The advent of the Romans to Britain was a military and not a spiritual victory, such as the coming of Christianity to pagan lands. The Roman occupation of Britain was eventually followed by the immigration of Anglo-Saxons and Jutes – Ireland missed both these events – and the word 'druid' was not used again in Britain, as far as we can tell, until a much later period. The word *drý*, probably from Irish *druí*, and compounds such as *drýcraeft* are employed regularly in Anglo-Saxon connoting 'magician', 'sorcerer', and used to translate Latin *magus* (Bosworth and Toller, *Anglo-Saxon Dictionary*).

However, some degree of druidic influence and authority must have survived the proscription of the order throughout the empire, in Britain as in Gaul. In some instances druids were referred to as *magi*. In Irish, for example, Simon Magus appears as Simon Druí. Pictish druids are also referred to as *magi* in Adamnan's *Vita Sancti Columbae*, for example, written in the seventh century, almost a hundred years after the death of the saint. When St Columba journeyed into the Inverness region of Pictland to convert the pagan Picts to the Faith, he had an encounter with Broichan, the hostile druid of the pagan Pictish king Brude. The royal fortress may have been sited on Craig Phadruig near Inverness, on which are the remains of a 'vitrified' fort. Just as St Patrick attacked Irish paganism at the court of the powerful king Loegaire, on the Hill of Tara, so did Columba attack Pictish paganism at the court of King Brude beside the river Ness.

When King Brude refused to open the gates of the fortress to Columba and his clerics, the saint made the sign of the cross and the bolts fell away. Alarmed, the druids (*magi*) exhorted their king to turn a deaf ear to the men of God; but Columba overcame all opposition and the king was converted to the Faith. Columba worked among the Picts for nine years after this, and mastered their language. However, Broichan, Brude's foster-father and tutor, remained hostile to the clerics, and did all he could to hinder their mission. One evening when the saint and his monks were chanting Evensong Broichan and his fellow druids tried unsuccessfully to hinder the service. But eventually the druid was converted by the superior magic of the saint. When Broichan became ill and no cure could be found, Columba was eventually summoned to cure him. The saint caused a white quartz pebble to be placed in some water, and the stone came to the surface of the liquid. A draught of the water was given to Broichan, then near death, and he recovered at once. In this context the druids are referred to as *magi*. However, in the metrical version of *Saint Columba's Prayer* we find the statement '*mo druí* . . . Mac Dé', 'My druid . . . the Son of God' (Fowler 1920).

So it is clear that after the Roman conquest of the southern half of Britain official druidism could not be acceptable to the imperial administration. However, native deities and their cults were countenanced; and native gods must have necessitated native priests, who could communicate with the gods in their own language. These are matters about which we have little knowledge to date, although archaeological work on Romano-British temples is constantly bringing more evidence to light with regard to native cult practices. Perhaps the Celtic priesthood was allowed to continue under another name, one which did not have the connotation of the word 'druid'. Functions would then be confined to the correct performance of such ritual as was permitted in the centuries following the Roman conquest.

The Vortigern (Welsh Gwrtheyrn) legend certainly indicates that druids (called *magi*) were still functioning in some parts of Britain after the end of Roman occupation. Possibly the earliest reference in Welsh literature to druids occurs in the tenth-century poem *Armes Prydein*, 'The Prophecy of Britain', from the *Book of*

Taliesin (Bromwich and Williams 1972: 12–13). The poem ends with the words *dysgogan derwydon meint a deruyd*, 'druids foretell all that will happen'. In the *derwydd* we have the root *wid*, 'to know' (Welsh *gwybod*, 'know'). The word which is cognate with druid is *dryw*, which also means 'wren', a druidic bird. The word came to be equated with druid in the eighteenth century, but the two instances in which *dryw* appears in the *Book of Taliesin* are ambiguous, although in one instance 'druid' rather than 'wren' would seem to be a more likely translation.

In 1632 John Davies of Mallwyd favoured the meaning 'oak' as a translation of the first part of the word *derwyd*. As the oak was a venerated tree among the Celts, 'knowledge of the oak' is a valid alternative for 'very great knowledge' for the Gaulish *druides* and the Insular counterparts. The Celts liked this sort of *double entendre*; the druids certainly had very great knowledge of their own *Discipline*, and according to Lucan they received their divinatory knowledge by means of a trance caused by their custom of chewing acorns (Ní Chatháin 1979–80: 211). In the Welsh poem *Cad Goddau*, 'The Battle of the Trees' – one of the 'futile battles' (*Tri Ouergat*) of the Island of Britain (Bromwich 1961: 206–8) – Taliesin (Bromwich 1991: 51) addresses certain druids of a 'Wise One' who may be Arthur, or the poet himself:

> Derwydon doethur
> Darogenwch y Arthur.
>
> 'Druids of a wise one
> Prophesy to Arthur.'

This may suggest that Arthur is present, waiting to hear the druids pronounce, as he did with the bards in *Breuddwyd Rhonabwy*, 'The Dream of Rhonabwy' (Jones and Jones 1974: 151). In both these passages the role of the druid is that of a prophet, which seems to have been a major and lasting function of the druids in general. The actions of kings in the early Celtic world depended upon the druids' knowledge of the future and the outcome of events; later the poets took over this role.

DRUIDS AND BARDS

We have no examples of the work of the continental bards, apart perhaps from the Chamalières and comparable inscriptions; but the account given by Athenaeus of the bard and Louernius the renowned Arvernian chieftain indicates that the role of the bard was the same in Gaul as it was to be in the British Isles (Tierney 1960: 24). Louernius made a great feast in an enclosure of vast size which he had prepared for the purpose. This was duly provisioned with huge vats of liquid and cauldrons of food, and the feast was served for many days to all who wished to partake of it. When the time came to end the feast, and Louernius was preparing to leave, a poet ran up to him singing a praise-poem in honour of Louernius and bewailing his own late arrival. Moved by this, and acting in accordance with accepted ritual, the chieftain had a bag of gold brought to him and threw it to the poet. In return, the poet sang another praise-poem, even more fulsome than the first, stating that even the tracks made by the chariot of Louernius gave 'gold and largesse to mankind'.

It is fitting to consider the rituals of the poets in the context of this chapter. As J.E. Caerwyn Williams so appositely comments in his Hallstatt Lecture (1991, Machynlleth):

> I have emphasized the authority and power of the Druids because the poets were a branch of the druidic order, and because the shadow of the Druids lay heavily on the poets of both Ireland and Wales even at a much later date when both countries had rejected paganism.
>
> (*Y Bardd Celtaidd*, 'The Celtic Bard': 7)

Prophets as indeed they were, and at all periods of recorded time, there can be little doubt that the druids were *primarily* priests of the Celtic religious cults. I believe that the great Celtic scholar J.G. MacCulloch, himself a churchman, was correct in stating: 'there is no reason to believe that Druids did not exist wherever there were Celts' (MacCulloch 1911: 298).

The Celts also had priests called *gutuatri*, whose functions would appear to have stemmed from the druids. The word seems to be derived from **ghutu-patèr*, 'Father (master) of the Invocation (to god)'. As Professor Caerwyn Williams suggests (1984: 23), '*Bardos* means "the singer of praise (?to men)", and it seems from the above that he had a priestly counterpart, "the singer of praise (to god)".' It is interesting to note that the medieval Welsh *pencerdd*, 'chief poet', must sing one song to God and another to the king. The Celtic poet exercised magical powers, as did the *fili* and the druid. He regarded himself as a shaman or a magician. He used words not only to praise those qualities he believed to be essential to a ruler, but he *called them into existence in him*. To quote the much-quoted words of the thirteenth-century Welsh poet, Phylip Brydydd, to his princely patron, *gwneuthum it glod*, 'I made fame for thee'. This indicates well the complex nature of Celtic society, where contract and offering and giving in return for privilege were all closely ordered and understood. We can imagine that the druids, by their chanting and by their rites of sacrifice and deposition, not only brought forth the desired results and benefits from the gods, they actually called them into existence, and 'made fame' for the deities by immortalizing them in words.

The most important of the tripartite learned orders – which could themselves clearly be divided within the group – were, of course, the druids. They were in charge of religion and its attendant ritual, and no matter what assistance they may have had from the other orders, the vates, bards and parasites – themselves an offshoot from the bardic order – the ability to communicate directly with the gods, and the power to know and interpret their will for the people, rested with the druids alone. They clearly correspond to the Brahmins of ancient India and the Flamines of early Rome; and all three must be seen as the representatives of and descendants from the ancient Indo-European priestly caste. As MacCulloch so pertinently comments: 'Druidism was not a formal system outside Celtic religion. It covered the whole ground of Celtic religion; in other words, *it was* that religion itself' (1911: 301).

Druidic teaching was oral. The Irish druids 'sang over' (*for-cain*, a word which can also mean 'prophesy, predict') their pupils; the pupils repeated the lesson in chorus. In the Irish texts there is an occasional reference to druidic books (McGrath 1979: 29f.). A script known as Ogam came into use about the fourth century AD, based on the Latin alphabet and consisting of strokes or notches which were cut into wood, bone or stone (McManus 1991: 1ff.). It seems highly likely that it originated as a system of magical symbols, and some scholars have maintained that it originated as long ago as *c*.500 BC as a sign language used by the continental druids. This argument is based on the fact that the symbols are clumsy as written letters but are well suited to mobile fingers (McManus 1991: 8f.). The Irish god Ogma is credited with having invented this system of writing.

Oaths sworn before druids were regarded as sacred and binding. Oaths were sworn on many things, including the elements, which, if the oath were to be violated, would be expected to turn upon the guilty one and destroy him. The magical power of the pagan oath made it unacceptable to the early Christian church. A reference to pre-Christian oath-taking occurs in the sixth-century First Synod of Saint Patrick. This synod ordained that a Christian who swore before a druid in the pagan manner had to do a year's penance (Kelly 1988: 198f.).

It is of especially great interest to consider the text of the Chamalières tablet. In 1971 a lead tablet with a Gaulish magico-religious text of some sixty words in Italic writing was found at the Source-des-Roches de Chamalières, Puy-de-Dôme, France. It has been dated to the early first century BC, an important period for pagan Celtic religion and rites. It is in the nature of a *defixio* (meaning 'bewitch', 'curse'), and is an important document for information on Celtic deities and magical formulae (Lejeune and Marichal 1977). The god Maponus is invoked as the Arvernian Maponus; and Lugus, the most widely venerated and important of all the Celtic deities, would seem to be present in the context of an oath, which is a kind of magical restraint, and had great powers in the early Celtic world. Perhaps the most striking feature is the magical formula for swearing by a god which, in Ireland, occurs as *tongu do dhia tonges mo thuath*, 'I swear by the god by whom my people swear'. The Old Irish word for oath is *lugae*, *luige*; and Sayers, in his important article on enchainment (1990), states: 'More attractive is the hypothesis . . . that Old Irish *lugae*, *luige*, 'oath', and the theonym *Lug* are related, with the latter possibly a tutelary divinity of contractual bonds' (1990: 234). There is a similar formula in Early Welsh, and the word for oath in Welsh is *llw*. In the Chamalières *defixio* we are in the very presence of active druidic ritual, and we are also able to envisage some small fragment of the myth of the pan-Celtic god Lugus.

ASSEMBLIES/ÓENAICH AND CALENDAR FESTIVALS

Caesar's comments on the religion of the Celts are astute, informed and well attested by the vernacular tradition. Perhaps his most important statement is his account of a great national assembly held annually under the aegis of the druidic orders. Its significance is such that it bears quoting in full:

> These Druids, at a certain time of the year, meet within the borders of the Carnutes, whose territory is reckoned as the centre of all Gaul, and sit in conclave in a consecrated spot. Thither assemble from every side all that have

disputes, and they obey the decisions and judgments of the Druids. It is believed their rule of life was discovered in Britain, and transferred thence to Gaul.

(Kendrick 1927: 77–8, 213)

It is, in fact, from the British Isles, especially from Ireland, that the best evidence of such seasonal assemblies is to be found. Before we examine a selection of these, it is appropriate to look at an important Gaulish document where mention is made of the most widespread and enduring of the seasonal assemblies or festivals, that known as Lughnasa in Ireland. The druids had a clear concept of time, and this is well evidenced by the fragments of a liturgical calendar dating to the turn of the Christian era, and thought to be a table of sacred times and festivals. Found in 1897 in a fragmentary state at Coligny, Ain, France, the fragments of a massive bronze panel had been engraved with a calendrical table in a Celtic language (Kendrick 1927: 116ff.). Presumably serving as a system of reckoning for use by the druids, it is drawn up in sixteen columns of months covering a period of five years. Most of the inscriptions are abbreviations, which are difficult to interpret, but the five-year period is of great interest in view of the observation by Diodorus Siculus that the continental Celts held quinquennial sacrifices. These we must suppose to have been of especial significance.

It is not possible in this context to examine the calendar in any detail, except to note that months and days are marked by the words *MAT*, 'good' (Irish *maith*, Welsh *mad*), and *ANM*, 'not good or lucky'. This is a concept which is encountered in the early Irish epic tale *Táin Bó Cúailnge*. Here Cathbad the druid, father of the king of the Ulaid, 'Ulstermen', Conchobor mac Nessa, is teaching his acolytes in his druidic school near Emain Macha, the royal stronghold. One of the pupils asks his master whether the omens for that day are good or bad: 'Iarfacht fer díb dia aiti ciaso sén 7 solud buí forin ló i mbatar, in ba maith fá in ba saich' (O'Rahilly 1967: 25–6).

Of great significance for the antiquity of the major Celtic calendar festivals is the fact that the pan-Celtic assembly of Lughnasa, 'Games or Assembly of Lugh', held on and around 1 August, a first-fruit feast, is indicated on the Coligny calendar under the name Rivros, 'great festal month'. Rivros has been equated with the Irish month Lughnasa; the notation at the thirteenth day of Rivros has been interpreted as 'great feast of the god' (McNeill 1962: 1). Coligny is not far from Lyons, which was allegedly founded by Lugus, the name Lugudunum meaning 'Fortress of Lugos'. It seems clear that the Celtic feast of Lughnasa was replaced by the feast of Augustus in the Roman period, this also being celebrated on 1 August. Lugos gave his name to several towns in Gaul, and it is probable that the great festival was held at or near these places also. In Britain, the earliest name for Carlisle is Luguvalium, 'Strong in the god Lugos', and here too we may expect to find traces of his festal month. The assembly in Ireland was founded, according to tradition, by Lugh in honour of his foster-mother the divine Tailtiu, or in memory of his wives, Nás and Búi. Two of the great Irish assemblies were held at Lughnasa, the Óenach Tailten and the Óenach Carmain. The first was celebrated at Teltown in modern County Meath. Óenach Carmain was connected with the kingship of Leinster, and is thought to have been sited somewhere in the plain known as the Curragh of Kildare. This ancient

Lughnasa festival is commemorated in a long poem in the metrical *Dindshenches*, 'Stories about Important Places', which gives the fullest and most detailed account of any of the ancient assemblies in the Celtic world. It illustrates the fact that, although matters of law were of great importance at these pan-tribal gatherings, many other events took place, especially competitive games and the horse-racing that still remains an Irish passion. Another word for *óenach* is *féis*, 'feast', and feasting and drinking as well as sacrifice and propitiation were important aspects of these assemblies. The Carman gathering would seem to be typical of all the archaic festivals (Best and O'Brien 1965, IV: 843ff.).

The ancient Celtic year was divided into two seasons, the cold season (Gaulish *giamon*, Irish *gaimred*, Welsh *gaeaf*) and the warm season (Gaulish *samon*, Irish *samrad*, Welsh *haf*). This division applied over the entire Celtic world; in antiquity it is noted in the Coligny calendar, and in modern times Welsh still knows Calan Gaeaf and Calan Mai. Each season was divided into two halves, and each of the quarter-days and the preceding nights were marked by a major assembly. It is of interest to note that these ancient days are still observed in some form in the British Isles down to the present time. Over and above the great national assemblies at which the individual tribes came together as one nation – Gaul, Ireland, the Island of Britain – there were numerous smaller regional and local festivals held to mark the major calendar feasts.

Samain

The Celtic New Year began on the eve of 1 November. It was the most dangerous and the most portentous of all the calendar festivals. At this time the gods moved freely in the world of mankind, and played cruel tricks on unsuspecting people. Men too could enter the Otherworld, but this was a hazardous undertaking. Many significant events took place at this time, according to tradition; for example, the great battle of the gods of Ireland, Cath Maige Tuired, is essentially a Samain myth (Gray 1982), the trinox Samoni, 'three nights of Samain', are noted in the Coligny calendar.

Óenach Temra

The Assembly of Tara, seat of the kings of Ireland, was the most prestigious of the Irish *óenaich*. It was held at Samain. We learn in the story of the *Battle of Crinna* that

> every king of Ireland (was in Tara) for the purpose of holding Tara's Feast; for a fortnight before *samain* that is to say, on *samain*-day itself, and for a fortnight after. And the reason for which they practised to gather themselves together at every *samain*-tide was this: because at such season it was that mast and other products were the best matured. Here too is the reason for which the Feast of Tara was made at all: the body of law which all Ireland enacted then, during the interval between that and their next convention at a year's end none might dare to transgress; and he that perchance did so was outlawed from *the men of Ireland*.

The national nature of the assembly is here made clear, and the reference to the laws tallies well with Caesar's observations (O'Grady 1982: 319, Irish text). In *The Taboos of the Kings of Ireland* we learn:

> For when those kings consumed the Feast of Tara they used to settle the affairs of Ireland for seven years, so that debts, suits and adjustments used not to be submitted for judgment until the next feast seven years later. [Ar in tan no tom-litis in rígh sin feiss Temruch no glétis dála Hérenn co secht mbliadna coná fuighlitis fíacho ná féchthemnusa ná coiccerta cusin feiss n-aile iar secht mblíadna].

> (Dillon 1951: 25)

The whole subject of Old Irish *geiss*, 'prohibition' (Welsh *tyghet*) and *búada* or *ada*, 'prescriptions', is archaic and essentially druidic. Traces of it appear on the Chamalières tablet.

Emain Macha

An important assembly was held at Samain here, the seat of the kings of the Ulaidh, modern Ulster, the centre of the province. It lasted for a week, and horse-racing was an important feature. Here the goddess Macha, who has clear equine aspects, raced the horses of the king, only to die afterwards giving birth to twins or triplets. This *óenach* was said to have been established in her honour. In *Scela Chonchobuir* it is recorded that:

> It was Conchobar himself who would give the Samain feast to them because of the assembly of the great host. It was necessary to provide for the great crowd because every Ulsterman who did not come to Emain Macha on Samain night would be deprived of his senses and his grave and his standing-stone would be put in place on the next day. [Conchobor im fessin no gaibed in samuin dóib fo dagin, terchomraic in tslúaig móir. Ba hecen in tsochaide mór do airichill. fo bith cech fer do Ultaib na tairchebad aidchi samna dochum nEmna. no gatta ciall de 7focherte a fert 7 a lecht 7 a lecht 7 a lie arnabarach].
> (*Book of Leinster* I, 402: Best and O'Brien 1956)

Samain, then, was a time of danger when the magic of the druids was required to control the hostility of the Otherworld beings by chanting and by sacrifice, spells and apotropaic formulae. A great assembly also took place at Tlachtga in modern County Meath at this season. Tlachtga was the daughter of the powerful druid Mug Ruith, originally a deity according to O'Rahilly (1946: 519). The ancient assembly site bearing her name is at the Hill of Ward, near Athboy.

Imbolc or Óimelc

This ancient name for the second festival of the pagan Celtic year has been discussed by Eric Hamp (1979). The word seems to mean 'purification', and the festival took place on the eve of 1 February and on the day itself, at a time when the sheep and other animals were beginning to lactate. Imbolc was sacred to the threefold Irish goddess Brigid, who was adored by poets, smiths and medical practitioners and who is clearly the goddess whom Caesar equated with Minerva. There are other claimants to this role in the Celtic mythology, but hers must be the place of honour. She was mother-goddess *par excellence*, a seasonal deity, and she presided over the important purification feast of Imbolc. As a Christian saint, many elements of her cult legend were taken over into Christianity, and her *cultus* is found widely over Europe. In Wales she is venerated as Sant Ffraid. Her festival was clearly acceptable to the church as, apart from anything else, it coincided with the Christian feast of the purification of the Virgin.

In Scottish Gaelic tradition the saint is venerated as the midwife of Mary, and in the Outer Hebrides her festival attracted a very ancient stratum of custom and belief. Of great interest is the fact that the recitation of Brigid's ancestry (*sloinntireachd*) was current in the Catholic islands until the nineteenth century, where it was believed to have efficacious powers. Imbolc was (and is) known as Latha Féill Bhrìde, 'The Day of the Festival of Bride', the Gaelic form of the name, and many legends and archaic customs adhered to this special day. She is 'said to preside over fire' (Carmichael 1928: 164), which is interesting in view of the fact that the Irish Brigid had a perpetually burning fire at Kildare, guarded by nineteen virgins, and no man might approach her shrine. Christ was known as Dalta Brìde in the southern Hebrides, 'the foster-son of Brìde'. Images of the goddess-saint were fashioned down to the twentieth century and adorned with greenery and early flowers, shells and pretty stones. These images were carried in procession by the girls round every house. A special bannock was made, known as *bonnach Brìde*, and this was consumed at a feast in her honour.

In Ireland the churn-staff was fashioned into the likeness of a woman, an interesting association with milk and dairy produce for which the saint was renowned; and this likeness was dressed as a woman called Brìdeog, 'Little Bride' (Danaher 1972: 13ff.).

Perhaps the most interesting and archaic of the Brigid rituals is that in which a serpent plays a central role (Carmichael 1928: 169). One is reminded of the Gaulish goddesses who are portayed holding or accompanied by serpents (Green 1989: 62, fig. 24, for example), and the relief of the goddess Verbeia, eponymous goddess of the river Wharfe in Yorkshire, which was found at Ilkley. She holds a serpent in either hand (Ross 1992: 279).

Brigid the saint was the daughter of a druid, Dubthach, and her future glory was prophesied by a druid named Mathgen. In spite of her pagan background she was welcomed into Christianity, and became one of the most popular and best loved of all the Celtic saints.

Beltain

Cormac, in his ninth-century Irish glossary, has two explanations for the name of the second great seasonal festival of Ireland, which is still called Beltain (Bealtain) in Scotland and Ireland, and Calan Mai in Wales. The first connects the fire with good luck (*bil-tene*) and says: 'that is, two fires which Druids used to make with great incantations', a piece of information on actual druidic ritual. Furthermore Cormac tells us that the druids used to bring the cattle as a safeguard against the diseases of each year to those fires. That is, they would drive the cattle between them. The second interpretation of the meaning of Beltain is that it is the fire of an idol god, i.e. Belenos: 'a fire was kindled in his name at the beginning of summer always, and cattle were driven between the two fires' (Stokes 1868: 19, 23). The festival is also known as Cétshamain, '1 May'.

Tara was the royal centre of Ireland; and Uisnech, in modern County Westmeath, was, like the sacred spot in the terrain of the Carnutes of Gaul, the druidic centre, sometimes called 'the navel of Ireland'. The chief assembly took place here at Beltain. This, too, was a fraught, potentially dangerous season, and many sacrifices had to be made to protect the young crops and stock from blight and evil forces.

It was a time of portentous happenings. According to the Irish Book of Invasions, *Lebor Gabála*, the incursions of the legendary Partholón, the Tuatha De Danaan, the gods of Ireland, and the sons of Míl, ancestors of the Gael, all took place at this season. The invasion of Nemed, too, seems to have happened at Beltain. It was then that Mide, chief druid of these people, and eponym of Meath, lit the first fire. It blazed for seven years, a significant number. Fire-lighting was very much a ritual act in the pagan Celtic world, and the Uisnech fire, lit ceremonially by the druids, was especially potent and magical. During Patrick's sojourn in Ireland he pre-empted the druids of Tara who were about to light their Beltain fire, and his great conflagration struck an ominous blow at the druids and at paganism in Ireland. It was a major triumph for the Christian faith (Stokes 1887: 41f.).

All the Celtic calendar festivals were in essence fire-festivals, and the druids were much concerned with fire-magic. Strabo observed that the druids maintained that the earth was indestructible, although 'both fire and water will at some time or other prevail' (*Geographica* IV.4.c.197 4[1]). The druids held that souls are likewise immortal. Fire and water were the two elements most revered and employed by the druids in their sacred rites. Young animals were sacrificed at this fraught season, and there is some evidence for human sacrifice in the traditions. When the druid Mide lit the huge Beltain fire, the great heat of which spread over the four quarters of Ireland, the indigenous druids were enraged. Mide responded by having them collected together in one dwelling where their tongues were cut out. The druids' tongues were then buried in the earth of Uisnech (*Metrical Dindschenchas* II.42).

The calendar festivals and the great assemblies which accompanied them were fundamental to Celtic social life, when the people met not as tribes but as a nation. The hosting of pre-eminent feasts was a visible sign of the wealth and authority of the kings and the druids.

There was an important Galatian meeting place where twelve 'tetrarchs' met annually with three hundred assistants at a place called Drunemeton, 'Oak Sanctuary' or 'Druid Sanctuary'. 'The Council decided murder cases, the tetrarchs and the judges all others' (Mitchell 1862: 27). This is reminiscent of the assembly in Gaul described by Caesar (*De Bello Gallico* VI.13), held annually, at which disputes of every kind were heard and settled by the druids. The tetrarchs may well have been priest-kings; like the druids of Gaul they were empowered to act as judges. The high-kingship of Pessinus, where Drumeneton may have been situated, was given to certain Celts in the second century BC. This suggests that some of the Celts at least were already in the habit of uniting the two offices of priest and king. The festival may have been held at Beltain (1 May) or Lughnasa (1 August), as it was customary to deck the dogs with flowers. Goats were sacrificed.

As mentioned above, Caesar refers to assemblages of the Carnutes at 'the centre of Gaul'. It seems probable that the holy place set aside for these formal gatherings was under or near Chartres Cathedral (Ross 1979–80: 260–9).

As would be expected, the *óenaich* or assemblies still had some place in the Irish laws in the eighth century. We learn from Kelly that the king 'also convenes the óenach, a regular assembly for political, social and perhaps commercial purposes. In the case of an overking, such an assembly may be attended by people from a number of *túatha* (tribes, peoples). For example, the Óenach Tailten, 'Fair of Tailtiu', is held each year at the festival of Lughnasad (early August), under the auspices of the king of Tara. An interesting fragment follows in Kelly (1988: 4) showing the close organization of these gatherings; 'by attendance at an óenach a person is evidently felt to have willingly exposed himself to the risk of being killed or injured by horses or chariots, and there is consequently no recompense for such accidents'.

The king of Meath (Mide) held the Samain *óenach* at Uisnech. At the same time, the king of Tara held his Samain assembly. The king of Meath was exempt from contribution to the Feast of Tara. *Mide* comes from the Celtic word **medion*, 'centre'. The *Metrical Dindshenchas* (IV.298–9) states: 'for it was great wealth for the king of Meath, alone among the kings of Erinn, not to contribute to the feast of Tara [ar ba mór an main do righ Midhe seach cach righ a nErinn cen imthuilled fessi Teamrach]'.

The word ritual in the context of the druids inevitably connotes the human sacrifice to which the Romans, newly freed from the same practice themselves, took strong exception. There can be no doubt whatsoever that the druids included this in their ritual repertoire, but to what extent, how frequently and on what occasions we have, to date, little knowledge. Archaeology can suggest but can rarely testify to the practice, but this may not always be the case. New techniques and scientific developments may provide us with more convincing evidence. Some of the bog bodies from northern Europe, including Lindow Moss, Cheshire, are generally accepted as sacrificial victims. Others are marginal cases, and may have been executions for social sins.

ANIMAL SACRIFICE

It is clear that animals were ritually slain for sacrificial purposes; there is much evidence both textual and archaeological for this widespread practice. Some of the most interesting examples of animal sacrifice come from Gaelic Scotland, where traditions of a clearly archaic nature have survived in remote and rural Celtic contexts. One of these, much abhorred by the church, persisted at least into the late eighteenth century. It took place in the month of August on Inis Maree, a little island in the loch of that name in Ross and Cromarty. The island is sacred to the saint Maelrubha. Clearly a Lughnasa ceremony, it consisted of sacrificing bulls to the saint by the people of the region. An invaluable account of this and other 'heathenish practices' is contained in the Dingwall Presbytery Records of 6 August 1778 (Mitchell 1862: 8–10, quoted in MacNeill 1962: 364 and in MacCulloch 1911: 243).

Pliny, in his famous description of the culling of mistletoe by the druids before a feast (*Naturalis Historia* XVI.249), states: 'Having made preparation for a sacrifice and a banquet beneath the trees, they bring thither two white bulls, whose horns are bound then for the first time. . . . Then they kill the victims.' In Ireland a bull-feast, *tarb-feis*, was used to determine by mantic means the rightful successor to the king of Tara. A bull was killed, and a druid ate of its flesh and drank of the broth in which it had been cooked. The druids sang a 'spell of truth' over him, and in his dreams he would 'see' the rightful king. Sometimes the prophet had to be wrapped in the hide of the slaughtered animal. The ritual slaughter of three bulls seems to be taking place on an inner plate of the Gundestrup Cauldron, where three warriors hold swords to the throats of huge animals, their immense size in comparison to the men suggesting their own divinity. Three surly dogs bound beneath the animals (Olmsted 1979: pl. 3D) (Figure 23.4).

The bull, and bovines in general, seem to have been regular sacrificial animals, and to have been included in the choice of animals thrown into the straw colossi and immolated, according to Strabo (*Geographica* IV.4.c.198.5). Brunaux mentions bovine sacrifice on a large scale revealed in the excavations of places such as Gournay, in Picardy, France, where the remains were deposited in a central pit (Brunaux 1988: 15, etc.).

There can be little doubt that animal sacrifice took place in Ireland at the great assemblies, as did human sacrifice. At the druidic site Uisnech, traces of the Beltain sacrifices have been found. In the centre of the enclosure on the top of the hill a large bed of ashes was exposed, relics of a series of fires, and charred skeletons of animals were found among them (Macalister 1931: 166ff.). Ann Woodward states in her *Shrines and Sacrifice* (1992: 78):

> It can be assumed that many of the sacrificed beasts would have provided meat for feasting, so the numbers of bodies and parts of bodies that have survived on Iron Age sites indicate that the practice of animal sacrifice in Celtic society must have been very widespread indeed.

All the evidence supports this statement. Cunliffe's discovery of the heads and legs of horses in various contexts at Danebury, Hampshire, is suggestive of the 'heads and hooves' ritual where the body of the animal was consumed and the hide used to wrap the seer in preparation for his mantic sleep (1968: 155ff.).

Pigs were choice animals for sacrifice and ritual consumption, and the pig heads in the Yorkshire iron age graves are indicative of this (Stead 1979: *passim*), as too is the scene on the Epona relief (Figure 23.5). A divinatory rite in early Ireland, recorded by Cormac, bishop of Cashel, in the ninth century, involved a process known as Imbas Forosnai, 'Knowledge that Enlightens':

> the *fili* chews a piece of the flesh of a red pig, or of a dog or a cat, and puts it afterwards on a flagstone behind the door, and pronounces an incantation on it, and offers it to idol gods.
>
> (O'Donovan and Stokes 1868: 94; Ford 1992: 14–15)

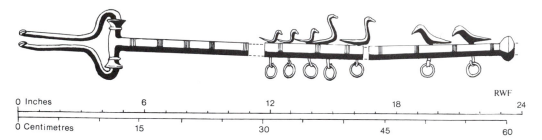

Figure 23.4 Incomplete bronze implement, probably a flesh-fork, ornamented with a pair of ravens and two swans with three cygnets. Dunaverney, Co. Antrim, Ireland. (R. Megaw and V. Megaw, *Celtic Art*, London 1989: 25, fig. 9.)

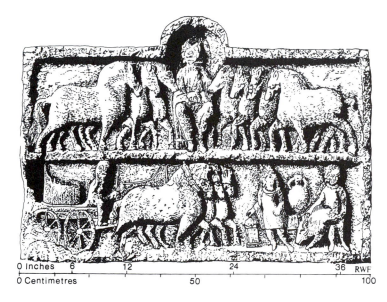

Figure 23.5 Epona with seven ponies, a tree-stump borne on a cart drawn by three horses, and two priests about to sacrifice a young boar which one priest holds by the back legs. Beihingen, Stuttgart, Germany. (E. Espérandieu, *Recueil général des bas-reliefs, statues et bustes de la Germanie romaine*, Paris and Brussels 1931: 404.)

Dog sacrifice is well attested archaeologically. Danebury produced several examples of this (Cunliffe 1968: 155f.), and there are numerous other occurrences of ritual deposits in Britain which contain the remains of dogs. At the religious site of Ivy Chimneys, Essex, a ditch contained dog teeth arranged in the form of a necklace. In the Upchurch Marshes, Kent, puppies were found buried in urns, one with an adult bitch; and these are paralleled by the pots containing dogs and dating to the pre-Roman Iron Age and earlier, which have been found in Jutland. Some of the bones were in pots, and some scattered generously round these (Todd 1975: 197ff.: for dog sacrifice, see Green 1986: 155, 168, 176). The shaft, with a depth of

200 ft (61 m), at the Romano-British shrine at Muntham Court, Sussex, contained a great many dog skeletons. The shrine is dated to the first century.

Animal sacrifice was much favoured by the Celts and the Germanic peoples alike, and the custom long persisted in the Celtic world, where, for example, one animal would be ritually slain in order to preserve the flock or herd from some decimating disease. Henderson (1911: 271–2) gives a personal account of such a custom:

> I well recollect how in the Highlands, when any loss occurred among the cattle in spring (*earchall*) the hooves and sometimes the head or parts of it were taken away to the wood and buried secretly in the soil under the great trees where nobody could possibly molest them. It was still better to bury them on an adjoining estate, and across a river. This was to put away the *earchall* and to prevent the loss of more animals. In some of the Isles there is still a memory of a cure for a species of cattle-plague. . . . The old people said if the heifer's head were struck off at a single blow with a clean or stainless sword that the plague would cease . . . this was done in the eighteenth century.

In Wales, according to the Revd John Evans in 1812, 'when a violent disease breaks out among the horned cattle, the farmers . . . give up a bullock for a victim, which is carried to the top of a precipice whence it is thrown down' (ibid.).

Celtic sacrifice, human and animal, is indeed well attested. More integral to druidism and to Celtic religion in general is the custom of deposition, which has a long ancestry in Europe. This was carried out into the earth, through which the deities could be reached in their Otherworld, known as Annwn or Annwfn and sited beneath the earth (*dwfn*) according to Welsh tradition. In Irish belief this subterranean Elysium was situated through the *sídh* (Otherworld) mounds, down wells or beneath lakes and pools or in rivers. The Celts did not love their deities; they made contracts with them as they did in their own society. By making offerings into pits, wells, springs, peat-bogs and all watery places, no doubt with solemn attendant ritual, the druids were in fact 'binding' the gods into making reciprocal gifts to mankind – including, no doubt, security against their own hostility (Figure 23.6).

A votive and, perhaps, sacrificial deposit, comprising four magnificent horns decorated with La Tène patterns and accompanied by human skulls, was recovered from Loughnashade, the lough which in all probability was connected with the nearby royal and sacred stronghold of Emain Macha, Navan Fort near Armagh, Ireland. Sacred places elsewhere in the Celtic world are often associated with lakes and pools. Here the whole surrounding landscape would seem to have been devoted to ritual, and the huge 130 ft (40 m) circular wooden structure – a kind of artificial oak grove, perhaps – destroyed by burning in 95 or 94 BC, provides evidence of druidic activity and ritual on an unprecedented scale. It must indeed be regarded as one of the most important religious iron age sites in Europe. It is contemporary with the traditions of the Ulster Cycle, with the Chamalières *defixio*, and with comments on the Celts and their religion by Poseidonios and, later, Caesar.

In an important article in *Emania* (1992: 41), C.J. Lynn asks:

> Who was the organiser, the master-mind, the motivator and the interpreter of this series of events? Who knew the secrets of the gods? Clearly there was a

specialist in religious beliefs and practices supervising the building of the Navan ritual construct. . . . It is reasonable to claim that 'historic' Druids (or a Druid) as described by Caesar were responsible for the initiation, planning, philosophy, specialist knowledge, supervision and religious organisation of this ritual sequence. Their supervision of the construction of a magico-religious, oak-post structure is particularly appropriate given that their name could well mean 'oak-wise'.

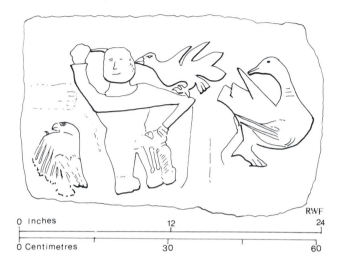

Figure 23.6 Very eroded relief of a beardless male, possibly a druid, holding up a knife in the right hand and with a small creature, a lamb or a young boar, in the left hand. A raven perched on the left shoulder addresses the socket which presumably once held the left ear; a goose turns to look back at the male from his left, while an eagle stands beside his right leg. Sault, Vaucluse, France. (E. Espérandieu, *Recueil général des bas-reliefs de la Gaule romaine* I, Paris 1907: 306.)

Ireland has long been thought to be a microcosm of the early Celtic world. It may well be that the Navan story, together with the many other important excavations of iron age sites in Ireland, will put the study of druidism and early Celtic religion in general on a new footing, and permit a fresh consideration of classical comments and archaeological discoveries both achieved and to come.

REFERENCES

Best, R.I. and O'Brien, M.A. (1956) *The Book of Leinster* II (Irish text) Dublin: Dublin Institute for Advanced Studies.

Bieler, L. (1953) *The Works of St Patrick, St Secundus, Hymn on St Patrick*, London.

Bromwich, R. (1978) *Trioedd Ynys Prydein* (2nd edn) Cardiff: University of Wales Press (first published 1961; reprint 1991).

Bromwich, R. and Williams, Sir Ivor (1972) *Armes Prydein*, Dublin: Dublin Institute of Advanced Studies.

—— (1991) *et al.* (eds) *The Arthur of the Welsh*, Cardiff: University of Wales Press.

Brunaux, J.-L. (1988) *The Celtic Gauls*, London.

Carmichael, A. (1928) *Carmina Gadelica* I, Edinburgh.

Cormac's Glossary – see O'Donovan and Stokes 1868.

Cunliffe, B. (1968) *Danebury*, London.

Danaher, K. (1972) *The Year in Ireland*, Cork.

Dillon, M. (1951) 'The taboos of the kings of Ireland', *Proceedings of the Royal Irish Academy* 54C(1).

Dunn C.W. (1969) *Ancient Irish Tales*, Dublin.

Fleuriot, Léon (1979) *Note Additionnelle sur l'Inscription de Chamalières*, Etudes Celtiques XVI 135–40.

Ford, P.K. (1992) *Ystoria Taliesin*, Cardiff: University of Wales Press.

Fowler, J.T. (1920) *Adamnani Vita S. Columbae*, Oxford.

Gray, E.A. (1982) *Cath Maige Tuired*, Dublin.

Green, M. (1986) *The Gods of the Celts*, Gloucester.

Gwynn, E. (1924) *The Metrical Dindshenchas*, part IV, R.I.A. Todd Lectures, Dublin.

Hamp, E.P. (1979) 'Imbolc, óimelc', *Studia Celtica* 14(1): 106–13.

Henderson, G. (1911) *Survivals in Belief among the Celts*, Glasgow.

Jones, G. and Jones, T. (1974) *The Mabinogion*, London.

Kelly, F. (1988) *A Guide to Early Irish Law*, Dublin: Dublin Institute for Advanced Studies.

Kendrick, T.D. (1927) *The Druids*, London.

Lambert, P.Y. (1951) 'La tablette gauloise de Chamalières', *Etudes Celtiques* 16: 141–69.

Lejeune, Michel and Marichal, Robert (1976–7) *Textes Gaulois et Gallo-Romain en Cursive Latine*, Etudes Celtiques, xv, 151–72.

Lynn, C.J. (1992) The iron age mound in Navan Fort', *Emania* 10: 33–57.

—— (1994) 'Hostels, heroes and tales: further thoughts on the Navan Mound', *Emania* 12: 5–20.

Macalister, R.A.S. (1931) *Tara*, London.

MacCulloch, J.A. (1992) *Religion of the Ancient Celts*, London (Edinburgh 1911).

MacEoin, G.S. (1962) 'Invocation of the forces of nature in the Loricae', *Studia Hibernica* 2: 212–17.

McGrath, F. (1979) *Education in Ancient and Medieval Ireland*, Dublin.

McManus, D. (1991) *A Guide to Ogam*, Maynooth Monographs 4, An Sagart, Maynooth.

McNeill, M. (1962) *The Festival of Lughnasa*, Oxford.

Ní Cathain, P. (1979–80) 'Swineherds, seers and druids', *Studia Celtica* 14–15.

O'Donovan, J. and Stokes, W. (1868) *Cormac's Glossary*, Calcutta.

O'Grady, S.H. (1892) *Silva Gadelica*, London.

O'Huiginn, R. (1989) 'Tongu do dia toinges mo thuath, and other related expressions', in *Sagas, Saints and Storytellers*, An Sagart, Maynooth.

Olmsted, G.S. (1979) 'The Gundestrup Cauldron', in *Collections Latomus* 162 (whole volume), Brussels.

O'Lochlainn, C. (1961) 'Luireach Phádraic, St Patrick's Breastplate', in *Studies 50*, Dublin.

O'Rahilly, C. (1976) *Táin Bó Cúailnge*, Recension I, Dublin.

O'Rahilly, T.F. (1946) *Early Irish History and Mythology*, Dublin.

Power, P. (1914) *Lives of Saints Declan and Mochuda*, London: Irish Texts Society.

Ross, A. (1979–80) 'Chartres: the *locus* of the Carnutes', *Studia Celtica* 14–15: 260–9.

Sayers, W. (1990) 'Images of enchainment in the Hisperica Famina and vernacular Irish texts',

Études Celtiques 27: 221–34.

Stead, I. (1979) *The Arras Culture*, York.

Stokes, W. (1887) *The Tripartite Life of Patrick*, London.

Thorpe, L. (ed.) (1966) 'Geoffrey of Monmouth', *The History of the Kings of Britain*, London.

Tierney, J.J. (1960) 'The Celtic ethnography of Posidonius', *Proceedings of the Royal Irish Academy* 60: 189–275.

Todd, M. (1975) *The Northern Barbarians*, London.

Williams, J.E. Caerwyn (1984) 'Gildas, Maelgwyn and the bards', in R.R. Davies *et al.* (eds) *Welsh Society and Nationhood*, Cardiff: University of Wales Press.

—— (1991) *The Celtic Bard*, The Hallstatt Lecture, Tabernacl Trust, Machynlleth.

Woodward, A. (1992) *Shrines and Sacrifices*, London.

FURTHER READING

Chadwich, N.K. (1966) *The Druids*, Cardiff: University of Wales Press.

Owen, A.L. (1962) *The Famous Druids*, Oxford and New York.

Piggott, S. (1968) *The Druids*, London and New York.

SANCTUARIES AND SACRED PLACES

——— •❖• ———

Jane Webster

A belief that Celtic rituals were centred on atectonic cult sites (Lewis 1966: 4) has for many years coloured archaeological attitudes to Celtic religion. This view is increasingly challenged by excavation, especially in northern France. At the same time, it is now recognized that evidence for some site categories, traditionally regarded as characteristic Celtic sacred spaces, is in fact poor.

Drawing on iron age texts and a critical examination of archaeological data, it is possible to suggest some key features of the sacred spaces among the Celts. Such is the aim of this brief review, which suggests some themes in the demarcation and function of sacred space among Celtic peoples. This study will concentrate less on rites within cult sites than on the structure of religious space.

WRITTEN EVIDENCE

As the iron age Celts made limited use of writing, textual accounts of Celtic peoples derive almost entirely from Graeco-Roman sources. Those classical texts contemporary with the Iron Age are most relevant to a discussion of iron age sites, and the present account concentrates on these. As the product of an external, conquering society, classical commentaries are in many ways a problematic source of data on the Celts (Nash 1978; Wait 1985: 192–3; Webster 1991: 1–87). But at the same time, such accounts are iron age artefacts (Webster 1991: 1–15), and when treated as such can yield much information.

Most classical accounts of Celtic sacred space date to the later Iron Age (i.e. La Tène D; *c*.120–0 BC). Greek colonization in the western Mediterranean, under way by the sixth century BC (Benoit 1955; Clavel-Lévêque 1977; Wells 1980), and Celtic expansion into northern Italy from the fourth to second centuries BC (Peyre 1979; Pauli 1980) and Asia Minor from the third (Mitchell 1974; Rankin 1981: 188–207) generated limited textual data on the Celts, but it was only from *c*.125–120 BC, with Roman intervention in the *Provincia*, that significant quantities of data emerged on Celtic peoples and practices. The date of these texts ensures that the question of Graeco-Roman influence, both on Celtic practices and on their literary depiction, is ever-present in assessing the literary evidence.

Not surprisingly, most classical accounts of Celtic cult sites employ Greek or Roman vocabulary. Equally, most writers give the standard classical terms for cult loci (Table 24.1).

Τέμενος and ἱερόν are Greek descriptors for temple complexes on the classical model. Τέμενος (a 'cut' or share of land apportioned to a god) defines a consecrated, enclosed area surrounding an altar, and ἱερόν the sanctuary at the heart of the enclosure. The Latin equivalents, *fanum* and *templum*, have similar meanings. The use of these terms in Celtic contexts could suggest structural similarities between Celtic and Graeco-Roman cult loci.

However, as with the use of Greek or Roman names in accounts of Celtic deities (e.g. Caesar *De Bello Gallico* VI.17), the use of classical vocabulary for Celtic cult sites is a form of *interpretatio*, the classical interpretation of alien gods and practices. Descriptive detail rarely accompanies *interpretatio*. It is thus uncertain whether the classical terminology in Table 24.1 represents a meaningful approximation to the nature of an alien cult site or simply the imposition of one frame of reference on another.

In this context, references to Celtic ἱερόν would appear to imply roofed structures. But Posidonius' account of the re-roofing of an ἱερον at the mouth of the Loire (Strabo *Geography* IV.4.6) is the single reference to suggest this unambiguously. In other cases, the issue remains uncertain, but it may be suggested that ἱερόν was often applied meaningfully. With the exception of the Loire account, all references to Celtic ἱερα are to northern Italy and the *Provincia*. It is probable, given the long classical influence in these regions, that some sites described in this way in the later Iron Age were constructed on the classical model. Equally, classical terms could have been felt appropriate for the Celto-Ligurian stone-built sanctuaries described below. It is certainly significant that ἱερόν references are largely restricted to zones of Mediterranean influence.

References to Celtic τέμενεα are equally difficult to assess. Although the iron age archaeological evidence suggests that enclosure was an important concept in Celtic sacred space, the standard τέμενος occurs infrequently, and is restricted to areas open to considerable Greek influence. As discussed below, there are significant differences between Graeco-Roman and Celtic usage of enclosures in sacred contexts. It is therefore conceivable that τέμενος was considered an inappropriate term for many Celtic enclosures. It is interesting, in this context, to find references to probable Celtic enclosures in which alternative vocabulary is employed (Table 24.2).

Posidonius's reference to σηκά (enclosures or shrines) is of great interest, as, according to Ammonius, σηκός specifies a site dedicated to a hero (*Diff.* 94.v). The Greeks heroized the dead, and it is surprising that the use of σηκός by a Greek commentator has not been noted by those arguing for a Celtic cult of the heroized dead (Benoit 1955: 16–27; Duval 1976: 21–2; Brunaux 1988: 38). Posidonius (Athenaeus, *Deipnosophistiae* IV.37) also documented a quasi-religious act of enclosure by the Arverni: Luvernius's construction of an enclosure 12 stades square in which to hold a feast.

Underlying most iron age texts is thus a common theme: a sacred area comprising or including an enclosure. How such enclosures were realized is nowhere specified, but the concept of sacred enclosure is clear. Ironically, given their interest to the

Table 24.1 Classical references employing standard vocabulary

Author	Reference	Location	Vocabulary
Polybius	II.32, 55	N. Italy (Insubres)	ἱερόν
Posidonius	Strabo IV.1.13	*Provincia* (Tolosa)	ἱερόν
Cicero	*Pro Fonteio* 13.30	Gaul	*arae ac templa*
Diodorus	V.27.4	*Provincia*	ἱερα και τέμενεα τέμενεα
Strabo	IV.4.6	Loire	ἱερόν
	XII.5.3	Asia Minor	τέμενοσ
Livy	XXII.28.9	Poenine Alps	*sacritum*
	XXIII.24.11	N. Italy (Boii)	*templum*

Table 24.2 Classical references employing non-standard vocabulary

Author	Reference	Location	Vocabulary
Posidonius	Strabo IV.1.13	*Provincia* (Tolosa)	σηκά
	Athenacus IV.152	Central Gaul (Arverni)	δωδεκάσταδιον τετράγωνον
Caesar	VI.13	N. Gaul (Carnutes)	*locus consecratus*
	VI.17	N. Gaul	*locus consecratus*
Strabo	XII.5.1	Asia Minor	Δρυνεμετον

excavators of the weapon-rich sites discussed below, almost the only texts for which enclosure remains an uncertainty are Caesar's references to *loci consecrati* (sacred spots). Caesar uses the term for the druidic meeting-place among the Carnutes of Gaul (VI.13) and for heaps of battle spoil dedicated to 'Mercury' (VI.17). In the latter case, Caesar simply says that booty was piled up in heaps; enclosure need not be implied. Elsewhere, Diodorus (*Bibliotheke* V.32) referred to booty being taken off the battlefield, without specifying its fate. Livy (*Historia* V.39) suggested spoils were heaped on the battlefield, apparently ruling out formal structure, but wrote with reference to the Celtic sack of Rome in 390 BC. As Brunaux (1988: 127) suggested, battlefield booty heaps may have been used in foreign territory, when spoils could not be moved to existing loci. Whatever the case, it is clear from Caesar's account (VI.13) that in later iron age Gaul booty heaps were conceptually bounded by their taboo status.

Interpretatio and the almost total absence of any detail on construction and use make it difficult to determine the nature of Celtic cult sites. But the formalized structuring of space, incorporating enclosing works, is suggested by most texts.

A 'NATURAL' RELIGION?

'Natural' loci such as woods, groves and trees are often advanced as Celtic cult loci *par excellence* (Henig 1984: 17; Green 1986: 19–22). This concept of Celtic sacred space derives in part from classical texts, but references on this theme do not commence before the first century AD (e.g. Mela, *Chorographia* III.2.18; Lucan, *Pharsalia* I.451–8, III.339–425; and Pliny *Natural History* XVI.103–4), when woodland sites are frequently associated with the druids. Iron age references to 'natural' loci are rare. In *c*.100 BC Artemidorus commented on a open-air ritual at Cape St Vincent in western Spain (Strabo III.1.4), and Poseidonios on the use of lakes as sacred repositories in the Toulouse area of the *Provincia* (Strabo IV.1.13). Strabo also stated that the Celtiberians worshipped a nameless god outside their houses (III.4.16). Although only Artemidorus makes explicit reference to the absence of structures, all three texts may imply rituals without use of formal (roofed) structures, or otherwise involving the restructuring of space; for example by construction of an enclosure. There are no other iron age references to such 'natural' cult sites.

The first-century AD change in emphasis to woodland sites is ignored by archaeological commentators except Wait (1985: 204), although we can advance reasons for a change in practice at this point. Imperial proscription of the druids could have forced the use of secluded locales. Equally, as Chadwick noted (1966: 38), the textual association of druids and groves could be the result of a spurious etymology, voiced in Pliny's suggestion (XVI.249) that 'druid' derives from the Greek word for oak (δρύς). It is not impossible that the association of groves with Celtic religion is a literary construct of the first century AD.

The concept of nature-based Celtic religion is also predicated on the apparent paucity of archaeological evidence for tectonic loci. As such sites would leave little archaeological trace, this proposition remains difficult to test, but it is important to note that the archaeological record is likely to be biased in favour of formal structures. Bearing this in mind, what evidence can be adduced for 'natural' loci?

Nemeton

Nemeton is a Celtic descriptor for sites of cult significance. Aside from one textual reference (Strabo XIII.5.1 on the Galatian Drunemeton), *nemeton* is attested mainly in post-conquest place-names and epigraphy, over a wide area. Place-names include Augustonemetum (Clermont-Ferrand) and Nemetodorum (Nanterre) in Gaul, Nemetobriga (near Ortense) in Spain, and Medionemeton (near the Antonine Wall) in Britain. Epigraphic attestations include Mars Rigonemetis from Britain (Nettleham, Lincs.) and Nemetona from Altripp (Spier).

Nemeton is commonly glossed 'sacred grove' (Green 1986: 111–12; Webster 1986; 107), with little indication that it principally denoted such sites. Rather, as Rivet and Smith suggest (1979: 254–5), *nemeton* had several meanings, including grove or clearing (Piggott 1968: 71–2) and small shrine or chapel (cf. the Irish *nemed*, glossed *sacellum*, suggestive of a small shrine). Formal structural associations are a possibility for some examples, as at Vaison-la-Romaine (Vaucluse, France; see Goudineau 1991: 252), where an inscription records the dedication of a *nemeton* to Belissama.

Goudineau's suggestion that this *nemeton* was a grove is unlikely, and the context suggests a structure or precinct. *Nemeton* thus remains enigmatic. The most acceptable gloss, MacCana's 'a sacred place' (1983: 14), simply emphasizes how little we may infer from the term regarding the form of Celtic cult sites.

TREES AND GROVES

Groves continue to be advanced as Celtic cult sites (Webster 1986: 107; Green 1986: 17), essentially by reference to *nemeton* attestations, and the first-century AD texts discussed above. Such sites would have little archaeological visibility, but some recent discoveries may suggest that representations of trees were employed in cult contexts. These are the finds of bronze leaves at the St-Maur sanctuary (Oise, France: Maier 1991: 249) and the remains of a golden tree from a pit at Manching (Bavaria: Maier 1991: 241–9). These finds are problematic; the Manching tree, which probably dates to the third century BC, and from which were suspended golden leaves and fruit, is apparently of Greek manufacture. The cult association of the find, which is not from one of the possible Manching cult foci, is also uncertain. Iron leaves, again designed for suspension, were found in a settlement context at Villeneuve-St-Germain (Aisne, France: Debord 1982: 213, 245). The positioning and use of such finds within sanctuaries (where related to these) are as yet unknown.

WATER

'Watery' loci such as a springs, lakes and bogs have traditionally been argued as important sacred spaces for Celts.

Springs

Springs are commonly seen as a focus for Celtic rituals (Ross 1967: 19–33; Thevenot 1968: 200–21). Textual evidence in this respect is very sparse. Hirtius' account of the diversion of a spring at Uxellodunum in 51 BC (*De Bello Gallico* VIII.43.4), and the subsequent surrender of the oppidum is a possible reference of iron age date (Brunaux 1988: 42), but a utilitarian function could well be implied for this spring (Webster 1991: 517–19). The one reference to springs in a clear iron age cult context is Lucan's overwrought account of a *lucus* near Marseilles, written in the first century AD with reference to the Civil War (*Pharsalia* III.339–425).

As noted by Brunaux (1988: 41) and Green (1986: 155), archaeological evidence for springs as pre-conquest cult foci is virtually non-existent. The argument for Celtic use of such loci is heavily dependent on the well-documented post-conquest use of springs for cult purposes (see e.g. Audin 1985; Webster 1991: 171–218). Finds of wooden statuary (a non-classical medium) at the Côte d'Or sites of Sources de la Seine (Martin and Grimaud 1953; Deyts 1983) and Essarois (Daviet and Daviet 1966) and at Chamalières (Puy-de-Dôme), and elsewhere in France, have been argued to show a Celtic presence at springs, but can nowhere be dated before the first century

AD (Deyts 1983; Webster 1991: 200–9). The recently excavated examples from Montlay-en-Auxois (Côte d'Or) were found in wooden catchment pools dated by dendrochronology to AD 86–119 (Dupont 1990: 154) .

On the other hand, cult activity occurred from the early post-conquest period at many springs: Luxeuil and St-Marcel (Indre), Avord and Sagonne (Cher), Vichy (Allier), Chateauneuf-les-Bains (Puy-de-Dôme), and Coren and Vic-sur-Cère (Cantal) have all produced early post-conquest coins or ceramics (Audin 1985). There are two ways to consider this phenomenon: either by the retrospective inference that such sites are close enough in date to the Roman intervention to suggest they represent the survival of pre-conquest practices; or as a veritable post-conquest phenomenon. On present evidence, the balance is in favour of the latter.

Lakes

Poseidonios, who visited Mediterranean Gaul in c.100 BC, refered to sacred lakes (λιμναι ιεραι) as repositories for treasures among the Tectosages of Toulouse (Strabo IV.1.13). This passage is often cited as evidence for a widespread use of sacred lakes by Celtic peoples, but the text is clearly specific to the Tectosages. Archaeological evidence for lakes in cult contexts is, however, more widespread. The deposition of high-value metal in watery contexts, including lakes, is well attested archaeologically in Atlantic Europe (Tobrügge 1971; Fitzpatrick 1984; Wait 1985: 15–50). This practice increased during the Iron Age in Britain, though on the Continent it declined after the second century BC (Wait 1985: 49). Numerous lakes are interpreted as depositional cult foci, including Llyn Cerrig Bach (Anglesey: Fox 1946: 58) and Carlingwark (Scotland: Curle 1932). A similar interpretation was originally advanced for the lake site at La Tène, Neuchâtel, Switzerland), where thousands of weapons and tools, and some jewellery and coins, were found (Piggott 1968: 76).

Bogs

Bogs also served as foci for metalwork deposits. This practice was not restricted to Celtic peoples, and features for example in Germanic cult (Glob 1969; Todd 1975: 163–89). The Gundestrup Cauldron, widely seen as the quintessential 'Celtic' cult artefact, was in fact found in a bog in Himmerland, Denmark (on the possible non-Celtic origins of this piece see Taylor 1992). Human remains are mainly known from Germanic contexts, but sometimes occur in Britain and Ireland. The Lindow bog body (Lindow Moss, Cheshire) is a recent example. Dating of the body is problematic (Gowlett et al. 1986; Otlet et al. 1986), but radiocarbon dates from the most recent analysis cluster around the first century AD (Ross and Robbins 1989: 17). Lindow man suffered a threefold death (by axe blows, garrotting and cutting of the throat). Whether or not he was a victim of human sacrifice (as Ross (1986) maintains), this triplication suggests a death with ritual links. Where datable, however, British bog bodies are mainly of bronze age or Roman date (Turner and Briggs 1986: 63), and their ritual associations unclear. The extent to which such deposits represent an iron age ritual phenomenon is thus uncertain.

Islands

There is some evidence that islands were favoured as cult sites by Atlantic Celtic peoples. Several texts may be noted in this context. Posidonius described a Gallic ιερον on an island off the mouth of the Loire (Strabo IV.4.6), served by female religious specialists. Tacitus, describing Suetonius' attack on Mona (Anglesey), associated the island with the druids and with women whom he compared to the Furies (*Annals* XIV.30). After the conquest, Mela (III.6.8) referred to virgin priestesses on the island of Sena (Brittany). Female religious specialists are linked to islands in all three passages. The implication is possibly of sexual boundedness (explicit in Strabo IV.4.6). Islands are also physically bounded, relating them conceptually to other forms of enclosure noted here. In Britain, archaeological evidence for an island sanctuary occurs in the form of a wooden circular temple on Hayling Island (King and Soffe 1991).

A link theme in the above discussion is that of water as a boundary. Brunaux (1988: 43) has suggested that lakes were natural sanctuaries, without enclosure or protection. This may not always have been the case, but water, or islands in water, clearly offer a ready-made form of enclosure.

Both textual and archaeological evidence for iron age 'natural' foci is thus very restricted, the latter being largely limited to certain water categories. It is very likely that Celtic peoples did employ natural forces as cult foci, without restructuring their space. In the Graeco-Roman world, for example, such loci co-existed with formal, public, cult centres (Ferguson 1970: 65–9), and the same is clearly probable for Celtic peoples. Indeed, it is possible to argue that our concept of Celtic religious life is distorted by the poor recognition of 'natural' cult loci by both classical commentators and archaeologists. In this context, the lack of textual data may reflect the fact that non-structural loci would not have been easily recognizable to external observers. But at the same time, natural forces, including trees and springs, were familiar cult foci in the Graeco-Roman world (Virgil, *Aeneid* VIII.352, 597; Ovid, *Metamorphosis* III.1.1, III.13.7 (groves); Pliny XII.3, XV.77, XV.137 (trees)), and such foci among the iron age Celts might have invited comment for precisely this reason. It remains significant that almost all iron age textual references suggest, with varying degrees of certainty, that the designation of Celtic cult sites involved the restructuring of space. Equally, while the difficulties of archaeological recognition of 'natural' sites must be borne in mind when assessing their importance to the Celts, it is also reasonable to expect some positive archaeological evidence in their favour. In many of the cases examined above, this is clearly lacking.

WELLS AND SHAFTS

Wells and shafts have long been argued as Celtic cult sites (Alcock 1965; Ross 1968; Ross and Feachem 1976; Wait 1985; Green 1986: 155–7). The British record has been comprehensively documented (Ross 1968: 255–85; Wait 1985: 51–82) but evidence for iron age usage is extremely poor (Webster 1991: 220–5). The present writer has argued (1991: 250–5) that wells and shafts have entered the British iron age cult site corpus as the result of an over-reliance on accounts of water worship in the medieval Irish literary sources. The appropriateness of these texts as evidence for iron age practices is highly questionable.

Stronger evidence for ritual wells and shafts comes from the continent. Shafts have been recovered, for example, inside or under the banks of southern German *Viereckschanzen*. Bavarian examples occur at Holzhausen (Schwarz 1962, 1975), Tomerdingen (Zürn 1971; Zürn and Fischer 1991), Schonfeld and Kreutzpullach (Schwarz 1962). Fellbach-Schmiden (Baden-Württemberg) may also be noted in this context (Planck 1985). At Holzhausen, three shafts up to 36.5 m deep were sunk in the Iron Age. The presence of organic material, burning within shafts, and the deliberate placement of a wooden stake and a flesh-hook in two shafts led the excavator to suggest these had been used for the disposal of sacrificial remains. At Fellbach-Schmiden fragments of three deer figurines were recovered from an oak-lined shaft (by dendrochronology to 123 BC). The cult interpretation afforded such shafts remains uncertain. Brunaux (1989: 13) and Mansfeld (1989: 31–2) have recently questioned Schwarz' interpretation of the Holzhausen shafts. At Fellbach, although the excavator suggested the enclosure itself served a cult function, the shaft was interpreted as a functional well, a role also suggested by Mansfeld (1989: 32).

Beyond southern Germany, shafts with iron age fills are rare. Gallic examples are mainly restricted to the *Provincia*. The fills of some Toulouse shafts date to the first century BC (e.g. the ceramic-filled shaft from Vieille-Toulouse: Fouet 1958), but none securely predates the Roman intervention. Pre-conquest fills occur elsewhere in the Provincia, as at Nîmes (Gard: Bessac *et al.* 1984: 187–222), but these shafts seem to have had utilitarian roles. Most Gallic examples postdate the Augustan era, as at Argentomagus (Indre) where shafts date to the first century AD (Allain *et al.* 1987–8: 105–14) and the first- to second-century AD examples at Chartres (Eure-et-Loir: *Gallia* 1978: 278–8; 1980: 319). Given this dating, it is important to recall that the use of shafts for cult purposes was common in the Graeco-Roman world (see e.g. Homer, *Odyssey* XI.25–50, 97–9; Philostratus, *Life of Apollonius* VI.2.18) and it seems very possible that wells and shafts are essentially post-conquest cult foci.

CELTO-LIGURIAN SANCTUARIES

These well-documented stone-built structures of Provence include Entremont (Benoit 1955), Roquepertuse (de Gerin-Ricard 1927) and Glanum (Salviat 1979). They comprise monumental propylaea, decorated with sculptured reliefs, frequently of the human head, and often associated with free-standing sculptures of cross-legged anthropomorphic figures. The dating of some examples is uncertain, but Entremont and Roquepertuse were probably destroyed during the Roman intervention in c.125 BC. These sites provide much information on sanctuary structure, but they represent an exceptional, localized development, owing much to the long Greek contacts in the Bouches-du-Rhône area, and, with the exception of a *dieu-accroupi* from Argentomagus (Indre: *Gallia* 1984: 320), do not appear to be replicated elsewhere in Celtic Europe.

ENCLOSURES AND THEIR RELATED STRUCTURES

Until recently, it was thought that prior to the second century BC, iron age Celtic peoples rarely constructed special cult sites, and possible early sites like the early third-century BC rectilinear enclosure at Libenice (Prague) were considered exceptions to this rule. Excavation in the last decade, particularly in northern France, has changed this position somewhat (the sanctuary at Gournay-sur-Aronde (Oise), for example, has fourth-century BC origins), but it remains true that the majority of excavated cult sites employing enclosures do not predate 250 BC.

Viereckschanzen

This term was originally applied to a series of Bavarian rectilinear enclosures delimited by an earth bank and ditch, enclosing an area of approximately 1 ha (Schwarz 1959). *Viereckschanzen* were classified on morphological and typological criteria by Schwarz (1959, 1962), who was influential in arguing for the cult function of such sites. In contrast to the 'Belgic' sanctuaries discussed below, the assemblages from excavated *Viereckschanzen* are generally very poor, and the cult function of most examples is uncertain.

Schwarz's (1962, 1975) excavation of one of two *Viereckschanzen* at Holzhausen (Lkr. Wolfratshausen, Bavaria) identified five constructional phases. Initially delimited simply by a palisade (phases 1–3) the 92 m sq area was later supplemented by an earth bank and ditch (phase 4). An internal structure was erected in phase 3 and rebuilt in phase 4 (Figure 24.1) and the three shafts noted above were sunk in phases 1, 2 and 4. The ensemble was dated to the later Iron Age. Largely on the basis of the shaft fills, noted above, Schwarz suggested a cult function for Holzhausen, an interpretation questioned recently by both Brunaux (1989: 13) and Mansfeld (1989: 31–2). Sites across Celtic Europe, from Gosbecks in Britain (Collis 1989: 15–18) to Mšecké Žehrovice in Bohemia (Venclova 1989) have been related to the Bavarian *Viereckschanzen* on morphological grounds (Büchsenschütz 1978, 1984, 1989). There has been a marked tendency to assume commonality of function across the series, and taking Holzhausen as an indicator, this role has often been argued to be a cult one. The recent doubts cast over Holzhausen are thus significant, not least because, despite numerous excavations, Holzhausen remains the sole site with a strong claim to a cult function. The excavators of *Viereckschanzen*-comparables in France, for example, have suggested utilitarian roles for enclosures at Montrollet (Charente Maritime: *Gallia* 1987–8; 250–2) and St-Arnoult (Yvelines: Baray 1989: 81–95). In addition, the perceived morphological and topographical similarities between the Bavarian sites and a set of proposed *Viereckschanzen*-comparables in the Limousin, France, have recently been shown to be statistically non-significant (Webster 1991: 293–308).

It is likely that some sites now placed in the *Viereckschanzen* class served a cult function, but it seems clear that the category subsumes a variety of monument groups. Without independent excavation criteria, as yet lacking, unexcavated sites, and the majority of excavated examples, cannot be seen as cult loci.

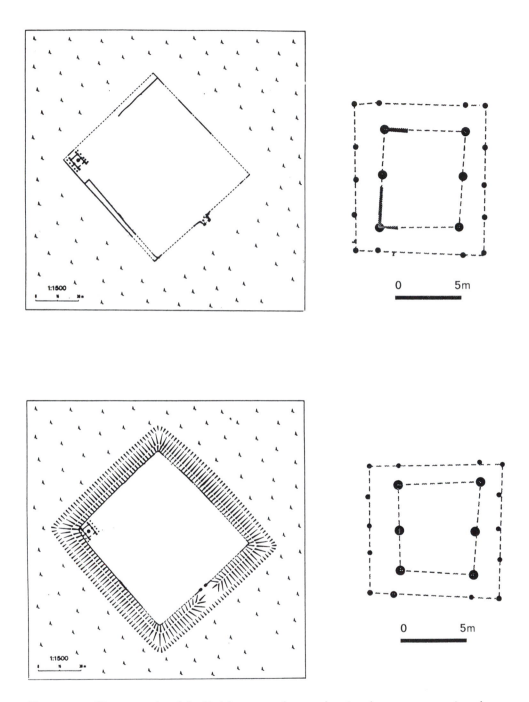

Figure 24.1 Phases 3 and 4 of the Holzhausen enclosure, showing the two construction phases of the interior structure. (After Schwarz 1962.)

Belgic sanctuaries

In the last decade, a series of excavations in the territory of the Bellovaci and Ambiani (Picardy, France) has substantially increased our knowledge of sanctuaries and attitudes to sacred space in Belgic Gaul. Sanctuary sites with features similar to those of Picardy occur beyond Belgic territory, but given the extent of excavation in Belgic Gaul, it is proposed to concentrate on that area here.

Belgic sanctuaries include Gournay-sur-Aronde (Brunaux, Meniel and Rapin 1985), Estrées-St-Denis (Woimant 1991), St-Maur (Brunaux and Lambot 1991) and Vendeuil-Caply (Piton and Dilly 1985) in Dept Oise; Ribemont-sur-Ancre (Cadoux 1984, 1991), Morviller-St-Saturnin (Delplace 1991) and Chilly (Brunaux 1986) in Dept Somme; and Mouzon (*Gallia* 1979: 808–10) in Dept Ardennes (Figure 24.2).

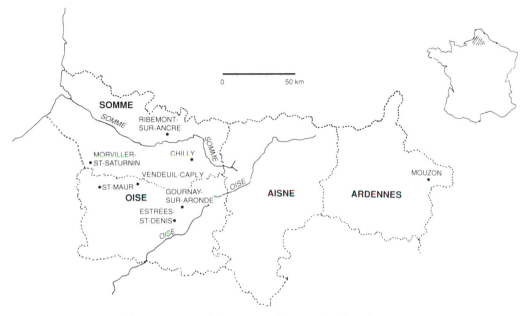

Figure 24.2 'Belgic' sanctuaries mentioned in the text.

One of the best-understood sequences is that for the sanctuary at the centre of the oppidum of Gournay-sur-Aronde (Oise) (Figure 24.3). The sanctuary site forms a rectilinear enclosure which in its first (fourth century BC) phase measured 45 × 38 m and was defined by a ditch and low bank. In the late fourth to mid-third century BC a palisade was added on the external edge of the ditch and in the late third to early second century BC a second ditch was added beyond the first. From its construction in the fourth century BC until *c*.30 BC, the primary ditch was used to deposit over 2,000 broken weapons and 3,000 animal bones. At the centre of the enclosure a group of pits was dug in the mid-third century BC. Nine roughly circular pits 1.2 m deep, surrounded a tenth, oval, pit in which cattle remains were allowed to decompose. Around the end of the third century BC these pits served as foundations for a wooden building, replaced by two subsequent first-century BC structures. The

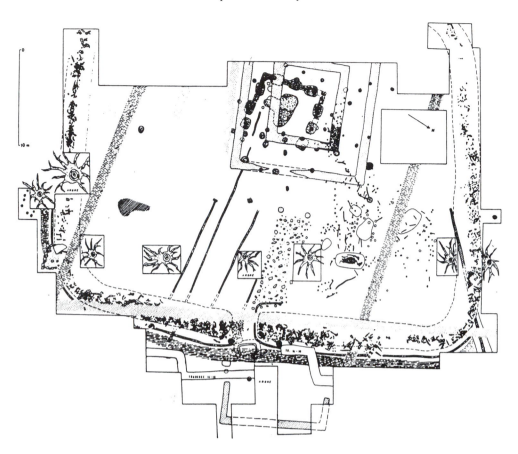

Figure 24.3 General plan of the structures of the sanctuary at Gournay-sur-Aronde. (After Brunaux 1988.)

latter, constructed *c.*30 BC, was of *fanum* form (Brunaux *et al.* 1980, 1985; Brunaux 1988).

Ditches serving as repositories for weapons, tools, and animal and human bone, associated with a central arrangement of pits which later saw structural formalization, occur at other Oise sites. These include St-Maur (Brunaux and Lambot 1991: 178) and Vendeuil-Caply (Piton and Dilly: 1985: 27–33) (Figure 24.4). At St-Maur, ritual activity commenced later than at Gournay, in *c.*250 BC.

Many variations on the Gournay pattern are known, even within Belgic Gaul. At some sites assemblages are characterized less by weapons than by jewellery; examples here are Estrées-St-Denis, Vendeuil-Caply and Morviller-St-Saturnin. Equally, certain sites, such as Estrées-St-Denis and Montmartin, are less clearly demarcated from their associated settlements than are others in the Belgic group.

A number of sites produce a high proportion of human bone. Among these is Ribemont-sur-Ancre (Somme), 50 km from Gournay. An iron age cult area was discovered here, near the principal temple of a vast Gallo-Roman cult complex. Over 200 long bones (mainly human, but also of horses) had been used to form a

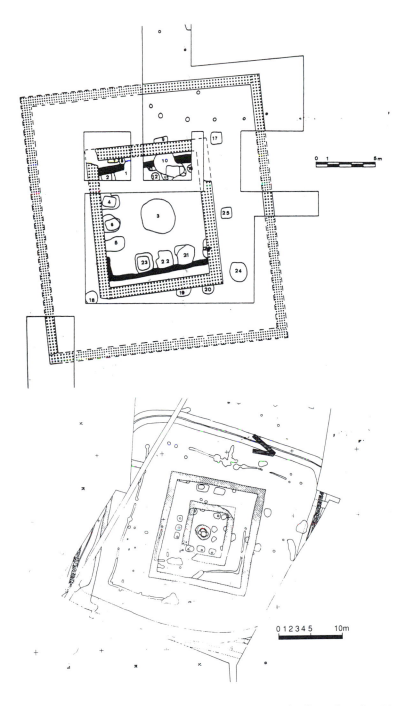

Figure 24.4 Pit groupings and subsequent structures at (1) Vendeuil-Caply (after Piton and Dilly 1985); (2) St-Maur (after Brunaux and Lambot 1991.)

box-like construction, 1.65 m sq, surrounding a post-hole filled with human ashes. Originally standing 1 m high, this ossuary was surrounded by iron weapons. A second ossuary has recently been excavated (*Gallia* 1989: 265–8). Both examples stood in corners of a ditch-and-bank quadrangular enclosure, itself set in a vast enclosure over 200 m in length. Weapons and bones had been placed along the edges of the former. Two distinct dating episodes are noted at Ribemont: the construction of the ossuaries *c.*200 BC, and a phase of deposition within the ditch, centred on the period of the Gallic War (Cadoux 1984: 71). The specific function of the site is unclear. The bone constructions could represent the massacre of prisoners, the remains of enemies killed in battle, or a collective sepulchre for the 'friendly' dead. A second site yielding a high proportion of human remains is Mœuvres, Cambrais (Pay-de-Calais: Cadoux 1984: 162).

Although Belgic sanctuaries thus exhibit considerable variety, two broad shared characteristics emerge: a rich assemblage of deposited material – weapons, often 'sacrificed' by deliberate damage (Brunaux and Rapin 1988), animal and human bones, and jewellery – and a palisaded/ditched enclosure. Many of the more fully excavated sites have also produced internal structures, but these generally postdate the enclosing works. This point is reconsidered below. Finally, whilst we know almost nothing of deity worship within these loci (or even whether this occurred), it is clear that deposition was a key ritual activity at such sites. These depositional acts were the culmination of a series of ritual processes, including the dismemberment and exposure of human and animal bone and the ritual sacrifice of weapons, well documented at Gournay-sur-Aronde (Brunaux and Rapin 1988) and Ribemont-sur-Ancre (Cadoux 1984, 1991).

Throughout the Celtic world, there are very numerous occurrences of pre-conquest horizons at Roman period *fana* (see e.g. Rodwell 1980). The structural associations of these levels are unfortunately often uncertain, obliterated by the subsequent buildings, but frequently comprise pits or pit groupings, similar to those of the Belgic area. A recently excavated example occurs at Vertault (Côte d'Or: Mangin, Mangin and Meniel 1991). Enclosures with affinities to those of Picardy include Mirebeau-sur-Bèze (Côte d'Or: Brunaux *et al.* 1985; Guillaumet and Barral 1991), Tronoën (Finistère: Duval 1990) and Lousonna-Vidy (Switzerland: Flutsch and Paumier 1991). Weapons assemblages recently reinterpreted as deriving from cult loci include Nanteuil-sur-Aisne and Roizy (Ardennes) in the territory of the Gallic Remi (Lambot 1991). In Britain, numerous enclosed loci are proposed as iron age sanctuaries (see Wait 1985 for a recent summary). Among these are a square palisaded enclosure surrounding a circular structure at Hayling Island (King and Soffe 1990), and a square, multi-ditched later iron age enclosure, overlain by a circular temple of the first century AD, at Gosbecks (Wait 1985:157). Other examples are Uley (Ellison 1980: 305–9), Lancing Ring (Bedwin 1981: 37–56) and Harlow (Selkirk 1968: 287–90).

The Importance of Enclosure

As Brunaux (1988: 25) rightly emphasizes, enclosure was the primary and indispensable feature of Celtic cult sites. Some general points may be offered on enclosures in Celtic religious contexts.

Enclosure is an act of boundary. Prior to the Late Iron Age, this boundedness was often underlined by the physical isolation of cult loci from settlement sites. The early La Tène quadrangular enclosure at the summit of the oppidum of Zavist (Bohemia) is one of earliest proposed cult sites to exhibit close settlement links. By the later Iron Age, many cult loci occur within settlement contexts. Others, like Ribemont, comprise rural foci which under the Roman hegemony develop into major cult complexes (Roymans 1988: esp. 63).

As the Belgic examples show, the early phases at most cult enclosures, delimited by a ditch and sometimes a palisade, had no accompanying internal structures. Crucially, in many cases, enclosure ditches were themselves a focus of ritual activity, serving as depositional zones. Brunaux (1988) has argued that among Celtic peoples enclosures served much the same purpose as the τεμενεα of the Graeco-Roman world, but this statement requires qualification. In the Celtic world, an enclosure ditch was often not simply a delimiter of sacred space; it was itself a primary focus of cult activity.

Weaponry, in particular, tends to be associated with ditches rather than with formal structures. The weapons assemblages of both Gournay and St-Maur were associated with the enclosure ditches; those of Ribemont with the ossuaries and the ditch edge, and during the first century BC weapons were also placed in the ditch. Formal structures occur at late stages in the history of these sites. Others may have had no structural phase at all, for example Mœuvres (Cadoux 1984: 75) and possibly also the poorly documented closed deposits of weapons and horse gear such as the *Massefund* at Tiefenau (de Bonstetten 1852) and Naillers (Vendée: Lejars 1989: 11).

Ditches, as depositional foci, were thus often intimately associated with cult activity. The relative chronology of enclosed cult foci merits stressing in this context. The perimeter – ditch and or palisade – tends to predate internal features. Later structures, often formalizing pit groups (as at Gournay and Vendeuil-Caply) tend to be square or rectangular in plan, culminating in square-plan *fana* in the first century BC. Brunaux (1988: 31) relates the form of internal structures to the plan of the enclosure itself, again emphasizing the pre-eminence of the enclosing works. Whether the development of formal structures is due to Mediterranean influence, as some commentators maintain (Brunaux 1988: 32; King 1991: 223) is open to debate. But it is clear that an essential feature of many Celtic cult loci is the act of enclosure, less as sacred delimiter than as itself sacred space.

SPACE AND SYMBOLISM

Our understanding of the beliefs which structured the organization of sacred space among Celtic peoples is very uncertain. But the characteristics of cult sites allow us to see some underlying principles at work, if not the reasons for them.

For example, many Celtic cult sites have east-facing entrances. This feature is by no means confined to sacred sites, but the frequent occurrence of easterly orientation suggests it was a symbolic referent informing spatial delimitation in many contexts. Posidonius, who says the Κελτοι revere the gods by turning to the right

(Athenaeus IV.152D), also recognized the symbolic importance of orientation, and may be describing a rite of circumambulation. In the first century AD Pliny (XXVIII.4) noted Gallic circumambulation, apparently in the opposite direction. Circumambulation is possibly reflected in Posidonius' comment on the Loire ἱερόν (Strabo IV.1.13), which was circled during a roofing rite. Similar rites have tentatively been evoked to explain the presence of an annular space, delimited by two palisades, at the St-Maur sanctuary (Oise: Brunaux and Lambot 1991: 178).

Other astronomical considerations may have influenced the structuring of space within enclosures. The internal structures at Libenice (Prague) were arranged with reference to the position of the sun and the solstices, and at Gournay (Oise) four posts at the centre of the enclosure marked the cardinal points.

Caesar's comment (VI.13) on the druidic meeting-place at the centre of Gaul may suggest the symbolic importance of centrality to Celtic peoples. This may also be reflected in the widespread occurrence of the element *medio-* (centre, middle) in Celtic place-names (Rivet and Smith 1979: 415). The British Medionemeton (ibid.: 417–18) is particularly relevant in this context. It is less clear whether this concept informed the structuring of sacred spaces on a microcosmic level, although Brunaux (1988) comments that most temples are placed at the centre of enclosures. Brunaux (1988) has also argued for a geography in which every natural phenomenon was deemed sacred by the Celts. At present, however, ideas on Celtic sacred geography remain speculative, articulated mainly by appeals to the medieval literature.

REFERENCES

Alcock, J.P. (1965) 'Celtic water cults in Roman Britain', *Archaeological Journal* 72: 1–12.
Allain, J., Faudet, I. and Dupoux, X. (1987–8) 'Puits et fosses de la Fontaine des Mersans à *Argentomagus*. Dépotoirs ou dépôts votifs?', *Gallia* 45: 105–12.
Audin, P. (1985) 'Les eaux chez les Arvernes et les Bituriges', in A. Pelletier (ed.) *La Médecine en Gaule*, Paris, 121–44.
Baray, L. (1989) 'Deux enclos quadrangulaires de l'âge du fer de l'independance Gauloise en Forêt de St Arnoult (Yvelines)', in O. Büchsenschütz and L. Olivier (eds) *Les Viereckschanzen et les enceintes quadrilatérales en Europe celtique* (Proceedings of the 9th colloquium of the AFEAF) Paris, 81–95.
Bedwin, O. (1981) 'Excavations at Lancing Down, West Sussex 1980', *Sussex Archaeological Collections* 119: 37–56.
Benoit, F. (1955) *L'art primitif méditerranéen de la vallée de Rhône*, Publications des Annales de la Faculté des Lettres, Aix-en-Provence NS 9.
—— (1957) *Entremont: capitale Celto-Ligure des Salyens de Provence*, Aix-en-Provence.
—— (1965) 'Recherches sur l'hellenisation du midi de la Gaule', *Annales de la Faculté des Lettres, Aix-en-Provence* 43.
Bessac, J.-Cl. *et al.* (1984) 'Découverte de deux puits antiques à Combas (Gard)', *Revue Archéologique Narbonaise* 17: 187–219.
de Bonstetten (1852) *Notice sur les armes et chariots de guerre découverts à Tiefenau, près de Berne, en 1851*, Lausanne.
Brunaux, J.-L. (1986) 'Le sacrifie, Le défunt et l'ancêtre', *Revue Aquitania*, Supp. 1.
—— (1988) *The Celtic Gauls: gods, rites and sanctuaries*, trans. D. Nash, London.
—— (1989) 'Les enceintes carrées, sont-elles des lieux de culte?', in O. Büchsenschütz and L.

Olivier (eds) *Les Viereckschanzen et les enceintes quadrilatérales en Europe celtique*, (Proceedings of the 9th Colloquium of the AFEAF), Paris, 11–14.

Brunaux, J.-L. and Lambot, B. (1991) 'Le sanctuaire celtique et gallo-romain de St-Maur', in J.-L. Brunaux (ed.) *Les Sanctuaires celtiques et leurs rapports avec le monde méditerranéen* (Proceedings of the Colloquium at St-Riquier 1990), Paris, 178–80.

Brunaux, J.-L., Meniel, P.L. and Popin, F. (1985) 'Gournay 1; les fouilles sur le sanctuaire et l'oppidum (1975–84)', *Revue Archéologique de Picardie*, special no.

Brunaux, J.-L., Meniel, P. and Rapin, A. (1980) 'Un sanctuaire gaulois à Gournay-sur-Aronde (Oise)', *Gallia* 38: 1–25.

Büchsenschütz, O. (1978) 'Faux camps romains … vraies enceintes cultuelles?', in 'Travaux militaires en Gaule romaine et dans les provinces du nord-ouest', *Caesarodunum* Supplement 28: 287–98.

—— (1984) *Structures d'habitats et fortifications de l'âge du fer en France septentrionale*, Paris: Mémoires de la Société Préhistoire Française 18.

—— (1989) 'Introduction', in O. Büchsenschütz and L. Olivier (eds) *Les Viereckschanzen et les enceintes quadrilatérales en Europe celtique* (Proceedings of the 9th Colloquium of the AFEAF), Paris, 5–9.

Cadoux, J.-L. (1984) 'L'ossuaire gaulois de Ribemont-sur-Ancre. Premières observations, premières questions', *Gallia* 42: 53–78.

—— (1991) 'Organisation spatiale et chronologie du sanctuaire de Ribemont-sur-Ancre', in J.-L. Brunaux (ed.) *Les Sanctuaires celtiques et leurs rapports avec le monde méditerranéen* (Proceedings of the Colloquium at St-Riquier 1990), Paris, 156–63.

Chadwick, N.K. (1966) *The Druids*, Cardiff.

Clavel-Léveque, M. (1977) *Marseille grecque, la dynamique d'un imperialism marchand*, Marseilles.

Collis, J. (1989) 'Viereckschanzen, enceintes carées et lapins en Angleterre', in O. Büchsenschütz and L. Olivier (eds) *Les Viereckschanzen et les enceintes quadrilatérales en Europe celtique* (Proceedings of the 9th Colloquium of the AFEAF), Paris, 15–20.

Curle, J. (1932) 'An inventory of objects of Roman and provincial Roman origin', *Proceedings of the Society of Antiquaries of Scotland* 116: 277–397.

Daviet, M. and Daviet, R. (1966) 'Réflexions sur le sanctuaire d'Apollon Vindonus à Essarois (Côte d'Or)', in R. Chevalier (ed.) *Mélanges d'archéologie offerts à André Piganoil*, Paris, 933–99.

Debord, J. (1982) 'Premier bilan de huit années de fouilles à Villeneuve-St-Germain', *Revue Archéologique de Picardie*, special no.

Delplace, C. (1991) 'La zone cultelle de Morviller-Saint-Saturnin', in J.-L. Brunaux (ed.) *Les Sanctuaires celtiques et leurs rapports avec le monde méditerranéen* (Proceedings of the Colloquium at St-Riquier 1990), Paris 196–8.

Deyts, S. (1983) 'Les bois sculptées des Sources de la Seine', *Gallia* Supp. 42.

Dupont, J. (1990) 'Le sanctuaire de Source de la Fontain Segrain à Montlay-en-Auxois', in *Il etait un fois la Côte d'Or, 20 ans de recherches archéologiques* 154.

Duval, A. (1990) 'Quelques aspects du mobilier métallique en fer anciennement recueilli à Tronoen, en St-Jean-Tromlimon (Finistère)', *Revue Archéologique Ouest*, Suppl. 3, 23–45.

Duval, P.M. (1976) *Les Dieux de la Gaule*, Paris.

Ellison, A. (1980), 'Natives, Romans and Christians on West Hill, Uley: an interim report on the excavations of a ritual complex of the first millennium AD', in W. Rodwell (ed.) *Religion in Roman Britain*, Oxford: British Archaeological Reports, British Series 77.

Ferguson, J. (1970) *The Religions of the Roman Empire*, London.

Fitzpatrick, A.P. (1984) 'The deposition of La Tène iron age metalwork in watery contexts in southern England', in B. Cunliffe and D. Miles (eds) *Aspects of the Iron Age in Central*

Southern Britain, Oxford: University of Oxford Committee for Archaeology, Monograph 2, 178–90.

Flutsch, L. and Paumier, D. (1991) 'Organisation spatiale et chronologie du sanctuaire de Lousonna-Vidy', in J.-L. Brunaux (ed.) *Les Sanctuaires celtiques et leurs rapports avec le monde méditerranéen* (Proceedings of the Colloquium at St-Riquier 1990), Paris, 169–77.

Fouet, G., (1958) 'Puits funéraires d'Aquitaine: Vieille-Toulouse, Montmaurin, *Gallia*, 16: 115–96.

Fox, C. (1946) *A Find of the Early Iron Age from Llyn Cerrig Bach, Anglesey*, Cardiff.

de Gérin-Ricard, H. (1927) 'Le Sanctuaire préromain de Roquepertuse', *Centenaire Société Statistique Marseille*.

Glob, P.V. (1969) *The Bog People*, London.

Goudineau, C. (1991) 'Les sanctuaires gaulois: relecture d'inscriptions et du textes', in J.-L. Brunaux (ed.) *Les Sanctuaires celtiques et leurs rapports avec le monde méditerranéen* (Proceedings of the Colloquium at St-Riquier 1990), Paris, 250–6.

Gowlett, J.A.J., Gillespie, R., Hall, E.T. and Hedges, R.E.M. (1986) 'Accelerator radiocarbon dating of the ancient human remains from Lindow Moss', in I.M. Stead, J.B. Bourke and D. Brothwell (eds) *Lindow Man: the body in the bog*, London, 22–4.

Green, M. (1986) *The Gods of the Celts*, Gloucester and New Jersey.

Guillaumet, J.-P. and Barral, P. (1991) 'Le sanctuaire celtique de Mirebeau-sur-Bèze', in J.-L. Brunaux (ed.) *Les Sanctuaires celtiques et leurs rapports avec le monde méditerranéen* (Proceedings of the Colloquium at St-Riquier 1990), Paris, 193–5.

Henig, M. (1984) *Religion in Roman Britain*, London.

King, A. (1991) 'The emergence of Romano-Celtic religion', in T.F.C. Blagg and M. Millett (eds) *The Early Roman Empire in the West*, Oxford, 220–41.

King, A. and Soffe, G. (1991) 'Hayling Island', in R.F.J. Jones (ed.) *Roman Britain: recent trends*, Sheffield: J.R. Collis Publications, Department of Archaeology and Prehistory, 111–13.

Lambot, B. (1991) 'Quelques aspects funéraires et cultuels chez les Rèmes', in J.-L. Brunaux (ed.) *Les Sanctuaires celtiques et leurs rapports avec le monde méditerranéen* (Proceedings of the Colloquium at St-Riquier 1990), Paris, 66–78.

Lejars, T. (1989) 'Les armes des sanctuaries Poitevins d'époque préromaine de Fay-l'Abbesse (Deux-Sèvres) et de Natalliers (Vendée)', *Gallia* 46: 1–39.

Lewis, M.J.T. (1966) *Temples in Roman Britain*, Cambridge.

Mac Cana, P. (1983) *Celtic Mythology* (revised edn), London.

Maier, F. (1991) 'Le petit arbre cultuel de Manching', in J.-L. Brunaux (ed.) *Les Sanctuaries celtiques et leurs rapports avec le monde méditerranéen* (Proceedings of the Colloquium at St-Riquier 1990), Paris, 240–9.

Mangin, N., Mangin, J.-M. and Meniel, P. (1991) 'Les dépôts d'animaux du sanctuaire de Vertault, Côte d'Or', in J.-L. Brunaux (ed.) *Les Sanctuaires celtiques et leurs rapports avec le monde méditerranéen* (Proceedings of the colloquium at St-Riquier 1990), Paris, 268–75.

Mansfield, G. (1989) 'Les Viereckschanzen dans le Baden-Württemberg', in O. Büchsenschütz and L. Olivier (eds) *Les Viereckschanzen et les enceintes quadrilatérales en Europe celtique* (Proceedings of the 9th Colloquium of the AFEAF), Paris, 27–35.

Martin, R. (1985) 'Wooden figures from the source of the Seine', *Antiquity* 39: 247–52.

Mitchell, S. (1974) 'The history and archaeology of Galatia', Ph.D. thesis, Faculty of Literae Humaniores, Oxford University.

Nash, D. (1976) 'Reconstruction Poseidonios' Celtic ethnography: some considerations', *Britannia* 7: 112–36.

Otlet, R.J., Walker, A.J. and Dadson, S.M. (1986) 'Report on radiocarbon dating of the Lindow

Man by ARERE, Harwell', in 'Lindow Man and the Celtic tradition', in I.M. Stead, Bourke, J.B. and D. Brothwell *Lindow Man: the body in the bog*, London, 27–30.

Pauli, L. (1980) *The Alps: archaeology and early history*, London.

Peyre, C. (1979) *La Cisalpine Gauloise du III au Ier siècle avant J.-C.*, Paris: Etudes d'Histoire et d'Archéologie 1.

Piggott, S. (1968) *The Druids*, London.

Piton, D. and Dilly, G. (1985) 'Le fanum des "Chatelets" à Vendeuil-Caply (Oise), *Revue Archéologique de Picardie* 1–2: 25–47.

Planck, D. (1985) 'Die Viereckschanze von Fellbach-Schmiden', in D. Plank (ed.) *Der Keltenfurst von Hochdorf: Methoden und Ergenbuisse dei landesarchäeologie*, Stuttgart.

Rankin, H.D. (1987) *Celts and the Classical World*, London and Sydney.

Rivet, A.L.F. and Smith, C. (1979) *The Place-names of Roman Britain*, London.

Rodwell, W. (ed.) (1980) *Temples, Churches and Religion in Roman Britain*, Oxford: British Archaeological Reports, British Series 77.

Ross, A. (1967) *Pagan Celtic Britain: studies in iconography and tradition*, London.

—— (1968) 'Shafts, pits, wells – sanctuaries of the Belgic Britons?', in J.M. Coles and D.D.A. Simpson (eds) *Studies in Ancient Europe* (Essays presented to Stuart Piggott), Leicester, 255–85.

—— (1986) 'Lindow Man and the Celtic tradition', in I.M. Stead, J.B. Bourke and D. Brothwell *Lindow Man: the body in the bog*, London, 162–9.

Ross, A. and R. Feachem (1976) 'Ritual rubbish? The Newstead pits', in J.V.S. Megaw (ed.) *To Illustrate the Monuments* (Essays presented to Stuart Piggott), 230–7.

Ross, A. and Robbins, D. (1989) *The Life and Death of a Druid Prince*, London.

Roymans, N. (1988) 'Religion and society in later iron age northern Gaul', in R.F.J. Jones *et al. First Millennium Papers*, Oxford British Archaeological Reports, International Series 401.

Salviat, F. (1979) *Glanum*, Paris.

Schwarz, K. (1959) *Atlas der Spätkeltischen Viereckschanzen Bayerns*, Munich.

—— (1962) 'Zum Stand der Ausgrabungen in der spätkeltischen Viereckschanzen von Holzhausen', *Jahresbericht der bayerischen Bodendenkmalpflege*, 22–72.

—— (1975) 'Die Geschichte eines keltischen Τεμενοσ im nördlichen Alpenvorland', *Ausgrabungen in Deutschland. Gefördert von der Deutschen Forschungsgemeinschaft, 1950–1975* 1: 324–58.

Selkirk, A. (1968) 'Harlow Roman temple', *Current Archaeology* 11: 287–90.

Taylor, T. (1992) 'The Gundestrup Cauldron', *Scientific American* 266(3): 66–71.

Thevenot, E. (1968) *Divinités et sanctuaires de la Gaule*, Paris.

Torbrügge, W. (1971) 'Vor- und Frühgeschichtliche Flussfunde zur Ordung und Bestimmung einer Denkmälergruppe', *Bericht der Römisch-Germanischen Kommisson* 51–2: 1–146.

Todd, M. (1975) *The Northern Barbarians 100 B.C. – A.D. 300*, London.

Turner, R.C. and Briggs, C.S. (1986) 'The bog burials of Britain and Ireland', in I.M. Stead, J.B. Bourke and D. Brothwell (eds) *Lindow Man: the body in the bog*, London, 144–61.

Venclova, N. (1989) 'L'enceinte quadrilatérale de Msecké Zehrovice (Bohême centrale)', in O. Büchsenschütz and L. Olivier (eds) *Les Viereckschanzen* (Proceedings of the 9th Colloquium of the AFEAF, Paris, 37–42.

Wait, G.A. (1985) *Ritual and Religion in Iron Age Britain*, Oxford: British Archaeological Reports, British Series 149.

Webster, G. (1986) *The British Celts and their Gods under Rome*, London.

Webster, J. (1991) 'The identification of ritual in the later Iron Age, with specific reference to selected themes in proto-historic Gaul and Britain', Ph.D. thesis, University of Edinburgh.

Wells, P.S. (1980) *Culture Contact and Culture Change: early iron age central Europe and the Mediterranean world*, Cambridge.

Woimant, G.-P. (1991) 'Organisation spatiale et chronologie du sanctuaire d'Estrées-St-Denis', in J.-L. Brunaux (ed.) *Les Sanctuaires celtiques et leurs rapports avec le monde méditerranéen* (Proceedings of the Colloquium at St-Riquier 1990), Paris, 164–8.

Zürn, H. (1971) 'Die keltische Viereckschanze bei Tomerdingen, Kreis Ulm (Württemberg)', *Proceedings of the Prehistoric Society* 37: 218ff.

Zürn, H. and Fischer, F. (1991) *Die Keltische Viereckschanze von Tomerdingen*.

THE GODS AND THE SUPERNATURAL

—— ·•· ——

Miranda J. Green

THE NATURE OF CELTIC RELIGION

Because the pagan Celts did not write about themselves, the only way that modern scholars can learn anything about their belief-systems is by constructing hypotheses based upon archaeological sources and historical documents written by contemporary, but alien, classical observers, who selected and often misunderstood what they recorded (Rankin 1987). There is another group of documents, those which tell of the earliest Welsh and Irish myths and written in the vernacular. But these have to be treated with extreme caution as sources for pagan Celtic religion, and as a strand of evidence which must be treated separately from contemporary data (Green 1992a: 18–21). This tradition is the work of Christian redactors writing in medieval times, and close links between the undoubted mythology it contains and the evidence which is synchronous with the pagan Celts (around 500 BC to AD 400) cannot usefully be made. Moreover, this vernacular tradition relates only to Wales and Ireland, far from the continental heartlands of the early Celts.

The picture painted by the evidence is of a rich and varied religious tradition. This variety and complexity is due largely to the essential animism which appears to have underpinned Celtic religion, the belief that every part of the natural world, every feature of the landscape, was numinous, possessed of a spirit. These natural forces were perceived as capable of doing humankind good or harm, and so they had to be controlled and their power harnessed by means of divination, sacrifice and other propitiatory rituals (see Chapter 23). Sacred space could take the form of built shrines, but equally important were natural cult foci such as lakes, springs and trees or open-air enclosures where worshippers were not cut off from the numinous land-scape around them (Chapter 23).

The perception of the supernatural as being present in the natural world penetrated all aspects of Celtic belief. Thus, the most popular, pan-tribal deities – the celestial gods and the mother-goddesses – were linked to their respective functions as providers of light, heat and fertility. The great healing cults of Romano-Celtic Gaul and Britain were centred upon the natural phenomena of thermal springs. Many divinities – such as Epona, Arduinna, Nodens and Cernunnos – had a close affinity with animals: indeed the horned and antlered gods took on the partial personae of bulls or stags. The perception of spirits in the landscape is amply demonstrated by the names of gods on epigraphic dedications of the Romano-Celtic period, which betray their topographical character, as personifications of places: the identity of gods such as Glanis of Glanum and Nemausus of Nemausus (Nîmes), both in Provence, were merged inextricably with their locality.

PROBLEMS OF EVIDENCE

Leaving aside the difficulties of the written sources for the present, we have a very real problem in the archaeological (that is the epigraphic and iconographic) evidence. This results from the fact that the great majority of inscriptions and images date to the Romano-Celtic rather than the free Celtic (i.e. pre-Roman) period. There is considerable overt Roman influence on indigenous religious expression. Gods in classical guise and bearing Roman names were adopted by the Celts but with subtle changes, such as the addition of a native surname to a dedication, or of Celtic symbols – like the wheel or torque – to the imagery of Jupiter or Mercury. Other divinities, like Cernunnos, the Mothers, Epona, Sequana and Sucellus, appear almost wholly indigenous in concept, but their imagery still owes something to Roman iconography and, of course, their names use Latin forms, even though their meaning may be Celtic. But even these apparently native gods are sometimes argued to be the products of romanization in that, with a few exceptions, they do not appear in the archaeological record until the Roman period. What is perhaps more likely is that the perceptions underlying the identity of these spirits were always present but only took the form of physical images once the stimulus of the great Mediterranean traditions of iconography took hold of the Celtic world. The lack of free Celtic epigraphy and the comparative paucity of pre-Roman religious imagery means that, inevitably, we have to observe Celtic gods through a window created by Rome.

PRE-ROMAN ICONOGRAPHY AND CULT EXPRESSION

Iconography

When an invading group of Celts overran and plundered the sacred Greek site of Delphi in the early third century BC their leader, Brennus, laughed at the anthropomorphic images of the Greek divinities which adorned the great sanctuary (Diodorus XXII.9.4). He was apparently scoffing at the naïvety of Mediterranean perceptions of the divine. But whilst it is undoubtedly true that religious iconography is comparatively scarce in Celtic lands before the intrusion of Graeco-Roman artistic traditions, images of Celtic divinities were nonetheless present in small numbers in the last few centuries before Christ.

Stone sculpture falls into two main distributional clusters: one in central Europe; the other in the area of southern Gaul known later by the Romans as The Province (Provence), because of their early conquest of the region (late second century BC). The central European group includes large stone male statues, dating between the sixth and third centuries BC, which are presumed to represent gods or dead heroes. One of the earliest such figures is a huge sandstone image from a late Hallstatt burial-mound at Hirschlanden near Stuttgart. He is naked but for a conical helmet, a torque, belt and dagger (Woodward 1992: fig. 45; Megaw 1970: no. 12). His original position may have been at the top of the mound, and he may represent the dead warrior himself or perhaps a war-god, patron of the deceased. The image at Holzerlingen, also in Germany and of similar date, almost certainly represents a god: a rough sandstone block was crudely hewn into a human torso, featureless except for a belt at the waist (Megaw 1970: no. 14). But the statue is janiform, surmounted by a dual head bearing horns, perhaps the earliest representation of a Celtic horned god. The carved head from Heidelberg comes from a statue or pillar-stone: dating to the fifth–fourth century BC, it bears a leaf crown consisting of two swelling lobes which meet above the head, and on the forehead is carved a motif which has been interpreted by some as a lotus bud, a Greek symbol of eternity (Megaw and Megaw 1989: 74). The two features of crown and lotus may signify divinity: both recur on the pillar-stone at Pfalzfeld in the Rhineland which dates to the same period, and which bears curvilinear foliate Celtic designs out of which peer four leaf-crowned human heads (*ibid.*: 74, fig. 83, left; Megaw 1970: no. 75). Further east is the third-century BC ritual site of Mšecké Žehrovice near Prague, which produced a carved stone head, originally from a life-size statue: the face is that of the typical Celt as stereotyped by classical writers (and more recently by the creators of Asterix): hair *en brosse*, staring eyes and flowing moustache (Megaw and Megaw 1989: 124, pl. XVII). The image bears a heavy buffer-torque, probably a symbol of divinity or, at least, high status. It is difficult to interpret the Mšecké Žehrovice head as representative of anything other than a god.

The Provençal group of sculptures dates to between the fifth and second centuries BC, and their presence may be due in part to the stimulus of mimetic representation provided by the nearby Greek (Phocean) colony of Marseilles. Such sanctuaries as those at Entremont and Roquepertuse in the lower Rhône valley have produced a rich iconography (Figure 25.1) (Benoit 1955, 1981), including sculptures of cross-legged male figures, some of whom wear armour, and who may be war-gods. The severed human head is a prominent iconographic theme at these shrines, and some of these 'warrior-gods' hold severed heads in their hands, as if reflective of the divine dominance over humans in life and death. Entremont produced a carved pillar of incised human heads; both this sanctuary and that at Roquepertuse had niches, filled with the human skulls of young men killed in battle, built into the structure of the temple. The sanctuary at Roquepertuse was guarded by a janiform head, perhaps that of the presiding deity, who gazed inwards and outwards from the gateway of his sacred place.

Other stone sculptures, presumed to represent divinities, come from elsewhere in the Celtic heartland: an important example is the boar-god at Euffigneix (Haute-Marne), an image which dates to the second or first century BC. The carving takes the form of a roughly hewn pillar depicting a beardless god wearing a heavy torque, with a boar in low relief striding up his torso. On the side of the pillar is an immense human eye, perhaps indicative of protection or omnipotence. The boar's dorsal crest is erect, as if to reflect aggression: for the Celts, the image of the boar was an important war

Figure 25.1 Stone frieze of horse-heads, from the Celtic sanctuary of Roquepertuse near Marseilles. Fifth–fourth century BC. Ht 32 cm. (Photo: author.)

symbol. The Euffigneix deity may himself be a god of war, or perhaps of hunting and wild nature (Espérandieu no. 7702; Pobé and Roubier 1961: no. 6; Green 1989: fig. 46).

Imagery in metal – usually bronze – also bears witness to the representation of divinities in the last few centuries BC. Small figures of warrior- or hunter-gods come from St Maur-en-Chaussée (Oise) (Rapin 1991: 330), Balzars in Liechtenstein (Green 1992a: 125) and Dinéault in Brittany (Abbaye de Daoulais 1982: no. 80.01), the last-mentioned a warrior-goddess with a goose-crested helmet. Images of animals are more common than are anthropomorphic depictions: bulls, like those from Býciskála (Czechoslovakia) (Figure 25.2) and Hallstatt (Austria), which date to the sixth century BC (Megaw 1970: no. 35), may symbolize the sacrifice of an animal which was central to the early Celtic economy. Boar figurines may reflect war symbolism: some, like those at Hounslow (Middlesex), Gaer Fawr (Powys) and Luncani in Romania, were probably helmet crests (Foster 1977; Green 1992b: fig. 4.19). But the bronze boars from Neuvy-en-Sullias (Loiret) are nearly life-size and almost certainly came from a shrine. The Neuvy hoard dates to the very end of the Gaulish Iron Age (Espérandieu nos. 2978, 2984; Megaw 1970: no. 238; Green 1989: fig. 59).

The Gundestrup Cauldron is one of the most important pieces of pre-Roman Celtic religious art. It is a large silver-gilt vessel made up of individual plates which bear a complex iconography, including depictions of divinities. The cauldron was found dismantled in a Danish peat-bog at Raevemose (Jutland), and was probably

Figure 25.2 Bronze figurine of a bull, Býciskála Cave, Czechoslovakia. Sixth century BC. Ht 11.4 cm. (Illustrator: Paul Jenkins.)

made in the second or first century BC. The circumstances of its manufacture, use and subsequent deposition have long been the subject of controversy. It was probably made in south-east Europe by Thracian or Dacian silversmiths. Many of the iconographic themes are exotic: lions, elephants and griffons adorn the plates. However, there are a number of unequivocally Celtic motifs: the weapons and armour belong to the Celtic world, and the deities represented may be paralleled in the later Romano-Celtic imagery of Gaul and Britain. These include the antlered god, sometimes identified as 'Cernunnos' because of a first century AD Parisian monument linking this name with a similar antlered figure (Espérandieu nos. 3132, 3133; *CIL* XIII: 3026). On the cauldron, the god is accompanied by a ram-headed snake, an idiosyncratic cult-animal which occurs consistently with the antlered god in Romano-Celtic Gaul. This serpent appears a total of three times on the cauldron. The antlered figure appears with two torques on the vessel, and he is thus represented on a number of later Romano-Gaulish depictions. Interestingly, as early as the fourth century BC, an antlered figure with torques and horned snakes is portrayed in the rock art of Camonica valley in north Italy (Anati 1965). Another undoubtedly Celtic divine representation on the Gundestrup vessel is the wheel-god, depicted on an outer plate. Once again, there is good evidence for this deity in Romano-Celtic imagery (Green 1984).

469

The mystery of the Gundestrup Cauldron may never fully be solved. It is possible that south-east European craftsmen were commissioned to make a great cult-vessel for a Celtic clientele. The cauldron could have been looted from Gaul by Teutonic raiders, perhaps the Cimbri, and later buried by them for safety or as an offering to their own gods (Green 1992a: 108–10; Olmsted 1979).

Vincent Megaw has pointed out (1989: 160) that the Euffigneix stone boar-god was perhaps carved by a craftsman who was more familiar with working in wood than in stone. There is no doubt that images of gods were made in wood, which usually does not survive. That they may have been common during the Iron Age is suggested by the chance preservation of these figures in waterlogged contexts (Coles 1990: 315–33). Five pinewood images of naked warriors with shields and detachable phalli, set in a simple boat model, were found at Roos Carr in the Humber estuary: they may date from as early as the seventh century BC. A wooden female image dating to the first century BC comes from a wicker structure at Ballachulish, Argyll (Green 1986a: fig. 5; Megaw and Simpson 1979: 477); and there are other stray British figures. Oak carvings of animals, dendro-dated to 123 BC, come from a shaft at the *Viereckschanze* of Fellbach-Schmiden in southern Germany (Figure 25.3) (Webster 1986a: 95; Planck 1982; Green 1992a: 96–7).

The first phase of the great healing sanctuary dedicated to Sequana, goddess of the source of the Seine at Fontes Sequanae near Dijon, dates to the interface between the free Celtic and Romano-Celtic periods. This primary, first century BC, phase is represented by more than 200 wooden votives, depictions of pilgrims and the parts of their bodies requiring a cure, which were offered to the power of the sacred spring. Of similar date (first century BC to first century AD) are the more numerous wooden images at Chamalières (Puy-de-Dôme), a holy place where two springs met (Deyts 1983, 1985; Vatin 1969: 103–14). We are reminded of Lucan's statement concerning a sacred grove near Marseilles, encountered by Julius Caesar's army:

> The images were stark, gloomy blocks of unworked
> timber, rotten with age, whose ghastly pallor
> terrified their devotees.
>
> (*Pharsalia* III.412–17)

We are unable positively to name or identify these pre-Roman gods whose images were carved in stone, wood or bronze because this iconography is unsupported by inscriptions or documents, although their accompanying symbolism may sometimes suggest their possible function.

Ritual Behaviour

It is clear that iconography is by no means the sole evidence for religious expression in the pre-Roman period. Discussion of ritual practices is properly the remit of Chapter 23 but here it is useful to allude briefly to recurrent cult activity which implies a relationship with specific elements of the supernatural world. Perhaps the most prominent iron age ritual behaviour concerns the deposition of prestigious objects, often of a martial nature, which were frequently buried on dry land or in watery contexts. These implements and weapons were often deliberately bent or

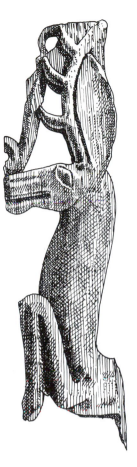

Figure 25.3 Wooden carving of a stag, from the *Viereckschanze* at Fellbach-Schmiden, Germany. Second century BC. Ht 77 cm. (Illustrator: Paul Jenkins.)

broken in order ritually to 'kill' them and thus render them appropriate as sacrifices to the spirits of the supernatural world. Examples of this practice are numerous: in Britain we may cite the deposit of metalwork, including swords and chariot fittings, in the marshy lake at Llyn Cerrig Bach on the island of Anglesey, which spans a period between the second century BC and the first century AD (Fox 1946). Broken weapons formed a substantial element of the offerings made at later pre-Roman iron age temples, such as Hayling Island (Hampshire) (Downey, King and Soffe 1980: 289–304; Woodward 1992: 66–7). This occurrence may be closely paralleled at Gournay (Oise) (Brunaux 1986). Deposits in Switzerland are particularly prolific: that at La Tène, on the shore of Lake Neuchâtel, is well known (Vouga 1923; Dunning 1991: 366–8), but the equally important deposit of weapons and chariot equipment at Tiefenau, in the oppidum of Bern-Engehalbinsel, is less familiar (Müller 1991: 526–7). This evidence of recurrent ritual behaviour may be interpreted as 'conspicuous consumption', but equally it may express behaviour associated with a warrior-cult, a practice essentially similar to that described by Caesar (*De Bello Gallico* VI.17):

> When they have decided to fight a battle, it is to Mars that they usually dedicate the spoils they hope to win.

CLASSICAL WRITERS ON CELTIC GODS

Although Greek and Roman writers recorded their perceptions of Celtic culture and religion, especially from the first century BC, they provide little evidence for the identity or function of Celtic deities. Indeed, such commentators as Caesar, Strabo and Diodorus Siculus are more concerned with ritual practices, such as head-hunting, or religious functionaries, like the druids, than with Celtic perceptions of the supernatural world. Caesar (*De Bello Gallico* VI.14) alludes to druidic lore concerning the transmigration of souls. Both Lucan (*Pharsalia* I.446ff.) and Diodorus (V.28.6) comment on this Celtic belief in a cycle of death and rebirth.

Where mention of the gods does occur, it is heavily overlaid by Roman conflation and misinterpretation. Thus Caesar (VI.17) speaks as if Celtic deities are identical with those of the Roman pantheon, giving them such names as Mercury, Mars and Jupiter. Does this mean that he was unaware of their native names, that they were deliberately

Figure 25.4 Altar of Romano-Celtic date dedicated to Taranucnus, a derivative of Taranis, the Celtic thunder-god; Böckingen, Germany. (Photo: Württembergisches Landesmuseum, Stuttgart.)

kept secret, or that the resemblance with his own gods was so strong that he was concerned to record this similarity? The first century AD Roman poet Lucan does allude to three gods with Celtic names who were apparently encountered by Caesar's army in southern Gaul in the first century BC (*Pharsalia* I.444–6). These are Esus, Taranis and Teutates, all of whom, states Lucan, demanded appeasement in the form of human sacrifice. Lucan implies that these were important Gaulish divinities, but this is not borne out by archaeological testimony. Taranis and Teutates each occur on a handful of dedications (Figure 25.4) (Green 1982: 37–44; 1986a: 111; 1992a: 209) which are scattered within the Romano-Celtic world, and the name Esus appears only once, on an early first-century AD monument in Paris (Espérandieu no. 3134; Green 1992a: 93–4). All three names are descriptive: Taranis ('Thunderer') is tied to function; Esus means 'Lord' or 'Master'; and Teutates probably refers to the divine leadership of a tribe or *tuath*. Esus and Teutates are therefore titles rather than names.

Sporadic references to Celtic gods appear in the literature of the Romano-Celtic period. Tertullian (*Apologeticus* XXIV.7) and Herodian (*History of the Empire after Marcus* VIII.3.6) allude to the cult of Apollo Belenus in Noricum and north Italy, and Ausonius alludes to sanctuaries dedicated to Belenus in Aquitaine in the fourth century AD (Zwicker 1934–6: 105). Grannus is referred to by Dio Cassius (*Historiae* LXXVII.15.5) who speaks of the emperor Caracalla's unsuccessful attempts to find a cure for his physical afflictions at the temples of Grannus, Aesculapius and Serapis. Reference is made to Epona's cult by a number of sources, including Apuleius (*Metamorphoses* III.27) and Minucius Felix (*Octavianus* XXVIII.7).

So the classical literary sources are of very little use in establishing the identities of Celtic gods and the nature of belief. Any detail concerning a Celtic pantheon must be sought from the epigraphy and iconography of the Romano-Celtic world.

THE ROMANO-CELTIC TRADITION

Celtic religious expression is represented during the Roman period by two main strands of material culture: epigraphy and iconography. Inscriptions give us the names of deities; imagery demonstrates how they were perceived as physical manifestations of the supernatural. One immediate problem lies in the fact that, very frequently, an epigraphic dedication to a god occurs without any accompanying image and vice versa. So it is usually impossible to marry images with their names or names with their images. Moreover, there is often a discrepancy between the ethnicity of a god as expressed by his name and by his appearance. Thus a being with a Celtic name – such as Sequana – may look very classical, whilst a god with a Roman name – Mars or Mercury, for instance – may be depicted in wholly native style.

Epigraphy

The names of indigenous Celtic gods may contain Roman and native elements or may be purely Celtic. Thus Mars and Mercury were frequently invoked with different Celtic surnames or epithets: Mars Lenus, worshipped among the Treveri, and Mars Corotiacus, invoked in Suffolk, are just two of numerous examples (Wightman

473

1970: 208–17; Thevenot 1968: 60–73; Duval 1976: 70; Green 1992a: 142–3; Collingwood and Wright 1965: 213). Mercury was equally diverse: his titles or surnames include Cissonius and Moccus (Duval 1976: 70; Thevenot 1968: 157). Jupiter was surnamed Brixianus in Cisalpine Gaul and Parthinus in north-east Dalmatia, both topographical names associated with high places: these are just two of many such titles (Pascal 1964: 76–83; Wilkes 1969: 165). Apollo was worshipped in Gaul mainly as a healer: Moritasgus, Grannus, Belenus and Vindonnus are among his epithets (Green 1992a: 30–2). Sometimes the Celtic name comes first: a good example is Sulis Minerva, the healer-goddess of Bath (Aquae Sulis). The pairing of Roman and Celtic god-names is confusing and difficult to interpret (Webster 1986b). Sometimes the Celtic surname is descriptive – hence Mars Rigisamus ('Greatest King') at West Coker in Somerset (Collingwood 1931: fig. 1, 2), or topographical, like Apollo Grannus at Grand in the Vosges (de Vries 1963: 82–3). But Sulis was clearly a goddess in her own right, equated in the Roman period with the classical Minerva.

Another method of epigraphic pairing concerns the linkage of male and female divinities (see Figure 25.12). A pattern may be discerned here, in that, very frequently, the male deity bears a Roman or Roman and Celtic name, whilst that of the female is wholly indigenous. Examples include Mercury and Rosmerta; Apollo Grannus and Sirona; Mars Loucetius and Nemetona. Sometimes both members of the divine couple have Celtic names: such is the case with Sucellus and Nantosuelta; Luxovius and Bricta, the local spirits of Luxeuil; or Ucuetis and Bergusia, the craft deities of Alesia (Green 1986a: 46; 1989: 46–54, 75–86; 1992a: 180–1, 160). Again the native element may often be interpreted as descriptive: 'Sucellus' means 'The Good Striker' (and his iconographic image is that of a man bearing a long-shafted hammer); Nantosuelta's name means 'Winding Brook'; Rosmerta is 'The Great Provider'; Nemetona 'The Goddess of the Sacred Grove'. Interestingly, goddesses like Rosmerta and Sirona may be invoked alone, without their partner, thus signifying their independent status within the Celtic pantheon.

Epigraphy gives us the names of many more purely native divinities, sometimes linked with images. Such is Epona, the great horse-goddess, worshipped all over the Celtic world (Figure 25.5) (Green 1992a: 90–2; Linduff 1979: 817–37; Magnen and Thevenot 1953; Oaks 1986: 77–84). The mother-goddesses or *deae matres* are interesting: often they are known merely by their Latin title 'matres' or 'matronae', but they may bear descriptive epithets which bear witness to localized versions of their cult. The Rhineland mother-goddesses bear outlandish-sounding topographical surnames, such as the Matronae Aufaniae or the Vacallinehae (Green 1992a: 146–7; von Petrikovits 1987: 241–54; Lehner 1918–21, 74ff.). The Celtic thunder-god Taranis is sometimes equated with the Roman Jupiter, but his occurrence alone on several inscriptions argues for his independent identity (Green 1982: 37–44; 1986b: 65–76). The god of the Lydney (Glos.) sanctuary, Nodens, is invoked on his own, but he is also linked with both Mars and Silvanus (Henig 1984: 51–6; Green 1992a: 162), as if the native god were perceived as possessing an affinity with the functions of both Roman deities. This apparent confusion in pairing recurs, for instance, with Mars and Mercury in Gaul, whose native surnames are sometimes shared: thus both Mars Visucius and Mercury Visucius were invoked on dedications (de Vries 1963: 150; Duval 1976: 88).

Figure 25.5 Stone relief of Epona, with fruit; Kastel, Germany. Second–third century AD. Width 25 cm. (Photo: author.)

The Evidence of Iconography

The imagery of Celtic religion in the Roman period is rich and varied. If it is accompanied by a dedicatory inscription, a sculpture or figurine may be positively identified; if not, the symbols accompanying the image must be used to attempt some classification in terms of character or function. A depiction may be associated with an inscribed name on only one or two stones, although the image itself may appear many times. In these instances, scholars have tended to use the inscribed name to identify similar images where the dedication is absent. Such is the case with Epona, the horse-goddess, whose image (a woman riding side-saddle on a horse or sitting between two or more horses) is far more common than are epigraphic dedications bearing her name. Likewise, the inscribed name 'Cernunnos' accompanies a depiction of an antlered, torque-bearing god on an early first-century AD stone in Paris. But there are many images of a similarly antlered being from Romano-Celtic Gaul which bear no name. Are we justified in assuming these portrayals also represent Cernunnos? The name itself merely means 'Horned One', and so it is less a true god-name than a descriptive title. The names Sucellus and Nantosuelta occur at Sarrebourg near Metz, on a carving of a male and female, the most distinctive accompanying symbol being the long-shafted hammer borne by Sucellus. But many other images of a similar divine couple were the focus of veneration in Gaul and the Rhineland, without the identifying names, although Sucellus is mentioned on one or two scattered dedications in Britain

475

and Gaul (*CIL* XIII: 4542; Green 1989: 46–54; Linckenheld 1929: 40–92; de Vries 1963: 99–100).

The symbols or motifs which accompany images of Celtic deities give some clues as to their function or identity, although our interpretation of these symbols may be open to misconception. The celestial god frequently carries a solar wheel as his main attribute (Figure 25.6) (Green 1984, 1991a). The fact that this wheel-god is sometimes invoked under the the name of Jupiter, the Roman sky-god, makes the native divinity's identification secure. The Celtic god of the sky and sun was sometimes invoked as a divine horseman, the horse symbolizing the prestige and swiftness appropriate to the high god of sun and firmament. Although this equestrian deity is entirely indigenous to the Celtic world, in terms of image and meaning, he is nevertheless venerated under the Roman name, Jupiter. The triple mother-goddesses may be represented by name, but their imagery alone betrays their responsibilities as promoters of fertility. Thus they may be portrayed with babies, children, fruit, corn or loaves. The Burgundian Mothers are often represented one with an infant at the breast, a second with a napkin, and the third with a bath-sponge and basin, and a

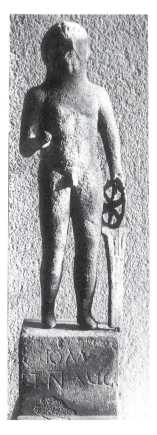

Figure 25.6 Bronze figurine of the celestial god with his solar wheel; Landouzy-la-Ville, France. Ht 22 cm. (Photo: author.)

cornucopia is frequently present in emphasis of the symbolism of abundance. Occasionally, this simple fertility imagery is subtly changed, so that the symbols of fecund plenty are accompanied or partially replaced by motifs of the Fates, such as a balance or spindle, reflective of the thread of life. In these images, the rolled napkin may instead be interpreted as a scroll, the Book of Life (Green 1989: 192–3; Espérandieu nos. 3377, 2081; Deyts 1976: no. 170; Thevenot 1968: 173–6). The Celto-Germanic mother-goddesses are distinctive in their imagery: they never reflect human fertility, but instead their attributes are those of fruit, bread or coins, symbolic of prosperity and commercial success (Figure 25.7). Moreover, these Rhineland goddesses may represent different ages of womanhood: the central goddess is always depicted as a young girl with flowing hair, whilst her flanking companions are older and wear huge beehive-shaped bonnets or headdresses (von Petrikovits 1987: 241–54; Green 1989: 194–8; Wild 1968: pl. 1). The triplistic character of many mother-goddess images expresses the power of 'three' in Celtic religion, a significance which transcends mere intensity of expression by means of repetition. Triplism is an important characteristic of Celtic religious iconography, and triadism may be observed in imagery other than that of the Mothers. The *Genii Cucullati* were hooded dwarves associated with fertility, and indeed with the Mothers themselves, and they usually occur in threes. Gods with triple heads were depicted especially among the Remi, the Aedui and Lingones; and a triple-horned bull was venerated particularly in north-east Gaul (Green 1991b: 100–8).

Figure 25.7 Pipe-clay group of the Rhenish mother-goddesses, with fruit, corn or coins in their laps; Bonn, Germany. Ht approx. 10 cm. (Photo: author.)

The symbolism of the healer-deities is varied and interesting. The Celtic Mars, at such therapeutic shrines as Mavilly (Côte d'Or) and Trier, is not a warrior in the true, Roman, sense, but instead he fights and protects against ill-health and barrenness. Sometimes, his image is that of a soldier, as at Mavilly (Figure 25.8) (Green 1989: 65, fig. 26; Thevenot 1968: 118). Frequently, the motifs of healing and fertility are blurred and merged. Thus curative goddesses such as Sirona and Damona are represented with ears of corn, eggs and snakes: the corn is a symbol of plenty; eggs have strong fertility associations, but may also represent death and regeneration (since the egg must be broken in order to release new life). Because of their habit of skin-sloughing, serpents were clear symbols of rebirth. Many curative deities were partners, such as Apollo and Sirona: in their imagery, it is often the goddess who possesses the symbolism evocative of function. But many healer-goddesses themselves carry no emblems which in themselves are indicative of their curative function: Sequana, the divine healer of the Seine at its spring-source near Dijon, is depicted as a woman in a long robe and a diadem, sailing in a duck-prowed boat to reflect her aquatic symbolism. But it is the presence of dedications and votive offerings that identify Sequana as a healer (Deyts 1985).

Perhaps the most powerful group of images is that associated with animals. The close relationship between god and beast is clearly reflected in iconography which

Figure 25.8 Stone relief from a pillar, depicting a healer-god in the guise of a Celtic warrior (fighter against disease), accompanied by a goddess and a ram-horned snake; from the curative spring-shrine at Mavilly, Burgundy. First century AD. Ht of monument 1 m 79 cm.
(Illustrator: Paul Jenkins.)

displays the ubiquity and cult importance of animal symbolism. Some creatures accompanied anthropomorphic images, presumably to demonstrate a particular quality or feature associated with the god's character, just as occurs in classical imagery. But there are indications that animals in Celtic religion achieved a status denied them in the Mediterranean world. Some divinities – and Epona is a prime example – are dependent upon animals for their iconographic and epigraphic identity. Thus, Epona is always depicted riding on a mare or accompanied by horses. Moreover, her name is philologically linked with *epos*, a Gaulish word for 'horse'. She was the goddess of the craft of horse-breeding, and she was revered by cavalry-men as a divine protectress of them and their animals. But she also possessed wider responsibilities as a deity of fertility and general well-being (Figure 25.9). There was even an underworld dimension to her cult (Green 1989: 10–16). Other, less widely known goddesses enjoyed a similar affinity with beasts: Arduinna, the boar-deity of the Ardennes Forest is one; Artio, bear-goddess of Muri in Switzerland, is another. It is difficult to establish whether or not the animals themselves possessed divine status; the likelihood is that they were sacred only inasmuch as they symbolized certain features of a particular cult. But there is debate over the status of certain creatures which appear in the iconography: monstrous animals, like the ram-horned serpent and the triple-horned bull, may well have been worshipped as beings of tremendous power, because of their hybrid or unnatural imagery. The triple-horned bull is not associated with any particular anthropomorphic god, but the snake

Figure 25.9 Stone statuette of Epona; from the Romano-Gaulish town of Alesia, Burgundy. First–second century AD. (Illustrator: Paul Jenkins.)

frequently accompanies the antlered god, and is also sometimes linked with Celtic versions of Mars and Mercury. Both images occur mainly in north-east Gaul, although outliers occur as far west as Britain (Colombet and Lebel 1953: 112; Boucher 1976: 170ff.; Thevenot 1968: 72–89, 154–6; Green 1992a: 53–4, 195–6; 1992b: 196–238; Bober 1951: 13–51; Drioux 1934: 67–72). Both these creatures are endowed with extra features in order to increase their potency: horns are symbols of power and fertility. Possibly linked with the triple-horned bull in some manner is Tarvostrigaranus, the 'Bull with Three Cranes', who is named and depicted on a first-century AD stone from Paris (*CIL* XIII: 3026; Duval 1961: 197–9, 264).

The sanctity of animals is seen at its least equivocal in the iconography of deities whose images, although essentially anthropomorphic, nevertheless incorporate animal features. Of these, the most important are the horned or antlered gods. Images with bull- or goat-horns appear all over the Romano-Celtic world. A particular group occurs in North Britain, among the Brigantes (Ross 1961: 59ff.), where local deities were depicted as naked warriors, often ithyphallic, with bull-horns (Figure 25.10). A god invoked especially in north-east Gaul is portrayed with antlers, and other recurrent features may also be discerned on these images: these include a cross-legged seating position; the possession of two torques (one worn, one carried); accompaniment by a ram-horned snake and/or stag; the possession of attributes of plenty, such as money, corn or fruit. As discussed above, a god with torques and antlers was invoked as Cernunnos on a Parisian monument, but all other images of

Figure 25.10 Bronze head of a bull-horned god; Lezoux, France. First century AD. (Illustrator: Paul Jenkins.)

an antlered god are without dedications. This image is particularly interesting because, unlike most Romano-Celtic iconography, there are examples which pre-date the Roman period: one of the iron age rock carvings at Val Camonica in north Italy, dating to the fourth century BC, depicts a standing figure with antlers, torques and a horned serpent (Anati 1965); and the same god appears on the Gundestrup Cauldron, as we have seen. The presence of semi-zoomorphic images serves to emphasize the lack of rigid boundaries between animal and human which is central to early Celtic religious perceptions (Green 1992b). Beasts were revered for their specific qualities (speed, virility, aggression or beauty) and these qualities were woven into the Celtic expression of the supernatural.

THE GODS OF THE EARLIEST WRITTEN MYTHS

The mythological traditions of Wales and Ireland are examined by Dr Sioned Davies (Chapter 39) and Professor Proinsias Mac Cana (Chapter 38). Here, I would like simply to draw attention to the deities themselves who are presented in this early Celtic literature. As mentioned at the beginning of this chapter, it is important to recognize the impossibility of making direct links between the gods of these western myths and those expressed by the images and inscriptions which are the main concern of this survey. There is a wide spatial and temporal chasm between the evidence for Romano-Celtic religion and the Insular divinities to whom we are introduced in – say – the Irish *Book of Invasions*. The early Welsh and Irish deities have names and characters, but no idea of cult or ritual associated with them is present in the documents. They are supernatural heroes rather than true objects of belief.

It is within the Irish vernacular tradition that the pagan gods are most clearly developed. The most important are those described in the *Book of Invasions*, the members of the Tuatha Dé Danann, the divine race of Ireland, the 'people of the goddess Danu' (Mac Cana 1983; Green 1993; Carey 1984: 1–22; O'Rahilly 1946: 141). The Tuatha Dé consist of deities with specific functions and responsibilities: these include the Daghdha, who was a specialist in druid lore and magic; Dian Cécht, the physician; Goibhniu, the divine blacksmith; Lugh, the warrior and god of light, who was also skilled in arts and crafts; Brigid, a triple goddess of poetry, prophecy and fertility. The *Book of Invasions* recounts a series of mythical occupations of Ireland (in order to explain the presence of the Gaels or Celts). The Tuatha Dé were one invading group, who inhabited the island until dispossessed by the Gaels and forced to create a new magical domain underground. This Otherworld was perceived as a mirror-image of earthly life, but better, a land of immortality, joy and plenty.

The Ulster Cycle, too, had its supernatural beings, though they are portrayed as heroes rather than gods *sensu stricto*. Chief of the Ulster tales is the *Táin Bó Cuailnge*, and here we are introduced to such characters as Cú Chulainn, the archetypal champion, and the warlike and promiscuous Medb, queen of Connacht, a euhemerized goddess (Lehmann 1989: 1–10; Kinsella 1969; Jackson 1964; Bhreathnach 1982: 243–60; Green 1992a: 70–2, 147–8). These beings are essentially similar to the heroic characters of the *Four Branches of the Mabinogi* and the *Tale of Culhwch and Olwen*. The Insular and Welsh mythological traditions contain many common elements: supernatural events; magical cauldrons of regeneration and plenty; beings of superhuman size, strength and wisdom; a brilliantly portrayed Otherworld; the potency of triads; supernatural animals, and the related phenomenon of shape-changing between human and animal form (Green 1992a: 150–1; 1992b: 162–195).

A CELTIC PANTHEON?

Leaving aside the separate and contentious issue of the vernacular mythology touched on above, we may legitimately pose the question as to whether it is possible to discern a hierarchy of Celtic divinities from the bewildering array of epigraphic dedications and iconographical forms of pagan Celtic Europe with which we are presented. Judging from frequency of occurrences and from distribution, it is possible to make some assessment of the popularity of various god-types. At the top are deities whose names and images appear widely and often throughout the Celtic world. These include the sky- and sun-god, although certain aspects of his cult, such as his depiction as a celestial horseman on the 'Jupiter columns' of eastern Gaul and the Rhineland, may cluster in specific regions (Green 1991a: 133–6). The mother-goddesses and Epona likewise transcend tribal boundaries and appear to have been venerated by many different communities. The cults associated with these deities not only spanned wide areas but their worship percolated down from the highest to the humblest echelons of society. For example, some of the Rhineland mother-goddesses were invoked by high-ranking officials in the Roman army or civil magistrates, whilst some Gaulish and British carvings of the goddesses were clearly commissioned by groups of rural people or by a single family for veneration in private shrines. Likewise, the 'Jupiter-Giant columns' set up in honour of the Celtic sky-god were the result of corporate religious activity (Figure 25.11), but the small pipe-clay figurines of the same god from Gaulish factories would have been purchased by individuals who perhaps could not afford an altar or a bronze statuette (Green 1991a: 136).

Less universal than the major, pan-tribal cults were those which had specific centres of popularity but which also occur sporadically elsewhere. The healers Apollo and Sirona had an important temple at Hochscheid in the Moselle Basin and were venerated particularly among the Treveri and the neighbouring Mediomatrici. But the couple appears also in Burgundy, at Mâlain (Figure 25.12), and Sirona was worshipped as far apart as Brittany and Hungary (Marache 1979: 15; Schindler 1977: 33; Dehn 1941: 104ff.; Szabó 1971: 66). Another important divine couple, Mercury and Rosmerta, were prominent especially in central and eastern Gaul, but with a cluster of British monuments among the Dobunni of Gloucestershire (Green 1992a: 180–1). Images of the antlered god occur mainly in eastern Gaul, appearing, for instance, among the Burgundian tribes at such places as Beaune and Etang-sur-Arroux (Espérandieu no. 2083; Thevenot 1968: 144–9) and among the Remi at Reims (Espérandieu no. 3653). But the Santones of Saintes in Aquitaine in western Gaul also venerated the antlered god (Espérandieu no. 1319) and his image is even known among the Dobunni of western Britain, at Cirencester (Green 1986a: fig. 86).

Certain Celtic divinities were the focus of cults which were of major importance but their veneration was centred upon a particular religious site of which the deity

Figure 25.11 Reconstruction of a Jupiter-Giant column; Hausen-an-der-Zaber, Germany. Ht approx. 13 m. (Photo: Württembergisches Landesmuseum, Stuttgart.)

Figure 25.12 Bronze group of Romano-Celtic date depicting Apollo and Sirona; the goddess's arm is encircled by a snake; Mâlain, Burgundy. (Illustrator: Paul Jenkins.)

was the resident spirit. Examples include Sequana at Fontes Sequanae (Figure 25.13) (Deyts 1985); Nodens at Lydney on the river Severn (Wheeler 1932) and Sulis at Bath (Cunliffe and Davenport 1985). Lenus Mars was a Treveran god, with major sanctuaries at Trier itself, at Möhn and Pommern (Wightman 1970: 208–17). But he was worshipped far away from his homeland, at Caerwent in Gwent and at Chedworth in Gloucestershire (Goodburn 1972: pl. 10; Collingwood and Wright 1965: 309). More localized still were the numerous obscure deities who are perhaps mentioned on only one or two dedications and who were apparently venerated solely by the inhabitants of one small settlement (Figure 25.14), or at the site of a particular spring or mountain. Such was Souconna, the spirit of the river Saône at Chalon (Green 1992a: 196), Vindonnus at Essarois (Thevenot 1968: 110–12) or Fagus ('Beech Tree') in the Pyrenees (*CIL* XIII, 223: 224).

CONCLUSION

One of the dangers of a survey such as this is the unwitting presentation of a picture which can assume a timeless continuum, spanning nearly a millennium. This is not the intention, but in part is the inevitable result of studying a period which is essentially prehistoric, where chronology is often imprecise, especially where iconography is concerned. Clearly, it is possible to make distinctions between religious behaviour

Figure 25.13 Bronze figurine of Sequana, goddess of the river Seine at its spring source, in her duck-shaped boat; from Fontes Sequanae near Dijon, Burgundy. First century AD. (Illustrator: Paul Jenkins.)

Figure 25.14 Stone head, presumably of local deity, from a shrine of late Roman date; Caerwent, South Wales. (Photo: Newport Museum.)

before and after the coming of Roman traditions to Celtic lands. It is possible to observe that imagery increased towards the end of the Iron Age, when Graeco-Roman concepts and customs were already intruding upon the Celtic world. Imagery and epigraphy which come from well-excavated sites offer an opportunity for close dating. But all too often, good archaeological contexts are absent for iconography, and dating by style alone is neither easy nor reliable. It is important, however, to acknowledge pagan Celtic religion as a dynamic force, which was constantly changing and responding to the stimuli of new concepts and ideas, whilst still retaining a core of conservatism. It is indeed the tension between tradition and innovation which gives Celtic religion its essential character of diversity and enigma.

REFERENCES

Abbaye de Daoulais (1987) *Aux temps des Celtes*, Quimper: Association Abbaye de Daoulais.

Anati, E. (1965) *Camonica Valley*, London: Jonathan Cape.

Anon. (1980) *Die Kelten in Mitteleuropa*, Hallein: Keltenmuseum.

Benoit, F. (1955) *L'Art primitif méditerranéen dans la vallée du Rhône*, Aix-en-Provence: Publications des Annales de la Faculté des Lettres.

—— (1981) *Entremont*, Paris: Ophrys.

Bhreathnach, M. (1982) 'The sovereignty goddess as goddess of death', *Zeitschrift für celtische Philologie* 39: 243–60.

Bober, J.J. (1951) 'Cernunnos: origin and transformation of a Celtic divinity', *American Journal of Archaeology* 55: 13–51.

Boucher, S. (1976) *Recherches sur les bronzes figurés de Gaule pré-romaine et romaine*, Paris/Rome: Ecole Française de Rome.

Brunaux, J.-L. (1986) *Les Gaulois: sanctuaires et rites*, Paris: Errance.

Carey, J. (1984) 'Nodens in Britain and Ireland', *Zeitschrift für celtische Philologie* 40: 1–22.

Coles, B. (1990) 'Anthropomorphic wooden figures from Britain and Ireland', *Proceedings of the Prehistoric Society* 56: 315–33.

Collingwood, R.G. (1931) 'Mars Rigisamus', *Somerset Archaeology and Natural History Society* 77: 112–14.

Collingwood, R.G. and Wright, R.P. (1965) *The Roman Inscriptions of Britain*, vol. 1: *Inscriptions on Stone*, Oxford: Oxford University Press.

Colombet, A. and Lebel, P. (1953) 'Mythologie gallo-romain', *Revue Archéologique de l'Est et du Centre-Est* 4(2): 108–30.

Corpus Inscriptiorum Latinarum (1861–1943), Berlin (= *CIL*)

Cunliffe, B.W. and Davenport, P. (1985) *The Temple of Sulis Minerva at Bath*, vol. I: *The Site*, Oxford: Oxford University Committee for Archaeology, Monograph no. 7.

Dehn, W. (1941) 'Ein Quelheiligtum des Apollo und der Sirona bei Hochscheid', *Germania* 25: 104ff.

Deyts, S. (1976) *Dijon, Musée Archéologique. Sculptures gallo-romaines mythologiques et religieuses*, Paris: Editions de la Réunion des Musées Nationaux.

—— *Les Bois sculptés des sources de la Seine*, Paris: *Gallia* Supplement 42.

—— *Le Sanctuaire des sources de la Seine*, Dijon: Musée Archéologique de Dijon.

Downey, R, King, A. and Soffe, G. (1980) 'The Hayling Island temple and religious connections across the Channel', in W. Rodwell (ed.) *Temples, Churches and Religion in Roman Britain*, Oxford: British Archaeological Reports British Series, no. 77: 289–304.

Drioux, G. (1934) *Cultes indigènes des Lingons*, Paris and Langres.

Dunning, C. (1991) 'La Tène', in O.-H. Frey *et al.* (eds), *The Celts*, London: Thames & Hudson, 366–68.

Duval, P.-M. (1961) *Paris antique*, Paris Hermann.

—— (1976) *Les Dieux de la Gaule*, Paris: Payot.

Espérandieu, E. (1907–66) *Recueil général des bas-reliefs de la Gaule romaine et pré-romaine*, Paris: Ernest Leroux.

Foster, J. (1977) *Bronze Boar Figurines in Iron Age and Roman Britain*, Oxford: British Archaeological Reports, British Series 39.

Fox, C. (1946) *A Find of the Early Iron Age from Llyn Cerrig Bach, Anglesey*, Cardiff: National Museum of Wales.

Goodburn, R. (1972) *The Roman Villa, Chedworth*, London: National Trust.

Green, M.J. (1982) 'Tanarus, Taranis and the Chester altar', *Journal of the Chester Archaeological Society* 65: 37–44.

—— (1984) *The Wheel as a Cult-Symbol in the Romano-Celtic World*, Brussels: Latomus.

—— (1986a) *The Gods of the Celts*, Gloucester: Alan Sutton.

—— (1986b) 'Jupiter, Taranis and the solar wheel', in M. Henig and A. King (eds) *Pagan Gods and Shrines of the Roman Empire*, Oxford: Oxford University Committee for Archaeology Monograph 8, 65–76.

—— (1989) *Symbol and Image in Celtic Religious Art*, London: Routledge.

—— (1991a) *The Sun Gods of Ancient Europe*, London: Batsford.

—— (1991b) 'Triplism and plurality: intensity and symbolism in Celtic religious expression', in P. Garwood et al. (eds) *Sacred and Profane*, Oxford: Oxford University Committee for Archaeology Monograph no. 32.

—— (1992a) *Dictionary of Celtic Myth and Legend*, London: Thames & Hudson.

—— (1992b) *Animals in Celtic Life and Myth*, London: Routledge.

—— (1993) *Celtic Myths*, London: British Museum Press.

Henig, M. (1984) *Religion in Roman Britain*, London: Batsford.

Jackson, K.H. (1964) *The Oldest Irish Tradition: a window on the Iron Age?*, Cambridge: Cambridge University Press.

Kinsella, T. (1969) *The Táin*, Dublin: Dolmen Press.

Lehmann, R.P.M. (1989) 'Death and Vengeance in the Ulster Cycle', *Zeitschrift für celtische Philologie* 43: 1–10.

Lehner, H. (1918–21) 'Der Tempelbezirk der Matronae Vacallinehae bei Pesch', *Bonner Jahrbücher* 125–6: 74ff.

Linckenheld, E. (1924) 'Sucellus et Nantosuelta', *Revue de l'Histoire des Religions* 99: 40–92.

Linduff, K. (1979) 'Epona: a Celt among the Romans', *Collection Latomus* 38, fasc. 4: 817–37.

Mac Cana, P. (1983) *Celtic Mythology*, London: Newnes.

Magnen, R. and Thevenot, E. (1953) *Epona*, Bordeaux: Delmas.

Marache, R. (1979) *Les Romains en Bretagne*, Rennes: Ouest France.

Megaw, J.V.S. (1970) *Art of the European Iron Age*, New York: Harper & Row.

Megaw, R. and Megaw, V. (1989) *Celtic Art*, London: Thames & Hudson.

Megaw, J.V.S. and Simpson, D.D.A. (1979) *Introduction to British Prehistory*, Leicester: Leicester University Press.

Müller, F. (1991) 'The votive deposit at Tiefenau near Berne', in O.-H. Frey *et al.* (eds) *The Celts*, London: Thames & Hudson, 526–7.

Oaks, L.S. (1986) 'The goddess Epona: concepts of sovereignty in a changing landscape', in M. Henig and A King (eds) *Pagan Gods and Shrines of the Roman Empire*, Oxford: Oxford University Committee for Archaeology, Monograph 8, 77–84.

Olmsted, G.S. (1979) *The Gundestrup Cauldron*, Brussels: Latomus.

O'Rahilly, T.F. (1946) *Early Irish History and Mythology*, Dublin: Dublin Institute for

Advanced Studies.

Pascal, C.B. (1964) *The Cults of Cisalpine Gaul*, Brussels: Latomus.

Petrikovits, H. von (1987) 'Matronen und Verwandte Gottheiten', *Ergebnisse eines Kolloquiums Veranstaltet von der Göttinger Akademiekommission für die Altertumskunde Mittel- und Nordeuropas*, Cologne/Bonn: Beihafte der Bonner Jahrbücher 241–54.

Planck, D. (1982) 'Eine neuentdeckte keltische *Viereckschanze* in Fellbach-Schmiden, Remsmurr-Kreis', *Germania* 60: 105–72.

Pobé, M. and Roubier, J. (1961) *The Art of Roman Gaul*, London: Gallery Press.

Rankin, H.D. (1987) *Celts and the Classical World*, London and Sydney: Croom Helm.

Rapin, A. (1991) 'Mercenary activity', in V. Kruta *et al.* (eds) *The Celts*, London: Thames & Hudson, 321–32.

Ross, A. (1961) 'The horned god of the Brigantes', *Archaeologia Aeliana*, series 4, 39: 59ff.

Schindler, R. (1977) *Führer durch des Landesmuseum Trier*, Trier: Selbstverlag des Rheinischen Landesmuseums.

Szabó, M. (1971) *The Celtic Heritage in Hungary*, Budapest: Corvina.

Thevenot, E. (1968) *Divinités et sanctuaires de la Gaule*, Paris: Fayard.

Vatin, C. (1969) 'Ex-voto de bois gallo-romain à Chamalières', *Revue Archéologique* 103: 103–14.

Vouga, A. (1923) *La Tène*, Leipzig: Karl W. Hiersemann.

Vries, J. de. (1963) *La Religion des Celtes*, Paris: Payot.

Webster, G. (1986a) *The British Celts and their Gods under Rome*, London: Batsford.

—— (1986b) 'What the Britons required from the gods as seen through the pairing of Roman and Celtic deities and the character of votive offerings', in M. Henig and A. King (eds) *Pagan Gods and Shrines of the Roman Empire*, Oxford: Oxford University Committee for Archaeology Monograph 8, 57–64.

Wheeler, R.E.M. (1932) *Report on the Excavations ... in Lydney Park, Gloucestershire*, London: Society of Antiquaries of London.

Wightman, E.M. (1970) *Roman Trier and the Treveri*, London: Hart-Davis.

Wild, J.-P. (1968) 'Die Frauentracht der Uber', *Germania* 46: 67–73.

Wilkes, J.J. (1969) *Dalmatia*, London: Routledge & Kegan Paul.

Woodward, A. (1992) *Shrines and Sacrifice*, London: Batsford/English Heritage.

Zwicker, J. (1934–6) *Fontes Historiae Religionis Celticae*, Berlin: Walter de Gruyter.

BURIAL AND THE OTHERWORLD

———— ·◆· ————

Gerald A. Wait

INTRODUCTION

It is a truism to observe that all people die. It is equally true to observe that the death of a loved one is one of the most traumatic events in life. Beliefs about the nature of life, death and what happens thereafter, are profoundly religious in nature. The study of burials brings the archaeologist into the closest possible contact with a vanished people and society – providing both the remains of the individuals and one of the very few enduring examples of very deliberate, and inherently meaningful, belief-laden activities. Jean-Louis Brunaux has phrased it thus: 'it would be more correct to see the [world of the dead] as the terrain of an ideology – not simply funerary, but more broadly religious and eschatological.' Burials and funerary practices are of unequalled value to the archaeologist.

There is a multitude of intervening factors between the archaeologist and an understanding of Celtic burial practices and Celtic beliefs about the Otherworld. These must be considered first, before discussing in rather more detail just what sources of information are available, and what those sources have to say about the Celtic world.

The first and most important point is that the archaeological record (which is almost all the information available over most of the time and area discussed) is of itself almost mute. The archaeological artefacts and contexts acquire meaning through a process of argument by analogy. It is therefore important that the analogies be selected with care.

A second and equally important point is that specific religious beliefs about death and the Otherworld need not be reflected in specific practices, and vice versa. Put simply, a belief in life after death may be instituted by the practice of cremation, but is equally likely to be implemented by inhumation burial. Lastly, the vagaries of survival that plague all archaeological evidence must be mentioned. It is all too likely that crucial evidence was made of perishable materials and is unlikely to survive in its usual context; therefore if it survives in an unusual context its relevance may not be recognized.

Sources

There are three principal sources of information available about Celtic burial practices and beliefs. The major source of information will always be archaeology. Two other sources require particular care in their use. The first is the writings about Celtic society by observers from the classical Mediterranean world (elsewhere referred to as Celtic ethnographies), and the second are tales and myths with religious meanings preserved in the Celtic vernacular literature of Ireland and Wales. Both of these sources should probably be used only to provide background, avoiding applications that are too specific (Wait 1985: 21–34).

In recent years the archaeological approach to the Iron Age and the Celts has altered radically. The 1970s and early 1980s were dominated by an interpretative framework that saw the Celts in relation to the classical world of the Mediterranean, reacting to stimuli originating in Greece or Italy. To a certain extent this generalizing approach was valid and useful, but it also created a view of the Celts as timeless and traditional, a monolithic entity across Europe and across more than a thousand years. An important goal of this short discussion is to discuss 'Celtic' burial practices while still recognizing the internal variability within the Celtic world.

The Literary Sources

The nature and descent of the Celtic vernacular literature has been discussed in some detail elsewhere (Wait 1985: 210–34). Here it may be sufficient to observe that Irish, and to a lesser extent Welsh, myths do contain a wealth of religious information deriving from a late and provincial Celtic society. This may legitimately be used as a source, but should not be extended to apply to Celtic societies widely separated in time and space.

One immediate limitation is that these sources contain virtually no direct references to typical Celtic funerals. There are, on the other hand, many passages about the Celtic Otherworld, or Otherworlds. One problem is that it is not made clear whether these Otherworlds are simply places where the gods dwelt, or included places where the Celtic dead went after death as well (e.g. Davidson 1988: 122–6, 167–76; MacCulloch 1949: 80–8). Another qualification is that the modern concept of the 'soul' may not be appropriate in the Celtic context.

What does seem very clear is that the Irish and Welsh Celts did believe in an Otherworld of superlative, Elysian nature, where the gods dwelt and which could be accessed through the Sidh mounds or by voyages. More common mortals (or their souls) journeyed to an Otherworld, called Tech Duinn, or the House of Donn. This Otherworld was ruled by Donn, a somewhat mysterious figure in mythology. Tech Duinn appears to be a more sombre place than the Sidh Otherworld, reached through the far south-west coastal land of Kerry. The 'mechanics' of travel to Tech Duinn are never stated.

Similarly, the observations by classical visitors about Celtic society in Gaul in the first centuries BC and AD have been widely discussed (e.g. Wait 1985: 191–209; Nash 1976, 1978). These sources have their own limitations, such as the motives of the Greek and Roman observers, but nonetheless are of considerable value in understanding Gaulish Celtic society during that crucial period of change.

One of the outstanding features of Celtic belief, as remarked on by these observers is that the Celts believed in an immortal soul (Wait 1985: 205–6):

> The belief of Pythagoras is strong among them, that the souls of men are immortal, and that after a definite number of years they live a second life when the soul passes to another body. This is the reason given why some people at the burial of the dead cast upon the pyre letters written to their dead relatives, thinking that the dead will be able to read them.
>
> (Diodorus Siculus, V.28; Tierney 1960: 250)

> They [the druids] are chiefly anxious to have men believe the following: that the souls do not suffer death, but after death pass from one body to another ... Funerals are on a large and expensive scale, considering the Gallic way of life; everything which they believe the dead man loved in life is given to the flames, even the animals.
>
> (Caesar V.14, IV. 19; Tierney 1960: 273)

Similar comments regarding the immortality of souls, and a further life in an Otherworld are echoed in Ammianus Marcellinus (quoting Timagenes), Pomponius Mela and Strabo (Chadwick 1966: 25, 30, 51–2).

An aspect of this belief which seems to have particularly impressed the observers was the concreteness of the afterlife. From all this emerges a conception of an Otherworld much like this world, where everyday objects would again have a place.

Ethnographic Analogy

Finally, mention should be made of a few aspects of the use of anthropological theory in interpreting archaeological evidence. The primary method is the ethnographic analogy – interpreting the archaeological record on the basis of parallels with the material culture of a society observed by modern ethnographers. This requires extensive parallels in many aspects of the two societies. Where such extensive parallelism cannot be demonstrated, a more general analogy may be employed (called general-comparative analogies). In this case a consistent relationship between burial practices and eschatological beliefs may be employed to explain a society observed archaeologically. In this mode of interpretation, it is clearly unwise to attempt too specific an explanation. There is a voluminous literature dealing with the 'archaeology of death' (e.g. Wait 1985: 235–40; Saxe 1970; Binford 1971; Tainter 1978; O'Shea 1984; Huntingdon and Metcalfe 1979) and the methodology is tolerably well understood.

Archaeology

Even overtly social dimensions such as political structure may also have ideological dimensions. In particular, much of the analysis of burial or mortuary practices rests upon the differential treatment of people as defined by the society itself. This may mean the differential treatment of political élites, economic groups, kin groups, or groups defined along ritual criteria. Within the burial traditions visible in the British Iron Age, several traditions appear to deal with a social majority (i.e. they are normative rites) while others apply to minority groups.

BRITISH CELTIC TRADITIONS

Central Southern England – the Pit Tradition

Within central southern England one tradition is now well studied – the 'Pit Tradition' (Wait 1985: 83–121; Whimster 1981: 4–36; Hill forthcoming). This tradition may be briefly described as the deposition of either whole or partial bodies in the nearly ubiquitous grain-storage pits found on sites on chalk hills and river terrace gravels. Up to six categories of burials may be distinguished depending on the number and treatment of individuals buried. It is, however, very difficult to assess what population these burials represent. Since these are the only type of burial known from this area for the whole of the Iron Age, it is tempting to conclude that they are in some way 'normal', but this simply is not convincing. On sites where it is possible to devise at least an order-of-magnitude estimate for the site's population through time, and then compare the number of expected burials with those found in the Pit Tradition, it is clear that the known burials represent a very small minority of the population, perhaps no more than 5 per cent. Furthermore, on most of the sites and for most of the period, few infants and children are represented although they should be numerically dominant. However, by the last century BC infants do become more common. Males and females are usually equally well represented.

The categories into which the range of burials may be divided also change in popularity through time. During the Early Iron Age most human remains occur as single bones, whereas by the end of the Iron Age, single complete inhumations predominate. Most are placed on the left side in a crouched or tightly flexed position, oriented with head between north and south-east. The partial bodies are always a rare occurrence, and are much more likely to occur on hill-forts than on other forms of settlement, and more likely to include juveniles and adolescents than the other categories.

These trends may be illustrated by examples at two recently well-excavated sites: the Hampshire hill-fort of Danebury, and the open village at Stanton Harcourt Gravelly Guy in Oxfordshire (Figures 26.1 and 26.2). At Danebury at least seventy individuals (from the 23 per cent of the site excavated) were represented by burials either complete or in a variety of partial states (Walker in Cunliffe 1984: 442–63). Most of the burials were found in the large pits usually interpreted as for grain storage but later reused for refuse disposal. This interpretation about refuse disposal has been challenged by J.D. Hill (forthcoming), whose detailed analyses of the pit contents suggest that the contents of many, if not most, pits were not normal rubbish, but rather follow discernible rules and may be better interpreted as ritual disposal.

The complete inhumations at Danebury number 25 individuals, comprising 11 adult males, 5 adult females, 2 children over 10 years, 2 children aged 5 to 10 years, and 5 infants. Fourteen of these were solitary burials, there was one double burial, two triples and two 'charnel pits' with larger mixed groups of corpses. All but one of the burials were crouched or flexed, and only one was extended. The tightly flexed bodies may have been bound prior to burial. The orientations vary widely, but a distinct preference for heads to the north is apparent. In addition there is a variety

Figure 26.1 Burial of a 35-year-old woman from the middle iron age occupation at Stanton Harcourt Gravelly Guy, Oxon. (Photo: Lambrick.)

Figure 26.2 Inhumation burials: deposits 28, 29, 30 in P829, Danebury. (Photo: Mike Rouillard, Institute of Archaeology, Oxford University.)

of partial bodies and skulls, and numerous single (complete or fragmentary) bones, with skull fragments and longbones from the right side of the body predominating.

The iron age site at Stanton Harcourt Gravelly Guy on the river Thames gravel terraces in Oxfordshire appears to be a typical open, undefended agricultural village during the Iron Age, with continued occupation from the Middle Iron Age into the early Roman period (Lambrick forthcoming). At least 70 individuals are represented, of whom 51 are infants (Wait in Lambrick forthcoming). There were 28 complete inhumations (23 infants, 1 child of 4–5 years, 3 adult females and 1 adult male), 1 single skull (an adult male), and 28 occurrences of infant bones (at least some of which are unrecognized burials), 1 adult male and 1 adult female longbone, and 11 unsexed adult bones. The adult burials were crouched, with 3 on the right side and

1 on the left, and among the infants 6 were crouched on the right and 3 on the left. Ten of the burials were placed with heads to the north (between north-west and north-east) and five with heads to the south.

The interpretation of the burials in the Pit Tradition is far from straightforward. The burials represent a small minority of the parent population, selected along criteria favouring adults but later broadened to include infants. Within this minority, several subgroups may be distinguished. Their characteristics do not match those of social or political élite minorities known from ethnographic study; such minorities are usually distinguished by burial with grave goods (indicative of their position) within restricted cemetery areas. Another possible minority group would be the victims of human sacrifice. It is certain that the Celts did practise human sacrifice (Caesar, Strabo, Lucan and Tacitus all mention the practice with a variety of details relating to method employed; see Wait 1985: 118–20, 235–45; Ross 1967), and it seems possible that the partial burials with overtones of violence and dismemberment are the results of sacrificial rites. The most likely explanation for most of these burials is that they are the remains of abnormal, outcast members of Celtic society. Within the ethnological literature, outcast groups usually receive a non-normative treatment of the body, a different mode of disposal, a different place of disposal, frequently associated with social rubbish and dirt, and rarely have a normal age/sex distribution – all true of the Pit Tradition. It is as if every effort had been made to differentiate these people from the social majority of 'normal' people, who may have been either cremated or had their corpses exposed, and then been disposed of either far from settlements or in rivers (Wait 1985: 118–20).

A major underlying theme is that the burials represent a belief in death as a transitional period (not an event) intervening between this world and the Otherworld. During this period the body and the soul are formless and stateless, objects of dread. This period is terminated with a formal ceremony marking the arrival of the soul in the Otherworld (Wait 1985: 235–45). The souls of those individuals denied the normal mortuary rite were prevented from following the normal after-death course, thus maintaining the purity of a society's Otherworld.

Who were these outcasts? A specific answer is probably unattainable, but a number of suggestions may serve as the basis for further investigation. In the ethnographic literature (e.g. the Asante), outcast people are defined either by life style or by type of death. Abnormal life styles include witches, sorcercers, criminals (especially murderers), religious heretics, and practitioners of ritually proscribed occupations. Abnormal deaths include drowning, murder, suicide, lightning, death in childbirth, or death outside the social group's territory.

It is interesting to speculate that if the Pit Tradition burials are abnormal burials consciously distinguished from the normal, then some of their characteristics may be a reversal of the social norm. For example, if these are usually buried on the left side, does this mean that the right side was considered favourable? If these are oriented to the north-east, what was the favoured direction? Was the placing of the bodies or body parts in a pit deliberately differentiated from a normal disposal by cremation or exposure, both of which methods would represent a clean, above-ground, or airy aspect? All of these extrapolations may be paralleled elsewhere in Celtic settlement structure and layout, and in ritual associations found in the Celtic vernacular literature.

Durotriges of Dorset

The Durotriges of Dorset on the southern coast of Britain appear to have adopted a new, possibly normative burial rite at the very end of the first century BC, which endured until it was replaced by the romanized cremation rite a century or so later (Whimster 1981: 37–59). The rite adopted was burial in simple earthen graves (and exceptionally in graves lined with stone to form a cist), and the regular provision of a limited but distinctive range of grave goods (Figure 26.3).

Burials seem to have been in defined cemeteries, probably with internal ordering (perhaps by family?). The corpses were usually placed in a flexed position, on the right side – placement on the left in 20–25 per cent of burials seems a deliberate variation – and oriented with heads between north-east and south-east. The age range excludes infants and young children but is otherwise 'normal', with both sexes represented. Grave goods most often include a restricted range of locally produced ceramic vessels, and less often joints of meat (beef with males, pig with females, and sheep with either sex), and very occasionally personal ornaments such as brooches or bracelets.

The general impression is of a fairly egalitarian distribution, with a low level of

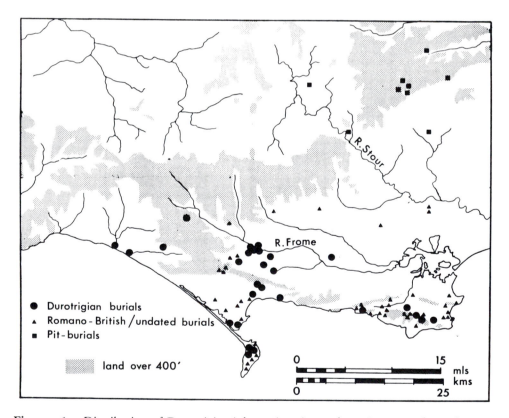

Figure 26.3 Distribution of Durotrigian inhumations in southern Dorset. (After Whimster 1981: fig. 15.)

496

social distinction replicated in grave goods. There are several notable exceptions. One is the well-known warrior burial from Whitcomb near Dorchester. This was a muscular young man in his twenties placed in typical position and orientation, but buried with a La Tène III sword, a La Tène II brooch, bronze belt-hook, and other subsidiary tools and weapons (cf. Whimster 1981: 50–1, 129–46). Equally exceptional are two cist-grave burials with mirrors from near Portland, and a third (of an elderly woman?) from Bridport – such mirrors were almost certainly family heirlooms of considerable age when buried.

This tradition superficially resembles what most modern observers would expect from a normative rite (the chronic absence of infants from the assemblages is commonly and probably correctly dismissed, as infants are very often not considered part of society until they survive a period of time and are 'baptized'). There are, however, very real problems with this conclusion. The principal problem is simply one of numbers – there are too few burials known. This could, of course, be a function of modern archaeological work, and Whimster makes this point (1981, 37), but even the more recently excavated examples are small clusters of burials. The strong suspicion must remain that this is in fact a burial rite adopted by or applied to only a sector of the population. The presence of grave goods may rule out a denigrated minority such as that represented in the Pit Tradition, but it may be either a social élite, or some other grouping such as a clan or lineage which for reasons unknown adopted a new rite.

Aylesford-Swarling Cremations

An apparently normative rite was introduced or adopted in Kent and the north Chiltern areas in the mid-first century BC, and thereafter spread to adjacent areas of eastern England (Figure 26.4). This is the much-discussed Aylesford-Swarling or 'Belgic' cremation tradition. One of its most controversial aspects is whether or not it represents an intrusive tradition – are these the invaders from Gaul recorded by Caesar? The literature on the subject is voluminous (cf. Stead 1976 and Whimster 1981: 147–66).

The Aylesford-Swarling rite appears in an early phase called 'Welwyn' *c.*50–40 BC (after Stead 1976) and later gains momentum in a 'Lexden' phase *c.*15–10 BC and merges into the early romanized tradition of cremation in the later first century AD. The rite involves cremation of the corpse (usually off-site but occasionally in the grave) and the collection of the calcined remains for burial, usually in a ceramic pot but alternatively in a simple pit or in a bucket of wood and metal. The graves cluster in cemeteries, usually very small but ranging up to the extraordinary King Harry Lane cemetery at St Albans (Stead and Rigby 1989) with over 472 burials. In the larger cemeteries there appears to be an internal arrangement of clusters, perhaps representing families or lineages.

Aylesford burials are frequently furnished with grave goods, the most frequent being a single pot (about 63 per cent of graves) derived from a restricted range of beakers or similar vessels. The vessels are stylistically derived from the Champagne-Ardennes and Normandy-Picardy areas of northern France (thus giving rise to the invasion hypothesis). A second tier of burials can be distinguished, furnished with

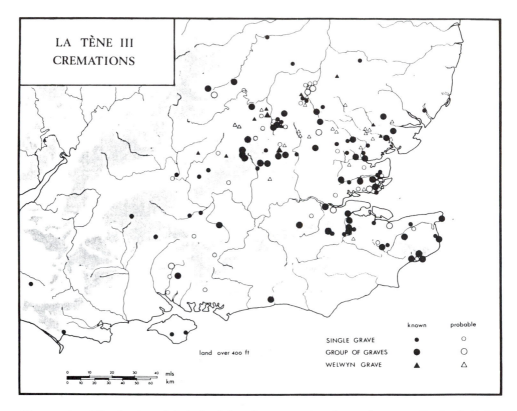

Figure 26.4 Distribution of Aylesford-Swarling cremations in south-eastern England. (After Whimster 1981: fig. 52.)

one to five pots or La Tène bow brooches, usually interpreted as belonging to a wealthier social group. In addition there are burials in wooden staved buckets, often provided with other valuable objects including imports. At the apex of this apparent pyramid is the Welwyn burial class, of unurned remains accompanied by an extraordinary range of imported amphorae, and bronze and silver vessels indicative of drinking and feasting, plus many items of locally produced wealth. More subtle variations in the size of grave pits, placement of remains within the pits, and distribution of goods within cemeteries may be suspected (e.g. Fitzpatrick 1991).

The King Harry Lane cemetery of 472 excavated burials is undoubtedly a major new source of information for study. This is interpreted as the cemetery for a stable population of about 200 people. However, the excavated sample is biased 3 to 1 in favour of males, and as usual contains very few pre-adults. This skewed sample is explained as a result of adoption of the rite by a particular (male-dominated) social group, later widened to include women and children in the Roman period. While this is certainly possible, it does reflect other peculiarities of the overall tradition. The vast majority of Aylesford cemeteries are clusters of less than a dozen burials, which cannot possibly represent stable populations. The Aylesford rite as presently documented appears to be one adopted by a social minority.

The Yorkshire Arras Tradition

Eastern Yorkshire presents a reversal of the typical British pattern, by containing a prolific burial record but a settlement record still largely unexplored (Whimster 1981: 75–128; Stead 1979). The burial record also presents another controversial example of possible migration/invasion. Sometime during the third/fourth century BC a tradition of burial appears on the Yorkshire Wolds (Figure 26.5) that bears many similarities with a contemporary shift in burial rites in the Champagne/Marne area of northern France, among people later known as Parisi. By the time of Caesar's invasion of Britain, the people of eastern Yorkshire were also known as Parisi.

The innovative burial tradition consists of burial underneath a barrow and sur-rounded by a square quarry ditch. Barrows vary greatly in size, and are often arranged into long linear barrow cemeteries. Burials were generally in a tightly flexed position, accompanied by a range of grave goods. The dead vary in apparent wealth and status from commoners with few grave goods to warriors with weapons to 'chieftains' buried with two-wheeled carts or chariots (Figure 26.6). Secondary burials were inserted into either the barrow or more commonly into the fill of the quarry ditches. Males and females appear in relatively equal numbers, though young children or infants are underrepresented. The square barrows were reserved for

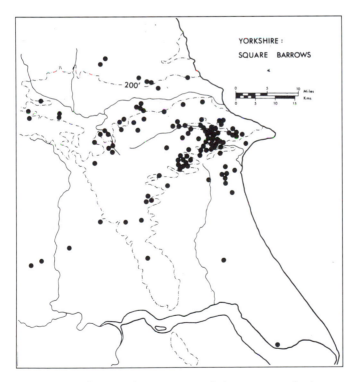

Figure 26.5 Distribution of square barrows recorded as crop-marks in eastern Yorkshire. (After Whimster 1981: fig. 31.)

adults of either sex – there is a small number of variant graves including simple flat graves and multiple (possibly familial) burials.

While nearly all the burials were crouched, a minority were placed in an extended position. This presents one point of variance from the possible continental homeland – Marnian burials are normally extended with heads to the west (see p. 505 below). About 80 per cent the burials were placed on their left side, with a minority of 20 per cent on the right side. Overall, about 70 per cent of the burials are placed with the head between north and north-east, with about 25 per cent buried with head to the south to south-west. The remainder are oriented east to west (with head to the east). Interestingly, the east–west burials are nearly always in an extended position rather than crouched. Such variations in position, orientation or preferences for left or right sides show no apparent correlation with age or sex. Thus the minorities represented are interpreted as normal social sub-groups.

The majority of Arras burials were accompanied by grave goods. These consisted of personal bronze jewellery, pottery vessels (small coarseware jars) and joints of pig meat. The extended burials have a distinctive inventory of goods, usually of iron (the jewellery with crouched burials is universally of bronze). This includes some burials of warriors with short swords and spears, as well as a variety of tools. The extended burials are not associated with ceramic pots, pig bones or personal ornamants.

At the top of the apparent range is a number of burials with two-wheeled carts or chariots (van Endert 1986). The carts are known from their iron fittings and wheel rims, and bronze horse trappings, and were usually dismantled for burial (whereas Marnian carts are usually complete). In the Arras tradition, cart-burials usually contain few subsidiary grave goods.

The Arras pottery is a local product, but the metalwork shows clear inspiration from northern France, albeit in very simple style and range. Most are in La Tène II style, but curiously appear not in the earliest series of burials but rather in a second phase. This may be interpreted as the second and third generations of an immigrant group burying family heirlooms, and thereafter carrying on with locally produced items.

Some speculation concerning this tradition may be hazarded in advance of the definitive excavation reports. The extended burials with iron objects including weapons may represent warriors. The crouched burials represent the majority of the population, subdivided by the use of body position and orientation into four subgroups. What is missing is the socially abnormal group so prominent in the surrounding traditions: if they existed they clearly received some other, archaeologically invisible form of disposal.

TRADITIONS OF NORTH-WEST EUROPE

Western Germany and Northern France

A generalized burial tradition developed during the Early Iron Age western Hallstatt period, and continued with local variations for several centuries. This tradition is based on simple extended inhumation in flat graves, and with east–west orientation (head to west). The burials are usually located in small cemeteries generally attributed to small villages or hamlets. The provision of grave goods is common and generally commensurate with a weakly ranked society.

This general tradition becomes elaborated in two distinct regions (during two phases) into quite extraordinary cultures that have given rise to an enormous amount of archaeological study (see Cunliffe 1988; Collis 1984; Wells 1980; Frankenstein and Rowlands 1978, and references there). Much of this information will be reviewed in other chapters, but some of the basic data will be repeated here to form the basis of a discussion of religious ideology.

Late Hallstatt South-western Germany and Eastern France *c*.600–450 BC

The south-western part of Germany and adjacent parts of France witnessed an explosive growth of late Hallstatt society during the Hallstatt D period. In the most general terms this was the rise of a centralized, highly hierarchical, complex chiefdom society. This was focused on the so-called *Fürstensitze* or chiefly residences, defended hilltop enclosures with evidence of dense permanent occupation and extensive and intensive craft specialization. In addition, there was evidence of extensive trade with the Mediterranean world (especially Greece and Etruria), probably by way of the Greek colony at Massalia (modern Marseilles). In the area surrounding these *Fürstensitze* is a wide variety of burial barrows, some of which contained extraordinary richness – the *Fürstengraber*, or chiefly graves (Kimmig 1969, 1975).

At the pinnacle of the chiefly complexes are the centres of Mont Lassois, with its associated burials at Vix and Ste Colombe, the Heuneburg with its Hohmichele burials, and the Hohenasperg with Grafenbühl. These are often interpreted as the residences and burials of 'paramount chiefs'. The paramount chief burials are characterized by inhumation in wooden chambers, accompanied by a four-wheeled wagon and horse trappings (van Endert 1987). In addition there is a wide range of prestige luxury goods, including Greek and Etruscan bronze and silver vessels for wine-drinking, gold (usually as jewellery such as torques, bracelets and leg-rings), glass, amber, coral and lignite (again as decoration or jewellery) and silk fabrics (Figure 26.6).

Surrounding these barrows is a periphery of less wealthy barrows, interpreted as vassal chiefs and subchiefs. These burials lack the imports; instead there are weapons with the men and jewellery with women, often of very high quality but probably produced at the *Fürstensitze*. Less wealthy village chiefs may also be distinguished. The possible social ramifications of this pattern have given rise to a number of strictly socio-economic interpretations, particularly variations on the 'prestige goods economy' model of Frankenstein and Rowlands (1978).

Inserted into the barrows of all levels of chiefly status are secondary burials (almost always inhumations). These burials are always far less well provided – men occasionally have weapons and women jewellery, but there are few pretensions about these mundane objects. Barrows occur in groups of 4 to 10, but one massive cemetery of 100 barrows is known. The numbers of secondary burials per barrow average 30 to 40, with the Magdalensburg (with 126 later burials) representing the upper limit.

The end of this flamboyant society *c.*450 BC was apparently quite sudden and violent, with some of the *Fürstensitze* destroyed. Few *Fürstensitze* can demonstrate any continuity into the subsequent La Tène I period.

La Tène I in the Hunsrück-Eifel and Champagne

Shortly after 450 BC the areas to the north-west of the Hallstatt heartland witnessed a *floruit* equally dramatic but different in detail. The La Tène resurgence occurred in the Hunsrück-Eifel along the Moselle river and further west in the Champagne-Marne region of France (Figure 26.7b). These areas had developed a tradition of warrior burial during the preceding Hallstatt period, perhaps in relationship with the Hallstatt heartland (e.g. Cunliffe 1988: 30–37). During La Tène I this was to develop radically (Bretz-Mahler 1971; Flouest and Stead 1979; Duval and Kruta 1977).

The La Tène culture in the Hunsrück-Eifel and Champagne differs from the Hallstatt D culture chiefly in that there are no parallels for the *Fürstensitze*. Only one of the Hallstatt *Fürstensitze* (the Hohenasperg with the Klein Aspergle burial) shows any continuity into the La Tène period. There are hill-forts, but these lack dense, specialized occupation, and there are many small open farming settlements instead. Another important difference from the Hallstatt predecessor is that the Mediterranean connections are with Etruria alone – the Greek connections via Massalia ceased with the decline of the Hallstatt centres.

The La Tène burial traditions continue earlier themes – extended east–west inhumation under barrows, some with square or rectangular quarry ditches.

Figure 26.6 Hallstatt *Fürstengraber* at Hochdorf. (From Biel 1985: fig. 33.)

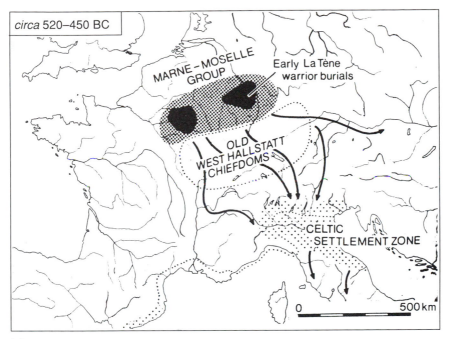

(a)

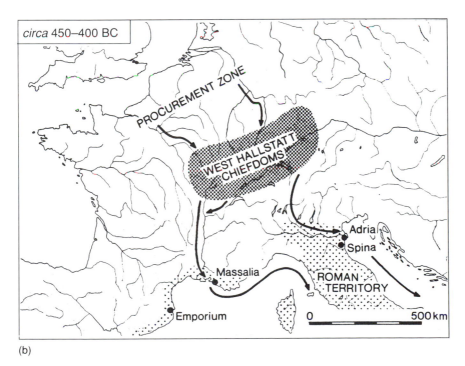

(b)

Figure 26.7 The (a) Hallstatt and (b) La Tène burial traditions. (After Cunliffe 1988: fig. 15.)

Secondary burials are frequently inserted into the barrows. Grave goods generally include bronze fibulae, bracelets for women and iron short swords and spears for men. Higher status burials, like the Reinheim barrow, are clearly set apart by gold jewellery, objects of shale, jet, amber, lignite and glass, two-wheeled carts/chariots, and imported Etruscan bronze vessels for wine-drinking. Unlike the dense Hallstatt barrow fields, the La Tène rich burials occur only once or twice per cemetery, while most burials were simple flat inhumations. Cemeteries with rich burials are not associated with any of the known hill-forts, but are well scattered (cf. Wells 1980: 104–11; Cunliffe 1988: 30–7; Collis 1984: 103–26).

More typical of cemeteries is Thely, with more than 37 burials in 18 barrows. One burial was unaccompanied, and 6 had only one pottery vessel each. Eight had weapons (swords and spears). Bronze bracelets/arm-rings occurring in pairs were the most common grave goods. There was no gold, jet, lignite, coral or glass, and no chariot or timber chamber.

The Champagne-Marne area in north-eastern France witnessed a contemporary development of burial traditions along very similar lines, probably closely related to the Hunsrück-Eifel focus and receiving imported goods via the Moselle. In Champagne two-wheeled carts/chariots are apparently more common, occurring in barrows in small cemeteries (Figure 26.8). Swords and spears appear with men (the typical complement is one pike and two javelins), occasionally with bronze helmets, and elaborate bronze chariot and horse harness fittings. Women are buried with bronze torques, bracelets and fibulae.

The Champagne cemeteries, of 30–40 burials on average, occur regularly across the landscape (with an unexpected congruence with modern parishes). The cemeteries are usually interpreted as serving farming hamlets or small villages.

The early La Tène Champagne culture, like its Hallstatt predecessor, seems to have come to a sudden end. Its collapse is contemporary with changes in the Mediterranean world (e.g. the rise of the Roman state), but it also probably had internal causes, including very rapid population growth and unrealistic expectations

Figure 26.8 Hallstatt *Fürstengraber* wagon. (From Biel 1985: fig. 42/3.)

of the élite regarding the supply of luxury items from Etruria. The final phase of the Champagne culture is intimately linked to the beginnings of folk movements culminating in the great Celtic migrations.

Later La Tène Traditions

The subsequent periods (*c.*200–100 BC; cf. Whimster 1981: 116–21; Cunliffe 1988: 33–6, 80–105; Collis 1984: 139–57; and Wells 1980: 104–42) reverted to simpler flat inhumation cemeteries (bodies extended with heads to the west) with weak social ranking indicated by grave goods of personal ornaments and weapons. There is a widespread (but poorly documented) tradition of decapitated burials throughout both the Hallstatt and La Tène traditions, hinting at complex social and religious distinctions. Cremation appears in northern France *c.*300 BC and gradually spreads south and eastwards. Throughout, both square and rectangular barrows occur alongside the simpler inhumations, and where present are usually associated with the 'richer' burials. The consistent incorporation of grave goods has been widely accepted as congruent with a belief in a concrete Otherworld where the dead will want and need symbols of their life and status from this world.

The true complexity of funerary practices has been demonstrated by the outstanding work of Brunaux and Meniel at Gournay-sur-Aronde (Brunaux 1987; Brunaux, Meniel and Poplin 1985). Gournay was a small ritual enclosure (about 45 × 38 m) set within a large later iron age *oppidum* of the Bellovaci. The enclosure was demarcated by ditches, and in the centre of the enclosure was a long sequence of cultic features and buildings. It is significant that the enclosure ditches and walls meant that the interior could not be observed from without, and that the cult features and buildings were not designed to accommodate large groups of people, such as worshippers or observers. The earliest phase was at the end of La Tène I (fourth century BC), and the site was deliberately and formally closed and dismantled in the mid-first century BC. A later Roman temple was subsequently built over the levelled remains of the Celtic temples, so some knowledge of the site's significance must have survived.

Gournay has provided an unprecedented wealth of information about Celtic ritual practices, and Brunaux (1987) is adept at teasing out elements of belief underlying the practices. Among the themes relevant to this discussion is the occurrence of some 2,000 sacrificed weapons and animals deliberately placed in the enclosure ditch (Brunaux 1987: 9, fig.), representing what Brunaux has described as 'an unbroken apotropaic cordon all the way around the sacred area' (1987: 32). Amongst the sacrifices are many human remains. These are consistently scored by fine knife marks, and Poplin was led to conclude that they represented the dismemberment of the corpse during a funerary ritual. This was not applied to the ordinary Gaul (buried or cremated) but rather to some small subset of the population. Brunaux prefers to link them to a long-standing cult of the head and an ancestor cult (for which he provides little evidence). The underlying belief was apparently that the soul of the deceased was contained in the skull or other bone, and that putting the bone in the enclosure ditch served to add the deceased's spiritual power to that of the weapons and animals also placed in the ditch. This has interesting implications about the nature of the people so treated – were they outcasts?

The nearby site at Ribemont-sur-Ancre (Picardy) adds another dimension to the retention of bones for ritual purposes. Excavations in 1982 revealed an ossuary composed of 2,000 human bones (mostly tibias, femurs and humeri) arranged in a criss-cross pattern to form a 1 m high hollow square, topped with human shoulder-blades. There is no concrete evidence for sacrifice, but there is evidence once again for the deliberate dismemberment of hundreds of individuals.

Celtic Gaul therefore provides evidence for a wide range of funerary practices. To understand the meaning of the rich burials in both late Hallstatt and early La Tène contexts, and sites like Gournay and Ribemont, it is necessary to consider both ethnolographic analogies and other archaeological evidence (cf. Wait 1985: 15–50; Fitzpatrick 1984; Torbrugge, 1971; von Brunn 1980). The ethnographic data were collected by Levy (1982) in relation to Danish Bronze Age hoards, but much of the material is relevant to iron age burials. One prime point is that the deposition of grave goods is in many ways similar to ritual hoard deposition – Levy's composite definition (1982: 20, 25) applies equally to either activity:

> A deposition made in a stereotypic way, of symbolically valuable objects (which may also be materially valuable, but this is incidental) with the conscious purpose of communicating with (by petition, blessing, thanking, propitiating) the supernatural world.
>
> (1982: 20)

Much of the message directed at the Otherworld through the performance of these rituals is carried by the objects used. Kuper (1973) has observed that personal ornaments and weapons are useful for symbolizing a social persona (in the sense of Saxe (1970) and Binford (1971)). Furthermore, according to Drennan (1976) rituals utilizing social symbols serve to sanctify or legitimate the social relationships which incorporate the symbolic object (cf. Müller 1990). In these types of rituals the general populace are neither observers nor participants, though keenly aware of what is happening.

A great deal of archaeological interpretation has been invested in constructing models of complex chieftains and politico-economic systems based on artefacts and activities symbolizing power and wealth. These interpretations have omitted to consider fully the symbolic messages inherent in the objects. It may be argued that the chieftains derived their political and economic authority by being linked to the Otherworld and the gods through the medium of the burial rituals. A chief held that position not only through the control of trade by diplomatic and mercantile skills, but also because the social group's authority was made obvious in the translation of the dead and their symbols of power into the Otherworld. Chiefs may therefore have held certain priestly authority in carrying out rituals on behalf of the larger society. Some elements of a cult of the ancestors may also have been involved.

Romano-Celtic Traditions in the First Millennium AD

Western Europe during the period of the Roman Empire is in many respects better understood than the prehistoric period, due in part no doubt to the fact that the period is historical as well as archaeological. The Roman period has recently benefited from a wide-ranging review (Wacher 1987) and only a very brief summary is needed here.

A consideration of Romano-Celtic burial traditions (and associated beliefs in an Otherworld) must be predicated upon some knowledge of Romano-Celtic religion (see for example Green 1976, 1984, 1986, 1989; Webster 1986; Piggott 1968; Vendryes 1948; Toynbee 1971; Sjoestedt-Jonual 1949; Ross 1967; Mac Cana 1970; Lambrechts 1942). One of the most important, but difficult aspects is the combination of beliefs and practices that occurred between the two parent religions to produce a unique hybrid. This blend was clearly not uniform across the Celtic world (e.g. Green 1986), a reminder that the preceding Celtic beliefs must have differed as well. Through this process of syncretism, formerly Celtic beliefs about the Otherworld would have undergone some changes. These may or may not be clearly reflected in burial practices. Romano-Celtic burial practices have been reviewed by Jones (1987) who was able to distinguish both a 'Roman' level of practice and more provincial variations that are likely to reflect a 'Celtic' component of belief and practice.

The most obvious 'Roman' contributions include the nearly universal adoption of cremation during the first centuries BC and AD. The anthropological literature makes it clear that specific practices may change radically without any change in belief or influence from another society: mortuary and burial practices may operate in the realm of changing fashion. Similarly, the switch to extended inhumation with an east–west orientation in the later third century was once confidently ascribed to the conversion of the Romano-Celtic world to Christianity – an interpretation clearly disproved. In spite of this caveat, Jones is probably correct to see the near-universal adoption of cremation and later inhumation as a reflection of the pervasiveness of Roman custom, if not an overlay of Roman belief (1987).

Some of the provincial practices that Jones recognized suggest that beliefs, at least at the level of defining social classes, certainly differed from region to region. Jones is clearly aware of this, as his work at Ampurias demonstrates (Jones 1984, 1987, forthcoming). Even without such basic information as age and sex for the Ampurias burials, it is clear that the rules governing the use of amphorae, tile, and grave forms are complex and idiosyncratic.

Another example of a regional practice is the occurrence of decapitated burials, in otherwise normal late Roman inhumation cemeteries in Britain. The normal cemetery contained inhumations placed in rows, generally aligned east–west. Grave goods are uncommon, limited to personal jewellery, hobnailed boots, and the provision of a coffin, providing limited scope for the interpretation of social status.

Four cemeteries in the Thames valley may be used to illustrate this custom, including Stanton Harcourt, Bloxham, Curbridge and Radley Barrow Hills (all in Oxfordshire) (Figure 26.9). There are 117 burials, of which there are approximately equal numbers of men and women. Infants are very few, though the distribution of ages at death is otherwise relatively normal. Most individuals were buried supine, and most were oriented with head to the north (a local preference). There are burials oriented east–west, and some burials are prone. Amongst the otherwise normal burials is a series of individuals with their heads removed and placed either between their knees or between their feet. Numerically, these represent about 8 per cent of the total. They are all post-adolescent, but this may not be statistically different from

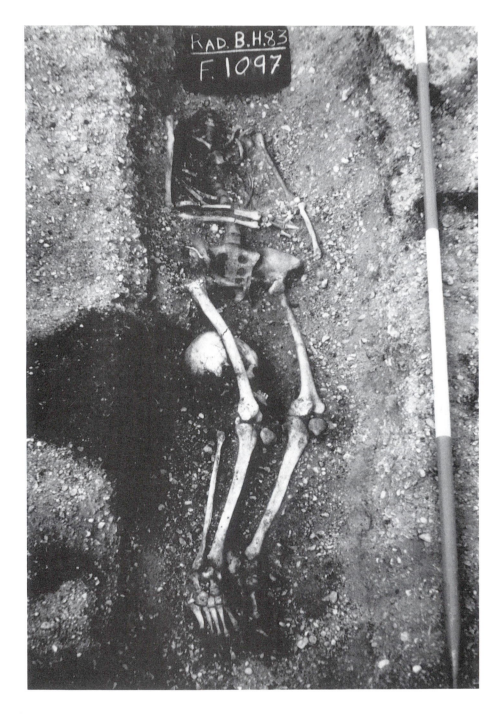

Figure 26.9 Romano-British decapitated burial from Radley Barrow Hills, Oxon. (Photo: R.A.C. Chambers.)

the rest of the burials. Just over half are identified as male – only one is definitely female. Most were buried supine and oriented to the north (partaking of some aspects of the normative traditions). Otherwise they appear normal. The purpose of the decapitation is unknown, but a convincing explanation is that the soul and body were prevented from participating in the normal transition from this life to the Otherworld. This has previously been attributed to the preservation of Celtic beliefs through three centuries of romanization, conceivably representing a class of people whose life style was reprehensible, such as witches or criminals.

SUMMARY

It is difficult to summarize this very brief review without falling into the trap of creating a misleadingly timeless and traditional picture of the Celtic world. The various themes touched upon are particular to the Celtic cultural context in which they appear, not to the whole of the Celtic world. Some key themes in Celtic beliefs include the concept of a familiar Otherworld of the dead, who possibly become 'ancestors' and possibly become associated with the gods. This may be reflected in the practice of providing grave goods; the use of objects symbolizing social relationships of power and authority in this world is most likely to indicate that those relationships derived legitimacy by being linked to the Otherworld. The belief in an Otherworld to which the dead go also has another ramification in practice. Many Celtic societies differentiated people according to both social and religious precepts, and access to the Otherworld was based upon those precepts. The élite were sent to the Otherworld with their symbols of worldly power; the ordinary Celt went as an ordinary soul; but the abnormal Celt was treated very differently, as if to keep that abnormal soul from polluting the Otherworld and jeopardizing the society's relationship to the Otherworld. It is likely that the precise ways in which people were differentiated varied through time and across space, and much work is required in order to understand either the practice or the belief. Detailed information about the age, sex, pathology, orientation, body position, etc. for both normal and abnormal mortuary practices is required before any single society's practices will be understood. It is through such study that progess is being made in the understanding of the Celtic world.

REFERENCES

Biel, J. (1985) *Der Keltenfurst von Hochdorf*, Stuttgart: Theis.
Binford, L. (1971) 'Mortuary practices: their study and potential' in J.A. Brown (ed) *Approaches to the Social Dimensions of Mortuary Practices*, New York, 6–29.
Bretz-Mahler, D. (1971) 'La civilisation de la Tène en Champagne', *Gallia*, Supplement 5.
Brunaux, J.L. (1987) *The Celtic Gauls: gods, rites and sanctuaries*, trans. D. Nash, Seaby.
Brunaux, J.L., Meniel, P. and Poplin F. (1985) 'Gournay I: les fouilles sur le sanctuaire et l'oppidum (1975–84)', Revue.
Chadwick, N. (1966) *The Druids*, Cardiff.
Collis, J. (1984) *The European Iron Age*, London.

Cunliffe, B.W. (1984) *Danebury: an iron age hillfort in Hampshire*, London: CBA Research Report 52.

—— (1988) *Greeks, Romans and Barbarians: spheres of interaction*, London.

Davidson, H.R.E. (1988) *Myths and Symbols in Pagan Europe: early Scandinavian and Celtic religions*, Manchester.

Dent, J. (1978) 'Wetwang Slack', *Current Archaeology* 6: 46–50.

Drennan, R.D. (1976) 'Religion and the social evolution in Formative Mesoamerica' in K. Flannery (ed.) *The Early Mesoamerican Village*, New York, 345–368.

Duval, P.M. and Kruta, V. (1975) *L'Habitat et la nécropole à l'âge du fer en Europe occidental et centrale*, Paris.

Fitzpatrick, A. (1984) 'The deposition of La Tène metalwork in watery contexts in southern England', in B.W. Cunliffe and D. Miles (eds) *Aspects of the Iron Age in Central Southern Britain*, Oxford, 178–90.

—— (1991) 'Death in a material world: the late iron age and early Romano-British cemetery at King Harry Lane, St Albans, Hertfordshire', *Britannia* 22: 323–8.

Flouest, J.L. (1979) *Iron Age Cemeteries in Champagne*, London: British Museum Occasional Paper 6.

Flouest, J.L. and Stead, I.M. (1977) 'Recherches sur des cimitières de La Tène en Champagne 1971–76', *Gallia* 35: 59–74.

Frankenstein, S. and Rowlands, M.J. (1978) 'The internal structure and regional context of early iron age society in southwest Germany', *Bulletin of the Institute of Archaeology* 15: 73–112.

Green, M. (1976) *The Religions of Civilian Roman Britain*, Oxford: British Archaeological Reports, British Series 24.

—— (1984) *The Wheel as a Cult Symbol in the Romano-Celtic World*, Brussels, Latomus.

—— (1986) *The Gods of the Celts*, Gloucester.

—— (1989) *Symbol and Image in Celtic Religious Art*, London.

Hill, J.D. (1993) 'Ritual and rubbish in the Iron Age of Wessex: a study in the formation of a specific archaeological record', Ph.D. thesis, University of Cambridge.

Huntingdon, R. and Metcalfe, P. (1979) *Celebrations of Death: the anthropology of mortuary ritual*, Cambridge.

Jones, R.F.J. (1984) 'The Roman cemeteries of Ampurias reconsidered', in T.F.C. Blagg, R.F.J. Jones and S.J. Keay (eds) *Papers in Iberian Archaeology*, Oxford: British Archaeological Reports, International Series 193, 237–65.

—— (1987) 'Burial customs of Rome and the provinces', in J. Wacher (ed.) *The Roman World*, London.

Kimmig, W. (1969) 'Zum Problem späthallstattischer Adelssitze', in K.-H. Otto and J. Hermann (eds) *Siedlung, Burg und Stadt. Studien zu ihren anfängen Festschrift Paul Grimm*, Berlin: Deutsche Akademie der Wissenschaften zu Berlin, Schriften der Sektion für Vor- und Früh-geschichte 25.

—— (1975) 'Early Celts on the upper Danube: excavations at the Heuneburg', in R. Bruce-Mitford (ed) *Recent Archaeological Excavations in Europe*, London, 32–64.

Kuper, H. (1973) 'Costume and identity', *Comparative Studies in Society and History* 15: 348–67.

Lambrechts, P. (1942) *Contributions à l'étude des divinités celtiques*, Bruges.

Lambrick, G. (forthcoming) *Stanton Harcourt Gravelly Guy*.

Levy, J. (1982) *Religion and Social Organisation in Bronze Age Denmark*, Oxford: British Archaeological Reports, International Series 124.

Mac Cana, P. (1970) *Celtic Mythology*, London.

MacCulloch, J.A. (1949) *The Celtic and Scandinavian Religions*, London.

Müller, F. (1990) *Der Massenfund von den Tiefenau bei Bern. Zer Deutung La Tenezeitlicher Sammelfunde mit Waffen*, Basle: Antiqua 20.

Nash, D. (1976) 'Reconstructing Poseidonios' Celtic ethnography: some considerations', *Britannia* 12: 111–26.

—— (1978) 'Territory and state formation in central Gaul', in D. Green, C. Haselgrove and M. Spriggs (eds) *Social Organisation and Settlement*, Oxford: British Archaeological Reports, International Series 47.

O'Shea, J. (1984) *Mortuary Variability*, New York.

Piggott, S. (1968) *The Druids*, London.

Ross, A. (1967) *Pagan Celtic Britain*, New York.

Saxe A.A. (1970) *The Social Dimensions of Mortuary Practices*, Ann Arbor.

Sjoestedt-Jonual, M.-L. (1949) *Gods and Heroes of the Celts* trans. M. Dillon, London.

Stead, I.M. (1976) *Excavations at Winterton Roman Villa*, London.

—— (1979) *The Arras Culture*, New York.

Stead, I.M. and Rigby, V. (1989) *Verulamium: the King Harry Lane site*, London: English Heritage Archaeological Reports 12.

Tainter, J.A. (1978) 'Mortuary practices and the study of prehistoric social systems', in M.B. Schiffer (ed.) *Advances in Archaeological Method and Theory*, vol. 1, New York.

Tierney, J.J. (1960) 'The Celtic ethnography of Posidonius', *Proceedings of the Royal Irish Academy* 60(c): 189–275.

Torbrügge, W. (1971) 'Vor- und frühgeschichtliche Flussfunde zur Ordnung und Bestimmung einer Denkmalergruppe', *Bericht der Römisch-Germanischen Kommission* 51/52: 1–146.

Toynbee, J.M.C. (1971) *Death and Burial in the Roman World*, London.

van Endert, D. (1986) 'Zur Stellung der Wagengraber der Arras-Kultur', *Bericht der Römisch-Germanischen Kommission* 67: 203–88.

—— (1987) *Die Wagenbeistattungen der späten Hallstattzeit in der Gebiet Westliche des Rheims*, Oxford: British Archaeological Reports International Series 355.

Vendryes, J. (1948) 'La religion des Celtes', *Les Religions de l'Europe III*, Paris.

Von Brunn, W.A. (1980) 'Eine Deutung Spätbronzezeitlicher Hortfunde zwischen Elge und Weichsel', *Bericht der Römisch-Germanischen Kommission* 61: 91–150.

Wacher, J. (ed.) (1987) *The Roman World*, London.

Wait, G.A. (1985) *Ritual and Religion in Iron Age Britain*, Oxford: British Archaeological Reports British Series 149.

Webster, G. (1986) *The British Celts and their Gods under Rome*, London.

Wells, P.S. (1980) *Culture Contact and Culture Change*, Cambridge.

Whimster, R. (1981) *Burial Practices in Iron Age Britain*, Oxford: Archaeological Reports, British Series 90.

PART IX

THE CELTS IN EUROPE

THE CELTS IN ITALY

—— ·•· ——

Otto-Herman Frey

In Italy, we find the oldest traces of a 'Celtic' settlement near the Lombardy lakes. In that region, the so-called Lepontic inscriptions occur, which date back to around 500 BC (Figure 27.1). Today it is generally believed that these inscriptions are in a Celtic language (Lejeune 1971; Prosdocimi 1991). The same area was occupied by the so-called Golasecca culture between the seventh and fifth centuries BC; it is named after a find-spot on the river Tessin, near its exit from Lake Maggiore. In order to place the culture in a wider perspective, it can only be viewed in the context of Italic developments. There is no sign of a break, by which one could conclude the massive immigration of a foreign ('Celtic') ethnic group. It is easy to demonstrate that the Golasecca culture developed from older local roots, which themselves go back to the so-called Fazies Canegrate group of about 1200 BC. On the other hand, the Canegrate culture complex is clearly related to Urnfield cultural developments beyond the Alps. This circumstance might explain the origins of the population, which is not 'Italic' in linguistic terms (Pauli 1971: 48ff.).

HISTORICAL SOURCES

The great wave of immigration by Celtic tribes into Italy in later times is reported on by numerous ancient historians. The main source is Polybius (Walbank 1957). He became a friend of Scipio Aemilianus after having been brought to Rome as a hostage; because of the friendship to Scipio, he became involved in politics in the second century BC. His universal *History* starts with Hannibal's war around 220 BC and the ascent of Rome to a 'world power'. He goes back to the more distant past to explain the growth and development of power politics. This is particularly relevant for his treatment of the wars against the Celts in Italy. From the relatively more recent past, he could look back to the Roman suppression of the Insubres and the other Gauls in the plain of the river Po after their defeat at Telamon in 225 BC, as well as the fighting with Hannibal, in which the Celts had been involved. Concerning Hannibal's crossing of the Alps, Polybius remarks (III.48.12) that he got his information from contemporaries and that he knew the area from personal observation. He had to use older sources for the Roman wars with the Celts before that

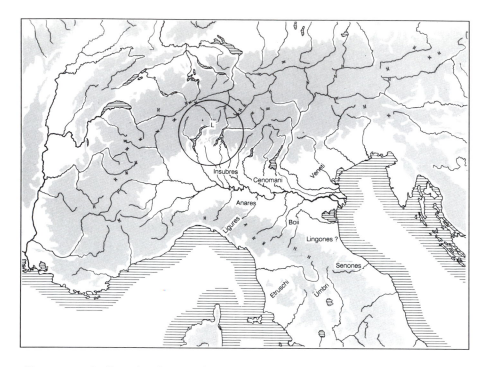

Figure 27.1 Italic and Celtic peoples in northern and central Italy. L = Lepontic area.

time: it is likely that the main source was the lost work of the Roman senator Fabius Quintus Pictor from fifty years earlier.

Polybius gives the date of 387/386 BC (the battle of Allia and the following conquest of Rome) as the starting-point of the fighting between Celts and Romans. Contemporary with this he mentions, among other things, the siege of Rhegion by Dionysius I (I.6.2). The two events are also connected by other ancient historians, too. Probably they had a common source in Timaios's *History of the Greek West*, which presumably derived information from Philistos.

Polybius gives an account of the migration of the Celts to Italy and their earlier history, 'which should touch only upon the main points, but goes back to the beginnings, when this people settled in the country' (II.14.1; 35.10). Thus there is only a general reference to the expulsion of the Etruscans, the former rulers of the plain of the river Po, the reasons for it and the immigration itself.

Of particular importance is the enumeration of the various Celtic tribes (II.17.4–7), which from west to east successively settled the land as far as the Adriatic Sea. Among others, he mentions the Insubres in western Lombardy, the Cenomani to the east as far as the river Adíge, the Boii in the area around Bologna, the Lingones as far as the Adriatic Sea and the Senones further to the south in the Picenum area, probably extending as far as the region around Ancona (Figure 27.1). The Insubres are described as the most numerous people among the Celts. In the whole of the northern Italian plain, only the area north of the river Etsch, controlled by the

Veneti, remained free from invaders. According to Polybius, this all happens only a 'short time' before the conquest of Rome (II.2.18.1).

Following Diodorus (XIV.113) and other sources, we may conclude that a rapid sequence of events ensued. Pliny, for example, gives us an account of a certain Cornelius Nepos, who came from the Transpadana, the north-west of Italy (*Natural History* III.125). It was reported that the old town of Melpum – presumably an Etruscan foundation – was conquered by the confederation of Boii, Insubres and Senones on the same day as the occupation of Veii by Camillus, i.e. in 396 BC. The intention, by this equation, to bring together the history of his country and that of Rome is unmistakable. It is, however, possible that the date is based on a similar chronology for the Celtic invasions as that of Polybius. The weakness of the historical tradition becomes clear from this biased report.

On the other hand, Livy gives a different account in his *Roman History*, which was written in the time of Augustus (V.34f.; cf. Ogilvie 1965: 700ff.). On the one hand, he lists the tribes of the Celts or 'Gauls' invading Italy in the same sequence as Polybius, so that a common source is likely. But, on the other hand, another tradition seems to have become incorporated into his account; thus he begins his report by stating that Ambigatus, the king of the Gaulish Bituriges, had sent his two nephews away with a great retinue in order to avoid overpopulation in his own country – and that had already happened under the rule of Tarquinius Priscus. This would bring us back to the sixth century BC. Following the signs of the flights of birds, one Bellovesus marched into Italy, accompanied by an entire population wave. The names of the groups are as follows: the Bituriges, Arverni, Senones, Aedui, Ambarri, Carnutes and Aulerci.

At first, the crossing of the Alps seems to have been impossible for this campaign. The Gauls, however, interpreted the arrival of Greeks looking for a homeland on the lower Rhône as a sign from the gods. They supported the Greek foundation of Massilia (Marseilles) against the efforts of the Salii, the rulers of this area. After this divinely favoured action, they succeeded in crossing the Alps. They defeated the Etruscans at the Tessin, as Hannibal later did the Romans. Since they heard that the region was called 'Insubrian', the same name as an area occupied by the Aedui in central Gaul, they regarded this as another divine omen that they should settle there. Thereupon they founded a town which they called Mediolanum (Milan). The Cenomani followed shortly afterwards; later the Boii, Lingones and Senones arrived.

Probably this report of the migrating groups under Bellovesus is founded on a Greek source (Grilli 1980). This conclusion is based on linguistic peculiarities and the association with the history of Massilia. Thus, the writings of Timagenes or Poseidonios come into question. In addition, traces of a Celtic migration legend are considered as a possibility (Dobesch 1989). Without any doubt, Livy's Roman history is influenced by the spirit of the Augustan era. It is in this context that the piety of the Gauls must be understood, a piety which finds its expression in their invariable obedience to signs of the gods. Internal discrepancies, which derive from the ideas of that time, can only be hinted at here.

The huge host of warriors under the leadership of Bellovesus consisted of a multiplicity of levies which, following later Roman reports, lived very close to each other in central Gaul. Therefore it is suspected that Livy, in this point, is influenced by the ideas of his time. In addition, the occupation of a country by founding a town is a Roman pattern, which should not be applied to the Gauls for such an early period since archaeological evidence is missing for towns north of the Alps at this time. More credible is the description of Polybius who, in his text *In the Beginnings*, states that the Celts lived in undefended villages and simple houses and that their occupation, apart from warfare, was agriculture alone. Thus, they lived a 'simple life'. 'Other knowledge and technical skills (which are preconditions for town life) were completely unknown' (II.17.9–10).

It could be suggested that Livy, by presuming such an early immigration, was trying to characterize in a positive light the descendants of the Insubres and Cenomani, who had already held Roman citizenship in his time. Did he want to contrast these two tribes with the later-arriving Boii and Senones, who had been expelled by the Romans after long hostilities? Yet questions of this kind cannot be further dealt with here. We do not have other texts which could verify Livy, even if there are sporadic indications of a Celtic presence in northern Italy as early as the sixth century BC (Dobesch 1989: 57). All in all, the sequence of the Celtic immigration to Italy remains problematic because of the contradictory and, in part, very fragmentary nature of the documentary evidence.

However, these sources yield other important details. The names of the major Celtic tribes, which had unquestionably settled in Italy and which are clearly mentioned in further sources, are met with in Caesar's Gallic War north of the Alps about 50 BC. We must conclude that only splinter groups from the tribes crossed the Alps. The correspondence of the names makes clear that the development of Celtic tribes had progressed considerably at the time of the immigration and that, in consequence, they possessed an awareness of their own identity.

The subsequent fate of the Celts in Italy can be readily documented after the military struggles for Etruscan Clusium (Chiusi), the first Roman defeat at the Allia and the conquest of Rome (397/386 BC) (e.g. Polybius I.6.2–3; II.18.2). Livy gives more details about the conquest of Rome. He informs us that it was carried out by the Senones (V.35.3), who later on were also at the centre of the fighting; he describes the events in vivid detail and with a bias towards Roman policy (V.37ff.). On the whole, the surviving historical sources concentrate predominantly on the fighting between Celts and Romans.

In the later fourth and early third centuries BC, numerous military expeditions were made according to the reports of Polybius and Livy, which make it clear that raiding and plundering was the everyday life of the Celts (see Dobesch 1982: 57f.). The statement of Polybius has already been noted: 'apart from agriculture, the Celts were exclusively dedicated to war' (II.17.10). 'In the beginning they had suppressed many of the neighbouring peoples' (II.18.1). In addition, the Celts often served as mercenaries, for example under the tyrants of Syracuse from Dionysius I onwards (Justin 20.5.6; Xenophon, *Hellenica* VIII.1.20, 28–32; Diodorus XV.70.1), or under the Carthaginians (Griffith 1935). On the other hand, the Celts, who became rich in Italy, were repeatedly attacked by the people of the Alps and by more distant tribes (Polybius II.18.4; 19.1). Time and time again, they recruited auxiliary troops from beyond the mountains for their battles in Italy (for example Polybius II.19ff.;

III.48.6). It is self-evident that such connections beyond the mountains presuppose further contacts of considerable extent.

In the course of time, Rome developed and strengthened its military affairs. Thus, a joint force of Senones and Samnites was utterly destroyed at Sentinum in 295 BC. Ten years later, after an initial reverse at Arretium (Arezzo), the Romans definitively conquered the Senones (Polybius II.19.7–12). In the middle of their old territory, the Roman colony at Sena (Senigallia) was founded. The final partition of the country, the 'Ager Gallicus', was carried out in 232 BC (Polybius II.21.7–8).

Conflict with the Boii and Insubres dragged on longer. Following an initially successful Gaulish campaign their forces, reinforced by Gaesatae from the Rhône valley, were destroyed at Telamon in 225 BC (Polybius II.27ff.). Shortly afterwards, the Romans advanced into the Po valley (Polybius II.31ff.) and inflicted further decisive defeats on these tribes. Then they founded the first colonies in the area: Placentia (Piacenza) and Cremona (Polybius III.40.3ff.; Velleius I.14.8). Hannibal was extensively supported by the Celts on his move to Italy (Polybius III.60ff.; Livy XXI.39ff.). But according to Livy's testimony, this revolt was quickly suppressed after the Second Punic War had ended. Surprisingly, the Cenomani, who up to then had avoided fighting, now turned against the Romans; they were, however, soon pacified. After many expeditions, the Insubres were finally defeated in 194 BC. The fighting with the Boii dragged on until 191 BC. They were hit hardest by their defeat because they were forced to vacate half of their lands (Livy XXXVI.39.3). We must, in all probability, reckon with a significant population withdrawal back across the Alps (Strabo V.213, 216). Already two years after their defeat, their capital Felsina (Bologna) was transformed into the Roman colony with Latin status, Bononia (Livy XXXVII.57.7–8). The two other tribes were treated less harshly. The process of 'romanization' extended rapidly to the whole of the Po valley. As early as 49 BC 'Gallia Cisalpina', the term by which the area was now known, obtained Roman citizenship (Dio Cassius XLI.36.3).

In 186 BC a Celtic group attempted to settle in the area where Aquileia was founded five years later; they were, however, forced to withdraw (Livy XXXIX.22.6–7, 54ff.). This also happened to another Celtic group shortly afterwards (Livy XL.53.5–6). A series of confrontations with the Alpine peoples continued into the time of Augustus.

The descriptions of the fighting by Polybius and Livy contain, in addition, numerous accounts which tell us more of the daily life of the Celts. We learn of their competitiveness, their personal appearance and their clothes, their golden bracelets and torques, as well as the weapons of their warriors (e.g. Polybius II.28ff.). Their long swords, only usable for slashing, were inferior to the Roman weapons in close combat (Polybius II.30.8; 33.5). Amongst other things, as for example their inferior defensive weaponry, this might have been one of the reasons why the Celts, as so often emphasized, had so little staying power in battle. But their attack was feared nonetheless. The references to standards and war trumpets (e.g. Polybius II.29.6; 31.5, and especially frequent in Livy) might point to the development of mobile warrior-bands. With this type of fighting, ambushes were common (Polybius III.71.2). A typical Celtic weapon, the chariot, seems no longer to have played a major role in the fighting in Italy (maybe still in the battle of Sentinum: Livy

X.28.9–11; chariots are only mentioned at the battle of Telamon: Polybius II.23.4; 28.5). Of importance too is the 'knightly' character of Celtic fighting, which is especially reflected in the single combats which precede battles (Livy VII.9f.; VII.26.1–6). Such a challenge was then unknown to the Romans and, therefore, filled them with consternation. An additional sign of such a 'knightly ethos' is the fact that whole bands swore an oath of allegiance to their leaders (Polybius II.17 12).

It is particularly significant that the social order was transformed during the Celtic rule in northern Italy. Kings are mentioned time after time during the initial battles. Yet the Boii, Insubres and Cenomani no longer had kings at the time of their defeat. Kings are only mentioned at this time with reference to the Celts beyond the Alps. Instead, a ruling aristocracy seems to have evolved. Polybius generally talks about 'leaders'. On the other hand, Livy repeatedly uses such terms as 'senate' or *principes* and *seniores* for the leading figures.

During the same period, the system of settlement was changing. While a rural population is frequently mentioned during the later battles, there is now a greater number of towns which may be considered as tribal capitals (Mediolanum: Polybius II.34. 10; Strabo V.1. 6; Brixia: Livy XXXII.30.6; Felsina: Livy XXXIII.37.4). In the case of Felsina (Bologna), it is evident that this was a development of an earlier Etruscan centre. The towns must also have had fortifications, as is apparent from the sieges of Acerrae and Clastidium (Polybius II.34.4–5; Livy also reports on the siege of Comum Oppidum (XXXIII.36.14). How the buildings within the towns looked and whether the shrines were situated within the walls (compare e.g. Polybius II.32.61) is not revealed to us.

It emerges clearly, however, that the Gauls adapted themselves gradually to the developed urban cultures which they encountered in northern Italy. It was inevitable that the initiation of such urban culture brought about not only social but also great economic changes.

ARCHAEOLOGICAL EVIDENCE

In contrast to the considerable evidence of the written sources, only briefly summarized above, the corresponding archaeological remains are far less extensive. Yet as early as 1871, at the international congress of anthropology and prehistoric archaeology in Bologna, E. Desort and G. de Mortillet were able to identify Celtic remains in the ruins of the Etruscan town at Marzabotto in the valley of the river Reno south of Bologna (*Congrès* 1873: 278, 476; see de Mortillet 1871). Comparable finds in their native countries, Switzerland and France, had been described by both scholars as 'Celtic'. Research continued, especially under E. Brizio who, as early as 1887, presented a synthesis of the Gaulish finds from the province of Bologna, which had come to light in the course of the intensive excavations there, and who also published a report on the great Senonian cemetery of Montefortino in the hinterland of Ancona (Brizio 1887, 1899). But a significant upsurge in the archaeological research of the Celts began only after the Second World War. The best indications of this are the exhibition 'The Gauls and Italy' held in Rome in 1978, and the great, wide-ranging exhibition which took place in Venice in 1991 (*I Galli* 1978; Moscati *et al.* 1991; further syntheses with bibliography: Peyre 1979; 'Les Celtes' 1987).

Nevertheless the available archaeological evidence remains inadequate, so that it is still difficult to build up a detailed picture. In the territory of the Boii and Senones, a greater number of graves is now known, including those published by Brizio, with the addition of some more recently excavated examples. Less satisfactory is the situation in the area of the Cenomani where only at the cemetery of Carzaghetto (Ferraresi 1976) is it possible to make sound interpretations. We know least about the Insubres. Most relevant finds date to the period of the Roman conquest. Remains of the fourth century BC which might be susceptible to detailed analysis are lacking. This applies also, in large measure, to the third century BC. The limited evidence available to us is insufficient to allow us to determine whether we are here dealing with Celts recently arrived from north of the Alps (perhaps imposed on an older 'Celtic' substratum) or not. There is more evidence only for the lake region and the adjacent alpine valleys (cf. e.g. *I Galli* 1978: 76ff.; Peyre 1979: 27ff.; Stöckli 1975).

Kruta-Poppi's distribution map of swords of Celtic type dating to the fourth and third centuries BC is informative (Figure 27.2) (Kruta-Poppi 1986). The territories of the Senones, Boii and Cenomani stand out clearly. The central area of the Insubres around Milan is, however, thinly settled in contrast to the situation along the foothills of the Alps. It is of great interest that the Ligures in the hinterland of Genoa/La Spezia, as well as the Umbrians, adopted this weapon characteristic of their feared neighbour. A few find-spots are even further dispersed. The Venetian area almost entirely lacks swords, although here, in particular, developing 'celticization' is evident. Thus, Polybius points out that, apart from their language, the Veneti are little different from the Celts in their customs and dress (II.17.5). The absence of swords must be

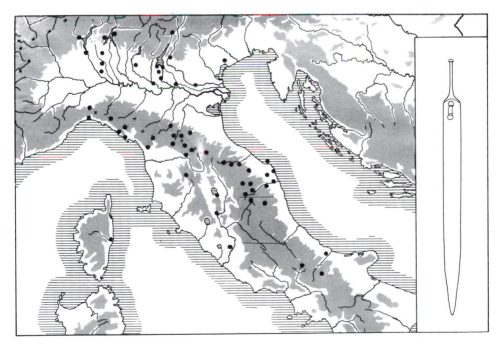

Figure 27.2 Distribution of swords of Celtic type in Italy. (After L. Kruta-Poppi.)

explained in terms of different burial ritual. Before the Gaulish invasion it was not customary, anywhere on the Po valley, to place weapons in the grave; this custom was retained by the Veneti.

While the finds already referred to belong to La Tène B and C1 according to the middle European chronological scheme, there is a number of earlier objects, which must also be linked to Celtic influences. These include torques, bracelets and fibulae, but above all openwork belt-hooks of bronze and iron, which were used to fasten the warrior's belt (Figure 27.3). North of the Alps, these hooks are typical of La Tène A, i.e. the fifth century BC. In northern Italy, too, finds dating approximately back to the fifth century BC occur. Undoubtedly such hooks and belt-rings were also produced in Italy, as is particularly well shown by a number of richly embellished bronze examples. Motifs such as 'birds and the tree of life' or a human figure between lyre-shaped gryphons ('lord of the beasts') hint at a long tradition in the Mediterranean. Occasionally, hooks with comparable decoration can be found north of the Alps. This leads to the conclusion that craftworking links across the Alps already existed (Figure 27.4). However, the earliest specimens seem to come from more distant areas of central and western Europe. Thus a number of Italian types are paralleled in France, i.e. in the possible areas of origin of the tribes invading Italy (Figure 27.4). On the other hand, other types are lacking in northern Italy, for example the mask ornament which we know from the area of the middle Rhine and

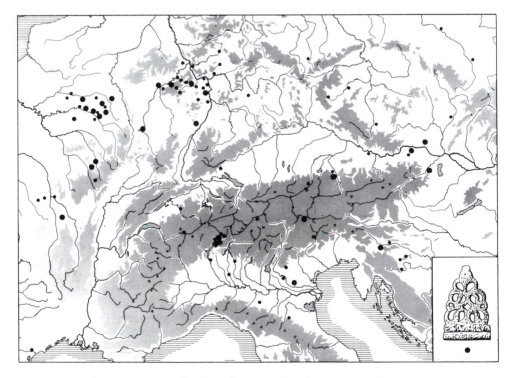

Figure 27.3 Distribution of openwork early La Tène belt-hooks.

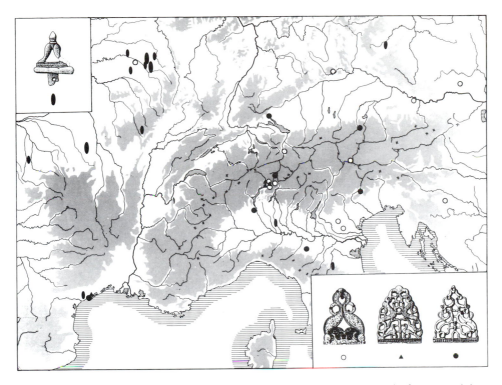

Figure 27.4 Distribution of belt-hooks with opposed 'dragon pairs' and of a type originating in northern France.

from regions further to the east. Since such belt-hooks can hardly be regarded as the products of normal trading activities, it seems reasonable to suggest that their dispersal came about through personal contact between those who wore them. Are they witnesses to an early phase of Celtic migration into Italy? (Frey 1987; 1991).

It is noticeable from their distribution that the hooks and associated rings occur frequently in the area of the Veneti, which the Celts supposedly did not invade. There are, however, signs that there it was not only men who wore such belt embellishment. Nevertheless, it might be that here we have an adoption of a typical part of the menacing Celtic warrior's apparel, without the accompanying weapons which have not come down to us because of the differing burial customs.

Likewise the belt-hooks and rings occur frequently in Ticino and in the region around Como. They are often found associated with swords. The novel custom of weapons as grave goods – as in the Celtic heartlands – indicates a change in burial ritual. As well as traditional forms, La Tène A fibulae are also relatively frequent. Since most cemeteries were in continuous use up to this period, it seems unlikely that the change in forms represents a change in population, a point also emphasized by the continuity of the 'Lepontic' inscriptions. More likely is the conclusion that Celtic weapons and personal ornament were taken over from outside. As these belt-hooks are absent in central Switzerland, it could be that it was the as yet poorly recognized Insubres, who settled in the plain around Milan, who inspired these innovations (Stöckli 1975).

In north Italy, there are still older, intrusive types, of late Hallstatt origin, especially fibulae, which derive from transalpine forms of personal ornament. The question is whether the fibulae, which were also copied locally, reached northern Italy together with those wearing them (Frey 1988). In any case, all these objects give ample evidence of relationships between central/western European and northern Italian population groupings, which extend back to the sixth century BC and increase in the following century.

The decline of the Etruscan towns is another sign of the invasion of the Boii in Emilia Romagna (Rivoldini 1960; *La formazione* 1987). The importation of Greek pottery ceases in Bologna and Marzabotto around 400/390 BC, in contrast to the port of Spina, situated at the estuary of the river Po, which was protected by its location in the lagoon. The same situation is evident at other Etruscan centres, giving us a date which fits well with the written accounts of the Celtic invasion. And, as early as the last third of the fifth century BC, there are gravestones in Bologna which depict battles between Celts and Etruscans (Figure 27.5) (Ducati 1928; 293ff.; Sassatelli 1983). The only conclusion to be drawn from these pictures is that Celtic bands were operating either as raiders or as mercenaries in the vicinity of the Etruscans as early as this.

The picture outlined above, though unclear in certain details, indicates that the great Celtic invasion, which affected the Etruscan towns, had been preceded by a much longer period of Celtic intrusions, which served as a prelude for it. We must assume a complex process, which, having taken place at an earlier period, was either simplified or distorted in the classical sources.

The way of life of the foreigners, who had adapted themselves to the circumstances in Italy, is displayed by grave goods of the fourth and third centuries BC in the area of the Boii and Senones. Let us take as an example the grave furnishings of a man in Montefortino in the hinterland of Ancona (Figure 27.6) (Brizio 1899). Here, although this is not a particularly rich grave, we find a substantial service for drinking and eating, consisting of various bronze containers as well as pottery of Greek and indigenous character. In addition, there are dices and gaming-pieces, as often occur in Etruscan graves. A *strigilis* shows us that the Celts took part in sports, as did the Greeks and Etruscans; the *strigilis* was used for scraping off the oil and sand after athletic exercises. Only the typical sword reveals the Celtic origin of the deceased. Similarly, Italian objects occur frequently in the graves of women.

Of all grave finds in the Senonian cemeteries, only various weapons display a 'Celtic' form (Kruta 1981). Many helmets are decorated in a mixed local style (as in Figure 27.8), which combines Celtic and Italian ornamental features. Two swords have bronze sheaths, which are embellished in a pure La Tène style and which, for example, have clear parallels in France (Figure 27.7) (Kruta *et al.* 1984). Apart from these weapons of the men, there are a few Celtic fibulae and rings, including a gold torc from a woman's grave at Filottrano (Grave 2) (Landolfi 1987: 452ff.), which also resembles artefacts from central Europe. All in all, there are only a few objects which are clearly related to the La Tène culture north of the Alps. Unfortunately, no associated settlements have as yet been investigated in this area. Therefore, the picture we have of the Senones remains one-sided, based as it is on burial evidence alone.

However, better evidence has recently been forthcoming in the region of the Boii. A new excavation in a small settlement in the Apennines to the south of Bologna gives

Figure 27.5 Etruscan grave stela from Bologna. The lower register shows a fight between an Etruscan on horseback and a Celt. (Museo Civico Archeologico, Bologna.)

us an idea of the process by which the settled Celts adapted themselves to the Italian environment (Vitali 1985, 1987). At the eastern downward slope of Monte Bibele, areas of settlement were uncovered which extend over several terraces. Foundations and remains of stone houses were uncovered which form built-up complexes clustered closely together and separated from each other by alleys. There is also a well. The first impression suggests that this is a small Etruscan centre. Remnants of iron and copper slag hint at metal prospection in the Apennines. The finds include various iron instruments as well as local pottery and black Firnis-wares from Etruscan Volterra. Sometimes the vessels have engravings, so-called graffiti which include Etruscan names. Only the fragments of a few glass arm-rings and several coins clearly indicate a Celtic presence. It is not yet clear whether the settlement was already in existence before 400 BC. It flourished in the fourth and third centuries BC.

Near the settlement a cemetery was discovered which was used for both cremations and inhumations. There was no discernible order in the arrangement of the male and female graves. It is noticeable that in the centre of the cemetery there are graves without weapons which contain, among other items, 'Italic fibulae', the

Figure 27.6 Grave goods of a Celt from Montefortino in the hinterland of Ancona.

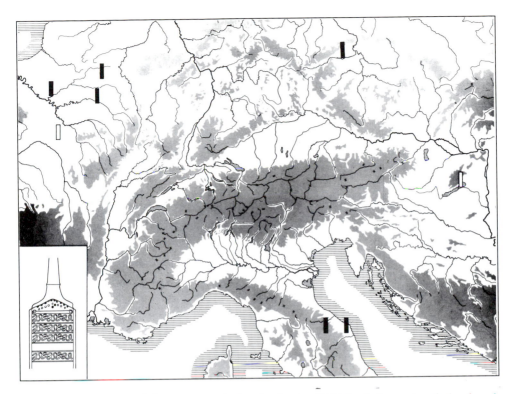

Figure 27.7 Decorated bronze sword sheaths in the Waldalgesheim style of the fourth century BC (solid symbols) and of later date (open symbols).

so-called Certosa fibulae; these are probably the oldest. They are surrounded by other graves, in which there are typical Italian objects including pottery, along with Celtic fibulae, beginning with examples belonging to La Tène B1. The men are now frequently accompanied by weapons such as the characteristic swords, spears and also helmets of 'Celtic' manufacture (Figure 27.8). Though these deceased give the impression of Gauls who became rich in the locality, the same is not so clear as regards the women, for many were excavated who were accompanied by pottery vessels upon which Etruscan names were engraved.

Similar finds have come from Bologna itself (e.g. Kruta 1980). They show clearly that a mixing of population had taken place which went beyond the simple adaptation by the Celts of the customs and the luxury items extant at that time in Italy.

In the territory of the Boii, too, settlement finds are unfortunately scarce. For Celtic Bologna in particular, we can reconstruct only a very vague picture. From burials in the immediate vicinity, however, or, for example, from the filling material of wells, it is evident that Celts lived there, having adapted to an urban way of life, and that the occupation of the towns continued, though in reduced form. Similar observations can be made in the suburbs of the Cenomanian Brixia (Brescia). To date we know least about Mediolanum (Milan) (e.g. Frey 1984).

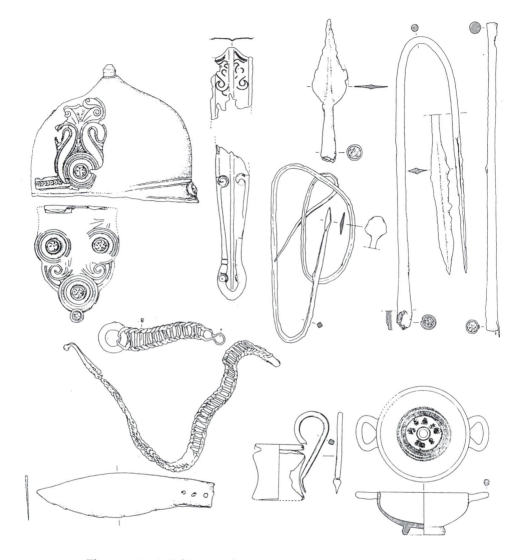

Figure 27.8 A Celtic grave from Monte Bibele in the Bologna region
(scale approx. 1:5).

The process of assimilation between the Celts and the Italian population stops abruptly in Picenum and the area of Bologna, after the Boii and the Senones had been defeated and largely expelled. For the area north of the river Po up to the valleys of the Alps, the picture, however, is different. Here continued development of Celtic culture in the second and first centuries BC is recognizable in the archaeological remains (Arslan 1991; Tizzoni 1981; 1984; 1985; Stöckli 1975).

Corresponding with the written sources, the archaeological evidence shows also that the Celts in Italy maintained close contact with their relations in western and central Europe. The development of personal ornament and of weapons parallels that in the areas north of the Alps. Conversely, reflux influences from the emigrating Gauls are recognizable in transalpine Europe. However, imported luxury goods from Italy are rare in central and western Europe in the fourth and third centuries BC. This may be the result of specific burial rituals or could reflect the fact that the towns of north Italy no longer had the capacity for surplus production and trade they had in Etruscan times. On the other hand, there are indications of cultural contacts – termed 'reflux cultural movements' by archaeologists – which go back to the assumed immigration of Celtic tribes. For example, several major burials in the Champagne have produced iron meat skewers which date to La Tène A, i.e. the fifth century BC (Déchelette 1914: 1412). These often occur in Italy from the late eighth century onwards; moreover, they are a recurring element in the graves of the Senones and the Boii. Should not this transfer of a burial rite be explained in terms of personal knowledge of the customs of another land ? Do we not have here an indication of the absorption of foreign ideas which is not mere coincidence?

As touched upon earlier, the relationships are clearer in the context of high-quality craftsmanship. These begin as early as the fifth century BC, the period of the characteristic belt-hooks. In the development of Celtic art, Italian influence is more marked in the second stylistic phase, in the fourth century BC. Even though the by now characteristic tendril style – the so-called 'Waldalgesheim-style', after a find-spot in the middle Rhine (Jacobsthal 1944: 94) – is, in basic conception, rooted in central Europe, strong influences from Greek/Italian 'plant ornament' are unmistakable (Frey 1976). Indeed, some scholars believe that the shaping of this style in fact originates in Italy (Kruta 1982; Peyre 1982). Such relationships in artistic production continue into the third century BC. The extent and intimacy of contacts across the Celtic world at this time is shown by swords with scabbards bearing a recurring dragon-motif (Figure 27.9) (Megaw and Megaw 1990).

Finally, the development of urbanization in Italy may well have had a lasting influence on the Celtic world (Figure 27.10) (Frey 1984). In this regard, there are, again, only a few signs of direct links. Among these, however, are certain types of location new to the major settlements of central Europe, including siting in the middle of a plain, as is indicated by the place-name 'Mediolanum', rather than their being protected by steep heights or by rivers. Above all are details of their fortifications for which the Italic *agger* is an obvious prototype. Of course this does not mean that the emergence of towns to the north of the Alps can only be explained in terms of relationships with Italy. Larger market-places near rivers or on the coast, as well as other sites, might well, with time, have developed an urban character. But the written sources, which give us plenty of detail about Italian towns, give also an impression of social organization and administrative institutions, which we can recognize later in Caesar's descriptions of the war in Gaul, and which form an essential element of Gaulish urban culture. Influences were thus already in place, later encountered by Caesar in Gaul, which formed the basis for a 'civilized' way of life and which paved the way for the rapid romanization of the whole country.

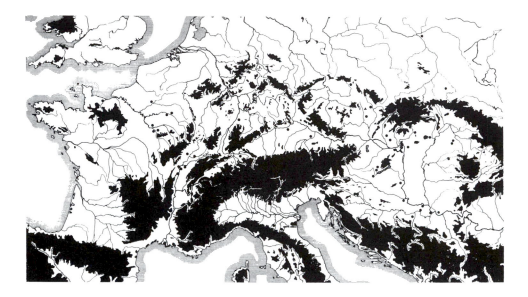

Figure 27.9 Distribution of sword sheaths with dragon pairs. (After J.V.S. Megaw.)

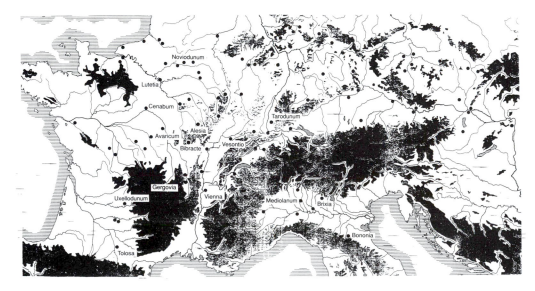

Figure 27.10 Distribution of the most important Celtic oppida.

REFERENCES

Arslan, E. (1991) 'I Transpadani', in S. Moscati *et al.*, *The Celts*, 461–70.

Brizio, E. (1887) 'Tombe e necropoli galliche della provincia di Bologna', *Atti e Memorie Deputazione di Storia Patria per le Province di Romagna*, series III, 5: 457ff.

—— (1899–1901) 'Il sepolcreto gallico di Montefortino presso Arcevia', *Monumenti Antichi* 9: 617–93.

Les Celtes en Italie (1987) Dossiers Histoire et Archéologie 112, Dijon: Archéologia.

Congrès international d'anthropologie et d'archéologie préhistorique. Compte rendu de la cinquième session à Bologne 1871 (1873), Bologna.

Déchelette, J. (1914) *Manuel d'archéologie préhistorique, celtique et galloromaine* II(3): *Seconde âge du fer ou époque de la Tène*, Paris: Picard (2nd edn 1927).

Dobesch, G. (1982) 'Die Kimbern in den Ostalpen und die Schlacht bei Noreia', *Mitteilungen Österreichischen Arbeitsgemeinschaft Ur- und Frühgeschichte* 32: 51ff.

—— (1989) 'Zur Einwanderung der Kelten in Oberitalien. Aus der Geschichte der keltischen Wanderungen im 6. und 5. Jh.v.Chr. 'Tyche', *Beiträge zur Alten Geschichte, Papyrologie und Epigraphie* 4: 35ff.

Ducati, P. (1928) *Storia di Bologna*, I: *I tempi antichi*, Bologna.

Duval, P.-M. and Kruta, V. (eds) (1982) *L'Art celtique de la période d'expansion IVe et IIIe siècles avant notre ère*, Proceedings of the Colloquium at Paris 1978, Geneva/Paris: Droz.

Ferraresi, A. (1976) 'Canneto sull 'Oglio. Frazione Carzaghetto (Mantova). Necropoli gallica', *Notizie degli Scavi di Antichità*, 5ff.

La formazione della città in Emilia Romagna. Catalogo della mostra, Bologna 1987–1988 (1987) Studi e Documenti di Archeologia 3, Bologna.

Frey, O.-H. (1976) 'Du premier style au style de Waldalgesheim. Remarques sur l'evolution de l'art celtique ancien', in P.-M. Duval and C. Hawkes (eds) *Celtic Art in Ancient Europe: five protohistoric centuries* (Proceedings of the Colloquium at Oxford (1972), London, New York, San Francisco: Seminar Press, 141–65.

—— (1984) 'Die Bedeutung der Gallia Cisalpina für die Entstehung der Oppida-Kultur', *Studien zu Siedlungsfragen der Latènezeit*, Marburg: Veröffentlichung Vorgeschichtliches Seminar Marburg, Special issue 3, 1ff.

—— (1987) 'Sui ganci di cintura celtici e sulla prima fase di La Tène nell 'Italia del Nord', in D. Vitali (ed.) *Celti ed Etruschi*, 9–22.

—— (1988) 'Les fibules hallstattiennes de la fin du VIe siècle au Ve siècle en Italie du Nord', in *Les Princes celtes et la Méditerrannée*, Recontres de l'Ecole du Louvre, Paris: La Documentation Française, 33–43.

—— (1991) 'Einige Bemerkungen zu den durchbrochenen Frühlatènegürtelhaken', in A. Halfner and A. Miron (eds) *Studien zur Eisenzeit im Hunsrück-Nahe-Raum*, Symposium at Birkenfeld 1987, Trierer Zeitschrift Beih. 13, Trier, 101ff.

I Galli e l'Italia (1978) Rome: Soprintendenza Archeologica di Roma.

Grassi, M.T. (1991) *I Celti in Italia*, Biblioteca di Archeologia 16, Milan: Longanesi.

Griffith, G.T. (1935) *The Mercenaries of the Hellenistic World*, London (reprint Groningen 1968).

Grilli, A. (1980) 'La migrazione dei Galli in Livio', *Studi in onore di F. Rittatore Vonwiller* Part II, Como, 183–92.

Jacobsthal, P. (1944) *Early Celtic Art*, Oxford: Clarendon Press (Reprint 1969).

Kruta, V. (1980) 'Les Boïens de Cispadane. Essai de paléoethnographie celtique', *Etudes Celtiques* 17: 7–32.

—— (1981) 'Les Sénons de l'Adriatique d'après l'archéologie (prolégomènes)', *Etudes Celtiques* 18: 7–38.

—— (1982) 'Aspects unitaires et faciès dans l'art celtique du IVᵉ siècle avant notre ère: l'hypothèse d'un foyer celto-italique', in P.-M. Duval and V. Kruta (eds) *L'Art celtique*, 35ff.

Kruta, V. *et al.* (1984) 'Les fourreaux d'Epiais-Rhus (Val-d'Oise) et de Saint-Germainmont (Ardennes) et l'art celtique du IVᵉ siècle av. J.-C.', *Gallia* 42: 1ff.

Kruta-Poppi, L. (1986) 'Epées laténiennes d'Italie centrale au Musée des Antiquités nationales', *Etudes Celtiques* 23: 33ff.

Landolfi, M. (1987) 'Presenze galliche nel Piceno a sud del fiume Esino', in D. Vitali (ed.) *Celti ed Etruschi*, 443–68.

Lejeune, M. (1971) *Lepontica*, Paris.

Megaw, J.V.S. and Megaw, M.R. (1990) '"Semper aliquid novum . . .", Celtic dragon-pairs re-reviewed', *Acta Archaeologica Academiae Scientificarum Hungaricae* 42: 55ff.

de Mortillet, G. (1870–1) 'Les Gaulois de Marzabotto dans l'Apennin', *Revue Archéologique* NS 22: 288ff.

Moscati, S., Frey, O.-H., Kruta, V. and Raftery, B. (1991) *The Celts*, London: Thames & Hudson.

Ogilvie, R.M. (1965) *A Commentary on Livy Books 1–5*, Oxford.

Pauli, L. (1971) *Studien zur Golasecca-Kultur*, Römisch Mitteilungen Ergh. 19, Heidelberg.

Peyre, C. (1979) *La Cisalpine gauloise du IIIᵉ au Iᵉ siècle avant J.-C.*, Etudes d'Histoire Archéologie, Paris: Presses de l'Ecole Normale Supérieure.

—— (1982) 'Y a-t-il un contexte italique au Style de Waldalgesheim?', in P.-M. Duval and Vikruta (eds) *L'Art celtique* 51ff.

Prosdocimi, A.L. (1991) 'The language and writing of the early Celts', in S. Moscati *et al.* (eds) *The Celts*, 51–9.

Rivoldini, M. (1960) 'La distribuzione della ceramica celtica nell'Etruria Padana', *Mostra dell'Etruria Padana e della città di Spina II*, Bologna: Repertori, 153ff.

Sassatelli, G. (1983) 'Le stele felsinee con "Celtomachie" in *Popoli e facies culturali celtiche a nord e a sud delle Alpi dal V al I secole a.C.*, Proceedings of the international colloquium at Milan 1980, Milan, 167–77.

Stöckli, W.E. (1975) *Chronologie der jüngeren Eisenzeit im Tessin*, Antiqua 2, Basle.

Tizzoni, M. (1981) La cultura tardo La Tène in Lombardia', Istituto unversitario di Bergamo, *Studi Archeologici* I, 3ff.

—— (1984) I materiali della tarda età del Ferro nelle Civiche Raccolte Archeologiche di Milano. Rassegna di Studi Civico Mus. Arch. e Civico Gabinetto Numismatico Milano, Suppl. 3.

—— (1985) I materiali della tarda età del Ferro al Museo Civico di Brescia ebd. 4.

Vitali, D. (1985) *Monte Bibele (Monterenzio) und andere Fundstellen der keltischen Epoche im Gebiet von Bologna*, Marburg: Kleine Schriften Vorgeschichtliches Seminar Marburg 16.

—— (1987a) *Celti ed Etruschi nell'Italia centro-settentrionale dal V secolo a.C. alla romanizzazione*, Proceedings of the International Colloquium at Bologna 1985, Imola.

—— (1987b) 'Monte Bibele tra Etruschi e Celti: dati archeologici e interpretazione storica', in D. Vitali (ed.) *Celti ed Etruschi*, 309–80.

—— (1991) 'Elmi di ferro e cinturoni a catena. Nuove proposte per l'archeologia dei Celti in Italia', *Jahrbuch Römisch-Germanisches Zentralmuseum Mainz* 35: 239ff.

Walbank, F.W. (1957) *A Historical Commentary on Polybius*, Oxford.

THE CELTS IN SPAIN

—— ·•· ——

Majolie Lenerz-de Wilde

The Danube rises in the land of the Celts near the town of Pyrene and flows through the middle of Europe, which it divides. The Celts live beyond the Pillars of Hercules and are neighbours of the Kynesii who, among the peoples of Europe, live furthest to the West.

(Herodotus II.33.3)

This account is one of the earliest in which Celtic people are mentioned; it leads us to the Iberian peninsula. These Celts are said to have lived beyond the Straits of Gibraltar. Herodotus obviously used a report of seafarers, who described the journey to the tin isles of Great Britain. For historical reasons, the report must be dated to the late sixth century BC (Fischer 1972; Koch 1979; Arribas (n.d.): Appendix, 190ff.). The model for the 'Ora Maritima' of Rufus Festus Avienus, a description of coastal travel, also dates to the late sixth century BC. In this document, reference is made to Celts – the tribe of the Beribraci – who probably lived inland from the northern Mediterranean coast.

The journeys of Pytheas in the fourth century BC considerably extended knowledge of western Europe. In the following period, the written sources refer to Celtic tribes in the north-west and south-west of the Iberian peninsula, and to the Celtiberians in the centre.

We know of the settlement of Celtic tribes in the Iberian peninsula not only from classical writers but also through linguistic research which supplies us with a rich body of evidence (Tovar 1961; Untermann 1961, 1965). Inscriptions, dedications, contracts, etc., which date from the last three centuries BC, are written in two different languages: a non-Indo-European one on the Mediterranean coast and in the Pyrenees, and an Indo-European one in the interior (Figure 28.1). The latter is mainly concentrated in Castillia and Lusitania. The Castillian inscriptions have been classed as Celtiberian, because the *idg.-p* fades away in the initial sound and between vowels, which is a characteristic feature of Celtic languages. The Lusitanian inscriptions appear to be in a related language. The Celtiberian, or Iberian, place-names which, for the most part reflect the situation in the Roman Imperial period, also divide the peninsula into two parts. Those names with the component *-briga-* (Celtic 'fortified hill') are distributed in the west and the centre, while they are absent

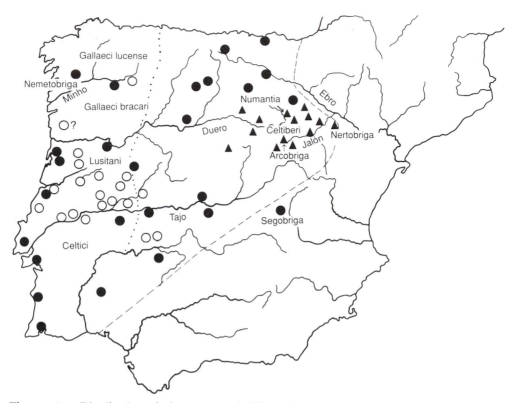

Figure 28.1 Distribution of place names of different languages in Iberia. After Untermann 1965, map 34, and Untermann 1984. **Key:** ● the placename element: 'briga'; ○ personal name 'Celtius'; ▲ Celtiberian settlements; — boundary between Indo-European and non-Indo-European language areas; - - boundary between Hispano-Celtic and Lusitanian divinity names and family names.

in Andalusia and the Mediterranean coastal region. Within the area of the *briga*-inscriptions, further subdivision is possible: this provides us with information on the social structure of the pre-Roman population (Albertos Firmat 1966): a type of name formula disseminated in the centre of the peninsula, which consists of the personal name, the name of the father and that of the clan. The west lacks such clan names. Votive inscriptions for local gods are to be found there, quite a few of which can readily be identified as Celtic deities. These inscriptions also contain information about social structure whereby the group identity of an individual is defined by worship of a particular tutelary god (Untermann 1985). These sources indicate that Celtic groups must have played an important role in the Iberian peninsula during the Iron Age. However, in settlement, burial customs, costume, weapons and pottery, a distinction can be made between the Celtiberian culture and the other iron age cultures of central Spain, on the one hand, and the late Hallstatt and La Tène cultures of central Europe, on the other (Lenerz-de Wilde 1991).

In the territory of the Meseta cultures of central Spain, several groups can be distinguished (Figure 28.2). In the earlier Iron Age, the process of settlement of the

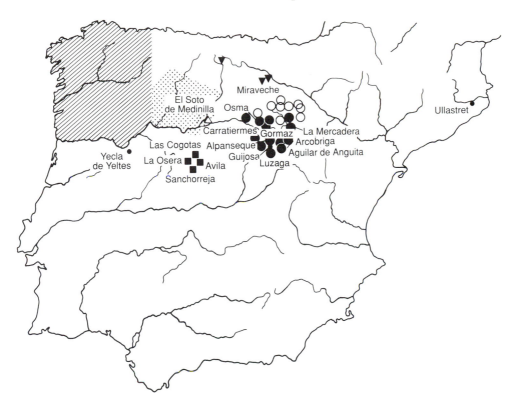

Figure 28.2 Different cultural groups in Northern Iberia. After Lenerz-de Wilde 1992, maps 5, 16 and 40; Lopez Monteaguo 1989, fig. 5; and Raddatz 1969, map 11. **Key:** ▨ Castro culture zone; ░ 'El soto de Medinilla' group; ▼ Miraveche group; ○ Settlements of the 'Castros sorianos' culture; ● Cremation cemeteries in the eastern Meseta, ■ Avila group.

mountainous regions of the upper Douro begins where the 'cultura de los castros sorianos' develops. Strategic places, which were easy to defend, were settled, mostly at a height of around 1250 m (Figure 28.3). The *castros* are always protected by walls with a thickness of up to 6 m; some are further protected by so-called *chevaux-de-frise* which consist of sharp, outward-facing stones, which prevented cavalry charges (Figure 28.4). Round and rectangular ground-plans of houses have been found. Mould fragments and a large quantity of iron slag are indicative of a flourishing metal industry. The economy was essentially pastoral, as is shown by the evidence of the animal bones. Burials are as yet unknown – the inhabitants must have disposed of their dead without leaving any archaeological traces. This calls to mind classical accounts which refer to the tribes of the Vaccaei and the Celtiberians who left their battle dead to be eaten by birds of prey (Silius Italicus, *Punica* II. 3; Aelian, *De Ore Natura Animali* X.22). The majority of the *castros* were deserted around 400 BC; only a third survived.

Extensive cremation cemeteries developed at the same time to the south of these *castros*. The urns are arranged partly in lines and marked above ground by standing

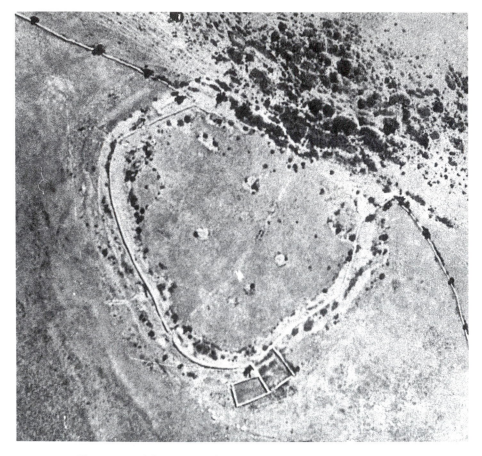

Figure 28.3 The castro 'El Castillo' Castilfrío de la Sierra, Soria.
(With kind permission of F. Romero Carnicero, University of Valladolid.)

stones. Round graves covered by cairns of stones are also known. Personal items, ornaments and weapons of bronze and iron were deposited both in and beside the urns. We have little knowledge about the associated settlements. Fortified settlements on hills exist near Aguilar de Anguita and Luzaga (Guadalajara). The Castro de Castilviejo was fortified by *chevaux-de-frise*, but this is an exception. The large cemeteries come into existence around 600 BC. Many end around 400 BC, such as Alpanseque and La Mercadara (both Soria), but others continue into the later Iron Age.

Settlements of the El Soto de Medinilla (Valladolid) type are situated in the fertile valleys of the middle Douro and its tributaries. The houses are built with clay bricks and are round in plan; occasionally they form small 'tells'. The population was mainly engaged in agriculture, but there are a few signs of animal husbandry, particularly of sheep and goats. Metallurgy was dominated by bronzeworking. Iron was unknown at the beginning of the period and remained rare later on. Here, too, burials are completely lacking.

The typologically distinct group known as the Miravecche Group is found in the

Figure 28.4 The castro of Yecla de Yeltes, Salamanca. (With kind permision of R. Martin Valls, University of Salamanca.)

north of the provinces of Palancia and Burgos; it is named after a major cremation cemetery. The hilltop settlements here are also fortified.

In Avila and Salamanca, the Castros Mesa de Miranda near La Osera and Las Cogotas date to this period. The hilltop settlements are associated with cremation cemeteries. They are arranged in zones and, in the case of La Osera, are partly covered by round or oval stone structures. Here, and also further to the west, the so-called *verracos* occur, granite sculptures in the shape of boars and bulls, which played an important role in the cult of the pre-Roman population (Lopez Monteagudo 1989).

The transition from the earlier to the later Iron Age is characterized first by the omnipresent use of iron in the production of weapons and tools and, second, by the emergence of wheel-turned pottery. But the two innovations did not appear at the same time: iron was used as a material everywhere from around 500 BC; wheel-turned pottery began to be made 100 years later. Only then was there a fully developed Celtiberian culture.

Numerous 'Sorianos' *castros*, as mentioned above, were deserted around 400 BC. On the other hand, new settlements were established, which were no longer situated at great heights, but still retained their fortifying walls. The economy was predominantly based on agriculture. Metallurgy, in particular iron-processing, became important. It has long been assumed that it was above all the iron deposits at Moncayo (Soria) which were now being exploited.

The *castros* in the region of Avila also exhibit radical changes. Generally the fortifications are dated to the fifth century BC. But while Sanchorreja was deserted around 400 BC, La Cogotas, for example, continued to flourish, as is shown by the extension of the settlement.

Similar upheavals are recognizable in the cemeteries of the eastern Meseta: some burial-grounds are abandoned, but new ones are laid out, such as Osma, Gormaz, Carratiermes (all Soria) and Luzaga (Guadalajara). Many finely decorated weapons and personal ornaments in the graves bear witness to specialized craftworking.

The settlements expand in the course of the later Iron Age. Numantia (Soria) had a planned street pattern and was urban in character by the time of the Roman conquest (133 BC). This urbanization developed from contacts with the Iberian area.

From the fifth century BC onwards, finds occur in the area of the Meseta cultures, which point to relationships with the cultures of Hallstatt and La Tène in central Europe: for example the many varieties of foot-decorated fibulae have good parallels in eastern France (Figure 28.5 nos. 1–2). Similarly, the so-called symmetrical fibulae clearly originate in fibulae with double masks and double bird-heads (Figure 28.5, no. 3), as is the case with the other fibulae of La Tène form. As well as specimens with parallels in central Europe (Figures 28.5, no. 4 and 28.6, no. 3), many variants emerge in the course of time, which are typical of the Celtiberian area (Figure 28.5, nos. 5–7).

The first La Tène swords with associated scabbards appear in the Meseta during the fourth century BC (Figure 28.6, nos. 1–2). Connections with the La Tène culture can also be found in ornamentation: silver-inlaid antenna-hilted daggers are embellished in a style which adopted elements of the 'Waldalgesheim Style' (Figure 28.7, no. 1). Torques and fibulae of precious metal were still produced in the La Tène character during the first century BC (Figure 28.5, no. 8).

While the bulk of the objects mentioned are distributed throughout the whole Meseta, as for example the symmetrical fibulae, some were concentrated in the upper reaches of the rivers Douro and Jalón (Figure 28.8). Certain things come from here which were undoubtedly produced in the La Tène area: two openwork belt-hooks, which had been later reworked to match a set of Iberian belt-plates (Figure 28.9, nos. 2–3). Such conversion can also be recognized on many sword sheaths. These still have the strap-shaped suspension loop from which the swords were suspended vertically on the belt, as was usual with Celtic swords, but possess two fittings which were added in order to facilitate carriage of the swords diagonally, as in the case of the Celtiberian daggers and slashing-swords (Figure 28.6, no. 1). Finally, in this region, a group of fibulae can be found which possess a genuine La Tène spring; all the other fibulae are either of composite construction or have an internal spiral. This is precisely the region which was settled by Celtiberians according to the testimony of ancient authors (see Figure 28.1). Yet the archaeological picture cannot be compared with the Celtic migration to Italy or to east-central Europe. Thus, there is a complete lack of flat inhumation cemeteries and the typical La Tène grave goods. A key to the understanding of the Celtic influences here might be supplied by an examination of the social structure of the iron age population, which can be determined on the basis of grave finds.

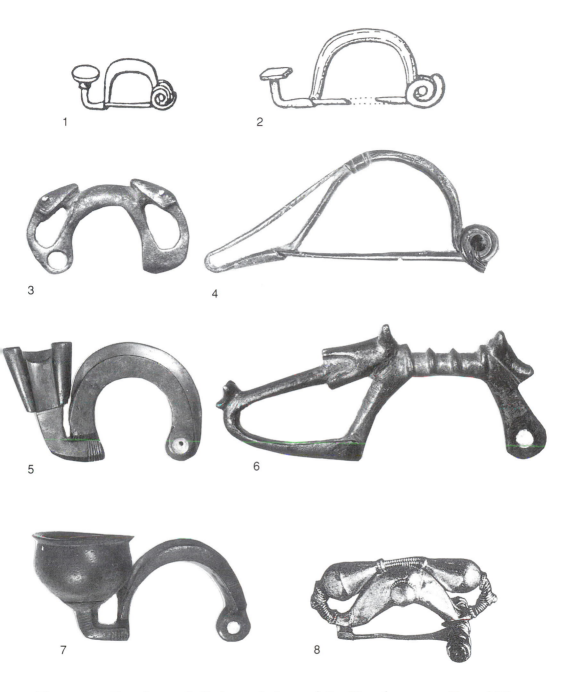

Figure 28.5 Foot-decorated fibulae and those of La Tène form. 1 – Torresabiñán (Guadalajara). 2 – La Mercadera (Soria). 3 – Findspot unknown. Burgos Museum. 4–6 – Findspot unknown. National Archaeological Museum, Madrid. 7 – Findspot unknown, Barcelona. 8 – Arrabalda (Zamora).

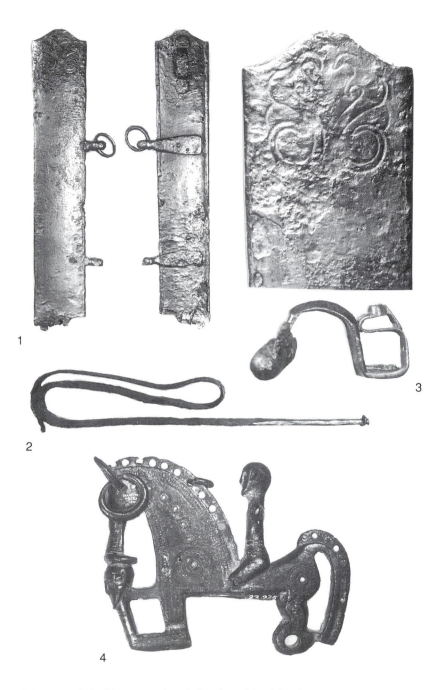

Figure 28.6 1–3 – A La Tène sword and sheath and bird-headed brooch from Quintanas de Gormaz (Soria). 4 – Brooch in the form of a cavalryman with a severed head under the horse's head. Findspot unknown. National Archaeological Museum, Madrid.

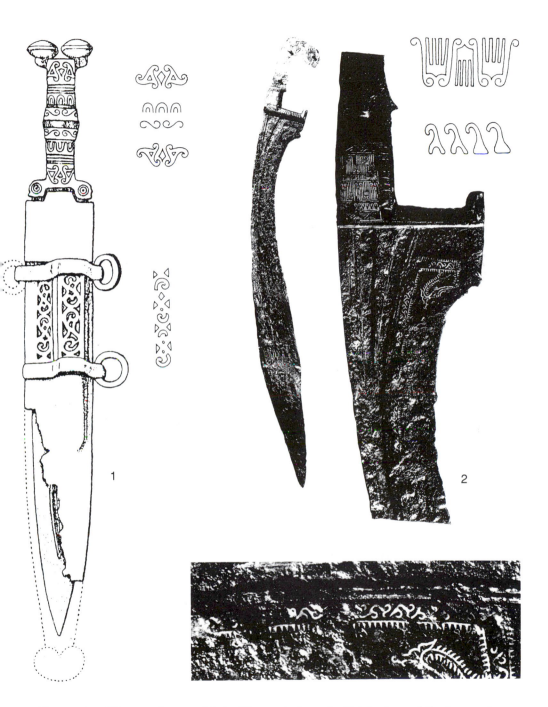

Figure 28.7 Weapons decorated in La Tène style from the Celtiberian and Iberian provinces. 1 – La Osera (Avila). 2 – Illora (Granada).

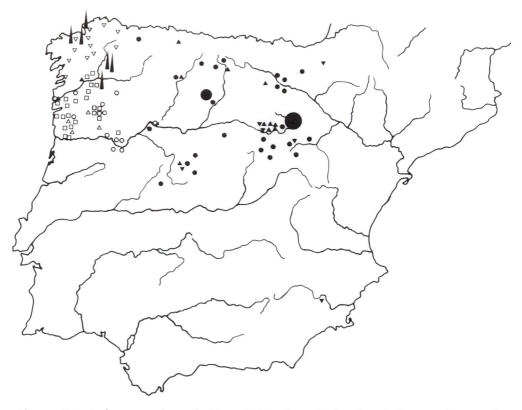

Figure 28.8 Sculptures and metal objects in Northern Iberia. **Key:** △ Stone sculptures of human figures; ○ Stone sculptures of animal figures; □ Guerreros galaicos; △ Torques with tulip-shaped terminals; ▽ Torques with conical terminals; • Symmetrical fibulae; ▼ Swords with sheaths; ▲ Foot-decorated fibulae with rectangular foot-plates.

Only 16.8 per cent of all graves in La Cogotas (Avila) contained finds, and of these, only 18 per cent had weapons; only five possessed a full warrior panoply, consisting of spears, dagger and shield (Kurtz 1987). In Sector VI of La Osera, which has been published, the proportions are similar: 355 out of 517 burials were without any finds. Only 65 of those with finds contained weapons, mostly 1–2 spears, with only a few possessing a dagger or a sword and shield. These rich graves otherwise contain horse-harness, fire-dogs, roasting-spits and large cauldrons. It is probable that the dead were the leaders of the clans. Daggers and swords were not only weapons but also status symbols. Thus it was the upper class of the Meseta population who wore elements of La Tène personal equipment and who used the La Tène sword as a prestige weapon. Many of these rich graves contain tools, which must be regarded as punches or awls and were possibly used in the decoration of belt-plates, dagger sheaths, etc. (Lenerz-de Wilde 1991: 211, with ill. 152). In Grave 60 at La Osera, which contained one of the most beautiful dagger sheaths, two small hammers were found, clearly the tools of a fine metalworker. Therefore it is possible that a

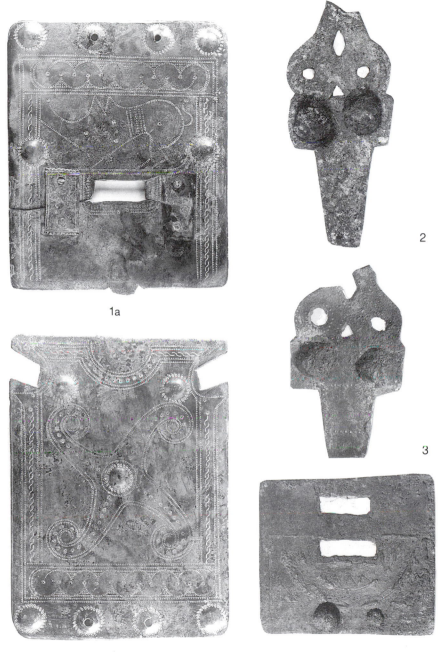

1a

1b

2

3

Figure 28.9 1 – Belt-plate with belt-fitments from Miraveche (Burgos). 2 – La Tène belt-hook from La Osera (Avila). 3 – La Tène belt-hook with flat clasp/belt-fitment from Osma (Soria.)

small number of Celtic immigrants came up the valley of the Ebro into the eastern Meseta, there to establish their knowledge of metallurgy, and were thus rapidly integrated into the local élite. They could be jointly responsible for the flourishing state of metallurgy, which can be seen at the Moncayo from the middle of the century onwards. The Moncayo is situated in the core of that region in which the biggest concentration of objects displaying Hallstatt and La Tène influences is found and which, at the time of the Roman conquest, was settled by the Celtiberians. Inscriptions testify to the worship of the Celtic deity Lugoves (in Osma, Soria). The potsherd with the portrayal of Cernunnos comes from Numantia (Figure 28.10, no. 1). It is, perhaps, no coincidence that it was just those gods who were patrons of craftsmanship who were worshipped.

The radical changes of 400 BC must be linked to military operations. It seems possible that there is a connection between these events and the breakdown of late Hallstatt culture and the start of the Celtic immigration which followed. For it is those very cemeteries which now develop, such as Luzaga (Guadalajara), and which contain La Tène fibulae in association with reworked La Tène swords, already mentioned (see Figure 28.6, nos. 1–3). Fibulae showing horsemen displaying severed heads suspended from the horse's neck are vivid testimony to the military clashes on the Meseta (Figure 28.6; see no. 4). The influence of Celtiberian culture spreads from the core area around the rivers Douro and Jalón to other groups. It is no coincidence that it was in the upper Ebro region (Miravecche Group) and in Avila that the adjacent copper deposits were being exploited.

The finds referred to above are not the oldest indications of links with the Celtic heartland. Contacts between the Iberian area and the region of late Hallstatt culture can be shown in different ways: a spectacular find was the Iberian belt-hook which was discovered in a secondary burial in the royal grave at the Magdalenenberg near Villingen (Figure 28.11, no. 7) (Spindler 1983; fig. 16). It belongs to a group which certainly dates to the sixth century BC and which was concentrated in the north of the Meseta, focused on the area between the rivers Douro and Jalón (Cerdeño Serrano 1978: 288, fig. 2). The golden earrings with hour-glass-shaped pendants from the royal grave at La Butte in Ste Colombe (Spindler 1983: 350, fig. 97) have a close parallel in the gold earring from Teruel (Schüle 1965) (Figure 28.11, nos. 3–4). The armbands from the gold find of El Carambolo (Carriazo 1973) bear a striking resemblance to those of the Hochdorf prince (Figure 28.11, nos. 1–2). The contacts between the Iberian peninsula and the Hallstatt princes were probably based on economic links: gold-types in the late Hallstatt royal graves have very good parallels on the Iberian peninsula (Hartmann 1970: 46ff.). It seems reasonable to assume that this gold was traded through Massilia and in this way contacts with the Hallstatt world were established. There are many signs that trading relations served not only for the exchange of goods but also brought about the mobility of people. Celtic groups later travelled to the Iberian peninsula along routes which had been established through these trading contacts, extending up the river Ebro into the Meseta region.

In the north-west of Spain and the north of Portugal, the so-called Castro culture occurs; this culture is named after the numerous fortified hill-settlements which are always found in easily defensible situations (Figure 28.1). There are considerable

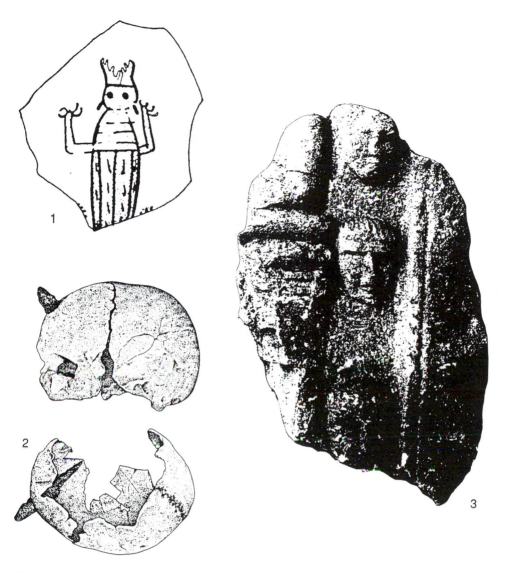

Figure 28.10 1 – Sherd with representation of Cernunnos from Numantia (Soria). 2 – Holed skull with iron nail from Ullastret (Gerona). 3 – Fragment of a pillar with severed heads from Sant Martí Sarroca (Barcelona).

problems concerning absolute and relative chronology, because the dead were treated in a way which is archaeologically undetectable. Because of the older excavations of many settlements, stratigraphical information is either suspect or non-existent. It is generally believed that the Castro culture flourished between the fifth and first centuries BC. But many settlements continued well into the Roman period and even to the Middle Ages. Moreover, it has been shown that some of the pottery formerly regarded as 'castro-ware' belongs in fact to the Roman period. The *castros* are

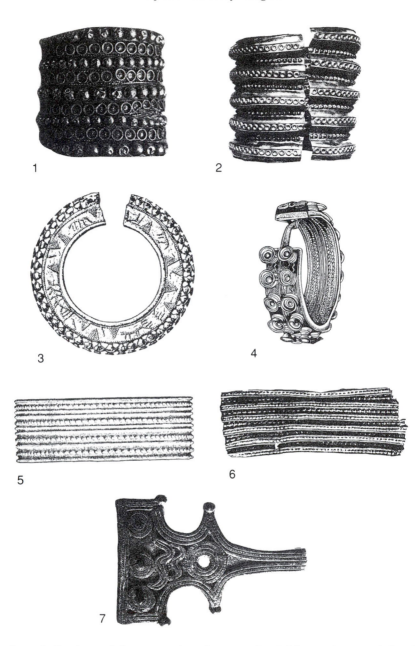

Figure 28.11 Indications of the connections between the Celtic provinces and the Iberian peninsula in the sixth century BC. 1–2 – Gold arm-bands (cuffs) from the El Carambolo hoard (Seville) and the Hochdorf princely grave (Kreis Ludwigsburg, Germany). 3–4 – Gold earrings with hour-glass-shaped details on their circumferences from Teruel and the princely grave at Sainte Colombe (Côte d'Or, France). 5–6 – Gold armlets from the province of Orense and the Kappel-am-Rhein princely grave (Kreis Ortenau, Germany). 7 – Iberian belt-hook from the princely grave at Magdalenenberg bei Villingen (Kreis Schwarzwald-Baar, Germany).

surrounded by stone walls; the houses have round or oval ground-plans. The basis of the economy was agriculture and livestock; the Roman sources especially emphasize horse-breeding in Galicia and Asturia. The extremely rich mineral resources, including copper, tin, gold and silver, for which the region was familiar in classical times, were doubtless already being exploited in the pre-Roman period. We are informed about personal appearance and weaponry only for the time immediately preceding the Roman conquest. The weapons were the spear, dagger and round shield. The social structure was different from that of the Meseta culture; clan names are not present here. The many votive inscriptions give us information about the indigenous divinities who, in the main, were worshipped on hilltops. Among them one finds names such as Lucubo, Lucoubu (Lugus), Teutates, Bormanus, who was venerated at thermal spring-sanctuaries in Gaul, and Adaegina, who may be equated with a goddess of night. *Têtes coupées*, stone heads with torques and multi-headed stone figures are also found. It is not in question that the north-west of the peninsula spoke a Celtic dialect. The tribal name Gallaeci is enshrined in the modern name of Galicia. Archaeological evidence for links with the Celtic world is particularly clear in prestige objects: heavy gold torques, which can be finely classified into subdivisions through the decoration on their terminals, occur frequently in gold hoards dating mainly to the first century BC (Figure 28.12, no. 2). Torques are often worn by the *guerreros galaicos*, life-size stone figures who are armed with daggers and round shields; they are found mainly in the entrance areas of *castros* (Figure 28.12, no. 1). In addition there are many variants of fibulae with an embellished foot, some of which are closely related to the western Hallstatt region, while others are of obviously local character. Almagro argues that Celtic influences were relatively late in reaching the north-west from the Celtiberian core area (Almagro Gorbea 1991: 401). This is, however, contradicted by the complete absence of long swords and La Tène fibulae. Even though the lack of swords might be explained by the find circumstances, the absence of fibulae is nevertheless odd. Perhaps the 'celticization' in fact took place at the same time as in the Meseta region. Philological evidence can be similarly interpreted, based on a comparison between Galician linguistic remains and those of the Celtiberian region and in Gaul (Albertos Firmat 1975: 52). Of course, this does not exclude the movements of groups in somewhat later times. Thus the proper name 'Celtiber' (which occurs only once in the north-west) proves that such an immigration took place.

A map, which contains the distribution of certain objects of the Castro culture such as sculptures and jewellery, shows a north–south division of the region, which approximately follows the course of the Rio Minho. Later, the Romans created the administrative units of *gallaeci bracari* and *gallaeci lucenses*, and it is clear that these are based on the old tribal areas (cf. Figures 28.1 and 28.8).

Hardly any archaeological evidence for Celtic links can be found outside the Celtiberian core region and the Galician–north Portuguese area of the Castro culture. Lusitania, between the rivers Tagus and Douro, is almost totally without finds. But here, the frequently occurring Celtic personal name 'Celtius' is evidence of the immigration of Celtic groups into originally non-Celtic territory (Figure 28.1). Pliny's account of the immigration of Celtiberians from Lusitania to Baetica refers to the western part of Andalusia (*Naturalis Historia* II.13). Untermann was able to

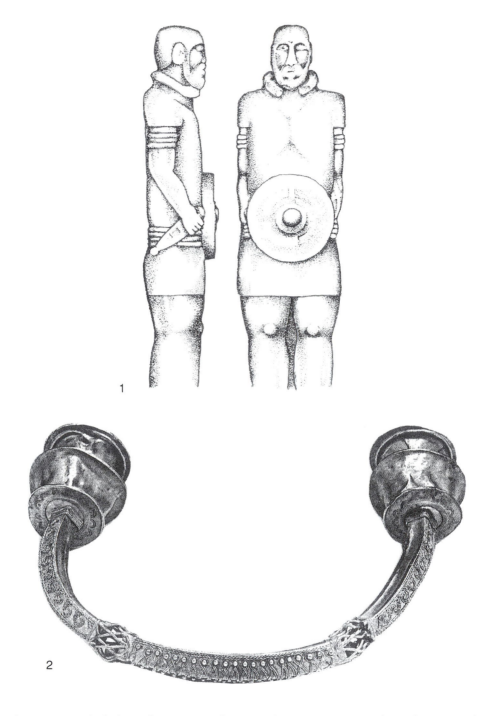

Figure 28.12 Finds from the Castro Culture province. 1 'Guerrero galaico' from Lezenho (Portugal). 2 Gold torque from Villa Boas (Portugal).

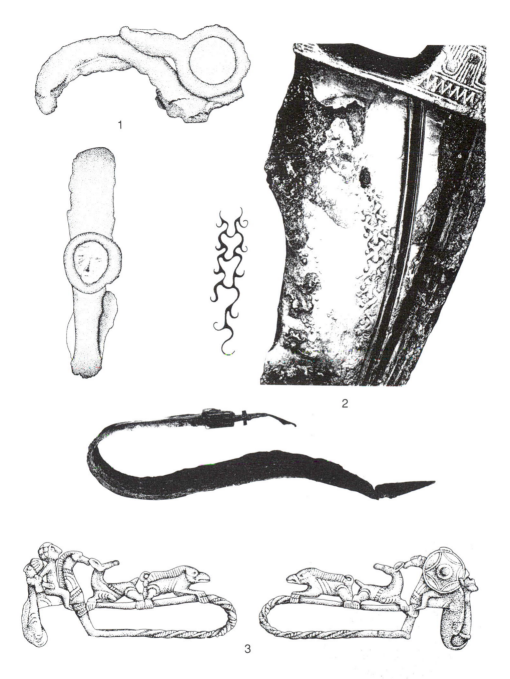

Figure 28.13 Finds of items related to the Celtic culture from the Iberian settlement area. 1 – Fibula of early La Tène style with a facemask from La Albufereta (Alicante). 2 – 'Falcata' (elaborate curved sword) with La Tène-style decoration from Almedinilla (Cordoba). 3 – Silver fibula of La Tène form, depicting a human figure and animals from Chiclana de Segura (Jaén).

show that this situation is reflected in place-names with the component *seg* (*sieg* = victory in the Celtiberian language), which indicate movement from the Celtiberian to the Iberian area (Untermann 1961: 16ff.). Such operations might have been carried out by Celtiberian mercenaries, who are mentioned repeatedly in the classical sources.

There is, however, also archaeological evidence of Celtic culture within the Iberian-speaking area: in historical sources, an Iberian–Ligurian mixed population is named in the north-east of Spain and in Languedoc, which occupied the Mediterranean coast on both sides of the Pyrenees and which absorbed Celtic elements of costume and weapons (Solier 1976–8: 211ff.). On French soil, there are shrines like Roquepertuse and Entremont, at which the Celtic cult of the head was practised. Closely similar finds have also come from Catalonia. Here, sculptures were discovered which depict *têtes coupées* on a pillar (Guitart Durán 1975) (Figure 28.10, no. 3). In the Iberian oppidum of Ullastret (Gerona), perforated skulls with iron nails *in situ* were found, indicating that the barbaric custom of displaying the skulls of dead enemies was practised here (Campillo 1976–8: 317ff.) (Figure 28.10, no. 2).

Finally, finds from the fourth century BC onwards, which witness the contacts with Celtic culture, can be brought together in the Iberian area of the south-east. These include numerous fibulae (Figure 28.13, no. 1) and an art form which contains elements of the 'Waldalgesheim Style' and is found on Iberian high-status weapons (Figure 28.13, no. 2). They show that Celtic craftsmanship was popular in the Iberian area and was integrated into the personal equipment of the indigenous people. Magnificent gold and silver fibulae of early and middle La Tène type still occur in the first century BC (Figure 28.13, no. 3). Incidentally, here, too, Celtic mercenaries were recruited by Iberian warrior-princes.

An entirely individual version of Celtic culture is thus found on the Iberian peninsula, one which is archaeologically most clearly evidenced in the Celtiberian core area of the Meseta; this culture is also a constituent element of the Castro culture and its influence is also detectable in the Iberian-speaking region.

The Romans, who had already begun to subjugate Iberian tribes in the third century BC, had to fight bloody wars in order to break the resistance of the population in the centre and the west of the peninsula. The war against Numantia lasted ten years; it was eventually completely isolated and was forced to give up its heroic battle in 133 BC after months under siege. Only with the conquest by Augustus of the Artabri in the north-west tip of Spain did the whole of the peninsula become a Roman province.

REFERENCES

Albertos Firmat, M.L. (1966) 'La onomástica personal primitiva de Hispania. Tarraconense y Betica', Theses et Studia Philologica Salmanticensia 13, Salamanca.

Almagro Gorbea, M. (1991) 'The Celts of the Iberian peninsula', in S. Moscati *et al.* (eds) *The Celts*, 389–405.

Arribas, A. (n.d.) *The Iberians: ancient peoples and places*, London: Thames & Hudson.

Campillo, D. (1978) 'Abrasiones dentarias y cráneos enclavados del poblado de Ullastret

(Baix-Empordà, Gerona)'. Simposi Internacional Els Origens del Món Ibèric. Barcelona-Empúries 1977, Barcelona 1976–8, Ampurias 38–40, 317 ff.

Carriazo, J.M. (1973) *Tartessos y El Carambolo*, Madrid: D.G. Belas Artes.

Cerdeño Serrano, M.L. (1978) 'Los broches de cinturón peninsulares de tipo céltico', *Trabajos de Prehistoria* 35: 279–306.

Ferreira da Silva, A.C. (1986) *A cultura castreja no noroeste de Portugal*, Pacos de Ferreira.

Fischer, F. (1972) 'Die Kelten bei Herodot', *Madrider Mitteilungen* 13: 109–24.

Guitart Durán, J. (1975) 'Nuevas piezas de escultura prerromana en Cataluna: restos de un monumento con relieves en Sant Martí Sarroca (Barcelona)', *Pyrenae* 11: 71 ff.

Hartmann, A. (1970) *Prähistorische Goldfunde aus Europa*, Studien zu der Anfängen der Metallurgie 3, Berlin.

Koch, M. (1979) 'Die Keltiberer und ihr historischer Kontext', in A. Tovar *et al.* (eds) *Actas del II. Colloquio sobre lenguas y culturas prerromanas de la Península Ibérica*, Tübingen 1976, Ediciones Universidad de Salamanca, Salamanca 1979, 387–419.

Kurtz, W. (1987) *La Necrópolis de las Cogotas I: Ajuares*. BAR International Series 344, Oxford.

Lenerz-de Wilde, M. (1991) *Iberia Celtica. Archäologische Zeugnisse keltischer Kultur auf der Pyrenäenhalbinsel*, Stuttgart: Steiner Verlag.

Lopez Monteagudo, G. (1989) *Esculturas zoomorfas celtas de la Península Ibérica*, Madrid: Consejo Superior de Investigaciones Cientificas.

Raddatz, K. (1969) *Die Schatzfunde der Iberischen Halbinsel vom Ende des 3. bis zur Mitte des 1. Jahrhunderts vor Christi Geburt*, Madrider Forschungen 5, Berlin: Walter de Gruyter.

Anon 1987, *I. Simposium sobre los Celtíberos*, Zaragoza: Institución Fernando el Católico.

Anon 1990, *II. Simposium sobre los Celtíberos. Necrópolis Celtibéricas*, Zaragoza: Institución Fernando el Católico.

Solier, Y. (1978) 'La culture ibéro-languedocienne aux VI-Veme siècles', *Simposi Internacional Els Orígens del Món Ibèric*. Barcelona: Empúries 1977 (Barcelona 1976–8). *Ampurias* 38–40, 211–64.

Spindler, K. (1983) *Die frühen Kelten*, Stuttgart: Philipp Reclam.

Tovar, A. (1961) *The Ancient Languages of Spain and Portugal*, New York.

Untermann, J. (1961) *Sprachräume und Sprachbewegungen im vorrömischen Hispanien*, Wiesbaden: Otto Harrassowitz.

—— (1965) *Elementos de un atlas antroponímico de la Hispania antigua*, Bibliotheca Praehistoria Hispana 7, Madrid: Consejo Superior de Investigaciones Cientificas.

—— (1984) 'Los Celtíberos y sus vecinos occidentales.'. *Lletres asturianes* 13: 6–26.

—— (1984) 'Los teónimos de la región lusitano-gallego como fuente de las lenguas indígenas', *Actas del III. Colloquio sobre lenguas y culturas paleohispánicas*, Lisboa 1980 (Salamanca 1985), 343–63.

Valdeón J, (ed.) *Historia de Castilia y León* 1, *La Prehistoria del valle del Duero*, Valladolid: Ambito Ediciones.

THE CELTS IN FRANCE

— ·•· —

Olivier Büchsenschütz

CELTIC FRANCE

The title of this chapter would suggest Brittany and the Celtic languages, rather than the ancient Gauls, to the contemporary French public. The success of the Asterix books (Goscinny and Uderzo 1960), which portray an idealized world peopled by very conventional Gauls with characteristics inherited from the Age of Romanticism, has only marginally increased the interest of the public in these obscure periods: the concepts of 'the Iron Age' and of 'protohistory' remain completely unknown to them. French archaeological research has concentrated on the Palaeolithic and on Gallo-Roman antiquity, the latter considered to be the principal source of French culture. Historians of the medieval period have failed to consider the protohistoric substratum of the country's occupation and it fell to F. Braudel, a modern historian, to suggest the development of a 'long-term history' in which the contribution of these far distant times might be taken into account.

Although the French of today take little interest in scientific research into Celtic culture, they do acknowledge the Gauls as their 'ancestors'. As is the case in several European countries, references to early, ancestral inhabitants first appear during the Renaissance, in works on genealogy which set out to link the royal dynasty to classical and biblical antiquity, drawing on – in this case – Gallic intermediaries. In subsequent centuries, a more scholarly analysis of the classical texts obliged writers to bring the Celts within the scope of acceptable 'history' which, at that time, did not extend back beyond the antiquity of Greece and Rome. In the explanations they offered, authors of this period tried to counterbalance the defeats of 52 BC at the end of the Gallic War by reference to the victorious raids during earlier centuries, when Gallic troops spread terror in Greece and Italy.

Not until the work of the Benedictines of Saint Maur (Dom Martin Bouquet 1738) do we find scientifically based critical analysis of the classical texts. At that time, however, archaeological finds were still regarded as little more than curiosities of interest only to antiquarians. The complete lack of any means of ordering chronological sequences for pre- and protohistoric periods led to the wholesale attribution to the Gauls of everything that was not recognizably Roman.

The archaeology of the Celts of Gaul effectively begins in the middle of the nineteenth century with the work of Napoleon the Third and the scholarly societies which then flourished widely in France. The high standards of fieldwork achieved by the teams sponsored by the emperor, and by a few notable individual excavators, such as J.-G. Bulliot at Mont Beuvray (Nièvre) or Castagné at Murcens (Lot) are remarkable for their date. As the identification of sites mentioned in Caesar's *De Bello Gallico* was the motivation behind much of this research, the final word as regards interpretation still invariably went to historians, to whom the indications provided by the written record remained the primary evidence. Thus was created a history and an image of the Gauls in which archaeological findings continued to play relatively little part.

The development of Celtic studies this century consists of a number of strands. In the universities, a historical perspective essentially informed by the classical texts remained dominant. It is clearly represented in the writings of scholars from C. Jullian to P.-M. Duval. Contrastingly, the recovery of archaeological evidence was the principal aim of the research programmes of learned societies and of enlightened amateurs, of whom the most outstanding was J. Déchelette. For over a century, personnel at the national archaeological museum at St-Germain-en-Laye, the Musée des Antiquités Nationales (founded in 1865), and three Paris-based institutions – the Ecole Pratique des Hautes Etudes (1869), the Ecole du Louvre (1882) and the Collège de France (1905) – have ensured that links between these two intellectual traditions have been maintained. Despite real successes in raising its profile in France's research community and with the general public, the study of the Iron Age is still only marginally represented in the universities, where it continues to be considered as a foundation myth rather than a vibrant component of the history of the country. As far as school textbooks are concerned, in many cases the Gauls 'may be considered as one of the topmost strata of the physical structure of France. With them, we find ourselves in a period before history began' (Guiomar 1982: 395).

The first significant archaeological discoveries last century were of burial-places – either flat graves as in the Marne area, or barrows covering burials – and of hill-forts which scholars were quite prepared to identify as examples of 'Caesar's camps'. The cemeteries of the Marne were unmethodically excavated, the sole aim being to gather objects which could enrich museum displays. With few exceptions, the contents of these cemeteries cannot now be reassembled into individual grave and cemetery groups. Furthermore, during the 1914–1918 war, some of these assemblages were destroyed. Even the sizeable collections dating from this period in the Musée des Antiquités Nationales can only really be used for typological analyses and similar exercises, since the contexts of many objects are not known in detail.

The search for the battlefields of Caesar's Gallic War obsessed researchers and fieldworkers throughout the nineteenth century. The efforts of both learned societies and the national commissions underpinned the production of coherent syntheses drawing on the archaeological material recovered in this pursuit. Many of these overviews appeared at the end of the nineteenth century. Though cultural and period subdivisions such as the 'Marnian' (early Second Iron Age: after the Marne cemeteries) and the 'Beuvraysian' (late Second Iron Age, named for Mont Beuvray) (Figure 29.1) developed by de Mortillet from French data were abandoned in 1900 in favour of the wider European period divisions devised by O. Tischler, the

Figure 29.1 Map of sites mentioned in this chapter.

publication of J. Déchelette's four-volume *Manual* underlines the importance of the French contribution to archaeological research on the Iron Age. This major archaeological synthesis of European prehistory from the earliest times until the expansion of the ancient civilizations was matched by the work of C. Jullian, especially the first volume of his *Histoire de la Gaule*. Published in 1907, this provided the philological and linguistic source for the later periods covered by Déchelette's *Manual* (Déchelette 1914).

These two syntheses seem to tower over the achievements of the inter-war generation. The most important work in France at this time was that of English researchers (in particular M. Wheeler in Normandy) or of individual amateurs. More recently, the establishment in the 1950s of the Centre National de la Recherche Scientifique has provided the framework for the recruitment of professional researchers. CNRS personnel can be attached to institutions such as those mentioned above, or to the universities of Strasbourg, Paris, Aix and Montpellier. A new generation of learned societies (Ogam, Société Préhistorique Française, Association Française pour l'Etude de l'Age du Fer) acted as a fresh focus for research. Lastly, the great increase in rescue excavations in the 1980s produced new information in quantity on the rural world of the Iron Age, in particular on its smaller settlements, its farms and its fields.

THE ENVIRONMENTAL SETTING

During the eighth century BC, the gradual change from the dry climate of the sub-Boreal to the more humid sub-Atlantic regime led to the abandonment of lake-margin villages around the Alps and of some high- and medium-altitude valleys. This trend does not appear to have been reversed until after the Roman conquest. Amongst forest trees, beech and hornbeam, sometimes accompanied by alder, spread westward. In the south-west, the vegetation still characteristic of this area became established: maritime pines and heathland with bracken. Pine, box and Mediterranean species covered the south-east. Pine, beech and alder spread into the Pyrenees. Fir became established in the Massif Central and were to be found along with beech in the northern Alps and in the Jura mountains.

MAJOR GEOGRAPHICAL ZONES IN THE FRENCH IRON AGE

The contrast which was already apparent during the Bronze Age in terms of material culture between Atlantic and continental groups persisted into the Iron Age. Stimulated by the establishment of the Greek colonies in Provence and by exchanges with the upper Danube valley, a culture with diagnostically Hallstatt traits developed on the Rhône–Saône–Rhine axis. In the north and the west of the Paris Basin, in the Massif Central and the south-west, recent research is helping to define a distinctive first iron age culture which was still in existence when La Tène culture became firmly established in the Marne area. The Armorican Iron Age has numerous characteristics which serve to distinguish it from the remainder of northern France: it remained untouched by second iron age La Tène influences until the last few centuries BC. The Languedoc region and Provence, their Mediterranean environment setting them apart from more northerly areas, equally developed indigenous cultures which were original not only in respect of their native origins but also in their reactions to Greek colonization.

With the exception of the spread of its characteristic iron and bronze items, La Tène culture was not archaeologically visible over much of Gaul for considerable periods. Celticization may thus be considered to have been a phenomenon of the second century BC in many areas. The early ancient geographers offer us little help: according to them the coasts of Gaul, from Biarritz to Dunkirk, were generally oriented east–west, and the great rivers flowed from south to north. Nevertheless, the Carcassonne Gap and the route to the Atlantic was well known at an early date, as was the link from Rhône to Danube. The modern reader needs to keep in mind the picture the ancient writers had of these northern territories when interpreting their writings on Gaul.

THE AISNE-MARNE CULTURE, A SOCIETY REVEALED BY ITS BURIAL RITE

Our knowledge of many iron age societies in France is based essentially on material recovered from cemeteries. Leaving aside a few intermediate cases, burials can often be categorized into distinct social or economic groups. We can usually distinguish ordinary burials in which the body, dressed according to sex and status, is accompanied by modest grave goods, from rich interments where numerous valuable objects display the important status the deceased held in life. This disparity in the apparent wealth of grave goods, very striking during the First Iron Age, continued throughout the Second Iron Age and into the Gallo-Roman period.

Rich tombs, remarkable both for their metal artefacts (including offensive and defensive weaponry and armour) and for the size of the mound which covers them, appear from Late Bronze Age times onward. Parade vehicles and Mediterranean imports, prestige goods monopolized by the élite, were soon added to the indigenous artefacts they contained. The sought-after imports are related to feasting and are represented mainly by drinking services for the consumption of imported wine or local mead. This burial rite is well documented in the Rhône valley, Burgundy, Alsace and in part of Lorraine. Further west (as in Berry or the middle Loire valley), these grave goods associated with prestige drinking occur either singly or at a later date. The sixth century is the golden age for rich tombs containing vehicles. These are usually associated with elaborate hill-forts considered to represent princely residences.

Research during the last twenty years has emphasized aspects of continuity between the cemeteries of the First and Second Iron Ages. This is apparent not only in the uninterrupted use of a number of burial sites but also in the recognition of the slow evolution in funerary rites, sometimes without wholesale change, and in the artefacts associated with these practices. Social changes are apparently in course throughout the Early and Middle La Tène periods, and there is no clear evidence for a major break in the fifth century, as was long believed.

Champagne remains the best documented region for the entire period between the fifth and first centuries BC. Cemeteries, generally some distance away from settlement sites, reunite in death the community which inhabited a large farm or a hamlet over several generations or even centuries. Inhumation is generally the dominant rite: the corpse was laid out in extended position on its back in a rectangular pit that was then infilled with black earth. Burials are usually oriented to conform to established customs, use of a common orientation often characterizing a particular group during a certain period.

The chariot graves of the La Tène period (presently estimated to number 250 examples in the Champagne) are both less extravagantly furnished and more numerous than those of the First Iron Age. They normally include the remains of a chief, buried on a two-wheeled vehicle that could have served in war. The pits used for burials, excavated into the chalk bedrock, often include subsidiary pits or slots to house the cart wheels and sometimes the chariot pole. These vehicle burials occur in the same cemeteries as other types of graves. A hierarchy is discernible among the latter.

Rich men were entombed with their weapons, generally a sword and thrusting spears: women of the same rank normally wore a torque. Then there are men's tombs with spears, but no swords, and women's tombs where the corpse is wearing bracelets. Finally, in the remaining half of the identifiable tombs, the deceased is simply accompanied by pottery. Superimposed on these patterns of social division is an evolution in grave goods through time which is quite well understood today. Taking weaponry as an example, spears and, in a secondary way, daggers, define the extreme end of the First Iron Age at the Jogasses cemetery: the following series of burials, those of the earliest La Tène horizon, usually contain three spearheads. Thereafter, the sword accompanied by a single spear and a sword belt is the usual panoply; finally, from the third century, shields are represented. Changing dress fashions, women's jewellery, and fighting gear provide a reflection of both evolution through time and of the the social and family status of individuals. Indications in the funerary record of specialists, such as traders or artisans, are very unusual. The burial evidence allows us to posit an essentially rural society, and seemingly a homogeneous one. Its weaponry illustrates both its independence from external influences and its wealth.

Several factors represent breakpoints in the gradual evolution of this rural society. Thus it has been possible to observe, particularly in the Aisne, that cemetery layout in the fifth century was based on family groupings in place of the sexual segregation that characterized the previous horizon (Demoule 1982). This is the main observable social change which occurs during the fifth century, apart from the gradual evolution from 'Hallstatt' to 'La Tène' in terms of material culture. The appearance of objects bearing pseudo-filigree decoration (Duval 1977) or of anklets in the women's tombs of the third century (Kruta 1985) is indicative of links with central Europe. Is this just a question of trade contacts or is it rather a matter of population movements as suggested by the Latin sources? Opinion remains divided. The introduction of cremation, which spread southward from the north Champagne region during the third and second centuries BC, is sometimes attributed to the Belgae. Material culture evolved further at this time and impressive structures began to be placed in cemeteries: square enclosures and buildings defined by heavy earthfast wooden posts. The grave, as such, lost importance as a focus for attention in favour of monumental superstructures. These latter heralded the development of traditions represented in due course by Gallo-Roman gravestones and funerary monuments.

BELGIC SANCTUARIES AND SETTLEMENTS

In the north of France, research and rescue work has by chance favoured the investigation of settlements and sanctuaries. The excellent quality of the results of aerial survey in Picardy and the early development of extensive excavations in the Aisne valley have combined to allow the collection of much information about settlement sites over the past twenty years. The discovery of the Gournay-sur-Aronde sanctuary (Oise) by accident has led to the excavation of numerous ritual sites, which have completely altered our perception of Celtic religion. But first we should discuss two groups of burials which complete the sequence we have identified in Champagne.

At the start of the Middle La Tène period, cremation burials appeared in this area: these may correlate with the arrival of Belgic tribes (Figure 29.2). These graves are surrounded by rectilinear ditches easily discernible by aerial survey. In a sizeable pit, probably wood-lined, the cremation was accompanied by deposits of food, pottery

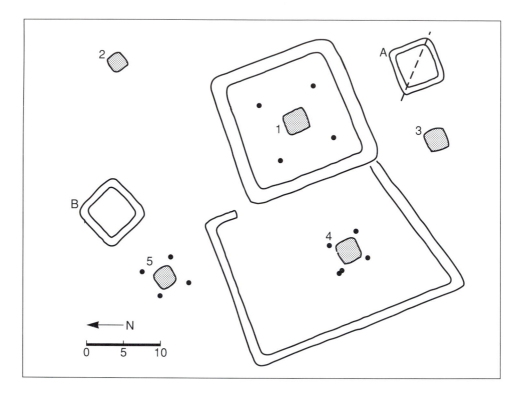

Figure 29.2 Plan of the middle La Tène cremation cemetery at Tartigny (Oise). (After J.-L. Massy and E. Mantel.) The five graves are numbered. The enclosures were identified from aerial photos; the shaded areas were excavated; • = post-hole.

artefacts, and a few metal objects, excluding weapons. The inclusion of all these kinds of objects in relation to this kind of burial is characteristic. The evidence suggests a complex yet standardized ritual which took place at the time of the deposition of the cremated remains, or possibly after it. We shall know more about this sequence when archaeologists have examined a more extensive series of examples.

The north of the country, the Paris region and west-central France all have chariot tombs datable from the Middle and Late La Tène periods and earliest Gallo-Roman times. The dismantled chariot was frequently burned, so that only a few elements have survived: parts of hubs or iron tyres, and perhaps a few items connected to the body of the vehicle or of horse harness. This fragmentary evidence explains why these burials have not been identified until recently. Weapons were offered in sacrifice, as happened in the sanctuaries discussed below, or were replaced by parade weapons such as anthropomorphic-hilted daggers. The most recent series of these tombs contains cooking utensils (iron grill frames), Italian amphorae, and imported metal jugs and other items from wine-drinking services, renewing the tradition of the banquet known earlier in the Iron Age. The Gaulish aristocracy is evidenced by these rich tombs which most often seem to be associated with large country estates rather than with the burgeoning agglomerations within each *civitas* (tribal area).

Elsewhere, weapons, no longer included amongst grave goods, were now disposed of in vast sanctuaries. Indeed it was the discovery of deposits of weapons that drew the attention of researchers to sanctuary sites. The excavation of a ditch filled with some 2,000 weapons and 3,000 bones at Gournay-sur-Aronde in Oise (Figure 29.3) by Jean-Louis Brunaux and his team led them to the reconstruction not only of a sanctuary but also of a complicated suite of rituals which indicates to us something of the strict formalization of Gallic religion. This sanctuary, set in the very centre of a fortified site, is demarcated by a ditched enclosure with a side length of 40 metres. Centrally placed within this enclosure there is a pit which has been covered at various times by a succession of wooden buildings, the last of these replaced by a small rectangular temple (*fanum*) during Roman times. Animals were sacrificed and their carcases placed in this pit: their remains were subsequently thrown into the enclosure ditch. Weapons, too, were exhibited in this sanctuary, before being deposited in the same ditch. These discoveries give rise more readily to comparisons with the Mediterranean world than with the primitive and bloody cults generally associated with Celts' ritual practices. The sacrifice of livestock, usually oxen, pigs and sheep, brings to mind the Roman *suovetaurilia*. Whereas the last-mentioned two species were eaten, the slaughtered oxen and some horses were exposed and not consumed, then eventually thrown into the ditch in the same way as the weapons. The replacement of

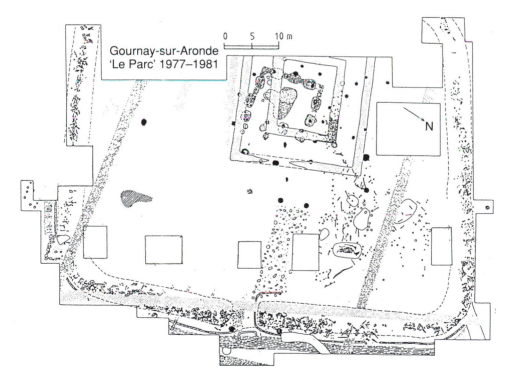

Figure 29.3 General plan of the excavations at the multi-phase sanctuary at Gournay-sur-Aronde (Oise). (After J.-L. Brunaux.)

the Gallic temple by a Gallo-Roman *fanum* after a long period during which the sanctuary had been closed, is not an isolated instance of such a sequence. The recovery of material from many Gallo-Roman sanctuaries has revealed the presence of Gallic weapons and, in the best-examined examples, further examples of wooden structures which pre-date their Gallo-Roman masonry buildings. Sequences like that encountered at Gournay have been identified not only in the north and in Normandy but also as far away as west-central France and in the Rhône valley.

Current excavations of the iron age levels at Ribemont-sur-Ancre (Somme), located beneath a huge Gallo-Roman architectural ensemble, have revealed evidence for ritual activity which was similar in format but different in its objectives from those identified at Gournay. At Ribemont, it is human bodies which have been cut up *post mortem*, then exhibited in the form of a construction made of human bone, with structures consisting of longbones forming the corners of an enclosure. In this case, the enclosure ditch still held both human remains and the weapons that were put in with them when both were in an advanced state of decay. These sanctuaries, which the Romans do not appear to have known about – perhaps as a result of a deliberate policy on the part of the Gauls – are sufficiently numerous in the north of Gaul for us today to be able to study their distribution across the tribal territories, in relation to both trade routes and frontiers.

More settlement sites (Figure 29.4) have been located in northern France than in the rest of the country. A first group is made up of native farms/*fermes indigènes* – as opposed to the Roman villa examples which initially monopolized the attention of aerial photographers. Consisting of large quadrangular or oval enclosures, interrupted here and there by in- or out-turned funnel-shaped gateways, these sites provide a clear indication of the occupation and use of extensive areas of landscape: individual enclosures could shelter living quarters, outbuildings and livestock. Internal structures are rarely visible and the results of test excavations are, on the whole, disappointing. But we can now say that the northern plateaux of France were occupied by large isolated farms, the forerunners of the *aedificia* (rural estate buildings) of the Gallic nobility which are mentioned by Caesar.

It is excavations in gravel quarries that have revealed most fully the complexity and density of the occupation of the valleys. The Aisne valley, in particular, is crammed with complex and interrelated agricultural establishments. We can identify dwellings and post-built granaries, surrounded by hundreds of pits of various kinds: for storage, work activities and water extraction, groups of such pits being associated with fences, stockades and enclosures of different types and sizes. As is the case with settlements in the Thames Basin in England, we can identify chronological and spatial variations; specialization in either stock-farming or in cereal production can be posited. The range of activities on these settlements, however, remains essentially agricultural until the end of the middle La Tène period.

The establishment of, or reoccupation of, fortifications on high ground – or on the valley floor – and the development of craft industries in specialized sectors in proto-urban settlements, occur during the Late La Tène and early Gallo-Roman periods. *Murus gallicus* walls and massive dump ramparts continued to be built after the conquest, by the Gauls and possibly also by troops in the service of Rome (see Chapter 5), on the high ground which dominates the valleys of the Somme and the

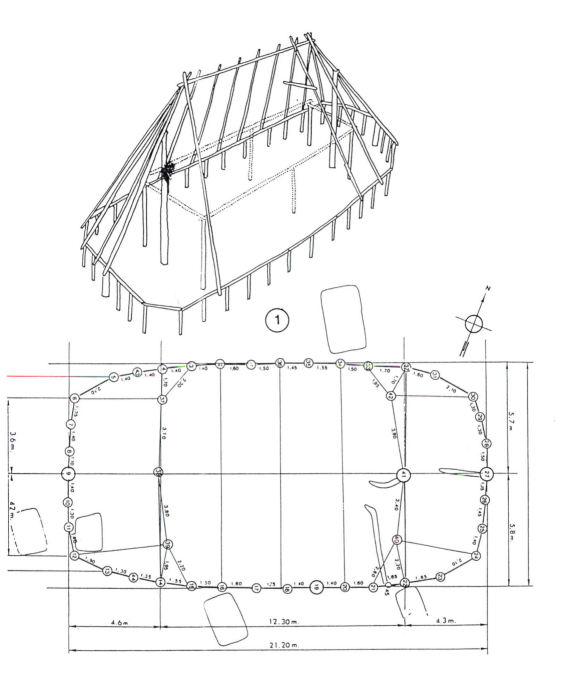

Figure 29.4 Plan and reconstruction of the substantial middle La Tène house at Verberie (Oise). (After J.-C. Blanchet, P. Meniel and O. Büchsenschütz.) This is the largest building seemingly corresponding to Caesar's description of an 'aedificium' excavated to date.

Figure 29.5 Reconstruction of the covered ditches at Villeneuve-Saint-Germain (Aisne), excavated by J. Debord. These subdivided an enclosed lowland settlement site set within a meander of the River Aisne. (Drawing by B. Lambot.)

Aisne. During the same period, in a valley-bottom setting at Villeneuve-Saint-Germain, surrounded by a meander of the Aisne, a town developed (Figure 29.5). Its industrial and residential areas were separated by a long, cruciform, roofed structure. This arrangement seems to represent a unique instance of urban planning, such as would be associated with the activities of Roman *aedili*, but executed in wood. The detailed chronology of these late pre-Gallo-Roman developments is probably easier to discern at present in east-central France than in the northern valleys.

THE ATLANTIC TERRITORIES

Before Caesar, the only texts that mention the Atlantic coastlands relate to the expeditions made by Himilco and Pytheas. It was primarily the search for tin which underpinned trade with these distant regions. This quest probably offers the best explanation for the presence of artefacts of Mediterranean origin as far north as the mouth of the Loire as early as the First Iron Age. Archaeological evidence of these contacts is thereafter difficult to perceive until the second century BC, when Campanian pottery was distributed to the Charente valley, but no further north-westwards. Slightly later, wine amphorae were exchanged as far as Armorica and southern England, but in small numbers. Distribution maps show concentrations at ports, but recent discoveries show that our information on the overall pattern is still very incomplete.

A number of traits are shared by the western peninsulas from Cornwall and Armorica to Galicia. It is thus possible to contrast a western community with a continental one. Current research, however, extends beyond simply contrasting an Atlantic tradition and continental Celtic influence, to define a range of indigenous cultures and their economic development at the local scale (Duval 1990).

The establishment of absolute chronology is the main difficulty facing the archaeologist working on these regions. The rarity of Mediterranean imports and the absence of large cemeteries with rich artefactual assemblages hinder the definition of the precise sequencing that is feasible in eastern France. In Armorica, M.-Y. Daire's research allows us to classify different ceramic traditions: graphite pottery; vases with stamped decoration; pot with red-painted decoration; and vases with internally channelled rims (Daire 1987). But the types of pottery thus defined are restricted to a few hundred items and the available typologies only indicate general trends. R. Boudet has put forward a chronology for Aquitaine which identifies five horizons between the sixth and first centuries BC (Boudet 1987). His scheme takes into account information from both settlements and tombs, the two stratified sites at La Lède du Gurp and Lacoste (both Gironde) providing stratigraphic controls. Although drawing attention to the fragility of this chronological scheme, which relies heavily on data from Languedoc, T. Lejars used it as the basis for his analysis of the western territories as a whole (Lejars 1987).

Our knowledge of the cultures of Armorica has made considerable progress during the past twenty years, thanks to very active research teams which have benefited from the examination of sites revealed as cropmarks by successive years of drought or identified through the requirements of rescue operations. The picture that we have thus gained of the Second Iron Age in Brittany is that it was distinctive and varied. The countryside of the time was deforested, an open landscape lacking the tissue of small hedged fields, formerly considered as typically Celtic in this region but now known not to predate the late Middle Ages. Leaving aside the heathland, the cultivated ground bore cereals and vegetables, among which must be noted the presence of buckwheat and beans. We know little of stock-farming as the soil is too acidic to preserve bone material. Both the discovery of bipyramidal ingots and the comments of Caesar and Strabo on the frequency of chains in the equipment of boats, bear witness to the working of iron on a substantial scale. From the north coast of Brittany to the Vendée region there is evidence of salt-working, salt being extracted from sea brine in ovens equipped with pans and then made into blocks.

The results of aerial survey have entirely changed our understanding of the settlement record. Settlement is dominantly dispersed: houses and associated out-buildings are often grouped within enclosures. As yet, villages are unknown, except on the Alet (Côtes-du-Nord) and Quiberon (Morbihan) peninsulas, where clusters of about ten dwellings are known. Hill-forts and associated categories of sites are not unknown in Brittany: there are small coastal cliff-castles and larger inland forts (Figure 29.6). Some date back to the First Iron Age and all, or nearly all, were occupied at the end of the Second. If the close links proposed by M. Wheeler between the use of these fortifications and various events during the Gallic War are now open to question, as first noted by Hawkes (1958), recent work has failed to tackle the definition of their functions, be it as simple refuges or as pre-urban centres. The architecture of houses is varied: we know of small post-built circular and rectangular structures. There are many buildings defined archaeologically by the presence of low dry-stone walls which are, with one exception, rectilinear in outline. Post-built granaries are attested, but most storage was done underground, in souter-rains which have long been known throughout the Armorican peninsula. This kind of structure seems to have been replaced by substantial, if no longer subterranean, pits in later times.

The funerary rituals are also distinctive. Cremation predominates and grave goods are generally limited to a few bracelets and sometimes some glass beads. The earliest phase is characterized by stone cists covered by small cairns. Later, larger mounds placed over stone circles are found, as are cremations without a covering mound. Stone cists for crouched inhumations add to this variety. On the other hand, much of Armorica is characterized by the presence of stone stelae; examples that are both low and almost spherical, or tall and sometimes faceted, are known. In several cases, it has been possible to link these pillars with cremations. These stelae, supplemented by the incised figure from Paule (Figure 29.7), are evidence that stoneworking techniques were better developed in Brittany than in many regions of the Celtic world at that time.

THE MASSIF CENTRAL AND THE HEARTLAND OF GAUL

The Massif Central, even today hardly touched by motorways and high-speed trains, was in ancient times both a refuge and a sanctuary as well as an inexhaustible reservoir

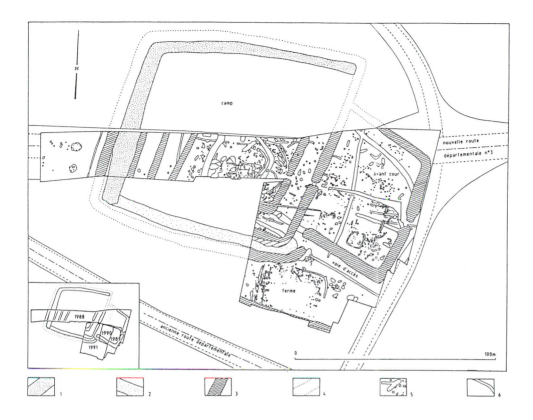

Figure 29.6 General plan of the fortified enclosure at Paule, Côtes d'Armor, Brittany. Continuing excavation of this site and its environs is prompting a reassessment of the significance of the roles of enclosed sites in Brittany. **Key:** 1 – rampart; 2 – ploughed out rampart; 3 – ditch; 4 – probable course of ditch; 5 – pits and post-holes; 6 – little ditch. (After Y. Menez.)

of open space and resources. Its position determines the ancient entry routes into Gaul, the isthmus between Narbonne and the Atlantic, and the Rhône valley, which it overlooks from the high plateaux of the Cévennes and Vivarais. Caesar understood this geography well, and carefully avoided entering the area during the first five years of the Gallic War. He had, however, eventually to resolve to confront the Arverni on their own territory but was only able to defeat them by drawing them as far as Burgundy, the home of their rival the Aedui, and ultimately to Alesia. In order to complete the conquest in 51 BC, Caesar had to overcome the resistance of the Cadurci, established around the Lot valley, who were posing a threat to the Province.

Innovations and new populations were slow to infiltrate this massif: its cultural substratum endured for centuries. Archaeological survey is difficult in the uplands: ploughed land is rare, as are the kinds of major development projects that can require rescue archaeological interventions. Moreover, the constraints imposed by the environment remain strong here: architectural changes have more to do with available raw materials than with technical developments. The information that we can muster remains quantitatively slight and statistically insufficient: it is not adequate to compose a lasting synthesis.

Traditionally, the Limousin region is attributed to the Lemovices, and the Auvergne to the Arvernes, while a series of small *civitates* (tribal areas) are scattered along the fringes of the south-west massif. Historical sources describe the Arverni as an important group who dominated Gaul politically at the time of the Celtic invasions in Italy, and whose power was only checked after their defeat at the hands of the Romans in 121 BC. The Lemovices seem to have kept aloof from the great European events until the time of the conquest itself. The First Iron Age in their area, characterized by burials under tumuli, and good-quality pottery with graphite-based decoration, displays a certain cultural unity in the western massif. But the characteristic elements of La Tène culture only penetrated this area very slowly. In the Auvergne, too, these appear somewhat tardily, during the second half of the fourth century, notably in the cemetery at Diou (Allier): about twenty burials in flat graves which yielded weapons, torques, bronze bracelets and also brooches or fibulae have been discovered. This short-lived cemetery bears witness to the links between Auvergne and the classic Celtic province, centred to the north and east.

(a)   (b)

Figure 29.7 (a) Stone sculpture from Paule (Côtes d'Armor, Brittany) compared with (b) sculpture from the open settlement at Levroux (Indre), excavated respectively by Y. Menez and collaborators and S. Krausz and collaborators. (Drawn by M. Dupré and S. Phillips.)

Gold coinage also links the Auvergne to historical evidence concerning the wealth of the Arverni. There is evidence of ancient mines in the region, and a recent project has shown that in Limousin the extraction of gold started no later than the Middle La Tène period (Cauuet 1991). Gold staters of Philip of Macedonia and, more particularly, imitations of them are very numerous in Puy-de-Dôme and in the south of the département of Allier. Remote from the great trade axes, the Auvergne drew its wealth from its own soil and the endeavours of its inhabitants.

Two pieces of evidence show us that the Auvergne participated fully in the economic changes that took place in the middle La Tène period. In the so-called 'tumulus' at Celles (Cantal), a structure the function of which remains unclear, a complete set of tools has been found which dates roughly from the middle or the beginning of the Late La Tène period. This specialized set of tools, designed for working in horn and bone, confirms the appearance of professional craftsmen (Guillaumet 1982) at this time.

At the same time, the hamlets that were scattered over the plains of the Limagne and Forez tended to coalesce to form villages, in which craft activities of a range of types played an important role. Trade with the Mediterranean became more intensive: it is mainly manifested in the archaeological record by the presence of heavy transport amphorae. These developments were sustained by a coinage of lower value than the staters, which was aligned on the contemporary issues of southern Gaul and Spain. Though by this time the Arverni had suffered political setbacks and may have been on the defensive in some ways, they nevertheless participated fully in the economic transformations that characterize this period.

The trend towards the establishment of large enclosed sites termed oppida affected the Massif Central, but in an uneven and often distinctive way. In the east and south, timber-laced walls of *murus gallicus* type have been identified, along with imported amphorae, and the artefacts which are characteristic of these proto-urban sites. In Limousin, the huge site at Villejoubert (Haute Vienne) seems to have consumed many of the resources of this tribal area (*civitas*), many of the other oppida-like sites here seeming to represent hasty refortifications of earlier hill-forts. An upland series of small enclosed sites could be the equivalent of the *aedificia* of the lowlands (Ralston 1992).

On the eve of the conquest several contrasting settlement patterns are thus to be found in the Massif Central. Oppida border the valleys of the south-west, such as the Lot and the Dordogne, or overlook the plains of Limagne, Forez and Allier, these latter densely occupied by settlements in which agriculture, craft industries and trade are all represented. In Limousin one immense oppidum dominated a tissue of farms and small hill-forts, in a more traditional, highland context; mining activity there has been too recent a discovery for it to have been integrated with other archaeological data. These perspectives remain provisional, as researchers have had to content themselves with putting forward interpretations in relation to those devised for the better-known regions of Berry and Burgundy, which we shall now look at.

EASTERN CENTRAL GAUL, AT THE CROSSROADS OF CELTIC EUROPE

Geography offers Burgundy a key position in both north–south and east–west contacts. At the western extremity of the Alpine arc, Vix, Autun, Vienne and Lyons are to be found at the apex of a fan-shaped zone which opens onto the valleys of the Loire, Seine, Saône-Rhône and Doubs, the last leading directly towards the Rhine. The historic record began earlier here than elsewhere in temperate France, and the phases of its development succeeded each other more rapidly.

Here, the First Iron Age had a remarkable final phase, being famous notably for its princely tombs. The Vix (Côte d'Or) princess was laid out in a burial chamber protected by a mound at the foot of the Mont Lassois fortified settlement. Next to a parade chariot encased in bronze fitments, which bears witness to the skills of local craftsmen, the famous vase tells of the close diplomatic links which linked local aristocrats to the distant Greek cities of southern Italy. Wine-drinking equipment and gold ornaments show the wealth and ostentatious way of life of an aristocracy which had taken advantage of its privileged relationship with Mediterranean societies in order to consolidate its power over the local population. We are at the heart of a 'prestige goods economy' which functioned perfectly in this area, readily open to commerce. At the foot of the Jura mountains and along the Doubs valley, burial mounds and neighbouring small upland fortified settlement sites have been identified, recalling the pattern known widely in the west Hallstatt province. Recent discoveries, at two locations within the town of Bourges, indicate that Greek pottery imports also reached Berry. Was the Avaricum of Caesar's text preceded by a major Hallstatt agglomeration? This hypothesis needs support from further discoveries, but is not at all unlikely.

Although the evidence from Hallstatt strongholds indicates aristocratic residences rather than proto-urban centres, such sites are, however, distinct from the mass of settlement units in the countryside because of a concentration on craft activities identifiable within them. One sees this in Germany at the Heuneburg, and the abundant artefacts recovered from Mont Lassois suggest a similar situation must have prevailed there.

A new perspective is offered by the results of excavations taking place at Bragny-sur-Saône (Saône-et-Loire). Here, evidence of the import of Mediterranean wares throughout the fifth century BC has been found on an unenclosed settlement set beside the river. This site is not merely a port for the break-in-bulk of materials which were destined for the hinterland. Craft activities were numerous and intensive, especially the iron-working industry. We may note on this site the beginnings of the combination of activities on a site which is clearly different from those which remain rooted in the traditional agricultural framework.

The extent of the influence of these long-distance exchanges has been shown by the discovery of a small hamlet at Lyon-Vaise. In a modest agricultural settlement near the Saône, Greek and Massaliote imports were discovered, demonstrating that imports were far from uniquely restricted to the princely sites.

In these eastern areas, the evidence from the early and middle La Tène periods is more diffuse than that of the late First Iron Age. Cemeteries have often been found through aerial survey, because of the cropmarks of the enclosures that surround the graves. A careful analysis of the contents of tombs allows regional fashions to be distinguished: grave goods, whether ceramics or weapons, vary from one group to another. During the past ten years, major rescue operations have revealed the presence of isolated farms and the indistinct remnants of field systems, but this evidence has not yet been adequately synthesized: its dating, too, is still subject to a considerable measure of uncertainty.

During the second century BC, the appearance of settlement agglomerations incorporating a mixture of agricultural and craft activities represented a new stage in the social and economic evolution of Gaul. Along the Saône, Doubs and Rhine but also away from the major river valleys as at Levroux (Indre) (Büchsenschütz 1988) or at Les Alleuds (Maine-et-Loire) (Dr Gruet, pers. comm.) field survey has by good fortune led to the identification of a series of settlements extending to 5 to 10 hectares which belong to this period. Close to the houses, which are generally poorly preserved, dozens of pits have been infilled with an extraordinarily abundant collection of objects: bones, pottery and also much evidence of craft activities. This last-mentioned is characterized first and foremost by the substantial quantities of associated waste that has been recovered. Iron slag and tapslag can be readily collected in quantity: tens of kilograms of such waste products are easily obtained. In addition, careful study of the material excavated from the pits reveals extremely specialized and standardized production. This applies not only to bronze- and ironworking, but also to the glass industry and to work in bone. Here, artisan production is no longer an individual activity of marginal significance in comparison with agriculture. The quantity and nature of the remains from these villages is indicative of the development of production by groups of artisans, representing a permanent activity conducted by an important group of individuals, who produced wealth by a new means. The increasing scale of metal production is marked, amongst other things, by the first substantial use of iron nails in assembling the timber frameworks of houses.

These settlements also provide us with clear evidence of active and strictly mercantile trade. Amphorae are the most obvious sign of this. Such containers are to be found in their thousands in the Saône valley, where one must picture river-ports at which the commodities were regularly unloaded. The numbers of amphorae are still substantial even at sites removed from the main river networks, as at Levroux or Les Alleuds. These are dominantly early, Republican amphorae (of Dressel 1a type), with some Graeco-Italic examples which indicate that this trade began as early as the second century BC. We have little information on the types of products which were exchanged for wine: doubtless cured pork, cloth, iron objects and slaves were important commodities. But the huge efforts of the Roman exporter to dispatch these heavy wine-jars north in substantial quantities is indicative of contacts of a wholly different nature from the glamorous presents sent by the Greeks to the Hallstatt princes to try to gain access to routes to the sources of tin.

The Gauls had entered into a rapidly developing economic system. The clearest indication of this is the production of coins in these little settlements. These are no longer heavy gold staters but lighter, less valuable, coinages struck in silver, with weights in line with western Greek and Roman standards so that they could be used in transactions. Many questions remain unanswered about the use and significance of these coinages. Were the flan-shaped moulds, which are frequently found on these settlements, used for the production of coins? What is the exact role of the cast bronze potin coinages which have distributions restricted precisely to central-east Gaul from an early date, possibly from the end of the second century BC? Did Massalia set these economic developments in train before the Roman annexation of Provence, or did that city manage subsequently to impose its standards, albeit temporarily, before the Roman merchants took over control of all the trade? It is in the fan-shaped area, centred on Lyons and defined above, that the answers to such questions will be found.

The tribal territory (*civitas*) of the Aedui lies in the heart of this zone. If one is to believe Caesar's evidence in *De Bello Gallico*, the Aedui made the most of the new economic situation, developing craft industries, long-distance trade links, and political alliances with Rome. The Sequani and Bituriges were not slow to follow this trend. This is borne out by the development of oppida in their territories, for such sites mark the last stage in the evolutionary development of still-independent Gaul.

For a long time, scholars considered that the development of craft industries and commerce, which we have just mentioned, were phenomena associated with the enclosed settlements termed 'oppida'. In this part of Gaul, at least, and as far east as the Rhine valley, oppida appear later than the artisan villages, with their ranges of diversified activities. At Levroux (Figure 29.8), for example, there is a physical shift from the lowland artisanal village upslope to the oppidum during the last century BC. The latter comes into existence as a result of a conscious move from the pre-existing settlement to a neighbouring hill, this latter surrounded by a rampart protecting about 20 hectares. The fortification of oppida is not limited to the weak points on their defensive circuits, those that natural topography does not protect. It is rather a matter of marking out the boundaries of a tract of territory with special characteristics than of simply ensuring defence. These sites maintained the tradition of fortification on high ground, perhaps because of its religious or symbolic value: permanent settlements were, however, installed within their enclosures, along with craft industries and commercial activities which seem paradoxical in such inaccessible places.

The case of Mont Beuvray (Saône-et-Loire/Nièvre), Caesar's Bibracte, is typical. A settlement, the inner enclosure around it covering 135 hectares, is perched on a summit in the Morvan uplands, at an altitude of 800 m 15 km from the neighbouring valleys. This enclosure is defined by a rampart forming an uninterrupted circuit and constructed in *murus gallicus* style – a prestige fortification with an internal timber framework into which thousands of long iron spikes have been augered. Its gates are gigantic, in the extreme case defined by a 20-m wide passage lying between two inturned sectors of fortification, over 40 m long (Figure 29.9). This effort to demarcate the settlement and to render the entrance to it so remarkable suggests that the settlement had a special status. A truly urban space has been isolated from the countryside, probably with its own laws and control over the movement of people and of merchandise. Within the settlement, crafts thrived, powerful inhabitants built themselves vast houses, and monumental collective constructions have been identified in the pre-Roman levels (Beck *et al.* 1987; Guillaumet 1987).

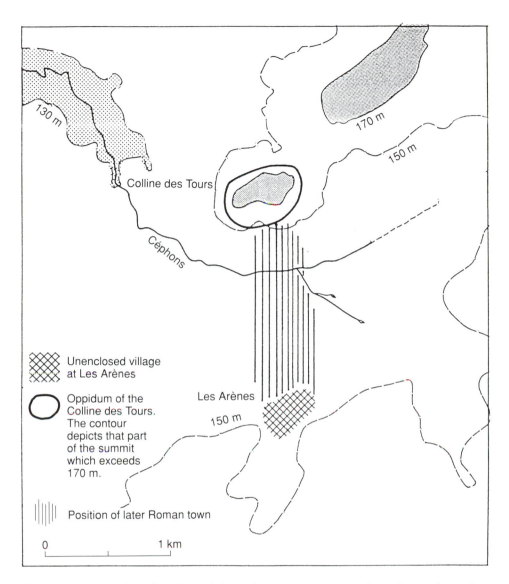

Figure 29.8 Successive relocations of the settlement at Levroux (Indre), after Büchsenschütz. Unenclosed settlement of middle/early Late (i.e. C/D1) La Tène date at Les Arènes; oppidum of the Colline des Tours; Roman town.

East-central Gaul is constantly mentioned in Caesar's text. It is where most of the oppida he names were located, where his allies were based, and also where the final act of the conquest was enacted. It would not have been possible to control the Germans, Belgae and Bretons for long, as they were tough fighters in battle and elusive on their own territories, if the east-central tribal territories (*civitates*), which were already partially integrated into the Mediterranean economy and heading towards urbanization, had not already been brought into line with the Roman political will.

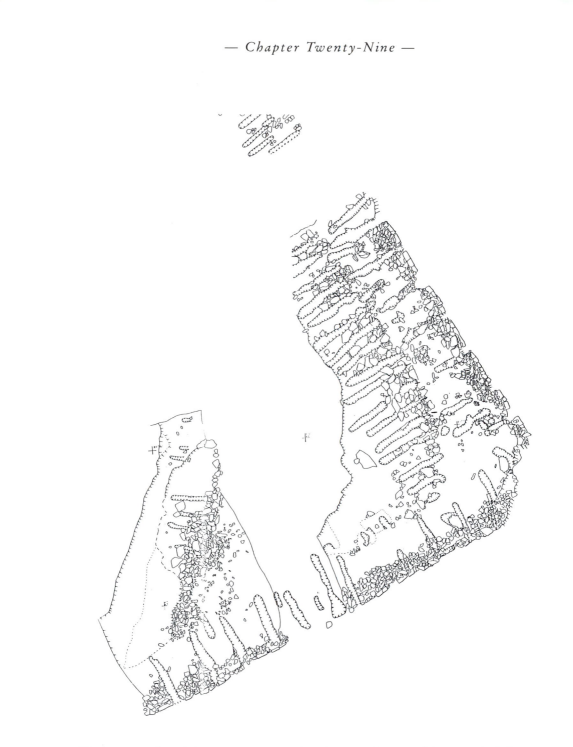

Figure 29.9 Plan of the *murus gallicus*-style defences at the start of the Porte du Rebout gateway at the oppidum of Mont Beuvray (Saône-et-Loire and Nièvre). The hachures ('tadpoles') define the positions of former timbering. (After O.Büchsenschütz, J.-P. Guillaumet and I. Ralston.)

The coalitions led by the Aedui, friends of the Roman people and active participants in international commerce, and the Arverni, the last Gallic champions of political and perhaps cultural resistance against the legions, were short-lived and opportunistic. On Caesar's testimony, the whole of Gaul was internally divided, both as regards its *civitates* (tribal units) and within individual families. The dilemma existed less at the scale of individual nations – an alliance with Rome being no more questionable than an accord with a neighbouring *civitas* – than at the level of the choice of life style. Urbanization or countryside, stone and mortar or earth and wood, Gallic ale or red wine? By 52 BC Gaul as far east as the Rhine had already oscillated in and out of the Mediterranean orbit for a long time, and thus the conquest was no more than a political and military formality to processes already long under way.

THE MEDITERRANEAN FRINGES

It would be an error to consider Celtic Gaul and the Mediterranean world as in absolute opposition. Gallic tribes and Mediterranean city-states, although divided by language and culture, had maintained close contacts for several centuries before the conquest led to their fusion. Provence and Languedoc, at the crossroads of the Rhône valley with the route between Italy and Spain, came under many influences. This is translated into an incredible wealth of archaeological remains in these areas, which display diverse cultural impacts. Research in this area has been advancing rapidly for forty years and here we can only outline the main results.

The indigenous population during the Iron Age was in contact with the colonizers, first the Phoenicians, and then with the Greeks who founded Massalia and Ampurias. Trading stations multiplied not only along the Mediterranean littoral, but also up the Rhône as far as Arles. The influence of these colonies on the indigenous way of life and its economy is very clear, even if the territory, up to the gates of Marseilles itself, was still controlled by the latter until the first century BC. The third-century Punic wars led Carthaginian and Roman armies to traverse the region and to conclude alliances that divided the local population, while favouring contacts with these Mediterranean cultures. Was it an extension of the Massaliote *chora*, or warlike tension on the part of the native population that provoked the conflicts of 125–120 BC? It was, in any case, a good pretext for the intervention of the Romans, who wanted to obtain a land link to their Spanish territories, to exploit a rich province and to ensure a base for their traders from which to extend northwards into the markets of Gaul.

The climate and vegetation of these southerly regions were different from those in the rest of the Celtic world, and geographical differences in themselves are sufficient to explain many differences between the way of life of their populations and those of more northerly residents. Thus the available building materials were stone and earth rather than wood. The need to erect structures to resist extremes of heat on one hand, and wind and storms on the other, led to an architecture which was radically different from that in more temperate parts of the country. It would be difficult for the archaeologist to identify cultural unity from material remains in the face of such different living conditions.

Archaeologists emphasize the modest dimensions of houses: a single room which hardly ever exceeded 15 square metres in the early period. Post-built structures were gradually replaced by those with weight-bearing walls, and wood was replaced by stone and above all earth-based materials. Recent excavations have uncovered numerous mudbrick or daub structures. Dwellings with several rooms or second storeys do not appear until the second century and become more common in the first century BC in the richer settlements.

Even though it has to be acknowledged that little is known about lowland settlements, because of difficulties in identifying them, the general tendency during the Iron Age seems to be towards the clustering of houses in hilltop sites. From the fourth century BC fortifications appear: their defences are nearly always dry-stone and enclose a large number of stone-built houses within a restricted area of, at most, several hectares. These buildings, identical in design and positioned in a clearly organized fashion along parallel streets, are indicative of the existence of established plans and by extension suggest highly organized societies. Forts like Nages (Gard) (Py 1978), Martigues (Bouches-du-Rhône) (Figure 29.10) (Chausserie-Laprée *et al.* 1985) and Lattes (Hérault) (Py 1988) show that this kind of pre-urban layout was widespread: it was also destined to continue in use for a very long time in these regions.

The recent resumption of excavations at Entremont (Bouches-du-Rhône) (Arcelin 1989) shows how this kind of settlement developed, at a late date, into a town. The earliest settlement at Entremont (190/170 BC), sometimes called the upper town, retained archaic charateristics, with small blocks of housing made up of identical huts backed onto a shared medial wall. In the more recent, lower town (laid out about 150/140 BC and surrounded by an imposing stone fortification), we can already see the organization of rooms into houses with three or four units, as well as working space for artisans, and the development of two-storey dwellings; public buildings make a first appearance. Specifically urban activities, such as craft industries and trade, appear before the Roman conquest here, but relatively late in the Iron Age. As elsewhere, these activities are focused on sites in regions that were nearest to the trade axes. In hundreds of little hilltop fortifications, scattered in the garrigue of Languedoc and especially in the hills of Provence, settlement continued on a modest scale and in the traditional manner.

Scholars have insisted on the survival of traditions inherited from the Bronze Age of the Midi. Society remained strictly family-based, and one can speak of a domestic economy dominated by agriculture. Though the Greek colonies could upset this autarchic set-up, they did not, however, manage to infiltrate the traditional social organization before the second century BC. A model of the economic development of these sites can be constructed on the basis of the identification of surpluses in local production and the quantification of the imported artefacts recovered from native settlements. At first, the presence of the Greeks stimulated production and exchange conferred benefits for both parties. In the middle phase of the Second Iron Age (400–100 BC), native settlements became poorer, indications of storage capacity for surpluses decreased and the tally of imports declined. M. Py sees a possible explanation for this in the intervention of Massalia, which would have gradually developed a more imperialistic policy towards the hinterland, putting a levy on its production and monopolizing trade (Py 1990: 199).

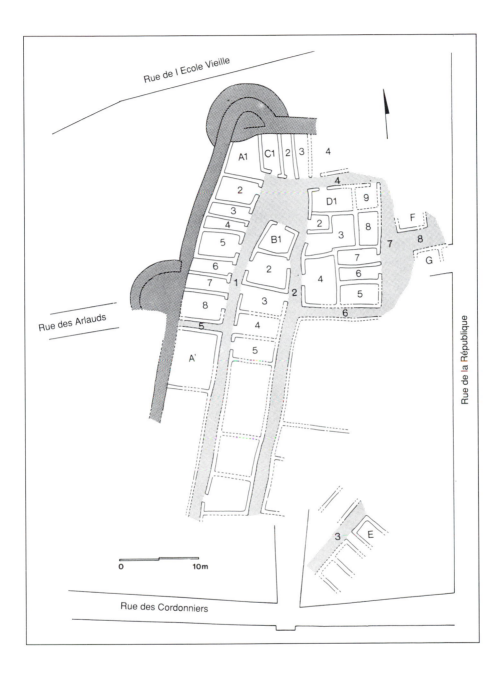

Figure 29.10 (a) General plan of the village at Martigues (Bouches du Rhône) and *overleaf* (b) reconstruction of a lane and of a house. (After Dessin D. Delpalillo, *Dossiers Histoire et Archéologie* No. 128, June 1988.)

(b)

Despite these distinctive characteristics, Languedoc and Provence have a number of points in common with the continental Celtic world. The development of craft industries, commerce and urbanization were characteristic of the second century BC in both areas. Numerous inscriptions on gravestones attest to the use of a Celtic language in Provence. The famous sanctuaries, such as those at Roquepertuse or Entremont, present an iconography, incised in stone, which is analogous with that of more northerly regions. In terms of more prosaic items, the metal artefacts from all periods of the Second Iron Age in the Midi are easier to parallel on the Swiss plateau than within Mediterranean cultures. Some objects may have been imported, but we know for example that bracelets and fibulae were produced in the Midi according to typical La Tène designs. In this respect, the south acted as an active, innovating province of La Tène culture.

To the west of this region, weapons from the cemetery at Ensérune, which are typical La Tène products, attest the permanent presence of warriors who fought like Celts. Should one deduce from this a borrowing of fighting styles by the local population, the presence of mercenaries, or the existence of a real colony of Celts? Recent research has shown that the local population had not fundamentally changed since the Late Bronze Age. It underwent and absorbed multiple influences, which were adapted to its distinctive natural environment. As often happens in Europe, as soon as the earliest written texts appear they describe the inhabitants as Celts. But we are not in a position to say whether the latter were native, whether they were mixed with an earlier population or whether they had replaced such groups.

THE PRINCIPAL RESEARCH DIRECTIONS

Against a rich and solid literary tradition, the archaeology of the Iron Age in France has revived, thanks to the development of aerial prospection and to the great increase in excavation and field research. In schoolbooks, parallels are no longer drawn between the benefits of French colonization and the opportunities that romanization conferred on Gaul. Increased appreciation of the fact that the flowering of Roman Gaul was underpinned by earlier developments in the country has also served to refocus research. Our views are based nowadays on a permanent dialogue between texts and archaeological evidence. The celticization of Gaul seems both earlier and more widespread than had previously been believed.

In Champagne and adjacent regions, cultural continuity from late Hallstatt to early La Tène has been demonstrated from cemetery evidence. Very similar burial traditions have been widely identified in Gaul, only Armorica and the south of Aquitaine retaining distinctive funerary rituals. Above all, our knowledge of the cemeteries of Middle and Late La Tène periods has advanced in recent years. The presence of enclosures and post-built structures within cemeteries suggests social distinctions which remain to be analysed in detail. Moreover, it is certain that aristocratic tombs, marked by the presence of a chariot and/or by the accoutrements of banqueting, continue throughout the Second Iron Age from Brittany to Alsace and from Picardy to Aquitaine.

This aristocracy was settled on big rural estates, which acted as the foci for the main economic and political strengths of the country, prior to the appearance of the oppida. Hill-forts, traditionally an element of protohistoric settlement patterns, seem to have been abandoned during the Early and Middle La Tène periods. The population was scattered across the countryside, where the expansion of agriculture ensured its wealth. It was not until the second century BC that settlements of 5 to 10 hectares – similar in size to the forts of the Midi – were created, in the middle of rich agricultural areas, such as happened at Levroux (Indre) or Aulnat (Puy-de-Dôme). New activities such as craft industries and commerce appeared there and were sufficiently important to have allowed some of the inhabitants to specialize in them. Iron tools, good-quality pottery, and standardized jewellery produced in multiple copies in complex moulds were made by professionals and sold, thanks to the appearance of low-value coins which facilitated trade, to families whose domestic production was rapidly withering.

Oppida develop in Gaul after the formation of these craft- and commerce-based villages. The presence of spectacular defences intimates a military role for these sites, of course, but this is not for us the essential element in the explanation of their development. There is no doubt that oppida represent a return to the hill-fort tradition. Such sites, since the Bronze Age, had acted as foci for the existence of communities, possibly enhanced by being the settings for festivals and meetings; they provided, too, for common defence. How else can one explain the placing of commercial and craft centres on summits which were distant from trade routes, as happened at Mont Beuvray, for example? Oppida display the characteristics of towns. They are deliberate foundations; complete circuits of enclosure separate the site from the surrounding countryside; monumental gateways giving access to the interior; agricultural, craft and business activities are all represented; and there is evidence for the construction of the first public buildings. But the frequent selection of locations on high ground to construct oppida meant that these sites were destined to be short-lived. Whilst their *floruit* in Gallia Comata is to be sought after, rather than before, the war with Caesar, they were generally abandoned in the first century AD in favour of settlements in the lowlands.

Sanctuaries, which form the third element in recent research about Gaul, display considerable similarities throughout the land (Brunaux 1991). Since the excavations at Gournay-sur-Aronde, discoveries of deliberately sacrificed La Tène weapons or of wooden structures under Gallo-Roman *fana* have multiplied. These sanctuaries are complex entities, with buildings, which would have required the presence of an active priesthood, for example to oversee sacrifices. Such a perspective is far from the traditional image we have – of the collection of mistletoe and visits to sacred springs. There is evidence of the rectangular enclosures known as *Viereckschanzen*, which survive more particularly in the forests of the west and in the south of the Paris Basin. Their function (as places of worship, for occasional meetings or for feasting) remains difficult to determine, but their date, whenever this has been obtained, is always within the La Tène period.

In none of these systems – settlements, funerary ritual, or religion – can we recognize an abrupt break with romanized Gaul. We have serious, if not conclusive, arguments to say that romanized villa farms succeeded their Gallic predecessors, the *aedificia* of Caesar, Roman cemeteries their Celtic predecessors, and the rural temples of Gallo-Roman times (*fana*), the earlier sanctuaries. It is the establishment of the major settlements in lowland settings, and the development of Roman-style – and especially masonry – architecture, that mark the most drastic change from what had previously been the norm. But the rural landscapes, and the buildings and people they contained, did not change. The mixing of traditions was rapid and complete, such that Roman troops soon left Gaul in order to ensure the defence of all its inhabitants on the Rhine frontier.

The celticization of nearly the whole of Gaul during the Iron Age seems evident. The movement of Celtic groups is also beyond question, but never during this period were they on such a scale that they led to the expulsion or annihilation of the indigenous populations. There are thus no complete breaks in the material culture record.

REFERENCES

Braudel, F. (1986) 'L'identité de la France', *Espace et Histoire*, Paris: Artaud. *The Identity of France*, vol. 1 *History and Environment*. Trans. Siân Reynolds, London: Collins.

Brunaux, J.-L. (1991) (éd.), *Les sanctuaires celtiques et le monde méditerranéen*, Dossiers de Protohistoire, 3, Paris: Editions Errance.

Büchsenschütz, O. *et al. L'évolution du canton de Levroux d'après les prospections et les sondages archéologiques*, *Revue Archéologique du Centre*, Suppl. Sér. 1, Tours.

Beck, F. *et al.* (1987) 'Les fouilles du Mont-Beuvray, Rapport biennal', *Revue Archéologique de l'Est et du Centre-Est*, 38, pp. 5–300; ibid. 39, 1988, p. 107; ibid. 1989, 40, p. 205.

Bellon, C. Burnouf, J., Martin, J.-M., Verot-Bourelly, A. (1988) 'Une occupation du premier Age du Fer à Lyon-Vaise', in F. Audouze and O. Büschsenschütz (eds) *Architectures des Ages de Métaux*: fouilles récentes, 2, Dossiers de protohistoire, Paris: Editions Errance, 55–66.

Bulliot, J.-G. (1899) *Les fouilles du mont Beuvray*, Autun, 2 vols.

Castagné, E. (1874) 'Mémoire sur les ouvrages de fortifications de Murcens d'Uxellodunum et de l'Impernal (Luzech), situés dans le département du Lot', *Congrès Archéologique de France*, 41, 427–538.

Cauuet, B. (1991) 'L'exploitation de l'or en Limousin, des Gaulois aux Gallo-Romains', *Annales du Midi*, 103, 149–81.

Chausserie-Laprée, J. *et al.* (1985) *Le quartier de l'île à Martigues, Musée d'Art et d'Archéologie*, Martigues.

Déchelette, J. (1914) *Manuel d'archéologie préhistorique, celtique et gallo-romaine*, 4, *Second Age du Fer ou époque de La Tène*, Paris: Picard.

Demoule, J.-P. (1982) 'L'analyse archéologique des cimetières et l'exemple des nécropoles celtiques', in G. Gnoli and J.-P. Vernant (éds) *La mort, les morts dans les sociétés anciennes*, Paris: Maison des Sciences de l'Homme, and Cambridge: Cambridge University Press.

Daire, M.-Y. (1987) 'Les céramiques armoricaines à l'Age du Fer', University of Rennes, unpublished Ph.D. thesis.

Dion, R. (1977) *Aspects politiques de la géographie antique*, Paris: Les Belles Lettres.

Dom Martin Bouquet, (1738–9) 'Rerum gallicarum et francicarum scriptores, Recueil des historiens de la Gaule et de la France', Paris, 1, 2, 1739.

Duval, A. (1977) 'Deux objets pseudo-filigranés de La Tène', *Antiquités nationales*, 9: 40–2.

—— (1990) 'L'Armorique vue du continent', in *La Bretagne et l'Europe préhistorique, mémoire en l'honneur de P.-R. Giot, Revue Archéologique de l'Ouest*, Suppl. Ser. 2, 279–86.

Duval, A., Le Bihan, J.P. and Menez, Y. (eds) (1990) *Les gaulois d'Armorique*, Actes XII Coll. HAFEAF, *Revue Archéologique de l'Ouest*, Suppl. Ser. 3, Rennes.

Goudineau, C. and Peyre, C. (1993) *Bibracte et les Eduens: A la découverte d'un peuple gaulois*, Paris: Errance.

Guillaumet, J.-P. (1987) *Bibracte, une ville gauloise sur le mont Beuvray*, Guides archéologiques de la France, Paris: Ministère de la Culture et de la Communication: Impréimerie Nationale.

Boudet, R. (1987) *L'Age du fer récent dans la partie méridionale de l'estuaire girondin*, Périgueux: Editions Vesuna.

Brunaux, J.-L. (1988) *The Celtic Gauls: gods, rites and sanctuaries*, London: Seaby.

Guillaumet, J.-P. (1982) 'Le matériel du tumulus de Celles, (Cantal)', in J. Collis *et al. Le deuxième Age du fer en Auvergne et en Forez*, Sheffield: Sheffield University, Centre d'Etudes Foréziennes, St Etienne, 189–213.

Guiomar (1982) 'Nos ancêtres les gaulois', Proceedings of the international colloquium of Clermont-Ferrand, P. Viallaneix and J. Ehard (éds), University of Clermont-Ferrand, 13.

Hawkes, C.F.C. (1958) 'The hill-forts of northern France', *Antiquity* 32: 154–62.

Jullian, C. (1907) *Histoire de la Gaule*, I, Paris.

Kruta, V. (1985) 'Le port d'anneaux de chevilles en Champagne et le problème d'une immigration danubienne au IIIe siècle avant J.-C.', *Etudes celtiques* 22: 27–51.

Lejars, T. (1987) *Quelques considérations sur le second Age du Fer dans le Grand Ouest*, D.E.A. University of Paris I, unpublished DEA dissertation.

Olivier, L. and Büchsenschütz, O. (éds) (1989), *Les Viereckschanzen et les enceintes quadri-latérales en Europe celtique*, Actes du IX Coll. HAFEAF.

Py, M. (1988) *Lattara* 1, Lattes: Edition de l'Association pour la Recherche Archéologique en

Languedoc Oriental.
—— (1990) *Culture, économie et société protohistoriques dans le région nîmoise*, Collection de l'Ecole française de Rome, 131, 2 vols, Rome.
—— (1993) *Les Gaulois du Midi*, Paris: Hachette.
Ralston, I.B.M. (1992) *Les enceintes fortifiées du Limousin*, D.A.F. 36, Paris.
Viallaneix, P. and Ehrard, J. (1982) *Nos ancêtres les Gaulois*, Proceedings of the international colloquium of Clermont-Ferrand, University of Clermont-Ferrand II, 13, 395–492.

CELTS OF EASTERN EUROPE

———— •◆• ————

Elizabeth Jerem

INTRODUCTION AND HISTORY OF RESEARCH

Before we start to look at recent developments in the study of eastern Celtic culture, it is necessary to review past discoveries.

At the beginning of this century, Reinecke (1902, 1911, [1965]) pointed out that Celtic artefacts show not only chronological but also regional differences. He was describing the earliest La Tène grave goods from north-east Bavaria; and by comparing these with chronologically similar materials he was able to conclude that the eastern provinces were quite distinct within the La Tène area. The most important characteristic of this eastern material is that it bears witness to strong links with Italy, especially with the Venetic culture (Jacobsthal 1944; Kruta 1986; Moosleitner 1985, 1991; Pauli 1991, 1994). The Veneti also functioned as middlemen through whom Etruscan cultural traits were transmitted to their Celtic neighbours north of the Alps.

It was not until much later that Reinecke's fundamental observations concerning the eastern early La Tène culture and its marked connection with the classical world were corroborated by later finds and new research. Kossack (1982) sums up the history of research in his study 'Südbayern im 5. Jahrhundert v. Chr. Zur Frage der Überlieferungskontinuität'. In this he draws particular attention to the rise of the Illyrian theory in the early 1930s (Kersten 1933). At about this time Bittel (1934) and later Giessler-Kraft (1942 [1950]) felt justified in proposing that a Celtic population could already be identified in the middle Rhine area and in south-west Germany during the Hallstatt period. They noted, like Kersten, that the Hallstatt cemeteries show a continuity of population. The same situation could not be readily assumed for the eastern area, since at that time no characteristic late Hallstatt or early La Tène material had been identified in those parts. For this reason and in particular because of the lack of comparable western early La Tène artefacts, it was generally believed that the Hallstatt culture, or the population groups with whom it was associated, had continued in the whole eastern area into the early La Tène. Only the individuals buried in 'flat cemeteries' were regarded as 'Celts', and considered to be immigrants in the sense of ethnically intrusive, the concept favoured by these authors (Hunyady 1944; Pittioni 1954, 1959; Willvonseder 1953). By way of a compromise it was believed that the Hallstatt culture had continued until the arrival of the 'Celts'. An alternative view of the Celts, held at the same time, was that they had appeared in the east with a distinct cultural assemblage which they brought with them from their 'Urheimat' and by means of which they could be identified. For this reason, scholars used to speak of a 'La Tène-ized Hallstatt population' of Celts, and of the continued co-existence of two separate cultures (Zürn 1942, 1952; and papers in: *Hamburger Beiträge zur Archäologie* 1972). An important publication in the field of Celtic study was that by Jan Filip (1956), later published in English as well (1976). He also carried out the typological and chronological evaluation of the material at his disposal at the time. This work provided the basis of all subsequent research for a long time.

Recent research has concentrated on establishing detailed fine chronologies of specific types of finds and of their particular characteristics, such as forms and decoration of pottery (Dehn 1951, 1962/3, 1964, 1969; Schwappach 1973, 1975, 1979; Gosden 1984, 1987), and on working out horizons characterized by the chronologically most sensitive types and assemblages of grave goods (Parzinger 1988).

An increasing number of excavations of settlements and cemeteries contemporary with them have offered improved opportunities to classify the artefacts according to chronological as well as functional principles. It became clear that there exists, in the eastern province, a number of sites where there is evidence for continuous occupation and where it is possible to distinguish the latest Hallstatt from the La Tène A phase. With regard to this, the Dürrnberg grave groups are of particular importance because here we can assume uninterrupted usage as well as witness the continuity of culture change from the late Hallstatt period onwards (Penninger 1972; Moosleitner *et al.* 1974; Pauli 1978, 1980). In addition, the key position of the site in topographical terms makes it possible to trace the influence of diverse cultures and to chart the widespread contacts of the local population. It is also of great importance that the assemblages of grave goods found at these cultural complexes, and the chronological indicators derived from them, serve as a link between the western and eastern territories. Results of intensive field surveys and settlement excavations not only provide an insight into everyday life in a traditional sense. Depending on the site's specific character, they also permit observations relevant to stratigraphy, architectural techniques and relative chronology. Excavations at the so-called 'industrial quarters' or workshops as well as in the salt-mines are worthy of mention here. The good preservation of artefacts (e.g. wooden vessels, various implements) and palaeoecological studies carried out in such areas can reveal entirely new aspects that enhance our previous observations (Fischer 1984; Maier 1974; Pauli 1974; Zeller 1984, 1989; Stöllner 1991; 1995). Figure 30.1 illustrates one of the most impressive products of local metalworking which has incorporated both stylistic and methodological elements (Moosleitner 1985, 1991; Megaw and Megaw 1989a).

Further to the east there is substantial evidence – mainly obtained from an increasing number of recent excavations – of the emergence of the early La Tène culture. In spite of local differences the overriding impression is of cultural similarity.

Figure 30.1 Bronze wine-flagon from Grave 112 at Dürrnberg bei Hallein, Austria (second half of the fifth century BC or early fourth century BC). Museum Carolino Augusteum, Salzburg. (After Moosleitner 1985.)

CELTIC BURIAL PRACTICE AND GRAVE GOODS

At this time in the west, early La Tène burials occur mostly as secondary deposits in burial mounds of the preceding Hallstatt period. For this reason this period is referred to as the 'Hügelgräber-LT' (burial-mound LT) (Krämer 1985). By contrast in the eastern province – in Bavaria, Austria, Bohemia, Moravia, south-west Slovakia and western Hungary – flat cemeteries appear in considerable numbers at the end of the sixth century BC, and some are much earlier than this (Jerem 1987). These cemeteries are characterized by the contemporary co-existence of inhumation and cremation burials. In the case of the latter, the cremated remains are either deposited in urns or else placed directly in the soil (Figure 30.2). These differences may reflect factors such as sex, age, social status or ethnic group (Neugebauer 1992; Jerem 1992). A detailed comparative analysis of cemeteries excavated under modern conditions is still outstanding, but when this is available it will provide the key to reinterpreting some of the earlier cemetery excavations. It is, nevertheless, possible to observe certain trends in burial rite. Cremation continued to be common in the eastern area throughout the Hallstatt period. Inhumations occur in parallel with cremations but increase in number during the second half of the phase.

Figure 30.2 Decorated terracotta vase with handles terminating in rams' heads of a cremation grave from Csobaj (third century BC). (After Hellebrandt 1989, courtesy of Hermann Ottó Múzeum, Miskolc.)

Large-scale cemetery excavations (for example Franzhausen, Reichersdorf, Herzogenburg, Oberndorf, Ossarn in the Traisen valley, Lower Austria; Bučany in southwest Slovakia; Sopron-Krautacker and Pilismarót-Basaharc in Transdanubia) provide material for statistical analysis which shows how the ratio of the two burial types changes over time. Cremation became rarer and towards the end of the La Tène A period it disappeared altogether. The custom came into fashion again at the transition between the early and middle La Tène (Bujna-Romsauer 1983; Čižmař 1970, 1975; Jerem 1981a, 1981b, 1986; Kutzián 1975, Neugebauer 1985, 1992; Pauli 1978; Waldhauser 1987).

The most important burials were enclosed by circular or rectangular ditches and were often marked by roughly finished stelae, or by simple stones. The grave pit (chamber) itself was often elaborately constructed using stone settings, lining with stones or covering with stones; wooden linings and wooden coffins were also common. Most of the burials show a regular south–north or south-west–north-west orientation (Lorenz 1978, 1980; Waldhauser 1987).

In cases in which the more recent early La Tène inhumations overlie older cremations or inhumations of the Hallstatt period, it is possible not only to make fine stratigraphic deductions, but also to show graphically how this orientation differs from the east–west direction favoured in Hallstatt times. The existence of multiple and consecutive burials in various forms allows one to begin to think in terms of family groups.

A recent analysis of the human skeletal material deriving from the eastern part of Austria furnishes valuable data not only of morphological or typological features but also regarding the population size and mortality rate of the early Celtic inhabitants (Renhart 1990a, 1990b, 1992). A continuity in both culture and population – similar to that observed among the western Celts – exists in the eastern province also. Here too there is significant typological heterogeneity and strong continuity of the earlier iron age population.

The major feature which distinguishes the eastern group from the west is the custom of providing the dead with food and drink (joints of meat, iron knives and pottery) (Figure 30.3); this is a continuation of Hallstatt rituals. Animal bones included in such deposits were always accompanied by a special knife (*Haumesser*) (Osterhaus 1981) and were most commonly from pig, followed by cattle, sheep and chicken. Sets of drinking vessels and sometimes cooking pots consisted mostly of types in use in domestic contexts and known from settlement excavations.

Pottery manufactured in local workshops shows a strong continuity of development until the introduction of new technology: the potter's wheel. This led to both an increase in productivity and standardization in form. Decoration now reflected the new technology – for example cordons and grooves – and was integral to the form of the pot rather than being applied after the pot itself was made. Wheel-thrown wares appear already during the course of the fifth century BC (Dehn 1962/3; Lang 1974, 1976). In addition to the flask-shaped vessels (*Linsenflasche*) (Voigt 1969; Schwappach 1975, 1979) and bowls characteristic of the eastern alpine region (Dehn 1951), there is a special form of cup decorated with high handles which terminate either in the form of animal heads or alternatively animal horns (Jerem 1981a, 1987).

Decoration typical of the Hallstatt period, such as graphite painting and burnishing, was used into the early La Tène period. At the same time, stamped decoration was very popular. This decoration occurred initially on the outer surface of the pots (particularly flasks and bowls) and on the interior of drinking vessels. These stamps comprise a combination of circles and other shapes; cylinder stamps were also used. The designs were imitations of classical decoration and particular to metal vessels. It is of interest to note that the stamped decoration was sometimes effected with metal working tools (e.g. punches) and that the pottery vessels themselves were often skeuomorphs closely imitative in both form and decoration of metal prototypes (Figure 30.4) (Schwappach 1973; Jerem 1974–5, 1984). Several manufacturing centres can be identified by means of analysing the fabric of the pots and their stylistic features and methods of decoration. Interdisciplinary investigation of the clay and inclusions used to temper it and of samples taken from pottery (petrographic and chemical analyses) conducted in Bohemia and western Hungary (Kardos *et al.* 1985; Gosden 1984, 1987; Jerem 1984; Salač 1992) prove that stamped ware is not only associated with particular workshops, but that it is also traded by means of a regional distribution network, which can, to some extent, be traced. There is certainly evidence of trans-regional contacts. Recently, the investigation of graphite-tempered pottery produced very similar results. In this case the relationship of sources of raw material, connected workshops and market areas has been analysed (Waldhauser 1992, 1994).

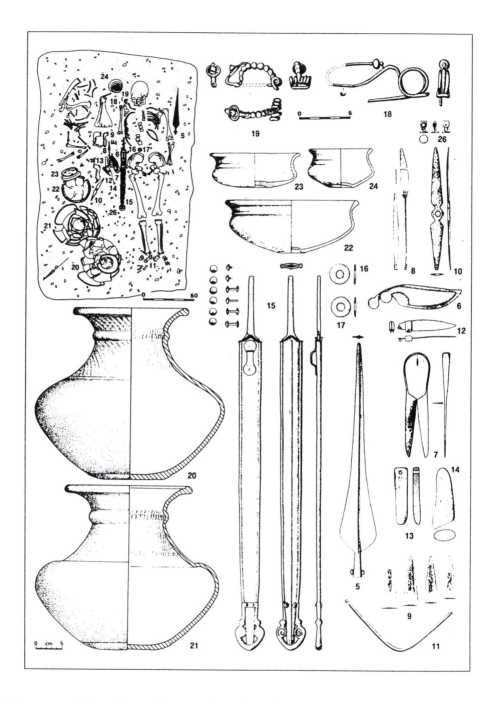

Figure 30.3 'Doctor's grave', no. 520 from Pottenbrunn cemetery. City Museum St Pölten, Lower Austria (fourth century BC). (After Neugebauer 1992.)

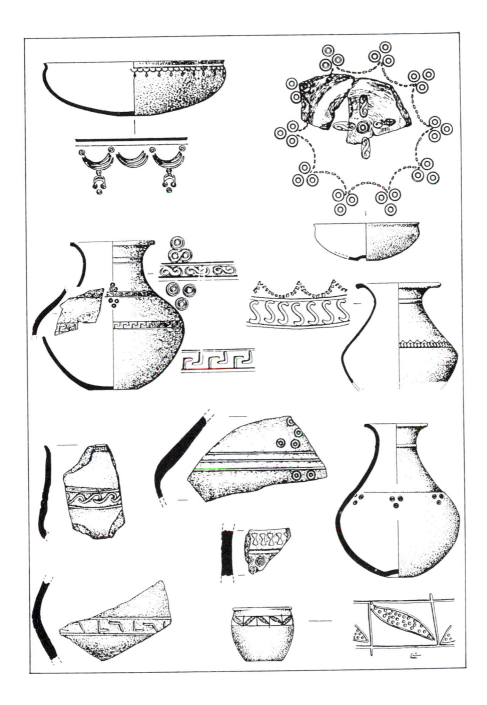

Figure 30.4 Early Celtic stamp-decorated pottery from Sopron-Krautacker workshop, Archaeological Institute of the HAS, Budapest, Hungary (fifth–third century BC).

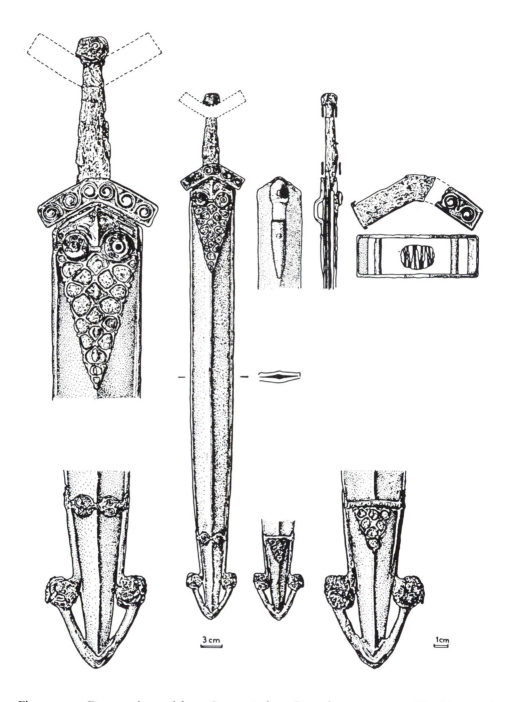

Figure 30.5 Decorated sword from Grave 562 from Pottenbrunn cemetery, City Museum St Pölten, Lower Austria (fourth century BC). (After Neugebauer-Gottringer 1984, also in Neugebauer 1991 and 1992.)

WEAPONRY AND DRESS

At the beginning of the early La Tène period, the grave assemblages can also be shown to retain Hallstatt cultural elements. This is true for weaponry and for style of dress – in both, close contacts with northern Italy and Slovenia are apparent. The addition of lances to the warrior's equipment in eastern Celtic graves accords well with male graves in other contemporary cemeteries. Lances are part of standard equipment for warriors, as can be deduced from representations of fighting men on situlae (Frey 1968, 1969; Stary 1981a, 1981b). Battle-axes were used predominantly in the south-east alpine regions; they occur less commonly in the north. Sword and scabbards from well-dated grave complexes were current from the fifth century BC onwards. The scabbard and chape-end were particularly finely decorated in many of the earlier examples (Figure 30.5). The sword was initially worn with a belt (Figure 30.6) and was only later suspended from a chain (Rapin and Brunaux 1988; Rapin 1993; Szabó-Petres 1992).

In early examples, triangular perforated belt-hooks were attached to the leather and often have decoration with an apotropaic function (Lenerz-de Wilde 1980; Megaw and Megaw 1989b; Serafini 1984, 1993). Their distribution has important centres in northern Italy and also in the eastern Alpine region. In recent years there has been a major controversy over the question of whether the previously mentioned artefactual assemblages described from Venetian cemeteries could be regarded as

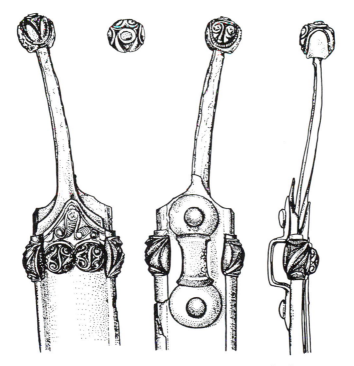

Figure 30.6 'Plastic'-decorated sword from the Szob cemetery (third century BC, Hungarian National Museum, Budapest). (After Szabó and Petres 1992.)

evidence for the early appearance of Celts in Italy (Frey 1987, 1991b). Alternatively, it has been suggested that the distribution of these objects may be a side effect of trade links of key importance. Trading between Italy and the areas north of the Alps intensified following the end of the sixth century BC. This latter region was of outstanding importance for the emergence of La Tène culture (Kruta 1983, 1986, 1991).

The same is true of rectangular belt-plates/plaques which, in addition to the masked figures, have certain motifs and decorative techniques which reflect cultural contact with the Etruscans and the Veneti (e.g. Ossarn, Stupava, etc.) (Megaw, Megaw and Neugebauer 1989). Box-shaped iron belt-hooks occur by the time of the most recent La Tène A horizon and are predominantly associated with early La Tène *Draht-* (wire) or bird-head fibulae (Parzinger 1988).

The range of fibulae in the Celtic east shows, as it did in the earlier part of the Iron Age, a strong affinity with eastern alpine types (Figure 30.7). People initially wore bow- or boat-shaped fibulae or the local variants of these, and later the various types

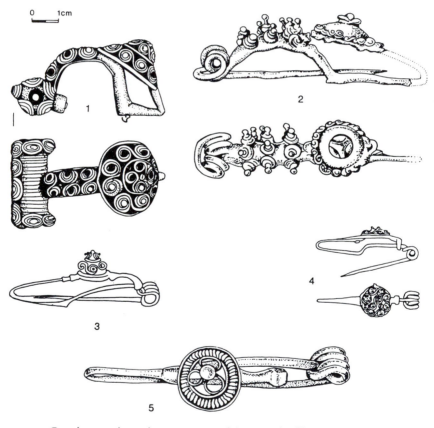

Figure 30.7 Cast-bronze brooches ornamented in 'pseudo-filigree' manner from flat grave cemeteries. 1 – Rezi, Balatoni Museum Keszthely, Hungary; 2 – Cluj, History Museum Cluj, Romania; 3, 5 – Osijek, Museum Osijek Hrvatska; 4 – Brežice, Posavski Museum, Slovenija (third–second century BC). (After Szabó 1992.)

of Certosa fibulae. The fibulae of the Hallstatt/La Tène transition are hybrid forms. They are correctly interpreted – like the La Tène foot-shaped fibulae – as distinctive variants of the latest Hallstatt crossbow fibulae. The fibulae with *bandförmigen Bügel*(?) and bent-back footplates are a similar case. They not only show advanced typological features, but they are also decorated with La Tène motifs.

The animal-form fibulae hybrid forms and so-called exceptional forms area of particular interest because they can often shed light on the development of particular stylistic elements (Pauli 1978; Binding 1993).

The late La Tène A phase is also characterized by the eastern alpine animal-head fibulae. Their distribution stretches as far as the periphery of the eastern early La Tène cultural province and is densely concentrated in the inner alpine region. They occur quite frequently at sites where a connection with the south and south-east is suggested by other finds (Jerem 1968; Parzinger 1988; Teržan 1976, 1990).

Women's and children's burials are characterized by a great variety of neck ornaments (Figure 30.8). The composition of bead necklaces (beads of glass, amber, coral and cowrie shells) allows different trade networks to be traced; while amulets may be suggestive of commonly held religious beliefs or superstitions (Pauli 1975; Venclová 1990).

Apart from the neck-rings, which may indicate special status in society or in the family, we have arm- and foot-rings too; their number and place within the graves shows regional differences (Lorenz 1978; Bujna 1982).

SETTLEMENT AND HOUSING

Early La Tène settlements present a rather uniform picture as far as topographical position and internal layout are concerned. The economy was based primarily upon agriculture and cattle-rearing. A variety of handicrafts (cottage industries) and the exchange of these products also contributed in large measure to the subsistence economy. Further information about the everyday life of the early Celtic population can be anticipated when the results of recent large-scale excavations are fully available for analysis. Fieldwalking and excavated sites have revealed that open settlements do not occur at a height of more than 300 m (for economic and agricultural reasons). The research on some micro-regions in Bohemia, Moravia and Lake Fertő has shown that the settlement network was extremely well ordered, with settlements laid out at regular distances from one another – between 1.5 and 3 km. Most of the villages have two or more cemeteries. The most common house form is a rectangular structure, with the substantial postholes in the short side (Figure 30.9). These huts measure between 12 and 25 square metres. The smaller sized ones may be workshops. The larger sized houses with hearths are assumed to be intended for habitation. They were sunk into the ground for 40–50 cm, had wattle-and-daub walls and probably had sloping roofs. Pits and four-post storage structures complete the picture (Figure 30.10) (Audouze and Büchsenschütz 1992; Meduna 1980; Jerem 1986; Waldhauser 1986, 1993).

Only indirect evidence of the field systems exists, i.e. cropmarks. No aerial photographs or excavations have been carried out with the aim of accurately

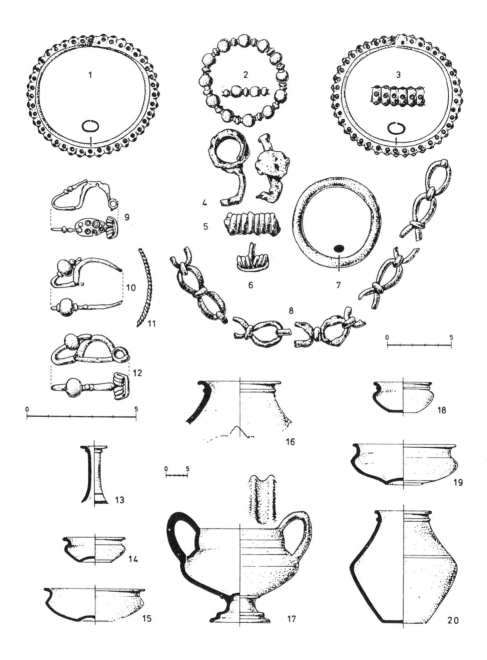

Figure 30.8 Grave goods of a female burial no. 21 from the flat grave cemetery at Chotin, District Komarno, Slovakia (early third century BC). (After Ratimorska 1981.)

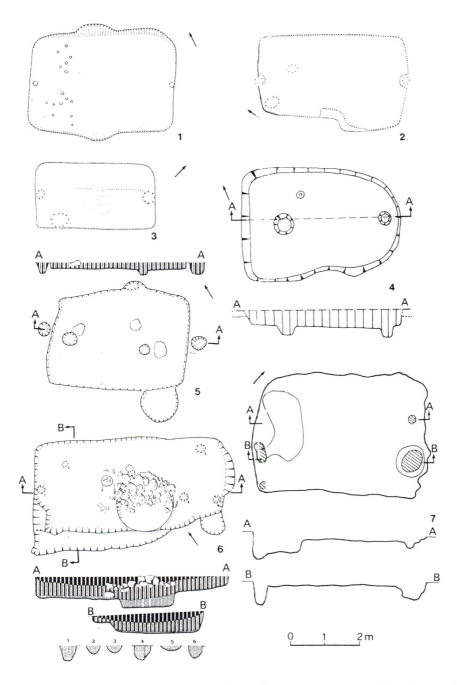

Figure 30.9 Rectangular structures from Celtic settlement sites. 1, 2, 3 – Velké Hosteradký (after Čižmař 1984); 4 – Lužice (after Salač and Smrž 1989); 5, 6 – Radovesice (after Waldhauser 1977); 7 – Sopron-Krautacker. (Combined by Jerem 1985.)

Figure 30.10 Model of the fortified settlement at Manching, Bavaria – based on excavation evidence. (After Gebhart 1993.)

surveying the topographical setting and the extent of cultivated land. Still, a relatively exact picture of Celtic crop cultivation may be reconstructed on the basis of samples gathered from water-sieving at more advanced excavations (Jerem *et al.* 1985; Jerem 1986; Waldhauser 1986, Waldhauser *et al.* 1993; Küster 1991, 1993; Gyulai 1994). The major crop was wheat, followed by rye, barley and millet. Vegetables included mostly pulses, beans, etc; of the industrial crops, flax was cultivated and pressed as well. Evidence for both the consumption and ritual interment of wild and domestic fruits is also known from this period. Some such plant remains are clearly recognizable among grave goods. Pollen diagrams contribute additional information concerning the natural vegetation and climate.

Animal husbandry was also a significant part of the economy. Excavations are chiefly characterized by meat consumption, while animal remains brought to light from graves seem rather to illustrate religious beliefs. Settlement debris revealed a dominance of bones of domestic pig and cow, followed by the remains of sheep and goat. In addition, domestic fowl also start to occur at this time. Hunted animals make up only a very small proportion of the refuse material but they include large game such as wild pig and red deer. These two wild animal species also had a cultic significance.

INDUSTRIAL ACTIVITY, HANDCRAFT

Stone and wood were worked on a small-scale basis in the settlements. There is evidence for iron industry only from La Tène D. The eastern alpine region (Burgerland) had an important role in iron production – roasting hearths to separate the worst of the dross from the ore-bearing rocks. We have evidence that the iron-ore roasting took place on hearths located outside the settlements whereas the smelting occurred inside. A furnace was found at the Sopron settlement. In Burgerland (eastern Austria) there is evidence of the roasting hearths outside the settlements. The smithing activity appears to have taken place in the settlement also – metalworking tools support this. There is no direct evidence for the bronze industry, but it must be remembered that few settlements have been excavated.

A change in settlement structure occurred during the first century BC. Some of the Hallstatt period fortified sites which had been abandoned were settled again and refortified. We know of perhaps one fortified settlement which has no predecessor in the Hallstatt period. The appearance of these defended sites may be connected with the internal fighting between tribes (Dacian wars, Bureebistas, etc.) or with the Roman occupation from the south-west.

These fortified settlements function as centres for industry, administration, re-distribution of products, trade and religion. This period marks the last flourishing of the iron industry, producing agricultural tools of a type used into the medieval period. Coinage is also connected with the fortified centres, which are mint sites (Szalacska, Regöly/southern Transdanubia). Imitations of Philip's tetradrachms in silver were the first coins minted by Celtic tribes – the Scordisci around Belgrade and the Boii around Bratislava. The inscriptions on these coins indicates a knowledge of Roman script (Figure 30.11).

The development of mass-produced pottery in a limited number of forms occurred in this period. Painted pottery resulted from western contacts (Manching, Basle). Pottery production was centred on oppida along the Danube, in contact with Manching and some of the Swiss sites. The most significant aspect of these well-developed industries is that they continue into the Roman period and are recognizable in the first century AD. Recently published work by D. Gábler indicates that some of the villages around the fortified oppida continued in operation into the Roman period.

Figure 30.11 Celtic silver coin, type of Réte (first half of the first century BC). (Courtesy of the Hungarian National Museum, Budapest.)

The possibility of synchronizing different types of evidence, the recently established chronological phases of the western and eastern find complexes, and the establishment of a relative chronology within each phase will continue to shed new light on the origin of the early La Tène culture.

REFERENCES

Audouze, F. and Büchsenschütz, O. (1992) *Towns, Villages and Countryside of Celtic Europe*, London: Batsford.

Die Ausgrabungen in Manching I–XV, Wiesbaden/Stuttgart.

Binding, U. (1993) *Studien zu den figürlichen Fibeln der Frühlatènezeit*, Universitäts-forschungen zur Prähistorischen Archäologie 16, Bonn.

Bittel, K. (1934) *Die Kelten in Württemberg*, Römisch-Germanische Forschungen 8, Berlin.

Bognár-Kutzián, I. (1975) 'Some new early La Tène finds in the northern Danube Basin', in *The Celts in Central Europe*, Papers of the 2nd Pannonia Conference, Székesfehérvár, *Alba Regia* 14: 35ff.

Bónis, E.B. (1969) 'Die spätkeltische Siedlung Gellérthegy-Tabán in Budapest', *Archeologica Hungarica* 47.

Božič, D. (1991) 'The Celts in Balkan area', in S. Moscati (eds) *The Celts*, 478–84.

Břeň, J. (1971) 'Das keltische Oppidum in Třísov', *Archeologické Rozhledy* 23: 294–303.

Bujna, J. (1982) 'Spiegelung der Sozialstruktur auf latènezeitlichen Gräberfeldern im Karpatenbecken', *Památky Archaeologické* 73: 312ff.

—— (1989) 'Das latènezeitliche Gräberfeld bei Dubnik I', *Slovenská Archeologia* 37: 245ff.

—— (1991) 'Das latènezeitliche Gräberfeld bei Dubnik. II. Analyse und Auswertung', *Slovenská Archeologia* 39: 221ff.

Bujna, J. and Romsauer, P. (1983) 'Späthallstatt- und frühlatènezeitliches Gräberfeld in Bučany', *Slovenská Archeologia* 31: 277ff.

M. Čižmař, (1970) 'Příspěvek k otázce počátku pohřbivání na plochych keltskych pohřebištích na Moravě', *Archeologické Rozhledy* 22: 196ff.

—— (1975) 'Relativní chronologie keltských pohřebišt na Moravě', *Památky Archeologické* 66: 417–37.

—— (1984) 'Laténské sídliště z Velkých Hostěrádek, okr. Břeclav', *Památky Archeologické* 75: 463–85.

—— (1989) 'Erforschung des keltischen Oppidums Staré Hradisko in den Jahren 1983–1988 (Mähren, ČSSR)', *Archäologisches Korrespondenzblatt* 19: 265–315.

—— (1993) 'Frühlatènezeitlicher Burgwall "Černov" in Mähren (Tschechische Republik)', *Archäologisches Korrespondenzblatt* 23: 207–12.

Dehn, W. (1951) 'Zur Verbreitung und Herkunft der latènezeitlichen Braubacher Schalen', *Bonner Jahrbuch* 151: 83–95.

—— (1962/3) 'Frühe Drehscheibenkeramik nördlich der Alpen', *Alt-Thüringen* 6: 372ff.

—— (1964) 'Zu den Lenzburger Kannen', *Germania* 42: 73ff.

—— (1969) 'Keltische Röhrenkannen der älteren Latènezeit', *Památky Archeologické* 60: 125–33.

Filip, J. (1956) *Keltové ve střední Evrope*, Prague.

—— (1976) *Celtic Civilisation and its Heritage*, Prague.

Fischer, F. (1984) 'Württemberg und der Dürrnberg bei Hallein', *Fundberichte aus Baden-Württemberg* 9: 223ff.

Frey, O.-H. (1968) 'Eine neue Grabstele aus Padua', *Germania* 46: 317ff.

—— (1969) *Die Entstehung der Situlenkunst. Studien zur figürlich verzierten Toreutik von Este*, Römisch-Germanische Forschungen 31.

—— (1985) 'Zum Handel und Verkehr während der Frühlatènezeit in Mitteleuropa', in K. Düwel *et al.* (eds) *Untersuchungen zu Handel und Verkehr der vor- und frühgeschichtlichen Zeit in Mittel- und Nordeuropa* I. Göttingen: Abhandlungen der Akademie der Wissenschaften, Phil.-Hist. Kl. 3 Folge, 143, 231–57.

—— (1987) 'Sui ganci di cintura celtici e sulla prima fase di La Tène nell'Italia del Nord', in D. Vitali (ed.) *Celti ed Etruschi nell'Italia centro-settentionale dal V secolo a.C. alla romanizzazione*, Proceedings of the International Colloquium, Bologna, 9–22.

—— (1991a) 'The formation of the La Tène culture in the fifth century BC', in S. Moscati *et al.* (eds) *The Celts*, 127–45.

—— (1991b) 'Einige Bemerkungen zu den durchbrochenen Frühlatènegürtelhaken', in A. Haffner and A. Miron (eds) *Studien zur Eisenzeit im Hunsrück-Nahe-Raum*, Symposium Birkenfeld 1987, *Trierer Zeitschrift* Supplement 13: 101–11.

Gabler, D. (1982) 'Aspects of the development of late iron age settlements in Transdanubia into the Roman period', in D. Gabler, E. Patek and I. Vörös (eds) *Studies in the Iron Age of Hungary*, International Series 144, Oxford: British Archaeological Reports, 57–127.

Gebhard, R. (1993) 'Ergebnisse der Ausgrabungen in Manching', in H. Dannheimer und R. Gebhard (eds) *Das keltische Jahrtausend*, Ausstellungskataloge der Präh. Staatssamml. München, Bd. 23, 113–19, Mainz.

Giessler, R. and Kraft, G. (1942 [1950]) 'Untersuchungen zur frühen und älteren Latènezeit am Oberrhein und in der Schweiz', *Berichte der Römisch-Germanischen Komission* 32: 20ff.

Gosden, C.H. (1984) 'Bohemian iron age chronologies and the seriation of Radovesice. *Germania* 62: 289–309.

—— (1987) 'The production and exchange of La Tène A wheel-turned pottery in Bohemia', *Archeologické Rozhledy* 39: 290–316.

Guštin, M. (1984) 'Die Kelten in Jugoslawien', *Jahrbuch Römisches–Germanisch Zentralmuseum Mainz* 31: 305–63.

Gyulai, F. (1995) 'Umwelt und Pflanzenbau in Transdanubien während der Zeit der Urnenfelder-, Hallstatt- und La-Tène Kultur', in E. Jerem and A. Lippert (eds) *Die Osthallstattkultur*, Archaeolingua 7.

Hamburger Beiträge zur Archäologie (1972).

Hellebrandt, M. (1989) 'Der keltische Kantharos in Csobaj und sein historischer Hintergrund', *Acta Archaeologica Academiae Scientiarum Hungaricae* 41: 33–51.

—— (1994) 'Kelta leletek Vácról. A Vác-kavicsbányai kelta temető [Keltische Funde von Vác. Das keltisches Gräberfeld von Vác-Kavicsbánya], *Váci Könyvek* 7: 7–84.

Hunyady, I. (1942–44) 'Kelták a Kárpátmedencében' [Die Kelten im Karpatenbecken] Budapest: Dissertations Pannonicae series II, no. 18 (Plates, 1942, text 1944.)

Jacobsthal, P. (1944) *Early Celtic Art*, Oxford (reprinted 1969).

Jansová, L. (1986) *Hrazany. Das keltische Oppidum in Böhmen* I. Prague

—— (1988) *Hrazany. Das keltische Oppidum in Böhmen* II. Prague

Jerem, E. (1968) 'The late iron age cemetery of Szentlörinc', *Acta Archaeologica Academiae Scientiarum Hungarica* 20: 159–208.

—— (1974–75) 'Stempelverziertes frühlatènezeitliches Gefäß aus Écs', *Mitteilungen des Archäologischen Instituts der Ungarischen Akademie der Wissenschaften* 5: 45-59.

—— (1981a) 'Südliche Beziehungen einiger hallstattzeitlichen Fundtypen Transdanubiens', *Materijali* 19: 201–20.

—— (1981b) 'Zur Späthallstatt- und Frühlatènezeit in Transdanubien', in *Die Hallstattkultur*, Symposium at Steyr 1980, Linz, 105–36.

—— (1984) 'An early Celtic pottery workshop in north western Hungary: some archaeological and technological evidence', *Oxford Journal of Archaeology* 3: 57–80.

—— (1986) 'Bemerkungen zur Siedlungsgeschichte der Späthallstatt- und Frühlatènezeit im Ostalpenraum', *Mitteilungen des Archäologischen Instituts der Ungarischen Akademie der Wissenschaften* Supplement 3, Hallstatt Colloquium at Veszprém 1984, Budapest, 107–18.

—— (1987) 'Die ältesten Körperbestattungen im Osthallstattkreis', *Mitteilungen Österreichisch Arbeitsgemeinschaft Ur- und Frühgeschichte* 37: 91-102.

—— (1992) Die östliche Latènekultur', in J.W. Neugebauer, *Die Kelten im Osten Österreichs.* Katalog. Wiss. Schriftenreihe Niederösterreich 92/93/94, St Pölten – Vienna 18ff.

Jerem, E., Facsar, G., Kordos, L., Krolopp, E. and Vörös, I. (1985) 'A Sopron-Krautackeren feltárt vaskori telep régészeti és környezetrekonstrukciós vizsgálata II. [The archaeological and environmental investigation of the Iron Age settlement discovered at Sopron-Krautacker. II] *Archaeológiai Értesítő* 112(1): 3–24.

Kardos, J., Kriston, L., Morozova, D., Träger, T., Zimmer, K. and Jerem, E. (1985) 'Scientific investigation of the Sopron-Krautacker iron age pottery workshop', *Archaeometry* 27: 83–93.

Kersten, W. (1933) 'Der Beginn der Latènezeit in Nordostbayern', *Prähistorische Zeitschrift* 24: 96–174.

Kossack, G. (1982) 'Südbayern im 5. Jahrhundert. Zur Frage der Überlieferungskontinuität', *Bayerische Vorgeschichtsblätter* 47: 9–25.

Krämer, W. (1985) *Die Grabfunde von Manching und die latènezeitlichen Flachgräber in Südbayern*, Die Ausgrabungen in Manching 9, Stuttgart.

Kruta, V. (1983) 'L'Italie et l'Europe intérieure du V siècle au debut du II siècle av. n. e.', *Savaria* 16: 203–21.

—— (1986) 'Le corail, le vin et l'arbe de vie: observations sur l'art et la religion des Celtes du Ve au Ie siècle avant J.-C.', *Études Celtiques* 23: 26ff.

—— (1991) 'The first Celtic expansion: prehistory to history', in S. Moscati *et al.* (eds) *The Celts*, 195–212.

Kruta, V. and Szabó, M. (1982) 'Canthares Danubiens du IIIᵉ siècle avant J.-C. en Bohême', *Études Celtiques* 19: 51–67.

Küster, H. (1991) 'The history of vegetation', in S. Moscati *et al* (eds) *The Celts*, 426–28.

—— (1993) 'Umwelt und Ackerbau', in H. Dannheimer and R. Gebhard (eds) Das keltische Jahrtausend, Ausstellungskataloge der Präh. Staatssamml. München, Bd. 23, 122–25, Mainz.

Lang, A. (1974) *Die geriefte Drehscheibenware der Heuneburg 1950–1970 und verwandte Gruppen*, Heuneburgstudien 3, Römisch–Germanische Forschungen 34, Berlin.

—— (1976) 'Neue geriefte Drehscheibenkeramik von der Heuneburg', *Germania* 54: 43ff.

Lenerz-de Wilde, M. (1980) 'Die frühlatènezeitlichen Gürtelhaken mit figuraler Verzierung', *Germania* 58: 61ff.

Lorenz, H. (1978) 'Totenbrauchtum und Tracht. Untersuchungen zur regionalen Gliederung in der frühen Latènezeit', *Bericht der Römisch–Germanischen Kommission* 59: 1–380.

—— (1980) 'Bemerkungen zum Totenbrauchtum', in *Die Kelten in Mitteleuropa*, Catalogue Hallein. Salzburg, 138ff.

Maier, F. (1974) 'Gedanken zur Enstehung der industriellen Großsiedlung der Hallstatt- und Latènezeit auf dem Dürrnberg bei Hallein', *Germania* 52: 326ff.

Meduna, J. (1980) *Die latènezeitlichen Siedlungen in Mähren*, Prague.

Meduna, J. (1991) 'The oppidum of Staré Hradisko', in S. Moscati *et al.* (eds) *The Celts*, 546–47.

Megaw, J.V.S. (1975) 'The orientalizing theme in early Celtic art: east or west?', in J. Fitz (eds) *The Celts in Central Europe*, Papers of the 2nd Pannonia Conference, Székesfehérvár *Alba Regia* 14: 15–33.

Megaw, J.V.S. and Megaw, M.R. (1988) 'The stone head from Mšecké Žehrovice: a reappraisal', *Antiquity* 62: 630–41.

Megaw, J.V.S. and Megaw, M.R. (1989a) *Celtic Art from its Beginnings to the Book of Kells*, London: Thames & Hudson (reprinted with corrections 1990).

—— (1989b) 'The Italian job: some implications of recent finds of celtic scabbards decorated with dragon pairs', in *Mediterranean Archaeology* 2: 85–100.

Megaw, J.V.S., Megaw, M.R. and Neugebauer, J.-W. (1989) 'Zeugnisse frühlatènezeitlichen Kunsthandwerks aus dem Raum Herzogenburg, Niederösterreich', *Germania* 67: 477–517.

Moosleitner, F. (1980) 'Handel und Handwerk', in *Die Kelten in Mitteleuropa*, 93–100.

—— (1985) *Die Schnabelkanne von Dürrnberg. Ein Meisterwerk keltischer Handwerkskunst*, Salzburg.

—— (1991) 'The Dürrnberg near Hallein: a center of Celtic art and culture', in S. Moscati *et al.* (eds) *The Celts*, 167–73.

Moosleitner, F., Pauli, L. and Penninger, E. (1974) *Der Dürrnberg bei Hallein II*, Münchner Beiträge zur Vor-und Frühgeschichte 17.

Moscati, S. *et al.* (1991) *The Celts*, Milan: Bompiani.

Motyková, K., Drda, P. and Rybová, A. (1990) 'Die Siedlungsstruktur des Oppidums Závist. Zum heutigen Forschungsstand', *Archäologisches Korrespondenzblatt* 20: 415–26.

—— (1991a) 'The hillfort and sanctuary of Závist', in S. Moscati *et al.* (eds) *The Celts*, 180–1.

—— (1991b) 'The oppidum of Zavist', in S. Moscati *et al.* (eds) *The Celts*, 542f.

Neugebauer, J.W. (1985) 'Neue Frühlatène-Fundkomplexe im Osten Österreichs', Mitteilungen Österreichische Arbeitsgemeinschaft Ur- und Frühgeschichte 35: 77–84.

—— (1991a) 'The St Pölten area in the fifth century BC', in S. Moscati *et al.* (eds) *The Celts*, 189–90.

—— (1991b) 'The cemetery near St Pölten', in S. Moscati *et al* (eds) *The Celts*, 296–7.

—— (1992) *Die Kelten im Osten Österreichs*. Katalog. Wiss. Schriftenreihe Niederösterreich 92/93/94, St. Pölten – Vienna.

Osterhaus, U. (1981) 'Zur Funktion und Herkunft der frühlatènezeitlichen Hiebmesser', *Kleine Schriften aus dem Vorgeschichte Seminar*, Marburg 9.

Parzinger, H. (1988) *Chronologie der Späthallstatt- und Frühlatène-Zeit. Studien zu Fundgruppen zwischen Mosel und Save*, VCH, Acta Humaniora, Weinheim.

Pauli, L. (1973) 'Ein latènezeitliches Steinrelief aus Bormio am Stilfser Joch', *Germania* 51: 85ff.

—— (1974) 'Der Goldene Steig: Wirtschaftsgeographische Untersuchungen im östlichen Mitteleuropa', in G. Kossack and G. Ulbert (eds) *Festschrift für Joachim Werner*, Münchner Beiträge zur Vor- und Frühgeschichte, supplementary volume 1, 115–39.

—— (1975) *Keltischer Volksglaube. Amulette und Sonderbestattungen am Dürrnberg bei Hallein und im eisenzeitlichen Mitteleuropa*, Münchner Beiträge zur Vor- und Frühgeschichte 28.

—— (1978) *Der Dürrnberg bei Hallein III*, Münchner Beiträge zur Vor- und Frühgeschichte 18.

—— (1980) (ed.) *Die Kelten in Mitteleuropa: Kultur, Kunst, Wirtschaft*, Catalogue Hallein, Salzburg.

—— (1985) 'Early Celtic society: two centuries of wealth and turmoil in central Europe', in T. C. Champion and J.V.S. Megaw (eds) *Settlement and Society: aspects of west European prehistory in the first millenium BC*, Leicester, 23–44.

—— (1991) 'The Alps at the time of the first Celtic migration', in S. Moscati *et al.* (eds) *The Celts*, 215–19.

—— (1994) 'Case studies in Celtic archaeology', in K. Kristiansen and J. Jensen (eds) *Europe in the First Millennium BC* Sheffield Archaeological Monograph 6: 67–80.

Penninger, E. (1972) *Der Dürrnberg bei Hallein I*, Münchner Beiträge zur Vor- und Frühgeschichte 16.

Petres, E. (1976) 'The late pre-Roman Iron Age in Hungary with special reference to oppida', in B. Cunliffe and T. Rowley (eds) *Oppida: the beginnings of urbanisation in barbarian Europe*, Oxford: British Archaeological Reports Supplementary Series II: 51–80.

Pittioni, R. (1954) *Urgeschichte des österreichischen Raumes*, Vienna.

—— (1959) ' Zum Herkunftsgebiet der Kelten', *Österreichische Akademie der Wissenschaften philosophisch-historische Klasse, Sitzungsberichte* 223(3): 3ff.

Rapin, A. (1993) 'Le ceinturon métallique et l'évolution de la panoplie celtique au IIIe siècle avant J.-C.', *Études Celtiques* 28: 349ff.

Rapin, A. and Brunaux, J.-L. (1988) *Gournay II. Boucliers et lances, dépôts et trophées*, Paris.

Ratimorska, P. (1981) 'Keltske pohřebisko v Chotine' (Das keltische Gräberfeld in Chotin), *Zapadné Slovensko* 8: 15ff.

Reinecke, P. (1902) 'Zur Kenntnis der La Tène-Denkmäler der Zone nordwärts der Alpen', *Festschrift zur Feier des fünfzigjährigen Bestehens des Römisch–Germanischen Zentralmuseum, Mainz*, Mainz, 53ff.

—— (1911a) 'Grabfunde der ersten La Tènestufe aus Nordostbayern', *Altertümer unserer Prähistorischen Vorzeit* 5: 281ff.

—— (1911b) 'Grabfunde der zweiten La Tènestufe Nordwärts der Alpen', *Altertümer unserer Prähistorischen Vorzeit* 5: 330ff.

—— (1965) *Mainzer Aufsätze zur Chronologie der Bronze- und Eisenzeit*, Bonn.

Renhart, S. (1990a) 'Zur Anthropologie der frühlatènezeitlichen Bevölkerung Ostösterreichs', dissertation, Vienna.

—— (1990b) 'Neue anthropologische Erkenntnisse zur Bevölkerung der frühen La-Tène-Zeit im ostösterreichischen Raum', *Archäologie Österreichs* 1(1–2): 73–6.

—— (1992) 'Die frühen Kelten aus der Sicht der Anthropologie', in J.-W. Neugebauer, *Die Kelten im Osten Österreichs*. Catalogue St Pölten, 131–9.

Rusu, M., (1969) 'Das keltische Fürstengrab von Çiumeşti in Rumänien', *Berichte der Römisch–Germanischen Kommission* 50: 267–300.

Rybová, A. and Drda, P. (1989) 'Hradiště de Stradonice – nouvelles notions sur l'oppidum celtique', *Památky Archeologické* 80: 383–404.

Salač, V. (1990a) 'Entwicklung und Struktur der hallstatt- und latènezeitlichen Eisenverhüttung und Eisenverarbeitung im Erzgebirgsvorland im Licht neuer Funde', *Památky Archeologické* 81: 208–32.

—— (1990b) 'Zu Untersuchungen über ein latènezeitliches (LT C2-D1) Produktions- und Distributionszentrum in Lovosice', *Archeologické Rozhledy* 42: 609–39.

—— (1992) 'Die Aussagen der Keramik zu Kontakten zwischen Böhmen und Mitteldeutschland in der Latènezeit', in *Beiträge zur keltisch-germanischen Besiedlung im Mittelgebirgsraum*, Weimarer Monographien zur Ur- und Frühgeschichte 28, Stuttgart.

Salač, V. and Smrž, Z. (1989) 'Laténské sídliště u Lužice v sz Čechách (Die latènezeitliche Siedlung bei Lužice in NW-Böhmen). Bemerkungen zur Siedlungskeramik der Stufe LT B im Erzgebirgsvorland und zum Bestehen eines Oppidums auf dem Berg Uhošt bei Kadan', *Archeologické Rozhledy* 41: 549–76.

Schaaff, U. (1974) 'Keltische Eisenhelme aus vorrömischer Zeit', *Jahrbuch Römisch–Germanisches Zentralmuseum Mainz* 21: 149–204.

—— (1988) ' Keltische Helme', *Antike Helme*, Mainz, 293ff.

Schaaff, U. (1990) *Keltische Waffen*, Mainz.

Schwappach, F. (1973) 'Frühkeltisches Ornament zwischen Marne, Rhein und Moldau', *Bonner Jahrbuch* 173: 53ff.

—— (1975) 'Zur Chronologie der östlichen Frühlatène-Keramik', in *The Celts in Central Europe*, Papers of the 2nd Pannonia Conference, Székesfehérvár, *Alba Regia* 14: 109–36.

—— (1979) *Zur Chronologie der östlichen Frühlatène-Keramik*, Die Keramik der Latène-

Kultur 2, Bad Bramstedt.

Serafini, R. (1984) 'Celtismo nel Veneto: materiali archeologici e prospettive di ricerca', *Études Celtiques* 21: 7–33.

Serafini, A.R. and Serafini, M. (1993) 'Un nuovo di cintura traforato da Montebello Vicentino (VI)', in Bianca Maria Scarfì (ed.) *Studi di archeologia della X regio in Ricordo di Michele Tombolani*, 157–69.

Stary, P.F. (1981a) *Zur eisenzeitlichen Bewaffnung und Kampfesweise in Mittelitalien (ca. 9. bis 6. Jh. v. Chr.)*, Marburger Studien z. Vor- und Frühgeschichte 3.

—— (1981b) 'Ursprung und Ausbreitung der eisenzeitlichen Ovalschilde mit spindel-förmigem Schildbuckel', *Germania* 59: 287ff.

Stöllner, T. (1991) 'Neue Grabungen in der latènezeitlichen Gewerbesiedlung im Ramsautal am Dürrnberg bei Hallein', *Archäologisches Korrespondenzblatt* 2: 255–69.

Szabó, M. (1983) 'Audoleon und die Anfänge der ostkeltischen Münzprägung', *Alba Regia* 20: 43–56.

—— (1988) *Les Celtes en Pannonie: contribution à l'histoire de la civilisation celtique dans la cuvette des Karpates*, Paris.

—— (1992) *Les Celtes de l'est: le second age du fer dans la cuvette des Karpates*, Paris: Editions Errance.

Szabó, M. and Petres, E.F. (1992) *Decorated Weapons of the La Tène Iron Age in the Carpathian Basin*, Inventaria Praehistorica Hungariae V, Budapest.

Teržan, B. (1976) 'Certoška fibula', *Archeoloski Vestnik* 27: 317–536.

—— (1990) *The Early Iron Age in Slovenian Styria*, Ljublijana: Catalogi et Monographiae, Narodni Muzej Ljubljana.

Urban, O. (1992) 'Oppidazeit (Spätlatènezeit)', in J.-W. Neugebauer (ed.) *Die Kelten im Osten Österreichs*, St Pölten/Vienna: Katalog. Wiss. Schriftenreihe Niedcrösterreich 92/93/94, 118–30.

Venclová, N. (1989) 'Mšecké Žehrovice, Bohemia', *Antiquity* 63: 142–6.

—— (1990) *Prehistoric Glass in Bohemia*, Prague.

—— (1993) 'Habitats industriels celtiques du IIIe siècle avant J.-C. en Bohême', *Etudes Celtiques* 28: 435ff.

Voigt, T. (1969) 'Zur Problematik der frühlatènezeitlichen Linsenflaschen', *Jahresschrift mitteldeutschen Vorgeschichte* 53: 415ff.

Waldhauser, J. (1977) 'Keltské sídliště u Radovesic v severozápadních Čechách' [Die keltische Siedlung bei Radovesice, Bez. Teplice in Nordwestböhmen] *Archeologické Rozhledy* 29: 144–77.

—— (1978) *Das keltische Gräberfeld bei Jenišuv Ujezd in Böhmen*, Teplice.

—— (1983) 'Závěrečny horizont keltských oppid v Čechác' [Schlußhorizont der keltischen Oppida in Böhmen], *Slovenská Archeologia* 31: 325–56.

—— (1986) 'Struktur und Ökologie der keltischen Besiedlung während der Stufen Ha D – LT D in Böhmen, Mitteilungen des Archäologischen Instituts der Ungarischen Akademie der Wissenschaften, Budapest: Hallstatt Colloquium at Veszprém 1984, 267–78.

—— (1987) 'Keltische Gräberfelder in Böhmen', *Berichte der Römisch–Germanischen Kommission* 68: 25–179.

—— (1990) 'Das Latènehaus von Roggendorf, p.B. Horn, HÖ', *Mannus* 56: 16–23.

—— (1992) 'Keltische Distributionssysteme von Graphittonkeramik und die Ausbeutung der Graphitlagerstätten während der Fortgeschrittenen Latènezeit', *Archäologisches Korres-pondenzblatt* 22: 377–92.

—— (1994) 'Ceramic variation, raw material supply and distribution areas during the last centuries BC (La Tène B2–D1) in Celtic Bohemia', in K. Kristiansen and J. Jensen (eds) *Europe in the First Millennium BC*, Sheffield Archaeological Monographs 6: 81–91.

—— (1993) *Die hallstatt- und latènezeitliche Siedlung mit Gräberfeld bei Radovesice in*

Böhmen I–II, Archeologický výzkum v severnich Čechách 21, Prague.

Willvonseder, K. (1953) 'Zur keltischen Besiedlung des Ostalpenraumes', *Beiträge zur älteren Europäisschen Kulturgeschichte 2, Festschrift für Rudolf Egger*, Klagenfurt, 90ff.

Zachar, L. and Rexa, D. (1988) 'Beitrag zur Problematik der spätlatènezeitlichen Siedlungshorizonte innerhalb des Bratislaver Oppidums', *Zbornik Slovenski Narodni Muzej 82, Historia 28*: 27ff.

Zeller, K. (1980) 'Kriegswesen und Bewaffnung der Kelten', in *Die Kelten in Mitteleuropa*, Catalogue Hallein, Salzburg, 111ff.

—— (1984) 'Latènezeitliche Gewerbebetriebe auf dem Dürrnberg bei Hallein', *Studien zu Siedlungsfragen der Latènezeit. Veröffentl. Vorgesch. Seminars Marburg 3*: 199ff.

—— (1989) 'Neue keltische Gewerbebauten auf dem Dürrnberg', *Salzburger Archiv 6*: 5ff.

Zirra, V. (1991) 'The cemetery of Çiumeşti and the chieftain's tomb', in S. Moscati *et al.* (eds) *The Celts*, 382–3.

Zürn, H. (1942) 'Zur Chronologie der späten Hallstattzeit', *Germania 26*: 116ff.

—— (1952) 'Zum Übergang von Späthallstatt zu Latène A im südwestdeutschen Raum', *Germania 30*: 38ff.

CELTS AND GERMANS IN THE RHINELAND

——— ·◆· ———

Colin Wells

When a people or peoples whom we can recognize as the Celts emerged from the Urnfield culture of the Late Bronze Age, their first cultural contribution to European history is labelled by archaeologists 'Hallstatt', from the type-site in Upper Austria. Although the Hallstatt culture of the Early Iron Age (Hallstatt C and D) was widely distributed throughout central and western Europe, its main centres, like the Heuneburg, were in the region of the upper Danube. Soon after 500 BC, however, they were largely abandoned, and the centre of gravity shifted northwards to the Hunsrück-Eifel region west of the Rhine on either side of the lower Mosel, just before it flows into the Rhine at Koblenz, the Roman Confluentes. Here were developed new decorative styles and new types of artefacts that archaeologists call 'La Tène', after the type-site on Lake Neuchâtel in Switzerland. It is not a good name, since, unlike Hallstatt, it is not central to the region in which the style evolved, but we are stuck with it.

The Hunsrück-Eifel uplands were not particularly good agricultural land, and the wealth of the area was based primarily on its mineral deposits, which included copper, gold and iron. Here and in the adjacent valleys of the Mosel and the Rhine, in the early fifth century BC, the grave goods suggest increasing wealth. Elite burials in two-wheeled chariots, evolving out of the four-wheeled wagon burials of the earlier period, are often associated with horse gear and warriors' equipment in men's graves, and gold torques and jewellery in women's, along with imported Greek and Etruscan luxury goods, such as beaked wine-flagons of a type that gives rise to local imitations (Figure 31.1).[1] Trade contacts with the Mediterranean world remain strong, and imported goods are also found in Champagne and Belgium, as well as beyond the Rhine, although not in such quantity as in the Hunsrück-Eifel region.

The La Tène style (La Tène Ia) evolved partly from the final phase of Hallstatt culture (Hallstatt D), partly under the orientalizing influence of imports. Although during the fifth century the potter's wheel was introduced into the Hunsrück-Eifel, the pottery types still follow their Hallstatt D predecessors. On the other hand, the La Tène metalworkers in particular begin to imitate and to transform imported shapes and motifs, so that motifs that originally emanated from the Near East and were mediated through the Greeks and the Etruscans evolve in the hands of La Tène craftsmen into the rich and elaborate abstract and semi-abstract or geometrical styles

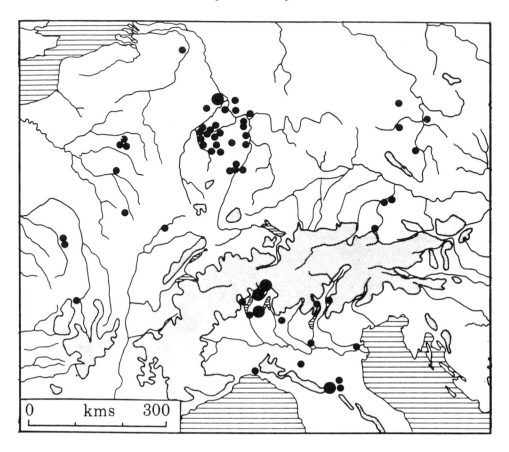

Figure 31.1 Distribution of imported Etruscan beaked flagons in early La Tène period. (From John Collis, *The European Iron Age*, London: Batsford, 1984.)

that have come to be regarded as typically 'Celtic'. Nowhere, however, do we find an abrupt break with earlier styles, and continuity from Hallstatt D into La Tène I can be demonstrated no less in central Europe than in the Hunsrück-Eifel region. By the end of the fifth century, the La Tène culture (La Tène Ib) extends throughout the upper Danube region and across the Alps into the Po valley. This was not achieved by conquest, and there are no major population shifts, although one factor in the spread of the new art style, particularly in styles of horse gear and weapons, must have been the widespread predatory activities of Celtic warrior bands, which broke the power of the Etruscans and in 390, traditionally, or 387, actually reached and sacked Rome itself.[2]

The absence of any break in the material culture of the Hunsrück-Eifel and adjacent regions must be stressed, since it is important for our understanding of the ethnicity of the region in later times. The Mosel valley was the stronghold of the Treveri, prominent in Caesar's narrative of his conquest of Gaul, and in the later history of the empire. In 279 BC, other Celtic warrior bands attacked the shrine of

Apollo at Delphi, and the following year, having crossed into Asia Minor, settled around Ancyra (Ankara) in Asia Minor, where they maintained their culture and their language for centuries, so that Jerome in the fourth century AD records that their language resembled that of the Treveri.[3] The Treveri in Caesar's day were still the great horsemen that the practice of chariot burial in the Early La Tène period shows their ancestors to have been.[4] Caesar does not include them among the Belgae, who were their neighbours to the north and west, nor among the *Germani cisrhenani*, the Germans who lived on the left bank of the Rhine, a somewhat anomalous group, discussed below, that did, however, include their clients, the Eburones and Condrusi; Hirtius, however, who completed Caesar's account of the Gallic War, says that the Treveri resembled the Germans in their behaviour and their ferocity because of continuous warfare against them, and Tacitus later reports that, like their Belgic neighbours, the Nervii, they claimed German ancestry as a status symbol that distinguished them from the more sluggish Gauls.[5] It is hard to see what this 'German' ancestry might have been, if 'Germanness' is also linked with origins east of the Rhine, as Caesar seems to suggest it is, since the Treveri appear to have been essentially autochthonous since the Bronze Age.[6]

It seems then that the start of the La Tène period in the Hunsrück-Eifel region is marked by increasing social stratification, to judge by the burials, but the region does not develop centres of population that stand out for their size and their wealth, such as marked the Hallstatt period on the upper Danube. There are some small hill-forts, but most of the population, including the wealthy élite, seem to have lived in the valleys, possibly in undefended settlements,[7] or in what were effectively the precursors of rural villas. Early in the fourth century, there may have been some depopulation of the area, and perhaps less social differentiation among the remaining population, and this may be connected with the migrations already referred to, but the evidence comes mostly from burials, and the fact that we find smaller cemeteries with fewer and poorer burials in La Tène II and III than in La Tène I may also be due to changes in fashion. Trade with the Mediterranean seems to decrease. This is the period in which La Tène culture reaches its largest extension throughout 'Celtic' Europe, but its old heartland seems to be suffering from a degree of economic decline and isolation, compared with the fifth century.

By the middle of the second century BC, however, the economy begins to revive. Trade contact with the Mediterranean is re-established, and Celtic coinage appears, based largely on Greek prototypes. Burial customs change, cremation replaces inhumation, and although grave goods comprise mostly local pottery, objects imported from Italy still appear. The living begin to group themselves into larger settlements, veritable urban agglomerations, to which we attach the term that Caesar used, 'oppida'. Just outside our area, one of the best-known of these is Bibracte, on the Mont Beuvray some 27 km from Autun in Burgundy, which Caesar describes as 'by far the largest and the best supplied of the oppida of the Aedui'.[8] It was on the basis of his excavations here that the great French archaeologist Joseph Déchelette, 'mort pour la patrie' in 1914 at the age of 52, recognized the essential unity of the La Tène world and, in initiating his great *Manuel d'archéologie préhistorique, celtique, et gallo-romaine*, of which the first volume appeared in Paris in 1908, made his great plea for an end to modern nationalistic bias in archaeology: 'Nos antiquités nationales ne sauraient être étudiées isolément . . . . Ce n'est plus seulement en Gaule et dans les Iles Britanniques, mais au delà du Rhin et des Alpes françaises que la culture celtique sollicite l'attention des archéologues'.

The oppida culture that in the Late La Tène period (La Tène III) subsisted throughout Gaul was rudely shattered by Caesar's invasion, and it is to Caesar's account that we must now turn to try to clarify the cultural and ethnic situation that he found along the Rhine when he got there in the 50s. Caesar, a political propagandist, not a trained ethnographer, uses three terms to refer to tribal groupings, namely 'Celts', also called 'Gauls' in Latin,[9] 'Germans', and 'Belgae', and any discussion of ethnicity involves us in trying to understand these terms. Caesar in the very first chapter of his work defines the Germans quite specifically as those 'who dwell across the Rhine', that is, east of the river, and seems to be trying to suggest as a result that the Rhine is a natural boundary.[10] He also emphasizes the difference between Celts and Germans, and insists upon the terror which the Germans inspire, 'by the huge size of their bodies, by their incredible courage and skill in arms'.[11] He argues, as it suits his political purpose, that if the Germans who had already invaded Gaul before he himself got there had not been checked and driven back across the Rhine where he claims they belonged, they might have overrun all Gaul and threatened Italy, 'as previously the Cimbri and Teutoni had done'.[12] The Cimbri and Teutoni had been turned back by Marius less than half a century before, so that there were Romans who could still remember the terror that they had inspired. It was a potent parallel.

Now in Caesar's account, it is clear that one way, and perhaps the most significant way, of distinguishing the Germans from the Celts is by the language they speak. This is most clearly shown in the case of Ariovistus, described as 'king of the Germans', *rex Germanorum*, who appears to belong to the Suebi, 'a people . . . by far the greatest and most warlike of all the Germans'. His Suebic origin is inferred from the fact that he had a Suebic wife 'whom he had brought with him from home', and he is said to speak Celtic only as the result of long practice in the language.[13] The name Ariovistus appears to be Celtic and turns up elsewhere belonging to a chieftain of the Insubrian Gauls, but this may only mean, as Rudolf Much argued, that it was transmitted to Caesar by Gaulish informants in a Celticized form.[14] Note too that the Cimbri, originally from Denmark, the Cimbric peninsula, are certainly not Celts, though their personal names too are transmitted through classical writers in a Celtic form. For Tacitus also, language was the prime distinguishing mark: the Cotini and the Osi, he argues, cannot be German, because the former speak a Gaulish and the latter a Pannonian language.[15] The Roman army must have been aware of this: even if other cultural distinctions that might interest a modern ethnographer escaped them, they could hardly have failed to notice when it was necessary to change the interpreter.

Now if the cultural differences between Celts and Germans were as great as Caesar suggests, and if the Rhine indeed formed the ethnic frontier, we are entitled to expect corresponding differences in material culture to show up in the archaeological record, thus making the Rhine the archaeological frontier also. The fact is that they do not:

1 Right across central Gaul and south Germany through Bohemia and into Yugoslavia we find, as Déchelette recognized, oppida such as those described by

Caesar at Bibracte, Alesia, and Avaricum. Examples include Tarodunum, Manching, Kelheim, Stradonice, Magdalensberg and Židovar.[16] All share a similar Late La Tène culture, and use the Celtic language.

2 Across Frisia and north Germany and into Scandinavia, we find the land covered with heavy forest, inhabited by people with a semi-nomadic way of life, different artefacts from those of the La Tène culture, no wheel-made pottery, and different burial rites: these people, whom we may call the 'northerners', correspond to what we should expect from Caesar's 'Germans'.

3 Between the two lies an intermediate zone, inhabited by people who can be called, as in the title of the seminal work on the subject, *Völker zwischen Germanen und Kelten*, with elements of both, so that it can be said that 'neither the Belgae west of the river nor the tribes east of it were fully German or Celtic in the normal sense'.[17]

The Belgae are either the key to the situation, or a confusing anomaly. In Caesar's usage, they are a group of tribes living in the northern part of Gaul, in the area west of the Rhine, bounded to the south by the Seine and the Marne.[18] In some contexts, they can be regarded as Gauls, but at the same time Caesar preserves a tradition that most of them originated east of the Rhine and were of German origin.[19] Five tribes in the north-east of the area inhabited collectively by the Belgae are also grouped together under the designation of 'left-bank Germans', *Germani cisrhenani*.[20] Philologists agree that the Belgae, like their neighbours to the south, such as the Treveri, spoke Celtic dialects, although there is some evidence for a substratum that is neither Celtic nor German, linguistically speaking, though allied to both.[21] North of the Belgae, amongst the low-lying swamps and the wandering channels of the lower Rhine, the Meuse and the Waal, there were certainly 'northerners', speaking German rather than Celtic dialects, but whether they were already there in Caesar's day, or came in during the warfare of the next thirty or forty years, discussed below, is unclear. The one reference in Caesar to the Batavi, who in Augustan times lived around Nijmegen (Oppidum Batavorum or Noviomagus) and whom Tacitus identifies as true 'northerners', formerly a branch of the Chatti, is unfortunately in a passage which may well be a later interpolation.[22] The same passage also mentions the Waal (Vacalus), later spelt Vahalis, in which form it is Germanic, or germanicized.[23]

So far on the middle Rhine we have largely confined ourselves to the left bank. But on the east bank there are also tribes whose names appear to be Celtic rather than German, and whose way of life is very different from that of the Suebi, who are archetypally 'German' in the later sense of the term. Such for instance were the Mattiaci, whom we find in the Augustan period on the lower Main and in the Wetterau, across from the Roman legionary base at Mainz (Mogontiacum), with their tribal capital in the first century AD at Wiesbaden (Aquae Mattiacorum). In the pre-Roman period, the La Tène culture extended throughout this area, although the further north one goes, the more impoverished it becomes, and there are some linguistic differences.[24] This was in fact a border zone, but the area has more cultural affinities with the Hunsrück-Eifel area on the opposite bank of the Rhine than it has with regions still further north. The Wetterau region is of great historical importance, because it yields evidence of peaceful Roman occupation and interchange in the years before and during Drusus's campaigns. There was an important Roman supply base at Rödgen, and at Bad Nauheim, just 2.5 km away across the valley, the extensive La Tène settlement around the saline springs not only continued to be occupied throughout and beyond the period when Rödgen was in use, but had access to Roman coins and artefacts, probably obtained by trade.

The La Tène settlement at Bad Nauheim was, however, abandoned later in the Augustan period, probably before Germanicus fortified the strong defensive position at Friedberg which blocks the route south out of the Wetterau, by which time 'German' finds have entered the area, and in this area and to the north of it at the time of Germanicus's campaigns in AD 14–16 we find the Chatti, whose very name is absent from Caesar's account.[25] The main settlement of the Mattiaci may originally have been on the Altenburg at Niedenstein, where the culture can be described as 'impoverished La Tène'.[26] It suits all the evidence if we assume that in the disturbances that followed the Varian Disaster, when Rome lost three legions, her prestige, and the territory and bases between the Rhine and the Elbe, the Celtic or celticized Mattiaci, peaceful allies of Rome, were attacked and driven southwards by the Chatti, hostile 'northerners', 'Germans' in the later sense of the term. The Cherusci are another tribe of 'northerners' with the initial Ch- characteristic of the way in which the Romans spelled that typical Germanic sound.[27] It is notable that they too, though prominent in Germanicus's campaigns, appear only once in Caesar, as remoter neighbours of the Suebi.[28] The evidence for a massive shift of population since Caesar's day seems unmistakable, even if we disregard the archaeological evidence.

Apart from the Mattiaci, other Celtic or celticized tribes on the right bank of the middle Rhine before the Romans came probably included the Usipetes, Tencteri and Ubii. The first two, like the Treveri, and quite unlike the Suebi, were notable for their cavalry, and the name of the Usipetes in Celtic actually means 'good horsemen' or 'well-horsed', cognate with the Greek *eu* and *hippos*, and though Caesar specifically describes them as 'German', we might wonder in what sense the term is used. The Ubii were notable farmers, and Caesar's account makes it clear that all three tribes are by choice settled agriculturalists, and none migrates except under pressure from the Suebi, who are themselves in a state of perpetual migration.[29] The Ubii moreover are 'accustomed to Gaulish manners' and have oppida which are refuges in time of danger, whereas the Suebi abandon their settlements when attacked to take refuge in the forests.[30] Harassed by the Suebi, the Usipetes and Tencteri tried to cross over to the left bank in 55 BC, but Caesar drove them off and they took refuge with the Sugambri, their right-bank neighbours. The Ubii put themselves under Caesar's protection, but some time between Caesar's departure from Gaul and Marcus Agrippa's arrival as governor in 39/38, they successfully crossed the river and Agrippa confirmed them in the lands on which they had settled around the site of what was to become Cologne (Oppidum Ubiorum, later Colonia Claudia Ara Agrippinensium).[31] The Usipetes and the Sugambri were still on the right bank when Drusus's campaigns started in 12 BC, but four years later the Sugambri were forcibly resettled on the left bank, and sometime between that date and AD 9, a cult of Augustus was established at Cologne with a Cheruscan priest.[32] This stretch of the right bank of the Rhine also belongs firmly to the La Tène world.[33]

The confusion that arises from Caesar's reference to Germans living on the left bank of the Rhine and to various tribes as having the tradition of German origins and of having come from beyond the Rhine can be resolved by supposing that there are in fact two types of 'German'. Caesar has either misunderstood the situation, or is perpetrating a politically advantageous deception. On the one hand there are the tribes along the Rhine, originally settled for the most part on the right bank, like the Usipetes, Tencteri and Ubii, who call themselves or are called by their neighbours 'German', whatever this means (the etymology is obscure), but who are in fact Celtic, or strongly celticized. In this sense 'German' is perhaps parallel to 'Gaulish' or 'Belgian' as a designation for a tribal grouping. On the other hand are the 'northerners' like the Suebi, who in Caesar's day are at a more primitive, semi-nomadic state of social and economic development, and who are already pressing on the margins of the late La Tène world before the Romans under Caesar irrupt into central and northern Gaul and the Rhineland and cause their own brand of disturbance. These 'northerners' speak, not Celtic, but what we now call a Germanic dialect, although Caesar is the first to pin the label 'German' on them. It is in his interest to fix in Roman minds the idea that the Rhine is a natural ethnic frontier, because that explains why his conquests go thus far and no further. From the statement that (some) Germans come from beyond the Rhine, certainly true of the Celtic Germans, like the Ubii and probably the *Germani cisrhenani*, we pass imperceptibly to the proposition that all tribes beyond the Rhine are 'German', including the intrusive 'northerners' like the Suebi and the Chatti, and because the latter by Augustus's day have come to dominate the area beyond the Rhine, they come virtually to monopolize the title 'German', which was not originally theirs, with resulting terminological confusion.

If then the culture and language on both banks of the Rhine seem to be alike before the Romans and the intrusive 'Germans', as we must henceforth call them, came in to disrupt the pattern, it should not surprise us, even if it conflicts with Caesar's evidence. Historically, rivers are not natural frontiers; they join rather than separate, and serve more readily as highways than as barriers. The history of post-colonial Africa has been bedevilled by frontiers inherited from the colonial powers, who were less concerned to respect tribal groupings and the cultural and linguistic unity of both banks of a river than they were to use the rivers, when they wished to negotiate a frontier, as convenient lines of demarcation. The Romans were not negotiating with barbarians as with equals; there was a 'moral barrier' on the Rhine and the Danube.[34] It was only when the Romans themselves had stabilized their frontier along these convenient rivers, and had set up forts and fortresses, with customs posts and artificial restrictions on natural freedom of movement along and across the river, that a real cultural gap was created between the provincial on the one side and the barbarian on the other, although even so there extended beyond the river a zone of Roman influence, if not in fact actual political control.[35]

Archaeological evidence for the disruption of the unity of the late La Tène world in the course of the first century BC by 'northern' elements, 'German' in Caesar's sense of the term, is not hard to find. Although no archaeological evidence has been found for Ariovistus's Suebi in Gaul, we have seen what happened in the Wetterau, and archaeology attests to the destruction of La Tène or 'Celtic' settlements in the

Vltava valley around Prague and Pilsen and between the Vah and Morava rivers around Bratislava, and this destruction is associated with newcomers whose cultural affinities are with the middle and lower Elbe. These were probably the Suebic Marcomanni and Quadi, driven out of the upper Main region by Drusus's campaigns in 12–9 BC.[36] Similar 'German' finds in the Main valley and Thuringia are also intrusive, since this area was previously fully integrated into the La Tène culture. On the other hand, the German settlements at Diersheim, north-east of Strasbourg, and elsewhere on the right bank of the Rhine are not earlier than the late Augustan period, and were apparently established under Roman protection, perhaps for German militia.[37]

The La Tène world, previously a cultural unit, was irreversibly split by Rome's irruption into it. Once the frontier settled down along the Rhine and the Danube in Tiberius's reign, the enormous area outside the frontier was recognized in Roman terminology simply as 'Germany', Germania. Gaul, Raetia and Noricum became Roman provinces and developed their distinct provincial-Roman culture. The Taunus region, the Wetterau and the Black Forest area become a military zone along the new frontier, which later in the first and early second centuries AD would expand to become the province of Germania Superior. The upper Main region, Thuringia, Bohemia and Moravia were abandoned to the incoming Germans. The lower Rhine became a military frontier, and no attempt was ever made to reconquer the lands between Rhine and Elbe lost in AD 9, but a buffer zone beyond the river was kept free of settlement and reserved for military use, and we know that outposts and taxation were maintained, at least along the Frisian coast.[38]

There was, however, a great deal of trade across the frontier, as across any Roman frontier,[39] and a clear distinction can be made between the zone of frontier trade (*Grenzhandel*) some 100 km wide and of long-distance trade (*Fernhandel*) beyond that.[40] Pliny and Tacitus reflect a changing sense of ethnicity in their writing about the Germans, though they seem to be puzzled by discrepancies with Caesar's account, discrepancies which a century and a half of change makes only natural in fluid tribal societies.[41] Archaeological evidence shows the Germans beyond the frontier influenced to greater or lesser degrees by contact with Roman provincial culture and trade. The so-called 'Weser-Rhein Germanen' were much influenced, the 'Elbe-Germanen' further east much less so, and different German cultural groupings developed.[42] Roman occupation of the area between the Rhine and the Elbe from 12/9 BC to AD 9 had, however, destroyed the power of the pre-existing tribes, thus opening up the area for the invading Germans, moving westwards up the same lines of penetration, such as the Lippe valley and the Wetterau, which the Romans had used in the opposite direction. The German newcomers had a great reservoir of manpower behind them. It was because Tiberius, who knew Germany and its peoples better than any other Roman, understood the numbers and the potential of these newcomers that he accepted Augustus's advice to keep the empire within its present limits,[43] and never tried to regain what had been lost.

What then happened to the Celts who thus found themselves incorporated willy-nilly into the empire and destined to become, though they did not know it, 'Gallo-Romans'? In 39/38 BC, Agrippa as governor of Gaul laid out a strategic road system that linked all of Gaul to Lyons (Lugdunum), the main centre of Roman administration. In the next twenty years, at least four Roman generals earned triumphs or imperatorial salutations for successes against rebellious tribes or invaders from across the Rhine, and Agrippa in his second governorship (19 BC) was again required to take military action. In 17, Marcus Lollius as governor suffered a defeat in a German raid, in which one Roman legion temporarily lost its eagle, but again order was restored, and over the next three years Augustus himself was in Gaul, supervising preparations for the great advance across the Rhine into Germany, which began in 12 BC under the command of his stepson Drusus. It was probably during these years, if not earlier, that semi-permanent legionary bases were established at key points on the left bank of the Rhine, and at least some advance supply depots were created, like the one already referred to at Rödgen in the Wetterau. In four years of operations, Drusus reached the Elbe and tried unsuccessfully to cross, but on his way back towards the Rhine he broke his leg in a riding accident and died a month later, 'to a great extent the conqueror of Germany'.[44] The conquests, consolidated by Drusus's brother, Tiberius, and others, were starting to be administered as a Roman province when in AD 9 a rebellion led by Arminius, a chief of the Cherusci, himself a Roman citizen, destroyed three Roman legions under the command of the governor, Quinctilius Varus, and wiped out the Roman garrisons between the Rhine and the Elbe. The territory thus forfeited was never reconquered.[45]

The Rhineland thus remained a perpetual frontier zone. It was linked to the rest of Gaul by Agrippa's road network and to Italy via Helvetia and over the Alps, and the road network was paralleled by a system of water transport using the rivers. The Rhine itself was a major artery, and goods from the south came up the Rhône and the Saône and then crossed a relatively short portage to descend the Mosel. Latin inscriptions recording guilds of boatmen (*nautae*) and shippers (*negotiatores*) show from the nomenclature that the men concerned were mostly of Gaulish origin, and north of Lyons the Belgae and especially the Treveri seem to predominate (Figure 31.2).[46] After the Varian Disaster, there were eight legions plus auxiliary troops stationed on the Rhine, making a total of between 80,000 and 100,000 men, who had to be kept fed and supplied, who spent their pay and sought their entertainments locally, and who often started families, retired, and settled just down the road from where they had spent their service. Their economic impact was enormous.[47] Civilian settlements grew up under the shelter of the bases, to such an extent that when civil war broke out in AD 69, 'The Year of the Four Emperors', the buildings which had been allowed to grow up during half a century of peace under the walls of the legionary base at Vetera, near Xanten on the lower Rhine, had to be torn down in a hurry in order to put the base into defensive order.[48] There were other legionary bases on the Rhine at Strasbourg (Argentorate), Mainz, Bonn (Bonna), Neuss (Novaesium) and Nijmegen. Regular municipalities developed, and Roman colonial status was conferred upon the most important towns, Cologne (Colonia Claudia Ara Agrippinensium) and Trier (Colonia Augusta Treverorum). There were native villages and villas on every scale, from humble farms to such grand establishments as the villa at Nennig, probably the home of some local Treveran notable, and on some sites there are hints of continuity from Late La Tène into Roman times (Figure 31.3).[49]

Figure 31.2 Ship carrying wine barrels. (Landesmuseum, Trier. Photo: H. Thörnig.)

The Celtic population, while adopting many aspects of Roman material culture, maintained also many of its Celtic attributes. We have already seen that Jerome testifies to the continued use of the Celtic language among the Treveri in the fourth century. Celtic religion too continued to flourish, alongside such imports as the imperial cult and the eastern cults, including Christianity, that soldiers and others introduced. Naturally the forms of the religion changed. Druids disappeared, but how important they had been, except in aristocratic circles, is in any event disputed.[50] Certainly their power and prestige did not long survive the end of Celtic independence, and Claudius actually proscribed them, Augustus having already forbidden Roman citizens to participate.[51] Human sacrifice and head-hunting, which had been features of Celtic society in pre-Roman times, clearly did not survive the conquest either. But the popular religious beliefs and practices that can be shown still to flourish after the conquest, often in a strongly syncretistic form, must have had very deep roots. Celtic religion attached great importance to natural features considered to be sacred, such as mountains, springs and rivers, and there are many references to sacred groves.

Celtic divinities were twinned with Roman counterparts, but the result is often 'hybrid and ambiguous', due perhaps to the contrast between 'Roman gods, defined strictly by function, and the ill-defined local spirits of the Celts'.[52] Did the Celts find it harder to accept the *interpretatio Romana* and to meld their beliefs with those of the Mediterranean world than most other peoples, the Jews being a notable

Hill-forts built or occupied in La Tène times • Other important hill-forts
✕ Other sites mentioned in text
⟶ Lines of communication probably available in Caesar's time

Figure 31.3 The Hunsrück-Eifel region in the late La Tène period. (From E.M. Wightman, *Roman Trier and the Treveri*, London: Hart-Davis, 1970.)

exception, who came under the empire? One might speculate that Celts more than most people would miss their own religious landscape. The conflated Romano-Celtic divinities turn up in the Rhineland as elsewhere in the Celtic world. The gods with double names are often linked with a purely Celtic consort, like Lenus Mars with Ancamna (Figure 31.4), or Mars Smertrius with the same goddess, Mars Loucetius

613

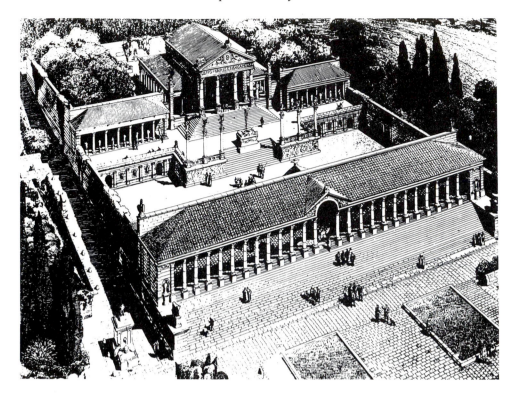

Figure 31.4 The Lenus Mars temple at Trier. (Landesmuseum, Trier.)

with a consort Nemetona, and Apollo Grannus with Sirona, but they also appear alone, as does Mercury in many guises, as Iovantucarus and Cnabetius and Abgatiacus.[53] Celtic cult centres continue to be frequented, and two specifically Celtic features that would strike any visitor to the area are the cult figures of the mother-goddesses or *matronae* and the Jupiter columns or *Gigantensäulen*, which are iconographically unique.

The iconography of the *deae matres* or *matronae*, Celtic though they are, is not fully developed before the Roman period. From this period, there are numerous representations, normally showing three female figures, seated side by side, dressed in matronly fashion, with attributes expressive of fertility and nurturing, such as fruit, loaves of bread, and indeed children. The Rhineland *matronae* are distinguished in inscriptions by local epithets, such as that on one of the finest of all extant *matronae* reliefs, found at Bonn and dedicated in AD 164 by a Cologne magistrate to the Matronae Aufaniae, whose cult is peculiar to the territory of the Ubii, between Cologne and Bonn (Figure 31.5).[54] Other epithets seem always to associate the *matronae* with a particular locality, and on the lower Rhine some of these epithets seem distinctly Germanic rather than Celtic, suggesting that this very Celtic cult won followers among the Batavi and other northerners who had settled there.[55] Equally un-Roman are the Jupiter columns or *Gigantensäulen*, about 150 of which are known, up to 15 metres high. Dedicated to Jupiter, sometimes in company with

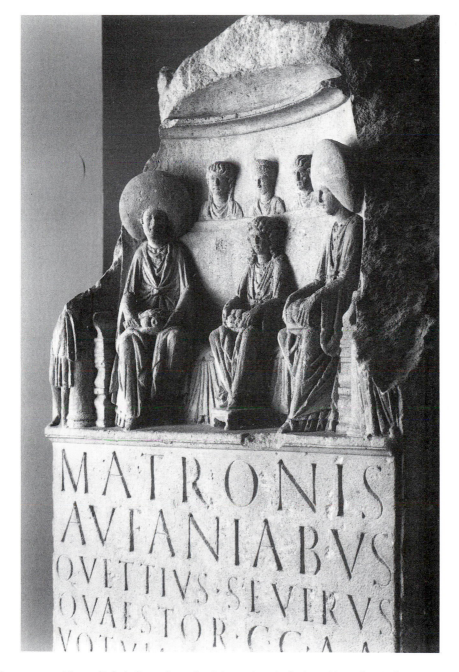

Figure 31.5 The relief dedicated to the Matroniae Aufaniae. (*Aus rheinischer Kunst und Kultur: Auswahlkatalog des Rheinischen Landesmuseums Bonn 1963*, Düsseldorf: Rheinland-Verlag, 1963, pl. 17.)

Figure 31.6 A Jupiter Column. (*Aus rheinischer Kunst und Kultur*, pl. 12.)

Juno, and set on a base covered with classical reliefs usually depicting such deities as Mercury, Minerva, Hercules and Juno, the column normally supports a horseman who is riding down a giant, part man, part serpent, although in the Rhineland the sculpture more often represents Jupiter enthroned (Figure 31.6). In either case, the total impression is wholly alien to classical iconography, like some crucifix from the early days of the Spanish conquest of Mexico, carved by sculptors trained in pre-Columbian styles and techniques.[56]

NOTES

1 The most lucid summary in English of the history and archaeology of the area at this period is by John Collis, *The European Iron Age* (London: Batsford, 1984), see especially pp. 114–15.

2 Polybius II.18; Livy V.32–49.

3 Jerome, *Commentary on the Epistle to the Galatians*, II.3.

4 *equites Treveri, quorum inter Gallos virtutis opinio est singularis,* (Caesar, *Gallic War* II.24).

5 Caesar, *Gallic War* I.1, II.4, IV.6, VI.2–3, VI.32; (Hirtius) VIII.25; Tacitus, *Germania* XXVIII.4.

6 *Germani qui trans Rhenum incolunt*, emphatic (Caesar, *Gallic War* I.1), discussed in more detail below. An earlier interpretation of the evidence thought in terms of 'an incoming aristocracy in the later Hunsrück-Eifel period' and possibly also 'a gradual movement of people westwards across the Rhine', the latter leaving no trace in the archaeological record: Edith Mary Wightman, *Roman Trier and the Treveri* (London: Hart-Davis, 1970), 17–18. This hypothesis is not however required since the rich graves are perfectly explicable as a local development, and need not have been introduced by newcomers.

7 Collis, *European Iron Age*, 114.

8 *oppido Aeduorum longe maximo et copiosissimo* (Caesar, *Gallic War* I.23).

9 *ipsorum lingua Celtae, nostra Galli appellantur* (Caesar, *Gallic War* I.1).

10 See n. 5; note also references to *Rhenum finesque Germanorum* (Caesar, *Gallic War* I.27), and continual emphasis on Germans *crossing* the Rhine, (I.31, I.33, I.37, I.43, I.44, I.53, etc.); see further C.M. Wells, *The German Policy of Augustus* (Oxford: Oxford University Press, 1972), 311–12.

11 *ingenti magnitudine corporum, incredibili virtute atque exercitatione in armis* (Caesar, *Gallic War* I.39).

12 *ut ante Cimbri Teutonique fecissent* (Caesar, *Gallic War* I.33).

13 Suebi as *gens . . . longe maxima et bellicosissima Germanorum omnium* (Caesar, *Gallic War* IV.1); Ariovistus's wives, *una Sueba natione quam domo secum duxerat*, and the other from Noricum, the sister of King Voccio, whose brother had sent her to him in Gaul to marry, (*Gallic War* T.53); Ariovistus speaking Celtic *longinqua consuetudine* (*Gallic War* I.47).

14 Insubrian chieftain, Florus I.20.4; on the name Ariovistus, D.E. Evans, *Gaulish Personal Names: a study of some continental Celtic formations* (Oxford: Oxford University Press, 1967), 54–5, 141–2; cf. R. Much, arguing against Sigmund Feist, *Germanen und Kelten in der antiken Überlieferung* (Halle: Niemeyer, 1927), in *Zeitschrift für deutsches Altertum und deutsche Literatur* 65 (1928): 11–13, 30–2.

15 *Cotinos Gallica, Osos Pannonica lingua coarguit non esse Germanos* (Tacitus, *Germania* XLIII.1).

16 John Collis, *Oppida: earliest towns north of the Alps* (Sheffield: Department of Prehistory and Archaeology, University of Sheffield, 1984), maps, with gazetteer and bibliography, 229–50.

17 Rolf Hachmann, Georg Kossack and Hans Kuhn, *Völker zwischen Germanen und Kelten* (Neumünster: Wachholtz, 1962); Wells, *German Policy of Augustus*, 23.

18 Caesar, *Gallic War* I.1.

19 Caesar, *Gallic War* II.4; cf. Tacitus, *Germania* II.5, *qui primi Rhenum transgressi Gallos expulerint ac nunc Tungri, tunc Germani vocati sunt.*

20 *Germani cisrhenani* (Caesar, *Gallic War* II.3, II.4, VI.32).

21 Kuhn in Hachmann, Kossack and Kuhn, *Völker zwischen*, 105–28.

22 Caesar, *Gallic War* IV.10, rejected by T. Rice Holmes (ed.) *C. Iulii Caesaris de bello Gallico I–VII* (Oxford: Oxford University Press, 1914, reprinted New York: Arno, 1979), 25–7; useful summary of arguments in Georg Hornig, *C. Iulius Caesar, Commentarii Belli Gallici, Erläuterungen zu Buch I–IV, B: Lehrerkommentar* (Frankfurt a.M., Berlin, Bonn: Moritz Diesterweg, 1965), 125–6; *Batavi ... Chattorum quondam populus*, Tacitus, *Germania* XXXIX.1; Lucan, *Pharsalia* I.431, includes Batavi among Caesar's auxiliaries, but this was written over a century later and may be an anachronism.

23 The fact that the passage preserves the spelling Vacalus may suggest that, if it is an interpolation, it is an early one; Vahalis in Tacitus, *Annals* II.6. See Kuhn in Hachmann, Kossack, and Kuhn, *Völker zwischen*, 121–2. The change from *c* to *ch* or *h* is part of the 'erste germanische Lautverschiebung', and words or names in which this sound-shift has not occurred 'sind nicht germanisch im strengen Sinn' (ibid., 116). Where it is found in toponyms west of the Rhine, as in Vahalis, does this betoken immigrants, or changes in local dialect? Cf. Wells *German Policy of Augustus*, 313–14.

24 Hachmann, Kossack and Kuhn, *Völker zwischen*, 134.

25 Tacitus, *Annals* I.55–6, II.7, II.25, etc.

26 Gerhard Mildenberger, 'Das Ende der Altenburg bei Niedenstein', *Fundberichte aus Hessen*, 1 (1969) (Marburger Beiträge zur Archäologie der Kelten: Festschrift für Wolfgang Dehn zum 60. Geburtstag am 6. Juli 1969) (Bonn: Habelt, 1969), 122–34; also id., *Germanische Burgen* (Veröffentlichungen der Altertumskommission im Provinzial-institut für Westfälische Landes- und Volksforschung, Landschaftsverband Westfalen-Lippe 6) (Münster: Aschendorff, 1978), 56; see Wells, *German Policy of Augustus*, 21, 312–13.

27 On the sound-shift that produced it, see Kuhn in Hachmann, Kossack and Kuhn, *Völker zwischen* 116.

28 Caesar, *Gallic War* VI.10.

29 Caesar, *Gallic War* IV.1–19; Ubii as farmers, Pliny, *Natural History* XVII.47.

30 *Gallicis moribus assuefacti* (Caesar, *Gallic War* IV.3); the different behaviour of the Ubii and the Suebi stressed by R. von Uslar, *Studien zu frühgeschichtlichen Befestigungen zwischen Nordsee und Alpen* (Bonner Jahrbücher, Beiheft 11) (Cologne and Graz: Böhlau, 1964), 10, n. 42.

31 Ubii in Appian, *Civil Wars* V.386; Dio, XLVIII.49.

32 Chief sources for Drusus's campaigns, Dio LIV.32–3, LIV.36, LV.6; Florus II.30.21–8; Livy, *epitome* CXXXVII–CXL; Orosius VI.21.15. On resettlement, Suetonius, *Augustus* XXI.1; *Tiberius* IX.2. On the altar at Cologne, Tacitus, *Annals* I.39, I.57.

33 U. Kahrstedt in E. Birley (ed.) *Congress of Roman Frontier Studies 1949* (Durham: University of Durham, 1952), 44: 'The material civilization of the Ubii and the Sugambri, prior to their transplantation, in no way differed from that of the Treveri and other Celtic peoples, except that they were a little poorer.'

34 A. Alföldi, 'The moral barrier on Rhine and Danube', in Birley, *Roman Frontier Studies*, 1–16.

35 Wells, *German Policy of Augustus*, 24–5, with further references.

36 Wells, *German Policy of Augustus*, 156–61.

37 Rolf Nierhaus, *Das swebische Gräberfeld von Diersheim: Studien zur Geschichte der Germanen am Oberrhein vom Gallischen Krieg bis zur Alamannischen Landnahme* (Römisch-Germanische Forschungen 28) (Berlin: de Gruyter, 1966), with review by C.M. Wells, *Journal of Roman Studies* 59 (1969): 303–5.

38 *agros vacuos et usui militum sepositos* (Tacitus, *Annals* XI.19, XIII.54); Frisian coast (*Annals* IV.72).

39 Compare the Numidian frontier, for instance, from which survives the list of customs duties on the Zaraï inscription (*CIL* 8.4508, cf. 18643): C.M. Wells, 'The problems of desert frontiers', in Valerie A. Maxfield and Michael J. Dobson (eds), *Roman Frontier Studies 1989: Proceedings of the XVth International Congress of Roman Frontier Studies* (Exeter: University of Exeter Press, 1990), 478–81.

40 Hans Jürgen Eggers, *Der römische Import im freien Germanien* (Atlas der Urgeschichte 1) (Hamburg: Hamburgisches Museum für Völkerkunde und Vorgeschichte, 1951).

41 Similar changes occurred along the St. Lawrence between the visits of Cartier in 1534 and Champlain early in the seventeenth century; see C.M. Wells, 'The ethnography of the Celts and of the Algonkian-Iroquoian tribes: a comparison of two historical traditions', in J.A.S. Evans (ed.), *Polis and Imperium: studies in honour of Edward Togo Salmon* (Toronto: Hakkert, 1974), 265–78.

42 Von Uslar *Studien*, 1–5; cf. Nierhaus, *Das swebische Gräberfeld*, 224–30.

43 *consilium coercendi intra terminos imperii* (Tacitus, *Annals* I.11).

44 *magna ex parte domitorem Germaniae* (Velleius II.97); for a more complete narrative of these events, with full references, see Wells, *German Policy of Augustus*, 93–5, 154–6.

45 Wells, *German Policy of Augustus*, 156–61, 237–45; the site of the Varian Disaster has now been identified north of Osnabrück, after generations of fruitless controversy: see Wolfgang Schlüter *et al.*, 'Archäologische Zeugnisse zur Varusschlacht? Die Untersuchungen in der Kalkrieser-Niewedder Senke bei Osnabrück', *Germania* 70 (1992): 307–402.

46 On this and other aspects of trade and economic life, see Edith Mary Wightman, *Gallia Belgica* (London: Batsford, 1985), chapter 6.

47 Cf. Ramsay MacMullen, 'Rural romanization', *Phoenix* 22 (1968): 337–41; C.M. Wells, 'The impact of the Augustan campaigns on Germany', in *Assimilation et résistance à la culture gréco-romaine dans le monde ancien: travaux du VIe Congrès international d'Etudes classiques* (Madrid, September 1974) (Bucharest: Editura Academiei, and Paris: Les Belles Lettres, 1976), 421–31.

48 Tacitus, *Histories* IV.22.

49 Wightman, *Gallia Belgica*, chapter 4.

50 The only druid that we know by name, Diviciacus, the pro-Roman Aeduan, was from a leading family and deeply involved in tribal politics: Caesar, *Gallic War*, 1.3, 1.16–20, etc.

51 Suetonius, *Claudius* XXV.5.

52 The phrase *interpretatio Romana* is from Tacitus, *Germania* XLII.4, and the quotations from Miranda Green, *The Gods of the Celts* (Gloucester and Totowa, N.J.: Alan Sutton, 1986), 36.

53 Wightman, *Roman Trier* 208–27.

54 *Aus rheinischer Kunst und Kultur: Auswahlkatalog des Rheinischen Landesmuseums Bonn 1963* (Düsseldorf: Rheinland-Verlag, 1963), 56–7, with bibliography, illustrated plate 17.

55 Green, *Gods of the Celts*, 78–85. For the language of the epithets, on the one hand, Ernest Babelon, *Le Rhin dans l'histoire: l'antiquité, Gaulois et Germains* (Paris: Leroux, 1916), 347–8, patriotically prejudiced (note the date of publication), with a long list of topographical epithets and the rather optimistic comment, 'Tous ces noms barbares de sanctuaires locaux ne sauraient s'expliquer par les langues germaniques. Ils paraissent bien

celtiques'; and on the other hand, H. von Petrikovits, *Rheinische Geschichte* I.1: *Altertum*, 2nd edn (Düsseldorf: Schwann, 1980), 154–5. Cf. also the goddess Nehalennia, recorded on votive altars dredged from the East Scheldt estuary, Celtic in iconography, the name itself ambiguous, though perhaps rather Germanic than Celtic, cf. J.E. Bogaers in *Deae Nehalenniae: Gids bij de Tentoonstelling Nehalennia de Zeeuwse Godin, Zeeland in de Romeinse Tijd, Romeinse Monumenten uit de Oosterschelde* (Middelburg: Koninklijk Zeeuwsch Genootschap der Wetenschappen, and Leiden: Rijksmuseum van Oudheden, 1971), 33–4.

56 Wightman, *Gallia Belgica*, 224–5; Green, *Gods of the Celts*, 61–5; Octavio Paz in *Mexico: splendors of thirty centuries* (New York: Metropolitan Museum of Art, 1990), 23–4, with crucifixes illustrated pp. 22 and 251, cf. mural and carvings, pp. 236, 248, 249, 255. Nancy M. Farriss, *Maya Society under Colonial Rule: the collective enterprise of survival* (Princeton: Princeton University Press, 1984), chapters 10 and 11, suggests parallels in the ways in which a conquered society adapts its worship to accommodate the conquerors' religion.

PART X

ON THE EDGE OF THE WESTERN WORLD

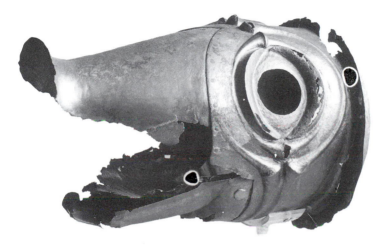

THE CELTIC BRITONS UNDER ROME

— ·•· —

Graham Webster

INTRODUCTION

It is very difficult to explain the process by which Britain became Celtic. Some scholars believe in the theory of successive waves of Celtic settlers from Europe. Others see British 'celticization' as a gradual process, involving European influences and the adoption of Celtic techniques and customs rather than invasion, other than in a few very specific and limited instances, exemplified by the 'Arras culture' of north-east Britain (Collis 1984). The presence of British Celts and their influences can be traced by their settlements, metalwork and changes in technology. The most significant of these changes was the discovery, probably in the Near East, of the technique of smelting iron from its own ore and its forging into tools and weapons (see Chapter 17) (Collis 1984: 15, 24, 28–32). By the fourth century BC, these techniques were well established in south-east Britain with the discovery of suitable ores from the limestone belt across Northamptonshire into Lincolnshire. This can be seen from the distribution of currency-bars which were used in trade-exchange (Allen 1967: 307–35, figs 1, 2). It has been assumed that these are the *taleis ferreis* mentioned by Caesar (*De Bello Gallico* V.12.4) as used by the Britons as 'money' (*pro nummo*). The Celts were great warriors and seized the opportunity to produce iron swords which, with tempering, became as fine as modern steel, well surpassing the earlier bronze weapons. They became master-craftsmen and even supplied the Roman army with its *gladii* and longer cavalry swords (*spathae*).

In the long period of the Iron Age in Britain, there were many changes. These were due perhaps to some movement of people from Gaul and the development of trade, especially in fine metalwork (Figure 32.1). The identification of particular communities can only be made by their burial customs and other religious rites. These were so deep a part of tribal tradition that changes took place only slowly over long periods and are not easily detectable. Unfortunately, there is a scarcity of recognized burials of their period (see Chapter 26).

Convincing evidence of cultural change can perhaps be studied in the appearance of defended enclosures, usually on hilltops, which is indicative of an unstable society (see Chapter 5). The different types and sizes of these enclosures must reflect changes in relationships between communities and their tribal hierarchies.

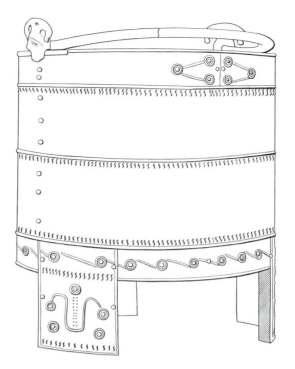

Figure 32.1 A reconstruction of a bucket from Baldock. (Copyright: British Museum.)

Cross-Channel trade routes had already been established for centuries before the Roman occupation, and some of the coastal tribes of northern Gaul had already well-founded trade relations with the peoples along the south coast of Britain. This has been shown by investigations at the ports of entry at Hengistbury Head (Cunliffe 1987) and Mount Batten (Cunliffe 1988) near Plymouth. The most important imports were olive oil and wine, to which the Gallic Celts had become addicted (Diodorus Siculus v.26.3), as the evidence from the distribution of amphorae shows (Peacock 1971: 168–88). More evidence of this trade is found from studying the ships of this period (see Chapter 15), especially from those wrecked off the British and Gallic coasts (Muckelroy 1981: 275–97). What is of great interest is that the wine was not confined to the Gallic producers but included products from north Italy as well (Galliou 1984), a factor which was to be of importance at a later date, as will be seen.

A problem to be faced by the British Celts was the payment for those imports. There was a limit to the quantity of gold bullion in the form of coins, especially as it was needed for internal uses. As a warrior society, there was always the possibility of capturing slaves in the inter-tribal frontier skirmishes which were almost annual events, but this too was limited and the only other marketable commodities were agricultural produce and livestock. The possibility of using such as surplus for trade has been discussed by Barry Cunliffe in relation to Danebury (Cunliffe 1983: 174–5). However much evidence excavation can produce, there remain too many imponderable factors to form a sound judgement. But the problem remains of the method of exchange for the wine consumed at Danebury on the evidence of the amphorae found in a late phase of the site (100–50 BC) (ibid.: 179).

This was suddenly changed, at least for south-east Britain, when this area came into direct contact with Rome, through the raids of Caesar in 55 and 54 BC. But before this is considered in detail, it is necessary to consider how and why Rome became interested in Celtic Britain through the operations of Caesar in Gaul.

ROME AND BRITAIN

At this period, the Roman image of Britain was of a remote island on the edge of the world, hidden in the Atlantic mists. There were stories brought back by intrepid Greek traders like Phytheas of the fourth century BC (Hawkes 1975) and from the Greek ethnographer, Poseidonios who wrote descriptions of the Celts. Although the text of his work has not survived, it is possible to recover some of it from others who quoted him. These include Athenaeus, Diodorus Siculus, Strabo and later, of course, Caesar (Tierney 1960: 189–275).

JULIUS CAESAR IN GAUL AND BRITAIN

After Julius Caesar's consulship in 59 BC, he first became governor of Cisalpine and then of Transalpine Gaul. Caesar chronicled his progress through Gaul in detail in the *Commentarii de Bello Gallico*. It was compiled for his dispatches to the Senate and can be seen as a skilful justification of his activities.

Caesar's interest in Britain was no doubt inspired by hopes of plunder, such as he had enjoyed in Gaul, but also perhaps to 'upstage' his Roman rival Pompey in venturing across the sea beyond the known world, but there was a more important factor. He had learnt from traders that the cross-channel trade was mainly controlled by the Veneti, a seafaring people occupying what is now the Cherbourg peninsula, which thrusts itself so intrusively into the Channel. So powerful was the control the Veneti possessed that, according to Caesar (III.8), they exacted tolls for all those who ventured into their waters. He was also informed that there was a long and well-established relationship between this tribe and those of southern Britain. According to Strabo (IV.4.1), the Veneti had even established a trading post in Britain. It has been argued from the excavations by Barry Cunliffe (Mays 1981: 55–7) that this could have been Hengistbury Head. The history and extent of this trade has been tentatively studied by Cunliffe (Cunliffe 1987). There is, however, more work needed at other points of entry such as Hamworth, Poole, before any considered assessment can be made. The Morini, who controlled the shorter route to the east, may have had trading relationships with the tribes of the area that is now Sussex and Kent. One of the obvious entry-points would have been Bosham Harbour, later to be occupied by the Roman fleet (Cunliffe 1971: 26–52).

Caesar became aware of the close relationship between the tribes of south-east Britain and north-east Gaul through cross-channel movements which had already been taking place and which were accelerated by his hostile activities in Gaul. Of the tribes affected, the Bellovaci had, according to Diviciacus, fled to Britain after Caesar's advance into north-east Gaul (II.14.2–5). This provided Caesar with a useful pretext to present to the Senate the evidence that those tribes now in Britain had been sending men and supplies to their distant relations (IV.20). There has even been a suggestion that the presence of a large number of Gallic coins in Britain was sent to pay for that help (Hawkes 1977: 142) though doubt has been expressed about this (Muckelroy 1981: 275–97). Strabo (IV.4.1) stated that the Veneti were prepared to attempt to hinder Caesar's projected campaign against Britain for fear of the loss of their monopoly, a suggestion explored by C.E. Stevens (1982: 3–18).

For Caesar to gain control over the Channel, it was essential that the Veneti and their fleet should be destroyed. The pretext for hostilities was the detention of the Roman officers sent to collect corn. Caesar probably made the offence seem far more serious by adding that they had been imprisoned (*in vincla*). Caesar had been collecting and hiring ships for his invasion of Britain, but he had come to realize that he could not compete seriously with the Veneti in the Channel. He began by attacking their cliff castles on the edges of the promontories. But he soon discovered that they were protected by the tides and they were also very difficult to approach by land, a completely new factor for one accustomed to the Mediterranean. Caesar describes in some detail the physical problems and also the type of ships used by the tribe (III.13). The only way the Romans could hope to capture and destroy the Venetic ships was by boarding them and he chronicles in detail the successful tactics that followed. Caesar's treatment of the Veneti was especially savage: the whole of their senate was put to the sword and all the able-bodied males sold into slavery. Thus the Channel trade monopoly was broken by the virtual destruction of the tribal leaders.

THE INVASIONS OF BRITAIN

The first reconnaisance of Britain took place late in the season of 55 BC as Caesar had first to deal with the Germans. Total ignorance of the neap tide almost led to disaster (IV.23–38). This could be considered, therefore, as no more than a raid, and the twenty days of thanksgiving decreed by the Senate must appear as an over-reaction or the result of misinformation. Caesar may have regarded it as one of his rare failures, to be rapidly expunged from the record. But he was more determined than before to seize the rich financial rewards which he calculated were available for the taking. He had been made aware of the difficulties of transporting a large army across the Channel, but he had also discovered that the Britons were still using war-chariots, long obsolete in Gaulish fighting practice. In the winter of 55–54 BC, he ordered more extensive and thorough preparations, which included the gathering together of 600 ships and building 28 men-of-war (V.2). After waiting twenty-five days for fair weather, he set sail with his legions and 4,000 Gallic cavalry. The Britons were so alarmed at the size of this armada that they withdrew from the coast; Caesar stated that 800 ships could be seen altogether and if 628 were used by the army, this leaves 172 hired or built by the traders (V.8; *annontinis privatisque quas sui quisque commodi fecerat*). One could have no clearer indication of Caesar's main intention, that of continuing to loot and plunder in hostile terrain, all of which would be skilfully disguised behind the glory of victories for Rome with the extra lustre of their being achieved in a far-off land beyond the stormy seas and any horizon familiar to Rome.

In this first season in Britain, Caesar had to rely on the tribal leader Commius to win over those Atrebates who had settled in Britain from Gaul but, in accomplishing this task, Commius had been captured by other Britons (IV.27). He was later returned to Caesar, but the net result was that only two of the British tribes sent hostages (IV.38). In 54, Caesar was better prepared since he now had a new ally in Mandubracius, a prince of the Trinovantes (V.20), whose father had been killed by Cassivellaunus. This information is only given by Caesar during the course of the campaign, almost as an afterthought, whereas his whole strategy was clearly based on the ability of this tribe to supply his army and for their territory to be used as a base for his operations on the north bank of the Thames.

The campaign had in fact been carefully planned when Mandubracius had visited Caesar at his winter quarters in Gaul. The tribal affiliation of the British Commander, Cassivellaunus, was not stated, only the information that the tribes hostile to Caesar had appointed him as their leader. It is stated that this tribe occupied a territory north of the Thames and it appears later in Caesar's narrative that it bordered that of the Trinovantes (V.21). His stronghold would therefore most probably have been in Epping Forest and would fit Caesar's phrase *cum silvas impeditas*.

Caesar lists the British tribes which had become his allies, i.e. the Cenimagni, Segontiaci, Ancalites, Bibroci and Cassi. Unfortunately, only one of these, the Cenimagni (the great Iceni), is known at a later date. There is a coin of Tasciovanus with the word SEGO (van Arsdell 1989: 385–7), which, if it refers to a tribe, may have been a shortened form of Segontiaci. If so, this tribe was later absorbed into one of the larger units. It must be assumed that the others also later became sub-units of the Catuvellauni or the Trinovantes.

To secure success in Britain, as in Gaul, it was Caesar's continued practice to form alliances. This enabled him to pursue a further aim, which was the deliberate breaking of the Gallic trading monopoly with the Britons, mainly in wine. He was then able to sell this valuable right to the Italian traders. Trading posts were set up in the territories of the friendly tribes for the sale and distribution of wine and fine silver utensils associated with its use. The evidence for this is quite positive since not only has one of the trading posts been discovered at Skeleton Green (Partridge 1981) on the river Lea but there are also the amphorae and other objects found in the rich burials of tribal notables found in the Welwyn area (Stead 1967: 1–62). This has enabled Barry Cunliffe to publish a map of their distribution, which clearly indicates a sudden shift in the direction of trade from the coast of northern Gaul to the shorter crossings to the east and even to the Rhine (Cunliffe 1984: fig. 9). The wine and the metal drinking utensils were now coming from Italy.

Although Caesar's immediate objective was personal financial gain, he must have been aware that this trade, once established, would be highly advantageous to Rome through the heavy export duty charged on goods leaving the empire. There was also a long-term effect of Britons becoming accustomed to Roman goods and with it the establishment of a currency and the more extensive use of it for commercial exchange. To that extent it could be seen as a 'softening-up' process towards eventual conquest.

But ninety-seven years were to elapse before conquest and the absorption of Britain into the Roman Empire were to become an actuality and during this time the British tribes of the south-east underwent considerable changes. They maintained contact with their compatriots and became aware of the advantages and disadvantages of becoming provincials under Rome. But the most important aspect which Romans may not have fully appreciated was the link between the Gaulish druids and Britain. Caesar had skilfully built up a programmed hostility towards these high priests and arbiters in Rome, mainly, perhaps, as a diversion for his own dubious practices. He was fully aware (VI.13) that they were the one and only unifying force among the Celts and thus a powerful force to combat his drive towards division of the tribes into friends or foes. The effect of this was that the Gaulish druids fled from their country and united themselves with those of Britain (whence, Caesar tells us, came the origins of druidism), where they began to instil a hatred of Rome in the ruling tribal families and especially into the children whom they educated. But Rome was always anxious to maintain a close contact with friendly client-rulers by flattery and rich gifts from the classical world. Another policy, developed by Augustus, was to require these rulers to send their children to Rome to be educated with the imperial family (Braund 1984: 9–22). They were then, in effect, hostages but also they became thoroughly romanized. An excellent British example of this policy was, most probably, Cogidubnus, whose aspirations as a builder on the grand roman scale are demonstrated by the Fishbourne palace and the Chichester inscription (Bogaers 1979: 243–5).

Concerning the tribal affiliations and boundaries of the Catuvellauni and the Trinovantes north of the Thames, the imported goods would seem to imply that the former were the more favoured recipients. But the coin distribution provides a more complicated pattern which has prompted van Arsdell to abandon any attempt to separate them. He considers that the two tribes can only be seen 'as a single economic group' (van Arsdell 1989: 319). There was a succession of rulers who put their names on coins; the first to do so was Addedomarus and the distribution of his coins spreads over what are assumed to be the areas of both tribes (ibid.: 494, map 67), but there is no help with mint names. Those of a successor or possibly contemporary, Dubnovellaunus, for a short time appear to be concentrated in the Trinovantian area. There followed a more powerful ruler, Tasciovanus, who controlled both tribes with mints at Camulodunum and Verulamium, as the names CAM and VERO on the coins clearly demonstrate (ibid.: 365). Another point of great interest is that some of the coins are modelled on Roman types. This can only indicate a close link with Rome, possibly the better trade opportunities being now officially recognized by the loan of Roman die-cutters with a range of coin types of the Republic offered for choice by the rulers.

After a brief interregnum, the most powerful of all British kings, Cunobelinos, took control. The coins were gradually improved in quality, but continued to copy Roman types (now of Augustus), Cunobelinos now being designated as REX, the Latin for king. His coinage was vast and is still in need of close study, but it must indicate a considerable increase in trade with the Roman Empire. There is even a hint of the introduction of a rudimentary currency, in the appearance of the strange potin coins, which may have been intended as small change.

Cunobelinos was a great statesman who was able to maintain a balance between the anti- and pro-Roman elements. He clearly saw the economic advantages of trade and also that maintaining a friendly relationship to Rome strengthened him politically. In AD 14–16 in the war against the Germans, some Roman soldiers were shipwrecked on the shores of his kingdom and he promptly sent them back to Gaul. Although his policy was opposed by the druids, they were forced to bide their time and concentrated on their influence on the sons of the king, Caratacus and Togodubnus. Their indoctrination was possible as they were responsible for the children's education. Their father had managed to avoid having to send them to Rome as he had presumably refused to become an actual client-king.

Cunobelinos must have exercised influence or even control over the neighbouring tribes, especially those south of the Thames. The succession of rulers whose names appear on coins offers a very confusing sequence of events. This applies particularly to the Atrebates–Regni alliance. The native ruler from *c.* AD 10 was Verica, who was deposed by Epaticcus, who claimed to be a son of Tasciovanus, thus bringing thus tribes under the Trinovantian control. This would probably have been the maximum extent of the influence of Cunobelinos. As the great king became enfeebled *c.* AD 40, the northern part of the kingdom of Verica was invaded by Epaticcus, whose Trinovantian origins appear on the coin-types he issued (van Arsdell 1989: 179). He pushed south and forced Verica out: as an ally of Rome, Verica fled there to seek help from Claudius for his restoration.

At this critical stage, Cunobelinos died and his great kingdom was inherited by his two sons Togodubnus and Caratacus. The former was presumably the elder since he held this homeland while his brother took over the Atrebatic/Regnian kingdom. The two brothers were radically opposed to Rome and it is possible that they ended the trading relationship with Rome which had been started by Caesar and developed under their father. This came at the very beginning of the reign of Claudius and he was faced with the loss of a lucrative trading partner and a client kingdom demanding restoration. Claudius himself was in a delicate position as he had been thrust into the purple by the praetorian guards. Meantime, the Senate had overlooked his existence, had annulled all the Imperial acts, and declared a republic. This august body was somewhat shocked when the praetorians marched into the Senate with a reluctant Claudius and demanded that he should be the new emperor. To Claudius, Britain would have been seen as a heaven-sent opportunity to divert public attention from his precarious position and also to gain the support of his frontier armies, thus reducing his dependence on the guards.

This was the background for the invasion of Britain in AD 43. In Britain there was considerable support for Rome. The old alliances created by Caesar had collapsed, although that with the Iceni probably survived, but for others Rome offered an escape from the dominance of Cunobelinos. Those who had suffered most were the Catuvellauni and the Atrebates/Regni but it would also appear that tribes on their western and northern boundaries had felt the strong arm of the British ruler. Plautius received supplication from the northern Dobunni on his arrival (Dannell 1977: 231). Many tribes saw Rome as their salvation against their British oppressors: the Catuvellauni in particular from the Trinovantes. They took the earliest opportunity of an alliance with Rome. This is demonstrated by the favours they later received and the hatred they incurred of the anti-Roman faction which was later responsible for the destruction of their capital, Verulamium, in the Boudican revolt of AD 60. The Dobunni had split into two tribes, due doubtless to an early dynastic quarrel. The southern half, south of the river Avon, were allied to the Durotriges, who had a bitter hatred of Rome, due mainly to Caesar's destruction of the Veneti with whom they had a close trading and possibly tribal relationship. The northern half of the tribe had felt the distant hand of Cunobelinos, according to Dio, and small-scale excavations at their great oppidum at Bagendon have produced evidence of early trade in the form of imported samian (Royal Commission on Historical Monuments 1976: 7). It is possible that they had been obliged to supply levies to the anti-Roman forces gathered together by Caratacus.

THE CLAUDIAN INVASION AND BEYOND

The fate of Britain was settled by the two-day battle on the Medway when Vespasian outflanked the Britons and established a bridgehead on the west bank. The army advanced to the Thames but remained on the south bank to await the arrival of Claudius to enable him to lead his victorious army into the enemy capital at Camulodunum. Here he received the surrender of eleven rulers, according to the surviving pieces of the inscription from his triumphal arch. What is surprising, however, is the inclusion of the phrase *sine ulla iactura* which, at that time, would have meant 'without bloodshed', which is grossly untrue. Caesar, a hundred years earlier, had used it in a totally different sense, since to him it meant 'without loss of honour'. The pedantic mind of Claudius may have seen an occasion to use an outdated phrase quite deliberately as an acknowledgement to his distinguished forebear. It would also have been legally correct, since it could have been said that Claudius invaded Britain in response to the request of a client-king, Verica.

The identity of the eleven rulers who surrendered is not known, but presumably it would have included those who had already come to terms with Rome, such as the northern Dobunni, the Catuvellauni, the Atrebates/Regni and most likely the old ally, the Iceni, and the powerful Brigantian confederacy of north Britain under Queen Cartimandua. It seems probable that, in the later reorganization of the tribes for administrative purposes, smaller tribes were absorbed into the larger units. This could be especially true of the Catuvellauni, who appear, in the Roman reorganization, to have occupied a territory larger than other tribes. This could also apply to the Corieltauvi (formerly and incorrectly known as the Coritani, Tomlin 1983: 353–5). The most interesting tribe is the Regni with its head of state, Cogidubnus. He had been given Roman citizenship by Claudius and took his name, Claudius Tiberius.

The Roman commander, Aulus Plautius, was evidently working to a predetermined plan to occupy only south-eastern Britain. The boundary of the new province was marked by the Fosse frontier which stretched from the Humber to Lincoln, then turned in a south-west direction to the south-west coast (Webster 1958: 49–98; 1993b: 159–67). It was a fortified zone some 30–40 miles in depth and included those tribes which had migrated to Britain from Gaul within the previous four centuries, the migration latterly accelerated by Caesar's conquest. These were the peoples who would have been expected to take most readily to the Roman way of life and especially to commerce and trade. The trading posts established in consequence of Caesar's trading arrangements had already intensified this process.

In the wake of the army, Gallic and other traders moved to Britain to supply the army and its followers and later to set up their workshops and markets. The British Celts of the south-east had hitherto built only in timber, but now the stone-masons arrived and rapidly found ample supplies of high quality stone. The two early military tombstones at Colchester (Collingwood and Wright 1965: 200, 201) are of Bath stone; Purbeck marble was very soon discovered and exploited, before its poor weathering qualities had been recognized. Tiles were an essential building material, especially for roof and heating systems and tile-wrights constructed their kilns where there were suitable amounts of clay and near enough to the demand for their products. The search for minerals by prospectors also rapidly followed the conquest, especially for silver and gold, which Tacitus regarded as *pretium victoriae* ('spoils of victory', *Agricola* 12). This almost precipitated a crisis in Rome when the Spanish lessees thought their prices would be seriously undercut. However, any fears were soon dissipated when it became known that the silver content in the British ore (*galena*) was low. This increased the production costs, but also provided a large lead resource, which was much needed for tanks, water-pipes and roof-flashings. That the Mendip mines were being worked by AD 49 is indicated by a stamped lead pipe (Collingwood and Wright 1990: II.2404.1) which must imply army involvement. The stamps also show that, at this stage, it was an imperial monopoly and under military protection in a potentially hostile area.

Thus the Britons of the south-east suddenly found themselves living in a capitalist state with large-scale exploitation of land and natural resources and urban building projects. This was an enormous change from life in tribal-centred communities totally unused to land ownership and a money economy. There is no evidence of their reactions, but one can assume that the kings, chieftains, their families and higher-ranking retainers would have quickly adapted to it with the help of any accumulated bullion which could now be changed into Imperial coinage. The craftsmen and trades-men would have had little difficulty in adapting to the new regime and in particular the Celtic smiths would have found many increased opportunities. But the bulk of the peasants remained tied to the land, with new masters who employed ruthless bailiffs and managers to introduce large-scale production methods. There would also have been a great demand for labourers in all trades.

In Celtic tribal society, the individual had a place and a feeling of belonging to a powerfully interknit family. The inevitable destruction of this basic way of life must have had serious effects on most individuals. This kind of process has been seen in recent times when our so-called civilization has descended on 'primitive' societies in many parts of the world and exploited their lands for commercial gain, with the sad result of total disintegration of tribal life. One of the most obvious and pitiful has been the fate of the Australian Aborigines and their treatment by the brash, ignorant settlers from Europe who regarded them only as savages. But the differences between the British Celts and the newcomers were not so extreme and many 'Romans' were Gauls who had close affinities with their fellow Celts of south-east Britain.

There remained strong anti-Roman elements, mainly in those tribes which had suffered in their encounters with the army. The Durotriges and southern Dobunni still nursed their grievances, which were kept alive by the druids, who saw their only hope of survival in forcing the Romans to give up Britain and, as will be seen, almost succeeding. They had retired to their sacred site on Anglesey (where they may have been responsible for the great ritual offerings of Llyn Cerrig Bach (see Chapter 25)) and now placed their hopes in the Trinovantian prince Caratacus, who had taken his warriors west into Wales. Here, through the influence of the druids, he was accepted by the Celtic chiefs there and started to recruit warriors for the battles ahead.

His first strike was in the winter of 48 when the governors were changing over. Plautius had left and was being replaced by the new governor, Ostorius Scapula. Caratacus led his men across the lower Severn to link up with the Durotriges and their allies. The word *turbidae* used by Tacitus (*Annales* XII. 31) had for him the meaning of internal dissension. Scapula ordered his troops out of their winter quarters and drove the Celts back over the Severn. He then realized that he was faced with a serious problem. He had no authority to invade Wales, but Caratacus posed a serious threat to the long frontier and could not be allowed the freedom to strike again. The governor was forced into a decision, which was to have most unfortunate consequences for Rome, in sowing the seed of the revolt of AD 60. In a corrupt sentence of the text, he appears to have attempted to disarm all the tribes within the province whose loyalty was suspect. This was designed to strike terror into the Britons, so that they would be too cowed to follow the call of the druids to rise. Only a section of the Iceni, hitherto loyal, revolted but having dealt with this incident, Scapula collected as many troops as he could for a search-and-destroy operation. This left some eastern areas very short of troops and he was obliged to create, with imperial authority, two client kings to be responsible for law and order in their kingdoms. They were Prasutagus of the Iceni and Cogidubnus of the Atrebates/ Regni. The latter is even credited by Tacitus as having been given an extended territory (*quaedam civitates*: *Agricola* 14) and his loyalty to Rome remained unstinting.

The subsequent battle and fate of Caratacus are also well recorded by Tacitus (*Annales*.XIII.33, 38; Webster 1993C: 28–32). Scapula was now faced with the problem of a frontier along the river Severn along the eastern border of the hill country. The basic concept was to block all the valleys to prevent the Celts from invading the province. They rejoiced at the sudden death of Scapula (probably resulting from stress) and had become so strong that a legion was defeated in the field (*Annales* XII.40). Didius Gallus, the new governor, managed to stabilize the situation, but a new trouble arose in the north because of the hostility of Venutius and the need to protect his wife, the client-queen Cartimandua.

Britain was now much on the agenda in Rome and the youthful Nero's elderly advisers, Seneca and Burrus, urged him to give up Britannia altogether, as it had become too expensive with heavy military losses and its mineral wealth was not as great as had been expected. This is based on an interpretation of a brief statement of Suetonius (*Nero* 18: *etiam ex Britannia deducere exercitum cogitavit*). Nero, however, refused to give up a province so dearly won by his distinguished forebear, thinking, of course, of Julius Caesar.

Quintus Veranius was sent to deal with the Welsh Celts and concentrated on the Silures, but it was his successor, Suetonius Paullinus, who eliminated the real source of anti-Roman activity, the druids and their sanctuary on Anglesey. But as soon as they realized they were the target, they attempted to divert the governor's intention by organizing a great revolt by the anti-Roman tribes, using Queen Boudica as the figurehead Paullinus was not to be diverted and ordered Legio XX, stationed on the Nene near Longthorpe, to deal with the problem before it got out of hand. The legion was ambushed and annihilated. The Britons then destroyed the much-hated *colonia* at Camulodunum, the depot and administration centre of Londinium and the British pro-Roman city of Verulamium. Drunk with success, they pushed up Watling Street to finish off the army of Paullinus. But the Roman legionaries showed their mettle and, although overwhelmed in number, hacked the British horde to pieces, and Paullinus, full of vengeance, swept through the lands of the hostile tribes destroying everything in sight. He had to be recalled before the damage was too great for recovery. This scarifying experience left deep wounds on the Britons and it was to be several generations before the province recovered, eventually to become a peaceful and prosperous member of the empire.

COLCHESTER.

Figure 32.2 A hunt cup scene.

Figure 32.3 A hunt scene on a beaker from Colchester. (Published by C. Roach Smith in 1857.)

REFERENCES

Allen, D.F. (1967) 'Iron currency bars in Britain', *Proceedings of the Prehistoric Society* 33: 307–35.

Arsdell, R.D. van (1989) *Celtic Coinage in Britain*, London: Spink.

Bogaers, J.E. (1979) 'King Cogidubnus in Chichester: another reading of RIB 91', *Britannia* 10: 243–5.

Braund, D.C. (1984) *Rome and the Friendly King: the character of the client kingship*, London: Croom Helm.

Collingwood, R.G. and Wright, R.P. (1965) *The Roman Inscriptions of Britain*, Oxford: Oxford University Press.

Collis, J. (1984) *The European Iron Age*, London: Batsford.

Cunliffe, B.W. (1971) *Fishbourne*, London: Society of Antiquaries.

—— (1982) 'Britain, the Veneti and beyond', *Oxford Journal of Archaeology* 1: 39–68.

—— (1983) *Danebury: anatomy of an iron age hillfort*, London: Batsford.

—— (1984) 'Relations between Britain and Gaul in the 1st century BC and early 1st century AD', in S. Macready and F.H. Thompson (eds) *Cross-Channel Trade between Gaul and Britain in the Pre-Roman Iron Age*, London: Society of Antiquaries Occasional Paper (NS) 4, 3–23.

—— (1987) *Hengistbury Head, Dorset*, Oxford: Oxford University Committee for Archaeology, Monograph 13.

—— (1988) *Mount Batten, Plymouth*, Oxford: Oxford University Committee for Archaeology, Monograph 26.

Dannell, G.B. (1977) 'The samian from Bagendon', in J. Dore and K. Greene (eds) *Roman Pottery Studies in Britain and Beyond*, Oxford: British Archaeological Reports, Special Series 30, 229–34.

Galliou, P. (1984) 'Days of wine and roses? Early Armorica and the Atlantic wine trade', in S. Macready and F.H. Thompson (eds) *Cross-Channel Trade between Gaul and Britain in the Pre-Roman Iron Age*, London: Society of Antiquaries Occasional Paper (NS) 4, 24–36.

Hawkes, C.F.C. (1975) *Pytheas, Europe and Greek Explorers*, Eighth J.L. Myres Memorial Lecture, Oxford: Oxford University Press.

—— (1977) 'Britain and Julius Caesar', *Proceedings of the British Academy* 63: 142.

Mays, M. (1981) 'Strabo IV, 4.1: a reference to Hengistbury Head?', *Antiquity* 55: 55–7.

Muckelroy, K. (1981) 'Middle bronze age trade between Britain and Europe: a maritime perspective', *Proceedings of the Prehistoric Society* 37: 275–97.

Partridge, C. (1981) *Skeleton Green*, London: Britannia Monograph Series no. 2.

Peacock, D.P.S. (1971) 'Roman amphorae in pre-Roman Britain', in D. Hills and M. Jesson (eds) *The Iron Age and its Hillforts*, Southampton: University of Southampton, 161–88.

Royal Commission on Historical Monuments (1976) *Ancient and Historical Monuments to the County of Gloucester I*, London: Her Majesty's Stationery Office.

Stead, I.M. (1967) 'A La Tène III burial at Welwyn Garden City', *Archaeologia* 101: 1–62.

Stevens, C.E. (1982) 'The *Bellum Gallicum* as a work of propaganda', *Collections Latomus* 11: 3–18.

Tierney, J.J. (1960) 'The Celtic ethnography of Posidonius', *Proceedings of the Royal Irish Academy* 60: 189–275.

Tomlin, R.S.O. (1983) 'Non Coritani sed Corieltauvi', *Antiquaries Journal* 63: 353–5.

Webster, G. (1958) 'The Roman military advance under Ostorius Scapula', *Archaeological Journal* 115: 49–98.

—— (1993a) *Boudica* (2nd edn) London: Batsford.

—— (1993b) *The Roman Invasion of Britain* (2nd edn) London: Batsford.

—— (1993c) *Rome against Caratacus* (2nd edn) London: Batsford.

IRELAND
A world without the Romans

—— ·•· ——

Barry Raftery

INTRODUCTION

The Roman general Agricola, advancing to western Scotland in AD 82, may well have glimpsed the coast of Antrim shimmering on a distant horizon to the west. He would certainly have been acquainted with Ireland which, according to his biographer Tacitus, was much like Britain 'in soil, in climate and in the character and civilization of its people' (*Agricola* 24). Agricola appears to have had no doubt that the country could be taken with a single legion and a small force of auxiliaries. This rash assertion was, however, never put to the test. As most of Britain succumbed to the iron embrace of Roman civilization, Ireland continued in its ancient ways, an Atlantic outpost of Celtic independence.

Ireland was not, however, aloof from Rome (Warner 1976, 1991) and there is ample evidence that extensive trade took place between the island and the Roman world. This is clear from the classical references, and many of the scattered items of Roman manufacture found in the country could have come in this way (Bateson, 1973). Undoubtedly, too, occasional travellers from provincial Rome set foot on Irish shores. Some were to die in Ireland as is shown by the classic Roman cremation burial in a glass urn found at Stonyford, Co. Kilkenny (Raftery 1981: 194, fig. 41, nos. 1–2; Bourke 1989) and by a series of coin-associated inhumations at Bray Head, Co. Wicklow (Bateson 1973: 45). Burials at Lambay, Co. Dublin, have been seen as those of refugees from Roman Brigantia (Rynne, 1976) while major hoards of silver and of coins, variously found in Limerick (ÓRíordáin 1947: 43–53), Antrim and Derry (Bateson 1973: 25), could represent payment made to Irish auxiliaries for service rendered to Imperial Rome. Alternatively, such hoards might be regarded as Roman booty brought home by Irish raiders.

Roman influences gradually percolated into the country and these are detectable in many aspects of material culture, in changing burial customs and, ultimately, in bringing about fundamental changes in religious beliefs. Ireland, however, remained Celtic and retained a prehistoric iron age society long after it had disappeared elsewhere.

The nature of this society and the processes by which 'celticization' took place continue to be a matter for intense debate among specialists. In recent years even the most deep-rooted assumptions have come under critical scrutiny. There is particular concern about the precise meaning of the term 'Celtic' in an insular context. In the narrowest sense the term is a purely linguistic one and thus there are problems when it is applied to the archaeological evidence.

At the beginning of history, around the middle of the first millennium AD, the country was wholly Celtic in its language and its institutions. For linguists, this can only have come about by means of a significant immigration of Celtic-speaking people at some time in later prehistory. Such an intrusion is not, however, reflected in the archaeological evidence. There is thus seeming conflict between the two disciplines.

It may be that these difficulties derive from the defective quality of the material record for, in truth, the Iron Age in Ireland is represented by only a small body of evidence, mainly consisting of scattered artefacts devoid of context and often even of provenance. Burials are few and settlements all but non-existent. There are also inherent weaknesses in the archaeological method which derive from the virtual impossibility of proving unequivocally from the archaeological record the presence in a given area of intrusive peoples, even in cases where an intrusion is historically documented.

These matters are not easily resolved and can scarcely be further debated here. From the perspective of archaeology the indications are, however, of very considerable population continuity throughout the last millennium BC. At the same time it is difficult not to see the profound changes in art and technology, which heralded the appearance of La Tène influences in Ireland, as indicative of the arrival of *some* foreigners in the land. These may well have been few in number, perhaps no more than a ruling caste with specialist metalworkers. Whether such hypothetical intruders could have been responsible for creating the Ireland of the earliest historical sources, however, will continue to be a matter for discussion.

IRON AGE BEGINNINGS

There is little to suggest that the earliest phase of the Irish Iron Age may be regarded as 'Celtic', however that term is applied. The Hallstatt culture is represented in Ireland by little more than a scatter of insular variants of the continental Gündlingen-type sword, a handful of winged chapes and a few other items (Raftery 1984: 8–14). None of these objects is iron with the rather doubtful exception of a corroded and fragmentary sword blade from the river Shannon at Athlone for which a Hallstatt date has been claimed (Rynne 1982; Scott 1991).

These remains undoubtedly show that Ireland was in touch with the Hallstatt world outside and that the country shared in the changing fashions of sword manufacture spreading across western Europe at this time (Champion 1982: 41). It seems too that experimentation in iron technology was also taking place in different parts of the country at about the same time. This is hinted at by two looped-and-socketed axeheads of iron from Co. Antrim and by a cauldron of riveted iron sheets from Co. Cavan (Raftery 1983, nos. 555, 567, 577). All are stray finds, however, so their dating is uncertain but the technique of their manufacture has generally been taken as showing the continuity of bronzeworking traditions in the new metal. Such a transitional phase is perhaps best illustrated at the second occupation level uncovered at crannóg 61, Rathtinaun, Lough Gara, Co. Sligo. This followed a primary level of wholly late bronze age character and was culturally indistinguishable from the latter apart from the presence in Level 2 of five iron artefacts (J. Raftery 1972). Of these, a shafthole axehead was most interesting (Raftery 1983, no. 583) for, though clumsily assembled from three forged iron plates, it nonetheless displays no small measure of technical skill, not least of which is the seemingly deliberate carburization of the blade to harden the cutting edge (Figure 33.1) (Scott 1991: 52–5).

The earliest Iron Age in Ireland is thus more properly regarded as merely an incipient Iron Age, a product of outside contacts and sporadic experimentation with the new metal by indigenous craftsmen. No population change is implied by the archaeological evidence. The transition from bronzesmith to blacksmith was slow and halting and doubtless it was the former who for a long time held sway.

In the centuries after about 600 BC major changes appear to have taken place in Ireland, changes which may well have been dramatic. The thriving and innovative industries of the later Bronze Age cease production and Ireland, as far as we can tell, lapses into a dark age. The causative factors responsible for this decline continue to elude us but climatic, social and economic reasons have variously been offered to explain the changes. The possibility that there was an upsurge of hill-fort construction at this time could well be significant. At any rate the country lapsed into a phase of introspective isolation preoccupied with its own internal crisis. Hallstatt D

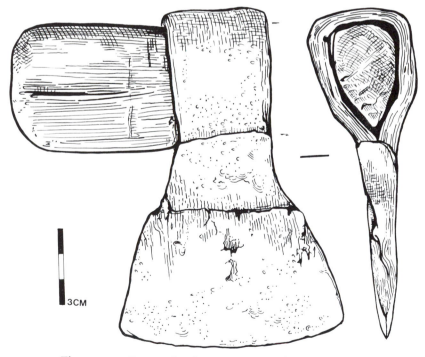

3CM

Figure 33.1 Iron axehead, crannóg 61, Rathtinaun, Co. Sligo.

influences are scarcely detectable in Ireland and the earliest phases of the continental La Tène culture are entirely absent. It was not until about 300 BC that the country began once more to renew its contacts with the outside world.

APPEARANCE OF LA TÈNE

By now, of course, the La Tène Celts had poured in all directions across the European mainland. Rome still trembled before them and the desecration of Delphi was imminent. Ireland was, however, far from these events and initial La Tène contacts were sporadic. Probably the oldest La Tène object from the country is a gold buffer torque of Rhenish origin (Figure 33.2), found with a ribbon torque of the

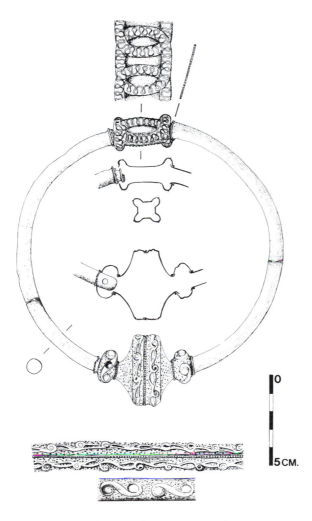

Figure 33.2 Gold torque of 'fused-buffer' type, Knock, Co. Roscommon. Scale 3:4.

639

same metal at Knock, Co. Roscommon (Raftery 1984: 175–81; Ireland 1992; formerly the Clonmacnois hoard). This marks the reawakening of links with the burgeoning iron age cultures of the European mainland but it is an isolated find and its cultural significance should not be exaggerated. It was not until later in the third century, or even in the second, that evidence of an established La Tène presence in Ireland is recognizable. This is best illustrated by a series of decorated bronze scabbard plates and associated items, from a bog deposit at Lisnacrogher, Co. Antrim (Figure 33.3), and from the river Bann in the north-east of the country (Raftery 1984: 74–107). These objects are unquestionably the products of local workshops. They demonstrate the existence in Ireland of craftsmen of the highest accomplishment, thoroughly in command of all the intricacies of La Tène technology and art. It is

Figure 33.3 Detail of decorated bronze scabbard plate, Lisnacrogher, Co. Antrim. (Photo: Ulster Museum, Belfast.)

difficult not to suppose that included in their number were master-craftsmen from abroad who played a part in the introduction of these complex innovations.

Archaeological studies of La Tène influences in Ireland tend to be preoccupied with detailed typological and stylistic examination of fine metalwork and, in consequence, our picture of the culture and the subsistence economy of the majority population is seriously flawed. This is, of course, to a very large extent a result of our continued inability to recognize the domestic habitation sites of the ordinary people. We can take it, however, that agriculture and animal husbandry were the main subsistence activities even though the details are scant. What little we can say of the former generally confirms the widely held assumption that cattle were dominant, though the surprisingly large percentage of pig bones at Navan Fort, Co. Armagh, is worthy of note (Lynn 1986). A large series of beehive quernstones (Caulfield 1977), a sickle and a number of wooden ards provide us with the principal evidence for tillage. Apart from a few domestic containers of wood and bronze, including a handful of cauldrons (Raftery 1984: 214ff.), there is little else in the surviving record to inform us of the lives of the general population.

It is the ruling élite who are reflected most clearly in the archaeological remains. The existence of a warrior aristocracy is certainly implied by the iron swords and the ornate scabbards referred to above. The shortness of the sword blades is, however, surprising and suggests that they were weapons of limited effectiveness (Raftery 1984: 62–73). Spears were also in use and their wooden shafts were often adorned with bronze butts of knobbed, tubular or conical shape (Raftery 1982, 1984: 110–28). A complete rectangular shield of leather-covered wood from a bog at Clonoura, Co. Tipperary (Raftery 1984: 129–33), its surface clearly battle-scarred, helps us dramatically to complete the picture of the fighting man's gear in La Tène Ireland.

There can be little doubt of the importance of the horse among the upper echelons of society at this time. Well over one hundred bridle-bits are known and at least another hundred fittings exist, including the curious, uniquely Irish Y-shaped objects, which are associated with the horse (Figure 33.4) (Raftery 1984: 15ff.). The bits have three-link mouthpieces and, with three or four exceptions, are all of cast bronze. Frequently the links are embellished with elegant curvilinear patterns or with enamel inlays. It is clear that these were prized and valuable objects, for great care and effort were expended to repair them, often repeatedly, after they became damaged through wear.

The majority of the bridle-bits are isolated specimens and from this it may be suggested that they were associated with riding. The wheel was, however, known by La Tène times, as is shown by the pair of block wheels found at Doogarymore, Co. Roscommon, for which there are radiocarbon dates centred on the fourth century BC (Lucas 1972). Wheeled transport is otherwise difficult to infer from the archaeological record (Raftery 1984: 57ff.). In a few instances matching pairs of horsebits have been found, indicating the use of paired draught, and the same is implied by examples with asymmetric decoration. Further indications of vehicular transport are provided by a bronze terret from Co. Antrim, a pair of possible yoke mounts of bronze and a single linchpin of the same material. A wooden yoke of probable Iron Age date from Co. Tyrone could also have been intended for a horse-pair.

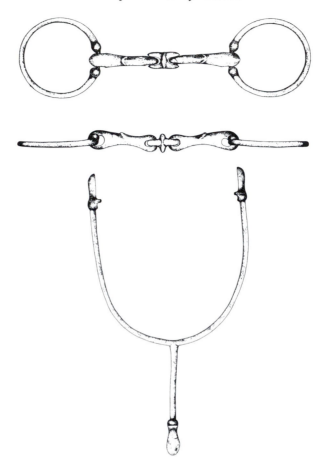

Figure 33.4 Three-link horse bit and Y-shaped object, both bronze. Urraghry, Aughrim, Co. Galway. Scale 1:4.

Horse-drawn vehicles are therefore likely to have been used in Iron Age Ireland but it is not certain to what extent we can describe such vehicles as chariots. It is probable that such existed but it seems likely that it is the rather staid reconstruction extracted from the early literature by Greene (1972) rather than the streamlined version based on the Llyn Cerrig Bach evidence (Fox 1946) which is closest to early Irish reality.

More dramatic evidence of the importance of vehicular travel in Iron Age Ireland is provided by the 2 km long road of massive oak planks which once extended across stretches of bogland in Corlea and Derraghan More, Co. Longford (Figure 33.5) (Raftery 1990). Tree-ring analysis indicates a felling date for the Corlea oaks in 148 BC. To construct this routeway thousands of oak planks, many up to 4 m in length, were laid edge to edge on longitudinally placed roundwood runners. The exceptional labour involved in the making of this road and its prodigious size leave little room to doubt that this was a significant artery of communication which must have been intended primarily for the passage of wheeled vehicles. Indeed, carved wooden

Figure 33.5 Section of bog roadway made of riven oak planks dated by dendrochronology to 148 BC. Corlea, Co. Longford.

fragments found as filling material under the roadway may well be the remains of such a vehicle.

Lavish personal ornament was a predilection of Celtic peoples in Europe and there are indications that for certain elements of society in Ireland this was also the case. The gold torque of early third-century BC date from Knock is unquestionably an outstanding item of personal adornment. It is not, however, a native piece. A second torque of gold is known from the country, found in association with other gold artefacts, the majority imported, at Broighter, Co. Derry. This specimen (Warner 1982), dating to the last century BC, is of Irish workmanship. Its ornament of raised, vegetal curves and prominent relief, snail-shell spirals, set against a background web of overlapping, compass-drawn arcs, is a magnificent example of indigenous La Tène artistic expression.

The Broighter collar (and perhaps also that from Knock) may, however, never have been intended to have been worn by mortal men. From the beginning they could have been meant for votive purposes and their final deposition in watery places is in keeping with this idea. More obviously secular ornaments (Raftery 1984: 144ff.) are the safety-pin fibulae and the ring-headed pins which were used as dress fasteners. Glass beads and bracelets of glass, bone, bronze and jet have also been found. Apart from a few minute textile fragments, however, archaeology tells us little of the clothing worn in Ireland in later prehistory.

Though the period in question is conventionally referred to as the Iron Age it is, as already noted, the work of the bronzesmith rather than of the blacksmith which dominates the surviving picture. Through the bronzes we can trace the development of Irish La Tène craftsmanship from its inception in the third century BC into the first Christian millennium. Outstanding skills in lost-wax casting, in repoussé and in engraved ornament are readily apparent and from the finished products we can infer a wide range of specialist tools, not one of which survives.

The objects of metal, allied to related material in bone and stone, illustrate the progress of native La Tène ornamentation. Initially this is represented by the free-flowing, vegetal designs of the Irish Scabbard Style whose ultimate roots lie in the continental Waldalgesheim Style. On the Broighter collar the vegetal elements are still recognizable but now the patterns are more formally geometric and entirely insular in concept and execution. Now the compass becomes increasingly dominant, as is particularly well illustrated on a series of bone flakes from Lough Crew, Co. Meath (Raftery 1984: 250–63) and this, along with the trumpet-and-lentoid curve, becomes the dominant characteristic of native La Tène art of the early historic centuries. Though overwhelmingly abstract, a recurring element in the art of the later La Tène phase in Ireland is the water-bird, which is most vividly seen in plastic form on the bronze cup handles from Keshcarrigan, Co. Leitrim, and Somerset, Co. Galway (Raftery 1984: 214ff.).

Native Irish craftsmen in the centuries spanning the birth of Christ created bronzes of the highest technical and artistic excellence (see Raftery 1984). The elegantly swirling, repoussé ornament on several of the so-called Monasterevin-type discs is of outstanding quality (Figure 33.6) as is the hand-cut openwork pattern on a cylindrical mount from Cornalaragh, Co. Monaghan. Even more exceptional is the delicacy and refinement of the fine, raised ornament on the object known as the

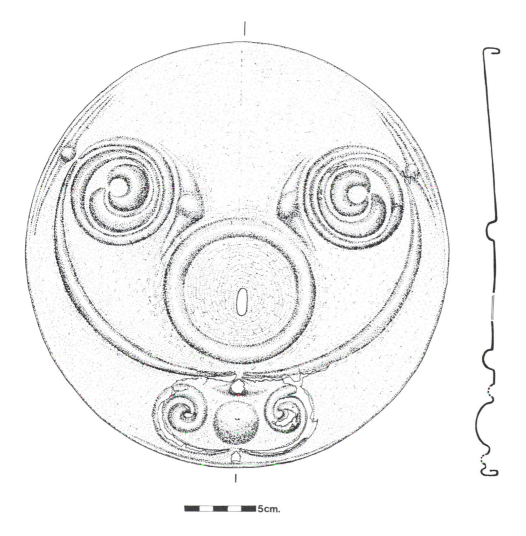

5cm.

Figure 33.6 Bronze disc with repoussé ornament, Monasterevin, Co. Kildare. Scale 1:2.

Petrie Crown and on the well-known disc from the river Bann which are apparently produced by background tooling of the bronze. In stone too, especially on the famous iron age monolith from Turoe, Co. Galway (Duignan 1976), the Irish craftsmen were of the highest calibre.

Among the finest of all the native bronzes, however, are the great bronze trumpets such as those from Ardbrin, Co. Down, and Loughnashade, Co. Armagh (Figure 33.7). These are large, elegantly curving instruments, formed by skilfully hammering and bending bronze sheets to tubular form and sealing the junction by internally riveted bronze strips. In the case of the Ardbrin example no fewer than 1,094 rivets were needed to keep the strips in place. These spectacular implements must have been display pieces intended to be blown on festive occasions or, perhaps, on the occasion

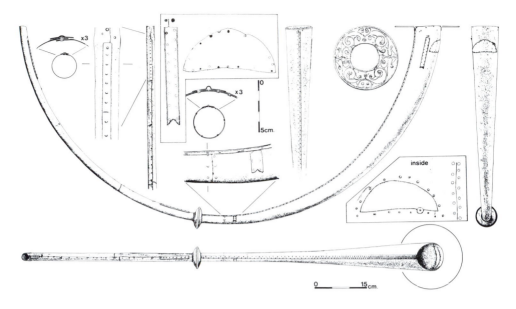

Figure 33.7 Sheet-bronze trumpet, Loughnashade, Co. Armagh.

of battle. They, above all, embody the pomp and ceremony and the barbaric splendour of pagan Celtic society in Ireland.

The Loughnashade trumpet was found with three other similar examples, along with human skulls, in a small lake in Co. Armagh. A ritual context for the find is scarcely in doubt. The location is thus significant, for overlooking this stretch of water is the hilltop site of Navan Fort (Emain Macha), the ceremonial centre of ancient Celtic Ulster.

ROYAL SITES

Navan is one of a number of sites reliably identified as tribal centres which were pre-eminent in the early Irish literature. The others are Dún Ailinne, Co. Kildare, Tara, Co. Meath, and Cruachain, Co. Roscommon. The last, the ancient centre of Connacht, is now an extensive complex of varied earthworks, spread over many acres of countryside. Each of the other three sites consists of a hilltop enclosure formed by a substantial earthen rampart with internal ditch. This defensively illogical feature reinforces the view that such sites were primarily ceremonial. Two – Navan and Dún Ailinne – have been excavated and the results of these investigations have been of great importance for Irish Iron Age studies.

At Navan, near the summit of the hill, two areas of excavation (Sites A and B) uncovered in each instance a complex sequence of overlapping, originally wooden, circular structures (Lynn 1986). Of these the most revealing was that discovered at Site B. Here an earth-covered cairn sealed evidence of activity covering most of the last pre-Christian millennium. Frequently replaced circular huts with attached annexes had once stood there and these dated to the later stages of the Bronze Age and the earlier Iron Age. They may have been purely domestic but it is not impossible that already at this period the site had acquired a ritual character. Few would, however, doubt that the great, multi-ringed circular building, which succeeded the annexed structures, was ritual in purpose. This construction (Figure 33.8), which may well have been roofed, was almost 40 m in diameter. It had an outer wall of horizontal planking, four concentric rings of internal posts and a huge central oak which seems to have been the focus of the monument. The latter timber was felled in 95/94 BC (Baillie 1986, 1988). Soon after it was built there are indications of the deliberate firing of this structure and its final, monumental sealing by the 5 m high mound of stones and earth.

All the evidence suggests that this is a temple for there were no traces of normal domestic activity there. Its systematic destruction and careful sealing also strongly support the view that this was a sacred place. The discovery there of the remains of a Barbary ape, transported to Armagh all the way from north Africa, further underlines the exceptional importance of Navan at this time.

Dún Ailinne was the centre of Celtic Leinster. Excavations on the summit of the hill there (Wailes 1990) have also revealed the former existence of large ringed enclosures of timber varying in diameter from 22 m to 37 m. Their dating falls wholly

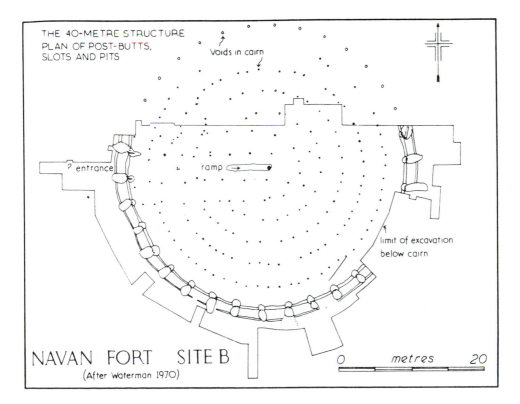

Figure 33.8 Plan of Phase 4 multi-ringed wooden structure, Navan Fort, Co. Armagh.

within the Iron Age and their resemblance to the circular constructions at Navan has been noted. There were three main constructional phases. The first was characterized by a single palisade trench, the second, which overlay the former, by three closely spaced concentric trenches, followed finally by a pair of similar trenches. A ring of large, free-standing posts was built within the third phase enclosure and inside this again there was a small circular hut. After the removal of all these timber constructions the hilltop at Dún Ailinne, in its final phase of use, was the scene of successive periods of outdoor feasting.

We can do little more than speculate as to the precise nature of the various phases of activity at Dún Ailinne. The excavator suggested that the ringed enclosures were the settings for ceremonial acts and that in the second and third stages some form of spectators' platforms may have existed. Whatever the details, however, the exceptional nature of the activities which took place on the hilltop is clear and few would question that here, as at Navan, we have archaeological indications of ritual happenings.

At Navan and Dún Ailinne archaeology and protohistory begin to merge. Although the details are unclear we can nonetheless begin to visualize those strutting Celtic rulers of the heroic tales engaged in their complex hilltop ceremonies. For theirs was a sacral kingship and correct ritual observance of the seasonal feasts was vital to the well-being of the tribe. The Navan temple, precisely dated to 95/94 BC, gives us a rare indication of the date at which such events were taking place. Dún Ailinne, though less closely dated, undoubtedly overlaps with Navan in time.

These major sites are not the only ones dating to this period. Several of the extensive travelling earthworks which run discontinuously for many kilometres across the country have been shown in recent years to belong to the same chronological horizon as that of the royal sites. The so-called Black Pig's Dyke in Co. Monaghan (Walsh 1987) and the Dún of Drumsna in Roscommon (Condit and Buckley 1989), for example, have yielded radiocarbon dates placing their construction late in the last pre-Christian millennium. More dramatic, however, is the dendrochronological evidence from an earthwork known as the Dorsey in south Armagh (Figure 33.9) which yielded oak timbers felled in almost precisely the same year as was the central post at Navan (Baillie 1988). The coincidence seems too great not to infer some link between the construction of the temple at Navan and the raising of the great earthen rampart at the Dorsey. It may thus be that during the second century BC, particularly its second half, the erection of major communal works reflects a phase of tribal expansion and consolidation on a grand scale. Indeed, it may well be that the enormous labour involved in the building of the Corlea roadway in 148 BC should also be considered in the same context. These are major achievements testifying to significant social organization and strong centralized leadership. It is not impossible that the development and spread of La Tène cultural influences across the land were related to such events.

FORTS

Navan, Dún Ailinne and Tara are obviously exceptional sites which can scarcely be regarded as shedding much light on the typical settlements of iron age Ireland.

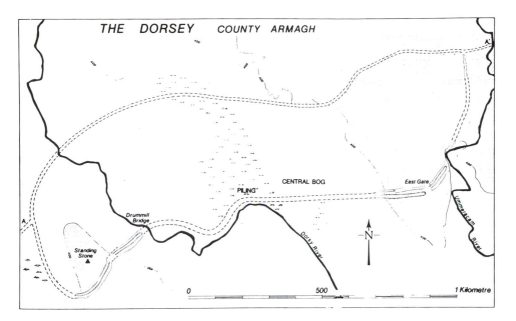

Figure 33.9 The Dorsey, Co. Armagh, linear earthworks. (After Lynn 1989.)

Indeed, it is, as already noted, our continued inability to recognize these settlements which is one of the greatest obstacles to our proper understanding of the period. A few occupation sites have been unearthed but these have not been illuminating in our search for information on the nature of secular settlement in iron age Ireland. Otherwise, the only possibility of pinpointing the settlements of the iron age occupants of Ireland is, at least for the moment, offered by an examination of fortified sites, both inland and coastal.

Because of the essentially non-defensive character of the royal sites it is not appropriate to refer to them as hill-forts in the strictest sense of the word. True hill-forts are, however, known in Ireland (B. Raftery 1972, 1976) even though they are far fewer than has sometimes been suggested in the past. Categorization of unexcavated sites is generally hazardous in Ireland but we can take it that there are at least three dozen sites which may be accepted into the hill-fort class. They are usually of fairly simple character, appearing in most instances as either a single rampart, or a series of widely spaced ramparts (Figure 33.10), encircling the summit of a hill. A few inland promontory forts, some with closely spaced multivallation, are also known. At some western sites the ground outside the defensive wall was protected by a band of tightly packed upright stone pillars, a device known as *chevaux-de-frise*.

Outside Ireland it has been established that hill-forts were an important settlement form of the Early Iron Age though in all areas of Europe it is clear that their origins stretch back into the later Bronze Age. For some reason, however, there has been a persistent tendency in Ireland to assume that the hill-fort in this country is a phenomenon of the Iron Age.

Hillfort excavations in Ireland have not been extensive and most of the questions

Figure 33.10 Multivallate hill-fort, Mooghaun, Co. Clare. (Photo: D.D.C. Pochin-Mould.)

concerning their dating and purpose remain open. Increasingly, however, it seems that it was during the later Bronze Age that hillfort construction became widespread. At Haughey's Fort in Armagh such dating was clearly established (Mallory 1988) and at Rathgall, Co. Wicklow, it is likely that hill-fort construction began in the same period (Raftery 1976). Several other hilltop sites have produced later bronze age remains. While a few have also produced evidence of occupation during the later phases of the Iron Age (e.g. Raftery 1969), in no case has the actual construction of a hill-fort during this period been demonstrated.

The immediate relevance of the hill-fort for a study of the Irish Iron Age is thus not clear and it must be admitted that further excavations may radically alter the present picture. It is, however, interesting to note the significantly southern concentration of hill-forts in areas where La Tène remains are virtually absent. Thus it would appear that the hill-fort in Ireland has little, if anything, to do with the cultural horizon represented by the La Tène metalwork.

This leads, of course, to one of the greatest problems concerning a study of the Irish Iron Age. With La Tène all but non-existent in the south what is there in the archaeological record to represent cultural developments there in the last centuries BC? The answer is, we do not yet know. Hill-forts may one day supply the answer but for the moment we can only assume that in the south, as elsewhere, an Iron Age existed but one wholly devoid of La Tène characteristics.

Coastal promontory forts, too, are enigmatic structures about which we have little information. While in most instances their dating is largely a matter of guesswork, it is likely that some at least of the 250 or so examples belong to the Iron Age. This can, however, only be demonstrated at a single site, at Drumanagh, Loughshinny, Co. Dublin, where a sherd of Gallo-Roman samian ware was found some years ago in association with occupation debris in disturbed soil within the fort (Raftery 1989: 139). Its east coast location and the presence of an excellent harbour there would have made this a choice site for trade between Ireland and the provincial Roman world and recently reported, as yet unpublished, finds from there appear to confirm its exceptional importance in this regard.

BURIALS

The burial record of iron age Ireland is not extensive (Raftery 1981). As far as we can tell cremation was the earlier rite. The remains of the dead were placed in simple pits which were sometimes inserted into earlier barrows, sometimes covered by contemporary tumuli. It seems that the modest ring-barrow, a low circular mound with enclosing ditch and external bank, was the most typical burial of the period. A simple mound or an embanked enclosure was also, on occasion, used to mark the interment. Grave goods are often absent. When present they amount to little more than a few personal ornaments, mostly brooches, beads or bracelets. As far as we can tell, inhumation, often in cist burials, becomes increasingly common in the centuries after Christ.

Most of the burials datable to the Iron Age are of essentially indigenous character. A few are, however, clearly exotic. A cremation found near Donaghadee, Co. Down at a place referred to as 'Loughey' contains a range of glass and bronze artefacts which undoubtedly represent the possessions of a southern English woman who was buried in Ireland around the birth of Christ (Jope and Wilson, 1957). Lambay and Stonyford have already been adverted to and there are several other burials of the early centuries AD which could well be those of foreigners from the provincial Roman world. Such contacts could have played a part in bringing about the change from cremation to inhumation which appears gradually to have been taking place at this time.

SUMMARY

Despite the fact that Ireland is generally regarded today as the Celtic country *par excellence* it is somewhat ironic that the archaeology of the period is so vaguely defined and so fraught with ambiguities. Hallstatt and La Tène, as defined on the European mainland, are terms of only marginal significance for Irish cultural developments in the last half-millennium or so BC. Despite some spectacular metalwork we know little of everyday society during this period. Debate continues as to the source or sources of the influences which underlie our native Iron Age without a general consensus emerging. It seems, however, abundantly clear that the ethnic stability of Ireland was not disturbed to any significant extent during the last pre-Christian millennium. Thus we return to the persistent conundrum of establishing the date, and defining the means, by which Ireland became 'Celtic'.

REFERENCES

Baillie, M.G.L. (1986) 'The central post from Navan Fort', *Emania* 1: 20–1.

—— (1988) 'The dating of the timbers from Navan Fort and the Dorsey, Co. Armagh', *Emania* 4: 37–40.

Bateson, J.D. (1973) 'Roman material from Ireland: a re-examination', *Proceedings of the Royal Irish Academy* 73C: 21–97.

Bourke, E. (1989) 'Stoneyford: a first-century Roman burial from Ireland', *Archaeology Ireland* 3(2): 56–7.

Caulfield, S. (1977) 'The beehive quern in Ireland', *Journal of the Royal Society of Antiquaries of Ireland* 107: 104–39.

Champion, T. (1982) 'The myth of iron age invasions in Ireland', in B.G. Scott (ed.) *Studies on Early Ireland*, 39–44.

Condit, T. and Buckley, V.M. (1989) 'The "Doon" of Drumsna – gateways to Connacht', *Emania* 6: 12–14.

Duignan, M.V. (1976) 'The Turoe Stone: its place in insular La Tène art', in P.-M. Duval and C.F.C. Hawkes (eds) *Celtic Art in Ancient Europe: five protohistoric centuries*, London, 201–18.

Fox, C. (1946) *A Find of the Early Iron Age from Llyn Cerrig Bach, Anglesey*, Cardiff.

Greene, D. (1972) 'The chariot as described in Irish literature', in C. Thomas (ed.) *The Iron Age in the Irish Sea Province*, 59–93.

Ireland, A. (1992) 'The finding of the "Clonmacnoise" gold torcs', *Proceedings of the Royal Irish Academy* 92C: 123–46.

Jope, E.M. and Wilson, B.C.S. (1957) 'A burial group of the first century AD from "Loughey" near Donaghadee', *Ulster Journal of Archaeology* 20: 73–94.

Lucas, A.T. (1972) 'Prehistoric block-wheels from Doogarymore, Co. Roscommon, and Timahoe East, Co. Kildare', *Journal of the Royal Society of Antiquaries of Ireland* 102: 19–48 .

Lynn, C.J. (1986) 'Navan Fort: a draft summary of D.M. Waterman's excavations', *Emania* 1: 11–19.

Mallory, J.P. (1988) 'Trial excavations at Haughey's Fort', *Emania* 4: 5–20.

ÓRíordáin, S.P. (1947) 'Roman material in Ireland', *Proceedings of the Royal Irish Academy* 51C: 35–82.

Raftery, B. (1969) 'Freestone Hill: an iron age hillfort and bronze age cairn', *Proceedings of the Royal Irish Academy* 68C: 1–108.

—— (1972) 'Irish hill-forts', in C. Thomas (ed.) *The Iron Age in the Irish Sea Province*, 37–58.

—— (1976) 'Rathgall and Irish hillfort problems', in D.W. Harding (ed.) *Hillforts, Later Prehistoric Earthworks of Britain and Ireland*, London, 339–57.

—— (1981) 'Iron Age burials in Ireland', in D. ÓCorráin (ed.) *Irish Antiquity: essays and studies presented to Professor M.J. O'Kelly*, Cork, 173–204.

—— (1982) 'Knobbed spearbutts of the Irish Iron Age', in B.G. Scott (ed.) *Studies on Early Ireland*, 75–92.

—— (1983) *A Catalogue of Irish Iron Age Antiquities*, Marburg.

—— (1984) *La Tène in Ireland: problems of origin and chronology*, Marburg.

—— (1989) 'Barbarians to the west', in J.C.Barrett, A.P. Fitzpatrick and L. Macinnes (eds) *Barbarians and Romans in North-West Europe*, Oxford: British Archaeological Reports, International Series 471, 117–52.

—— (1990) *Trackways Through Time*, Dublin.

Raftery, B. (1994) *Pagan Celtic Ireland*, Thames & Hudson.

Raftery, J. (1972) 'Iron Age and Irish Sea: problems for research', in C. Thomas (ed.) *The Iron Age in the Irish Sea Province*, 1–10.

Rynne, E. (1976) 'The La Tène and Roman finds from Lambay, Co. Dublin: a re-assessment', *Proceedings of the Royal Irish Academy* 76C: 231–44.

—— (1982) 'A classification of pre-Viking Irish swords', in B.G. Scott (ed.) *Studies on Early Ireland*, 93–7.

Scott, B.G. (ed.) (1982) *Studies on Early Ireland: essays in honour of M.V. Duignan*, Belfast.

—— (1991) *Early Irish Ironworking*, Belfast.

Thomas, C. (ed.) (1972) *The Iron Age in the Irish Sea Province*, London: Council for British Archaeology Research Reports 9.

Wailes, B. (1990) 'Dún Ailinne: a summary excavation report', *Emania* 7: 10–21.

Walsh, A. (1987) 'Excavating the Black Pig's Dyke', *Emania* 3: 5–11.

Warner, R.B. (1976) 'Some observations on the context and importation of exotic material in Ireland from the first century BC to the second century AD', *Proceedings of the Royal Irish Academy* 76C: 267–92.

—— (1982) 'The Broighter hoard: a reappraisal, and the iconography of the collar', in B.G. Scott (ed.) *Studies on Early Ireland*, 29–38.

—— (1991) 'The earliest history of Ireland', in M. Ryan (ed.) *The Illustrated Archaeology of Ireland*, Dublin, 112–16.

THE EARLY CELTS IN SCOTLAND

Euan W. MacKie

INTRODUCTION

Before embarking on this short description of the early Celts in northern Britain it is necessary to review again briefly what we mean by 'Celts' or 'Celtic' (MacKie 1970: 12: Baker 1974: ch. 15). This is particularly important in this chapter because people speaking a Celtic language and following a prehistoric-looking and allegedly Celtic tribal way of life – albeit one which was gradually changing under the impact of an urban society in the lowlands – were living in the highland and island regions of Scotland at least until the middle of the eighteenth century. What is more, this tribal life style was observed and described by many educated travellers before its final demise. Thus of all the parts of Europe once inhabited by prehistoric Celts, however defined, highland Scotland is unique in that this ancient world existed there in an evolved form until – like the stone age societies of the Pacific which were also discovered and described in the later eighteenth century – it could be recorded and studied by the precursors of modern anthropologists. It is intriguing that this remarkable fact seems so little regarded by many iron age archaeologists who – seeking parallels and analogies for their excavated material among tribal cultures in other parts of the world – tend to ignore the late survival of the real thing in their own backyard. One long-noted sign of this is that the study of recent Scottish highland society still tends to be regarded as 'folk life' and quite distinct from ethnography and is rarely taught in departments of archaeology (that in Glasgow University being an exception).

Broadly 'Celtic' is used to describe *first* a language; *second* objects (artefacts or human remains) which have a connection with the historically documented iron age peoples of central and north-western Europe and their characteristic material culture; *third* any distinctive racial or ethnic group of people which can be isolated as speaking a Celtic language or who created the iron age society mentioned; and *fourth* by custom a person of modern highland Scottish or Irish descent. Since there are very few iron age burials from Scotland, and none from the highland-island zone, nothing can be said about the ethnic question for which the evidence from southern Britain and the Continent has been discussed in some detail (Baker 1974: ch. 15). This chapter will therefore review briefly the linguistic and material cultural evidence for prehistoric Celts living in Scotland, and the final section will try to show how a study of recent highland society can throw light on that of its iron age forebears.

CELTIC LANGUAGES IN NORTH-WEST EUROPE

As is explained more fully in Chapter 2 the modern Celtic languages divide into two families; the *p*-Celtic group includes Welsh, Cornish and Breton while the *q*–Celtic group includes Scottish and Irish Gaelic and the old Manx language of the Isle of Man. A simple illustration of the difference is the Old Welsh *map* meaning 'a youth' which is equivalent to the Gaelic *mac*, originally *maquos* (Watson 1926: 2). When the two language groups split apart in this way is not so clear but it must have been well before the Iron Age since both the continental Celtic names recorded by classical writers and the Celtic place-names surviving in those parts of Europe and Britain showing archaeological traces of the Celts are of *p*-Celtic type (Piggott 1965: 173 and figs 95–7: Jackson 1953). This was first demonstrated more than four centuries ago by the Scot George Buchanan (1582).

It will immediately be obvious that there is a problem with linking the historical Celtic peoples of Ireland and highland Scotland – who spoke *q*-Celtic Gaelic dialects – with the iron age *p*-Celtic-speakers who (if language is a good guide) had been separated from them since at least as far back as the Bronze Age. One can only provisionally assume that the long linguistic separation did not cause other aspects of the two groups of Celtic societies to diverge too much.

Early Accounts

There are a number of early historical traditions about who the first peoples of Scotland were. After the movement into Argyll of Gaelic-speaking Scots from Ireland from about AD 500 onwards (and before the coming of the Norsemen) it was understood that the other peoples of Alba (then meaning Britain as a whole) were the Cruithne, the Saxons and the Britons (Watson 1926: ch. 1). *Cruithne* later meant 'Picts' but originally meant 'Britons', or 'Pretani' in the original form. The Cruithne, or 'northern Britons', were also apparently in north-east Ireland before being supplanted by the Gaels, and such close links with Ulster may be confirmed by the fact, known from a contemporary source, that the powerful Brigantes tribe lived both in northern England and eastern Ireland at the end of the first century (Rivet 1978: fig. 1).

Early Place-names in Scotland

There is also abundant evidence from surviving place-names that a people speaking a *p*-Celtic language inhabited the southern and eastern lowlands of Scotland in ancient times and this is confirmed by historical evidence, both from the Iron Age itself (below, p. 656) and for the existence of the British kingdom of Strathclyde in south-western Scotland until well on in the first millennium AD (Duncan 1975: 63ff.). Watson gave the first systematic account of the subject (1926: ch. II), both in terms of historical references and surviving British names, and Nicolaisen presents some of the data more clearly as distribution maps (1976: ch. 8). For example, the region of the distinctive early historic people known as the Picts is well defined by the distribution of the place-name element *pit* (ibid.: 153, map 17); these are heavily concentrated immediately north of the river Forth (in Fife and Aberdeenshire and adjacent regions), east of the central highland massif and south of the Dornoch Firth; the far northern mainland is almost free of them. The early British place-name element *carden* is also found restricted to a very similar area, as are the monumental stone slabs carved in the distinctive Pictish style and dated to the mid and late first millennium.

However, apart from one striking form of post-Roman bronze armlet (p. 659), this region is beyond the zone of iron age Celtic decorated metalwork, presumably the clearest indication of the presence of prehistoric Celts. As we shall see, there is archaeological evidence for a specific population living in what later became Pictland and whose roots lie very far back, at least as early as the Late Bronze Age.

Other early British names are more widespread and include the elements *pert*, *lanerc*, *pevr* and *aber* (Nicolaisen 1976: 163, map 20). These are found throughout Pictland but also in southern Scotland, especially in the central lowlands, and they give a clearer indication of a more widespread ancient population which spoke a *p*-Celtic tongue akin to ancient Welsh. However it is striking that these place-names are almost completely absent from the highlands north-west of the Great Glen and from all the islands.

Iron Age Tribal Names in Scotland

In fact we know that this absence is not due to *p*-Celtic speakers never having been in these north-western regions because of the evidence of iron age tribal names. The Greek geographer Ptolemy compiled his well-known verbal descriptions of the British Isles – by means of place-names and geographical features identified by latitude and longitude – in the second century and included information about the native tribes in the various regions (Thomas 1876; Rivet 1978; Mann and Breeze 1988). It is generally agreed that the information he had about Scotland dates from the late first century and was obtained from officers and others who had campaigned in the north with Gnaius Julius Agricola, Roman governor of Britain, between about AD 79 and 86. During its campaigning the army had penetrated far up the east coast and the navy went right round Scotland, calling at many islands including the Orkneys. Most of these names are of *p*-Celtic type. 'The ancient tribal names recorded by Ptolemy and others are all of the same type as the tribal names of Gaul – plural in form' (Watson 1926: 15; Powell 1962).

Another important piece of evidence given by the tribal names is of clear connections between Scotland and the south. For example the Damnonii of south-western Scotland must surely be connected with the Dumnonii of south-western England and the Cornavii of Caithness seem identical to those of North Wales (Rivet 1978: fig. 1).

The Coming of Gaelic Speakers

The study of modern Scottish place-names confirms that ancient Britons inhabited Scotland before the Irish Gaels who penetrated the country from the south-west in the fifth century; the very early Gaelic name *sliabh* 'a hill' (anglicized to 'Slieve' or 'Slew') shows this clearly, being dense in the islands of Islay and Jura in Argyllshire and very dense in the extreme south-west of Scotland (Nicolaisen 1976: 41–4 and map 1); it appears to mark the areas of the primary settlements from Ireland. *Cill* meaning 'church' is another early Gaelic name (probably before AD 800) concentrated in the western part of the country while *baile*, a 'farm', is more easterly and evidently marks a later stage in the settlement; others like *achadh*, 'field', are universal and must have been coined throughout the colonization (ibid.: ch. 7). The density of this Irish Gaelic settlement evidently obliterated all British place-names from the north-western areas, which in any case were presumably fairly thinly populated; the *p*-Celtic speakers may moreover have been ruling minorities among aboriginal populations (see pp. 665–8).

IRON AGE ARCHAEOLOGICAL PROVINCES

How does the archaeological evidence fit with the picture presented by these linguistic data? This suggests that the iron age peoples of Scotland – or at least their leaders – at the beginning of the first millennium spoke *p*-Celtic dialects and that some tribes among them could have had strong links with southern and western England. In broad terms one can detect among the available iron age sites and artefacts three distinct archaeological zones (Figure 34.1); the geographical terms for these 'provinces' used are those suggested by Piggott (1966).

The Tyne/Forth and Solway/Clyde Provinces

This area comprises that part of Scotland south of the Forth/Clyde line (including some of north-east England) and it is distinguished from the rest of Scotland in one important way, by the presence of decorated bronze metalwork in the British La Tène style (Thomas 1963; Stevenson 1966). Many of these objects – sword scabbards, bridle bits and early penannular fibulae together with three unique craftsmen's objects (the Deskford carnyx head (Piggott 1959: 24–32) the Torrs chamfrein (Atkinson and Piggott 1955) and the Balmaclellan mirror (Fox 1949) (Figure 34.2)) – were strays or found in hoards; except in Roman forts systematic excavations have given few signs of the existence of such objects and have revealed only a simple material culture which probably goes back to the Late Bronze Age.

The distribution of Piggott's Group III and IV swords and scabbards is particularly interesting, extending as they do from the La Tène vehicle graves in Yorkshire – the only archaeologically attested example of the settlement of these continental Celts in Britain (Stead 1979) – mainly west and north-west into Brigantia, southern Scotland and Ulster (Piggott 1950: figs. 6 and 12; Thomas 1963: fig. 2) (Figure 34.1). Presumably only the most optimistic anti-diffusionist would maintain that these aristocratic weapons had been traded from hand to hand, and a movement of chiefly members of the Yorkshire La Tène lineages to dominate new areas seems indicated.

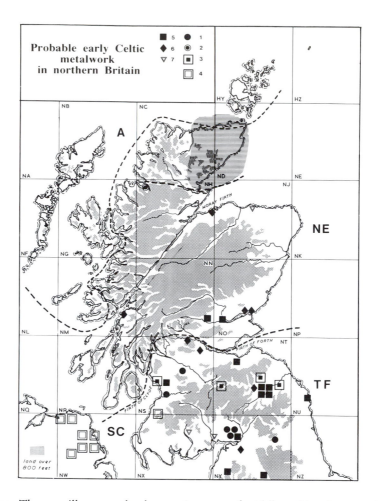

Figure 34.1 The map illustrates the three main zones of middle and late iron age Scotland. In the southern mainland – the Tyne/Forth (TF) and Solway/Clyde (SC) provinces – are most of the examples of early La Tène metalwork (below), most of the bun-shaped rotary querns and most of the glass armlets.

In the North-eastern province (NE) – which may be said to include most of Argyllshire until about the first century BC – are about three-quarters of the timber-framed hill-forts (all save one vitrified), perhaps nine-tenths of the Pictish stones of Class I (pre-Christian) and II and most of the *pit* place-names. Most of the late La Tène-derived metalwork is here, namely the massive armlets, spiral armlets and the 'Donside' terrets.

The maritime Atlantic province (A – including Shetland) is adjusted here to include only the zone of fine pottery and the main broch concentrations. The shaded area (Caithness and Sutherland) is an intermediate zone where the fine pottery is mainly absent but where there are large numbers of brochs and, in the south-east, many Pictish stones (a few of which also occur in Orkney).

Symbols: 1 – straight-jointed bridle bits; 2 – iron single-jointed bridle bit from Dun Lagaidh; 3 – Group III swords and scabbards; 4 – Group IIIa swords and scabbards; 5 – Group IV 'Brigantian' swords and scabbards; 6 – penannular fibulae of Type Aa; 7 – the Deskford carnyx, the Torrs pony cap and the Balmaclellan mirror.

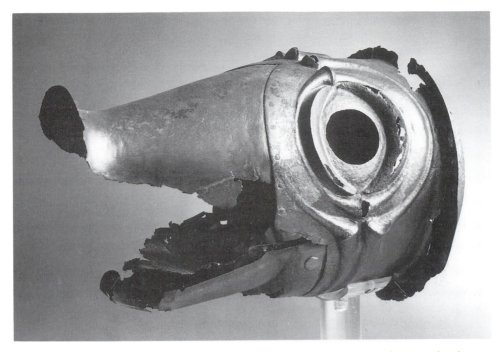

Figure 34.2 This decorated bronze carnyx – part of a horn in the form of a boar's head – was found in about 1816 about 6 ft down in peat on Liecheston Farm, near Kirkton of Deskford, Banffshire, in the northern part of the North-eastern province. It has been stylistically dated to the first century BC. (Piggott 1959.)

Likewise derivatives of the the 'Arras' three-link bronze bridle bits – the 'straight bar snaffles' (Palk 1984) – show an exactly similar spread into southern Scotland, as do the early Type Aa penannular fibulae (Palk 1984; Fowler 1960, esp. 161ff.) and their derivatives (Stevenson 1966, n. 46). With one striking exception this early metalwork does not extend north of the rivers Forth and Clyde; the boar's head trumpet from Deskford in Banffshire is far up in the north-east (Piggott 1959) (Figure 34.2). The only objects with Celtic curvilinear decoration which do are the massive bronze arm-lets and the decorated terrets, both found concentrated in Aberdeenshire (Stevenson 1966: fig. 5), and these are explicable as the final (second century) products of Celtic craftsmen, and their local imitators, who fled north with their chiefly patrons after the heavy defeat of the iron age tribes by the Romans at the battle of Mons Graupius in AD 86. It may not be too fanciful to see this concentration of La Tène-descended tribal leaders in Aberdeenshire in the second century as resulting eventually in the coalescence of the tribes of lowland Pictland into a powerful cultural unity.

The rotary quern is another important indicator of the cultural distinctiveness of the southern Scottish iron age population, and of its albeit increasingly tenuous links with continental La Tène cultures. There are two types of iron age querns in Scotland, one being the non-adjustable bun-shaped form the distribution of which is almost entirely confined to below the Forth/Clyde line (MacKie 1971: fig.1); it was probably operated on the ground by some kind of wooden turning mechanism

(MacKie 1989: 7ff.). The same thing seems to apply in Ireland where the bun-shaped querns are found in broadly the same area as decorated La Tène metalwork; both are markedly absent from the southern half of the country (Caulfield 1977: fig. 24) and several of the Irish stones bear La Tène curvilinear ornament (ibid.: fig. 21).

Another clear indication of the continental links of the middle iron age peoples of southern Scotland – in which they contrast with the tribes both north and south of them – is seen in the liking of their leaders for translucent glass armlets inlaid with coloured patterns (Stevenson 1966: 28 and fig. 3; MacKie 1989: 3–4). The great majority of these ornaments are made of ice-green Roman glass so they clearly could not exist until this became available after the conquest. Yet the tribes of southern England and the midlands, conquered first, have hardly any; the concentration is heavily in central and south-eastern Scotland and in north-east England with a few outliers in the North-eastern and Atlantic provinces. Glass armlets are characteristic of the La Tène cultures northern and north-western France (Giot *et al.* 1979), and of course of their Yorkshire relations (Stead 1979), and it is difficult not to conclude that the armlets suggest the same as the decorated metalwork, that the south Scottish tribes had an unusually strong continental La Tène heritage. It is curious, however, that no complete armlet has been found on a settlement site; the ends of the fragments have often been carved as if to be mounted on something.

The North-Eastern Province

The iron age cultures of the region between the river Forth and the Moray Firth, and east of the great central highland massif, are not as well understood as those further north and west. Partly this is because, with one or two exceptions, the few excavated sites have not yielded either long sequences of occupation or rich and informative material cultures; neither has the Royal Commission on the Ancient and Historical Monuments of Scotland yet surveyed this vast area fully. However, there are a number of clues which suggest that this province had a distinctive culture at the end of the first millennium BC.

The most striking of these are the stone-walled hilltop strongholds known collo-quially as vitrified forts but more accurately as timber-framed forts (MacKie 1977a). The archaeological evidence obtained from excavated sites like Finavon, Abernethy and Sheep Hill shows a sparse but consistent material culture, the most important components of which seem to be barrel- and bucket-shaped urns of thick, gritty pottery and jet ring-pendants and bracelets; later iron age bronze ornaments – for example three La Tène Ic brooches (for which V.G. Childe suggested a Swiss origin) and a few spiral bronze finger-rings – appear on some sites. Radiocarbon dates indicate that the oldest of these timber-framed forts probably belong to the eighth century BC, making highly plausible the hypothesis – offered by Piggott before C-14 dates were available (1966: 7–8) – of their origin among the late bronze age Urnfield cultures of the Continent. An analysis of their distribution by size strongly suggests an eastern origin with the forts becoming smaller as they spread west into the mountains (MacKie 1977a: 444, fig. 6). Only the presence of some strangely early thermoluminescence dates for the vitrified rock on some of these hill-forts disturbs this rather clear picture (Sanderson *et al.* 1988).

There are hints in the local late bronze age metalwork and pottery of strong contacts between Aberdeenshire and north Germany in the seventh century BC (Coles 1960) and the timber-framed hill-forts are now known to be suitably early to be part of that foreign influence brought directly across the North Sea. Such origins would perhaps explain the early presence in the north-east of a *p*-Celtic dialect, later to become Pictish, which is distinct from other such in north Britain and appears to have closer links with Gaul (Jackson 1955) although the picture is not at all straightforward (MacKie 1970: 17–21).

However, signs of the influence of the classic iron age La Tène cultures are absent except, as we have seen, for some late items which can explained as the result of Roman conquests further south and which are not associated with the hill-forts mentioned. Likewise at a late date appear the distinctive underground galleries or souterrains, concentrated immediately north of the river Tay and in central Aberdeenshire; Stevenson has persuasively argued that these also represent the activities of proto-Pictish tribes galvanized by the influx of tribal élites from the south (1966). In early historic times the area evolved the distinctive Pictish kingdom with its unique art style (Henderson 1967). Thus the iron age tribes of the area – Maeatae, Caledonii and the rest – could be described as Celtic-speaking but with a distinctive cultural and genetic ancestry (Mackie and Mackie 1984); they seem to have had no links with the La Tène cultures until very late.

The Atlantic Province

This is the name given to the maritime highland and island zone west and north of the highland massif, an area always open to invasion and settlement by sea and one of the last places except Iceland to which a fugitive from further south or further east could go. This is well seen in Early Neolithic times in the distribution of the chambered cairns (Henshall 1972, end maps) and in early historic times by that of Norse place-names, indicating where the Vikings settled (Nicolaisen 1976: ch. 6). In the Middle Iron Age the province is equally well, though slightly differently, defined by the distribution of brochs – a form of defended wooden round-house with a high, thick dry-stone wall containing a remarkable series of hollow-wall architectural features unique to Scotland and giving the whole tower-like proportions (MacKie 1965). By contrast with the rest of Scotland the associated material culture is rich and informative and the pottery styles numerous and well made.

The hollow-walled brochs, with superimposed tiers of galleries inside the wall, appear to constitute the great majority of the sites about the architecture of which anything useful can be said (themselves a small proportion of all known and suspected brochs) and none have been plausibly dated to before the first century BC. A few broch-like buildings, and some slimmer stone round-houses, have been explored in Orkney and Caithness and the latter do go back to the end of the Bronze Age (Hedges and Bell 1980; Hedges 1990). Likewise there are plausible hollow-walled broch prototypes in the Western Isles which go back somewhat earlier (MacKie 1992). However the crucial point here is that all these stone structures seem to have been locally developed; only the two- or three-storeyed wooden round-house enclosed by the hollow-walled brochs (but not by the others) could be said to be an imported idea, presumably from iron age cultures further south in Britain (although determined anti-diffusionists doubt that also – Armit 1991).

The iron age material culture of the Atlantic province is exceptionally rich and diverse, the many well-made and finely decorated pottery styles for example not only provide a sharp contrast with the sparse sherds of plain undistinguished wares which are found on contemporary mainland sites but could be providing many clues to the influences that impinged on this maritime province from several different regions beyond the seas. The richness of the material culture makes it possible to formulate some tentative hypotheses about the origins of the middle iron age populations which lived there. Moreover, several excavated sites – like Jarlshof in Shetland (Hamilton 1956), Howe in Orkney (Carter *et al.* 1985), Crosskirk in Caithness (Fairhurst 1984) and Dun Mor Vaul on Tiree (MacKie 1974) – proved to have been occupied for many centuries, beginning at the end of the local Bronze Age. These show clearly that there was an early iron age horizon with a sparse material culture quite distinct from the middle phase that followed and to which the brochs and allied structures belong. This early horizon typically shows carinated pottery, very occasionally black-burnished, resembling comparably dated ware in southern and eastern England; however, much of the pottery seems to be local.

The radiocarbon dates for the early iron age horizon cluster in the sixth and fifth centuries BC (uncorrected) and those for the middle phase in the first centuries BC and AD (MacKie in press: table 1); the latter horizon is also clearly tied to the Roman occupation of southern Scotland between about AD 80 and 180, samian sherds having been found on several sites near the top of the primary middle iron age occupation levels. Thus despite a number of valiant recent efforts (Armit 1991) it is really not possible to argue for complete continuity between the two phases, although some important pottery styles are clearly locally descended; the Middle Iron Age sees a wholesale transformation of the buildings and the associated pottery and artefacts which – unless one rules out the possibility on theoretical grounds (Renfrew 1990) – seems to argue for the arrival of an influential if not substantial new population and the galvanizing of the flourishing local cultures in various ways.

Allowing at least for the possibility of the arrival of some new dominant tribal élites – either to form dynastic alliances with relations in the north (Fitzpatrick 1989) or avoiding the Romans and looking for new territories – at the start of the Middle Iron Age (probably in the first century BC), where might they have come from? The first striking aspect of the province in this period is the complete absence of decorative bronze metalwork in the La Tène style. No bronze or iron bridle bits, or decorated sword scabbards or early penannular fibulae of the Aa type have been found in the many excavated brochs, wheel-houses and allied sites. The one iron three-link bit known from north of the Forth/Clyde line – from Dun Lagaidh on Loch Broom (MacKie 1977a: 515, X) – comes from a dun (small dry-stone fortified house with comparatively low walls) of Argyllshire type which lacked the Atlantic material culture. Also completely absent from the maritime zone are fibulae of La Tène type, though, as noted, a few early ones have been found in the southern and eastern lowlands (Stevenson 1966: 20, 25 and figs. 1 and 2).

It may be mentioned at this point that some of the items on Thomas's map of 1963 purporting to show the spread of La Tène influence from Yorkshire into Scotland can now be seen to be irrelevant in that context, and they include the two objects which appeared to extend this zone of influence into the Atlantic province (Thomas 1963: fig. 1). The bronze and iron bent ring-headed pins are now known from pottery impressions at Dun Mor Vaul to go back to the Early Iron Age (MacKie 1974: fig. 11, no. 16 and fig. 12, no. 87), and the same is probably true of the long-handled 'weaving combs', seen at the early iron age site of Bu in Orkney (Hedges *et al.* 1987: fig. 1.14). Thus the maritime province is in that sense more distinct from the lowlands than used to be thought.

On the other hand there are artefacts clearly of southern English type – the bronze spiral finger-rings and the various types of glass beads – which are consistently found in Atlantic middle iron age layers but not before, but are also common in the southern lowlands. As always with such small 'exotic' ornaments it is hard to tell whether these signify more than trade, or gifts between lineages forming alliances. However, there are two important artefacts which, together with the absence of La Tène-derived metalwork already mentioned, suggest that any exotic population elements in the Atlantic middle iron age cultures are truly distinct.

Rotary querns seem not to pre-date the Middle Iron Age here and are of a quite different type from the beehive and bun-shaped stones of the southern mainland (MacKie 1972, 1989: 5ff.). Not only are they larger, flatter and thinner – hence the term 'disc querns' – but they appear to have had a sophisticated adjusting mechanism for coarse and fine grinding, as outer Hebridean and Orkney and Shetland querns did until very recently (Curwen 1937; Fenton 1978: 392). This means that they rested on a table rather than on the ground. The crucial element is the lower stone, with a complete perforation through which the movable spindle passes, raised and lowered from below; the spindle slots into the bridge or rind fixed across the bottom of the hole of the upper stone and thus alters slightly the distance between the stones and the fineness of the flour produced. A non-adjustable quern has only a socket in the lower stone for a fixed spindle and the vast majority of the pre-Roman bun-shaped and beehive querns in Britain and France appear to have this (MacKie 1989: fig. 1). However, no disc quern with a socketed lower stone has ever been found among the scores recovered from excavations on Atlantic middle iron age sites. Such adjustable disc querns are thus quite distinct from those of the entire western La Tène province and their origin is as yet unclear. A preliminary assessment, however, does suggest that we may have to look to Brittany and ultimately to Iberia for the origin of this 'non-La Tène' rotary quern.

The second element is a pottery style – black or plain, bulging-waisted jars with sharply everted rims and *omphalos* bases, some with a curious decoration of horizontal fluting along the inside of the rim. These fluted-rimmed jars – especially the black-burnished examples – strongly resemble late Hallstatt cremation jars in north-west France (Giot *et al.* 1979: 261ff.) and they appear suddenly with the earliest defended (pre-broch) site at Clickhimin in Shetland (Hamilton 1968: ch. 5 and figs 42–4) and with the broch at Dun Mor Vaul, Tiree (MacKie 1974: 19ff; 1970: map 3). Only at the Shetland site are the jars numerous and the date of this occupation – discovered before C-14 dating was applied in the north – is disputable; a case can be made out for the first century BC rather than the excavator's estimate of the fifth (MacKie 1969b).

In the Hebrides an appearance in the first century BC seems very likely and these few jars seem quickly to have developed into a common local hybrid – everted-rim Clettraval ware – on which is decoration of an horizontal, applied waist cordon and sometimes concentric curvilinear channelled arches above this. These last resemble the arches on the bowls of the later Iron Age in southern England and indeed a local imitation of such a one may have been found at Dun Mor Vaul (MacKie 1969: pl. Vc).

Only here, among the brochs and wheel-houses of parts of the Outer Hebrides, and at Clickhimin is this everted-rim pottery, with its apparently exotic origins, at all common. Elsewhere in Atlantic Scotland it is rare and the common pottery styles are firmly local, sometimes with origins going back several centuries. Moreover no middle iron age cremation burials, or indeed any burials, have been found in Atlantic Scotland so the significance of the pottery is unclear.

Discussion

What can be said about these three archaeological zones of iron age Scotland in the light of the questions posed at the start? It is clear that we are asking two different questions, the first being whether there was a Celtic-speaking population in Scotland in the pre-Roman Iron Age. It appears that there was if the *p*-Celtic place-names and the Ptolemaic tribal names are good guides. However, tribal names could simply reflect the ancestry and military prowess of tribal chiefs and warrior élites and do not necessarily imply that all the tribesmen were of the same origin (below, p. 667). Place-names are more difficult; the date of their first application to natural features cannot be discovered and the question of who in a tribe or clan had the right to give names to geographical features arises. However, the existence of a historical British-speaking kingdom in Strathclyde in the mid-first millennium AD surely confirms that the iron age population of the Tyne-Forth province was largely *p*-Celtic speaking. Yet one may doubt whether the same applied to the apparently *p*-Celtic tribes in the highlands and islands; here perhaps were larger populations of aborigines and a small number of early British-speaking élites. Hardly any *p*-Celtic place-names survive.

With all its imperfections the archaeological picture matches the linguistic one quite well. The presence of tribal élites with direct links with the Yorkshire La Tène groups is surely implied by the scatter into southern Scotland of sword scabbards, bridle bits and early penannular brooches, and the local rotary quern provides a clear link between the more ordinary households and their presumably *p*-Celtic-speaking neighbours further south and on the Continent. It also shows that there was a profound cultural and probably political frontier at the highland boundary through which the bun-shaped querns rarely penetrated.

The North-east province is archaeologically distinct with a strong suggestion of early origins going back to the end of the Bronze Age, yet a clearly *p*-Celtic form of language was used there, as well as words quite unlike any others known (Jackson 1955). It is difficult to resist the conclusion that this is partly explicable by the fleeing north to, and settling in, Aberdeenshire and adjacent areas by thousands of southern tribal chiefs, gentry and warriors and their families after their crushing defeat by the Romans in AD 86. No doubt it was this genetic and cultural mixing that resulted in the emergence of the dynamic kingdom of the Picts two or three centuries later.

Atlantic Scotland is even more distinct from the southern mainland in the Middle Iron Age, cut off from it by mountains and sea and having many peculiar, locally originating dry-stone structures and an array of individual artefacts and pottery styles which are not matched elsewhere and many of which also seem to be local. Absent from this array are signs of links with the La Tène provinces in the broadest sense, except perhaps for the glass beads, spiral bronze finger-rings and curvilinear ornament on Clettraval jars, which suggest a connection of some kind, perhaps brief, with the Wessex area. On the other hand the adjustable disc querns and the fluted everted-rimmed jars might suggest a link with the devolved Hallstatt cultures of Brittany or even Iberia, and links with Ireland are apparent too (Warner 1983).

Pace Renfrew (1990: 250), the great broch tower residences themselves indicate the presence of highly organized tribal societies (MacKie 1989 and below), the leading elements of which may well have arrived from elsewhere (though there are signs in some places – Caithness and Sutherland for example – of their being adopted by indigenous cultures). These élites may have spoken *p*-Celtic dialects but it seems doubtful if many of their clansmen did; the whole province seems to have been a world apart from lowland Scotland and the rest of the sub-La Tène provinces – a mixture of very long-established aborigines and sea-borne tribal élites from the western fringes of Europe who established themselves among them, anticipating the Vikings by eight hundred years.

SOCIAL STRUCTURE

As implied above, it may be possible to construct from archaeological evidence a plausible outline of the basic social organization of some of the iron age tribes of Scotland even though – since we are dealing with pre-literate times and there are no known laws linking material culture with social structure – such a feat is normally considered to be impossible without resorting to analogy (Hodder 1982: 11ff.; MacKie 1977b: 10–12). Also there is fairly clear evidence for the social structure of the late medieval highland clans of Scotland with which the iron age evidence may reasonably be compared. It is unfortunate, however, that our most detailed information comes from the Atlantic province – remotest from the iron age Celts in the classical sense; for the area closest to the La Tène province we can really only argue from analogy.

Iron Age Society

The case has recently been set out in some detail (MacKie 1989) so may be summarized here; in essence there are four independent strands of evidence for social structure which seem to mesh well together.

The oldest and best known of these strands is the architecture of the hollow-walled broch towers which must be regarded as a highly sophisticated development with several ingenious defensive features (MacKie 1965). If the broch builders did use a standard measuring system and geometry to set out the towers, this impression of sophistication is reinforced (MacKie 1977b: 62). What evidence there is for the amount of labour involved in building one of the dry-stone towers seems to confirm that only the wealthy and powerful could have afforded one; Dun Carloway in Lewis probably took a gang of sixty men seven months to build (Thomas 1890: 414–15).

The second strand consists of the results of the only systematic, statistically based geographical fieldwork yet carried out on a group of brochs, in this case in Shetland (Fojut 1982). The method of this work was to study the links between all known sites – about seventy – and various aspects of the landscape such as rock type, soil type, drainage, distance from the sea and so on. By analysing a set of randomly chosen, non-archaeological sites in the same way it was possible to estimate how important – negatively or positively or not at all – each of these features was to the people who chose the sites on which brochs were built.

It became clear in this way that each broch was sited in a distinct, economically useful territory with arable land, pasture and usually some sea coast. Using as a basis the productivity of the Shetland land in pre-Improvement times it seemed clear that each of these territories could have supported between about 200 and 400 people in the Iron Age. Since only a fraction of that number could have lived comfortably in a broch the implication must surely be that the tower was the fortified farmhouse of the leading family of the territory and that the rest lived in simple dwellings of wood and thatch round about.

A picture of a stratified iron age society emerges, having a number of subchiefs, each of whom lived in a broch and had a number of dependent clansmen and their families owing allegiance to him. Since there are no giant brochs (technically impossible) or even ordinary hill-forts in most of Atlantic Scotland it is not possible to say from archaeological evidence alone whether these 'broch lairds' owed allegiance to a tribal chief although it seems highly likely. Some brochs have suggestive names, like Cunningsburgh, or 'King's borg', in Shetland; Clickhimin, moreover, has a carved stone footprint which suggests that it was a royal site at some stage (Hamilton 1968: fig. 70 and pl. XVIIId).

The third and fourth strands consist of evidence from two excavated brochs which is relevant in this context. Dun Mor Vaul broch is on Tiree in the Inner Hebrides and was excavated long before the Shetland fieldwork was carried out, and at a time when brochs were considered to have been forts rather than defended farmhouses. The stratigraphy was clear and the finds numerous and the analysis of the pottery styles over the six phases of occupation strongly suggested that there was a leading family with one style, who owned the broch, and numerous subordinates, using a much older pottery (MacKie 1974: 164–5; 1977b: 213–14).

Leckie broch in Stirlingshire was excavated during the 1970s and, though producing hardly any native pottery, had large quantities of native ornaments and imported Roman luxuries (MacKie 1982). Because of violent destruction most of this was preserved and it gives a clear impression of a wealthy iron age family (there was a central hearth) of the mid-second century AD. Also well preserved were many iron tools, and also weapons like sword blades and spearheads. The latter confirmed the élite nature of the inhabitants of the broch but the former included sheep shears and an ard point, indicating that the inhabitants of Leckie were active farmers as well as, presumably, the leaders of the community.

It is striking how all four separate and independent strands of evidence seem best explained by similar pictures of a stratified iron age society with an élite group inhabiting the brochs and having authority over a larger class of ordinary clansmen who sometimes – as at Dun Mor Vaul – seem to be of different origin if the pottery is a reliable guide. The existence of tribal chiefs cannot be confirmed from this material but seems indisputable from general considerations as well as from the evidence for the tribal structure of Scottish middle iron age society supplied by Roman writers.

Recent Highland Clan Society

A brief look at the highland clan system in the seventeenth and eighteenth centuries AD may help us to decide whether the picture built up of iron age society is plausible. It is also of general interest because, as noted, it was the last Celtic tribal culture surviving in Europe, albeit one of different origins, judging from the language, from that of the iron age La Tène cultures. One may reasonably suppose that much of the late medieval population was genetically and culturally descended from the iron age inhabitants of the same area although many drastic changes had occurred in the intervening centuries, notably the arrival of the Christian church and the stamping out of paganism, the settlement in strength first of Gaels in the west and south-west and, later, of Norsemen in the Western Isles, the development of an urban society with a money economy in the lowlands and the rise of feudalism in Scotland with a king claiming to have a higher authority than that of the clan chiefs (although he was often not able to exercise it) (Duncan 1975: 106ff.).

We know from early English witnesses of the highland way of life – like Edmund Burt who was stationed with the army in Inverness in the mid-1720s (Burt 1754) – that the basis of the late clan system was the inherited authority of the chief (the *ceann cineil* or 'chief of kin') over his *clann* ('children' in Gaelic) rather than over a tract of territory, which was the feudal system (Skene 1902; MacInnes 1972). It is also clear that there was a clan gentry – sometimes called the *fine* (Macinnes forthcoming) – composed of the collateral descendants of the chief's family, the subchiefs among whom would have had their own estates and rents. In late medieval times there was another class in the hierarchy, the tacksmen, who were more distant relatives whose job it was to collect the rents for the chiefs and subchiefs. Rents in cash or kind were a relatively recent innovation arising from the spread of the money economy from the lowlands.

Because of invasions of various kinds foreigners often took over ancient clans or started their own. A good example are the Stewarts of Appin whose origins lie in the aristocratic Anglo-Norman FitzAlan family in Wales in the twelfth century (Anon 1901: 9ff.). One Walter eventually moved to lowland Scotland under King David I and became High Stewart (i.e. 'Steward') and his descendant John Stewart became Lord of Lorn (northern Argyllshire) in the fifteenth century by marrying the heiress of clan MacDougall, residing at Dunollie near Oban. This link by marriage to an old highland family was essential if the Stewarts were to have legitimacy in the eyes of the highlanders.

After various conflicts the Stewarts were able to hold on to only part of Lorn, namely Appin, and by 1745 there was a clan chief and five major subchiefs each with his own estate and known by the names of these; they were Ballachulish, Ardsheal, Achnacone, Invernahyle and Fasnacloich. Indeed the Stewarts of Appin were apparently the only branch of that powerful family that adopted the true highland clan structure (Stewart of Achnacone 1979) and learned to speak the Gaelic of their clansmen. To emphasize the legality of his highland descent the chief was addressed as 'MacIain Stiubhart', that is 'son' (or 'descendant') 'of John Stewart'.

Each of these cadet families, as well as that of the chief, would have a number of male relatives making up a fairly numerous Stewart gentry whose names appear as officers in the Order Book of the Appin Regiment which was raised to fight for Prince Charles Edward Stewart (Livingstone of Bachuil 1984). The majority of the clansmen had different names – like McColl, Black, MacInnes and so on – and were descended from people who already lived in Appin when the Stewarts arrived to take over or who joined them there; they appear as 'other ranks' in the Order Book.

The picture presented by this branch of the Stewart family matches well with that inferred directly from the iron age archaeological evidence; it is of a clan gentry, presumably members of a single family lineage, having dominion over a much larger number of ordinary farmers and living in grander houses than the commoners. These last had become tenant farmers by the eighteenth century but back in the Iron Age they were doubtless true clansmen, paying tribute in kind and owing allegiance and support in war in return for being looked after like *clann*. In late medieval times the gentry with a few exceptions did no work – physical labour being thought unworthy of a gentleman. In the Iron Age, however, we have a glimpse of a different state of affairs at Leckie broch – of an élite family who were nevertheless engaged in everyday farming and domestic activities. In those remote times the elements of tribal society may have been closer together.

REFERENCES

Anon (1901) *The Story of the Stewarts*, Edinburgh.

Armit, I. (1991) 'Epilogue: the Scottish Atlantic Iron Age', in I. Armit (ed.) *Beyond the Brochs*, Edinburgh, 194–210.

Atkinson, R.J.C. and Piggott, S. (1955) 'The Torrs "Chamfrein"', *Archaeologia* 96: 197–235.

Baker, J.R. (1974) *Race*, Oxford.

Buchanan, G. (1582) *Rerum Scoticarum Historiae*, Edinburgh.

Burt, E. (1754) *Letters from a Gentleman in the North of Scotland . . .*, London.

Carter, S.P. *et al.* (1985) 'Interim report on the structures at Howe, Stromness, Orkney', *Glasgow Archaeological Journal* 11: 61–73.

Caulfield, S. (1977) 'The beehive quern in Ireland', *Journal of the Royal Society of Antiquaries of Ireland* 107: 104–38.

Coles, J.M. (1960) 'Scottish late bronze age metalwork: typology, distributions and chronology', *Proceedings of the Society of Antiquaries of Scotland* 93: 16–134.

Curwen, E.C. (1937) 'Querns', *Antiquity* 1: 135–51.

Duncan, A.A.M. (1975) *Scotland: the making of the kingdom*, Edinburgh.

Fairhurst, H. (1984) *Excavations at Crosskirk broch, Caithness*, Society of Antiquaries of Scotland, Monograph Series no. 3, Edinburgh.

Fenton, A. (1978) *The Northern Isles: Orkney and Shetland*, Edinburgh.

Fitzpatrick, A.P. (1989) 'The submission of the Orkney Isles to Claudius: new evidence?', *Scottish Archaeological Review* 6: 24–33.

Fojut, N. (1982) 'Towards a geography of Shetland brochs', *Glasgow Archaeological Journal*: 9: 38–59.

Fowler, Elizabeth (1960) 'The origin and development of the penannular brooch in Europe', *Proceedings of the Prehistoric Society*, 26: 149–79.

Fox, C. (1949) 'Celtic mirror handles in Britain with special reference to the Colchester handle', *Archaeologia Cambrensis* 100: 24–44.

Giot, P.R., Briard J. and Pape, L. (1979) *Préhistoire de la Bretagne*, Rennes.

Hamilton, J.R.C. (1956) *Excavations at Jarlshof, Shetland*, Edinburgh.

—— (1968) *Excavations at Clickhimin, Shetland*, Edinburgh.

Hedges, J.W. (1987) *Bu, Gurness and the Brochs of Orkney*, 3 vols, Oxford, British Archaeological Reports 163.

Hedges, J.W. (1990) 'The broch period', in C. Renfrew (ed.) *The Prehistory of Orkney*: BC 4000–1000 AD (sic), Edinburgh, 150–75.

Hedges, J.W. and Bell, B. (1980) 'That tower of Scottish prehistory: the broch', *Antiquity* 54: 87–94.

Henderson, Isobel (1967) *The Picts*, London.

Henshall, A.S. (1972) *The Chambered Tombs of Scotland*, II, Edinburgh.

Hodder, I. (1982) *The Present Past: an introduction to anthropology for archaeologists*, London.

Jackson, K.H. (1953) *Language and History of Early Britain: a chronological survey of the Brittonic languages, first to twelfth century AD*, Edinburgh.

—— (1955) 'The Pictish language', in F.T. Wainwright (ed.) *The Problem of the Picts*, Edinburgh, 129–66.

Livingstone of Bachuil, A. *et al.* (1984) *The Muster Roll of Prince Charles Edward Stewart's Army 1745–46*, Aberdeen.

Macinnes, A. (in press) 'Crown, clan and *fine*: the "civilising" of Scottish Gaeldom 1587–1638', in K.M.Brown (ed.) *The Scottish Nobility from the Renaissance to the Reformation*.

MacInnes, J. (1972) 'Clan unity and individual freedom', *Transactions of the Gaelic Society of Inverness* 47 (1971–2): 338–73.

MacKie, E.W. (1965) 'The origin and development of the broch and wheelhouse-building cultures of the Scottish Iron Age', *Proceedings of the Prehistoric Society* 31: 93–146.

—— (1969a) 'Radiocarbon dates and the Scottish Iron Age', *Antiquity* 43: 15-26.

—— (1969b) 'Review of *Excavations at Clickhimin, Shetland*', *Proceedings of the Prehistoric Society* 30: 386–8.

—— (1970) 'The Scottish "Iron Age"', *Scottish Historical Review* 49(147): 1–32.

—— (1971) 'English migrants and Scottish brochs', *Glasgow Archaeological Journal* 2: 39–71.

—— (1972) 'Some new quernstones from brochs and duns', *Proceedings of the Society of Antiquaries of Scotland* 104 (1971–2): 137–46.

—— (1974) *Dun Mor Vaul: an iron age broch on Tiree*, Glasgow.

—— (1977a) 'The vitrified forts of Scotland', in D.W. Harding (ed.) *Hillforts: later prehistoric earthworks in Britain and Ireland*, London, 205–35.

—— (1977b) *Science and Society in Prehistoric Britain*, London.

—— (1982) 'The Leckie broch, Stirlingshire: an interim report', *Glasgow Archaeological Journal* 9: 59–72.

—— (1989) 'Leckie broch: impact on the Scottish Iron Age', *Glasgow Archaeological Journal* 14 (1987): 1–18.

—— (1992) 'The iron age semibrochs of Atlantic Scotland: a case study in the problems of deductive reasoning', *Archaeological Journal* 148 (1991): 149–81.

—— (in press) 'On misinterpreting Scottish brochs: Gurness and Midhowe in Orkney', *Archaeological Journal* 149.

MacKie, E.W. and Rona, M. (1984) 'Red-haired "Celts" are better termed Caledonians', *American Journal of Dermatopathology* 6 (Suppl. 1), 147–9.

Mann, J.C. and Breeze, D. (1988) 'Ptolemy, Tacitus and the tribes of northern Britain', *Proceedings of the Society of Antiquaries of Scotland* 117: 85–92.

Nicolaisen, W.F.H. (1976) *Scottish Place-names*, London.

Palk, Natalie (1984) 'Iron Age Bridle Bits from Britain', *University of Edinburgh Archaeological Occasional Papers* 10, Edinburgh.

Piggott, S. (1950) 'Swords and scabbards of the British Early Iron Age', *Proceedings of the Prehistoric Society* 16: 1–28.

—— (1959) 'The carnyx in early iron age Britain', *Antiquaries Journal* 39: 13–32.

—— (1965) *Ancient Europe*, Edinburgh.

—— (1966) 'A scheme for the Scottish Iron Age', in A.L.F. Rivet (ed.) *The Iron Age in Northern Britain*, Edinburgh.

Powell, T.G.E. (1958) *The Celts*, London.

—— (1962) 'The coming of the Celts', in S. Piggott (ed.) *The Prehistoric Peoples of Scotland*, London, 105–24.

Renfrew, C. (1990) 'Epilogue', in C. Renfrew (ed.) *The Prehistory of Orkney: BC 4000–1000 AD (sic)*, Edinburgh, 243–61.

Rivet, A.L.F. (ed.) (1966) *The Iron Age in Northern Britain*, Edinburgh.

—— (1978) 'Ptolemy's geography and the Flavian invasion of Scotland', *Studien zu den Militärgrenzen Roms* 2: 46–64.

Rivet, A.L.F. and Smith, C. (1979) *The Place-names of Roman Britain*, London.

Sanderson, D.C.W. *et al.* (1988) 'Scottish vitrified forts: TL results from six study sites', *Nuclear Tracks Radiation Measurements* 14(1/2): 307–16.

Skene, W.F. (1902) *The Highlanders of Scotland*, Stirling.

Stead, I. (1979) *The Arras Culture*, York.

Stevenson, R.B.K. (1966) 'Metalwork and some other objects in Scotland and their cultural affinities', in A.L.F. Rivet (ed.) *The Iron Age in Scotland*, Edinburgh, 17–44.

Stewart of Achnacone, I.M. (1979) 'Clan Stewart of Appin', *The Stewarts* 15: 225–35.

Thomas, C. (1963) 'The animal art of the Scottish Iron Age and its origins', *Archaeological Journal* 118: 14–64.

Thomas, F.W.L. (1876) 'Analysis of the Ptolemaic geography of Scotland', *Proceedings of the Society of Antiquaries of Scotland* 11 (1874–76): 198–225.

—— (1890) 'On the duns of the Outer Hebrides', *Archaeologica Scotica* 5: 365–415.

Warner, R.B. (1983) 'Ireland, Ulster and Scotland in the earlier Iron Age', in Anne O'Connor and D.V. Clarke (eds) *From the Stone Age to the 'Forty-five: studies presented to R.B.K. Stevenson*, Edinburgh, 160–87.

Watson, W.J. (1926) *The History of the Celtic Place-names of Scotland*, Edinburgh.

THE EARLY CELTS
IN WALES

—— •◦• ——

Jeffrey L. Davies

Tacitus's *Annals* (xii.32) record how in AD 48 the governor of Britannia, Ostorius Scapula, led the army against the Decangi (*sic*): the first historical reference to a Celtic tribe inhabiting Wales. Thereafter Rome was to become embroiled in protracted warfare with two other militarily powerful Welsh tribes, the Silures and Ordovices, conferring particular fame upon the former. Tacitus's physical description of the Silures as *colorati* and with curly hair (*Agricola* xi) forms part of a precious body of documentary evidence which allows us to glimpse first-century AD Welsh communities for whose wartime behaviour we can find echoes in contemporary Britain from Kent to Caledonia, or earlier in Caesarian Gaul. The origins of these Celtic communities inhabiting the principality are to be sought not in a pattern of migration and interaction with indegenes but rather in a protracted phase of social and economic change affecting sedentary communities over at least a millennium. It is this process of adjustment and evolution, coupled with the workings of 'cumulative Celticity' (Hawkes 1979), which gives rise to the fully developed insular socio-economic systems of the western British pre-Roman Iron Age (PRIA).

Wales is topographically a mountainous area but upland is unevenly distributed; hence the dramatic contrasts between Snowdonia and offshore Anglesey, or the Cambrian range and lowlands of Glamorgan and Dyfed and the broken hill-country and fertile valleys of the Marches. Geomorphological and pedological differences are critical in comprehending the settlement base and social development of this distinctive geoclimatic region, whilst geography has fostered a strong regional and sub-regional identity which crystallized in the territorial divisions of late prehistoric and early historic times.

By the early first millennium BC the region was characterized by agricultural communities of family or extended family size which were sufficiently sedentary to require permanent settlements encompassing a variety of habitats. Some occupied classic pastoral upland typified by the flimsy huts and 'field systems' on the Denbigh Moors, of which Graig Felen is a good example (Manley 1990b). The majority, though, occupy lowland settings exemplified by the early to late bronze age (EBA–LBA) settlement complex at Atlantic Trading Estate, Barry (Glam.) (Price and Wardle 1987; Wardle 1988), or those built on the stable peat of the Severn foreshore at Cold Harbour (Mon.), with nearby Chapeltump 1 and 2 probably representing successive timber settlements of the seventh to ninth centuries BC (Whittle 1989). More remarkable still is the waterlogged complex at Caldicot Castle Lake (Mon.) with its worked timbers and wide artefactual range, including the remains of plank-built boats and a Wilburton chape incorporated in deposits of the eighth century BC (Parry 1988; Parry and Parkhouse 1989, 1990) (Figure 35.1). In south Pembrokeshire a middle to late bronze age (MBA–LBA) multifocus agricultural settlement at Stackpole was abandoned to sanding in the eighth century BC (Benson *et al.* 1990). All were apparently unenclosed. In this respect Meyllteyrn Uchaf (Caerns.), a concentric enclosure with two timber round-houses dated *c.* 1950–1380 BC (Kelly 1990, 1991a, 1992), is an exciting new discovery. None continued in occupation beyond the onset of the climatic deterioration of the sub-Atlantic phase.

THE LATE BRONZE AGE CRISIS

Much has been written on the issue of climatic deterioration beginning just before 1250 b.c. accelerating after 850 and reaching its coolest and wettest about 650, with a period of climatic amelioration from *c.* 450 (Lamb 1981; Harding 1982). The impact will have been most severe in areas of high precipitation, especially the exposed western hills and classic uplands where vegetational coupled with anthropogenic changes led to leaching and podsolization, and at worst to extensive peat formation. Though the effects are thought to have been less severe in the rain-shadow zone of eastern Wales, overall a massive loss of exploitable land and a dramatic curtailment of agricultural potential is envisaged, precipitating a protracted crisis which can only have led to a primitive economic recession and certainly pressure on population, if not a demographic decline in some areas (Burgess 1985).

It is thought that one response to the crisis was a retreat from the uplands and the realignment of settlement in favour of more sheltered locations. However, pollen sequences from the Brenig valley (Denbs.) seem to conflict with the general hypothesis that the Welsh uplands were wholly abandoned soon after 800 b.c. (Lynch 1993: 167). What is significant is the wholesale failure of many LBA settlements – even those in lowlands – to continue in occupation into the EPRIA, clearly indicating dislocation and thus far-reaching socio-economic change. The starkness of climatic variation between the Welsh regions – broadly eastern and western – eventually led to different subsistence systems and social frameworks which are manifest in the settlement archaeology of the LBA/EPRIA transition.

One response, perhaps universal but better represented in eastern Wales, was conflict leading to a growing investment in the physical security of groups of families and their chattels by the construction of fortified villages. The relationship between climatic deterioration, the process of nucleation and fortification is complex. In a Welsh dimension the eastern bias is perhaps explicable by the fact that this interface between upland and lowland supported a habitually larger population, but one which suffered proportionally greater stress because of a reduction in agricultural yields which could not be remedied through normal expansion; and if, as is suggested, there was a switch of emphasis to pastoralism, which demands proportionately even more land, sources of conflict would have multiplied.

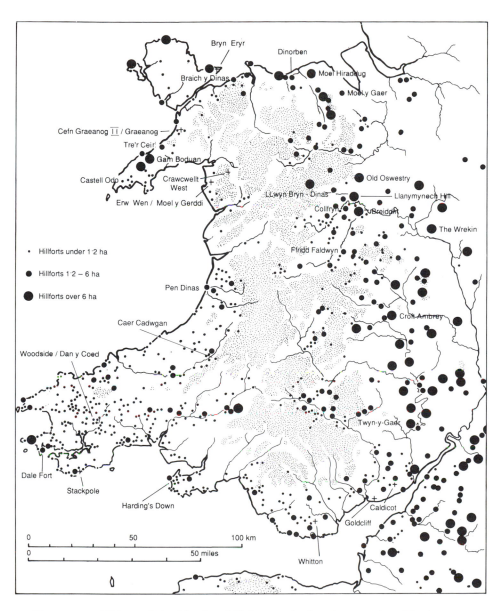

Figure 35.1 Wales and the Marches: hill-forts and other sites mentioned in the text.

Fortification takes a number of forms: a timber-reinforced rampart of *c*. 800 BC at the Breiddin (Mont.) (Figure 35.2) (Musson 1991); an eighth-century BC stone-revetted earthwork at Llwyn Bryn-dinas (Musson *et al.* 1992); but palisades dominate as at Moel y Gaer (Guilbert 1976) (Figure 35.3a), Dinorben (Guilbert 1979b), Old Oswestry (Varley 1948), Dale Fort (Pembs.) (Benson and Williams 1987) and possibly Ffridd Faldwyn (Mont.) (Guilbert 1981). Such sites, normally on hilltops, represent a fundamental reappraisal of the needs of communities which hitherto do

673

Figure 35.2 The Breiddin, Mont.: simplified plan of the late bronze age and iron age defences and internal features at the south-western end of the hill-fort. (Source: Musson 1991.)

not seem to have inhabited defensible, nucleated settlements. Whilst most are of the order of 3–5 ha, the Breiddin, with probably 28 ha enclosed, is an exception, with clear implications in terms of population and social organization. The site was apparently permanent with timber buildings and four-posters (Figure 35.2) and, judging by the presence of Broadward complex weapons, tools and items of personal adornment, of high status. Its occupation ended within the eighth century BC with its burning. At Llwyn Bryn-dinas, too, occupation terminated within the century, whilst at Coed y Cymdda (Glam.) (Owen-John 1988) the defences were left unfinished.

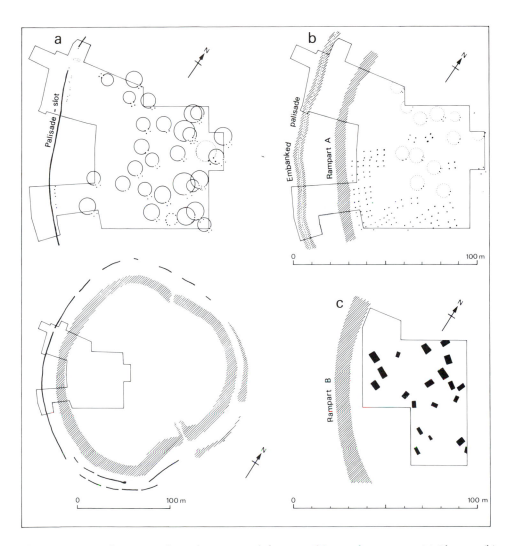

Figure 35.3 Moel y Gaer, Flint.: the western defences and internal structures: (a) Phase 1; (b) Phase 2; (c) Phase 3. (Sources: Guilbert 1976, 1982.)

The general tendency for these community settlements to be abandoned suggests that social stress may have been transient and/or spasmodic. Nevertheless, they seem to have been the harbinger of a need to enclose and protect communities; hence the hierarchy of defended settlements which is the hallmark of the PRIA. Despite the apparent sharp breaks exhibited in the settlement record some of the essential components of MBA/LBA settlement, especially structural and artefactual, continue, though economic strategies were changing in response to the prevailing conditions, whilst in the emergence of a more markedly hierachical social system we can discern one of the dominant forces of the PRIA.

Climatic amelioration after *c.* 450 b.c. allowed communities to establish an agricultural balance leading to a population recovery, with eastern areas benefiting soonest. The north and west may have suffered a more prolonged hiatus (Williams 1988), with the loss of upland grazing necessitating an increase in forest clearance, archaeologically recognizable only after *c.*400 b.c. (Turner 1970; Taylor 1980; Kelly 1991b).

SETTLEMENT IN THE PRE-ROMAN IRON AGE

On the one hand a trend towards fortified community settlement continues whilst on the other we discern clear sub-regional trends in the development of settlement type and hierarchy, reflecting differential socio-economic systems. Hill-forts – widely distributed over the principality – loom large in this story.

Hill-forts

New data allow us to appreciate regional trends within their development sequences, and it is no longer possible to generalize about their function and chronology on the basis of morphology or size, or necessarily apply the chronologies and socio-economic strictures of the southern English hill-fort sequence to Wales (Savory 1976a). Yet there are clear general trends. For example, palisaded enclosures which often underlie hill-forts, as at Castell Odo (Alcock 1960), Caer, Bayvil (James 1987), Bryn Maen Caerau (Williams 1988) and Moel y Gaer (Guilbert 1976) may be superseded by sixth–fifth-century BC timber-laced defences or earthworks, whilst timber-lacing itself is not normally employed after the fourth century BC – Phase 3 at Moel y Gaer (Figure 35.3c), post-dating 180 BC, being an exception. Similarly, early gates tend to be simple portals, with more sophisticated guard-chambered gates coming into fashion in the Marches and north-east Wales in the fifth century BC (Guilbert 1979a). Multivallation and enlargement are also features of the MPRIA and LPRIA.

By virtue of the fact that hill-forts reflect investment of energy in their building, maintenance of defences and internal structures, then size and complexity should relate directly to permanence, population density and the socio-political situation prevailing within a given area. Long-term settled occupation is certainly implied at the Breiddin where, despite its incongenial position, occupation is intense and continuous from the later third to first century BC (Figure 35.2). Yet apparent permanence may be belied in the archaeological record, for at Moel y Gaer the late fourth/early third century BC Phase 2 settlement, with 2.7 ha enclosed, with its stake-walled round-houses and rows of four-posters, is a short-lived plantation (Figure 35.3b). At this site, at least, the three phases in its history, each separated by interludes of centuries, is surely related to a sub-regional cycle of socio-political unrest (Guilbert 1975).

The question of functional similarity or dissimilarity in terms of hill-fort occupation is one which cannot be pursued here, yet there are clear hints that hill-forts were socially, if not economically, significant. The distribution pattern of many of the larger forts on the upland margins such as the Vale of Clwyd suggests that they acted as nodal points from which the control of valley resources could be organized and integrated with upland grazing. Whether this necessarily assumes a redistributive function is unclear, though some possibly served as the social and political focus of a community through the residence there of an élite group, with non-resident members tied to a major hill-fort through links of kinship or patronage. In support of such a claim we might note the incidence of high-status metalwork from Moel Hiraddug (Brassil *et al.* 1982) and Pen-coed-foel (Cards.) (Savory 1976b).

Sub-regional differences in hill-fort development, resulting in part from geomorphology, but more particularly from economic and social differences, are typified by the contrast between those of the northern Marches and south-west Wales.

The Welsh Marches, a 50 km wide belt of broken country, is studded with hillforts whose density is greater in the south-central hills prompting Stanford (1991) to suggest that 'Hillfort settlement was better suited to the social and economic needs of the hill tribes than those people of the northern plains'. At the northern extremity of the March Dinorben had passed through a phase of palisaded defence to timber lacing in the fourth/fifth century BC (Guilbert 1980) whilst the 10.5 ha Clwydian fort on Moel Hiraddug developed from a single enclosure to a multiple enclosure fort with a guard-chambered main inner gate by the early fifth–mid-fourth century BC (Brassil *et al.* 1982; Guilbert 1979a). Further south in the valleys of the Severn and its tributaries the hill-fort sequence as presently known is later. At Llwyn Bryn-dinas the LBA rampart was refurbished in the fourth/third century and again in the second/first century BC. The 28/40 ha stone-walled fort on the Breiddin was built after 270 ± 90 b.c. and was packed with round-houses and four-posters, the latter often replacing houses (Figure 35.2). Llanymynech Hill, at 57 ha one of the largest hill-forts in Britain, impressively sited in the fringe of the Shropshire plain, was in existence by the late second century BC (Musson and Northover 1989). If it was as densely occupied as the Breiddin then in these instances we must be dealing with settlements which not only have the attributes of defensive strongholds but function as hill-towns, and by implication centres of power.

In south-west Wales hill-forts are of more modest size, the majority lying on the fringes of the uplands. Some, such as Dale Fort (Benson and Williams 1987), Llanstephan Castle (Guilbert 1974) and possibly Caer Cadwgan (Austin *et al.* 1984–8), may have been in existence by the mid-fifth century BC. Others such as Merlin's Hill, the third largest hill-fort in Dyfed, initially an univallate enclosure of 1 ha, was enlarged to 3.8 ha sometime after 360 ± 60 b.c. (Williams *et al.* 1988), whilst the successive enlargement of Pen Dinas, Aberystwyth, with Phase IV associated with third- to first-century BC Malvernian ceramics (Figure 35.9f), suggests an early origin (Forde *et al.* 1963). Despite its relatively unimpressive size Moel Trigarn at 2.8 ha is covered in building platforms, c.220 in all, suggesting a substantial population at some stage in its history (Baring Gould *et al.* 1900); but sites of over 2.5 ha are exceptional. Pembrey Mountain (Williams 1981), Holgan Camp (Williams 1984), Castell Henllys (Mytum 1989) and Coygan Camp (Wainwright 1967) represent the norm, with C–14 dates suggesting that the majority were being built from the fourth century BC, and in some instances, as at Holgan, apparently having a short life.

Elsewhere in Wales the study of hill-forts is bedevilled by minimal excavation and few C–14 dates. In the south-east only Coed y Bwnydd (Babbidge 1977) and Twyn-y-Gaer (Probert 1976) have produced C–14 dates which suggest that the former at

1.4 ha was extant by *c.*400 b.c., whilst at the latter the earthwork annexe was built soon after 294–231 BC. The region abounds with powerful 2–5 ha hill-forts, both coastal such as The Bulwarks, Porthkerry (Davies 1973b) and Sudbrook (Nash-Williams 1939) or dominating tracts of fertile vale such as Castle Ditches, Llancarfan (Hogg 1976), and Llanmelin (Nash-Williams 1933). On ceramic grounds these were occupied in the first century BC to the first century AD, but the chronology of developmental sequences such as at Castle Ditches remains unknown. Similarly, of the multiple-enclosure forts which occupy the upland margins of South Wales only Harding's Down West has been examined (Hogg 1973) and their broad chronologies remain undetermined. Finally, in the north-west the position is just as grim. The only dates available are for minor sites; the weak double ringwork at Castell Odo (2390–2215 B.P.) and an origin sometime before *c.*100 BC for the 0.1 ha stone fort at Bryn y Castell (Mer.) (Crew 1984). Despite the impressive size and obvious complexity of the larger hill-forts such as Garn Boduan and Braich y Ddinas whose dimensions, if not morphology, are broadly akin to those of north-eastern Wales, their development and broader relationships are presently unclear.

Non-hillfort Settlement

Though hill-forts loom large, the dominant type of settlement throughout the first millennium BC was the farmstead, normally delimited by any of several enclosure techniques. Unenclosed settlements are also known. Indeed in some areas we may be seeing only a fraction of the actual settlement evidence. Though there is undoubtedly a broad relationship between hill-fort and farmstead, a simplistic model of it may be misleading given the chronologically and spatially variable pattern of hill-fort building and the many different types of broadly contemporary settlements which can exist.

This situation is well illustrated in south-west Wales where Williams (1988, 1991) notes a duality in the settlement pattern; the north and east with a dominant hill-fort element; the inland south and west pattern comprising promontory forts, 'ringforts' and concentric antenna enclosures (James 1990) of less than 0.5 ha (Figure 35.4). Rectilinear ditched and embanked enclosures of the Penycoed type are common to both areas (Davies 1994) and appear to date to the second century BC and later. Penycoed (Figure 35.5) is interpreted as a farm (Murphy 1985). The incidence of unenclosed settlements such as Stackpole (Benson *et al.* 1990) is problematical. This second-century BC and later coastal site appears not to be marginal and may well be characteristic of what has not survived agricultural practices elsewhere in the region. What is particularly interesting is that defensibly postured settlements of the sixth to fourth centuries BC in the inland south-west give way in the third to second centuries BC to a proliferation of 'ringfort'-type sites, possibly either indicating population growth resulting in the fragmentation of social groups and tenurial units, or the consequence of partible inheritance (Williams 1988). Both causal factors may be applicable. Certainly, a settlement explosion seems to have occurred by the last centuries BC.

In north-west Wales the non-fortified element has been intensively studied and subject to recent recension (Smith 1974, 1977; Kelly 1988, 1991b). Stone-built 'hut-

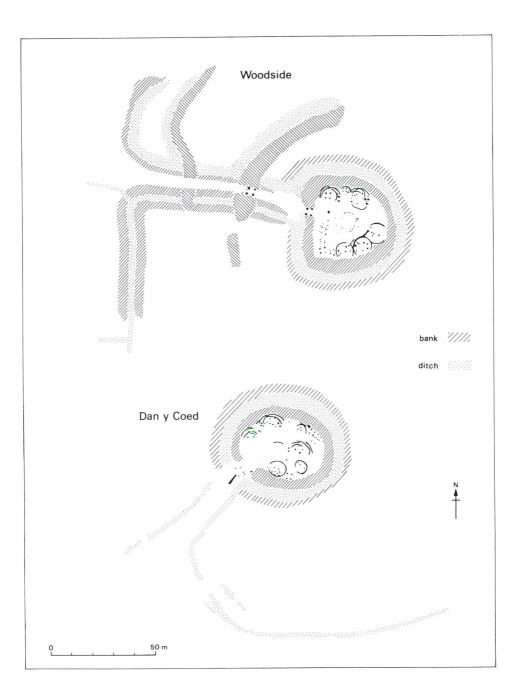

Figure 35.4 Woodside and Dan y Coed 'ringforts', Pembs. (Source: Williams 1988.)

679

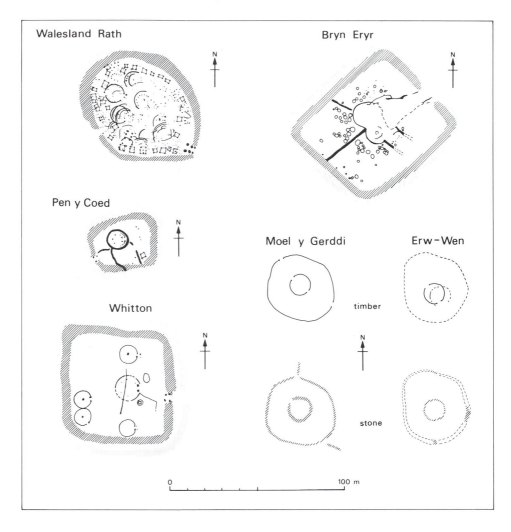

Figure 35.5 Non-hillfort settlements: Walesland Rath, Pembs. (Source: Wainwright 1971); Bryn Eryr, Ang. (Source: Longley, forthcoming); Pen y Coed, Carm. (Source: Murphy 1985); Whitton, Glam. (Source: Jarrett and Wrathmell 1981); Moel y Gerddi and Erw-Wen, Mer. (Source: Kelly 1988).

circle' settlements of enclosed and open type, with associated field enclosure systems, survive in considerable numbers. Enclosed forms can now be seen to originate within the PRIA and have timber precursors, whilst the possible bronze age date of un-enclosed, upland huts and enclosures has been cast into doubt as a result of work at Crawcwellt West (Mer.) (see p. 687). In addition other types of settlement have been recognized: two large timber round-houses and four-posters within Henge A at Llandegai (Caerns.) (Houlder 1967) may be an abberation, but at Bryn Eryr (Ang.) (Longley 1988) a timber round-house was transformed into a rectangular, embanked and ditched farmstead after the fourth/third century BC (Figure 35.5). It is, however, the stone-built settlements, presently surviving only in marginal landscapes, which predominate and for which a fairly consistent pattern of development is now emerging. At Erw Wen (Mer.) clearance was followed by the construction of a timber round-house and concentric palisaded enclosure, then translated into stone, all within the period 770–400 b.c. A similar sequence occurs at Moel y Gerddi c.330–190 b.c. (Kelly 1988) (Figure 35.5). On the Graeanog ridge (Caerns.), where settlement is long-lived and multi-focus, clearance coincides with an initial phase of agricultural activity – a field system of c.400–200 BC at Cefn Graeanog II and Graeanog – probably associated with a timber settlement (Kelly 1991b). Sometime about 200–150 BC the first stone farmstead was built against a lynchet at Graeanog II, only to be abandoned until the first century AD. The trend, then, seems to be the gradual replacement of timber farmsteads in stone as timber became exhausted, though in areas already lacking timber such as Ty Mawr (Ang.) (Smith 1987) settlements were already being built in stone well before the third century BC. If the pattern recognized on the Graeanog ridge is generally applicable, then there was a massive phase of land clearance and settlement after c.500 BC and, although not always successful, seems to indicate an expansion of settlement, if not population increase, particularly in the last centuries BC.

Prior to the application of aerial photography to the central region of the Welsh Marches the dominance of hill-forts gave a seriously unbalanced picture of later prehistoric settlement. That picture has been rectified and a balanced landscape of fortified/unfortified, hilltop, hillside and valley-bottom settlement exhibited by diverse types of cropmark enclosures has emerged (Whimster 1989). The majority of these are of less than 0.5 ha enclosed and appear to be farmsteads. Morphologically diverse, their chronology and economies are only known in a few instances, as at Sharpstones Hill (Shrops.) Site A, where a rectilinear enclosure apparently succeeds an LBA/EPRIA settlement of more dispersed character sometime before the third century BC, and Site E, where a bivallate rectangular farmstead was occupied from the third century BC into the Roman period (Barker *et al.* 1991); or Arddleen (Mont.), where an LPRIA origin is suggested for a lowland concentric enclosure (Britnell and Musson 1984). It is an untested assumption that the great majority of these enclosures were constructed between the fourth to third century BC and the Roman period. Curvilinear forms are more prevalent in the western Marches, rectilinear in the east; but whether morphological variation represents fundamental differences in date, function or simply cultural preferences is uncertain. Multiple-ditched enclosures such as Collfryn (Mont.) (Figure 35.6), however, *are* seemingly different, not only being more defensively sited but having much longer and complex structural sequences which Musson (1991) suggests may place them in a hierarchically higher slot as 'pioneering' settlements, sometimes succeeded by less overtly defensible settlements.

Non-hillfort settlement in north-east Wales has also benefited from an aerial photographic input (Manley 1990a, 1991) and shows a settlement pattern akin to that of the central Marches, particularly in the Tanat valley and the upper Clwyd. The presence of unenclosed settlement is also vouched for by the discovery of a second- to first-century BC farm at Prestatyn (Flints.) (Blockley 1989) and an apparently similar site at Rhuddlan (Blockley 1989: 223), whilst an apparently isolated timber

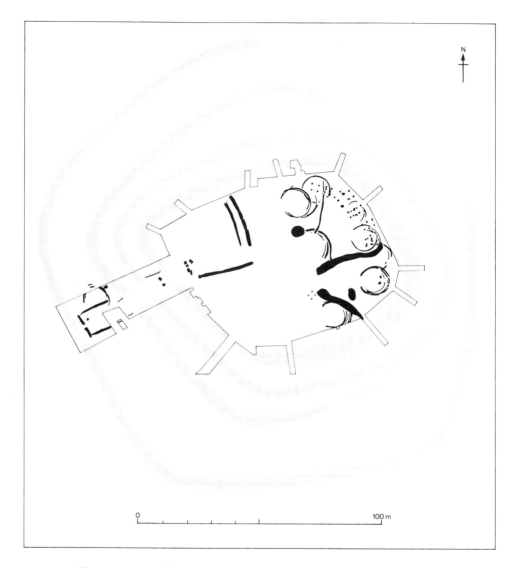

Figure 35.6 Collfryn, Mont.: iron age features. (Source: Britnell 1989.)

round-house associated with second-century BC Malvernian pottery appears to represent something more than seasonal occupation on moorland at Nant y Griafolen, Brenig (Denbs. (Lynch 1993: 159–61).

In south-east Wales non-hillfort settlement is largely constrained to the lowlands of Glamorgan and Gwent, though pastoral enclosures occupy upland margins. Most of the investigated settlements belong to the LPRIA. Some, such as Mynydd Bychan (Savory 1954, 1956), have a defensive potential, as does the second-century BC to first-century AD rectilinear hilltop enclosure at Cae Summerhouse (Davies 1973a, 1982; Robinson 1988: xvi–xvii), now seen to be bivallate. A similar situation pertains at the rectilinear early first-century AD farmstead at Whitton (Jarrett and Wrathmell 1981) (Figure 35.5). Many LPRIA settlements manifestly underlie those of Roman date, as is the case at Llandough, Biglis and Caldicot (Robinson 1988), though our knowledge of them is woefully poor. The PRIA artefactual range at the above is unequivocally first century BC to first century AD (Figure 35.7). Though 'Glastonbury Ware' sherds from Llandough and Biglis hint at occupation prior to *c.*50 BC, pre-first-century BC settlement sites are elusive. That such must exist is demonstrated by exciting new discoveries from the Severn foreshore where a rich PRIA sequence is emerging. This involved the laying down of trackways such as the Upton Track (470±70 b.c.) (Whittle 1989), and the building of settlements after a long hiatus. At Magor Pill (Whittle 1989) a dump of third- to first-century BC ceramics (Figure 35.9d,e,g) indicates the proximity of a settlement, perhaps akin to that remarkably preserved at Goldcliff (Bell 1992, 1993), where three to four rectangular timber buildings were built on a peat shelf. Building 1 (Figure 35.8) produced an uncalibrated C–14 date of 2120±90 b.p. Environmental data indicate an association with grazing and the utilization of estuarine resources, perhaps on a seasonal basis. Such structures are highly unusual, even in a wider British context, and in Wales have broad parallels only at Moel y Gaer, Phase 3 (Figure 35.3c). Such evidence serves to demonstrate the large-scale but perhaps seasonal exploitation of the Wentlooge Levels in the LPRIA as well as the probable character of undefended settlements on drier land.

SUBSISTENCE

The mode of PRIA subsistence was deeply rooted in prehistory with the pattern of settlement and social organization dependent upon it (Caseldine 1990). Mixed agriculture was the norm with regional variation in microclimate and topography determining overall subsistence strategies. Though climatic deterioration accentuated the bioclimatic diversity of the principality, the pattern of settlement, even in lowland settings, represents land-use systems which rely upon both pasture and arable. The needs of both were met by woodland clearance from *c.*400 b.c. for cultivation on the Graeanog ridge, and for pasture in the vicinity of Tregaron Bog (Cards.) (Turner 1970; Williams *et al.* 1987) and the Ystwyth Forest (Taylor 1973, 1980).

Cereal cultivation is held to have been more important in some areas than others (Williams 1988) though its incidence on marginal landscapes such as Moel y Gerddi and Erw Wen demonstrates the tenacity of agriculturalists. Evidence for field systems, that primary mechanism of land division, is patchy. Small, squarish relict fields survive extensively in north-west Wales, but rarely elsewhere, though examples exist at Stackpole and Pembrey Mountain in the south-west and at the Breiddin and Collfryn in the Marches. Pre-rampart plough-marks are known at Woodbarn Rath (Vyner 1986), whilst wooden ard-tips come from Walesland Rath (Pembs.) (Wainwright 1971) and a possible iron bar-share from Llanstephan Castle (Guilbert 1974). However, agricultural tools such as reaping-hooks and sickles (Figure 35.7) are rare, which suggests that iron tools never became commonplace among the agricultural community. In contrast food-processing equipment, normally querns of the saddle

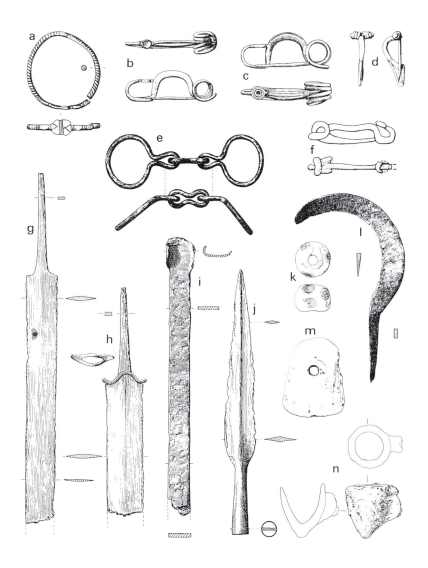

Figure 35.7 (a) La Tène-style copper alloy bracelet, Coygan Camp, Carm.; (b)–(c) La Tène I-style copper alloy brooches from Moel Hiraddug, Flint. and Merthyr Mawr Warren, Glam.; (d) La Tène-style copper alloy brooch, Caldicot, Mon.; (e) iron horse bit, Llyn Cerrig Bach, Ang.; (f) late La Tène I–II-style iron brooch, Breiddin, Mont.; (g)–(h) iron swords, Llyn Cerrig Bach; (i) 'currency bar', Llyn Cerrig Bach; (j) iron spearhead, Llyn Cerrig Bach; (k) blue glass bead with spiral decoration, Collfryn, Mont.; (l) iron sickle, Llyn Cerrig Bach; (m) clay loom-weight, Breiddin; (n) crucible, Llwyn Bryn-dinas, Denb. (Sources: (a) Wainwright 1967; (b) Brassil *et al.* 1982; (c) Grimes 1951; (d) Robinson 1988; (e), (g), (h), (i), (j), (l) Fox 1946; (f)–(m) Musson 1991; (k) Britnell 1989; (n) Musson *et al.* 1992.) Scale (a)–(d), (f), (k) ½, remainder ¼.

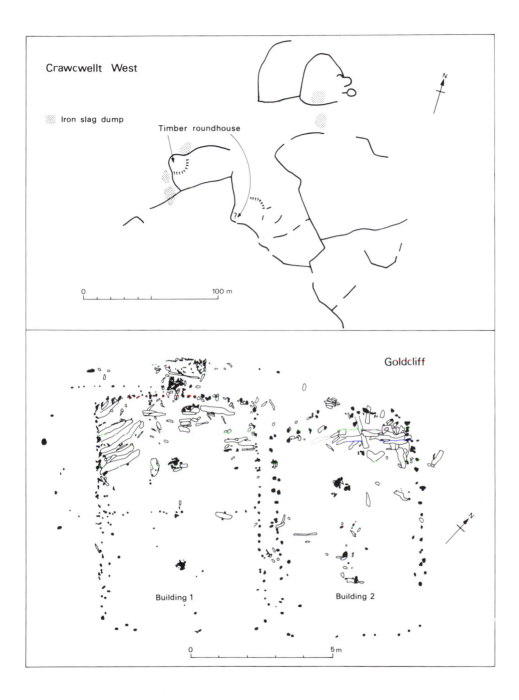

Figure 35.8 Crawcwellt West, Mer.; late iron age ironworking settlement (Source: Crew 1989); Goldcliff, Mon., later iron age rectangular timber buildings. (Source: Bell 1992.)

variety, is mandatory and frequently renewed, even on farms such as Penycoed where the environmental data produce little indication of arable. At Twyn-y-Gaer saddle querns were being replaced by beehive types in LPRIA contexts. The main crops were wheat – spelt and emmer varieties – and barley. Spelt eventually predominates from Cefn Graeanog II to Woodside, though emmer was the main crop at Ty Mawr and probably also at the Breiddin and Collfryn. Barley was grown everywhere, except in areas of poor drainage and high acidity, and was the secondary crop at Cefn Graeanog II. Of oats and rye there is some evidence at Penycoed, but there is none for bread wheat or legumes. The crops were most likely stored in the ubiquitous four-, sometimes five- or six-post structures, common everywhere except in the north-west, though the stored commodity could have varied over time and place.

It was a long-held view that the dictates of topography, soils and climate would have led to a dominance of pastoralism in the subsistence strategy of PRIA communities in Wales. However, recent research demonstrates pastoral and arable activities at the great majority of settlements, without prejudicing their relative importance – always difficult to assess. The role of pastoralism may often be indicated in settlement morphology – the concentric enclosures, embanked track-ways and antenna-ditches of the south-west (Figure 35.4), or annexes attached to hill-forts such as Ffridd Faldwyn (Mont.), or most graphically at Twyn-y-Gaer, where no fewer than eight successive fence alignments of an annexe were recorded before its transformation into earthwork (Probert 1976). A relatively poor database makes it difficult to establish the relative importance of species, but the ubiquity of droveways and enclosures suggests a greater concern with cattle management, and where bone assemblages are sufficiently large cattle are either dominant – for example, Coygan Camp (Wainwright 1967) – or occur in broadly equal numbers to sheep – Dinorben and Collfryn. Though sheep were dominant at Croft Ambrey in the southern Marches (Stanford 1974), there is no evidence of a switch to large-scale sheep farming characteristic of the LPRIA of southern England. The ubiquity of spindle-whorls, and loom-weights at the Breiddin (Figure 35.7m), Castle Ditches, Biglis and Prestatyn do, however, highlight the importance of these animals. Pigs too were kept – apparently in some numbers at Coygan – whilst the importance of horses for traction and riding is evidenced by numerous examples of horse-gear and cart and chariot fittings in the archaeological record. Finally, though there is reliable evidence for the production of surpluses, there is none for agricultural intensification or specialization.

PRODUCTION AND EXCHANGE

Metalworking

In Wales the study of PRIA metalworking in copper alloy (bronze) and iron has received a heightened profile consequent upon research into their primary production and an on-going programme of metal analysis (P. Crew, pers. comm.). These analyses have served to demonstrate that conceptual models of metal production are of small value unless tested against an empirical framework, and that in the case of ironworking some traditional views have been shown to be invalid (Crew 1991).

With the collapse of the insular bronze industry there was a dramatic reduction in the range and scale of bronze object production. Large, luxury objects are rare before the second century BC, and only really come into their own in the first century BC to early first century AD; for example, the shield fitments from Moel Hiraddug (Brassil *et al.* 1982) and Tal-y-Llyn (Savory 1964; Spratling 1966). Bronzeworking was limited in scale, and judging by the distinctive handled crucibles (Figure 35.7n) and residues from a variety of sites was probably catering for the needs of local communities and only relatively small objects were being produced. Such appears to be the case at copper-rich Llanymynech Hill, itself a focus of metal extraction and working in the second to first century BC, and Llwyn Bryn-dinas, where the casting and finishing of objects was undertaken on a small scale within a timber smithy (Musson *et al.* 1992). The high zinc content Llanymynech ores were certainly being exploited from the third century BC and served the needs of numerous communities from nearby Four Crosses (Warrilow *et al.* 1986) and the Breiddin to Old Oswestry and Croft Ambrey. Copper of diverse origins (or the finished pieces) were certainly being traded about. A high antimony ore, possibly of continental origin, was used in the Cerrig-y-drudion 'bowl' as well as a piece from Tal-y-Llyn, whilst two horse-bits and sheet-metal fragments from Llyn Cerrig Bach have a high cobalt content and a south-western English source is proposed (Northover 1991). Other examples of copper from Llanymynech are to be found in a shield fitting from Moel Hiraddug and a horse-bit from Llyn Cerrig Bach.

Ehrenreich (1985) suggests that ironworking was introduced via Atlantic routes, became established in areas such as south-western England which had existing metallurgical significance, and was then transferred to south Wales. Though iron technology was already in a dynamic state from *c*.700 BC, as indicated by the competence of a smith in fashioning copies of a bronze sickle and spearhead from Llyn Fawr (Glam.), it is assumed that bronze tools and weapons continued to be used until a sufficient number of smiths had mastered the new technology. Hence, in the EPRIA iron objects were rare and expensive and the scale of production small, leading to a recycling of objects (Alexander 1981). In Wales, as elsewhere, there is an increase in its frequency after *c*.300 BC, with a consequent decline in recycling; for example at Twyn-y-Gaer (Probert 1976). Only with the apparently massive increase in the supply of iron in the first century BC was it used for the fashioning of large objects such as the Capel Garmon fire-dog (Savory 1976b: pl.VI) or the cauldron-chain in the Lesser Garth hoard (Savory 1966a). By this stage, as Alexander (1981) has suggested, there were two social levels of ironworking (as was doubtless the case with bronze); low-level smithing producing utilitarian goods, and prestige smithing producing high-quality metal and finished objects, particularly military equipment as evidenced at Llyn Cerrig Bach.

Much of this LPRIA iron may have been of Welsh origin. Whilst Dinorben (Gardner and Savory 1964) has produced evidence of primary production, most of the evidence for ironworking (for example, at Llwyn Bryn-dinas) relates to forging, and current opinion suggests that hill-forts were not principal centres for iron production. It is in the context of the scale and chronology of primary production that Crew's work at Bryn y Castell (Crew 1984, 1991 and forthcoming) and Crawcwellt West (Mer.) (Crew 1989, 1991 and forthcoming) is of such significance.

At a 0.1 ha stone fort on the one hand, and a 4 ha upland settlement of scattered timber round-houses and stone enclosures on the other (Figure 35.8), bog ores were being exploited to produce bar iron in increasing quantities in the first century BC and first century AD. Crew has suggested that the economic basis of Crawcwellt may have been founded primarily on iron production, and notes the frequency of such sites in the locality. Clearly LPRIA iron production was extensive in the north-west, the early first-century AD increase satisfying a huge demand; whether in response to the necessity of equipping war-bands for internecine war, or the threat from Rome is unclear.

Iron production in Wales was seemingly decentralized, and the same may apply to smithing. What is significant is the fact that iron was clearly being traded because of its special properties. Harder, high-phosphorus iron – the bog-iron product – is good for weapon production, and in this respect it is notable that a ploughshare-type 'currency bar' in the Llyn Cerrig Bach deposit (Figure 35.7i) is probably a north-western product (Crew and Salter 1992) as other objects in the hoard may be. If north Welsh iron was being exchanged – with a reciprocal trade in low-phosphorus and high-carbon iron for the production of some of the tyres and a 'Malvern'-type currency bar at Llyn Cerrig Bach – as a valued and distinctive product, then we are some way towards explaining other archaeologically manifest exchange systems.

Salt

The production and distribution of this commodity is evidenced by its characteristic briquetage containers – 'VCP' (Figure 35.9c) (Morris 1985). The principal sources of western British salt lay outside the principality at Nantwich (Ches.) and Droitwich (Worcs.), whose products have differential distribution patterns over the sixth to fifth century BC and fourth century BC and later. Cheshire salt has a later distribution in north and north-west Wales, whilst Droitwich salt has a southerly distribution to the Wye at Twyn-y-Gaer and the Severn at Sudbrook, though these are marginal (Figure 35.10d). Though the scale of production and distribution varied over time, a more or less mutually exclusive distribution pattern emerges by the third to first century BC, with some Cheshire salt reaching the southern Marches. Neither product reaches south and south-west Wales, where sea-salt may have been utilized, which begs the question as to why Cheshire salt reached maritime north-west Wales. Was it due to a reciprocal exchange for another commodity, raw metal?

Pottery

Generally speaking, pottery is rare through much of Wales, that of the EPRIA and MPRIA being the most scarce. The region was essentially aceramic and wooden vessels (Figure 35.9j, k) must have sufficed for most purposes other than cooking, whilst metal cauldrons will have graced élite households.

The LBA/EPRIA is characterized by the production and distribution of highly localized pottery with broadly similar forms but different fabrics; for example, at the Breiddin and Llwyn Bryn-dinas. Local production of coarse wares may then have

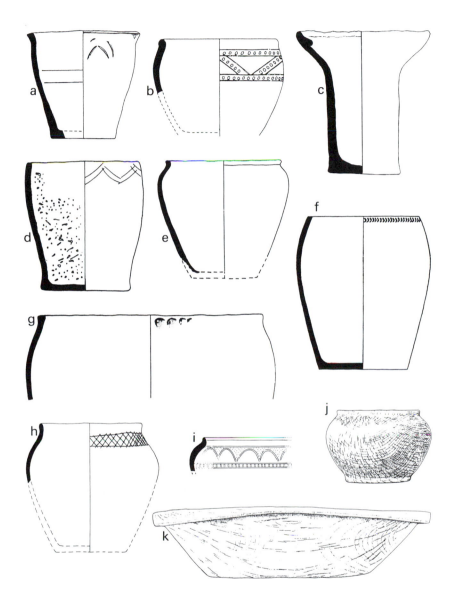

Figure 35.9 Ceramic and wooden containers: (a) Coygan Camp, Carm.; (b) Lydney, Glos.; (c) Collfryn, Mont.; (d), (e), (g) Magor Pill, Mon.; (f) Pen Dinas, Card.; (h) Breiddin, Mont.; (i) Castle Ditches, Llancarfan, Glam.; (j), (k) wooden bowls, Breiddin. (Sources: (a) Wainwright 1967; (b) Cunliffe 1991; (c) Britnell 1989; (d), (e), (g) Whittle 1989; (f) Forde *et al.* 1963; (h), (j), (k) Musson 1991; (i) Hogg 1976.) Scale: (a)–(i) 1/4, (j), (k) 1/5.

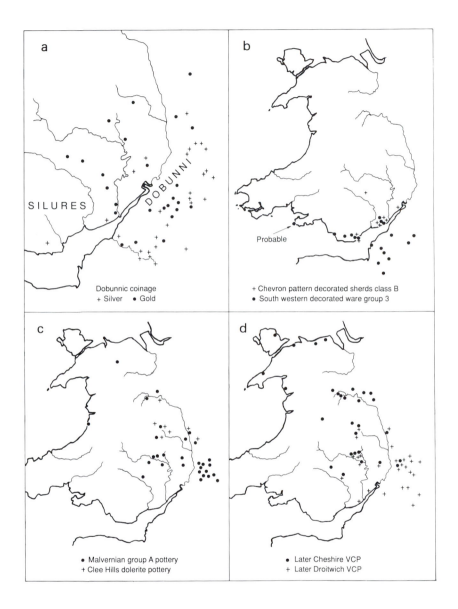

Figure 35.10 (a) Distribution of Dobunnic coinage. (Source: Manning 1981); (b) distribution of chevron/'eyebrow'-decorated pottery and Group 3 South-western Decorated pottery. (Sources: author; Peacock 1969 and author); (c) distribution of Malvernian Group A and Clee Hills pottery. (Sources: Morris 1981, 1982); (d) distribution of later Cheshire and Droitwich briquetage ('VCP'). (Source: Morris 1985.)

continued in the Marches to judge by the restricted distribution of dolerite-tempered Clee Hills ware (Figure 35.10c) (Morris 1981). In the LPRIA a pattern of coarseware production is evident in Spencer's (1983) Class A products, distributed from west Gloucestershire to the Gower, whilst unspecified plain wares of probably comparable age exist in small quantities in south-west Wales (Williams 1991). By the time that the Breiddin was refortified in the third/second century BC only a little locally produced pottery was being used; the remainder was being imported from at least two sources just north of the Malvern hills (Figure 35.9h) (Musson 1991). Stamped and linear-tooled Malvernian wares appear in a variety of fabrics from c.300 BC as specialist, high-quality products with a distinctive distribution related to their social value, which though focused on the Marches has outliers at the Brenig and Pen Dinas, Aberystwyth (Figures 35.9f, 35.10c) (Morris 1981; Cunliffe 1991: 462–3). Similarly, second- to mid-first-century BC 'Glastonbury' or South-Western Decorated Wares (Peacock 1969) of Group 3 (Figure 35.9i), with a distribution concentrated upon the Mendips, have coastal outliers in south-east Wales from the Knave, Rhosilli (Gower) to Sudbrook (Figure 35.10b). The well-defined LPRIA Lydney-Llanmelin style (Cunliffe 1991: figure A.18), more especially those forms with chevron/'eyebrow' decoration (Figures 35.9a,d, 35.10b), may imply an ethnic linkage (see p. 695).

WIDER HORIZONS

Though production and exchange of commodities on a local and regional basis was an enduring feature, Wales was never isolated from wider British and continental exchange networks. The continental origins and nature of the objects in the Parc-y-Meirch (Savory 1976b) and Llyn Fawr hoards – weaponry, equestrian and feasting equipment and items of personal hygiene – indicate that the Welsh LBA/EPRIA aristocracy were as conscious of what was *de rigueur* as their counterparts elsewhere in Britain and Ireland. Maritime links via the Atlantic routes are vouched for by the unique sherd in so-called 'Braubach' style from Merthyr Mawr Warren (Glam.) (Savory 1976b), similar to stamp-ornamented Armorican imports of the fifth century BC from Carn Euny, Cornwall (Christie 1978: figure 34.4). Metalwork in early La Tène (ELT) style, of which the most common examples are Marzabotto-type fibulae (Figure 35.7b,c), is rare in Wales, but no fewer than three brooches come from Merthyr Mawr. This concentration, coupled with the evidence for metalworking, suggests that the Ogmore estuary was perhaps of significance in articulating these Atlantic contacts. Savory (1990) has suggested that the Osismi of western Brittany may have had a role in spreading metalwork and a little pottery to south Wales, citing a pot from Bacon Hole (Glam.) (Savory 1976b), a mould from Worm's Head (Glam.) (Savory 1974), the Clynnog (Caerns.) collar (Savory 1976b) and the La Tène I or II bracelets from Coygan Camp (Figure 35.7a). Though the direct importation of larger items of metalwork was uncommon, the Cerrig-y-drudion 'bowl', one of the finest pieces of Celtic art found in Britain, and recently reconstructed as a lid (Stead 1982), may be an exception. In the middle La Tène continental links waned, to re-emerge in a small way in La Tène III, though the imported prestige items found in southern England are absent. Whereas imports may have been necessary to sustain the expansive economies of southern England they may have been an irrelevance amongst the highly fragmented societies of the west (Nash 1984). Yet the peripheral zone to which Wales belonged was a source of mineral wealth which may, in part, have helped sustain the dynamic economies of the core – continental as well as British. In this context first-century BC Gaulish coins, of a type widely distributed in northern and western France, from Merthyr Mawr, Caerwent and Weston-under-Penyard, and an issue of the Coriosolites found in an iron mine at Scowles, Lydney (Glos.) (Boon 1980b), may indicate that Gaulish intermediaries were seeking metal sources. Indeed it is not impossible that the Porth-Felen lead anchor-stock (Boon 1977), typologically of second- to first-century BC date, may be a relic of a shipwreck linked to classical sources pertaining to the exploration of western sea-routes in connection with a search for metals c.90–70 BC (Strabo III.5.11).

BURIAL AND RITUAL

Rituals connected with death were apparently not being widely observed in LBA Wales, when most of the evidence for burial disappears. Thereafter this trait, common to northern and western Britain, is perpetuated. Yet a scattering of burials, encompassing a variety of rites, is known, with the probability that 'normal' burials are grossly underrepresented either because they are unfurnished, are cremations, or because of the principality's predominantly acid soils.

Few authentic cemeteries are known. About six inhumations of LPRIA date were found at a bronze age barrow complex at Four Crosses (Warrilow et al. 1986), with a similar focus at Plas Gogerddan, Aberystwyth (Murphy 1992), where an unfurnished cremation was apparently followed by two inhumations with La Tène III fibulae. The Ogmore Down (Glam.) inhumations with their ELT helmets remain an enigma (Savory 1976b), but if these are dubious high-status burials, then authentic examples do exist. Gelliniog Wen (Ang.) (Savory 1976b) is the only Welsh example of an LPRIA 'warrior' burial; the Cerrig-y-drudion 'bowl' is said to have been found with an inhumation, whilst there are two possible instances of La Tène III burials with mirrors – Llechwedd du bach (Mer.) (Fox 1925) and Llanwnda (Pembs.) (Boon 1980c). The 'spoons' found at Ffynnogion and at Castell Nadolig (Savory 1976b) may either have accompanied burials or form ritual deposits on their own. Inhumed remains within caves associated with PRIA material, as was certainly the case at Big Covert (Savory 1951) and probably at Nant y Graig (Davies 1949: 445–8) and Culverhole (Boon 1980a), may represent other ritual practices rather than a funerary rite.

Of more interest because of its likely general applicability is burial within or close to settlements. As to the former, inhumations, largely of LPRIA date, are known at Moel Hiraddug, Coygan Camp, Mynydd Bychan, Stackpole and Llanmelin, whilst unfurnished inhumations – some encisted, others beneath cairns – exist at Merthyr Mawr. Two cremation deposits, just outside the 'ring-fort' of Castle Bucket (Pembs.), provide one of the earliest dates for PRIA burial – 390±60 bc – though the inclusion of animal bones suggests the faint possibility of ritual deposits (Williams 1985).

PRIA ritual practice in Wales is largely manifest in the form of the deposition of offerings to the gods in watery places. However, comparative data suggests the probability of PRIA shrines beneath those of Romano-British date, as seems likely at Gwehelog (Gwent.) (Wilson 1991), or where Roman cult objects point to the existence of a healing shrine as at Llys Awel (Denbs.). Cult activity may also be indicated at hill-forts such as Dinorben where numerous fragments of human skulls are known (Gardner and Savory 1964: 221–2), or less convincingly at those spots where reputedly PRIA or Romano-British carved stone heads have been found.

Tacitus's reference to 'groves devoted to Mona's barbarous superstition' (*Annals* xiv.30) being felled in AD 60/1 relates to another well-known Celtic custom of practising ritual in an arboreal setting, where the druids (a Tacitean reference to their presence on Anglesey) will have officiated. Until such cult centres have been identified, it is only in the case of the 'cult of watery offerings' that we may gain some insight into a focus of religious observance. The LBA practice of bog, lake and river deposits is continued into the PRIA, as instanced at Llyn Fawr, but it is not until the last centuries BC that metalwork was deposited in any quantity. Though the great deposit at Llyn Cerrig Bach (Fox 1946) is the best known, the Capel Garmon fire-dog is also reputed to have been found in a pool, and the Trawsfynydd tankard in a bog. Fitzpatrick (1984) notes a continuing bias towards the deposition of weaponry, which Llyn Cerrig Bach has in plenty – 11 swords, 7 spears, shield fitments, at least 10 horse-bits (Figure 37.7e, h, j) and up to 22 iron tyres, some of which qualitatively are likely to belong to chariots. Such items, some possibly the spoils of war, he suggests were deliberately selected as élite status symbols made consecrate to the gods in public ceremonies, with faunal assemblages – cattle, sheep, pig, horse and dog bones at Llyn Cerrig Bach – as the appropriate contribution of the plebs, thereby cumulatively ensuring group security and prosperity. The ceremonies at Llyn Cerrig Bach were probably recurrent since the metalwork spans the second century BC to the first century AD. Its diverse origin, with a putative continental blade with an armourer's mark (Figure 35.7g) (Savory 1966b) and an Irish bronze trumpet, begs the question of whether the lake had, as Fox suggested, a significance as a cult focus well beyond Anglesey. The recognition of a widespread pattern of exchange in finished products as well as raw metal (Northover 1991) makes such a question desperately difficult to answer.

CELTIC SOCIETY IN WALES

There are numerous indicators which suggest that Welsh PRIA society shared traits common to the Celtic world at large, with power articulated through social hierarchies based upon tribute networks, whose basis will have been aristocratic lineage, status or prowess in war. Both economy and society, then, will have been centred upon the aristocratic household where status-building activities – feasting and the patronage of the arts – were focused. The recognition of such in the archaeological record, against a background of gradations in absolute ranking and clear differences in social organization over time as reflected in settlement archaeology, is a major challenge.

Recent research has suggested the existence of two basic socio-economic systems: an eastern redistributive economy in those zones dominated by large hill-forts, where agricultural surpluses were stored and exchanged, and a western clientage economy in those where hill-forts are few and where a dichotomy exists between producer farmsteads and consumer settlements of higher status (Cunliffe 1991: 394–8). Certainly the large, complex hill-forts of the Marches imply a much higher population density and one more amenable to manipulation and organization. A multifocal system may be envisaged here, with the biggest as the strongholds of the most powerful clans; and, though absolute power was fragmented, common cultural traits and lively exchange networks imply a strongly knit alliance of clans. Hidden social distinctions may lie within the settlement range of powerful hill-forts and producer farms, and within the structural range of individual settlements as exemplified at the Breiddin and Collfryn (Musson 1991). Defensive complexity and house dimensions at the latter (Figure 35.6) suggest an élite residence, and whilst the Breiddin apparently has smaller houses it has proportionately four times as many four-posters as Collfryn, suggesting a key role at least as a central repository of agricultural produce.

In south-west Wales Williams (1988) perceives two contrasting social systems: a redistributive system based upon the larger hill-forts of the north and east, with a clientage system in the inland south and west – certainly from the third century BC – based upon producer farms, and small promontory forts and 'ring-forts' which were high-status consumers of agricultural produce. If the latter were indeed residences of élite family groups, then their sheer numbers imply no regional political focus in the MPRIA and LPRIA and we may envisage a system of small clans who rarely acted in concert. However, though no central authority is visible in the settlement record or any other tangible indicator of PRIA political allegiance, it did exist by the time that the *civitas Demetarum* was in being by the later second century AD.

If conditions in Wales were seemingly inimical to the creation of centralized tribal communities on the southern or north-eastern English model, by the later second century AD Roman sources show that it was divided into a minimum of four tribal areas – Ordovices, Deceangli, Demetae and Silures (Jarrett and Mann 1969; Rivet and Smith 1979) – roughly approximating to the broad geographical divisions. Several writers have mused on the possibility that this political division was already reflected in the four main 'cultural provinces' of the LBA (Burgess 1980; Savory 1980) though Jones (1984: 33) warns against an uncritical acceptance of such views and writes, 'The same geographical elements as helped to form the earlier cultural provinces by influencing the distribution of LBA metalwork are also likely to have influenced the later pattern of trade and settlement, and of social and political cohesion.' The tribal distribution of the second century AD is likely to hold good at least for the immediate pre-Roman period, but although there is a broad consensus as to their geographical placement – the Ordovices excepted – recognizing these entities is difficult. They were most probably composed of clans who only came together at times of stress; instanced in the first century AD by the Roman threat. The distribution of ceramics, a traditional means of recognizing ethnicity or 'identity-conscious interest groups', is a less reliable guide to clan or tribal distribution in Wales for reasons stated above, though the chevron/'eyebrow'-decorated Lydney-Llanmelin pots (Figure 35.9) have a tight distribution which may conceivably define a 'Silurian' heartland (Figure 35.10b). Where tribal coinage impinges upon Wales we can attempt to be more specific. Both Manning (1981) and Sellwood (1984) define a region west of the lower Severn which did not share the monetary system of the Dobunni *c.*35 BC–AD 43 (Van Arsdell 1989) and must have been excluded from it (Figure 35.10a). Whether this formed part of Siluria or represented a border zone is speculative.

The recognition of the Silures and Demetae as *civitates* may either reflect their precocity or a higher level of political consciousness, and by implication the continuation of an essentially PRIA form of power structure. Furthermore, the Silurian and Demetian élites were sufficiently wealthy to create an urban focus, which in turn presupposes a substantial agricultural surplus and the possibility that such was also the case in the LPRIA. The absence of *civitas* development elsewhere in the principality may be a silent commentary upon the inability of the agrarian base in those areas to produce the necessary surplus, which together with geographical constraints which inhibited political co-operation fostered the continuance of highly segmented societies.

ACKNOWLEDGEMENTS

The writer would like to thank W.J. Britnell, P. Crew, R.S. Kelly, F. Lynch and K. Murphy for unstinting access to unpublished information, including illustrations. Mr Geoffrey Ward prepared the drawings, and the University of Wales, Aberystwyth, provided a generous Sir David Hughes Parry Award for the financing of the same.

REFERENCES

Alcock, L. (1960) 'Castell Odo. An embanked settlement of Mynydd Ystum, near Aberdaron, Caernarvonshire', *Archaeologia Cambrensis* 109: 78–135.

Alexander, J.A. (1981) 'The coming of iron-using to Britain', in H. Haefner (ed.) *Frühes Eisen in Europa*, Schaffhausen.

Austin, D. *et al.* (1984–8) *The Caer Cadwgan Project Interim Reports 1984–8*, Lampeter.

Babbidge, A. (1977) 'Reconnaissance excavations at Coed y Bwnydd, Bettws Newydd, 1969–1971', *Monmouthshire Antiquary* 3: 159–78.

Baring Gould, S., Burnard, R. and Anderson, I.K. (1900) 'Exploration of Moel Trigarn', *Archaeologia Cambrensis* 1900: 189–211.

Barker, P.A., Haldon, R. and Jenks, W.E. (1991) 'Excavations at Sharpstones Hill, near Shrewsbury, 1965–71', in M. Carver (ed.) *Prehistory in Lowland Shropshire, Transactions of the Shropshire Archaeological and Historical Society* 67: 15–74.

Bell, M. (1992) 'Goldcliff excavation 1991', *Severn Estuary Research Committee Annual Report 1991*, Lampeter, 13–19.

—— (1993) 'Goldcliff', *Archaeology in Wales* 32: 59–62.

Benson, D.G. *et al.* (1990) 'Excavations at Stackpole Warren, Dyfed', *Proceedings of the Prehistoric Society* 56: 179–245.

Benson, D. and Williams, G. (1987) 'Dale Fort', *Archaeology in Wales* 27: 43.

Blockley, K. (1989) *Prestatyn 1984–5: an iron age farmstead and Romano-British industrial settlement in North Wales*, Oxford: British Archaeological Reports, British Series 210.

Boon, G.C. (1977) 'A Graeco-Roman anchor-stock from North Wales', *Antiquaries Journal* 57: 10–30.

—— (1980a) 'Two iron-age glass beads in the National Museum', *Bulletin of the Board of Celtic Studies* 28: 745–6.

—— (1980b) 'A Gaulish coin from Merthyr Mawr Warren, Glamorganshire', *Bulletin of the Board of Celtic Studies* 29: 345.

—— (1980c) 'A neglected late-Celtic mirror-handle from Llanwnda near Fishguard', *Bulletin of the Board of Celtic Studies* 28: 743–4.

—— (1988) 'British coins from Wales', in D.M. Robinson (ed.) *Biglis, Caldicot and Llanough*, 92.

Brassil, K.S. *et al.* (1982) 'Rescue excavations at Moel Hiraddug between 1960 and 1980', *Journal of the Flintshire Historical Society* 30 (1981–2): 13–88.

Britnell, W. (1989) 'The Collfryn hillslope enclosure, Llansantffraid Deuddwr, Powys: excavations 1980–1982', *Proceedings of the Prehistoric Society* 55: 89–134.

Britnell, W.J. and Musson, C.R. (1984) 'Rescue excavation of a Romano-British double-ditched enclosure at Arddleen, Llandrinio, northern Powys', *Archaeologia Cambrensis* 133: 91–9.

Burgess, C. (1980) 'The Bronze Age', in J. Taylor (ed.) *Culture and Environment*, 243–86.

—— (1985) 'Population, climate and upland settlement', in C. Spratt and C. Burgess (eds) *Upland Settlement in Britain: the second millennium BC and after*, Oxford: British Archaeological Reports, British Series 143, 195–230.

Burnham, B.C. and Davies, J.L. (eds) (1991) *Conquest, Co-existence and Change: recent work in Roman Wales* (*Trivium* 25 (1990): Lampeter).

Caseldine, A. (1990) *Environmental Archaeology in Wales*, Lampeter.

Christie, P.M.L. (1978) 'The excavation of an iron age souterrain and settlement at Carn Euny, Sancreed, Cornwall', *Proceedings of the Prehistoric Society* 44: 309–434.

Crew, P. (1984) 'Bryn y Castell hillfort – a late prehistoric iron working settlement in north-west Wales', in B.G. Scott and H. Cleere (eds) *The Crafts of the Blacksmith*, Belfast, 91–100.

—— (1989) 'Crawcwellt West excavations, 1986–1989: a late prehistoric upland iron-working settlement', *Archaeology in Wales* 29: 11–16.

—— (1991) 'Late iron age and Roman iron production in north-west Wales', in B.C. Burnham and J.L. Davies (eds) *Conquest, Co-existence and Change*, 150–60.

—— (forthcoming) 'Decline or prohibition: the end of prehistoric iron-working in north-west Wales'.

Crew, P. and Salter, C. (1992) 'Currency bars with welded tips', in A. Espelsund (ed.) *Bloomery Ironworking during 2000 Years*, vol. 3, Proceedings of the Budelseminaret, Trondheim.

Cunliffe, B. (1991) *Iron Age Communities in Britain* (3rd edn) London.

Cunliffe, B. and Miles, D. (eds) (1984) *Aspects of the Iron Age in Central Southern Britain*, Oxford: Oxford University Committee for Archaeology, Monograph 2.

Davies, E. (1949) 'Appendix to the prehistoric and Roman remains of Denbighshire', in *The Prehistoric and Roman Remains of Flintshire*, Cardiff.

Davies, J.L. (1973a) 'Cae Summerhouse, Tythegston', *Morgannwg* 17: 53–7.

—— (1973b) 'An excavation at the Bulwarks, Porthkerry, Glamorgan', *Archaeologia Cambrensis* 122: 85–98.

—— (1982) 'Cae Summerhouse', *Archaeology in Wales* 22: 15.

—— (1994) 'The Iron Age', in J.L. Davies and D.P. Kirby (eds) *Cardiganshire County History* vol. 1. *From the Earliest Times to the Coming of the Normans*, Cardiff.

Ehrenreich, R.M. (1985) *Trade, Technology and the Ironworking Community in the Iron Age of Southern Britain*, Oxford: British Archaeological Reports, British Series 144.

Fitzpatrick, A.P. (1984) 'The deposition of La Tène iron age metalwork in watery contexts in southern England', in B. Cunliffe and D. Miles (eds) *Aspects of the Iron Age*, 178–91.

Forde, Daryll C. *et al.* (1963) 'Excavations at Pen Dinas, Aberystwyth', *Archaeologia Cambrensis* 112: 125–53.

Fox, C.F. (1925) 'A late Celtic bronze mirror from Wales', *Antiquaries Journal* 5: 254–7.

—— (1946) *A Find of the Early Iron Age from Llyn Cerrig Bach, Anglesey*, Cardiff.

Gardner, W. and Savory, H.N. (1964) *Dinorben: a hillfort occupied in Early Iron Age and Roman Times*, Cardiff.

Grimes, W.F. (1951) *The Prehistory of Wales*, Cardiff.

Guilbert, G.C. (1974) 'Llanstephan Castle: 1973 Interim Report', *Carmarthenshire Antiquary* 10: 37–48.

—— (1975) 'Planned hillfort interiors', *Proceedings of the Prehistoric Society* 41: 203–21.

—— (1976) 'Moel y Gaer (Rhosesmor) 1972–1973: an area excavation in the interior', in D.W. Harding (ed.) *Hillforts*, 303–17.

—— (1979a) 'The guard-chamber gateways at Dinorben and Moel Hiraddug hill-forts, and the problem of dating the type in north Wales', *Bulletin of the Board of Celtic Studies* 28: 516–20.

—— (1979b) 'Dinorben 1977–8', *Current Archaeology* 6: 182–8.

—— (1980) 'Dinorben C14 dates', *Current Archaeology* 6: 336–8.

—— (1981) 'Ffridd Faldwyn', *Archaeological Journal* 138: 20–2.

—— (1982) 'Post-ring symmetry in round-houses at Moel y Gaer and some other sites in prehistoric Britain', in P.J. Drury (ed.) *Structural Reconstruction*, Oxford: British Archaeological Reports, British Series 110, 67–86.

Harding, A.F. (ed.) (1982) *Climate Change in Later Prehistory*, Edinburgh.

Harding, D.W. (ed.) (1976) *Hillforts: later prehistoric earthworks in Britain and Ireland*, London.

Hawkes, C.F.C. (1979) 'Cumulative Celticity in pre-Roman Britain', *Etudes Celtiques* 13 (2): 607–28.

Hogg, A.H.A. (1973) 'Excavation at Harding's Down West Fort, Gower', *Archaeologia Cambrensis* 122: 55–68.

—— (1976) 'Castle Ditches, Llancarfan, Glamorgan', *Archaeologia Cambrensis* 125: 13–39.

Houlder, C.H. (1967) 'Llandegai', *Current Archaeology* 5: 116–19.

James, H. (1987) 'Excavations at Caer, Bayvil, 1979', *Archaeologia Cambrensis* 136: 51–76.

James, T. (1990) 'Concentric antenna enclosures – a new defended enclosure type in west Wales', *Proceedings of the Prehistoric Society* 56: 295–8.

Jarrett, M.G. and Mann, J.C. (1969) 'The tribes of Wales', *Welsh Historical Review* 4: 161–71.

Jarrett, M.G. and Wrathmell, S. (1981) *Whitton: an iron age and Roman farmstead in south Glamorgan*, Cardiff.

Jones, M.L. (1984) *Society and Settlement in Wales and the Marches 500 BC to AD 1100*, Oxford: British Archaeological Reports, British Series 121.

Kelly, R.S. (1988) 'Two late prehistoric circular enclosures near Harlech, Gwynedd', *Proceedings of the Prehistoric Society* 54: 101–51.

—— (1990) 'Meyllteyrn Uchaf', *Archaeology in Wales* 30: 43.

—— (1991a) 'Meyllteyrn Uchaf', *Archaeology in Wales* 31: 16.

—— (1991b) 'Recent research on the hut group settlements of north-west Wales', in B.C. Burnham and J.L. Davies (eds) *Conquest, Co-existence and Change* 102–11.

—— (1992) 'Meyllteyrn Uchaf double ditched enclosure', *Archaeology in Wales* 32: 58.

Lamb, H.H. (1981) 'Climate from 1000 BC–AD 1100', in M. Jones and G.W. Dimbleby (eds) *The Environment of Man: the Iron Age to the Anglo-Saxon period*, Oxford: British

Archaeological Reports, British Series 87, 53–65.

Longley, D. (1988) 'Bryn Eryr', *Archaeology in Wales* 28: 57.

Lynch, F. (1993) *Excavations in the Brenig Valley: a mesolithic and bronze age landscape in north Wales*, Loughborough: Cambrian Archaeological Association Monographs 5.

Manley, J. (1990a) 'A preliminary survey of some undated small settlements in north-east Wales', *Archaeologia Cambrensis* 139: 21–55.

—— (1990b) 'A late bronze age landscape on the Denbigh moors, north-east Wales', *Antiquity* 64: 514–26.

—— (1991) 'Small settlements', in J. Manley, S. Grenter and F. Gale (eds) *The Archaeology of Clwyd*, Mold.

Manning, W.H. (1981) 'The territory of the Silures', *Report on the Excavations at Usk 1965–1976: the fortress excavations 1968–1971*, Cardiff, 15–23.

Morris, E.L. (1981) 'Ceramic exchange in western Britain: a preliminary view', in H. Howard and E.L. Morris (eds) *Production and Distribution: a ceramic viewpoint*, Oxford: British Archaeological Reports, International Series 120, 67–82.

—— (1982) 'Iron age pottery from western Britain: another petrological study', in I. Freestone, C. Johns and T. Potter (eds) *Current Research in Ceramics: thin section studies*, London: British Museum Occasional Paper 32, 15–27.

—— (1985) 'Prehistoric salt distributions: two case studies from western Britain', *Bulletin of the Board of Celtic Studies* 32: 336–79.

Murphy, K. (1985) 'Excavations at Penycoed, Llangynog, Dyfed, 1983', *Carmarthenshire Antiquary* 21: 75–112.

—— (1992) 'Plas Gogerddan, Dyfed: a multi-period burial and ritual site', *Archaeological Journal* 149: 1–38.

Musson, C.R. (1991) *The Breiddin Hillfort: a later prehistoric settlement in the Welsh Marches*, London: Council for British Archaeology Research Report.

Musson, C.R. *et al.* (1992) 'Excavations and metal working at Llwyn Bryn-dinas hillfort, Llangedwyn, Clwyd', *Proceedings of the Prehistoric Society* 58: 265–83.

Musson, C.R. and Northover, J.P. (1989) 'Llanymynech hillfort, Powys and Shropshire: observations on construction work, 1981', *Montgomeryshire Collections* 77: 15–26.

Mytum, H. (1989) 'Excavations at Castell Henllys, 1981–89: the iron age fort', *Archaeology in Wales* 29: 6–10.

Nash, D. (1984) 'The basis of contact between Britain and Gaul in the late pre-Roman Iron Age', in S. Macready and H. Thompson (eds) *Cross-Channel Trade between Gaul and Britain in the Pre-Roman Iron Age*, London: Society of Antiquaries Occasional Paper 4, 92–107.

Nash-Williams, V.E. (1933) 'An early iron age hill fort at Llanmelin, near Caerwent, Monmouthshire', *Archaeologia Cambrensis* 88: 232–315.

—— (1939) 'An early iron age coastal camp at Sudbrook, near the Severn tunnel, Monmouthshire', *Archaeologia Cambrensis* 94: 42–79.

Northover, P.J. (1984) 'Iron age bronze metallurgy in central southern England', in B. Cunliffe and D. Miles (eds) *Aspects of the Iron Age*, 126–45.

—— (1991) 'Analysis of iron age bronze metalwork from Llyn Cerrig Bach', in F. Lynch, *Prehistoric Anglesey* (2nd edn) Llangefni, 392–3.

Owen-John, H. (1988) 'A hill-slope enclosure in Coed y Cymdda, near Wenvoe, south Glamorgan', *Archaeologia Cambrensis* 137: 43–98.

Parry, S.J. (1988) 'Caldicot Castle lake', *Archaeology in Wales* 28: 55–6.

Parry, S.J. and Parkhouse, J. (1989) 'Caldicot Castle lake', *Archaeology in Wales* 29: 47–8.

—— (1990) 'Caldicot Castle lake', *Archaeology in Wales* 30: 48–9.

Peacock, D.P.S. (1968) 'A petrological study of certain iron age pottery from western

England', *Proceedings of the Prehistoric Society* 34: 414–27.

—— (1969) 'A contribution to the study of Glastonbury ware from south-western Britain', *Antiquaries Journal* 49: 41–61.

Price, C. and Wardle, P.A. (1987) 'Atlantic Trading Estate, Barry', *Archaeology in Wales* 27: 40–1.

Probert, L.A. (1976) 'Twyn-y-Gaer hill-fort, Gwent: an interim assessment', in G.C. Boon and J.M. Lewis (eds) *Welsh Antiquity*, Cardiff, 105–20.

Rivet, A.L.F. and Smith, C. (1979) *The Place Names of Roman Britain*, Cambridge.

Robinson, D.M. (ed.) (1988) *Biglis, Caldicot and Llandough: three late iron age and Romano-British sites in south-east Wales. Excavations 1977–79*, Oxford: British Archaeological Reports, British Series 188.

Salter, C. and Ehrenreich, R. (1984) 'Iron age metallurgy in central southern Britain', in B. Cunliffe and D. Miles (eds) *Aspects of the Iron Age*, 146–61.

Savory, H.N. (1951) 'Burial cave at Llanferres', *Bulletin of the Board of Celtic Studies* 14: 174–5.

—— (1954) 'The excavation of an early iron age fortified settlement on Mynydd Bychan, Llysworney (Glam.) 1949–50 Pt I', *Archaeologia Cambrensis* 103: 85–108.

—— (1956) 'The excavation of an early iron age fortified settlement on Mynydd Bychan, Llysworney (Glam.) 1949–50 Pt II', *Archaeologia Cambrensis* 104: 14–51.

—— (1964) 'The Tal-y-Llyn hoard', *Antiquity* 38: 18–31.

—— (1966a) 'A find of early iron age metalwork from the Lesser Garth, Pentyrch (Glam.)', *Archaeologia Cambrensis* 115: 27–44.

—— (1966b) 'Armourer's mark from Llyn Cerrig Bach (Ang.)', *Bulletin of the Board of Celtic Studies* 21: 374–6.

—— (1971) *Excavations at Dinorben, 1965–9*, Cardiff.

—— (1974) 'An early iron age metalworker's mould from Worms Head', *Archaeologia Cambrensis* 123: 170–4.

—— (1976a) 'Welsh hillforts: a reappraisal of recent research', in D.W. Harding (ed.) *Hillforts*, 237–92.

—— (1976b) *Guide Catalogue of the Early Iron Age Collections*, Cardiff.

—— (1980) 'The Early Iron Age in Wales', in J.A. Taylor (ed.) *Culture and Environment*, 287–310.

—— (1990) Review of Cunliffe 1988: *Greeks, Romans and Barbarians: spheres of interaction* (London), *Archaeologia Cambrensis* 139: 82–3.

Sellwood, L. (1984) 'Tribal boundaries viewed from the perspective of numismatic evidence', in B. Cunliffe and D. Miles (eds) *Aspects of the Iron Age*, 191–204.

Smith, C.A. (1974) 'A morphological analysis of late prehistoric and Romano-British settlements in north-west Wales', *Proceedings of the Prehistoric Society* 40: 157–69.

—— (1977) 'Late prehistoric and Romano-British enclosed homesteads in north-west Wales: an interpretation of their morphology', *Archaeologia Cambrensis* 126: 38–52.

—— (1987) 'Excavations at the Ty Mawr hut-circles, Holyhead, Anglesey. Part IV – Chronology and discussion', *Archaeologia Cambrensis* 126: 20–38.

Spencer, B. (1983) 'Limestone-tempered pottery from south Wales in the Late Iron Age and early Roman period', *Bulletin of the Board of Celtic Studies* 30: 405–19.

Spratling, M.G. (1966) 'The date of the Tal-y-Llyn hoard', *Antiquity* 40: 229–30.

Stanford, S.C. (1974) *Croft Ambrey*, Hereford.

—— (1991) *The Archaeology of the Welsh Marches* (2nd edn) London.

Stead, I.M. (1982) 'The Cerrig-y-drudion "hanging bowl"', *Antiquaries Journal* 62: 221–34.

Taylor, J.A. (1973) 'Chronometers and chronicles: a study of the palaeoenvironments of west central Wales', *Progress in Geography* 5: 248–334.

—— (ed.) (1980) *Culture and Environment in Prehistoric Wales*, Oxford: British

Archaeological Reports, British Series 76.

—— (1980) 'Man–environment relationships', in J.A. Taylor (ed.) *Culture and Environment*, 311–36.

Turner, J. (1970) 'Post-neolithic disturbance of British vegetation', in D. Walker and R.G. West (eds) *Studies in the Vegetational History of the British Isles*, Cambridge, 81–96.

—— (1981) 'The Iron Age', in I.G. Simmons and M.J. Tooley (eds) *The Environment in British Prehistory*, London, 250–81.

Van Arsdell, R.D. (1989) *The Celtic Coinage of Britain*, London.

Varley, W.J. (1948) 'The hill-forts of the Welsh Marches', *Archaeological Journal* 105: 41–66.

Vyner, B.E. (1986) 'Woodbarn, Wiston: a Pembrokeshire rath', *Archaeologia Cambrensis* 125: 121–33.

Wainwright, G.J. (1967) *Coygan Camp*, Cardiff.

—— (1971) 'The excavation of a fortified settlement at Walesland Rath, Pembrokeshire', *Britannia* 2: 48–108.

Wardle, P.A. (1988) 'Atlantic Trading Estate, Barry', *Archaeology in Wales* 28: 52.

Warrilow, W., Owen, G. and Britnell, W. (1986) 'Eight ring-ditches at Four Crosses, Llandysilio, Powys, 1981–85', *Proceedings of the Prehistoric Society* 52: 53–87.

Whimster, R. (1989) 'The Welsh Marches', in *The Emerging Past: air photography and the buried landscape*, London, 35–65.

Whittle, A.W.R. (1989) 'Two later bronze age occupations and an iron age channel on the Gwent foreshore', *Bulletin of the Board of Celtic Studies* 36: 200–23.

Williams, G. (1981) 'Survey and excavation on Pembrey Mountain', *Carmarthenshire Antiquary* 17: 3–32.

—— (1984) 'Holgan Camp', *Archaeology in Wales* 24: 46–8.

—— (1985) 'An iron age cremation deposit from Castle Bucket, Letterston, Pembrokeshire', *Archaeology in Wales* 25: 13–15.

—— (1988) 'Recent work on rural settlement in later prehistoric and early historic Dyfed', *Antiquaries Journal* 68: 30–54.

—— (1991) 'Recent work on rural settlement in south-west Wales', in B.C. Burnham and J.L. Davies (eds) *Conquest, Co-existence and Change*, 112–22.

Williams, G., Darke, I., Parry, C. and Isaac, J. (1988) 'Recent archaeological work on Merlin's Hill, Abergwili', *Carmarthenshire Antiquary* 24: 5–13.

Williams, G., Taylor, J.A., Hunt, C., Heyworth, A. and Benson, D.G. (1987) 'A burnt mound at Felin Fullbrook, Tregaron, Ceredigion', *Bulletin of the Board of Celtic Studies* 34: 228–43.

Wilson, D.R. (1991) 'Air-reconnaissance of Roman Wales 1969–88', in B.C. Burnham and J.L. Davies (eds) *Conquest, Co-existence and Change*, 16, pl. 8.

PART XI

CELTIC BRITAIN
POST AD 400

—◆—

LANGUAGE AND SOCIETY AMONG THE INSULAR CELTS
AD 400–1000

—— •◆• ——

Thomas Charles-Edwards

In this chapter I shall discuss three relationships in the world of the Insular Celts: of language to nationality; of language to status; of language to the connections between the Insular Celts and the wider world, first of the Roman Empire and then of Latin Christendom.[1] The three relationships cannot be separated. This is obvious enough for the first and the third, for they are two sides of a single issue: how far did language convey a sense of difference, or of community, between the peoples within the British Isles and even within western Europe? The second relationship is also directly germane, for a crucial question both in the late Roman period and afterwards is how far élites, political, religious and intellectual, were distinguished by their linguistic behaviour. Under the Roman Empire a British noble was far more likely to speak Latin than a British peasant.[2] Our understanding of the shape of British society after the Romans will be considerably aided by finding an answer to the question of when a British noble ceased to speak Latin. A related question is why the Britons who settled in Gaul in the fifth century were not accepted as fellow citizens of the empire. Was language something which divided them from their Gallic neighbours? If one judges only by the languages their medieval descendants spoke – French and Breton - then of course it was. But the distinction may not have been that clear, especially if it is true that many Welsh continued to speak Latin at the very time when their fellow Britons were settling in Armorica.[3] Or, again, if we cross the Irish Sea, what sustained the existence of Old Irish as a standard language almost without dialect variation? In an island notorious for its many small kingdoms one would expect numerous dialects. Was Old Irish the form of the language spoken, or just written, by religious and intellectual élites? Was it also used by the secular nobility?

---

1 I am much indebted to Oliver Padel and Paul Russell for their comments on a draft of this chapter.

2 This was already happening within a generation or two of the Claudian conquest: Tacitus, *Agricola* c. 21; cf. E. Hamp, 'Social gradience in British spoken Latin', *Britannia* 6 (1975): 150–61.

3 I shall occasionally, as here, use 'Welsh' for British inhabitants of what later became Wales. This is anachronistic but convenient.

The relationship of language to both nationality and status underwent major changes in the early medieval period, just as the languages themselves were transformed in the late Roman and post-Roman periods. I shall take the kingdom of Dyfed in the south-west of Wales as a specimen case, for it is easy to show that, early in the period, Dyfed was a land of three languages, while by the end it was, for most purposes, a land of only one. The early medieval kingdom of Dyfed was heir to the Romano-British *civitas* of the Demetae: reflecting this inheritance, the early inscriptions of the area are predominantly in Latin. Moreover, the character of the Latin used in the inscriptions demonstrates that it was then a spoken language, not merely a language of the quill and the chisel. On the other hand, from at least the sixth century until the ninth Dyfed was ruled by a dynasty for which Irish ancestry was claimed.[4] In much of the kingdom, in the county of Pembroke and the western part of Carmarthenshire, an Irish presence in the early Middle Ages is confirmed by inscriptions written in the ogam alphabet and in an early form of the Irish language.[5] The inscriptions show therefore that Dyfed was far from being just a British kingdom.

Yet by the mid-tenth century another view of the past had been developed for a new royal kindred of Dyfed. It shows how the Irish presence in Dyfed had come to an end, but also how a British identity was partly defined in terms of an expulsion of Irish settlers in western Britain. Early in the tenth century Dyfed was drawn into the conglomeration of lands ruled by the descendants of Merfyn Frych (*ob.* 844) and his son, Rhodri Mawr (*ob.* 877).[6] Both Merfyn and Rhodri were kings of Gwynedd and founders of the dynasty called by modern scholars the 'Second Dynasty of Gwynedd'. This dynasty, however, soon extended its power beyond Gwynedd into Powys and later into Ceredigion and Dyfed. The earliest surviving collection of Welsh genealogies takes as its initial focus Owain ap Hywel ap Cadell ap Rhodri, the king of Dyfed.[7] First it gives his patriline and then the descent of his mother from the old kings of Dyfed who ruled before the sons of Rhodri gained control over the south-west. So much is the normal genealogical testimonial of the time: first the agnatic descent and then prestigious connections through females. What is more surprising is that the line of the old kings of Dyfed is traced back, not to any Irish settlers, but to an evidently fictitious 'Nyfed son of Dyfed son of Maxim Wledig'. The personal name Nyfed perhaps echoes the Irish use of *nemed* 'sacred' for a person of high status as well as for a sanctuary.[8] Dyfed is the name of the people transmogrified into the name of a distant ancestor.[9] Nyfed, therefore, was probably chosen simply to rhyme with Dyfed. Maxim Wledig (later Maxen Wledig), on the other hand, is an

4 *Tairired na nDésse*, ed. and transl. K. Meyer, 'The expulsion of the Déssi', *Y Cymmrodor* 14 (1901): 112–13, § 11; T. Ó Cathasaigh, 'The Déissi and Dyfed', *Éigse* 20 (1984): 1–33.
5 M. Richards, 'Irish settlements in south-west Wales: a topographical approach', *Journal of the Royal Society of Antiquaries of Ireland* 90 (1960): 133–62, discusses the place-name as well as the epigraphical evidence.
6 J.E. Lloyd, *A History of Wales from the Earliest Times to the Edwardian Conquest*, 3rd edn (London 1939), 333.
7 *ob.* 988, *Annales Cambriae* (MSS *B, C*) (ed. J. Williams ab Ithel (Rolls Series; London, 1860), 21). The Harleian Genealogies of the tenth century are edited by P.C. Bartrum, *Early Welsh Genealogical Tracts* (henceforward *EWGT*) (Cardiff, 1966), 9–13.

entirely genuine historical person (Magnus Maximus), but for the genealogists he was the link between Britain and its Roman past: Gildas's tyrant who removed the military force of Britain and so laid it open to Saxon attack was still the man 'who killed Gratian the king of the Romans',[10] but he was also made into a descendant of Constantine the Great and the ancestor of the dynasty of Dyfed as well as of other royal lines. *Romanitas* was now like an ancient title-deed: it was important that descent from Christian Roman emperors could be displayed in case of need, but the claim looked to another age and the title-deed usually gathered dust in the archive. Yet if *romanitas* was not a present force, Roman descent was at least not Irish descent. The line of Irish kings with their *dofreth* 'billeting' (< Early Irish **damreth*) which they imposed upon the land of Dyfed had been pushed aside.[11] Tenth-century Dyfed was a British kingdom whose kings enjoyed the high dignity of descent from Constantine and from his mother Helen, 'who went from Britain as far as Jerusalem to seek the Cross of Christ, and she brought it with her to Constantinople, and there it remains to the present day'.[12] There had been a conscious rejection of the Irish past of Dyfed and a conscious stress on a Roman past.

Already by the mid-tenth century, therefore, the surviving evidence of Irish settlement consisted of the odd fossil – some place-names, some inscriptions in an alphabet now probably unintelligible, some loan-words. It was known that there had been Irish settlers, but now they were often not considered people with whom good men consorted. A version of Rhigyfarch's Life of St David tells his readers that, in order to found St David's, the saint had been obliged to deal with an Irish chieftain Boia and his formidable wife.[13] The origin of the premier church of Wales lay in a

---

8   The latter sense is attested in the Continental and British Celtic *nemeton*, A. Holder, *Altceltischer Sprachschatz* (1891–1913), s.v. *nemeton*; *Bechbretha*, ed. T. Charles-Edwards and F. Kelly (Dublin, 1983), pp. 107–8. Compare also *Nemetes, Nemetu*, J. Whatmough, *The Dialects of Ancient Gaul* (Cambridge, Mass., 1970), pp. 1093, 1290, Ednyfed < Iudd Nyfed 'lord of a sanctuary' or, perhaps, 'sacred lord'.

9   This may have been encouraged by biblical precedent, for example Israel, both the people and the alias for the ancestor, the patriarch Jacob. Cf. Glywys, probably from *Gleuenses*, the people of Gloucester and its region, which also appears as a personal name, *ECMW* no. 255 (and possibly no. 239). *Demetus* was likewise used as a personal name in *ECMW* no. 390, but the Dyfed supposed to be a person and the ancestor of the kings of Dyfed must be a counterpart to the biblical habit of naming peoples by the ancestors of their kings.

10 Gildas, *De Excidio Britanniae*, c.13; *EWGT*, p. 10, § 4. Compare *ECMW* no. 182 and *EWGT*, p. 2 (the Pillar of Eliseg), *qui occidit regem Romanorum*, and J.F. Matthews, 'Macsen, Maximus, and Constantine', *Welsh History Review* 11 (1982–3): 431–48.

11 Irish *dámrad* < **dámreth* was used for the company of a king or other great lord; but in Dyfed, betraying the point of view of the subject, *dofreth* came to mean the obligation to provide quarters for men, notably from the company of the king, who were billeted upon his subjects.

12 *EWGT* 10, § 2.

13 The identification of Boia (or Baia) as an Irishman is found in the Vespasian Recension of the Life and its Welsh offshoot, *Buchedd Dewi*: see Rhigyfarch, *Life of St David*, ed. J.W. James (Cardiff, 1967), 9; *Buchedd Dewi*, ed. D.S. Evans (Cardiff, 1965), 7; but it is also found in the poem by Gwynfardd Brycheiniog, *Hen Gerddi Crefyddoi*, ed. H. Lewis (Cardiff, 1931), p. 50 (XVIII, 225).

triumph over Irish resistance.[14] In Ireland, however, as late as the beginning of the ninth century, the name of David of Cell Muine (the Irish form of Mynyw, St David's) was preserved together with those of the saints of Ireland.[15] The Irish Sea had for long linked churches and peoples: in 836 the Annals of Ulster record 'the first prey taken by the heathens from southern Brega, that is from Telcha Dromáin and from Durrow of the Britons'.[16] Another monastery in Ireland, Mayo 'of the Saxons', is well known as a link between the English and the Irish in the pre-Viking period; its bishop subscribed the decrees of the provincial synod of York in 786, held at the instance of the papal legate, George, bishop of Ostia, and his Frankish assistant, Wigbod.[17] The entry in the annals suggests that there were British counterparts to Mayo, less well recorded but perhaps no less influential in fostering relations between Ireland and Britain.[18] By the tenth century, however, these relations were no longer sustained by the presence within Britain of an Irish dynasty and settlers who spoke Irish.

A celebration of British victory over Irish immigrants is offered by three out of four versions of the Cunedda legend, each one of which has a different story to tell. A consideration of the story in its various forms will provide an understanding of changing Welsh perceptions of the former Irish presence in Britain. The first and second versions are preserved in the *Historia Brittonum*, written in 829/30, within the reign of Merfyn Frych (king of Gwynedd 825–44), the founder of the Second Dynasty of Gwynedd.[19] A third version appears in the reign of a great-great-grandson of Merfyn, Owain ap Hywel Dda, king of Dyfed.[20] Merfyn probably stemmed from the Isle of Man, a land which had been occupied by both Britons and Irish at different periods.[21] From the early ninth century Cunedda and his sons were sometimes perceived as the pre-eminent leaders of a British counter-offensive against

---

14 An utterly different view is suggested by the tenth-century *Armes Prydein Vawr*, ed. I. Williams, Engl. version by R. Bromwich (Dublin, 1972), lines 127–30.

15 *The Martyrology of Oengus the Culdee*, ed. W. Stokes (Henry Bradshaw Society; London, 1905), March 1 (p. 80).

16 Durrow of the Britons, in South Brega, is not to be confused with the Durrow founded by St Columba, which lay further west, or Dairmag Ua nDuach in the north of the king-dom of Ossory (namely the Durrow on the main road from Dublin to Cork).

17 ed. E. Dümmler, MGH *Epistulae* IV = *Epistulae Karolini Aevi* II (Berlin, 1895), 19–29, transl. D. Whitelock, *English Historical Documents* I (London, 1955), no. 191.

18 Compare *The Annals of Ulster*, ed. S. Mac Airt and G. Mac Niocaill (Dublin, 1983), s.a. 823. 9: Galinne na mBretan exhaustum est o Feidlimtidh cum tota habitatione sua ₇ cum oratorio. A similar example of an English house in Ireland is Tulach Léis na Saxan (Tullylease on the boundary between Cork and Limerick (grid ref. R 34 18).

19 D.N. Dumville, 'Some aspects of the chronology of the *Historia Brittonum*', *Bulletin of the Board of Celtic Studies* (hereafter BBCS) 25 (1972–3): 439–45.

20 N.K. Chadwick, 'Early culture and learning in North Wales', in N.K. Chadwick (ed.) *Studies in the Early British Church* (Cambridge, 1958), 32–6; D. Dumville, 'Sub-Roman Britain: history and legend', *History* 62(1977): 181–3. R.G. Gruffydd, 'From Gododdin to Gwynedd: reflections on the story of Cunedda', *Studia Celtica* 24/25 (1989/90): 1–14.

21 J.E. Lloyd, *History of Wales*, 3rd edn (London, 1939), I.323–4; N.K. Chadwick, 'Early culture and learning in North Wales', 79–82. The clearest evidence is from the *Kyuoesi*

the Irish which had occurred many centuries earlier. In this form, the legend of Cunedda implied that British territory had been purged of Irish intruders. It thus perceived relations between both the languages and the peoples of Britain and Ireland as fundamentally hostile and as issuing in a British victory.

The earliest versions of the story, then, are those in the *Historia Brittonum* of 829/30. In chapter 14 of the *Historia Brittonum* it is said that 'the sons of Liethan took land within the territory of Dyfed and also in other territories, namely Gŵyr and Cedweli, until they were driven out by Cunedda and his sons from all British lands'.[22] In the Harleian Genealogies of the mid-tenth century there is a radically different version: here there is no mention of the Irish but only of a migration of Cunedda with eight sons and one grandson from Manaw Gododdin and of a land-division between the sons and the grandson embracing territories from the Dee to the Teifi.[23] The southern boundary of the activities of Cunedda and his family in this account is the traditional northern boundary of Dyfed. Yet the latter was the principal theatre of their activity in the version given in chapter 14 of the *Historia Brittonum*.

Chapter 62 of the *Historia Brittonum* and the *Vita Secunda* of St Carannog (probably of the twelfth century) offer different intermediate versions. The *Historia Brittonum* says that Cunedda, the great-great-great-grandfather of Maelgwn king of Gwynedd,

> had earlier come with his sons, of whom there were eight, from the northern part [of Britain], that is from the district which is called Manaw Gododdin, 146 years before the reign of Maelgwn, and they drove out the Irish with very great slaughter from those districts, and they [the Irish] never returned to dwell there again.

Myrdin a Gwendyd y Chwaer (*Myvyrian Archaiology*, 110, Stanza 36 = *The Poetry in the Red Book of Hergest*, ed. J. Gwenogvryn Evans (Llanbedrog, 1911), 578.40), which provides a king-list of Gwynedd in verse, initially going up as far as the tenth century but with a stanza which may refer to Gruffudd ap Cynan. Cf. *Llawysgrif Hendregadredd*, transcribed by Rhiannon Morris-Jones, ed. J. Morris-Jones and T.H. Parry-Williams (Cardiff, 1933), 65.15 (*marwnad* for Owain Goch ap Gruffudd ap Llywelyn), 'hil g6ra6 breinhya6l brenhin mana6', 'most courageous privileged lineage of the king of Manaw'; this is not a reference to the later marriage connection between Rhodri ab Owain Gwynedd and a daughter of the king of Man, for Rhodri was not Owain's ancestor. There can be no question of linking Merfyn with Manaw Gododdin since that Manaw had been lost by the Britons more than a century and a half before Merfyn's time. The Second Dynasty of Gwynedd is regularly called by the poets *Merfyniawn* after Merfyn. See also P.M.C. Kermode, 'A Welsh inscription in the Isle of Man', *ZCP* 1 (1897): 48–53, J. Rhys, 'Note on Guriat', ibid. 52–3; P.M.C. Kermode, *Manx Crosses* (London, 1901), no. 48 (pp. 121–3); R.A.S. Macalister, *Corpus Inscriptionum Insularum Celticarum* (hereafter *CIIC*) (Dublin, 1945–9), no. 1066. For the mixed character of the Isle of Man see J.M. Wallace-Hadrill, *Bede's Ecclesiastical History of the English People: a historical commentary* (Oxford, 1988), 223.

22 *Historia Brittonum*, c. 14.
23 *EWGT* 13.

There is ambiguity in this passage: the only Welsh *regio* named is Gwynedd, but it also says that Cunedda and his sons drove out the Irish *ab istis regionibus*, suggesting either that Gwynedd was not the only land to be freed from the foreign settlers or that it was perceived as a collection of *regiones*.[24] All one can say is that in terms of the territories named, chapter 14 and chapter 62 look to the south-west and the north-west of Wales respectively. Chapter 62 of the *Historia Brittonum* likewise differs from the Harleian Genealogies: although it mentions eight sons of Cunedda, it makes no reference to any land-division between them. The *Vita Secunda* of St Carannog quotes the Harleian version almost verbatim, in a corrupt form, but then goes on to say that the Irish fought against one of the sons of Cunedda, Ceredig (the eponym of Ceredigion), and conquered all his territory.[25] The defeat of the Irish, so we are left to assume, was the work of Ceredig's successor. These differences may be tabulated as follows:

	HB c. 14	*HB* c. 62	*Harl. Gen.*	*Vita II S. Car.*
Migration:	—	Yes	Yes	Yes
Irish expelled:	Yes	Yes	—	Later
Where from:	Dyfed Gŵyr Cedweli	Gwynedd (+ other *regiones*?)	—	Ceredigion
Land-division:	—	—	Yes	Yes

There are some very puzzling things about these texts. It will be noticed that the version which has Cunedda and his sons expelling the Irish from Dyfed is contemporary with Merfyn Frych, who ruled Gwynedd, while the version which is contemporary with Owain ap Hywel Dda, who was ruler of Dyfed, specifically excludes Dyfed from the territories shared out among Cunedda's sons. In other words, there is no consistent relationship between the location of a ninth- or tenth-century kingdom and the location of the land-taking activities of Cunedda and his sons. To regard the story, in all its versions, as essentially an origin legend justifying the position of the Second Dynasty of Gwynedd is to ignore the layout, geographical and chronological, of the evidence. These versions may have been contemporary with rulers belonging to the Second Dynasty, but there is no good reason to suppose that they were sponsored by kings to justify their power.

Information from the other side of the Irish Sea does not simplify matters. The story of the 'Expulsion (or Migration) of the Déissi' claims that one branch of the Déissi founded the royal dynasty of Dyfed; Cormac's Glossary places the fortress of the sons of Líathán in Cornwall, not in Dyfed as in the *Historia Brittonum*, c. 14,

---

24 On the one hand there is in *regione Guenedotae*, *Historia Brittonum*, c. 62, and the *ab omnibus Britannicis regionibus* of c. 14, which may include Dyfed, Gŵyr and Cedweli; on the other hand there is the possiblity that districts such as Rhos, Mon, Arfon, etc. might also be regarded as *regiones*.

25 *Vitae Sanctorum Britanniae et Genealogiae*, ed A.W. Wade-Evans (Cardiff, 1944), 148 (§§ 2–3); the only significant change is that the southern boundary is the Gwaun, not the Teifi.

and says nothing of the Déissi.[26] The former existence of Irish settlements in western Britain is apparently common knowledge. The details, however, are far from being agreed. The period of Irish power on both sides of the Irish Sea is clearly seen as something in the past by Cormac, as it is by the Welsh sources, but this is not surprising since the Glossary, in so far as it is the work of Cormac mac Cuilennáin (*ob.* 908), is a text of the Viking period.[27] The whole body of evidence, British and Irish, gives the impression of an old but muddled tradition, not propaganda newly devised on behalf of an intrusive dynasty.[28]

By the tenth century the Irish settlements were receding into a more remote past. The Harleian Genealogies ignore the anti-Irish role of Cunedda. For them what matters is land-division, and in particular the way in which, if a son dies before his father, the grandson can step into his shoes and share the patrimony along with his uncles. On the other hand, the grandson is to assume the position of the youngest son, even if he is the son of the eldest son; it is, therefore, his duty to divide the patrimony and to take the last share.[29] In terms of the succession of one son to an undivided kingship of Gwynedd – which can co-exist with a territorial division by which the other brothers receive lordship but not kingship – the grandson of the

26 K. Meyer, 'The expulsion of the Déssi', § 11; *Sanas Cormaic: an old Irish glossary*, ed. K. Meyer (Anecdota from Irish Manuscripts, ed. O.J. Bergin *et al.*, IV: Halle, 1912) (hereafter *Sanas Cormaic (YBL)*, no. 883; M. Dillon, 'The Irish settlements in Wales', *Celtica* 12 (1977): 1–11; T. Ó Cathasaigh, 'The Déisi and Dyfed', 1–3, 18–28 (on pp. 18–19 the versions of Rawlinson B 502 and Laud Misc. 612 are both given); on p. 26 he suggests that the composite material in the Déisi material suggests a further migration to Dyfed from Leinster.

27 The most likely interpretation is that the shorter version of Cormac, as found in *Lebor Brecc* and fragmentarily in Bodleian MS Laud Misc. 610, is at least of Munster origin about the time of Cormac: cf. P. Russell, 'The sounds of a silence: the growth of Cormac's Glossary', *Cambridge Medieval Celtic Studies* 15 (Summer 1988): 1–30, especially 10–11.

28 Mrs Chadwick, 'Early culture and learning in North Wales', 34–5, maintains that the Cunedda story is antiquarian speculation based on the genealogies and stimulated by a new sense of nationalism associated, in Wales, with the reign of Rhodri Mawr. Against this is the priority in date of attestation of the versions of the story in the *Historia Brittonum* as against the version in the Harleian Genealogies: the genealogical version is the later. Also the versions in the *Historia Brittonum* both antedate Rhodri Mawr; and, moreover, the intellectual character of Merfyn's court, in so far as it can be reconstructed, shows no sign of any rise in nationalism, if one excludes the Cunedda story itself. David Dumville, 'Sub-Roman Britain', 182, sees the point of the story as being (1) an explanation of the close relationship between Wales and the British kingdoms of what is now southern Scotland; (2) to provide a parallel to the intrusion of an outside dynasty into the kingdom of Gwynedd; (3) to explain how the sub-kingdoms of 'Greater Gwynedd' came into existence. This view rests on the unspoken assumption that all the versions of the story can be assimilated into a single tradition. My view is that they cannot.

29 The alternative interpretation is that the new king was supposed to assign shares to his brothers, as he appears to do in the *Vita Sancti Gundleii*, § 1, *Vitae Sanctorum Britanniae et Genealogiae*, ed. Wade-Evans, p. 172; this would imply that Meirion succeeded his father Cunedda, whereas the line of Maelgwn Gwynedd is traced from Einion Yrth, *EWGT*, p. 11.

eldest son will presumably not succeed to the kingship if his father predeceased his grandfather.[30] We are dealing with a model of royal succession applied to a very specific issue; the presence or absence of Irish settlers is, for this question, of no concern.[31]

By the tenth century, therefore, the Irish settlements may have ceased to be of more than antiquarian concern even to those who told the story of Cunedda. That is not to say, however, that relationships between the Irish and Welsh languages were no longer of any interest. On the other side of the Irish Sea, Cormac's Glossary (c.900) betrays considerable knowledge of Welsh; and it also shows how the relative positions of the two languages had been transformed since the sixth century. As befits a lexicographer, Cormac is interested in loan-words. Moreover he came closest of anyone in the Middle Ages to realizing that Welsh and Irish are cognate languages (it has to be remembered that while any well-informed person in the early Middle Ages knew that English was related to the languages of Germany, no one made the same connection between Irish and Welsh until the Renaissance).[32] He maintains that Irish *brath* is a loan from Welsh *brawd*, which he explains as meaning *iudex*, 'judge'.[33] He makes the point by saying that *brath* is *Combrec*; in other words, he uses an early form of the modern term for the Welsh language, *Cymraeg*, probably borrowed into Irish no later than the early seventh century.[34] On the Irish name Cathal he wrote as follows:[35]

> Cathal is the name of a Briton. That is, it is Welsh (*Combrec*), i.e. Catell. *Cat* in Welsh is *cath* in Irish (*Scottica*); *ell* is *ail*. Cathal then is *ail chatha* 'rock of battle'.

The final etymology leaves something to be desired, but the equation of Cathal and Cadell is plausible, while that of *cad* and *cath* is correct. The most interesting thing about this passage, however, is the identification of the Briton with his language, *Combrec*. Because Cormac thinks Cathal is a Welsh name, therefore he thinks it is the

---

30 On royal succession see J. Beverley Smith, 'Dynastic succession in medieval Wales', *BBCS* 33 (1986): 199–232.

31 Cf. the model offered by the Preface to the Life of St Cadog, *Vitae Sanctorum Britanniae et Genealogiae*, ed. A.W. Wade-Evans, p. 24, and the more elaborate version in § 1 of the Life of St Gwynllyw, ibid. p. 172.

32 The references to Welsh all belong to the shorter version of Cormac.

33 *Sanas Cormaic (YBL)*, no. 110 (very possibly extracted from no. 850).

34 The earliest attestation in Welsh is early twelfth-century: *Llyfr Du Caerfyrddin*, ed. A.O.H. Jarman (Cardiff, 1982), no. 4, line 3. The regular preservation of the old -*mb*- in *Combrec* (compare OE *Cumbraland* alongside *Cumerland*) suggests that the word was borrowed into Irish before -*mb*- > -*mm*- in British (a slow change beginning in the fifth and ending in the seventh century, K.H. Jackson, *Language and History in Early Britain* (Edinburgh, 1953), p. 511). The corresponding change in Irish is late eighth to ninth century, but I have no examples of Irish *Com(m)reg* suggesting that Cormac's consistency in spelling the word with -*mb*- reflects the earlier Old Irish pronunciation. *Combrec* is thus likely to be have been borrowed into Irish during the period of maximum British influence in the late fifth and sixth centuries.

35 *Sanas Cormaic* (YBL), no. 206.

36 Cf. *Sanas Cormaic* (YBL), no. 883 for *Bretnas*.

37 *Sanas Cormaic* (YBL), no. 124.

name of a Briton. He is wrong in fact: Cathal is good Irish, and, moreover, it is his habit of explaining correspondences between Irish and Welsh by supposing borrowings from Welsh into Irish which prevents him from perceiving that the languages themselves are cognate. Nonetheless we have one crucial conclusion: for him British nationality is linguistic; Britishness has to do with *Combrec*.

The equation of *Combrec* with the language of the Britons, also called *Bretnas*,[36] is found elsewhere in Cormac.[37] The implications of this usage are worthy of consideration. *Cymraeg* is derived from *Cymro*, and the latter is the person of the same *bro*, by contrast with the *allfro*, the person of another *bro*. Yet the normal meaning of *bro* was 'district'.[38] One might therefore suppose that *Cymraeg* should have meant 'dialect', the language of a local district, whereas in fact it can be used as much of the British language of southern Scotland as of Welsh (Cormac identifies *Combrec* with *Bretnas*, the language of the Britons, and there is no doubt that the men of Strathclyde were Britons and also Cumbrians, 'Cymry'). In other words, *Cymro* corresponds to the wider but rarer sense of *bro*, as in *bro Frython*, 'the land of the Britons', rather than to the commoner and more local sense, such as *bro Gadfan*, 'the district of Cadfan' (around his church at Tywyn).[39] What is therefore especially in need of explanation is why *Cymry* should invariably correspond to the wider sense of *bro* and never to the more local one. It is not the case that the wider sense of *bro* is the older one; on the contrary, the more local sense is indubitably older.[40]

---

38 Bro does not seem to be a normal term either of Middle Welsh narrative or legal prose: it is never used in the Four Branches, in *Culhwch ac Olwen*, *Breudwyt Ronabwy* or *Llyfr Cyfnerth*. In *Llyfr Iorwerth* it is only used once, in a proverb (§ 81/9: *ny eyn em bro ny rodho guyr*, 'there is no room in a *bro* for one who does not concede justice'). In *Llyfr Blegywryd*, ed. S.J. Williams and J. Enoch Powell (Cardiff, 1942), it occurs only in the phrase *maenawr vro* as opposed to *maenawr wrthtir* (71. 16–7); here it means 'lowland' as opposed to 'upland'. It is not even used in the lists of countries in *Delw y Byd*. On the other hand it is quite common in the early poetry, often followed by (a) a personal or (b) a place-name, or (c) preceded by a possessive pronoun: (a) e.g. *bro Gaduan*, *Gwaith Llywarch ap Llywelyn 'Prydydd y Moch'*, ed. E.M. Jones and N.A. Jones (Cardiff, 1991), no. 12, line 36; (b) e.g. *Carno 6ro*, 'district of Carno', ibid. no. 28, line 3; (c) e.g. *Llyfr Du Caerfyrddin*, ed. Jarman, 18. 147 = T. Jones, *Proceedings of the British Academy* 53 (1967), 126–7, *hydir y wir in y bro*, 'whose justice was strong in his land'. When the proper name requires it, the area denoted by *bro* can be extensive: e.g. *broyd Asya ac Affrica*, 'the lands of Asia and Africa', *Red Book Poetry*, 1229. 23–4; *bro Frython*, 'the land of the Britons', *Myfyrian Archaiology*, 222 a 16. The second meaning distinguished in *GPC*, namely 'boundary', is not well attested: in *Canu Aneirin*, line 574, *Heilyn achubyat pob bro*, *bro* may equally well be 'land'; in Judith 3: 8, *efe a ddifwynodd eu holl frôoedd hwynt, brôoedd* translates Greek *hória* (sg. *hórion*), originally 'boundaries', but often used in the Septuagint and in the New Testament for 'district' or 'neighbourhood' (in the NT it is translated by *cyffiniau, terfynau, tueddau, parthau, goror*). Although the NT translation tends to preserve the older meaning of *hória*, it cannot be inferred that the translation of Judith did likewise.

39 See n. 38.

40 It explains the development of *breyr* 'noble' (from **brogorix*, 'king of a *bro*'). Compare the Cornish name Pembro, which probably marks the edge of a district, O.J. Padel, *Cornish Place-Name Elements* (English Place-Name Society, lvi/lvii; 1985), 32, and the Breton use

In the tenth-century *Armes Prydein Fawr*, the poet envisages a formal alliance between the *Cymry*, on the one side, and the men of Dublin and the Irish on the other.[41] The Irish and the Hiberno-Norse were therefore merely allies. The men of Cornwall and Strathclyde, however, will be 'included among us', namely among the *Cymry*;[42] they will therefore participate in the resharing of the land of Britain that will follow the expulsion of the foreigner, the *allmon* or *allfro*.[43] Moreover the leaders of the *Cymry* are to be both Cadwaladr of Gwynedd and Cynan of Brittany.[44] The poet can thus use the terms *Brython* and *Cymry* without distinction.[45] What is striking about his terminology is that he seems at one point to distinguish the Cornish and the men of Strathclyde from the *Cymry*, from 'us', and yet he says that the other Britons will be 'included among us'.[46] They have perhaps not been 'among us' but this will change in the future.[47] In the thirteenth century, *cynnwys* 'include' is used in the laws for bringing in a distant kinsman and giving him a share in an inheritance.[48] Such a nuance fits the context in *Armes Prydein* perfectly.[49] Moreover, the apparent double sense of *Cymry* – 'Welsh' but also 'Britons' – corresponds exactly with the double sense of *Britannia* in Asser's Life of Alfred, both 'Wales' and 'Britain'.[50] Therefore, in the wider sense of both terms, just as the *Cludwys* 'men of the Clyde' are *Brython*, so

of *bro*, normally equivalent to French *pays*, perhaps exceptionally 'holding of land', *Trois Poèmes en Moyen-Breton*, ed. R. Hemon (Dublin, 1962), stanza 242 (and see note); also, more distantly, Irish *mruig*.

41 *Armes Prydein*, ed. I. Williams, lines 9–10, where I would translate *cymod* by 'alliance' rather than 'reconciliation'.

42 Ibid., line 11; for *cynnwys* see n. 45. Whereas the *Cymry / Brython* will possess everything from Manaw to Brittany, line 172, the men of Dublin, allies though they were, will return home, line 177. For the priority of honour given to the *Gwyr Gogled*, cf. the similar claims made for the men of Arfon in the *Breiniau Gwyr Arfon*, *Ancient Laws and Institutes of Wales*, ed. A. Owen (London, 1841), Venedotian Code, II.ii.

43 *Armes Prydein*, ed. I. Williams, lines 171–7.

44 Ibid., lines 81–95, 163–70, 182–4.

45 Ibid., lines 42–4: the land of the Britons is the land of the *Cymry* where they should never suffer 'homelessness', *diffroed* (= *di-fro-edd*, 'the state of being deprived of one's *bro*). On this compare *Hen Gerddi Cryefyddol*, ed. H. Lewis (Cardiff, 1931), XIV.12: *A chymro diuro diurad weti*.

46 With line 11 compare lines 151–4. I take it that the 'us' of *genhyn*, line 11, are the *Kymry* of line 9.

47 This is shown by the role of Cynan of Brittany and by the phrase *o Vynaw hyt Lydaw*, line 172. There is no need to assume a legend of a quarrel between Cynan and Cadwaladr and a subsequent need for reconciliation: see D.N. Dumville, 'Brittany and "Armes Prydein Vawr"', *Etudes Celtiques* 20 (1983): 145–59, esp. 156–8.

48 *Llyfr Iorwerth*, ed. A.Rh. Wiliam (Cardiff, 1960), § 85/6, which corresponds to the context of *Armes Prydein*, line 11 (distant kinship, yet inclusion).

49 Note the presentation of the future British revival as the pursuit of a land-suit against the English in lines 132–46.

50 In the dedication to Alfred, the latter is *omnium Britanniae insulae Christianorum rector*, but in c. 79 Asser agrees with Alfred that he will spend six months of every year with the king, six months in *Britannia: Asser's Life of King Alfred*, ed. W.H. Stevenson, rev. edn by D. Whitelock (Oxford, 1959), pp. 1, 64.

are they *Cymry*. Moreover we know from a contemporary English source, the Anglo-Saxon Chronicle, that the land of the *Cludwys* is *Cumbraland*, the land of the *Cymry*, Cumbria.[51] Since, for Cormac, *Combrec* and *Bretnas* are synonyms, and, for the English, the Britons of southern Scotland were *Cumbras*, *Cymry*, we can add the further point that the language of the *Cludwys* was *Combrec*, *Cymraeg*.

The puzzle remains: a word whose literal meaning is 'the language of a district' is used for the language spoken down the western side of Britain from Loch Lomond to the Lizard. To make matters worse, a man of Cormac's time may well also have regarded Breton as *Combrec*.[52]

The most likely answer lies further back in time, in Roman and sub-Roman Britain; and the clue is the word *Deutsch* (Old High German *diutisk*, *thiutisk*).[53] In 786 two papal envoys, George, bishop of Ostia, and Theophylact, bishop of Todi, were sent to England to secure reforms in the church. When they came to a council of the Mercians, they had with them Alcuin and a man who was later his deacon, Pyttel, probably also a Northumbrian. There the decrees which had been accepted by a Northumbrian synod earlier in the same year were read out and explained both in Latin and *theodisce*. The account of these proceedings survives in the form of a letter from the bishop of Ostia to Pope Hadrian.[54] George had, for some time, been resident in Francia and had undertaken his mission with the help of Wigbod, a Frank sent as his companion by Charlemagne.[55] The context of his use of *theodisc* is thus as much Frankish as it is English.

The best known Frankish example of the term is later, in the account given by Nithard (*ob.* 844) of a treaty made between Charles the Bald and Louis the German on 14 February 842, at which Nithard was himself very probably present.[56] Oaths were sworn to confirm the treaty, both by the kings and by their supporters. On both sides the leaders were Franks, but Charles swore his oath in *teudisca lingua* (here German), while Louis swore in *romana lingua* ('the Roman tongue', in this instance Old French). The purpose was to make the crucial oath intelligible to the Frankish supporters of the other king. Both kings first addressed their own men in their own language, Charles in the *romana lingua*, Louis in *teudisca*; similarly, when their followers took the oath, Louis's men swore in *teudisca* while Charles's swore in *romana*. The speeches were naturally meant to be comprehensible to their own side, while the kings' oaths were intended to be understood by the other side.

51 *Anglo-Saxon Chronicle* in *Two of the Saxon Chronicles Parallel*, ed. C. Plummer and J. Earle (Oxford 1892), i, s.a. 945; cf. 1000 (E); G.W.S. Barrow, *Kingship and Unity: Scotland 1000–1306* (London, 1981), 11–13. I assume that the English used *Cumbras* of the Strathclyde Britons because the latter used *Cymry* for themselves.
52 Just as Cynan of Brittany could be a leader of the *Cymry*.
53 L. Weisgerber, *Deutsch als Volksname: Ursprung und Bedeutung* (Stuttgart, 1953).
54 *Epistolae Karolini Aevi*, ii (=MGH *Epistolae*, iv; Berlin, 1895), ed. E. Dümmler, no. 3, transl. D. Whitelock, *English Historical Documents. c. 500–1042* (London, 1955), no. 191.
55 P. Wormald, 'In search of King Offa's "Law-Code"', in I.N. Wood and N. Lund (eds) *People and Places in Northern Europe 500–1600: essays in honour of P.H. Sawyer* (Woodbridge, 1991), 28–9.
56 *Nithard: histoire des fils de Louis le Pieux*, ed. Ph. Lauer (Paris, 1926), 100–8.

Teudisca is derived from the word for a people, Old English *theod*, Old High German *diot*, *thiot*. *Teudisca* is thus the language of the people, but it is not easy to say which people was the *thiot* that spoke *teudisca*. The Franks were on both sides of this linguistic divide, speaking *romana lingua* as well as *teudisca lingua*: *teudisca lingua* was not just Frankish. Moreover, we have already seen that someone coming from Francia could use the word without hesitation of English. *Teudisca*, therefore, does not define the *thiot* of the Franks; Frankishness, quite simply, was not a matter of language. In the letter of George of Ostia to Hadrian, the context of the word is public reading of the decrees both in Latin and in *theodisc*. *Deutsch*, then, is in origin the language of the people in the sense of the local population, whether English or East Frankish, as opposed to Latin. It is not applied to Old French because of the still evident relationship between *lingua romana* and *lingua Latina* and because, to Germanic speakers, Romance was known as *walhisk* (cognate with 'Welsh' but applied to Romans).[57] East of the Rhine, and in a context in which western Franks were not involved, matters were different. Here the local language could be characteristic of a people. Thus Old High German glosses on Latin texts could be marked by the letter .f. standing for *franciske*, (East) Frankish.[58]

Cymraeg has a similar origin. It was not necessarily the language of every *bro* in Roman Britain, but only of those districts whose principal language was not Latin (just as *theodisc* was not the language of every *theod* in Britain or in the Frankish empire). In those districts it was 'the local language', *Cymraeg*, as opposed to Latin. It so happened, however, that only one language, apart from Latin, was widely spoken in Roman Britain, namely British. This identity of British with the native language of Roman Britain explains the equivalence for Bede of the Britons with speakers of British, and for Cormac of *Bretnas* and *Combrec*. The notion of *Cymraeg* derives, therefore, from a Romano-British contrast between the language of government, of the church and of the aristocracy – the language of the empire as a whole – and the language spoken locally. By the dominant side this contrast would have been seen as one between *lingua Latina* and *lingua vulgaris*, but by the locals, the *Cymry*, as one between Latin and *Cymraeg*.

The roots of a sense of nationality among the *Cymry* were then largely linguistic and cultural and depended on a contrast between 'us' and the Romans. This contrast we find already taken for granted in the sixth century in Gildas: the *Romani* came from overseas to subdue the *Britanni* to good laws;[59] the Romans are one *gens*, the Britons another.[60] *Cives*, 'fellow-citizens', in this island can be contrasted with those subject to 'the kings across the sea', *transmarini reges*.[61] What then made the *Cymry*, the locals, into one people, was the plain fact that whether they lived in Penwith in Cornwall or by the banks of the Clyde, their local language, when contrasted with

---

57 L. Weisgerber, 'Walhisk: die geschichtliche Leistung des Wortes Welsch', *Rheinische Vierteljahrblätter* 13 (1948): 87–146; *id.*, *Deutch als Volksname*, 115–251.

58 W. Braune, K. Helm and W. Mitzka, *Althochdeutsche Grammatik*[12] (Tübingen, 1967), p. 11, § 6 d, n. 1.

59 Gildas, *De Excidio Britanniae*, 5.

60 Ibid., c. 25.

61 Ibid., c. 4.

Latin, was seen as a single British tongue: *Combrec*, 'the local language', was therefore *Bretnas*, 'the language of the Britons'. Formally, *Cymraeg* is derived from *Cymro*; semantically, *Cymro*, meaning 'Briton' rather than 'fellow local', is derived from *Cymraeg*. It was *Cymraeg* 'British' which ensured that *Cymro* meant 'Briton'.

With this in mind we may turn back to Dyfed, and to the sixth century to the time of Voteporix, perhaps Gildas's Vortiporius, *Demetarum tyrannus*.[62] He is commemorated in a bilingual (Latin/Irish) inscription at Castell Dwyran in the west of Carmarthenshire in the heartland of early medieval Dyfed.[63] The Latin, in square capitals, runs as follows: MEMORIA / VOTEPORIGIS / PROTICTORIS. The other, containing only the name, is in the ogam alphabet and in an early form of Irish, VOTECORIGAS. In what is, therefore, the commemorative stone of a person of very high rank,[64] even if he is not Gildas's ruler of the Demetae, Irish is admissible alongside Latin; Welsh does not appear at all.

In discussing the term *Cymraeg*, I have up to now tacitly assumed that the only vernacular language spoken alongside Latin was British. For most of Britain for most of the Roman period, that was true; but along the western seaboard, including Dyfed, it ceased to be true in the fourth and fifth centuries. A further problem is that it is not clear for how long Latin was still a spoken language in Britain. On both these points the inscriptions offer decisive evidence.[65] They show quite unambiguously the

---

62 Cf. D. Dumville, 'Gildas and Maelgwn', in *Gildas: new approaches*, ed. M. Lapidge and D. Dumville (Woodbridge, 1984), 57.

63 *ECMW* no. 138.

64 On the term *protector* see A.H.M. Jones, *The Later Roman Empire* (Oxford, 1964), 53–4, 597, 636–40; it was used for one of the two corps of élite bodyguard troops (*domestici* and *protectores*) entitled 'to adore the purple'. In effect, the *protectores* served as staff officers and were likely to receive high military office as the next step in their careers. Cassiodorus, *Variae* XI.31 (ed. Th. Mommsen, MGH, Auctores Antiquissimi, XII.348), is the formula by which, for Ostrogothic Italy, a *primicerius singulariorum* (head of the messenger service) was advanced to the company of the *domestici et protectores*, in that he was *sacram purpuram adoraturus*. This is an example of the practice whereby deserving veterans or officials received the honour of adoring the sacred purple on retirement. As the Ostrogothic example shows, the practice could survive in a barbarian kingdom. If Voteporix was Gildas's tyrant of the Demetae, it would be surprising to find him being called a *protector* since that would imply a recognition of imperial authority of some kind, such as the purple worn by the parents of Ambrosius Aurelianus, Gildas, *De Excidio*, 25.3. On the other hand, it would also be surprising if there were someone called Voteporix flaunting the right 'to adore the purple' in the heart of Vortiporius's kingdom. He might conceivably have been a kinsman of Vortiporius (so explaining the close similarity of the names) of a slightly earlier generation (so explaining the adoration of the purple).

65 On dating see Jackson, *Language and History in Early Britain*, pp. 158–62; I do not, however, share his opinion that the Catamanus stone is likely to be later than *c*.625: square capitals did not evolve into half-uncials within Britain; rather square capitals were replaced by half-uncials as a form of lettering appropriate for inscriptions. There is no need to allow time for a gradual evolution of letter-forms; since the change was a matter of fashion, it may have happened very fast. It certainly extended to the whole of Wales. Jackson's appeal to the date of foundation of Llangadwaladr depends on the text of *Bonedd y Saint* printed in the *Myfyrian Archaiology*. The reference there to Llangadwaladr is editorial: see Bartrum's edn, *EWGT*, p. 56.

presence of Irish; with rather more difficulty they can also indicate approximately how long Latin remained a spoken language in Britain. By this I mean how long it was a language used in a wide variety of styles and registers; Latin remained a spoken language in the liturgy, for example, throughout the Middle Ages, but that is only a use restricted to one register and will not count for this discussion.

It is characteristic of the spoken Latin of Late Antiquity that the quantitative distinction between long and short vowels, to which differences in the point of articulation were ancillary, disappeared. Instead, differences in the point of articulation, formerly secondary, were now crucial. So *vīvo* gives Italian *vivo*, but *bibo* gives Italian *bevo*, because a Latin short *i* was more open than a long *ī*, and hence *i* > *e*, but *ī* > *i*.[66] The way in which this process worked itself out varied between the individual Romance languages, but the direction of change was fundamentally the same. At a rather earlier period the diphthongs, *ae*, *oe*, had become simple vowels.[67] Among the changes to consonants is the disappearance of final *-m* (very early) and *-s* (late and only in some areas of Romance, including British Latin).[68] The consequences for morphology were far-reaching: there was no distinction between, for example, *Petrus*, *Petrum*, *Petrō* (all > *Petro* or *Pedro*). All these changes are attested in the British Latin inscriptions of the fifth and sixth centuries:

> VASSO for *vassus*, ADQUAE for *atque*[69]
> CONGERIES for *congerie*[70]
> CIVE for *civis*, CONSOBRINO for *consobrinus*[71]
> MULTITVDINEM for *multitudine*[72]

The genitive singular ending of the second declension in *-i* was used without any attention being paid to the syntax. We have both:

> SENACVS / PRESBYTER HIC IACIT[73]

and

> DOMNICI / IACIT FILIVS / BRAVECCI[74]

or

> CORBALENGI IACIT / ORDOUS[75]

---

66 V. Väänänen, *Introduction au latin vulgaire* (Paris, 1967), §§ 42–6.
67 Ibid., § 59.
68 Ibid., §§ 127–9; cf. C. Smith, 'Vulgar Latin in Roman Britain: epigraphic and other evidence', in H. Temporini and W. Haase, *Aufstieg und Niedergang des römischen Welt. II. Prinzipat*, 29.2, *Sprache und Literatur*, ed. W. Haase (Berlin, 1983), 925–6.
69 *ECMW*, no. 33; cf. Smith, 'Vulgar Latin in Roman Britain', 911–12.
70 *ECMW*, no. 101.
71 *ECMW*, no. 103.
72 *ECMW*, no. 78.
73 *ECMW*, no. 78.
74 *ECMW*, no. 122.
75 *ECMW*, no. 126.

The idea that the genitive might be being used elliptically – '(the stone) of Domnicus' – can hardly account for the second and third of the examples just given. It is not much more plausible for the following:

BROHOMAGLI / IC IACIT / ET VXOR EIVS CAVNE[76]

Late British Latin must have been in the same situation as the one we find in modern Italian: *-i* was the mark of the plural of second-declension nouns, but no longer of the genitive singular. British, by the fifth century, was in the same position.[77] This is what explains the numerous relics of the plural in *-i* (for example, early Welsh *meip* from British **mapi*) as opposed to the very few relics of the genitive singular in *-i*. We may contrast this linguistic situation with that of a man who learnt his Latin from grammars, for example the Anglo-Saxon Bede or the Irishman Tírechán. The former writes much better Latin than the second, but both have learnt in the same way. The kind of mistakes made by Tírechán are of two types: one is familiar to all those who have had to learn a second language after childhood – he makes simple grammatical errors;[78] the second is more interesting – he writes a Latin in which Irish constructions or idioms prevail over their Latin counterparts.[79] Tírechán, however, is perfectly well aware of the distinction between Latin cases, even if he makes mistakes. Many of those who were responsible for the texts of the inscriptions were unaware of any case system at all. They had not learnt their Latin from grammars. Latin was, therefore, in the time of Voteporix, a spoken language, alongside Welsh and, as I shall now try to show, Irish.

The clearest evidence that Irish was a spoken language in Wales comes from Kenfig in Glamorgan, many miles to the east of the main Irish settlements in Dyfed. A bilingual inscription runs as follows:[80]

Ogam: POPIA[ ] // ROL[..]N M[AQ]I LL[E]NA
Latin: PVMPEIVS / CARANTORIVS

The Latin inscription is in square capitals. There is nothing in the form of the inscription to suggest that Pumpeius and Carantorius are different persons. The ogam inscription, however, appears to be in two parts: one, on the left of the Latin inscrip-

---

76 *ECMW*, no. 183.

77 J.T. Koch, 'The loss of final syllables and loss of declension in Brittonic', *BBCS* 30 (1983): 201–33.

78 For example, Tírechán, *Collectanea*, 6. 1, ed. L. Bieler, *The Patrician Texts in the Book of Armagh* (Dublin, 1979), 126, *possimus* for *possumus*, *acciperunt* for *acceperant*.

79 For example, 24. 1 (p. 140), *quae tenuit pallium apud Patricium et Rodanum = gaibes caille la Pátraic ⁊ Ródán*.

80 *ECMW*, no. 198, now in the Margam Museum; the stone is damaged and the reading therefore uncertain, but Nash-Williams's reading is a distinct improvement on that of Macalister, *CIIC* no. 409. See also McManus, *A Guide to Ogam*, § 6.20, who confirms P[.]P[, and The Royal Commission on Ancient and Historical Monuments in Wales, *An Inventory of the Ancient Monuments in Glamorgan*, 1.3 *The Early Christian Period* (Cardiff, 1976), p. 38, no. 849, reads P[O *or* A]P[...]. On the form of ogam used for /p/ see P. Sims-Williams, 'The additional letters of the ogam alphabet', *Cambridge Medieval Celtic Studies* 23 (1992): 39–44, esp. 42.

tion, reading upwards; the other, on the right, reading downwards. Only the left-hand ogam text corresponds to the Latin. The other may be quite separate and may have been cut at a different time. PVMPEIVS shows, in the first syllable, the Late Latin confusion of *u* and *o*. Like the other Latin name it is in the nominative case. POPIA is an Irish form of the same name which has been assimilated both to the phonology and the morphology of Primitive Irish.[81]

In the next major kingdom to the north, Brycheiniog in the centre of South Wales, two inscriptions, about five miles apart, each of which is bilingual, are of particular interest.

Trallwng[82]   Ogam: CUNACENNI [A]VI ILVVETO
        Latin: CVNOCENNI FILIVS / CVNOGENI HIC IACIT

Trecastle[83]   Ogam: MAQITRENI SALICIDUNI
        Latin: MACCVTRENI + SALICIDVNI

In the Trallwng ogam inscription the initial CUNA- shows, by his choice of -*A*-rather than -*O*- (namely CUNA- rather than CUNO-), the development of Irish whereby the link vowel -*o*- was lowered and unrounded to -*a*-; this -*a*- subsequently lowered the preceding -*u*- to -*o*- and was itself lost (**cuno-* > **cuna-* > **cona-* > *con-*).[84] This independence of the ogam-cutter *vis-à-vis* the Latin suggests that Irish was for him a spoken language. On the other hand, on the Trecastle inscription a few miles further west, the form of the name in the ogam inscription, MAQITRENI, is more archaic than the Latin MACCVTRENI, since it preserves the old *q*, and *i* as against the later *c(c)* and *u*.[85] Here the Latin form of the name – still, of course, an Irish name even though in a Latin inscription – is closer to the probable pronunciation at the time. In this inscription, therefore, we have evidence in the ogam of an Irish orthographical tradition surviving in Brycheiniog independently both of the Latin tradition and of the pronunciation of Irish at that period.

In the sixth century, therefore, both Latin and Irish were spoken languages in Wales. Brycheiniog as well as Dyfed was a kingdom of three languages. Both Latin and Irish enjoyed a higher social status than did British. By the ninth century, however, neither Latin nor Irish were normal spoken languages used for all purposes. Latin was a language of liturgy and learning; Irish was probably not spoken at all apart from the occasional immigrant or the churchman who had studied in Ireland. The best indication of the relationship of the three languages is the eighth- and

---

81 It shows -*omp*- > -*ōb*-; the last syllable -*IA*[is probably for -*ijah*, the primitive Irish nominative singular of a *io*-stem.

82 *ECMW*, no. 70, situated in the church at SN 965 295; Nash-Williams reads CVNACEN-NIVI, following Macalister, *CIIC*, no. 342, but the first V is merely a slip for U. Jackson, *Language and History in Early Britain*, p. 185, suggests *CUNACENNI [A]VI ILVVETO* and he is followed by D. McManus, *A Guide to Ogam* (Maynooth, 1991), § 4.11 (p. 62).

83 *ECMW*, no. 71; *CIIC* no. 341. Nash-Williams reads MAQUTRENI but the U is a slip for I, as shown by the drawing. The stone is now in the British Museum.

84 McManus, *A Guide to Ogam*, § 5.23.

85 Ibid. § 5.32, 5.33.

ninth-century Juvencus manuscript (Cambridge University Library Ff. 4. 42). This reveals the existence of a group of scholars, including Irishmen as well as Britons, whose primary language for scholarly purposes was Latin, but who accepted Welsh as a written language at least for the purpose of glossing and entering marginalia.[86] The latter include the Juvencus *englynion*, the earliest Welsh verse to survive in a manuscript close to the date of composition. Another, perhaps overlapping, group of scholars was patronized by Merfyn Frych, king of Gwynedd, whose family probably came, as we have seen, from the Isle of Man, where Irishman and Briton may have lived side by side for centuries.[87] A further symptom of the status of Latin solely as a learned language is the relatively good grammar and innocence of Late Latin rhetorical preciosity shown by the two main Welsh writers of the ninth century. The *Historia Brittonum* from the first half of the century and Asser from the second both show a good command of Latin, considerably superior to many of their English contemporaries.[88]

In some circles, then, a scholarly Latin survived. There were, however, churches of which this cannot be said. Ninth- and tenth-century inscriptions from Margam, Merthyr Mawr and Llanilltud Fawr (all in Glamorgan) suggest a highly imperfect grasp of Latin. Moreover, one or two of the errors made indicate that such knowledge as remained stemmed in part from sources outside Wales. An inscription, perhaps of the late ninth century, from Llanilltud Fawr has PROPE[RA]BIT for *praeparauit*.[89] An inscription from Margam has PROPARABIT.[90] The use of *b* rather than *u* suggests continental influence (compare *avoir* and *habere*). Another Llanilltud inscription was commissioned by the abbot, Samson, as an act of intercessory prayer for himself and for the king, Ithel; it thus lacked nothing in solemnity of purpose, yet it demonstrates fundamental ignorance of Latin grammar.[91]

---

86 M. Lapidge, 'Latin learning in Dark Age Wales: some prolegomena', in *Proceedings of the Seventh International Congress of Celtic Studies, Oxford, 1983*, ed. D. Ellis Evans *et al.* (Oxford, 1986), 97–101; A. Harvey, 'The Cambridge Juvencus glosses – evidence of Hiberno-Welsh interaction', in *Proceedings of the Eighth International Symposium on Language Contact in Europe, Douglas, Isle of Man, 1988*, ed. P. Sture Ureland and G. Broderick (Tübingen, 1991), 181–98, esp. 190–4. Harvey's paper is an attempt to sift the evidence for scribes in the MS who knew both Irish and Welsh, as opposed to a group of scribes some of whom knew Irish, some Welsh. The uncertainties are great especially because of the difficulty in knowing when a gloss has been copied and also in distinguishing hands which only occur in a few glosses. The suggestion (p. 190) that the main scribe Nuadu need not have known Irish because some Anglo-Saxons bore names of British origin (Cædmon and Ceadwalla) seems to me very weak: the issue is whether Welshmen bore Irish names, not whether, in very different circumstances, some Englishmen bore British names.

87 M. Lapidge 'Latin learning in Dark Age Wales', 92; N.K. Chadwick, 'Early culture and learning in North Wales', 94–103.

88 N. Brooks, *The Early History of the Church of Canterbury* (Leicester, 1984), 171–4.

89 *ECMW*, no. 220.

90 *ECMW*, no. 233.

91 *ECMW*, no. 223.

IN NOMINE D(e)I SUMMI INCIPIT. CRUX. SALUATORIS. QUAE
PREPARAUIT SAMSONI :. APATI PRO ANIMA SUA: [ET] PRO ANIMA
IUTHAHELO REX :. ET ARTMALI :. ET TEC[AI]N

The grammar more or less survives as long as the inscription keeps to formulae – the bookish *incipit*, *crux saluatoris* and *pro anima* – but as soon as it goes further it betrays a complete ignorance of Latin morphology. Yet, however incompetent the *magistri* of Llanilltud Fawr may have been in the ninth and tenth centuries, they used Latin, not Welsh, for such weighty purposes as the commemoration of abbots and kings.

The relationship between Latin and Welsh had, therefore, changed fundamentally since the sixth century. As a spoken language Welsh cannot have had low status in the ninth century for the good reason that it was spoken by all native inhabitants of every British kingdom, whatever their rank. As a written language, however, it reached only as far as the margins and the interlinear spaces of surviving manuscripts. Evidence of any wider use of written Welsh is uncertain and confined to poetry.[92] In Brittany and Cornwall the situation was even less favourable to the wide use of a written vernacular. A high social status was attained by the Brittonic languages once the aristocracy and even churchmen ceased to use Latin as their normal means of communication; this did not, however, make much difference to the predominance of Latin over Welsh as a language of written learning. *Legenda*, Welsh *llên*, 'things which ought to be read', remained in Latin.

On the rise in the status of Welsh (or British, *Combrec*), Cormac again offers valuable evidence. As we have already seen, he was interested in loanwords. This interest led him to a concern with the phonological changes undergone by a word when it was borrowed from one language into another. Following a Latin tradition, he saw this process as one of deformation, *corruptio* – the result of the speaker adapting a foreign word to fit the sound-system of his own language. In this perception of linguistic borrowing, the source of loan-words and the source of *corruptio* are necessarily opposed. *Corruptio* stems from the speech-habits of the recipient, while the pronunciation of the donors is automatically correct. The word belongs to the ultimate donor-language.

One of the clearest examples of Cormac's perception of the linguistic traffic between Ireland and Britain is his account of Patrick's oath.[93] The head-word is *modebroth*, but Cormac went on to explain that this was an incorrect pronunciation on the part of the Irish: 'it ought to be pronounced thus: *muin duiu braut*'. Cormac's rendering of an Old Welsh version of the oath gave him what he believed ought to be the pronunciation, as opposed to the corrupt version of the Irish: linguistic corruption is thus contrasted with how something should be said.

---

92 D.N. Dumville, 'Early Welsh poetry: problems of historicity, in B.F. Roberts (ed.) *Early Welsh Poetry: studies on the Book of Aneirin* (Aberystwyth, 1988), 4–7.

93 *Sanas Cormaic (YBL)*, no. 850; how far Patrick could have said any such thing is not my concern: for this see Ifor Williams, *The Beginnings of Welsh Poetry*, 14–15; Jackson, *Language and History in Early Britain*, 633; J.T. Koch, 'The loss of final syllables and loss of declension in Brittonic', 212–14.

When the examples of linguistic borrowing in Cormac's Glossary are assembled, it soon becomes clear that the traffic, in general, is one way. It may be tabulated as follows:

Latin > Welsh > Irish: no. 211, *presbyter > premter > cruimther*.
Welsh > Irish: no. 124, *bracaut > brocóit*.
Latin > Welsh: no. 327, *consilium > cusyl*.
Latin > Irish: no. 852, *mater > máthair*.

For Cormac, then, Latin was always the donor, Irish always the recipient; Welsh was both. Put another way, Irish corrupts, Latin is corrupted, while Welsh both corrupts and is corrupted. In these terms, we may say that, although Latin was evidently the language which enjoyed the highest prestige, Welsh now shared to some extent in that prestige in that it offered a staging-post for the journey from Latin to Irish, as well as being an independent source of loans. That Latin was, as one would expect, of higher status than Welsh, is suggested by a contrast between Cormac's treatment of two words, *dobar* and *máthair*. *Dobar*, as he rightly says, is a word common to Irish and Welsh.[94] Neither language is said to have borrowed the word, and therefore neither has corrupted it. On the other hand, Irish *máthair* is said to be a corruption of Latin *mater* rather than, as it is, a word common to the two languages.[95] Latin is inevitably seen as the donor, whereas Welsh may be put upon the same level as Irish.

Two developments may lie behind the improved status of *Combrec* in Cormac's eyes. The first is its association with Patrick, already regarded, even in Munster, as the apostle of the Irish. Patrick the Briton may have been, along with thousands of his compatriots, the slave of an Irishman, but in the eyes of Heaven the shepherd-boy of Miliucc was of higher rank than any Irish king or druid. Second, whereas in Patrick's day the Irish dominated the western sea-approaches to Britain, by the end of the seventh century the Britons appear to have established a grip on the Irish Sea.[96] Britons were now able to invade the very areas in the province of Ulster where Patrick was believed to have served Miliucc.

In spite of its acknowledged debt to Patrick, Ireland offered a sharp contrast with Britain in the matter of language. What is more, it did so from the start. The ogam alphabet was probably invented in the late Roman period by an Irishman who knew Latin well but wished his own language to enjoy a status equal to that of the language of Imperial Rome.[97] The peoples across the frontiers of the empire were both attracted and repelled by Roman civilization. They might desire to take what they wanted

---

94 *Sanas Cormaic (YBL)*, no. 311.
95 *Sanas Cormaic (YBL)*, no. 852.
96 *Annals of Ulster*, ed. S. Mac Airt and G. Mac Niocaill (Dublin, 1983), s.a. 697.10; 702.2; 703.1; 711.5; 717.5.
97 A recent discussion of the conditions in which the ogam alphabet must have been created is A. Harvey, 'Early literacy in Ireland: the evidence from ogam', *Cambridge Medieval Celtic Studies* 14 (Winter 1987): 1–15; his arguments about Latin literacy in Ireland only hold if ogam was not invented by an Irishman in Britain, as suggested by Jackson, *Language and History in Early Britain*, p. 156. There is still much of value in Harvey's argument (notably p. 14, n. 51) even if one subscribes to Jackson's view.

– subsidies, trade, even office within the empire – but they also desired to remain distinct.[98] The ogam alphabet was created under just these twin impulses of attraction and repulsion. It was to be an alphabet fit for the commemoration in stone of a king or a *protector*. In Wales and the south-west it normally appears alongside Latin.[99] Sometimes the ogam has the same information as the Latin,[100] sometimes it has different information,[101] sometimes less.[102] What it never has is more information. Moreover, there are one or two inscriptions in which the Latin seems to have influenced the wording of the Irish.[103] As an inscriptional language, therefore, Irish remained the junior partner. Yet the contrast with Welsh remains: Welsh was not a partner at all.

The same relationship of semi-independent and junior status is exemplified by one of the central texts of early Irish learning, *Auraicept na nÉces*, 'The Primer of the Poets'.[104] It is the business of the *Auraicept* to raise Irish to the same level as Latin; and grammar is to be the means by which this elevation of status is to be achieved. Latin has so many letters; so does Irish. Latin has its declensions; so does Irish. In the *Auraicept*, the writer of Irish is always looking over his shoulder at his elder brother, the *Laitneóir*. The only early medieval counterpart to the *Auraicept* is the grammar of his native language commissioned by Charlemagne;[105] in that instance, too, the purpose was plain: the language of the Franks was, like Latin, to have the dignity of grammar. But, unlike the *Auraicept*, Charlemagne's grammar does not survive.

It is difficult to believe that a principal stimulus to this elevation and cultivation of Irish as a partner to Latin was not the experience of the Irish settlers in Britain in the last period of Roman rule. If I had to guess where the ogam alphabet was invented, I should, without hesitation, opt for South Wales.[106] The example of Gildas demonstrates that in post-Roman Britain, alongside spoken Latin, there was a grammatically correct and highly wrought form of the language – a Latin in which a prophet might denounce the sins and follies of kings and bishops.[107] The gap

---

98 For examples see the account of the Alamanni in J.F. Matthews, *The Roman Empire of Ammianus* (London, 1989), 306–18, and that of the Goths in P. Heather, *Goths and Romans, 332–489* (Oxford, 1991), esp. 121.

99 *ECMW*, no. 300 is an exception.

100 *ECMW*, nos. 71, 142.

101 *ECMW*, no. 70.

102 *ECMW*, nos. 84, 127, 354.

103 *ECMW*, no. 142 and possibly no. 169.

104 Edited by A. Ahlqvist, *The Early Irish Linguist: an edition of the canonical part of the Auraicept na nÉces* (Societas Scientiarum Fennica, Commentationes Humanarum Litterarum, 73; Helsinki, 1982).

105 Einhard, *Vita Karoli*, c. 29; Einhard's *inchoauit* perhaps suggests that the plan came to nothing.

106 Following Jackson, *Language and History in Early Britain*, p. 156, in preferring Britain to Ireland; South Wales is chosen simply because it is the part of Roman Britain in which there was the most extensive contact between Irish and Latin.

107 M. Lapidge, 'Gildas's education and the Latin culture of sub-Roman Britain', in *Gildas: new approaches*, ed. M. Lapidge and D. Dumville (Woodbridge, 1984), 27–50, and F. Kerlouégan, *Le De Excidio Britanniae de Gildas: les destinées de la culture latine dans l'île de Bretane au VIᵉ siècle* (Paris, 1987), ch. 1.

between the two – between the language of a Gildas and the spoken Latin, the *lingua Romana* of Britain – implies the continuance of effective schools of grammar and rhetoric; and that continuance, in its turn, implies the enduring high prestige of standard Latin. In several parts of western Britain the Irish were established as rulers. The anxiety of some of them to be commemorated in stone, both in Latin and in Irish, shows an appreciation of the position of Latin: it remained the language of the empire and of the church, and it may well also have been the language spoken, at least in their grander moments, by the native aristocracy among whom they came to rule. The insistence on the part of the settlers on using Irish as a language enjoying a status equal to that of Latin is likely to have been a deliberate statement of the cultural legitimacy as well as the distinctiveness of their rule in Britain.[108]

The very name of Irish, *Goídelc*,[109] borrowed from Welsh *Gwyddeleg*, points to western Britain.[110] A clear sense of linguistic nationality of the connection between *Goídel* and *Goídelc*, between the Irishman and the Irish language, would naturally predominate in a multilingual community, and, therefore, as *Goídelc* suggests, in Britain rather than in Ireland.[111] The name is unlikely to have been borrowed before c.600;[112] it thus attests the continuance into the seventh century of linguistic contact and of a consciousness of distinct linguistic communities within western Britain. Names for languages, *Combrec*, *Goídelc*, *Laitin*, were imported from multilingual Britain into monolingual Ireland.[113]

In Ireland also, however, we must allow for a considerable difference between the language refined and elevated by the grammarian and the language of ordinary people. This was true both of the imported Latin and of the native Irish. The Welsh and Irish words for Lent, *carawys* and *corgus*, illustrate the less correct form of Latin. Both derive from *quadragesima* via some such Late Latin spoken form as **quaragēss(a)*; neither can be explained as a direct borrowing from standard Latin.[114] At the other extreme is an author such as Columbanus (*ob.* 615).[115] His grammar and style were evidently taken by him to Burgundy where he settled c.591, since he was already an educated man when he became a monk at Bangor (near the modern

---

108 This point is well made by A. Harvey, 'Early literacy in Ireland', p. 14, n. 51.

109 *Auraicept na nÉces*, ed. Ahlqvist, *The Early Irish Linguist*, §§ 1. 11, 12; 5.

110 David Greene, *The Irish Language* (Dublin, 1966), 11; cf. Welsh *wy* for Irish *oí* in a borrowing going the other way, *macwyf < macc coím*).

111 But see T.F. O'Rahilly, 'The Goidels and their predecessors', *Proceedings of the British Academy* 21 (1935): 323–7 (also publ. separately), for the view that a Brittonic language was once spoken in Ireland; also his *Early Irish History and Mythology* (Dublin, 1946), 85–91.

112 It postdates w- > –gw in British, the date of which is uncertain and may have varied as between Welsh, Cornish and Breton; see *Language and History in Early Britain* § 49 (especially pp. 389–91).

113 As Paul Russell has pointed out to me, an earlier Irish form of 'Latin' survives in the gen. sg. in the title *Dúil Laithne*.

114 D. Greene, 'Some linguistic evidence relating to the British church', in M.W. Barley and R.P.C. Hanson (eds) *Christianity in Britain, 300–700* (Leicester, 1968), 82.

115 C. Mohrmann, 'The earliest continental Irish Latin', *Vigiliae Christianae* 16 (1962): 216–33.

Belfast).[116] It was apparently some years later that he formed a plan to travel to Gaul so as to live as a *peregrinus*, far from homeland and kin.[117] By then his linguistic habits were well formed. He can profitably be compared with another monastic exile of the previous century, the Briton Faustus of Riez.[118] They have the same grammatical correctness and the same ability to vary their style according to genre or context. The best example is the way they can write in a grand style at the beginning of a letter, whereas, once the substance of the matter in hand has been reached, the style becomes far less elevated.[119] The reason is straightforward: at the beginning of the letter what is at issue is the relationship of two men, the writer and his correspondent. The more the writer perceives, or chooses to be seen to perceive, himself as inferior in rank to his correspondent, the more elevated is the style. Such elevation of style in these two monastic writers is, at one and the same time, a recognition of the claims of high rank in the correspondent and an expression of monastic humility in the writer. In Columbanus's case, much more than in Faustus's, the elevation is achieved through unusual vocabulary rather than through elaborate syntax: there are Greek words such as *theoria* 'contemplation', calques instead of Greek words, when the latter had been fully assimilated, such as *speculator* for 'bishop' (rendering the literal sense of *episcopus*, 'overseer'), rare or even unique Latin words such as *castalitas* 'chastity' (from *castus* as if via **castalis*, or by analogy with such words as *liberalitas*). And then, once the perception of relative status has been fully conveyed and the writer gets down to issues rather than personalities, the style immediately comes down to earth. The appropriate virtues sought by the writer are now clarity and persuasiveness, not a flattering sensitivity to high rank.

Such linguistic expressions of social hierarchy are not surprising either in Faustus's Gaul where the British monk corresponded with senatorial aristocrats such as Ruricius, men whose support for the ideals of Lérins was crucial, or in Columbanus's Gaul where the Irish monk needed to kindle the enthusiasm of Burgundian and Frankish nobles. Similar phenomena were, however, also found in Ireland and in the Irish-settled districts of Britain; for Ireland, more even than Gaul, was a land of minute distinctions of rank, especially among the learned. There were, broadly speaking, two societies living intermingled, one sometimes called the *áes trebtha* 'the

---

116 Jonas, *Vita Columbani*, c. 3 (ed. B. Krusch, MGH Scriptores rerum Germanicarum in usum scholarum; Hanover, 1905), 157–8.

117 *peractis itaque annorum multorum in monasterio circulis*, ibid., c. 4 (ed. Krusch, 159).

118 A. Loyen, *Sidoine Apollinaire et l'esprit précieux en Gaule aux derniers jours de l'empire* (Paris, 1943), 124–9, distinguishes between practical letters and 'lettres d'art'. The letters of Faustus and Columbanus fall principally into the first class, but the introductions and conclusions are often closer to the second.

119 e.g. Columbanus, *Ep.* 1.1–2 (introductory high style) (ed. G.S.M. Walker, *Sancti Columbani Opera* (Scriptores Latin Hiberniae, II; Dublin, 1957), p. 3), whereas c. 3 begins the straightforward discussion of the issues and the style relaxes (in spite of *calcenteris* in the first sentence), *Fausti Reiensis . . . Opera*, ed. A. Engelbrecht (CSEL xxi; Vienna, 1891), *ep.* 8 to Ruricius (pp. 208–11); on Faustus's Latin see the introd., p. xxxiii.

120 *Cóir Anmann*, ed. W. Stokes, *Irische Texte*, III.2 (Leipzig, 1897), § 149; *Táin Bó Cúailnge Recension*, ed. C. O'Rahilly (Dublin, 1976), line 2045, contrasts the *áes trebtha* with one category within the *áes dana*, the magicians, *áes cumachta*.

people of husbandry', the other the *áes dána* 'the people of craft'.[120] The *áes dána* necessarily derived their sustenance from the *áes trebtha*, in exchange for which they exercised crafts ranging from the skills of a smith to those of a poet-seer and a teller of tales. Within the *áes dána* there was a restricted group of men skilled in words – poets and scholars – and those whose sacramental or judicial functions were exercised linguistically – priests and judges. All these crafts, both verbal and non-verbal, were arranged in elaborate hierarchies of rank, the seven grades of the poet-seer, the three of the judge, the seven of the clergy.[121] Among the crafts of the word, the minute distinctions of rank, based upon verbal skill, had immediate linguistic consequences.

Among the 'scholastic colloquies' published by W.H. Stevenson, one, the 'Hisperic Colloquy', reveals the social and linguistic conditions under which a *Laitneóir* worked.[122] The colloquy is not solely Irish in background: the craftsmen of the Latin word may move from one country to another within the British Isles. The text therefore includes a passage in which a junior scholar from another land, a *discipulus peregrinus*, approaches a master and his pupils. This device requires the stranger to identify himself not merely as an individual but as a scholar. It corresponds to the practice found both in Irish vernacular narrative and in Latin Saints' Lives whereby the stranger is asked, usually by a king or other dignitary, to identify himself. Particularly elaborate versions of this practice occur in Adomnán's Life of St Columba;[123] this custom of the world, therefore, lost nothing of its significance in the monastery. In one of Adomnán's personal identifications the stranger declares himself to be a student of scripture although he is not yet a monk.[124] In this way he reveals his *conversatio*, manner of life. The situation of the stranger in the Hisperic Colloquy was, therefore, governed by recognized conventions. Yet until the stranger has been securely placed within the social categories of the natives, the relationship between the two sides – stranger and native – is uncertain and strained. In the Hisperic Colloquy the consequence of this uncertain and strained relationship is linguistic competition. Will the stranger's Latin put the disciples of the native master to shame? Worst of all, could a foreign *discipulus* rival a native *magister* and so shame not just individuals but an entire scholastic tradition?[125] Such competitiveness and the extraordinarily elaborated language to which it gave rise is attested both in the Hisperic Colloquy and in Aldhelm's letter to Heahfrith arguing the inferiority of Irish scholarship to that offered at Canterbury by Theodore and

---

121 For the Church see the *Collectio Canonum Hibernensis*, ed. H. Wasserschleben, *Die irische Kanonensammlung* (Leipzig, 1885), Books I–IX; *Corpus Iuris Hibernici*, ed. D.A. Binchy (Dublin, 1978), 2269.35–2270.5, 2279.16–29; for the poets see *Uraicecht na Ríar*, ed. L. Breatnach (Dublin, 1987).

122 W.H. Stevenson, *Early Scholastic Colloquies* (Oxford, 1929), 12–20; what follows is heavily dependent on M. Winterbottom, 'On the *Hisperica Famina*', *Celtica* 8 (1968): 126–39.

123 e.g. I.2, II.39, ed. A.O. and M.O. Anderson, *Adomnán's Life of Columba* (revised edn, Oxford Medieval Texts; Oxford, 1991), pp. 20, 154.

124 I.2.

125 See esp. the foreign pupil's remarks, p. 14, lines 29–32, and the reply of the native pupil, lines 33–4.

Hadrian.[126] At Aldhelm's level issues of scholarly and national prestige came together. The competition in the Hisperic Colloquy is on a humbler, more local scale. The principal weapon used by the contestants is just what we should expect from reading Columbanus: rare and exotic vocabulary. Such a competition explains the purpose of the *Hisperica Famina*, indeed the function of Hisperic Latin itself. The scholar of high status does not merely speak Latin, he faminates *Ausonica dictamina*.[127] For someone approaching this linguistic phenomenon from outside, the result seems ludicrous self-advertisement. It is only within a society divided into numerous ranks and within an *áes dána* governed by competition that such linguistic behaviour makes sense.

A similar phenomenon appears in Old Irish. In the laws, and occasionally in prose tales, we meet text marked by unusual vocabulary, allusive turns of phrase, including kennings, and some syntactical peculiarities.[128] Several devices, therefore, distance such text from normal prose whether it is exposition of the law or narrative. Using a term which has been employed for some examples of consciously elevated and rarefied text, I shall call this form of the language 'rhetorical Old Irish'.[129] In the Hisperic Colloquy, as we have seen, the social situation which called for exotic Latin was uncertainty in the relative status of two or more persons. This characteristically arose from the arrival of a stranger whose learning might pose a threat to the native. In *Tochmarc Emire*, the Wooing of Emer (by Cú Chulainn), there are passages of rhetorical Old Irish, including kennings and riddles, at the point at which Cú Chulainn first approaches Emer.[130] Within these passages there are clear echoes of Latin, but, curiously, not so much of Hisperic Latin as of the style of elementary grammars.[131] In this instance, display of Latin learning, however rudimentary, marked Irish as rhetorical. This is not true for didactic Old Irish (law, exegesis, grammar) in which elementary Latin style appears in equally elementary contexts. In *Tochmarc Emire*, it should be noted, rhetorical language marks the opening of Cú Chulainn's courtship of Emer, not its success. When the relationship between them is most uncertain – when it most urgently calls for clarification – the language

---

126 Aldhelm, Letter 5, ed. R. Ehwald, *Aldhelmi Opera Omnia*, MGH, AA xv (Berlin, 1919), no. 5 (pp. 486–94); transl. in M. Lapidge and M. Herren, *Aldhelm: the prose works* (Ipswich, 1979), 163.

127 *The Hisperica Famina: I. the A-text*, ed. M. Herren (Toronto, 1975), lines 37–41.

128 D. Greene, 'Archaic Old Irish' in *Indogermanisch und Keltisch*, ed. K.H. Schmidt (Wiesbaden, 1977), 11–33; L. Breatnach, 'Canon law and secular law in early Ireland: the significance of *Bretha Nemed*', *Peritia* 3 (1984): 439–59, esp. 452–9.

129 P. Mac Cana, 'On the use of the term *retoiric*', *Celtica* 7 (1966): 65–90, argues that the original use of the marginal abbreviation *.r.* was not for *retoiric* but for *rosc* or *roscad*; for another suggestion, see D. Melia, 'Further speculation on marginal *.r.*', *Celtica* 21 (1990): 362–7. I am not trying to revive a discredited interpretation but only to characterize a type of Old Irish which had affinities with a type of Latin. It is the third type of text marked by *.r.* distinguished by Mac Cana, p. 89.

130 *Tochmarc Emire*, §§ 17–27, ed. A.G. Van Hamel, *Compert Con Culainn and Other Stories* (Dublin, 1933), 26–32.

131 *Ceist*, § 26, and *ní hansae*, §§ 20, 22. On these see T.M. Charles-Edwards, 'Review article: the Corpus Iuris Hibernici', *Studia Hibernica* 20 (1980): 147–50.

is most rhetorical. In *Táin Bó Cúailnge* the situation which gives rise to rhetorical language is different but even more ambiguous.[132] Ailill and Medb have gone on an expedition to seize the Bull of Cúailnge. They have been accompanied by Fergus, an exile from Ulster, indeed former king of Ulster, whose heroism as a warrior was as exceptional as his virility as a lover. Medb and Fergus make a secret assignation but fail to escape the notice of Ailill who sends his charioteer to spy on them. The charioteer removes Fergus's sword from its scabbard while the couple are making love. Fergus is compelled to make a wooden sword which he puts in his scabbard in place of the sword which has been removed. When the couple reappear and meet Ailill, the latter laughs at Fergus and reproaches Medb and they defend themselves, all in highly obscure rhetorical dialogue. The substitution of the wooden sword in the sheath provides an opportunity for embarrassing riddling, but riddles are only one element in a general heightening of the language.

Rhetorical Old Irish is not, however, the only form of the language which needs to be set in its social context. One way to elevate the language is to use archaism. This is more important in Old Irish than in Latin because the latter has a wider variety of ways in which to render prose exotic: poetic vocabulary, Greek loans and even the odd Hebrew item. In general, Irish had to make do with its own resources and archaism was therefore a most useful device. This had probably long been the case. A fair proportion of the ogam inscriptions date from a time when the form of the language they use – called Primitive Irish by modern scholars – was no longer spoken. Just as the Latin of post-Roman Britain stretched all the way from the grammatically correct and highly wrought prose of Gildas to phrases betraying a radical ignorance of the elements of Latin grammar, so too some ogam inscriptions are consistent in language while others combine features from different periods. The latter appear to be not only artificial in language but also incompetent in their archaism; the former may sometimes be just as artificial but at least they were inscribed in accord with the rules of a form of Irish which sometimes already lay in the past.[133] Archaisms in rhetorical Old Irish may be just as artificial and just as genuine as Primitive Irish in an ogam inscription: the tradition of using ancient language to elevate the style of a text has been an enduring feature of Irish from the ogam period to modern times.

Even ordinary, non-rhetorical Old Irish is unlikely to represent the normal spoken language of the people.[134] It is notoriously free of dialect. How odd this is can be seen from a comparison with Welsh, Old English and Old High German. Modern Welsh dialect differences sometimes go back to the OW period:[135] English

---

132 *Táin Bó Cúailnge, Recension I*, ed. C. O'Rahilly, lines 1030–1146.

133 D. McManus, *A Guide to Ogam*, §§ 5.6, 5.7 (pp. 80–2).

134 On the learned character of Old Irish see K. McCone, 'Zur Frage der Register im frühen Irischen', in S.N. Tranter and H.L.C. Tristram (eds) *Early Irish Literature – media and Communication/Mündlichkeit und Schriftlichkeit in der frühen irischen Literatur* (Tübingen, 1989), 84–7.

135 Old Welsh *ceintiru* (plural), in the Oxoniensis Prior glosses on Ovid's *Ars Amatoria*, *St Dunstan's Classbook*, ed. R.W. Hunt (Amsterdam, 1961), fo. 38^r, line 4, is South Welsh as against *cefndyrw*: cf. T.M. Charles-Edwards, 'Some Celtic kinship terms', *Bulletin of the Board of Celtic Studies* 24 (1970–2): 107–8.

was already divided into distinct dialects, recognized as different by contemporaries, as early as the time of Bede.[136] Yet English had only developed dialects since the Anglo-Saxon settlement of eastern and southern Britain.[137] Their political divisions – evidently crucial in the development of dialect – were few compared with those of the Irish. Both because of the longer period since the language was introduced into Ireland, and because political morcellation was more advanced, one would expect Irish to have more dialect than English. Yet apart from one or two uncertain items, it has none.[138] In Old High German it almost seems that every monastery had a different form of the language.[139] In Ireland, therefore, one might have expected an Iona form of Irish distinct from the Armagh or the Clonmacnois forms. Indeed, given the multiplicity of small kingdoms in Ireland and the barriers against travel – for the *áes trebtha*, but not for the *áes dána* – it is safe to assume that there were dialects; the problem is simply why these differences do not surface in the standard form of the language, which, because it alone was written, is the only form we have. Because it is the only form we have, I shall use the term 'Old Irish' for the standard form of the language between *c.*600 and *c.*900.

The uniformity of Old Irish does not show that it was merely a fossilized *Schriftsprache*, written but not spoken. It changes through time. Moreover, it was not a standard of the same kind as Classical Modern Irish in which forms from different dialects were admitted, for example both synthetic and analytic forms of the verb. If that had been the case, the presence of dialects would have been clear from the written evidence. It is more likely that Old Irish began as a single dialect which was then given a special status. That is to say, it was more like Standard Late Old English (probably based on the dialect of Winchester) than Classical Modern Irish.[140] Also orthographic distinctions prove that, in its written form, it was not uniform; the differences, however, were orthographic rather than phonological.[141] The uniformity of the language is thus clearer in its phonology and grammar than its orthography. Yet if Old Irish had simply been a *Schriftsprache* in which an early form of some dialect was preserved solely in a written form long after it had ceased to be spoken even in the area of its origin, the orthography should have been the most uniform aspect of the language. Old Irish was, therefore, a spoken language.

It was not just the language of the *áes dána* as opposed to the *áes trebtha*, nor was it just the language of the craftsmen in words.[142] When the latter wish to display their

---

136 Bede, *Historia Ecclesiastica*, II.5, ed. B. Colgrave and R.A.B. Mynors (Oxford Medieval Texts, 1969), p. 148, on Caelin versus Ceaulin.

137 A. Campbell, *Old English Grammar* (Oxford, 1959), p. 3; J. Hines, 'Philology, archaeology and the *Adventus Saxonum vel Anglorum*', in A. Bammersberger and A. Wollmann (eds) *Britain 400–600: language and history* (Heidelberg, 1990), 30–1.

138 R. Thurneysen, *A Grammar of Old Irish* (Dublin, 1946), § 16.

139 W. Braune, K. Helm and W. Mitzka, *Althochdeutsche Grammatik*, 12th edn (Tübingen, 1967), §§ 3–6.

140 H. Gneuss, 'The origin of Standard Old English and Æthelwold's School at Winchester', *Anglo-Saxon England* 1 (1972): 63–83.

141 For example, *ro-*, *do-*, as against *ru-*, *du-*.

142 McCone appears to regard Irish as simply the language of the *áes dána*, 'Zur Frage der Register im frühen Irischen', 86–7.

distinctive skills, plain Old Irish is not enough. They have to elevate their language by the devices I have already discussed. In other words, when they display their word-craft, they distance themselves from ordinary Old Irish. In straightforwardly didactic texts, however, such as homilies, in which a language immediately intelligible to the audience was appropriate, ordinary Old Irish is the medium. The natural deduction is that standard, non-dialectal Old Irish was the language of the social élite whether of the *áes dána* or of the *áes trebtha*. This language was itself not uniform: it has been shown that even in the Würzburg and Milan glosses, the main contemporary sources of Old Irish, forms characteristic of Middle Irish occur.[143] Yet even here there are no clear signs of dialect. A natural interpretation is that the later forms were close to the ordinary spoken language of the élite *c.*800, while the more standard forms represent a higher and more conservative style, normal in written texts, but not always observed in glosses.[144] That Old Irish was the language of the nobility, and not just of church-men, poets and judges, is also suggested by the close familial links between the nobility and these more privileged elements in the *áes dána*.[145] Its uniformity must reflect the ability of the *áes dána* to move around the country, but its grip on Irish society as a whole suggests that the upper ranks of the *áes trebtha* considered standard Old Irish to be a mark of status. My suggestion, therefore, is that Old Irish as we have it, namely in a standard form, with occasional non-dialectal variations, is the language both of those elements in the *áes dána* whose skills were verbal and of the nobility. Members of both these groups may well also have used their own local dialects, but in any competitive context they would be much more likely to use the standard.[146]

An instructive contrast is offered by the fate of the numerous Britons who passed under English rule in the post-Roman period. Of all the insular Celtic peoples in the early medieval period, least is known about them; yet their fate was crucial for the future shape of Britain. The British language of lowland Britain disappeared almost without trace. True, there are some British place-names; but they are remarkably few even as far west as Shropshire.[147] The British loan-words in English are even

---

143 K. McCone, 'The Würzburg and Milan glosses: our earliest sources of Mid Irish', *Ériu* 36 (1987): 85–106.

144 I have modified McCone's conclusion according to which the later forms belonged to 'a sub-literary register approximating to popular speech', ibid. 102. One would not expect glosses to exhibit 'high style', but they still do not reveal dialect.

145 Compare L. Breatnach's discussion of the Uí Buirechán in his 'Canon law and secular law in early Ireland', *Peritia* 3 (1984): 439–44, and the general rule discussed by T.M. Charles-Edwards, 'The *Corpus Iuris Hibernici*', *Studia Hibernica* 20 (1980): 161–2.

146 Note here P. Russell's suggestion, *Celtic Word-Formation: the velar suffixes* (Dublin, 1990), 109–10, that nouns in *-óc* occur only rarely in Old and Middle Irish because they were formed according to 'a sub-literary derivational pattern'. Since *-óc* is best attested in Old Irish as a way of creating hypocoristic forms of personal names, it is likely that its use was in informal, non-competitive speech. One may compare the way in which Adomnán's Columba, when speaking to peasants, uses an unusually high proportion of Latin diminu-tive forms in *-ul-*, *bocula*, *pauculus*, *uaccula* (*Vita S. Columbae*, II.20, 21 (perhaps also compare the *misellus homuncio* of II.37).

147 M. Gelling and H.D.G. Foxall, *The Place-Names of Shropshire*, I (English Place-Name Society, LXII/LXIII, 1990), xii–xvi.

more rare – a mere ten in Max Förster's list.[148] Yet Welsh showed no inhibitions in borrowing from English.[149] The exiguous traffic the other way, from British into English, cannot be explained by any paucity of contacts between the two peoples or by any mass extermination or migration of Britons. This is demonstrated very simply by considering the character of Old English both within and without the areas of the country settled by the English in any numbers. To judge by cemetery evidence, relatively few English settled west of a line running from Dorset along the Cotswolds north to the Pennines. Yet the English language west of this line was no less English than the language east of the line. There are very few Anglo-Saxon graves north of the Tees. The bulk of the inhabitants of Bernicia therefore appear to have been Britons by descent, yet Lothian became as English in language as Kent. The direct implication is that English showed an ability to assimilate tens of thousands of Britons so thoroughly that hardly a trace of British remained in the English they spoke. The relationship of English to both the cognate Scandinavian language of the Vikings and the much more distant French of the Normans was to be utterly different. The English dialects of Yorkshire and Lincolnshire betray Scandinavian influence to an even greater extent than does standard English. French had a wide impact on English from the Channel to northern Scotland. These examples suggest that what determined relations between English and the languages with which it came in contact was the social and political status of the languages concerned. Probably the number of Scandinavians settling in England was greatly inferior to the number of Britons who had earlier passed under English rule. Scandinavian linguistic influence was vastly greater because the political power and social status of the settlers were high.

The Britons were *wealas*, foreigners; and because they were foreigners they had lower status. The treatment of the *wealh* in Wessex in the late seventh century was essentially the same as that which the Salian Franks offered to their Roman subjects in the early sixth century.[150] This makes it likely that, give or take the odd detail, we have here a common approach adopted by the Germanic settlers within the empire on either side of the Channel. For the Franks the Gallo-Romans were *walas* just as the Britons were *wealas* to the English. They had a legal status, but their wergilds were around half those enjoyed by the corresponding Frankish or English rank. A Frank who entered the *trustis* or war-band of his king had a wergild of 600 *solidi*.[151] The corresponding Gallo-Roman was the *conviva regis*, the man admitted

---

148 M. Förster, 'Keltisches Wortgut im Englischen', in H. Boehmer *et al.*, *Texte und Forschungen zur englischen Kulturgeschichte. Festgabe für Felix Liebermann* (Halle, 1921), 119–41; also published separately (Halle, 1921); the list has hardly changed in D. Kastorsky's chapter, 'Semantics and vocabulary', in R.M. Hogg (ed.) *The Cambridge History of the English Language*, I *The Beginnings to 1066* (Cambridge, 1992), 318–19.

149 T.H. Parry-Williams, *The English Element in Welsh: a study of English loan-words in Welsh* (Cymmrodorion Record Series X; London, 1923), ch. 2.

150 Ine, 23.3, 24.2, 32, 46.1, 74 (ed. F. Liebermann, *Die Gesetze der Angelsachsen* (Halle, 1903–16), I.100–20) compared with *Pactus Legis Salicae*, ed. K.A. Eckhardt (MGH, Leges Nationum Germanicarum, IV. i Hanover, 1962), XLI.8–10 (note the Malberg glosses, *uualaleodi*, versus the simple *leodi* of XLI.1 and 5), XLII.4.

151 *Pactus Legis Salicae*, XLI.5.

to feast at the table of the king; he had a wergild of only 300 *solidi*.[152] Similarly the West Saxon nobleman had a wergild of 1,200 shillings, but the Welsh noble within the West Saxon kingdom had a wergild of 600 shillings. The further use of *wealh* for a slave is only a more extreme expression of the low status accorded to the alien.

The linguistic situations north and south of the Channel were, however, quite different. In Gaul the native Celtic language was all but extinct by the sixth century. The Bretons spoke British although many of them may also have spoken Latin. They were a people distinct in language, dress and social custom both from their new overlords, the Franks, and from the Gallo-Romans. Former fellow citizens of the empire though they were, the Gallo-Romans found it easier to reach an accommodation with the Franks than they did with the Bretons.[153] This may, of course, have been because the Gallo-Romans had little choice but to come to terms with Frankish power. Also, because the Bretons were much less disposed to submit to the Franks, a Gallo-Roman alliance with the Franks entailed Gallo-Roman separation from the Bretons.[154] The survival of the Breton offshoot of British is the clearest evidence that the native language survived in southern Britain in the late Roman period. Whereas, therefore, in sixth-century Gaul (outside Breton and Burgundian areas) Latin was the only widely spoken language apart from Frankish, in Britain there were three languages in competition, Latin, British and English. (I assume here that the various Germanic dialects of the invaders of Britain were so intermingled by the processes of war and settlement that a new, relatively uniform variety of Germanic was produced, namely English. It is, in any case, doubtful whether any of the dialect differences in Old English go back beyond the Germanic settlement of Britain.) Latin was spoken even in what became Wales, but British was also the language of many in lowland Britain.

The division between Latin and British was, therefore, not so much geographical as social. This is implied first by the inscriptions of post-Roman Wales and second by the different attitudes adopted by the English to Latin and British. Already in the Old English period there were numerous loans from Latin into English, whereas there were hardly any from British. As we have seen, the social and political status of the languages in contact determined the flow of loan-words. The English settlers were faced by one language, of high status but probably less widely spoken, namely Latin, and by another, British, more widely spoken but of lower status. It is not surprising that they retained their Germanic language, while the Franks of Neustria – confronted by only one language, Latin, a language spoken by aristocrats, and also the liturgical language of the Catholic church – came to abandon their native Frankish in favour of *lingua romana*.

---

152 *Pactus Legis Salicae*, XLI.8.

153 This is apparent from the treatment of the Bretons in Gregory of Tours's *Histories*, IV.4; V.16, 29, 31; IX.18,24; X.9. Similarly, Venantius Fortunatus praises Felix, bishop of Nantes, by saying that he is *iura Britannica uincens*, *Venantii Fortunati Opera Poetica*, ed. F. Leo (MGH Auctores Antiquissimi, IV.1; Berlin, 1881), III.5 (p. 154); cf. *insidiatores Britannos*, ibid, III.8 (p. 59).

154 Compare the Breton *Excerpta de Libris Romanorum et Francorum (Canones Wallici)*, A version, c. 61 (ed. L. Bieler, *The Irish Penitentials* [Dublin, 1963], p. 148).

British as a language was, therefore, losing speakers in the post-Roman period on a scale not to be matched until the twentieth century. By the same token, the nascent English formed from the various Germanic dialects introduced by the settlers was showing a remarkable capacity to assimilate large numbers of Britons without any appreciable influence from British on its grammar or vocabulary.[155] The problem is all the greater since one explanation of the uniformity of the earliest English depends on the role of the Britons who abandoned British for English. *Koinē* Greek offers a parallel. The relatively uniform Greek learned by non-Greeks in the empire of Alexander and its successor states became the standard form of the language. The numerical preponderance of the *koinē* eventually ensured that it superseded even the dialects of Greece itself. So, one might suggest in Britain: the language of Angles may have differed from that of Jutes, the language of Frisians from that of Saxons, but what survived to become English was the *koinē* learnt by the Britons under English rule. Yet if this explanation is to have any chance of being accepted, it will be necessary to explain why Old English is so lacking in any symptoms of British influence.

Bede shows in his Ecclesiastical History that two things were common knowledge about the English of his day. It was well known that English differed according to region and according to social status. He remarks in passing that the West Saxon king Cælin was known to his own people as Ceaulin.[156] The story he tells about the wounding of the Northumbrian noble Imma at the battle of the Trent in 679, and his subsequent fate at the hands of his Mercian captors, is one of the most important passages of the entire work for anyone wishing to understand early English society.[157] Imma, once in the hands of the Mercians, pretended to be a *rusticus*; he was, however, revealed to be a noble by, among other things, his language. We do not know whether the nobility of his language consisted in its phonology, grammar or vocabulary or a mixture of more than one of these, but we do know that a man's status could be indicated by the way he spoke. Indeed we know rather more since Imma's status was recognized across the boundary of a kingdom and of a dialect. A Mercian could tell the status of a Northumbrian from the way he talked. From this hard information some modest speculation may proceed. To judge by the archaeological, and indeed the historical, evidence, Northumbria was, of all the major Anglo-Saxon kingdoms, the least widely and heavily settled by Anglo-Saxons.[158] Major segments of Northumbrian territory had been British in political

155 If similarities between Welsh and English syntax, for example in the use of auxiliary verbs, are to be attributed to British influence on English, as claimed by H. Wagner, *Das Verbum in den Sprachen der Britischen Inseln* (Tübingen, 1959), 143–51, nevertheless the similarity did not emerge until the later Middle Ages. Moreover, they may well be examples of phenomena affecting neighbouring languages without the direction of influence being at all clear.

156 *Historia Ecclesiastica*, II.5 (ed. Colgrave and Mynors, p. 148).

157 *Historia Ecclesiastica*, IV.22 (20) (ed. Colgrave and Mynors, pp. 400–4).

158 L. Alcock, *Economy, Society and Warfare among the Britons and the Anglo-Saxons* (Cardiff, 1987), ch. 17.

terms, not merely in language, only a generation before Imma's experiences among the Mercians.[159] We have seen already that the overriding disadvantage suffered by British as against its rivals was its low social standing. This was particularly true when British was the language of defeated and dishonoured *wealas*. And, finally, it is safe to assume that the first generation or two of Britons to use English would certainly not use an English uninfluenced by British. On this basis it can be immediately deduced that prominent among the features of rustic, low-status English avoided by men such as Imma, were any elements of Northumbrian English associated with the Britons. To speak a language in any way reminiscent of *Wilisc* was to be marked out as a *wealh*.

It may be objected that in a small-scale agricultural society few would think of language in grand national terms. They might have a keen awareness of local dialect differences, but only scholars such as Bede would have thought of the languages of whole nations. In some periods this may be true, but in the early Middle Ages, in the exceptional conditions created by the Anglo-Saxon settlement of Britain, horizons were necessarily wider. True, it is Bede who provides some of the clearest evidence linking language and national identity, but he is not alone.[160] The very terms for language and nation in Old English – and also in Welsh and Irish – betray the same link.[161] One must also take into account the surprising fact that the earliest laws of a Saxon king, the West Saxon code promulgated by Ine, use *Englisc* not *Seaxe* whenever the context involves a contrast with the Britons, the *Wealas*.[162] It was this contrast with British and the Britons, a contrast of direct local significance all the way from the Channel coast to the frontiers of Dál Riata and Pictland, which made English the linguistic bond of a nation. By the same token, once the descendants of a Briton had passed from speaking British as their first language to speaking an English coloured by British, and then on to a purer form of English, they would have conclusively thrown off British nationality. The social and political disadvantages of being a *wealh* were such that the population of much of lowland Britain took this road. They probably did so all the more easily because the low status of British *vis-à-vis* English only continued its earlier low status *vis-à-vis* Latin. In what was to become England British had been under attack for centuries; the linguistic nationalism of the new settlers was only the final blow.

The story of Cunedda and his sons first appeared as a tale of British revival.[163] Even on the eastern frontier of Wales there could be smaller-scale recoveries of

---

159 Notably Elmet conquered by Edwin, *Historia Brittonum*, c. 63, and Lothian, probably conquered by Oswald: K. Jackson, 'Edinburgh and the Anglian occupation of Lothian', in *The Anglo-Saxons: studies presented to Bruce Dickins*, ed. P. Clemoes (London, 1959), 35–47.

160 *Historia Ecclesiastica*, I.1 (ed. Colgrave and Mynors, p. 16); III.6 (ed. Colgrave and Mynors, p. 130); *Felix's Life of St. Guthlac*, ed. B. Colgrave (Cambridge, 1956), ch. 34.

161 In Old English while þeod is the people, geþeode is both language and people (compare geþeodan 'to unite'). In Welsh iaith is both language and nation, cyfiaith, literally 'joint-language' is both the people sharing the same language and the person who is a fellow countryman.

162 Ine 24, 46.1, 54.2, 74 (ed. Liebermann, I.100, 110, 114, 120).

163 *Historia Brittonum*, cc. 14, 62.

territory, as the Pillar of Eliseg proudly claims for Powys in the eighth century.[164] Within Wales, however, the status of Welsh was transformed. Gildas rebukes Maelgwn, the pupil of 'the *magister elegans* of almost all Britain',[165] for abandoning the religious life, murdering his way back to the throne, and then allowing himself to be praised, in spite of his flagrant sins, by a yelling mob of encomiasts.[166] These have generally, and I believe rightly, been taken to be poets praising Maelgwn in British. It is not clear, however, that they were repellent in Gildas's eyes because they sang Maelgwn's praises in British; the crucial point was rather that they poured glory on such a notorious sinner. Nevertheless the contrast which Gildas allows to be drawn but does not emphasize is between a *magister* whose refined learning was indubitably in Latin and a crowd of sycophants whose praises of Maelgwn were as physically repulsive in delivery as they were unmerited by their subject. Gildas's words suggest that even if British, unlike Latin and Irish, was not admitted to the distinction of being carved in stone, it was admitted to court. While Voteporix was probably praised in Irish and was certainly commemorated in both Latin and Irish, Maelgwn was probably praised in Welsh.

One of the most obscure questions about the Britons in the post-Roman period is how far there was a reaction against the cultural depreciation of the British language, a depreciation which had been a central aspect of romanization and was inherited both by the English and by the Irish settlers in Britain. It cannot have been a far-reaching reaction since Gildas and Maelgwn's *magister elegans*, as well as the Latin inscriptions of the period, demonstrate the survival of a high Latin culture alongside a spoken form of the language. The claim that Cadfan, king of Gwynedd in the early seventh century, was *sapientissimus* suggests that the cultural values of late Roman Christianity had not been abandoned.[167] Similarly, the few surviving Welsh manuscripts of the pre-Norman period admit Welsh, as we have seen, only to the margins or the interlinear spaces of the parchment page. It looks as though the continued prestige of Latin caused the rise in the status of Welsh to be confined largely to poetry. The rise was therefore in a primarily oral form. Poetry was sometimes written down, as the Juvencus *englynion* and, probably, the textual history of the *Gododdin* show.[168] If there had been a less miserable survival rate of early medieval Welsh manuscripts, there might even have been more evidence for Welsh prose. The marginalia in the Lichfield Gospels show that Welsh, interspersed with Latin, could be used for weighty purposes such as the attestation of land-grants or of manumissions.[169] Apart from such rare appearances of Welsh prose, the existence

164 *EWGT* 2.
165 Gildas, *De Excidio*, c. 36.
166 Ibid., c. 34. 6; on which see P. Sims-Williams, 'Gildas and vernacular poetry', in *Gildas: new approaches* (Woodbridge, 1984), 169–92.
167 *ECMW* no. 13.
168 I. Williams, *The Beginnings of Welsh Poetry*, 89–121; D.N. Dumville, 'Early Welsh poetry: problems of historicity', 4–7.
169 *The Text of the Book of Llan Dâv*, ed. J. Gwenogvryn Evans (Oxford, 1893; reprinted Aberystwyth, 1979), xliii–xlvii; D. Jenkins and M.E. Owen, 'The Welsh marginalia in the Lichfield Gospels', *Cambridge Medieval Celtic Studies* 5 (Summer 1983): 37–66; 7 (Summer, 1984): 91–120.

of a recognized orthography for Welsh shows that it had a widely acknowledged status as a written language.

The contrast, however, with Irish remains. While Irish was, from the fifth and sixth centuries, admitted to a dignity second only to that of Latin, whether in inscriptions or in grammars, Welsh scarcely appears in inscriptions at all and the earliest grammar is late medieval. Irish soon became a language written for all purposes – law, poetry, narrative, exegesis – while the range of surviving written Old Welsh is much more limited. Poetry seems to have been the principal early medium in which Welsh attained high status, to be followed only later by law and prose narrative. The explanation of the contrast lies in the historical conditions of the fifth and sixth centuries. While Irish entered Britain in the late Roman and post-Roman periods as the language of a conquering people, British had long been greatly inferior in status to Latin and was to remain so for centuries. There was perhaps a rise in the status of British in the sixth and seventh centuries as the Britons gained some control of the Irish Sea, but on their eastern frontier the great movement from British to English speech, and therefore from British to English nationality continued apace until the eighth century. Even in Brittany, the Gallo-Roman neighbours of the Bretons preferred to throw in their lot with the long-haired Merovingians rather than with their former fellow citizens of the empire, exemplary in their *Romanitas* though the hair-cuts of Breton laymen may have been.[170]

Because British had low status by comparison with Latin, Irish and English, it was more subject to external influence. Much the most important such influence was that of Latin. In vocabulary and even in grammar, British was strongly marked by the centuries of political subjection to Rome and cultural subjection to Latin. The existence of a pluperfect in Welsh, Cornish and Breton, but not in Irish, has been attributed to the example of Latin.[171] While such a theory cannot be demonstrated, it is a serious possibility. Similarly, the use of compound prepositions is widespread in Late Latin and in the Brittonic languages, as in Welsh *oddiwrth* or Latin *usque ad in* and *desuper*.[172] More generally, British lay within two linguistic zones. The first was constituted by the Latin-speaking part of the empire; British, together with all varieties of Late Latin, but unlike Irish and English, shared the loss of distinctive vowel length and extensive loss of declension. The second linguistic area was a northern European zone to which the Insular Celtic and Germanic languages

---

170 As suggested by the *Excerpta de Libris Romanorum et Francorum* (*Canonesa Wallici*), c. 61 (ed. Bieler, *The Irish Penitentials*, p. 148).

171 P. Mac Cana, 'Latin influence on Brittonic: the pluperfect', *Latin Script and Letters: Festschrift presented to Ludwig Bieler on the occasion of his 70th Birthday* (Leiden, 1976), 194–203. Paradigms are given by H. Lewis and H. Pedersen, *A Concise Comparative Celtic Grammar* (Göttingen, 1961), § 460 = H. Pedersen, *Vergleichende Grammatik der keltischen Sprachen*, 2 vols (Göttingen, 1909–13), § 615.

172 D. Greene, 'Some linguistic evidence relating to the British church', 76, following A. Sommerfelt, 'External versus internal factors in the development of language', *Norsk Tidsskrift for Sprogvidenskap* 19 (1960): 304; M. Leumann, J.B. Hofmann and A. Szantyr, *Lateinische Grammatik*, II: *Syntax und Stilistik* (Munich, 1965), § 160; Väänänen, *Introduction au latin vulgaire*, § 203 (on adverbs); D.S. Evans, *A Grammar of Middle Welsh* (Dublin, 1964), e.g. § 223.

belonged – a zone characterized by apocope, syncope and associated umlaut phenomena, all occurring within a period stretching from the fourth to the eighth century. The two zones are thus of slightly different date: the Latin zone was obviously a consequence of the empire, while the distinctive characteristics of the northern area were acquired in the immediate post-Roman period, at a time when Britain was subject to invasion and settlement both from the west and from the east. The development of British therefore reveals, in outline, the history of north-western Europe in the Roman and post-Roman periods.

The Irish language was much less deeply influenced by Latin than was British. Yet, because Irish enjoyed a higher status than did British, and because the *áes dána*, the men of craft and learning, enjoyed a privileged position in society, the prestige of Latin as a written language encouraged them to give their native language a similar standing. Their language, too, was to be worthy of stone monument and parchment book. The richness of Early Irish literature is a paradox: it owes its existence to the example and challenge of Latin, but also to the independence of Ireland from the Roman Empire. If Ireland had been part of the empire, Irish would have had a status similar to that of British, one local language among many, overshadowed by the immense cultural prestige of Latin.

Abbreviations

CSEL   Corpus Scriptorum Ecclesticorum Latinorum.
EWGT   *Early Welsh Genealogical Tracts,* ed. P.C. Bartrum (Cardiff, 1966)
ECMW   *The Early Christian Monuments of Wales,* V. E. Nash-Williams (Cardiff, 1950)
GPC   *Geiriadur Prifysgol Cymru*
MGH   Monumenta Germaniae Historica
ZCP   *Zeitschrift für celtische Philologie*

EARLY CHRISTIANITY AND ITS MONUMENTS

——— •◆• ———

Mark Redknap

HISTORICAL BACKGROUND

Of all the developments to take place following the meeting of Roman and Celtic worlds, it was Christianity that had the most profound effect on Celtic society and material culture. Centred on the Life of Christ, the Bible and numerous commentaries, and supported by strong codes of ethics and morality, it introduced writing to regions in which it had hitherto been absent, and through its active ministry promoted education and the arts.

The Irish sources for the early medieval period are rich in comparison with those for other regions, and this imbalance has resulted in a popular Hibernocentric view of early medieval Christianity, mythologized to some degree into a 'Celtic church', with Irish characteristics extended to other regions. However, this view is changing in the light of recent research, and much regional diversity is now recognized within Celtic areas.

Christianity appears to have been well established in Roman Britain during the fourth century as one of the state-tolerated religions in a pantheistic society. The structure and organization of the early church were based on that of the state – provinces under bishops, who were to begin with 'local spiritual chairmen'. Towns and congregations may have been served by bishops, and it has been argued that, as elsewhere in the late Roman Empire, the church was organized into territorial dioceses. During this period, native pagan cults continued to be followed, and some resurgence of deity worship at pagan temples is suggested. At Caerwent, for example, there is limited evidence for the presence of a Christian community side by side with paganism.[1]

In some areas of Britain romanization had little lasting impact, and in regions remote from Roman administration a form of Celtic social order may have persisted, leading, in the fifth century, to the re-emergence of native aristocracy in some areas, and to the development of princely kingdoms that may echo former tribal patterns. A number of presumptions may be made about early Christianity in fifth- to eighth-century Britain from the literary sources, though hard facts are rare, and often biased. Our view of its early history is coloured by Gildas's denunciation of the church and society among the Britons, calling it complacent and corrupt. His *De Excidio et*

Conquestu Britanniae mentions monks, abbots and deacons, suggesting the existence of an episcopally organized church with roots in late Roman Britain, and he criticizes the bishops and priests for supporting tyrants such as Vortipor and Maelgwyn Gwynedd.

Certainly there was British missionary work in Wales, Scotland and Ireland in the fifth and early sixth centuries, and there were ascetic holy people withdrawn from society. Such characteristics were not exclusive to the Celtic West, and similar activity can also be found in England and on the Continent at this period (Davies 1992: 14). In 431 Palladius, a deacon of the important church at Auxerre, was sent by Pope Celestine as the first official bishop to the growing Christian community (the 'believers in Christ') in Ireland in order to counteract the Pelagian heresy, which claimed that man's free will was independent of divine grace. Patrick, following his consecration as a bishop, returned to Ireland (the scene of his boyhood enslavement by raiders) to minister to the Christian community there. Patrick said that 'many thousands' were taken into captivity alongside himself, suggesting the existence of numerous Christians in Ireland in the late fourth century (certainly by the first decades of the fifth century). It is not hard to imagine an earlier process of gradual acculturation and limited conversion supported by a ruling class, initially by direct contact with the Continent and Christian parts of western Britain such as south-west Wales, via trade or mercenary activity, before the stimulus provided by Palladius and Patrick from the continental and British churches respectively. Indeed, the role of missionaries and martyrs has been exaggerated to some degree in the historical records. Much conversion may have been at a kin-based and local level via returning inhabitants, as well as via conversion of the aristocracy. The nature of 'Celtic' society in fifth- and sixth-century Ireland, Wales and Scotland was of small independent tribal kingdoms, with a rural, hierarchical and familial character. It appears that, by the sixth century, ecclesiastical organization in Celtic-speaking Britain was being modified to fit local circumstances, under external influences.

By the sixth century Christianity had become established in Ireland, though it co-existed with pagan society (Figure 37.1). The extent of Christianity in lowland England at this time remains a subject of debate. It is thought that in sub-Roman Wales and Cornwall and those parts of England not occupied by pagan Germanic settlers, bishops and sub-Roman dioceses may have continued in a form related to the emergent native kingdoms. It is unclear whether Christianity in the fifth–sixth century attained more than local importance in southern Scotland, as suggested by a few commemorative stones. Dioceses have been suggested based at Carlisle and Whithorn (for Rheged), the south side of the Forth (for the area of the Gododdin), Glasgow (associated with St Kentigern for Strathclyde) and the Tweed valley (for Bernicia). Bede, writing in the 720s, records the tradition that the British bishop Ninian, who had been regularly instructed in Roman Christian practice, preached at Whithorn, a principal settlement near the Galloway coast, where he built a stone church in the Roman fashion, called *Candida Casa* (or 'the White House').[2] In general, Christianity appears to have spread across most of southern Scotland among the British and southern Picts by about 600. The situation amongst the Scotti of western Scotland and northern Picts is clearer. Following the establishment by St Columba of the community at Iona in 563 or shortly thereafter, the monastery

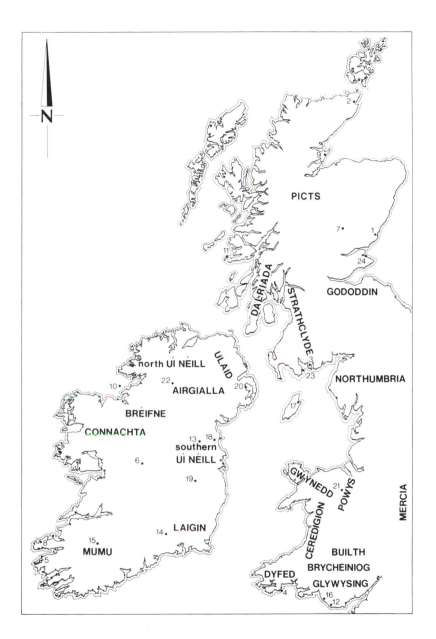

Figure 37.1 Selected sites mentioned in the text, and kingdoms: 1 – Aberlemno; 2 – Ackergill; 3 – Ardwall Island; 4 – Caldy Island; 5 – Church Island; 6 – Clonmacnois; 7 – Dunfallandy; 8 – Gallarus/Reask; 9 – Hilton of Cadboll; 10 – Inishmurray; 11 – Iona; 12 – Llantwit Major; 13 – Kells; 14 – Kilkieren/Ahenny; 15 – Kilmacoo; 16 – Margam; 17 – Maughold; 18 – Monasterboice; 19 – Moone; 20 – Nendrum; 21 – Valle Crucis; 22 – White Island; 23 – Whithorn; 24 – St Andrews.

became one of the most influential centres of missionary activity and learning in Europe, and principal church for the kingdom of Dalriada, sending missionaries to the Picts, and establishing communities in Ireland, Scotland and England. One result was Aidan's foundation of Lindisfarne (Holy Island), famous for its role in the conversion of Northumbria, and the original monastery of Melrose (Mailros), referred to by Bede in 731.

Recent studies of the early religious communities in post-Roman Britain have moved from a polarized debate on whether church organization was episcopal or monastic towards an examination of the level of pastoral care and methods of ministry (Blair and Sharpe 1992). The old distinctions between the clichés of the 'Celtic' and Roman church, of monastic and episcopal dioceses, and of wandering monks are now being reassessed by comparative study.

The deliberate withdrawal of individuals from material affairs – the solitary or eremitical form of monasticism – was practised from an early time, as evidenced by Patrick, Ninian and St Germanus of Auxerre (d. 448). St Samson of Dol moved from the busy monastery of Llantwit Major to Caldey Island, then as a hermit to a cave near the Severn, and ultimately as a bishop established three monasteries (*monasteria*) in Cornwall and Brittany. That he baptized converts in Cornwall, according to the Breton Life of St Samson, suggests that he probably performed the same sacrament in South Wales when bishop (Pryce 1992: 42). The sacrament of baptism required only the availability of water, and it is not difficult to envisage in the initial phases baptism taking place in lakes or rivers, or at springs in the open air. The Christian rite of baptism, involving purification and spiritual refreshment by water, readily merged with pre-Christian Celtic tradition. The veneration of springs and wells, many of which were miraculously created for a saint to baptize, is common in Ireland, Cornwall, Wales, Scotland and Brittany. Water was (and is) seen as a symbol of purification and life, and some sites with antecedent well worship may have been important venues of pre-Christian ritual activity.

Dedications to Celtic saints were widespread, as they are today, and suggest the influence of religious centres and the popularity of their cults. The early cult of saints was usually associated with early Christian martyrs, and dedications to universal saints such as Peter can illustrate links with Rome. A wider veneration of individual saints had evolved throughout the Christian world from the fourth century. In Celtic areas, they came to be associated with principal ecclesiastical figures, including missionaries such as Patrick or founders of ecclesiastical sites such as Columba. Places or relics associated with these saints were venerated (a practice with pagan roots), and Gildas records that veneration of martyrs' tombs was taking place in Britain in the sixth century. Some Celtic saints may have been international (e.g. Columba), national (e.g. Patrick) or local (e.g. Iestyn, Cadog and Cynog). By the seventh–eighth century this had developed to the extent where the veneration of relics of *local* saints was common. The discovery in early cemeteries of special graves respected by subsequent activity may indicate foci for such special devotion. Bones were seen to have great powers, and the whole body of the saint appears to have been important; in Wales at least (though not necessarily Ireland), there seems to have been opposition to its division (N. Edwards, in litt.).

Secondary relics and places associated with saints were also viewed as being endowed with healing properties. Bells, books and croziers were important secondary relics characteristic of Celtic areas, and oaths sworn on holy books, bells and the remains of saints (often head, arm or hand bones) in particular were considered to have great power. Many cults were centred on churches promoted by the royal house, unifying royal and saintly power.

Groups of monks living in one fixed community, subject to regular rule and under an abbot were in existence by the sixth century. The concept of such a 'communal hermitage', closely linked to eremitical monasticism of the solitary monk (the distinction between the two was not always sharp) may have arrived as a result of contact with the Mediterranean and Gaul.

Recent work has shown that there was no institutional church structure encompassing all Celtic countries, but rather regional differences and regional synods where bishops met and decided church affairs. There was no universally recognized 'Celtic church', and the lack of unity is illustrated well by the disputes concerning the differing methods of calculating the date of Easter, and the gradual adoption of the nineteen-year cycle of Dionysius. Following the Frankish Council of Orleans in 541, it was adopted by different regions at different dates: in southern Ireland in the 630s, some parts of Britain by 703, in others by 731, on Iona and in Pictland in 716, and in Wales in 768 (Davies 1992: 14).

Church and monastic organization in Ireland have been shown to be complex, with arguments for mother-churches or head churches of the *tuath* ('people' or small kingdom), staffed by pastorally active communities (Sharpe 1992: 81). Similarly the distinction formerly made between 'monastic' and pastoral roles is no longer possible in Wales, where monasteries had a variety of royal, episcopal and proprietary origins (Blair and Sharpe 1992: 6).

The evidence from authors such as Gildas for the presence of these Christian leaders and thinkers in the fifth century is complemented by the presence in Wales of early inscribed stones of Christian association. From the sixth century religious establishments are attested there under a variety of terms.[3] While churches in Celtic areas were largely without archbishops and metropolitan provinces, occasionally honorific titles were held, and prominent bishops sometimes behaved as if they sought archiepiscopal authority (Davies 1992: 14), though authority in most areas lay with bishops and abbots. It appears that monastic communities contained both secular and monastic clergy, some under a bishop, as at St Davids, some under an abbot, who could in the later period be a layman as at Llanbadarn Fawr in 1188 (Pryce 1992: 53). Up to the eighth century, the term *monasterium* was in use in Wales, but later the word *clas* (pl. *clasau*) was used for a mother-church. Unlike England, Benedictine monasticism did not take root in Wales until the eleventh century.

Ecclesiastical centres were established in Cornwall certainly by the mid-tenth century, and probably earlier (possibly by the sixth century, indicated by the *Vita Samsonis*). In Ireland, some monasteries were established by the middle of the sixth century, such as Clonmacnois by Ciarán (d. 549), and c.563 Iona in western Scotland was founded by Columba. The new institutions of the church appear to have been absorbed successfully into Irish society, though the structure known elsewhere in western Europe was less suited to Irish social and political life, which lacked a Roman administrative precursor. The result was the growth of monastic churches with holdings scattered all over the country. Influential Irish missionary activity, in the form of *peregrinationes* through Europe, began *c.*590 with the departure of Columbanus, first Irish missionary to the Continent, from Bangor (Co. Down) to Burgundy. His three Irish foundations at Luxeuil, Fontaine and Annagray were to become influential centres in Merovingian Gaul. The charisma of such personalities led to a growth in the number of Frankish houses under disciples influenced by Columbanus ('Hiberno-Frankish' monasticism). It should at the same time be remembered that a complex network of connections developed between *scriptoria* in Ireland and the Celtic West, and Northumbria and the Continent, from the middle of the seventh century. The influence of the Irish church, which was active alongside the Anglo-Saxon church on the Continent, must be set alongside that of other non-Celtic missionary activity.

The degree of monastic dominance in church affairs, and the deviation of Ireland from regular church administration, are under debate (Sharpe 1984). Conflict was supposed between the two diocesan and monastic systems of ecclesiastical organization with the records indicating eventual monastic supremacy. The conventional view has been of a weak episcopal church, contrasted to the growth in the sixth and seventh century of monastic churches or federations (called *paruchiae*, the word originally used to designate a diocese) linked to the emergence and fortunes of dynastic families, who provided both kings and church leaders. This was thought to have resulted in differences in organization between Ireland and her neighbours, with primacy of the authority of the abbot rather than bishop, and tribal bishoprics/monastic federations rather than territorial dioceses. A model has recently been proposed of communities of priests and other clergy (some monks under vows) in mother-churches as centres of pastoral care, which was provided at a more local level through small churches, each under a single priest.[4] Monastic life in eighth- and ninth-century Ireland can be seen as of collegiate or communal rather than of private, contemplative Benedictine form.

Davies has pointed out that diversity in religious practice was common in Europe and within Celtic areas in the seventh–eighth century, that private penance cannot be seen as exclusively characteristic of Celtic churches, and that there were deviations in the adoption of the tonsure (crown-like or ear-to-ear).

> Not only was there diversity within Celtic churches but a constant tendency for the Welsh to be the most conservative (*vide* the Easter controversy), and for a party of the Irish (often southern Irish) to be most clearly influenced by Roman practice.
>
> (Davies 1992: 18)

In short, it would appear that around this time regional characteristics were emerging, and that by the eleventh century all Celtic regions looked 'deviant' to the leaders of the newly reformed western church, being only slightly changed by continental reform (Davies 1992: 20).

The importance of the church within Celtic society, coupled with the scholarship of individual churchmen, and the development of learning in a shared Latin culture, are reflected in the artistic achievements of the different ecclesiastical centres. One of the most profound changes brought about in Celtic society was the development of literacy – in some areas such as Wales a continuation of Romano-British practice, in Ireland a new introduction (see below on ogam).[5] Monastic centres, endowed with royal patronage and protection, formed foci in manpower, skills, and resources for local improvements, and (as at royal sites) bases for craftsmen in stone, metal and other materials: centres such as Armagh, Clonmacnois, Clonard and Glendalough in Ireland, Iona and St Andrews in Scotland, Llancarfan, Llanilltud Fawr, Llanbadarn Fawr in Wales, and St Petroc's monastery, Bodmin, in Cornwall. It was in the monastic *scriptoria* that manuscripts were adorned with characteristic decoration and lettering in half-uncial, a development of the older uncial script. Pilgrimage, described by a Carolingian writer as second nature to the Irish, resulted in the preservation of many valuable manuscripts and books written in 'Insular' script (*libri Scottici scripti*) in continental libraries. The role of the church as an important repository for secular goods, as well as place of pilgrimage and recipient or donor of gifts, resulted in a new powerful Christian authority whose support the ruling aristocracies needed: the monasteries.

THE ARCHAEOLOGICAL EVIDENCE

While later religious foundations may be indicated by historical evidence from charters and Saints' Lives, archaeological evidence has provided a more detailed picture of earlier foundations through survey and excavation.

Early ecclesiastical sites may be identified by concentrations of early inscribed stones, types of burial and field monuments such as cemetery enclosures. Unmarked sites in Wales may be indicated by place-name elements: *llan* (enclosure), or *merthyr* (Latin *martyrium*), denoting a site where a saint was buried. Aerial photography has assisted the recognition of curvilinear graveyard enclosures which may represent early ecclesiastical boundaries. In contrast to the cremation of earlier periods, Christian burial involved inhumation, usually without grave goods, and orientated with the head to the west. Early burials may have been isolated or in open groups; circular banks and ditches forming the enclosure (*llan*) may be a secondary development of a Christian burial area. Graves may take several forms: long cist graves made up of stone slabs are characteristic of British rather than English areas, though unlined graves are known, as is clustering of graves around a specially marked burial. Burial near to that of a saint or martyr was thought to give more assurance of participation in the Resurrection, and on some sites the tomb shrine of the founder saint became a focus for ritual. It could take several forms, being marked in the open by cross-decorated pillars or cross slabs, A-roofed tombs or box shrines of decorated stones (the latter from the end of the seventh century) or even tomb-shrines set apart from the principal church on the site (Herity 1993: 194). Some specially marked graves, such as those recently excavated in Wales, may be aristocratic: at Tandderwen, Clwyd, a small proportion of graves had been enclosed by square-plan ditches (the cemetery is associated with radiocarbon dates of ad 510 and ad 860: Brassil, Owen and Britnell 1990: 46f.), and prominent graves have been identified at Llandegai and Cae Capel Eithin, Gwynedd.

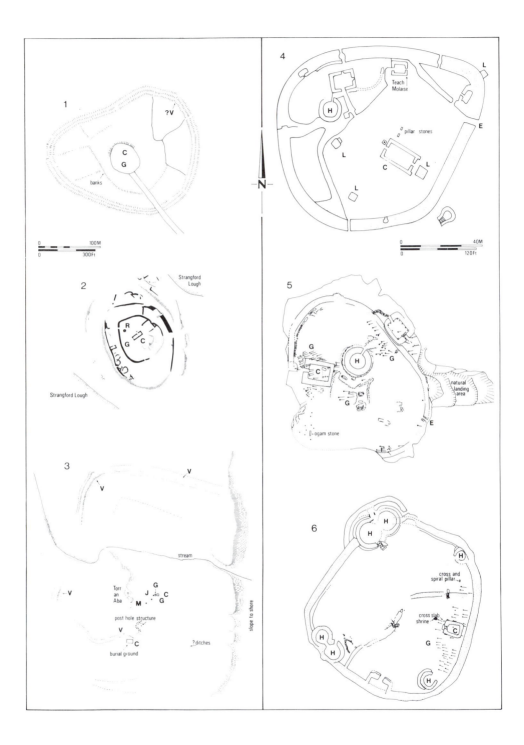

Small Ecclesiastical Sites

Early religious centres probably conformed in general physical appearance to a similar pattern throughout western and northern Britain. The earliest churches and associated buildings were probably of wood, which continued to be used well beyond the tenth century.[6] Churches of large size appear comparatively early, as indicated by the seventh-century description of the wooden church at Kildare (Radford 1977: 5–6). The larger church sites are characterized by multiple churches used for different purposes. Small churches, less suitable for large congregations, are associated with small ecclesiastical sites of uncertain status, such as Church Island, Co. Kerry (Figure 37.3).

In Ireland, a range of small church sites has now been recognized which probably provided some level of pastoral care in the rural community.[7] It has been estimated that the known pre-ninth-century place and tribal names in Ireland include those of approximately 250 churches, using elements such as *dumach* (grave-mound), *cell* (*cella, cellola, aecclesia*), *senchell* (*sen chell*, 'old church'), *domnach* (*dominicus*, 'little church') (Sharpe 1992). It would appear that as late as the seventh century, lay people were buried in the traditional burying place of the kin group – Christians, distinguished by crosses, may have lain side by side with pagans. Burial in consecrated ground need not have been usual or normal at this date (O'Brien 1992), though in Ireland every church was expected to have a burial ground (Rule of Patrick, 6).

Many early ecclesiastical sites are still places of Christian devotion, either with continuing use of the cemetery, or visits to holy wells (such as St Seiriol's well, Penmon, Gwynedd, and Holywell, Clwyd) or to the tombs of founding saints. This has often limited archaeological work to rescue investigations, and more extensive excavation is needed before their development can be fully understood. The general form and layout of some smaller eccelesiastical sites may be illustrated by a few published examples (Figure 37.2).

Church Island (Co. Kerry; Figures 37.2, no. 5) is a small ecclesiastical site on a tidal islet on the north side of Valencia Island. The first of the two main phases

---

Figure 37.2 Plans of some early ecclesiastical sites (no phasing is shown).

Key: G = graves, C = church, V = vallum, E = entrance, L = leacht, H = house or *clochan*, R = round tower, J = St John's cross, M = St Martin's cross

1 – Probable ecclesiastical site at Kilmacoo, Co. Cork (redrawn from Hurley 1982; fig. 18.7); 2 – Nendrum, Co. Down (redrawn from Archaeological Survey of Northern Ireland 1966); 3 – Iona, where Adomnán mentions a church (*ecclesia; oratorium; sacra domus*), a number of huts for monks (*cubicula*), a hut where Columba slept with bare rock for couch and stone for a pillow (*domus; hospitium; hospitiolum*), one in a higher place for writing (*tegoriolum; tegorium*), a building for guests (*hospitium*), a communal building probably with kitchen (*domus; monasterium*), a barn (*horreum*) and shed (*canaba*). The plan is based on ground and geophysical survey and excavation (Royal Commission on the Ancient and Historical Monuments of Scotland); 4 – Inishmurray, Co. Sligo (redrawn from Wakeman 1893: 13); 5 – Church Island, Co. Kerry (redrawn from O'Kelly 1958: pl. XVII); 6 – Reask, Co. Kerry (redrawn from Fanning 1981: fig. 2).

Figure 37.3 *Above:* Gallarus oratory, Co. Kerry. *Overleaf:* St McDara's Church, Cruach Mac Dara, Galway, prior to restoration by the Office of Public Works, Ireland. Certain Irish stone churches have distinctive gable finials and antae (projections of the side walls beyond the gable ends), and it has been suggested that the earliest examples are those displaying wooden skeuomorphic features (i.e. borrowed from wooden structures). Few bear elaborate architectural carving, in contrast with those in Northumbria, and it is likely that early stone buildings were rare, most surviving examples probably dating to the eleventh or twelfth centuries. The boat-shaped, corbelled oratories such as Gallarus are probably of similar date, though the earlier (possible eighth-century) beehive cells of Skellig Michael, Co. Kerry, may represent a stone version of timber buildings. (Photos: The Office of Public Works, Ireland.)

comprised some thirty-three burials aligned on a small wooden structure, interpreted as a tiny chapel or oratory. Evidence for a small wooden round-house was found to the east. Phase 2 involved the replacement of the chapel with a larger, stone church, on which some eight burials were aligned. The wooden round-house appears to have been replaced about the same time with one of stone. The presence of a female amongst the phase 1 burials suggests that the buildings may have served the local people, under a priest. A seventh–eighth-century ogam stone on the site was not found *in situ*, and the stone church may be as late as the twelfth century.

At Reask, on the Dingle peninsula (Co. Kerry; Figure 37.2, no. 6) early activity is indicated by postholes possibly belonging to a circular structure whose hearth has been radiocarbon-dated to between the late third and mid-seventh centuries. The

stone-walled enclosure around cist and unlined graves may be contemporary. A cross-and-spiral decorated pillar of sixth- or seventh-century date may mark the edge of the cemetery. Later phases include corbelled stone huts (*clochans*), one containing evidence for ironworking. The second phase included the construction of a stone church partially over the earlier cemetery. Without the evidence of the inhumation bone which has not survived, the precise religious function of this site, and whether it was monastic, remains unclear. However, the fine collection of sculpture does indicate that it was an important ecclesiastical site.

Evidence for early Christian activity at the monument popularly known as Dunmisk Fort, Co. Tyrone, comprises a timber building (possibly a small church or shrine), debris associated with glass- and metalworking, an industrial area, and a burial ground which shows distinct burial patterns: in the centre, well-spaced graves in lines running south-west/north-east focused around a large pit which may originally have held a cross or pillar stone. To the east of the church, a number of large, elaborate graves were found, some marked with kerbstones or cappings of white pebbles. The site has been interpreted as that of a small monastic community, though the presence of mixed burial (all ages and both sexes) suggests that it may have served the surrounding area, perhaps also through the manufacture of goods (Ivens 1989; Henderson and Ivens 1992: 56). The elaborate graves may be those of abbots or ecclesiastics, or important lay persons. Sometimes the evidence is less definite. At Tullylish, Co. Down, where the Annals of Ulster record a community as early as AD 809, excavations have revealed a massive ditch in use in the seventh century, filled by the ninth century and replaced by a large outer, steep-sided rock-cut ditch (Ivens 1988: 55–6). Both may relate to monastic occupation, but this is not certain.

Large Ecclesiastical Centres

Many important ecclesiastical sites (*monasteria*) were located close to land or water routes, giving easy access to good communications (either close to the coast, or on navigable rivers). Such centres from the seventh–eighth centuries possessed similar, simple layouts – usually within a sub-circular enclosing bank (*vallum*) or stone wall symbolizing the boundary between sacred and profane, and invested with properties of sanctuary and divine protection. These were sometimes set inside earlier enclosures, or constructed as new, occasionally rectilinear earthworks (favoured where no other boundaries existed). The area enclosed was often organized into two or three concentric areas, each with its own enclosing wall, for the particular needs of the population. The church (or multiple churches in the case of larger ecclesiastical sites) may be sited within a central enclosure (or within small separate enclosures). Early cross-marked pillars may mark separate graves, or graves in the cemetery, an important part of every early monastery, often positioned close to the principal church. Such cemeteries may have served the needs of both community and local royal and noble families. Cross-marked stones were in some areas later replaced by more elaborate recumbent grave slabs. Some Irish monasteries were enclosed by two or more walls, separating the inner enclosure (which often contained an abbot's house, round tower, stone churches, cemetery and large freestanding crosses) from the outer area, an enclosure for industrial, commercial and domestic activities, all of which were essential for the prosperity of the community. Round towers (called *cloigtech* or belfry in Irish texts) served as belfries and also for storage of valuables and refuge in time of trouble. Most of these probably date from the tenth–twelfth centuries, being constructed to reflect the status and wealth of monasteries, rather than as a late response to Viking attack. The *leacht*, a small rectangular altar-like stone mound occasionally marked by cross-slabs, may have been associated with the demarcation of special graves, or served as an open-air altar, though their date is often uncertain.

The multi-period monastery at Nendrum, Co. Down, traditionally founded by St Mochaoi, was the subject of excavation in the 1920s, and is now difficult to interpret (Figure 37.2, no. 2). It comprises three concentric walls, the inner enclosure containing a stone church, fragmentary round tower, and cemetery. Traces of round huts were found in the middle enclosure, and a rectangular stone building may have been used at one time for craft activities, to judge from the finds associated with it.

Armagh is a well-documented site, with references to ecclesiastical buildings in the annals from *c.* AD 800. By the eighth century it had become the paramount ecclesiastical centre in Ireland on the assertion that St Patrick had himself designated it as his chief centre. The first reference to a stone church here is of one in 789, and several churches stood on the hill as well as an abbot's house, library, kitchen and dwellings, most within an enclosure with an entrance on the east, close to a high cross whose remains are dated to the late ninth or tenth centuries. The activity on the hill (the *Rath*) was divided into three districts or thirds. Excavations within the inner enclosure have revealed a substantial ditch, the first phase of which has been radiocarbon-dated to between *c.* ad 180–560, filled in between the fifth and eighth centuries and used as a tip for metalworking debris. Excavations since 1975 in the supposed area of Patrick's church of *na ferta* (of the graves or grave-mounds) have produced evidence for transient fifth-century activity (a charcoal/ash-filled pit), followed by an early, apparently Christian, cemetery, with shallow burials in groups laid in irregular rows, one grave appearing to be marked by a pair of wooden uprights at its western end – possibly the 'cemetery of the martyrs' said to occupy the site first used by Patrick. It is possible that there were pagan burials in the vicinity, or that some Christian burials were originally marked by mounds/ditches in pagan manner. It has been suggested that visible prehistoric monuments on the knoll may have given the area an aura of sanctity, and provided an appropriate ritual focus for the early ecclesiastical centre (the reuse of pre-Christian sites of long-standing ritual use, such as the placing of burials or memorials on barrows, can be found elsewhere). Craft industries – amber, glass, bronze and bone working – took place in this area in the tenth century, with some evidence for masonry building before the end of the Early Christian period. This evidence for craft activity is commonly found on such sites, and latterly will have included those skilled in working stone.

At Clonmacnois, Co. Offaly, a low bank and ditch which runs for some 400 m to the south of the present buildings and then runs for a similar distance at right angles towards the river may represent an enclosure of uncertain age. Most of the present buildings are eleventh/twelfth-century or later, but limited excavation has now shed light on the early medieval site. Trenches inside the western perimeter wall of the modern cemetery have uncovered early evidence of occupation in the form of postholes for post-and-wattle houses (King 1992: 12–14). Above these lay the low stone wall, hearth and clay floor for a round-house, with a path or gravelled surface outside the house. An ogam stone found on the ground immediately outside its east wall appears to have been reused as a sharpening stone. Two circular corn-drying kilns were located to the south of the house, and evidence for other industrial activity in the area included iron, bronze, gold and antler working. The finds indicate a pre-eleventh-century date for this activity, much being seventh–ninth century.

The famous monastery of Iona in Argyll (Figure 37.2, no. 3) shows interesting parallels with similar sites in Ireland. Survey and excavation has revealed a complex network of pre-Viking enclosures belonging to several phases. A large vallum, still visible on the north and west of the site, enclosed an area of over 8 ha (20 acres, comparable with Clonmacnois), the east side being either open or enclosed in a different manner towards the sea. A smaller enclosure has been detected within the larger one, on the northern side, while another smaller enclosure seems to have enclosed the Reilig Odhrain, one of the cemeteries. One ditch close to the north of the Reilig Odhrain was V-shaped, and peat deposits formed within it gave radiocarbon dates of sixth–seventh centuries (Barber 1981). Some evidence for timber structures has been uncovered: two possible circular buildings, and part of a rectangular structure made with sill beams or vertically set planking. One building which post-dated an early seventh-century pit may have stood within a circular fenced enclosure (Royal Commission on the Ancient and Historical Monuments of Scotland 1982: 41). Postholes and slots which may perpetuate an earlier structure were also found beneath and around 'St Columba's Shrine', a small stone building with antae similar to the very smallest Irish churches (Redknap 1976), though no coherent pattern could be identified. It has not been possible to recover complete building plans or establish the function of any of these timber structures. The grouping of the large freestanding crosses, which appear to be *in situ*, suggests that by the eighth century a church was situated close to or beneath the site of the present medieval abbey church and 'St Columba's Shrine', and support a tradition that the 'Shrine' was the founder's burial-place. As at other monastic centres, evidence for craftworking has been found, including metalworking and the working of glass (the production of decorative glass studs). Excavations at Iona also have shed light on the economy and environment of an early monastery. Animal bones recovered from pre-Viking levels suggest a preponderance of cattle, with some red deer, sheep, pig, seal and various fish, suggesting that not all visitors or members followed austere diets. Cereals appear to have been grown close to the enclosure ditch by the Reilig Odhrain with a break about the mid-seventh century, perhaps at a time of reorganization to the layout of the monastery. Holly may have been grown in hedges, and may have been used for the manufacture of ink (Royal Commission on the Ancient and Historical Monuments of Scotland 1982: 14). Grave slabs lie in the area around St Columba's Shrine and in the Reilig Odhrain, but it is unclear whether any are *in situ*.

EARLY CHRISTIAN MONUMENTS

The inscribed stones or early Christian monuments of various kinds are the most numerous visible relics of the Christian Celts. The term 'Celtic' in this context is interpreted in the loose sense of 'belonging to the (non-Germanic) early medieval British Isles', and the term 'Insular' is generally applied to material belonging stylistically to this period and area. The different regional studies of stone monuments have produced differences in terminology, though the main groupings are similar.[8] These can be grouped into (1) commemorative stones inscribed in Latin or ogam (fifth- to seventh/eighth century); (2) cross-marked grave markers without inscriptions; (3) recumbent grave slabs with crosses and inscriptions; (4) cross-marked stones which served other functions such as boundary markers; (5) freestanding crosses/freestanding Pictish slabs; (6) architectural stonework. The collection at Iona is one of the largest in Britain, with over 100 stones described in the Royal Commission inventory (Royal Commission on the Ancient and Historical Monuments of Scotland 1982), eclipsed only by Clonmacnois, Co. Offaly, and in Scotland approached only by the series of monuments at St Andrews, Fife.

Figure 37.4 *Top left:* Nineteenth-century view of the Latin and ogam-inscribed stone in use as a gatepost at Little Trefgarne, St Dogwells, Dyfed. (Photo: National Museum of Wales.) *Top right:* Fragment of eighth-century slab discovered in a later grave fill during excavations on the south side of 'St Columba's Shrine', Iona. Part of a long-shafted cross, it is inscribed [OROIT] DO ERGUS ('A prayer for Fergus'). (Photo: author.) *Bottom:* Base stone of St John's Cross, Iona, marked out with circular groove apparently for a millstone (millstones were also reused as recumbent slabs and cross bases at Clonmacnois). (Photo: author.)

The Earlier Monuments

The first group, and the earliest carved stones with Christian significance, are generally dated to the fifth–seventh centuries (though some later examples are known) (Figure 37.4 *top left*). There are some 150 early stones inscribed in Latin or ogam with Christian associations known from Wales (Nash-Williams's Group I) from the period, about 50 from Cornwall and Devon, and a smaller number from southern Scotland and the Isle of Man. The earliest inscriptions are in Roman capital letters, while the later ones are in half-uncials, a form of letter copied from manuscripts. The stones vary in size and shape, but most are undressed boulders chosen for their natural regularity. As with those from Ireland and Scotland, those from Wales acted as grave-markers, memorials or boundary markers between territories. The inscriptions are thought to record individuals of high standing, and the dead person's father is often also named (reflecting the importance of kinship in Celtic society). These stones have been found in a wide range of locations: beside earlier roads, tracks, or ridgeway routes, in churchyards, or incorporated in recent times into walls or buildings. Some are associated with cemeteries, where they are often found in reused positions or where there has been a custom of incorporating them into grave backfill.

Ogam script was probably developed and first used in Ireland, though precisely when is under debate (see below). Approximately 330 stone memorials have been recorded in Ireland, concentrated in the south-west. This distribution extends to south-west Wales, Cornwall and to a lesser extent the Isle of Man, North Wales and Dalriada, and is taken to illustrate the early presence of Irish-speaking or Irish-descended people. Some of the stones are clearly Christian, bearing crosses (some are certainly later additions) or references to Christian offices.[9] Unlike the stones in Wales where the use of Latin and ogam side by side suggests a degree of contact between the two traditions, Irish ogam-inscribed stones are normally monolingual (an exception being one from Killeen Cormaic, Colbinstown, Co. Kildare) (Figure 37.5).

Figure 37.5 *Top left:* Two faces of the Tywyn stone, Gwynedd. The half-unical text, uncertain in detail, has been rendered by the late Sir Ifor Williams as follows:

(a) Cengrui (or Tengrui) cimalted gu(reic)/adgan/ant erunc du but marciau/ ('Ceinrwy wife of Addian (lies here) close to Bud (and) Meirchiaw)

(b) cun ben celen:/tricet nitanam ('Cun, wife of Celyn: grief and loss remain')

Top right: Stone from Ackergill, Caithness, with an ogam inscription which reads NEHTETRI . . . , possibly an abbreviated form of the name Nechton. (Photo: The Trustees of the National Museums of Scotland.)

Bottom left: The Trecastle stone from Capel Ilud, Cwm Crai, Powys. The other side bears the fifth/sixth-century inscription in Latin: [M]ACCVTRENI + SALICIDVNI, and ogam (read upwards): MAQITRENI SALICIDVNI ('The stone of Maccutrenus Salicidunus'). (Photo: British Museum.)

Bottom right: Tenth-century cross-slab from Meifod, Powys, bearing a crucifix, ring cross, Celtic plaits and Scandinavian knots and animals. (Photo: National Museum of Wales.)

In Scotland, early inscribed stones bearing British names are found in Galloway, Lothian, and the Borders.[10] Similar to those from Wales and Cornwall, they bear Latin in Roman capitals, and indicate the presence of Christian communities in the fifth–sixth century. The Picts, living in the region north of the Forth and Clyde, may have been a mixture of Britons and earlier non-Celtic peoples with different language and customs. The movement of the Scotti from Ulster into Argyll and the Western Isles led to the formation of the kingdom of Dalriada, and following the foundation of the monastery on Iona and the extension of its activities, both the Picts and the Angles of Northumbria were converted to Christianity. There is considerable debate about the date of the so-called Pictish symbol stones, and the degree to which they had Christian associations (some may have originated before the adoption of Christianity). They represent abstract symbols or identifiable animals or objects drawn in profile, and comprise Romilly Allen's Class I stones (some of which may have been carved as early as the sixth or seventh century: Allen and Anderson 1903; Henderson 1967; Jackson 1984).

The second group of inscribed stones (Nash-Williams's Group II in Wales) are decorated with incised crosses in many forms, usually without inscriptions. The execution of the symbolic design was often very crude, and the stones are frequently like those of the earlier period – upright pillars or slabs of natural or roughly prepared stone, often plain slabs scratched with two lines in the sign of the cross. The so-called 'primary cross-marked slabs' or 'primary grave-markers' are difficult to date because of long survival, though they may include the earliest cross-marked stones. The cross forms are thought to have regional significance, and occur widely from the sixth century onwards, many being assigned to the seventh century.

The third group, recumbent grave slabs with crosses and inscriptions, are usually dated from the seventh to late ninth or early tenth centuries, though their use continues to a later date. They are often decorated with crosses which may extend the full length of the stone, either incised or in low relief, as a simple linear form, or with ring-and-hollow devices, or ring crosses, some embellished with interlace. The lettering is usually in half-uncial, common on Irish examples, and the inscription often follows a formula, requesting a prayer for 'so and so'.

Cross-slabs similar to those in Ireland and Wales also appear on the Isle of Man, and they were divided by Kermode into Class I (pre-Scandinavian), and Class II (Scandinavian: from second half ninth century). Recent research br R. Trench-Jellicoe indicates that fewer of the cross-slabs pre-date the main period of Viking settlement on the island than previously thought (Ian Fisher, in litt.). The pre-Scandinavian crosses are skilfully executed. The series begins with five ogam-inscribed stones of various date.[11] Late seventh-century cross-slabs with cross-of-arcs hexafoils, marigolds or maltese cross designs are particularly well represented at Maughold, the main ecclesiastical centre on the island.

Cornwall has few cross-slabs, and there is an apparent gap between the inscribed stones of the early period and the freestanding crosses of the ninth–tenth century. The range of cross-carved stones and pillars from Ireland has not been published in detail. Most occur in the west of Ireland, and it has been suggested that this absence in the east may be because in this area they were commonly fashioned in wood. Some may have been made over a short period, some over a long period, overlapping with freestanding cross production in areas where stone was less suited for the production of larger crosses. Most cross-carved stones are extremely difficult to date because chronology relies on the typology and ornamental style of the cross symbol.[12]

The Later Monuments

In general, the simple form of monument gave way to more elaborate freestanding carved stones associated with the development of ecclesiastical centres. Crosses were no longer partly modified gravestones, but the elaborate monuments of workshops under monastic or royal patronage. Dating of freestanding crosses is problematic and the subject of continuing debate, which depends on a few inscriptions dated by reference to persons historically attested elsewhere, art-historical comparisons and theoretical progressions.[13] Most have cross-head and shaft carved in one, and Irish examples may be topped by a capstone in the form of a cone, a roof-shape or house-shaped shrine. Cross bases may take the form of truncated pyramids (sometimes stepped), though a number have rough boulders for bases, and some no bases at all. It has recently been pointed out that almost 30 per cent of Irish crosses have no ring, and that one characteristic which distinguishes most crosses from Anglo-Saxon examples is the cross form, based on an extended Latin cross, as opposed to an equal-armed cross on a pillar (Kelly 1993: 221).

Local traditions of carving soon developed, probably in the late eighth century. Some craftsmen, presumably with instructions from patrons, concentrated on abstract interlace ornament of Insular tradition, others on elaborate figural iconography,[14] and some on aspects of both. A characteristic shared by many is the organization of figural scenes and abstract ornament into discrete panels. In Wales the custom of erecting freestanding crosses in stone from the ninth century is thought to have spread from adjacent parts of Britain. Structurally the monuments fall into two basic types – cross-slabs and high crosses – within which regional groups can be identified. Most surviving freestanding crosses from Cornwall are of more recent date (late eleventh–thirteenth century), and Langdon divided his 260 examples into Class A: unornamented crosses, Class B: ornamented crosses, and Class C: miscellaneous monuments. The latter includes five early cross-slabs.[15]

Romilly Allen's Class I symbol stones in Pictland have no crosses, but the eighth-century Pictish stones had adapted the Christian symbol of the cross in low relief, usually in the Anglo-Saxon form of a cross-on-a-pillar, as a main motif on their large cross-slabs with straight or gable-shaped tops (Romilly Allen Class II). They are difficult to date – this is usually reliant on ornament and the typology of the cross symbol – and some may overlap chronologically with those of Class I. Most are thought to date from the early eighth century onwards (generally eighth–ninth century). These slabs provided a greater area for ornamentation, and their skilful composition in stone has been compared with great carpet pages of illuminated manuscripts such as the Book of Durrow or Lichfield Gospels, possibly involving a similar degree of forethought and planning. On the front would be the Cross symbol bearing interlace and cruciform ornament, flanked by figures, while the back would bear Pictish symbols and figure sculpture, often including riders, hunts or biblical scenes. The relief sculpture of the Picts may derive from early Northumbrian

Figure 37.6 *Top left:* Stone from Mullaghmast, Co. Kildare, with 'Celtic' spiral motifs. (Photo: National Museum of Ireland.) *Top right:* Warrior effigy from White Island, Co. Fermanagh. (Photo: Crown Copyright, by permission of the Controller of HMSO.) *Bottom left:* Cross-slab from Dunfallandy, Perthshire. (Photo: Trustees of the National Museums of Scotland.) *Bottom right:* Hilton of Cadboll. (Photo: Trustees of the National Museums of Scotland.) Horsemen and hunting scenes appear on Pictish, Irish and a few Welsh monuments, and along with figures provide a glimpse of native costume and dress sense – Celtic moustaches, tunics, cloaks and penannular brooches, and for ecclesiastics use of the tonsure. The Hilton of Cadboll stone shows a Pictish lady riding side-saddle with her husband beside her. The proximity of mirror and comb symbols suggests that the monument may have been erected for her. The White Island figures which include an ecclesiastic with bell and crozier, and a representation of King David, suggest that ambitious architectural schemes were also undertaken. Sockets in the tops of the heads may have supported steps for a pulpit or similar structure. Though stylized, interesting details of dress are depicted, which suggest a date around ninth–tenth century.

carving. Freestanding monumental crosses are known in southern Scotland, in particular in areas of Northumbrian influence. Romilly Allen's Class III is a mixed group, including those crosses erected in south Scotland during Northumbrian occupation, and the tenth–eleventh-century Whithorn school of sculpture, which under Irish-Norse influences produced disc-headed crosses similar to later examples from Wales, Cumbria and Cornwall.

The architectural effect of some crosses on Irish cross-slabs[16] recalls similar features on cross-slabs from Pictland and Wales. Freestanding crosses began to appear with Irish influence from the late eighth or ninth century in west Scotland, where all three classes of Irish cross form appear – those with pierced rings (e.g. Kildalton, Islay, Argyll), those with solid rings, and unringed crosses (e.g. Kilmartin, Argyll and Hamilton, Lanarkshire), and in east Scotland (e.g. Dupplin, Perthshire). The monastery at Iona, with its easy communications by sea, was a meeting place of many traditions, lying between Pictland and Ireland, and close to Northumbria. It was an important artistic centre working in other media (not just stone), and it is generally believed that it received knowledge of working stone from Northumbria, alongside knowledge of Irish traditions and of Pictish artistic inspiration, which found expression in its own form and style of freestanding crosses (Royal Commission on the Ancient and Historical Monuments of Scotland 1982; Hamlin 1987: 19). Some of the Iona crosses have been regarded as an experimental group, though the degree of influence on them by Pictish and Northumbrian sculpture is a subject of continuing debate. Iona transferred to Kells, Co. Meath, as a result of early ninth-century Viking raids. From the early ninth century a tradition of monumental ringed crosses developed in Ireland, perhaps inspired in part by influences from Iona. Its famous crosses of St John, St Martin and St Oran are now considered to date to the second half of the eighth century (Royal Commission on the Ancient and Historical Monuments of Scotland 1982: 18f.), and it has now been argued that the *fully* developed Irish high cross is no earlier than *c*.800 (Edwards 1985: 407).

While ornament drew on Celtic tradition from the ninth century, Scandinavian-style interlace, animals, figures and occasionally runes were incorporated on stones found on the Isle of Man. The disc-headed cross-slab was also developed there, bearing Celtic rather than Norse decoration.[17]

Early Inscriptions

The inscriptions carved on the stones reveal much about individual people in the different Celtic areas, and the development of the Celtic tongues. The majority of the early Welsh stones have inscriptions in Latin, often following the wording and well-formed style of inscriptions in early Christian Gaul and the Rhineland. Inscriptions ascribed to the late fourth and fifth century are horizontal and use the formula HIC IACIT, a late vulgar Latin form of the classical Latin HIC IACET ('here s/he lies'), popular in southern and central Gaul in the fifth century. The western maritime distribution of stones bearing the IN PACE MEMORIAE formula, common on the Continent, suggests contact with Cornwall and north-west Wales, while early inscribed stones bearing the HIC IACIT formula from Bodmin Moor and Dartmoor[18] may indicate a late fifth-/early sixth-century movement of

Christian settlers from south-west and south-central Wales, where the formula is commonly found, across the Bristol Channel to Cornwall. In a recent survey of early stones from south-west Britain, Okasha has argued that her Category 1 shares characteristics of script, layout, language and formulae with Nash-Williams's Groups I and II to form a south-west tradition 'akin to but not identical to that of Wales', subject to similar influences (Okasha 1993: 40).

Irish learning was traditionally by oral transmission and recitation, but a form of writing eventually developed, called ogam, based phonetically on consonant and vowel clusters which were established by Roman grammarians (Jackson 1953: 159), rather than our present ABC alphabet (Figure 37.7). This alphabet is generally considered to have developed by the third century in Ireland, where about 330 ogam-inscribed memorial stones are known.[19] They are linguistically of great importance, providing the earliest form of Old Irish (Goidelic) names such as Moinena, Ronan, Comgan, Oilacon. This development of a cipher, giving monuments special powers, has been associated with the use of wooden notched talley sticks, or a manual sign language using fingers and thumbs;[20] most recently it has been described as a system of incremental tallies devised *c.*AD 300 ± 50 by someone familar with Latin and Roman script (McManus 1991).

Ogam was used up to about the end of the eighth century, the period of Christian growth in Ireland. The stress on kinship and family links recorded on many Christian stones should be seen as a Celtic practice rather than a particularly pagan characteristic. Over 100 examples in Macalister's 1945 *Corpus* occur on sites with ecclesiastical associations (*c.*34 per cent), and approximately 14 per cent bear crosses, most of which appear to be contemporary with the ogam and not added at a later date. The names of ecclesiastics have been identified amongst the inscribed names. Inscriptions are usually short, and record a name and family group, following a formula 'so & so, son of so & so',[21] which parallels the Latin on bilingual stones found outside Ireland. As previously mentioned, some refer to Christian offices, such as the seventh-century stone from Arraglen, Co. Kerry. It has been suggested that the apparent seventh-century demise of orthodox ogam may have been the result of Christian disapproval, rather than replacement by a more effective system. A modified form of ogam is found on a few Pictish symbol stones and cross-slabs in the eighth–ninth century. They are so far untranslated, but some words, mainly personal names, have been identified.[22]

Later Inscriptions

Later Latin inscriptions ascribed to the sixth–seventh centuries are inscribed vertically (top to bottom) in Celtic fashion similar to ogam script. The style of lettering, having initially followed standard Roman capital and cursive letter forms, becomes gradually debased, so that by the end of the sixth century new letter forms based on bookhand were being employed, called half-uncial and minuscule. These were probably introduced and spread by manuscripts and adapted for use on stone.[23]

The Tywyn stone, Gwynedd, may bear the earliest example of the Welsh language inscribed on stone (Figure 37.5). The half-uncial lettering of the inscription is comparable with eighth-century epigraphic forms, and the influence of manuscripts

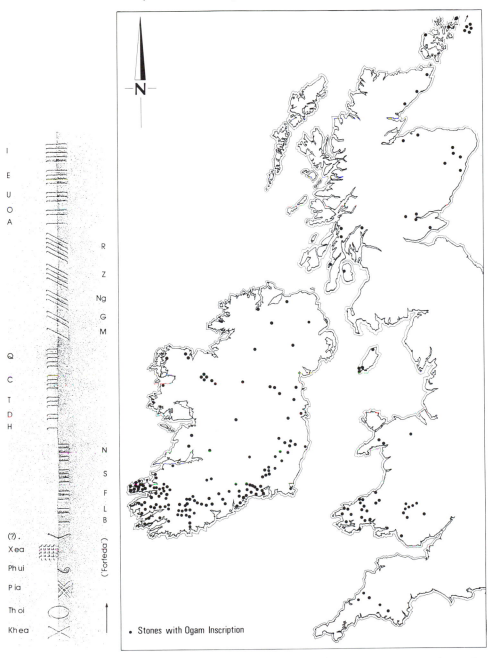

Figure 37.7 *Left:* The ogam alphabet. Ogam was a system of representing twenty letters by inscribing strokes or grooves set at different angles on either side of, or crossing, a vertical stem-line, usually the edge of an object or stone. It was usual for the inscription to be placed on a stone so that it could be read from the bottom up. *Right:* Ogam-inscribed stones in Wales, Ireland and Scotland. (Based on R.A.S. Macalister, Nash-Williams and work by Katherine Forsyth.)

is evident in the tendency of the lettering to run together. One formula found particularly on recumbent grave slabs in south-west Wales (Dyfed) as well as Ireland is CRUX XRI (Cross of Christ). On later freestanding crosses, panels of horizontal text appear. Many stones in Ireland and Scotland bear inscriptions in Irish recording the person's name, and a request for a prayer for his soul – the irregularity and arrangement often indicating their hasty addition to previously prepared stones. An inscription in Greek uncials, on the slab from Fahan Mura, Co. Donegal, is probably copied off a Greek manuscript, and illustrates the influence of continental contact on sculpture.

Schools of Sculpture

For an understanding of the creation of such monuments, we are reliant on examination of their technical and design construction. For the early stones, natural boulders were modified to varying degrees. Some are unhewn pillar stones, and many are cut on a dressed and prepared face, though in areas such as Wales Roman material was occasionally reused.[24] Few early stones show evidence for being dressed to a regular shape, but later cross-incised slabs show greater preparation of the stone.

The appearance of elaborate large freestanding monuments with locations centred on postulated or proven early ecclesiastical centres suggests that workshops or schools of craftsmen had been established by the ninth century (Figure 37.8). To judge from the characteristics of the various regional styles and their localised distribution, such workshops were under primary patronage of the church. For example, the crosses at Penmon and Dyserth (Gwynedd) and at Whitford (Clwyd) share characteristics of the Chester school of sculpture, as well as iconography and abstract ornament which is paralleled in the Barrow valley in Ireland, illustrating a fusion of multicultural influences. In Cornwall the ecclesiastical sites at St Buryan near Lands End, and St Petroc, Bodmin, are thought to have had schools of sculpture attached to them, as are the south Welsh monasteries. Early groups in the Irish Midlands, dated to the late eighth or early ninth century, centre on Clonmacnois and Ahenny/Kilkieran, and display an emphasis on Insular ornament.

At least two individuals would be associated with the creation of a monument – an instigator (patron, dedicant) and an executor (artist, craftsman), both having a role in determining the type of monument and form of inscription or ornament. It is not always possible to state with certainty whether the choice of a particular motif was up to date, or a revival. Some craftsmen may have been catering for a local taste influenced by external styles, others may have been working under external influences brought in by travelling craftsmen. Some sculptors may have been working within external (Northumbrian, Scandinavian) traditions, or within a local fashion for art-styles and ideas from abroad. Decorative patterns could also have been copied or borrowed and modified from illuminated manuscripts and portable works of art travelling between monastic houses. On the later Welsh monuments, one finds examples of plant-scroll (vine-scroll) patterns favoured by the Northumbrian Anglo-Saxons, and twin beasts, animals and birds found on sculpture from Mercia and Northumbria. Constructional grids were used (sometimes horizontal, sometimes diagonal) for the laying out of abstract ornament. Complex key- and fretpatterns and interlace (in the form of plaitwork and knotwork) have parallels in Ireland, and

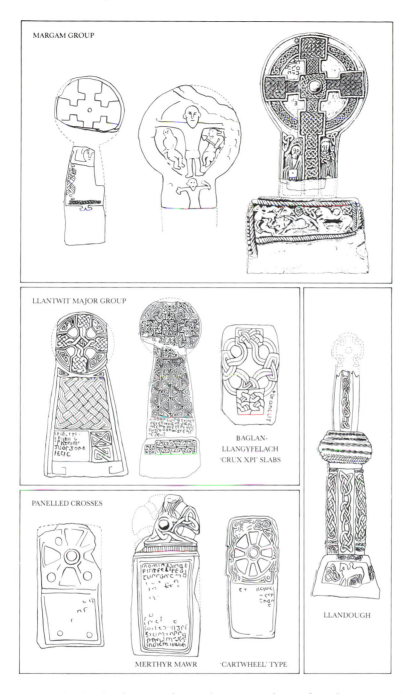

Figure 37.8 Local schools of carving from Glamorgan, where a form known as a 'panelled' or 'cartwheel' slab emerged in the late ninth century (the 'Margam' group). Another distinctive form was the disc-headed cross (from Margam and Llantwit Major). No Celtic cross-heads with perforations are known, though disc-heads with Celtic cross designs in low relief occur.

Anglo-Scandinavian style ring-chain and key-patterns of the tenth century can be found on many sites around the Irish Sea. The regional or 'workshop' production must be seen as a differing response to varied accumulations of influences.

When suitable, locally available stone was selected by the stone carvers; otherwise it was imported from the nearest source (some composite crosses have been manufactured from more than one type of stone).[25] The sculptors of the later slabs would have used a similar array of tools and techniques (such as pocking and smoothing) to the earlier, individual craftsmen, though the removal of considerable amounts of stone to create deeper relief designs required greater input of time, and labour, and the more complex designs suggest access to pattern books or motif pieces, as well as specialized tools such as compasses and dividers. An unfinished cross at Kells gives some indications that patterns were probably first sketched out on the stone and then blocked out in rough relief. Once the background had been deepened and interlace executed,[26] the head of the cross and figures would be completed. One cross at Sancreed near St Buryan, Cornwall, has interlace of tenth-century type, and is inscribed with the name RUNHOL, believed to be the name of the sculptor. A cross at Andreas, Isle of Man, is inscribed: 'Gaut Bjornson of Kuli made it'.[27] The tenth-century cross by Gaut at Kirk Michael is inscribed 'Maibrikti, son of Athakan the smith, raised this Cross' – a man with a Celtic name (as was his father's) commissioning a Norse sculptor to carve a Christian memorial.

Once the carving was finished, it is likely that the final work was undertaken by the painter. Though all traces of such paint have generally now been weathered away, it is likely that many later stones were richly painted in different colours, sometimes on a surface smoothed with lime-based whitewash. A number of apparently uninscribed stones may have borne painted texts. Some stone crosses copied to differing degrees compositions in metal and wood, and it has been suggested that the Ahenny North cross (Co. Tipperary) may have been painted to give the impression of a great golden cross, studded with enamel and glass studs (copying closely the metal cross form (Figure 37.12)).[28]

It is impossible to estimate the number of wooden crosses, pillars, slabs and freestanding crosses which once existed. Adomnán in his Life of St Columba c.688–92 describes a cross which has been set up in a millstone, and was still extant in his own day. Some depictions of cross-slabs appear to show simple wooden crosses (either those made from two laths of wood at right angles to each other,[29] or with pointed or spiked bases.[30] The construction of some composite crosses and in particular of two of the Iona crosses (Figure 37.9) in segments using mortice and tenon joints may represent the application of carpentry techniques to a special problem (I. Fisher, in litt.) rather than conscious copying of either freestanding wooden crosses, or smaller wooden crosses covered in metal plates (for example, the eighth-century Anglo-Saxon 'Rupertus Cross'). Some of the rounded shaft crosses (such as the Pillar of Eliseg, Powys and Gosforth Cross, Cumberland) give the impression of being based on wooden prototypes, as modified tree trunks, while the interlace-decorated wooden boss found at Wood Quay, Dublin, may have been originally attached to a wooden cross (Lang 1988: 4). This also occurs in related stonework, such as the decorated stone pillar shafts from Llantwit Major, Glamorgan, which resemble in form architectural columns with vertical V-shaped grooves to hold planks or panels, possibly as part of

Figure 37.9 The crosses of St John (*left*) and St Martin (*right*) on Iona. St John's cross appears to have been designed without a ring, which was added using mortise and tenon, perhaps after a fall. (Courtesy of The Royal Commission on the Ancient and Historical Monuments of Scotland.) Iona became the most important centre for 'cultural exchange' between Ireland and Britain in the late sixth and seventh centuries, and its abbots exercised great influence. Abbot Adomnán of Iona (d. 704) was a friend of King Aldfrith of Northumbria and older contemporary of Bede; he wrote a biography of Columba (*Vita Columba*), one of the earliest saints' lives and manuscripts to survive. When Oswald, educated at Iona, became king of Northumbria (*c*.635), he looked to Iona to provide a bishop to complete the Christian conversion begun by Paulinus.

a chancel screen. It is likely that similar woodcarvings, now lost, formed an important influence on stone ornament and design, whether secular or religious.

The Purpose of the Stones

The exact purpose and sequence of events leading up to the erection of most monuments remain obscure.

Most of the inscriptions on stones are commemorative, recording the name and frequently the kinship of individuals, usually seen as members of the well-to-do upper class, and occasionally their status (such as king or priest).[31] Little is known about the burial rite associated with early memorials.[32] Amongst the early inscribed stones which appear to represent Christian burial, there are isolated examples which may mark the position of early cemeteries which are no longer visible, lying outside but close to existing churchyards. Such early burials in isolated places are commemorated in poetry such as the 'Stanzas of the Graves' ('The graves which the rain wets . . . Whose grave is on the mountain.').[33] Only gradually did burials become associated with churches, as they gained authority and organization to insist on or provide for churchyard burial. Cross-marked stones and pillars probably served different functions – undoubtedly some as grave-markers, or to act as foci of worship, or to mark out an area of sanctuary. Some stones are clearly meant to lie flat, above a grave, while others are no more than beach pebbles bearing incised crosses which may have been placed in or over a grave.

The functions of freestanding crosses were probably complex. In Ireland, the entrance to a monastery was often marked by a cross, and cemeteries and enclosures would frequently have focal points marked by a cross or founder's tomb. A schematic drawing in the *Book of Mulling* marks a number of crosses inside and outside concentric circles, with the dedications of some to prophets and evangelists (recalling the names of some of Iona's crosses), probably to invoke their protection and power for the monastery. Some crosses may have illustrated the united power of church and state, and it is likely that they also played a role in the liturgy as stations for processions, or marking points where Mass was said.

Some monuments record grants of land, achievements or possibly events such as battles. An early ninth-century cross-slab from Maughold, Isle of Man, is inscribed: IHS XPS/ BRANCUI /HOC AQUA/ DIRIVAVIT ('. . . Brancui led off water to this place'), recording his provision of a water supply to the *monasterium*. Exceptional is the inscription on the 'Pillar of Eliseg' at Valle Crucis, Powys, which records and praises the achievements and kinship of Cyngen's great grandfather Eliseg ('. . . who annexed the inheritance of Powys . . . throughout nine [years?] from the power of the English, which he made into a sword-land by fire . . .'). Concenn (Cyngen ap Cadell, who died in 854) and his great-grandfather Eliseg were kings of Powys.

The purpose of the Pictish symbol stones remains obscure (see p.765), but Class II Pictish stones provide evidence for thriving Christian culture. No written records of Pictish exist to verify the various interpretations placed on the older Class I symbols, which on Class II stones rarely appear on the front with the cross, being relegated to the back. The Aberlemno churchyard cross-slab (Tayside) bears a large cross in low relief, giving it an architectural presence similar to freestanding crosses. Figural representations on Class III stones, minus symbols, appear subordinate to the cross, being confined to the decorative panels. While the secular imagery appears tightly controlled, the patterns frequently mimic fine metalworking techniques seen on objects adorning both court and altar – one effect being a unifying of church authority with that of the ruling élite (Driscoll 1988: 186).

Inscriptions on later freestanding monuments are commonly set in panels, often defined by borders. It has been suggested that some were set low down on the shaft so that they could be conveniently viewed and read when kneeling. It is probable that the majority could not read the simple requests for prayers or the records of patrons and deceased, and some important inscriptions may have needed reading or interpreting by those versed in the skill. Some appear to invite the reader to recite the text out aloud, such as a cross-slab from Llanwnnws, Dyfed, which asks for a prayer from those who are able to explain the inscribed name, and the ninth-century example from Caldey Island asks 'all who walk there that they pray for the soul of Catuoconus'. Sometimes phrases resemble those used in charters and manuscripts, for example the inscription from Merthyr Mawr (ECMW 240) ... IN.GRE/ FIUM.INPRO/PRIUM ... ('in writing, in perpetuity') which may have recorded the transfer of land to a religious body.

Inscriptions on Irish sculpture similarly indicate that some stones were either dedicated to apostles, or commemorated events or individuals. Some crosses are dated by deciphering and interpreting of their inscriptions. The cross at Bealin, Co. Westmeath, possibly from Clonmacnois, Co. Offaly, asks passers-by in Irish to pray for Tuathgal who set up the cross.[34] Inscriptions on the cross at Kinnitty ask the reader to pray for King Maelsechnaill, king of the Southern Uí Neill from 846 to 862, and son of Maelruanaid, and for Colmán 'who made the cross for the King of Ireland' (probably the abbot of Kinnitty; de Paor 1987).

Symbolism on the Stones

Symbols occur repeatedly on early Christian monuments as a language linking motif with idea, both to enhance and identify an image, and to emphasize a message. Selection would have been by those familiar with the most appropriate means of communicating the message to the audience, literate or otherwise. In general, the divergence from classical or Carolingian naturalism of art style on many stones may in part result from experimentation by Celtic craftsmen with borrowed forms and motifs imbued with specific Christian concepts, adapted and enhanced to indigenous taste. Under Christian (and continental) influence, Celtic symbolism and love of pattern were absorbed, and adapted to the new belief system and its monuments. Mystical beliefs may have continued to some degree the Lives of the Saints suggest an association between magic and Christianity in relic pagan form, still evident in folklore today.

Few overtly Celtic symbols are employed on the early stones. Known examples of crosses on prehistoric menhirs or Roman monuments, perhaps symbolizing the victory of Christ over paganism, or simply the reuse of convenient materials, are known but rare.

On some early stones from Ireland, 'Ultimate La Tène' scrollwork remained a vital decorative element. Some stones bear Celtic curves and spirals related to ornament on sixth-/seventh-century metalwork, such as the carved stone from Mullaghmast, Co. Kildare (Figure 37.6), illustrating residual pre-Christian ornament in an increasingly converted world. Spirals are used in combination with chi-rhos and crosses on later cross-slabs. The adoption of curvilinear and spiral patterns from indigenous Celtic tradition can be seen on the pillar stone from Reask, Co. Kerry, in a design reminiscent of a *flabellum* or liturgical fan (Figure 37.11). Spiral patterns are found in particular on pillar stones in the Dingle peninsula, as well as in manuscripts

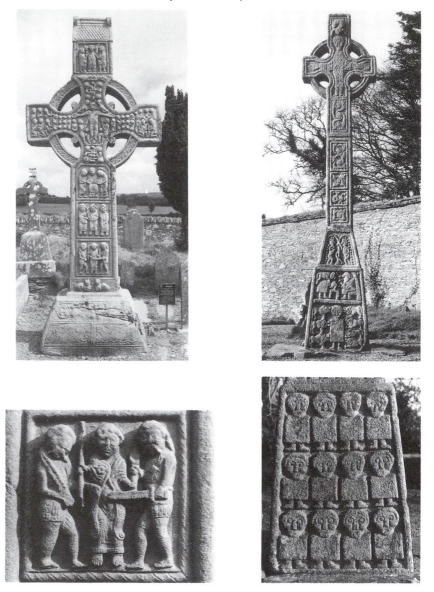

Figure 37.10 *Top left:* The fine cross of Muiredach, Monasterboice, Co. Louth, Ireland, and (*below*) detail, showing the arrest of Christ in naturalistic style. (Photo: Office of Public Works, Ireland.) *Top right:* Cross of Moone, Co. Kildare, and (*bottom right*) detail showing twelve apostles. (Photo: Office of Public Works, Ireland.) The naive nature of some sculpture, such as the tall, ninth-century cross at the ecclesiastical centre at Moone, contrasts with the naturalism of others, for example, the cross of Muiredach. On the west side of the base of the Moone cross, a simple Crucifixion is placed above a remarkable panel of the apostles, each with conventionalized body in simplified style. The style may have been influenced by the difficulty of working the stone, but the arrangement indicates deliberate stylization to create a sequence of patterns.

such as the *Cathach* of Columba, and on metalwork. Geometrical patterns using compass arcs (the so-called cross-of-arcs or Maltese cross, related to marigold patterns common on Merovingian sculpture) are common during the early period, and it has been suggested that the ambiguity of the design (flower or cross) may have appealed to Celtic taste. There is little direct evidence for the fusion of pagan mythology with Christian scripture in the early period, though curvilinear designs do re-emerge later.

New motifs were also introduced by the new religion. The Constantinian monogram of Chi-Rho/Christogram, representing the first two letters of Christ's name in Greek combined into a cross (also known as the monogrammatic chi-rho) appears in the fourth century almost as an official Christian badge of state on various objects. The monogrammatic chi-rho is exemplified by the African Red Slipware base from Dinas Emrys with pendant alpha and omega letters which appear in similar positions beneath the cross arms on some stones (Figure 37.11, no. 6). The Carausius stone from Penmachno bears a chi-rho monogram without a circle, while the later pillar-stone from Kirkmadrine, Galloway, with its INITIUM / ET FINIS ('Beginning and end') inscription (an allusion to Revelation) bears a later 'open rho' symbol within a circle. The chi-rho forms suggest a wide range of portable sources or models while the reversal of the imagery on some stones illustrates either the occasional misunderstanding or in some cases the poor comprehension on the part of the executor.

The so-called 'Celtic cross' which characterizes many later large freestanding crosses also appears on metalwork and cross-slabs from the eighth century. It has been taken to be derived from some form of triumphal victory wreath honouring the Cross of Redemption, but typological explanations based on the encircled chi-rho have also been developed. The cross, as a sign of victory and symbol of protection, became popular in western Europe in the seventh century and was important in Insular, Anglo-Saxon and Hiberno-Norse art. Simple crosses were produced over a long time, and the designs are difficult to date. Some cross-decorated monuments increase in complexity and monumentality in the seventh–early eighth century, possessing slab-like shapes in low relief ornament, and many Welsh upright monuments fall into this category. Many bear similar cross designs over wide areas, but there is the suggestion of regional variations. Some are contemporary equivalents to freestanding crosses, such as the ninth- or tenth-century Crucifixion-inscribed slab from Carndonagh, Co. Donegal, or the decorated slab from Llanhamlach, Powys, and the tenth-century cross-slab from Nash Manor, South Glamorgan. An eleventh-century cross-slab at Llowes, Powys, bears a high-relief wheel cross decorated with triangular panels, and gives the architectural effect of a freestanding cross in the same way as some Pictish slabs.

As with the chi-rho the impetus for many of the cross designs may have come from several sources – from tiny initial crosses in manuscripts to cross-marked portable objects from Britain, the Continent and the Mediterranean. The influence of metalwork has been cited in the form and ornament of some Irish crosses from Ahenny, Kilkieran, Killamery and Kilree which, with their chip-carving, hatched edge mouldings and bosses in the locations of rivet heads, resemble metalwork crosses translated into carved stone (Figures 37.12 and 37.13). Similar influences can be seen in the Pictish cross-slab at Dunfallandy, Tayside, with full development of a boss-style on the cross, which appears to imitate metalwork (a late feature possibly derived from Iona; Figure 37.6. Some Iona crosses share with the Kildalton cross, Islay, the use of bosses containing internal pellets, serpent-and-boss ornament, elaborate spiralwork and a style of carving which may also be derived from metalwork, and which distinguishes them from the Ahenny group of similar date.

Some forms are unusual in having ornamentation which may have had symbolic significance such as the cross-slab from Meifod, Powys (Figure 37.5), which bears an unusual dedication, including triquetra and other knots taken to represent the Trinity as well as snakes and a fearsome rodent taken to represent the force of evil. Similar triquetra knots appear on the base of the 'Conbelin' stone at Margam, Glamorgan, beside riders in a hunting scene. Christian interpretations have

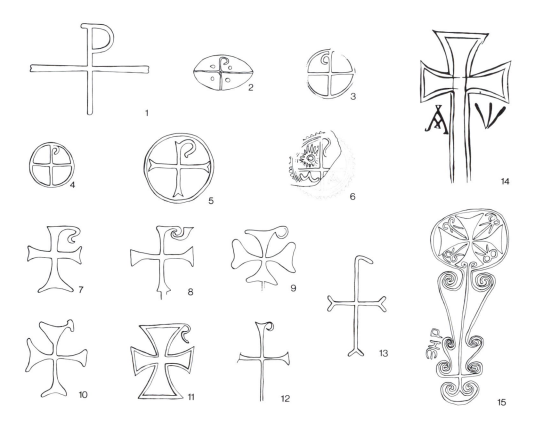

Figure 37.11 Chi-rho and alpha/omega symbols from Ireland, Wales and Scotland (not to scale). 1 – Penmachno, Dyfed; 2 – Kilcorban, Co. Kerry; 3–4 – Drumaqueran, Co. Antrim; 5 – Kirkmadrine; 6 – Dinas Emrys (on North African Red Slipware); 7 – St Endeileo, Cornwall; 8 – Iniscealtra, Co. Clare; 9 – Knockane, Co. Kerry; 10 – Arraglen, Co. Kerry; 11 – Iona, Argyll; 12 – Kilshannig, Co. Kerry; 13 – Treflys, Gwynedd; 14 – Loher, Co. Kerry; 15 – Reask, Co. Kerry.

Figure 37.12 The north cross at Ahenny, Co. Tipperary. (Photo: Office of Public Works, Ireland.)

been placed on hunt scenes: for example, the deer has been interpreted as Christ the victim or as the Christian soul, persecuted by devils (the hounds and riders). The horse was important in Celtic society, and is often the dominant animal form on stones, appearing frequently in profile, stylized but powerful and appearing united with rider (suggesting power by association). The complex 'knotting' which appears from the mid-seventh century in illuminated manuscripts seems to have been an Insular development, though not restricted to Celtic areas. The Picts, partially Celtic, enthusiastically adapted a great variety of interlace, key and spiral patterns to their cross-slabs.

Figure 37.13 The Kildalton cross, Islay. (Photo: Royal Commission on the Ancient and Historical Monuments of Scotland.)

The meaning of the unique Pictish symbols on some 200 Class I and II stones remains obscure. The earliest are thought to be seventh century (possibly earlier), and most are generally dated to the eighth century, with some later survivals. Some symbols depict everyday objects, or animals in realistic profile. They are thought to have had social rather than religious significance – rare inscriptions in ogam comprise personal names. Hicks has summarized a number of complex interpretations of the animal symbols as 'hunter's art', as 'a magic art drawing on Celtic cult animals', as a 'totemic system of references surviving from an Iron Age society' and 'a form of discourse, including reference to pagan mythological animals, devised to secure the status of the elite' (Hicks 1993: 199). A symbolic connection has been suggested between the animals, representing the different orders of creatures as distinguished by Genesis. They have been interpreted not as a secret code, but as part of the recurrent tradition of animals on both pagan and Christian monuments. The debate is complex, and the Christian significance of the early stones is unclear. They may have acted as gravestones or memorials, the symbols conveying information on the genealogy of the person commemorated (such as tribal affiliation, rank, lineage or occupation).[35]

Iconography

Celtic art is often seen as stylized, abstract and aniconic, and it is not surprising that early cross-decorated stones only rarely depict human or animal figures, the emphasis being on abstract ornament or Christian symbolism. Where human representations occur on the early stones, they tend to show 'orant' figures with arms raised in the ancient attitude of prayer. These images are far removed in style from Mediterranean concepts of realism or artistic convention, and may have been copied and adapted from early Gospel books.

Few of the decorative characteristics developed without strong influence from other regions, in particular Anglo-Saxon England, and the Continent. During the late eighth/early ninth century, scriptural iconography that may have had Carolingian models appears on sculpture, mainly in Ireland. This developed into complex cycles of iconography. On some crosses of this period, the emphasis is on Insular ornament of spirals, interlace, step-patterns, zoomorphic and anthropomorphic motifs.

Unlike Ireland and Scotland, figure sculpture is poorly represented in Wales. The tenth-century cross of Briamail Flou from Llandyfaelog Fach, Powys, is a rare example of possible labelling in half-uncial of the important warrior figure depicted. In common with Celtic imagery, many depictions are simple schematic outlines, symbolic rather than realistic, naturalism becoming subservient to overall artistic design and pattern. A small number of stones show unusual depictions. For example, the figure of a man on the shaft of the Whitford cross, Clwyd, may be a representation from Viking mythology. After being reset, the 'Trecastle' stone (Figure 37.5) was inscribed with pictographs which have been interpreted as Christian doctrines and scenes, with a figure holding a crozier or shepherd's crook at the bottom. The precise meanings of the panels are uncertain.

The stylized square bodies and hair (tonsured?) of the twelve apostles on the base of the cross at Moone (Figure 37.10) resemble depictions in enamel- and metalwork of the eighth century, and some manuscript art. The east panel of the base of the late tenth- or eleventh-century Llandough cross depicts five human figures in a row, seated facing front, each with ?vestments and holding a cross-headed staff or sceptre. As at Moone, the heads are so formalized and naive as to be far removed from any primary classical sources, and may echo an earlier Celtic concept of the head as the most significant part of the body, seat of understanding and the spirit, and source of strength.

Figural iconography begins in the late eighth or ninth century, and most crosses bear it by the tenth century in Ireland, though it is still rare in Wales. The Crucifixion usually occupies the centre of the head, Christ depicted wearing a loincloth or long/short-sleeved robe, sometimes flanked by sponge- and spear-bearers (in the manner of some metalwork plaques). Recurring scenes include representations of the Last Judgement, David playing the lyre, St Michael weighing a soul, Saul, as well as salvation themes such as David and Goliath, Daniel in the lions' den, Cain and Abel, Jonah and the whale. An important aspect of Christianity was that it offered individual hope of salvation through faith and action, baptism, communion, proper burial, and the hope of resurrection.

It is clear that the early Christian monuments, many of which are now seen as great artistic achievements, are great in variety and diverse in style; this is also true for the sites, and the term 'Insular' has been applied in a non-ethnic sense to encompass this diversity, a legacy which continues to inspire scholars and public alike.

NOTES

1 The temple at Caerwent is late fourth-century in date. Evidence for Christianity here is in the form of large numbers of east–west burials together with the discovery of an inscribed chi-rho monogram on a flanged pewter bowl found associated with a collection of late fourth-century vessels and interpreted as one of the vessels used in the early Christian supper known as the *agape* (Boon 1992: 17).

2 It has been argued that this implies that a group of Christians had asked for a bishop, and that Ninian was sent by the sub-Roman diocese of Carlisle. Recent excavations have unearthed evidence for the early Northumbrian monastery, ascribed to the period c.730–836 and later. Indirect evidence from these excavations has also been taken to support the possibility of the presence of a lime-washed building on the crown of the hill in the fifth-century period of activity on the site.

3 *Ecclesia, locus, monasterium, podum, llog* (Latin *locus*), *llan.*

4 It has been pointed out that the word *manach* for monk is used equally of a layman or anyone to whom the church provided pastoral care, and from whom tithes were received (Sharpe 1992).

5 Certainly in the early days of Christianity, as recorded by Irenaeus of Lyons, many 'believed in Christ without the benefit of writing and ink, having salvation in their hearts through the Holy Spirit' (Irenaeus, *Adversus Haeres* III. 4).

6 The Irish term *dairthech* or 'oakhouse' is used. Adomnán describes the use of large timbers from the mainland for construction and repair work at Iona, where excavations have revealed postholes and wooden architectural elements (Barber 1981; Karkov 1991: 32–3).

7 Bishop Tirechan, writing in the second half of the seventh century, describes St Patrick's supposed missionary work in Ireland, and records the names of the churches he founded, and of the priests and bishops installed, as well as the effects of plague on the church (Sharpe 1992: 87).

8 For Wales, Nash-Williams (1950) produced a classification and general chronology of the monuments which still forms the basis of their study today – Group I inscribed stones (fifth to seventh century), Group II cross-marked stones (seventh to ninth century), and Group III cross-slabs and freestanding crosses (ninth to thirteenth century). This classification has now been amplified by Gwyn Thomas's addition of new classes for the Royal Commission Inventory of the Early Christian Monuments of Glamorgan (though this has

not been universally adopted). Macalister compiled a gazetteer of all the inscribed stones from Ireland, Wales, England, the Isle of Man, and Scotland (1945, 1949), which he classified by type of inscription into Latin- and ogam-inscribed stones, and those in half-uncial script. His corpus on the large collection of grave slabs at Clonmacnois (1909) grouped them by cross type: Latin, Greek, in square panels, in circular panels, Celtic crosses, and those with looped terminal expansions (see also Lionard 1961: 95f.). The range is similar to Wales: the early ogam-inscribed stones, carved pillars, cross-inscribed slabs and recumbent slabs (in that order). The Irish stones have been the subject of early lists by Crawford (1912, 1913, 1916) and important reviews and regional studies (Henry 1965, 1967, 1970; Harbison 1986, 1992; Hamlin 1976, 1982; de Paor 1987; Lacy 1983; Cuppage 1986; Edwards 1983, 1985). Most recently Harbison has published a complete corpus of all the high crosses of Ireland, with a discussion of their iconography by subject (1992). The Scottish stones, which are more rarely inscribed, were grouped by Romilly Allen and Anderson (1903) by form and style, and many western examples are catalogued in the various Royal Commission volumes on Argyll (Royal Commission on the Ancient and Historical Monuments of Scotland).

9 Such as the seventh-century example from Arraglen, Co. Kerry, inscribed 'Ronan the priest, son of Comgan' (Macalister 1945: 140–1).

10 For example the stone from Liddel Water, Roxburghshire, inscribed HIC IACIT/ CARANTI FIL(I)/ CVPITIANI ('Here lies (the body) of Carant(i)us; of the son of Cupitianus'). For a recent discussion of the Scottish stones, see Thomas 1991–2: 1–10.

11 The fifth-century example from Ballaqueeney, Rushen, is inscribed: BIVAIDONAS MAQI MUCOI CUNAVA, 'The stone of Bivaidu, son of the tribe of Cunava', possibly a reference to the Conaille, a sub-kingdom in east Ireland (Cubbon 1982: 259).

12 A rare exception may be the pillar from Kilnasaggart, Co. Armagh, with a dedication by Ternhoc mac Cernan Bic, who died according to the Annals in 714 or 716. This dates the slab to *c.*700 (Hamlin 1982: 291).

13 The cross from Cardonagh, Co. Donegal, was considered by Henry as the first freestanding cross in Ireland (1965: 118–31). Its form is composed of broad interlaced ribbons, and below it an outline figure interpreted as Christ in Glory, or the Crucifixion. Unusual small pillars flanking the cross are inscribed with a head emerging from a fish's mouth (Jonah?) and a warrior (David?). It has more recently been argued that this cross represents a regional development rather than an early example, a contemporary equivalent rather than forerunner of the ringed cross form (Edwards 1985; 1990: 163), and redated to the ninth–tenth century.

14 Such as the early tenth-century Muiredach's cross, Monasterboice, Co. Cork.

15 The Doniert stone near St Cleer has been thought to commemorate the Doniert mentioned in an Early Welsh source as late ninth-century king of Cornwall. Wheel-headed crosses such as that at Sancreed near St Buryan became established in Cornwall. The Perranporth stone near the former church of St Piran is mentioned in a charter of 960, making it one of the few Cornish crosses which can be given a secure early date.

16 Such as the stones from St Kevin's Church, Glendalough, Co. Wicklow, Fahan Mura, Co. Donegal, and Gallen Priory, Co. Offaly.

17 A good example is the ninth/tenth-century slab from Lonan, which resembles the 'Conbelin' stone from Margam, West Glamorgan. Particularly fine is the late eighth-century stone altar frontal depicting the Crucifixion, from a chapel on the Calf of Man, which depicts a robed Christ flanked by lance-bearer and (now missing) sponge-bearer, with ornament suggesting copying from a metalwork of Irish type.

18 LATINVS IC IACIT/ FILIVS MACARI (Worthyvale, Cornwall); BROCAGNI IHC IACIT NADOTTI FILIVS (Doydon, St Endellion, Cornwall); DRVSTANVS HIC

IACIT/ CVNOMORI FILIVS (Castle Dore, Cornwall: the first occurrence of the name of Tristan).

19 At least 125 are known in Kerry, over 80 in Cork, 47 in Waterford and a few to the north (Hamlin 1982: 283). It has been recently argued that ogam may have developed earlier, in the first or second century (Stephenson 1989; Harvey 1990).

20 A medieval key to the script can be found in the fourteenth-fifteenth-century manuscript *The Book of Ballymote*. Ogam has sometimes been found scratched onto portable materials such as slate, bone or metal, along a drawn stem-line.

21 For example, DOTETTO MAQI MAGLANI, 'The stone of Dottetto, son of Maglani', from Aghascrebagh, Co. Tyrone.

22 That from Bressay, Shetland, has an inscription on its sides reading upwards: CRROSCC: NAHHTVVDDADDS:DATTRR:ANN/ BENNISES:MEQQDDRROANN. *Crossc* or cross and *maqq* (of the son of) are Gaelic words, while *dattr* is the Norse word for daughter. The other words are believed to be Pictish with punctuation borrowed from Norse runes and double consonants of Irish ogam, indicating a Christian community speaking a very mixed dialect.

23 Literacy may have been passed on by meetings held at outdoor meeting places. On the sixth-century pillar stone from Kilmalkedar, Co. Kerry, the letters of the alphabet have been added vertically to the original stone carving, namely a cross with spiral terminals and DNI (Domini).

24 For example an altar from Loughor, West Glamorgan, with a damaged ogam inscription on one angle and a milestone from Port Talbot, with a sixth-century inscription commemorating CANTVSVS PATER PAULINVS ('Here lies Cantusus. His father was Paulinus').

25 For example, on Iona Torridonian sandstone from the shore to the east of the Abbey, and mica schists from the Ross of Mull are used, together with large blocks from mainland Argyll more suitable for the freestanding crosses; in Glamorgan, South Wales, local Pennant sandstone is often used; different types of stone may sometimes used for head and shaft, as on the Carew cross, Dyfed.

26 The decoration on some stone appears incomplete, indicating possible haste in erecting the monument (e.g. Llandyfaelog Fach, Powys).

27 Kuli has been tentatively identified with Coll in the Hebrides, and Gaut as the son of a Hebridean Norseman who had moved to the Isle of Man.

28 The 'Pillar of Eliseg' (Valle Crucis, Powys) actually records the person responsible for writing the text of the inscription: + CONMARCH PINXIT HOC/ CHIROGRAF(I)U(M) REGE SUO POSCENTE ('Conmarch wrote (literally 'painted') this text at the command of his king'). An elaborate cross was carved over an earlier inscription on a stone from Defynnog (Powys), which would have been hard to see clearly unless the earlier inscription had been whitewashed over, and the carving coloured.

29 As at Ardwall Island, Holm of Noss (Shetland), and Staplegorton (Dumfries).

30 Such as the spiked feet on the outline cross set in the buttress of the church at Llangeinwen, Gwynedd.

31 In Wales, for example, the Latin name CATAMANUS on the Cadfan stone from Llangadwaladr, Gwynedd (ECMW 13), is described as REX SAPIENTIS(S)I/MUS OPINATISSIM/US OMNIUM REG/UM ('wisest and most renowned of all kings'). The stone may have been erected after his death by his grandson Cadwaladr, who died in 664. The early inscription from Aberdaron, Gwynedd, is inscribed VERACIVS PBR HIC IACIT ('Here lies the priest Veracius'); one from Kirkmadrine, Galloway, is inscribed HIC IACENT/ SCI ET PRAE/ CIPVI SACER/ DOTES ID EST/ VIVENTIVS/ ET MAVORIVS ('Here lie the holy (sancti) and outstanding priests (sacerdotes) . . .').

32 A lead sarcophagus of probable fifth-century date unique for Wales, from Rhuddgaer, Gwynedd, indicates that burial practice was initially consistent with that of Roman Britain in some areas. Two of the side sheets bear the raised inscription CAMVLORIS, and the letters HOI on one side have been expanded to H(IC) O(SSA) I(ACENT) ('Here lie the bones of Camuloris'; Williams 1878: 136).

33 The stone from Penmachno (Gwynedd) records the burial of Carausius beneath a cairn or burial mound (CARAVSIUS/ HIC IACIT/ IN HOC CON/ GERIES LA/ PIDUM).

34 OROIT AR TUATHGAIL LAS DERNATH IN CHROSSA. Probably the abbot of Clonmacnois who died in 811 (for a discussion, see Kelly 1992: 74–5).

35 It has recently been suggested that symbols, often in pairs, may have been used to convey pictorially the bipartite names of the commemorated built upon themes (Samson 1992). Interestingly, a Class I stone from Inchyra, Perth, also bears ogam inscriptions.

ACKNOWLEDGEMENTS

This chapter has relied heavily on the scholarship of others, many of whom are cited in the bibliography. I am particularly grateful to Ian Fisher and Dr Nancy Edwards for reading a draft of the text and making valuable comments. I would also like to thank Raghnall ÓFloinn, Katherine Forsyth and Mike Spearman for information, Tony Daly for preparing the line drawings, and the following bodies for permission to reproduce their illustrations: the Royal Commission on the Ancient and Historical Monuments of Scotland; the National Museum of Ireland; the Office of Public Works, Ireland; the National Museums of Scotland; the National Museum of Wales, and the Controller of Her Majesty's Stationery Office.

REFERENCES

Allen, J.R. and Anderson, J. (1903) *The Early Christian Monuments of Scotland*, 3 parts, Edinburgh.

Archaeological Survey of Northern Ireland 1966, *An Archaeological Survey of County Down*, Belfast: Her Majesty's Stationery Office.

Barber, J.W. (1981) 'Excavations on Iona, 1979', *Proceedings of the Society of Antiquaries of Scotland* 111: 282–380.

Blair, J. and Sharpe, R. (eds) (1992) *Pastoral Care Before the Parish*, Leicester: Studies in the Early History of Britain.

Boon, G.C. (1992) 'The early church in Gwent, I: the Romano-British church', *The Monmouthshire Antiquary* 8: 11–24.

Brassil, K.S., Owen, W.G. and Britnell, W.J. (1991) 'Prehistoric and early medieval cemeteries at Tandderwen, near Denbigh, Clwyd', *Archaeological Journal* 148: 46–97.

Crawford, H.S. (1912) 'A descriptive list of early cross-slabs and pillars', *Journal of the Royal Society of Antiquaries of Ireland* 42: 217–44.

—— (1913) 'A descriptive list of early cross-slabs and pillars (cont.)', *Journal of the Royal Society of Antiquaries of Ireland* 43: 151–169, 261–5, 326–34.

—— (1916) 'Supplementary list of early cross-slabs and pillars', *Journal of the Royal Society of Antiquaries of Ireland* 46.

Cubbon, A.M. (1982) 'The early church in the Isle of Man', in S.M. Pearce (ed.) *The Early*

Church in Western Britain and Ireland, 257–82.

Cuppage, J. (1986) *Archaeological Survey of the Dingle Peninsula. A description of the field antiquities of the Barony of Corca Dhuibhne from the Mesolithic period to the 17th century A.D.*, Ballyferriter.

Curle, C.L. (1940) 'The chronology of the early Christian monuments of Scotland', *Proceedings of the Society of Antiquaries of Scotland* 74: 60–116.

Davies, W. (1982) *Wales in the Early Middle Ages*, Leicester.

—— (1992) 'The myth of the Celtic church', in N. Edwards and A. Lane (eds) *The Early Church in Wales and the West*, Oxford, 12–21.

de Paor, L. (1987) 'The high crosses of Tech Theille (Tihilly), Kinnitty and related sculpture', in E. Rynne (ed.) *Figures from the Past*, Dun Laoghaire, 131–58.

Driscoll, S.T. (1988) 'The relationship between history and archaeology-artefacts, classments and power', in S.T. Driscoll and M.R. Nieke (eds) *Power and Politics in Early Medieval Britain and Ireland*, Edinburgh, 162–87.

Edwards, N. (1983) 'An early group of crosses from the kingdom of Ossory', *Journal of the Royal Society of Antiquaries of Ireland* 113: 5–46.

—— (1985) 'The origin of the freestanding stone cross in Ireland: imitation or innovation?', *Bulletin of the Board of Celtic Studies* 32: 393–410.

—— (1990) *The Archaeology of Early Medieval Ireland*, London.

Fanning, T. (1981) 'Excavation of an early Christian cemetery and settlement at Reask, County Kerry', *Proceedings of the Royal Irish Academy* 81: 67–172.

Hamlin, A. (1976) 'The archaeology of early Christianity in the north of Ireland', Ph.D. thesis, Queen's University, Belfast.

—— (1982) 'Early Irish stone carving: contact and context', in S.M. Pearce (ed.) *The Early Church in Britain and Ireland*, 283–96.

—— (1984) 'The archaeology of the early Irish churches in the eighth century', *Peritia* 4: 279–99.

—— (1987) 'Iona: a view from Ireland', *Proceedings of the Society of Antiquaries of Scotland* 117: 17–22.

Harbison, P. (1986) 'A group of early Christian carved stone monuments in County Donegal', in J. Higgitt (ed.) *Early Medieval Sculpture in Britain and Ireland*, 49–85.

—— (1970) 'How old is Gallarus oratory? A reappraisal of its role in early Irish architecture', *Medieval Archaeology* 14: 34–59.

—— (1992) *The High Crosses of Ireland*, Römisch-Germanischen Zentralmuseums Mainz and Royal Irish Academy.

Harvey, A. (1990) 'The ogham inscriptions and the Roman alphabet: two traditions or one?', *Archaeology Ireland* 4(1): 13–14.

Henderson, I. (1967) *The Picts*, London.

—— (1987) 'The Book of Kells and the snake-boss motif on Pictish cross-slabs and the Iona crosses', in M.Ryan (ed.) *Ireland and Insular Art A.D. 500–1200*, Dublin, 56–65.

Henderson, J. and Ivens, R. (1992) 'Dunmisk and glass-making in early Christian Ireland', *Antiquity* 66 no. 250, 52–64.

Henry, F. (1965) *Irish Art in the Early Christian Period (to 800 AD)*, London.

—— (1967) *Irish Art during the Viking Invasions (800–1020 AD)*, London.

—— (1970) *Irish Art in the Romanesque Period (1020–1170 AD)*, London.

—— (1980) 'Around an inscription: the cross of the Scriptures at Clonmacnois', *Journal of the Royal Society of Antiquaries of Ireland* 110: 36–46.

Herity, M. (1993) 'The forms of the tomb-shrine of the founder saint in Ireland', in R.M. Spearman and J. Higgitt (eds) *The Age of Migrating Ideas*, Edinburgh, 188–95.

Hicks, C. (1993) 'The Pictish Class I animals', in R.M. Spearman and J. Higgitt (eds) *The Age of Migrating Ideas*, Edinburgh, 196–202.

Higgitt, J. (ed.) (1986) *Early Medieval Sculpture in Britain and Ireland*, Oxford: British Archaeological Reports 152.

—— (1986) 'Words and crosses: the inscribed stone cross in Britain and Ireland', in J. Higgitt (ed.) *Early Medieval Sculpture*, 125–52.

Hughes, K. (1966) *The Church in Early Irish Society*, London.

Hughes, K. and Hamlin, A. (1977) *The Modern Traveller to the Early Irish Church*, London.

Hurley, V. (1982) 'The early church in the south-west of Ireland: settlement and organisation', in S.M. Pearce (ed.) *The Early Church in Western Britain and Ireland*, 297–332.

Ivens, R. (1988) 'Around an early church', in A. Hamlin and C. Lynn (eds) *Pieces of the Past*, Belfast, 55–6.

—— (1989) 'Dunmisk Fort, Carrickmore, Co. Tyrone. Excavations 1984–1986', *Ulster Journal of Archaeology* 52: 17f.

Jackson, A. (1984) *The Symbol Stones of Scotland*, Kirkwall.

Jackson, K. (1953) *Language and History in Early Britain*, Edinburgh.

Karkov, C. (1991) 'The decoration of early wooden architecture in Ireland and Northumbria', in C. Karkov and R. Farrell (eds) *Studies in Insular Art and Archaeology*, American Early Medieval Studies 1, 27–48.

Kelly, D. (1992) 'The high crosses of Ireland. A review article', *Journal of the Royal Society of Antiquaries of Ireland* 122: 67–78.

—— (1993) 'The relationships of the crosses of Argyll: the evidence of form', in R.M. Spearman and J. Higgitt (eds) *The Age of Migrating Ideas*, Edinburgh, 219–29.

Kermode, P.M.C. (1907) *Manx Crosses*, London.

King, H. (1992) 'Excavations at Clonmacnoise', *Archaeology Ireland* 6(3): 12–14.

Knight, J.K. (1970–1) 'St Tatheus of Caerwent: an analysis of the Vespasian Life', *Monmouthshire Antiquary* 3: 29–35.

—— (1984) *Glamorgan AD 400–1100: Archaeology and History*, Glamorgan County History 2.

Lacy, B. (ed.) (1983) *Archaeological Survey of County Donegal. A description of the field antiquities of the county from the Mesolithic period to the 17th century AD*, Lifford.

Lang, J. (1988) *Anglo-Saxon Sculpture*, Aylesbury.

Langdon, A.G. (1896) *Old Cornish Crosses*, Truro.

Lionard, P. (1961) 'Early Irish grave-slabs', *Proceedings of the Royal Irish Academy* 61: 95–170.

Macalister, R.A.S. (1909) *The Memorial Slabs of Clonmacnois King's County: with an appendix on the materials for a history of the monastery*, Dublin.

—— (1945) *Corpus Inscriptionum Insularum Celticarum* I, Dublin.

—— (1949) *Corpus Inscriptionum Insularum Celticarum* II, Dublin.

McManus, D. (1991) *A Guide to Ogam*, Maynooth Monographs 4.

Nash-Williams, V.E. (1950) *The Early Christian Monuments of Wales*, Cardiff.

O'Brien, E. (1992) 'Christian burial in Ireland: continuity and change', in N. Edwards and A. Lane (eds) *The Early Church in Wales and the West*, Oxford.

Okasha, E. (1993) *Corpus of Early Christian Inscribed Stones of South-west Britain*, London: Studies in the Early History of Britain.

O'Kelly, M.J. (1958) 'Church Island near Valencia, Co. Kerry', *Proceedings of the Royal Irish Academy* 59: 57–136.

Pearce, S.M. (ed.) (1982) *The Early Church in Western Britain and Ireland*, Oxford: British Archaeological Reports 102.

Pryce, H. (1992) 'Pastoral care in early medieval Wales', in J. Blair and R. Sharpe (eds) *Pastoral Care*, 41–62.

Radford, C.A.R. (1977) 'The earliest Irish churches', *Ulster Journal of Archaeology* 40:

1–11.

Redknap, M. (1976) 'Excavation at Iona Abbey, 1976', *Proceedings of the Society of Antiquaries of Scotland* 108: 228–53.

—— (1991) *The Christian Celts. Treasures of late Celtic Wales*, Cardiff: National Museum of Wales.

Royal Commission on the Ancient and Historical Monuments of Scotland (1982) *Argyll, an Inventory of the Monuments*, vol. 4: *Iona*, Edinburgh: Her Majesty's Stationery Office.

Royal Commission on Ancient and Historical Monuments in Wales (1976) *An Inventory of the Ancient Monuments of Glamorgan*, vol.I, part III: *The Early Christian Period*, Cardiff: Her Majesty's Stationery Office.

Samson, R. (1992) 'The reinterpretation of the Pictish symbols', *Journal of the British Archaeological Association* 145: 29–65.

Sharpe, R. (1984) 'Some problems concerning the organization of the church in early medieval Ireland', *Peritia* 3: 230–70.

—— (1992) 'Churches and communities in early medieval Ireland: towards a pastoral model', in J. Blair and P. Sharpe (eds) *Pastoral Care*, 81–109.

Stephenson, J. (1989) 'The beginnings of literacy in Ireland', *Proceedings of the Royal Irish Academy* 89: 127–165.

Stokes, W. (1887) *The Tripartite Life of Patrick*, 2 vols, London.

Thomas, C. (1986) *Celtic Britain*, London.

—— (1991–2) 'The early Christian inscriptions of southern Scotland', *Glasgow Archaeological Journal* 17: 1–10.

Wade-Evans, A.W. (ed.) (1944) *Vitae Sanctorum Britanniae et Genealogiae*, Cardiff.

Wakeman, W.F. (1893) *A Survey of the Antiquarian Remains on the Island of Inismurray*, London and Edinburgh.

Westwood, T.J. (1876–9) *Lapidarium Walliae*, Oxford.

Williams, W.W. (1878) 'Leaden coffin, Rhyddgaer', *Archaeologia Cambrensis* 9: 136–40.

Woodward, A. (1992) *Shrines and Sacrifice*, London: Her Majesty's Stationery Office.

MYTHOLOGY AND THE ORAL TRADITION
Ireland

Proinsias Mac Cana

One of the matters on which Celticists have failed most signally to achieve consensus is the degree to which the extant corpus of medieval Irish literature may be accepted as a reliable index of native mythology and religion: apart from the diverse special interests of the scholars themselves – constituents of the literary evidence which appear to stand forth in high relief when viewed from one academic or ideological perspective may be less prominent when seen from other points of view – there is the very real problem posed by the nature of the evidence itself and by the manner of its survival. First one must have regard to the chronological gap which separates the Irish materials from the information on the beliefs and practices of the continental Celts that survives in inscriptions, iconography and the commentaries of various classical authors and which furnishes a vital complement to the Insular evidence. Near the beginning of the twentieth century Camille Jullian commented on this difficulty from the standpoint of a historian of Gaul. Even if it could be proved that Irish tradition and Gaulish civilization were historically related, is it justifiable to interpret the one by recourse to the other? Can one, he asks, really rely on documents written in Ireland so many centuries later than the independent Gaul of the pre-Christian era?[1]

His problem was a very real one, but somewhat exaggerated in its formulation. In the first place, while the extant manuscript collections of vernacular literature only commence about the end of the eleventh century, a large proportion of their contents are linguistically older by two or three centuries. Second, the substantial conversion of Ireland from paganism did not take place until the fifth century, and there is no evidence to suggest that Christianity might have had a foothold anywhere in the country before the fourth. However, as a corollary to this Jullian raised another issue which was – and still is – of greater consequence: the extant mythological texts are, he believed, largely the creation of storytellers and learned authors and as such do not represent faithfully either Ireland itself or its beliefs and traditions.[2] This argument has considerable substance; just how much is still a matter for lively debate among students of Irish antiquity, though naturally the range of material and detail now involved goes far beyond anything Jullian had in mind. But essentially the central issue remains the same: to what extent does the literature written in a Christian environment in the Old Irish period truly reflect the traditions and institutions of an earlier time when Ireland was still innocent of Christianity and of writing?

Written Irish – if we discount the ogam alphabet, which was not suited to the recording of extended discourse – dates from the sixth century. It originated in a monastic milieu and to all intents and purposes it remained a monastic monopoly for the next six hundred years. In its early stages it seems to have been confined mainly to historical and panegyric verse and to short formulistic legal texts. One group of poems, commonly referred to as the 'Leinster poems' because of their concern with Leinster history, is considered particularly significant for the evolution of the orthodox presentation of native history and genealogy during the first couple of centuries of Christianity. In particular it exemplifies the great monastic design of grafting native historical and genealogical tradition on to Christian world history, so that the ancestor of the Leinstermen, Labraid Loingsech, is himself made the descendant of Noah and Adam; the enterprise in learned ecumenism first glimpsed in these poems was subsequently extended and elaborated by generations of scholars until its final culmination in the eleventh and twelfth centuries in the great synthetic history of *Leabhar Gabhála*, literally 'The Book of the Taking'. The conscious and sustained shaping of this amalgam of ecclesiastical learning and native tradition throughout the period of Old and Middle Irish is in itself the clearest caution against assuming any consistent correspondence between the extant corpus of text and the oral learning and literature of the pre-literate era. The same monastic milieux and in large measure the same *literati* who from the seventh century on produced a substantial learned and ecclesiastical literature also generated a rich manuscript corpus of heroic and mythico-historical literature conforming broadly to traditional genres and categories. That the individual texts which make up this literature were shaped in varying degrees by the intellectual ambience in which they were composed and by the exotic learning of their monastic authors is beyond dispute; there is clear enough evidence of it in their vocabulary and content. Where agreement falters is with regard to the extent of this monastic innovation and the degree of continuity, or discontinuity, between the new written literature and the oral literature which preceded it and later coexisted with it.

James Carney (1914–89), a scholar of great literary and philological insight, reacted to what he perceived as an exaggerated regard for the role of tradition on the part of some of his older colleagues whom he dubbed 'nativists' by seeking to demonstrate that the written literature of Old Irish was largely a new creation deriving much of its motivation and substance from the Latin learning of the monasteries.[3] Whether the academic divisions of opinion were anything like as constant and clear-cut as he implies is open to question – from a different vantage-point, that of the anthropologist-mythologist observing the ingrained preconceptions of the philologist, Alwyn D. Rees remarks of Celtic scholars in general, including at least some of those whom Carney takes to task, that 'they seem to have a predisposition to minimize the *continuity* of the native tradition ... into historical times.'[4] Yet undoubtedly Carney's critical revisionism provided a healthy deterrent and counterbalance to uncritical acceptance of the traditional character of the new literature, even if his vivid advocacy of his views has had the effect of polarizing the terms in which the argument continues to be prosecuted, thereby imbuing it with a polemical element which sometimes has the effect of distorting rather than clarifying the questions at issue. One of Carney's major contributions to Irish studies was his series of valuable commentaries on the style, motivation and structure of early Irish verse, and here again he was often concerned to stress the importance of its contemporary and sometimes personal motivation. By contrast, however, when dealing with some of the 'Leinster poems' already referred to he tended increasingly to ascribe them to dates rather earlier than had been customary, and in a couple of instances even to within the pre-Christian period: this kind of verse, he suggested, constituted 'the oral archives of the kingship of Tara'.[5]

Prose, on the other hand, was a more fluid medium and its literal continuation from oral to written correspondingly less likely, which, given that Irish (and Welsh) narrative is characteristically in the form of prose, is a matter of considerable importance in assessing the relative roles of the traditional and the exotic in its composition. It is in its externals that early written narrative betrays most clearly its literate origins. When Carney refers to its use of words borrowed from Latin, he is pushing an open door; after all, the commonest of its terms for 'hero', *láech*, derives from Latin *laicus*, and, it would indeed be surprising if the working vocabulary of the monastic *literati* did not affect the texts they composed.[6] Even its characteristically terse diction is a typically written style, though one that has almost certainly been evolved from the less constrained medium of oral storytelling.[7] It is when one turns from the externals to considerations of theme and content that one finds sharp differences of interpretation and presentation, not surprisingly perhaps. On the one hand the use of Latin borrowings and the development of a distinctive written style do not in themselves imply that the matter of the narrative is not, as it purports to be, largely or essentially traditional. On the other, the considerable interaction and collaboration evidenced from the sixth century onwards between vernacular and monastic learning and between *filidh* and *literati* must inevitable have left its mark on the matter as well as the form of written secular narrative. Authors and redactors trained in biblical precedent would have been quick to see its analogies with native tradition, as – to take only one example from many – when they compared Cormac mac Airt with Solomon and, if we accept Gwynn's plausible suggestion, perceived the analogy between the great hall of Tara and Solomon's House and Temple.[8]

While some of Carney's assertions of borrowing from Latin/classical and ecclesi-astical sources are at the very least evidentially improbable – for example that the (seating) arrangement at formal gatherings in texts like *Táin Bó Cuailnge* derive from the seating arrangement in heaven as presented in the vernacular religious text *Fís Adomnán* 'Adomnán's Vision', that the Otherworld tree is taken from the Tree of Life in Genesis, and that the familiar 'watchman device' is borrowed from Homer (*Iliad* III.161ff.) '*through whatever intermediaries*'[9] (my italics) – the fact remains that Irish thought and learning from the sixth century on was an interweave of native and exotic, monastic constituents. One need only instance – apart from the Bible itself – the remarkable impact of Isidore's *Etymologiae* on Irish learning, or the close blend of native and 'external' concepts of the nature of art and poetic inspiration in Old Irish didactic texts such as *Immacallam in dá Thuarad*, 'The Converse of the Two Sages'. As I have observed on other occasions, this confluence was probably inevitable given the convergence and considerable overlapping of the professional interests of traditional poet-scholars and monastic *literati* and given the fact that both groups would have issued largely from the same social class and even from the same families. In this context one can readily endorse and even enhance Kim McCone's observation that 'Continuity with the pre-Christian past by no means precludes significant changes on the way'.[10] The problem is, of course, that the literary results of this amalgam are now accessible to us only to the extent that they have survived in texts written and transmitted in monastic schools and by monastic scholars. Of the learned oral tradition which preceded the written and which continued alongside it, obviously we know nothing except by written reference or by extrapolation from the written texts. One may easily be inclined therefore, while not denying it, largely to discount it, on the grounds that in Old Irish we have a homogeneous corpus of learning and literature created solely in terms of the written text, a tendency this that is all the stronger when accompanied by certain preconceptions about oral tradition.

James Carney speaks of '*primitive* oral tradition' (my italics) and gratuitously assumes a contrast between a dynamic written text and a 'stereotyped' oral text.[11] In the sense in which he uses them these terms are of doubtful relevance – for one thing, the evidence of comparable situations elsewhere in the world is that oral 'histories' have their own dynamic and are adapted to the requirements of contemporary or local taste and circumstance just as often and as freely as written ones – but their effect as used by Carney is to exaggerate the actual discontinuity, or mutation, occasioned by the transition from the oral to the written phase. The nature of this discontinuity is perhaps most easily summarized by indicating briefly what early Irish literature as we know it is. Excluding its specifically ecclesiastical component it is a corpus of texts in prose and verse comprising a wide range of matter and genre – historical and genealogical, mythico-heroic, lyrical, dramatic, and so on – all of it drawing upon secular tradition and all of it composed and written by monastic scholars and inevitably influenced by the broad sweep of their ecclesiastical experience and learning. The creative dynamic of this combination is attested in the sheer volume and variety of the literature it generated, in the rich diversity of metre it produced, in the stylistic experimentation that produced written Old Irish narrative prose, in the infusion of Christian and personal values and perspectives into traditional themes, in the aesthetic and philosophical preoccupation of certain monastic *littérateurs* with the relativities of time and space in traditional tales of the Otherworld, and so on. One cannot gratuitously assume that a corresponding oral tale lies behind each written one, and one can think of other texts analogous to the Old Irish store of Deirdre, *Longas mac nUislenn*, which is so finely crafted within its compact frame that one feels it was probably first composed as a written tale.

Paradoxically, it is precisely these tales that seem most subtly and cunningly to exploit the resources of traditional literature to invest their laconic prose with its peculiar sense of complex allusion and resonance. But it is also true that the whole corpus of Old Irish secular narrative supposes such a diversified oral tradition. On this there is a broad measure of agreement: even a work such as Kim McCone's *Pagan Past*, which is a thoroughgoing, articulate essay in maximizing the Latin and biblical element in the literature, does in one way or another acknowledge the substantial continuity from pre-literate and pre-Christian tradition.[12] How this continuity is realized in writing will vary from one text to another: the early recension of Cú Chulainn's birth-tale is a coherent mythico-heroic text and is evidently a tersely phrased version of an oral narrative;[13] the 'Death of Conchobor', as James Carney pointed out, comprises 'a genuine traditional story' and an extension relating his death to Christ's crucifixion;[14] the centre-piece of the Ulster cycle, *Táin Bó Cuailnge*, though rich in heroic forms and ideology, need not as a whole presuppose a close equivalent in pre-literate tradition; the story of 'Cú Chulainn's Boyhood Deeds' which forms part of the extant text of the *Táin* is a highly skilful essay in written narrative, not a didactic account of ritual, yet it offers a consistent and, as Georges Dumézil has shown, remarkably archaic view of heroic initiation.

The modern convention of classifying the literature into four cycles – the mythological cycle, the Ulster cycle, the Finn cycle and the king cycle – is indeed modern and, so far as mythology is concerned, quite misleading, since the whole corpus is in varying degrees mythological. The traditional mode of classification was not by cycle but instead grouped the individual tales together under such heading as 'birth-tales', 'death-tales', 'wooings', 'elopements', 'plunderings', etc. which did not explicitly distinguish 'mythological' from other tales. Of those tales which deal specifically with the gods *Cath Maige Tuired*, 'The Battle of Mag Tuired', has a central role, featuring as it does virtually the whole Irish pantheon in the archetypal victory of the divine Tuatha Dé Danann over the demonic Fomoiri, a theomachy that has familiar analogues in the mythology of Scandinavia, Greece and India; the fact that it has in its approximately ninth-century written form been accommodated to the new synthetic history of *Leabhar Gabhála* does not of course invalidate it as evidence for the nature of Irish mythology. Indeed it is remarkable how the testimony of this and other Irish texts matches and complements the continental (and British) evidence on the Celtic gods despite the glaring disparities and deficiencies of the extant sources. Lugh and Brighid (Brigid) are only the two most conspicuous of those Irish deities who are identifiable as pan-Celtic either by name or function, or both, and it is some measure of the tenacity of custom and oral tradition that residual popular lore and ritual associated with them continued to flourish virtually to our own day.

The primary reason why there was such a carry-over from the oral to the written phase was that oral literature and learning enjoyed high status long before the coming of writing, and that mainly because, in their more formal mode, they were cultivated and controlled by an élitist and privileged class of semi-sacred savants and poets: the druids and, subsequently, the *filidh*, who were closely associated with religion and ideology and had their close counterparts in Wales and, earlier still, among the Celts of Britain and the Continent. The extent to which their repertoire was transmitted in writing depended on factors beyond their immediate control: the motivation and priorities of individual monastic scribes and authors for example, or the hazards by which manuscripts perished or survived to our own time.

Given the pivotal role of sacred kingship in early Irish society it is hardly surprising that the mythology, and to some extent the ritual, of sovereignty bulks large in the extant literature, even if trimmed of some their most uncivil features. Yet even here, despite the richness of the extant material, its incompleteness as a record of the oral tradition is evidenced by the casual or fortuitous manner in which some items are attested. When, for example, in the twelfth century Giraldus Cambrensis describes a 'barbarous and abominable' rite of inauguration practised in what is now

Donegal, one can hardly dismiss it as an unsympathetic fiction, considering how vividly it recalls the great inauguration rite of the horse-sacrifice, the *aśvadmedha*, in ancient India.[15] If indeed they are analogous, then where must one seek the source of Giraldus's report? That the rite was then obsolete in his time is indicated by other accounts of roughly contemporary inauguration, and one can only conclude that it reached Giraldus as an item of *seanchas*, or oral tradition, which remains wholly unattested elsewhere.

NOTES

1 *Histoire de la Gaule* II (Paris, 1908), 13 n. 5.

2 'Ces documents de langue britannique [*sic*], cycle mythologique irlandais, etc., sont en grande partie des œuvres artificielles, dues à l'imagination ou à l'érudition de conteurs ou de demi-savants, et sont loin de donner l'écho fidèle de l'Irlande elle-même, de refléter ses croyances ou de conserver ses traditions. Trop de fantaisies individuelles ont pu s'y glisser, trop de remaniements s'y sont produits.' Here and elsewhere Jullian uses the term *britannique* as if it included the Irish language.

3 Cf. especially his *Studies in Irish Literature and History* (Dublin, 1955, repr. with index 1979).

4 'Modern evaluations of Celtic narrative tradition', *Proceedings of the Second International Congress of Celtic Studies*', Cardiff, 1963 (Cardiff, 1966) 31–61 at 39.

5 'The dating of archaic Irish verse', in Stephen N. Tranter and Hildegard L.C. Tristram (eds) *Early Irish Literature – Media and Communication: Mundlichkeit und Schriftlichkeit in der frühen irischen Literatur* (Tübingen, 1989) 39–55 at 41.

6 cf. Carney, *Studies* 278; P. Mac Cana, 'On the word *láech* "warrior"', *Celtica* 11 (1976): 125–6.

7 Mac Cana, *Ériu* 23 (1972): 102–42 at 107–17.

8 Edward Gwynn, *The Metrical Dindshenchas* I (Dublin, 1903, repr. 1941, 1991), 70–4.

9 On the 'watchman device' see Gerard Murphy, *Éigse* 8 (1955–7): 157 n. 3; Jan de Vries, *Heroic Song and Heroic Legend* (London, 1963), 75–7; Patrick Sims-Williams, *Studia Celtica* 12–13 (1977–8): 84–5.

10 *Pagan Past and Christian Present in Early Irish Literature* (Maynooth, 1990), 17.

11 *Studies*, 298, 319. Referring to variants of the 'watchman device' in the written literature he comments that they indicate 'that we are dealing with a technique which is developing rapidly from generation to generation within the literary period rather than with one that was inherited in a stereotyped form from an oral tradition immemorially old'. In fact a wider comparison of relevant material elsewhere shows that the supposed progressive development of the topic in Irish is at best doubtful (cf. P. Sims-Williams, *Studia Celtica* 12–13: 84 n. 5).

12 *Pagan Past, passim*.

13 Mac Cana, *Ériu* 23 (1972): 102–42 at 107–14.

14 Carney, *Studies*, 296–7.

15 *Topographia Hibernica* III, 25; *Giraldi Cambrensis Opera*, ed. James F. Dimock, v (London, 1967), 169; *The First Version of the Topography of Ireland by Giraldus Cambrensis*, transl. John J. O'Meara (Dundalk, 1951) 93–4.

MYTHOLOGY AND THE ORAL TRADITION
Wales

——— ·•· ———

Sioned Davies

Classical authors have left us with several references to the eloquence of the early Celts (Chadwick 1970: 45–7). Traces of this eloquence have survived into medieval Welsh literature which, although accessible only in written form, reflects much of the oral tradition of the period. Many stylistic features of medieval Welsh poetry and prose betray an oral background, while certain mythological themes and characters in eleventh- and twelfth-century tales are recognizably Celtic in origin, the material having been transmitted orally for centuries before reaching its extant form.

Before the twelfth century, literacy in Wales was probably confined to the monastic environment. Side by side with a church learning, however, there existed a tradition of native learning, transmitted orally at first. This would have included history, genealogies and origin narratives, topography, boundaries and geography, religious myths, tribal and family lore, antiquities and legends, social and legal procedures, and medicine (Roberts 1988: 62). This corpus of traditional lore was known as *cyfarwyddyd*, a term connected etymologically with 'guidance, direction, instruction, knowledge', while the *cyfarwydd* was 'the guide, well-informed person, expert' (Mac Cana 1980:139). Various classes of learned men would have been responsible for the different aspects of *cyfarwyddyd*, including the lawyers, mediciners and bards. Indeed, the bards (*beirdd*, singular *bardd*), like their Irish counterparts, seem to have played a central role in native Welsh learning at this period. However, poetry does not seem to have been the medium for narrative in medieval Wales. Rather, tales were related in prose, and it is to this corpus that we must turn if we are to find any substantial evidence of Celtic mythology in medieval Welsh literature.

Cyfarwyddyd was also a term for 'story' in medieval Welsh, and the storyteller was known as the *cyfarwydd* (plural *cyfarwyddiaid*). As suggested by Mac Cana (1980: 139), what may have happened is that the semantic range of the word *cyfarwydd* used as a quasi-literary term became gradually narrowed until in the end it was virtually confined to one, and that a lesser one, of its older connotations. We know very little of the *cyfarwydd* and his functions in medieval Welsh society. In medieval Ireland, there is evidence to suggest that the composition of both prose and poetry was linked to that of the *fili* (poet), although storytelling was not one of his main functions. In Wales there is no direct evidence regarding the relationship between the *bardd* (poet) and *cyfarwydd* (storyteller). One-much quoted passage in an eleventh-century tale tells of Gwydion and his companions visiting the court of Pryderi in the guise of poets:

> They made them welcome. Gwydion was placed at Pryderi's one hand that night. 'Why,' said Pryderi, 'gladly would we have a tale [*cyfarwyddyd*] from some of the young men yonder.' 'Lord,' said Gwydion, 'it is a custom with us that the first night after one comes to a great man, the chief bard [*pencerdd*] shall have the say. I will tell a tale gladly.' Gwydion was the best teller of tales [*cyfarwydd*] in the world. And that night he entertained the court with pleasant tales and story-telling [*cyfarwyddyd*] till he was praised by everyone in the court.
>
> (Jones and Jones 1976: 56–7; for Welsh edition see Williams 1930: 69)

On another occasion Gwydion, in the guise of a poet from Glamorgan, is made welcome at a North Wales court and narrates *cyfarwyddyd* (stories) after feasting. Both passages are open to interpretation regarding the role and significance of the poet/storyteller in medieval Wales. The implication is that the poet would travel from court to court, even from north to south of the country; he was a welcome guest and would be honoured with the seat next to the ruler of the court; the *pencerdd* (chief poet) was accompanied by a retinue of lesser poets; it was not the rule for the *pencerdd* to narrate stories, rather this was the domain of the lesser poets; and finally, the purpose of the *cyfarwydd* was to entertain. Even so, this does not necessarily equate the poet with the storyteller – one could argue, with Mac Cana (1980: 138), that the term *cyfarwydd* is an occasional title which primarily denotes a function rather than a social or professional class.

Few native medieval Welsh tales have survived – eleven in all – and although the extant tales are the product of a literary culture, the inherited rules of oral art no doubt played an essential role in their composition. As Robert Kellogg states (1991: 137), the earliest vernacular texts represent a collaboration between the two cultures, oral and literate. The texts have been preserved mainly in two Welsh collections, the White Book of Rhydderch (*c*.1350), and the Red Book of Hergest (*c*.1400). Fragments also occur in manuscripts earlier by a hundred years or so, while certain of the stories must have been known in their present redaction well before the time of the earliest of these manuscripts. The tales are known today as the *Mabinogion*. This collective title was first given to the tales by Lady Charlotte Guest who translated them into English between 1838 and 1849. However, the word *mabinogion* occurs only once in the original text, and is almost certain to be a scribal error. Yet, *mabinogion* has become a convenient term to describe this corpus of prose tales, although we should not perceive them as a unified collection of any kind – they vary in date, background and content (for an English translation, see Jones and Jones 1976). The earliest tales seem to be *Pedeir Keinc y Mabinogi* (The Four Branches of the Mabinogi), generally referred to as *Pwyll, Branwen, Manawydan, Math*, dated *c*.1060–1120; *Culhwch ac Olwen* (Culhwch and Olwen) is the earliest Arthurian prose tale, dated *c*.1100; *Breuddwyd Maxen* (The Dream of Maxen) and the three Welsh Arthurian Romances of *Owein, Peredur, Gereint* with their counterparts in the French poems of Chrétien de Troyes belong to the twelfth and thirteenth centuries; *Cyfranc Lludd a Llefelys* (The Encounter of Lludd and Llefelys) first appears in the thirteenth century when a Welsh translator of Geoffrey of Monmouth's *Historia Regum Britanniae* (History of the Kings of Britain) inserted it into his translation – the episode then appears as an independent tale in the Red Book and the White Book manuscripts; *Breuddwyd Rhonabwy* (The Dream of Rhonabwy) is the latest of all and is a parody on the Arthurian age. These then are the only surviving examples of traditional Welsh narrative – obviously much has been lost as testified by allusions in these and other sources, especially the bardic triads *Trioedd Ynys Prydein* (The Triads of the Island of Britain).

A scattering of mythological characters, motifs and allusions are to be found throughout these narratives. Shape-shifting, for example, occurs in *Culhwch ac Olwen* – the supernatural wild boar is a king who has been transformed because of his wickedness, while Menw has the ability to change himself into a bird. Magical objects such as a hamper and a horn of plenty feature in the tale, and many of Arthur's men possess supernatural powers. It has been argued that the three Romances contain traces of a Celtic mythological sovereignty theme, involving a symbolic marriage between king and goddess, and combats with Otherworld powers (Bromwich 1983). In the tale of *Owein*, the keeper of the forest who has power over all the animals, may well be analogous to the Celtic god Cernunnos, an antlered deity (Green 1992: 59–61; Mac Cana 1983: 39–42). However, of the extant tales, the Four Branches of the Mabinogi are of greatest importance in the context of Celtic mythology. Many of their characters are Otherworld beings, and their world is one where the supernatural impinges on the lives of everyday mortals. It is generally held that the Four Branches are the work of one individual, a deliberate artistic piece of literature (Davies 1992). Indeed, the author may well have been Sulien, bishop of St David's, or his son Rhigyfarch. Even so, the author is clearly drawing on traditional sources for his material. He states this categorically on two occasions:

> And that is what this *cyfarwyddyd* says of their encounter. 'The men who set forth from Ireland' is that.
> (Jones and Jones 1976: 40)

> And according to the *cyfarwyddyd*, he was lord thereafter over Gwynedd.
> (Jones and Jones 1976: 75)

In other words, he is trying to distance himself from the traditional material. As Kellogg says of the compiler of a thirteenth-century Icelandic manuscript (1991: 139), he is aware of himself as occupying a boundary between two worlds – his own rational, scholarly, literary world and the more fantastic world of ancient myth and legend from which the tales have come down. However, as emphasized by Green (1986: 16), it is evident that the author of the Four Branches and other writers of the period were fairly ignorant of the actual beliefs of the people about whom they wrote. Yet a careful examination of the texts can enrich our general understanding of Celtic mythology.

The first branch tells of Pwyll prince of Dyfed and his encounter with Arawn, king of Annwfn, the Otherworld. They exchange places for one year during which time Pwyll kills Arawn's enemy – an example of an Otherworld figure invoking the help of a mortal. Upon his return to Dyfed, Pwyll encounters Rhiannon, who appears riding a white horse. They are eventually married after tricking Gwawl, her betrothed, and a son is born to them. He disappears on the night of his birth and Rhiannon is falsely accused of killing him. Her punishment is to sit at the horseblock outside the court gate and to carry all visitors to court on her back. Meanwhile, Teyrnon lord of Gwent Is-Coed discovers the boy and rears him for seven years before returning him to his parents, whereupon the child is named Pryderi. It has been suggested that Teyrnon (from *Tigernonos, 'Great, or Divine, Lord') was originally a divine figure and played a more important role in the tale, while Rhiannon (from *Rigantona, 'Great, or Divine, Queen') with her equine associations is to be equated with Epona, the Celtic horse-goddess (Gruffydd 1953: 98; Mac Cana 1983: 80–1). Moreover, in the third branch and in *Culhwch ac Olwen* she is assigned magical birds who 'wake the dead and lull the living to sleep' (Jones and Jones 1976: 115–16). Attempts have also been made to equate Pryderi and Rhiannon with Mabon (from *Maponos, 'Divine Son') and Modron (from *Matrona, 'Great Mother') (Gruffydd 1953). Mabon son of Modron appears in the role of a huntsman in *Culhwch ac Olwen* and 'was taken away when three nights old from his mother' (Jones and Jones 1976: 118). Hamp (1975) has even argued that the term *Mabinogi* itself is to be understood as originally the material, or doings pertaining to (the family of) the divine Maponos, and has nothing to do with youth, son, story of youth, as is commonly held.

The family of Llŷr is central to the second branch, namely Brân or Bendigeidfran (Brân the Blessed), king of Britain, his brother Manawydan and sister Branwen. Her hand is given in marriage to Matholwch king of Ireland, whereupon Efnysien, Branwen's half-brother, insults Matholwch by mutilating his horses. Brân offers gifts to pacify him, including a magic cauldron whose virtue is that when dead men are placed in it they will rise the following day, but will not have the power of speech. On their return to Ireland Branwen is punished for the insult done to her husband in Wales. She rears a starling and sends it to Wales with news of her plight, where-upon Brân wages war against the Irish. In the ensuing battle, Brân is mortally wounded in his foot – he orders his head to be cut off and taken for burial to the White Mount in London where it will serve as a talisman to keep away invaders. Following Brân's instructions, the seven survivors spend seven years feasting at Harlech, and a further eighty years on the island of Gwales before burying the head. There is no evidence that Branwen was ever a divine figure, but her brother Brân certainly possessed magical qualities. We are told that he was a man of immense stature – no house could ever hold him – and when the Welsh discover that the Irish have destroyed the bridge over the Llinon (probably Shannon), Brân lies across the river, forming a bridge for his men to cross. After his death his severed head remains uncorrupted and is excellent company for his men, the implication being that it speaks to them.

The Otherworld is an interesting feature of the second branch – it is portrayed as a happy and welcoming place. In the first branch, the Otherworld court is perfection itself, but there is no detailed description. Neither is there an exact location – Annwfn is a land in close proximity to Dyfed, but no clear boundary separates them. In the second branch, it is a wonderful place by the sea in both instances. The magical birds of Rhiannon sing to the company at Harlech, while Gwales is a time-less land where the sorrows of the mortal world are forgotten (a common theme in Celtic literature). There is also a taboo connected with life there – in *Branwen* the enchantment will be destroyed once a certain door is opened (Gruffydd 1958). In Irish literature the Otherworld was often perceived as an island or group of islands in the sea (Mac Cana 1983: 122–31); other times it was a land beneath the earth, compare the Welsh *Annwfn* (from *an* (in/under) + *dwfn* (world)). At the turn of this century a tale was recorded by John Rhŷs (1901: 158–60) concerning *Plant Rhys Ddwfn* (The Children of Rhys Ddwfn), a corruption it would seem of *Plant yr Is-Ddwfn* (The Children of the Underworld). According to the tale these fairies inhabited an island off the coast of Dyfed. This is also the location of Gwales (Grassholm Island) in the tale of *Branwen* where the Otherworld feasting takes place. In the *Pembroke County Guardian* of 1896 Captain John Evans claimed to have seen a 'floating island' just off Grassholm, while according to the *Cambrian Superstitions* (1831), the people of Milford Haven believed that the off-shore islands were populated with fairies. Therefore, over the centuries, the belief has survived that Gwales and its neighbouring islands were places of magic and enchantment, thus linking the eleventh century with the twentieth.

Manawydan is the brother of Branwen and the central figure of the third branch. Pryderi gives his mother, Rhiannon, as wife to Manawydan. An enchantment falls on Dyfed, Pryderi and his mother disappear in a magic fort, but Manawydan succeeds in freeing them by capturing the wife of Llwyd, the magician who has placed the enchantment on Dyfed. Manawydan may be the Welsh equivalent of the Irish sea-god Manannán son of Lir (Mac Cana 1983: 78–80). However, there is no connection between him and the sea in Welsh tradition. The enchantment falls on Dyfed while the characters are seated on *Gorsedd Arberth* (The Mound at Arberth). It is from the same spot that Pwyll sees Rhiannon, having first been warned of the peculiarity of the mound:

> whatever high-born man sits upon it will not go thence without one of two things: wounds or blows, or else his seeing a wonder.
>
> (Jones and Jones 1976: 9)

This reflects the dual nature of the Otherworld – Pwyll sees a wonder, but Manawydan and his companions are less fortunate. The mound, therefore, serves as a marker between two worlds in the Four Branches as, indeed, does the colour white. Rhiannon first appears mounted on a white horse; Arawn's dogs are shining white with red ears; Pryderi's dogs are lured into the Otherworld fortress of the third branch by a shining white boar. Once inside the fortress, Pryderi is transfixed by a fountain and 'a golden bowl fastened to four chains . . . and the chains ascending into the air, and he could see no end to them' (Jones and Jones 1976: 46). His hands stick to the bowl and he loses his power of speech (compare the effect of the cauldron in *Branwen*). Shape-shifting also occurs in this third branch – Llwyd transforms his war-band and subsequently the ladies of his court into mice so that they may destroy Manawydan's corn.

Metamorphosis is most apparent in the fourth branch which tells of the family of Dôn, the equivalent perhaps of the Irish Tuatha Dé Danann (Mac Cana 1983: 78).

Math son of Mathonwy is lord over Gwynedd, and must rest his feet in the lap of a virgin unless he is at war. His sister's son, Gilfaethwy son of Dôn, falls in love with the virgin, and through trickery and magic Gilfaethwy's brother Gwydion succeeds in waging war between Math and Pryderi in order to free the virgin. (Pryderi is actually tricked into giving Gwydion pigs which his father received as a present from Arawn, king of Annwfn.) She is raped, and Gwydion and Gilfaethwy are punished – Math transforms them into animals for three years. At the end of each year they produce an offspring until finally their own human form is restored to them. Arianrhod, daughter of Dôn, is the new virgin foot-holder offered to Math, but as she steps over Math's magic wand as a test of her virginity she gives birth to two sons. The first is named Dylan Eil Ton (Dylan son of Wave) – he immediately makes for the sea whereupon 'he received the sea's nature and swam as well as the best fish in the sea' (Jones and Jones 1976: 63–4). Arianrhod places three curses on the other boy: he is to have neither a name nor arms unless provided by her, nor a wife of humankind. Through Gwydion's magic (including shape-shifting), she is tricked into giving him a name, Lleu Llaw Gyffes (The Bright One of the Skilful Hand – cognate with the Irish Lugh), and also arms. With the help of Math, Gwydion finally conjures up a wife for him out of flowers who is called Blodeuwedd (Flower-face). She, however, proves unfaithful to Lleu and plots to kill him with her lover although Lleu is almost immortal. Lleu is transformed into an eagle, but Gwydion succeeds in disenchanting him. The lover is killed by Lleu and Gwydion transforms Blodeuwedd into an owl.

It is apparent, therefore, that the author of the Four Branches is drawing on traditional stories ultimately derived from earlier primary Celtic mythology. However, the author is using these tales and traditions from the past as a vehicle for his own ideas – underneath the magic and enchantment we are aware of his emphasis on a moral code of conduct which he tries to communicate to his medieval audience. The Four Branches have, in their turn, inspired twentieth-century novelists and playwrights who have interpreted them according to their own personal vision. This is proof of the lasting appeal of these medieval tales and ultimately of Celtic mythology itself.

REFERENCES

Bromwich, R. (1983) 'Celtic elements in Arthurian Romance: a general survey', in P.B. Grout, R.A. Lodge, C.E. Pickford and E.K.C. Varty (eds) *The Legend of Arthur in the Middle Ages*, Cambridge: D.S. Brewer, 41–55.
Chadwick, N. (1970) *The Celts*, Harmondsworth: Pelican Books.
Davies, S. (1992) *Pedeir Keinc y Mabinogi – The Four Branches of the Mabinogi*, Llandysul: Gomer Press.
Green, M.J. (1986) *The Gods of the Celts*, Gloucester and New Jersey: Alan Sutton.
—— (1992) *Dictionary of Celtic Myth and Legend*, London: Thames & Hudson.
Gruffydd, W.J. (1953) *Rhiannon*, Cardiff: Wales University Press.
—— (1958) *Folklore and Myth in the Mabinogion*, Cardiff: Wales University Press.
Hamp, E.P. (1975) 'Mabinogi', *Transactions of the Honourable Society of Cymmrodorion*, 243–9.

Jones, G. and Jones, T. (1976) *The Mabinogion*, London: Everyman. First published 1948.

Kellogg, R. (1991) 'Literary aesthetics in oral art', *Oral Tradition* 6: 137–40.

Mac Cana, P. (1977) *The Mabinogi*, Cardiff: Wales University Press.

—— (1980) *The Learned Tales of Medieval Ireland*, Dublin: Institute for Advanced Studies.

—— (1983) *Celtic Mythology*, London: Newnes.

Rhŷs, J. (1901) *Celtic Folklore, Welsh and Manx*, Oxford: Oxford University Press.

Roberts, B.F. (1984) 'From traditional tale to literary story: Middle Welsh prose narratives', in L.A. Arrathoon (ed.) *The Craft of Fiction*, Rochester: Solaris Press, 211–30.

—— (1988) 'Oral tradition and Welsh literature: a description and survey', *Oral Tradition* 3: 61–87.

Williams, I. (1930) *Pedeir Keinc y Mabinogi*, Cardiff: Wales University Press.

PART XII

THE SURVIVAL OF
THE CELTS

—◦◆◦—

LANGUAGE AND IDENTITY IN MODERN WALES

Wynne Lloyd

I had better declare my position at the outset. I cannot conceive of a Welsh identity kit without the language. I do not imply that the Welsh language is, of itself, the sole means of identity, but I do believe that a meaningful Welsh identity is not credible or indeed possible without the language.

As a contributor to this volume I find myself very much a layman in the shadow of a constellation of academics. I suspect that, in the name of academic integrity, it is possible for them to consider their chosen topic with a high degree of objectivity. I, however, do not have that categoric objective. I am not an academic; neither do I pretend to be one for the purpose of this volume. My views and opinions are subjective. They reflect the standpoint of someone who has, apart from the war years, lived and worked in Wales. They also reflect the attitudes of someone who was born into a Welsh-speaking community, who subsequently lost the language and who, eventually, regained it.

I am only too conscious of the fact that I am in a minority within my own country. I belong to that fifth part of the population which calls itself bilingual. The non-Welsh-speaking majority are the monoglots. The only bilingual people in Wales are the Welsh speakers.

In this chapter my main concern is the fundamental link between the Welsh language and Welsh identity in contemporary Wales. It would appear, therefore, that I am not concerned with what has become to be known as 'the unspoken-for majority'. Not so. It is a matter which I cannot avoid, let alone ignore. Any consideration of the relationship between the two linguistic communities in Wales does hinge on one issue of critical importance.

The bilingual speaker is far better equipped to appreciate the position of the monoglot English speaker. The converse is not true simply because the monoglot does not have access to the other language which, in my view, is the indigenous mother tongue. In this sense I would argue that the non-Welsh speaker is deprived in his or her own country. There are various reasons for this, some of which are historical, others sociological.

I live in the real world of bilingualism. My home is in Cardiff, the capital city of Wales. The home language is Welsh, our near neighbours are English-speaking and our Welsh-speaking friends and acquaintances are dispersed throughout the city and its environs. I do not live in a linguistic ghetto or in anything which can be thought of as *y fro Gymraeg* (the Welsh heartland). Yet I have to handle day by day two languages and, in varying degrees, two cultures. Both are often kept on the boil though there are times when one or other is on the back burner.

This duality can lead to a sense of ambiguity. Constant movement and traffic across two cultural frontiers can blur the border line. On the other hand, this line of demarcation can become more tangible. Whichever way it works there is no doubt that living in such a society does make life interesting. If I may be permitted a sweeping generalization I would suggest that the English are congenitally incapable of understanding that there is another indigenous language and culture in Britain which is not Anglo-Saxon. This imperial vocation dies hard.

I still continue to be amazed that the Welsh language has survived at all. Since the Act of Union in 1536 when it was virtually banned, it has been subjected to direct and indirect bombardment which should have demolished it once and for all. It has been demeaned and neglected, derided and discouraged for over four hundred years yet it is still very much alive. Today, it is tolerated by many, rejected by many. It is used by a large number of people as a natural means of communication. It is actively pursued by some and is being learnt as a second language by an ever-increasing number. For those of us who cannot imagine being Welsh without it life is all the richer for it. Coupled with this feeling is the constant shadow of frustration of a society which is, like the dear old ant in Culhwch and Olwen, lame. The fundamental flaw is that no Welsh speaker can live life totally through the Welsh language. It is possible to go a long way towards this ideal but there are huge gaps. Nevertheless, there is no reason why it should be abandoned. Despite the problems and irritations, the patronizing attitudes and intolerance, there are too many of us who can say with the poet T.H. Parry-Williams, 'Duw a'm gwaredo, ni allaf ddianc rhag hon'. These words end his sonnet 'Hon' in which he seeks to come to terms with his natural means of expression and he ends with the words 'God help me, I cannot escape her'.

I am, therefore, clear in my own mind that the Welsh language is fundamental to the Welsh identity. A Welsh accent is not enough, neither is living in Wales sufficient of itself. To have been born in Wales or, for that matter, anywhere else, of Welsh parents is not necessarily a sufficient qualification. It is a matter of will. It is a question of commitment to a language and culture. It is not ethnic, neither is it exclusive. It is simply different, of significance in the European context and of value within the spectrum of human society throughout the world.

It is easier to define the lack of Welsh identity in the light of the fact that the country has no political identity as a nation state. Consequently, it does not have any real tangible political institutions which are the hallmarks of any modern nation state. Its language is not, therefore, a language of the state. It does not function as an official medium of state simply because there is no state. There is no machinery of state of which it is an integral part. As a result, all the efforts for its survival, its use and its recognition have depended, over the centuries, on the will of its speakers. Government has had to be reminded of its existence. The impetus for its use in public, in education, in administration has come from below, from the grass roots. Government has rarely, if ever, initiated anything towards its well-being. It has merely responded.

Consequently, there are a number of 'institutions' which have established themselves as protectors, defenders and promoters of the language. Since the Second World War there has been a heightening of awareness and concern about the language and this has been matched with a proliferation of supporting organizations.

One of the most important of these is the National Eisteddfod, officially known as The Royal National Eisteddfod of Wales (Figure 40.1). The Eisteddfod is a peculiar Welsh institution which has its origins in mediaeval times. It is a competitive festival of the arts in music and poetry. It began as an ornament of the culture of the nobility but it has become democratized and since its revival in the nineteenth century has become an integral part of our culture. It is an annual event and visits North and South Wales in alternate years. It is a travelling cultural circus which costs well over £1 million annually.

In 1948 the Eisteddfod authorities made a fundamental decision about its future. They reasserted Welsh as the sole official language of the Eisteddfod; a means of safeguarding and promoting the language. Since then it has flourished and the first week of August is a fixed feast for anyone interested in the Welsh cultural scene at its amateur best and worst. Attendances during the week average 150,000.

If the competitive element is paramount this is not to the exclusion of other activities of a non-competitive nature. All in all, it is an arts festival where pride of place is given to literature, music and drama, to the visual arts and tactile crafts and to the Welsh pop culture. Superimposed on to this cultural trunk are all manner of related branch activities to be found in tent and caravan on the Eisteddfod field. It is a microcosm of an ideal world where it is possible to live out one's life entirely in

EISTEDDFOD GENEDLAETHOL FRENHINOL CYMRU

Figure 40.1 National Eisteddfod logo.

Welsh. Nevertheless, it is productive, inspiring, reassuring and stimulating. If it is a week of fantasy and creatively artificial it is a powerful manifestation of the virility and vitality of a minority language and culture which is not echoed in the cultural life of the majority. It may be exclusively Welsh but it excludes no one.

There is one element in the presentation of the National Eisteddfod which does provide a sense of ritual and drama. The Gorsedd of Bards is a strong lobby within the Eisteddfod structure. It may be an admixture of fiction, fantasy, fancy and fact but it does have a broad appeal. It controls both major poetic ceremonials – those of the Chairing and the Crowning of the winning bards. These are two of four prestigious occasions when the members, dressed in robes of white, blue and green, assemble to honour the successful poets.

The pseudo-Celtic origins are reflected in the symbolism of its ritual, which is more a fruit of late Celtic romanticism than that of the true Celts. Nevertheless, in a country which is very short on colourful ceremonial the Gorsedd of Bards does seek to fill a gap in the Celtic–Welsh relationship.

The other major Welsh competitive festival is an offspring of the 'National'. The Urdd Eisteddfod – Eisteddfod Genedlaethol yr Urdd – is the cultural apex of Urdd Gobaith Cymru – the Welsh League of Youth – founded in 1921 (Figure 40.2). Held in May alternately in North and South Wales, it is firmly based on the competitive element. Competitors arrive at this Eisteddfod after a sifting process at local and county level. Its aims are broadly those of its parent but the competitive curriculum is targeted at children and youth.

Both these annual events make great demands on the localities which host them.

URDD GOBAITH CYMRU

Figure 40.2 Urdd logo.

There is a formidable financial commitment, the programme has to be prepared and published, a site has to be found and accommodation sought. The work involves a great deal of effort from volunteers over a period of two to three years. The overall effect on the locality is to consolidate and to encourage the perception of Welshness in a variety of ways but, primarily, in terms of the language. Both of these Eisteddfodau are unashamedly clear in their intention to declare the interdependence between language and identity.

Since the end of the Second World War there has been a remarkable growth in the establishing of Welsh-medium schools. These schools have been the result not of government or even local authority initiative but of parental demand. The need arose, initially, for education within school to be conducted in most, if not all, subjects through the medium of Welsh. This was a bold departure from the orthodoxy which was practised by education authorities throughout the whole of Wales. Education in Wales was not only modelled on that of England but its language was English. Not only was the content of education English with little, if any, reference to Wales, but this imperial blessing was to be conveyed in the imperial language. The second half of this century has seen a sea change in the servile yet understandable attitude of the Welsh to formal education. English was the key to success, the language of progress and elevation, with Welsh as a vernacular outside the temples of education. By today there is a huge network of schools at all levels where Welsh is the primary means of instruction. This growth has been particularly striking in the anglicized areas in the south-east and the north-east. There is progression from play group to nursery school to primary school to secondary school (Figure 40.3). From thereon the provision in Welsh at the higher education institutions is sporadic. What is significant about the bilingual school is that Welsh is the prime language in both classroom and corridor. It is the lingua franca of the school whereas, in the others, Welsh is a second language heard only in the Welsh lesson.

gyda chyfarchion
Mudiad Ysgolion Meithrin

Mudiad Ysgolion Meithrin

NATIONAL ASSOCIATION OF WELSH MEDIUM NURSERY SCHOOLS AND PLAYGROUPS

Figure 40.3 MYM logo.

This amazing growth has made life difficult for local authorities, who have had to respond to demand. The situation is all the more amazing in that the demand for this kind of education very often comes from parents neither of whom speaks Welsh. Most bilingual schools are attended by children from non-Welsh-speaking homes. Welsh schools in the anglicized urban areas have shown the way and schools in the so-called 'heartland' areas westwards have moved in the same direction. This has had to be done because of the massive immigration into rural Wales of monoglot English families, too many of whom are unsympathetic to the native language and culture.

With the assertive development of bilingual schools in the anglicized areas and the defensive development in the traditionally Welsh-speaking areas, the link between language and identity is unquestioned.

The role of the media in sustaining identity is of the utmost importance. There is no national daily Welsh language newspaper but there are a number of weeklies, monthlies and quarterlies written entirely in Welsh. One particular development has been the rapid increase in the number of 'local' newspapers in Welsh. These have arisen as a reaction against the single article in Welsh in the local journal serving a predominantly Welsh-speaking area. The new *papurau bro* have proliferated and, in addition to enhancing a local identity, they have also strengthened a linguistic identity. They are to be found all over Wales and if the content is local the language of each and every one is part of the corporate national language.

Broadcasting is another potent force in the Welsh situation. There is a Welsh language radio network, Radio Cymru, provided by the BBC, which broadcasts some 100 hours a week entirely in Welsh. The Welsh language television output is found on S4C, Sianel Pedwar Cymru (Figure 40.4). This service was established in 1982. In it all the Welsh programmes, previously transmitted as opt-outs on other channels, are contained on this one channel. S4C does not of itself produce programmes but acts as a commissioning body. Its programmes are drawn from two main sources – BBC Cymru and the independent commercial companies, particularly those in Wales, which have mushroomed since S4C was set up. The channel has to be all things to all men and it is funded largely by central government grant supplemented by its own advertising and marketing income. It is in a unique situation in terms of its independent status, its funding and its programming. Whatever its virtues, and they are many, whatever its weaknesses, of which there are some, S4C does fly the flag of linguistic identity. It was intended to be a coherent Welsh language service at peak viewing hours and it came as the result of a long campaign of agitated and heated canvassing. It now transmits some 30 hours of Welsh language television per week flanked by programmes from the UK Channel 4 output.

Figure 40.4 S4C logo.

The setting up of S4C was a seminal achievement for Cymdeithas yr Iaith Gymraeg – Welsh Language Society – which was in the vanguard of the campaign. This society was founded in 1962 and, over the years, has conducted an active programme for the recognition of the language by government, local authorities and agencies (Figure 40.5). It is spearheaded by a constant turnover of college students who have succeeded in sustaining considerable pressure on officialdom and who have

Figure 40.5 WLS logo (Cymdeithas y Iaith 'tafod y ddraig (dragon's tongue)).

kept the Welsh consciousness alive among the generations. Condemned by the conservative, praised by the radical, it continues to agitate, infuriate and inspire and no authority, whatever its level, is immune to its proddings.

Ever since Roman times Wales has been governed from afar. The Roman *caer*, the Norman *castell* and the English castle have all, in turn, been the tangible presence of a central power based outside Wales. The modern equivalent of this arm of central government is Y Swyddfa Gymreig, the Welsh Office. Headed by the Secretary of State, it is an extension of central government and its fortress is a formidable white building in Cardiff's Cathays Park. It is a bureaucratic hive of civil servants among whose many functions is its concern for the Welsh language. The Welsh Office is not known for its initiatives concerning the language. In fact, were it not for the conscience of enthusiasts, very little, if anything, would have been achieved. In order to assist him in his deliberations the Secretary of State creates a plague of nominated bodies known as quangos. One of these is Bwrdd yr Iaith Gymraeg, the Welsh Language Board (Figure 40.6)

**BWRDD
YR IAITH
GYMRAEG**

**WELSH
LANGUAGE
BOARD**

Figure 40.6 Bwrdd Yr Iaith logo.

Established by the then Secretary of State in 1988 the Board was asked 'to advise on matters which called for legislative or administrative action, to assist and advise on the use and promotion of Welsh, to consider complaints and to reconcile differences'. The Board, chairman and eight members, are supported by five specialist working groups each chaired by a Board member. The Board and its working groups are serviced by its own secretariat. The Board is of considerable importance if only in its role as advisor on financial support for the numerous organizations throughout Wales committed in some way or other to the language cause. The position and status of the Board is, however, dependent on the political will not of Wales but of central government whatever its colour.

Hopes ran high in 1993 with the prospect of a new Welsh Language Act which would give Welsh official legal status. In the event the measure was subjected to all manner of governmental ploys and suspect devices which would ensure that the new act would fall short of even the Board's own recommendations. It certainly falls short of what is now a consensus, not hitherto articulate among both language communities, that Welsh should be given official status. Already, there is agitation for another language act of a more positive nature. Under the new act the Welsh Language Board will become a statutory body nominated by the Welsh Office. After five years of considerable and significant work it is a matter of regret that government did not take the Board's proposals as a baseline for the new act.

I suspect that when the new chairman of the Board was approached to consider the post, which he subsequently accepted, he had good reason to believe that the act would be far more powerful than the diluted version which has reached the statute book.

The devious arm of central government has, once again, prevailed, adding another component to the democratic deficit.

The governmental and bureaucratic mills grind 'exceeding slow' and are in constant need of lubrication by individuals and groups at grass-root level. It is felt that the Welsh Office does not truly identify itself with the language cause. It has been forced to recognize it, compelled to respond to it and persuaded, somewhat reluctantly, to be active in its support and promotion. Despite positive gestures, of which there have been many, the establishment is still suspect. After all, politics is so much a matter of expedience, whereas the language is a matter of survival for the committed.

In order to discover the linguistic identity of the kind which I have sought to articulate one has to dig beneath the surface. The superficial gloss is obvious enough in the tourist shops, the tourist publications and the predictable clichés (Figure 40.7). Beneath this layer of veneer lie veins of encouragement and significance.

There are thousands of adults who are attending classes to learn Welsh as a second language. At the other end of the age range is the phenomenal growth of Welsh language medium education notably in the traditional anglicized areas of industrial south-east and north-east Wales. The fulcrum of the concern for the language has shifted from what was the 'heartland' of the west.

Figure 40.7 Welsh dragon.

I like to think that this awareness and concern for language is derived from the Celtic background. It is not without significance that poetry and the delight in words still play a prominent role in the culture at all levels. The intricate interweaving and tracery seen on the Celtic crosses have resurfaced in the metrical complexity of the strict verse. Bards, great and small, are still revered and respected and versifying in all its alliterative glory is a source of enjoyment. Whatever the case for a Welsh identity without the language I have to say that anyone who claims to be Welsh is indebted, knowingly or not, to *Canu Aneirin*, the *Mabinogion*, Dafydd ap Gwilym, Gruffydd Robert of Milan, Bishop Morgan, Goronwy Owen, Pantycelyn, O.M., Saunders Lewis and Dafydd Iwan. This heritage is unique and it is the hallmark of a language and culture clearly and irrevocably identifiable in the modern world with its increasingly uniform, plastic culture.

THE CELTIC LANGUAGES
TODAY

— ·•· —

Glanville Price

Six Celtic languages survived into post-medieval times. Of these, three, namely Scottish Gaelic, Manx and Irish, belong to the Gaelic or Goidelic branch of Celtic and are closely related to one another. The other three, Breton, Cornish and Welsh, constituting the Brittonic or Brythonic branch, are less closely related to one another than are the Gaelic languages. Cornish died out towards the end of the eighteenth century but Manx survived until well into the second half of the present century (the last native speaker died at the age of 97 in 1974).

The situation of all four remaining Celtic languages is precarious, leaving few grounds for optimism as to their long-term future. In widely differing respects, to varying extents, and with markedly divergent practical effects, official attitudes towards and public awareness of and concern for all four have improved in recent decades and significant numbers of non-native speakers have achieved considerable competence in them, but the decline in the number of native speakers goes on.

We have, with the proviso noted below, reasonably accurate figures for the numbers of speakers of Scottish Gaelic and of Welsh, but, for different reasons, not for Irish and Breton.

The decennial censuses held in the United Kingdom have, since 1891, included in Scotland and Wales a question relating to each individual's ability to speak (and, in recent censuses, to understand, read or write) Gaelic or Welsh respectively. The statistics derived from the answers to these questions can be taken as a fairly safe indication of the state of the language at the dates in question, provided always that one makes allowance for the fact that it is not always easy, or possible, to give a straight 'yes' or 'no' answer to the question: 'Do you speak a given language?' It is quite certain that some individuals whose knowledge of Gaelic or Welsh is very limited have claimed, on census returns, to be speakers of the language, whereas it is more than likely that some (perhaps many) others who have a real, if limited, conversational competence in the language and whose usual medium of communication is English have been enumerated as non-speakers of Gaelic or Welsh respectively. There is the further consideration that no corresponding question is asked in England, where there have been throughout this century and still are substantial numbers of Welsh speakers.

However, if statistics relating to linguistic competence derived from the censuses cannot be taken as having an absolute value, they nevertheless provide a valid basis for comparative purposes. On the one hand, they reveal the extent of the progressive decline of the language, while on the other hand they indicate the relative strength or weakness of the language in different parts of the country. All figures and percentages given below should be interpreted with these considerations in mind.

Wales is the area where any form of Celtic speech is best maintained both in the sense of having (with the possible exception of Breton) the highest number of speakers and in the sense of enjoying the greatest and most effective measure of public support and public use.

At the turn of the century, Welsh was still spoken by 50 per cent of the total population of Wales, including 15 per cent who claimed to speak Welsh only, and the total number of bilingual and monolingual speakers of Welsh was well over 900,000. Ten years later, the total had risen and was approaching a million (977,366), but, since there had meanwhile been an increase in the total population, the proportion of that population claiming to speak Welsh had dropped significantly, to 43.5 per cent. Thereafter, the decline in both absolute numbers and percentages has seemed irreversible.

By 1951, the proportion of those claiming to speak Welsh only had dropped to 2 per cent and thereafter has remained at around 1 per cent, but it is known that, in reality, some bilinguals have entered themselves on the census forms as speaking Welsh only and it can safely be assumed that all Welsh speakers, apart from some young children who will inevitably learn English later in life, have at least an adequate competence in English. The truly monoglot community has, in effect, disappeared. In what follows, the term 'Welsh speakers' includes both the declared bilinguals and those who claim to speak Welsh only. The following are the data provided (for the population aged 3 years and over) by the four post-war censuses for which statistics are available (a further census was held in April, 1991, but, at the time of writing, the results thereof have not been published):

	Welsh-speakers	% of total population
1951	714,686	29
1961	656,002	25
1971	542,425	21
1981	508,207	19

The most optimistic interpretation one can place on these figures is that, although the decline continues, the rate of decline seems to have slowed down significantly, perhaps as a result of positive action taken in recent decades to encourage the use of the language.

The geographical distribution of the still largely (which does not necessarily mean predominantly) Welsh-speaking areas also reflects the weakened state of the language. It comes as no surprise to see[1] that the area where less than 50 per cent can now speak Welsh covers the eastern zone, bordering England, and the greater part of Glamorgan and the long-anglicized southern part of Pembroke. What is more worrying is the fact that, all around the coast, in what had long been strongly Welsh-speaking areas such as Anglesey, Merioneth, Cardiganshire and northern Pembroke, there are sizeable pockets, mainly in and around urban centres such as Holyhead, Beaumaris, Aberdyfi, Aberystwyth and Fishguard, where the proportion of the population able to speak Welsh is in the 40–55 per cent band. There are even parts of Anglesey that fall within the 25–40 per cent band. Already on the basis of the results of the 1971 census, Professors E.G. Bowen and Harold Carter drew attention to the presence of an 'anglicized corridor' in mid-Wales, whereby the concurrence of the anglicizing influence of the university town and tourist resort of Aberystwyth in the west and 'a long established drive' proceeding up the valley of the Severn and across the valley of the Dyfi seemed likely to drive a wedge through the Welsh-speaking heartland:

> From the point of view of those concerned with the preservation of the language this corridor is a geographical feature of great concern, for there are clear indications that its extension will leave the country in the near future with its Welsh-speaking area irrevocably divided into two separate sections, the north-west and the south-west.
>
> (Bowen and Carter 1975: 6)

If Welsh is to be preserved as a living language, the decline must of course not only be slowed down but halted and, if at all possible, reversed. This is inevitably a long-term task, but there are signs that it might perhaps be successfully accomplished. It is, after all, possible to extrapolate from existing census figures, to the extent that these provide a break-down by age-groups. As we have seen, 19 per cent of the total population aged 3 years and over were recorded as Welsh-speaking in 1981 but, not unexpectedly, there are wide differences among age-groups.[2] Whereas 27.4 per cent of the population in the age-group '65 and over' were Welsh-speaking, the proportion for the group aged 45–64 was 20.7 per cent, and that for the age-group 25–44, which we may classify as 'young adults', was 15.5 per cent and that for the age-group 15–24, whose pattern of linguistic competence may be considered to be more or less firmly established, was 14.9 per cent. However, that of the critical age-groups 10–14 and 5–9 was 18.5 per cent and 17.8 per cent respectively, corresponding to 17 per cent and 14.5 per cent respectively in 1971, this suggests that the increased encouragement and teaching of Welsh in schools in the intervening decade was having an appreciable effect. Whether this will be maintained it is too early to say but, at the very least, it is as yet too early to abandon hope.

We have dwelt at some length, but even so only in summary fashion, on the situation of Welsh as revealed by census reports. The other remaining Celtic languages will have to be dealt with even more summarily.

The census figures for Scottish Gaelic reveal that, whereas over a quarter of a million (254,415) claimed to speak the language in 1891, this had been reduced by over two-thirds to 79,307 by 1981, i.e. within one (if lengthy) human lifetime. To give percentages for the whole of Scotland would be pointless, given that Gaelic has never been the language of the whole of Scotland and that many parts of the country, particularly in the south-west, that were once Gaelic-speaking have long been totally bereft of the language. We can, however, trace the decline, often to the point of virtual extinction, of Gaelic in those parts of the Highlands and Islands where the language was well maintained and, indeed, in many cases flourished a century ago.

The collapse of the language is most evident in north-eastern and central Scotland. In two representative north-eastern parishes, Loth (Sutherland) and Fearn (Ross and Cromarty), for example, the proportion of Gaelic speakers declined from 51 per cent and 63 per cent respectively in 1891 to 3 per cent and 4 per cent respectively in 1981.[3] A similar decline is evidenced for the 'Highland District' of Perthshire, i.e. the north and west of the county, in central Scotland. Meanwhile, a similar if less catastrophic decline had taken place on much of the west coast of the mainland, even in the far north where the proportion of Gaelic speakers in the sparsely populated parishes of Tongue, Durness, Eddrachillis and Assynt in north-western Sutherland, declined from 85 per cent on average in 1891 to 34 per cent on average in 1981.

Further south, one mainland parish, Applecross (in the county of Ross and Cromarty), had a majority of Gaelic speakers (54 per cent) in 1971, but by 1981 this had declined to little more than a third (36 per cent). In the four other mainland parishes (from north to south, Gairloch, Lochcarron, Glenshiel and Ardnamurchan), where the proportion of Gaelic speakers ranged from 43 per cent to 45 per cent in 1971 (no other mainland parish then exceeded 40 per cent), the proportion had dropped in 1981 to 35 per cent, 22 per cent, 37 per cent and 38.5 per cent respectively.

Census statistics for Irish exist for the Republic of Ireland (but not for Northern Ireland) but they cannot be taken at their face value. The numbers of those claiming to speak Irish rose from 540,802 (= 19.3 per cent of the population) in 1926, i.e. in the first census after southern Ireland achieved its independence, to 1,018,413 (= 31.6 per cent) in 1981.[4] This would suggest that the number of speakers of the native language was rather more than twice that of speakers of Welsh and that the proportion of the total population speaking the language was also considerably higher than in Wales. This is very obviously not the case: whereas there are still extensive areas of Wales where the native language is widely spoken on a normal everyday basis, this is not so in Ireland (see below). The overwhelming majority (i.e. some 95 per cent at least) of those recorded as Irish speakers have acquired a degree (in many cases a high degree) of competence in Irish as a second language through the educational system, and informed sources by no means hostile to the Irish language now put the number of native speakers as low as 50,000 (some estimates would put it substantially lower). It appears, therefore, that native speakers of Irish are probably fewer than those of Scottish Gaelic. It is by no means improbable that the native speakers of both languages taken together number little more than 100,000, if that.

Even in the Gaeltacht, the officially Irish-speaking areas, the language is in a gravely weakened condition. Comparing the data provided by the two most recent censuses for which figures are available, Máirtín Ó Murchú comments (1985: 29):

> In 1971 the total population of the Gaeltacht areas was 65,982, of whom 54,940 were returned as Irish speakers, or 83.3% of the total. By 1981 the population of the Gaeltacht areas was exactly 75,000. This represents an increase of more than 9,000 over the 1971 figure, due in part to boundary changes effected in 1974, but the proportion of Irish speakers at 58,026 had by 1981 declined to 77.4% of the total. Apart from that, it is necessary to distinguish between the

incidence of competence to speak the language and the incidence of actual use. It is fairly reliably estimated that no more than 25,000 of the Gaeltacht population now use Irish consistently in day-to-day communication.

Territorially, Irish has long been in an even worse situation than that which is feared for Welsh, should a wedge be driven between the northern and southern parts of Welsh-speaking Wales. The three main Gaeltacht areas are to be found in Donegal in the north-west, in Co. Mayo and Connemara in the west, and in the Dingle and Inveragh peninsulas in south-west Munster. These three areas are separated from one another by extensive English-speaking areas and, furthermore, are themselves to some extent fragmented.

Questions as to linguistic competence have never been put in French censuses. A number of private surveys, on differing methodological bases and with varying degrees of reliability, have, however, been made for Breton. One of the most recent is by H.Ll. Humphreys who, by taking the population figures provided by the 1962 French census and making carefully judged assumptions, based on close personal knowledge of Brittany, about the likely extent of Breton speaking in different areas, arrives at an estimate of 686,000 speakers, which, as he says (1991: 113), is 'more or less in line with other estimates'. More recently still, another estimate based on an audience research survey carried out by Radio Bretagne Ouest in 1983 gives a total of some 615,000, 'of whom 40% were very frequent speakers and 40% occasional speakers' (ibid.: 115). It is, however, possible that these figures overestimate the numbers of those who have a good spoken competence in Breton.

Taking the most optimistic realistic figures for native speakers of any form of Celtic speech at the present time, we may conclude that they almost certainly number in excess of a million.

The future of these languages depends on a number of factors, including their role in official and administrative life, in education and in the media. We shall return to these topics below. The crucial factor, however, though one that is inevitably conditioned by other factors such as those we have just mentioned, is the attitude towards the language of its own native speakers. Ó Murchú, for example, immediately after his comment quoted above on the situation of Irish in the Gaeltacht, adds (1985: 29) that 'a new decline appears to have set in over the last 15 years [i.e. since about 1970]' and that 'many Irish-speaking parents in Gaeltacht areas have been using English only with their children'.

Two recent questionnaire-based surveys (Lyon and Ellis 1991; Roberts 1991) of parental attitudes towards the teaching of Welsh and Scottish Gaelic respectively in areas where the language is still in widespread use indicate a high degree of support for such a policy. Lyon and Ellis's survey relates to the parents of all children born in Anglesey in the year ending February 1989. Of those (45 per cent of the total) who responded, 86 per cent wished their children to learn Welsh in school and 62 per cent wished them to be 'fluent in Welsh' (defined as a step beyond learning Welsh at school). It is noteworthy that, though the level of enthusiasm was predictably highest among parental couples both of whom were Welsh-speaking, positive attitudes predominated even among couples of whom neither was Welsh-speaking (71 per cent in favour of Welsh at school, with 26 per cent wishing for fluency in Welsh). There does, however, seem to be some difference in motivation between groups, in that 'integrative' reasons (representing a positive attitude towards Welsh culture and the Welsh language as such) were high among those where one or both parents were Welsh-speaking, while non-Welsh-speaking couples tended to lay greater emphasis on 'instrumental' reasons (the advantages, particularly in terms of job prospects, of having a knowledge of Welsh).

Roberts (1991) bases his conclusions on a questionnaire sent to the parents of all children in the area covered for the purposes of education by Comhairle nan Eilean ('The [Western] Isles Council'), i.e. the islands of Lewis and Harris, North Uist, Benbecula, South Uist, Eriskay and Barra, and achieved a 61 per cent response rate. One disturbing feature that emerges, almost incidentally, from the survey is that 'in the Western Isles as a whole, a clear majority of children are now coming to school from homes where Gaelic is not "normally" spoken' (Roberts 1991: 255). Despite that, the same percentage as in the Anglesey survey, namely 86 per cent, wished their children to be bilingual, and 71 per cent supported Gaelic-medium education as a part of the Western Isles bilingual policy – though how far this should be taken, i.e. for how many years of a child's primary education, was much more controversial.

If we assume that positive attitudes towards a language are a necessary, though not a sufficient, condition for its survival, we can perhaps draw some encouragement from these two surveys.

There are wide differences among Celtic languages in respect of their legal and official status at the present time.

In the Republic of Ireland, the Constitution asserts that 'the Irish language as the national language is the first official language' and an active interventionist policy has been adopted with a view to encouraging the use of the language in education, in the media and, to some extent, in the field of industrial development. In 1978, the Irish Language Board (Bord na Gaeilge) which had come into being in 1975 was 'established by Act of the *Oireachtas* (Legislature) as the official State agency for planning and policy-making in relation to the Irish language' (Ó Murchú 1985: 36).[5] Irish is also an official language of the EC but not a working language, i.e. there is no requirement for the provision of an Irish-language version of all working documents of the Community's institutions, committees, etc.

The public and official use of Irish, at least outside the Gaeltacht areas, is very often little more than tokenism. In reality, the Celtic language that has achieved the greatest degree not only of formal recognition but of actual use in public life generally is incontrovertibly Welsh.

As far as the legal and official status of Welsh is concerned, the situation has been completely transformed within the last thirty years. Until fifty years ago, Welsh had no official status whatsoever. A first, though minimal and in practice more or less ineffectual, step towards acceptance of the language for use in the courts of law was made by the Welsh Courts Act of 1942 which enacted that 'the Welsh language may be used in any court in Wales by any party or witness who considers that he would otherwise be at any disadvantage by reason of his natural language of communication being Welsh': this, it must be observed, fell far short of allowing any participants in a trial the option of expressing themselves in Welsh as a matter of right and merely because they preferred to do so.

A major step forward was made in 1967 when, after the publication in 1963 of an official *Report on the Welsh Language Today* and, in 1965, of a further official report on the *Legal Status of the Welsh Language*, the first Welsh Language Act was passed. This provides *inter alia* that 'in any legal proceeding in Wales ... the Welsh language may be spoken by any party, witness or other person who desires to use it', that Welsh versions of official documents or forms 'may' (i.e. not 'must' or 'shall') be provided at the behest of the appropriate minister, and that 'anything done in Welsh' on the basis of such documents 'shall have the like effect as if done in English'. The 1967 Act has had far-reaching effects, extending beyond the field of the use of Welsh in legal and official business to which its scope is technically limited. One effect has been a vastly increased use of Welsh by such public or recently privatized bodies as the Post Office, British Rail, electricity and gas companies, by banks and building societies, by political and other organizations in their publicity material, and, though as yet only to a limited extent, by supermarkets and other commercial concerns.

Though much was achieved for Welsh in the wake of the 1967 Act, proponents of the language feel that it has not ensured a totally satisfactory role for the language in public life. The next step forward occurred in July 1988 with the setting up by the Secretary of State for Wales of the Welsh Language Board, whose terms of reference were stated as being 'to promote and develop the Welsh language and advise on matters requiring legislative action'. This the Board has interpreted as entrusting to it, *inter alia*, the tasks of 'assisting public and private bodies and individuals in the use of the language, and of promoting it in their activities' and of 'advising the Secretary of State on matters relating to the Welsh language' (Welsh Language Board 1989: 2). In February 1991, the Board published specific proposals for a new Welsh Language Act. It identified as particular inadequacies of the 1967 Act 'its failure to declare that in Wales the Welsh language shall be equal in status to the English language' and 'its failure to make effective provision for greater use of the language in the public sector' (Welsh Language Board 1991: 3).

The position accorded to Scottish Gaelic in public life is in no way comparable to that enjoyed by Welsh. The Western Isles Islands Council, which covers most of the Gaelic-speaking area, has in the last ten years adopted a policy of encouraging the use of the language in those fields for which it has responsibility, but as far as central government is concerned, and outside the field of education (see below), it is almost as if the language did not exist. The position is fairly summarized in a 1986 document prepared for the European Commission by the Istituto della Enciclopedia Italiana (Commission of the European Communities 1986: 176):

> Certificates of civil status and publications regarding the same are not available in Gaelic. ... Gaelic has virtually no place in Government. ... Citizens with an understanding of English ... are not entitled as of right to use Gaelic when defending themselves in court.

The status of Breton is inferior even to that of Gaelic in that, quite simply, 'Breton has no official role in administration' (Humphreys 1992: 259) apart from 'its rather cosmetic use on signs'. The most that the author of the words just quoted can find to say on the positive side is that the *département* of Côtes d'Armor 'has gone some way towards bilingualizing roadsigns in the Breton area, while certain banks issue bilingual cheque-books' (ibid.), adding, not without irony, that 'these show that the symbolic use of Breton has extended beyond war-memorials'.

In the field of education, Welsh is now well provided for, at least at primary and secondary levels. Welsh has long been taught as a subject in Welsh-speaking parts of Wales and already before the Second World War was used to some extent as a medium of instruction in primary schools. The first specifically Welsh-medium primary school within the state system was opened in 1947 and the first bilingual secondary school (Welsh being both the administrative language and the medium of instruction for most subjects) in 1956. There are now nearly seventy such schools in the primary sector and sixteen in the secondary sector. A more recent – and very important – development has been the growth in the last twenty years of Welsh-language nursery schools, which could prove an effective factor in slowing down the decline in the use of the language. At the other end of the scale, some provision is made for teaching through the medium of Welsh in some departments in the University of Wales but, although there are demands for further expansion in this direction and even for the establishment of an entirely Welsh-medium college within the university, there seems little likelihood that this will prove to be feasible.

As in other fields, the provision for Gaelic within the educational system is greatly inferior to that of Welsh. Gaelic is, however, widely taught as a subject in the Gaelic-speaking areas and the sympathetic attitude towards it taken by the Western Isles Islands Council is likely to lead to a substantial improvement.

The attitude of the French authorities towards Breton, as towards all minority languages under their jurisdiction, has long been one of considerable hostility. In 1951, strictly limited provision for the teaching of Breton (and of Basque, Catalan and Occitan) in state secondary schools was granted by act of parliament but this was hedged around by highly discouraging constraints as to the circumstances in which the languages in question could be taught. Some progress has been made since, at both secondary and tertiary levels, but the most significant development has been the rise, since 1977 and outside the state system, of a number of nursery and primary schools in which Breton is not only taught but, to some extent, used as a medium of instruction. However, 'in 1984, only a little over 5 per cent of all pupils [i.e. in schools in the Breton-speaking part of the country] had any instruction in Breton' (Humphreys 1991: 101), and the situation is unlikely to have improved markedly since.

The picture in the Republic of Ireland is a very different one. There, in the two decades following the establishment of the Irish Free State in 1922, an extensive policy of gaelicization of the educational system was pushed through, with much stress not only on the teaching of Irish but on teaching through the medium of Irish. Views differ both as to the success of this policy measured by its influence on the 'restoration' of Irish and as to its possible harmful effects on the general educational development of the children. However that may be, the policy has been largely abandoned: an Irish Language Board report dated 1986 comments that the number of Irish-medium primary schools, outside the designated Gaeltacht areas, declined from 232 to 43 between 1957–8 and 1969–70, and to only 20 by the mid-1980s (though there was later a small increase). In the same period, the number of Irish-medium post-primary schools outside the Gaeltacht fell from 81 to 15 (Bord na

Gaeilge [1986]: 42), and the proportion of those attending Irish-medium secondary schools fell from 28 per cent in 1937–8 to 17 per cent in 1957–8 and to a mere 1.4 per cent in 1981–2 (ibid.: 28).

The problems of publishing books and periodicals in minority languages are, of course, immense and few such publications can be viable in the absence of public or private subsidies or commercial sponsorship. State subsidies are, in fact, available for Irish, Welsh and Scottish Gaelic and, in the case of Welsh, a wide range of both books and periodicals continues to appear. Inevitably, however, these represent only a small fraction (and an even smaller one in the case of Irish and Scottish Gaelic) of what is available in English. Such factors as the definition of what counts as a book and fluctuation from year to year mean that precise figures, unless given for a period of several years and accompanied by a detailed commentary, could be misleading. It would not, however, distort the picture unduly to say that, in recent years, the average number of books published annually has been about thirty for Scottish Gaelic, forty to fifty for Breton, about a hundred for Irish, and between four and five hundred for Welsh.

In the broadcasting media, only Welsh has achieved a level of diffusion generally considered by the linguistic community in question to be more or less satisfactory. The BBC's Radio Cymru broadcasts in Welsh for an average of twelve or thirteen hours per day while there is a daily average output of some five hours in Welsh on television. To give daily or weekly averages for the other three languages would serve little purpose, given that the situation is constantly changing, that there is much variation according to season, and that some programmes can be received only in parts of the relevant areas. It can, however, fairly be said that they all compare most unfavourably with Welsh and that, in the case of TV, each of them has substantially less (often less than half) in an average week than Welsh has per day.

One important stronghold of the languages has been the churches and, in general, the use of Welsh, Scottish Gaelic or Irish in churches in a given area corresponds more or less to the extent to which the languages are still in use in everyday life in that area. The case of Breton is, however, different.[6] Up to the First World War, Breton was extensively used both in sermons and for teaching the catechism, but more recently there has been a catastrophic decline: '[French] took over the catechism almost completely by 1950. Breton preaching survived a little longer but was generally abandoned in the 1960s . . .; hymns often survived only in connection with annual festivals' (Humphreys 1992: 256).

Although, thanks to the initiatives of groups of individuals (clergy and lay), the liturgy and the Bible have been translated and occasional Breton masses are still held, 'the church as an institution seems to have no place for Breton, beyond the inclusion of a Breton appendix in the three diocesan hymnals' (ibid.).

The pessimistic conclusion to any survey of the Celtic languages in the late twentieth century must be that they are all at risk. Numbers of native speakers of both varieties of Gaelic may well have declined beyond the point of no return and Breton is in a distressingly disadvantageous position. Welsh probably still has a chance of more than short-term survival: it has a substantial number of native speakers, the numbers of those who achieve considerable competence in it as a second language are increasing significantly, its role in official and public life, in education, and in the media, is much improved. It is certain that many children who will be born in the early decades of the twenty-first century will be brought up to speak Welsh as either a first or a second language: it will depend on them whether or not, by the end of the century, Welsh is in a stronger position than Irish and Scottish Gaelic are now.

NOTES

1 The distribution of the language according to the 1981 census is presented with stark clarity by the maps and accompanying commentary in Aitchison and Carter 1985.
2 See Office of Population Censuses and Surveys 1983.
3 See Registrar General Scotland 1983.
4 See Central Statistics Office 1985.
5 For a fuller coverage of the fields dealt with in this paragraph see Ó Murchú 1985: 35–6, and 1992: 48–9.
6 For a survey of the use of Breton in the Catholic Church throughout the twentieth century, see Humphreys 1991: 106–11.

REFERENCES

Aitchison, J. and Carter, H. (1985) *The Welsh Language 1961–1981: an interpretative survey*, Cardiff: University of Wales Press.
Bord na Gaeilge (1986) *The Irish Language in a Changing Society*, Dublin: Bord na Gaeilge.
Bowen, E.G. and Carter, H. (1975) 'The distribution of the Welsh language in 1971: an analysis', *Geography* 60: 1–15.
Central Statistics Office (1985) *Census of Population of Ireland, 1981*, vol. 6: *Irish Language*, Dublin: Central Statistics Office.
Commission of the European Communities (1986) *Linguistic Minorities in Countries belonging to the European Community*, Luxembourg: Office for Official Publications of the European Communities.
Humphreys, H.L. (1991) 'The geolinguistics of Breton', in Colin H. Williams (ed.) *Linguistic Minorities, Society and Territory*, Clevedon: Multilingual Matters, 96–120.
—— (1992) 'The Breton language', in Glanville Price (ed.) *The Celtic Connection*, Gerrards Cross: Colin Smythe, 245–75.
Lyon, J. and Ellis, N. (1991) 'Parental attitudes towards the Welsh language', *Journal of Multilingual and Multicultural Development* 12: 239–51.
Office of Population Censuses and Surveys (1983) *Census 1981: Welsh Language in Wales*, London: HMSO.
Ó Murchú, M. (1985) *The Irish Language*, Dublin: Department of Foreign Affairs and Bord na Gaeilge.
—— (1992) 'The Irish language', in Glanville Price (ed.) *The Celtic Connection*, Gerrards Cross: Colin Smythe, 30–64.
Registrar General Scotland (1983) *Census 1981: Gaelic report*, Edinburgh: HMSO.
Roberts, A. (1991) 'Parental attitudes to Gaelic-medium education in the Western Isles of Scotland', *Journal of Multilingual and Multicultural Development* 12: 253–69.
Welsh Language Board (1989) *The Welsh Language: a strategy for the future*, Cardiff: Welsh Language Board.
—— (1991) *Argymhellion ar gyfer Deddf Iaith Newydd / Recommendations for a New Welsh Language Act*, Cardiff: Welsh Language Board.

INDEX

—◆—